The Cambridge Handbook of Japanese Linguistics

The linguistic study of Japanese, with its rich syntactic and phonological structure, complex writing system, and diverse sociohistorical context, is a rapidly growing research area. This book, designed to serve as a concise reference for researchers interested in the Japanese language and in typological studies of language in general, explores diverse characteristics of Japanese that are particularly intriguing when compared with English and other European languages. It pays equal attention to the theoretical aspects and empirical phenomena from theory-neutral perspectives, and presents necessary theoretical terms in clear and easy terms. It consists of five thematic parts including sound system and lexicon, grammatical foundation and constructions, and pragmatics/sociolinguistics topics, with chapters that survey critical discussions arising in Japanese linguistics. *The Cambridge Handbook of Japanese Linguistics* will be welcomed by general linguists, and by students and scholars working in linguistic typology, Japanese language, Japanese linguistics, and Asian Studies.

YOKO HASEGAWA is Professor of Japanese Linguistics in the Department of East Asian Languages and Cultures at the University of California, Berkeley. Her research interests range over the great diversity of Japanese linguistics. Her publications include: *Japanese: A Linguistic Introduction* (2014, Cambridge University Press), *Soliloquy in Japanese and English* (2010), and *Nihongo kara mita nihonjin: Shutaisei no gengogaku*, with Yukio Hirose (2010).

CAMBRIDGE HANDBOOKS IN LANGUAGE AND LINGUISTICS

Genuinely broad in scope, each handbook in this series provides a complete state-of-the-field overview of a major sub-discipline within language study and research. Grouped into broad thematic areas, the chapters in each volume encompass the most important issues and topics within each subject, offering a coherent picture of the latest theories and findings. Together, the volumes will build into an integrated overview of the discipline in its entirety.

Published titles

The Cambridge Handbook of Phonology, edited by Paul de Lacy
The Cambridge Handbook of Linguistic Code-switching, edited by Barbara E. Bullock and Almeida Jacqueline Toribio
The Cambridge Handbook of Child Language, Second Edition, edited by Edith L. Bavin and Letitia Naigles
The Cambridge Handbook of Endangered Languages, edited by Peter K. Austin and Julia Sallabank
The Cambridge Handbook of Sociolinguistics, edited by Rajend Mesthrie
The Cambridge Handbook of Pragmatics, edited by Keith Allan and Kasia M. Jaszczolt
The Cambridge Handbook of Language Policy, edited by Bernard Spolsky
The Cambridge Handbook of Second Language Acquisition, edited by Julia Herschensohn and Martha Young-Scholten
The Cambridge Handbook of Biolinguistics, edited by Cedric Boeckx and Kleanthes K. Grohmann
The Cambridge Handbook of Generative Syntax, edited by Marcel den Dikken
The Cambridge Handbook of Communication Disorders, edited by Louise Cummings
The Cambridge Handbook of Stylistics, edited by Peter Stockwell and Sara Whiteley
The Cambridge Handbook of Linguistic Anthropology, edited by N. J. Enfield, Paul Kockelman and Jack Sidnell
The Cambridge Handbook of English Corpus Linguistics, edited by Douglas Biber and Randi Reppen
The Cambridge Handbook of Bilingual Processing, edited by John W. Schwieter
The Cambridge Handbook of Learner Corpus Research, edited by Sylviane Granger, Gaëtanelle Gilquin and Fanny Meunier
The Cambridge Handbook of Linguistic Multicompetence, edited by Li Wei and Vivian Cook
The Cambridge Handbook of English Historical Linguistics, edited by Merja Kytö and Päivi Pahta
The Cambridge Handbook of Formal Semantics, edited by Maria Aloni and Paul Dekker
The Cambridge Handbook of Morphology, edited by Andrew Hippisley and Greg Stump
The Cambridge Handbook of Historical Syntax, edited by Adam Ledgeway and Ian Roberts
The Cambridge Handbook of Linguistic Typology, edited by Alexandra Y. Aikhenvald and R. M. W. Dixon
The Cambridge Handbook of Areal Linguistics, edited by Raymond Hickey
The Cambridge Handbook of Cognitive Linguistics, edited by Barbara Dancygier
The Cambridge Handbook of Japanese Linguistics, edited by Yoko Hasegawa

The Cambridge Handbook of Japanese Linguistics

Edited by
Yoko Hasegawa
University of California, Berkeley

CAMBRIDGE
UNIVERSITY PRESS

University Printing House, Cambridge CB2 8BS, United Kingdom

One Liberty Plaza, 20th Floor, New York, NY 10006, USA

477 Williamstown Road, Port Melbourne, VIC 3207, Australia

314-321, 3rd Floor, Plot 3, Splendor Forum, Jasola District Centre, New Delhi - 110025, India

79 Anson Road, #06-04/06, Singapore 079906

Cambridge University Press is part of the University of Cambridge.

It furthers the University's mission by disseminating knowledge in the pursuit of education, learning and research at the highest international levels of excellence.

www.cambridge.org
Information on this title: www.cambridge.org/9781316636411
DOI: 10.1017/9781316884461

First published 2018
First paperback edition 2020

A catalogue record for this publication is available from the British Library

Library of Congress Cataloging in Publication data
Names: Hasegawa, Yōko editor.
Title: The Cambridge handbook of Japanese linguistics / edited by Yoko Hasegawa.
Description: Cambridge ; New York : Cambridge University Press, 2018. | Series: Cambridge handbooks in language and linguistics | Includes bibliographical references and index.
Identifiers: LCCN 2017061575 | ISBN 9781107185456 (hardback)
Subjects: LCSH: Japanese language | BISAC: FOREIGN LANGUAGE STUDY / General.
Classification: LCC PL523 .C35 2018 | DDC 495.6–dc23
LC record available at https://lccn.loc.gov/2017061575

ISBN 978-1-107-18545-6 Hardback
ISBN 978-1-316-63641-1 Paperback

Contents

Figures

Maps

Tables

Contributors

Haruko Minegishi Cook, University of Hawaii at Manoa
Florian Coulmas, University of Duisburg-Essen
Bjarke Frellesvig, University of Oxford
Seiko Fujii, University of Tokyo
Nobuko Hasegawa, Kanda University of International Studies
Yoko Hasegawa, University of California, Berkeley
Michael Haugh, University of Queensland
Yukio Hirose, University of Tsukuba
Kaoru Horie, Nagoya University
Yosuke Igarashi, Hitotsubashi University
Shoichi Iwasaki, University of California, Los Angeles
Wesley M. Jacobsen, Harvard University
Taro Kageyama, Doshisha University
Hideki Kishimoto, Kobe University
Haruo Kubozono, National Institute for Japanese Language and Linguistics
Yoshiko Matsumoto, Stanford University
Emi Morita, National University of Singapore
Wataru Nakamura, Tohoku University
Heiko Narrog, Tohoku University
Kyoko Hirose Ohara, Keio University
Shigeko Okamoto, University of California, Santa Cruz
Masayoshi Shibatani, Rice University
Michinori Shimoji, Kyushu University
Mitsuaki Shimojo, University at Buffalo, The State University of New York
Rumiko Shinzato, Georgia Institute of Technology
Polly Szatrowski, University of Minnesota
Kiyoko Toratani, York University
Timothy J. Vance, National Institute for Japanese Language and Linguistics

Abbreviations

#	unacceptable
?	questionable acceptability
*	ungrammatical
@	laughter
ABL	ablative
ACC	accusative particle
ACOP	adjectival copula
ADD.HON	addressee honorific
ADN	adnominal
ADV	adverbial
AGT	agent
ALL	allative
ANP	adnominal present
ASP	aspect
ATT	attributive
AUX	auxiliary
BEN	benefactive
BOU	boulomaic modality
CAUS	causative/cause
CL	classifier
CNJ	conjectural
CNCL	conclusive
CNT	contrast particle
COM	comitative
COMP	complementizer
COND	conditional
CONJ	conjunctive
COP	copula
CPV	completive

CSL	causal converb
CTR	contrast
DAT	dative particle
DECL	declarative
DEM	demonstrative
DEO	deontic modality
DES	desiderative
DIR	directional
DYN	dynamic
EMPH	emphasis
EPI	epistemic modality
ERG	ergative
ESS	essive
EVID	evidential
EX	exalting prefix
EXCL	exclamative
EXM	exemplative
FIL	filler
FIN	finite form
FOC	focus
FRG	fragment
FS	false start
FUT	future
GEN	genitive
GER	gerund
GOAL	goal
HON	honorific
HORT	hortative
HUM	humilific
HYP	hypothetical
ICVP	imperfective converb
IMP	imperative
INF	infinitive
INFR	inference
INSTR	instrumental
INT	interrogative particle
INTNT	intentional
INTJ	interjection
INTR	intransitive
IP	interjectional particle
IPFV	imperfective
IRR	irrealis
LIT.	literal
LK	linker
LOC	locative

MIM	mimetic
MOD	modality
MPST	modal past tense
NEG	negative
NMLZ	nominalizer/nominalization
NMNL	nominal
NOM	nominative
NP	noun phrase
NPST	non-past
OBJ	object
OPT	optative
PASS	passive
PERF	perfective
PL	plural
PLN	plain form
POL	polite form
POT	potential form
PRED	predicative
PRES	presumptive
PRF	perfect
PRO	pronoun
PROG	progressive
PROPOS	propositive
PROV	provisional
PRS	present
PRT	particle
PST	past
PTCP	participle
PURP	purposive
Q	question/interrogative
QFOC	interrogative focus
QP	question particle
OPT	optative
QUOT	quotative
REF	reflexive
RES	resultative
RESP	respect
SBJ	subject
SEQ	sequential
SFP	sentence-final particle
SPEC	speculative
SPST	simple past
STAT	stative

SUF	suffix
TERM	terminative
TMP	temporal
TOP	topic particle
TR	transitive
VBZ	verbalization
VOC	vocative
VOL	volitional
VP	verb phrase

Part I

Overview

1

Introduction

Yoko Hasegawa

1 Overview

Designed to serve as a concise reference book for researchers interested in the Japanese language and/or in typological studies of language in general, *The Cambridge Handbook of Japanese Linguistics* explores diverse characteristics of Japanese that are particularly intriguing when compared with English and other European languages. It consists of five thematic parts: (i) overview (Chapters 1 –6), (ii) sound system and lexicon (Chapters 7–11), (iii) grammatical foundation (Chapters 12–18), (iv) grammatical constructions (Chapters 19–24), and (v) pragmatics/sociolinguistics topics (Chapters 25–29). In the hope of stimulating readers to participate in and carry on these dialogs, many chapters survey critical discussions arising in Japanese linguistics. This preliminary chapter introduces subsequent chapters as well as providing background information, knowledge of which is often taken for granted.

Japanese is the native language of virtually all Japanese nationals, over 127 million as of 2015,[1] the ninth largest native-speaker population among the world's languages.[2] As of 2015, approximately 192,000 non-native speakers residing in Japan were studying Japanese as a foreign language;[3] overseas, approximately 3.65 million in 137 countries studied the language in 2015.[4]

Japanese is a "rigid" SOV language (Greenberg 1963: 79). It is also commonly classified as an *agglutinative language* because units of

All contributors to this *Handbook* gratefully acknowledge Professor John H. Haig for his meticulous proofreading of our manuscripts and invaluable advice regarding both content and style. This project was supported in part by grants from the University of California, Berkeley Academic Senate and the Center for Japanese Studies.

[1] The Statistics Bureau of Japan: www.stat.go.jp/data/kokusei/2015/kekka/pdf/youyaku.pdf.

[2] The SIL Ethnologue: www.ethnologue.com/statistics/size.

[3] The Agency for Cultural Affairs: www.bunka.go.jp/tokei_hakusho_shuppan/tokeichosa/nihongokyoiku_jittai/h27/pdf/h27_zenbun.pdf (p. 5).

[4] The Japan Foundation: www.jpf.go.jp/j/about/press/2016/dl/2016–057-1.pdf.

meaning are "glued" on one after another, as exemplified in (1). (Abbreviations appearing in the glosses are listed at the beginning of this *Handbook.*)

(1) *kotae-* *sase-* *rare-* *taku-* *na-* *katta-* *ra* ...
answer CAUS PASS DES NEG PST COND
'if (you) don't want to be made to answer...'

Kotae- is the root of the verb *kotaeru* 'to answer'; *sase-* is the causative auxiliary; *rare-* is the passive auxiliary; *taku-* is the adverbial form of the desiderative auxiliary *-tai* 'want to do ~'; *na-* is the root of the negative auxiliary *nai* 'not'; *-katta* can be considered as the past tense marker; *-ra* is a conditional connective particle. Kaoru Horie's Chapter 4, "Linguistic Typology and the Japanese Language," elaborates on a typological profile of Japanese regarding its structural and functional-cognitive characteristics. Specifically it analyzes two typologically noteworthy linguistic phenomena (one grammatical and the other lexico-grammatical) which highlight the interpretive flexibility of grammatical constructions and the innovative creativity of borrowing phenomena in Japanese.

Although SOV is undeniably canonical, the word order in Japanese is remarkably flexible. Mitsuaki Shimojo's Chapter 18, "Word Order and Extraction: A Functional Approach," demonstrates that the actual order is determined according to the information structure of the utterance, especially that which pertains to focused elements.

It is fortunate that Japanese has been recorded since the eighth century CE, which enables us to fathom its diachronic development and synchronic variations. A succinct account of the history of the Japanese language is provided by Bjarke Frellesvig in Chapter 2, "The History of the Language," and Michinori Shimoji's Chapter 5 "Dialects" takes up divergent variations of contemporary Japanese. Readers are likely to be inspired to broaden their perspectives on Japanese linguistics by the information supplied in these chapters.

A brief explanation of the notion of "Standard Japanese" is pertinent here. After two hundred years of isolation, Japan opened its doors to the West in the mid-nineteenth century, in the midst of the predatory colonial period when many Asian countries had been colonized. In order to preserve independence, the most pressing matters for the government were industrialization of the nation and strengthening of the military as rapidly as possible. When people from all over Japan were recruited to work for factories, the military, and the government, communication problems occurred because many, possibly most, of those recruits spoke mutually unintelligible dialects.

A movement to establish *hyōjungo* 'Standard Japanese' commenced. However, due to the presence of the great number of dialects, achieving a consensus about which dialect should serve as the basis of standardization was a formidable problem. Eventually, it was decided that *hyōjungo* would be a refined variation of the dialect spoken by intellectual Tokyoites (Ueda 1895).

The government aggressively enforced use of the standard as part of the newly established compulsory education, whereby dialects were viewed as social evils. This biased view made many dialect speakers feel inferior (Shibata 1958: 90–139). Nevertheless, most people did not actually have opportunities to hear how intellectual Tokyoites spoke, so *hyōjungo* was considered by them as a kind of written language detached from daily life. However, 1925 brought the beginning of national radio broadcasting, and announcers were trained to speak only in *hyōjungo*, thus accelerating the spread of *hyōjungo* as a spoken language.

After World War II, the term *kyōtsūgo* 'common Japanese' gained popularity in order to remedy the negative impact of the authoritarian enforcement of *hyōjungo*. Today, the term *hyōjungo* is rarely used in mass communication for political correctness, although younger generations do not suffer from this dark history surrounding *hyōjungo* and tend to use the term without reservation.

2 Sound System

Organization of Japanese phonology is fairly simple. Nevertheless, it is an indispensable stock language in phonology courses for illustrating the concept of mora (vis-à-vis syllable). This is the theme of Timothy Vance's Chapter 7, "Moras and syllables." It also addresses the important issue of whether Japanese has diphthongs. Haruo Kubozono in Chapter 8, "Pitch Accent," discusses another frequently addressed phonological topic. Japanese is known for its diverse pitch accent systems found in regional dialects. Kubozono describes and analyzes this diversity with Tokyo Japanese as a reference point. Unlike English, in which suprasegmental prominence is distinguished by pitch, duration, amplitude, and articulatory precision, only pitch is critical in the Japanese accentual systems. This leads to an interesting issue concerning the interaction between pitch accent and intonation – the topic of Yosuke Igarashi's Chapter 9, "Intonation" – both of which are manifested by manipulation of the voice fundamental frequency.

3 Writing System

Compared with its plain phonology, the Japanese writing system is astonishingly complicated, as epitomized by Sampson (1985: 173): "One reason why Japanese script deserves its place in this [Sampson's] book is as an illustration of just how cumbersome a script can be and still serve in practice." As concisely described by Florian Coulmas's Chapter 6,

"Writing and Literacy in Modern Japan," this notoriety is ultimately due to the fact that Japanese writing evolved from that of Chinese, a language with substantially different sound and word formation systems.

Another consideration at this point is romanization. Two schemes (and their variations) are concurrently in use when representing Japanese in the Roman alphabet: the *Hepburn system*, invented by the American missionary James Curtis Hepburn (1815–1911), based on English writing conventions, and the *Kunreishiki* 'Cabinet Ordinance System.' The former is widely employed for general purposes, while the latter is selected almost exclusively by linguists, *sans* researchers in pragmatics, because of its systematicity (cf. Hasegawa 2015: ch. 4). They are similar, and yet, they differ in a crucial way, as shown in (2).[5]

(2)

	Hepburn	*Kunreishiki*
[ɕ]	*sha, shi, shu, sho*	*sya, si, syu, syo*
[t͡ɕ]	*cha, chi, chu, cho*	*tya, ti, tyu, tyo*
[t͡sɯ]	*tsu*	*tu*
[d͡ʑ]	*ja, ji, ju, jo*	*zya, zi, zyu, zyo*
[ɸɯ]	*fu*	*hu*

This *Handbook* utilizes the modified Hepburn system, except Chapter 7, "Moras and Syllables." Long vowels are designated by the use of macron (ā, ī, ū, ē, ō), except for well-known proper nouns used in an English context; for example, *Tokyo, Osaka*. Chapter 2, "The History of the Language," Chapter 7, and Chapter 8, "Pitch Accent," use duplication of vowels (aa, ii, uu, ee, oo) for expository purposes.

4 Lexicon

In lexical categorization schemes, the following are commonly recognized: nouns, verbs, adjectives (and adjectival nouns), adverbs, particles, interjections, conjunctions, and mimetics. Some noteworthy characteristics are described below.

4.1 Nouns

There is no grammatical distinction between singular and plural in Japanese. The so-called *verbal noun* can co-occur with the verb *suru* 'do' to form a verb – for example, *ito* 'an aim' + *suru* 'to aim,' *meiwaku* 'annoyance' + *suru* 'to be troubled.' While this formation permits some flexibility as to which nouns can participate in it, and innovative combinations can occasionally be observed, not all semantically plausible nouns can function as verbal nouns. For example, *mokuhyō* 'an aim' cannot co-occur with *suru* to mean 'to aim' nor can *giwaku* 'suspicion' co-occur with *suru* to mean 'to

[5] [ɕ] (voiceless alveolo-palatal fricative); [t͡ɕ] (voiceless alveolo-palatal affricate); [t͡sɯ] (voiceless alveolar affricate); [d͡ʑ] (voiced alveolo-palatal affricate); [ɸ] (voiceless bilabial fricative); [ɯ] (close back unrounded vowel).

suspect.' English, by contrast, is highly adaptable in this respect; many, if not most, nouns can be used as verbs – for example, *to pen this comment, Let's seafood.* Foreign loanwords can be used as verbal nouns, as exemplified in (3).

(3) *kyanseru suru* 'to cancel,' *rikabā suru* 'to recover,' *sabaibu suru* 'to survive'

4.2 Verbs

With two exceptions (*kuru* 'come' and *suru* 'do'), Japanese verb stems end either in a consonant (e.g. *tor-* 'take') or in the vowel /i/ or /e/ (e.g. *mi-* 'see,' *tabe-* 'eat'). The suffix for consonant-ending stems to make the *shūshikei* 'conclusive form' (which appears in dictionaries as entry labels and serves as the default non-past tense marker) is *-u*; thus, in teaching Japanese as a foreign language (TJFL), they are called *u-verbs*. For vowel-ending stems, the suffix is *-ru*, and they are called *ru-verbs*.[6] According to Kokuritsu Kokugo Kenkyūjo (1964: 64), approximately 63% of verbs are *u*-verbs, 32% are *ru*-verbs, and the remaining 5% includes variations and compounds of the two irregular verbs.

The following forms are commonly recognized in TJFL (cf. Hasegawa 2015: ch. 6):

(4)
a. Negative — *tor-ana-* — 'not take'
b. Adverbial — *tor-i* — 'taking'
c. Conclusive — *tor-u* — 'take'
d. Hypothetical — *tor-eba* — 'if (someone) takes'
e. Imperative — *tor-e* — 'Take (it)!'
f. Volitional — *tor-ō* — 'I shall take (it), let's take (it)'
g. *Te*-form — *tot-te* — 'taking'
h. *Ta*-form — *tot-ta* — 'took'
i. Causative — *tor-ase-* — 'make (someone) take'
j. Passive — *tor-are-* — 'be taken'

In the traditional grammar taught at schools in Japan, only the following conjugations are recognized:

(5)
a. *Mizen* — 'irrealis' — *tor-a-*
b. *Ren'yō* — 'adverbial' — *tor-i*
c. *Shūshi* — 'conclusive'[7] — *tor-u*
d. *Rentai* — 'attributive' — *tor-u*
e. *Katei* — 'hypothetical' — *tor-e-*
f. *Meirei* — 'imperative' — *tor-e*

Forms listed in (4), but not in (5), are considered to be derived from (5). For example, the volitional form is derived from the irrealis form plus the

[6] In traditional Japanese grammars, *u*-verbs are called *go-dan katsuyō* 'five-tier conjugation' verbs, whereas *i*-ending *ru*-verbs are called *kami-ichi-dan katsuyō* 'upper one-tier conjugation,' and *e*-ending *ru*-verbs *shimo-ichi-dan katsuyō* 'lower-one-tier conjugation' verbs.

[7] The conclusive and attributive forms were distinct in classical Japanese, but in Modern Japanese, they are identical, except for the copula: *da* (conclusive) versus *na* (attributive). This issue is discussed in Chapter 2, Section 4.1; Chapter 4, Section 3.1; Chapter 19, Section 1; and Chapter 20, Section 2.

auxiliary suffix *-u* (i.e. *tor-a-u* > *torō*) by euphony, and the *te*-form from the adverbial form plus the conjunctive particle *-te* also by euphony (*tor-i-te* > *totte*). The verbal negative form (for clausal negation) is derived from the irrealis form plus the negative auxiliary. Unlike English *not*, clausal negation in Japanese is not expressed by a negative adverb but by auxiliaries. As discussed by Hideki Kishimoto in Chapter 14, "Negation," it exhibits various morphosyntactic constraints.

Although it is usually taught in TJFL that the *ta*-form indicates the past tense, and the conclusive form the non-past tense, whether or not Japanese has tense markers comparable with those in European languages has been highly controversial. In Chapter 15, "Tense and Aspect," Wesley Jacobsen shows how this controversy is rooted in the close interrelationship that exists between the order that events have in time with respect to other events, called tense, and the structure that events describe as they unfold in time, called aspect. While both kinds of meaning are present in most temporal forms in Japanese, a careful analysis of their use allows us to identify the existence of both markers of tense and markers of aspect in Japanese.

There is also a group of words that are collectively referred to as the *copula*. Among several variations, the most common forms are *da* (plain non-past) and *datta* (plain past), while its polite counterparts are *desu* (non-past) and *deshita* (past), with no singular–plural distinction.

4.3 Adjectives

Japanese has two kinds of adjectives. *I*-adjectives (so called because its non-past form ends in *-i*) are native Japanese adjectives that cover semantically primary vocabulary, as in (6):

(6)	*akaru-i*	'bright'	*kura-i*	'dark'
	hiro-i	'spacious'	*sema-i*	'small (space)'
	omo-i	'heavy'	*karu-i*	'light'
	taka-i	'high'	*hiku-i*	'low'

Unlike English adjectives, they do not need copula-support, that is, they can stand by themselves as a predicate (e.g. (7a)), and, like verbs, they conjugate (e.g. (7b–c)):

(7) a. *Kono heya wa akaru-i.*
this room TOP bright-NPST
'This room is bright.'

b. *Kono heya wa akaru-k-atta.* (*ku-atta* > *katta*)
bright-ADV-PST
'This room was (once) bright.'

c. *Kono heya wa akaru-ku-te hiro-i.*
bright-ADV-CONJ spacious-NPST
'This room is bright and spacious.'

The second type is called *na*-adjectives (e.g. (8)), because they require the attributive form of the copula (*na*) when they modify an NP, as in (9a). When used predicatively, they need the conclusive form of the copula (*da/desu*), as in (9b).

(8) *benri* 'convenient,' *kōka* 'expensive,' *zenryō* 'law-abiding'

(9) a. *benri na kuruma* 'convenient car,' *kōka na hon* 'expensive book,' *zenryō na shimin* 'law-abiding citizen'

b.

Kono	*hon*	*wa*	*kōka*	*da.*
this	book	TOP	expensive	COP.NPST

'This book is expensive.'

Semantically appropriate foreign words can be treated as *na*-adjectives, as in (10):

(10) *janbo na takarakuji* 'jumbo lotto,' *risukī na torihiki* 'risky deal,' *rūzu na hito* 'loose person'

4.4 Postpositional Particles

Japanese has four groups of particles (i.e. dependent formatives that are invariant in form and do not belong to such main classes of lexemes as nouns, verbs, adjectives, and adverbs); viz. *case, adverbial, conjunctive*, and *sentence-final*. Case particles comprise nominative, accusative, and dative, which designate grammatical relationships between the predicate and the nominal constituent that they accompany. Wataru Nakamura's Chapter 12, "Case," discusses the complexity of the Japanese case-marking system. He provides a historical overview of the generative accounts of the nominative, accusative, and dative particles and suggests a functional alternative.

Adverbial particles also indicate relationships between the NP and the predicate but do not specify case – for example, *wa* (topic marker), *mo* 'also,' *dake* 'only,' *sae* 'even.' Chapter 13, "Subjects and Topics," by Yoko Hasegawa explores the uses of the particles *ga* and *wa*, both of which can mark grammatical subjects.

Conjunctive particles join phrases or clauses – for example, *ga* 'and/but,' *kara/node* 'because,' *keredo/noni* 'although,' *nagara* 'while,' *shi* 'and.' Those pertaining to conditionality (e.g. *ba, nara, (ta)ra, to*) are discussed by Seiko Fujii in her Chapter 24, "Conditionals."

Sentence-final particles, some of which can also occur sentence-medially, play a particularly important role in spoken Japanese. Maynard (1997: 88) reports that in her 60-minute conversation data, sentence-final particles occurred approximately once in every 2.5 phrase-final positions (about 40.0% of the utterances). Emi Morita explores this topic in Chapter 25, "Sentence-final Particles."

4.5 Mimetics

One of the defining characteristics of human language is its arbitrariness. That is, there is no logical or natural relationship between the word and its meaning. However, some vocabulary in human languages is not so arbitrary. Albeit vaguely and sometimes synesthetically,[8] we can intuitively perceive some correspondences between sound and meaning. Words created as a result of such experience are called *mimetics* (sound-symbolic words). Japanese is well known for its rich inventory of mimetics, as illustrated in (11):

(11) a. Auditory
kokekokkō 'cock-a-doodle-doo' *wanwan* 'bow-wow'
b. Visual
meramera 'flare up' *pikapika* 'glitter'
c. Glossal (taste)
kotteri 'rich/heavy' *sakusaku* 'crisp'
d. Tactile (touching)
nebaneba 'sticky' *subesube* 'smooth'

This is the topic of Kiyoko Toratani's Chapter 10, "Semantics and Morphosyntax of Mimetics."

4.6 Predication

Taro Kageyama's Chapter 11, "Events and Properties in Morphology and Syntax," has a unique place in this *Handbook*, for its ultimate interest is form–meaning mismatch. Arguing for the significance of the distinction between event and property predication that underlies linguistic phenomena that challenge theories concerning the interface of morphology, syntax, semantics, and possibly pragmatics, Kageyama scrutinizes two issues: (i) agent compounding, which is claimed to be prohibited universally, **student-writing of a letter*, and (ii) *suru* 'do' when it appears in a description of physical attributes – for example, *Naomi wa aoi me o shite iru* 'Lit. Naomi is doing blue eyes,' that is, 'Naomi has blue eyes.'

5 Subjectivity

In the Japanese linguistic tradition, sentences are commonly analyzed in terms of a layered structure that locates propositional content at the core, subjective elements surrounding it, and intersubjective expressions in the

[8] Synesthesia is a condition in which one type of sensation (e.g. sound) evokes sensation of different modality (e.g. color).

outermost layer. Chapter 3, "Layered Structure, Positional Shifts, and Grammaticalization" by Rumiko Shinzato, accounts for this structural organization with reference to Western diachronic studies of grammaticalization. It is demonstrated that semantically heavy, contentful constituents are likely to move to the left periphery, while semantically light lexemes tend to move to the right periphery.

In the same tradition, *modality*, the topic of Heiko Narrog's Chapter 16, is often understood in terms of subjective elements. In this case, *modality* can include a wide variety of categories, such as topic and focus marking, tense, politeness, sentence moods, illocutionary marking, and evaluative adverbs. Narrog argues that it is best instead to define modality in terms of factuality, with expressions of possibility and necessity at the core. Subcategorizing such expressions, Narrog teases out this often intangible concept of modality.

Yukio Hirose also examines subjectivity in Chapter 17, "Logophoricity, Viewpoint, and Reflexivity." He analyzes the reflexive pronoun *jibun* 'self' from a cognitive-semantic perspective and argues that it has three related but distinct uses (viz. logophoric, viewpoint, and reflexive). He discusses the kind of self encoded in each use and its characteristics in relation to other subjectivity-related phenomena in Japanese.

6 Grammatical Constructions

Part IV of the *Handbook* consists of six chapters. It begins with Masayoshi Shibatani's Chapter 19, which navigates the labyrinth of "Nominalization." He argues that the products of nominalization are like nouns by virtue of their *metonymic* association with denotations and referents, for example, *tachi* 'standing' + *nomi* 'drinking' → 'establishments that let customers drink while standing.' He criticizes the tendency to concentrate on lexical nominalizations and neglect grammatical nominalizations, despite the latter's theoretical importance.

Yoshiko Matsumoto explores another highly complex phenomenon in her Chapter 20, "Clausal Noun Modification," where she demonstrates that Japanese provides only one construction (involving a head noun and its modifying clause) that corresponds to several different constructions in English; for example, relative, noun complement, infinitival (*things to do*), gerundive (*the result of practicing everyday*), and participial (*burnt toast*) clauses.

Japanese is equipped with an uncommon construction, which is the topic of Kyoko Hirose Ohara's Chapter 21, "Internally Headed Relativization and Related Constructions." Example (12) is adapted from Furui Yoshikichi's *Seto no saki* 'beyond Seto.'

(12) *Sono yoku-yoku-nen no aki ni, [hahaoya ga machi*
that next-next-year GEN autumn in mother NOM town

no byōin no shujutsu.shitsu kara nakanaka dete.ko-nai
GEN hospital GEN operating.room from considerably come.out-not

no] o sue no musuko wa ikameshige.na ki no tobira
? ACC end GEN son TOP daunting wood GEN door

no mae de matte.ita.
GEN front at was.waiting

Lit. 'Two years later, in autumn, the youngest son was waiting outside the daunting wooden door for [his mother was in the operating room at the town hospital for quite some time].'

Here, the main clause asserts that the youngest son was waiting for his mother, who did not emerge from the operating room for a long time. The direct object of *wait* (i.e. the head noun) is apparent semantically; however, it appears inside the relative clause with no syntactic identification. Hence the term "internally headed relativization." This is a widely accepted analysis of this type of sentence. Nonetheless, a quite different perspective is proposed by Shibatani in Chapter 19, Section 4.2.1.

One of the salient differences between Japanese and English language use occurs in expressions pertaining to one's subjective evaluation of a described event. Such expressions are sometimes mandatory in Japanese, but never in English. For example, (13a) sounds indifferent, and, therefore, can potentially be regarded as inappropriate. Its English translation, on the other hand, exhibits no negative qualities.

(13) a. *Chichi wa watashi ni kuruma o katta.*
father TOP I DAT car ACC bought
'My father bought me a car.'

If the speaker is grateful for her father's buying a car for her, it is idiomatic to add the auxiliary verb *kureru* 'give' to express this feeling of gratefulness.

b. *Chichi wa watashi ni kuruma o kat-te kureta.*
father TOP I DAT car ACC buy-CONJ gave
Lit. 'My father gave me a favor of buying a car.'

Because this type of construction describes actions or events from which someone receives benefit, it is called a *benefactive (construction)*. Nobuko Hasegawa's Chapter 22, "Benefactives," inspects their structural aspects and addresses the question as to the possibility of representing the speaker's empathy or point of view in syntax.

Discussions of Japanese passive constructions are frequently heard in linguistics classrooms because they differ conspicuously from their

English counterparts. Most notoriously, many find bewildering passives with intransitive verbs, for example, *shinu* 'die' (I was died by my father?!). In Chapter 23, "Passives," Shoichi Iwasaki lays out peculiarities of Japanese passive constructions from structural, functional, and discourse perspectives and scrutinizes the concept of "adversity" frequently associated with them.

The "Grammatical Constructions" section concludes with Seiko Fujii's Chapter 24, "Conditionals." She investigates multifaceted families of Japanese conditionals (in both form and meaning) as well as neighboring semantic domains (temporals, causals, and concessives). The chapter also discusses the use of Japanese conditionals as discourse markers.

7 Pragmatics

Japanese is one of the most extensively studied languages in the field of pragmatics. This *Handbook* devotes the five final chapters to its essential topics. These chapters all convincingly demonstrate the methodical importance of scrutinizing how given expressions are used in actual, naturalistic settings.

As mentioned earlier, sentence-final particles (SFPs) are ubiquitous and are an indispensable part of spoken Japanese, and yet they defy precise characterizations. Emi Morita describes in Chapter 25, "Sentence-final Particles," the complexity of their uses and proposes a future research direction: only a detailed analysis of actual interactional context, she argues, will enable us to understand how meanings of SFPs are derived, and ultimately how SFPs verbally structure Japanese social interactions.

The most extensively studied aspect of Japanese pragmatics is arguably *politeness*, that is, display of respect and consideration for the feelings of interlocutors. Because Japanese furnishes "fossilized" politeness expressions (*honorifics*), making politeness research is tremendously complex. Michael Haugh's Chapter 26, "Linguistic Politeness," provides a comprehensive account of Japanese politeness research in various academic traditions. He suggests that, although the study of honorifics has an important role to play in politeness research, Japanese linguists can also contribute to politeness research through analyzing both the (meta)language that underpins different conceptualizations of politeness in Japanese and the role that the specific linguistic composition of turns at talk play in the interactional accomplishment of politeness.

The intricacy of Japanese linguistic politeness is also manifested in speech style shifts between addressee honorifics (the *desu/masu* style) and their non-honorific counterparts (the plain style) even during a single span of conversation, in which the interlocutors' social relationships can hardly be altered. Haruko Minegishi Cook accounts for this perplexing phenomenon in her Chapter 27, "Speech Style Shift."

Researchers in pragmatics commonly utilize concepts and techniques developed in discourse analysis and/or conversation analysis. In Chapter 28, "Discourse/Conversation Analysis," Polly Szatrowski surveys outcomes since the 1970s related to discourse/conversation units, devices, strategies, utterance functions and discourse structure, sequential organization, and multimodality (gaze and body movements). Recurring themes include ellipsis/zero anaphora, aizuchi 'back channel,' turn-taking, postposing, and co-construction.

In the final chapter of the *Handbook*, Chapter 29, "Language, Gender, and Sexuality," Shigeko Okamoto reviews previous research, addressing the questions of how linguistic gender norms have been constructed and how men and women negotiate such norms and choose linguistic forms in specific social contexts. She emphasizes the multiplicity and variability of meanings of linguistic forms in situated practice.

2

The History of the Language

Bjarke Frellesvig

1 Introduction

Japanese has a written history of just over 1,200 years, going back to the beginning of the eighth century AD, customarily divided into the following periods, which largely coincide with major political periods in Japanese history (showing also the usual Japanese terms):[1]

Old Japanese (OJ; 上代語) 700–800	Nara, 712–784
Early Middle Japanese (EMJ; 中古語) 800–1200	Heian, 794–1185
Late Middle Japanese (LMJ; 中世語) 1200–1600	Kamakura, 1185–1333
	Muromachi, 1336–1573
Modern Japanese (NJ; 近世語, 現代語) 1600–	Edo/Tokugawa, 1603–1868, etc.

The OJ, EMJ, and LMJ reflected in the written record is the language of the Kansai area, particularly of the capitals of Nara and Kyoto. Present-day Japanese is "cNJ" ("contemporary" NJ), and in this chapter I assume that readers have some knowledge of Standard (or common) cNJ. Standard cNJ was established and codified in the course of a concerted language policy effort as a linguistic norm in the early twentieth century, mainly based on the language of the educated middle and upper classes of Tokyo (which had been set up as the de facto capital from the beginning of the Edo period and which, under its new name "Tokyo," became the constitutional capital with the Meiji Restoration) as an emblem of the emerging Japanese nation state and as a vehicle for efficient nationwide education (and conscription).[2] This

I am grateful to the National Institute for Japanese Language and Linguistics (NINJAL) for hosting me over summer 2016 when the bulk of this chapter was written. This chapter forms part of the NINJAL research project "Construction of Diachronic Corpora and New Developments in Research on the History of Japanese."

[1] In the past, other terms have been used (e.g. "Ancient Japanese" for OJ (Syromiatnikov 1981) or "Late OJ" for EMJ (Miller 1967), but the terms used here are now the standard English terms. "NJ" ("new" Japanese) is used for Modern Japanese in order to avoid confusion with MJ, "middle" Japanese. Some people prefer to abbreviate Modern Japanese as "ModJ" rather than "NJ."

[2] The spread and enforcement in educational and other official and public settings of Standard Japanese was pursued aggressively and oppressively by the state – to the detriment of other varieties of Japanese – and today the word *hyōjungo* 'standard language' has negative and nationalistic connotations for many, especially older, Japanese people.

took place together with vernacularization of the written language (cf. Chapter 6, this volume), which until the end of the nineteenth century mainly had been a form of "Classical Japanese," a loose written norm which had fossilized from around 1100 onwards.

Examples (1) and (2) are of premodern Japanese: (1) is a poem from OJ from the poetry anthology *Man'yōshū* ("MYS"), and (2) is the beginning of one of the fables of Aesop, translated into Japanese and published by the Jesuit press in 1593 under the name *Esopo no fabulas*, that is to say, a text from the very end of LMJ.

(1) *Maturagapa kapa no se pikari ayu turu*
Matsuragawa river GEN rapids shine.INF sweetfish fish.CNCL

to tata-s-eru imo ga mo no suswo
PURP stand-RESP-STAT.ADN young.girl GEN skirt GEN hem

nure-nu.
become.wet-PERF.CNCL

'The rapids of the Matsuragawa shine, and the hems of the skirts of the young girls who are standing there in order to fish sweetfish will get drenched.'

(MYS 5.855)

(2) *ookame ip-piki aru fi emono ga nɔɔte u'e ni*
wolf one-CL some day food NOM not.exist.GER up DAT

oyoode, koko-kasiko o kake-meguri, aru yama-zato
reach.GER here-there ACC walk-go.around.INF some mountain-village

no sidu ga i'ori no nokiba ni yori-soote
GEN lowly.person GEN hut GEN eaves DAT approach-be.close.to.GER

kikeba,
hear.PROV

tiisa-i ko no naku o sukasu tote, sono
small-NPST child GEN cry.NPST ACC calm.down.NPST PURP his

fawa "kama'ete nakaba, ookame ni yarɔɔzu" to yuu
mother really! cry.COND wolf DAT give.INT COMP say.NPST

niyotte ookame kore o kiki, makoto ka to omoote,
because wolf this ACC hear.INF true Q COMP think.GER

"appare kore wa yo-i siawase ka na" to
wow this TOP good-NPST fortune Q SFP COMP
exist.PROV day

matikakete ireba, fi mo yɔɔyɔɔ kure-yuita.
wait.expectantly.GER exist.PROV day also gradually grow.dark-go.PST

'One day a wolf came up [out of the woods] as there was no food, and he went about here and there; as he went up close to the eaves of the hut of a lowly person in a mountain village and listened, a mother said, in order to calm down her child who was crying: "if you must cry [if you don't stop crying] I will give you to the wolf," and therefore the wolf heard that. As he was waiting expectantly, believing it was true [and thinking] "wow, this is really good fortune," the day gradually grew dark.'

Comparing (1) with cNJ, it is easy to see that the language since OJ has changed appreciably, if by no means dramatically, in both phonology and grammar.

Now, comparing (2) with cNJ tells us two things. First, we see that Japanese has not changed very much since the end of the LMJ period: Differences between the language in (2) and cNJ are limited to a few phonological differences and minor differences in some verb morphology and syntax (such as nominalization without *no* (here in an internally headed relative clause *tiisai ko no naku o*), cf. Chapters 19 and 21, this volume). Second, we understand that there is direct continuity between LMJ and Standard cNJ, despite the apparent geographical discontinuity: The language of (2) is explicitly the language of Kyoto at the end of the sixteenth century, and it does not display any major dialectal differences from cNJ, apart from a little variation in verbal gerund and past tense and adjectival gerund forms. This substantiates that the educated upper and middle classes of Tokyo of the late nineteenth century spoke a variety of Japanese which was a continuation of the educated common language used by the upper and administrative classes in Kyoto, which is the language in *Esopo*. Thus, we find no significant break in tradition between the language reflected in premodern sources and the current common/standard language, despite the fact that the capital was moved from Kyoto to Tokyo; bearers of the variety which became the basis for Standard cNJ moved with the capital.

In this chapter I describe the main changes that Japanese has undergone from its written beginnings until its present-day shape.[3] I focus on structural, internally motivated changes in phonology (Section 3) and grammar (Section 4), with a short section on contact-induced change (from Chinese and from European languages, Section 5). I do not address the cognation of Japanese to other languages or its reconstructed pre-history (see, e.g., Frellesvig and Whitman 2008 about this). First of all, Section 2 gives a brief overview over writing and sources.

2 Writing and Sources[4]

The sources for OJ are primarily from the eighth century AD. There are a few epigraphical materials on stone and metal from the eighth century and earlier; in addition, a large amount of wooden slips with writing on them (*mokkan* 木簡) from the seventh and eighth century have been excavated over the past half century, valuable mainly for the study of the history of writing. The great majority of sources, however, are texts which have been handed down in

[3] Frellesvig 2010 provides both more detail and further references. In this chapter I will generally not reference information or analyses which may be found in Frellesvig 2010, but only provide references where the exposition therein is insufficient or wrong. Other analyses or perspectives on Japanese language history may be found in, for example, Martin 1987, Seeley 1991, Takeuchi 1999, Tranter 2012, Vovin 2003, 2005–2009.

[4] The OJ texts are available online through the Oxford Corpus of Old Japanese (OCOJ): http://vsarpj.orinst.ox.ac.uk/corpus/. The main texts from EMJ and increasingly also texts from LMJ are being made available online through the Corpus of Historical Japanese (CHJ) published by the National Institute of Japanese Language and Linguistics, Tokyo: http://pj.ninjal.ac.jp/corpus_center/chj/overview-en.html.

copies from later periods. Some texts were compiled in the eighth century from older, since lost, texts or from oral tradition, with the earliest texts represented thought to date from the late fifth century. A small proportion of text reflects Eastern OJ dialect features, but overall the language represented is that of the central region of the capital Nara.

Japan has no indigenous script and all OJ texts are written in Chinese characters (*kanji*), adapted to be used in principle in two ways: *logographically* (to represent words or morphemes) and *phonographically* (to represent sound, specifically syllables). Phonographically used *kanji* are called *man'yōgana* '*man'yō* letters' after the poetry anthology *Man'yōshū* (万葉集 'Collection of Myriad Leaves,' compiled sometime after 759), which consists of around 4,500 poems (approximately 90,000 words) spanning three centuries but with a large proportion of text from the eighth century. In practice, OJ writing is very varied, with some texts written exclusively phonographically and some logographically, but most in a mixture of logographic and phonographic writing, and with many examples of playful or deliberately complex writing. Much of logographically written text is open to some interpretation, and some of it can only be read for sense in a general way.

The EMJ period saw the development of the *kana* script still in use today, which arose through graphic simplification of the *man'yōgana* –for example, 安 > あ and 阿 > ア – eventually with codification of two distinct fonts (or types) *hiragana* and *katakana*. The *kana* letters provided a straightforward direct phonographic representation of the language,[5] and the development of the *kana* letters accompanied a surge in writing in Japanese. We have a much greater volume of text from EMJ than from OJ, both poetry and a large body of important and well-known literature written almost exclusively in *kana*, including the *Genji monogatari* 'The tale of *Genji*' and the *Makura no Sōshi* 'The pillow book,' both from around 1000 AD produced at the court in the capital (which in 794 had moved to Kyoto). Other writing used a mix of *kana* and logographically used *kanji*, including warrior tales such as the *Heike monogatari* 'The tale of the *Heike*' and didactic tales such as the *Konjaku monogatarishū* 'Collection of tales now past.' Thus, until near the end of the EMJ period we have a large volume of material which provides a fairly close record of the contemporary language of the court and the educated classes.

Toward the end of the EMJ period, the written language starts fossilizing and a loosely normative "classical Japanese" language emerges which remained the main medium of writing in Japanese until the end of the nineteenth century, and during that long period contemporary spoken language features are in most texts reflected only sporadically and incidentally. This makes it difficult to trace in detail many of the grammatical changes which took place through the LMJ period. However, we have

[5] With the exception that the *kana* letters, as opposed to the *man'yōgana*, did not represent the distinction between tense and lax obstruents and, for example, /ka/ and /ga/ were written by the same *kana* letter. It was only from the beginning of the NJ period that the use of diacritics became widespread in general use to represent, for example, /ka/ and /ga/ differently (か and が respectively).

a good-sized valuable body of printed texts, dictionaries, and grammars produced by Portuguese and Spanish missionaries in Japan, dating from the turning point between LMJ and NJ, around 1600. These texts are written in the Latin alphabet and reflect the spoken language of Kyoto, providing an accurate picture of the language at the time.

3 Phonology

OJ had the following phoneme inventory:

(3) Vowels

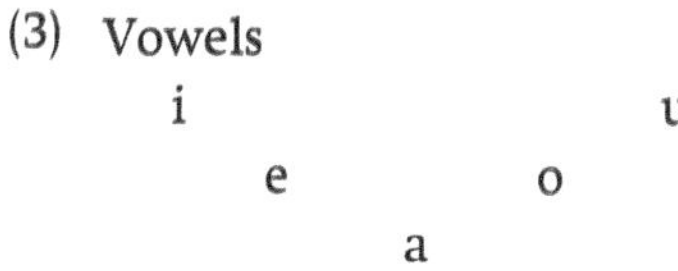

This system of five short vowels has remained unchanged to the present day in most varieties of Japanese, including the main descendants of OJ, EMJ, and LMJ: Kyoto and Tokyo cNJ.

(4) Consonants

Tense	p	t		k	s
Lax	b	d		g	z
Nasal	m	n			
Liquid		r			
Glide	w		y		

The lax obstruents and the liquid, /b, d, g, z, r/, were not used in initial position in lexical words of native wordstock or older assimilated loans. The intake of Sino-Japanese vocabulary (see Section 5.1) overruled this phonotactic restriction, but even today word-initial /b, d, g, z, r/ is largely limited to Sino-Japanese and other borrowed vocabulary, as well as a few native forms which result from sporadic sound change, for example, loss of initial vowel, NJ *das-* 'put out' < OJ *idas-*.

Tense /p, t, k, s/ were distinct from lax /b, d, g, z/. Voicing was not phonemically distinctive, as the tense obstruents were allophonically voiced ([-b-, -d-, -g-, -z-]) intervocalically (this is generally referred to as "medial voicing"). Conversely, lax /b, d, g, z/ were prenasalized ([^{m}b, ^{n}d, ^{ŋ}g, ^{n}z]). Thus /pata/ 'banner' and /pada/ 'skin' were pronounced [pada] and [pa^{n}da], respectively. The prenasalization reflects the diachronically secondary status of the lax obstruents, which derive from pre-OJ contractions of nasal + (tense) obstruent, sometimes following vowel reduction and loss. In some cases, the etymological source is readily recoverable, for example, *yama**d**i* 'mountain path' < *yama* + ***m**i**t**i* 'mountain + path.' The origin of the lax obstruents makes their non-occurrence in word-initial position readily understandable. Sibilant (strident) /s, z/ were distinct from non-sibilant (mellow) /p, t, k, b, d, g/. Both sibilants and non-sibilants exhibited allophonic variation with respect to *continuousness*

Table 2.1 *Old Japanese syllables*

a	ka	ga	sa	za	ta	da	na	pa	ba	ma	ya	ra	wa
i	ki	gi	si	zi	ti	di	ni	pi	bi	mi		ri	wi
	kwi	gwi						pwi	bwi	mwi			
u	ku	gu	su	zu	tu	du	nu	pu	bu	mu	yu	ru	
e	ke	ge	se	ze	te	de	ne	pe	be	me	ye	re	we
	kye	gye						pye	bye	mye			
o	ko	go	so	zo	to	do	no	po	bo	mo	yo	ro	wo
	kwo	gwo	swo	zwo	two	dwo	nwo			mwo	ywo	rwo	

(under conditions that are not entirely clear), such that sibilants had both fricative and affricative variants – for example, /s/ [s, ^{t}s] – and non-sibilants had both stop and fricative variants – for example, /p/ [p, ɸ]. Other important allophonic variation includes palatalization of consonants before /i, e, y/ – for example, /kimi/ '(my) lord' realized as [k$_j$im$_j$i] – and nasalization of vowels before nasals and (prenasalized) lax obstruents – for example, /uma/ 'horse' [ũma].

OJ syllable structure was very simple, with only open syllables and with only few complex syllable onsets (Cy-, Cw-, with restricted distribution). The total number of distinct syllables in early OJ was eighty-eight, as shown in Table 2.1. Vowel-initial syllables were only found in word initial position.

Cye, Cwi, and *Cwo* type syllables were lost and merged with *Ce, Ci*, and *Co* type syllables in the transition to and the early part of the EMJ period and they are not reflected or represented in the EMJ *kana* script. The existence of the *Cye, Cwi*, and *Cwo* type syllables was only finally discovered in the 1910s and at the time they were described and thought about in terms of "extra" syllables in OJ, paired with the syllables they later merged with and labeled in relation to them, see (5). In Japanese these "syllable pairs" are referred to as *kō-rui* (甲類 "type A") and *otsu-rui* (乙類 "type B") syllables.

(5) OJ EMJ

/Cye/	($Ce_{A/1/\text{甲}}$)	/Ce/
/Ce/	($Ce_{B/2/\text{乙}}$)	/Ce/
/Ci/	($Ci_{A/1/\text{甲}}$)	/Ci/
/Cwi/	($Ci_{B/2/\text{乙}}$)	/Ci/
/Cwo/	($Co_{A/1/\text{甲}}$)	/Co/
/Co/	($Co_{B/2/\text{乙}}$)	/Co/

Some transcription systems use diacritics or subscript numbers or letters (e.g. $Ce_{A/1/\text{甲}}$) to distinguish between these syllable types, rather than a phonemic transcription. Until the 1960s it was commonly thought that the differences between these syllable types resided in differences in vowel quality, rather than the presence or absence of a glide. Such descriptions would posit unitary vowel phonemes for /-wi, -ye, -wo/ and talk about an "eight vowel" system in OJ.

3.1 Phonological Changes

From the end of OJ through Early Middle Japanese (EMJ; 800–1200), phonological changes took place, both in syllable structure and in segmental phonology. At the end of EMJ, the phonological structure of Japanese was largely as it is today.

3.1.1 Syllable Structure

A major structural phonological change took place in the transition between OJ and EMJ, namely the introduction of the distinction between metrically *short* (or light) and *long* (or heavy) syllables. This is the main structural sound change to have affected Japanese in its attested history. Thus, EMJ acquired long syllables of the shape CVV and CVC. Through this change Japanese became *quantity sensitive* and the *mora* became a relevant unit in the language, with short CV syllables counting as one mora, but long CVV or CVC syllables counting as two moras (cf. Chapter 7, this volume). The phonemes which occur in the new syllable position, and which therefore contribute extra syllable length (or weight), are mainly the two high vowels /-i, -u/, forming diphthongs or long vowels (/CVi, CVu/), and the two obstruents /-N-, -Q-/ which formed word medial closed syllables. /N/ and /Q/ were mutually distinguished only by nasality and would copy place and manner of articulation features from the immediately following consonant, just like their reflexes /N, Q/ in cNJ. /N/ later came to be found in word final position and before vowels and is in that position usually pronounced as an unreleased, uvular, nasal, sometimes described as an approximant.

The change in syllable structure came about in the main through a set of non-automatic sound changes (known as *onbin* 'euphony'), which took place in the transition between OJ and EMJ, in which a short syllable with a high vowel (/Ci, Cu/) was phonetically reduced and subsequently phonologically reinterpreted as a single segment incorporated into the preceding syllable, for example, (6) which shows EMJ syllable boundaries by a period.

(6)

OJ		EMJ	
/ni**pi**(-)ta/ 'new(-)field' proper name	>	/ni**Q**.ta/ (*nit.ta*)	/ni**u**.ta/
/ka**gu**pasi/ 'fragrant'	>	/ka**N**.ba.si/ (*kan.ba.si*)	/ka**u**.ba.si/
/yo**bi**-te/ 'call-GER'	>	/yo**N**.-de/ (*yon.de*)	/yo**u**.-de/
/yo**mi**-te/ 'read-GER'	>	/yo**N**.-de/ (*yon.de*)	/yo**u**.-de/
/na-**ki**/ 'not.exist-ACOP.ADN'	>		/na-**i**/
/paya-**ku**/ 'fast-ACOP.INF'	>		/pa.ya-**u**/

As shown, in some cases both consonantal and vocalic forms resulted. When the reduced syllable had initial (prenasalized) lax or nasal consonant, a following tense consonant became lax (prenasalized), as in *kagupasi* 'fragrant' > *kan**b**asi, kau**b**asi; yo**b**ite* 'call'> *yon**d**e, you**d**e*; and *yo**m**ite* 'read' > *yon**d**e, you**d**e*. As shown in some of the examples in (6), both verbal inflected forms and forms of the adjectival copula were affected by this set of changes, which therefore also had an impact on morphophonology, in particular resulting in new stem variants for consonant base verbs (e.g. *yob-* 'call' and *yom-* 'write' acquiring *yoN-* and *you-* as derived stems for use with certain suffixes) and also changed forms of the adnominal and infinitive of the adjectival copula.

3.1.2 Segmental Sound Changes

Segmental sound changes through the EMJ and LMJ periods had almost no effect on the inventory of onset consonants, with the exception of the split of /p/ into /p, f/, most likely in early LMJ, and the subsequent change of /f/ to /h/ in NJ, after 1700. However, in the course of EMJ and early LMJ a series of changes involving conditioned loss, change, and split applying to the glides /w, y/ and to /p/ appreciably changed the phonemic shape of a large number of words.

(7) a. Over several centuries, from very late eighth through to the thirteenth century, OJ /w, y/ were lost in many environments: /w/ as lost before /o, i, e/, first in /Cwi, Cwo/ and later in syllable initial position, and /y/ was lost before /e/ first in /Cye/, later in syllable initial position.

b. OJ /p/ lenited: Intervocalic /-p-/ changed to /-w-/ in the tenth century (and was subsequently lost before /u, o, i, e/, cf. immediately above); later, at some point during LMJ, initial /p-/ changed to /f/,[6] which changed to /h/ in NJ, at some point after 1700.

Some examples of changes in phonemic word shapes resulting from these two sets of changes are given in (8), showing the OJ, the current, present-day forms in bold, and the period during which the present-day forms reached their current shape.

(8)

OJ	EMJ	LMJ	NJ
/**kwo.pwi**/ 'love' >	/kwo.pi/ > /ko.pi/ > /ko.wi/ > /**koi**/		
/**winokwo**/ 'boar, pig' >	/winoko/ >	/**inoko**/	
/**wotokwo**/ 'man' >	/wotoko/ > /**otoko**/		
/**mapye**/ 'front' >	/mape/ > /mawe/ > /**mae**/		
/**yeda**/ 'branch' >	/**eda**/		
/**nuye**/ 'thrush' >	/**nue**/		
/**kapo**/ 'face' >	/kawo/ > /**kao**/		
/**kapa**/ 'river' >	/**kawa**/		
/**para**/ 'stomach' >		/fara/ >	/**hara**/

These changes resulted in a different phonotactic distribution of /p, w, y/ such that /w/ only was found before /a/, /y/ only before /a, o, u/,[7] and /p/ only in initial position (later changing to /f/),[8] and they therefore also resulted in

[6] We know from the alphabetic Jesuit materials from around 1600 that /p-/ > /f-/ had taken place by then, as they consistently write "f" for earlier /p/, for example 'stomach' as "fara," but other than that this change is difficult to date as it found no written expression in *kana* writing: はら would write EMJ /para/ and later LMJ /fara/, as it today is used to write /hara/.

[7] While /Cwo/, /Cwi/, and /Cye/ were lost in the course of these changes, adoption of Sino-Japanese loanwords resulted in the introduction of /kwa, gwa/ and /Cya, Cyo, Cyu/ syllables, such that complex syllable onsets were not lost from the language.

[8] Note that /p/ was retained after /Q/ and thus was never completely lost from the language. In cNJ a number of mimetics have initial /p/ (e.g. *pika-pika* 'sparklingly') but it is not entirely clear whether such forms have retained /p/ or whether they are innovations.

a reduction in the number of different short syllables. Conversely, however, they also resulted in an increase in vowel sequences, as intervocalic consonants were lost. Of these, /Vi, Vu/ became metrically long, single syllables within the new syllable structure (e.g. monosyllabic /koi/), whereas /Ve, Vo/ remained disyllabic and were pronounced with an onglide on the second vowel: /ma.e/ [ma^{j}e], /ka.o/ [ka^{w}o]; this feature of pronunciation was only lost in the nineteenth century. During LMJ /Vu/ diphthongs in long syllables (/iu, eu, ou, au/) changed to long vowels (/yuu, yoo, oo, ɔɔ/), which remained metrically long and which therefore usually are interpreted and transcribed as double vowels, as in (9).

(9) OJ		EMJ		LMJ		NJ
/nipita/ 'proper name'	>	/n**iu**ta/	>	/n**yuu**ta/		
/kyepu/ 'today'	>	/kepu/ > /k**eu**/	>	/k**yoo**/		
/kinopu/ 'yesterday'	>	/kinopu/ > /kin**ou**/	>	/kin**oo**/		
/kagupasi/ 'fragrant'	>	/k**au**basi/	>	/kɔɔbasi/	>	/k**oo**basi/

In NJ, /ɔɔ/ changed to and merged with /oo/, but for some time long vowels appear to have had a height distinction between back vowels which was absent among short vowels (with long /ɔɔ/ ≠ /oo/ ≠ /uu/, but only short /o/ ≠ /u/). This is often remarked upon as being a typologically unusual feature of LMJ phonology, but rather than having a typologically anomalous vowel system, it is more likely that LMJ and early NJ /ɔɔ/ also synchronically was a derived realization of underlying //au// (=>/ɔɔ/).

A few further changes took place in NJ. In early NJ, /d, z/ merged as /z/ before /u/ and as /d/ before /i/, that is /du, zu/ > /zu/ and /di, zi/ > /di/, (10), and later, probably in the eighteenth century, NJ /f/ changed to /h/.

(10) OJ		EMJ	NJ
/mi-zu/ 'see-NEG; not seeing'	>		/mizu/
/midu/ 'water'	>		/mizu/
/kizi/ 'pheasant'	>		/kidi/
/kwi-di/ 'Kii road; the road to the Kii province'	>	/kidi/	/kidi/

In addition to phonemic changes, the prominent allophonic realization rules of OJ were lost: medial voicing of tense obstruents was lost at some point during LMJ and prenasalization of lax obstruents was lost in NJ (although both intervocalic voicing and prenasalization are preserved dialectally today). These two interrelated phonetic changes had no visible phonemic consequences, but resulted in a significant change in the phonetic sound texture of Japanese, as illustrated here in the pronunciation of the word /tanabata/ 'Vega, the Weaver,' which has remained phonemically unchanged from OJ into cNJ, but whose pronunciation has changed significantly.

(11)	OJ	NJ
/tanabata/	[tãnã^{m}bada]	[t^{h}anabat^{h}a]

Internal phonemic change has not affected the phoneme inventory of Japanese much, cf. the onset phoneme inventories of OJ/EMJ, LMJ and NJ until around 1850.

(12) OJ and EMJ /p, t, k, b, d, g, s, z, m, n, r, w, y/
LMJ /p, t, k, b, d, g, f, s, z, m, n, r, w, y/
NJ (until mid-nineteenth century NJ) /p, t, k, b, d, g, s, z, h, m, n, r, w, y/

However, since the middle of the nineteenth century sudden, large-scale intake of loanwords from European languages took place, and in the course of the phonological adaptation of the loanwords, a number of new onset phonemes arose, largely through phonemicization of what until then had been allophonic variation. Thus /f/ is now distinct from /h/ (e.g. *fairu* 'file' versus *hairu* 'enter'), and several palatal and affricative sounds have become distinctive, rather than conditioned by a following vowel or palatal glide. Phonemic analyses of these sounds differ, but some posit unitary phonemes such as /ɕ, tɕ, dʑ/ (see further Vance 1987: 17ff.).

4 Grammar

4.1 Verb Morphology

In a segmentational model, the structure of Japanese verb forms may in general be described as follows, for any stage of Japanese, with three main morphemic layers. This is illustrated in Table 2.2 with the verb *sak-* 'come into bloom' (appearing in different stem shapes), for NJ (*saita* '(it) bloomed,' *sakasemashita* '(I) made (it) bloom') and OJ (*saku* '(it) comes into bloom,' *sakyerikyeri* '(it) was blooming').

Flectives express the obligatory, paradigmatically opposed categories of which any verb form must express one and only one, for example, NJ past tense or OJ conclusive. Auxiliaries are bound inflecting suffixes.[9]

Table 2.2 *Three morphemic layers*

	1	2		3
	verb stem-	auxiliary-		flective
NJ	sai-			*ta* PST
	saka-	se- CAUS	mashi- POL	ta PST
OJ	sak-			*u* CNCL
	sak-	yeri- STAT	kyer- MPST	i CNCL

[9] The term "auxiliary" is unfortunate, as these morphemes are not auxiliary verbs by any stretch of the imagination, but it has become common as the English term used for the Japanese *jodōshi* 'helping verb.'

Auxiliaries are optional and express a variety of verbal categories (e.g. NJ causative, polite, OJ stative, modal past tense, see 4.1.1 below). Some auxiliaries can combine, whereas others are mutually exclusive; the last auxiliary in a chain carries the inflection of the whole verb form. Although this basic morphological structure has been the same throughout the attested history of Japanese, the range of obligatory inflectional categories and the inventories of auxiliaries, the categories they express and their combinatory possibilities changed profoundly between OJ and the end of LMJ (and NJ).

4.1.1 Old Japanese and Early Middle Japanese

OJ verbs obligatorily inflect for the following categories.[10] Inflection is mainly for *syntactic, modal,* and *conjunctional* categories (as opposed to LMJ and NJ which inflects for tense and aspect). OJ has eight verbal conjugation classes which fall into two major groups: *consonant* base verbs (approximately 75% of all verbs) and *vowel*-base verbs (approximately 25%), each with a number of subclasses. The inflected forms are here exemplified with verbs from the two main verb classes, regular *sak-* 'come into bloom' and *ake-* 'dawn' and irregular *ar-* 'exist' and *se-* 'do' (both of which have important grammatical functions) (Table 2.3).

The non-finite, or converb, forms conclude non-final, mostly subordinating, clauses. They include a range of specific subordinations (continuative 'while,' conditional 'if,' provisional 'as, when,' concessive 'although'), as

Table 2.3 *OJ verb forms*

Base	sak-	ar-	ake-	se-
Finite				
Conclusive	*saku*	*ari*	*aku*	*su*
Adnominal	*saku*	*aru*	*akuru*	*suru*
Exclamatory	*sake*	*are*	*akure*	*sure*
Imperative	*sakye*	*are*	*ake(yo)*	*se(yo)*
Negative conjectural	*sakazi*	*arazi*	*akezi*	*sezi*
Optative	*sakana(mu)*	*arana(mu)*	*akena(mu)*	*sena(mu)*
Non-finite				
Infinitive	*saki*	*ari*	*ake*	*si*
Gerund	*sakite*	*arite*	*akete*	*site*
Continuative	*sakitutu*	*aritutu*	*aketutu*	*situtu*
Conditional	*sakaba*	*araba*	*akeba*	*seba*
Provisional	*sakeba*	*areba*	*akureba*	*sureba*
Concessive	*sakedo*	*aredo*	*akuredo*	*suredo*
Nominal	*sakaku*	*araku*	*akuraku*	*suraku*

[10] Some readers will be more familiar with the Japanese *katsuyōkei* 'conjugation' system for describing Japanese morphology. While that is one way of describing formation of some inflected forms, it is not a description of inflectional paradigms, such as Table 2.3, and it is completely unsuited for describing and understanding the morphological changes which have taken place in Japanese.

well as two general non-finite forms, infinitive and gerund, which can be both subordinating and coordinating. The infinitive also derived a verbal activity – for example, *kwopwi-* 'to love' => *kwopwi* 'loving' – which could be predicated by *se-* 'to do' and which in some cases were lexicalized as common nouns – for example, *kwopwi* 'love.' The nominal, which was lost as a productive form early in EMJ, expresses abstract nominalizations ('(the fact) that'). Example (13) exemplifies the provisional and the nominal.

(13)	*Aki*	*tukeba*	*momiti*	*tiraku.*
	autumn	arrive.PROV	autumn.leaves	scatter.NMNL

'The scattering of the autumn leaves when autumn comes.'
(MYS 19.4161)

Apart from the nominal form, the system of non-finite forms is not greatly different from NJ, which has more or less the same categories as OJ, although the morphological expression of some of them has changed over time.

Finite forms can conclude a main clause. As opposed to the non-finite forms, the system of finite forms has undergone major changes between OJ and LMJ (and NJ), such that the morphological categories obligatorily expressed in finite verbs changed profoundly between OJ and LMJ. In OJ, in addition to primarily modal categories (exclamatory, imperative, negative conjectural, and optative), a main distinction is between conclusive and adnominal. The distinction between conclusive and adnominal verb forms is functionally important in OJ and EMJ. However, it is important to bear in mind that while this distinction has morphological expression in most verb classes, and for most auxiliaries, there is syncretism between the conclusive and the adnominal in the largest verb class of all, the regular consonant base verbs which make up close to 75% of all OJ verbs, for example, *saku* 'come into bloom' being both conclusive and adnominal.

The conclusive was used to conclude declarative main clauses (14) (as well as being followed by modal extensions and final particles). The adnominal was used as (i) in relative clauses (15), (ii) to form headless nominalizations ('the one who') (16), and (iii) as the predicate in exclamative and interrogative main clauses or main clauses which involve focus (17–19).

(14)	*Nwosima*	*ga*	*saki*	*ni*	*opori*	***su*,**	*ware*	*pa.*
		GEN	cape	DAT	lodging	do.CNCL	I	TOP

'Me, I make a hut on the cape of Noshima.' (MYS 15.3606)

(15)	*[Tama*	*no*	*ura*	*ni*	*asari*	***suru*]**	*tadu.*
		GEN	bay	DAT	foraging	do.ADN	crane

'A crane fishing in the Tama bay.' (MYS 15.3598)

(16) *[Kadi no oto* **suru***]* *pa ama-wotomye kamo.*
rudder GEN sound do.ADN TOP fisher-girl Q
'The one making the sound of a rudder, is that a fisher-girl?'
(MYS 15.3641)

(17) *Wa ga kwopuru* **kimi** **so** *kizo no ywo ime*
I GEN love.ADN my.lord FOC last.night GEN night dream
ni **mi-ye-turu***.*
DAT see-PASS-PERF.ADN
'It was you, my beloved lord, that appeared (to me) last night in a dream.'
(MYS 2.150)

(18) *Ume no pana* **tare ka** **ukabe-si** *sakaduki no pe ni.*
plum GEN flower who QFOC float-SPST.ADN saké.cup GEN top DAT
'The plum blossoms, who (is it who) has floated them, on top of my sake cup.'
(MYS 5.840)

(19) *Tukwi wo sirwotape no* **kumo ka** **kakus-eru***.*
moon ACC white.cloth like cloud QFOC hide-STAT.ADN
'Is it white clouds that are hiding the moon?' (MYS 7.1079)

It is the contrast between usages such as (14) and (15) after which the conclusive and adnominal forms are named, but in fact the general characteristic of the "adnominal" form is that it forms a nominalized predicate, as for example in the headless nominalization in (16). That is also what underlies the use of the adnominal in focus constructions, traditionally known as *kakari-musubi*,[11] in which the focused element is marked by a focus particle (*so* ~ *zo* (> EMJ *zo*), *namo* (> EMJ *namu* ~ *nan*) and interrogative focus *ka, ya*) and the adnominal form concludes the sentence, as in (17–19).

It is the fact that the adnominal is used to conclude main clauses of this type that is the reason it is included among finite forms. These focus constructions are mono-clausal and have a semantic effect similar to *it*-clefts in English, as reflected in the translations of (17–19). A focus construction can be thought of as establishing a copular, predicative relation between a nominalized presupposition (*kizo no ywo ime ni mi-ye-turu* '(what) appeared to me in a dream last night') and focus (*wa ga kwopuru kimi so* 'you, my beloved lord'), like that between subject and nominal predicate, and that is probably the diachronic explanation for the use in the presupposed predicate of the nominalizing "adnominal" form. These focus constructions are a conspicuous and prominent feature of both OJ and EMJ but disappear in LMJ.

A number of verbal morphological categories, including voice, aspect, negation, and tense, are optionally expressed by "auxiliaries" (inflecting suffixes) (see Table 2.4).

[11] *Kakari-musubi* means 'hanging-tying,' expressing that one element is set ("hung") up and the predication completed ("tied up") by use of a particular verb form. A variant of *kakari-musubi* uses the focus particle *koso* and concludes the sentence by the exclamatory form.

Table 2.4 *OJ auxiliaries*

	sak-	ake-
Respect (***-s-***)	*saka-**su***	–
Voice		
Causative (-***sime***-)	*saka-**simu***	*ake-**simu***
Passive (-***ye***-)	*saka-**yu***	–
Passive (-***re***-)	*saka-**ru***	–
Aspect/Negation		
Perfective (-***te***-)	*yaki-**tu***	*tuke-**tu***
Perfective (-***n***-)	*saki-**nu***	*ake-**nu***
Stative (-***yer***-)	*sak-**yeri***	–
[EMJ Stative (***-tar-***)]	[*saki-tari*]	[*ake-tari*]
Negative (-***zu*** /-***n***-)	*saka-**zu***	*ake-**zu***
Tense/Mood		
Simple past (-***ki*** / -***kye***- / -***si*** / -***se***-)	*saki-**ki***	*ake-**ki***
Modal past (-***kyer***-)	*saki-**kyeri***	*ake-**kyeri***
Conjectural (-***m***-)	*saka-**mu***	*ake-**mu***
Subjunctive (-***masi*** / -***mase***-)	*saka-**masi***	*ake-**masi***

Auxiliaries inflect for a subset of the categories which lexical verbs inflect for; most auxiliaries belong to one of the verbal conjugation classes, but a few (negative, simple past, subjunctive) have highly irregular and/or suppletive paradigms. For example, modal past *-kyer-* belongs to an irregular consonant base verb conjugation class (like *ar-* 'exist') and has the forms conclusive *-kyeri*, adnominal *-kyeru*, exclamatory *-kyere*, provisional *-kyereba*, concessive *-kyeredo*, nominal *-kyeraku*; the negative auxiliary inflects largely as a verb, but has some suppletive forms – conclusive *-zu*, adnominal *-nu*, exclamatory *-ne*, infinitive *-zu* ~ *-ni*, gerund *-zute* ~ *nito*, conditional *-zupa*, provisional *-neba*, concessive *-nedo*, nominal *-naku*; the simple past has its own idiomatic, suppletive and quite irregular paradigm – conclusive *-ki*, adnominal *-si*, exclamatory *-sika*, conditional *-seba* ~ *-kyeba*, provisional *-sikaba*, concessive *sikado*, nominal *-siku* ~ *-kyeku*.

Auxiliaries attach to the basic stem of vowel-base verbs, and for consonant base verbs either to one of two derived stems (ending in /a/ or /i/) or to the basic stem. They are shown in Table 2.4 in their basic stem form in the leftmost column, and in the conclusive form when attached to verbs.

As shown, some auxiliaries (respect, passive, stative) do not combine with the regular vowel-base verbs; this reflects that that verb class is younger in the language and was only formed shortly before the OJ period. From EMJ onwards the passive, which changed to *-rare-*, could combine with verbs from all verb classes, and stative *-yer-* and respect *-s-* were lost as productive auxiliaries.

The stative auxiliary is used about both progressive and resultant states. Etymologically the stative incorporates the existential verb *ar-*, for example, *sak-yer-* 'be blooming' < *saki ar-. This construction was morphologized prior to the formation of the main vowel-base verb classes and therefore the stative was not used with these verb classes. It is supplemented by a productive periphrastic stative, formed by the gerund and an existential verb – for example, *iki-te ara-ba* [live-GER exist-COND] 'if you are alive' – which was used with all verb classes. Through EMJ the periphrastic stative replaced the stative auxiliary and itself morphologized to give a new stative auxiliary, *-te ar-* > *-tar-*; for that reason *-tar-* is included in square brackets in Table 2.4, although it was not yet a morphologized auxiliary in OJ.

The stative construction consisting of non-finite verb + existential verb is pervasive throughout the history of Japanese and has gone through several cycles of morphologization followed by innovative analytic formation, and it is also the way in which statives are formed in NJ, with the new animate existential verb *i-* (*suwatte i-* 'be sitting'), and dialectally a number of variants are found.

The two perfectives are selected by different verbs, *n-* by unaccusatives (e.g. *sak-*, *ake-*) and *-te-* by unergatives (e.g. *wem-* 'laugh') and transitives (e.g. *yak-* 'burn,' *tuke-* 'attach' which have been added to Table 2.4). Perfective auxiliary selection is the main expression of split intransitivity in OJ. The modal past tense contains an element best characterized as "speaker commitment," which is absent in the simple past. The modal past is thus paradigmatically opposed both to the simple past and to the conjectural, whereas simple past and conjectural could combine to give a past conjectural *-kye-m-*.

Generally, auxiliaries can combine between (but not within) the main groups (respect, voice, aspect/negation, and tense/mood (apart from the combination of simple past and conjectural)) to form longer syntagms; for example, *apa-**sa-zu*** [meet-**RESP-NEG**.CNCL] 'you do not meet (me),' *uwe-**te-kyer**-i* [plant-**PERF-MPST**-CNCL] '(you) have planted,' *pupum-**yeri-ki*** [bud-**STAT-SPST**.CNCL] '(the cherry trees) were budding,' *asipuma-**si-na-m**-u* [step-**RESP-PERF-CONJ**-CNCL] 'you will end up stepping.' Auxiliaries occur in a fixed order, respect being closest to the verb stem, tense/mood being rightmost, although far from all seemingly possible combinations are attested.

4.1.2 Late Middle Japanese

LMJ saw large-scale changes in verbal morphology and by the end of the period the grammatical categories expressed by finite inflection and by auxiliaries had changed profoundly (whereas the system of non-finite, converbal forms remained largely as before), and the overall system then was more or less as in NJ today.

Table 2.5 presents the finite inflected verb forms from the end of LMJ and from cNJ.

The only finite form from the OJ paradigm which survived in shape and function from OJ into LMJ is the imperative. The OJ/EMJ exclamatory, optative, and negative conjectural were lost, whereas volitional, intentional, and past conjectural were acquired. The volitional remains a core inflected form in NJ, but the intentional was lost during NJ and also the past conjectural is now no longer used productively in cNJ. Apart from regular sound change (/ɔɔ/ > /oo/), other differences between LMJ and NJ are in the shape of the

Table 2.5 *LMJ and NJ verb finite forms*

	sak-		***ake-***	
Base	LMJ	NJ	LMJ	NJ
Non-past	*saku*	*saku*	*akuru*	*akeru*
Past	*saita*	*saita*	*aketa*	*aketa*
Imperative	*sake*	*sake*	*akei ~ akeyo*	*akero*
Volitional	*sakɔɔ*	*sakō*	*akyoo*	*akeyō*
Past conjectural	*saitarɔɔ*	*(saitarō)*	*aketarɔɔ*	*(aketarō)*
Intentional	*sakɔɔzuru*	–	*akyoozuru*	–

forms of vowel-base verbs, where the basic stem now appears in all inflected forms and the imperative changed.[12]

The OJ/EMJ distinction between conclusive and adnominal forms was lost, as the two forms merged, probably before the middle of the LMJ period. The outcome of the merger had the shape of the OJ/EMJ adnominal (OJ/EMJ *aku, akuru* > LMJ *akuru* > NJ *akeru*). The resulting system included a non-past opposed to a past tense. This is a major morphological shift, in which morphological expression of the distinctive syntactic functions associated with the OJ/EMJ conclusive and adnominal forms (OJ/EMJ *aku* versus *akuru*) was lost and was replaced by a system with obligatory expression of tense (LMJ *akuru* versus *aketa*, NJ *akeru* versus *aketa*) as the core of verb inflection (whereas the expression of tense in OJ/EMJ by means of auxiliaries was optional). The past tense flective *-ta* attaches to the stem of the consonant base verbs which arose in the course of the *onbin* 'euphony' sound changes, for example, EMJ *sai-* (< OJ *saki-* <= *sak* + *i*).

Through the LMJ period a set of changes in syntax took place which are in some way related to or involve the loss of the conclusive/adnominal distinction in verb inflection. With the merger of those two forms (and the emergence of tense as an obligatory inflectional category), the expression by verbal morphology of the distinctive functions of the two forms was lost.

Both the non-past and the past forms reflect the conclusive and the adnominal (*aku, akuru* > *akuru; ake-tari, ake-taru* > *ake-taru* > *aketa*), see further below. In LMJ both the non-past and past each combined the functions of the conclusive and adnominal forms and thus both came to function as:

(20) a. predicates in all types of main clause types (except imperatives), *odyaru* in (21),
  b. predicate in adnominal clauses, *yuu* in (21),
  c. predicates in (headless) nominalized clauses, *yuuta* in (22), *kuyamu* in (23), and *naku* in (24) (which has an internally headed relative clause).

Examples (21–27) are all from the translation into Japanese of Aesop's fables, produced and printed in 1593 in Japan by Jesuit missionaries as *Esopo no fabulas.*

[12] The imperative of vowel-base verbs, ending in *-ro*, is the only morphological feature in standard cNJ which is attributable to direct substratum influence from an eastern dialect variety which reflects Eastern OJ.

(21) *[Amonia to yuu] sato ga odyaru.*
QUOT call.NPST village NOM exist[POL].NPST
'There is a village called Amonia.'

(22) *[Sisi no yuuta] wa ware wa arufodo no kedamono no*
lion GEN say.PST TOP I TOP all COP.ADN animal GEN
ɔɔ nareba
king COP.PROV
'(What) the lion said: As I am the king of all animals...'

(23) *[Kurusyuude kuyamu] wa tikusyɔɔ no waza zo.*
suffer.GER regret.NPST TOP beast GEN job EMPH
'It is the burden of the beast to suffer and feel regret.'

(24) *[Tiisai ko no naku] o sukasu tote*
small child GEN cry.NPST ACC calm.down.NPST in.order.to
'In order to calm down a small child who was crying...'

The past and non-past forms of NJ are still used in main clauses and in adnominal clauses, but they no longer form direct nominalizations. In this function, and thus in examples corresponding to (22–24), NJ uses *no* as a nominalizer. This use of *no*, which only developed in the seventeenth century, in NJ, served to re-establish expression of one of the nominalizing functions of the OJ/EMJ adnominal, but it is important to note that there is no direct replacement, as there are several centuries between the loss of the conclusive/adnominal distinction and the emergence of *no* as a nominalizer (see Wrona 2012).

The *kakari-musubi* focus construction was lost in the course of LMJ. This is often said to be directly related to the loss of the conclusive/adnominal distinction, but the fact that the largest of all verb classes had syncretism between those two forms shows that the availability of a distinct adnominal form was not a prerequisite for the *kakari-musubi* construction, and so it is difficult to accept a causal link between those two changes. Of the focus particles, *ya* now means 'and, or, or the like' and *namu* was lost completely. Both *ka* and *zo* changed to final particles: *zo* was in late LMJ used in exclamatives and wh-questions and *ka* in yes/no questions (25–27). This suggests that one important function of the adnominal verb form, namely to mark sentences as exclamative or interrogative, was taken over after the conclusive/adnominal merger by two former focus particles: first of all *zo*, but in yes/no questions by *ka*. In NJ this has changed, so that *zo* is exclamative and *ka* is used in both wh- and yes/no questions.

(25) *Ookame no kuru zo.*
wolf GEN come.NPST SFP
'The wolf is coming!'

(26)	*Ware*	*wa*	*doko*	*e*	*yuku*	*zo.*
	I	TOP	where	ALL	go.NPST	SFP
	'Where do I go?'					

(27)	*Kisyo*	*wa*	*yakusoku*	*wa*	*wasureta*	*ka.*
	you	TOP	promise	TOP	forget.PST	SFP
	'Did you forget your promise?'					

Most of the OJ/EMJ auxiliaries have been lost. However, two of them are sources of new inflected forms: stative *-tar-* and conjectural *-m-*. As the conclusive/adnominal distinction and also the exclamatory form were lost, these auxiliaries thereby lost their own main, finite inflection, and they were in turn reinterpreted as flectives expressing new inflectional categories. The EMJ stative *-tar-*, which in the course of MJ changed to become a perfect tense, is the source of the past tense, *-ta* (which lost the final /ru/ of its original adnominal form, *-taru*), for example *aketa*, which was reinterpreted as a past tense flective in opposition with the outcome of the merger of the conclusive and adnominal of verbs without auxiliaries, for example *akuru*, which was reinterpreted as a non-past. Conjectural *-m-* is reflected in the volitional: EMJ *saka-mu* (adnominal of the conjectural attached to *sak-* 'come into bloom') > LMJ *saka-u* => *sakɔɔ*> NJ *sakō*; EMJ *ake-mu* > LMJ *ake-u* => *akyoo* > NJ *akeyō*.[13]

All of OJ respect (*-s-*), perfective (*-te-* ~ *-n-*), stative (*-yer-*), simple past (*-ki/-si*), modal past (*-kyer-*), and subjunctive (*-masi/-mase-*) were completely lost from the language. Thus, the category of perfective disappeared, but stative was retained as a category, expressed analytically (gerund *-te* + *i-* 'exist').

Late LMJ had the following auxiliaries. As shown in (28), the categories expressed by auxiliaries is the same as in NJ, as is to a large extent also the morphological material.

(28)	LMJ	NJ
Causative	*-sase-*	*-sase-*
Passive	*-rare-*	*-rare-*
Potential	*-e-*	*-re-*
Negative	*-n-*	*-na-*
Polite	*-marase-*	*-mas-*
Desiderative	*-ta-*	*-ta-*
Evidential	*-ge-/-sɔɔ-*	*-sō-*

The OJ causative and passive auxiliaries were reshaped and replaced during EMJ, but the categories remained, in the shape they still have today. As opposed to OJ, causative and passive became able to combine (*-sase-rare-* 'be made to') from EMJ, and the restrictions on combination with particular verb classes were also lost in EMJ. The only auxiliary to survive directly as such into LMJ was the OJ negative, whose inflectional paradigm,

[13] The LMJ past conjectural (*aketarɔɔ*) reflects EMJ stative + conjectural: EMJ *-tara-mu* LMJ > *-tara-u* > *-tarɔɔ*. Also the intentional reflects a construction with the conjectural.

however, underwent significant change and remained irregular. In NJ, the negative has been further reformed significantly and the OJ/EMJ negative auxiliary, which was mainly verbal in conjugation, has been replaced by an auxiliary *-na-* which morphologically is an adjective (cf. Chapter 14, this volume): *saka-na-i* [bloom-NEG-NPST] 'does not bloom.' A potential auxiliary, *-e-*, arose during LMJ, used first with consonant base verbs (*nom-e-ru* 'can drink'), but in NJ spreading to vowel-base verbs, in the shape *-re-* (*mi-re-ru* 'can see'). New categories expressed by auxiliaries arose: polite (NJ *nomi-mas-u*), desiderative (*nomi-ta-i*), and evidential (*nomi-sō-da*).

4.2 Case Particles, Grammatical Roles, and Word Order

The core Japanese case particles are as in (29).[14] As shown, OJ/EMJ had no nominative case, but instead two genitives, of which *ga* in late LMJ changed to become a nominative.

(29)	OJ/EMJ	LMJ/NJ
Nominative		*ga*
Accusative	*wo* > *o*	*o*
Genitive	*ga, no*	*no*
Dative	*ni*	*ni*

The two OJ/EMJ genitives were used for possession, or adnominal modification, and for subject marking in certain clause types, with no difference in function between them. The details of their distribution have yet to be understood fully, but overall they were lexically selected by different nouns, determined to a large extent by animacy and close personal relation, with demonstratives (*ko, so*) and most common nouns taking *no*, but personal pronouns (*wa, a, na, si, ta, ono*) and a smaller set of nouns, some very frequent, mainly referring to people close to the speaker taking *ga*; for example, *kimi* '(my) lord,' *imo* 'sister, my beloved,' *sekwo* 'older brother, beloved (male).' A few nouns, for example, *kwo* 'child, dear' or *matu* 'pine-tree,' select both *ga* and *no*, and not all nouns referring to people take *ga*: for example, *pito* 'person,' *opokimi* 'great lord,' *tukapi* 'messenger,' or *masurawo* 'gentleman' all take *no*. The distributional tendencies are clearer with genitive marked subjects than with genitive marked possessors (or noun modifiers), partly, though not exclusively, because some head nouns modified by genitives always select *ga*, overriding the lexical properties of the genitive marked noun; for example, always X *ga ne* 'the sound of X,' never *X *no ne*.

4.2.1 Subject and Object Marking

Extensive pro-drop, topicalization, and right dislocation, combined with widespread use of relative clauses from which arguments are extracted, means

[14] Other particles include ablative ('from, along' etc.) *ywori* (> EMJ/LMJ/NJ *yori*) ~ *ywo* ~ *yuri* ~ *yu*, comitative *to*, ablative *kara*, and allative *pye* (> EMJ *pe* > *we* > LMJ/NJ *e*). Apart from the OJ *ywo* ~ *yuri* ~ *yu* variants, these are all still in use.

that most clauses in Japanese do not overtly express all their arguments within the clause. For that reason, the details of clause-internal case marking of subjects and objects and word order are not straightforwardly observable, especially in OJ where the available materials are limited. A further complicating factor is that it is difficult to distinguish systematic differential case marking of arguments from simple case drop, which for example is frequent in NJ. It does seem clear that all stages of Japanese have accusative alignment and that the dominant word order is SOV, but it is further possible to discern important changes within that overall frame that have taken place in the marking of subjects and objects between OJ and NJ. This is, however, an area where much further research is both possible and needed.

In OJ, subjects of declarative, imperative, or optative main clauses were not case marked. However, subjects of subordinate, relative, and nominalized (including focused and interrogative) clauses could receive genitive case marking, by one of the two genitive particles *ga* (30), and *no* (31), subject to the distribution described above. Not all subjects in these types of clauses were genitive marked, but the distribution of bare and genitive marked subjects has not yet been fully described and it is not clear whether some regularity was involved, or whether all cases of bare subjects in these clause types simply have case drop.

(30)	*Urasima*	*no*	*kwo*	*ga*	*tamakusige*	*ake-**zu***	***ari**-seba*
		GEN	child	GEN	jewel.box	open-NEG.INF	exist-SPST.COND

'If (only) the child from Urashima had not opened the jeweled box.'
(Fudoki 15)

(31)	*opo-kimi*	*no*	*myesi-si*	*nwobye*
	great-lord	GEN	see[RESP]-SPST.ADN	field

'The field that my great lord saw.'
(MYS 20.4509)

The use of the two genitive particles *no* and *ga* changed in the course of LMJ: The use of *no* to mark subjects in subordinate clauses was gradually curtailed. As seen in several of the LMJ examples above, *no* could mark subjects in adnominal and directly nominalized clauses, but that was no longer possible in other subordinate clauses, and in NJ *no* can only mark subjects in a subset of relative clauses. *No* continued to have possessive and other adnominal uses as a genitive case particle. Conversely, *ga* lost use as a (possessive or adnominal) genitive, while retaining and eventually expanding use as a subject marker to include use in declarative main clauses, as in (21) above. At the end of LMJ *no* remained as the sole genitive particle, whereas *ga* had all but completed the transition from a genitive to a nominative case particle, marking subjects in all clause types.

Objects were in OJ accusative case marked in accordance with a system of *differential object marking*, in which only objects which were *specific* (definite and otherwise discourse linked) were accusative case marked, whereas non-specific objects were bare (Frellesvig, Horn, and Yanagida

2015), such as here where context makes clear that (32) is specific and (33) non-specific, as reflected in the translations.

(32)

Kwomatu	*ga*	*sita*	*no*	***kaya***	***wo***	*kara-sane.*
small.pine	GEN	under	GEN	grass	ACC	cut-RESP.OPT

'I want you to cut **some of the grass** under the small pine.'

(MYS 1.11)

(33)

Akami-yama	***kusane***	*kari*	*soke*
Akami-mountain	grass	cut	remove

'cutting and removing **grasses** at Mount Akami. . .'

(MYS 14.3479)

This system of differential object marking was lost in EMJ where also non-specific objects can be marked by *wo*. The OJ system is further complicated by the fact that some specific objects were bare, due to case drop, the precise conditions of which are not yet clear. Case drop continued in EMJ and subsequent stages of the language, so that also today not all objects are accusative case marked.

NJ has basic SOV word order, subject to scrambling and pro-drop which are also frequent in OJ, EMJ, and LMJ. While OJ also appears to have had dominant SOV word order, there is one significant systematic exception (Yanagida and Whitman 2009): *wo*-marked objects usually appear to the left of a subject, and always to the left of *ga*-marked subjects, as in (34), which has a nominalized predicate in a focus construction and therefore allows genitive subject marking.

(34)

Ware	***wo***	*yamwi*	*ni*	*ya*	***imo***	***ga***
I	ACC	darkness	DAT	QFOC	my.beloved	GEN
kwopwitutu	*aru*	*ramu.*				
yearn.CONT	exist	PCONJ.ADN				

'Would my beloved be longing for me in the darkness?'

(MYS. 15.3669)

This word order rule was lost in EMJ, and from then on *ga*-marked subjects regularly precede *wo*-marked objects and case marking appears to have no impact on word order.

4.3 Pronouns, Demonstratives, and Interrogatives

OJ had a set of personal pronouns and a morphological system of two-way demonstratives + interrogative.

(35) Personal pronouns

	short	long
1st	*wa, a*	*ware, are*
2nd	*na*	*(nare)*
3rd	*si*	–
interrogative	*ta*	*tare*
reflexive	*ono*	*(onore)*

(36) Demonstratives

	short	long	locational
proximal	*ko*	*kore*	*koko*
non-proximal	*so*	*(sore)*	*soko*
interrogative	*i-/idu-*	*idure*	*iduku*

The short forms are used in compounds and derivatives (e.g. *ko-yopi* 'this night,' *wa-dori* 'my bird' (*tori* 'bird'), *i-ka* 'how'), or with a following particle, by far the most frequently genitive particles, for example, *wa ga kokoro* 'my heart.' The long forms are used in isolation, for example as topics, and with various particles, but never with a genitive particle (except *idure* which has no corresponding free short form). Of the two genitive particles, personal pronouns take *ga* and demonstratives take *no*. *Nare, onore*, and *sore* are very rare in OJ, but became full members of the system in EMJ.

Although most descriptions of OJ project the three-way demonstrative system (proximal, mesial, distal) found in EMJ and onwards in Japanese on to OJ, there is no proper attestation of the distal terms in OJ, and the system is in fact a two-way system: *proximal* referring to what is within the speaker's domain of direct sensory perception or experience, versus *non-proximal* referring to what is outside of the speaker's domain of direct experience (see Hashimoto 1966). The non-proximal forms were very often used anaphorically, whereas the proximal forms mostly were used deictically.

The simple system of personal pronouns in OJ was lost in the course of EMJ. Some of the forms continued to be used, for example, *ware* 'I,' *wa-ga* 'I-GEN' and *tare* 'who,' but the system as such disappeared. Already in OJ the pronominal system was supplemented by a number of lexical terms of address, and in EMJ such usage grew to displace the pronominal system, with a number of terms of address and of speaker- and self-reference, including speaker – *maro, mi* ('body' < OJ *mwi*), *onore-ga-mi/ono-ga-mi, ware, wa-ga-mi, midukara*; hearer – *nandi, kimi, omape* (> *omawe* > *omae*), *gozen*. *Kimi* and *omae* are still used today for hearer reference; *anata*, which originates in a distal demonstrative ('that person,' supposedly < *(k)ano kata*), was used for third person reference in EMJ and LMJ and only changed to hearer reference in the eighteenth century. The NJ speaker reference *watakushi* ('he/she' in EMJ) and *ore* (hearer reference in EMJ) came to be used from LMJ.

From EMJ a three-way demonstrative + interrogative system develops and by the end of the LMJ period the system is close to that found in NJ:

(37)

	Modifier	Noun	Location
proximal	*kono*	*kore*	*koko*
mesial	*sono*	*sore*	*soko*
distal	*ano*	*are*	*asoko*
interrogative	*dono*	*dore*	*doko*

The short forms of OJ lexicalized with genitive *no* to become modifiers. EMJ did not have forms for all the slots in the set, but over time forms arose which filled the empty slots to make up what is now a full and consistent paradigm.

The shape of the forms has shown some change which may be thought to be due to paradigmatic pressure: The distal forms were *kano, kare, kasiko* in EMJ, but eventually changed, with higher differentiation from proximal *kore*. More significantly, all the interrogative forms have undergone changes such as *iduku* > *iduko* > *idoko* > *doko* (which are all attested), acquiring the same vocalism and length as the proximal and mesial forms. The initial /d/ of the interrogative forms was in NJ extended to the interrogative personal pronoun which changed from *tare* to *dare*, and the interrogatives today form a neat morphophonological class with initial /d-/ which is the result of leveling over time.

5 Significant External Influences

Japanese has undergone two major waves of external influence, from Chinese (Section 5.1) and from European languages (Section 5.2).

5.1 Sinification

In the course of EMJ we see the impact of influence from Chinese, first of all in vocabulary, resulting in a significant Sino-Japanese component in the language. Well-assimilated *loanwords* from Chinese may be identified within OJ, which were acquired through direct spoken language contact. However, of far more profound impact was the influence from Chinese which arose primarily from reading practices in Japan of Chinese texts. This originated from before the OJ period and certainly such influence is seen already in the OJ texts, but it is from EMJ that this influence manifests on a large scale.

There are two kinds of influence. One reflects the dissemination into the common language of practices which arose in the translation of Chinese texts into (or "rendition" in) Japanese (*kanbun-kundoku* (漢文訓読) 'reading Chinese in Japanese'). The full extent of the lasting influence of *kanbun-kundoku* practices on Japanese remains to be charted and described, but it includes loan translation collocations such as *ame-tuti* 'heaven and earth; the world' and *ko no yo* 'this world (as opposed to before- and after-life),' the noun modifiers *iwayuru* 'so-called' and *arayuru* (lexicalized from the adnominal forms of the passives of *iw-* 'say' and *ar-* 'exist'), the adverb *osoraku* 'likely, probably' (from the nominal form of *osor-* 'to fear'), as well as extensive use of sentence initial and modal adverbs; for example, *imada* '(even) now' (> NJ *mada*) in correlation with a negative verb form to mean 'not yet,' or *sikasite* 'and, then.'

More conspicuous and manifest is the intake of direct loanwords from Chinese, again through the medium of Chinese texts. Early Sino-Japanese (SJ) loanwords include court titles, Buddhist or philosophical terms, or words for technology, but there is also from early on common nouns such as *niku* 'meat,' *nikki* 'diary,' *neti* ~ *net* 'fever.' Also the Chinese numerals 1–10, 100, 1,000, and 10,000 were borrowed, and while the native numerals 1–10 are still in use today, they are restricted and the SJ numerals are the main, unmarked numerals. Most SJ loanwords are nouns, and verbs were usually taken in as verbal nouns, predicated by *se-* 'to do'; for example, *gu-se-* 'furnish, be furnished (with),' *si-se-* 'die,' *rongi-se-* 'debate.'

On the whole, it is difficult to judge the dissemination of SJ vocabulary among the general population in EMJ, or the extent to which SJ vocabulary primarily was a written form. It is clear, though, that a fair number of everyday SJ words were common, and from around 1600 the missionary materials clearly show a large SJ vocabulary which was in widespread use and seems to have been fully assimilated at the time.

In the *Tale of Genji* from around 1000 AD, just under 5% of distinct words and 12.5% of words in running text are SJ, while on the other hand, SJ vocabulary was normatively excluded from poetry. This shows both that SJ vocabulary was in fairly common use among people at court (such as Murasaki Shikibu, the author of *Genji*) and that SJ to a large extent remained identifiable. This is also reflected in the fact that SJ vocabulary in some genres (though not in the *Tale of Genji*, for example) often would be written in the *kanji* used to write them in Chinese. In NJ, a much larger proportion of the vocabulary is Sino-Japanese, but that is due to the large amount of loan translations of words from European languages, especially English, into Sino-Japanese (see below).

A few phonological features were innovations introduced through SJ vocabulary, further contributing to the identifiability of some SJ vocabulary (although these features obviously were not shared by all SJ vocabulary): syllable final /-t/ (lost in NJ), new complex syllable onsets /kwa, gwa/ (now lost in most dialects of NJ) and /Cya, Cyo, Cyu/ (which subsequently also arose in the native wordstock through sound change, and which are frequent in NJ), and use of word initial /b, d, g, z, r/ (also in NJ found in loans from other languages).

5.2 Westernization

Loanwords from European languages appear from the first extensive contact with Europeans in the sixteenth century.[15] Early loans still in use include *pan* 'bread' and *tabako* from Portuguese, and *hōku* ~ *fōku* 'fork' from Dutch. However, since the Meiji Restoration in 1868, NJ has been affected to a much larger and significant extent by contact with European

[15] See Irwin 2011 for detail about European loanwords in Japanese.

languages in the course of the rapid economic and political modernization which took place in the late nineteenth and early twentieth centuries, and later also as a result of the increasing globalization of the language. This contact has affected both phonology and vocabulary through large-scale intake of loanwords. Until the end of World War II, loanwords were taken in from variety of European languages, although at that time English was already the main donor language. Since the end of World War II, English has become the overwhelmingly dominant source of borrowing, with large numbers of words from English used in everyday life. Phonologically, the intake of loanwords from English has resulted in the introduction of several new phonemes, alongside innovations in phonotactics.

However, rather than direct borrowing, the main, conscious strategy adopted in the linguistic modernization of Japanese was the coining of loan translations (calques) from European languages, using Sino-Japanese wordstock, for new notions, institutions, and things that were introduced in the course of the Meiji period modernization. A few examples are *shakai* 'society,' *tetsugaku* 'philosophy,' *kaisha* 'firm, company,' *yūbin* 'post,' *jidōsha* 'automobile,' *tetsudō* 'railway,' *denwa* 'telephone,' *bungaku* 'literature,' *shōsetsu* 'novel,' *kokka* 'nation,' and *kokumin* 'people.'

This coinage often consisted of finding some word, or *kanji* combination, in one of the Chinese Classics, which could be drafted in to write the new word, which was vocalized by using the SJ reading, or alternatively of reviving or adapting SJ words from earlier or specialized usage; however, free coinage from Sino-Japanese was also frequently used. SJ words deliberately coined, revived or adapted in this way during the Meiji period make up the great majority of SJ words in use today, and the overwhelming majority of academic, political and intellectual vocabulary used in Japanese today, and not a few of these words were later adopted in China and Korea, with Chinese or Sino-Korean vocalization. Thus, SJ loan translations are the core of the lexical, terminological modernization, the linguistic Westernization, of the Meiji period, which would scarcely have been as successful as it was if it had had to rely on direct loans. SJ coinages are short and in some cases provide educated readers with clues to their meaning, and in addition, SJ coinages have the important function of giving the (albeit false) impression that these words were part of and belonged in an East Asian intellectual and cultural tradition.

3

Layered Structure, Positional Shifts, and Grammaticalization

Rumiko Shinzato

1 Introduction

This chapter aims to synthesize primarily synchronic Japanese linguistic studies of modality with Western diachronic studies of grammaticalization. In the former tradition, the syntactic organization of Japanese sentences is often captured in a layered structure model, which expands from the inner to the outer layers in Figure 3.1. In grammaticalization research, it is now well-accepted that source lexemes shift from the Core (Levels A and B in Figure 3.1) to peripheries (LP, left periphery, or RP, right periphery) in their grammaticalization processes, resulting in more (inter)subjective target lexemes (e.g. Traugott and Dasher 2002: 40, precise definitions are given in Section 2). These two independently evolved approaches obviously differ in their analytical orientations, with one synchronic and the other diachronic, but they also share a common ground in that both recognize the significance of outer layers, or peripheries. In both frameworks, the peripheries are recognized as more (inter) subjective than the Core, which is discerned as objective and referential.

The grammaticalization research centered on the LP/RP functional distinctions is fast growing (e.g. Beeching and Detges 2014). With the focus primarily on how the same source lexeme grammaticalizes as two functionally different target lexemes in LP/RP, investigations into the likely directionality of shifts of source lexemes to either periphery has not yet garnered much attention.[1] The goal of this chapter is to respond to such

I would like to thank Yoko Hasegawa for her guidance and valuable input throughout the process, Seiko Fujii for her thorough and thoughtful review, and John Haig for his superb editing. I am also indebted to John Bentley, Yuko Higashiizumi, Noriko Onodera, Satoko Suzuki, and Foong Ha Yap for their discussion and feedback.

[1] Traugott (2010: 20) poses the following as one of the future research questions: "Can the establishment of more fine-grained distinctions at LP and RP give us a better handle on predicting direction of shift to one edge or the other?" In a similar vein, Onodera (2011: 624) states "One unsolved assignment is the issue of periphery . . . What kind of expressions in terms of structure and meaning occur in initial and final positions?"

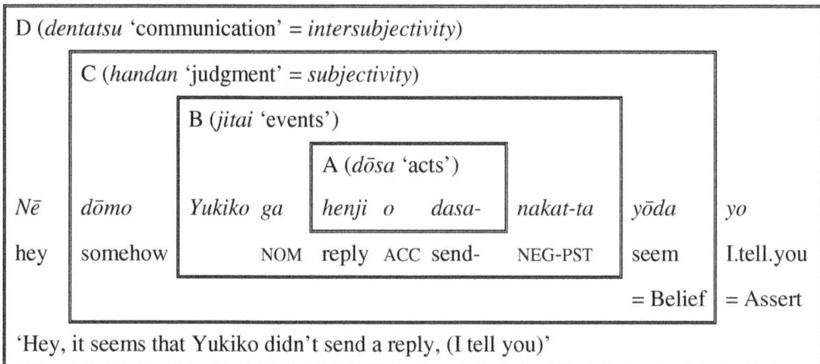

Figure 3.1 Layered structure model (Shinzato 2007: 177) based on Minami (1974), Takubo (1987), and Noda (1997)

directionality issues by tying them in with the Japanese syntactic organization. Specifically, it addresses the questions below:

(1) a. Is the directionality of source lexemes to either periphery predictable? If so, in what way?
  b. Are there peripheral-specific meanings?
  c. Do the Japanese patterns of grammaticalization have cross-linguistic relevance?

The organization of this chapter is as follows. Section 2 provides an overview of *kokugogaku* (the traditional Japanese linguistic) studies of *jojutsu* versus *chinjutsu*, or roughly, proposition versus modality, and the layered structure model of Japanese sentences. Section 3 sketches the background of grammaticalization studies related to periphery issues. Section 4 deals with the directionality of the movements of Japanese source lexemes: Core to LP, Core to RP, and Core to both LP and RP. Questions (1a–b) are dealt with in this section. In addition, the addressee honorifics, *desu* and *masu*, are highlighted for the seeming mismatch of their syntactic positions (Core) and their generally conceived semantic characteristics of intersubjectivity. To address (1c), Section 5 places the Japanese grammaticalization cases in a broader cross-linguistic context with regard to Beeching and Detges's (2014) Functional Asymmetry Hypothesis. Section 6 concludes the chapter.

2 *Kokugogaku* Studies and the Layered Structure

In *kokugogaku*, it is common to view Japanese sentences in a layered model as in Figure 3.1, synthesized from Minami (1974: 131–139),[2] Takubo (1987: 38), and Noda (1997: 209). In this model, the most referential part of

[2] In concept, Minami's (1974) analysis is extremely similar to but predates the layered syntactic clause structure in Western linguistics such as Foley and Van Valin's Role and Reference Grammar, Cinque's functional head hierarchy, Rijkhoff's NP hierarchy, and Hengeveld's layered model. For more detailed discussion, see Shinzato (2006).

a sentence is situated in the Core, and the sentence extends to both peripheries in order of increasing subjectivity.

The core is referred to as *jojutsu* 'proposition' and the outer layers as *chinjutsu* 'modality' (Watanabe 1953; Chapter 16, this volume; inter alia). The *chinjutsu* is often divided into two: the more subjective part called *juttei/ handan* 'judgment' and the more intersubjective portion referred to as *dentatsu* 'communication' (Haga 1954; Takubo 1987). Haga (1954: 58) defines *juttei* and *dentatsu* as "the speaker's attitude toward the proposition" and "communication of proposition and propositional attitude to the addressee," respectively. Minami (1974: 137) sees a parallel between his Levels C and D and Haga's *juttei* and *dentatsu*, respectively: his Level C expresses "self's attitude," while his Level D conveys "self's appeal to the addressee." Crucially, their distinction matches Benveniste's (1971: 299) definition of subjectivity (= the attitude of the speaker with respect to the statement he is making) and intersubjectivity (= "what constitutes communication as an exchange between the speaker and his addressee").

This layered model elegantly depicts the Core to peripheral extensions as well as the correlation between the LP and RP elements. For instance, the agreement between the S-initial modal adverb *dōmo* 'probably' and the S-final inferential auxiliary *yōda* 'seem' shows a syntactic (both at Level C), and semantic (both exhibiting the speaker-oriented supposition) correspondence. Likewise, at Level D, the S-initial attention getter *nē* agrees with the S-final addressee-oriented particle *yo* 'I tell you,' both of which are intersubjective. This speaks to the symmetry of the Japanese syntactic organization (more in Section 5).

Building on the *kokugogaku* studies, the relevant notions of Core versus Peripheries and (inter)subjectivity are defined as below. It should be clarified that this chapter considers the utterance/sentence-final positions rather than clause-final positions to be the peripheries, as clause-final positions can still be inside the scope of negation and tense.

(2) Core: Levels A and B
Peripheries: Levels C and D

(3) Subjectivity: Speaker's evaluative stance toward the propositional content.
Intersubjectivity: Speaker's alignment with the addressee in co-building discourse (i.e. textual cohesion) and solidifying interpersonal relationship.

3 Issues of Peripheries in Grammaticalization

The term "grammaticalization" had traditionally been associated with a unidirectional cline of change as in discourse > syntax > morphology > morphophonemic > zero (Givón 1979: 209), or with Givón's famous slogan "yesterday's syntax is today's morphology" (ibid.). From the standpoint of syntactic scope, this type of change is an example of scope decrease. In contrast to such a position, semantic changes of (inter)subjectification point to scope increase (Traugott and Dasher 2002: 40). As noted in Hansen and Visconti (2009: 9), the development of pragmatic markers embraces "scope increase, greater syntactic freedom, optionality, and strengthening of their pragmatic import."[3]

Since pragmatic markings are categorized with numerous labels[4] such as Discourse Marker (Schiffrin 1987: 328), Pragmatic Marker (Brinton 1996: 29), Pragmatic Particle (Martin 1975: 914), and Modal Particle (Degand, Cornillie, and Pietandrea 2013: 6–7), it is imperative to define them at this point. The terms and definitions adopted are similar to Detges's (2015: 132) definitions of discourse markers (DMs) and modal particles (MPs).[5]

(4) DM (Discourse Marker) marks a textual cohesion sentence-initially, and roughly corresponds to sentence-conjunctions.

(5) MM (Modal Marker) marks the speaker's attitude toward the proposition and/or toward the addressee sentence-finally, and roughly equates to final particles.

As syntactic scope expansion necessarily hinges upon syntactic peripheries, it is natural that inquiry into the relationship between LP/RP with pragmatic meanings has begun in recent grammaticalization studies. A pioneering undertaking in LP/RP research is Beeching and Detges's (2014) edited volume, in which their Functional Asymmetry Hypothesis (to be discussed in detail in Section 5) is presented and tested cross-linguistically. For instance, Degand (2014: 166–167) observes that French *alors* 'then, at that time, so' functions as a "turn-taking device" at LP, and at RP it requests confirmation of the conclusion from the hearer. On the other hand, Traugott (2014) challenges their hypothesis with her study of *surely* and *no doubt*. She (2014: 86) states that "where *surely* and *no doubt* are concerned, subjectivity or intersubjectivity appears to be correlated more closely with their inherent meaning and immediate context than with use at LP/RP." Related to the LP/RP asymmetry proposed in Beeching and

[3] Some scholars call this type of diachronic change pragmaticalization, and treat it differently from grammaticalization. For a further discussion concerning grammaticalization, pragmaticalization, and scope increase, see Hansen and Visconti (2009: ch. 1.4).

[4] Sometimes, labels are contradictory and confusing. Fraser (1999: 940) regards both clausal and sentence conjunctions equally as discourse markers, while Schiffrin (1987: 328) designates DM functions only to sentence conjunctions. Regardless of "striking similarities" between German Modal Particles (= MP) and Japanese sentence-final particles (Izutsu and Izutsu 2013: 218), assigning the MP label to Japanese sentence-final pragmatic markers may be problematic to German linguists because German MPs occur sentence-internally. Thus, the label MM (=Modal Marker) is adopted in this chapter.

[5] Detges (2015: 132) states: "Unlike DMs which indicate two-place relations between sequentially ordered chunks of discourse, MPs mark a relationship between a speech act and some element in the common ground, usually a belief ('a proposition') attributed to the addressee."

Detges's hypothesis, Degand (2014: 153) raises a question of whether there is something like "peripheral-meaning" that would add up to the coded meaning(s) of source lexemes.

4 Directionality of Positional Shifts

In the Japanese context, it is natural that (inter)subjectification goes hand in hand with scope expansion as the (inter)subjective elements occur at the periphery, as in the layered model in Figure 3.1. As for the directionality of shifts, this chapter identifies (6i–iii) and one non-shift (6iv) as below:

(6) a. Core to LP
    b. Core to RP
    c. Core to both LP/RP
    d. Non-shift

Examples of source lexemes corresponding to (6) are listed as (7).

(7) Patterns of positional shifts and non-shift:
    a. Connectives of cause/condition/concession/contrast (= 4Cs, or four-Cs, as in Couper-Kuhlen and Kortmann 2000), Sino-Japanese nouns, etc.
    b. Connectives of enumeration (e.g. *shi* 'and'), formal nouns (e.g. *no* 'one'), etc.
    c. Adverbs (e.g. *yahari* 'as expected') and quotatives with an integrated *say* verb, etc.
    d. Honorifics (e.g. *desu* 'polite counterpart of the copula *da*')

Admittedly in no way exhaustive, this list may reveal noteworthy differences between groups (7a) and (7b), which are composed of categorically similar source lexemes, and interesting attributes in group (7c). For instance, 4C connectives (7a) shift to LP while the enumerative connectives (7b) move to RP. Close examination of such contrastive movement may shed light on what motivates the distinct directionality of shifts (i.e. the predictability of directionality as whether (1a) and if there are peripheral-specific meanings (1b).

4.1 Core to LP

4.1.1 Clause Connectives of 4Cs (Cause, Condition, Concession, and Contrast)

The first source lexemes to be highlighted for the shift to LP are 4C connectives. Example (8), derived from Onodera (2004) with slight changes in glosses, portrays the development of the clause connective *-te mo*/*-de mo* 'although, even if' to the sentence conjunction *demo* 'but.' As shown in (8a), *-te mo* was a bound connective expressing concessive condition. In (8b) and (8c), *demo* is a full-fledged sentential conjunction. Example (8b) expresses the speaker's (= the retainer) intention to refute his interlocutor (= the lord) (Onodera 2004: 95) and is thus subjective. In (8c), *demo* resumes a prior topic, which had not been discussed for a while. Onodera (2014: 109) considers this conversation-opening function without a referential contrast as intersubjective.

(8) a. *Jinen koji* (before 1384)

*Mi o kokkani kudaki-***te** ***mo***, *kano mono o*
body ACC now break-GER but that person ACC

tasuken tame nari, . . .
save purpose COP

'Although my body would fall apart, it (my body falling apart) is to save that person...' (Onodera 2004: 90)

b. Nō kyōgen: *Suehirogari* (1792)

Lord: *Sore wa daidokoro ni nanbon mo aru kasa ja.*
that TOP kitchen in several exist umbrella COP

Sore o motomete kuru to iu koto ga aru
it ACC get come QUOT NMLZ NOM exist

mono ka.
thing Q

'That is an umbrella, several of which are in our kitchen. You shouldn't have brought it back.'

Retainer: ***Demo*** *miyako no mono ga, 'suehirogari'*
but capital GEN people NOM fan

ja to mōshita ni yotte motome-te maitta.
COP QUOT say-PST because get-GER come-PST

'But, because people in the capital told me that it was suehirogari (a fan), I brought it back.'

(Onodera 2004: 95)

c. present-day Japanese

Demo, nihon ni kaettara tanoshimi desu ne
but, Japan To go.back fun COP SFP

'But, it will be fun, won't it, when you go back to Japan?'

(Onodera 2004: 79)

Similar developments to the examples of concession in (8) are also seen with other clause connectives of contrast, cause, and condition, as in (9).

(9) *da* (COP) + *ga* 'conjunctive particle' → *daga* (but)
da + *kara* 'conjunctive particle' → *dakara* (so) (Onodera 2014: 101)[6]
da + *ttara* 'conditional form' → *dattara* (if) (Fujii 2013: 98–100)

[6] Onodera (p.c. 8/31/2016) also stated that the intermediate stage with the demonstrative *so(o)* was likely in the development of *d*-connectives as shown in footnote 11.

Because of the commonality of incorporating the copula *da* or its gerundive form *de*, Onodera calls these grammaticalized conjunctions *d*-connectives. She asserts that the copula's functions to *replace* and *recover* the predicate or situation in the preceding discourse are suitable for these *d*-connectives to link the subsequent discourse with the previous one, thereby establishing them as DMs.

4.1.2 Sino-Japanese Nouns

The second group of source lexemes that shift to LP are a group of Sino-Japanese nouns such as *kihon* 'principle,' *gensoku* 'principle,' *kekka* 'result,' *shōjiki* 'honesty,' (*aru*) *imi* '(in a) sense,' *jissai* 'actuality,' and *jijitsu* 'fact' (Takahashi and Higashiizumi 2013: 196). Interestingly, the degrees of grammaticalization of these nouns are not the same and present the following gradation.

(10) Degree of grammaticalization

kihon	*kekka*	*shōjiki*	*jissai*
gensoku		(*aru*) *imi*	*jijitsu*
inception stage as a sentence-conjunction		←——————→	in-progress/final stage as a sentence-conjunction

Derived from a corpora-based study, Takahashi and Higashiizumi (2013) point out the development of the sentence conjunction *kekka* 'result' as in (11c). The precursors to this new usage are (11a) where *kekka* is used as the head noun of a relative clause, or (11b) in which *kekka* is preceded by the demonstrative *sono* (*sono kekka* (*toshite*)). This appears to be a shift from an utterance-internal (or clause-final) position to an utterance-initial position, like the case of *-te mo*, delineated in (8). The utterance-initial *kekka* is shown in (11b) and (11c). According to Takahashi and Higashiizumi, the meaning of *kekka* in (11c) is closer to the coordinate conjunction *soshite* 'and,' rather than 'result.' That is, *kekka* in (11c) functions like a DM.

(11) a. *Itsutsu* *no* *hoteru* *ni* *shiborimashi-ta* ***kekka*** ...
five GEN hotel to narrow-PST result
'**As a result of** our narrowing it down to five hotels, ...'

b. *Itsutsu* *no* *hoteru* *ni* *shiborimashi-ta.* ***Sono kekka*** ...[7]
five GEN hotel to narrow-PST that result
'We narrowed it down to five hotels. **As a result of that**, ...'

[7] Blog entry 6/9/2016: www.tripadvisor.jp/ShowTopic-g298184-i861-k9349858-5-Tokyo_Tokyo_Prefecture_Kanto.html.

c. . . . *kyojūsha* *no* *shōdaku* *o* *tora-zu* *mudande* *tachiitta*
resident GEN consent ACC get-NEG w/o.notice search-PST

anken *ga* *arimashi-ta.* ***Kekka***, *kyojūsha* *wa*
case NOM there.is-PST and resident TOP

sanbyakuman *sōtō* *no* *udedokei* *to* *yubiwa*
3,000,000 worth GEN wrist.watch and ring

ga *nakunat-ta* *to* *shuchōshi* . . .
NOM be.gone-PST QUOT claim

'There was a case where residences were searched without the consent of the residents. **And** the residents claimed that a watch and a ring worth 3,000,000 yen were missing. . .'
(Higashiizumi and Takahashi 2013: 200)

Below is an additional example of DMs (on their way to being) grammaticalized from Sino-Japanese nouns. Here, a sentence which DMs introduce elaborates on the previous one, as DMs often do. The interchangeability between *jijitsu* 'fact,' which appeared in the original texts, and *jissai* 'actuality' in (12) pointed out by Saegusa (2013: 54) is interesting as they also assume the identical position in the gradation scale (10).

(12) {***Jijitsu/Jissai***} *sono* *yōna* *koto* *wa* *kakuchi* *de*
fact/actually that kind.of situation TOP everywhere in

kansatsusa-rete-iru.
observe-PASS-COP

'(It can be speculated that the number of Malaria patients will increase rapidly.) {**The fact of the matter is/Actually**} that kind of situation is observed everywhere.' (*Kokkai Gijiroku*, Saegusa 2013: 54)

4.2 Core to RP

4.2.1 Connectives of Enumeration

In contrast to the 4C connectives (cause/condition/concession/contrast), which shift to LP, the connectives of enumeration move to RP. Some such examples include *tari suru* 'do things like ~,' *toka* 'things like ~' and *shi* 'and.' Here are earlier examples of enumerative connectives.

(13) a. *Omoki* *mono* *wo* *ofu-**tari**,* *idafi-**tari*** *shite-ire-ba* *koso*
heavy thing ACC carry-TARI hold-TARI do-be-since EMPH

shizu-me.
sink-INFR

'Since they were carrying or holding heavy things (on top of a heavy armor), therefore they must have sunk.' (*Heike monogatari*)

b. *O-yashiki* *e* *deru* ***toka*** *zashiki* *ga* *aru*
EX-residence to attend TOKA entertainment NOM there.is
toka *iu* *to* ...
TOKA say QUOT
'When I said things like I attend to [things] at the residence, or there is a duty at the entertainment quarter ... ' (*Shunshoku umegoyomi*)

c. ... *nari-mono* *ni* *obie-nu* *mo* *are-ba,* *obieru*
resound-thing by threaten-NEG also exist-COND threaten
ko *mo* *arō* ***shi,*** ... *sōrei* *no* *kowameshi*
child also would.exist SHI funeral GEN rice
o *ku-u* *no* *mo* *arō* ***shi,*** ...
ACC eat NMLZ also would.exist SHI
'[Even for children in entertainment quarters], there are those who do not get frightened at the percussion, and also those who would be, [as for members of a temple], there are those who would eat rice served at a funeral (but also it is not necessary to think that is the case).' (*Yūgiri awanaruto*)

In recent developments, these connectives have shown three common syntactic/functional/semantic changes as in examples (15–17): (i) a movement to the utterance/sentence-final positions to decategorize as sentence-final particles;[8] (ii) a change from a multiple-item listing to a single-item listing; and (iii) an emergence of (inter)subjective meanings.

According to S. Suzuki (2008: 163–165), the single-item listing *tari suru* exudes emotive connotations such as jocularity as in (14), lightness, and contempt.

(14) *Otagai* *onaji* *kangae* *no* *mono* *dōshi,* *tama ni*
we similar ideas GEN people each.other once.in.a.while
mōsō *(shō)* *shi-**tari shite*** ...
fantasize (laugh) do-TARI SURU
'(I really like you (Haruna) just the way you are now!!) We have similar ideas, we might fantasize (ha ha ha) about each other once in a while...'
(S. Suzuki 2008: 162)

She argues that the list with *tari suru* is inexhaustive and vague, and as a result, it facilitates the speaker's lack of commitment to, and his/her detachment from, his/her own statement. She (2008: 165) states: "One

8 Whether to categorize grammaticalized connectives as sentence-final particles or not is sometimes controversial. For instance, in the case of the causal connective *kara*, controversy surrounds the absence/existence of the implied causal relationship with an implied main clause. Thompson and Suzuki (2011: 675–676) consider some cases (e.g. *atode donnani kuyandemo shiranai kara ne* 'No matter how much you regret later, I won't care (about you guys)') involve "neither an explicit 'main clause' nor a clear 'hanging implication'" but expressing "an assertion/warning," and thus they are "well on its way to being a final particle." Regarding *shi*, Kurihara (2009) also argues that *shi* is not a full-fledged sentence-final particle if its interpretation is bound to, and restricted by, the implied/related main clause. In the case of connectives of contrast, Shirakawa (1996) considers some cases of *kedo* with the elided main clauses as sentence-final particles instead of clausal connectives.

can joke about something only when one is psychologically distanced from it."

Taylor (2015: 150) claims that *toka* has been "decategorized and reconstructed in utterance-final position to become a pragmatic particle that softens the whole sentence." She argues that it is impossible to interpret the *toka* usage in (15) as exemplification as there is no item comparable to *genki ni nattari* 'becoming well' to create a list. For her it is a hedge to make the already completed utterance without *toka* end in a less assertive way.

(15) *Soshitara sugoku yappari genki ni nattari* ***toka***.
then very after.all energetic DAT become:tari TOKA
'(Because it seemed that he didn't have stamina when I called him, I said "O.K." and sent (the soup to him).) Then, (he) became really well [*toka*].'
(Taylor 2015: 151)

A similar pathway (S-internal connective to S-final particle) is also applicable to *shi*.

(16) a. (Watching people in a café)
Wain nonderu ***shi***.
wine drink-be
'(They're) drinking wine *shi*.'
(McGloin and Konishi 2010: 568)

b. *Okotteru* ***shi***.
be.angry
'You are angry *shi*.'
(McGloin and Konishi 2010: 569)

According to McGloin and Konishi (2010: 568), example (16a) is uttered by a speaker who is somewhat irritated by the fact some people are enjoying wine, while she has to study. They note that the utterance without *shi* is a simple objective statement, but *shi* conveys her "negative affect." Example (16b) is uttered in a situation in which the interlocutor responds to the speaker's comment on her computer screen being weird. They (2010: 569) take *shi* to be expressing "the effect of mildly criticizing the interlocutor's action with a teasing and playful tone." They characterize (16a) and (16b) as cases of subjectification and intersubjectification, respectively.

In a stark contrast with the 4C connectives, which developed into sentence-initial DMs, the enumerative connectives, *tari suru*, *toka*, and *shi* moved to a sentence-final position to grammaticalize as sentence-final particles, or MMs. When they list *single*, instead of *multiple* items, contrary to the expected *enumerative* function, they invite an inference that there is more to be said about the singled-out item. This line of inference is conducive to the various connotations noted above:

Subjective meanings, expressing the speaker's attitude toward the proposition as in (14) and (16a), and the intersubjective functions involving the addressee as in (15) and (16b). It is of interest that the above studies explicitly point out intersubjective meaning in these grammaticalized MMs at RP, however, none of them mention the turn-yielding or response-inviting functions of these markers, which may be an indication that these functions are insignificant (contra Beeching and Detges's hypothesis in Section 5).

4.2.2 Japanese Formal Nouns

In contrast to Sino-Japanese nouns discussed earlier, so-called formal nouns (*keishiki meishi*) in traditional Japanese linguistics have very general abstract meanings such as *mono* 'thing/person,' *no* 'one,' *koto* 'matter,' etc. As shown in (17), at the first stage, they appeared utterance-/sentence-internally as a lexical head noun with a preceding sentential modifier. When grammaticalization proceeded, they shifted positionally to RP, and further combining with the copula *da*, became utterance/sentence-final modal auxiliaries (e.g. 18). When the copula was dropped at the next stage, they resulted in more (inter)subjective utterance/sentence-final MMs (e.g. 19) (cf. R. Suzuki 2006; Ujiie 1992).

(17) lexical noun > formal noun + *da* (Modal Auxiliary) > formal noun (= MM)

According to Kitamura (2008), *mono da* 'thing COP' started to show the subjective meaning of surprise/exclamation in *Hanashi-bon*, a collection of comical anecdotes and stories compiled in the eighteenth century, as in (18). Note here that the first *mono* in (18a) is a lexical head noun with a referential meaning, while this referential meaning is bleached in the second *mono da* in (18a) as well as (18b).

(18) a. (Hearing a wooden flute producing insect-like chirping sounds)

Kimyōna	***mono***	*mo*	*deru*	***mono***	***da***.
strange	thing	also	come.out	MON	DA

'Strange sounds come out (from this), (to my surprise).'
(*Fukuwauchi*, Kitamura 2008: 455)

b.

Naruhodo	*sakura*	*ni*	*mo*	*iroiro-na*	*yatsu*	*ga*
I.see	cherry.blossoms	for	also	various	one	NOM

aru	***mono***	***da***.
exist	MON	DA

'I see. Even among cherry blossoms, there are many different varieties!' (*Kokin shūku otoshi banashi*, Kitamura 2008: 454)

In addition to the surprise effect of *mono da*, the new copula-less form *mo(no)* appears in present-day Japanese as a marker of *amae* 'dependence (on the addressee).' In (19), Speaker E's conversation partner is laughing at

Speaker E's clumsiness in handling the abacus.[9] The sentence-final *mon* communicates E's emotional dependency on and full trust of the addressee that her clumsiness with the abacus could be understood and accepted as the result of her lack of experience with it in grade school.

(19) E: *Shiranai* *n* *da* ***mon***
know-NEG NMLZ COP MON
'I don't know (how to use an abacus) MON'
E: *Yat-ta* *koto* *nai* *n* *da* ***mon***
do-PST things NEG NMLZ COP MON
'I've never learned abacus MON'
(Fujii 2000: 105)

Yet another such formal noun is *no* 'one.' According to Ujiie (1992: 561), the utterance-final *noda* established itself around the eighteenth century. In present-day Japanese, Noda (1997) recognizes two types of *noda*: what she calls *taiji-teki* 'event-oriented' and *taijin-teki* 'addressee-oriented' *noda* as in (20–21). The former embodies a sense of discovery with no addressee involvement, and is thus considered subjective, while the latter is directed to the addressee as an explanatory statement (21a) or as a directive (21b) and therefore is analyzed as intersubjective. Noda (1997: 68) notes that the event-oriented *noda* (20) is not interchangeable with *no*, but *no* is interchangeable with the addressee-oriented *noda* as in (21a') and (21b'). This supports the claim that just like the *mono da*/*mon* differences, the copula-less *no* is more intersubjective than *noda*.

(20) ***Taiji-teki*** (event-oriented) *noda*: subjective
Yamada-san *ga* *ko-nai* *nā.* *Kitto* *yōji* *ga* ***aru*** ***nda (= no da)***
NOM come-NEG SFP surely errands NOM exist NODA
'Yamada's not here I'm sure he has some errands to do.'
(Noda 1997: 68)

(21) ***Taijin-teki*** (addressee-oriented) *noda*: intersubjective
a. *Watashi* *ashita* *wa* *ko-nai* *yo.* *Yōji* *ga* ***aru*** ***nda (= no da).***
I tomorrow TOP come-NEG SFP errands NOM exist NODA
a'. *Watashi ashita wa ko-nai yo. Yōji ga* ***aru no.***
'I'm not coming tomorrow. I have some errands to do.'
b. *Kono* *suitchi* *o* ***osu*** ***nda!***
this switch ACC push NODA
b'. *Kono suitchi o* ***osu no!***
'Push this switch!'
(adopted from Noda 1997: 68–69)

Given the above, it is evident that these formal nouns grammaticalized as MMs in RP, marking an unequivocal contrast with the Sino-Japanese nouns, which grammaticalized as DMs in LP. Further, it appears that the

[9] The collocational affinity of *mon* with the DM *datte* is pointed out by Fujii (2000: 105). This is reminiscent of the concordances of the sentence-initial C/D item to the corresponding sentence-final C/D item (e.g. *dōmo* . . . *yōda*, see Section 2).

grammaticalized "formal nouns+*da*" are more subjective, while the copula-less formal nouns are more intersubjective. Of note here is that even though they are intersubjective, these MMs do not explicitly signal turn-yielding (cf. Section 5).

4.3 Contrastive Pathways of Change: An Explanatory Account

The previous two sections have identified the contrastive directionality: The 4C connectives and the Sino-Japanese nouns move to LP, while the connectives of enumeration and the Japanese formal nouns shift to RP. Recognizing such an opposing directionality of the same/similar categorical items, questions regarding the predictability of the directionality (1a) and the existence of peripheral-meanings of LP/RP (1b) now come into focus.

4.3.1 LP versus RP

Starting with query (1a), three factors are crucial: (i) clausal cline types (i.e. subordinate/hypotactic/paratactic as in Hopper and Traugott (2003: 179)), (ii) the combinability with the deictic *sore/sono/sō* 'that' and (iii) the contentfulness of nouns.

The 4C connectives are subordinate in nature, while those of enumeration are paratactic. In the $Clause_1$-4C connective-$Clause_2$ structure, the relationship between CL_1 and CL_2 is tight syntactically and semantically, and neither CL_1 nor CL_2 by itself can express the whole proposition fully. For instance, for the 4C connective *cause* CL_1 (cause) is part and parcel with CL_2 (result). However, in CL_1-enumerative connective-CL_2, CL_1, and CL_2 are paratactic, and loosely joined syntactically and semantically. Thus, CL_1 is readily separated from CL_2 to form a full sentence or proposition by itself.

The second factor, the combinability with *sore/sono/sō* relates to the first factor and the nature of DMs. It is noted that DMs indicate two-place relations between sequentially ordered chunks of discourse (Fraser 1999: 938; Cuenca 2013: 192; Detges 2015: 132). Naturally, the two-place relations call for two clauses as in cause (CL_1) and result (CL_2) as argued above. From these two tightly connected clauses, neither is dispensable, and as such they serve as ready candidates for DMs, which straddle two clauses. Consistent with Diewald's (2013: 25) characterization of DMs as "indexical elements relating items of discourse to other items of discourse," it is not surprising that the deictic *sore/sono/sō*+DM, which precedes CL_2 points to CL_1. What the demonstrative *sore* does is to refer to, or replace the previous discourse (CL_1 CL_2 $\rightarrow$ *sore*+connective S_2), thereby reinforcing the two place relations and creating a textual cohesion between the two sentences. Thus, the source lexemes' combinability with the deictics may predict the likelihood for connectives to serve as DMs. As shown in (22), the 4C connectives can combine with *sore/sono/sō* naturally, while the enumerative connectives yield unnatural or extremely awkward sequences as in (23).[10]

(22) 4C Connectives:
A: *Tesuto wa iya da na.* 'I hate tests!'
B: (a) ***Sore dakara**, itsumo tesuto ga dekinai nja nai no?* **'Because of that**, *you always get low marks, right?'*
(b) ***Sore demo**, ukenakya ikenai nda yo ne.* '**Even so**, we must take them, right?'
(c) ***Sō dakedo**, ukenakya ikenai nda yo ne.* '**However (= in contrast to that)**, we must take them, right?'

(23) Enumerative connectives:

A: *Hanako-san, kyūni nakidashite . . .* 'Hanako starts crying all of a sudden. . .'
B: (a) ***Sore-dat-tari**, warattari, okottari . . .* 'She does things like laughing, getting mad, **and that**. . .'
(b) ****Sore da toka**, warau toka, okoru toka . . .* 'She laughs, gets mad, **and does things like that**. . .'
(c) ****Sō-da shi**, warau shi, okoru shi. . .* 'She laughs, gets mad, **and does things like that**. . .'

The intermediate stages with the deictics (e.g. *Soredemo* → *Demo* and *Soredakara* → *Dakara*) are hypothesized by Onodera (2004: 87). Furthermore, it is also attested in Higashiizumi's (2015: 141) study as a "layering" stage (Hopper and Traugott 2003: 49) where both *sore dakara* and *dakara* (with and without *sore*) coexisted.[11]

(24)

Sore-da-kara	*mā*	*chitto-bakari*	*demo*	*tore-ba*	*yokat-ta*
DEM-DA-KARA	INTJ	a.little.bit-some	even.if	steal-if	good-was

mono	*o,*	. . .
NMLZ	ACC	

'Because it is (so), uh, (I) should have stolen a little bit, but. . .'
(*Kiruna* 1785, in Higashiizumi 2015: 141)

[10] The acceptability judgments here are based on an informal survey of twenty-two native speaker informants. The average rates of acceptability for (22) are as follows: (a) 91%, (b) 95% and (c) 91%. For (23): (a) 0%, (b) 9%, and (c) 0%.

[11] Higashiizumi (p.c. 9/6/2014) notes the demonstrative *so(o)* is also involved in the following grammaticalization processes (*kekka* 'result'; *daro(o)/desho(o)* 'conjectural auxiliary'):

(1) CL_1-*kekka*-CL_2	>	CL. *Sono-kekka-toshite*, CL	>	*Kekka* CL
(2) CL-*daro(o)/desho(o)*	>	CL. *Sō -daro(o)/desho(o)*	>	*daro(o)/desho(o)*

A similar tendency with conditionals is also noted by Fujii (2013: 93–94).

Sō/sore-nara 'so-if'	→	*Nara* 'if that is the case, then'
Sō-da-to-shi-tara 'so-COP-QUOT-do-if'	→	*Datoshitara* 'if that is case, then'
Sō-suru-to 'so-do-when'	→	*Suruto* 'when that happened, then'

To recapitulate, two factors, clausal cline types and the combinability with *sore/sono/sō* 'that,' enlighten the propensity of the 4C (subordinate) instead of enumerative (paratactic) connectives to move to LP to grammaticalize as DMs.

The third factor, contentfulness, illuminates the distinct behavior of the two types of nouns. "Contentfulness" refers to the quality of being able to stand alone and yet still be meaningful. Formal nouns are so abstract and semantically "light" that they require a preceding modifying clause to be meaningful (Matsumura 1971: 193). Indeed, without one, ill-formed sentences result, as in (25b).[12] But the opposite is true for the Sino-Japanese nouns, as in (25a). They also embody meanings which readily evolve to introduce elaboration on the preceding sentence (e.g. S_1 *kekka* S_2 'S_1. As a result S_2'; S_1 *jissai* S_2 'S_1. Actually S_2').

(25) a. *{Kekka / Kihon / Shōjiki / Jissai} wa ii.*
result principle honesty actuality TOP good
'{The result/The principle/Honesty /Reality} is good.'

b. *{*No / *Koto / ?Mono} wa ii.*
One thing thing TOP good
'{Ones/Things/ ?Things} are good.'

The modifying clause for these formal nouns varies in length and content, and thus is unpredictable. For this reason, it is unlikely that the 'modifying clause+formal noun' will compact itself to become a short sentence conjunction, or a DM. Brinton (2010: 285) states that generally agreed formal features of discourse markers are "phonologically 'short' items that preferentially occur in sentence-initial position." On the other hand, already compact and contentful Sino-Japanese nouns could easily turn into DMs. Example (26a) shows this possibility, while (26b) is both structurally and semantically anomalous if these formal nouns are intended to be read as DMs.

(26) a. S_1 (*Kekka / Kihon / Shōjiki / Jissai*) S_2
'S_1 (As a result / In principle / To be honest / In reality) S_2.'

b. S_2 (**No / *Koto / *Mono*) S_2
'S_1 (*Ones / *Things / *Things) S_2.'

To recap, the contentfulness of the Sino-Japanese nouns helps them achieve their structural brevity and semantic readiness to express two-place relations needed for DM functions in a meaningful way.

So far, three factors have been explored in an effort to account for the source lexemes' likeliness to shift to LP. But the lack of them does not logically entail the opposite directionality. Thus, one may rightfully ask if there is any positive driving force for them to shift to RP. Instructive in this regard is Cuenca's (2013: 192, 195) view: "discourse markers ... are two

[12] For (25b), if *mono* means the abstract noun 'quality,' it can stand by itself.

position operators, that is, units typically linking two content segments, whereas modal particles are one position operators that modify the illocution of an utterance."

It is possible to see RP-bound source lexemes (enumerative connectives and the formal nouns) as possessing such MM attributes in Japanese. The enumerative connectives are basically paratactic and dealing with one independent content segment, therefore, they are like MMs, which are "one position operators" using Cuenca's term. Likewise, the formal nouns are one position operators, as they involve only one preceding modifying clause. Furthermore, since what precedes them are complete sentences, it is possible for these preceding sentences to be reanalyzed as main clauses and propositions (i.e. Level B). With this syntactic and semantic reanalysis, the connectives and nouns following the proposition could be reanalyzed as RP elements. Because illocutions and speaker attitude are generally expressed in Levels C/D, or RP, it is natural for these RP-bound connectives and the nouns to acquire emotivity and be decategorized as MMs.[13]

4.4 Core to Both LP/RP

A group of words and constructions, which shift both to LP and RP, includes adverbs (e.g. *yahari* 'as expected'), quotative constructions, particles (*ne*, *na*, and *yo* as LP/RP elements as noted in Onodera 2014), etc. The historical pathways of adverbs and quotative constructions are delineated below with an account of why such bi-directionality is possible.

4.4.1 Yahari

The adverb *yahari* started as a sentence-internal manner adverb meaning "being still" as in (27). Later, it developed a morphophonological variant, *yappari*, and also acquired modal adverbial usage 'as expected/after all/at any rate' (still > predictable > as expected) as in (28a). At this point, the original manner adverbial function fell into disuse. Later, yet another morphophonological variant, *yappa* as in (28b) came into the picture (Shinzato 2011).[14]

(27) *Omote* *wo* *ba* ***yahari*** *owite* *te* *wo*
face ACC EMPH still hold hand ACC

atikoti *suru* *wa* *minikui* *zo.*
here.and.there do TOP unsightly SFP

'Keeping the head still when facing (someone), yet with hands unsettled is unsightly.'

(*Hyaku jō shingi*, 1462)

[13] This is similar to R. Suzuki's (2006: 37) account of *wake*: "what happened diachronically is the reanalysis of the preceding clause modifying the noun *wake* as the main clause of an utterance with a modality marker (*wake* and related forms) at the end. The syntactic reanalysis leads to the pragmatic uses of *wake* today."

[14] Shinzato (2014) found that the adverbs of degree *amari* 'not much' and *bakari* 'about' have gone through developmental paths parallel syntactically (positionally), semantically, and morphophonologically to *yahari*.

(28) a. *Nara* *wa* ***yappari*** *yaezakura* *kana.*
TOP as.expected cherry.blossom SFP
'Speaking of Nara, (what comes to mind) as expected, is cherry blossoms!' (*Haikai okina gusa*, 1696)

b. *Nanisa* ***yappa*** *Yagura* *ka* *Susotsugi* *ga* *yō* *gozensu.*
IP as.expected or NOM good COP
'Well, as expected, Yagura or Susotsugi (amusement quarters) is good.' (*Sharebon Fukagawa shinwa*, 1776)

Core to LP

In present-day Japanese, *yappa(ri)* developed a DM usage. This parallels a well-known cline of "Clause-internal Adverbial > Sentence Adverbial > Discourse Particle" (Traugott 1995). Example (29) illustrates a DM usage of *yappa* in LP (*so* < *as you know* < *as expected*), as it signals a turn change, instead of conveying the meaning of "as expected." Here, when Speaker B slows down by uttering several fillers, Speaker A initiates her turn with *yappa*, which unexpectedly coincided with Speaker B's utterance of *kawa*↑ 'leather.' Realizing immediately that she was interrupting Speaker B, Speaker A stops suddenly, then continues with the topic prompted by B instead, thereby giving up the topic change she originally intended with *yappa, koinu no toki*... '**So**, when he was a puppy....'

(29) B: *Kubiwa* *wa* *nani,* *ano=* *[kawa]*↑
collar TOP what well leather
'His collar is what, well leather...'

A: ***[Yappa***, *koinu* *no* *toki].*
DM puppy gen time
'**So**, when he was a puppy //stops suddenly//'

A: *Kawa* *na* *nda* *kedo,* <u=n> *koinu* *no* *toki* *kat-ta* *yatsu*
leather COP it's.that but hmm puppy GEN time buy-PST thing
'It's leather. It's the one we bought when he was a puppy...'
(Gendai Nihongo Kenkyūkai 1997, *Female Corpus*: 5105)

Core to RP

In contrast to its move to LP, the adverb *yappari* also shifts to RP to express the speaker's stance toward the proposition and to the addressee. In (30), A is emphatically defending her likes, despite B's criticism. In (31), B is forcefully telling the addressee to alter her behavior. These two adverbs are fully grammaticalized as sentence-final particles. Placing them sentence-internally would be unnatural or would not connote similar emotive effects of coercion or insistence.[15]

[15] According to Shinzato's (2011) survey, at least half (in the second case, three-quarters) of thirty-five Japanese informants found the sentence-internal version of (30) and (31) unnatural, and several of them explicitly stated that

(30) B: *Omae-tte sōiu yatsu na nda yo.*
you-TOP that.kind.of fellow COP it's.that SFP
'It's that you are that kind of (pathetic) fellow.'
A: *Sō na no kana?*
so COP NMLZ SFP
Sōiu no ga sukina nda yo, ***yappari****.*
that.kind.of things NOM like it's.that SFP YAPPARI
'Do you think so? It's that I like such things, **you know**.'
(Gendai Nihongo Kenkyūkai 1997, *Female Corpus*: 273)

(31) B: *Omae no baai, sōiu fūni itte kokoro no naka*
you LK case that way say heart LK inside
ni samui kaze ga fuite-ru baai ga aru kara,
in cold wind NOM blow-PROG time NOM exist so
sonna hanashi o kiite-ru-nja nai nda yo, ***yappa****.*
that things ACC listen-PROG-COP NEG it's.that SFP YAPPA
'In your case, you say that way, (but) cold wind is blowing in your heart. So, you shouldn't listen to such talk, **you know**.'
(ibid.: 264)

After the bi-directional shift delineated above, *yappari/yappa* was grammaticalized as a DM with a turn-taking function at LP, while at RP, it acquired MM functions of expressing the addressee-oriented meanings.

4.4.2 Quotative Constructions

Quotative constructions (e.g. quotative conditionals as below) also shift bi-directionally.[16]

(32) S_1 *to + it-tara + ba* S_2 S_1 QUOT + say-PERF + COND S_2
S_1 *to + ie + ba* S_2 S_1 QUOT + say + COND S_2

Core to LP

Taking the *to ifi-tara-ba* (QT say-PERF-COND), the following developmental stages can be constructed (Stages 1–3 are from Shinzato and Suzuki (2007)). Stage 4 shows an ongoing grammaticalization.

the emphatic or insistent tone lessened if these adverbs were placed internally. The translation of *yappa(ri)* with 'you know' was suggested by several informants.

(30′) *Sō na no kana? Sō iu no ga yappari suki na n da yo.*

(31′) *Omae no baai, . . . samui kaze ga fuite-ru baai ga aru kara, yappa kiiterunja nainda yo.*

[16] R. Suzuki's (2007) study of the quotative construction, *tte+iu/omou* 'quotative particle+say/think' also offers a similar bi-directional shift. The construction grammaticalized as a sentence-final particle in RP, while the amalgamation of *tte* and the alternative question particle *ka* (i.e. *tte yūka* 'or rather') decategorized as a DM in LP.

(33) Stage 1 S-internal quotative conditional: X *to it-tara(ba)* 'if/when saying X'
Stage 2 As a topic marker: X *to it-tara-(ba)* 'Speaking of X (X = prompted)'
Stage 3 As an emotive topic marker, with a phonologically reduced form: X *ttara*[17] (indicating the speaker's evaluative attitude, surprise or animosity)
Stage 4 Pseudo-sentence conjunction, with demonstrative *sō: sō-it-tara* 'if (you) say so'

Examples (34)–(36) represent Stages 1, 2, and 3, respectively. The prompted topic X for Stage 2 is underlined in (35).

(34) *(...) senaka o nagashite-kudasē* ***to it-tara*** *babāme ga*
back ACC wash-give.IMP QUOT say-when hag NOM
tawashi o motte kiyagatte o-senaka o araimashō ka to
scourer ACC bring came HON-back ACC wash QP QUOT
nukashiyagaru.
say
'(...) When I said, "Please wash my back," an old hag came with a scourer and said, "May I scrub your back?"'
(*Tokaidōchū hizakurige* 1802–1809)

(35) A: *Keiko no iranē mono nishite...*
rehearsing GEN need-not thing as
'Something which needs no rehearsing...'
B: *Keiko no kakara-n mono* ***to-iu-tara,***
rehearsing GEN take-not thing QUOT-SAY-TARA
Chūshingura, Hiragana, ...
<name> <name>
'Speaking of things which need no rehearsing, they are Chushingura, Hiragana, ...'
(*Ukiyoburo* 1809)

(36) ... *otōsama-**ttara** kinō katte-oide-ninat-ta no yo [...]*
father-TTARA yesterday buy-come-HON-PST NMLZ SFP
Okashina otōsama deshō?
funny father right
'(I don't know when I will be able to wear it, but) my father, (to my surprise), bought a hat for me yesterday. Isn't he funny?'
(*Kaze tachinu* 1938)

Below is an example of Stage 4. The difference between this and Stage 2 is that here the phrase *sō ittara* in toto refers to the entire utterance, not just

[17] The robust elision of 'say' verbs in the development of 'say' constructions with pragmatic uses is also noted in Ahn and Yap (2014).

a phrase in the preceding discourse like the underlined one in (35). The exchanges in (37) follow interviewer A's explanation of the purpose of her interviews as the solicitation of male doctors' opinions about balancing work and family together with their physician spouses. The opener *sō it-tara* by Speaker C does not mean "speaking of the word '*sō*'" (as in 'X' in Stage 2 of (33) and the quoted phrase in (35B), but it means "in that case" or "then," that is, the function of a DM.

(37) B: *Sō* *desu.*
correct COP
'(Asked if B is the husband of Dr. Isoko Negishi) Yes, that's correct.'
C: ***Sō it-tara***, *boku* *nanka* *kekkonshite-inai* *ndesu* *kedo.*
then I like marry-NEG it.is.that but
'**In that case/Then**, (I'm not qualified as) I'm not married.'[18]

Core to RP

The same quotative conditional shifts to RP to become a sentence-final particle (Shinzato 2015).

(38) Stage 1 S-internal quotative conditional: X *to it-tara(ba)* 'if/when saying X'
Stage 2 Formulaic quotative conditional: X *to it-tara* X 'If I say X, it's X'
Stage 3 Sentence-final particle: X *ttara* '*You* confirm/comply with X'

Stage 2 is exemplified in the formulaic expression (39) where the predicate *oide* 'come' is repeated, and appears twice both before and after *ttara*. At Stage 3, *ttara* is added to the already completed utterance. The function of *ttara* is to express emotivity directed to the addressee, such as the speaker's coercion on the addressee to comply (40a), or his insistence (40b). These pragmatic meanings are indicative of their statuses as MMs.

(39) *Oide* *yo.* *Oide* *to* *i-**ttara*** *oide* *yo.*
come.IMP SFP come.IMP QUOT say-when come SFP
'Come. If I tell you to come, come.' (*Ukigumo* 1887)

(40) a. *Chotto* *omoi* *wa* *yo.* *Doite-**ttara**.*
hey heavy SFP SFP get.off.IMP-TTARA
'Hey. You're heavy, you know. Get-off me (already, I'm telling you)!' (*Isogashii hanayome*)
b. (Asked what he is cooking up with his friend behind the addressee's back)
Marude *kyōhaku* *da* *na.* *Warui* *koto* *ja* *nai-**ttara***
like accusatory COP SFP bad things COP NEG-TTARA
'Your tone is so accusatory. It's nothing bad (I tell you)!' (*Shōnen no umi*)

[18] www.yokohama.kanagawa.med.or.jp/woman_physician/interview-no11.html (5/29/2016).

To recap, after the bi-directional shifts, the grammaticalized adverbs and quotative constructions both exhibit textual functions at LP in a broad sense, while at RP, they both show more modal functions. This functional bifurcation affirms the existence of the peripheral-specific meanings (1b).

4.4.3 An Account of the Bi-directional Shifts

Why are such bi-directional shifts possible? As for the modal adverbs, the bi-directional shifts may be possible because they are morphologically unbound and compact, semantically full, and functionally equipped for modifying functions. Their morphological brevity facilitates the freedom of their positional shifts. Like Sino-Japanese nouns but unlike formal nouns, adverbs are contentful, thus can modify *others* without the need to be modified by other lengthy clauses. In fact, modal adverbs are already able to modify an entire sentence (cf. Matsumura 1971: 720; Traugott 1995 on Adverbial Cline).

As for the quotative conditionals, their move to LP is in line with the other 4C connectives (Section 4.3, footnote 11). However, unlike the regular conditionals, the quotative conditionals also shift to RP and grammaticalize there as sentence-final particles or MMs (Shinzato 2015). It seems that the key for this RP pathway is the fact that the embedded *say* verb appends to a complete sentence like the RP-bound enumerative connectives and formal nouns. In the series of developments below, when the phrase *to ittara* gets phonologically reduced and absorbs the *say* verb as *ttara*, the original conditional meaning also becomes obscure. When the construction further loses its apodosis, the conditional meaning comes to be bleached and irrelevant. This leads to the emergence of the sentence-final particle (41c).

(41) a. $[X]_S$ *to ii tara(ba)* $[Y]_S$ 'When/If saying X, then Y.'
b. $[X]_S$ *to it-tara* $[X]_S$ 'When/If I say X, it's X.'
c. $[X]_S$ *ttara* 'You confirm/comply with X.'[19]

Regular conditionals without the *say* verb go through a similar development as in (42). In the second stage (42b), formulaic expressions are formed, and in the third stage (43c), the apodoses are deleted. However, there is a difference between (41c) and (42c): the apodoses in (42c) are still extremely relevant. It is only after the deleted apodoses are recovered by contextual and phonological cues (e.g. rising intonation for suggestion) that the utterance-final *tara* (42c) can be interpreted appropriately. In other words, the conditional meaning is not completely bleached. For this reason, the S-final *tara* is not regarded as a fully grammaticalized sentence-final particle in RP (see footnote 8). Subsequently, the *tara*'s case was not taken as a bi-directional shift.[20]

[19] Foong Ha Yap (p.c. 6/25/2016) suggests "Confirm/Comply with X, I say" as a bridge context between (41b) and (41c).

[20] Suspended clauses (Ohori 1995), or *iisashi yōhō* (Kurihara 2009) are seen in other 4C connectives such as *kara* (see footnote 8). Scholars' views are not uniform as to whether to discern such cases as fully grammaticalized sentence-final particles. According to Kurihara's litmus test, if a target lexeme could be replaced with other sentence-final particles, then they are categorized as sentence-final particles. For instance, the *ttara* in (41c) or (40a) can be replaced

(42)	a.	X-*tara(ba)* [Y]$_S$	'When/If it's X, then Y.'
	b. (i)	X-*tara*, ***dō suru***?	'How(What) {would you do/ would that be} if it's X?'
	(ii)	X-*tara*, ***dō***?	'How would it be if you do X?'
	(iii)	X-*tara*, ***ii***.	'It would be good if it's X'
	c. (i)	X-*tara?*	'What if it's X?'
	(ii)	X-*tara?*	'Why don't you X?'
	(iii)	X-*tara*	'I hope/wish it's X'

4.5 Japanese Honorifics: *Desu* and *Masu*

The Japanese honorifics, *desu* and *masu*, are generally analyzed to express deference to the addressee. Below, the b-sentences are polite counterparts of the a-sentences.

(43) a. *Un*, *taberu* *yo*. (plain)
b. *Ē*, *tabe**masu*** *yo*. (polite)
yes eat SFP
'Yes, I'm going to eat.'

(44) a. *Shimekiri* *wa* *ashita* *da* *yo*. (plain)
b. *Shimekiri* *wa* *ashita* ***desu*** *yo*. (polite)
due.date TOP tomorrow COP SFP
'The due date is tomorrow.'

Both *desu* and *masu* were originally verbs (Martin 1975: 1032), but in the course of development, their original lexical meanings were bleached, and they came to be grammaticalized as so-called addressee honorifics. The addressee honorifics are considered Level D (in the layered structure) elements for its assumed intersubjectivity, yet unexpectedly, *desu* and *masu* remain as the Core items (A and B), as they are within the scope of tense and negation as in (45). Thus, they present a mismatch between syntax and semantics.

(45) a. *tabe-**masu*** (positive) vs. *tabe-**masen*** (negative)
b. *tabe-**masu*** (present) vs. *tabe-**mashita*** (past)

However, the assumed mismatch is not a mismatch according to Kindaichi (1953), who disputes the claim that the *desu/masu* is an addressee honorific. For him, it is a *stylistic* variation, as succinctly captured by the Japanese term, *desu/masu tai* 'the *desu/masu* style.' Japanese prose has to be written either in the polite *desu/masu* style or in the plain style, and mixing of the styles is not allowed. Thus, he concludes that the use of the *desu/masu* endings is not the result of the speaker's desire to express exaltation toward the addressee, but

by *yo* as in *doite ttara* 'Get off me!' → *doite yo*, but not those in (42c) because of *doi tara?* → **doi-yo* 'Why don't you get off me?' Similarly, *toka* in (15) can be replaced by *ne*. However, it is not the case with *tari shite* in (14). This may show the gradation in grammaticalization (cf. footnote 8).

rather that it is the formality of the situation that dictates it. Consistent with Kindaichi's view, Ide (1992) does not consider *desu/masu* as volition-based addressee honorifics, but as an instance of *wakimae* 'discernment.' *Wakimae* is the social/cultural norms that members of the society are brought up to observe (cf. Chapter 26, this volume). For her, the use of *desu/masu* is comparable to automatic person, number, and gender agreement in European languages.

Kindaichi, however, considers the newer usage of *desu* as in (46) to be the addressee honorific. *Desu* follows *masu/mashita* endings whether they are tensed or negated, but *desu* itself cannot be tensed or negated. Thus, syntactically, this usage of *desu* has a scope wider than *masu/masita*. Martin (1975: 1030) also states, "Sometimes one gets the feeling that *desu* can be added to just about anything to lend a touch of politeness."

(46) *Jōgen* *ga* *kimatteori-**masu*** ***desu*** *ne.*
ceiling NOM be.decided-ADD.HON(?) ADD.HON SFP
'The ceiling of the budget has been decided.'
(Tamura and Kitazawa 2011: 8)

The new usage of *desu* indeed exhibits the correlation of syntax and semantics. Syntactically, it qualifies as an RP item for its inability to be negated and tensed (Levels C or D), and semantically, it satisfies the volitionality aspect of addressee-honorifics, unlike the original *wakimae*-driven politeness markers. The controversy over the classification of the original *desu* and *masu* as addressee honorifics may very well be a reflection of their syntactic and semantic mismatch.

5 Beeching and Detges's Functional Asymmetry Hypothesis

Table 3.1 below summarizes Beeching and Detges's Functional Asymmetry Hypothesis.

In part, Japanese data are consistent with Beeching and Detges's hypothesis.

Table 3.1 *Hypothesized usages of linguistic items on the left and right periphery*

LP	RP
Dialogual	Dialogic
Turn-taking/attention-getting	Turn-yielding/end-marking
Link to previous discourse	Anticipation of forthcoming discourse
Response-marking	Response-inviting
Focalizing, topicalizing, framing	Modalizing
Subjective	Intersubjective

(Beeching and Detges 2014: 11)

(47) a. Japanese lexical items (4C connectives/Sino-Japanese nouns vis-à-vis enumerative connectives/formal nouns) show an asymmetrical pattern of grammaticalization: the former grammaticalizes as DMs in LP, while the latter decategorizes as MMs in RP.
b. In the case of the bi-directional shift (e.g. *yappari* 'as expected'), functional bifurcation is observed: the target lexemes are functionally aligned with DMs at LP, and MMs at RP.

On the other hand, Japanese data deviate from their hypothesis:

(48) a. Contrary to their equation of LP to intersubjectivity and RP to subjectivity, both peripheries are equally subjective and intersubjective (e.g. subjective and intersubjective usages of *demo* in LP, and those of *shi* in RP, and also see Onodera 2014: 109–111).
b. Unlike their claim, RP turns out to be more response marking, and not overwhelmingly response-inviting.
c. A symmetry of LP and RP is also seen in the concordance of elements at the same levels (e.g. collocation patterns of subjective elements at Level C in LP/RP in Figure 3.1).

6 Conclusion

In the grammaticalization literature, research focusing specifically on the relationship between the structure of the target language and the issues of LP/RP is scarce. Even less studied is the relationship between source items and the likely directionality of their movement. In an attempt to fill such a gap, this chapter has shown the intricate correlation of structure (layered model), semantics ((inter)subjectivity) and positional shifts in the grammaticalization of Japanese source items. It has argued that semantically heavy, contentful constituents (4C connectives and Sino-Japanese nouns) are likely to move to LP, while the opposite (movement to RP) is expected for the semantically light source lexemes (connectives of enumeration and formal Japanese nouns). It has also highlighted adverbs and quotative conditionals as examples of bi-directional movement and offered an account for such bi-directionality. Finally, it has also touched upon the addressee honorifics for their seeming mismatch of structure and semantics.

In conclusion, this chapter has provided affirmative answers to the questions posed in the introduction (1a–b). As for (1c), it explored the Japanese case in the context of Beeching and Detges's Functional Asymmetry Hypothesis. It confirmed the overall tendencies, but at the same time, pointed out some deviations from it.

It is hoped that this chapter will stimulate this line of research in general/Japanese grammaticalization studies. In closing, it lists the following as future research questions:

(49) a. Not all source lexemes are grammaticalized equally as target lexemes, but show some gradation (e.g. *ttara* was categorized as a full-fledged sentence-final particle, but *tara* was not. See (41–42)). What would be the proper characterization of such a gradation? (see also (10), footnotes 8, and 20)
b. How do we deal with the secondary shift? For instance, in some Japanese dialects, the sentence-initial *soshite* 'and' back-shifts to the sentence-final position with more modal-like functions (Izutsu and Izutsu 2013: 224–226): *Kore shimatte-kite* ***soshite*** 'Go and put this aside, **anyway**.'
c. How do we properly characterize fillers, which are intersubjective, but are apparently sentence-internal elements? Related to this, should RP be clause-final instead of sentence-final?

4

Linguistic Typology and the Japanese Language

Kaoru Horie

1 Introduction

Linguistic Typology, the cross-linguistic study of grammatical, lexical, and phonological systems, has revealed the structural "standing" of an individual language relative to other languages in the world (Comrie 1989; Whaley 1997). In the past, the Japanese language has often been labeled by non-linguists (and occasionally even by linguists) as a "unique" language, rather impressionistically, due to the existence of linguistic features such as honorification and the seemingly complex writing systems consisting of *hiragana, katakana* (two types of native Japanese syllabaries respectively used to represent native Japanese morphemes and foreign loanwords other than from Chinese), and *kanji* (Chinese characters). However, thanks to the findings of typologically oriented research (e.g. Shibatani 1990), a more precise, relativized description of the Japanese language has become possible.

Informed by cognitive-functional and sociopragmatic approaches to the form–meaning mapping across languages (e.g. Croft 2001; Talmy 2000; Trudgill 2011), Linguistic Typology has been successful in identifying the unique manner in which a language selects and projects grammatical meaning onto its structural resources and conventionalizes the form–meaning mapping as constructions.

Inspired by the recent findings in Linguistic Typology and its related disciplines, this chapter is intended to provide a structural and functional typological profile of the Japanese language. It first provides a general typological sketch of the Japanese language in terms of structural properties such as word order, agglutinating morphology, case marking, and the degree of differentiation between noun and verb. It then probes the prominent grammatical and lexical features of the Japanese language that are

My deep thanks go to Yoko Hasegawa for extensive and constructive criticism, and to Koyomi Takahashi and An Hyeryeon for the data presented in Section 3.2. Thanks also go to John Haig and Nathan Hamlitsch for stylistic comments. The usual disclaimer applies.

closely linked to discourse-pragmatic and rhetorical practices and language-particular lexicalization patterns in the language from the perspectives of Comparative Typology and Cognitive Typology. The latter two analytical frameworks, mutually independent, have been developed from Linguistic Typology to address cross-linguistically variable form–meaning interactions more precisely than was possible in traditional Linguistic Typology (see Section 2 for details).

The organization of this chapter is as follows. Section 2 introduces three cross-linguistic analytical perspectives adopted in this chapter. Section 3 discusses two linguistic phenomena in Japanese that are worthy of attention typologically. Section 4 presents the conclusion.

2 Three Cross-linguistic Analytical Perspectives: Linguistic, Comparative, and Cognitive Typologies

It is not easy to identify the prominent lexico-grammatical features of a language, which can be identified only through a comparison with other languages. Linguistic Typology is concerned with classifying, or "typologizing," languages of the world based on their formal properties, for example, phonological, morphological, lexical, or syntactic. The primary research interest of Linguistic Typology is cross-linguistic generalization. As such, Linguistic Typology, the theoretical foundation of which was established by Joseph Greenberg (see Greenberg 1978), excels in identifying whether a particular linguistic phenomenon in a language is cross-linguistically common or rare.

In terms of word order, for instance, Japanese is by no means unique among the languages of the world. In fact, the basic word order of Japanese is Subject–Object–Verb (SOV), the most common word order type cross-linguistically. Morphologically, Japanese is categorized into an agglutinating language in which free and bound morphemes are tightly glued, as it were, in a strict co-occurrence order, while keeping the morpheme boundaries distinct, with each bound morpheme coding a different grammatical meaning, as shown in (1):

(1) a. *Chichi-ga* *haiku-o* *hajime-mashi-ta.*
father-NOM poem-ACC begin-POL-PST
'My father started composing haiku poems.'

b. *Watashi-igai-no* *kazoku* *zen'in-ga* *odoroki-{mashi-ta/*ta-masu}.*
I-except-GEN family all-NOM be.surprised-POL-PST/PST-POL
'All the family members except I were surprised.'

c. *Demo* *watashi-{ni-wa/*wa-ni}* *chichi-no* *kimochi-ga* *yoku* *wakari-masu.*
but I-{DAT-TOP/TOP-DAT} father-GEN feelings-NOM well understand-POL:NPST
'But I could understand my father's feelings very well.'

As shown in (1), the morpheme boundaries are clear and each bound morpheme encodes a distinct grammatical meaning. Crucially, the order of occurrence of bound morphemes is fixed, as illustrated in two bracketed portions, that is, the order of tense and addressee politeness suffixes in (1b) and that of case and topic markers in (1c). Examples in (1) also show that Japanese, like many languages of the world, has a nominative–accusative case marking system where the transitive subject *chichi* (1a) and the intransitive subject *kazoku zen'in* (1b) are commonly marked by the same case marker *ga* (nominative) in contradistinction to the transitive object *haiku* marked by a different case marker *o* (accusative). Furthermore, it indicates that nouns and verbs are morphosyntactically distinguished in Japanese. Nouns like *chichi, haiku,* and *kimochi* are immediately followed by case markers such as dative *ni*, accusative *o*, and genitive *no*, while verbs like *hajimeru, odoroku,* and *wakaru* change their shapes by attaching various grammatical suffixes such as politeness and tense.

On the other hand, from the perspective of the presence of grammaticalized honorification systems, Japanese belongs to a small minority league of "haves," along with Korean. While Linguistic Typology is undoubtedly a useful tool in highlighting the typological profile of a language, it may need to be complemented by a more fine-tuned cross-linguistic analytical approach.

Comparative Typology, a typological analytical framework proposed by John Hawkins (1986), is geared to revealing more subtle cross-linguistic contrasts between two or more languages that superficially have similar typological profiles. Specifically, Comparative Typology has been successful in capturing the differential degrees of a fit between morphosyntactic structure and semantic representation between such pairs of languages as Japanese and Korean (e.g. Horie 1998, 2012) and English and German, as shown in (2) (Hawkins 1986: 121, partially modified):

(2) English-German morpho-syntactic and semantic contrasts

	English	**German**
a. Grammatical morphology	Less	More
b. Specific selectional restrictions	Less	More
c. Word order freedom	Less	More
d. Semantic diversity of grammatical relations	More	Less
e. Raising	More	Less
f. Extraction	More	Less
g. Pied piping	Less	More
h. Deletion of NPs	More	Less

Comparative Typology complements the generalized discipline of Linguistic Typology in that it enables the in-depth comparison between languages that share much overall typological similarity possibly due to genetic relatedness.

Finally, this chapter also adopts the analytical viewpoint of Cognitive Typology, a typological framework inspired by the discipline of Cognitive Linguistics (e.g. Croft 2001; Spring and Horie 2013). Specifically, this chapter is intended to delve into the cognitive and communicative foundations governing the form–meaning correspondence in Japanese grammatical and lexical structures. This approach will help uncover and identify some motivations for the preference of particular grammatical and lexical resources in Japanese for depicting a given situation.

Previous studies attempted to identify the prominent characteristics of mood and modality systems in Japanese through a comparison with Korean, English, and German (Moriya and Horie 2006; Horie and Narrog 2014). This cross-linguistic comparison made it possible to capture the characteristics of Japanese mood and modality systems in relativistic terms. Concretely speaking, Japanese modality is characterized as having an elaborate modal system of deontic, epistemic, and evidential auxiliaries, and a prominent discourse system of sentence-final particles designed to convey the speaker's communicative stance relative to her addressee.

This chapter adopts the same typologically comparative approach based in part on my previous studies. The topics to be covered will include the following:

(3) a. subordination and insubordination in Japanese
  b. pattern replication through the Japanese language contact with English

The two phenomena, one grammatical and one lexico-constructional, serve to represent cross-linguistically interesting and prominent features of Japanese.

3 Grammatical and Lexico-Constructional Phenomena in Japanese from a Typological Perspective

3.1 Subordination and Insubordination in Japanese

Complex sentences, that is, coordinate and subordinate clauses, have understandably been a target of typological studies (e.g. Haiman and Thompson 1998; Shopen 2007). Recently, complex sentences, as a prime example of syntactic complexity, have received focused attention from not only typologists but also child acquisition researchers, discourse linguists, and researchers working on the evolution of human language (e.g. Givón and Shibatani 2009). Figure 4.1 illustrates the cross-linguistic coding variation of complex sentences proposed by Croft (2001), an insightful cognitive typological finding applicable to many languages including Japanese.

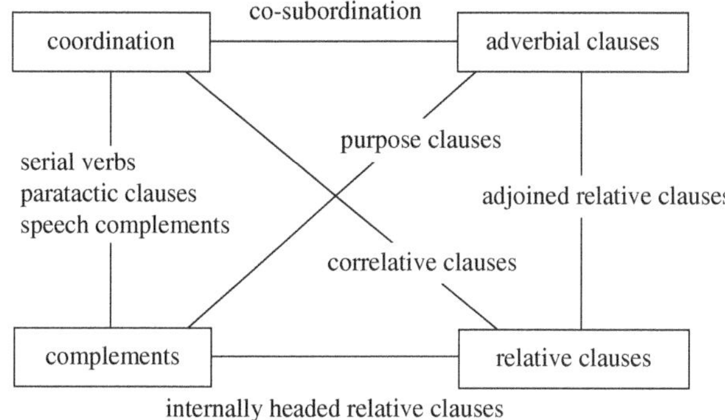

Figure 4.1 Continuum of complex sentence (Croft 2001: 322)

It serves to inform us that not all languages have four distinct complex sentence types, that is, relative clauses, complement clauses, adverbial clauses, and coordinate clauses, and that there are various "intermediate" constructions situated between different complex sentence types, for example, internally headed relative clauses (cf. Chapter 21, this volume).

Complex sentences in Japanese have been traditionally classified into two macro-categories, that is, those with a nominal head (*rentai fukubun kōbun*), which cover both relative clauses and complement clauses (4a), and other complex sentences (*renyō fukubun kōbun*), which cover both adverbial and coordinate clauses (4b). From the cognitive typological perspective inquiring into the continuum of complex sentences advocated by Croft (Figure 4.1), Japanese complex sentences are broadly categorized into the following two structures:

(4) a. [$_{\text{MATRIX CLAUSE}}$ [$_{\text{CLAUSE}}$ Predicate] {NOUN} Case Marker Matrix Predicate].
b. [$_{\text{CLAUSE}}$ Predicate] {Conjunction}, [$_{\text{MATRIX CLAUSE}}$ Matrix Predicate].

Relative and complement clauses in Japanese, which are both encoded as in (4a), are illustrated below:

(5) a. *[Kishatachi wa [seifu ga happyō shita] {koto} o*
reporters TOP government NOM announced matter ACC
sono mama hōdō shimashita]. (relative clause)
literally reporting did
'The press reported verbatim what (= the content which) the government announced.'

b. *[Kishatachi wa [seifu ga jijitsu to chigau happyō*
reporters TOP government NOM fact with different presentation
o shita] {koto} o shirimashita]. (complement clause)
ACC did matter ACC learned
'The press learned that the government announced what was factually not true.'

In (5), the same noun *koto* is employed in both examples. In (5a), *koto* is a lexical noun with the abstract meaning 'matter, content' which serves as the head of a relative clause. In (5b), *koto* serves as a complementizer heading the complement clause.

Adverbial and arguably coordinate and co-subordinate (dependent yet non-embedded) clauses in Japanese are illustrated in (6):

(6) a. *[Yuki ga takusan furu] {node}, [fuyu no unten wa*
snow NOM much fall because winter GEN driving TOP
kowai desu]. (adverbial clause)
scary is
'As it snows a lot in winter, it is scary to drive in winter time.'

b. *[Yuki ga takusan fut]{te}, [kōtsū wa daijūtai shimashita].*
snow NOM much fall-TE traffic TOP heavy.congestion did
'It snowed a lot (and so) there was heavy traffic congestion.'
(co-subordinate clause, see Hasegawa 1996: 16–17)

c. *[Yuki wa takusan furimasu] {shi}, [ame wa ame de*
snow TOP much fall and rain TOP rain COP
takusan furi-masu]. (coordinate clause)
much fall
'It snows a lot, and as for the raining, it rains a lot.'

Complex sentences in Japanese exhibit some interesting structural and functional continuity with main clauses internally and externally. Internally, subordinate, co-subordinate, and coordinate clauses can become less formally distinct from main clauses by allowing some prototypically matrix-clause grammatical phenomena to be manifested therein. This phenomenon is generally known under the name of "main clause phenomena" (Hooper and Thompson 1973: 473). Languages differ in terms of the morphosyntactic differentiation between main clauses, on the one hand, and subordinate, co-subordinate, and coordinate clauses, on the other. In English, for instance, relative clauses, complement clauses, adverbial clauses, and coordinate clauses all allow for finite predicate forms to occur internally, and as such they do not seem to differ from main clauses in terms of the finiteness marking of the predicates used.

(7) a. *The news [which **surprised** everyone] **was** Nixon's resignation.* (relative clause)

b. *The news [that Nixon **resigned**] **surprised** everyone.* (complement clause)

c. *[When Nixon **resigned**], everyone **was surprised**.* (adverbial clause)

d. *[Nixon **resigned**] [and everyone **was surprised**].* (coordinate clause)

It should be noted, however, that the predicate forms in some types of subordinate clauses are formally more restricted and hence are not fully finite, as shown below:

(8) a. *They insisted [that she* ***turn*** *in her resignation immediately].*
b. *We'll need to go home [before he* ***comes*** *back].*

Does Japanese manifest any morphosyntactic differentiation between subordinate and main clauses? One of the candidates for the differential marking between subordinate and main clauses is the so-called predicate conjugation form (*katsuyōkei*), particularly the distinction between attributive forms (*rentaikei*) and final form (*shūshikei*). Another candidate is the selection of the nominative marker *ga* or the topic marker *wa*. In subordinate clauses modified by lexical nouns or grammaticalized nouns/complementizers (9a), attributive forms (in this case *kireina*) are selected, which are distinct from their main final predicate counterparts (9b) (*kireida*). These two predicate forms cannot be switched. In the nominalized complement clause, the topic marker *wa* is not fully acceptable and needs to be changed to the nominative marker *ga* (cf. Chapter 13, this volume). In the main clause, there is no such restriction and either the topic marker or the nominative marker is possible, conveying different pragmatic meanings (topicality versus exhaustive listing).

(9) a.

[Kanojo	*no*	*hanarabi*	*{*?**wa**/**ga**}*	*{**kireina**/***kireida**}]*
she	GEN	teeth	TOP/NOM	beautiful.ATT/be.beautiful.FIN

koto	*o*	*shittemashita*	*ka?*
COMP	ACC	knew	Q

'Did you know that her teeth were well aligned?' (complement clause)

b.

Kanojo	*no*	*hanarabi*	*{**wa**/**ga**}*	*{**kireida**/***kireina**}.*
she	GEN	teeth	TOP/NOM	be beautiful.FIN/beautiful.ATT

'As for her teeth, they are well aligned./Her teeth are well aligned (which is her quintessential feature).' (main clause)

The formal distinction between attributive and final predicate forms is not consistently maintained, however. In Modern Japanese, except for nominal adjectives such as *kireida* (9) and the copula *da*, the majority of predicates, that is, verbs and regular (non-nominal) adjectives such as *yomu* 'read' and *omoshiroi* 'be interesting' have no formal distinction between attributive and final forms, as shown below:

(10) a.

[Kōkō	*no*	*toki*	*ni*	***yonda**]*	*hon*	*o*
senior.high.school	GEN	time	LOC	read.ATT	book	ACC

saido	***yonda**.*
again	read.FIN

'I read the book again which I had read when I was a senior high school student.'

Table 4.1 *Merger of attributive and sentence-final predicate forms*

	EMJ		LMJ	
	Attributive	Final	Non-past	
r-irregular (*ra*-hen)	*aru*	*ari*	*aru*	'exist'
n-irregular (*na*-hen)	*shinuru*	*shinu*	*shinuru*	'die'
Lower bigrade (*shimo nidan*)	*akuru*	*aku*	*akuru*	'get bored'
Upper bigrade (*kami nidan*)	*okuru*	*oku*	*okuru*	'wake up'
s-irregular (*sa*-hen)	*suru*	*su*	*suru(~su)*	'do'
k-irregular (*ka*-hen)	*kuru*	*ku*	*kuru*	'come'
Quadrigrade (yodan)	*kaku*	*kaku*	*kaku*	'write'
Upper monograde (*kami ichidan*)	*miru*	*miru*	*miru*	'see'
Lower monograde (*shimo ichidan*)	*keru*	*keru*	*keru*	'kick'

(Based on Frellesvig 2010: 329, modified)

b. *[Kōkō no toki ni* ***omoshirokatta****]* *hon* *wa* *yahari*
was.interesting.ATT book TOP indeed

***omoshirokatta*.**
was.interesting.FIN
'The book which was interesting to me when I was a senior high school student was indeed interesting even now.'

This is a result of a diachronic change wherein the formal distinction between the two forms, which was maintained through the stage of Early Middle Japanese (EMJ, 800–1200), was lost during Late Middle Japanese (LMJ, 1200–1600), as shown in Table 4.1. Crucially, the merger took place in such a way that attributive forms expanded their functional domain and replaced final forms. As a result, the final forms in Modern Japanese (e.g. *aru* 'exist') are the EMJ attributive forms. The independently existing final forms in EMJ (e.g. *ari* 'exist') thus disappeared.

In the absence of the attributive-final distinction with the majority of predicates in Modern Japanese, (addressee-oriented) polite predicate forms, that is, *masu* and *desu*, are likely candidates of prototypical main clause elements, as shown below:

(11) a. *[Kōkō* *no* *toki* *ni* ***{yonda/*yomi-mashita}****]*
senior.high.school GEN time LOC read.ATT/read-POL.PST

hon *o* *saido* *yomi-mashita.*
book ACC again read-POL.PST
'I read the book again which I had read when I was a senior high school student.'

b. *[Kore* *ga* *kōkō no toki ni yonda hon* ***{dearu/?desu}****]*
this NOM COP.ATT/COP.POL

koto *o* *ima* *omoidashita* *tokoro* ***desu*.**
COMP ACC now remembered place COP.POL
'It just came to my mind that this is the book I read when I was a senior high school student.'

The (addressee-oriented) polite forms *masu* and *desu* are disfavored in subordinate clauses such as (11) arguably because there is no communicative need to mark politeness within sentence-medial subordinate clauses. The polite forms serve their due politeness-marking functions in sentence-final positions. However, adverbial clauses appear to provide more main-clause-like environments; they are more prone to accommodate polite forms, as shown below:

(12) a. *[Kōkō no toki ni kono hon o* ***{yonda/yomi-masita}]*** *ga, sukkari*
read.PST/read-POL.PST but completely
*wasurete i-**mashita**.*
forget.POL.PST
'I read this book when I was a senior high school student, but I completely forgot about it.'

b. *[Mada kōkōsei* ***{datta/deshita}]***
still senior.high.school.student COP.PST/COP.POL.PST
kara, sono hon no naiyō wa chotto
because that book GEN content TOP a.bit
muzukashikatta ***desu***.
be difficult.PST COP.POL.NPST
'As I was still a senior high school student, I found the content of the book a bit difficult.'

The distinction between adverbial clauses and other subordinate clauses is a matter of degree. If there is sufficient pragmatic reason to be tactfully polite to the addressee, as in a telephone conversation between the customer service operator and the customer, politeness marking becomes available within a relative clause, as shown in (13):

(13) *[Kochira kara o-okuri shi-**masu**] yōshi ni go-shomei*
this side from humbly.send do-POL.NPST form in HON-sign
no ue o-kaeshi kudasai mase.
GEN after HON-return give(me) POL.IMP
'Could you kindly send me back the form [that we humbly send to you] after signing it?' (Matsumoto 2009: 206)

While the distinction between subordinate and main clauses in Japanese is not very rigidly maintained, there are other languages that consistently keep them separate. Korean is such a language. Unlike Japanese, Korean distinguishes attributive and final forms of all predicates. Final forms are not employed in subordinate clauses, including relative, complement, and adverbial clauses. Compare the attributive and final forms in Korean and Japanese:

(14) Korean attributive and final predicate forms ('read (NPST)')
 a. *ilk-nun* (attributive)
 b. *ilk-nun-ta.* (final)

(15) Japanese attributive and final predicate forms ('read (NPST)')
 a. *yomu* (attributive)
 b. *yomu.* (final)

Unlike Japanese, Korean subordinate and main clauses are formally distinguishable in terms of the co-occurring predicate form. Attributive forms are restricted to nominalized subordinate clauses such as relative clauses (16). Final forms, including (super) polite forms, are employed in main clause environments, and are not interchangeable with attributive forms.

(16) *[Kotunghakkyo* *ttay* *{ilk-un/*ilk-ess-ta}]* *chayk-ul*
 senior.high.school time read-ATT.PST/read-PST-DECL book-ACC

 tasi *hanpen* *{ilk-ess-ta/*ilk-un}.*
 again one.time read-PST-DECL/read-ATT.PST
 'I read again the book that I had read when I was a senior high school student.'

The subordinate clause and the main clause in Japanese – though separated by the presence of such elements as lexical nouns, grammaticalized complementizers, and conjunctions – are continuous to varying degrees. Adverbial clauses in general are likely to be less distinct from matrix clauses compared to relative and nominalized complement clauses, the latter of which are more restricted in terms of the co-occurring elements (e.g. the predicate form used therein). However, as shown previously, pragmatic motivations can overrule grammatical convention.

With the distinction between subordinate and main clauses rather blurry, it is not altogether surprising that subordinate clauses, separated from the main clauses, can take on a life of their own and become main clauses themselves. The following two examples from English and French illustrate the mild directive use of conditional clauses, which are conventionalized in the respective languages:

(17) TA 3: *If you go down to the bottom left hand corner of your page,*
 TB 4: *Aha.*
 TA 5: *do you have a van?* (Yoshida 2015: 180)

(18) *Si* *on* *allait* *se* *promen-er?*
 if one went REF walk-INFR
 'What if we went for a walk?' (Evans 2007: 380)

This phenomenon has recently started to receive intensive attention from typologically oriented researchers under the heading of "insubordination," ingeniously labeled by Evans (2007), who opened the door to this line of cross-linguistic inquiry (e.g. Evans and Watanabe 2016). It should be noted, however, that insubordination phenomena, referred to as *iisashi* 'suspended speech,' have long been the target of focused research of Japanese linguistics and Japanese pedagogy (e.g. see papers in Ohori 1998 and Shirakawa 2009) as they are very frequently observed in Japanese conversation as communicative devices. For instance, consider the following types of insubordination in Japanese:

(19) a. *[Chotto tabako katte kuru]* ***{kara**//Ø}*.
a.bit tobacco buy.and come because
'I'll go and buy tobacco; I'll be right back.'

b. *[Kaigi ga mō hajimaru sō desu]* ***{kedo**/Ø}*.
meeting NOM already begin.NPST I.hear COP.POL.NPST but
'I hear the meeting will start any moment.'

These insubordinate clauses (19) behave as main clauses. In fact, without any subordinating conjunctions, they serve as full-fledged main clauses. There are some rather subtle, context-dependent pragmatic differences between insubordinate clauses and simple main clauses. Insubordinate clauses respectively convey some additional pragmatic nuances such as casual explanation for the speaker's action (19a) and the speaker's lack of total confidence (19b). Crucially, these insubordinate clauses serve to end a sentence instead of the usual sentence-final predicate forms (i.e. the ϕ options in (19)). In (19), the sentence-finally occurring conjunctions *kara* and *kedo* indeed function practically as sentence-final particles, for example, *ne, yo*.

Adverbial clause type insubordination is rather easy to identify cross-linguistically (17–19), and it was these types that had been the focus of attention in past Japanese linguistics and pedagogical research. However, in Japanese, there is a tendency to avoid ending a sentence with a bare verb (i.e. its sentence-final non-polite form) due to unwanted pragmatic implications (e.g. sounding impolite or rude); therefore, insubordination is used to soften the speaker's assertion. Consequently, practically any type of complex sentence, that is, not only subordinate but also arguably co-subordinate and coordinate clauses, can be used independently as main clauses, as illustrated below:

(20) a. [MATRIX CLAUSE [CLAUSE Predicate] {Noun} Case Marker Matrix Predicate].
→ [CLAUSE Predicate] {Noun}.

b. [CLAUSE Predicate] {Conjunction}, [MATRIX CLAUSE Matrix Predicate].
→ [CLAUSE Predicate] {Conjunction}.

Each type comes in varieties, and a full-scale investigation into the formal and functional characteristics of each type is beyond the scope of this chapter. Some illustrative examples not mentioned previously will follow:

(21) a. Relative clause type

Genba *wa* *[shadanki* *no* *nai]*
site TOP crossing.gate GEN not.exist
fumikiri. (newspaper report)
railroad.crossing
'The site of the accident is a railroad crossing which has no crossing gate.'

(Onishi 2013: 27, partially modified)

b. Complement clause type

[Hanarabi *ga* ***kireina/kireida]*** *koto!*
teeth NOM beautiful.ATT/be.beafutiful.FIN COMP
'How beautifully aligned her teeth are!'

c. Adverbial clause type (19)

d. Co-subordinate clause type

[Ōyuki *ga* *furi-mashi]-te.*
heavy.snow NOM fall-pol-CONJ
'It snowed a lot, so.'

e. Coordinate clause type

[Jibun *no* *chikara* *de* ***yare]*** *shi!*
self GEN power INST do.IMP CONJ
'Do it on your own!' (originally Yamanashi dialect, now popularized among youth)

The relative clause type comes in great varieties, and (21a) is just one instance of an independently occurring relative clause used in the media (e.g. news being reported on a website).

The complement clause type (21b) also has various subtypes, and the complementizer *koto* functions as a sentence-final particle as it can occur not only with attributive (*kireina*) but also final forms (*kireida*).

Finally, the coordinate clause type (21e) presents an interesting example where the conjunction *shi*, which has become a sentence-final particle, occurs with the imperative form.

3.2 Pattern Replication of the Japanese Counterpart of the English *See*-construction

Lexical and grammatical borrowing have received focused attention in linguistic typology and contact linguistics (e.g. Matras 2009: 1–2). Since the ancient times, the Japanese language has been in contact with neighboring East Asian languages and more recently with European languages like Dutch, English, French, German, Italian, Russian, Spanish, and Portuguese. The uniqueness of lexical borrowing in Japanese lies in the manner in which foreign words are adopted and categorized into different lexical layers, that is, Sino-Japanese words (*kango*), which are written in Chinese characters, and non-Sino foreign words (*gairaigo*), which are written in the *katakana* syllabary.

What is particularly noteworthy about lexical borrowing in Modern Japanese is the fact that it has borrowed nouns, verbs, and adjectives massively from English. Cross-linguistically, verbs are known to be less likely to be borrowed between languages (Moravcsik 1978: 111), but since the ancient times, Japanese had borrowed a great number of Chinese verbs as "verbal nouns" and nativized them as Japanese verbs by attaching a verbalizing suffix *-suru*. In a similar manner, Modern Japanese has borrowed numerous verbs from English and has nativized them. Some of the nativized Japanese verbs originally borrowed from Chinese and English are as follows:

(22) Sino-Japanese verbs: *setsudan-suru* ('severing-do'; sever), *iji-suru* ('maintenance-do'; maintain)
English verbs borrowed into Japanese: *katto-suru* ('cut-do'; cut), *kīpu-suru* ('keep-do'; keep)

The propensity of the Japanese language to borrow foreign verbs on a massive scale is all the more conspicuous when it is contrasted with Korean, which has also borrowed a great number of Chinese and English verbs. A systematic comparison between the two languages in terms of the extent to which English verbs are borrowed is provided in Table 4.2.

The results obtained in Table 4.2 indicate that Japanese has borrowed and nativized approximately twice as many verbs from English as Korean.

In what follows, I will present an instance of "pattern replication" (Matras 2009: 234) at the constructional level, arguably through language contact between premodern Japanese and English.

English has a construction consisting of visual perception verb *see* which encodes *the materializing of an event* when it co-occurs with (i) a subject NP

Table 4.2 *Verbs borrowed from English into Japanese and Korean*

English	Japanese	Korean
To access	*akusesu-suru*	*(*)*
To advise	*adobaisu-suru*	*etupaisu-hata*
To appeal	*apīru-suru*	*ephil-hata*
To approach	*apurōchi-suru*	*ephulochi-hata*
To arrange	*arenji-suru*	*eleyinci-hata*
To assist	*ashisuto-suru*	*esisuthu-hata*
To attack	*atakku-suru*	*
To back up	*bakkuappu-suru*	*paykep-hata*
To block	*burokku-suru*	*
To boil	*boiru-suru*	*
To boycott	*boikotto-suru*	*poikhos-hata*
[Verbs beginning with letters C through Z are omitted due to space limitations]		
Total	143(Japanese)	74(Korean)

* indicates non-existence
(*) unacceptability by two native consultants
(Horie 2002: 93–97)

encoding broadly construed "Setting," for example, location, time (Langacker 1991: 232–233), and (ii) an event-encoding object NP.

(23) a. Over a three year span Mississippi has ***seen*** an increase in HIV and STD infections among the population.
(*Journal of Behavioral Health* 2012, 1: 118)

b. *The last decade* ***has seen*** *cooperation among scholars, as well as new theories and discoveries.* (*Publication Information* Mar/Apr 2010, Vol. 63)

c. *. . . the clearer it became that the EC could not, the less eager the United States was to* ***see*** *the alliance.* (*Foreign Affairs*, Jul/Aug, 1994)

Interestingly, Japanese also has an analogous construction, a virtual translational equivalent of the English construction:

(24)
KEDO	*rijikai*	*ga*	*raigetsu*	*igo,*	*jūyu*	*no*	*kyōkyū*	*o*
	board	NOM	next.month	after	crude.oil	GEN	supply	ACC
teishi-suru	*koto*	*de,*	*itchi*	*o*	*mi-ta. . .*			
stop-do	NMLZ	INST	agreement	ACC	saw			

'The KEDO board has reached an agreement (Lit. seen an agreement) in their decision to stop the supply of crude oil after next month. . .'
(*Tokyo Shinbun*, Nov 116, 2002)

(25)
Kokusai	*shakai*	*wa . . .*	*aratana*	*kadai*
international	society	TOP	new	problem
no	*hassei*	*o*	*mi-teimasu.*	
GEN	emergence	ACC	see-PROG.POL	

'The international society is witnessing the emergence of new problems. . .'
(*Chūnichi Shinbun*, Jan 22, 1993)

(26)
Taiwan	*kaikyō*	*ryōgan*	*no*	*kōryū*	*ga*	*saikin*	*tokuni*
	strait	both.sides	GEN	exchange	NOM	recently	especially
shinten	*o*	*mi-teiru*	. . .				
progress	ACC	see-PROG					

'The exchange between both sides of the Taiwan strait is witnessing the recent accelerated progress. . .'
(Ibid., Aug 26, 1988)

Similar to its English counterpart, the Japanese construction consists of a visual perception verb *miru* which encodes *the materializing of an event* when it co-occurs with (i) a subject NP encoding broadly construed "Setting" (e.g. location, time) and (ii) an event object NP.

What enables such usage is an interesting cognitive linguistics question. Arguably the construction is made possible through some metaphorical process which crucially concerns the argument structure of visual perception verbs such as *see* and *miru*. Cross-linguistically, perception verbs are known to encode the Experiencer's perception of an ongoing event by taking a complement:

(27) a. *John {saw/heard} [Mary shouting angrily].*
b. *[Onna no ko ga hitori de piano o hii-te iru no o] {mita/kiita}.*
girl NOM alone piano ACC play-PROG NMLZ ACC saw/heard
'(I) saw/heard a girl playing the piano by herself.'

The constructional template of perception verbs taking a complement is as follows:

(28) EXPERIENCER Subject NP + Perception Verb + EVENT Object (complement clause)

Visual perception verbs exhibit rather uniquely distinct lexico-semantic characteristics from other perception verbs (e.g. *hear*) cross-linguistically (e.g. Viberg 1983: 136), arguably as a reflection of the relatively higher degree of directness involved in obtaining the target sense data through vision. For instance, visual perception verbs are observed cross-linguistically to take on cognition/inference senses (e.g. Viberg 1983: 156) unlike other perception verbs:

(29) a. *I saw that John was crossing the street.* (cognition)
b. *Keiji wa sono otoko ga uso o tsui-te iru to mita.*
detective TOP that man NOM lie ACC tell-PROG COMP saw
'The detective judged the man to be a liar.' (inference)

It is thus not surprising that visual perception verbs such as *see* mediate the following kind of metaphorical extension:

(30) a. EXPERIENCER Subject NP + SEE (visually perceive) + EVENT Object (typically complement clause)
(28a) *John saw [Mary shouting angrily].*
b. SETTING Subject NP + SEE (< materialize) + EVENT Object (NP)
(23a) *Mississippi has seen an increase in its wild-hog population...*

In this process, a prototypically human experiencer subject NP of *see* is extended to a non-human setting subject NP and concomitantly the lexical meaning of *see* is arguably changed into 'materialize.'

That such a metaphorical extension was possible in English is closely related to a comparative typological characteristic of English pointed out by Hawkins in (2), that is, greater semantic diversity of grammatical relations (as compared with German). English subject NPs are known to be capable of encoding various semantic roles such as instrument, location, and time, where German subjects NPs fail to occur felicitously (Hawkins 1986: 58–59):

(31) Instrument
a. *A few years ago a pfennig would buy two or three pins.*
b. **Vor einigen Jahren kaufte ein Pfennig zwei bis drei Stecknadeln.*

(32) Location
a. *This hotel forbids dogs.*
b. **Dieses Hotel verbietet Hunde.*

(33) Time

a. *Tomorrow will be rather cold and showery in most places.*

b. **Morgen verspricht meistenorts ziemlich kalt zu sein und Regenschauer zu geben.*

In view of the semantic variability of subject NPs in English, the setting/experiencer subject NP with the visual perception verb *see* does not seem to be an entirely abnormal innovation in English.

Unlike English, however, Japanese has a strong tendency to avoid inanimate subject NPs such as instrument and location. In these instances, locative adpositional phrases are likely to be selected, and concomitantly transitive verbs are changed into intransitive (and potential) or passive verb forms:

(34) Instrument

a. **Sūnen mae de are-ba, ichi penī ga 2, 3 bon no pin*
a.few.years before COP if a.penny NOM CL GEN pin
o ***katta*** *mono da.*
ACC bought used.to
'A few years ago a penny would buy two or three pins.'

b. *Sūnen mae de areba, ichi penī de 2, 3 bon no pin o* ***kaeta*** *mono da.*
INST could.buy used.to
'A few years ago, with a penny, it would be possible to buy two or three pins.'

(35) Location

a. **?Kono hoteru wa inu o* ***kinji-te iru***.
this hotel TOP dog ACC forbid-RES
'This hotel forbids dogs.'

b. *Kono hoteru de wa inu ga* ***kinji-rare-te iru***.
this hotel LOC TOP dog NOM forbid-PASS-RES
'In this hotel, dogs are forbidden.'

How did the *see*-construction come into existence in Japanese, which has a strong tendency to disfavor inanimate subject NPs unlike English?

Interestingly, the *see*-construction was attested in Japanese texts as early as the late nineteenth century:

(36) *Waga kuni wa mottomo ichijirushiki zōka o miru.*
our country TOP most remarkable increase ACC see
'Our country sees the most remarkable increase.'
(*Taiyō* 'The Sun' 1895, Vol. 10)

(37) *Shikōshite dokkoku no ikō hanahada taenara-zu,*
however Germany GEN intent quite innocent-NEG
nochi tsuini sangoku dōmei o miru-ni itare-ri.
later finally triple alliance ACC see-to reach-PERF
'And then, Germany wasn't quite satisfied, which resulted in (the world) *witnessing* (the formation of) the *triple alliance*.' (Ibid., Vol. 12)

(38) *Waga gaikoku bōeki ga, kono gotoki chōsoku no shinpo o*
our foreign trade NOM this like rapid GEN progress ACC
miru ni itari-shi ...
see DAT reach-PAT
'Our foreign trade has made (Lit. seen) rapid progress like this...'
(Ibid., Vol. 2)

The late nineteenth century was the time when Japan underwent the Meiji Restoration and reopened its doors to the outside world. At that time, a great number of lexical items (mostly nouns, and a few verbs and adjectives) were borrowed from European languages, among which English was by far the largest donor. The *see*-construction is presumed to have been borrowed from English into Japanese, with the following kind of English instances of *see* as a model template. These instances were attested prior to the putative earliest attestation of their Japanese equivalents (36–38).

(39) *Europe was astonished to see the re-union of Moreau and Pichegru.*
(*The Times*, Jun 14, 1804)

(40) *The year 1861 saw an increase of 49 percent. in the number of burglaries and 56 percent. in its cases of housebreaking.* (Ibid., Feb 20, 1863)

It is an interesting cognitive typological question why Japanese borrowed this particular construction from English. Borrowing of a construction, which involves both a verb and its co-occurring subject and object NPs in this instance, is deemed to be cognitively more complex than that of lexical items such as nouns. There is no definitive answer to this question, but the greater propensity of Japanese to borrow verbs from English as compared with Korean (Table 4.1), an indication of progressiveness toward borrowing of foreign words, may be suggestively relevant. It may have been that this particular rhetorical device was first literally translated from English into Japanese and may have gradually gained attention and popularity, eventually leading to the conventionalization of the construction. It is interesting to note that in Korean, the less progressive recipient of the two languages, the *see*-construction appears to be more severely restricted, as shown below:

(41) *Twu salam-i uykeyn-uy ilchi-lul po-myen...*
two person-NOM opinion-GEN agreement-ACC see-if
'If two people reached (Lit. seen) an agreement...'
(*Taycen Ilpo*, May 11, 2009)

(42) *Ppalli hapuy-lul po-psita.*
quickly agreement-ACC see-PROPOS
'Let's solve this issue quickly.' (Lit. Let's see an agreement.)

It is another interesting cognitive typological question how the visual perception verb *pota* 'see' has acquired this usage, which shows partial resemblance to its Japanese counterpart *miru*. Similar to its Japanese equivalent, Korean *pota* takes as its object NP such abstract event nouns as *ilchi* 'agreement' and *hapuy* 'agreement.' Unlike Japanese, however, Korean *pota* almost always occurs with a human experiencer subject NP and rarely with a setting/inanimate subject NP.

In this connection, it is noteworthy that, though inanimate subject NPs are still disfavored in various environments (34a, 35a), many inanimate transitive subject NPs are indeed observed in Modern written Japanese texts (e.g. novels, newspapers, etc.), for example (43), as pointed out by Xiong (2009: 53):

(43) *Kanshi kamera ga yōgisha o ichihayaku waridashita.*
surveillance camera NOM suspect ACC immediately identified
'*The surveillance camera* identified the suspect right away.'
(*Sankei newspaper* July 21, 2005)

This putatively recent stylistic change has arguably been caused by the introduction of inanimate subject NPs through contact with European languages, most influentially English. The *see*-construction in Japanese is arguably a precursor of such stylistic innovation.

The construction, which has been in existence for more than ten decades, has undergone some diachronic change, especially in terms of the semantic range of event object NPs. In its putatively earliest instance, for example (37), it was possible for *miru* 'see' to take 'the triple alliance' as its direct object:

(37) *Shikōshite dokkoku no ikō hanahada taenara-zu,*
however Germany GEN intent quite innocent-NEG
nochi tsuini sangoku dōmei o miru-ni itare-ri.
later finally triple alliance ACC see-to reach-PERF
'And then, Germany wasn't quite satisfied, which resulted in (the world) *witnessing* (the formation of) the *triple alliance*.'
(*Taiyō* 1895, Vol. 12)

This option is no longer available; it is not possible to 'see' the triple alliance directly in Modern Japanese (37'), though it is possible to 'see' its establishment (37"):

(37') *. . . *sangoku dōmei o mita.*
'. . . saw (witnessed) the triple alliance.'

(37") . . . *sangoku dōmei no seiritsu o mita.*
'. . . saw (witnessed) the establishment of the triple alliance.'

The construction underwent some change in terms of its selectional restriction of the co-occurring object NPs, as shown in (37') and (37"). In present-day Japanese, *miru* is capable of taking, as its object, an abstract event noun, mostly Sino-Japanese verbal nouns such as *itchi* 'agreement' and *zōka* 'increase.' Semantically, the construction encodes the inception or endpoint of an event, or an event in progress, as illustrated below (examples repeated):

(25) Inception of an event

Kokusai	*shakai*	*wa ...*	*aratana*	*kadai*	*no*	*hassei*
international	society	TOP	new	problem	GEN	emergence

o	*mi-teimasu.*
ACC	see-PROG.POL

'The international society is witnessing the emergence of new problems...'

(*Chūnichi Shinbun*, Jan 22, 1993)

(26) Event in progress

Taiwan	*kaikyō*	*ryōgan*	*no*	*kōryū*	*ga*	*saikin*	*tokuni*
	strait	both.sides	GEN	exchange	NOM	recently	especially

shinten	*o*	*mi-teiru...*
progress	ACC	see-PROG

'The exchange between both sides of the Taiwan strait is witnessing the recent accelerated progress ... '

(Ibid., Aug 26, 1988)

(24) Endpoint of an event

KEDO	*rijikai*	*ga*	*raigetsu*	*igo,*	*jūyu*	*no*	*kyōkyū*	*o*
	board	NOM	next.month	after	crude.oil	GEN	supply	ACC

teishi-suru	*koto*	*de,*	*itchi*	*o*	*mi-ta...*
stop-do	NMLZ	INST	agreement	ACC	saw

'The KEDO board has reached an agreement (Lit. seen an agreement) in their decision to stop the supply of crude oil after next month...'

(*Tokyo Shinbun*, Nov 16, 2002)

The *see*-construction in Japanese, arguably an instance of "pattern replication" (Matras 2009: 234) inspired by its analogue in the donor language (English), has a well-established status in present-day Japanese. The range of different types of event representation appears to have become diversified compared to its earlier usage in the late nineteenth century even if some earlier usages are no longer available, and this is an attestation of creative ingenuity on the part of the recipient language.

In fact, this is not an isolated instance of ingenious pattern replication, nor creation mediated by language contact in Japanese. Japanese not only borrowed and nativized a massive quantity of characters and lexemes from Chinese but also created a novel pattern of Sino-Japanese verbal noun and relational noun combinations which, in spite of the lack of overt tense marking, are interpreted as tensed verbal phrases, as shown below (the original observation on the Japanese-Korean contrast and the examples to follow are due to Tsukamoto (1997); the romanization, glosses, and translations are from Horie and Pardeshi (2009: 110–111)):

(44) *Hikarigō* *ga* *Shizuoka eki* *o* *[tsūka-go]* *ni, ...*
Super.express.Hikari NOM Station ACC passing-after LOC
Lit. 'After Hikari('s) passing of Shizuoka station ... '; (intended meaning: 'After Hikari passes/passed Shizuoka station...')

The Sino-Japanese combination of verbal noun *tsūka* 'passing' and relational noun *go* 'posterity, after' lacks overt tense marking, but it behaves as a tensed verb and can co-occur with the nominative case-marked subject *Hikarigō* and the accusative case-marked *Shizuoka eki*. Interestingly, this innovative Sino-Japanese noun–noun combination co-exists with the alternative tensed-equivalent structure (45):

(45) *Hikarigō* *ga* *Shizuoka eki* *o* *[tsūka-**shita***
Super.express.Hikari NOM station ACC passing-did
nochi] *ni...*
after LOC
'After Hikari passes/passed Shizuoka station...'

The creation of tense-unmarked Sino-Japanese structures in Japanese is in sharp contrast with the neighboring language Korean, which strongly favors a tense-marked Sino-Korean structure (46) over its tense-unmarked counterpart (47):

(46) *Hikhaliho-ka* *Sicuokha yek-ul* *[thongkwa-**ha-n**-hwu]-ey ...*
Super.express.Hikari-NOM Shizuoka station-ACC passing-do-PST-after-LOC

(47) *?Hikhaliho-ka* *Sicuokha yek-ul* *[thongkwa-hwu]-ey...*
Super.express.Hikari-NOM station-ACC passing-after-LOC
'After Hikari passes/passed Shizuoka station...'
(Horie 2002: 92)

Finally, let us revisit the *see*-construction in English as it has developed some novel usages. According to Peter Hook (personal communication), Googling the phrase "Sunday saw" yields the following kinds of sentences especially in Australian and New Zealand varieties:

(48) a. *Sunday saw the Cycle Club race a mini Tour de France.* (griffithcycleclub.com)
b. *Sunday saw me racing the same 50 mile course.* (highaltitudetraining.com)
c. *Sunday saw me being the MOST UNPROFESSIONAL ever!* (volig.multiply.com/journal)

This usage appears to be conventionally observed, not with any kind of setting subject NP, but primarily with the special setting subject "Sunday" only. However, it shows that English, as an arguably donor language of the *see*-construction, can go one step ahead of Japanese, the recipient language in terms of further extended usage, as illustrated below:

(49) a. EXPERIENCER Subject NP + SEE (visually perceive) + EVENT Object (typically complement clause) (English, Japanese)
(27) a. John *saw* [Mary shouting angrily].
b. SETTING Subject NP + SEE (< materialize) + EVENT Object (NP)
(23) a. Mississippi ***has seen*** an increase in HIV and STD infections among the population. (English, Japanese)
c. SETTING Subject NP + SEE + EVENT Object (complement clause)
(48) a. *Sunday* saw *the Cycle Club race a mini Tour de France.* (English only)

The *see*-constructions in English and Japanese present an interesting case of pattern replication arguably induced through language contact. Comparative Typology (Hawkins 1986) informs us that languages can differ in terms of the extent to which surface grammatical structures match semantic structures. Inspired by Hawkins's comparative typological generalizations, Muller-Götama (1994) proposes the scale of lowest to highest transparency of form–meaning correspondence across languages based on various syntactic and semantic processes that can involve the rearrangement of the argument structure of a sentence (see (1)), e.g. greater/lesser semantic variability of grammatical relations, passive, raising, WH-extraction, deletion of NPs. Muller-Götama makes the following remarks on the cross-linguistic variation that relate to three languages discussed in this section, that is, English, Japanese, and Korean:

> Whereas Babungo, Sawu, and Russian have a highly transparent organization across all properties tested, English is characterized by the lowest overall transparency. Yet other languages display a split distribution, scoring high on one dimension and low on another. (1994: 144)

> Summing up, Japanese has a considerable level of semantic transparency. As a language with a rich case-marking system, it uses scrambling to encode pragmatic information and has the semantically narrow grammatical relations typical of highly transparent languages ... passivization is a frequently used means of rearranging the argument structure of a sentence. In these ways, Japanese falls somewhat short of semantic transparency found in Korean and Malayalam. (1994: 105)

Based on these observations, the three languages can be plotted on the scale of transparency relative to each other:

(50) Cross-linguistic variation in semantic transparency

English > ····························· Japanese ≧ Korean ·····
Lower transparency ←————→ Higher transparency

In view of the relative positions of the three languages on the semantic transparency scale, it is natural that English, which is located toward lowest transparency, manifests the most flexible semantic extension of the *see*-construction. Japanese is an interesting case in point. Despite having "a considerable level of semantic transparency" (Muller-Götama 1994:

105), Japanese manifests creative ingenuity in language contact situations with Chinese and English. Not only are lexical items borrowed and nativized but also constructional patterns are created or replicated, based on the form–meaning pattern of the donor language. Compared to Japanese, Korean, which manifests even higher semantic transparency than Japanese, is more restricted in terms of lexical borrowing and pattern replication.

4 Conclusion

This chapter highlights the importance of approaching lexico-grammatical phenomena in Japanese from a broadly construed typological perspective. Specifically, it probes into two linguistic phenomena, that is, subordination and insubordination in Japanese, and the pattern replication of the *see*-construction through language contact with English, as they serve to reveal what is cross-linguistically noteworthy about Japanese.

While the two phenomena look very different superficially, they both instantiate the flexibility of semantic or pragmatic interpretations which lexico-grammatical resources in Japanese can be extended to receive. The cross-linguistically variable degree of semantic/pragmatic interpretability of lexico-grammatical resources is not easy to capture in the traditional Greenbergian linguistic typological framework. However, with the insights from the more interdisciplinary typological analytical frameworks such as Comparative and Cognitive Typologies, this chapter has succeeded in highlighting the semantic or pragmatic dimension along which lexico-grammatical resources in typologically different languages can be compared.

5

Dialects

Michinori Shimoji

1 Introduction

Under the term "Japanese dialects" are subsumed both the local varieties of Japan's mainland (spoken in the areas from Hokkaidō to mainland Kyūshū) and Ryukyuan (spoken in Amami Islands of Kagoshima Prefecture, Kyūshū and Okinawa Prefecture). It should be emphasized here that Ryukyuan is usually regarded as an independent language (or even a group of languages) by domestic as well as international researchers because there is no mutual intelligibility between the mainland dialects and Ryukyuan. It is spoken in an area that was once an independent country (Ryukyuan kingdom, 1429–1869). The reason that the mainland dialects and Ryukyuan are dealt with in a single chapter is simply because the two languages constitute the Japonic Family and are worth discussing together in understanding the typological diversity of Japonic Family.

There is no officially established "Standard" Japanese, but the de facto standard language is a written language based on the Tokyo dialect, which is usually simply referred to as Japanese in the linguistic literature. In this chapter, this Tokyo-based (written) language will be called Standard Japanese (SJ) to distinguish it from Japanese dialects. SJ is one of the most well-known languages in the typological literature. By contrast, Japanese dialects have largely been ignored in typological studies. The World Atlas of Language Structure (WALS, Dryer and Haspelmath 2013) of the Max Planck Institute for Evolutionary Anthropology, the world's largest typological database, does not contain the data from Japanese dialects other than SJ except for Shuri, which is the dialect of the former capital of the Ryūkyū kingdom. This by no means indicates that Japonic Family is typologically homogenous. Rather, just as SJ is a typologically interesting language and is worth a separate chapter (see Chapter 4, this volume), Japanese dialects are also worth a detailed typological characterization in their own right.

The present chapter focuses on one aspect of the typological diversity of Japanese dialects – the alignment of the case marking of three major core arguments: intransitive subject (S), transitive subject (A), and transitive direct object (P). The alignment typology of Japanese dialects allows readers who are unfamiliar with the dialectal variation of Japanese to gain a basic understanding of the structural diversity in this language family. It will be shown that there is a wide range of alignment patterns, including cross-linguistically uncommon ones such as split intransitive, tripartite, and marked nominative.

The organization of this chapter is as follows. In Section 2 a brief overview of Japanese dialects is provided. Section 3 introduces various terms and concepts necessary for the subsequent discussion of alignment typology. Section 4 sets out to discuss the typology of alignment by drawing on the available data from both mainland and Ryukyuan dialects. Section 5 focuses on the phenomenon outlined in Section 4 and discusses it in detail from a cross-linguistic perspective. Section 6 concludes the discussion and suggests future research topics.

2 Japanese Dialects: An Overview

2.1 Genealogical Classification

The mainland dialects are spoken in a chain of islands stretching from Hokkaidō to the Tokara Islands of Kagoshima Prefecture. Ryukyuan is spoken on the Ryūkyū Islands, which stretch from Kikaijima Island to Yonaguni Island. As briefly noted in Section 1, the two dialect groups constitute a single genetic group (Japonic Family; see Map 5.1).

A widespread view on the genetic subgrouping of Ryukyuan is that it divides into Northern Ryukyuan and Southern Ryukyuan, and that Northern Ryukyuan further divides into Amami and Okinawan, and Southern Ryukyuan further divides into Miyako and Yaeyama, which consists of Nuclear Yaeyama and Yonaguni (Pellard 2015). The genetic subgrouping of the mainland dialects and the positioning of Ryukyuan within the Japonic Family has continued to be a matter of debate, and there are several competing hypotheses. One widespread hypothesis divides Japonic into Ryukyuan and Japanese, the latter of which further divides into the Eastern and Western groups. The Hachijōjima dialect, which is spoken on the Hachijōjima Island of Tokyo, is treated either as a part of the Eastern group, or as a distinct branch in a sister relationship with Eastern and Western, or as a distinct branch in a sister relationship with Japanese.

Map 5.1 Japan's mainland, Hachijōjima, and the Ryūkyū Islands

2.2 Geolinguistic Classification

Based on various lexical, phonological, and morphosyntactic variations, several major dialectal groupings (isoglosses) have been suggested (Tojo 1966; Kindaichi 1964; Hirayama 1968; inter alia). The foundational classification is Tojo's work, to which minor and major revisions have been made subsequently by a number of researchers. According to Tojo's classification, Japanese dialects divide into two major areas: the mainland dialect area and Ryukyuan area (Map 5.2). The former further subdivides into (a) Eastern dialects (Hokkaidō, Tōhoku, Kantō, Tōkai-Tōsan, Hachijōjima), (b) Western dialects (Hokuriku, Kinki, Chūgoku, Shikoku), and (c) Kyūshū dialects. Ryukyuan subdivides into (a′) Amami, (b′) Okinawa, and (c′) Sakishima. Hirayama (1968) later revised Tojo's classification and treated Hachijōjima (which belongs to (a) above) as a distinct group which is in a sister relationship with the mainland dialects and Ryukyuan. He also made changes to Ryukyuan subgrouping, dividing (c′) Sakishima into Miyako, Yaeyama, and Yonaguni.

	Area	Dialect Group
1	Hokkaidō	Eastern
2	Tōhoku	
3	Kantō	
4	Tōkai-Tōsan	
5	Hachijōjima	
6	Hokuriku	Western
7	Kinki	
8	Chūgoku	
9	Shikoku	
10	Kyūshū	
11	Amami	Ryukyuan
12	Okinawa	
13	Sakishima	

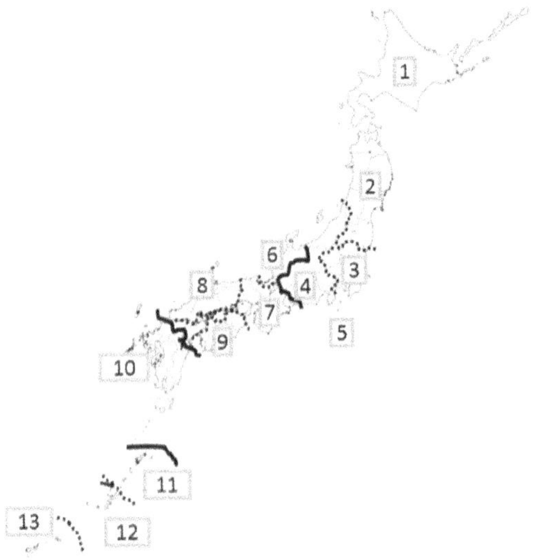

Map 5.2 Geolinguistic classification of Japanese dialects

Note that the geographic classifications suggested here roughly correspond to the genealogical subgrouping outlined in Section 2.1. However, it must be emphasized here that the geolinguistic classification suggested in Japanese dialectology is distinct from a genetic classification as outlined in Section 2.1, which is strictly based on shared innovations. Rather, the geolinguistic classification is based on structural (or lexical) similarities and yields a synchronic grouping of different dialects. For example, it is often suggested that the Eastern and Western dialects differ in the following set of structural variables.

(1) Oft-cited structural variables of Eastern versus Western dialects
   a. /u/: Unrounded [ɯ] versus Rounded [u]
   b. Negative morpheme: *-nai* versus *-n(u)*
   c. Morphophonological fusion of the adverbial form of adjective: non-fused (e.g. /takaku/ 'high') versus fused (/takō/)
   d. Imperative form of the verb (vowel-final stem class): *mi-ro* versus *mi-yo* 'Look!'
   e. Existential verb: *iru* versus *oru*
   f. Copula: *da* versus *ja*

Thus, a given dialectological area should be understood in terms of prototype, with one dialect having more Eastern (or Western, or any given dialectal area) features than others. This prototype-based grouping is in sharp contrast to a genetic subgrouping, where a group is defined by a set of shared innovations that are both necessary and sufficient conditions for a language to be classified under the group.

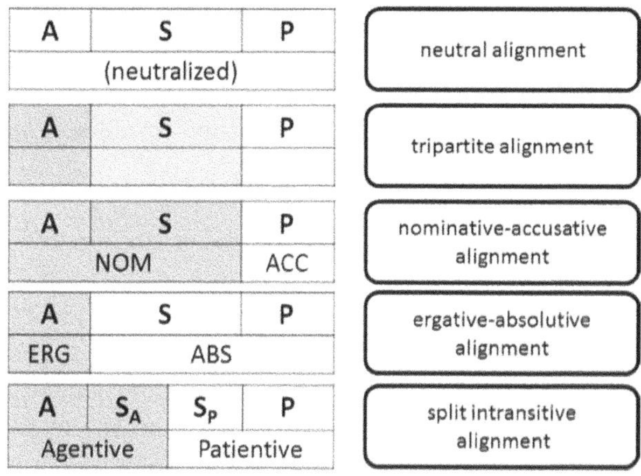

Figure 5.1 Major alignment types

3 Preliminary Remarks on the Typology of Alignment

3.1 Alignment

Alignment is the identical or distinct grouping of S, A, and P with a certain coding device: case marking on NPs (flagging), verbal agreement morphology (indexing), or word order. In the present chapter, our focus will be on the alignment of case marking, the major coding device for alignment in Japonic.

As schematized in Figure 5.1, there are five major types of alignment of case marking. Neutral alignment is an identical coding of S, A, and P (typically with no overt case marking on the three arguments). Tripartite alignment is a distinct coding for each of S, A, and P, with S being usually unmarked and the other two being distinctly coded. Nominative–accusative alignment treats P distinctly from S/A, typically with the unique case marking for P (accusative) and no case marking for S/A (nominative). Ergative–absolutive alignment treats A distinctly from S/P, typically with the unique case marking for A (ergative) and no case marking for S/P (absolutive).

The split intransitive alignment differs in nature from the other four, in that S splits into two categories (Agentive S, or S_A, and Patientive S, or S_P). The essential feature of the split intransitive system is that the alignment pattern is semantically based, that is, the coding of an argument is based on its semantic role (e.g. whether it is (like) an agent), not on its syntactic role (whether it is S, A, or P) as in the case of the other four systems.

3.2 Alignment Patterns and the Function of Case-marking

The major alignment patterns outlined in Figure 5.1 are not randomly arranged but are highly principled and largely explainable and motivated by the functions of the case-marking. Case-marking has two basic functions: to identify the semantic (or pragmatic) role of the NP and to distinguish A and P in a transitive clause. The former function opts for an explicit marking of the NP in question, as the lack of case-marking would lead to the failure to identify the semantic-pragmatic role of the NP. By contrast, the latter opts for the principle of economy: for distinguishing purposes, there is no need for the explicit marking of S (as it is the sole argument), and the explicit marking of both A and P is redundant and marking of either argument suffices. Case-marking of core arguments (S, A, and P in this chapter) is more associated with the distinguishing function than the identifying one, whereas the case-marking of peripheral arguments (adjuncts) is associated with the identifying one alone. For example, in (2) from colloquial Japanese, the case marking of either A (*aitsu*) or P (*bīru*) may be dispensable whereas the case marking of the peripheral argument (*reizōko*) may not, indicating that the former has to do with the distinguishing function and the latter with the identifying one.

(2) *Aitsu* *ga* *bīru* *o* *reizōko* *kara* *toridashita.*
that.guy NOM beer ACC refrigerator ABL took.out
'That guy took out beer from the refrigerator.'

It is noted that if S/A is focused, then the nominative marking becomes obligatory even when the accusative marking is present, indicating that the nominative marker *ga* has the identifying function of marking focus as well as the distinguishing function between S/A and P.

The principle of economy associated with the distinguishing function is reflected in the attested patterns of alignment in Figure 5.1. In the first four patterns, S is usually unmarked, as the overt marking of S does not help disambiguation between A and P, and the most common patterns are those in which either A or P is marked, that is, nominative–accusative or ergative–absolutive patterns. Tripartite alignment is unusual in that both A and P are overtly marked, but it is very often the case that S is still left unmarked. In neutral alignment, the principle of economy is maximally respected. Here, the distinction between A and P is secured by other means such as context, an animacy restriction (which predicts that A is higher in animacy than P), indexing, or word order.

The split intransitive alignment, where S (typically S_A (agentive S)) is overtly marked, is unusual in terms of the distinguishing function, but the overt case marking of S in split intransitive alignment makes sense in terms of the identifying function whereby the semantic feature (i.e. agentivity) of the NP is explicitly indicated.

3.3 Information-structure and Alignment

It is often suggested that Japanese in general is a topic-prominent rather than a subject-prominent language. This means that the coding of core arguments is sensitive to information-structure. In SJ, for example, topic-comment structure requires topic marking (*wa*) on the topic element, and the topic marking on S, A, and P replaces the case-marking for the core arguments (nominative *ga* and accusative *o*), resulting in neutralization of the case-marking of core arguments. *Ga* is the nominative case marker in the sense that it marks S/A, but it is also an "anti-topic" marker which indicates that the subject so marked is not a topic. That is, *ga* appears if the subject is focused (Argument-Focus), if it is within the broader scope of sentential focus (Sentence-Focus) with no particular focus on the subject itself, or if it is in the domain of presupposition (in adnominal clauses, etc.), again with no particular focus on the subject. Note that all three usages of *ga* have in common the fact that the subject is not a topic.

As will be shown below, information-structure also plays a significant role in the alignment patterning of Japanese dialects. It will be shown that in many, Argument-Focus often results in a radically different alignment pattern than Sentence-Focus (where no particular focus is put on any argument), resulting in the split of alignment into one pattern for Sentence-Focus and another for Argument-Focus.

4 A Typology of the Alignment Patterns in Japanese Dialects

4.1 An Overview

This section presents a typology of the alignment patterns in Japanese dialects. The data for the present typology range from published works to my own field data. The data of Irabu (Section 4.5), of Shiiba (Section 4.6.2) and of Yonaguni (Section 4.7.1) are from my own field data.

Table 5.1 is a summary of the typology of alignment patterns attested in Japanese dialects. Each type will be briefly discussed in the following sections. If there is a split of alignment (e.g. neutral and nominative–accusative) due to a specific factor (e.g. animacy), the attested patterns are indicated by "α/β" in the left-most column, which reads "the alignment splits into the α pattern and β pattern." In the third column, the factor motivating the split is indicated. Focus and animacy are two common factors of alignment split in Japanese dialects. If a dialect has the nominative–accusative alignment either as its sole pattern or one of the possible patterns, a further specification is made in the middle column as to what subtype of nominative–accusative alignment is observed. In nominative–accusative alignment where S/A is coded distinctly from P, three logically possible patterns are distinguished: (a) marked nominative (Marked Nom in the table), which marks A/S alone, (b) marked accusative (Marked Acc), which marks P alone,

Table 5.1 *Alignment typology of Japanese dialects*

Type	Subtype of Nom–Acc	Factor of split	Dialect
Neutral			Hateruma
Neutral/Nom–Acc	Marked Nom	Focus	Kinki
Neutral/Nom–Acc	Marked Acc	Animacy and focus	Tōhoku
Nom–Acc	Marked Nom–Acc		Irabu
Nom–Acc	Marked Nom Marked Nom–Acc	Animacy, focus, adjacency	Chūūgoku, Kyūshū, Amami
Nom–Acc/Split intransitive	Marked Nom	Animacy, focus	Yonaguni, Okinawan
Nom–Acc/Split intransitive/ Tripartite	Marked Nom–Acc	Animacy	Koshikijima

and (c) marked nominative–accusative (Marked Nom–Acc), which marks both A/S and P with two distinct overt case markers.

Note that all the major alignment patterns but ergative–absolutive alignment are attested in this single language group, including cross-linguistically uncommon patterns such as split-intransitive and tripartite. The lack of ergative–absolutive alignment is a conspicuous typological feature of Japanese dialects.

Table 5.1 tells us another important feature of the alignment patterns in Japanese dialects. That is, if there is no alignment split in a given alignment system, the sole alignment pattern is a cross-linguistically common pattern, that is, neutral or nominative–accusative. In other words, if a dialect has a cross-linguistically rarer pattern like split intransitive or tripartite, then it implies the existence of a more common pattern(s) in the dialect. Thus, the present chapter suggests the following implicational hierarchy, which regulates the possible alignment patterning in a given dialect.

(3) Nominative–accusative > Split intransitive > Tripartite
Neutral

According to this hierarchy, the existence of tripartite alignment in a dialect implies the existence of split intransitive and a more basic alignment pattern, that is, nominative–accusative or neutral. The existence of split intransitive implies the existence of neutral or nominative accusative, but it does not necessarily imply the existence of tripartite. What is significant about this hierarchy is that it roughly reflects the relative frequency of the five major alignment patterns in the world's languages. A survey of WALS Online (98A: Alignment of case marking of full NPs) reveals that neutral alignment is the most common cross-linguistically (98 out of 190 sample languages), followed by nominative–accusative (52/190), ergative–absolutive (32/190), split intransitive (4/190) and tripartite (4/190).[1]

[1] WALS Online, ch. 98 (http://wals.info/chapter/98).

A final remark on Table 5.1 is about the structural diversity of nominative–accusative alignment in Japanese dialects, where all possible patterns of nominative–accusative alignment are observed, that is, marked nominative (where only S/A are marked), marked accusative (where only P is marked), and marked nominative–accusative (where both are marked). Cross-linguistically, the marked nominative pattern is known to be extremely rare (Handschuh 2014: 1). This pattern is unusual in terms of the distinguishing function of core case marking (Section 3.2). Since S is expected to be always left unmarked in terms of the distinguishing function, it is predicted that if there is an unmarked case for any of S, A, and P, then it must be used (at least) for S, a prediction known as Greenberg's Universal 38 (Greenberg 1963). The prediction is then made that if A or P is left unmarked in a system, S must also be unmarked. The marked accusative pattern (where only P is marked) and the marked nominative–accusative pattern (where S, A, and P are all marked) do not contradict this prediction, whereas the marked nominative alignment clearly goes against this prediction. It is therefore important to ask what is going on in those dialects where the marked nominative alignment is attested. This issue will be discussed in Section 6.

4.2 Neutral Type

The strict neutral alignment with no optional overt case-marking is not found in the mainland dialects. It is also extremely rare in Ryukyuan, and the only dialect that exhibits the strict neutral system is Hateruma, a dialect of Yaeyama (Southern Ryukyuan). The following data come from Aso (2015).

(4) *Fumon* *ndan.*
cloud appeared
'Clouds have appeared.'

(5) *Fumon* *shina* *hakosutan.*
cloud sun hid
'The cloud hid the sun.'

(6) *Aboa* *fumon* *miri* *biryatan.*
mother cloud look.SEQ PROG.PAST
'(My) mother was looking at clouds.'

As is common in languages with neutral alignment, word order is crucial in Hateruma (Aso 2010: 200), where the APV order is considered as the default. This is based on the fact that, without any contextual information, the first NP is identified as the subject, although it is logically possible for the latter NP to be the subject.

(7) *Aboa* *iya* *miri* *biryatan.*
mother father look.SEQ PROG.PAST
'(My) mother was looking at (my) father.'

(8) *Iya* *aboa* *miri* *biryatan.*
father mother look.SEQ PROG.PAST
'(My) father was looking at (my) mother.'

4.3 Neutral/Nominative–accusative (Marked Nom)

In this pattern, S/A/P are left unmarked in the Sentence-Focus environment while overt marking for S/A (but not P) is obligatory when the subject (S/A) is focused, displaying the split of alignment between neutral (Sentence-Focus) and nominative–accusative (Argument-Focus). Kinki dialects (spoken in Hyōgo, Osaka, Kyoto, Shiga, Wakayama, and Nara) are known to exhibit this pattern. The following example is from the Kyoto dialect (Takeuchi and Matsumaru 2015b: 4).

(9) *Tanaka* *Yamada* *oshidashita.*
pushed.out
'Tanaka pushed out Yamada.'

The overt marking of S/A by *ga* is rare but seems possible in the Sentence-Focus environment (ibid.). It is still clear that neutral alignment is default as the overt marking of S/A is conspicuously infrequent.

(10) *A,* *tsuki* *ga* *deteru.*
oh moon NOM rose
'Oh, the moon has risen.'

(11) *Yōyaku* *Tanaka* *(ga)* *Yamada* *oshidashita.*
at.last NOM pushed.out
'Tanaka pushed out Yamada at last.'

According to Takeuchi and Matsumaru, if S/A is focused, the neutral pattern disappears and the overt A/S marking by *ga* becomes obligatory. So, the nominative marking for (9) becomes obligatory, as in (12), if it is a response to a question like "Who pushed out Yamada?"

(12) *Tanaka* *ga* *Yamada* *oshidashita.*
NOM pushed.out
'(It is) Tanaka (who) pushed out Yamada.'

As in the case of Hateruma, word order is crucial in identifying A and P in a transitive clause. In (9), the first NP is interpreted as the subject without any context, indicating that APV order is the default. However, if there is a context whereby Yamada is the agent, the order of arguments must reflect this fact (Takeuchi and Matsumaru 2015b: 4).

(13) *Yamada Tanaka oshidashita.*
pushed.out
'Yamada pushed out Tanaka.'

4.4 Neutral/Nominative–accusative (Marked Acc)

In this pattern, the alignment splits into neutral (where S, A, and P are all unmarked) and nominative–accusative (where only P is marked). The factor of the split (i.e. the factor motivating the overt marking of P) is animacy in most dialects, but focus also plays a key role in some dialects. The pattern is common in the eastern part of Japan (Tōhoku and northern Kantō), where there is a well-known alignment split, known as differential object marking (DOM), which is an overt versus zero marking of P depending on the referential status (typically animacy) of the P argument. See Section 5 for a detailed discussion of DOM.

In the eastern dialects, S/A is left unmarked[2] and P is usually also left unmarked or may be uniquely marked by one of the following accusative markers: *godo/dogo* (in most Tōhoku and northern Kantō), *ba* (in coastal Hokkaidō, Aomori, Akita, Yamagata, etc.) or *to(ba)* (Aomori).[3] The overt P marking is typically conditioned by the animacy of P, in such a way that animate Ps can be marked whereas inanimate Ps are always unmarked. The following example is from the Mitsukaidō (Ibaraki) dialect (Sasaki 2006: 7, 19). Depending on the presence or absence of the overt P marking, we get either the neutral alignment where S/A/P are unmarked ((14) versus (15)) or the marked accusative alignment where only P is marked ((14) versus (16)) in the single language system.

(14) *Are hadaraederu.*
he is.working
'He is working.' [intransitive: S is unmarked]

(15) *Mango garasu watta.*
grandchild glass broke
'The grandchild broke the glass.' [transitive: A and P are unmarked]

(16) *Ano yarō ore godo bukkurashita.*
that guy I ACC struck
'That guy struck me.' [transitive: A is unmarked, P is marked]

[2] In some dialects such as Aomori, the subject NP that ends in a front vowel may be followed by /a/ (e.g. *Amea furu* 'The rain falls (i.e. it rains),' K. Sato 2003: 33), and it might be a historical remnant of the former nominative **ga*, which is lost in the current system of these dialects.

[3] The accusative marker *godo/dogo* is the cognate of *koto* in SJ. Unlike *koto* in SJ, which is a formal noun that heads an NP, *godo/dogo* cannot be followed by the accusative case *o* (**godo o*) or any other case (**godo ni*), indicating that it does not head an NP, but has become a case marker which is in paradigmatic relationship with other case markers.

In some dialects such as Aomori and Yamagata, the overt P marking is also conditioned by focus. In Aomori (K. Sato 2003: 34), where the overt P marker may be *ba, toba, to*, or *godo*, the inanimate P *sage* 'alcohol' is unmarked if it is not in focus (17), whereas it is overtly marked if it is in focus (18). According to Sato, (18) would be appropriate answers to the question "What do you want to drink?," which induces Argument-Focus.

(17) *Sage nomu.*
alcohol drink
'(I) drink alcohol.'

(18) *Sage godo/toba/ba nomide.*
alcohol ACC want.to.drink
'(I) want to drink alcohol.'

4.5 Nominative–accusative (Marked Nominative–accusative)

In this pattern, all core arguments are obligatorily marked with the nominative marker of S/A and the accusative marker of P. The obligatory marking of both S/A and P as the sole alignment pattern is extremely rare in Japanese dialects, and the only unambiguous example of this pattern is found in a restricted set of dialects of Ryukyuan (Miyako). In what follows, the Irabu dialect of Miyako Ryukyuan is examined for illustration.

The nominative marking is either *ga* or *nu* (cognates of *ga* and *no* in SJ, respectively), and the differential subject marking is largely based on the animacy of the subject NP. *Ga* is used when the subject is higher in the Animacy Hierarchy (only human: a pronoun or an address noun like a proper name or a (elder) kinship term, a restricted set of human nouns such as *shinshī* 'teacher') whereas *nu* is used elsewhere.

(19) *Aza ga du bijūr.*
older.brother NOM FOC is.sitting
'An older brother is sitting.' [S: human (older kinship term)]

(20) *Ffa nu du bijūr.*
child NOM FOC is.sitting
'A child is sitting.' [S: human (common noun)]

(21) *In nu du bijūr.*
dog NOM FOC is.sitting
'A dog is sitting.' [S: animal]

(22) *Aza ga du munu u faiur.*
older.brother NOM FOC thing ACC1 is.eating
'An elder brother is eating something.' [A: human (older kinship term)]

(23) *Ffa* *nu* *du* *munu* *u* *faiur.*
child NOM FOC thing ACC1 is.eating
'A child is eating something.' [A: human (common noun)]

(24) *In* *nu* *du* *munu* *u* *faiur.*
dog NOM FOC thing ACC1 is.eating
'A dog is eating something.' [A: animal]

The accusative marking is either *u* (accusative 1, default) or *a* (accusative 2, non-canonical), and the differential object marking is loosely explained in terms of the aspect (perfective versus imperfective) of the clause in which the P occurs. The non-canonical *a* occurs mostly in a sequential converbal clause (which is similar in function to the *-te* clause in SJ) with imperfective aspect. Since the sequential converb is contextual and ambiguous with regard to the aspectual interpretation (narrative/perfective versus modifying/imperfective), the non-canonical object marking disambiguates the aspectual value of the clause in which it occurs, explicitly indicating the imperfective aspect. For example, in the following pair of examples, the bracketed sequential clause has the modifying/imperfective interpretation when *a* is used, whereas the aspectual interpretation of the same clause is ambiguous when *u* is used.

(25) *[Is* *sa* *turī]* *du* *bijūr.*
stone ACC2 take.SEQ FOC is.sitting
'Holding a stone (in his hand), (the man) is sitting.' [imperfective interpretation]

(26) *[Is* *su* *turī]* *du* *bijūr.*
stone ACC1 take.SEQ FOC is.sitting
'(The man) took a stone, and (now) (the man) is sitting.' [perfective interpretation]
'Holding a stone (in his hand), (the man) is sitting.' [imperfective interpretation]

Very few, if any, case ellipses occur in natural speech. Whereas the marked nominative–accusative pattern as observed in Irabu is clearly redundant in terms of the distinguishing function, it is clear that the obligatory overt marking for both S/A and P is motivated by the identifying function of the case marking: the differential subject marking is an explicit marking of the animacy of S/A, and the differential object marking is an explicit marking of the aspect of the clause in which P occurs.

4.6 Nominative–accusative (Marked Nominative–accusative/ Marked Nominative)

In this pattern, the overall alignment pattern is of the nominative–accusative type, but the split occurs between marked nominative (where only S/A is marked) and marked nominative–accusative (where P is additionally marked), depending on whether there is an overt marking of P, which is conditioned by the animacy of P and/or the adjacency of P to the verb with which it occurs. This pattern is very common in the western part of Japan (especially in Kyūshū and Chūgoku) and in Ryukyuan, especially in Amami.

4.6.1 Ryukyuan Dialects

In most Amami dialects (Northern Ryukyuan), S/A is marked by either *ga* (higher in animacy) or *nu* (lower in animacy), while P is marked by *ba* or left unmarked. The marking of S/A is obligatory, and this obligatory marking may be explained in the same vein as for Irabu (Section 4.5): the nominative marking is sensitive to the semantic feature of the subject NP and is therefore motivated by the identifying function of case marking, which is in favor of explicitness.

As for the case marking of P, the relevant factor is typically animacy, and adjacency to the verb might also be relevant. In Yuwan (Niinaga 2014: 157), for example, the overt P marking is almost obligatory if P is a personal pronoun, a human demonstrative, or an address noun (i.e. a kinship term or a proper name), while the P marking is optional (and often absent) with inanimate nouns.

(27) *Mattaku wakaranba ura ba abɨranbō.*
at.all not.understand.CSL you ACC call.NEG.COND
'If (I) don't call you, (I) won't understand (what I should do) at all.'

Thus, the overt versus zero marking of P in Yuwan (and Amami Ryukyuan in general) is a typical animacy-driven DOM as in the case of Tōhoku dialects (Section 4.4), although the overt P marking in the latter is strictly limited to animate nouns.

Although Niinaga does not mention it explicitly, an additional factor of adjacency might also be relevant. In (28–29), the inanimate P, which is adjacent to the verb with which it occurs, is left unmarked (28), whereas the same inanimate P is marked by *ba* when it is not adjacent to the verb (29).

(28) *Ujī ga daibangɨ: nantɨ nashi mutun wake.*
old.man NOM big.tree LOC pear be.picking SFP
'An old man is picking pears off on a big tree.' [P (*nashi*): unmarked]

(29) *Nashi ba tˀɨ: tˀɨ: mutun wake yo.*
pear ACC one one be.picking.up SFP SFP
'(The old man) is picking up pears one by one.' [P (*nashi*): marked by *ba*]

However, due to the lack of data including Ps not adjacent to the predicate in the corpus, it is difficult to conclude that the adjacency condition is relevant in Yuwan.

4.6.2 Kyūshū Dialects

In most Kyūshū dialects, S/A is marked by *ga* or *no*, while P is either unmarked or marked by *ba* (or *oba, o*). P is marked by one of *ba, oba* (less common), or *o* (less common) or is left unmarked, displaying a DOM pattern.

As in the case of many Ryukyuan dialects such as Irabu (Section 4.5) and Amami (Section 4.6.1), the differential case marking of S/A is conditioned by the animacy of the subject NP. *Ga* is attached to nouns higher in animacy (human nouns, especially pronouns), while *no* is attached to nouns lower in animacy (typically animal or inanimate).[4] Again, the marking of S/A is almost obligatory as in the Ryukyuan dialects noted in Section 4.5 and 4.6.1, indicating that the identifying function prevails in the subject marking of Kyūshū dialects.[5]

In the Shiiba dialect of Miyazaki Prefecture (Shimoji 2016: 40), S/A is obligatorily marked by *ga* if it is a pronoun (30), or very likely to be marked by *ga* if it is a human (31).

(30) *Ore ga kokē oru.*
I NOM this.place.LOC exist
'I stay here.'

(31) *Kodomo ga(/no) kokē oru.*
child NOM this.place.LOC exist
'There is a child here.' [S: human]

S/A is more likely to be marked by *no* if it is an animal or an inanimate (32a, b). Note here that the existential verb differs depending on whether the subject is animate (32a) or inanimate (32b), as in the case of SJ.

(32) a. *Arimushi no oru.*
ant NOM exist
'There is an ant.' [S: animal]

b. *Hon no aru.*
book NOM exist
'There is a book.' [S: inanimate]

[4] Unlike the differential subject marking in Ryukyuan, there is no restriction on the occurrence of *ga* in Kyūshū dialects, probably due to the heavier influence from SJ where uniform *ga* marking is the norm in main clauses. So, in (32–33) *ga* may also be used.

[5] In many Kyūshū dialects, there is an additional factor that overrides the animacy-driven differential marking, that is, honorification. Thus, if a human referent which opts for *ga* is honorified (by the verb inflection), it is likely to be marked by *no* instead of *ga*. The honorification-driven subject marking with *no* is common in the mainland dialects that have the differential subject marking. In the Izumo dialect of Shimane Prefecture (Unpaku), honorification is the only relevant factor for the differential marking by *no* rather than *ga* (Hirako 2016: 75).

As in many other Kyūshū dialects, A is slightly more prone to take *ga* for animal nouns than S. Compare (33) and (34):

(33)

Akko	*de*	*inu*	*no*	*hoetoru.*
that.place	LOC	dog	NOM	is.barking

'A dog is barking over there.' [S: animal]

(34)

Inu	*ga/no*	*chō*	*o*	*ūte*	*tobiagatta.*
dog	NOM	butterfly	ACC	chase	jumped

'Chasing the butterfly, the dog jumped.' [A: animal]

P is obligatorily marked if it is a pronoun, as in (35). However, P may be marked or unmarked with other kinds of noun, although inanimate nouns are very often left unmarked (36).

(35)

Gedō	*ga*	*ore*	*ba*	*hikkokashita.*
bastard	NOM	I	ACC	pushed

'That bastard pushed me (into a cliff).' [P: pronoun]

(36)

Ano	*hitaa*	*ore*	*ga*	*e*	*e*	*saifu*	*(ba/oba/o)*	*wasureta*
that	person.TOP	I	GEN	house	LOC	wallet	(ACC)	left
fū	*wai.*							
EVID	SFP							

'That person seems to have left (his/her) wallet at my house.' [P: inanimate]

The comparison between (35) and (36) reminds us of the animacy-driven DOM in Tōhoku dialects (Section 4.4) and Amami (Section 4.6.1). However, the P marking in Kyūshū dialects is more complicated, and it is difficult to make a precise prediction if we only rely on the animacy of P. See Section 5 for a detailed account of the P marking of Shiiba, where it will be argued that it is not the animacy of P but the *relative animacy* of P and A that matters in the presence or absence of the overt P marking, making the DOM in this dialect typologically highly noteworthy.

The adjacency of P to the verb is another important factor of overt P marking. That is, whereas overt P marking is optional if P is adjacent to the verb with which it occurs (37), it is almost obligatory if P is remote from the verb (38).

(37)

Uma	*ga*	*kusa*	*(ba/oba/o)*	*kwīoru.*
horse	NOM	grass	(ACC)	is.eating

'The horse is eating grass.'

(38)

Uma	*ga*	*kusa*	*ba/oba/o*	*umasō*	*ni*	*kwīoru.*
horse	NOM	grass	ACC	keen.relish	DAT	is.eating

'The horse is eating grass with keen relish.'

4.6.3 Chūgoku Dialects

In most Chūgoku dialects, S/A is marked by *ga*, and P is either marked by *o* or left unmarked. Even though it is often claimed that S/A is always marked in these dialects, there is no empirical study that demonstrates its validity. Let us examine this claim by taking up the Tottori dialect from the Chūgoku area, which has the nominative *ga* and the accusative *o* (which may fuse with the final vowel of the object noun). I examined the folktale *Tsuru no ongaeshi* 'The Grateful Crane' listed in Hirayama (1998), and counted all the examples of S, A, and P in the Sentence-Focus environment. According to this count, S and A were regularly marked by *ga* (N = 19) and there was no example of an unmarked S/A. This is in sharp contrast to the overt P marking. Among all the attested examples of P (N = 25), only half were overtly case-marked (14/25). Thus, the brief examination of the Tottori texts reveals that S/A is obligatorily marked whereas P is not, instantiating the alignment pattern claimed for Chūgoku dialects in general.

With regard to P marking, whereas both animacy and adjacency play an important role in Kyūshū dialects (and possibly Amami Ryukyuan, Section 4.6.1), in Chūgoku dialects adjacency is an important factor but animacy seems irrelevant. For example, the Hiroshima dialect (Konishi 2015) exhibits a nominative–accusative alignment pattern which further splits into marked nominative (A/S: *ga*, P: unmarked) and marked nominative–accusative (A/S: *ga*, P: *o*).[6] Konishi claims that the adjacency of P to the verb is relevant in the overt marking of P based on the fact that 85% of all the tokens of unmarked Ps (twenty-two out of twenty-six) were adjacent to the predicate. The following example (Konishi 2015: 19) illustrates an overtly marked P (*enshō* 'gunpowder') that is remote from the verb (*yarō* 'will give').

(39) *Soryā mukasha-a ano enshō o ikkin yarō omōtara,*
then old.times-TOP well gunpowder ACC one.kin will.give think.COND
'In those days if (one) wants to give a *kin* (= 4 grams) of gunpowder…'

4.7 Nominative–accusative/Split Intransitive

4.7.1 Yonaguni

In Yonaguni (Southern Ryukyuan), alignment splits into (a) split intransitive (where A/S_A is marked and S_P/P is unmarked) and (b) nominative–accusative (where A/S is marked and P is unmarked, displaying the marked nominative pattern). The split between (a) and (b) occurs depending on whether only S_A is marked (a) or S is consistently marked (b). The factors motivating

[6] The accusative *o* may be fused with the stem-final vowel of the noun to which it is attached, which is in certain conditions realized as the prolongation of the stem-final vowel. This feature is typical in Chūgoku dialects.

the split marking are animacy (whether S/A/P is pronominal) and focus (whether S/A is focused).

In any environment where S/A/P is not topic-marked, A is always marked by *nga*, whereas P is always left unmarked. If the subject is either a pronoun or is focused, S aligns with A, with the obligatory *nga*. These two environments thus yield nominative–accusative alignment in which only S/A is marked.

In the Sentence-Focus environment with non-pronominal core arguments, a clear split intransitive pattern emerges. S splits into two semantically based categories: S_A (agentive S) and S_P (patientive S). S_A aligns with A with the overt marking by *nga*. A set of activity verbs (most of which are volitional motion verbs, WALK, MOVE, LEAVE, RUN, etc.) take S_A, always requiring their subjects to be marked by *nga*.

(40) *Munu* *nga* *uiti* *du* *buru.*
living.thing AGT move.SEQ FOC PROG
'Some living thing is moving.' [S_A: agent]

S_P aligns with P with no overt marking. A set of non-volitional change-of-state verbs (SPROUT, CRACK, FALL, BEND, BREAK) take S_P, always requiring their subjects to be left unmarked.

(41) *Nai* *uti* *du* *buru.*
nut fall.SEQ FOC RSL
'The nut is fallen.' [S_P: patient/theme]

All other verbs allow their subjects to be marked by *nga* (as S_A) or left unmarked (as S_P), depending on whether the subject is more agentive or more patientive.

(42) *Ija* *(nga)* *khaguri* *du* *buru.*
father (AGT) hide.SEQ FOC PROG
'The father is hiding.' [in favor of *nga*: agent]

(43) *Ija* *(?nga)* *khutandi* *du* *buru.*
father (?AGT) get.tired.SEQ FOC PROG
'The father is tired.' [in favor of zero marking: patient/theme]

Thus, the Yonaguni speakers treat the volitional motion verbs as S_A, the few non-volitional change-of-state verbs as S_P, and the rest either as S_A or S_P.

4.7.2 Okinawan

It is much less straightforward to argue for split intransitivity in Okinawan (Northern Ryukyuan), and careful argumentation is required. The currently widespread view is that they display an unambiguous marked nominative pattern, whereby S/A is obligatorily marked by *ga* or *nu* (depending on the animacy of the subject NP just as in the case of

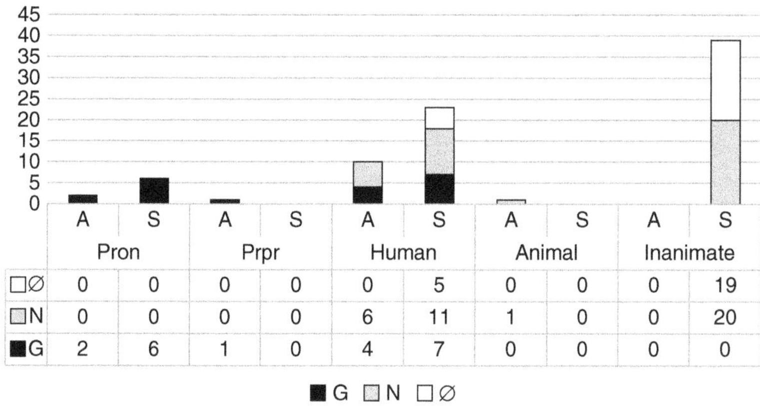

	A	S	A	S	A	S	A	S	A	S
	Pron		Prpr		Human		Animal		Inanimate	
Ø	0	0	0	0	0	5	0	0	0	19
N	0	0	0	0	6	11	1	0	0	20
G	2	6	1	0	4	7	0	0	0	0

Figure 5.2 Subject marking in five narrative texts of the Sesokojima dialect

Miyako (Section 4.5) and Amami (Section 4.6.1)), whereas P is always unmarked. However, a closer look at these dialects reveals a different pattern: S often lacks overt marking (henceforth "zero marking"), a fact which calls into question the marked nominative analysis. In what follows, the Sesokojima dialect will be taken up to illustrate the problem of zero marking in Okinawan. There are two reasons for taking up this dialect as a representative Okinawan dialect. First, the S/A marking and P marking of this dialect demonstrate a typical Okinawan pattern, with the differential subject marking sensitive to animacy (*ga* and *nu*) and with the zero marking of P. Second, the data of this dialect is available online,[7] and it is easy for one to analyze the case-marking patterns of this dialect with empirical data. I examined five narrative texts. The total number of occurrences of S/A that are not topic-marked is eighty-two. As shown in Figure 5.2, they are sorted according to animacy (Pronoun, Proper name, Human, Animal, and Inanimate) and transitivity (S versus A).

As is clear from Figure 5.2, zero marking (Ø) is very common, especially for inanimate subjects. Before examining the zero marking, let us first discuss the distribution of the two overt subject markers, *ga* (G) and *nu* (N). The choice is largely explainable by referring to the animacy of S/A: *ga* distributes from the left end of the Animacy Hierarchy to the middle (human), whereas *nu* distributes from the right end of the hierarchy to the middle, with an overlap of the two forms in the middle. It seems that in many dialects honorification plays some role for the case marking of human nouns (as in Kyūshū dialects and Izumo; see footnote 6), in that the use of *nu* is induced when the predicate is in the honorific form. Thus, the honorification factor overrides the animacy factor in such a way that human nouns, which opt for *ga* by animacy, may opt for *nu* by the additional honorification factor.

[7] http://kikigengo.sakura.ne.jp/motobu/motobu.html.

As is common in most Okinawan dialects (Shimoji 2015: 111), the zero marking is limited to S in Sesokojima. Now, the question arises whether the zero marking is syntactically based whereby S is consistently zero-marked, that is, the syntactic category S is relevant, or semantically based whereby zero marking is limited to a non-agentive S. If the former, then the language is said to have an ergative–absolutive pattern, as in (44). If the latter, then the language is said to have a split intransitive pattern where the distinction between agentive S (S_A) and non-agentive S (S_P) is relevant, as in (45).

(44) A: G/N
S: Ø
P: Ø

(45) A: G/N
S_A: G/N
S_P: Ø
P: Ø

There is no evidence that zero marking is syntactically based, and, therefore, the ergative–absolutive analysis is not supported. According to the data, most of the zero-marked Ss are inanimates, but one cannot say that inanimate S is systematically zero-marked. Inanimate Ss may also be marked by *nu* (see Figure 5.2). Conversely, it is possible to find zero-marked animate Ss, as in (46):

(46) *Inagungwa* *chui* *ʔmaariti* ...
woman.DIM one was.born.SEQ
'A baby girl was born, and...'

On the other hand, it is possible to argue for the split intransitive analysis. All available descriptions that report zero marking in individual Okinawan dialects show a striking similarity with regard to the kind of verbs that take a zero-marked S: a restricted set of non-agentive verbs, especially the verbs that denote existence and emergence. Such verbs include (a) existential verbs (EXIST, NOT EXIST) and (b) verbs that pertain to emergence (BE BORN, EMERGE, APPEAR, COME OUT, BEGIN, DAWN, etc.).[8] In the Sesokojima texts, almost all of the attested examples of zero marking are found with the verbs of these two types. Several examples are listed below:

(47) *arashī: ijīchi* 'a battle occurred, and...'
waku nēnu '(there) is no water'
nagungwa ʔmāriti 'a baby girl was born, and...'
ju: akirūshi 'until the night gets light'

[8] This is a special class of unaccusative verbs in Levin and Rappaport Hovav's (1995) theory of unaccusativity.

Table 5.2 *Alignment of the Okinawan type*

	Pronoun/Proper name	Human	Animal/Inanimate
A		GA/NO	NO
S_A	GA		
S_P		NO/Ø	NO/Ø
P	Ø	Ø	Ø
alignment	Nominative–accusative	Split intransitive	

The subjects that these verbs take are clearly non-agentive, since they lack volition or control. Thus, it is reasonable to consider that zero marking is determined by the semantic feature of the verb, rather than the animacy of S. That is, zero marking is possible if the verb in question is of existence-emergence whose S is categorized as S_P in most Okinawan dialects. Zero marking is mostly found in inanimate S because most of the verbs of the type take inanimate subjects, not because the zero marking is determined by animacy.

Unlike S_P in Yonaguni, the Okinawan system restricts the S_P category to the S of the verbs of existence-emergence, and this lexical restriction makes it difficult to see the split intransitivity of this dialect. Moreover, these classes of S may also be overtly marked by *nu*, showing fluidity of zero marking. For example, the S of the verb *nēnu* 'not exist' may be zero-marked or marked by *nu*.

In sum, in Sesokojima, like most other Okinawan, pronouns and proper names are always marked by *ga* (and P is always unmarked), and therefore the marked nominative pattern holds for these classes of nouns. For other classes of nouns, the split intransitive pattern holds in the sense that S is subcategorized into S_A and S_P, although S_P is restricted to the S of the verbs of existence-emergence (Table 5.2).

4.8 Nominative–accusative/Split Intransitive/Tripartite

Split intransitive alignment is extremely rare in the mainland dialects, and it is only partially integrated into the entire alignment system of the dialects that are claimed to have such a pattern. Split intransitive is found in two Kyūshū dialects: the Kumamoto dialect and the Sato dialect of Koshikijima Island in Kagoshima. In what follows, the alignment of Sato is briefly discussed, based on Sakai (2015).

In the Sato dialect, A/S are marked either by *ga* or *no*, whereas P is marked by *ba* (or *o*, which is a form introduced under the influence from SJ). As discussed in Section 4.6.2, *ga* has no restriction in Kyūshū dialects, so the region of *no* in Table 5.3 also allows *ga* marking. If this uniform subject marking by *ga* is taken seriously, the Koshikijima dialect is claimed

Table 5.3 *Alignment in the Sato dialect of Koshikijima Island*

<table>
<tr><th></th><th>Pronoun</th><th>Kin/Proper/Human</th><th>Animal</th><th>Inanimate</th></tr>
<tr><td>A</td><td rowspan="3">GA</td><td rowspan="2">GA</td><td>GA</td><td rowspan="3">NO</td></tr>
<tr><td>S_A</td><td rowspan="2">NO</td></tr>
<tr><td>S_P</td><td>NO</td></tr>
<tr><td>P</td><td>BA</td><td>BA</td><td>BA</td><td>BA</td></tr>
<tr><td>alignment</td><td>Nom–Acc</td><td>Split intransitive</td><td>Tripartite</td><td>Nom–Acc</td></tr>
</table>

(Based on Sakai 2015)

to display the marked nominative–accusative/marked nominative pattern which is observed in Kyūshū and Chūgoku as noted above. However, this section is concerned with the alignment system that is less influenced by SJ, paying attention to the occurrence of *no* and leaving aside the potential *ga* marking for all nouns.

Here, two factors affect the alignment pattern: animacy and agentivity. If the arguments are pronominal, S/A is uniformly marked by *ga*, and P is marked by *ba*, displaying the marked nominative–accusative pattern.[9] If the arguments are inanimate, the same alignment pattern emerges, with A/S marked by *no* and P by *ba*. That is, at the two edges of the Animacy Hierarchy, we get the same alignment pattern, even though the subject marking takes two different forms (*ga* for pronouns, *no* for inanimates).

The tripartite alignment pattern, which is cross-linguistically very rare, emerges when the arguments are animal nouns. Here, A is distinctly marked by *ga*, whereas S is marked by *no*. P may be marked by *ba* or left unmarked.

(48) *In ga garasu ba wai dō.*
dog NOM glass ACC break SFP
'The dog will break the glass.' [transitive]

(49) *In no dete kita.*
dog NOM exit.SEQ came
'The dog came out.' [intransitive; S_A]

In (48) A (*in* 'dog') is marked by *ga* and P (*garasu* 'glass') is marked by *ba* or left unmarked. In (49), S (*in*) is marked by *no*. Unlike the cross-linguistically well-known tripartite pattern, where S is unmarked (e.g. Hindi), the tripartite alignment in Sato has an overt marker for S.

Split intransitive alignment occurs elsewhere, that is, when the arguments are kinship terms, proper names, or other human nouns. S is not uniformly treated, but it splits into S_A marked by *ga* and S_P marked by *no*.

9 According to Sakai (2015: 91), the accusative *o* is borrowed from SJ and not a native form, which is *ba*.

(50) *Otōto* *ga* *iku* *dō.*
younger.brother NOM go-NPST SFP
'The younger brother will go.' [intransitive; S_A]

(51) *Mago* *no* *nmareta* *na.*
grandchild NOM was.born SFP
'A grandchild was born.' [intransitive: S_P]

5 Differential Object Marking

As noted in Sections 4.4 and 4.6, differential object marking (DOM) is very common both in mainland and Ryukyuan dialects. There are several major factors that trigger DOM: animacy, focus, and adjacency of P to the verb. In what follows, animacy, the most common factor in both mainland and Ryukyuan dialects, is discussed in detail. A typologically uncommon feature of DOM in some dialects has theoretical implications for the typology of DOM (Bossong 1985).

The overt marking of P in Tōhoku is typically induced by the animacy of P. That is, the overt marking (*godo/dogo/ba*) is typically restricted to those that are animate (especially human), exhibiting a cross-linguistically common DOM pattern. In traditional analyses, the relevant factor has been believed to be the animacy of P, and the animacy of A has been simply ignored. However, there are at least two dialects where the overt P marking is conditioned by *relative animacy*, which is based on the comparison of the animacy of A and P with respect to the Animacy Hierarchy (Human > Animate > Inanimate). The Shiiba dialect (Miyazaki Prefecture, Kyūshū) is an example. Shiiba has three accusative markers, *ba*, *oba*, and *o*, and the overt marking may be absent, exhibiting a typical DOM pattern.

(52) *Ora* *mari* *(ba)* *ūta* *koto* *ga* *aru.*
I.TOP ball (ACC) chased fact NOM exist
'I have once chased a ball.' [P: inanimate]

(53) *Ora* *saru* *(ba)* *ūta* *koto* *ga* *aru.*
I.TOP monkey (ACC) chased fact NOM exist
'I have once chased a monkey.' [P: animal]

(54) *Kono* *nekaa* *saru* *ba* *ūta* *koto* *ga* *aru.*
this cat.TOP monkey ACC chased fact NOM exist
'This cat has once chased a monkey.' [P: animal]

The overt accusative marking in these examples is *ba*, which may be freely replaced by *o* or *oba*. The animacy of P differs in (52) and (53), but the P marking is equally optional. The overt marking of P is obligatory only in (54), although its animacy is the same as (53). This cannot be explained by referring to the animacy of P alone as in the case of the

Table 5.4 *DOM in Shiiba*

		Animacy of P		
		Human	Animal	Inanimate
Animacy of A	Human	Acc	(Acc)	(Acc)
	Animal	Acc	Acc	(Acc)
	Inanimate	[Acc]	[Acc]	Acc

DOM of Tōhoku dialects (see Section 4.4). Rather, in Shiiba relative animacy plays a crucial role, whereby the overt P marking is obligatory if P is equal or higher in animacy than A. The DOM of Shiiba is schematically shown in Table 5.4.

In Table 5.4, 'Acc' indicates the obligatory accusative marking (as in (54)), and '(Acc)' indicates that such a marking is optional (as in (52–53)). '[Acc]' indicates that the obligatory marking is theoretically predicted but such an instance is ungrammatical due to the strong animacy constraint that bans inanimate subjects in this dialect.

The Tome dialect of Miyagi Prefecture (Tōhoku) shows a similar DOM but the effect of relative animacy is less conspicuous. According to Takeuchi and Matsumaru (2015a), in Tome the animacy of NPs falls into two categories: High (Human and Animal) and Low (Inanimate). Relative animacy works in such a way that the High-Low combination (i.e. where A is High and P is Low) blocks overt P marking (as in (55)), whereas the other combinations induce the obligatory P marking by *dogo*.

(55) *Sasaki-san jitensha kattat cha.*
bicycle bought SFP
'Mr. Sasaki bought a bicycle.' [High–Low]

(56) *Sasaki-san ano buta dogo oshidashitara adashi no kachi dat cha.*
that pig ACC push.COND I GEN win COP SFP
'If Mr. Sasaki pushes off the pig (in a game where the one who pushes off the other is supposed to win), then (it indicates) I will win.' [High–High]

(57) *Ano buta Sasaki-san dogo oshidashitara adashi no kachi dat cha.*
that pig ACC push.COND I GEN win COP SFP
'If that pig pushes off Mr. Sasaki, then (it indicates) I will win.'
[High–High]

(58) *Tama bōshi no hisashi dogo tsuranuitara sasugani*
bullet hat GEN brim ACC penetrate.COND certainly

tamagetcha nē.
get.surprised SFP
'If a bullet penetrates the brim of a hat, (I) would certainly get surprised.' [Low–Low]

(59) *Jishin* *demo* *ogide* *hondana* *ano* *ko* *dogo*
earthquake etc. happen.SEQ bookshelf that child ACC
oshitsubushidara *najo* *sun* *no?*
crush.COND how do Q
'If earthquake occurs and the bookshelf crushes that child, what would you do?' [Low–High]

Unlike Shiiba, where (56) would allow the optional P marking (as A is higher than P in animacy), Tome requires it to have the obligatory P marking, as both A and P arguments of this example belong to High.

If we compare the DOM in Shiiba (Table 5.4) and that in Tome (Table 5.5), we immediately find that the latter is more familiar where the overt marking is determined by the animacy of P alone, in such a way that P is overtly marked if it is of the High category. However, this generalization fails to explain why (58) has the overt P marking even when P is of the Low category. It is in this case that relative animacy is a key notion.

The two types of animacy-driven DOM in Japanese dialects (Tome and Shiiba) can be roughly characterized as the local DOM and global DOM. The terms *local* and *global* are from Silverstein (1976b), which distinguished between the local factor of case-marking (the referential status of individual arguments) and the global factor (relative animacy that holds between the two arguments in a transitive clause). The local DOM is common in Japanese dialects, whereas the global DOM is reported in very few dialects such as Shiiba. The Tome DOM is somewhere in between, exhibiting both features.

A number of researchers point out that there is an ongoing diachronic shift from the (local) DOM pattern to a stable accusative marking pattern in Tōhoku dialects, giving birth to the canonical marked accusative alignment. Hidaka (2005: 82–84) demonstrates that both inanimate and animate Ps are marked by the accusative *godo*/*dogo* in northern Tōhoku such as Aomori, Akita, and Yamagata. For example, the Tsuruoka dialect (Yamagata Prefecture) allows P marking on inanimate nouns as shown in the following examples (adopted from Onishi and Matsumori 2012: 318).

Table 5.5 *DOM in Tome*

			Animacy of P		
			High		Low
			Human	animal	inanimate
Animacy of A	High	Human		Acc	*Acc
		Animal			
	Low	Inanimate		Acc	Acc

(Based on Takeuchi and Matsumaru 2015a)

(60) *Kāchan* *dogo* *mida.*
mother ACC saw
'(Someone) saw the mother.'

(61) *Inu* *dogo* *kusari* *sa* *tsunaida.*
dog ACC chain LOC linked.
'(Someone) put the dog to a leash.'

(62) *Ano* *e* *dogo* *mida.*
that house ACC saw
'(Someone) saw the house.'

A similar pattern of spreading the overt marking to inanimate Ps is observed for dialects where the overt P marker is *ba* (e.g. the Tsugaru dialect of Aomori Prefecture), indicating that this language change is not limited to *godo*/*dogo* but should broadly be understood as a change from a restricted accusative marking to a consistent accusative marking.

This way of approaching the DOM systems allows us to capture the possible (unidirectional) path of diachronic development of DOM in Japanese dialects as follows:

(63) Global DOM > Local DOM > Stable accusative marking

The Global DOM is represented by the DOM of Shiiba, and the Local DOM is represented by the DOM of Tōhoku dialects. It is argued that the intermediate stage between the Global to Local shift is represented by the Tome dialect and that the intermediate stage between the Local to the Stable accusative marking shift is represented by a subset of Tōhoku dialects such as Tsuruoka. This suggested process of development is a series of simplifications of the determining factor of DOM. That is, in the process of shifting from Global DOM to Local DOM, the relative animacy that holds between A and P is simplified to the absolute animacy of P (with the Tome DOM in the middle of the two phases), and in the process of shifting from Local DOM to Stable accusative marking, the semantically based animacy feature is lost altogether in favor of the more abstract and syntactic feature of direct object.

6 Summary and Suggestions for Future Research

This chapter has presented typological characteristics of Japanese dialects with a special focus on alignment. The structural and typological diversity is quite evident, and almost all possible alignment patterns recognized in the typological literature are attested, except for the ergative–absolutive pattern. Furthermore, cross-linguistically rare patterns have been noted, such as split intransitive, tripartite, and marked nominative. Based on the attested alignment patterns, this chapter has suggested a hierarchy of alignment for Japanese dialects as in (3):

(3) Nominative–accusative > Split intransitive > Tripartite
Neutral

This hierarchy predicts that if there is a cross-linguistically rare pattern like split intransitive and tripartite, there must be a more basic and cross-linguistically common pattern in the dialect. This implicational hierarchy must be tested against the vast dialectal data in future research.

There are additional topics for future research on the typological study of alignment of Japanese dialects. One is to examine the underpinnings of the marked nominative alignment pattern, which is claimed to be extremely rare cross-linguistically (Section 4.1). It was noted that the rarity of marked nominative is explained in terms of the distinguishing function of case-marking whereby S should be left unmarked. The typology of alignment in the present chapter has revealed that marked nominative constitutes a possible and in fact common pattern within the alignment system in a number of Japanese dialects: Kinki, Chūgoku, Kyūshū, Amami and Yonaguni Ryukyuan, and Okinawan.

Even though marked nominative is unusual in terms of the distinguishing function of case-marking, a close look at the marked nominative of the above-mentioned dialects (except for Chūgoku dialects) reveal that it is the identifying function of case marking (whereby the explicit marking of S (and A) is required) that induces the overt marking of S. In Kinki dialects, the obligatory overt marking of S/A is induced by focus. In Amami Ryukyuan and Kyūshū dialects, the overt S/A marking by *ga* or *no*/*nu* identifies the animacy of the subject NP to which they are attached. In Yonaguni, the obligatory overt marking of S/A by *nga* is induced by animacy (whereby pronouns are obligatorily marked) and focus. In Okinawan, the obligatory overt marking of S/A by *ga* is induced by animacy just like Yonaguni, although it is still unclear whether focus plays a role here. Thus, if a dialect displays the marked nominative pattern, it is usual for the case-marking of S/A to be motivated by the explicit identification of a semantic (animacy) or pragmatic (focus) feature of the NP in question. The only dialects for which this generalization does not seem to hold are Chūgoku dialects, where the factor motivating the obligatory S marking is still unclear. It is therefore necessary to examine the factor of the obligatory S marking in these dialects, or to reexamine whether S (and A) is really obligatorily marked in the first place.

6

Writing and Literacy in Modern Japan

Florian Coulmas

1 Introduction

This chapter describes and explains the relationship between spoken and written Japanese at present with recourse to recent history where necessary. It begins with a summary account of the systematic differences between alphabetic writing systems and writing systems centered on or derived from Chinese characters. A discussion of the attitudes, (mis)conceptions, and ideologies associated with both kinds of writing systems follows.

Against this background, this chapter will then provide an account of the Movement to Unify Spoken and Written Language (*genbun itchi undō*) which played a significant role in Japan's modernization efforts during the eventful Meiji period (1868–1912). The idea that the written language should closely correspond to speech was imported from Europe, as was the notion of a "national language" (*kokugo*) that would unite ruler and ruled. In the agrarian society of feudal Japan, there was not much need for the power elite to communicate with the rest of the population. Accordingly, most written documents of any consequence were redacted in a language far removed from common people's speech. Regional varieties of Japanese were very diverse and *kanbun* (= Chinese *hánwén*), the Japanese variety of Classical Chinese, served an important function for exercising government control throughout the Tokugawa state (Edo period, 1603–1868) of premodern Japan. A sense of unity of language, nation, and state was brought about only through general education institutionalized in the early Meiji period.

Yet, the question of what the national language taught at school should look like was not yet settled. Extensive discussions about both the writing system and the written language continued until the mid-twentieth century, the question of what role Chinese characters should play for writing Japanese being at the center of the debate. The effects on the use of Chinese characters of computer-mediated communication will be dealt with in the final section of the chapter.

2 Units of Language and Units of Writing

Writing systems can be characterized by the units of which they consist. These units do not determine all systematic properties of writing systems, but they allow for a rough and ready categorization. For instance, Chinese characters and Sumerian cuneiform signs are interpreted[1] as words or morphemes, *kana*, the units of the Japanese syllabaries *katakana* and *hiragana*, are interpreted as syllables (technically speaking as short syllables or mora), and Greek letters are interpreted as speech sounds. Words, syllables, sounds – these units are easy to distinguish and form important linguistic building blocks for the construction of writing systems, but they do not completely control their makeup. There are no pure writing systems of one type or another (Coulmas 2003). Rather, fully developed writing systems tend to be mixed systems that integrate features of different structural levels. This is true of alphabetic writing systems, many of which contain logographic elements and deviate from the supposedly ideal one-to-one correspondence of graphemes (letters) and phonemes (sounds). It is also true of the seemingly uniform Chinese script which contains many elements that violate the simple one-character-one-syllable-one-morpheme principle.[2] *Kana* is a strong candidate for a purely syllabic system, mapping, as it does, neatly onto the syllable structure of (standard) Japanese; however, a caveat has to be added immediately, for individual *kana* are not interpreted as syllables, but as moras, the rhythmic units of speech which coincide with short syllables (cf. Chapter 7, this volume). This implies that two-syllable words, if they contain geminate consonants or long vowels, are written with three or four *kana* (e.g. はっぱ *ha.p.pa* 'leaf,' とうきょう *to.u.kyo.u* 'Tokyo'). What is more, while it is possible to write Japanese in *kana* only, in practice this is not done except in special cases, such as children's books.

Another important feature that distinguishes writing systems from each other is the numerical strength of their sign inventories. In all languages, words are more numerous than morphemes, morphemes more numerous than syllables (or moras), and syllables are more

[1] I use the term "interpret" rather than "represent" for genealogical reasons. No writing system was designed to represent words, syllables, or individual speech sounds, but graphical signs came to be associated with, hence interpreted as, words, syllables, or speech sounds. For a detailed discussion of this distinction cf. Coulmas (2003: 10–17).

[2] For example, 蛛 *zhū* 'spider,' a bound morpheme which does not occur outside the compound 蜘蛛 *zhīzhū* 'spider.' Pirani (2008) provides many examples of bound morphemes in Chinese – e.g. 电子 *diàn zǐ* 'electron,' 脑力 *nǎo lì* 'intelligence,' which she compares with neo-classical compounds in European languages, such as *semi-* as in *semi-autonomous* and *neuro-* as in *neurology*, which cannot be used independently.

numerous than phonemes. Assuming that there is a relatively systematic mapping relationship between the units of writing and the units of language, the size of the set of signs allows us to make an educated guess as to the nature of the writing system. Yet, again a caveat must be added because the simple inventory of elementary signs may be deceptive. The set of twenty-six letters is in no way indicative of the complexity of the English writing system which is more meaningfully described by hundreds of phoneme-grapheme correspondences including digraphs (<th> as in *think* [θɪŋk]) and trigraphs (<igh> as in *high* [haj]), as a proficient reader of English knows (Venetzky 1995). Similarly, the Devanagari script, as used for Hindi among other languages, has forty-seven primary characters, a number that puts it into the category of phonemic (actually, alphasyllabic) writing systems. In contradistinction to alphabetic systems, an alphasyllabary is a segmental writing system that uses consonant vowel sequences as units. The basic set of primary CV units makes Devanagari for Hindi look simple. However, over time hundreds of ligatures have been formed adding graphic complexity to the script and undermining the simplicity of its basic structure.

The analysis of any writing system has to consider the nature of the basic graphic signs, their number, and the rules for relating them to units of language in two directions (for writing and reading).

3 Writing System and Literacy

The number of basic signs is the most conspicuous characteristic of any writing system and, therefore, not surprisingly features prominently in popular discourse about writing, often as the sole basis of comparison. Chinese characters are many and hence difficult to write/read; the letters of the ABC are few and hence easy. Putting it this way is exaggerating only slightly. In arguments for the reform of the Japanese written language, to which we will return below, this kind of reasoning plays a central role. The reason for this is the implicit but hard to substantiate assumption that there is a causal relationship between the nature of writing systems and literacy rates. It stands to reason that high literacy rates are more easily accomplished with a writing system consisting of a small set of basic signs and simple rules than with a highly involved writing system made up of thousands of characters. But what is the evidence? In the present context it must suffice to note that this line of reasoning, above all else, betrays ignorance not just of the Chinese writing system but also of the potential and factual complexities of alphabetic writing and the general phonocentrism characteristic of European thinkers from Hegel to Saussure (Harris 2000: 142).

Current scholarship pays more attention to the linguistic fit of different writing systems, conceding that isolating languages (e.g. Chinese), agglutinating languages (e.g. Japanese), and inflecting languages (e.g. Greek) favor the development of different types of writing systems (Fayol and Jaffré 2014: 12; Rogers 2005: 13; Coulmas 2003: 18). Also, writing systems are seen as major cultural achievements serving a variety of functions in addition to the communication of information by visual means. Rather than assume that the Latin alphabet is per se superior and will and should eventually drive out all other writing systems of lesser utility, it is now widely accepted that a meaningful comparison of different writing systems cannot be limited to purely structural analyses, but must include historical linguistic features as well as social, cultural, and symbolic functions.

Yet, when it comes to literacy, it is not uncommon that the discourse is reduced to structural features of the writing system and the unquestioned assumption that the nature of the writing system has an influence on the spread of literacy. The argument, put forth by Protestant missionary J. C. Gibson, that in China the "ideographic script had limited literacy to an upper-class minority" (Goody 1968: 23), has been repeated in various guises many times. It is based on an "autonomous view of literacy" that ignores its social embeddedness (Street 1995). On one hand, we know that "despite the relative simplicity of the Greek alphabet, literacy never became the norm in ancient Greece" (Gnanadesikan 2009: 217); and on the other, literacy rates in the sinographic world differ widely. In nineteenth-century Japan, Chinese characters were used in ways more complex than Chinese writing proper (see below). Yet, Japan had literacy rates that were commensurate with Western European countries, and much higher than China. It may also be noted that prior to the People's Republic of China's literacy campaign as of the 1950s, Taiwan was far ahead of China in the spread of literacy (UNESCO 1957). These observations cast serious doubts on the supposed causal relationship between technical (structural) properties of writing systems and literacy rates. Other factors, such as urbanization, the school system, literary traditions, and a culture of letters seem to be far more consequential.

4 Writing in Japan

Japanese makes use of a highly involved mixed writing system that integrates logograms (i.e. Chinese characters), phonograms (i.e. two sets of *kana*), and, nowadays, roman letters. Writing in Japan has a long history, expertly documented by, among others, Seeley (1991) and Lurie (2011), which explains the complexity of the system. Having learnt the art of linguistic inscription from the Chinese, the Japanese had from the start to grapple with the difficulties of adapting a system that evolved for an isolating language to writing an agglutinating one. This typological difference between Chinese and Japanese has many implications for

1、孔子聖人

2、孔子ハ聖人ナリ

3、孔子は聖人なり

Figure 6.1 Kanbun example sentence, "Confucius is a sage." 1. Chinese characters only; 2. Japanese grammar annotated in katakana, ハ *ha* 'topic marker,' ナリ *nari* 'copula, is'; 3. corresponding hiragana は *ha* and なり *nari* integrated into the sentence.

writing the Japanese language with Chinese characters, the most consequential and general one being that in isolating languages words do not change their form, whereas in agglutinating languages they are modified by formative elements indicating grammatical relationships between them as well as semantic information, such as tense and aspect. Accordingly, Japanese has a rich morphology consisting of grammatical morphemes which are hard to express by means of Chinese characters. The ensuing peculiarities still characterize the Japanese writing system today.

The written language, too, bears witness to the Chinese origin of Japanese writing. Ever since writing became a fixed part of Japan's culture, new varieties and styles came into existence that were characterized by function-specific text types, lexical registers, and syntactic patterns. They did not necessarily supersede each other, but following genre differentiations were practiced next to each other. They ranged between purely logographic styles consisting of Chinese characters exclusively, *kanbun* (Figure 6.1), on the one hand, and phonographic styles close to vernacular speech written with *kana* (*wabun*, Figure 6.2), on the other.

In between there is an epistolary style known as *sōrōbun*, so called for the frequently used verb 候 *sōrō/soro* 'to serve,' which consist of a mixture of Classical Japanese and a heavily sinicized vocabulary as well as Chinese word order. The example in (1) is derived from *Wagahai wa neko de aru* ('I'm a Cat') by NATSUME Sōseki (1867–1916):

(1) *Sōrōbun* (候文)
今度御光来の節は久し振りにて晩餐でも供し度心得に御座[候]。寒厨何の珍味も無
之[候]えども、せめてはトチメンボーでもと只今より心掛居[候]。

Kondo	*gokōrai*	*no*	*setsu*	*wa*	*hisashiburi*	*nite*
next.time	visit	GEN	occasion	TOP	after.a.long.time	because

bansan	*demo*	*kyōshi-taki*	*kokoroe ni*	***gozasoro.***	*Kanchū*
dinner	EXM	offer-DES	in.the.feeling	COP	winter.larder

nan no	*chinmi*	*mo*	*kore*	*naku*	***sōrae***	*do mo,*	*semete*
no	delicacy	even	this	exist.NEG	COP	although	at.least

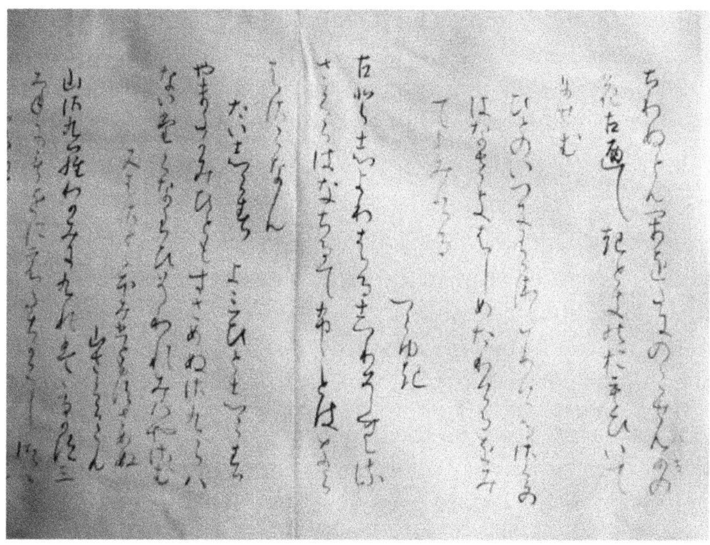

Figure 6.2 Wabun. Literary text written in hiragana, *Sekidobon, Kokinshū* (*Collection of Japanese Poems of Ancient and Modern Times*, Sekido edition), 905 CE.

wa	*Tochimenbō*	*demo*	*to*	*tadaima*	*yori*	*kokorogake ori*	***soro*.**
TOP		EXM	QUOT	now	from	bear.in.mind	COP

'Next time when I'm honored to receive your visit after a long absence, I'd like to serve a dinner. Although there is no special delicacy in my winter larder, I hope at least to be able to offer Tachimenbo [a fictitious dish], and I've already have started preparation for it.'

Because few people in Japan were conversant in Chinese, a peculiar literary practice, called *hentai kanbun* 'variant Chinese' or *kundoku* 'explanation reading' evolved whereby the characters in a text were rearranged and read in the order required by Japanese syntax, as exemplified in (2):

(2) Hentai Kanbun (variant Chinese). A phrase from *Kojiki*, eighth century CE. (Aldridge 2011)

Chinese characters	名	賜	曙立	王	
Meaning of characters	name	give	Aketatsu	prince	
Japanese reading	*na-wo*		*Aketatsu-no*	*Opokimi-ni*	*tamapi-te*
	name-ACC		Aketatsu-GEN	prince-DAT	give-CONJ

'(He) gave a name to Prince Aketatsu, and...'

The pronunciation was in Japanese. Several styles with and without auxiliary diacritics attached to the Chinese characters indicating the necessary transformations evolved. Common to all is the basic principle of producing from a Chinese input a Japanese output. Thus, what *kundoku* amounts to is reading as translation.

Since in the course of time, both the Chinese and Japanese languages continued to change, the intricacies of Japanese letters increased rather than diminished. The interaction of a variety of factors was responsible for this, among them:

(3) a. language change and linguistic incongruities,
b. the prestige of participating in the high culture of Chinese learning, Buddhism, and Confucianism,
c. a ceaseless influx of Chinese loanwords into Japanese,
d. and the guiding power of the path once chosen.

It is remarkable that in spite of these complexities, near the end of the Tokugawa period, in the early nineteenth century, Japan had literacy rates commensurate with Western European countries. In some 11,000 so-called temple schools (*terakoya*) about 750,000 students were taught the basics of literacy and numeracy (Dore 1965). Through the Dutch trading post in Nagasaki in western Kyūshū, the Japanese elite had known the Latin alphabet for two hundred years and some specialists had learnt to use it for the Dutch language. Education was important in Tokugawa Japan, and an urban elite cultivated a vivid and multifarious literary life, but even though many different writing styles were developed, the idea of abandoning Chinese characters only entered the intellectual debate in the nineteenth century. Rationalizing the writing system and established writing practices was not part of the Tokugawa agenda to promote education, which was largely successful nevertheless.

Although these are well-known facts, the idea that a structurally simple writing system promotes the spread of literacy and that, therefore, every language community would naturally prefer a simple system and be in favor of simplifying reforms seems hard to abandon. For example, discussing modern Japanese, Brown (1985: 533) expresses his astonishment that "this outrageously otiose and cumbersome writing system persists into the present" – just as if efficiency maximization, in a very narrow sense, were the sole force at work in the history of writing. Both the Japanese writing system and literacy in Japan are vivid testimony that this is not the case. Japan has shared the literary and calligraphic traditions of China for some sixteen centuries, a heritage that involves more than communicating a message in writing as cost-effectively as possible. In modern history, Japan stood twice at the crossroads of parting from this tradition, but after much deliberation did not, limiting changes to adjustments of the extant system. We now turn to attempts at changing the traditional ways of writing.

5 Correspondence of Speech and Writing: The *Genbun Itchi* Movement

In the momentous years of the Meiji Restoration (restored imperial rule to Japan), Japan embarked on a series of reforms touching on multiple aspects of social life and state responsibilities, including education and language. They were all intended to serve the overarching purpose of turning feudal Japan into a modern nation state to follow the Western model. Writing and language were a major concern. NISHI Amane (1829–1897), who studied philosophy in Leiden, Netherlands and upon his return to Japan became one of the intellectual champions of modernization, introduced in 1874 the inaugural issue of the enlightenment journal *Meiroku zasshi* 'the magazine of the sixth year of Meiji' with a lengthy article about "Writing Japanese with the Western alphabet." In it he expounded the idea that there should be a close match between speech and writing, as he had got to know it in Europe. He left no doubt about his reasons for advocating such a measure. "The Europeans," he wrote, "now lead the world ... nothing has contributed more to their world pre-eminence in science, the arts, and letters than the twenty-six letters of the 'ABCs'" (Nishi n.d.: 15).

Nishi's high regard for the Latin alphabet echoes views prevalent in Europe at the time.[3] The underlying general assumption of a causal link between type of writing system and level of civilization/social progress does not bear scrutiny, but his blunt thesis is indicative of the intellectual atmosphere of early Meiji as well as of the great importance attached to letters in Japanese culture. His strong belief in the formative power of the writing system prompted him to advocate the adoption of the Latin alphabet for writing Japanese. "Since the trend to import from the West is already so strong that we cannot leave three after taking seven out of ten, I think it best to adopt their entire alphabet" (p. 6). His expectations of such a step were high: "If we adopt their system, all things of Europe will be entirely ours" (p. 9). Other advantages he foresaw included "the convenience of writing sideways" and that "technical words in translations can be employed directly without translation" (pp. 8–9).

Nishi himself called his proposal "a strange plan" (p. 5), and strange it must have appeared to his readers, but then the early Meiji years were a time of strange plans. A couple of years earlier, leading intellectual MORI Arinori (1849–1889), another who would be Japan's Minister of Education, ventilated the idea of changing not just the writing system but the language, replacing Japanese by English (Saito 1977: 15). This Nishi would not espouse because, in his view, "the language of a nation is innate" (Nishi n.d.: 7) and, therefore, must not be abandoned.

[3] For instance, in his "Philosophy of spirit" (the work quoted here is organized in numbered articles. The reference is to article number 459), philosopher G. W. F. Hegel called alphabetic writing "on all accounts the more intelligent."

Verbalizing another sentiment that was common in his day, Nishi considered the integration of Chinese vocabulary into Japanese exemplified in particular by *sōrōbun* as destroying "our innate tongue" (p. 7). The obvious argument against adopting the Western alphabet for similar reasons of posing the danger of contamination he pre-empted as follows:

> My response is that I would only write Japanese with the Western alphabet and then read it in accordance with established rules of pronunciation. This is not something, however, that can be taught under compulsion or achieved by strict command. The reform will be accomplished through months and years of gradual learning. (p. 7)

With his article of 1874, Nishi anticipated the debate about vernacularization that climaxed in the 1880s. He gave expression to the widely held view that Japanese letters were in need of reform, and he understood that more was involved than the writing system. The great variety of more or less sinicized styles of writing should be replaced with a new style bringing spoken and written Japanese closer together.

In 1885, Kanda Takahira (1830–1898), a scholar of Western learning, coined the term *genbun itchi* 'unified spoken and written language,' which became the name of the language reform movement that lasted until the turn of the nineteenth century (Heinrich 2012: 44–48). Reform proposals concentrating on writing system and spelling were advanced by individual scholars and associations. The Kana Club (*Kana no kai*), picking up the thread of the *kokugaku* 'national study' movement which was committed to the study of the native literature and culture as distinct from the Chinese heritage, was founded in 1883, and the Western-oriented romanization Club (*Rōmaji kai*) followed two years later. Advocating the abolition of Chinese characters and a written language that made use of *kana* and the Latin alphabet, respectively, these societies published bulletins and leaflets, such as the *Mainichi hiragana shinbun* and *Rōmaji zasshi*, that put their schemes into practice and discussed various issues of orthography. An important question for the Kana Club was whether *kana* usage should be historical or based on current pronunciation, and if the latter, which pronunciation. Similarly, the Romanization Club discussed the specifics of romanization.

In the end, both projects came to naught, as Japanese continued to be written with Chinese characters and *kana*. This is, however, not to say that these discussion circles had no effect. They helped to bring the importance of language and script reform to public attention. The Romanization Club settled on a romanization scheme leaning on common sound-letter correspondences of English which gained prominence in James Curtis Hepburn's Japanese–English dictionary *Wa-ei gorin shūsei* of 1886 and thus came to be known as the Hepburn system.

The deliberations of the Kana Club paved the way for the standardization of *kana*. Until the end of the Edo (Tokugawa) period, there was no one-to-one graph per mora correspondence for *kana*. Although the *gojūonjun* 'fifty sounds order' modeled on Sanskrit phonology goes back to the fifteenth century, and although many primers and textbooks for the teaching of reading and writing appeared throughout the Edo period, a normative regulation of *kana* usage had not taken hold. Two different historical *kana* spellings were in use (Seeley 1991: ch. 6).

The writing system was just one of the objectives of the reform; the other no less important one was the written language. The leading intellectual and founder of Keiō Gijuku University, FUKUZAWA Yukichi (1835–1901), realized its importance early on and published a three-volume reader for children that made do with less than one thousand different Chinese characters (Fukuzawa 1873). Though addressed to children, this work helped to popularize the concept of limiting the number of Chinese characters in use. In the twentieth century, this became the major theme of script reform, but initially opposition against it was strong. Elegant writing in the minds of most who considered themselves elegant writers meant having command of a huge set of Chinese characters and writing long sentences without punctuation marks. A rich vocabulary of Chinese characters was proof of erudition and indispensable for sophisticated writing. As NISHI Amane had predicted in the article quoted above, developing a vernacular style and building support for it was a long-term project that could not be implemented overnight. Conservative opponents of reform had to be appeased and the government had to be persuaded that the simplification of the written language was in the best interest of Japan.

Exactly what the language reform should accomplish was a matter of fierce debates among intellectuals, many of whom practiced in their own writing what they preached. Heinrich (2012) noticed some conspicuous stylistic differences in the writings of proponents and opponents of *genbun itchi*. Advocates used the copulas *desu* and *da*, whereas their adversaries used no copulas, formulating sentences without punctuation marks that were much longer than those of the modernizers. In the most famous *genbun itchi* debate, the texts contributed by the principal *genbun itchi* advocate, YAMADA Bimyō (1868–1910), averaged thirty-one characters per sentence, while his main opponent KOJIMA Kenkichirō (1866–1931) had 407 characters per sentence (Heinrich 2012: 50). This stunning contrast is indicative of very disparate ideals of the written language entertained by traditionalists and reformers.

Opponents of *genbun itchi* considered a written language modeled on vernacular speech as ugly and unrefined and, consciously or not, a threat to their status as literati that was based on years of strenuous study necessary to master the bookish styles of *kanbun*, *wabun*, and *sōrōbun* with all their sub-varieties. They favored a modified but still heavily sinicized style called *futsūbun* 'regular writing,' which persisted for some time and was even used for official and semi-official functions in the early decades of the twentieth century. Yet, by the turn of the century, the debate about *genbun itchi* had died down because the vernacular style, *zokubun*, had largely carried the day. Various measures had brought the written language much closer to contemporary colloquial speech. *Kanbun* no longer commanded the authority it once had, and the notion that a Classical Chinese education was a precondition for aspiring to be a writer had lost credibility. *Genbun itchi* had become the preferred style taught at school, that is, the language taught to the nation.

Crucially important for the success of *genbun itchi* was the notion of "national language," *kokugo*, imported from Europe. It was UEDA Kazutoshi (1867–1937) who brought the notion to Japan and founded a scientific discipline for its study. He had studied from 1888 to 1892, mainly in Germany with a stint in France, and upon his return became the first professor of linguistics at the Imperial University in Tokyo. Impressed by European linguistic nationalism, he was convinced that a proper country needed a national language and spent the rest of his life in various functions and offices to make this idea a reality (Tanaka 1978; Lee 1996; Heinrich 2012). As Tanaka (1978: 246) put it, a national language

> requires the recognition of its standards by all people. That is to say, such recognition has to pay tribute to the nation-state with regard to obedience, respect and loyalty toward the ideological structure of the nation state.
>
> (Quoted from Heinrich 2012: 68)

The diversity of written styles and their distance from vernacular speech in premodern Japan marked distinctions, that is, distinctions of social class, of region, and of genre. These distinctions were very pronounced. The national language, by contrast, was supposed to create a unified bond across all distinctions. The general dynamics of deliberate language change epitomized by *genbun itchi* can thus be described as a movement from distinction to convergence and from separation to standardization. Compulsory education institutionalized in the early Meiji years was the agent to bring this about.

Many writers, novelists, poets, as well as non-fiction writers, journalists, and publishers contributed to the formation of the national language. Among academics who guided its development, UEDA Kazutoshi occupied a special position (Coulmas 2016: 169–182). As a university professor, he taught several generations of disciples; he published many books and scholarly articles. In 1898, he established the Society for the Improvement of the National Language (*Kokugo kairyō kai*), and he advised the government as a member of several committees and agencies. At the pinnacle of his career, he served as head of the Temporal National

Language Investigation Committee (*Rinji kokugo chōsa kai*), which, in 1922, compiled a list of 1,962 Chinese characters for daily use, which became an important reference point for further reforms of Japanese writing and literacy education.

Another matter of concern was *kana* usage. Both *hiragana* and *katakana* originate from *man'yōgana*, a set of Chinese characters used in early Japanese literature for their sound values rather than their meaning. Attempts at regulating *kana* usage go back to the twelfth century. The best-known proposals are *Teika kanazukai*, so named after Fujiwara no Teika (1162–1241), the seventeenth-century *rekishiteki kanazukai* (historical usage), and the *Jion kanazukai* (pronunciation of characters) put forth by the *Kokugaku* school of "national learning," which in the later Edo period dedicated itself to recapturing the "authentic" Japanese heritage. Thus, Motoori Norinaga (1730–1801) studied the *Kojiki* in an attempt to reconstruct the sound system of medieval Japanese. Reforms of *kana* spelling were necessitated by perpetual sound change, as they would be in any writing system that aims at a simple correspondence between graphic and phonetic units. However, in spite of the high level of insight into the nature of the kana system on the part of scholars, no effective unification of *kana* usage was accomplished in premodern times.

The "current orthography" (*gendai kanazukai*) is based on a government regulation of 1946 (Cabinet Announcement), which was designed to adjust *kana* usage to contemporary Japanese phonology. Thus, hiragana ゐ /wi/ and katakana ヰ /wi/ fell out of use because the syllable /wi/ had become indistinguishable from /i/, and both were henceforth to be written い andイ, respectively. By the same logic, hiragana へ and katakana ヘ would have been eliminated because the syllable /he/ had in some contexts been reduced to /e/, but grammatical particles for topic は/ハ /ha/, direct object を/ヲ /o/ and direction へ/ヘ /e/ were retained, notwithstanding the phonological changes that had turned /ha/ into /wa/, /wo/ into /o/, and /he/ into /e/. Some other irregularities and uncertainties persist, such as the writing of long vowels – for example, おうand おお for /ō/ – but on the whole *gendai kanazukai* is a systematic orthography that is easy to learn and functions as a relief for those with limited literacy in Chinese characters.

6 Literacy

After Japan's defeat in the Pacific War, literacy became an issue of education reform. For obvious reasons, traditional ways were called into question, much like during the early Meiji years, or were outlawed by the occupation forces. Romanization and character limitations were back on the agenda, for some intellectuals saw a link between the complex writing system and uncritical obedience and, therefore, called for the abolition of Chinese characters as a measure to boost literacy rates which would be conducive to democratization (Gottlieb 1995: 123). The democracy argument also reverberated in occupation circles after the 1946 United States Education Mission to Japan had submitted its report, which states among other things that

> [t]he problem of the written language is fundamental to all modifications in educational practice . . . It is recommended that some form of Romaji be brought into common use.
>
> (United States Education Mission to Japan 1946: 22)

As a result of these recommendations and the ongoing discussions about romanization, the Japanese Ministry of Education even sponsored an experimental program of *rōmaji* education over three years from 1948 to 1950. Unger (1996) offers a thorough account of the background and the specifics of this program, which, however, like earlier proposals came to nothing. Discussions about the suitability of three rival romanization systems – Hepburn, *Kunreishiki*, and *Nipponshiki* – continued, but using any of them for replacing the mixed Chinese character cum *kana* writing system was never seriously considered by political decision-makers. However, two other measures came to pass, an official limitation of characters and a literacy assessment survey.

Based on earlier proposals, the *Tōyō kanjihyō* 'list of Chinese characters for current use' was officially promulgated together with the new standard of *Modern kana usage* in November 1946. A significant simplification of writing as compared to what was common practice until 1945 was thus accomplished. Further modifications of the character list continued, concerning additional characters, Sino-Japanese (*on*) and Japanese (*kun*) readings, special characters for given names, characters with irregular readings (*ateji*) for loanwords, and characters used in graphically different forms. In 1981, the *Tōyō kanji* were replaced by the *Jōyō kanji* list of 1,945 characters, which was last revised in 2010 and now comprises a total of 2,136 characters. The general principle of restricting the number of characters for common use is universally accepted, although writers of belletrist literature are free to use characters not in the list.

The *Jōyō kanji* list also defines educational objectives: Senior high school graduates should be able to read and write the characters, and junior high school graduates (compulsory education) should be able to read them. Hence it also defines a standard of Japanese literacy. Discussions about script reform and education following the defeat in World War II motivated heightened attention to literacy. According to educationalists and government officials, illiteracy was not a problem, but data confirming this widely held belief were lacking. It was thus decided to conduct a nation-wide literacy survey. After careful preparation by members of the National Institute of Education, the National Institute of Japanese Language, and the Institute of Statistical Mathematics, who cooperated with the Civil Information and Education Section of the US occupation, it was carried out in August 1948. A questionnaire of ninety questions was administered to 16,814 subjects between 15 and 64 years of age. When the results were published three years later, they were accompanied by a salutary message from John Campbell Pelzel, an American cultural anthropologist who participated in the project as liaison officer from the occupation's Civil Information and Education Section (Yomikaki Nōryoku Chōsa Iinkai, 1951: 3–4). It was entirely in romanized Japanese, which could be understood as an expression of the author's hope that one day Japanese would be written with the Latin alphabet.

This day never came because the results of the survey reassured the defenders of the time-honored writing system, or more accurately, were presented in such a way as to allow them to feel reassured, that there was no reason to depart from the trodden path. To their great satisfaction, just 1.7% of the sample turned out to be illiterate, and 2.1% partially illiterate. Accordingly, the survey committee concluded that "what UNESCO calls 'fundamental education' is not a problem in Japan" (p. 336).

The sample of 16,814 randomly selected respondents was large, and the statistical methods applied to its analysis were highly sophisticated. From the 900-odd page report, it is possible to derive a differentiated picture of literacy in Japan. (The table of contents alone covers fourteen pages.) The questionnaire items were arranged in seven groups as follows: (1) writing *kana*, (2) writing numerals, (3) reading *kana* and numerals, (4) reading Chinese characters, (5) writing Chinese characters, (6) word comprehension, and (7) sentence and paragraph comprehension (p. 339). The 1.7% illiterates in the sense of the survey were those who were unable to answer a single question and thus scored 0 points. At the opposite end of the scale, just 4.4% achieved perfect scores of ninety points and only 49.1% scored eighty points. The data show a marked gap between reading and writing proficiency as well as significant regional differences, the Tōhoku (north-east) region lagging behind the rest (p. 342).

A wealth of many other facts can be gathered from the report, but the one figure that caught media attention and was subsequently quoted so frequently that Yamashita (2011: 98) called it "the very basis of the Japanese myth of literacy" was "1.7 percent illiterates" – fewer than in most countries for which literacy rates were available at the time. It was what traditionalists were hoping to find, something to be proud of, and a pretext for closing their eyes to less agreeable findings. Illiteracy, that was the upshot, was not a problem in Japan. This idea took hold and is largely responsible for the fact that to date no other nation-wide literacy proficiency assessment has been carried through.

Yamashita (2011) offers a critical appraisal of the 1948 survey, discussing its methodological weaknesses as well as the social functions of the optimistic presentation of its results by the media and the consequences for literacy education and writing reform. It certainly helped to push whatever literacy problems there were, for example by marginalized groups, into the background of educational policy making. Japan's persistent high rankings in the OECD Programme for International Student Assessment (PISA) as of the 1990s only reinforced this attitude. Japan has a very effective school system which, however, does not mean that no one falls through the cracks. Enrolment and graduation figures cannot be equated with literacy rates, but for lack of other evidence often have been.

To conclude this section, the winds of renewal that blew through Japan in the post-war years also rekindled discussions about script and language reform. Official approval of limiting the number of Chinese characters and further standardization of *kana* usage continued the simplifying tendencies initiated in the Meiji period while avoiding a radical beak with the past. The principal dynamics of language development from the decades of reconstruction until the Internet revolution were marked by further standardization and narrowing the gap between speech and writing, as the influence of the (written) national language on the spoken language grew stronger.

7 The Impact of Computer Mediated Communication (CMC)

The Unicode Standard[4] comprises 80,388 CJK unified characters used in China, Japan, and Korea. This is just slightly less than the number of characters in the largest printed Chinese character dictionary, the 1994 *Zhōnghuá Zìhǎi* (中華字海) consisting of 85,568 different characters. The Japanese software *Konjaku mojikyō* (今昔文字鏡) lists even twice as many characters, that is, eighty times the number of *Jōyō kanji*. How many Chinese characters were ever produced and used nobody knows (Kokoma 2014: 45). Whatever the number may be, the characters coded by Unicode, synchronized with International Standard Organisation ISO/IEC 10646, are made available to Internet platforms and computer applications, taking different national typographic traditions into account. Obviously, no one ever uses that many characters, yet, the question is whether the effortless accessibility of many thousands of characters has any noticeable effect on how Japanese is written today.

Word-processing technology meant a shift from writing to recognizing and selecting characters correctly. Employing obscure, historical, and otherwise unconventional characters has become much easier, but has

[4] www.unicode.org/cldr/charts/27/collation/ja.html

this worked as an incentive to deviate from the conventions laid down in official policies and taught at school since the adoption of *Tōyō kanjihyō*? New writing technologies can be expected to alter the appearance and perhaps contents of the written language, in Japan as elsewhere. Given that Internet penetration in Japan is almost total[5] and that, in a space where standards seem partially or wholly suspended, virtually everyone receives and sends dozens if not hundreds of emails, text messages, and social media posts every day, it would hardly be surprising if the written language itself would be affected. However, it is not easy to substantiate this assumption.

Gottlieb (2011) has convincingly argued that wordplay, script play, unconventional language use, and bending and breaking the rules of the written language deliberately using mistaken (e.g. homophonous characters, modifying the appearance of characters[6]) have been part of normal written discourse for a long time and should not be seen as a side-effect of computer-mediated communication. Many spellings not officially recognized and not listed in dictionaries are in current use. For example, transferring the reading of synonyms is a common practice. To illustrate, 幸福 *kōfuku* 'happiness' read as *shiawase*, 運命 *unmei* 'fate' read as *sadame*, and 本気 *honki* 'earnest' read as *maji* are widely known but ignored in dictionaries. It has always been possible to assign idiosyncratic readings to characters by annotating them with reading aids (*furigana*). These and many other peculiarities are enabled by the nature of the Japanese writing system, which is complex but also fascinating and therefore a cultural icon of central importance. Chinese characters have always been and still are an indispensable element of it. Their abolition today seems more remote than ever, and computer-mediated communication (CMC) has done nothing to make it more likely. Quite the contrary, for CMC has made it easier to use uncommon characters in unconventional ways.

Gottlieb's reasoning about the long-standing tradition of inventive character usage notwithstanding, CMC has brought with it new ways of writing and engendered new types of text and written varieties. Miyake (2014: 194) therefore speaks of a "style beyond the unification of spoken and written language" (*chō-genbun itchi tai*), directly alluding to the *genbun itchi* notion of the Meiji era. This style is "not just 'exactly like speech,' but is a written language formed by including elements that cannot be expressed in speech," that is, it transcends the quasi-orality of vernacular speech typical of CMC in social media by adding components that do not and cannot exist in the spoken language.

5 For some recent statistics of Internet use in Japan, cf. the website of the Ministry of Internal Affairs and Communications at www.soumu.go.jp/johotsusintokei/whitepaper/ja/h26/html/nc253120.html.

6 For example, タヒる for 死ぬ.

This new style, which originates with the digital-happy young generation, is characterized by two distinctive features: its visual quality and its norm deviance. The term "quasi-orality" was introduced (Coulmas 2013: 146) to describe a style that combines the visual mode that is characteristic of writing and hence a spatial and temporal distance between sender and recipient and real-time communication. It thus includes elements that supposedly compensate for eye contact, facial expressions, gestures, volume and tone of voice, such as spelt out back channel signals (ねえええ, *n.e.e.e*), emphasis (はあああい, *ha.a.a.a.i*), *kao-moji* 'face character' (≧∇≦)b 'OK,' d(⌒o⌒)b 'happy,' that are not used in traditional writing. In that quasi-orality suggests a co-presence in spite of the physical separateness of conversation participants, it differs from other forms of written word play that are not predicated on real-time feedback and the possibility of asking for immediate clarification.

Two other examples of new, CMC induced varieties discussed by Miyake (2014) are *gyaru-moji* 'gal character,' a playful register popular with high school girls during 2001 to 2005, and the special vocabulary of 2 Channel (*ni channeru*), an online discussion site where users can post messages anonymously.[7] Both varieties display typical features of in-group slang whose users express solidarity and claim to membership by means of a lexicon of abbreviations, acronyms, and metaphors not readily understood by outsiders.

Some of these features depend on the visual medium, such as special fonts, unconventional use of Chinese characters, *kana*, roman letters, and numerals, the integration of special characters such as *e-moji* 'picture character,' *kao-moji* 'face character,' mathematical and logical symbols, as well as the occasional letter of different alphabets, Cyrillic, for example. While mannerisms of this sort would be possible, in principle, by putting pen to paper, many are unlikely to occur in other than computer-mediated communication. For instance, without access to Unicode (hex), the typical Japanese high school student can hardly be expected to use the lower case Greek letter *tau* (τ) for its graphic similarity to hiragana *te* (て) in combination with quotation marks (") to write *desu*, as in好τ"す *suki desu* 'I like you,' in *gyaru-moji*. The decomposition of characters we see here which is also done with Chinese characters (日+寺=時, that is, *toki* 'time' decomposed into the two constituent parts which happen to be characters in their own right) and is a hallmark of *gyaru-moji*, has no real equivalent in speech (although one might think of pig Latin and similar language games). This mannerism is of particular interest because in it reverberates, consciously or not, the history both of Japanese writing and

[7] Illustrations can be found by searching the two names, ギャル文字 and 2ちゃん (or 2chan). http://mizz.lolipop.jp/galmoji/v2.cgi is a website that offers conversion of regular script into *gyaru-moji*, and http://pmakino.jp/channel5/misc/2chbible.html is a glossary of terms commonly used on 2 Channel.

playing with it, going back more than one thousand years when Chinese characters were first disjointed and used for their phonetic values. The revitalization of this playful practice can be called, as Gottlieb (2011) would have it, "old wine in new bottles," except that it occurs a century and a half after *genbun itchi*.

As explained above, *genbun itchi* was intended to narrow the gap between spoken and written language and was largely successful, primarily through the vernacularization of writing. However, the standardization of speech throughout the country as an effect of national language education was part of the unification, too. Eventually, the *genbun itchi* style of writing, rather than being a truthful image of speech, became a model for it. What we are witnessing nowadays is the emergence of written varieties that do not reflect anything in speech and can, therefore, be described, with Miyake (2014: 184), as a "style *beyond* the unification of spoken and written language." In addition to the visual peculiarities of CMC writing style, she emphasizes its dialogical quality. In the past, most writing was monologic in the sense that narrative, descriptive, expository, and even epistolary texts were autonomous (Olson 1977) in the sense of being comprehensible by themselves in the absence of the author. By contrast, CMC in text forums, online chats, SMS exchanged over smartphones, etc. has many dialogic characteristics reminiscent of conversations, since in many instances the interlocutors are "online together." Their contributions to the thread are connected and often meaningless or incomprehensible if extracted from it. "Chat" is an apt metaphor for a "long distance dialog" without the co-presence of interlocutors. However, the visual nature of this kind of dialog still distinguishes it from spoken interchange. The media, or rather the material realizations of verbal messages, follow their own, distinct laws. As described in conversation analysis long ago (Sacks, Schegloff, and Jefferson 1974), speakers do not alternate sequentially in natural conversation. In dialog, multi-party meetings, and telephone conversations they frequently overlap. This is not possible in writing, on paper or on smartphone displays. In view of the huge volume of Internet traffic in Japan, which is still growing, it is to be expected that new forms of writing and a style beyond *genbun itchi* will emerge with many features of colloquial conversation, but the distinction in the turn-taking organization of speech and writing will remain.

8 Conclusion

This chapter has shown how writing system, written language, and literacy interact to constitute Japan's literate culture. Mutual influences among these three components were never straightforward in the past and are not today. Over many centuries, the writing system and written styles evolved to become more diverse and complex until, in the Meiji era, deliberate efforts were undertaken to achieve a measure of simplification and standardization. This trend continued in the wake of World War II in conjunction with educational reforms, which encompassed an official scheme for the limitation of Chinese characters in common use. The new standard, welcomed by progressive educators and condemned by conservative intellectuals who feared a degeneration of the nation's language and culture, is still recognized today, but with the advent of the age of CMC the cards of the literacy game have been reshuffled. The changes in progress are visible, but hard to assess, for it is early days yet.

Part II

Sound System and Lexicon

7

Moras and Syllables

Timothy J. Vance

1 Introduction

This chapter discusses the small pronunciation units into which the segments (i.e. consonants and vowels) of words seem to be organized: *moras* and *syllables*. Speakers of English and many other languages have an intuitive understanding of what syllables are, but moras are unfamiliar, and researchers disagree about whether it is appropriate to analyze English as having moras. Speakers of Japanese, in contrast, have an intuitive understanding of what moras are, while syllables are unfamiliar. Researchers who work on Japanese disagree about whether there are syllables distinct from moras.

Problems of definition are taken up in the remainder of this section. Section 2 provides a basic explanation of how the notion of mora has ordinarily been applied to Japanese, and Section 3 does the same for the notion of syllable. Section 4 deals with vowels that are adjacent to each other, with no intervening consonant. Such sequences can be problematic in the sense that it is sometimes uncertain whether or not the second vowel is a "special mora" (i.e. dependent on the immediately preceding mora). Section 5 looks at some generalizations that have usually been stated in terms of syllables and argues that they can also be stated in terms of moras. The brief conclusion in Section 6 suggests that there is an interaction between Japanese writing system and native speakers' intuitions about moras.

1.1 Syllables

Most linguists would agree that syllables seem to be basic units of speech production and perception (Abercrombie 1967: 37; Lieberman 1977: 120–121), but syllables are notoriously difficult to define either articulatorily or auditorily (Laver 1994: 113–114; Rogers 2000: 267–268; Zec 2007:

161). In prototypical cases, the number of syllables in an utterance matches the number of peaks of sonority (Goldsmith 2011: 194), where sonority is taken to be a scale of intrinsic audibility on which individual segments can be ranked (Laver 1994: 503–505; Parker 2008). Syllables also seem to be intuitively natural units for ordinary native speakers of most languages, at least in the sense that there is general agreement on how many syllables a word contains, although not necessarily on where the boundary is between one syllable and the next (Clark and Yallop 1990: 97; Steriade 2003: 193; Duanmu 2009: 1–2).

There is also a consensus that phonotactic constraints apply to syllables (Pike 1947: 180–181; Fudge 1969: 254; Zec 2007: 162). For the most part, any string of phonotactically admissible syllables in a language is a phonotactically admissible word in that language, although not all phonotactic generalizations are syllable based (Zec 2007: 192).

Most researchers today who would identify themselves as phonologists analyze Japanese (i.e. modern Tokyo "standard" Japanese) as having both moras and syllables: one-mora light syllables (short syllables), two-mora heavy syllables (long syllables), and even three-mora superheavy syllables (extra-long syllables), although this last category is marginal. There is, however, no colloquial Japanese word that denotes a Japanese syllable in this sense, and ordinary native speakers know how to count moras but not how to count syllables (Vance 2008: 115–116; Labrune 2012b: 116).

1.2 Moras

A mora is understood as a unit of syllable weight (i.e. quantity) in languages that distinguish between light (i.e. short) and heavy (i.e. long) syllables (Trubetzkoy 1969 [1939]: 173–181; Davis 2011: 103–108). Japanese moras are intuitively isochronous units of rhythm for native speakers, and scholars familiar with traditional Japanese language research often use the musical term *haku* 'beat.' Thus, in a well-known categorization of languages into rhythmic types (Pike 1943: 35; Abercrombie 1967: 96–98), Japanese is the textbook example of a mora-timed language, in contrast to syllable-timed languages such as Spanish and stress-timed languages such as English (Ladefoged 1982: 226; Rogers 2000: 270–271; Kubozono and Honma 2002: 20–21).

Languages do not, however, exhibit a straightforward relationship between syllable weight and duration (Davis: 2011: 132–133), and experimental work on Japanese has not been able to demonstrate even approximate isochrony of moras. Of course, no linguist would maintain that every mora has precisely the same duration, even at a fixed tempo. Phonetic research on mora timing in Japanese has focused on trying to show that compensation effects make average mora durations more nearly equal than would be expected from inherent segment durations. A thorough review of this research concludes that the evidence for such compensation is not persuasive (Warner and Arai 2001), and it has even been suggested that moraic isochrony in Japanese is merely an illusion caused by the relative proportion of vowels and consonants in utterances (Ramus, Nespor, and Mehler 1999).

The remainder of this chapter assesses Japanese moras and syllables as psychological units. The arguments that researchers offer involve language-internal phenomena and behavior on psycholinguistic tasks. Moraic isochrony is not at issue.

1.3 Subsyllabic Constituents

The standard terminology for the parts of syllables presupposes that the boundaries between syllables can be determined, although it can accommodate ambisyllabicity, that is, a segment that is both the end of one syllable and at the beginning of the next. The nucleus of a syllable is the portion with the highest sonority (Zec 2007: 163) and is prototypically a vowel, although many languages allow at least some consonants to function as nuclei (i.e. syllabic consonants). A syllable must have a nucleus, and some languages allow syllables with only a nucleus, as in the monosyllabic English word /ɔ/ *awe*. The non-nuclear segments in a syllable make up the margins. Consonants in the margin preceding the nucleus are the onset, and those in the margin following the nucleus are the coda. In the monosyllabic English word /plænt/ *plant*, for example, the nucleus is /æ/, the onset is /pl/, and the coda is /nt/. A syllable with a coda is closed, and a syllable without a coda (e.g. /pli/ *plea*) is open.

It is often claimed that in English and many other languages, the nucleus and the coda in a closed syllable form a unit and that syllables therefore have the hierarchical structure in Figure 7.1 (Fudge 1969: 268; Blevins 1995: 212–216; Treiman and Kessler 1995). (The symbol σ stands for a syllable.) The unit containing the nucleus and the coda (if there is a coda) is called the rhyme.

Two main types of evidence are usually cited for the rhyme. First, English shows a strong preference for dividing between the onset and the rhyme in speech errors (Fromkin 1971: 32; Kubozono 1989: 266), as in /ren trɛk/ *rain trek* for intended /tr^en r^ɛk/ *train wreck*, in intentional blends, as in /brʌnč/ [brʌ̃ntʃ] *brunch* from /br^ɛkfəst/+/l^ʌnč/ *breakfast+lunch*, and in language games (Haraguchi 2003: 49), as in Pig-Latin /ɪtsple/ *it-splay*

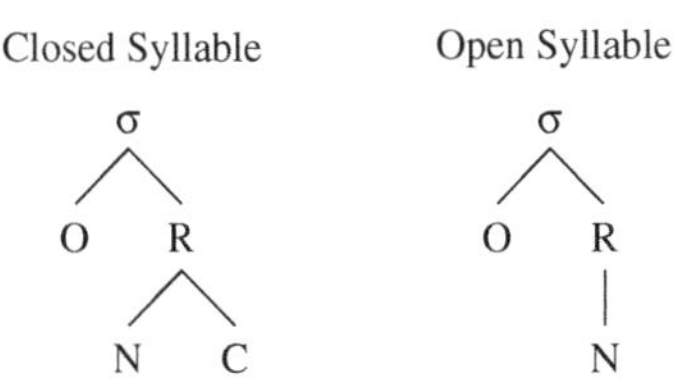

Figure 7.1 Hierarchical structure: onset + rhyme

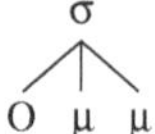

Figure 7.2 Hierarchical structure with moraic nodes representing weight

for /spl^ɪt/ *split*. (The symbol ^ marks onset-rhyme division points in the source forms.) Not all phonologists regard such phenomena as persuasive evidence for the rhyme as a constituent (Davis 1989; Goldsmith 2011: 172).

The other type of evidence involves phonotactics, specifically, the claim that phonotactic restrictions are much more stringent between the nucleus and the coda than between the onset and the nucleus (Fudge 1969: 272–283; Haraguchi 2003: 48; Duanmu 2009: 40). For example, /au̯/ is an admissible English nucleus, as in /kau̯nt/ *count*, and /mp/ is an admissible coda, as in /kæmp/ *camp*, but this nucleus and this coda cannot co-occur (Haraguchi 2003: 48): */kau̯mp/. (A preceding asterisk indicates that a form is deviant.) Nonetheless, it is not true in every language that an admissible onset followed by an admissible rhyme is always an admissible syllable, and some phonologists therefore find the phonotactic evidence for the rhyme unconvincing (Zec 2007: 177).

In languages with weight distinctions, the fact that onsets are never relevant to syllable weight (Hyman 1985: 6; Davis 2011: 117) has been used to motivate structures like the one in Figure 7.2, with the onset attached directly to syllable node and weight represented straightforwardly by the number of mora nodes (Zec 2007: 176; Duanmu 2009: 8). (The symbol μ stands for a mora.) The first mora in a heavy syllable is often called the head mora, and it typically has a higher sonority threshold than the non-head mora (Zec 2007: 183), that is, the class of segments that can fill the head mora position is limited to a higher portion of the sonority scale.

2 Japanese Moras

The psychological reality of moras in Japanese is beyond dispute. Native speakers learn to count moras as small children, and moras are the units of traditional Japanese poetic meters. Furthermore, since Japanese has quite restrictive phonotactics, there is no uncertainty about the boundaries between moras in the sense that every phoneme in a traditional linear transcription is unambiguously a member of one particular mora.

A prototypical Japanese mora consists of a single consonant followed by a short vowel, as in the three moras of /mi$_{\mu}$zo$_{\mu}$re/ *mizore* 'sleet' (using a subscript μ to mark the boundary between one mora and the next).[1]

[1] As in most of this handbook, this chapter uses the Hepburn system of romanization for transcribing Japanese words. Except for using /R/ to represent vowel length, the phonemic representations in this chapter follow the system described in Vance (2008: 53–114), that is, /š/ for [ɕ] (voiceless alveolo-palatal fricative), /ǰ/ for [d͡ʑ] (voiced alveolo-palatal affricate), /c/ for [t͡s], /č/ for [t͡ɕ].

Table 7.1 *Phonetic realizations of moraic and non-moraic nasals*

kan'i 'easy'	*kami* 'paper'	*kani* 'crab'
/ka$_{\mu}$N$_{\mu}$i/	/ka$_{\mu}$mi/	/ka$_{\mu}$ni/
[kɑ̃ɰ̃ːi]	[kɑmʲi]	[kɑɲi]

In some phonemic analyses, including the one adopted here, there are also moras with a two-consonant cluster preceding the vowel. The second consonant can only be /y/, as in the first mora of /kya$_{\mu}$ku/ *kyaku* 'guest.'[2] There are also moras consisting entirely of a vowel, as in the first and last moras of /e$_{\mu}$ga$_{\mu}$o/ *egao* 'smiling face.'

Departing even further from the CV prototype are the two moraic consonants. The moraic nasal /N/ has a wide range of phonetic realizations, but its place of articulation and aperture (stop or approximant) are determined by the immediately following segment (Vance 2008: 96–105).[3] The second mora in /te$_{\mu}$N$_{\mu}$po/ *tenpo* 'tempo' (phonetically [tẽmːpo]) is a typical example. A moraic nasal can immediately precede a vowel or a semivowel, and so can the non-moraic nasals /m/ and /n/, but there is no ambiguity in the phonetic realizations, as shown in Table 7.1.[4] The odd-looking transcription [ɰ̃ː] in the left example in Table 7.1 is intended to convey the fact that the moraic nasal in this environment is realized as a long, nasalized approximant, that is, a vowel-like segment that functions as a consonant. The important point is just that /Ni/ is clearly distinguishable from /mi/ and /ni/.

When a moraic nasal immediately precedes a non-moraic nasal, the phonetic realization of the two-phoneme sequence is an extra-long nasal with no auditory dividing point between one mora and the next. For example, /sa$_{\mu}$N$_{\mu}$ma/ *sanma* 'saury' is phonetically [sɑ̃mːːɑ]. Intuitively, the three moras correspond to [sɑ̃](/sa/), [mː] (/N/), and [mɑ] (/ma/), but [sɑ̃mːmɑ] is misleading because it implies that there is some sort of phonetic boundary between the end of the second mora and the beginning of the third mora. The two length marks in [sɑ̃mːːɑ] are intended to convey the idea that long [mː] realizes the moraic nasal and that the remaining portion of the bilabial nasal (i.e. the second [ː]) realizes the onset of the following mora.

The moraic obstruent /Q/ usually occurs immediately preceding a non-moraic obstruent and assimilates totally to that following obstruent.[5] For example, /ba$_{\mu}$Q$_{\mu}$ta/ *batta* 'grasshopper' is realized as [bɑtːːɑ], and /re$_{\mu}$Q$_{\mu}$ša/ *ressha* 'train' is realized as [ɾeɕːːɑ]. Here again, there is no auditory dividing

[2] Some speakers may have /kw/ and /gw/ clusters in a few recent loans such as /kwo$_{\mu}$R$_{\mu}$cu/~/ku$_{\mu}$o$_{\mu}$R$_{\mu}$cu/ 'quartz.'

[3] Recent studies indicate that the realization of /N/ is unpredictably variable when immediately followed by a pause (Hashi et al. 2014; Nogita and Yamane 2015).

[4] In conservative varieties of "standard" Japanese that have mora-initial velar nasals (Hibiya 1999), [kɑ̃ɰ̃ːi] 'easy' is also distinct from [kɑŋʲi] 'key.'

[5] There are marginal instances of the moraic obstruent immediately preceding a sonorant or a pause, and these are realized as a glottal stop. When an immediately following non-moraic obstruent is phonologically voiced, the phonetic extra-long consonant is often partially devoiced (Kawahara 2006: 540–544).

point within the extra-long consonant, although the three moras in the former intuitively correspond to [bɑ] (/ba/), [t:] (/Q/), and [tɑ] /ta/. The transcription [bɑt:tɑ] is misleading, however, because it implies that there is some sort of phonetic boundary between the end of the second mora and the beginning of the third mora, and [bɑttɑ] is even worse because it implies both a phonetic boundary and a short [t] as the realization of /Q/. The two length marks in [bɑt::ɑ] are intended to convey the idea that long [t:] realizes the moraic obstruent and that the remaining portion of the voiceless alveolar stop (i.e. the second [:]) realizes the onset of the following mora. (The transcription [bɑt:ɑ], with only one length mark, could be taken as suggesting the deviant phonemic form */baQa/.) When the non-moraic obstruent in such a sequence is an affricate, only the stop portion is elongated, as in /ma$_{\mu}$Q$_{\mu}$ča/ *matcha* 'powdered green tea' realized as [mɑt::ɕɑ].

There is also an intuitive boundary between moras within a long vowel, but once again no auditory division. For example, using /R/ to represent moraic vowel length, /to$_{\mu}$R$_{\mu}$ka/ *tōka* 'ten days' is realized as [to:kɑ]. The question of whether vowel length should be represented with a length phoneme or with a double vowel (as in /to$_{\mu}$o$_{\mu}$ka/ rather than /to$_{\mu}$R$_{\mu}$ka/) requires consideration of syllables and will therefore be postponed until Section 4.1.

Japanese has no restrictions on hiatus, that is, any two vowels can occur in sequence with no intervening consonant. In a sequence of two short vowels, the second constitutes a V mora, as in the second moras of /ši$_{\mu}$o/ *shio* 'salt' and /ta$_{\mu}$i/ *tai* 'sea bream.' A sequence of two identical short vowels is phonetically distinct from a long vowel. For example, /ki$_{\mu}$R/ *kī* 'key' is pronounced [kʲi:], with a long vowel, but /ki$_{\mu}$+i/ *ki-i* 'strange' is pronounced [kʲiˇi] in careful speech, with two short vowels separated by a brief dip in intensity known as vowel rearticulation (Bloch 1950: 105–106; Martin 1952: 13), transcribed here as [ˇ].[6] There is almost always a morpheme boundary (at least arguably) where vowel rearticulation appears, but a word meaning 'flame' is an exception. This word is synchronically monomorphemic, but some speakers have vowel rearticulation where there used to be a boundary, that is, some speakers treat it as /ho$_{\mu}$no$_{\mu}$o/, realized as [honoˇo], although others treat is as /ho$_{\mu}$no$_{\mu}$R/, realized as [hono:].

3 Japanese Syllables

In traditional Japanese language research in Japan, the term *onsetsu* (the usual translation of *syllable*) was used to denote the moras described above in Section 2 (McCawley 1968: 131; Kubozono and Honma 2002: 18).

[6] Vowel rearticulation can be hyperarticulated as a glottal stop. Ladefoged and Maddieson (1996: 76–77) adopt the non-IPA symbol [*] for transcribing vowel rearticulation in the Papuan language Gimi, but to avoid confusion with asterisks marking deviant forms (see Section 1.3), [ˇ] is used in this chapter.

ikada 'raft'	*konkyo* 'evidence'	*totte* 'handle'	*kinō* 'yesterday'
/ikada/	/koNkyo/	/toQte/	/kinoR/
σ σ σ	σ σ σ	σ σ σ	σ σ σ
i ka da	ko N kyo	to Q te	ki no R

Figure 7.3 Model A: Moras as syllables

Influential American Descriptivists followed this tradition and used the English word *syllable* to denote these same units (Bloch 1950: 90–92; Martin 1952: 12; Hockett 1955: 59). These syllables/moras do not correspond exactly to the weight units in moraic analyses like the one in Figure 7.2 because the traditional units incorporate onsets, as in model A in Figure 7.3. Model A does not quite faithfully reflect the now standard version of the traditional analysis, because all the syllables in Figure 7.3 have equal status. In this tradition, the moraic nasal /N/, the moraic obstruent /Q/, the vowel-length phoneme /R/, and (for some researchers) the second vowel in some V_1V_2 sequences are categorized as "special" moras (*tokushu-haku*). The crucial characteristic that makes them special is that they are less independent than "ordinary" moras. Although Japanese allows monomoraic words, such as /ka/ *ka* 'mosquito' and /u/ *u* 'cormorant,' there are no words consisting entirely of a single special mora. This systematic gap is unsurprising, since pronouncing special moras in isolation is unnatural (to varying degrees). In the remainder of this chapter, the term *mora-qua-syllable analysis* will refer to an analysis like model A in Figure 7.3.

One way of dealing with the dependent character of special moras is to draw a distinction between phonological and phonetic syllables (Arisaka 1959 [1940]: 106–107). The idea is that in very slow and careful pronunciation, each mora can be pronounced as a separate syllable, although a special mora combines with the preceding mora into a single phonetic syllable in normal pronunciation. It has been suggested that this same distinction can be extended to handle so-called vowel devoicing, which often results in the complete absence of any vowel-like acoustic interval. For example, /ašita/ *ashita* 'tomorrow' is normally pronounced [ɑɕtɑ], but it can be hyperarticulated as [ɑɕitɑ], so [ɑɕtɑ] can be described as three phonological syllables (/a$_\sigma$ši$_\sigma$ta/) but only two phonetic syllables ([ɑɕ.tɑ]). This description has encouraged some researchers to treat CV moras that have undergone vowel devoicing/deletion as an additional type of dependent mora (Terakawa 1941: 18–21; Labrune 2012b: 135–136). On the other hand, the distinction between phonetic and phonological syllables has been used to handle vowel devoicing without treating special moras as phonological syllables (Hattori 1954: 32).

In any case, the appeal to unnaturally careful, mora-by-mora pronunciation is problematic for at least two reasons. First, because of the close (although not quite perfect) correspondence between moras and the individual letters of *kana* writing, mora-by-mora pronunciation is arguably just a way of spelling words out loud. Second, there is an important distinction between careful pronunciation and "elaborated" pronunciation (Linell 1979: 54–56), although it is not always easy to draw. Careful pronunciation has a special status in phonological analysis because it appears to provide the basis for native-speaker intuitions (Jakobson and Halle 1962: 466–467; Lass 1984: 294–295). Elaborated pronunciation, on the other hand, introduces a kind of unnaturalness, and pronouncing special moras as separate syllables should probably be discounted as misleading elaboration (Kawakami 1977: 76).

Labrune (2012b: 139–140) advocates an analysis very similar to the one in model A in Figure 7.3 (see Section 6 below), but she calls the three units in each example word moras and rejects the idea that moras are the syllables of Japanese. One could certainly argue that treating Japanese special moras as syllables is at odds with the notion that syllables correspond fundamentally to a "sonority cycle" (Clements 1990: 299), that is, the "wave-like recurrence of peaks of sonority" (Goldsmith 2011: 194). If Japanese moras are syllables, all special moras are anomalous syllables, and many are highly anomalous.

Most phonologists who analyze Japanese as having light and heavy syllables adopt something like model B in Figure 7.4 (Kubozono 1989: 254; Terao 2002: 47–48). Model B represents the dependence of special moras directly by grouping each special mora into a syllable with the preceding mora. Syllable structure can be indicated in a linear phonemic transcription by using a subscript σ to mark the boundary between one syllable and the next and a subscript μ to indicate the boundary between two moras within the same syllable, as in /$\text{to}_{\mu}\text{Q}_{\sigma}\text{te}$/ and /$\text{ki}_{\sigma}\text{no}_{\mu}\text{R}$/ in Figure 7.4. A syllable boundary in this model always coincides with a mora boundary. In the remainder of this chapter, the term *mora-plus-syllable analysis* will refer to an analysis like model B in Figure 7.4.

The moras in model B, like the mora-size units in model A in Figure 7.3, incorporate onsets and thus do not correspond exactly to the weight units in moraic analyses like Figure 7.2. This structure is not usually argued for explicitly, but the rationale presumably is that "the initial C and V display strong solidarity" (Labrune 2012b: 133), that is, there are phonotactic

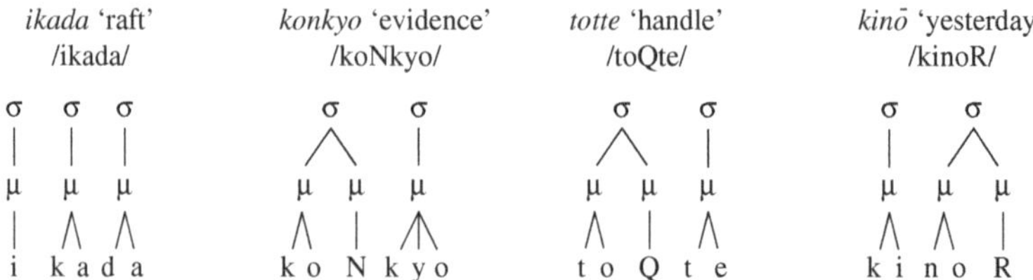

Figure 7.4 Model B: Moras as subsyllabic constituents

restrictions on onset-nucleus combinations but not on nucleus-coda combinations. To give just a few examples, */wu/ and */yi/ are prohibited, and so is */ye/ for most speakers. Assuming a phonemic analysis that treats [ɸ] as /f/ and [h]/[ç] as /h/ (Vance 2008: 80–82), */hu/ is prohibited. In contrast, any permissible ordinary mora can be followed by any permissible special mora (Labrune 2012b: 121).

Whether consonant+glide onsets, as in the /kyo/ of /ko$_{\mu}$N$_{\sigma}$kyo/ *konkyo* 'evidence' in Figure 7.4, are grouped into a single onset constituent is a question that has not attracted any attention, and the answer has no important consequences here.[7]

4 Vowel Sequences

4.1 Vowel Length and Sequences of Identical Vowels

As noted in Section 2, there is a phonetic distinction in Japanese, at least in careful pronunciation, between a long vowel and a sequence of two identical short vowels, as the words /ǰiR/ *jī* 'G' ([dʑiː]) and /ǰi+i/ *ji-i* 'intention to resign' ([dʑi˘i]) illustrate. Intuitively, the second mora of /ǰiR/ behaves like a special (i.e. dependent) mora, but the second mora of /ǰi+i/ behaves like an ordinary (i.e. independent) mora, and traditional accounts in Japan treat most or all V moras as ordinary moras. For example, in the commentaries included in successive editions of the pronunciation dictionary issued by Japan's public broadcasting corporation (NHK), Kindaichi (1966: 17–18, 1985: 20–21, 1998: 105–106) consistently recognizes only three special moras: /N/, /Q/, and /R/.

For Kindaichi (1966: 10), a special mora is just a mora consisting of one of the three "special phonemes" (*tokushu-onso*), that is, /N/, /Q/, or /R/. As he himself pointed out many years ago (Kindaichi 1950a), the phonetic distinction between a long vowel and two identical short vowels in sequence is a problem for any phonemic analysis that treats long vowels as double short vowels, and he saw this as a decisive argument in favor of the vowel-length phoneme /R/. A syllable advocate could argue that /ǰi+i/ has two light syllables and /ǰiR/ has one heavy syllable, allowing the difference to be represented as /ǰi$_{\sigma}$i/ versus /ǰi$_{\mu}$i/ (Vance 2008: 60–61), but this analysis violates a widely accepted principle, namely, that "lexical items do not contrast minimally in their syllabic divisions" (Steriade 2003: 190).[8] Since sequences of two identical short vowels almost always straddle a morpheme boundary (see Section 2), the difference between [dʑiː] and [dʑi˘i] could be attributed to the difference between /ǰii/ and /ǰi+i/, with a syllable boundary corresponding to the morpheme boundary in the

[7] In a phonemic analysis that treats such onsets as distinctively palatalized single consonants, there are no onset clusters in Japanese.

[8] Kindaichi's (1967: 70–71) view of syllables was essentially the one in model A in Figure 7.3, so this analysis involving long versus short syllables was not possible for him.

latter, but this solution will not work for /honoo/ 'flame' pronounced [hono˘o] (see Section 2). In any case, not all phonologists agree that lexical items cannot differ minimally in syllabification (Duanmu 2009: 59).

4.2 V_1V_2 Sequences Ending in a High Vowel

V_1V_2 sequences are problematic when V_2 is a high vowel (i.e. /i/ or /u/). Most phonologists who ascribe light and heavy syllables to Japanese recognize a fourth type of special mora in addition to /N/, /Q/, and /R/, namely, "the second half of diphthongal vowel sequences" (Kubozono 1999: 32). Most such sequences end in /i/, but some end in /u/. A diphthong can be described as a change in vowel quality within a syllable that is noticeable enough to make it sound as if there is a sequence of two phonetically distinct vowels. Depending on the language, a diphthong like [ai̯] can be a single phoneme (/ai̯/) or a sequence of two phonemes (/ai/ or /ay/), just as a stop+fricative sequence like [ts] can be an affricate (one phoneme) in some languages but a cluster (two phonemes) in other languages (Hyman 1985: 2; Duanmu 2009: 6–7). Nonetheless, there is a tendency to misinterpret the term *diphthong* as implying a single-phoneme analysis, and Kubozono's phrase *diphthongal vowel sequence* is presumably an attempt to avoid such misunderstanding. There is no question that all Japanese diphthongs should be analyzed phonemically as sequences of two vowels, and the more compact term *quasi-diphthong* will be used in the remainder of this chapter to denote the Japanese two-vowel sequences in question.[9]

In a mora-plus-syllable analysis, like model B in Figure 7.4, it is often hard to tell whether a V/i/ or V/u/ sequence is a quasi-diphthong because it is hard to tell whether the two vowels are in the same syllable. In an analysis with no distinction between syllables and moras, like model A in Figure 7.3, a quasi-diphthong can be defined as a V/i/ or V/u/ sequence in which the second vowel behaves like a dependent mora, and the corresponding challenge is deciding whether there is such dependence. If all onsetless V moras were dependent, then all V_1V_2 sequences would be quasi-diphthongs. The remainder of this section is devoted to arguing that there is a distinction between dependent and ordinary V moras, although some instances of /i/ in V/i/ and /u/ in V/u/ are not readily categorizable.

The evidence for quasi-diphthong status involves accent patterns, so a brief introduction to the (modern Tokyo) Japanese pitch-accent system is necessary here (see also Chapter 8, Section 2.1, this volume). Some words are accented and others are unaccented, and the intonation pattern on a phrase is determined in part by whether or not the word(s) it contains are accented and, if so, by the location of the accent(s). An accent is manifested by

[9] The term *quasi-diphthong* is adopted from a presentation by Rei Fukui at a symposium ("Japanese and Korean Accent: Diachrony, Reconstruction and Typology") hosted by the Tokyo University of Foreign Studies (July 2, 2016).

a steep fall from a relatively high pitch to a relatively low pitch. The smallest intonational units in Japanese are accent phrases, and an accent phrase has at most one accentual fall. Most of the examples cited in this chapter consist of a content word in isolation or followed by a particle, and these are all pronounced as accent phrases. An unaccented accent phrase has no steep pitch fall.

In the remainder of this chapter, the location of an accent is marked in phonemic transcription by a downward-pointing arrow.[10] In /ka↓makiri/ *kamakiri* 'praying mantis,' for example, there is a relatively high pitch on /ka/ and a relatively low pitch on /ma/, /ki/, and /ri/, and /ka/ is the accented mora (or accented syllable). Virtually all textbooks and pronunciation guides for Japanese use a phonetically imprecise system for describing the pitch patterns on accent phrases that categorizes each mora as either high-pitched (H) or low-pitched (L), and in this system, the pitch pattern on /ka↓makiri/ is HLLL.[11] In an accent phrase that begins with an ordinary mora and is not initially accented, the first mora is L and the second mora is H, as in /pori+bu↓kuro/ *pori-bukuro* 'plastic bag' (LHHLL). This phrase-initial LH pattern is sometimes called initial lowering.

In principle, a noun consisting of *n* ordinary moras (or, equivalently, *n* light syllables) can have any of *n*+1 accent patterns: it can have an accent on any one of its *n* moras or it can be unaccented. Special moras, on the other hand, cannot ordinarily bear accent. Consequently, in a mora-plus-syllable analysis like model B in Figure 7.4, the number of possible accent patterns for a noun is one more than the number of syllables, regardless of whether the syllables are heavy or light, and this relationship is the basis for saying that syllables, not moras, are the accent-bearing units in Japanese (McCawley 1968: 59; Kubozono and Honma 2002: 37–38), as illustrated in the examples in Table 7.2. The downward-pointing arrow appears between the two moras of an accented heavy syllable because,

Table 7.2 *Possible accent locations in disyllabic nouns*

Light syllables	Heavy syllables
2 Moras	4 Moras
/ha↓ši/ *hashi*	/se↓N+niN/ *sen-nin* 'thousand people'
/haši↓/ *hashi* 'bridge'	/seN+ni/ ↓N *sen-nin* 'hermit'
/haši/ *hashi* 'edge'	/seN+niN/ *sen-nin* 'full-time work'

[10] When manuscripts were still prepared using typewriters, it became common practice in books and articles written in English to use apostrophes to mark accent locations. This tradition remains strong, despite the potential confusion with a different use of apostrophes in romanized representations, as in *kin'yū* (/kiNyuH/) 'financing' versus *kinyū* (/kinyuH/) 'writing in,' both of which are unaccented. Given the ubiquity of personal computers today, it is easy to opt for a symbol like ↓ that is unambiguous and more iconic.

[11] Pierrehumbert and Beckman (1988), among others, provide phonetically more realistic descriptions.

according to traditional descriptions, the first mora of such a syllable is H and the second mora is L. Phonetically, however, the pitch just falls smoothly from the beginning to the end of an accented heavy syllable.

It is resistance to bearing accent that has led researchers to treat some V/i/ and V/u/ sequences as quasi-diphthongs. If onsetless high-vowel moras repelled accent consistently (or at least nearly consistently), they could simply be identified as special moras, always dependent on an immediately preceding ordinary mora. In fact, however, there is no such consistency. Onsetless /i/ and /u/ often bear accent, and in a mora-plus-syllable analysis, such instances are treated as separate syllables, as in /hi$_{\sigma}$ro$_{\sigma}$i$^{\downarrow}{}_{\sigma}$zu$_{\sigma}$mu/ *hiroizumu* 'heroism.' In a mora-qua-syllable analysis like model A in Figure 7.3, the phonemic transcription would be the same, but an onsetless /i/ or /u/ that carries accent is clearly not dependent on a preceding ordinary mora.

If accent falls on the first mora or on neither mora of a V_1V_2 sequence, the accent pattern usually provides no information about whether V_2 is syllabic (i.e. independent). For example, there is no reliable way to tell whether (in a mora-plus-syllable analysis) /ka$^{\downarrow}$i+ro/ *kai-ro* 'circuit' should be treated as /ka$^{\downarrow}{}_{\mu}$i$_{\sigma}$ro/ or as /ka$^{\downarrow}{}_{\sigma}$i$_{\sigma}$ro/ and whether /ni+kai+me/ *ni-kai-me* 'second time' should be treated as /ni$_{\sigma}$ka$_{\mu}$i$_{\sigma}$me/ or as /ni$_{\sigma}$ka$_{\sigma}$i$_{\sigma}$me/. Initial lowering can be diagnostic if the second mora of a word is an onsetless V and the first mora does not bear accent, since initial lowering is optional in words that begin with a heavy syllable (see Section 5.1). For example, /dai+gaku/ *dai-gaku* 'university' would be /da$_{\sigma}$i$_{\sigma}$ga$_{\sigma}$ku/ if initial lowering is obligatory (LHHH) and /da$_{\mu}$i$_{\sigma}$ga$_{\sigma}$ku/ if initial lowering is optional (LHHH~HHHH).[12]

It has been noted many times that the default location for accent in recent borrowings and foreign names is the syllable containing the antepenultimate mora (or the first syllable if the word is shorter than three moras) (McCawley 1968: 133–134; Kubozono 1999: 43; Kubozono and Honma 2002: 36–38). In many loanwords, a sequence of the form (C)V/i/ arguably behaves like a heavy syllable with respect to default accent. For example, /taipura$^{\downarrow}$itaR/ *taipuraitā* 'typewriter' has default accent if it is syllabified as /ta$_{\mu}$i$_{\sigma}$pu$_{\sigma}$ra$_{\mu}{}^{\downarrow}$i$_{\sigma}$ta$_{\mu}$R/, with /i/ treated as a special mora.

Comparable examples involving (C)V/u/ sequences are much harder to find, but verb forms provide some relevant data. When the citation form of a verb or adjective combines with the interrogative particle *ka* and the particle has a low and non-rising pitch, the combination expresses a kind of acquiescence. For example, *Kowareru ka* means something like 'So (it's) going to break.' When the verb form is accented, like /koware$^{\downarrow}$ru/ *kowareru* 'to break,' its accent is retained before *ka* in this pattern: /koware$^{\downarrow}$ru ka/. When the verb form is unaccented, an accent appears immediately preceding *ka*, as

[12] Labrune (2012a: 155) says that words beginning with (C)V/i/ "behave like words beginning with CVCV" in the sense that initial lowering is obligatory, but the consensus seems to be that the initial lowering in relevant phrase-initial (C)V /i/ sequences is optional (Tanaka and Kubozono 1999: 60): /kai+ša/ *kai-sha* 'company' (LHH~HHH), /haibo$^{\downarrow}$Rru/ *haibōru* 'highball' (LHHLL~HHHLL).

Table 7.3 *Accentuation of verb and adjective forms followed by* ka

Citation form	
/čigau/ *chigau* 'to differ'	/čiga↓u ka/
/sasou/ *sasou* 'to invite'	/saso↓u ka/
/akai/ *akai* 'red'	/aka↓i ka/
/omoi/ *omoi* 'heavy'	/omo↓i ka/
/usui/ *usui* 'thin'	/usu↓i ka/

in /agaru↓ ka/ (cf. unaccented /agaru/ *agaru* 'to rise') and /susumu↓ ka/ (cf. unaccented /susumu/ *susumu* 'to advance'). The examples in Table 7.3 show what happens when *ka* in this meaning follows the citation form of an unaccented verb ending in (C)/au/ or (C)/ou/ or follows the citation form of an unaccented adjective ending in (C)/ai/, (C)/oi/, or (C)/ui/. In such combinations, the accent falls on the penultimate mora rather than the final mora. This is the expected result if the verb or adjective form ends in a heavy syllable (on the mora-plus-syllable analysis) or, equivalently, in a dependent (i.e. special) mora (on the mora-qua-syllable analysis).

There are, however, V/i/ and V/u/ sequences that do not behave like quasi-diphthongs. Pronunciation dictionaries (NHK Hōsō Bunka Kenkyūjo 1998; Kindaichi and Akinaga 2001) give /fukui↓+ši/ for *Fukui-shi* 'the city of Fukui,' with /u/ and /i/ in separate syllables (/fu$_{\sigma}$ku$_{\sigma}$i↓$_{\sigma}$ +ši/), although many speakers seem to prefer /fuku↓i+ši/ (implying (/fu$_{\sigma}$ ku↓$_{\mu}$i$_{\sigma}$+ši/). There are foreign province and state names that show the same kind of variability. When such a name combines with /šuR/ *shū* 'province,' name-final accent appears. Typical examples are /arubaRta↓ +šuR/ *Arubāta-shū* 'the province of Alberta' (where /ta/ is a short syllable and an ordinary mora) and /orego↓N+šuR/ *Oregon-shū* 'the state of Oregon' (where /goN/ is a long syllable or a sequence of an ordinary mora followed by a dependent mora). In /hawai↓+šuR/~/hawa↓i+šuR/ *Hawai-shū* 'the state of Hawai'i' and /irinoi↓+šuR/~/irino↓i+šuR/ *Irinoi-shū* 'the state of Illinois,' however, many speakers prefer the form in which the onsetless /i/ mora carries the accent. In general, there is considerable variability and uncertainty regarding the dependent status of the second vowel in (C)V/i/ sequences and, to a lesser extent, (C)V/u/ sequences (which are relatively uncommon).

When there is good reason to treat a high front vowel as a dependent mora, it is not uncommon to see it transcribed phonemically as /J/ (see, e.g., Kubozono 1993: 73; Kawahara 2016: 170), as in /taJpura↓JtaR/ for *taipuraitā* 'typewriter.' This phonemic distinction between /i/ and /J/ has the same basic motivation as the distinction between ordinary vowel phonemes and /R/. As noted earlier in this section, if long vowels and V$_1$V$_1$ sequences are both analyzed phonemically as two identical vowel phonemes in a row, lexical items can differ minimally in syllabification or, equivalently, in the dependence versus independence of an onsetless V mora. In the same way, if V_1V_2 sequences ending in a high front are all analyzed phonemically as ending /i/, the door is open to violations of the widely (but not universally) accepted principle that minimal pairs differing only in syllabification are not possible (Section 4.1). For example, although /ha↓ir-u/ *hairu* 'to enter' and /oi↓-ru/ *oiru* 'to grow old' are not a minimal pair, if they are treated as /ha↓$_{\mu}$i$_{\sigma}$ru/ and /o$_{\sigma}$i↓$_{\sigma}$ru/, they both have penultimate accent (the regular accent pattern for an accented citation form of a verb). The problem of contrastive differences in syllabification disappears if these two words are phonemically /ha↓Jru/ and /oi↓ru/, because /J/, like /R/, implies dependence.

It would be preferable to be able to transcribe all onsetless high front vowel moras as /i/ and use other information to determine which instances of /i/ are dependent. If this were possible for all onsetless vowel moras, there would be no need for the phonemes /J/ and /R/, and the claim that lexical items do not differ minimally in syllabification could still be maintained. The same logic applies to the much less common instances of a high back vowel behaving as a dependent mora. If dependence is not predictable, then in addition to /R/ and /J/ a phoneme /W/, distinct from /u/, would presumably be necessary in examples like /dona↓W+gawa/ *Donau-gawa* 'Danube River' for speakers who have this pronunciation. River names ending in /gawa/ are generally accented on the syllable immediately preceding /gawa/ (or, in a mora-qua-syllable analysis, the last ordinary mora preceding /gawa/), as the examples in Table 7.4 illustrate. According to one authoritative accent dictionary (Kindaichi and Akinaga 2001), *Donau-gawa* can be either /donau↓+gawa/ or /dona↓u+gawa/ (the same kind of variability exhibited by state names such as /hawai↓+šuR/~/hawa↓i+šuR/ *Hawai-shū* 'the state of Hawai'i').

5 Syllable-based Generalizations

This section reviews four generalizations that have usually been stated in terms of syllables, presupposing a mora-plus-syllable analysis. In each case, it is not difficult to capture the same generalization if one assumes a mora-qua-syllable analysis instead. In fact, there do not appear to be any decisive empirical differences between the two analyses as long as they treat the same subset of moras as special (i.e. dependent). The upshot is

Table 7.4 *Accentuation of river names*

Isolation form	
/te↓muzu/ *Thames*	/temuzu↓+gawa/
/mišiši↓Qpi/ *Mississippi*	/mišišiQpi↓+gawa/
/a↓mazoN/ *Amazon*	/amazo↓N+gawa/
/ma↓reH/ *Murray*	/mare↓H+gawa/
/do↓nau/ *Donau* 'Danube'	/donau↓+gawa/~/dona↓u+gawa/

that the choice between the two analyses rests on the researcher's view of language in general, that is, what properties are taken to be universal and what degree of language-specific variability is regarded as plausible.

5.1 Initial Lowering

In an accent phrase that is not initially accented, initial lowering (i.e. the rise from a low pitch on the first mora to a high pitch on the second mora; see Section 4.2) is optional in some cases. In a mora-plus-syllable analysis, the generalization is that initial lowering is optional when the initial syllable is heavy (Hattori 1954: 246; McCawley 1977: 262; Kubozono 2006b: 14). The facts may actually a bit more complicated (Labrune 2012b: 123–124), but in a mora-qua-syllable analysis, the same generalization can be captured by saying that initial lowering is optional when the second mora of a word is a special mora. It is not clear in either analysis what the motivation is for this optional flattening of the LH contour.

5.2 Accent-bearing Units

In a mora-plus-syllable analysis, as explained above in Section 4.2, it is syllables, not moras, that are the accent-bearing units of Japanese. In a mora-qua-syllable analysis, needless to say, moras are the accent-bearing units, but since special moras ordinarily resist carrying accent, there is usually "a leftward shift of the accent when they occupy a prosodic position where an accent would be expected to occur" (Labrune 2012b: 124). Accented special moras do sometimes occur, however, and only /Q/ is indisputably incapable of carrying accent (ibid.: 125, n. 10).

One example of accent on /N/ involves a compounding pattern in which a place name combines with an emphatic /Q/ and /ko/ 'child' to form a noun denoting a person from that place. Most compounds that follow this pattern are accented on the penultimate syllable. When the place name is /ro$^{\downarrow}$NdoN/ *Rondon* 'London,' the compound is /ro$_{\mu}$N$_{\sigma}$do$_{\sigma}$N$^{\downarrow}$$_{\mu}Q_{\sigma}$ ko/ *Rondon-kko* 'born and bred Londoner' in a mora-plus-syllable analysis, with the accent carried by the first mora of the unusual heavy syllable /N$_{\mu}$Q/. The alternative would be /ro$_{\mu}$N$_{\sigma}$do$^{\downarrow}$$_{\mu}N_{\mu}Q_{\sigma}$ko/, with the accent carried by the first mora of the superheavy syllable /do$_{\mu}$N$_{\mu}$Q/, but Kubozono (1999: 50–55) argues that such trimoraic syllables are universally dispreferred and that Japanese usually avoids creating them or repairs them when they arise. In a mora-qua-syllable analysis, the atypical accent on the second /N/ in /roNdoN$^{\downarrow}$Qko/ could be accounted for on the assumption that a special mora is dependent on the nearest preceding ordinary mora. Treating /N/ as independent and allowing it to bear accent can be understood as a way to avoid having the two special moras in /doNQ/ both dependent on the same ordinary mora /do/.

Labrune (2012b: 125) claims that /R/ can also bear accent, but the example she cites is not persuasive. Accent dictionaries (NHK Hōsō Bunka Kenkyūjo 1998; Kindaichi and Akinaga 2001) give two alternative patterns for a loanword meaning 'chain store': /če↓RN+teN/~/čeR↓N+teN/ *chēn-ten*, both represented in a way that implies accent-bearing /R/ in the latter. However, in the audio recording that accompanies this entry in electronic editions of the NHK dictionary, the latter alternative is pronounced /čee↓NteN/ [tɕeˇẽnːtẽɴː], with clear vowel rearticulation, implying the sequence /ee/ rather than the long vowel /eR/. Furthermore, initial lowering (Section 5.1) is obligatory when the latter form appears phrase-initially (*HHLLL), as expected if the first two moras are in separate syllables (/če$_\sigma$e···/). In contrast, the unequivocal long vowel /eR/ in /čeRsu+gi↓NkoR/ *Chēsu-ginkō* 'Chase Bank' does not require (and typically lacks) initial lowering.

On a mora-plus-syllable analysis, the form of *chēn-ten* with a second-mora accentual peak can be treated as /če$_\sigma$e↓$_\mu$N$_\sigma$+te$_\mu$N/, with no trimoraic syllable. On a mora-qua-syllable analysis, this same form can be treated as /če$_\sigma$e↓$_\sigma$N$_\sigma$te$_\sigma$N/, with no sequence of two special moras both dependent on the same ordinary mora. In neither case is there an accent-bearing special mora. However, if the second mora were /R/ rather than /e/, mora-plus-syllable /če$_\mu$R↓$_\mu$N$_\sigma$te$_\mu$N/ and mora-qua-syllable /če$_\sigma$R↓$_\sigma$N$_\sigma$te$_\sigma$N/ would both have two dispreferred characteristics. The former has an accent-bearing special mora and a trimoraic syllable, and the latter has an accent-bearing special mora and two special moras (/R/ and /N/) both dependent on the ordinary mora /če/. It would be hard to explain why a form that violates two constraints would ever arise, given that the alternative (mora-plus-syllable /če$_\sigma$e↓$_\mu$N$_\sigma$te$_\mu$N/ or mora-qua-syllable /če$_\sigma$e↓$_\sigma$N$_\sigma$ te$_\sigma$N/) avoids both violations. In short, it appears that /R/ cannot carry accent.[13]

5.3 Accent Loss Before */no/*

Some lexically accented nouns lose their accent immediately preceding the genitive particle *no* (Martin 1975: 23–24). On a mora-plus-syllable analysis, this loss affects only nouns of two or more syllables that are lexically accented on the last syllable, which can be either light or heavy. For example, /a$_\sigma$ši$_\sigma$ta↓/ *ashita* 'tomorrow' (with a light final syllable) and /ki$_\sigma$no$_\mu$↓R/ *kinō* 'yesterday' (with a heavy final syllable) retain their lexical accents when followed by nominative *ga* (/ašita↓ ga/, /kino↓R ga/) but become unaccented when followed by *no* (/ašita no/, /kinoR no/).

[13] Higurashi (1983: 33–34) reports accent-bearing /R/ preceding a negative-polarity meaning 'only' for speakers who treat this particle as "preaccenting" (/↓šika/), but the relevant pitch patterns have not been studied systematically because most Tokyo speakers treat it as initial-accented /ši↓ka/ or unaccented /šika/.

There are many exceptions, and accent retention before *no* may actually be the default (Labrune 2012b: 129–130), but the fact remains that every noun that does undergo this accent loss is lexically accented on its final syllable. Furthermore, the accent loss never affects monosyllabic nouns, regardless of whether the lone syllable is light or heavy. On a mora-qua-syllable analysis, the nouns in question can be characterized as (1) containing more than one ordinary mora and (2) having a lexical accent on the last ordinary mora.

If one is willing to posit underlying/input accents in locations where they never surface, it is possible to claim that a noun ending in a special mora that loses its accent before *no* has its lexical accent on that last mora (Labrune 2012b: 130). For example, /nihoꜜN/ *Nihon* 'Japan,' which loses its accent (/nihoN no/), would be ^{LEX}/nihoNꜜ/, whereas /hoRgeꜜN/ *hōgen* 'dialect,' which does not lose its accent (/hoRgeꜜN no/), would be ^{LEX}/hoRgeꜜN/. Since a special mora cannot ordinarily bear accent (see Section 4.2), the accent shifts leftward onto the preceding ordinary mora to yield the actual output form /nihoꜜN/ when not followed by *no*. No shift is necessary for /hoRgeꜜN/, since the output matches the input. This approach cannot account for nouns ending in an accented ordinary mora that fail to undergo accent loss. The fact that /cugiꜜ/ *tsugi* 'next,' for example, retains its accent (/cugiꜜ no/) while /yamaꜜ/ *yama* 'mountain' does not (/yama no/) cannot reasonably be attributed to an underlying difference in accent location.

The same sort of analysis is possible for some compounds with a second element (E2) ending in a special mora (Labrune 2012a: 227–231). For example, in descriptions that assume syllables distinct from moras, it is frequently claimed that in a compound with an E2 that is three moras or longer and accented on its final syllable as an independent word, the compound will be accented on the first syllable of E2 (Kubozono 2008: 177). A typical example with a light final syllable is /tera+oꜜtoko/ *tera-otoko* 'temple assistant' (cf. /otokoꜜ/ 'man'), and one with a heavy final syllable is /aka+čoꜜRčiN/ *aka-chōchin* 'red lantern' (cf. /čoRčiꜜN/ 'lantern'). If the word for 'lantern' is underlyingly ^{LEX}/čoRčiNꜜ/, the accent in /aka+čoꜜRčiN/ can be attributed to the underlying accent on the final mora of E2, just as in ^{LEX}/otokoꜜ/, making it unnecessary to refer to syllables distinct from moras. As a word on its own, of course, ^{LEX}/čoRčiNꜜ/ surfaces as /čoRčiꜜN/ in order to avoid an accent on a special mora. On this approach, the accent in compounds like /koRčoR+seNseꜜi/ *kōchō-sensei* 'school principal' (cf. /seNseꜜi/ 'teacher') indicates that the word for 'teacher' is underlyingly ^{LEX}/seNseꜜi/, with the accent on the penultimate mora.

A major problem for an abstract analysis involving underlying accents on word-final special moras is that accent loss before *no* and E2-initial accent in compounds do not necessarily go together. For example, /nihoꜜN/ *Nihon* 'Japan' loses its accent before *no* (as noted above), indicating that the underlying form is ^{LEX}/nihoN↓/, but compounds like /niši+niho↓N/ *nishi-Nihon* 'western Japan' indicate that the underlying form is ^{LEX}/niho↓N/. On the other hand, /čoRči↓N/ *chōchin* 'lantern' retains its accent before *no* (/čoRči↓N no/), indicating that the underlying form is ^{LEX}/čoRči↓N/, but compounds like /aka+čo↓RčiN/ *aka-chōchin* 'red lantern' (cited above) indicate that the underlying form is ^{LEX}/čoRčiN↓/.

To summarize, the necessary (but not sufficient) conditions for accent loss before *no* can be stated either in terms of a mora-plus-syllable analysis (more than one syllable and accent on the final syllable) or in terms of a mora-qua-syllable analysis (more than one ordinary mora and accent on the last ordinary mora). It does not appear that either analysis offers any advantage in dealing with the irregularity of this accent-loss phenomenon.

5.4 Names ending with /taroR/

The name /ta↓roR/ *Tarō* is a traditional favorite for first-born sons, and it is also popular as a second element in longer names. Assuming a mora-plus-syllable analysis, these longer names are unaccented if the first element (E1) is monosyllabic, accented on the second syllable if E1 is two light syllables, and accented on the first syllable of /ta↓$_{\sigma}$ro$_{\mu}$R/ if E1 is three moras or longer (Kubozono 1999: 45–46). This pattern is clearly productive and applies, for example, to /kyu$_{\mu}$R$_{\sigma}$+ta$_{\sigma}$ro$_{\mu}$R/ *Kyū-tarō* (the name of a cartoon character), in which E1 is a single heavy syllable. Additional examples are given in Table 7.5. There are also a few common nouns ending with *Tarō*, and in these as well, light and heavy monosyllabic E1s are treated the same: /yo$_{\sigma}$+ta$_{\sigma}$ro$_{\mu}$R/ *yo-tarō* 'dunce,' /pu$_{\mu}$R$_{\sigma}$+ta$_{\sigma}$ro$_{\mu}$R/ *pū-tarō* 'day laborer.'

To formulate the generalization in terms of a mora-qua-syllable analysis, one can say that names ending in *Tarō* are unaccented when E1 is either a single mora or a sequence of an ordinary mora followed by a special mora (Labrune 2012b: 131). The same set of E1s could also be specified as those that contain only one ordinary mora. It is not clear why this set of E1s should be a natural class in a mora-qua-syllable analysis (Kawahara 2016: 186), but the generalization is not difficult to state.

Table 7.5 *Names ending with /taroR/*

E1 = $(\mu)_{\sigma}$	E1 = $(\mu\mu)_{\sigma}$	E1 = $(\mu)_{\sigma}(\mu)_{\sigma}$	E1 $\geq 3\mu$
/ya+taroR/ *Ya-tarō*	/kiN+taroR/ *Kin-tarō*	/momo↓+taroR/ *Momo-tarō*	/čikara+ta↓roR/ *Chikara-tarō*
/ki+taroR/ *Ki-tarō*	/šoR+taroR/ *Sō-tarō*	/kuni↓+taroR/ *Kuni-tarō*	/kareR+ta↓roR/ *Karētarō*

6 Conclusion

This chapter has not attempted to catalog all the phonological properties of Japanese that researchers have described in terms of moras or in terms of syllables, since comprehensive reviews are readily available (Kubozono 1999; Kubozono and Honma 2002: 25–96; Vance 2008: 117–138). Instead, the focus here has been on the long-running controversy over whether or not Japanese has heavy syllables as well as light syllables, that is, syllables distinct from moras. As noted at the beginning of Section 5, both a mora-plus-syllable analysis and a mora-qua-syllable analysis are capable of capturing the same generalizations, provided that certain moras can be categorized as dependent (i.e. "special"). The crux of the debate is the fact that heavy syllables are not psychologically salient units for ordinary native speakers of Japanese. As Labrune (2012b: 114) puts it, "the syllable is rather inconspicuous" in Japanese, and this lack of salience is presumably the reason that such speakers do not have a folk category for the units treated as syllables in a mora-plus-syllable analysis (as noted at the beginning of Section 1).[14]

If, however, syllables are basic units of speech production and perception in all languages, as suggested in Section 1.1, then Japanese must have syllables, regardless of whether ordinary native speakers have a name for them. One possibility is that moras are the syllables of Japanese, as in a mora-qua-syllable analysis like model A in Figure 7.3. The drawback to this approach is that it treats Japanese as aberrant from a cross-linguistic point of view, with many anomalous syllables (Section 3). A more appealing possibility is that Japanese has both light and heavy syllables but that some language-particular factor prevents syllables from becoming psychologically salient units. The most likely candidate for a language-particular factor is the Japanese writing system, specifically the mora-based *kana* subsystems (*hiragana* and *katakana*) that children learn first on the path to literacy. It seems highly plausible that learning to read and write *kana* might cause or at least enhance the strong moraic intuitions of adult speakers (Kubozono 1999: 57). There is also experimental evidence that pre-literate children find it natural to treat syllables as units instead of or in addition to moras, and that their behavior becomes more mora-based as they learn *kana* (Inagaki, Giyoo, and Otake 2000).

[14] Labrune (2012b) actually takes the radical position that Japanese simply does not have syllables; instead, she groups moras into feet with no intervening level of organization. Kawahara (2016) rebuts Labrune's claim, but both Kawahara and Labrune concede that it is not possible to prove the existence or non-existence of syllables in Japanese (Kawahara 2016: 17; Labrune 2012b: 145; cf. Hyman 1985: 27).

8

Pitch Accent

Haruo Kubozono

1 Introduction

The pitch accent system of standard Tokyo Japanese is well known in the literature, but it represents only one type of Japanese pitch accent system. In fact, many regional dialects have systems that are strikingly different from the Tokyo system. This chapter aims to describe the diversity of Japanese pitch accent systems with the Tokyo system as a reference and, thereby, to illuminate the nature and range of pitch accent systems in the language.

To achieve this goal, this chapter is organized as follows. Section 2 discusses the number of pitch accent patterns permitted in the system as well as the functions that pitch accent plays therein. The peculiar accent class known as "unaccented words" is also sketched. Section 3 analyzes the phonetic correlate of pitch accent. In Tokyo Japanese and many other dialects, an abrupt pitch fall manifests the word-level phonological prominence, but there are also some dialects in which pitch rise plays the same role.

Section 4 focuses on the domain within which pitch accent patterns are defined. Tokyo Japanese and some other dialects use the *word* as this domain, while other dialects define pitch accent patterns within a larger domain. A hybrid system involving the two domains is also discussed. This is followed by a discussion of culminativity, the question of whether the system permits only one prominence or more than one prominence within the domain of lexical pitch accent (Section 5). This discussion bears crucially on the roles that the word-level prominence plays in each pitch accent system.

The work reported in this chapter was supported by the NINJAL collaborative research project "Cross-linguistic studies of Japanese prosody and grammar" and JSPS KAKENHI grants (Grant no. 25580098 and 26244022).

Sections 6 and 7 are concerned with the ways in which the word-level phonological prominence is assigned. Section 6 examines the linguistic unit that is used to determine the position of the prominence as well as the unit that bears the prominence. Tokyo Japanese is known to be a typical mora-counting language, but it relies crucially on the syllable when actually assigning pitch accent.[1] Moreover, some dialects use the syllable as a counting unit. As McCawley (1978) demonstrated, the choice between the mora and the syllable is entirely independent of the distinction between counting and accent-bearing units. Japanese dialects vary remarkably in this respect, depending on which unit they use as a counting unit and which unit they actually assign pitch accent to.

Section 7 discusses the direction in which the phonological prominence is determined. Tokyo Japanese typically determines the prominent position from the end of the word, but there are other systems in the language that choose the opposite directionality.

Section 8 expands the scope of our analysis to compound words, or words that consist of two or more words. Tokyo Japanese has a typical right-dominant accent rule whereby compound accent patterns are determined with reference to the phonological structure of the rightmost element. This contrasts with the left-dominant compound accent rule found in many other Japanese dialects. Moreover, some dialects exhibit a hybrid system where both the rightmost and leftmost elements are referred to by the compound accent rule. The final section gives a summary of the chapter as well as some agenda items for future work. Map 8.1 shows the locations where the main dialects that are discussed in this chapter are spoken.

2 Multiple-pattern Versus *N*-pattern Systems

2.1 Tokyo Japanese

Based on the number of pitch patterns observed or permitted in the system, Uwano (1999, 2012a) proposed classifying Japanese pitch accent systems into two major groups, accented systems and accentless ones, with the former further divided into two groups, multiple-pattern and *N*-pattern systems. Of these, the accentless group refers to systems that have no fixed pitch pattern for words, namely, those where pitch is not

[1] In Japanese, as in many languages of the world, syllables can be defined as a phonological unit consisting of a vowel and one or more optional consonants; for example, /tookyoo/ 'Tokyo' and /kyooto/ 'Kyoto' are disyllabic words since they both contain two vowels, either short or long. On the other hand, moras are usually defined as a unit of phonetic duration or phonological length in general (Hyman 1985; Hayes 1995). Since short and long vowels count as one and two moras, respectively, /tookyoo/ has four moras, whereas /kyooto/ has three. Mora and syllable counts often differ from each other since long vowels and diphthongs count as one unit by syllable count, but as two units by mora count. Similarly, syllables with coda consonants (moraic nasal or obstruent) count as one syllable, but as two moras: /nissan/ 'Nissan,' for example, is a disyllabic, four-mora word, whereas /honda/ 'Honda' is a disyllabic, three-mora word. See Kubozono (1999, 2006c) and Chapter 7 of this volume for more details.

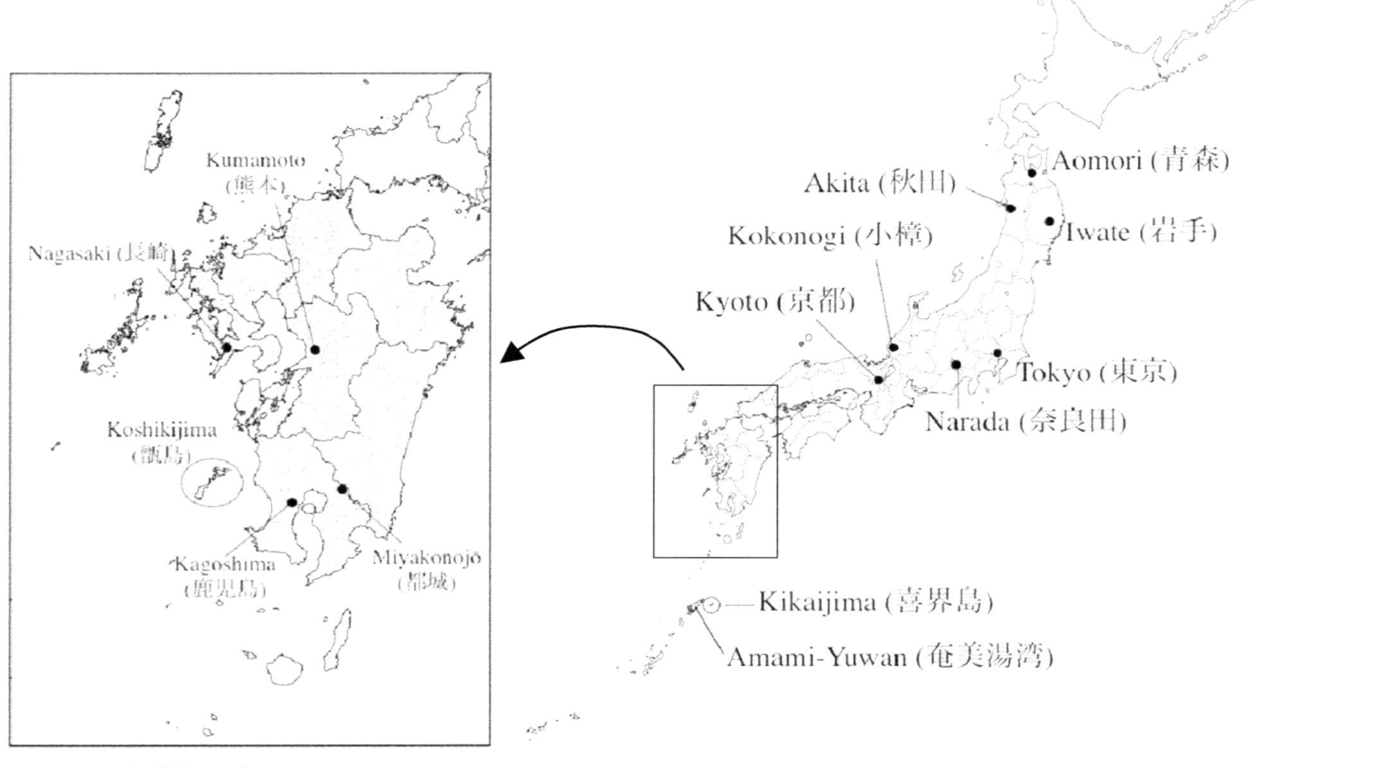

Map 8.1 Main dialects of Japanese

specified at the lexical level. Accented systems, on the other hand, have pitch specifications at the lexical level. Among this latter group, multiple-pattern systems refer to those in which the number of pitch patterns increases as the word becomes longer, whereas the number is fixed to a certain integer in *N*-pattern systems, typically ranging between one and four, independent of the length of the word.

Of these three types, Tokyo Japanese belongs to the multiple-pattern group since it exhibits two pitch patterns for monosyllabic nouns, three patterns for disyllabic nouns, and four patterns for trisyllabic nouns. This is illustrated in (1–3). In (1–3) and the rest of the chapter, pitch accent in Tokyo Japanese is denoted by an apostrophe, whereas superscript /°/ is added to unaccented words to clearly distinguish them from accented words. Dots indicate syllable boundaries, wherever necessary, and /ga/ is a grammatical particle denoting the nominative case (NOM).

(1) Monosyllabic nouns
- a. hi'-ga 'fire-NOM'
- b. hi°-ga 'sun-NOM'

(2) Disyllabic nouns
- a. ha.'na-ga 'Hana (female name)-NOM'
  - a'me-ga 'rain-NOM'
  - a.'ki-ga 'autumn-NOM'
- b. ha.na'-ga 'flower-NOM'
  - a.ki'-ga 'weariness-NOM'
- c. ha.na°-ga 'nose-NOM'
  - a.me°-ga 'candy-NOM'
  - a.ki°-ga 'vacancy-NOM'

(3) Trisyllabic nouns
- a. ka'.bu.to-ga 'helmet-NOM'
- b. ko.ko'.ro-ga 'heart-NOM'
- c. o.to.ko'-ga 'man-NOM'
- d. sa.ka.na°-ga 'fish-NOM'

As shown in (1–3), each syllable can bear an accent, yielding *n*-patterns for *n*-syllable nouns.[2] Tokyo Japanese permits one additional pattern for each word length, hence (*n+1*) patterns for *n*-syllable words. This additional pattern is called the unaccented pattern, which involves no sudden pitch fall even if the noun is followed by a grammatical particle. This pattern apparently violates the principle of obligatoriness, or the idea that every lexical word must have at least one prominence or prominent position (Hyman 2006), and may differentiate Tokyo Japanese from many pitch

[2] The syllable rather than the mora functions as an accent-bearing unit in Tokyo Japanese because bimoraic syllables such as /too/ 'ten' and /ton/ 'ton (a unit of weight)' do not show an accentual contrast between the accent on the initial mora, that is, /to'o/ and /to'n/, and the accent on the second mora, that is, /too'/ and /ton'/ (McCawley 1978). See Section 6 for more details.

accent languages in the world (Kubozono 2012a). In phonetic terms, it is often difficult to distinguish this accent pattern from the finally accented pattern shown in (2b) and (3c) when words are pronounced in isolation or in utterance-final position (Vance 1995), but they can be readily distinguished when followed by a grammatical particle since pitch suddenly falls immediately before the particle in one case but not in the other. Because of the unaccented pattern, moreover, the multiple-pattern system illustrated in (1–3) as a whole displays a contrast in accentedness – presence or absence of a pitch accent – in addition to accent position.

Four points must be noted here. First, while nouns thus exhibit multiple pitch patterns in Tokyo Japanese, verbs and adjectives permit only two patterns, as shown in (4): (a) a pattern with an accent on the penultimate mora and (b) the unaccented pattern.[3] Since accent position is fixed in accented verbs and adjectives, pitch accent can only be contrastive in terms of accentedness in these types of words.

(4) Verbs and adjectives in Tokyo Japanese

a. Accented

ki'.ru	'to cut'
su'.ru	'to print'
mo.to.me'.ru	'to request'
a.o'i	'blue, green'[4]
u.ma'i	'tasty'

b. Unaccented

ki.ru°	'to wear'
su.ru°	'to do'
ma.to.me.ru°	'to sum up'
a.kai°	'red'
a.mai°	'sweet'

Second, the multiple pitch accent patterns displayed by nouns are not equally distributed across the vocabulary. On the contrary, there are only two accent patterns that are popular across nouns of different lengths: the antepenultimate pattern with an accent on the third mora from the end of the word, as in (3a), and the unaccented pattern as in (2c) and (3d) (Haraguchi 1991; Kubozono 2006a). For example, these two accent patterns combined account for more than 90% of trimoraic nouns (Kubozono 2006b). Moreover, the (*n*+1) rule does not work in relatively long words; for example, there are very few six-mora words, if any, that are initially accented or finally accented. This led Kubozono (2008) to propose that

[3] Jita, one of the Bantu languages spoken in Africa, shows a similar asymmetry between nouns and verbs (Downing 2011).

[4] The status of diphthongs, or tautosyllabic vowel sequences, in Japanese is not clear (Hasegawa 2015: 40), but recent phonological studies present several independent pieces of evidence that the language has only three diphthongs, /ai/, /oi/, and /ui/ (Kubozono 2015a).

Tokyo Japanese basically has a two-pattern system for nouns as it does for verbs and adjectives and that nouns differ from verbs/adjectives in the extent to which lexical exceptions are permitted.

Third, since there are only two dominant patterns in nouns in Tokyo Japanese, the contrastive function of pitch accent in this system naturally involves an opposition in accentedness. That is, most pairs of words that contrast in pitch accent show a contrast between the accented and unaccented patterns. This is exemplified in (5).

(5) Accented and unaccented pairs in Tokyo Japanese
a. Accented words
mi.ya.gi'.san 'Mt. Miyagi'
ko'o.koo 'filial piety'
ta'n.go 'Tango (place name), the tango (dance)'
i'.on 'ion (in chemistry)'
b. Unaccented words
mi.ya.gi.san° 'produce of Miyagi'
koo.koo° 'high school'
tan.go° 'word'
i.on° 'allophone'

Finally, and related to the third point, the contrastive function of pitch accent in Tokyo Japanese is not as high as might be assumed: it only accounts for 14% of all pairs of words that are segmentally homophonous, while the remaining 86% are pairs of words that are also homophonous accentually (Sibata and Shibata 1990). This has two implications. For one thing, it implies that accentuation in Tokyo Japanese is rule-governed to a considerable extent: accent patterns are more or less predictable if the structure of the word is given. Second, it also implies that the primary function of pitch accent in Tokyo Japanese is not a distinctive one but rather a demarcative or culminative one, that is, the function of signaling the unity of words in the sentence or in connected speech. This view is supported by the fact that the default position of pitch accent is the antepenultimate mora irrespective of the length of the word: an abrupt pitch fall signals that it is almost the end of the word.

2.2 *N*-pattern Systems

While the number of accent patterns increases as the word becomes longer in Tokyo Japanese, there are also many dialects – especially in the southern part of Japan – that have *N*-pattern systems, or systems where the number of accent patterns is independent of the length of the word. The number may vary from one to four, with the two-pattern system being by far the most common (Uwano 1999). One of the most well-known two-pattern systems is that of Kagoshima Japanese, which has a high (H) tone on the penultimate syllable (Type A) or on the final syllable

(Type B) for both nouns and verbs/adjectives (Hirayama 1951; Kibe 2000; Kubozono 2006b, 2010). The choice between the two accent patterns is mostly lexically determined in short words, although it becomes more predictable as the word becomes longer or morphologically more complex (Kubozono 2011; see also Section 8 below). In (6) and the rest of the chapter, high-pitched portions are denoted by capital letters.[5] Parentheses describe an alternative accentual analysis of this system whereby Type A is regarded as accented and Type B as unaccented (Haraguchi 1977; Shibatani 1990; Kubozono 2012a; see also Section 3 below for more details).[6]

(6) Two accent patterns in Kagoshima Japanese

a. Type A

NA.tsu (na'.tsu)	'summer'
A.ka (a'.ka)	'red'
na.tsu.ya.SU.mi (na.tsu.ya.su'.mi)	'summer holiday'
KI.ru (ki'.ru)	'to wear'
ma.to.ME.ru (ma.to.me'.ru)	'to sum up'

b. Type B

ha.RU (ha.ru°)	'spring'
a.O (a.o°)	'blue, green'
ha.ru.ya.su.MI (ha.ru.ya.su.mi°)	'spring holiday'
ki.RU (ki.ru°)	'to cut'
mo.to.me.RU (mo.to.me.ru°)	'to request'

Note that this system resembles the two-pattern accent system of verbs and adjectives in Tokyo Japanese illustrated in (4) above, although surface pitch patterns are often different between the two systems.

2.3 Accentless Systems

In addition to the multiple-pattern and *N*-pattern systems, Uwano (1999) posits an independent type called an accentless system. This is a system where word prosody does not use pitch. In the Kumamoto dialect spoken near Kagoshima, words are usually produced with a more or less flat pitch in utterances (Maekawa 1997a). Pitch is used at the sentence level in this system, too, to differentiate interrogative sentences from declarative ones, for example. However, it is not specified at the lexical level, so a single word may be produced with several pitch patterns depending on the syntactic and/or pragmatic context, without changing its lexical meaning.

[5] This notation is used since word-level prominence in Kagoshima-type pitch accent systems is usually defined in terms of the high tone rather than the abstract notion of pitch accent as used in the description of Tokyo-type systems.

[6] As far as native words are concerned, the accentedness of words tends to be reversed between Tokyo and Kagoshima Japanese: most words that are accented (pronounced with a pitch fall) in Tokyo are unaccented (pronounced without a pitch fall) in Kagoshima, and vice versa.

The accentless systems should not be confused with one-pattern systems that represent a subtype of *N*-pattern systems. A typical one-pattern system is found in the Miyakonojo dialect, which is also adjacent to Kagoshima (Haraguchi 1977; Shibatani 1990). In this system, all words are pronounced in the same way, usually with a high pitch in phrase-final position so that pitch is not used distinctively in this system just as in accentless systems. However, pitch must nevertheless be specified at the lexical level in this system since words would sound awkward if they were pronounced with different pitch patterns, for example, with an H tone in their initial position. Moreover, the H tone is usually bound by *bunsetsu*, the basic syntactic phrase consisting of a content word and one or more function words. A typical pitch pattern of a sentence is illustrated in (7).

(7) bo.ku-WA ni.hon-ka.RA ki.TA
I-TOP Japan-from came
'I came from Japan.'

3 Distinctive Feature: Pitch Fall Versus Pitch Rise

As mentioned above, the pitch accent system of Tokyo Japanese is sensitive to a pitch fall, processing words with an abrupt pitch fall as accented and those without it as unaccented. Accented words may also contrast with each other in terms of the position of the accent. In this type of system, pitch fall functions as the distinctive phonetic feature of pitch accent. While this feature is shared by many dialects of the language, there are also some dialects that exceptionally display sensitivity to pitch rise rather than pitch fall (Uwano 2012a). These dialects are found mainly in the Tohoku area of northern Japan such as Aomori, Akita, and Iwate Prefectures. One geographical exception to this is the Narada dialect spoken in Yamanashi Prefecture, which is surrounded by Tokyo-type dialects where pitch fall is distinctive (Uwano 2012a).

Narada, which is a highly endangered dialect spoken in a mountainous area, is similar to Tokyo Japanese in permitting (n+1) accent patterns for n-syllable nouns. However, it crucially differs from the standard variety in using pitch rise as a distinctive feature. This can be seen from the comparison of the two systems given in (8): the original data of Narada are cited from Uwano (2012a: 1427) although in a different notation.

(8) Tokyo versus Narada (surface pitch patterns)

Tokyo	Narada	
KA.bu.to	ka.BU.to	'helmet'
KA.bu.to-ga	ka.BU.to-ga	'helmet-NOM'
ko.KO.ro	KO.ko.RO	'heart'
ko.KO.ro-ga	KO.ko.RO-ga	'heart-NOM'

o.TO.KO	O.to.ko	'man'
o.TO.KO-ga	O.to.ko-GA	'man-NOM'
sa.KA.NA	SA.ka.na	'fish'
sa.KA.NA-GA	SA.ka.na-ga	'fish-NOM'

Comparison of the surface pitch patterns in (8) reveals that the two systems are more or less mirror-images of each other. Specifically, the Narada patterns exhibit a pitch rise in the positions where the Tokyo patterns show a pitch fall. Uwano (2012a) interpreted this as evidence that pitch rise rather than pitch fall is distinctive in Narada. Using /ɹ/ as an accent mark for pitch rise, he interpreted the data in (8) as in (9). This analysis captures the basic identity between the two systems as well as their crucial difference: they are identical to each other with respect to the position where an abrupt pitch change occurs, but are different in the direction involved in the pitch change. The system of Narada Japanese is thus different from that of Tokyo Japanese in using pitch rise rather than pitch fall as a distinctive feature of pitch accent.[7]

(9) Tokyo versus Narada (phonological analysis)

Tokyo	Narada	
ka'.bu.to	kaɹ.bu.to	'helmet'
ka'.bu.to-ga	kaɹ.bu.to-ga	'helmet-NOM'
ko.ko'.ro	ko.koɹ.ro	'heart'
ko.ko'.ro-ga	ko.koɹ.ro-ga	'heart-NOM'
o.to.ko'	o.to.koɹ	'man'
o.to.ko'-ga	o.to.koɹ-ga	'man-NOM'
sa.ka.na	sa.ka.na	'fish'
sa.ka.na-ga	sa.ka.na-ga	'fish-NOM'

We have seen two types of pitch accent systems so far, one sensitive to pitch fall and the other to pitch rise. This classification may seem simple, but it is not as easy or straightforward as it might appear to be. To take one example, the two-pattern system of Kagoshima Japanese described in (6) may be interpreted either way. The traditional analysis assumes that the two patterns contrast with each other in terms of the position of the H tone, that is, penultimate versus final (Hirayama 1951; Kibe 2000). This analysis implies that it is the position of a pitch rise that is relevant, that is, that pitch rise is the phonetic correlate of pitch accent in this system. However, this is not the only analysis that one could propose for this system.

Looking at the same data, Haraguchi (1977) and Shibatani (1990) put forth an entirely different analysis whereby the system is sensitive to pitch fall rather than pitch rise: Type A has a pitch fall, whereas Type B does not.

[7] Other pitch features are lexically redundant in both dialects. Specifically, the initial mora is low-pitched in Tokyo Japanese unless it is accented. Similarly, the same mora is high-pitched in Narada Japanese unless it is accented.

This led Haraguchi (1977) and Shibatani (1990) to propose an accentual analysis whereby Type A is labeled as accented and Type B as unaccented (as shown in the parentheses in (6) above), just like the two major accent types in Tokyo Japanese described in (5).

One and the same set of data from a single dialect can thus be analyzed in two different ways, either as evidence for a system where pitch rise is distinctive or as evidence for a system involving pitch fall as a distinctive feature. This poses difficult questions in many cases. However, a more careful analysis might favor one analysis over the other. In the case of Kagoshima Japanese, the two competing analyses can be compared with each other in an objective way by considering a wider range of data. The most important is the fact that this dialect displays a tonal contrast in monosyllabic words as well: a pitch fall occurs within the sole syllable in Type A words, for example, /hi/ 'sun' and /ha/ 'leaf,' while no abrupt pitch fall occurs in Type B words, for example, /hi/ 'fire,' /ha/ 'tooth.' These two types of monosyllables are distinguished from each other not in terms of the position of a pitch rise but in terms of the presence or absence of a pitch fall (Kubozono 2011; see Ishihara 2004 and Kubozono 2007a for additional arguments for this view).

4 Domain of Pitch Accent Assignment

Our discussion so far has assumed that word accent patterns are defined within the domain of the word across Japanese dialects. This is correct to the extent that pitch accent is a property of a particular word or morpheme in Japanese in general. However, this does not mean that the word is the domain of pitch accent assignment in all dialects. Japanese pitch accent systems actually fall into two groups in this respect, those whose pitch accent is manifested within the domain of the word per se and those that use a larger domain for the same purpose. Tokyo Japanese and other multiple-pattern systems belong to the first group, while *N*-pattern systems generally belong to the second. This difference can be understood by comparing Tokyo and Kagoshima Japanese.

In Tokyo Japanese, pitch accent does not change its position whether the word is pronounced in isolation, as in (10a), or in combination with the following grammatical particle(s), as in (10b–d). This reveals the nature of pitch accent in the dialect (see Akinaga 1985 and Poser 1984 for some exceptional cases where the grammatical particles affect the pitch accent of the preceding content word).

(10)	a. ko.ko'.ro	'heart'
	b. ko.ko'.ro-ga	'heart-NOM'
	c. ko.ko'.ro-ka.ra	'from (the) heart'
	d. ko.ko'.ro-ka.ra-mo	'from (the) heart, too'

In Kagoshima Japanese, in contrast, the position of the prominence is not fixed on a particular syllable of the word but shifts rightward if the word is followed by one or more particles. This occurs in both accent types, as shown in (11–12).

(11) Type A
  a. sa.KA.na 'fish'
  b. sa.ka.NA-ga 'fish-NOM'
  c. sa.ka.na-KA.ra 'from (the) fish'
  d. sa.ka.na-ka.RA-mo 'from (the) fish, too'

(12) Type B
  a. ko.ko.RO 'heart'
  b. ko.ko.ro-GA 'heart-NOM'
  c. ko.ko.ro-ka.RA 'from (the) heart'
  d. ko.ko.ro-ka.ra-MO 'from (the) heart, too'

What is invariant in (11–12) is that the prominence appears on the penultimate and final syllables, respectively, within the *phrasal* domain: the H tone apparently moves rightward as the phrase becomes longer. This is the domain generally referred to as *bunsetsu* (the minimal syntactic phrase consisting of a content word plus one or more grammatical particles). Positing the *bunsetsu* as the relevant domain where pitch accent patterns are manifested, the two accent patterns can be described in a principled way. This Kagoshima-type property can be found across dialects with an *N*-pattern accent system (Uwano 2012b).

To account for the difference between the Tokyo-type and the Kagoshima-type systems, Hayata (1999) proposed to divide Japanese pitch accent into two types: word-accent and word-tone systems. In word-accent systems, a particular syllable or mora is chosen as the prominent position of the word; since the prominent position is marked at the lexical level, it will not change even if the word is placed in a larger domain. In word-tone systems, on the other hand, it is the pattern of prominence, not the prominent position per se, that is lexically specified. This pattern may naturally spread to a larger domain and be subsequently realized within each *bunsetsu*.

This analysis can explain why the two parameters pertaining to pitch accent – that is, the multiple versus *N*-pattern distinction and the word versus *bunsetsu* distinction – are largely correlated with each other (Kubozono 2012b). In a word-accent system, where the prominent position is lexically marked, the number of loci (moras or syllables) for the prominence may increase as the word becomes longer. Moreover, the lexically marked position will not change whether the word is pronounced in isolation or in a phrase. In a word-tone system, in contrast, a particular prominence pattern rather than a particular position is lexically specified. In such a system, the number of distinctive pitch accent patterns should not increase in principle as the word becomes longer. Moreover, since the prominence is not specified for a certain position, the prominence pattern is permitted to spread beyond the word.

This situation is complicated by the fact that the word and the *bunsetsu* may both be the domains of pitch accent assignment in one and the same system. The Wan dialect of Amami-Kikaijima Ryukyuan is such a dialect (Uwano 2000).[8] As illustrated in (13), this dialect has a two-pattern system like Kagoshima Japanese, but unlike Kagoshima, one accent pattern is realized within the word and the other pattern in the *bunsetsu* domain, both on a moraic basis. Specifically, one accent pattern – Type α in Uwano's analysis – involves a low (L) tone on the penultimate mora within the *bunsetsu* domain, while the other pattern – Type β – has an L tone on the antepenultimate mora and an H tone on the penultimate mora in the *word* domain.

(13) Wan dialect of Amami-Kikaijima

a. Type α	HA.sa.MI	'scissors
	HA.SA.mi-GA	'scissors-NOM'
	HA.SA.MI-ka.RA	'from the scissors'
	KAN.na.RI	'thunder'
	KAN.NA.ri-GA	'thunder-NOM'
	KAN.NA.RI-ka.RA	'from the thunder'
b. Type β[9]	ha.TA.na (~ha.TA.NA)	'sword'
	ha.TA.NA-ga (~ha.TA.NA-GA)	'sword-NOM'
	ha.TA.NA-KA.ra (~ha.TA.NA-KA.RA)	'from the sword'
	MEe.RA.bi (~MEe.RA.BI)	'young girl'
	MEe.RA.BI-ga (~MEe.RA.BI-GA)	'young girl-NOM'
	MEe.RA.BI-KA.ra (MEe.RA.BI-KA.RA)	'from the young girl'

This system is arguably a hybrid system which has combined the two types of systems found in other Amami-Kikaijima dialects, that is, a system where accent patterns are realized in the word domain and a system where they are manifested in the *bunsetsu* domain (Kubozono 2015b).

5 Culminativity

In prosodic systems with a lexical accent, whether pitch accent or stress accent, a certain constituent (mora or syllable) is generally marked as the phonological head of the word so that the prominence associated with the head constituent signals the peak or edge of the word. However, Japanese permits two major exceptions to this culminative function of word accent. One is the existence of unaccented words discussed above, which do not

[8] Amami-Kikaijima belongs to the Northern Ryukyuan dialect group of the Ryukyuan language if Ryukyuan is regarded as a language independent of Japanese.

[9] Type β ends in a low-toned mora in the sentence-final position and a high-toned mora in non-final positions.

have a phonologically prominent position. The other exception is the existence of words that have more than one pitch peak.

Tokyo Japanese permits unaccented words but not words that have more than one phonological peak or pitch accent. Thus, one word may have at most one pitch accent no matter how long it may be, as long as it is realized in one prosodic word.[10] In phonetic terms, this dialect does not allow pitch to rise again after it has fallen within the word domain: /ka'.ma.ki.ri/ 'mantis' and /ka'n.sai/ 'Kansai,' for example, show a pitch fall immediately after the first mora, /ka/, but no pitch rise after that. If the pitch should rise again, it would signal the beginning of the next word.

While this feature is shared by many Japanese dialects, including Kagoshima, it is not shared by all of them. In fact, there are several dialects, especially in the southern part of Japan, where one word permits more than one pitch peak. Koshikijima Japanese spoken on a small island in Kagoshima Prefecture is one such dialect. A sister dialect of Kagoshima Japanese, this endangered dialect permits two (and only two) accent types, Type A and Type B, and realizes them within the domain of *bunsetsu* rather than the word. Unlike its sister dialect, however, it permits two pitch peaks – or two H tones – in three-mora or longer words (Kamimura 1937, 1941; Kubozono 2012c, 2016). This is illustrated in (14), where the Teuchi dialect of Koshikijima Japanese is compared with Kagoshima and Tokyo Japanese.

(14)	Koshikijima-Teuchi	Kagoshima	Tokyo	
Type A	A.me	A.me	a.ME	'candy'
	ba.REe	BA.ree	BA.ree	'volleyball'
	o.NA.go	o.NA.go	o.NA.GO	'woman'
	KA.ma.BO.ko	ka.ma.BO.ko	ka.MA.BO.KO	'boiled fish paste'
	KE.da.MOn	ke.DA.mon	ke.DA.MON	'wild animal'
	NA.TSU.ya.SU.mi	na.tsu.ya.SU.mi	na.TSU.YA.su.mi	'summer holiday'
Type B	a.ME	a.ME	A.me	'rain'
	MI.kaN	mi.KAN	MI.kan	'orange'
	KO.ko.RO	ko.ko.RO	ko.KO.ro	'heart'
	A.SA.ga.O	a.sa.ga.O	a.SA.ga.o	'morning glory (flower)'
	A.NI.saN	a.ni.SAN	A.ni.san	'elder brother'
	HA.RU.YA.su.MI	ha.ru.ya.su.MI	ha.RU.YA.su.mi	'spring holiday'

As these examples show, Koshikijima Japanese has an H tone on the penultimate mora (Type A) and on the final mora (Type B), respectively, but it permits an additional H tone at the beginning of relatively long words. The two H tones are usually separated by one low-toned *syllable* as in (15).

[10] See Section 8 below for some compound words realized in two or more prosodic words; see also Kubozono (1988, 1995b) and Ito and Mester (2015) for full discussion of these multiphrasal compounds.

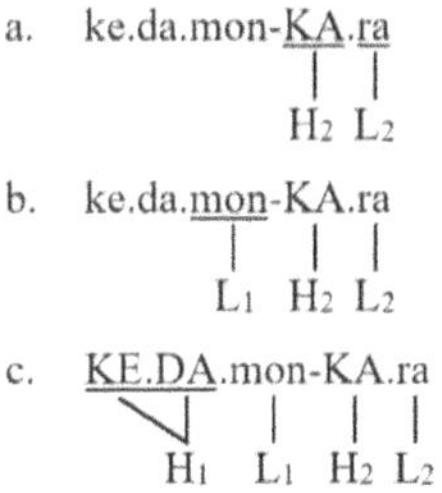

a. ke.da.mon-KA.ra
H_2 L_2

b. ke.da.mon-KA.ra
L_1 H_2 L_2

c. KE.DA.mon-KA.ra
H_1 L_1 H_2 L_2

Figure 8.1 Pitch accent assignment in Koshikijima Japanese

(15)			
	a. Type A	KE.da.MOn	'wild animal'
		KE.da.MOn-ga	'wild animal-NOM'
		KE.DA.mon-KA.ra	'from the wild animal'
		KE.DA.MON-ka.RA-mo	'from the wild animal, too'
	b. Type B	A.NI.saN	'elder brother'
		A.NI.san-GA	'elder brother-NOM'
		A.NI.SAN-ka.RA	'from the elder brother'
		A.NI.SAN-KA.ra-MO	'from the elder brother, too'

These accent patterns can be accounted for if one assumes that the dialect has two melodies – $/H_1L_1H_2L_2/$ (Type A) and $/H_1L_1H_2/$ (Type B) – and that these melodies are associated with the segmental material from the right edge of the domain. This pitch accent assignment process can be described in a derivational way as in Figure 8.1 (Kubozono 2012c).

One may wonder here if the secondary prominence at the beginning of the word may be a phrasal tone signaling the beginning of the phrase just like the phrase-initial pitch rise in Tokyo Japanese (e.g. /a.ME.RI.KA/ 'America'). This interpretation seems correct in the old system of Koshikijima that Kamimura (1937, 1941) described eighty years ago, where H1 was linked only to the second mora in both accent classes (Kubozono 2016). In the present-day system of Koshikijima-Teuchi, however, the same H tone is realized over multiple moras/syllables. Moreover, this tone signals not only the onset of a new *bunsetsu*, but also the Type A/B distinction in connected speech (Kubozono 2012c). More specifically, H2 disappears in non-final position of the sentence, while H1 survives as the sole prominence. This is illustrated in (16), where /. . ./ means that the phrase is followed by another phrase in the same utterance.

(16) H2 deletion in connected speech in Koshikijima-Teuchi Japanese
a. Type A
KE.da.MOn. . . → KE.da.mon. . . 'wild animal. . .'
KE.DA.mon-KA.ra. . . → KE.DA.mon-ka.ra. . .
'from the wild animal. . .'
b. Type B
A.NI.saN. . . → A.NI.san. . . 'elder brother. . .'
A.NI.SAN-ka.RA. . . → A.NI.SAN-ka.ra. . . 'from the elder brother. . .'

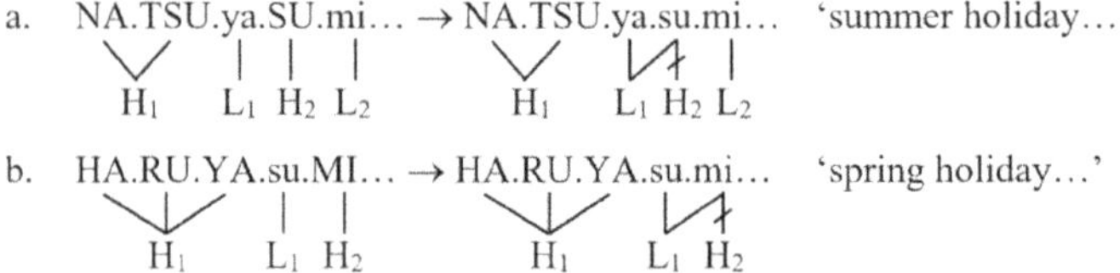

Figure 8.2 H2 tone deletion in connected speech

This H tone deletion is a peculiar phenomenon involving the deletion of the lexically dominant H tone (H2) and the subsequent promotion of the secondary H tone (H1) as the dominant tone at the post-lexical level. Since this process applies to both Type A and Type B alike, the lexical tonal contrast comes to be signaled by the domain of H1 in non-final phrases in connected speech. This is shown in Figure 8.2. What this means is that, like H2, H1 is a lexical tone rather than a phrasal one in this system.

6 Counting and Accent-bearing Units

Japanese dialects also show diversity with respect to the phonological units used in pitch accent assignment. McCawley (1978) proposed a two-way classification of word accent systems whereby accent-bearing units are distinguished from the unit used to measure phonological distances. According to this classification, Tokyo Japanese is a "mora-counting, syllable language": the mora is used as the basic unit to measure phonological distances, whereas the syllable actually bears the accent. The famous antepenultimate rule, for example, is formulated as in (17) (McCawley 1968), which accounts for the accent position of most accented nouns including loanwords, as exemplified in (18) (Kubozono 2006a).

(17) Antepenultimate rule
Nouns are accented on the syllable containing the third mora from the end of word.

(18) a. ba'.na.na 'banana'
b. pa.re'e.do 'parade'
c. i'n.do 'India'
d. pi'i.man 'green pepper'
e. ba.do.mi'n.ton 'badminton'
f. e.re.be'e.taa 'elevator'

The reason for the discrepancy between the syllable and the mora in Tokyo Japanese is that non-head moras of bimoraic syllables – for example, the moraic nasal /n/ as in /ba.do.mi'*n*.ton/ and the second half of the long vowel as in /e.re.be’e.taa/ in (18) – cannot bear the accent.[11] When accent falls on such moras by rule, it automatically shifts one mora to the left, that is, onto the head mora of the same syllable. This interaction between the mora and the syllable can be accounted for by generalizing the accent rule with the notion of bimoraic foot (see Poser 1990 and Kubozono 1999 for more evidence for this constituent). This generalization is given in (19) and exemplified in (20), where foot boundaries (parentheses) are minimally given. In (20a), for example, the accent is placed on /ba/, which is the head mora of the bimoraic foot whose right edge is not aligned with the right edge of the word.

(19) Nouns are accented on the head mora of the rightmost, non-final foot.

(20) a. (ba’.na).na ‘banana’
b. pa.(re’e).do ‘parade’
c. (i’n).do ‘India’
d. (pi’i).(man) ‘green pepper’
e. ba.do.(mi’n).(ton) ‘badminton’
f. e.re.(be’e).(taa) ‘elevator’

Note that this foot-based generalization does not dispense with the notion of syllable since, as the examples in (20) show, foot formation respects syllable boundaries (see Kubozono 1999; Ito and Mester 2015; and Kawahara 2016, among others, for more evidence for the syllable in Tokyo Japanese).

While the syllable and the mora are both indispensable units in the description of lexical pitch accent in Tokyo Japanese, only one of them is needed for the description of some other dialects. Nagasaki Japanese, for example, has a two-pattern pitch accent system like Kagoshima, but unlike this sister dialect, it uses the mora both to measure phonological distances and to bear the accent, which is realized as the prominent H tone in this dialect. Specifically, this system assigns an H tone on the second mora of the word – or the *bunsetsu*, to be more precise – in one class of word (Type A), while assigning a flat pitch pattern to the entire word/phrase in the other accent class (Type B) (Sakaguchi 2001; Matsuura 2014).[12]

(21) a. ba.NA.na ‘banana’
b. pa.REe.do ‘parade’
c. iN.do ‘India’
d. piI.man ‘green pepper’
e. koN.saa.to ‘concert’

[11] Non-head moras group into four kinds in Tokyo Japanese: the moraic nasal /n/, the first half of geminate (or long) consonants, the second half of long vowels, and the second half of diphthongs. The first two constitute the coda of closed syllables, while the latter two form the second half of a bimoraic nucleus in open syllables. See Kubozono (1999) and the references cited therein for the roles of the syllable, mora, and foot in Tokyo Japanese.

[12] The coda nasal in (21c, e) is a moraic nasal and not a syllabic one. Since there is no independent evidence that the coda nasal counts as one syllable in this dialect, treating it as syllabic would result in an entirely circular argument.

In this system, Type A words have an H tone on their second mora, be it a head mora as in (21a–b) or a non-head mora as in (21c–e). These accent patterns can be formulated by the mora alone, without reference to the syllable or syllable boundaries. Nagasaki Japanese can therefore be labeled as a "mora-counting, mora language."

While Nagasaki Japanese relies solely on the mora, Kagoshima Japanese uses only the syllable in pitch accent assignment. As already mentioned in (6) above, this system assigns an H tone on the penultimate *syllable* in Type A, whether this syllable is monomoraic or bimoraic. Likewise, it assigns an H tone on the final *syllable* in Type B. Alternatively, if a pitch fall rather than the H tone itself is postulated as the distinctive phonetic feature of pitch accent, as assumed by Shibatani (1990), this system bears an accent on the second syllable from the end of the word/phrase. In either case, the syllable is used both as a unit to measure phonological distances and as the bearer of the prominence. There is no evidence for the mora in this dialect.[13] It is highly interesting to ask why the two sister dialects – Nagasaki and Kagoshima – thus use different units for pitch accent assignment.

It is worth referring to a hybrid system here, a system where both the mora and the syllable are used to measure phonological distances (and to bear phonological prominences). The Koshikijima-Teuchi dialect sketched in (14–15) above, for example, bears two H tones in both accent classes and assigns them in different ways – assigning the lexically more dominant H tone (H2) by counting the number of *moras* from the end of the word/phrase, while spreading the less dominant H tone (H1) to all *syllables* preceding H2 except the *syllable* immediately preceding it.

The peculiarity of this hybrid system may be understood by comparing it with the simpler pitch accent system of Amami-Kikaijima Ryukyuan. The Nakasato dialect of Amami-Kikaijima, for example, assigns an HLHL melody to loanwords *mora by mora* from the end of the word. This system consistently uses the mora both as a counting and an accent/tone-bearing unit, although it is otherwise very similar to Koshikijima-Teuchi Japanese. Example (22) shows the differences between the two systems.

(22) Kikaijima-Nakasato versus Koshikijima-Teuchi

Kikaijima-Nakasato	Koshikijima-Teuchi	
TAN.ba.RIn	TAN.ba.RIn	'tambourine'
TEE.PU.RE.KOo.DAa	TEE.PU.RE.koo.DAa	'tape recorder'
E.SU.Oo.E.su	E.SU.oo.E.su	'SOS'
PII.PIi.E.mu	PII.pii.E.mu	'PPM'

[13] This dialect appears to permit a mora-based tone assignment in sentence-level prosody such as vocative and question intonation, but this is an epiphenomenon resulting from the interactions between lexical and post-lexical tones (Kubozono 2018).

7 Directionality

Directionality is another parameter that can be used to demonstrate the diversity of languages in general (Hyman 1977). This is also true of Japanese pitch accent systems. As the foregoing discussion shows, Tokyo Japanese determines the position of word-level prominence from the *end* of the word. The antepenultimate accent rule illustrated in (18) and (20), for example, places pitch accent on the third or fourth mora counted from the end of the word. The same directionality is employed in all other accent rules of the dialect, including the compound accent rule (McCawley 1968; Kubozono 1995a, 1997). Word-level prominence is measured in the same way in Kagoshima Japanese, too, where H tones are associated with the penultimate syllables (Type A) or the final syllables (Type B), as illustrated in (6) above. Koshikijima-Teuchi Japanese described in (14–15) also exhibits this directionality.

While this right-to-left procedure is very popularly found in Japanese dialects, there are also some dialects where the position of the word-level prominence is determined from the beginning of the word. Nagasaki Japanese is a typical example. As shown in (21) above, this dialect assigns an H tone on the second mora in Type A words, based on a left-to-right procedure – note that Type B words do not show any evidence for directionality since they exhibit a rather flat pitch pattern (Sakaguchi 2001; Matsuura 2014). Again, it is very interesting to ask why the directionality of accent assignment differs between Kagoshima and Nagasaki Japanese, two sister dialects both with two-pattern systems.

The situation is further complicated by the existence of a hybrid system where the two directionalities – left to right and right to left – are both involved. The Kokonogi dialect spoken in Fukui Prefecture, for example, has three distinctive pitch patterns based on pitch fall (Nitta 2012), one of which is obviously defined from the left edge of the word and another from the right edge, both on a moraic basis. Thus, a group of words including /hi.da.ri/ 'left' and /no.ko.gi.ri/ 'saw, handsaw' involve a pitch fall between the second and third moras in each *bunsetsu*, whereas another group including /ku.ru.ma/ 'car' and /ya.ma.za.ku.ra/ 'wild cherry blossoms' have a pitch fall between the final two moras in the same domain. These two patterns are illustrated in (23–24), respectively. A third group of words are pronounced with a flat pitch pattern involving an initial pitch rise, for example, /ma.KU.RA/ 'pillow.' This third pattern can be interpreted as involving either a left-to-right or right-to-left procedure.

(23) One accent pattern in the Kokonogi dialect
a. hi.DA.ri 'left'
hi.DA.ri-ga 'left-NOM'
b. no.KO.gi.ri 'saw'
no.KO.gi.ri-ga 'saw-NOM'

(24) Another accent pattern in the Kokonogi dialect
a. ku.RU.ma 'car'
ku.RU.MA-ga 'car-NOM'
b. ya.MA.ZA.KU.ra 'wild cherry blossoms'
ya.MA.ZA.KU.RA-ga 'wild cherry blossoms-NOM'

The same kind of hybrid system can be found in the Yuwan dialect of Amami Ryukyuan, spoken in the south of Kagoshima Prefecture.[14] With three distinctive pitch patterns, this system exhibits a pitch fall immediately after the syllable containing the second mora counted from the beginning of the *bunsetsu* in one accent pattern, and immediately after the syllable containing the penultimate mora in another pattern (Niinaga and Ogawa 2011). Although a little more complicated than the Kokonogi system in (23–24), this dialect, too, has a hybrid system involving both the left-to-right and right-to-left procedures.

This situation is even further complicated by the Kuwanoura dialect in Koshikijima Japanese, which exhibits a hybrid situation within one and the same word (Kubozono 2016). This dialect has a two-pattern system just like all its sister dialects of Koshikijima Japanese as well as Kagoshima and Nagasaki Japanese. It also permits two H tones within relatively long words just like most other dialects of Koshikijima Japanese. However, it differs from all its sister dialects in assigning the first H tone (H1) from the beginning and the second H tone (H2) from the end of the *bunsetsu*. Thus, H1 is usually associated with the first two moras from the *beginning* in both Type A and Type B words,[15] while H2 is linked basically to the penultimate and final moras counted from the end in Type A and Type B, respectively. Unlike the Koshikijima-Teuchi dialect sketched in (14–15) above, this dialect determines the positions of the two H tones independently and allows them to clash with each other as in /KA.ZAI.MO.no/ in (25).[16] The pitch patterns of the Koshikijima-Teuchi dialect are given for comparison.

[14] Like the Amami-Kikaijima dialect discussed in Section 4, this dialect belongs to Northern Ryukyuan of the Ryukyuan Family.

[15] The initial mora may optionally be low. Moreover, H1 spreads to the third mora if the second and third moras form one syllable.

[16] This system also undergoes H2 deletion in non-final phrases in connected speech, but this H tone deletion occurs only in Type B words, thereby keeping the accentual contrast between Type A and Type B in connected speech (Kubozono 2016).

(25)	Koshikijima-Kuwanoura	Koshikijima-Teuchi	
Type A	KA.ZA.ri.MO.no	KA.ZA.ri.MO.no	'decoration'
	KA.ZA.ri.mo.NO-ga	KA.ZA.RI.mo.NO-ga	'decoration-NOM'
	KA.ZAI.MO.no	KA.zai.MO.no	'decoration' (colloquial)
	KA.ZAI.mo.NO-ga	KA.ZAI.mo.NO-ga	'decoration-NOM'
Type B	I.NA.bi.ka.RI	I.NA.BI.ka.RI	'lightning'
	I.NA.bi.ka.ri-GA	I.NA.BI.KA.ri-GA	'lightning-NOM'
	I.NA.bi.kaI	I.NA.BI.kaI	'lightning' (colloquial)
	I.NA.bi.kai-GA	I.NA.BI.kai-GA	'lightning-NOM'

8 Compound Accent

Japanese dialects fall into two groups according to the ways accent patterns of compound words are determined. One group, which is represented by Tokyo Japanese, looks at the *rightmost* element of the compound and preserves the accent of this element as much as possible. The other group is represented by Kagoshima Japanese and refers to the accent pattern of the *leftmost* element in determining the accent pattern of the compound (Uwano 1997).

8.1 Right-dominant Compound Rule

The right-dominant nature of compound accentuation in Tokyo Japanese is illustrated in (26–28). Whether the rightmost element is 'short' (monomoraic or bimoraic) or 'long' (trimoraic or longer) (McCawley 1968), the basic principle underlying this rule is to preserve the accent of the rightmost element if it is lexically accented, unless it violates the non-finality constraint prohibiting the preservation of any accent on the word-final syllable (Kubozono 1995a, 1997; cf. Poser 1990). Thus, the lexical accent of the rightmost element is readily preserved if it does not violate this constraint as in (26). If this accent cannot be preserved due to the non-finality constraint or if the rightmost element has no accent to preserve, a default compound accent emerges on the rightmost, non-final bimoraic foot of the compound.[17] This is exemplified in (27a, b), respectively, where foot structure is minimally shown.

[17] This default accent pattern can be attributed to a constraint prohibiting the head foot, or the bimoraic foot containing the accented syllable, from occurring in word-final position.

(26) o.na.ga° + sa'.ru → o.na.ga-(za'.ru)
'long tail + monkey; long-tailed monkey'
koo.so.ku° + ba'.su → koo.so.ku-(ba'.su) 'highway + bus; highway bus'
ku'.ro + ka'.ra.su → ku.ro-(ga'.ra).su 'black + crow; black crow'
ryuu.kyu'u + a.sa'.ga.o → ryuu.kyuu-a.(sa'.ga).o
'Ryukyu + morning glory (flower); Ryukyuan morning glory'

(27) a. a'.ki.ta + i.nu' → a.ki.ta')-(i.nu) 'Akita + dog; Akita Dog'
me'.ron + pa'n → me.(ro'n)-(pan)
'melon + bread; melon flavored bread'
te' + ka.ga.mi' → te-(ka'.ga).mi 'hand + mirror; hand mirror'
b. ku.gu.ri' + to° → ku.gu.ri')-do 'to go through + door; side door'
o.na.ga° + to.ri° → o.na.ga')-do.ri 'long tail + bird; long tailed cock'
ku'.ro + ga.ra.su° → ku.ro-(ga'ra).su 'black + glass; black glass'
mi.na.mi° + a.me.ri.ka° → mi.na.mi-(a'.me).(ri.ka)~
mi.na.mi a.(me'.ri).ka 'south + America; South America'

A major exception to the generalization illustrated in (26–27) is unaccented compounds, most of which occur due to the deaccenting nature of so-called deaccenting morphemes (McCawley 1968; see Giriko 2009 and Kubozono 2017 for other factors triggering unaccented compounds in Tokyo Japanese). Thus, native morphemes such as /i.ro'/ 'color' and /ka.ta'/ 'type' as well as Sino-Japanese morphemes including /to'o/ 'political party' and /se'n/ 'line' have an effect of deaccenting the entire compounds of which they form the final member.[18]

(28) a. pi'n.ku + i.ro' → pin.ku-i.ro° 'pink + color; pink'
ne.zu.mi° + i.ro' → ne.zu.mi-i.ro° 'rat + color; gray'
b. e'e + ka.ta' → ee-ga.ta° 'A + type; blood type A'
ha'.mu.ret.to + ka.ta' → ha.mu.ret.to-ga.ta°
'Hamlet + type; the type of Hamlet'
c. kyoo.san° + to'o → kyoo.san-too°
'common wealth + political party; Communist Party'
roo.doo° + to'o → roo.doo-too° 'labor + political party; Labor Party'
d. too.ka'i.doo + se'n → too.kai.doo-sen°
'Tokaido + line; Tokaido Line'
yo.ko.su.ka° + se'n → yo.ko.su.ka-sen°
'Yokosuka + line; Yokosuka Line'

Compound accentuation in Tokyo Japanese is thus determined by the rightmost member of compounds, including the deaccenting morphemes in (28). One potential exception to this general rule is the accentuation of "dvandva" compounds, or compounds involving a coordinate structure. This type of compound tends to preserve the lexical accent of the initial

[18] Note that almost all deaccenting morphemes are accented on the final syllable when pronounced in isolation (Poser 1984) although not all finally accented morphemes yield unaccented compounds, for example, /a.ki.ta'-i.nu/ 'Akita Dog' in (27a).

member and lose the accent (if any) of the second member if they consist of two short members as in (29a) (Akinaga 1985). If they consist of relatively long members, on the other hand, they tend to split into two accentual units or prosodic words instead of being fused into one unit (Kubozono 1988, 2017). This latter pattern is illustrated in (29b), where {} denotes prosodic word boundaries.

(29) a. a'.sa + ban° → {a'.sa-ban} 'morning + evening; morning and evening'
a'.me + ka.ze° → {a'.me-ka.ze} 'rain + wind; rain and wind'
ta' + ha'.ta → {ta'-ha.ta} 'rice field + farm; the fields'
b. che'.ko + su.ro.ba'.ki.a → {che.'ko}{su.ro.ba.'ki.a}
'Czecho + Slovakia; Czecho-Slovakia'
bik.ku'.ri + gyoo.ten° → {bik.ku.'ri}{gyoo.ten°}
'being astonished + being stunned; being astonished and stunned'
i'p.pu + ta.sai° → {i'p.pu}{ta.sai°}
'one husband + many wives; polygamy'
to'o.zai + na'n.bo.ku → {to'o.zai}{na'n.bo.ku}
'east & west + south & north; all directions, everywhere'

8.2 Left-dominant Compound Rule

While compound accentuation in Tokyo Japanese is basically right-dominant, there are many dialects whose compound accent patterns are left-dominant. The two-pattern accent systems found in Kyūshū – for example, Kagoshima, Nagasaki, and Koshikijima Japanese – are typical examples (Hirayama 1951; Uwano 1997; Hayata 1999; Kibe 2000). To take some examples from Kagoshima Japanese, compound words in this dialect take the Type A pattern (an H tone on the penultimate syllable) if their initial member is lexically Type A, while they take the Type B pattern (an H tone on the final syllable) if the initial member is Type B. This is exemplified in (30a, b), respectively.

(30) a. NA.tsu + ma.TSU.ri → na.tsu-ma.TSU.ri
'summer + festival; summer festival'
NA.tsu + ya.su.MI → na.tsu-ya.SU.mi
'summer + holiday; summer holiday'
b. ha.RU + ma.TSU.ri → ha.ru-ma.tsu.RI
'spring + festival; spring festival'
ha.RU + ya.su.MI → ha.ru-ya.su.MI 'spring + holiday; spring holiday'

One naturally wonders here if the right-dominant and left-dominant nature of compound accentuation may have to do with the distinction between multiple-pattern and *N*-pattern systems discussed in Section 2, which, in turn, may be linked to the typological categorization of Japanese pitch accent into "word accent" and "word tone" discussed in Section 4 (see Kubozono 2012b for arguments for this idea). Whether these parameters correlate with each other is a very important and interesting topic for future work.

8.3 Hybrid System

Interestingly, there also exists a pitch accent system that exhibits both the right-dominant and left-dominant features in its compound accentuation. This system is widely found in Kinki Japanese (Uwano 1997; Hayata 1999). In the Kyoto dialect, for example, compound words display two major prosodic features, one concerning the pitch height of their initial position – high or low – and the other regarding their accentedness – accented or unaccented. Of these two features, the second one is shared by Tokyo Japanese as shown in (26–28). Kyoto Japanese is, in fact, quite similar to Tokyo Japanese in that compounds look at their *final* member to determine whether they are accented or unaccented. They also tend to preserve the lexical accent of their final member as much as possible, subject to the non-finality constraint.

In addition to this, compounds in Kyoto Japanese refer to their *initial* member to determine whether they begin with a high or low pitch. If the initial member begins with a high pitch when pronounced in isolation, this feature is inherited by the compound, as in (31a). Likewise, the compound begins with a low pitch, as in (31b), if the initial member is a low-beginning morpheme (Wada 1942).

(31) a. NA.tsu + YA.su.mi → NA.TSU-YA.su.mi
'summer + holiday; summer holiday'
KYA.be.tsu + ha.TA.ke → KYA.BE.TSU-BA.ta.ke
'cabbage + field; cabbage field'
b. ha.RU + YA.su.mi → ha.ru-YA.su.mi 'spring + holiday; spring holiday'
ya.saI + ha.TA.ke → ya.sai-BA.ta.ke 'vegetable + field; vegetable field'

Compound accentuation in Kyoto Japanese thus shows a hybrid system combining the right-dominant nature of compound accentuation found in Tokyo Japanese and the left-dominant one found in Kagoshima Japanese.[19] To use Hayata's (1999) terminology, Kyoto Japanese has both "word accent" and "word tone" and its compound accentuation involves the right-dominant preservation of "word accent" (pitch fall) and the left-dominant preservation of "word tone" (word-initial pitch pattern in this particular dialect).

9 Conclusions

9.1 Summary

This chapter has considered the diversity of pitch accent systems in Japanese with the system of Tokyo Japanese as a reference. It has shown

[19] Historically, the Kagoshima-type left-dominant compound rule discussed in Section 8.2 is believed to have developed from the left-dominant rule in Kyoto described in (31) (Uwano 1984).

that Japanese dialects differ from each other in many features pertaining to word accent. For example, Tokyo Japanese permits multiple accent patterns for nouns – two patterns for monosyllabic nouns, three patterns for disyllabic ones, four patterns for trisyllabic ones, etc. On the other hand, *N*-pattern systems permit a fixed number of accent patterns irrespective of the length of the word: Kagoshima Japanese and its sister dialects, for example Nagasaki and Koshikijima Japanese, exhibit only two patterns (Type A and Type B) no matter how long the word may be (Section 2).

Japanese dialects also show variability with respect to the distinctive phonetic feature of lexical pitch accent (Section 3). Tokyo Japanese and many other dialects employ pitch fall to differentiate one accent pattern from another, whereas some like the Narada dialect exceptionally use pitch rise for the same purpose.

Japanese dialects also display variability in how accent patterns are determined. First, they differ in the domain where pitch accent patterns are defined: Tokyo Japanese uses the word as the domain, whereas many dialects such as Kagoshima and Nagasaki Japanese realize pitch accent patterns in the domain of the *bunsetsu*, 'the basic syntactic phrase' (Section 4). Second, many dialects including Tokyo, Kagoshima, and Nagasaki Japanese permit only one prominence or underlying H tone per domain, whereas some dialects such as Koshikijima Japanese permit more than one prominence or H tone in the same domain (Section 5). Third, Tokyo and Nagasaki Japanese use the *mora* as the basic unit to measure phonological distances in pitch accent assignment, while Kagoshima Japanese measures phonological distances with the *syllable* (Section 6).

Fourth, Japanese dialects may vary in the directionality of pitch accent assignment (Section 7). Tokyo Japanese as well as Kagoshima and Koshikijima Japanese count the number of moras (or syllables) from the *right* edge of the domain. In contrast, Nagasaki Japanese determines the position of the word-level prominence from the *left* edge.

Finally, Japanese dialects display variability regarding compound accentuation, too (Section 8). Tokyo Japanese has a typical right-dominant compound accent rule by which the phonological structure of the rightmost element plays the key role in determining compound accent patterns. In contrast, Kagoshima Japanese and its sister dialects have a left-dominant accent rule whereby the prosodic property of the leftmost element is inherited by the entire compound.

These observations, which are summarized in Table 8.1, show how and to what extent pitch accent systems of Japanese differ from each other. They clearly demonstrate that Tokyo Japanese represents only one type of system among various Japanese pitch accent systems.

The situation summarized in Table 8.1 is complex enough. However, it is further complicated by the existence of hybrid systems involving

Table 8.1 *Summary of various parameters and dialects*

Dialect	Pitch patterns in nouns	Distinctive feature	Domain	Prominence peak	Unit	Direction	Compound
Tokyo (Tokyo)	multiple ($n+1$)	pitch fall	word	one	mora +syll	R → L	R-dominant
Kyoto (Kyoto)	multiple ($2n\pm1$)	pitch fall	word	one	mora	R → L	R-dominant +L-dominant
Kokonogi (Fukui)	N-pattern (N=3)	pitch fall	*bunsetsu*	one	mora	R → L L → R	?
Nagasaki (Nagasaki)	N-pattern (N=2)	pitch fall	*bunsetsu*	one	mora	L → R	L-dominant
Kagoshima (Kagoshima)	N-pattern (N=2)	?	*bunsetsu*	one	syll	R → L	L-dominant
Koshikijima-Teuchi (Kagoshima)	N-pattern (N=2)	?	*bunsetsu*	two	mora +syll	R → L	L-dominant
Koshikijima-Kuwanoura (Kagoshima)	N-pattern (N=2)	?	*bunsetsu*	two	mora +syll	R → L L → R	L-dominant
Amami-Yuwan (Kagoshima)	N-pattern (N=3)	pitch fall	*bunsetsu*	one	mora +syll	R → L L → R	?

Note: Parentheses after the dialect show the prefecture where it is spoken. 'syll' stands for 'syllable,' whereas R and L denote right and left, respectively. Question marks indicate that data and/or analyses are inconclusive.

two seemingly competing features pertaining to one and the same parameter. For example, a single dialect may use both the *word* and the *bunsetsu* as the domain of pitch accent assignment: it defines one accent pattern within the *word*, while defining another pattern within the *bunsetsu* domain (Section 4). Similarly, a single system may use both the syllable and the mora as counting units: Koshikijima-Teuchi Japanese counts the number of moras to determine the position of the primary H tone, while counting syllables to define the position/domain of the secondary H tone (Section 6).

Moreover, while most dialects determine the position of word-level prominence from either the left edge or right edge of the word or *bunsetsu*, some dialects use both the left-to-right and right-to-left procedures in the same system or even within the same word (Section 7). Finally, the left-dominant and right-dominant compound accent rules may coexist within a single prosodic system (Section 8). The existence of these hybrid systems makes Japanese pitch accent look more complex, but even more interesting and fascinating at the same time.

9.2 Future Agenda

This chapter has raised as many questions as it has solved. One interesting question for future work concerns the relationship between the various parameters that are used to describe the pitch accent systems. It was suggested in passing that the distinction between multiple-pattern and *N*-pattern systems is closely related to the domain parameter (word versus *bunsetsu*) (Section 4) and also to the nature of compound accentuation (left-dominant versus right-dominant) (Section 8). On the other hand, our analysis has shown that the multiple-pattern versus *N*-pattern distinction is independent of other parameters regarding the distinctive feature (Section 3), culminativity (one prominence versus two prominences) (Section 5), the basic prosodic unit (mora versus syllable) (Section 6), and the directionality of pitch accent assignment (left to right versus right to left) (Section 7). The foregoing discussion has clearly shown that *N*-pattern systems display variability in these parameters: Nagasaki, Kagoshima, and Koshikijima Japanese, for example, all have two-pattern systems, but they exhibit different features with respect to culminativity, the prosodic unit, and directionality. It will be interesting to examine in more depth how these parameters interact with each other and other parameters.

To answer this interesting question, it will be necessary to look at more data from a wider range of Japanese dialects. Given that many regional dialects are at the risk of extinction like the Koshikijima and Kikaijima dialects, it is indeed vital to expand our data in order to better understand the diversity of pitch accent systems, while we also continue to examine the pitch accent system of Tokyo Japanese.

Expanding the scope of analysis is another dimension in which our research on Japanese pitch accent can be extended. Most research on Japanese pitch accent in the past has concentrated more or less on the analysis of word accent within the word or *bunsetsu*. On the other hand, how word accent patterns are manifested in sentences and connected speech remains a largely understudied topic. If word accent studies are expanded in this direction, they might reveal new aspects of lexical accent such as the loss of word accent or accentual contrasts in focus and other constructions beyond the word and phrase.

Research along these lines will inevitably call for cross-linguistic comparisons between Japanese and other languages. The diversity of Japanese pitch accent systems is certainly an interesting topic by itself, but it will be more interesting to consider it from cross-linguistic and typological perspectives to see what insight and implications the diversity has for the nature of word accent and prosodic typology.

9

Intonation

Yosuke Igarashi

1 Introduction

The last three decades have witnessed explosive development in the phonological study of languages' intonation structure. Pierrehumbert's (1980) thesis on English intonation is undoubtedly the most influential contribution to intonational phonology. The intonation systems of the Japanese language have been extensively investigated, beginning from the 1980s (e.g. Poser 1984; Pierrehumbert and Beckman 1988; Kubozono 1993). Findings from Japanese have contributed to the development of a widely accepted framework for describing the intonational phonology of numerous languages (Ladd 2008; Gussenhoven 2004).

This chapter aims to present an overview of the intonation structure of Japanese. Section 2 provides the background, defining what intonation is and briefly describing prosodic phrasing and boundary pitch movements. Sections 3 and 4 describe two major components of Japanese intonation, boundary pitch movements and prosodic phrasing, respectively. Section 5 discusses intonational contrasts, and Section 6 concludes this chapter. All illustrative utterances of Tokyo Japanese have been produced by the author (a native speaker). The speakers of the dialectal utterances discussed in Section 5.4 are native speakers of the corresponding dialects.

2 Intonation and Its Components

2.1 What is Intonation?

Ladd (2008: 4) defines intonation as "the use of suprasegmental phonetic features to convey 'post-lexical' or sentence-level pragmatic meanings in

The study reported in this chapter was supported in part by Grant-in-Aid for Encouragement of Young Scientists (B) #26770143, Grant-in-Aid for Scientific Research (A) #26244022, Grant-in-Aid for Scientific Research (A) #16H01933, and the collaborative research projects hosted by NINJAL "Endangered Languages and Dialects in Japan" and "Cross-linguistic Studies of Japanese Prosody and Grammar."

a linguistically structured way." *Suprasegmental features* are commonly defined as fundamental frequency (F0), intensity, and duration. F0 corresponds to the rate of complete cycles of vibration of the vocal folds per unit of time. A higher F0 value gives listeners the auditory sensation of a higher pitch. Thus, F0 is a physical property of speech, whereas pitch is its perceptual correlate (however, these two terms are used interchangeably in this chapter). In Japanese and many other languages (Cruttenden 1997; Gussenhoven 2004), pitch is the primary feature in intonation; therefore, this chapter focuses on the F0 contours of the utterance.

Meanings conveyed by intonation apply to phrases or to an utterance as a whole. They include, according to Ladd (2008), sentence type, speech act, focus, or information structure. A prototypical sentence-type distinction signaled by intonation is statement versus question, which in many languages is achieved by a rising boundary pitch movement at the end of the question sentence. Intonation contrasts with lexical tones (generally called "lexical pitch accents" in Japanese linguistics), which distinguish word-level meanings. In the distinction between *háshi* 'chopstick' and *hashí* 'bridge,' for example, a high pitch (denoted by the acute accent marker) falls on the first syllable in the former but on the second syllable in the latter. In Japanese, lexical pitch accent constrains prosodic phrasing above the word level; therefore, this chapter especially focuses on lexical pitch accent in Section 2.

Intonation conveys meanings in a structured way as a phonological organization (e.g. Ladd 2008: 3–42; Gussenhoven 2004: 49–70). Pitch variation conveying non-linguistic information (e.g. sex, age, and emotional state) is excluded from intonation as defined here. This information can be interpreted even by listeners who do not know the language because forms and functions are directly correlated. For example, the more excited a person is, the higher is the pitch of his/her voice. In the currently defined meaning of intonation, in contrast, forms and functions are phonological in the sense that the phonetic dimension is mediated by the language's phonological system. To confirm that intonation differs from non-linguistic pitch variation, Gussenhoven (2004: 49–70) demonstrates that intonation and other language components share the three design features that Hockett (1958) identifies for human language: *arbitrariness, discreteness*, and *duality of structure*.

In fact, the form-function relation in intonation tends to be non-*arbitrary*. In many languages, rising or high pitch signals question while falling or low pitch signals statement (Ohala 1984). Moreover, a word produced with a higher pitch tends to be interpreted as being more informative than another produced with a lower pitch. Utterance-final rising, or high pitch in general, conveys continuation while falling or low pitch conveys finality (Gussenhoven 2004: 71–96). Even though in most cases intonation lacks an arbitrary relation between form and function, this is not always the case. In Chickasaw, for example, the interrogative contour is falling, whereas the declarative contour is rising (Gussenhoven 2004: 53–54), thus indicating the arbitrariness of the form-function relation in this language. While it is not easy to find evidence for arbitrariness in Tokyo Japanese, aspects of certain regional varieties of Japanese defy the non-arbitrary tendency. In the Kagoshima dialect, for example, a rising pitch contour does not signal interrogativity; the pitch contour in a question sentence is virtually identical to that in a statement (Kibe 2010). Furthermore, in the Imaichi dialect, the focused word bears the lowest pitch and the location of the pitch peak in the utterance is not associated with the focused word at all.[1]

Most contemporary researchers agree that intonation has a *discrete* form-function relation, indicating that phonetic dimensions are not directly correlated with semantic ones. This can be illustrated by the case in which two phonetically similar pitch contours are interpreted as signaling discrete meanings. Pierrehumbert and Steele (1989) demonstrate that the phonetic continuum of English rise–fall–rise contours is interpreted by native speakers as two discretely different intonation patterns. However, we frequently observe cases in which a certain putative linguistic message is signaled by continuously variable pitch. For example, Liberman and Pierrehumbert (1984) show that in English, the degree of emphasis and pitch range size are correlated, with more emphatic utterances having a wider pitch range. This message (i.e. the degree of emphasis conveyed by a pitch range) cannot be considered to be the meaning that the intonation as defined here conveys. Instead, the pitch range variation at issue is considered to be a phonetic modification of a single phonological category of intonation. In fact, establishing discreteness in intonation is one of the most challenging issues in the study of intonation. In Japanese as well, the question of the number of intonation patterns is yet to be resolved. We will return to these issues in Section 3.3, which concerns the inventory of Japanese boundary pitch movements.

Duality of structure is the most controversial issue in intonation. According to Gussenhoven (2006), the existence of duality in intonation is suggested by the English calling contour or "vocative chant" (like *Jo-ohn!*) in which two phonological elements embody one intonational morpheme. However, we will not discuss duality of structure in this chapter.

2.2 Major Components of Japanese Intonation

We describe the Japanese intonation system in terms of two major components: boundary pitch movements (BPMs) and *prosodic phrasing above the word level* (*prosodic phrasing*).

BPMs are tones that occur at the end of the prosodic phrase and contribute to the pragmatic interpretation of the utterance (Venditti,

[1] This is illustrated in the utterances of the Imaichi dialect shown in Figures 9.20 and 9.21. Here, the interrogative word *doko* 'where' or *dare* 'who' is focused, but the F0 peak is located in the post-focal word.

Maekawa, and Beckman 2008: 471), for example, as showing questioning, continuation, or emphasis. This information is sometimes regarded as "modality," which is defined as the mental attitude that a speaker assumes when s/he produces an utterance with a certain intention. According to Kori (1997: 190), modalities include questions, strong insistence, incredulity, and emphasis, which can be distinguished solely by intonation. For example, when *Ichirō ga hōmuran o utta* (Ichiro NOM homerun ACC hit.PAST 'Ichiro hit a homerun') is articulated with a rising pitch at utterance-final mora (i.e. with a rising BPM), the sentence is interpreted as a question, whereas it is interpreted as a statement without this BPM. While BPM is sometimes referred to as "sentence-final intonation" (Kori 1997: 190), this terminology is avoided in this chapter as BPM occurs not only sentence-finally but also sentence-medially.

Prosodic phrasing is defined as the grouping of words in an utterance through suprasegmental features. In Japanese, prosodic phrasing can signal the focused word in the sentence, the syntactic constituency, and so forth. For example, when the NP *utsukushii suishagoya no musume* (beautiful miller GEN daughter) is divided into two prosodic phrases, {*utsukushii*} {*suishagoya no musume*}, it is interpreted as 'the miller's beautiful daughter' (curly brackets indicate boundaries of prosodic phrases). When, in contrast, the NP is produced with a single prosodic phrase, {*utsukushii suishagoya no musume*}, it is interpreted as 'the daughter of the beautiful miller.' These two interpretations are a consequence of differences in the syntactic structure. The former has the structure [*utsukushii* [*suishagoya no musume*]] in which the adjective *utsukushii* 'beautiful' modifies the extended NP *suishagoya no musume* 'miller's daughter' (square brackets indicate syntactic boundaries). In contrast, the latter has the structure [[*utsukushii suishagoya no*] *musume*] in which the adjective modifies only the immediately following noun *suishagoya*.

3 Boundary Pitch Movements

3.1 Introduction

BPMs are tones that occur at the end of prosodic phrases. They include a slightly concave rising pitch movement, transcribed as LH% in the X-JToBI scheme (see Section 3.2), which typically occurs at the end of a question sentence. The sentence ending with a verb in a predicative form shown in Figure 9.1 is interpreted as a question when accompanied by LH% (left), whereas the same sentence is interpreted as a statement without LH% (right) (Uemura 1989; Japanese utterances can also have no BPM at all).

While LH% typically appears in question sentences, it does not always indicate a question. This is shown in Figure 9.2 where the sentence is

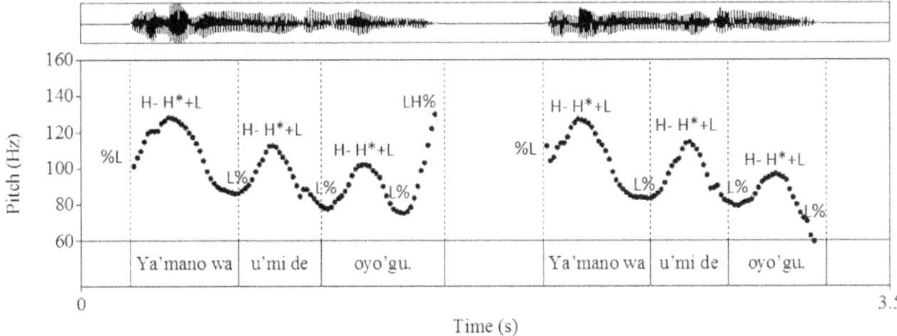

Figure 9.1 Question utterance with BPM and statement utterance without BPM. *Ya'mano wa u'mi de oyo'gu.* (LH%) (Yamano TOP sea LOC swim) 'Will Yamano swim in the sea?' (left) and 'Yamano will swim in the sea' (right). The mora assigned a BPM is /gu/, which is underlined in this caption.

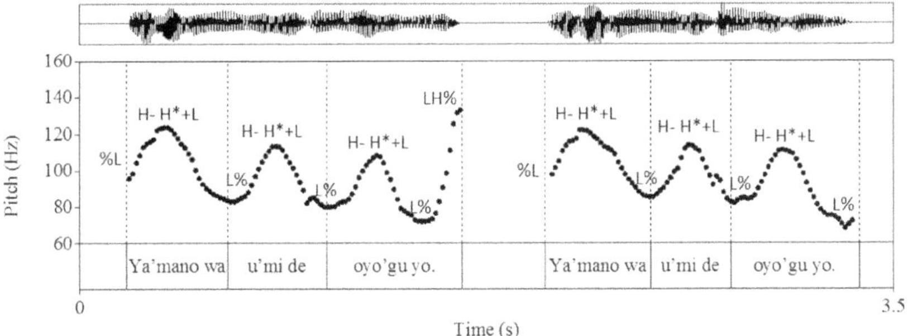

Figure 9.2 Statement utterances with and without BPM (LH %). *Ya'mano wa u'mi de oyo'gu yo.* (Yamano TOP sea LOC swim SFP) 'Yamano will swim in the sea.' The mora assigned a BPM is /yo/, which is underlined in this caption.

interpreted as a statement even with LH%, indicating that the meanings of BPM are more abstract, as will be described in the following section.

3.2 The BPM Inventory

LH% is not the only BPM in the inventory of Japanese BPM. As discussed in Section 3.4 below, there is disagreement over the number of BPMs. Figure 9.3 depicts the four main types of BPM indicated by the X-JToBI framework (Maekawa et al. 2002), the extended version of Japanese Tone and Break Indices, or the J_ToBI system (Venditti 2005), which owes its theoretical foundation to Pierrehumbert and Beckman's (1988) study. The four main types of BPM are H% (simple rise), HL% (rise–fall), LH% (scooped rise), and HLH% (rise–fall–rise). All the BPMs in this figure are attached to a phrase comprising a single word.

H% differs from LH% mainly in its F0 shape. In the case of H%, F0 starts rising at the beginning of the phrase-final mora, whereas in the case of LH% it starts in the middle of the final mora. In addition to this alignment

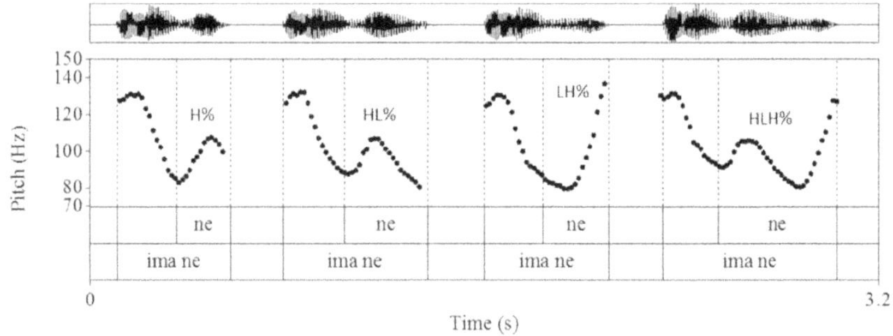

Figure 9.3 Main types of BPM. *Ima ne* (now SFP) 'Now.' The boundaries of the final mora /ne/ are marked.

difference, pitch range is generally (but not necessarily) smaller in H% than in LH% (Venditti, Maekawa, and Beckman 2008). The resultant F0 shape for H% is a linear rise with a smaller excursion while that for LH% is a concave or scooped rise with a larger excursion.

H% in the utterance-final position generally does not signal a question interpretation. Instead, it provides information, for example, that the speaker is insisting (Venditti, Maeda, and van Santen 1998) or that he is firmly persuading the listener to agree with what has been said (Uemura 1989). As will be discussed in Section 3.5, H% is sometimes referred to as an "emphatic" rise in other frameworks (Kori 1997; Uemura 1989) as it emphasizes the phrase to which it is attached. H% is also used, according to Uemura (1989), when the speaker is seeking approval, convincing the listener, inviting the listener's attention, or blaming. H% can appear utterance-medially, and, in this case, it can also lend prominence to the phrase in which it appears (Kori 1997; Yoshizawa 1960). It also signals a continuation of speech (Kori 1997).

LH% is most often observed at the ends of utterances and typically expresses a question. However, as mentioned in Section 3.1, LH% does not always convey the meaning of a question. Uemura (1989) summarizes the functions of this BPM as an expression of intimacy or a friendly attitude toward the listener.

HL% is a rise–fall BPM in which the beginning of the rise is at the onset of the phrase-final mora with the peak at the end of the rise aligned with the middle of the mora (close to its onset). After the rise, F0 falls at the end of the mora, and its duration is lengthened. The function of HL% is akin to H%: it imparts a prominence to the phrase that the BPM is attached to. In their perception study, Venditti, Maeda, and van Santen (1998) showed that HL% is perceived by the listener as explanatory and emphatic, and it is judged to signal continuation. Citing this study, Venditti, Maekawa, and Beckman (2008) summarize the functions of HL% by stating that listeners expect speakers to use HL% when they are explaining a certain point and want to focus attention on a particular phrase in their explanation.

The choice of H% or HL% at least partly depends on speaking style and spontaneity. An analysis of the impression rating assigned to talks in the Corpus of Spontaneous Japanese (CSJ, Maekawa 2003) showed that the rate of H% positively and negatively correlates with speaking style and spontaneity, respectively, while the rate of HL% negatively and positively correlates with speaking style and spontaneity, respectively (Maekawa 2006). In other words, listeners judge H% to be more formal and less spontaneous than HL%.

The F0 configuration of the former part of HLH% is akin to HL%; however, F0 rises again after the fall in the case of HLH%. The final mora is considerably lengthened. Venditti, Maekawa, and Beckman (2008) suggest that HLH% may be particularly characteristic of infant-directed speech (IDS) as it can give a wheeling or cajoling quality to the utterance to which it is attached. Indeed, an analysis of Japanese infant-directed speech using the RIKEN Japanese Mother–Infant Conversation Corpus (Mazuka, Igarashi, and Nishikawa 2006), which contains IDS and adult-directed speech (ADS) in Japanese, revealed a higher occurrence of HLH% in IDS than in ADS (Igarashi et al. 2013). However, this type of BPM occurs much less frequently than other types, even in IDS. It occurs only twelve times in eight hours of IDS produced by twenty-one mothers. The low frequency of HLH% is also confirmed by the CSJ analysis. It occurs only fourteen times in the forty-five hour core portion of the CSJ (Venditti, Maekawa, and Beckman 2008).

The X-JToBI framework describes types of BPM other than the four types discussed here (H%, LH%, HL%, and HLH%). These types are operationally considered to be variants of the main types of BPMs in X-JToBI (for details, see Igarashi 2015: Section 3.4).

The meanings of the BPMs described here are merely a first approximation. Unfortunately, no analysis of the meanings conveyed by BPMs is uncontroversial, and a comprehensive description is beyond the scope of this chapter. However, it is reasonable to point out here that the relations between forms and meanings in Tokyo Japanese BPMs seem to lack arbitrariness, and they fit comfortably into Gussenhoven's theory of *biological code* concerning form-function relations based on the effects of the production process's physiological properties on the speech signal (Gussenhoven 2004) (for a full discussion, see Igarashi 2015: 548–550).

3.3 How Many BPMs Does Japanese Have?

No consensus has emerged regarding the number of BPMs in Japanese. Moreover, few quantitative analyses have been conducted for BPMs. In the following paragraphs, we will discuss the extent to which researchers agree or disagree on the inventory of BPMs. Figure 9.4 is a schematic representation of the categorical boundaries of the rising BPMs.

Most researchers distinguish two types of rises: *information-seeking question rise* (InfoQ rise) and *prominence-leading rise* (Prom rise) (Venditti, Maeda,

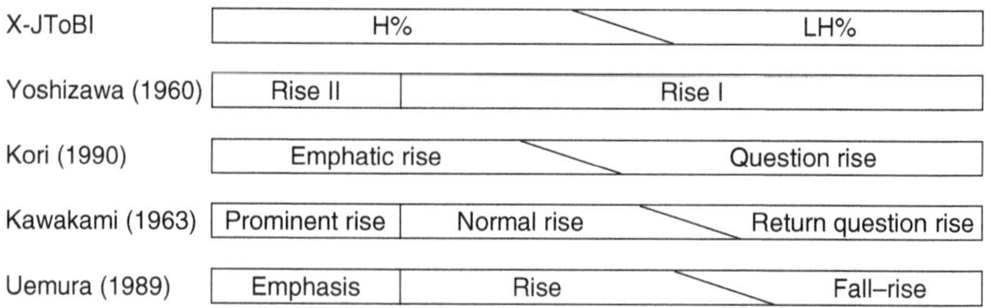

Figure 9.4 Schematic representation showing correspondences among categories of the rising BPMs identified by different researchers

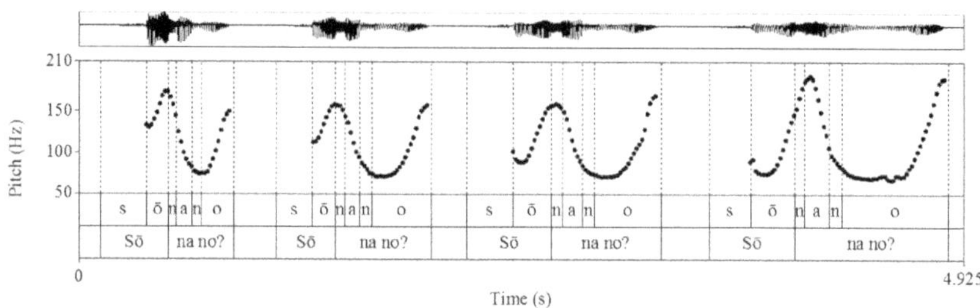

Figure 9.5 An InfoQ-IncreQ continuum. *Sō na no* (so COP NMLZ) 'Is it so?'

and van Santen 1998). The InfoQ rise typically occurs in a question ending, whereas the Prom rise typically occurs when a speaker is making an insistent statement, such as *Yameru!* 'I will definitely quit!'

In addition to these two rises, Kawakami (1963) and Uemura (1989) distinguish the InfoQ rise from what we may call the "incredulity question rise" (IncreQ rise) (Venditti, Maeda, and van Santen 1998). The IncreQ rise is typically observed in a question where the speaker is expressing disbelief, such as *Yameru?* 'Will you quit??' However, Venditti, Maekawa, and Beckman (2008) suggest that the InfoQ and IncreQ rises are the extreme endpoints of a continuum that includes many intermediate degrees of emphatic lengthening. The continuum between InfoQ and IncreQ is shown in Figure 9.5. They also point out that the gradient nature of the relation between the phonetic dimensions and the continuum of contrasting degrees of incredulity suggests an analysis analogous to the one proposed by Hirschberg and Ward (1992) for the uncertainty versus incredulity interpretations of the English rise–fall–rise contour (transcribed as L*+H L- H%).

Thus, defining the inventory of BPMs is far from trivial, and we cannot always rely solely on native speakers' intuition as their intuition in the case of intonational contrasts is less sharp than in the case of lexical tone contrasts (Gussenhoven 2004: 60). As exemplified in the InfoQ–IncreQ continuum, it is difficult to decide whether two phonetically different contours convey two categorically distinct intonational patterns or are merely phonetic variants of a single pattern. Researchers have recently been attempting to develop experimental methods for establishing intonational categories (for a discussion of the experimental approaches, see Gussenhoven 2004: 62–70).

4 Prosodic Phrasing

4.1 Double-layered Model

Prosodic phrasing is the grouping of words in an utterance. Although controversies still exist on the number of levels of prosodic phrasing in Japanese and their organization (for review, see Ishihara 2015: 570; Igarashi 2015: 527–529), this chapter, based on the X-JToBI framework, adopts the double-layered model, with the hierarchically organized *Accentual Phrase* (at the lower level) and *Intonation Phrase* (at the higher level).

4.2 Accentual Phrase

Japanese has two types of words: *accented* and *unaccented*. The former exhibit a pitch contour with a steep fall from high (H) to low (L) somewhere in the word while the latter show no such fall. In this chapter, the term *pitch accent* refers to this lexically specified pitch fall in the accented words. For example, *a'me* 'rain' has an accent on the initial syllable and is, therefore, an accented word, whereas *ame* 'candy' has no pitch accent and is, therefore, an unaccented word (the accented vowel is post-marked by an apostrophe). In addition to the presence or absence of pitch accent, its location in the word is also lexically specified; for example, *na'mida* 'tear' has an accent on the initial syllable, *nomi'ya* 'pub' on the second, and *atama'* 'head' on the final.

An Accentual Phrase (AP) is defined as having a delimitative rise to high around the second mora and a subsequent gradual fall to low at the end of the phrase and as having at most one lexical pitch accent. While a typical AP comprises one lexical word plus a following particle or multiple particles (e.g. *yama' ga* 'mountain NOM,' *niwa ni' wa* 'garden LOC TOP'), a single AP can often contain two or more lexical words. For instance, a noun with a genitive particle followed by another noun, such as *Hiroshima no omiyage* (Hiroshima GEN souvenir) 'a souvenir from Hiroshima,' often forms a single AP. Moreover, a particle can form its own AP. For example, in a sequence of an accented noun and a following accented particle, such as *nomi'ya ma'de* (pub up-to) 'to the pub,' the noun and the particle are often merged into a single accented AP, with the accent of the particle being deleted, as in *nomi'ya made*. Deaccenting of particles is, however, not obligatory (see Igarashi 2015: 538). When the accent is maintained, the particle forms its own AP.

The intonation contours of a single AP are described as a sequence of tones: an unaccented AP (1a), and an accented AP (1b).

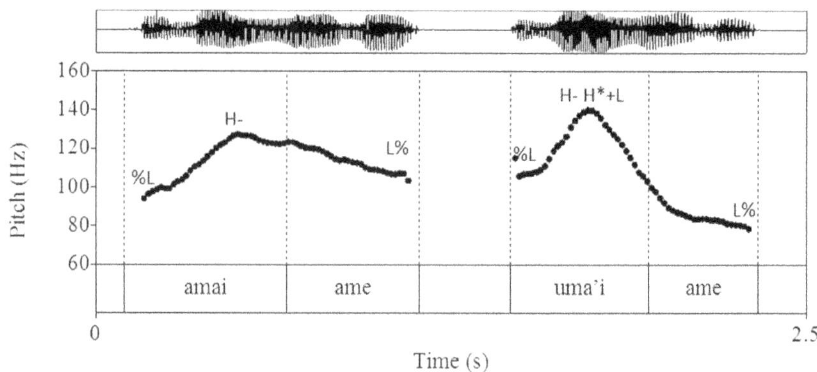

Figure 9.6 An unaccented AP *amai ame* 'sweet candy' (left), and an accented AP *uma'i ame* 'tasty candy' (right)

(1) AP tones
  a. Unaccented AP: %L H- L%
  b. Accented AP: %L H- H*+L L%

"H*+L" stands for pitch accent, where the asterisk indicates the tone associated with the mora that is governed by the accented syllable. (An accent is assigned to a syllable, but the accentual H is associated with a mora.) Henceforth, the mora with which the H tone of H*+L is associated will be referred to as the accented mora.

L tones with a "%" symbol are called *boundary tones*, with %L and L% being the initial and final boundary tones, respectively. The low tone found at the beginning of the AP is sometimes called the *initial lowering* in some frameworks (e.g. Haraguchi 1977). The H-tone is called the *phrasal high*. The %L and H- function as starting and ending points, respectively, of the AP's initial rise. The L% serves as the endpoint of a gradual pitch fall from H- in the case of an unaccented AP, or from L of H*+L in the case of an accented AP. In Figure 9.6, the unaccented adjective *amai* 'sweet' is combined with the following unaccented noun *ame* 'candy' into a single unaccented AP, where the %L H- L% pattern can be clearly observed.

4.3 AP Sequences

When a speaker produces fluent utterances of the sentences in (2), s/he groups the words into several APs. The syntactic branching structure is [A [N_1 N_2]], where A is an adjective and N is a noun followed by a particle but not [[A N_1] N_2]. The grouping of words into APs depends on the interaction of various factors such as word accentuation, syntactic branching, focus, and/or discourse structure (Venditti 2005). A typical prosodic phrasing of these sentences is shown in

Figures 9.7–9.10.[2] The rise at the end of these utterances is a LH% BPM, which was discussed in Section 3.

(2) a. *Amai jagaimo no nimono wa do're desu ka?*
sweet potato GEN stew TOP which COP INT
'Which are the sweet stewed potatoes?'

b. *Uma'i jagaimo no nimono wa do're desu ka?*
tasty potato GEN stew TOP which COP INT
'Which are the tasty stewed potatoes?'

c. *Amai zuwa'igani no nimono wa do're desu ka?*
sweet snow.crab GEN stew TOP which COP INT
'Which is the sweet stewed snow crab?'

d. *Uma'i zuwa'igani no nimono wa do're desu ka?*
tasty snow.crab GEN stew TOP which COP INT
'Which is the tasty stewed snow crab?'

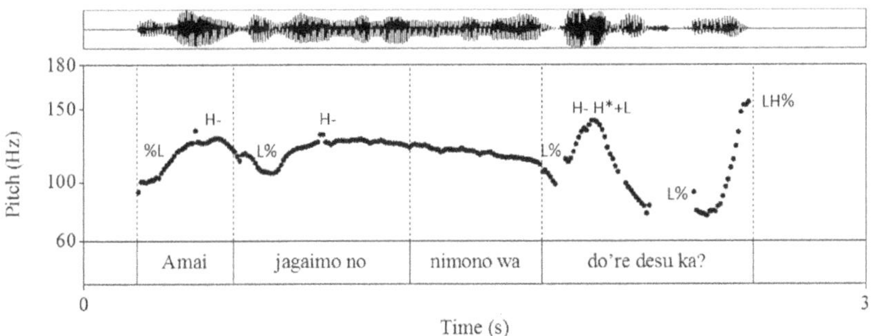

Figure 9.7 Phrasing at the AP level. *Amai jagaimo no nimono wa do're desu ka?* (sweet potato GEN stew TOP which COP.POL INT) 'Which are the sweet stewed potatoes?'

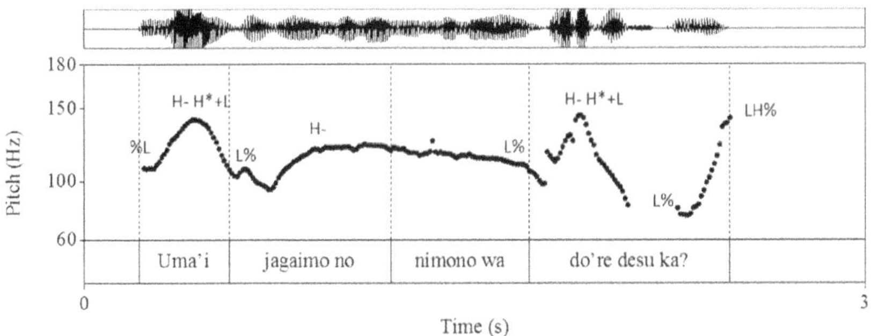

Figure 9.8 *Uma'i jagaimo no nimono wa do're desu ka?* (tasty potato GEN stew TOP which COP.POL INT) 'Which are the tasty stewed potatoes?'

[2] For a brief and specific description of intonation contours for combinations of unaccented and accented APs, see Vance (2009: Section 7.6).

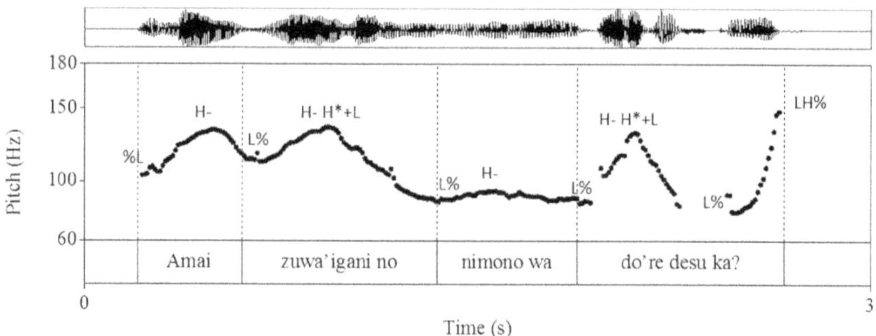

Figure 9.9 *Amai zuwa'igani no nimono wa do're desu ka?* (sweet snow_crab GEN stew TOP which COP.POL INT) 'Which is the sweet stewed snow crab?'

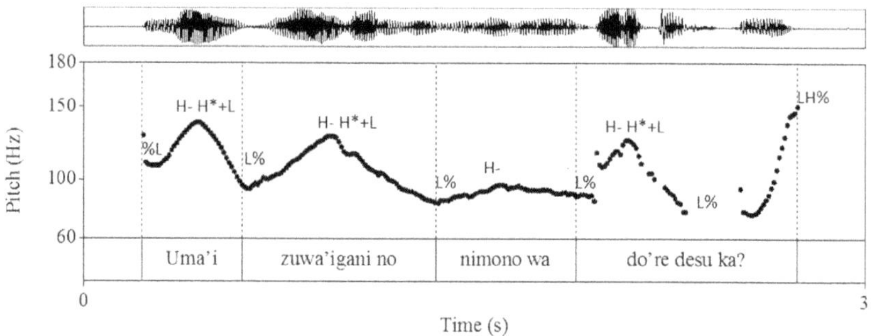

Figure 9.10 *Uma'i zuwa'igani no nimono wa do're desu ka?* (tasty snow_crab GEN stew TOP which COP.POL INT) 'Which is the tasty stewed snow crab?'

When a right-branching syntactic boundary exists, an AP boundary is frequently inserted. Thus in (2), the adjective *amai* or *uma'i* forms a single AP. When no right-branching boundary intervenes, an unaccented word and the word that follows it tend to be conjoined into a single AP. In (2a–b), therefore, two NPs *jagaimo no* and *nimono wa* are conjoined into an AP. When an accented word is followed by another word, the latter often forms its own AP (Vance 2008: Section 7.6) even if there is no right-branching boundary. Thus, in (2c–d), two NPs *zuwa'igani no* and *nimono wa* form separate APs. In all the examples in (2), the VP *do're desu ka* constitutes a single AP. Thus, prosodic phrasing in (2) can be couched in the form of (3), where parentheses denote the AP boundaries.

(3) Prosodic phrasing in (2)

a.	(amai)	(jagaimo no nimono wa)	(do're desu ka)
b.	(uma'i)	(jagaimo no nimono wa)	(do're desu ka)
c.	(amai)	(zuwa'igani no) (nimono wa)	(do're desu ka)
d.	(uma'i)	(zuwa'igani no) (nimono wa)	(do're desu ka)

4.4 Downstep and Intonation Phrase

The *Intonation Phrase* (IP) is defined as the prosodic phrase immediately above the AP in the hierarchy within which pitch range is specified. At the beginning of each new IP, the speaker chooses a new pitch range that is independent of the specification of the preceding AP (Venditti 2005: 175). This process is called *pitch reset*. The pitch range specification of IPs is closely connected with a phonological process called *downstep*. Through this process, the pitch range of each AP is compressed when it follows an accented AP. Downstep is displayed in Figure 9.11. The peak of the third AP is significantly lower when preceded by an accented AP (right) than when preceded by an unaccented AP (left).

When multiply accented APs form a single IP, downstep occurs iteratively, thus resulting in a staircase-like F0 contour, as demonstrated in Figure 9.12. However, in a sequence of four APs (in a syntactic phrase with a uniformly left-branching structure), as in Figure 9.11, the pitch range of the third AP is frequently expanded so that a staircase-like F0 is not

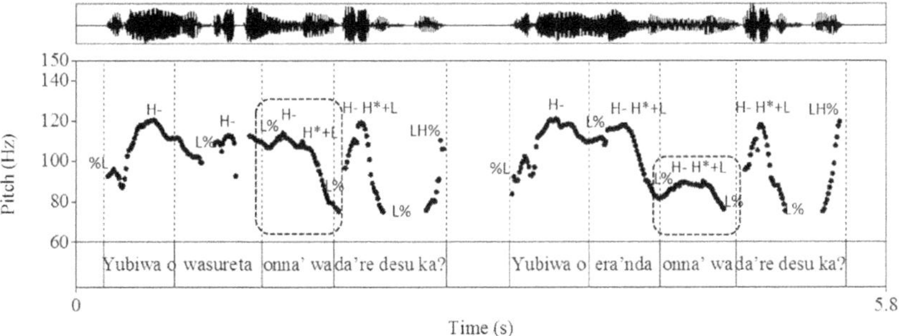

Figure 9.11 Downstep. An utterance without a downstep: *Yubiwa o wasureta onna' wa dare desu ka?* (ring ACC forgot woman TOP who COP.POL INT) 'Who is the woman that left the ring behind?' (left), and an utterance with downstep on the third AP: *Yubiwa o era'nda onna' wa da're desu ka?* (ring ACC chose woman TOP who COP.POL INT) 'Who is the woman that chose the ring?' (right). The relevant portions of the F0 contours are marked by broken-line boxes. Dotted vertical lines symbolize AP boundaries.

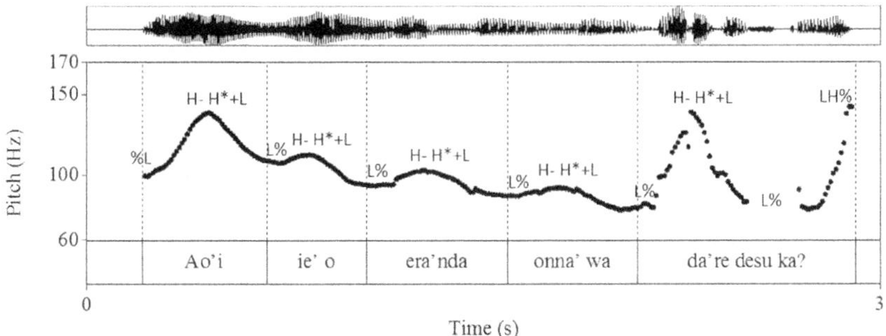

Figure 9.12 Successive downstep: *Ao'i ie' o era'nda onna' wa da're desu ka?* (blue house ACC chose woman TOP who COP.POL INT) 'Who is the woman that chose the blue house?' without the rhythmic effect. Vertical lines indicate AP boundaries.

observed. This effect is known as "rhythmic boost" (Kubozono 1988 [1993]: 220–223) and is shown in Figure 9.13, in which the pitch range of the third AP is larger than the preceding AP.

When the IP boundary is inserted, downstep is blocked at this boundary; that is, pitch reset occurs, and a new pitch range is specified to the IP. Various linguistic factors result in pitch reset at the IP boundary, including syntactic constituency and focus (Kawakami 1957; Kori 1997; Ishihara 2007; Kubozono 2007b). The pitch ranges of post-focal words in accented APs are significantly reduced, a process called *post-focal compression.* Pitch reset and post-focal compression are shown in Figures 9.14 and 9.15, respectively. The prosodic phrasing in the utterances in these figures is shown in (4), in which curly brackets represent the boundaries of the IPs.

(4) The prosodic phrasing in the utterances in Figures 9.14 and 9.15. Focused words are capitalized.
  a. {(na'oya no) (ane ga)} {(nomi'ya de) (no'nda)} (Figure 9.14, left)
  b. {(na'oya no)} {(ANE GA nomi'ya de) (no'nda)} (Figure 9.14, right)
  c. {(na'oya no) (a'ni ga)} {(nomi'ya de) (no'nda)} (Figure 9.15, left)
  d. {(na'oya no)} {(A'NI GA) (nomi'ya de) (no'nda)} (Figure 9.15, right)

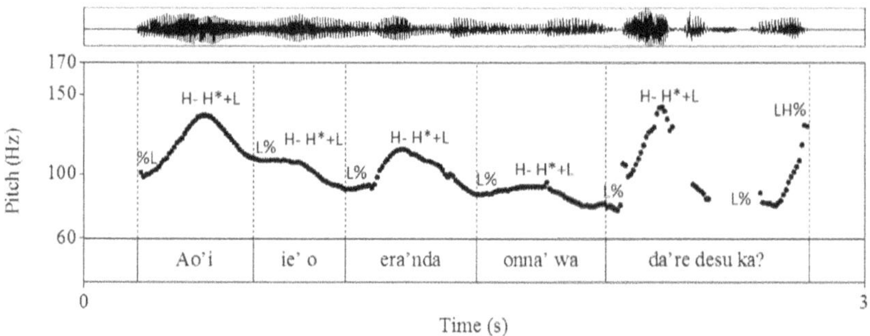

Figure 9.13 Successive downstep: *Ao'i ie' o era'nda onna' wa da're desu ka?* (blue house ACC chose woman TOP who COP.POL INT) 'Who is the woman that chose the blue house?' with the rhythmic effect. Vertical lines indicate AP boundaries.

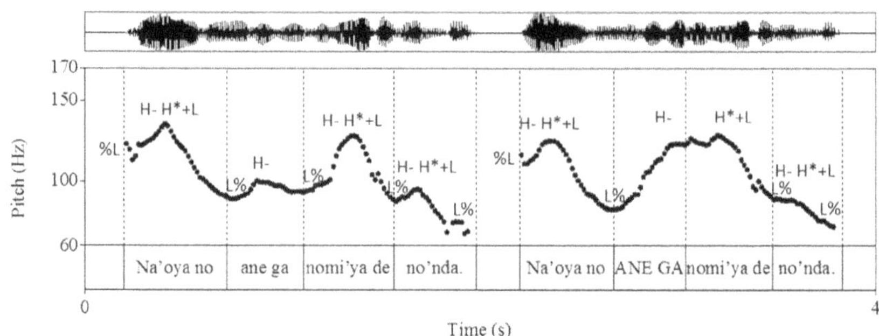

Figure 9.14 Pitch reset and post-focal compression: *Na'oya no ane ga nomi'ya de no'nda* (Naoya GEN sister NOM pub LOC drank) 'Naoya's sister drank in the pub,' without (left) and with (right) focus on the second unaccented AP *ane ga.* Focused words are capitalized.

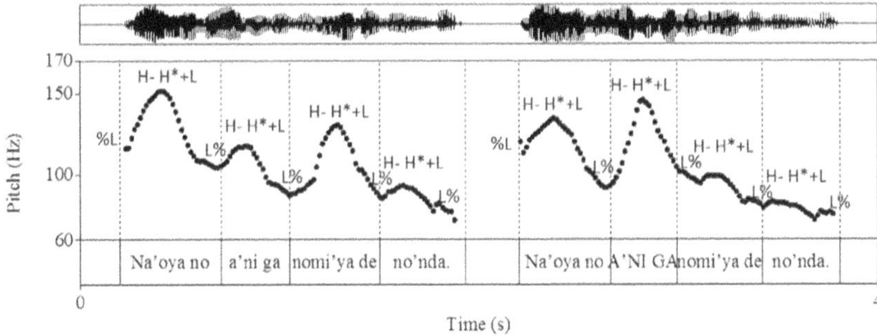

Figure 9.15 *Na'oya no a'ni ga nomi'ya de no'nda* (Naoya GEN brother NOM pub LOC drank) 'Naoya's brother drank in the pub,' without (left) and with (right) focus on the second accented AP *a'ni ga.*

5 Other Possible Intonational Contrasts

5.1 Intonational Contrasts in Phrasal Edges

Thus far, we have described the Japanese intonation system in terms of BPM and prosodic phrasing. They are both boundary-related prosodies, meaning that BPM is localized at the edges of prosodic phrases, which are signaled by a pitch movement localized at the phrasal edges. In other words, the locations where intonational tone occurs are not typically found in the middle of prosodic phrases in Japanese.

A marginal case is the presence or absence of downstep as discussed in Section 4.4. Downstep is manifested as the manipulation of the pitch range of the AP, which may be considered a global prosodic characteristic specific to the AP as a whole rather than a local event at the phrasal boundary. However, downstep is simultaneously a cue for the presence or absence of the IP boundary and thus may also be considered a prosodic event localized at the phrasal boundary.

On the other hand, more obvious intonational contrasts that can be described in terms of types of tones (such as H% versus HL%) or the presence or absence of tones (such as with versus without BPM) are undoubtedly localized in the phrasal edges. This restriction may be considered to be one of the typological characteristics of Japanese (for a full discussion regarding these putative typological characteristics, see Igarashi et al. 2013: 1286–1288 and Igarashi 2015: 556–563).

5.2 Possible Intonational Contrasts at the Beginning of the Phrase

In most studies of Japanese intonation, it is assumed that intonationally contrastive tones are localized at the phrasal *end* but not its beginning. However, Kawakami (1956) observed variability in the timing of the initial rise of the utterance-initial AP: rise aligned earlier or later with respect to

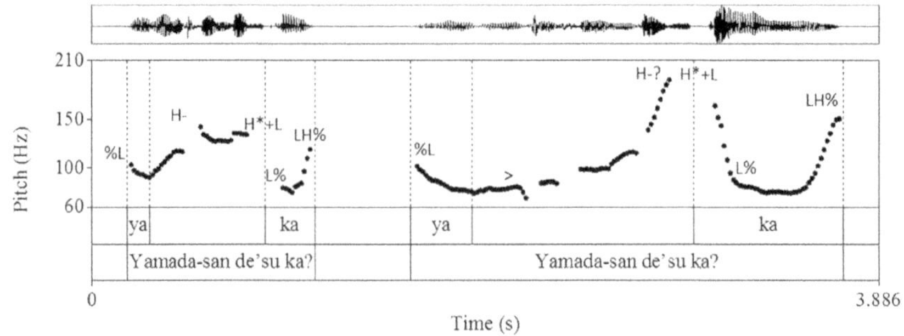

Figure 9.16 Utterances produced with a neutral attitude (left) and with suspicion (right). *Yamada-san de'su ka?* (Yamada COP.POL INT) 'Is it Mr. Yamada?' The boundaries of the first and final moras (/ya/ and /ka/, respectively) are marked to indicate their lengthening in the utterance with suspicion.

the phrasal boundary. He also proposed that the alignment varies according to the speaker's "emotions." In their experimental studies, Maekawa and Kitagawa (2002) showed that the F0 contour at the beginning of the utterance varies significantly depending on the speaker's attitude and intentions ("paralinguistic information," in their terms), such as admiration, disappointment, and suspicion. For example, in an utterance produced with suspicion, the beginning of the initial rise is delayed considerably, thus yielding a long stretch of low F0 before the rise, and the contour exhibits a concave shape in the rising movement (BPM at the end of the phrase is what is referred to as IncreQ rise in Section 3.3). An example of strong suspicion is shown in Figure 9.16 (left).

The delay of the initial rise, or the long low-pitched stretch at the beginning, may be considered a manifestation of intonational contrast. Further research is required to investigate whether this pattern is indeed contrastive or a mere variant of a single pattern. If the two contours shown in Figure 9.16 (i.e. non-delayed and delayed rise) are two contrastive intonational patterns, then we need to posit an intonational contrast at the beginning of the phrase as well. One possibility may be to posit a contrast in phrasal tones, such as a H- versus LH- contrast. Another may be to posit a %L vs. %LL contrast for the initial boundary tone.

5.3 Possible Intonational Contrasts in the Middle of the Phrase

Even if there is an intonational contrast at the beginning of the phrase, it is nevertheless localized at the phrasal edge. It must be noted, however, that the Japanese intonational contour is known to exhibit variability in the middle of the phrase.

In Section 4.2, we have seen that an unaccented phrase shows a gradual fall. The fall is accounted for by interpolation between H- and L% in the X-JToBI framework. However, Sugahara (2003), based on the inter-speaker variation found in her experimental results, claims that unaccented

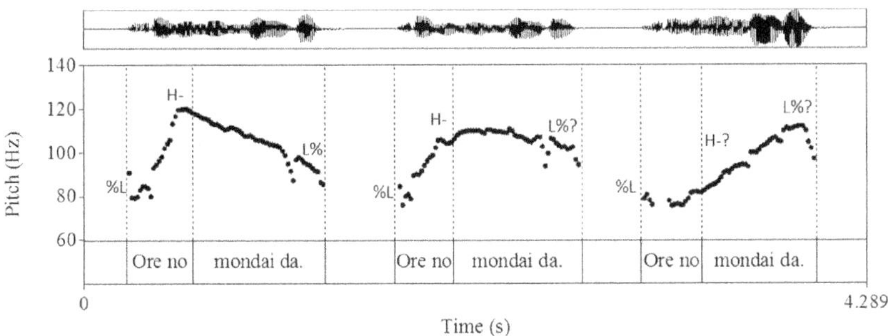

Figure 9.17 Variations in the contour of unaccented APs *Ore no mondai da* (I GEN problem COP) 'It's my problem.' An ordinal contour (left), a contour that would be accounted for by tone spreading (middle), and a rising contour without an apparent tone target (right).

phrases may have no gradual fall at all and may show a high plateau instead. Indeed, in Japanese spontaneous speech, it is not difficult to find unaccented phrases without a gradual fall. An example of a high plateau in an unaccented AP is shown in Figure 9.17 (middle). Gradual pitch fall (Figure 9.17 [right]) could merely be regarded as one possible realization of the pitch pattern. Future research should address whether the two contours (with a gradual fall and with a high plateau) are indeed due to two categorically distinct intonation patterns. If they are contrastive, then Japanese intonation should be regarded as having intonational contrast in the middle of an AP.

In addition to a high plateau (Figure 9.17 [middle]), a gradual rise without any turning point in the contour is also observed in an unaccented AP. Figure 9.17 (right) exemplifies an F0 rise from the beginning of the unaccented AP to the final mora, without apparent targets for H- and L% (although F0 rises throughout the utterance, it is interpreted as a statement rather than a question). If this contour results from the deletion of H-, then we need to define the contrast between L% and H% for the final boundary tone (not for BPM), in addition to the tone deletion rule for H- (thus, the contour may be interpreted as a combination of the initial boundary tone %L and a final boundary tone H%). In contrast, if the contour results from the dislocation (or delay) of H-, we must posit a tone deletion rule for L% and a rule modifying the alignment of H- (thus, the contour may be interpreted as a combination of the initial boundary tone %L and the phrasal H- without a final boundary tone). In any case, given that the contour is contrastive, we may need to assume an intonational contrast in the middle of the phrase, although these putative contrasts can still be regarded as those at the phrasal edges since edge tones such as phrasal high and boundary tones are involved in the contrasts.

Intonational contrasts existing in the middle of an AP, if any, have rarely been investigated. The reason for the scarcity of research can, in my view, be attributed to the low flexibility in variability in pitch contours in the middle of an AP. The middle of an AP in Japanese is allocated to lexical tone contrast, which is manifested as the location of a sharp pitch fall, if any. To preserve lexical tone contrasts, it is impossible to delete a sharp fall in the case of an accented AP or to implement an additional sharp fall in the case of an unaccented AP. In general, it is not usual for intonational effects to cause the neutralization of lexical tone contrasts in Japanese (Kawakami 1956).[3]

However, there are regional dialects of Japanese without any lexically contrastive tones; these are generally called "accentless dialects." They are expected to show more intonational contrasts as there are no restrictions imposed by lexical tones. Indeed, recent studies reveal that accentless dialects show more flexibility in varying the contours that may be involved in intonational contrasts (Maekawa 1997b; Igarashi 2014). Some of the contrasts occur in the middle of APs, as we will see in the following subsection.

5.4 Intonational Contrasts in the Accentless Dialects

Accentless dialects are widely scattered in non-contiguous areas of the Japanese archipelago. The high variability in the pitch contour of the accentless dialects is reported by Maekawa (1994, 1999) for the Kumamoto dialect spoken in Kyūshū in which the AP basically has a rise–fall contour, %L H- L%. However, this rise–fall shape shows considerable variability. First, the alignment of H- varies. As shown in Figure 9.18a, H- can appear on virtually any syllable within the AP while in Standard Japanese it is generally aligned with the second mora. This unstable H- is called a "wandering high" by Maekawa (1994). Second, a high plateau can be observed between the rise and fall in Figure 9.18b. Maekawa (1994) accounts for this plateau by assuming the spreading of H-. Finally, the fall at the end of the phrase can be unrealized as shown in Figure 9.18c. Henceforth, these three phenomena will be called *H wandering*, *H spreading*, and *L deletion*, respectively.

Igarashi (2014) demonstrated that the Koriyama dialect spoken in Fukushima Prefecture also shows H wandering. Figure 9.19 illustrates the contours of six tokens of the same wh-question 'What do you see?' produced by a single speaker. Each utterance comprises a single AP, and the rise at the end of the AP is due to a BPM: %L H- L% LH%. We see that the location of H- in the AP varies from one token to another.

[3] There is an obvious case in present-day Tokyo Japanese in which a specific intonational pattern causes lexical tone neutralization. It is the so-called "jumping intonation" (*tobihane inton shon*) (Tanaka 1993), which is used in an utterance ending with the word *na'i*, such as *Kawai'ku na'i?* 'It's cute, isn't it?,' and which, accompanying a variant of H% (called "hooked rise" by Kawakami 1963), deletes a pitch accent in what immediately precedes the word *na'i* as well as the one in *na'i*. Thus, the utterance *Kawai'ku na'i?* is produced with a single unaccented phrase *Kawaiku nai?* Jumping intonation has been diffused throughout the areas around Tokyo since the 1990s.

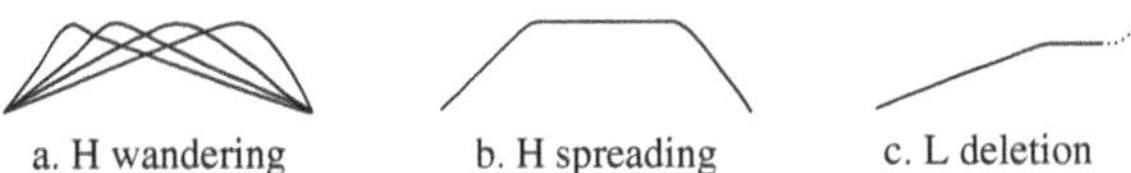

Figure 9.18 Variations in pitch contours in AP in the Kumamoto dialect

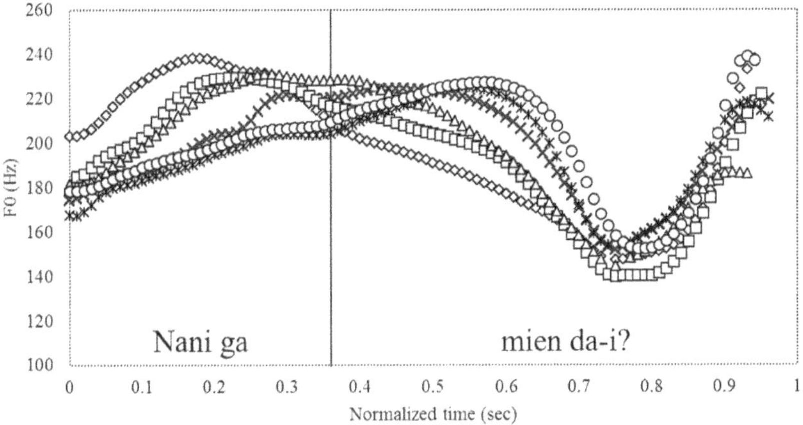

Figure 9.19 H wandering in the Koriyama dialect: *Nani ga mien da-i?* (what NOM visible. NMLZ COP-SFP) 'What do you see?,' produced by a female speaker born in 1957. Six tokens normalized along the temporal scale are overlaid.

H spreading can be observed in other accentless dialects. The two panels in Figure 9.20 contrast utterances without (left) and with (right) H spreading in the same wh-question produced by a single speaker in the Imaichi dialect spoken in the Northern Kanto district (Igarashi 2014: 482). Both utterances comprise a single AP with a BPM (LH%) at its end. The AP in this dialect also has a rise–fall contour (%L H- L%), although the rise tends to be more concave than that in the Kumamoto dialect. In the utterance in the top panel, F0 continuously rises from the beginning of the AP to around the middle of the third word and then falls toward the end of the AP. In the utterance in the bottom panel, a sharp initial rise ends around the beginning of the second word, followed by a high (slightly rising) plateau that persists until approximately the middle of the final word.

L deletion is also observed in the Imaichi dialect (Igarashi 2014: 482). Figure 9.21 shows two tokens of the same wh-question produced by the same speaker. Both utterances comprise two APs with a BPM at the end of the second AP. They differ, however, in that the fall seen in the second AP in the left panel is not found in that in the right panel.

As the observed variability in the contours is much more obvious here than in Tokyo Japanese, especially in the case of L deletion, it seems reasonable to assume that they are not merely phonetic variants of a single intonational category but are involved in intonational contrasts, conveying distinct pragmatic meanings. Issues concerning meaning differences in these

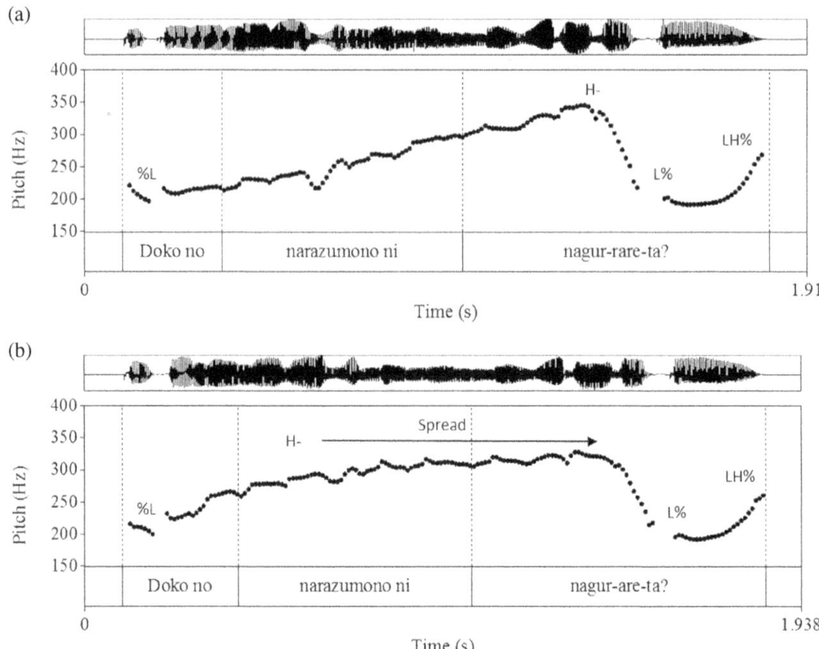

Figure 9.20 Utterances without (top) and with (bottom) H spreading in the Imaichi dialect: *Doko no narazumono ni nagur-are-ta?* (where GEN gang DAT punch-PASS-PST) 'What gang were you punched by?,' produced by a female speaker born in 1984.

contours are addressed in Maekawa's (1999) perception study of the Kumamoto dialect in which differing H- alignments affect the perceived politeness of the utterance, with a later alignment yielding more "polite" judgments. The utterance with the L deletion in combination with the latest H- alignment led to most "polite" judgments. Although further research is necessary to establish categorically distinct intonational patterns in the accentless dialects, it is suggested that intonational contrasts are involved in the different contours under investigation. This in turn suggests that more intonational contrasts exist in the accentless dialects than in Tokyo Japanese.

6 Conclusion

This chapter has provided an overview of the intonation system of Japanese. Japanese intonation can basically be described in terms of two edge-related components: BPM and prosodic phrasing. However, as discussed in Section 5, Japanese may have intonational contrasts in the middle of prosodic phrases; this aspect requires further investigation. An examination of the regional dialects of Japanese, as was conducted in Section 5.3, may shed new light on these issues.

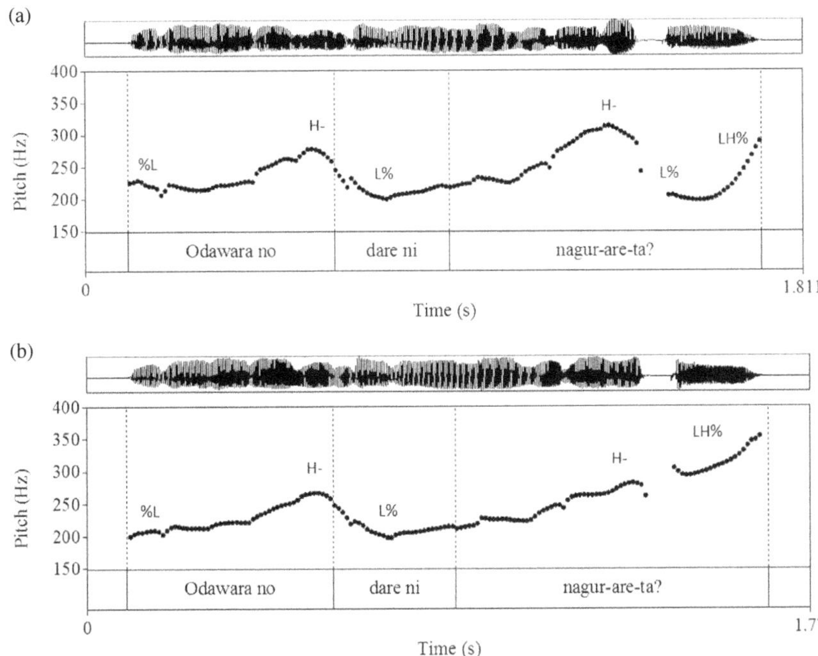

Figure 9.21 Utterances without (top) and with (bottom) L deletion in the Imaichi dialect: *Odawara no dare ni nagur-are-ta?* (Odawara GEN who DAT punch-PASS-PST) 'Who in Odawara were you punched by?,' produced by a female speaker born in 1984.

The inventory and meanings of Japanese BPMs discussed in Section 3 also require further investigation. Quantitative analysis based on the experimental methods discussed in Gussenhoven (2004: 62–70) will help resolve this issue.

Due to space limitations, the present chapter could not adequately discuss principles that may govern prosodic phrases in Japanese. In general, prosodic phrasing cannot be predicted from syntax alone (Bolinger 1972) and there can be multiple options for phrasing utterances with the same syntax. It is also known that extra-syntactic factors, such as utterance rhythm and length, as well as non-linguistic factors, such as speech rate, play a role in determining prosodic phrasing (see Shattuck-Hufnagel and Turk 1996) (for a review of recent discussions on issues in prosodic phrasing in Japanese, especially the prosody–syntax interface, readers may refer to Ishihara 2015).

10

Semantics and Morphosyntax of Mimetics

Kiyoko Toratani

1 Introduction

The late 1990s to 2000s marked an important turning point in mimetics research, with researchers moving toward investigating mimetics from a theoretical standpoint and away from the traditional descriptive approach. Topics investigated also diversified to include exploration of what role mimetics play in the lexicon and how they function in the grammar of Japanese. Despite numerous publications, however, many aspects remain unaccounted for. Important remaining topics include: how similar and dissimilar mimetics are to non-mimetic words (e.g. how mimetics participate in "verbal alternations" (see Section 4)) and whether to account for such similarities and differences the adopted linguistic theories can be applied without modification or whether some adjustment is required.

This chapter takes up some of recent developments, focusing on the semantic and morphosyntactic characteristics of Japanese mimetics.[1] Section 2 introduces fundamental characteristics of mimetics, with a focus on their unique morphophonology and semantics. It touches on the notion of lexical category, showing how it is difficult to determine. The chapter then turns to some much-discussed issues, honing in on three topics. Section 3 discusses the controversy centering on Kita (1997), who treats mimetics as constituting a word group *sui generis*. Section 4 outlines different approaches to the semantics of mimetic verbs and the realization of their arguments in clause structure. Section 5 critiques work on the

I am grateful to the two reviewers for their insightful comments, as these substantially improved the quality of the chapter. Unfortunately, many of their points remain unaddressed due to space limitations. I also thank Kimi Akita for his valuable comments, and Elizabeth Thompson for her editorial suggestions. The remaining errors, omissions and shortcomings are, of course, solely my responsibility.

[1] An alternative survey of literature on mimetics with different foci and topics can be found in Akita and Tsujimura (2016).

optionality of the quotative particle *to* with reduplicated mimetics. Section 6 contains concluding remarks.[2]

2 Characteristics of Mimetics

2.1 Morphophonological Characteristics

In the literature of traditional Japanese grammar, mimetics have been grouped together with native Japanese words (cf. Kageyama and Saito 2016). In recent literature, however, it is more common to treat mimetics separately from Japanese native words, following McCawley (1968), who treats Japanese vocabulary as constituting four types of lexical strata: native Japanese words, mimetics, Sino-Japanese words, and foreign words (loanwords from Western languages). This stratification is primarily based on phonological characteristics.

However, there are other reasons to suggest mimetics should be distinguished from native words. For example, mimetics have distinctive morphophonological forms. Akita (2009: 107–109) shows that mimetics fit into one of the fifteen "morphophonological templates," arguing that the templates can be used to differentiate mimetics from non-mimetic words. The templates cover information on accent, root types (mono- versus bimoraic) and morpheme types (reduplicated, suffixed). Table 10.1 shows the templates in square brackets, preceded by examples of mimetics.

In the table, the representations are adjusted from Akita's original. First, the templates are simplified by removing the pitch fall symbols (^). An acute accent is placed on some reduplicated mimetics (e.g. *gúigui* 'jerking'), thus contrasting accented and the unaccented forms. Second, the templates are rearranged from Akita's root-type-based organization to

Table 10.1 *Morphological types of mimetics*

(I) Reduplicated:		(II) Non-reduplicated	
Accented (Place of accent: Initial vowel):			
a. *búubuu* 'oink-oink'	[CVV-CVV]	h. *niQ(-to)* 'grinning'	[CVQ]
b. *púNpuN* 'reeking'	[CVN-CVN]	i. *zuN(-to)* 'zank'	[CVN]
c. *gúigui* 'jerking'	[CVi-CVi]	j. *poiQ(-to)* 'tossing'	[CViQ]
d. *méramera* 'blazing up'	[CVCV-CVCV]	k. *kaa(-to)* 'caw'	[CVV]
		l. *kuraQ(-to)* 'dizzy'	[CVCVQ]
Unaccented:		m. *doroN(-to)* 'vanishing'	[CVCVN]
e. *paNpaN* 'bursting'	[CVN-CVN]	n. *niyari(-to)* 'grinning'	[CVCVri]
f. *booboo* 'weedy'	[CVV-CVV]	(III) CVCCVri	
g. *betobeto* 'sticky'	[CVCV-CVCV]	o. *jiNwari* 'warmly moved'	[CVCCVri]

[2] Different terminology has been employed to refer to sound-symbolic words, mostly depending on the geographic region. "Mimetics" is commonly used for Japanese and Korean and *ideophones* for African languages and the indigenous languages in the American continents. Although a newer tradition uses the term *ideophone* to cover all regions, including Japan, this chapter follows the older tradition, using *mimetics*.

morpheme-type-based, grouping mimetics into three major morphological types: (I) reduplicated, (II) non-reduplicated, and (III) the CVCCVri forms (C=consonant, V=vowel).

Reduplicated mimetics have reduplicated roots, indicated by the presence of the morpheme boundary, which are represented by the hyphenation in the template (e.g. CVV-CVV). While many reduplicated mimetics are accented (on the initial vowel) as in (a–d), some are unaccented as in (e–g). The same sequence may be accented or unaccented, in which case, there is usually a contrast in meaning (e.g. *gátagata* 'rattling sound' versus *gatagata* 'rough (surface)').

Non-reduplicated mimetics, alternatively called "suffixed mimetics," consist of a root with a suffix: *N* (=mora nasal), *Q* (=mora obstruent), *V* (=Vowel), or *ri*.[3] As indicated in the parentheses following the examples in the table, mimetics in this group must be marked by the quotative particle *to* when they appear in a sentence (cf. (3)).

The CVCCVri form, sometimes labeled "emphatic" or "*ri*-suffixed," is similar to the reduplicated form in that it consists of four moras, but the internal structure is distinct: in the CVCCVri form, the accent falls on the last vowel before *ri*, and the consonant following the initial vowel is moraic (N or Q) as in *jiNwári* 'warmly moved.'

One of the most interesting characteristics of mimetics is that many denote an event or state (Kita 1997), whose function is normally carried out by verbs. Like verbs, mimetics express aspect (Hamano 1998) but unlike verbs, mimetics indicate aspect by their overall morphological form rather than by means of a particular aspectual morpheme.

While there is no coherent form–aspect correspondence in the CVCCVri form, there is a regular correspondence between the form and the aspectual meaning in both the reduplicated and non-reduplicated forms. Reduplicated mimetics, accented or non-accented, express unboundedness, which is characterized by various terms depending on the situation, such as: iterativity (*pókapoka* 'hitting repeatedly'), continuity or durativity (*kírakira* 'glittering continuously'), and atelicity (*zarazara* 'being coarse'). By contrast, non-reduplicated mimetics express boundedness, which may be characterized by terms such as: brevity (*kaa* 'a short cry of a crow'), completion of one cycle (*pokaQ* 'hitting once'), punctuality (*baN* 'a bang'), and telicity (*koroQ* '(someone) dies'). Moreover, the repetition of the form with a short phonological break iconically depicts the number of occurrences of the event. For example, *toN* expresses the sound of 'a knock,' but *toN toN* expresses 'two knocks,' or *toN toN toN* 'three knocks,' and so forth. Furthermore, if the form contains a prolonged vowel, it represents a prolonged duration. For instance, while *gyuQ* expresses a brief contracting motion of a hand, *gyuuuuuuQ* expresses that this contraction is maintained for a longer period. Most CVCCVri forms are aspectually non-specific. Although some may

[3] The form with *ri* in this group differs from the mimetics in III, as the latter must occur in the CVCCVri structure.

express boundedness if they have non-reduplicated counterparts, as in *paQkuri* 'split open' (cf. *pakuQ* 'pop open'), most express meanings other than aspect proper, such as degree (*meQkiri* 'considerably') and quantity (e.g. *taQpuri* 'a lot').

2.2 Semantic Characteristics

According to Hinton, Nichols, and Ohala (1994: 1), sound-symbolism refers to "the direct linkage between sound and meaning." As convincingly shown in Hamano (1998), Japanese mimetics are a quintessential example. For instance, in a CV-root-based mimetic, palatalization means "childishness" or "excessive energy," or the word initial *p* expresses the meaning of "taut surface; explosive movement" (p. 99), or the final *-ri* of a CVCV-root-based mimetic expresses "quiet ending" (p. 174). Japanese mimetics also display what Hinton, Nichols, and Ohala call "imitative sound-symbolism" wherein the word itself mimes the meaning, as with "onomatopoeic words and phrases representing environmental sounds" (p. 3), but the entire system goes far beyond the category of onomatopoeia.

In traditional Japanese grammar, mimetics are frequently classed into semantic groups (cf. Kindaichi 1978). The most common grouping is a tripartite classification of *giongo* 'phonomimes,' *gitaigo* 'phenomimes,' and *gijōgo* 'psychomimes' (translations due to Martin 1975: 1025). This classification is adopted in many recent linguistic studies.

(1) a. Phonomimes (*giongo*):

Animal cry:	*kórokoro*	'croaking of a frog'
Human voice:	*géragera*	'guffawing'
Sound:	*bashaQ*	'sound of a splash'
	páchipachi	'popping sound'

b. Phenomimes (*gitaigo*)

Manner:	*hírahira*	'fluttering'
	gúruguru	'going round and round'
Condition:	*kushakusha*	'being all crumpled'
	betobeto	'sticky'

c. Psychomimes (*gijōgo*)

Bodily sensation:	*múzumuzu*	'itchy'
	chíkuchiku	'prickling'
Psychological state:	*íraira*	'irritatedly'
	gaQkari	'feeling disappointed'

Phonomimes cover mimetics expressing an animal cry, a human voice, and sounds more generally. Japanese abounds in mimetics representing environmental sounds; for example, *bashaQ* 'sound of a splash,' *kátakata* 'rattling sound,' *páchipachi* 'popping sound.' Phenomimes cover expressions of manners (dynamic events) and conditions (states). Japanese has a variety of mimetics expressing manner of motion; for example, *pyókopyoko* 'hopping,' *gúruguru* 'spinning,' and *zúruzuru* 'sliding.' Japanese is also rich in mimetics expressing conditions that rely on tactility; for example, *betobeto* 'sticky,' *tsurutsuru* 'smooth' (Kindaichi 1978). Psychomimes cover two groups of mimetics: those expressing bodily sensations (e.g. *hírihiri* 'smarting pain,' *múkamuka* 'feel nauseous') and those expressing a psychological state (e.g. *íraira* 'irritatedly'). As implied by the translations, mimetics usually have detailed meanings (e.g. *yóchiyochi* 'toddling'). Because of this, they are sometimes characterized as "hyponyms" and contrasted with verbs which tend to have a more neutral meaning (*aruku* 'walk'). The three types with detailed meanings in (1) constitute the semantic prototypes of mimetics.

It is essential to recognize three points about these semantic categories. First, the relationship between a mimetic and its categorical affiliation is not necessarily one-to-one, as mimetics may simultaneously express what is gathered through different senses. For instance, *kórokoro* can be categorized as a phonomime or a phenomime, as it can simultaneously express what is sensed from both audition (a light sound an object emits as it rolls) and vision (the manner of a small object rolling). This sharply contrasts with a non-mimetic word like *mawaru* 'roll'; this vision-based descriptive word leaves the sound the object emits unexpressed, even if it has emitted a sound. Second, many mimetics extend their meanings across (sub-)categories. For instance, mimetics expressing bodily sensation are often extended to denote a psychological state, as in *dókidoki*, which can mean 'heart pounding' (sensation) or 'feeling nervous' (psych.), or a phonomimic sense is extended to a phenomimic sense, as in *káchikachi*, which can mean 'click click' (sound) or 'being very hard' (condition) (see Akita 2013 for more on this topic). Third, a small group of "demimeticized" (Akita and Usuki 2016: 255) mimetics resides outside the tripartite classification in (1). Many take the CVCCVri form, expressing concepts such as quantity *taQpuri* 'a lot,' degree *meQkiri* 'considerably,' or pace *yuQkuri* 'slowly.' It is important to make note of their presence when making a generalization about mimetics in Japanese; they do not fit into the semantic prototypes in (1), even though they are mimetics in terms of their morphophonological forms.

2.3 Lexical Category

Among the forms introduced in Table 10.1, there is a major division in the pattern of how the mimetics behave in a morphosyntactic context (there are exceptions, notably CVCCVri),[4] with each group associated with a different lexical category.

[4] Exceptions include the following: some CVCCVri mimetics, which usually occur as adverbs or verbs, can take copula *da* (*doNyori da* 'be gloomy,' *yuQkuri da* 'be slow'), or have a prenominal usage marked by *no* (*doNyori no tenki* 'gloomy weather,' *yuQkuri no peesu* 'slow pace'), suggesting an adjectival or nominal status; some of the accented reduplicated mimetics, usually classed as adverbs, behave as nouns when they are used nomenclaturally (*kúnekune (-san)* '(Mr./Ms.) *wiggling* (person)') or in children's language (*wáNwaN* 'doggy' (cf. Tamori and Schourup 1999: 59)).

The unaccented reduplicated mimetics (e.g. *tsurutsuru* 'being slippery') occur in some of the same environments as nouns [N] and adjectival nouns [AN], although semantically, they are adjectival in that they express a state.

(2) a. *Kore wa tsurutsuru (/ki/gōka) da.* [N/AN]
this TOP MIM wood/gorgeous COP.NPST
'This is *slippery* (/wood/gorgeous).'

b. *Tsurutsuru (/gōka/ mizu) ni natta.* [N/AN]
water COP.ADV became
'It became *smooth* (gorgeous/water)'

c. *tsurutsuru (/ki) no yuka* (cf. *?tsurutsuru na/*ki na yuka*) [N]
COP.ATT floor
'*slippery* (/wooden) floor'

d. *gōka na yuka* (cf. *gōka *no yuka*) [AN]
gorgeous COP.ATT floor
'gorgeous floor'

e. *Yoru made sono tsurutsuru ga tsuzuita.* [N]
night till that MIM NOM continued
'That *smoothness* continued till night (after brushing my teeth with the toothpaste).'

In the predicate position, the unaccented reduplicated mimetic is accompanied by the copula *da* as in (2a). This follows the pattern of N such as *ki* 'tree' and AN such as *gōka* 'gorgeous,' both of which require *da*. Similarly, as a complement of *naru* 'become,' the mimetic requires *ni*, following the pattern of both N and AN (see (2b)). In contrast, the mimetic in the prenominal position follows the pattern of nouns, requiring *no* to modify the head noun (see (2c)). The AN's pattern, which usually requires *na* (see (2d)), seems less acceptable, though an Internet search indicates the form with *na* is also used, albeit much less frequently (see Uehara 1998 for the similar characteristic displayed by non-mimetic ANs). Further, the mimetic can be preceded by the demonstrative *sono*, following the pattern of nouns (e.g. *sono hon* 'that book') (see (2e)), but many ANs cannot be preceded by a demonstrative (**sono gōka* 'that gorgeous'). This distribution suggests that, overall, unaccented reduplicated mimetics more closely follow the morphosyntactic patterns of nouns.

The remaining large majority (accented reduplicated, non-reduplicated and CVCCVri forms) are usually classed as adverbs, as they syntactically modify the verb or adjective that co-occurs with them in the sentence. As adverbs, mimetics appear marked by the quotative particle *to*, which is obligatory for non-reduplicated forms (3a) but syntactically optional for the accented reduplicated (3b) and the CVCCVri forms (3c), as indicated by the parentheses around *to* (Tamori and Schourup 1999: 65–68).

(3) a. *Kodomo ga nikoQ to waratta.* [Non-reduplicated] [Adv.]
child NOM MIM QUOT laughed
'The child laughed *with a smile.*'

b. *Kodomo ga níkoniko (to) waratta.* [Reduplicated, accented] [Adv.]
MIM QUOT
'The child laughed *smilingly.*'

c. *Ocha o yuQkuri (to) nonda.* [CVCCVri] [Adv.]
tea ACC MIM QUOT drank
'I drank tea *slowly.*'

Furthermore, these three forms can be used as verbs, as exemplified below; in such cases, the mimetics are followed by a light verb *suru* 'Lit. do.' These forms are usually called "mimetic verbs" with *suru* carrying the tense.[5]

(4) a. Non-reduplicated: *mukaQ to suru* 'get angry,' *shiN to suru* 'become quiet,' *pitaQ to suru* 'fit,' *karari to suru* 'dry'

b. Reduplicated, accented: *múkamuka suru* 'feel angry,' *píNpiN suru* 'be healthy,' *húsahusa suru* 'be affluent,' *pásapasa suru* 'dry'

c. CVCCVri: *gaQkari suru* 'get disappointed,' *hiQsori suru* 'be quiet,' *huNwari suru* 'be fluffy,' *gaQshiri suru* 'firm'

Beyond this major division, it is not easy to assign a category to mimetics. For one thing, it is unclear whether the mimetics in (4) (without *suru*) should be assigned a category at all, when the entire sequence with *suru* is already classed as verb (see Sells 2017 for more on this topic). For another thing, mimetics can appear in a sentence without any verbs as in (5a–b) or in isolation as in (5c).

(5) a. *Shachō wa uriage-zō ni niNmari.*
president TOP sales-increase at MIM
'The president (is) *grinning* (looking) at the increase in sales.'

b. … *totsuzen no kōtsūjiko no shirase ni urouro.*
sudden GEN car.accident GEN news to MIM
'(The mother got into) *panic* to hear the sudden news of (her son's) car accident.'
(Tamori and Schourup 1999: 88)

c. *SutoN.*
MIM
'(Something) fell.'

[5] The verb *iu* 'say' can occur in a fashion similar to *suru*: when the mimetic is more iconic to the event it depicts (*hyúuhyuu iu* '(the wind) howls'), *iu* is used, but if it is less iconic (*iraira suru* 'become irritated'), *suru* is used (see Hamano 1988: 138–139; Toratani 2015: 135–137). In addition, a small group of mimetics may co-occur with other semantically lighter verbs, such as *naru* 'become' and *kuru* 'come' (e.g. *kaQ to naru* 'flare up in anger,' *mune ni guQ to kuru* 'be pierced to the heart').

The puzzle is whether the mimetic is an adverb in (5a–b), as Tamori and Schourup (1999: 88) assume (in their view, the clause-mate verb has simply been elided), or all the mimetics in (5) are verbal, since they are, arguably, the constituting element of the predicate, even though the mimetic has no morphosyntactic indications of a verbal element (i.e. there is neither an inflectional morpheme nor a verbal element such as *suru* or *iu*).

Given the heterogeneous patterns, it does not seem appropriate to accept the existence of a lexical category called "mimetics," despite claims to the contrary in references to sound-symbolic words in other languages (cf. Newman 1968). The inquiry must remain open as to whether mimetics have a lexical category at all, as questioned in Tsujimura (2001). Alternatively, can mimetics be grouped into a traditional lexical category, such as noun and verb (or even a new hybrid category)? A final unresolved point of inquiry is how forms are related in the word-formation process.

3 Semantic Uniqueness of Mimetics

3.1 Two-dimensional Semantic Representation

Kita's work (1997) is an important cornerstone in the research history of the semantics of mimetics. It paved the way for a reoriented focus, moving from a morphophonological descriptive account of the word group – mimetics – to an explanatory investigation of why mimetics are "unique," with a special focus on their semantics. His discussion illuminated various characteristics of mimetics hitherto taken for granted, trivialized, or simply neglected. These include: (i) the underlying principle of the form-meaning relationship of mimetics is iconicity; (ii) the semantics of mimetics have a direct appeal to sensory, motor, and affective aspects. Both characteristics clearly set the semantics of mimetics apart from those of prosaic words.

To capture the unique semantics of mimetics, Kita claims that it is necessary to posit what he calls a "two-dimensional semantic representation," whereby the semantics of mimetics are distinguished from those of non-mimetic words. Namely, non-mimetic words belong to "the analytic dimension" in which "[a] thought or experience is represented as a proposition," whereas mimetics belong to "the affecto-imagistic dimension" where "different facets of an experience are represented [which] include the affective, emotive, and perceptual activation in an experience" (p. 387). To defend the two-dimensional model, Kita argues that "the semantics of a mimetic and that of other parts of a sentence are not fully integrated with each other despite the fact that they are syntactically integrated" (p. 388).

While Kita's contribution cannot be emphasized enough, his arguments are not problem-free. First, Kita's proposal is a direct challenge to Jackendoff's "The Conceptual Structure Hypothesis," which states:

"There is a *single* level of mental representation, *conceptual structure*, at which linguistic, sensory and motor information are compatible" (1983: 17, emphasis in original). Kita simply says this "*single* level of mental representation" is only for non-mimetic words (1997: 380, 409), naturally assuming the conceptual structure is unable to cover the semantics of mimetics. He takes no notice of Jackendoff's point that the conceptual structure is expected to "be rich enough in expressive power to deal with all things expressible by language . . . [and] to deal with the nature of all the other modalities of experience as well" (1983: 17). This seems to imply that Jackendoff's system is intended to be able to cover the semantics of mimetics. Kita neither explains why Jackendoff's model is inadequate nor elucidates why having some unique semantic characteristics alone guarantees an independent dimension for mimetics. Second, Kita (1997) claims that, while the semantic representation of mimetic adverbs belongs to the affecto-imagistic dimension, that of "nominal mimetics" belongs to both the analytic and the affecto-imagistic dimension.[6] As Tsujimura (2001: 416) aptly notes, the use of the categorial status (the notion belonging to the analytic dimension) as a key criterion for assigning mimetics to the affecto-imagistic dimension is irrational. Third, Kita makes a generalization about mimetics without encompassing all types of mimetics. As noted in Section 2.2, some mimetics express prosaic word-like meanings, deviating from the semantic prototypes. For these mimetics, the dimensional assignment leads to a clash. For instance, *taQpuri* 'a lot' must belong to the affecto-imagistic dimension since it is a mimetic, but at the same time, it must belong to the analytic dimension since it is a quantifier. Fourth and finally, when there is a certain linguistic behavioral difference between mimetic and non-mimetic words, Kita automatically attributes it to the dimensional difference, without exploring other possible causes. Examples include a phenomenon of negation, a semantic redundancy, and certain selectional restrictions, as elaborated below.

3.2 Linguistic Evidence of the Need to Separate the Dimension for Mimetics

3.2.1 Negation

Some earlier work on sound-symbolic words argues sound-symbolic words and negation are incompatible. For instance, Diffloth notes: "[In Korean] one cannot negate the ideophone itself but only the appropriateness of a given ideophone to describe a certain situation" (1972: 446, note 4). Interpreting Diffloth's comment to mean "metalinguistic negation is the only possible interpretation" for mimetics, Kita uses an example like (6) to substantiate his argument.

[6] Another category (mimetic verbs) is added as an element represented in both dimensions in Kita (2001).

(6) a. *Tama ga shizukani korogatta no de wa nai.*
ball NOM quietly rolled NMLZ COP TOP NEG
(i) 'It was not the case that a ball rolled quietly.'
(ii) 'It was not a ball that rolled quietly.'
(iii) 'It was not rolling quietly that a ball did.'

b. *Tama ga gorogoro to korogatta no de wa nai.*
ball NOM MIM QUOT rolled NMLZ COP TOP NEG
(i) *'It was not the case that a ball rolled *gorogoro*.'
(ii) ??'It was not a ball that rolled *gorogoro*.'
(iii) *'It was not rolling *gorogoro* that a ball did.'
(adapted from Kita 1997: 390)

Example (6) contains the negated *no da* construction, wherein the content of the clause marked by the nominalizer *no* is negated entirely or partially. The two sentences minimally contrast in the element expressing the manner: (6a) has a non-mimetic adverb *shizukani* 'quietly,' and (6b) contains a mimetic *gorogoro* 'manner of a heavy object rolling.' According to Kita, with the non-mimetic adverb, negation can apply to various parts of the sentence, thus yielding different interpretations, such as (i–iii) in (6a), but the same is not true of the sentence with the mimetic, as indicated by the marks representing downgraded degrees of acceptability, such as (i–iii) in (6b). Kita explains (6b) is acceptable if the mimetic is prosodically emphasized, in which case, the sentence can be given a metalinguistic negation interpretation.[7] Though he does not provide the entire sequence, it is understood that (6b) can be followed by a sentence like *Korokoro to korogatta no da* 'It was *korokoro* ('manner of a light object rolling') that (it) rolled,' which rejects the heaviness of the weight of the ball but not the occurrence of the ball's rolling per se. The contrast between (6a) and (6b) obtains, he argues, because "logical negation ... [is] an operation in the analytic dimension" (1997: 390); that is, (6a), with all the elements from the analytic dimension, can participate in logical negation, but (6b) cannot, as it contains a mimetic, an element which does not belong to the analytic dimension.[8]

For Tamori and Schourup (1999: 156), (6a) and (6b) are not qualitatively very different, and they provide examples like (7), showing logical negation is indeed operative.

(7) a. *Gorogoro to korogatta no wa tama de wa naku, taru datta.*
MIM QUOT rolled GEN TOP ball COP TOP NEG barrel was
'It was not a ball that rolled *gorogoro*, but was a barrel.'

[7] It remains to be examined if the presence/absence of *to* affects the interpretation of negation in (6b), as questioned by one of the reviewers.

[8] A few mimetics accompany negation (*nai* NEG), often obligatorily; for example, *manjiri to mo shi-nai* 'cannot get a wink of sleep,' *ochiochi nemure-nai* 'cannot get a good night's sleep' (cf. Akita 2012: 81). Needless to say, these negation-friendly mimetics run counter to Kita's proposal.

b. *Tama ga shita koto wa gorogoro to korogaru koto*
ball NOM did event TOP MIM QUOT roll event
de wa naku, ikioiyoku hazumu koto de atta.
COP TOP NEG vigorously bounce event COP existed
'What the ball did was not rolling *gorogoro*, but was bouncing vigorously.' (Tamori and Schourup 1999: 157)

These examples show that the negation of part of the proposition is possible for the semantic argument *tama* 'ball' in (7a) and for the event including the manner expressed by the mimetic in (7b), even though Kita questions such interpretations, as in (6b-ii) and (6b-iii) (for a fuller range of examples in Japanese and English, see Tamori and Schourup 1999: 154–160).

Tamori and Schourup (1999: 158) rightly conclude that if (6b) is awkward at all, it stems from the violation of a general pragmatic condition that the sentence should have one focus. Example (6b) is awkward as it has two focus-bearing elements: the negation and the mimetic.

3.2.2 Semantic Redundancy

The second piece of evidence which leads Kita (1997) to claim the need to distinguish between the two dimensions is the absence of semantic redundancy observed in an example like (8). In the description of a fast-walking event, (8a) contains a mimetic *sutasuta to* 'manner of walking hurriedly,' and (8b) has a non-mimetic adjunct *isogi-ashi de* 'with hurried steps,' with both modifying the verbal phrase *haya-aruki o shita* 'did a fast-paced walking.'

(8) a. *Tarō wa sutasuta to haya-aruki o shita.*
TOP MIM QUOT haste-walk ACC did
'Taro walked hurriedly.'

b. *#Tarō wa isogi-ashi de haya-aruki o shita.*
TOP hurried-feet with haste-walk ACC did
'Taro walked hastily hurriedly.' (adapted from Kita 1997: 388)

According to Kita (1997: 389), even when the mimetic co-occurs with a verbal phrase with a similar meaning, as in (8a), the sentence remains felicitous without being wordy (because the mimetic comes from the affecto-imagistic dimension, distinct from the analytic dimension to which the other phrase belongs). But if the mimetic is replaced by an adjunct as in (8b), the sentence becomes infelicitous, as it causes semantic redundancy (because all elements belong to the analytic dimension).

Tsujimura (2001) points out that the wordiness in (8b) is caused by the repetition of virtually the same meaning in *isogi-ashi de* and *haya-aruki o*, that is, "both refer to feet and describe the manner of fast walking" (p. 411).

Meanwhile, the lack of wordiness in (8a) can be explained by the fact that "*sutasuta to* refers to fast walking but also expresses smoothness of movement" (p. 411), that is, two different things are expressed. Accordingly, the sentence is rendered felicitous. Tsujimura's point is corroborated in the following constructed example.

(9) #*Uta ga umai hito wa goman-to gorogoro iru.*
song NOM skilled person TOP large.numbers-in MIM exist
'There are many people in large quantities who are good at singing.'

Example (9) has a mimetic *gorogoro* and a non-mimetic adverb *goman-to*, both meaning 'in large numbers.' Kita's theory would predict the sentence to be felicitous, as the semantic representations of the words belong to different dimensions, but this is not the case; the sentence sounds redundant, as both the mimetic and the non-mimetic have practically the same meaning. As this example implies, the semantic coverage of the two words must be first examined to determine redundancy before considering semantic dimension.

3.3 Selectional Restrictions

Kita claims mimetics impose "selectional restrictions" on the theme objects, but "[i]n general, mimetics never impose restrictions on [the] agent" (1997: 404).[9] Accordingly, in (10) *gorogoro* 'manner of a heavy object rolling' requires that the object be heavy but the heaviness cannot refer to the weight of the agent, as the acceptability contrast in the translation below indicates.

(10) *Dareka ga tama o gorogoro to korogashita.*
someone NOM ball ACC MIM QUOT rolled
a. 'Somebody rolled a heavy ball.'
b. *'Somebody heavy rolled a ball.' (adapted from Kita 1997: 403)

Tsujimura (2001: 412) cogently points out that the oddity of the (10b)-reading comes from the fact that the mimetic is simply inappropriate to describe the subject. That is, *gorogoro* in (10) describes a motion of an object that rolls. Even if it is used in a transitive sentence like (10), the fact remains that it describes something about the object, not about the subject. Naturally, the (10b)-reading is unavailable.

Tsujimura further shows that the unavailability of the (10b)-reading is not because the mimetic never imposes a restriction on the agent, as in some instances, the mimetic does precisely that.

(11) *Gamu o kuchakucha suru*
chewing.gum ACC MIM do
'Somebody is chewing gum.' (adapted from Tsujimura 2001: 413)

[9] The term is revised from "selectional restrictions" to "compatibility requirements" in Kita (2001).

In (11), Tsujimura notes, "the agent must be a human being. If the mimetic does not impose a selectional restriction on the agent, it could be a dog or a bird, or even a car, none of which would be acceptable" (2001: 413).

In short, not all Kita's arguments are convincing. This does not require us to deny that mimetics have unique semantics. Far from it. Kita's work has caused other researchers to take the semantics of mimetics very seriously. The influence of mimetics on the interpretation of event participants or "argument structure" is an important issue, especially when the mimetic is used as a verb, as discussed in the next section.

4 Mimetic Verbs and Verbal Alternations

One of the major concerns of work dealing with the theories of the syntax-semantics interface is how to account for the ability of one verb to co-occur with a different set of arguments or with a set of arguments realized in distinct encoding, depending on the morphosyntactic context. This phenomenon is sometimes called "verbal alternation" and can take several forms. For instance, in valency alternation, a labile verb such as *eat* can be used monovalently, as in *Kim ate*, or bivalently, as in *Kim ate the apple* (cf. Kulikov and Lavidas 2014). In locative alternation, such as *Lee spread paint on the wall* versus *Lee spread the wall with paint*, the two arguments – the entity being acted upon (*paint*) and the location affected by the action (*wall*) – appear in distinct morphosyntactic codings in the respective portrayals, keeping the actor (*Lee*) constant (e.g. Iwata 2005).

Verbal alternations have been approached from two theoretical standpoints, *projectionist* and *constructionist* (cf. Levin and Rappaport Hovav 2005; Van Valin 2013). According to Levin and Rappaport Hovav, "the fundamental assumption [of projectionism is] that a verb's lexical entry registers some kind of semantically anchored argument structure, which in turn determines the morphosyntactic expression – or projection – of its arguments" (2005: 186). In contrast, constructionist theorists posit that "the lexical entry of the verb registers only its core meaning . . . and this core meaning combines with the event-based meanings which are represented by syntactic constructions themselves or are associated with particular syntactic positions or substructures" (2005: 190). In other words, on the one hand, projectionist theories posit a specific representation for the lexical entry of the verb, and this determines the syntactic structure of the clause (e.g. Foley and Van Valin 1984); constructionist theories, on the other hand, posit an underspecified representation for the verb while postulating the construction as the supplier of the rest of the necessary information (e.g. Pustejovsky 1995).

Tsujimura (2005) is perhaps the first to extend these two positions to discuss the syntactico-semantic characteristics of mimetic verbs, a verbal form in which a mimetic is followed by *suru* (cf. (4)). She discusses the case of multiple sets of arguments attributed to the polysemy of a mimetic verb. She offers a constructionist account, addressing the difficulty of decomposing the image/iconicity-based meaning of mimetic verbs, in comparison with prosaic verbs: "The so-called 'meaning' of a mimetic verb should not be attributed solely to the mimetic word itself, but rather it results from more global information obtained throughout a sentence in which the mimetic verb appears" (2005: 139). To prove her point, she discusses an instance like (12).

(12) a. *Doa no totte ga burabura-suru.*
door GEN knob NOM MIM-do
'The door knob is loose.'
b. *Tarō ga kōen o burabura-shita.*
NOM park LOC MIM-did
'Taro strolled leisurely in the park.'
c. *Tarō ga uchi de burabura-shi-te iru.*
NOM home at MIM-do-CONJ exist
'Taro is being lazy at home.'
d. *Tarō ga ashi o burabura-suru.*
NOM leg ACC MIM-do
'Taro swings his legs.' (adapted from Tsujimura 2005: 147)

This example features the mimetic verb *burabura-suru*. As the translation suggests, the mimetic verb can have multiple meanings, depending on the context: (i) to sway to and fro, (ii) to stroll, or (iii) to idle the time away. Tsujimura argues that without the aid of co-occurring NPs and the morphological cues on the nouns and the verb, the verb's meaning cannot be determined. For instance, (12a) and (12d) have the same verbal form, both expressing the sense of swaying.[10] The precise meaning is attained by referring to the co-occurring NPs: (12a) shows the intransitive frame with an inanimate NP; together they yield the stative meaning of the object being loose. By contrast, (12d) shows the transitive frame with the nominative-marked agent and the accusative-marked body part; together they yield the dynamic sense of the agent's swinging action. If the agent NP co-occurs with an *o*-marked NP expressing a spacious place where people usually take a walk, as in (12b), the verb yields the sense of strolling, but with a *de*-marked NP expressing the sense of a home where someone usually stays and relaxes, the verb yields the idling sense as in (12c). In short, "these varying 'meanings' are not attributed to the mimetic verb alone, but should be deduced from the construction in which it appears" (2005: 148).

Eschewing the constructional argument, Kageyama (2007) articulates a projectionist view whereby "mimetic words are inherently outfitted

[10] Tsujimura's (2005) original example lists the causative morpheme *sase* but this is removed here so the discussion can focus on the non-causative form *suru* 'do.'

with rather clear-cut conceptual meanings" (p. 30). In his proposal, Kageyama decomposes the meaning of a mimetic verb into two parts, the mimetic and *suru* 'do,' each represented by a Lexical Conceptual Structure (LCS). The LCS of *suru* has a skeletal representation and serves as the template into which the LCS of the mimetic is "integrated" via "Semantic Incorporation" (p. 46). Kageyama divides the LCS for *suru* into two groups: one with Agent or Experiencer subjects (subdivided into Type 1 through Type 4), and the other with Theme subjects (subdivided into Type 5 through Type 7). For instance, one of the senses of *burabura suru* (introduced in (12b), glossed as 'stroll leisurely') is classed as Type 3; it contains "verbs of locomotion designating continuous movement in random directions in a place" (p. 54). Example (13) illustrates the LCS for the mimetic verb.

(13) a. Type 3 *suru*: [$_{\text{EVENT}}$ x CONTROL [. . .]]
b. Mimetic: x MOVE $_{\text{<Manner } \alpha\text{>}}$ [$_{\text{Route}}$]
(e.g. *burabura*: [x MOVE $_{\text{<Manner SWAYING>}}$ [$_{\text{Route}}$ the park]])
c. Mimetic verb: [$_{\text{EVENT}}$ x CONTROL [$_{\text{EVENT}}$ x MOVE $_{\text{<Manner } \alpha\text{>}}$ [$_{\text{Route}}$]]]
(adapted from Kageyama 2007: 56, 59)

Type 3 *suru* has a skeletal meaning of an event controlled by the subject x, as represented in (13a). To this, the meaning of a mimetic, shown in (13b), is integrated. Here, the LCS indicates that x moves in a particular manner (where the variable α is replaced by the specific manner expressed by the mimetic such as 'swaying' in the case of *burabura*) in a certain place, to be indicated after "route" (e.g. the park). Example (13c), the LCS of the mimetic verb, presents the outcome of Semantic Incorporation, yielding the reading, "the subject x controls his own movement along a Route" (p. 59). In his in-depth discussions of examples like (13), then, Kageyama shows the semantic composition of mimetic verbs can be achieved "without resorting to the notion of Construction" (p. 34).

Elsewhere, I offer another projectionist view, working within the framework of Role and Reference Grammar (RRG) (Toratani 2013). RRG is, categorically, a projectionist theory, but it does not alienate the notion of "constructions." Following Van Valin's (2013) analysis of verbal alternations, which incorporates Pustejovsky's (1995) constructional theory or "co-composition," I take a consolidating position; the seemingly opposing views that center on mimetic verbs are, in fact, complementary, that is, the projectionist account corresponds to information-processing from the speaker's perspective, and the constructionist account corresponds to information-processing from the hearer's perspective. In other words, in the former, the speaker knows exactly which verb to use, pulling it from the lexicon to make the utterance (represented as semantics-to-syntax linking). By contrast, in the latter, the hearer must rely on the morphosyntactic or constructional clues, as well as the meanings of the lexical items, to arrive at the precise meaning of the verb and the entire sentence (represented as syntax-to-semantics linking).

As far as semantic representation is concerned, the meaning of mimetic verbs can be decomposed, in step with Kageyama (2007), but the representation differs from Kageyama's in that the mimetic verb is analyzed as having a lexical entry of its own, not as having two components: the LCS of the mimetic and the LCS of *suru*. For instance, the third sense of *burabura-suru* introduced in (12c) '(someone) is being lazy (at home),' is represented as **do´** (x, [**loaf.around´** (x)]) (Toratani 2013: 52).

Meanwhile, Tsujimura revisits her constructional view of mimetic verbs to posit two types of mimetics: those that parallel prosaic verbs with the "conventionalized and fossilized" (2014: 304) meanings typically listed in (mimetic) dictionaries, and those that do not. In the former case, Tsujimura agrees with Kageyama (2007): a "unified analysis for mimetic and prosaic verbs" is valid (Tsujimura 2014: 304). But in the latter, she emphasizes a difference, saying they "exhibit a high degree of extension to innovative meanings and a relative freedom of argument structure possibilities, far beyond the level to which prosaic verbs have access." For instance, speakers may use a mimetic verb, such as *gachagacha-suru* on the fly, *mutatis mutandis*, intending to mean "some chaotic situation such as doing odds-and-ends that lack organization" (2014: 307), presumably basing it on the dictionary meaning of 'a rattling/clattering noise.'

As this summary indicates, verbal alternations involving mimetic verbs require more intense investigation. The two works adopting the projectionist position (Kageyama 2007; Toratani 2013) make a good start, but both rely on a rather simple decomposition to represent the meaning of mimetics. While it may be sufficient for the purpose of syntax-semantics linking, it is likely not fine-grained enough to encapsulate the detailed and elastic aspects of the meanings of mimetic verbs which distinguish them from prosaic verbs, as Tsujimura (2014) argues. A challenge for projectionist theorists, then, is to develop a richer representational system, capable of handling the unique aspects of the meanings of mimetic verbs. A similar challenge should be issued to constructionist theorists. To date, to the best of my knowledge, no work has formally illustrated the precise mechanism whereby the underspecified meaning of a mimetic verb can receive a specific reading when placed in a specific context.

Whichever stance is taken, how the verbal alternations of mimetic verbs relate to those of non-mimetic verbs and what the (non-)relatedness implies to semantic and morphosyntactic theories, in general, remain unclear.

5 Marking Alternation on Reduplicated Mimetics

Another topic now generating considerable interest is the optionality of marking by the quotative particle *to* on reduplicated mimetics used adverbially. As introduced in (3), *to* is obligatory for non-reduplicated mimetics but is syntactically optional for reduplicated mimetics. The central question is what determines the choice of one marking over the other. The literature to date suggests different factors are at work, independently or intertwiningly. Some syntactic and semantic factors are introduced below.

5.1 Syntactic Condition

The relevance of the marking distinction to syntactic realization of mimetics is first discussed in Tamori (1980). He notes *to*-marking is usually optional for reduplicated mimetics in normal clause-internal position, such as *pakupaku* 'munch-munch' (cf. (14a)), but it becomes obligatory at the postposed position (cf. (14b)) and a preferred choice at the preposed position (cf. (14c)).[11]

(14) a. *Jon ga pakupaku to/Ø pan o tabeta.*
NOM MIM QUOT bread ACC ate
'John ate the bread, with a *munch-munch.*'

b. *Jon ga pan o tabeta, pakupaku to (*Ø).*
NOM bread ACC ate MIM QUOT
'John ate the bread, with a *munch-munch.*'

c. *Pakupaku to (??Ø) Jon ga pan o tabeta.*
MIM QUOT NOM bread ACC ate
'With a *munch-munch* John ate the bread.'

(adapted from Tamori 1980: 165)

While Tamori (1980) pioneers in relating the mimetic's marking distinction to the syntactic position, his discussion focuses on the clause-external positions, leaving the clause-internal positions untreated.

Following up on the topic, elsewhere I examine literary texts (309 tokens) to investigate how reduplicated mimetics distribute within a clause. I find a more dominant pattern of Ø-marked forms occupying the immediately preverbal position (151/187=81%) than *to*-marked forms (58/122 = 48%) (Toratani 2006).[12] Although the results reveal a tendency, a critical question remains unconsidered. Is *to*- or Ø-marking obligatory for some mimetics at the immediately preverbal position, and if so, what types of mimetics are they? Section 5.2 partially addresses the issue, but for more on the topic, see Akita and Usuki (2016) and Toratani (2017).

5.2 Semantic Condition

The literature suggests that the distinction of *to*/Ø-marking is related to different semantic factors. For instance, mimetics expressing abstract notions tend to be Ø-marked (e.g. frequency: *chokuchoku-Ø iku* '*frequently* go,' degree: *meQkiri-Ø heru* '*drastically* reduces' (Tamori and Schourup 1999: 68–69). In addition, the marking can help identify which verb/adjective the mimetic is modifying (Toratani 2006: 419). For instance, (15) has a mimetic *gorigori* 'sound of grating' with two potential hosts: *futoi* 'thick' and *mawasu* 'turn.'

[11] Although (14c) is judged awkward by Tamori (1980) as indicated by his two question marks, the (14c)-type sentences where reduplicated mimetics are preposed are found in literary texts, albeit infrequently: *Kusukusu okāsan wa waratta* '*Stifle-stifle* Mom laughed.' (Source: Yoshimoto, Banana. 1991. *Kitchin* [Kitchen]. Tokyo: Kadokawa, p. 27.)

[12] The group difference is endorsed as statistically significant in Akita and Usuki (2016: 251).

(15) a. *Mata* *gorigori* *to* *futoi* *kubi* *o* *mawasu.*[13]
again MIM QUOT thick neck ACC rotate
'Again, (he) rotated his thick neck *gorigori* (= with audible noises).'

b. #*Mata* *gorigori* *futoi* *kubi* *o* *mawasu.*
again MIM thick neck ACC rotate
'Again, (he) rotated his *noisily* thick neck.'

If the mimetic is bare (i.e. Ø-marked) as in (15b), it favors a reading in which the element next to it is taken to be its host, yielding an infelicitous reading (as *gorigori* and *futoi* are semantically incompatible), but if it is *to*-marked as in (15a), it allows a reading whereby the verb in the distance is interpreted as its host, yielding the felicitous reading (as *gorigori* and *mawaru* are semantically compatible).

Beyond these, another much-discussed semantic factor is concerned with the mimetic-host predicate relation. Elsewhere, I argue that the distinction of *to*/Ø-marking indicates whether the mimetic co-occurs with a particular type of host predicate.

(16) *To*-marking indicates a "semantic mismatch between the predicted host and the host that actually co-occurs, whereas Ø-marking suggests a match" (Toratani 2006: 419).

This applies to the contrast observed in (17).

(17) a. *Kare* *wa* *nikoniko* *warat-te* *iru.*
he TOP MIM laugh-CONJ exist
Lit. 'He is laughing *smilingly* (He is smiling).'

b. *Kare* *wa* *nikoniko* *to* *akarui.*
he TOP MIM QUOT cheerful
Lit. 'He is cheerful, smiling.'

Example (17b) has a bare (i.e. Ø-marked) mimetic. This is consistent with (16) because the mimetic–host relation is considered a match. Mimetics typically co-occur with a verb belonging to the mimetic's superordinate category. *Warau* 'laugh' is considered to belong to the superordinate category of the mimetic as it subsumes the meaning of the mimetic *nikoniko* 'smilingly,' thereby qualifying as the predicted host of the mimetic. Example (17b) has a *to*-marked mimetic. This is also consistent with (16). Here, the mimetic–host relation is considered a mismatch, as the host *akarui* 'cheerful' does not belong to the superordinate category of the mimetic; naturally it is an "atypical host," or an unpredicted host.

Although the marking distinction in (16) seems intuitively reasonable, the distinction turns out to be less straightforward. Example (16) suffers from a vague usage of the term "predicted host," which, in turn, builds on

[13] The text comes from: Murakami Haruki. 2006. *Afutā dāku* [After dark]. Tokyo: Kōdansha, p. 112.

an unexplained term "typical host." Without clear definitions, the task of prediction concerning *to*/*Ø* marking is practically impossible.

That said, if the criteria can be set, the empirical validity of (16) can readily be tested. For the sake of argument and for present purposes, I searched literary texts and gathered 317 instances of reduplicated mimetics that occur at the immediately preverbal position; I then examined whether the marking of the mimetics conforms to the prediction made by (16), assuming "typical hosts" refer to the verbs/adjectives listed as part of the entry in a mimetic dictionary; for example, *mawaru* 'turn' is the typical host for the mimetic *kurukuru* 'roll-roll.'[14] If (16) is tenable, we should expect two types of reduplicated mimetics: Ø-marked mimetics co-occurring with their typical hosts, and *to*-marked mimetics co-occurring with their typical hosts. This turns out not to be the case, however. When the two variables (the marking and the host) have two values each (*to*/*Ø*, typical/atypical, respectively), we get four logical combinatory possibilities. As Figure 10.1 shows, all combinations are found in my examples (the number represents token frequency or the ratio to the total).

Examples for each combination are shown as follows:[15] (a) Ø-marked mimetics with typical hosts (*níkoniko warau* 'laugh *smilingly*,' *óioi naku* 'cry *boohoo*,' *púkapuka uku* 'float *bobbingly*'); (b) Ø-marked mimetics with atypical

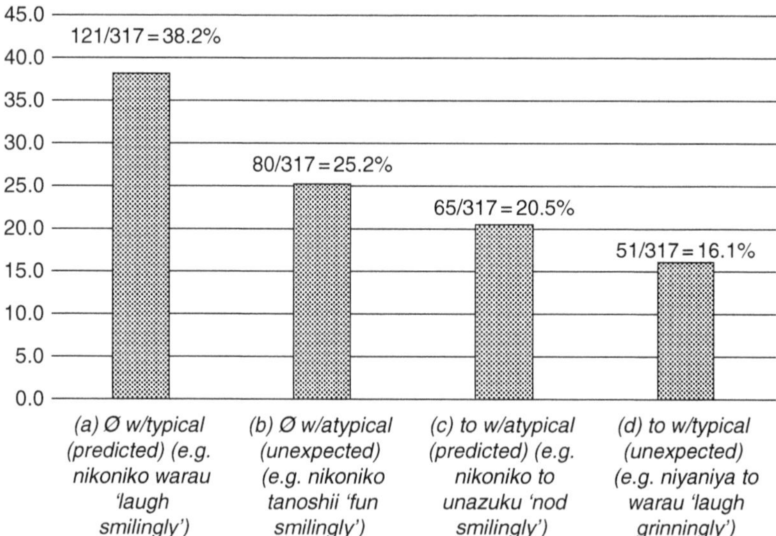

Figure 10.1 Distribution of *to/Ø*-marked mimetics

[14] The data exclude: (i) mimetics expressing an abstract concept such as *sorosoro* 'be about time to do something,' as these are usually not associated with any particular verbs; (ii) mimetics co-occurring with *iu* 'say,' *suru* 'do' and their causative counterparts, as these are posited to form a tighter morphosyntactic unit than mimetic adverbs (Akita and Usuki 2016: 269).

[15] One of the reviewers of this chapter asked how the Ø-marked mimetics relate to mimetic verbs with *suru*. One response is provided in Akita and Usuki (2016). They argue that the two forms take different constructions: the bare mimetic predicate construction (*búrabura yureru* 'sway *danglingly*') and the mimetic-'do' construction (*búrabura suru* 'dangle'), with the former syntactically looser than the latter.

hosts (*níkoniko tanoshii* 'fun *smilingly*' [instead of *warau* 'laugh'], *nóronoro kurasu* 'live *sluggishly*' [instead of *susumu* 'move forward'], *hírahira oyogu* '(goldfish) swim *wavingly*' [instead of *chiru* 'scatter']); (c) *to*-marked mimetics with atypical hosts (e.g. *níkoniko to unazuku* 'nod *smilingly*' [instead of *warau* 'laugh'], *kúnekune to aruku* 'walk *meanderingly*' [instead of *ugoku* 'move'], *súrusuru to shimaru* 'close *smoothly*' [instead of *suberu* 'slide']); and (d) *to*-marked mimetics with typical hosts (e.g. *níyaniya to warau* 'laugh *grinningly*,' *súyasuya to neru* 'sleep *peacefully*,' *pyónpyon to tobihaneru* 'jump *frisking around*'). Of these, the combinations in (a) and (c) are expected from (16), but those in (b) and (d) are not expected.[16]

The puzzle is why there are (b)- and (d)-type combinations at all.[17] In the case of the latter, some suggest the mimetic is *to*-marked when it is the focus-bearing element of the sentence (e.g. Toratani 2006: 419–420). In other words, the mimetic is the sole carrier of new information, with the verb carrying old information, introduced in the immediately preceding discourse (Lambrecht 1994). Even if all the instances in (d) can be assumed to be motivated by the notion of focus, the (b)-type combination, such as *níkoniko tanoshii* 'fun *smilingly*,' remains unexplained. At least, the dictionary-based determination of typicality of host does not work well for an account of the distribution of *to*/*Ø*-marked reduplicated mimetics. That is, their distribution is not as simple as (16) assumes. A closer examination of the contexts may shed more light on the issue.

6 Concluding Remarks

This chapter outlines some fundamental characteristics of mimetics and provides a critical survey of recent literature. While many issues remain unsettled, the past two decades have seen some much-needed research breakthroughs. Among other things, researchers have worked to situate the discussion cross-linguistically, to diversify the methods of inquiry by incorporating experiments and corpora (e.g. Shinohara and Uno 2013), and to appeal to different theoretical frameworks and notions (e.g. Iwasaki, Sells, and Akita 2017). Such endeavors inspire new questions while shedding welcome light on certain characteristics of mimetics likely to have gone unnoticed in the descriptive accounts dominating earlier studies. As most current work resorts to a small set of cognitive-functional-based theories, future work may glean different insights from other linguistic theories and approaches.

[16] The predicted group contains more instances ((121+65)/317=59%) than the unexpected group ((80+51)/317=41%) ($\chi^2(1)=7.81$, $p<.01$).

[17] It is possible to consider the (b)-type examples showing the influence of "colloquial particle drop," following Akita and Usuki (2016: 253, note 7).

11

Events and Properties in Morphology and Syntax

Taro Kageyama

1 Introduction

Based on a semantic distinction between stable properties and dynamic events, this chapter attempts to open up a new perspective on the interaction of form and meaning observed in certain unruly phenomena in Japanese that constitute a major challenge for general theories of morphology and syntax. The term *property* (also called *quality* or *attribute* in the literature on lexical aspect) refers to stable features of an entity that are supposed to remain intact through the passage of time, whereas the term *event* (also called *eventuality* or *situation*), when paired with property, is intended as a general notion covering dynamic events/actions and temporary states that may change as time progresses. This opposition can be readily understood by comparing two English sentences: (i) *The rope broke all of a sudden*, with the ergative *break* representing an event that happened at a particular place at a particular time; and (ii) *This rope won't break easily*, with the middle verb *break* describing an inherent quality of the rope that holds regardless of place and time.

In Western linguistics, the event-property distinction has been extensively discussed under the heading of "stage-level predicates" and "individual-level predicates" (e.g. Milsark 1974; Carlson 1977; Krifka et al. 1995), as illustrated in (1).

(1) a. Stage-level predicates: *The doctor is {available/sick/drunk} today.*
b. Individual-level predicates: *The doctor is {tall/intelligent/altruistic} (*today).*

In (1a), the occurrence of the time adverbial *today* indicates that the doctor's being available/sick/drunk is a temporary state, whereas in (1b) the infelicity of the same adverb suggests that the doctor's property of being tall/intelligent/altruistic is not affected by the passage of time. The same kind of contrast is known to be overtly manifested by two *be*-verbs in some languages, such as Spanish *ser* for properties and *estar* for temporary states (Arche 2006). Aomori dialects of Japanese also embody the same opposition by means of two copula forms.

(2) Goshogawara dialect of Aomori Prefecture (Yakame 2008: 132)

Property: *Tanaka-san ekichō* ***da***. 'Mr. Tanaka is a station
station.manager COP manager.'

Event: *Tanaka-san ekichō* ***dera***. 'Mr. Tanaka is a temporary station manager.'

Presumably due to its topic-prominent character, Japanese boasts a broader variety than European languages of syntactic and morphological constructions that pertain to the description of a property of a subject/topic, as in (3).

(3) a. Topic-predicate construction
Kanojo wa chōshin da/ aisō ga yoi.
she TOP tall COP affability NOM good
'She is tall/affable.'
b. Generic subjects
Zō wa hana ga nagai.
elephant TOP nose NOM long
'Elephants have a long trunk.'
c. Generic tense
Kono inu wa hito ni kamitsuka-nai.
this dog TOP people DAT bite-NEG
'This dog will never bite.'
d. Resultative aspect with *-te iru* or *-ta*
Kono futon wa fuka-fuka shi-te iru.
this TOP fluffy do-GER is
'This futon is fluffy.'

fuka-fuka shi-ta futon
fluffy do-PST
'a fluffy futon'

Since the event-property distinction is determined by the interpretation of an entire sentence, not just by the lexical meaning of the verb or adjective, we will employ the term *predication* instead of *predicate. Event predication* thus largely corresponds to stage-level predication, and *property predication* to individual-level predication.

This chapter proceeds as follows. By sketching the history of the relevant research in both Western and Japanese linguistics, Section 2 lays the foundation of theoretical concepts necessary for the discussion in the subsequent sections centering on peculiar phenomena that are recalcitrant to standard analyses in morphology and syntax. In particular, Section 3 presents a novel type of compounding, called *agent compounding*, that combines a transitive predicate with its subject in direct violation of the putatively universal prohibition on such combinations. It will be demonstrated that the deviant nature of this compounding finds a rationale in its special function as property predication. Section 4 turns attention to a unique construction in Japanese that depicts human physical attributes with the verb *suru* 'do,' as in *Naomi wa aoi me o shite iru* 'Lit. Naomi is doing blue eyes,' that is, 'Naomi has blue eyes.' The seemingly idiosyncratic use of *suru*, it will be shown, has a reasonable motivation if it is viewed as a special construction depicting an inborn trait of the subject. Overall, the major finding of the present chapter is that sentences of property predication are subject to different grammatical conditions from sentences of event predication. This generalization regarding the form–meaning mismatch calls for a reconsideration of the basic tenet of lexical semantics that the syntactic behavior of words is largely predictable from their lexical meanings. Section 5 concludes this chapter.

2 Research on Events and Properties in Japanese and Western Linguistics

Preliminary to a probe into particular constructions in Japanese, this section presents an overview of the history of the relevant research in Japanese and Western linguistics. Apart from Bolinger's (1973) seminal paper pointing out that Spanish *ser* and *estar* respectively depict "essence" and "accident," in the tradition of generative syntax and formal semantics, Milsark (1974) was the first to point out the pertinence of the distinction between transitory states and unalterable properties to the English existential construction illustrated in (4).

(4) a. *There were several people {shot/awake/undressed/tired}.* [temporary states]
b. **There were several people {tall/foolish/intelligent/talkative}.* [properties]

Sentences of perception report like *Martha saw the policemen X* constitute another test frame to separate states, which fit in the construction (*Martha saw the policemen shot*), from properties, which do not (**Martha saw the policemen tall*).

Milsark's observation was extended by Carlson (1977) to a classification of predicates into stage-level predicates (SLPs, Milsark's "states"), individual-level predicates (ILPs, Milsark's "properties"), and kind-level predicates (such as *extinct* used to refer to a kind of things). *Stage* in Carlson's terminology suggests that an event, action, or state is conceived of as a cluster of different stages that develop as time moves on, whereas the term *individual-level* implies a property or quality of

Table 11.1 *Diagnoses of SLP and ILP*

	Compatibility with punctual time adverbials	Compatibility with progressive aspect	Occurrence in complements to direct perception verbs
SLP	Yes: *Firemen were not available at that time.*	Yes: *The service is being available only in the daytime.*	Yes: *I saw John drunk.*
ILP	No: *Firemen are altruistic (*at this moment).*	No: *He is (*being) intelligent.*	No: **I saw John intelligent.*

an individual entity that persists over time. The basic diagnoses of SLP and ILP are summarized in Table 11.1 (see Krifka et al. (1995) and Fernald (2000) for details).

The semantic notions of SLP and ILP espoused by Milsark and Carlson were integrated into syntactic structure by Diesing (1992), who proposed to set the subject of an ILP in the Specifier of IP (outside of VP) while relegating the subject of a SLP to the Specifier of VP. Remarkable progress was achieved by Kratzer (1995), who, by consolidating Diesing's syntactic bipartition of SLP/ILP subjects and Davidson's (1967) idea of an "event argument," proposed that SLPs do but ILPs do not have an event argument (in addition to the regular arguments such as agent and theme).

In traditional Japanese grammar, on the other hand, inquiries into the semantic modes of sentences more or less comparable to the SLP/ILP distinction started much earlier than in Western linguistics and have been carried out until recently totally independent of the Milsark–Carlson–Kratzer line of research. Sakuma (1941) was the first to classify diverse construction patterns from the viewpoint of functions in communication. Among other modes of sentences, he specifically distinguished *monogatari-bun* (storytelling sentences), which describe the progress or development of events, from *shinasadame-bun* (characterizing sentences), which express the characteristics or properties of entities.

What is notable is that Sakuma's storytelling sentences mark the subject phrase with the nominative (*ga*), while his characterizing sentences mark the subject phrases with the topic marker (*wa*) in the copula construction "X *wa* Y *da*." With hindsight, Sakuma's differentiation of subject marking presents an amazing resemblance to Diesing's (1992) theory of partitioning the subject positions of SLPs and ILPs: the nominative subject is parallel to the VP-internal subject of SLPs in Diesing's theory, and the topic phrase to the VP-external subject of ILPs. The *ga*/*wa* distinction in Sakuma's theory merits further attention because of its similarity to Kuroda's (1972) distinction between "thetic judgment" with *ga*-marked subjects and "categorical judgment" with *wa*-marked subjects (cf. Chapter 13, this volume), which Ladusaw (2000) identifies with the SLP/ILP bipartition.

Sakuma's modes of sentences were taken over by Mikami (1953) and more recently by Masuoka (1987, 2004, 2008), who has developed what appears to be the most detailed classification of Sakuma's characterizing sentences. Masuoka proposes to view Sakuma's modes of sentences as different types of predication, thereby subsuming the variety of storytelling sentences under the rubric of event predication and the variety of characterizing sentences under the rubric of property predication, with each type of predication divided into subcategories. Particularly important among Masuoka's subcategories of property predication is the distinction between "categorical" properties (inherent or inborn properties that serve a classificatory function) and "experience-based" properties (properties acquired through one's experience).

The notion of acquired properties, which appears absent from discussion in Western linguistics, has the potential for universal applicability. For example, the formation of adjectival passives in English, which is characterized by Levin and Rappaport (1986) as being targeted only at an internal argument (theme) of the base verb, as in *baked potatoes* (from the transitive *bake*) and *an expired passport* (from the unaccusative *expire*), actually applies exceptionally to the external arguments (agents) of certain unergative verbs, as in *a much-traveled man* and *a well-read scholar*. Problematic as they are to Levin and Rappaport's theory, these exceptional adjectival passives receive a natural account if they are interpreted as representing an acquired property of the agent. In *a much-traveled man*, the man, due to his extensive travel experiences, is characterized as being knowledgeable about foreign countries, and in *a much-read scholar*, the scholar is characterized as being erudite as a result of his numerous experiences of book-reading.

This brief survey shows that domestic Japanese grammarians and Western theoretical linguists have investigated similar phenomena with similar treatments, but quite independently. Although Western linguistics excels in the depth of abstract theorization in formal terms, Japanese grammarians appear more advanced in the breadth and richness of the empirical data they deal with. Of special importance is the fact that, while the SLP/ILP distinction in Western linguistics is primarily motivated by a classification of adjectives and similar lexical categories, the studies on event and property predications in Japanese linguistics have an all-embracing coverage extending to all lexical categories and to whole sentences in discourse.

As hinted at by the English adjectival passive examples, the semantic distinction of events and properties exerts substantial influence on morphological and syntactic forms. To be more specific, morphological and syntactic structures that ought to be ruled out by general principles governing sentences of event predication gain acceptability when viewed as property predications. Such a claim was already adumbrated by Masuoka (1987: 188), who pointed out that Japanese has a passive of property predication which takes a different agent marking from regular passives of event predication.

(5) a. *Kono shōsetsu wa jū-nen-mae ni Tarō* {**niyotte**/***ni**} *kak-are-ta.*
this novel TOP ten-years-ago LOC {by/*DAT} write-PASS-PST
'This novel was written by Taro ten years ago.'

b. *Kono shu no suiri-shōsetsu wa nihon no sakka* ***ni*** *wa*
this kind GEN mystery-novel TOP Japan GEN novelist DAT TOP

ichido mo kak-are-ta koto ga nai.
once even write-PASS-PST NMLZ NOM be.NEG
'This kind of mystery novel has never been written by Japanese novelists.'

The passives of creation verbs such as *hon o kaku* 'write a book' generally call for the agent marker *niyotte* 'by' rather than the simple dative *ni*, as shown in (5a). Contrary to this regularity, however, the passive sentence in (5b) with the same verb is fully acceptable with the agent marked by the dative *ni*. What distinguishes these two sentences is that, while (5a) is a mere storytelling sentence, (5b) is construed as a characterizing sentence denoting a unique property of the subject as a 'new type of mystery story' on the basis of the information provided by the passive predicate. The property interpretation is schematically represented in (6).

(6) Semantic representation of property reading
[Topic phrase] [semantic concept denoting a property] + *da*.
To be interpreted as 'The topic is such that it is endowed with such and such a property.'

3 Agent Compounding as Property Predication

This section introduces a novel morphological process termed *agent compounding*, where an agent (external argument) is compounded with a transitive predicate in direct violation of the universal principle of verbal compounding or noun incorporation that bans the morphological combinations of a volitional agent and a transitive verb. This phenomenon, which was discovered only recently (Kageyama 2006b), provides perhaps the most apposite and most forceful illustration of the kind of division of labor between event and property predications.

3.1 Exclusion of Agents from Compounds of Event Predication

In the literature on lexical semantics it is generally agreed that how the arguments of a verb are realized in syntactic structure is generally predictable by the lexical semantic representation of the verb and/or the

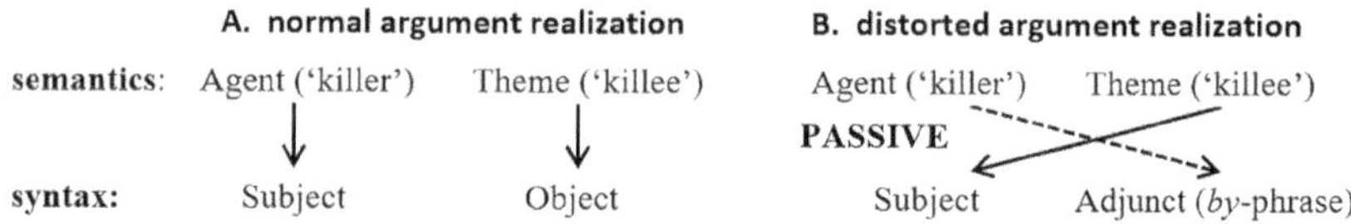

Figure 11.1 Normal and distorted argument realization

semantic roles borne by its arguments (Levin and Rappaport Hovav 2005). The core linking rule holds that the agent argument of a transitive verb is realized as subject in syntactic structure, and the theme argument as direct object. The linking pattern of the canonical transitive verb *kill*, for example, is schematically shown in A of Figure 11.1. Only when implemented by a special operation like passive can a distorted argument realization as in B be accepted.

Generalizations on argument linking are formally stated in terms of argument structure configurations where the agent argument is situated in an external argument position (*x*) and the theme argument in an internal argument position (*y*).

(7) Argument structure
  a. transitive verbs: (x <y>)
  b. unaccusative verbs: (<y>)
  c. intransitive (unergative) verbs: (x < >)

Besides the argument structure of transitive verbs (7a), those of unaccusative verbs (non-volitional intransitive verbs that have only an internal argument) and unergative verbs (volitional intransitive verbs that are characterized as having only an external argument) are represented as in (7b) and (7c), respectively. For some researchers, an event argument is added on top of the thematic argument structures in (7).

Word-formation processes that are based on verbs as the head are generally sensitive to the distinction of external versus internal argument of the base verbs. As formulated by Lieber (1983: 272), for example, English deverbal (synthetic) compounding applies either to the internal argument of a verb if it has one, as in *letterwriting*, or to an adjunct if it does not, as in *sleepwalking*. This principle correctly rules out compounds that involve a transitive verb and its external argument, as shown by the ungrammaticality of **student-writing of a letter* (meaning 'Students write a letter'). The exclusion of external arguments is in fact deemed a universal constraint that holds for noun incorporation in polysynthetic and other languages (e.g. Mithun 1984: 875).

Japanese N-V compounding complies with this universal restriction faithfully. Limiting attention to the argument realization in three major types of N-V compounds that function as predicates as summarized in Table 11.2, we find that there is no unequivocal instance of compounds consisting of a transitive verb and its subject.

Table 11.2 *Argument restrictions on N-predicate compounds*

	A. Trans. object	B. Trans. subject	C. Unaccusative subj.
I. native N + V compounds	*tema-doru* [time-take] 'to take time'	None	*nami-datsu* [wave-rise] 'to billow'
II. Sino-Japanese V + N compounds	*doku-sho* [read-book] 'book-reading'	None	*shuk-ka* [fire-break.out] 'outbreak of fire'
III. post-syntactic compounds	*erebētā : shiyō* [use : elevator] 'to use an elevator'	None	*chōnan : tanjō* [first.son : be.born] 'one's first son be born'

Examples like *kaeru-oyogi* [frog-swim] 'breaststroke' and *inu-kaki* [dog-paddle] 'dog-paddle' that apparently involve an agent as the first member of a compound do not denote an action in which the named animals actually participate but only a particular manner of conventionalized action that is typically associated with these animals. On this interpretation, since the animal nouns do not represent an agent argument, they are irrelevant to the constraint on agent compounding.

In contrast to English, where compounds headed by verbs are hardly productive, Japanese abounds in productive compounding rules that apply to verbs and other predicates as the head. Among them, what Shibatani and Kageyama (1988) call *post-syntactic compounding* (Row III in Table 11.2) exhibits by far the highest productivity, freely applying to any combination of a VN (Verbal Noun; nouns that have argument structure and case but do not inflect for tense by themselves) and its internal argument. Corresponding to the clausal structure in (8a), for example, a post-syntactic compound is formed as in (8b), where the compound is enclosed by square brackets, with the colon (:) inside signaling a short phonological break. The same kind of phonological break is observed with other types of complex words using Sino-Japanese elements as in prefixed words (e.g. *datsu : genpatsu* 'de-nuclear power generation,' *zen : daitōryō* 'ex-president') and compound nouns (e.g. *bōeki-gaisha : shachō* 'president of a trading company').

(8) a. *daitōryō ga Howaito-Hausu de pātī o kaisai no sai*
president NOM White-House LOC party ACC host GEN time
'when president hosted/hosts a party at the White House'

b. *daitōryō ga Howaito-Hausu de [pātī : kaisai] no sai*
president NOM White-House LOC [party : host] GEN time

In Japanese, the order of arguments and adjuncts may be altered by scrambling as in (9a), with the consequence that the subject argument shows up in front of the predicate 'host.'

(9) a. *Howaito-Hausu de pātī o daitōryō ga kaisai no sai*
White-House LOC party ACC president NOM host GEN time
(Same meaning as (8a), with the word order changed by scrambling)

b. **Howaito-Hausu de pātī o [daitōryō : kaisai] no sai*
White-House LOC party ACC [president : host] GEN time

Despite the linear adjacency, compounding the agent (president) with the following predicate yields an illegitimate result in (9b). This indicates that post-syntactic compounding is constrained by the composition of argument structure rather than by surface order.

3.2 Compounding of External Arguments in Property Predication

Surprisingly, the systematic exclusion of an external argument explained in Section 3.1 is flatly contradicted by a fairly productive process of compounding an agent (external argument) with a Sino-Japanese VN. The total ungrammaticality of the post-syntactic compound in (9b) should thus be compared with the well-formedness of compounds like those in (10).

(10) a. *[daitōryō : shusai] no pātī*
[president : host] GEN party
'a/the party hosted by the president'

b. *[ichiryū-kenchikuka : sekkei] no bijutsukan*
[first.class-architect : design] GEN museum
'a/the museum designed by a/the first-class architect'

In (10), transitive VNs *shusai* 'host' and *sekkei* 'design' are combined with the external arguments 'president' and 'first-class architect,' while leaving the internal arguments 'party' and 'museum' outside of the combinations. By using diagnoses of "lexical integrity" showing that words make up an integral unit whose internal structure cannot be manipulated by syntactic means, it is easily confirmed that these combinations of agent nouns and VNs truly constitute morphological compounds. For example, their internal structure cannot be interrupted by insertion of a focus particle between the two members. Likewise, deletion of only the noun members results in total ungrammaticality, as in **shusai no pātī* 'Lit. a/the party hosted' and **sekkei no bijutsukan* 'Lit. a/the museum designed.' Such genuine agent compounds thus exhibit a striking contrast to spurious agent-VN combinations due to particle ellipsis, such as *fan : taibō (no shinsaku)* '(a new work) awaited by fans,' which permit deletion of the agent noun, as in *taibō (no shinsaku)* 'a long-awaited (new work).'

Given that agent compounds like those in (10) are robust morphological constructs, how could the asymmetry in argument realization between them and the post-syntactic compounds in (8b) be accounted for? A first conceivable analysis will be to hypothesize that the predicates in agent compounds are passives derived by an invisible passive morpheme. This suggestion sounds plausible in view of the fact that comparable compounds in English use adjectival passives, as in *architect-designed (homes)*. Under this analysis, the Japanese agent compounds do not violate the universal ban on external argument compounding, because the erstwhile agents – 'president' and 'first-class architect' in (10) – are demoted to adjuncts. The passive analysis, however, does not seem to be supported empirically. First, postulation of an invisible passive morpheme is dubious because VNs themselves cannot be passivized due to their noun morphology. Second, the agent nouns in (10) refuse paraphrases using an adjunct agent phrase with *niyotte* 'by'; instead, they are most plausibly paraphrased with a nominative marking, as shown in (11).

(11) a. *[daitōryō {ga/*niyoru} shusai] no pātī*
[president NOM/by host] GEN party
b. *[ichiryū- kenchikuka {ga/*niyoru} sekkei] no bijutsukan*
[first.class-architect NOM/*by design] GEN museum

While the passive analysis can be dismissed as infeasible, a second approach, suggested to me by Akira Watanabe (p.c. 2010), has some validity. Watanabe's idea was that what we call agent compounds might be a special case of post-syntactic compounding applied to relative clause structure, where relativization of an object argument renders the transitive subject linearly adjacent to the predicate and hence compounding takes place. This analysis, it will be shown, is relevant only to one type of agent compound, that is, Class C in (12) below.

The two approaches mentioned above are based on the assumption that the relevant data involving external arguments constitute a uniform class with no internal variation. Careful scrutiny, however, reveals that the data are not monolithic but should be split into a few distinct classes. Kobayashi (2004) gathered a large number of actually occurring examples from newspaper articles and attempted to confirm their compound status by applying certain diagnostics for lexical integrity such as modifiability of the noun members by external adjectives and deletability of the VN members on identity. Kageyama (2004) closely inspected Kobayashi's as well as other data and proposed to tease apart three classes of expressions that share the formal appearance of an external argument combined with a transitive VN. The three classes (A to C) are exemplified in (12), with their essential features cataloged in Table 11.3.

Table 11.3 *Four classes of agent-transitive predicate combinations*

Class	Compound status	Copula construction	Spatiotemporal adverbs
A	Yes	Yes [inborn property]	No [property predication]
B	Yes	No [acquired property]	No [property predication]
C	Marginal	No	Yes [event predication]
D	No	No	Yes [event predication]

(12) A. *[Supirubāgu-kantoku : seisaku] no eiga* ([Spielberg-director : produce] GEN film) 'a/the film(s) produced by Spielberg,' *[Andō-Tadao-shi : sekkei] no hoteru* ([Ando-Tadao-Mr : design] GEN hotel) 'a/the hotel (s) designed by Architect Tadao Ando'

B. *[Warutā : shiki] no Koronbia-kōkyōgakudan* ([Walter : conduct] GEN Columbia-Symphony.Orchestra) 'Columbia Symphony Orchestra conducted by Bruno Walter,' *[josei-untenshi : sōjū] no shinkansen* ([female.driver : operate] GEN Shinkansen) 'a/the Shinkansen train operated by a female driver'

C. *[kishōchō : happyō] no taifū-jōhō* ([meteorological.agency : release] GEN typhoon-information) 'typhoon information released by the Meteorological Agency,' *[Seki-Tsutomu-shi : hakken] no shin-shōwakusei* ([Seki-Tsutomu : discover] GEN new-asteroid) 'a/the new asteroid discovered by Mr Tsutomu Seki'

Only Classes A and B qualify as full-fledged morphological compounds consisting of an external argument and a transitive VN. A typical diagnosis for testing the compound status is to see whether a given sequence is interruptible by a syntactic element. Classes A and B are equipped with the hallmark of lexical integrity, that is, non-interruptibility, while Class C appears to have a marginal status as compounds. Although the examples given in (12C) are collected from Japanese web pages, I conjecture that their acceptability will diverge among individual native speakers. Their questionable status can be ascribed to their irregular production by an aberrant operation. Recall that post-syntactic compounding rules out combinations of a transitive VP and an external argument, as shown by (13b).

(13) a. *kishōchō* *ga* *[taifūjōhō : happyō]* *chokugo*
meteorological.agency NOM [typhoon.info : release] right.after
'right after the Meteorological Agency released typhoon information'

b. **taifūjōhō* *o* *[kishōchō : happyō]* *chokugo*
typhoon.info ACC [meteorological.agency : announce] right.after

However, if the accusative object is relativized, its object position becomes invisible (being occupied by a trace), as in (14).

(14) *Kishōchō* *ga* t_i *happyō* *no* *taifūjōhō*
meteorological.agency NOM release GEN typhoon.info
'the typhoon information released by the Meteorological Agency'

In this structure, the subject argument (Meteorological Agency) is linearly adjacent to the transitive VN 'release' (ignoring the trace of the relativized noun). Given this surface order, the condition on post-syntactic compounding may be relaxed (for some speakers) in such a way that it can work on linearly adjacent words to give rise to a compound-like unit. This rather irregular implementation of post-syntactic compounding, I suspect, accounts for the marginal status of Class C compounds. Their questionable status is confirmed by the fact that, unlike the full-fledged compounds of Classes A and B, Class C compounds are incapable of participating in an iterative application of compounding with the theme nouns they modify, as shown in (15).

(15) A: *[[Supirubāgu-kantoku : seisaku] bōken-eiga]* (OK as a compound)
[[Spielberg-director : produce] adventure-film]
B: *[[Warutā : shiki] Koronbia-kōkyōgakudan]* (OK as a compound)
[[Walter : conduct] Columbia-Symphony.Orchestra]
C: **[[kishōchō : happyō] taifūjōhō]* (Bad as a compound)
[[meteorological.agency : release] typhoon.info]

3.3 Inherent versus Acquired Properties in Agent Compounding

Having delineated the range of relevant data, we will now grapple the vital question of why Classes A and B compounds are acceptable despite their ostensible violation of the universal constraint on external argument compounding. The key to the problem lies in the compatibility or incompatibility with spatiotemporal adverbials that designate a particular time or place when/where the event denoted by a compound takes/took place. This point is made clearer by comparing compounds of Classes A and B with Class C compounds. Observe first that Class C compounds, for those speakers who accept them at all, are fully compatible with such adverbials, as demonstrated in (16).

(16) a. *gogo san-ji ni [kishōchō : happyō]*
p.m. three-o'clock at [meteorological.agency : release]

no taifūjōhō
GEN typhoon.info
'the typhoon information that the Meteorological Agency released at 3 p.m.'

b. *kyō no gikai de [yatō-giin : teishutsu]*
today GEN Diet LOC [opposition-dietmen : present]

no shitsumonsho
GEN written.inquiry
'the written inquiry the opposition party presented at today's diet meeting'

The acceptability of (16) contrasts dramatically with the total incompatibility of such adverbials with compounds of Class A (17a) and Class B (17b).

(17) a. *Sono eiga wa (*2001-nen ni *Hariuddo de)*
the film TOP (*2001-year in Hollywood LOC)

[Supirubāgu-kantoku : seisaku] da.
[Spielberg-director : produce] COP
'That film was produced by Spielberg in Hollywood in 2001.'

b. *(*1958-nen ni *Nyūyōku no sutajio de) [Warutā : shiki]*
(*1958-year in New.York GEN studio LOC) [Walter : conduct]

no Koronbia-kōkyōgakudan
GEN Columbia-symphony.orchestra
'the Columbia Symphony Orchestra conducted by Walter in 1958 in a studio of New York'

The disparity between (16) and (17) is exactly parallel to the one we saw in Section 2 between stage-level predication (as in *My doctor is not available today*) and individual-level predication (as in **My doctor is tall today*). This is tantamount to saying that Class C compounds, compatible with spatiotemporal adverbials, are event predications describing the occurrence of a particular action or event along the time dimension, whereas the compounds of Classes A and B, which are incompatible with such adverbials, are property predications depicting a more or less constant quality attributed to the theme nouns they modify.

For example, (17a), with the adverbials left out, characterizes the particular film as one of superior quality on the basis of the pragmatic knowledge that Spielberg is a celebrated film director with outstanding expertise. Since, however, the quality of the film is a permanent attribute, the time and place adverbials that refer to the process of film-making are rendered irrelevant. Likewise, (17b) evaluates the performance of the Columbia Symphony Orchestra as having been excellent when it was under the baton of Bruno Walter, a conductor of eminent reputation in the early 1900s. Although the referential NPs do not necessarily refer to leading figures like Spielberg or Walter, they are indeed required to convey cogent information that helps to assign a noteworthy quality to the theme noun that the compound modifies. Nouns that do not convey information semantically or pragmatically sufficient to uniquely characterize the quality of a theme noun, such as 'my son' in (18a) or 'a certain composer' in (18b), are not suitable as the noun members in agent compounding.

(18) a. **[chōnan : seisaku] no ehon*
[first.son : create] GEN picture.book

b. **[bō-sakkyokuka : sakkyoku] no gasshō-kyoku*
[certain-composer : make] GEN chorus-music

So far, it has been established that compounds of Class A and Class B are acceptable because of their semantic function as property predication. What distinguishes between the two classes then? They can be sharply differentiated from each other by the simple test of whether a given compound can fit into the copula construction 'X (theme noun) *wa* COMPOUND *da*.' Class A compounds comfortably fit into the copula construction, while Class B compounds do not.

(19) Class A compounds in the topic-copula construction

a. *Kono eiga wa [Supirubāgu-kantoku : seisaku] da.*
this film TOP [Spielberg-director : produce] COP
'This film is one that was produced by Spielberg.'

b. *Kono bijutsukan wa [Andoo-Tadao-shi : sekkei] da.*
this museum TOP [Ando-Tadao-Mr : design] COP
'This museum is one that was designed by Tadao Ando.'

(20) Class B compounds in the topic-copula construction

a. **Kono kōkyōgakudan wa [Warutā : shiki] da.*
this symphony.orchestra TOP [Walter : conduct] COP
'The symphony orchestra is one that was conducted by Walter.'

b. **Kono shinkansen wa [josei-untenshi : sōjū] da.*
this Shinkansen.train TOP [female-driver : operate] COP
'This Shinkansen train is one that is operated by a female driver.'

The discrepancy between (19) and (20) can be attributed to the archetypical function of the copula construction of the form "X *wa* Y *da*," which serves to describe an inherent property of the theme noun realized as the topic.

As briefly noted in Section 2, Masuoka (2004) distinguishes two types of property: (i) property inherent in a category and (ii) property acquired from a past experience. The former refers to an inherent property, and the latter to an acquired or derived property. Since the copula construction prototypically denotes an inherent, classificatory property, the Class A compounds are construed as representing inherent properties of a topic noun. Strong evidence for this construal derives from the lexical meaning of VNs employed in these compounds. Specifically, the VNs qualified for Class A compounds, such as *shusai* 'host,' *sekkei* 'design,' and *sakusei* 'create,' are all accomplishment verbs that converge on the core meaning of production and creation. With the aid of the agent nouns, which mostly represent eminent figures in a particular field of activity, the VNs of creation and production assign an inborn quality to the topic phrase. The meaning of inborn properties is also activated by compounds like those in (21), where the noun members denote producing centers for artifacts, food, and other commodities.

(21) a. *Kono kagu wa [Itaria : chokuyunyū] da.*
this furniture TOP [Italy : direct.import] COP
'This furniture is imported directly from Italy.'

b. *Kono ise-ebi wa [sanchi : chokusō] da.*
this lobster TOP [producing.district : direct-send] COP
'This lobster is sent directly from the producing center.'

By metonymic extension, a noun designating a famous place of production is naturally conceived of as its "creator" or agent. Notice that the VNs in (21) express 'acquisition' or 'arrival' of the goods, which are broadly equivalent to the lexical meaning of 'production.'

The delineation of the semantic range of VNs in Class A compounds as having the meaning of production and creation strongly indicates that these compounds bear a classificatory function, assigning an inherent property to the topic phrase they are predicated of. By contrast, Class B compounds, which are unable to occur in the topic-copula construction, represent the kind of property that has been acquired through the action or event denoted by its modifying compound. Since past experiences that motivate the assignment of an acquired property are variegated, the VNs that may participate in this class of compounds exhibit diverse lexical meanings in diverse aspectual classes.

This section has shown that Masuoka's distinction between inherent property and acquired property, which is not known in Western linguistics, is neatly reflected in the Japanese agent compounds of Class A and Class B. It remains to be seen how the distinction is formally represented and exploited in theories of event semantics. A plausible proposal is to attribute the difference of the two classes to different modules of grammar in which each of them is generated. Class A compounds denoting inborn properties are formed in the lexicon, whereas Class B compounds representing acquired properties are formed in syntax (Kageyama 2006b). Telling evidence for this distinction is found in the availability or unavailability of the honorific prefix *go-*, which normally cannot be embedded inside lexical words. As predicted, Class B compounds in syntax permit this prefix on the VNs inside compounds, while Class A compounds in the lexicon do not.

(22) A: *Kono kyoku wa [Takada-Saburō-sensei : (****go***-)sakkyoku] desu.*
this music TOP [Takada-Saburo-Mr : (*HON-)compose] COP
'This music was composed by Mr. Saburo Takada.'

B: *[Heika :* ***go***-*hōmon] no chi*
[emperor : HON-visit] GEN place
'the place(s) visited by the emperor'

To recapitulate, agent compounding in Japanese is a robust rule of creating compounds that depict a characteristic property/quality of the theme noun they are predicated of by combining a transitive VN with its external argument. Given that agent compounding is allowed only in property predication, we must ask whether the convergence of its morphological peculiarity and its property-predication function is a mere coincidence or a logical consequence of some abstract principle relating them to each other. Probably it is not an accidental idiosyncrasy because there are many other phenomena in which property predication is associated with the violation of otherwise valid constraints in syntax and morphology, as reported by Kageyama (2006a, 2009). Those phenomena that look disorderly when viewed from event predication become orderly when regarded as belonging to the realm of property predication that is distinct from the more familiar realm of event predication.

4 The Physical Attribute Construction Using the Verb *Suru* 'Do'

This section tackles thorny issues surrounding the form–meaning mismatch presented by another curious construction in Japanese, schematically represented in (23). Let us call this the *physical attribute construction.*

(23) [Subject TOP] [adjective + body part noun] ACC do-GER be.
Naomi wa aoi me o shi-te iru
'Naomi has blue eyes; Naomi is blue-eyed.'

Extremely common in colloquial as well as written language, as contrasted with the formal style associated with the agent compounding discussed in Section 3, the physical attribute construction describes a noteworthy physical/personal attribute of a human subject with the verb *suru* 'do.' From a theoretical standpoint, it has an array of intriguing and probably mutually intertwined properties ranging from morphology to syntax to semantics and pragmatics that are foreign to regular sentences predicated by the action verb *suru.* Although the curious behavior of the construction has long been noted by Japanese grammarians, there have been very few attempts so far to unravel the interaction of the puzzling properties in a principled way. This section will suggest a direction for an integrated analysis by associating the peculiarities of the construction with the notion of property predication.

The most fundamental problem of this construction is why *suru* 'do,' an archetypical action verb meaning a dynamic action when it takes an accusative object, is exploited to designate a static attribute of the subject/topic. In the template of (23), while the slots for subject, adjective, and body part noun are freely occupied by appropriate lexical items, the verb *suru* cannot be replaced by any of its synonyms like *okonau* 'carry out,' *yaru* 'do,' and *dekiru* 'be able to do' (suppletive for the potential form of *suru*), nor with possessive verbs like *motsu* 'have' and *aru* 'exist, have.' The tense and aspect of *suru* are also strictly limited to the resultative *-te iru* in concluding a sentence or to the resultative *-ta* in noun-modifying (i.e. relative) constructions, as in *aoi me o shi-ta shōjo* 'a girl who is blue-eyed.' The physical attribute construction thus counts as a "constructional idiom" in the terminology of Jackendoff (2010: 272–274). The idiomatic nature of the construction will be highlighted by the selectional restriction that only human nouns are fully qualified for its subject (topic), as suggested by the degraded acceptability of sentences like ?*Zō wa nagai hana o shite iru* 'Elephants have a long trunk' and **Sono ie wa akai yane o shite iru* 'This house has a red roof.' The subsequent discussion will attempt to disentangle the intertwined characteristics of this constructional idiom by teasing them apart into three groups as follows:

(24) Characteristics related to *suru* 'do'
 A. Why is the verb *suru* employed in this construction?
 B. Why are the verb forms restricted to *shite iru* or *shita*?

(25) Characteristics related to objects and adjuncts
 C. Why are nouns like 'wart' and 'mole' excluded from the construction?
 **Naomi wa ōkina hokuro o shite iru.*
 'Naomi has a big wart.'
 D. Why is the construction incompatible with particular spatiotemporal adverbials?
 **Naomi wa kyō wa kyōshitsu de aoi me o shite iru.*
 Lit. 'Naomi has blue eyes in the classroom today.'
 E. Why is an adjective or other kind of modifier mandatory for the object noun?
 *Naomi wa {aoi me/*me} o shite iru.*
 'Naomi is {blue-eyed/*eyed}.'

(26) Characteristics related to the definiteness restriction
 F. Why must the object NPs be 'indefinite'?
 **Naomi wa sono aoi me o shite iru.*
 Lit. 'Naomi has the blue eyes.'
 G. Why do the object NPs resist syntactic movement?
 **Naomi ga shite iru no wa aoi me da.*
 Lit. 'What Naomi has are blue eyes.'

Each of the characteristics cataloged in (24–26) will be discussed in Sections 4.1, 4.2, and 4.3, respectively.

4.1 Characteristics Related to the Verb *Suru* 'Do'

We begin our discussion with the question of why *suru* turns up in this construction. Tsunoda (1996) provides a descriptive observation on the distribution of possession verbs along what he calls the inalienability cline: *shoyū-suru* 'own' is used for objects representing nouns of alienable possession such as 'car,' *motsu* 'have' for kinship terms such as 'wife' and 'son' as well as nouns of alienable possession, *aru* 'exist, have' for acquired properties such as *hokuro* 'mole' as well as kinships, and finally *suru* for inborn attributes. Tsunoda, however, gives no account of why the action verb *suru* is employed to represent static properties. A conceivable analysis might be to regard *suru* in the physical attribute construction as an extension of the same verb used for wearing accessories on one's body.

Japanese is known to have a set of special dressing verbs that are distinguished by the body part to which a clothing item is applied: *kaburu* for covering one's head or face with items like a hat or a mask; *haku* for covering one's feet, legs, or lower body with items like shoes, socks, stockings, pants, or skirts; and *kiru* for covering one's upper body or whole body with such items as clothes, pullover, jacket, shirt, or suit. While these three verbs are dedicated to dressing actions ('putting on' and 'wearing'), there are no dedicated verbs of wearing that refer to other small parts of a body such as a waist, neck, or finger. For these body parts, *suru* comes into play as an elsewhere verb, thus serving as a surrogate verb for *shimeru* 'fasten' (a necktie, a belt), *hameru* (a ring, gloves), *kakeru* (glasses), and *maku* (a scarf, a sash). The suggested analysis of identifying *suru* in the physical attribute construction with the same verb used as a wearing verb cannot be upheld, however, because they exhibit distinct aspectual properties, the former (as a non-volitional verb) depicting a permanent and unchanging feature of the subject and the latter (as a volitional verb) describing a temporary state. In Section 4.3 it is suggested that the *suru* in the physical attribute construction might be a variant of *suru* in light verb constructions.

Concerning the aspectual properties of verbs, Kindaichi (1950b), a pioneering work on Japanese lexical aspect, classifies Japanese verbs into four groups: (i) stative verbs such as *aru* 'exist' and *dekiru* 'be able' (incompatible with the "progressive" *-te iru* in the conclusive form), (ii) continuative verbs such as *hataraku* 'work' and *kaku* 'write' (expressing an ongoing action or event when followed by *-te iru*), (iii) instantaneous verbs such as *shinu* 'die' and *tsuku* '(light) come on' (expressing a resultant state of an event when followed by *-te iru*), and (iv) Type 4 verbs such as *sobieru* 'soar' and *sugureru* 'excel' (which express an unalterable state that obtains as a result of some sort of change and always occur with *-te iru* in the conclusive form or with *-ta* in prenominal modification).

The verb *suru* 'do,' which falls under Type 2 (continuative verbs) in its typical usage as an activity verb, is actually indeterminate in terms of aspectual class and is versatile enough to acquire different aspectual properties depending on the combinations with particular objects or adverbs. Thus, *suru* behaves as a continuative verb when it takes as its object such activity nouns as *shukudai* (homework)/*tenisu* (tennis)/*onigokko* (tag)/*kyōshi* (teacher) *o shite iru* 'He is doing homework/tennis/tag/[Lit.] a teacher.' If the object designates items for wearing, the same verb behaves as an instantaneous verb, as in *nekutai o shite iru* meaning either 'He is putting on a tie' (progressive) or more plausibly 'He has a tie on' (resultative). The latter interpretation is made possible by the fact that a necktie has an intrinsic purpose of being worn (the Telic role in Pustejovsky's (1995) theory of qualia structure). Since neckties and other kinds of accessories can be put on or taken off volitionally, *shite iru* can also express an ongoing action in addition to the resultative state.

Now, if body part nouns show up in the object position of *suru*, the *-te iru* construction is no longer ambiguous. The example in (23), *Naomi wa aoi me o shite iru*, cannot express an ongoing action like 'Naomi is in the process of putting on blue eyes,' but only the permanent state of Naomi being blue-eyed. When put in relative clauses, the same verb can be set in the past (i.e. resultative) form *-ta*, as in *aoi me o shita shōjo* 'a blue-eyed girl.' This provides good reason to assume that *suru* in the physical attribute construction belongs to the class of Type 4 verbs, as in fact, Kindaichi (1950b) identifies a physical attribute construction *takai hana o shite iru* 'has a prominent nose' as an example of Type 4.

4.2 Characteristics Related to Objects and Adjuncts

Previous studies were mostly concerned with the lexical semantic properties of the nouns that do and do not fit in with the physical attribute construction. Details aside, only certain nouns of inalienable possession qualify as the object of the construction under discussion. Thus, nouns like those in (27), denoting alienable objects, are ruled out, while those in (28), denoting alienable possession, are acceptable.

(27) **Sensei wa {akai kuruma/tayorininaru musuko/kireina okusan} o shite iru.*
Intended meaning: 'My teacher has {a red car/a reliable son/a beautiful wife}.'

(28) *Sensei wa {ōkii me/hosoi ashi/utsukushii koe/yōkina seikaku} o shite iru.*
'My teacher has {big eyes/slender legs/a beautiful voice/a cheerful character}.'

The last two examples in (28) suggest that the nouns qualified for this construction are not limited to body parts but may include physical and mental traits intrinsic to the subject, such as voice and character. Drawing on previous studies, Takuzo Sato (2003) presents an almost exhaustive list of eligible nouns and characterizes them as denoting an essential attribute of the subject, that is, an intrinsic property that cannot be externally added after the person in the subject is born. Sato's characterization is sufficient to exclude from this construction nouns like *hokuro* 'mole,' *ibo* 'wart,' *shiraga* 'white hair,' and *yakedo no ato* 'burn scar,' which are accidentally acquired after one's birth.

Let us now consider the marked contrast in the compatibility with spatiotemporal adverbials between temporary facial expressions as in (29), which are event predications, and permanent attributes as in (30), which are property predications.

(29) a. *Kanojo wa sono toki totsuzen fukuret-tsura o shita.*
she TOP that time suddenly sullen-look ACC did
'She suddenly put on a sullen look at that time.'

b. *Kanojo wa chichioya no mae de wa itsumo fukuret-tsura o*
she TOP father GEN front LOC TOP always sullen-look ACC

shi-te iru.
do-GER be
'She always look sullen in front of her father.'

(30) a. **Kanojo wa sono toki totsuzen hosoi yubi o shita.*
she TOP that time suddenly slim fingers ACC did
Lit. 'She suddenly put on slim fingers at that time.'

b. **Kanojo wa chichioya no mae de wa itsumo hosoi yubi o*
she TOP father GEN front LOC TOP always slim finger ACC

shi-te iru.
do-GER be
Lit. 'She always has slim fingers in front of her father.'

Another diagnostic to distinguish properties from events is susceptibility to adversative passive formation. Regardless of whether the verb is transitive or intransitive (unergative), sentences of event predication can form adversative passives, although sentences predicated by unaccusative verbs such as *aru* 'exist' and *okoru* 'occur' are excluded because they lack an external argument. Sentences of property predication are also resistant to adversative passive. The total ungrammaticality of (31b) indicates that the physical attribute construction lacks an external argument (in other words, it is uncontrollable).

(31) a. *Watashi wa sensei ni nemusōna me o s-are-ta.*
I TOP teacher DAT sleepy eye ACC do-PASS-PST
'I was disturbed by my teacher's sleepy look.'

b. **Watashi wa sensei ni aoi me o s-are-ta.*
I TOP teacher DAT blue eye ACC do-PASS-PST
Lit. 'I was disturbed by my teacher's having blue eyes.'

It is thus shown that the physical attribute construction presents property predication, where an inherent bodily feature of the subject is described by the verb *suru* in the resultative forms *-te iru* or *-ta*. The nature of the construction as characterizing sentences naturally accounts for why the verb *suru* 'do' exhibits idiosyncratic behavior that deviates from the archetypical usage of the same verb as a volitional and self-controllable activity verb in event predication sentences.

The outstanding problem with this construction is why the object noun should be accompanied by an adjective or other modifier in syntactic structure.

(32) a. **Kanojo wa {me/yubi/kami} o shi-te iru.*
she TOP {eye/finger/hair} ACC do-GER is.
Lit. 'She is {eyed/fingered/haired}.'

b. *Kanojo wa {sunda me/hosoi yubi/nagai kami} o shi-te iru.*
she TOP {clear eye/slim finger/long hair} ACC do-GER is.
'She has {clear eyes/slim fingers/long hair}.'

The reason for the ill-formedness of sentences like (32a) is not pragmatic because addition of meaningful information by way of morphological compounds as in (33) does not improve the grammaticality (see Tsujioka (2002: 140) for related discussion).

(33) **Kanojo wa {chō-hatsu/chijire-ge/tare-me} o shi-te iru.*
she TOP {long-hair/curly-hair/droopy-eye} ACC do-GER is
'She has long hair/curly hair/droopy eyes.'

My proposal is that the contrast between (32a) and (32b) is syntactic in nature. The syntactic composition of 'adjective+noun' in the object phrase is a logical necessity to provide an appropriate semantic representation for property predication. Specifically, the body part noun used in the physical attribute construction does not refer to the body part as a physical entity but to the noun's characteristic state expressed by the adjectival modifier. For example, *aoi me* 'blue eyes' does not refer to the entity itself (eyes that are blue) but instead represents a state of the eyes being blue, namely, *me ga aoi* 'the eyes are blue.' In other words, *aoi me o shite iru* is paraphrasable as *me ga aoi*. Actually, such a reversed interpretation of a prenominal modifier as a predicative element is not rare in Japanese. Some "exocentric" compounds of the form "A+N" are also interpretable in the same vein as a predication of the form "N is A" (Kageyama 2010). For example, *futop-para* [big-stomach] 'big-hearted, generous' does not refer to a big stomach itself but to the quality of being generous paraphrased as *Hara ga futoi* 'The heart [stomach] is big.'

To sum up, the object noun in the physical attribute construction calls for an adjectival modification in syntactic structure. This syntactic structure is motivated to productively obtain the "subject+adjective" predication in reversed order in semantic representations. The form–meaning mismatch found in the physical attribute construction is thus generalized as a shift from prenominal modification in syntactic structure ('blue eyes') to predicative structure in semantic representation ('eyes are blue'). This analysis renders the semantic contribution of the verb *suru* minimal.

In fact, the meaning of the *aoi me o shite iru* sentence can be easily paraphrased as (34a), where the verb *suru* is dispensed with in an overt topic-copula construction.

(34) a. *Naomi wa (*itsumo) aoi me da.*
TOP (*always) blue eye COP
'Naomi is (*always) blue-eyed.'

b. *Naomi wa itsumo fukuret-tsura/katsura da.*
TOP always sulky-face/wig COP
'Naomi always looks sulky/Naomi is always wigged.'

The inappropriateness of the time adverb *itsumo* 'always' in (34a) reinforces the claim that the construction is a property predication, as opposed to the compatibility of the same adverb in (34b) with *fukuret-tsura o suru/ fukuret-tsura da* 'wear a sulky face' and *katsura o suru/katsura da* 'wear a wig,' which are event predications.

4.3 Syntactic Behavior of Object NPs

The object phrases of the construction under discussion must be indefinite NPs rather than definite or referential NPs. This is indicated not only by incompatibility with definite determiners like *sono* 'that' but also by incompatibility with any kind of quantifier.

(35) a. *Naomi wa (*sono/*kanojo no) aoi me o shi-te iru.*
TOP (*those/*she GEN) blue eyes ACC do-GER is

b. *Naomi wa (*takusan/*jup-pon/*zenbu) hosoi yubi o shi-te iru.*
TOP (*many/*ten-CL/*all) slender fingers ACC do-GER is

One might be tempted to attribute the impossibility of determiners in (35a) to the fact that the object (eyes) is lexically bound by the subject phrase. However, this account does not go through for (35b), where both weak quantifiers ('many,' 'ten') and strong quantifiers ('all') are excluded. Notably, this restriction is shared by the topic-adjective construction in (36).

(36) *Naomi wa (*takusan/*jup-pon/*zenbu) yubi ga hosoi.*
TOP (*many/*ten-CL/*all) fingers NOM slender
Lit. 'Naomi has many/ten/all slender fingers.'

On the other hand, the quantifier *juppon-tomo* 'all of ten,' as in (37a), appears acceptable in the *shite iru* construction in parallel with the acceptability of the same quantifier in the topic-adjective construction (37b).

(37) a. *Naomi wa juppon-tomo hosoi yubi o shi-te iru.*
TOP ten-CL-all.together slender finger ACC do-GER is
'All of Naomi's ten fingers are slender.'

b. *Naomi wa juppon-tomo yubi ga hosoi.*
TOP ten-CL-all.together finger NOM slender
(Same meaning as 38a)

The reason (37) is acceptable in contrast to (35–36) will be sought in the special function of *-tomo* 'all/both of,' which quantifies the whole proposition instead of the noun phrase it is directly associated with, as in "The proposition that Naomi's fingers are slender holds true of all of her fingers."

The object phrase in the physical attribute construction thus lacks referentiality just because it is semantically construed as a predicate in a topic-adjective construction. Its predicative status correctly prohibits the object NP from undergoing syntactic movement rules like relativization and topicalization, as shown in (38).

(38) a. **Naomi ga shi-te iru* ***hosoi yubi*** *wa haha-yuzuri desu.*
NOM do-GER is slim fingers TOP mother-inherited COP
'The slim fingers that Naomi has are inherited from her mother.'

b. ****Hosoi yubi*** *wa Naomi ga shi-te iru.*
slim fingers TOP NOM do-GER is

Given the property predication function of the construction under discussion, the question remains which of inborn properties and acquired properties it represents. Observe that there are a variety of expressions that exhibit much the same behavior with respect to their meaning and syntactic realization with the verb *suru*. These include expressions like *gotsu-gotsu suru* 'be rugged' and *geijutsukazen to suru* 'be a prototypical artist' which, categorized in Kindaichi's Type 4, appear obligatorily in the resultative aspect with *-te iru* when used as predicates of finite sentences. Kindaichi (1950b: 49) characterizes the basic meaning of Type 4 verbs as "the taking on of a state" rather than "being in a state." In other words, Type 4 verbs imply that the current state has been achieved gradually over time. Support for this characterization derives from the compatibility with adverbs like *masumasu* 'increasingly' when accompanied with the auxiliary *-te kuru* 'come to.' Example (39) thus denotes an incremental change.

(39) *Yamada-san wa masumasu geijutsukazen to shi-te kita.*
Yamada-Mr TOP increasingly true.artist QUOT do-GER came
'Mr Yamada is increasingly acquiring the air of as a true artist.'

By contrast, the physical attribute construction is wholly incompatible with such adverbs.

(40) **Naomi wa masumasu aoi me o shi-te kita.*
TOP increasingly blue eye ACC do-GER came
Lit. 'Naomi increasingly came to have blue eyes.'

The total unacceptability of (40) leads us to conclude that the physical attribute construction of 'blue-eyed' type is distinct from Type 4 verbs and constitutes a pure representation of inborn properties whose process of acquisition has no relevance to the speaker.

In closing this chapter, I will briefly mention how all the idiosyncratic features of the construction and their intricate interaction can be accounted for in a unified manner. While Tsujioka (2002) entertains a generative-syntactic analysis, Kageyama (2004) explores an approach exploiting "semantic incorporation" – a process reported in diverse languages – whereby syntactically immobile indefinite objects are analyzed as being semantically incorporated with the head verb. Under this analysis, the indefinite and non-referential character of body part nouns in the physical attribute construction falls out as a natural consequence of the formation of abstract composite predicates consisting of accusative NPs and the "light" verb *suru*.

5 Conclusion and Future Research Perspectives

By highlighting certain idiosyncratic phenomena that have been largely neglected in the mainstream research on Japanese grammar, this chapter has argued that the distinction between event predication and property predication that lies at the heart of these phenomena has far-reaching implications for theories dealing with the interface of morphology, syntax, semantics, and possibly pragmatics – much more so than has previously been thought in Western linguistics. Specifically, it has been argued that sentences of property predication constitute a realm of their own that is distinct from the realm of event predication sentences on the grounds that these two realms are governed by different rules and principles. The rules and principles that determine the well-formedness of sentences of event predication often fail to apply to sentences of property predication. Whereas sentences of event predication are interpreted on the basis of the predicate's argument structure, sentences of property predication are fundamentally built on the topic-copula structure, which is prevalent in the grammar of Japanese as a topic-prominent language.

The universal validity of this line of thought can be found in a wide array of phenomena from various languages that have eluded satisfactory accounts in the past studies focused on event predication but are susceptible to a systematic account on the interpretation that they represent property predication. These allegedly idiosyncratic phenomena include peculiar passives in Japanese and English, middle constructions in English and Japanese, peculiar reflexive constructions in Spanish and other languages, adjunct subject constructions in English and Chinese, potential forms in some Japanese dialects, and many others (Kageyama 2006a, 2009).

Given the reality of the event-property distinction, then, a number of questions remain for future research. One of them is how to capture the distinction in formal terms. A possible approach is to consider sentences of event predication to be turned to sentences of property predication by "suppressing" the event argument. An alternative approach would be to dissociate syntactic constructions from their semantic structures and allow a non-one-to-one correspondence between them.

Another non-trivial question is whether events and properties make a dichotomous bipartition or constitute a continuous cline. The possibility suggested here is that the two predication types basically constitute distinct realms of grammar, without denying the possibility of shifting one predication type to the other by certain grammatical means. Masuoka (2008), on the other hand, holds that several subcategories he sets up for each of event and property predication are related to each other in a continuous manner. This question has to do with how events, states, and properties can be related to each other. On the assumption that verbs describe events that are temporally unstable, nouns describe objects whose character is stable, and adjectives have an intermediate status, Givón (1984) contends that these three categories are arranged on a continuous scale of temporal stability. The assumption that events and properties are continuous concepts, however, cannot easily account for the disparity in their syntactic and morphological behavior as evidenced by agent compounds, the physical attribute construction, and many other phenomena. The papers collected in Kageyama (2012) will serve as a good point of departure for future research.

Part III

Grammatical Foundation

12

Case

Wataru Nakamura

1 Introduction

The aim of this chapter is threefold: (i) to provide an overview of the case system of "Standard" Modern Japanese (SMJ); (ii) to present a set of case frames borne by constructions that have presented a challenge to contemporary syntactic theories; and (iii) to account for some of such case frames in generative and functional terms as a guide for further research.

The Japanese case system has been classified as accusative, despite recent controversies over how to characterize the case system of Old Japanese (OJ) (e.g. Vovin 1997; Yanagida and Whitman 2009).[1] SMJ implements its accusative case system by postpositional particles, which have been referred to as *kaku-joshi* 'case particles' by traditional Japanese grammarians. These case particles are phonologically bound to the preceding words, but the fact that other elements may intervene between the case particles and the nouns they mark and that their scope may extend over more than one NP when they are coordinated (as illustrated in (1)) indicates that the case particles are phrasal clitics rather than nominal declensions:

(1) *Tarō-to* *Hanako-dake-ga* *eki-kara* *arui-ta.*
Taro-and Hanako-only-NOM train.station-ABL walk-PST
'Only Taro and Hanako walked from the train station.'

One of the prominent features of the SMJ case system is that more than one nominative-marked NP may occur within a clause when the clause-initial one may be taken as being characterized by the remaining part of the clause (Takami and Kamio 1996: 217), as illustrated in (2):

1 Yanagida and Whitman (2009: 131–132) argue that *ga* was mostly restricted to mark *A arguments* (i.e. agentive arguments of transitive verbs) and agentive *S arguments* (i.e. subject arguments of intransitive verbs) of nominalized and other dependent clauses and propose that the case system of OJ involves a split between the accusative and active system, that is, the one that groups A arguments and agentive S arguments together as opposed to *O arguments* (i.e. patientive arguments of transitive verbs) and patientive S arguments (the three-way distinction among A, S, and O is originally due to Dixon (1979)).

(2)

Tarō-ga	*hahaoya-ga*	*hyōban-ga*	*ii.*
Taro-NOM	mother-NOM	reputation-NOM	good

'Taro is such that his mother has a good reputation.'

Such multiple-nominative case frames are the hallmark of *topic-prominent languages* including Japanese, Korean, and Mandarin Chinese (Li and Thompson 1976) and have been a major problem for descriptions of the SMJ case system.

This chapter is organized as follows. Section 2 outlines the primary functions of the following case particles: *ga* (nominative), *o* (accusative), *ni* (dative), *no* (genitive), *e* (allative), *kara* (ablative), *yori* (ablative), *made* (terminative), *de* (instrumental), and *to* (comitative). Section 3 introduces a set of non-canonical case frames borne by Dative-Subject, Multiple-Nominative, Genitive-Subject, Causative, and Desiderative Constructions. Section 4 provides a summary of selected generative accounts of the nominative, accusative, and dative case assignment. Section 5 outlines an alternative functional account of case frames. Section 6 concludes the chapter.

2 Case Particles

The case particles in SMJ are listed in (3). *Ga, o,* and *ni* are distinguished from the other particles, in that they are omissible in colloquial speech, as illustrated in (4):[2]

(3) Case Particles in SMJ: *ga, o, ni, no, e, de, yori, kara, made, to*

(4) a.

Tarō(-ga)	*kesa*	*daigaku(-ni)*	*it-ta?*
Taro(-NOM)	this.morning	university(-DAT)	go-PST

'Did Taro go to university this morning?'

b.

Onigiri(-o)	*soto-de*	*taberu-no?*
rice.ball(-ACC)	outside-INSTR	eat-SFP

'Are (we) going to eat rice balls outside?'

It has been the standard practice to treat *no* as in (5a) as an instance of the genitive particle, but *no* also functions as a marker of adnominal modification, as illustrated in (5b–c):[3]

[2] *Ni* is omissible in limited contexts including when it marks goal arguments of motion verbs, as illustrated in (4a).

[3] *No* may also function as a nominalizer or a pro-form that refers back to an entity that is recoverable from the discourse context:

(i)

Tarō-ga	*hitoride*	*gaishutsu-suru-no-o*	*yame-ta.*
Taro-NOM	alone	going.out-do-NMLZ-ACC	stop-PST

'Taro stopped going out alone.' (nominalizer)

(ii)

Sono	*akai-no-o*	*sute-nasai.*
that	red-one-ACC	throw.away-IMP.HON

'Please throw away that red one.' (pro-form)

(5) a. *Tarō-no* *atama/musume/hon*
Taro-GEN head/daughter/book
'Taro's head/daughter/book' (genitive case)

b. *Tarō-ga* *itsumo-no* *basu-de* *kitaku-shi-ta.*
Taro-NOM always-GEN bus-INSTR going.home-do-PST
'Taro went home by the bus he always rode.' (attributive marker)

c. *Tarō-ga* *jinja-e-no* *michi-o* *mitsuke-ta.*
Taro-NOM shrine-ALL-GEN way-ACC find-PST
'Taro found a way to the shrine.' (attributive marker)

The particle *no* in (5a) relates the possessor noun to the head noun, while *no* in (5b–c) turns the adverb *itsumo* 'always' and the postpositional phrase *jinja-e* 'to/toward the shrine' into adnominal modifiers. In either case, *no* makes an element that it is attached to serve as an adnominal modifier. It remains an open question whether such uses of *no* as the one illustrated in (5a) may be analyzed as the genitive case marker or as a subtype of the adnominal modifier.[4]

The major uses of the nominative *ga* are illustrated in (6a–d):

(6) a. *Tarō-ga* *hon-o* *yon-da.*
Taro-NOM book-ACC read-PST
'Taro read a book.'

b. *Tarō-ni/ga* *eigo-ga* *wakar-u.*
Taro-DAT/NOM English-NOM understand-PRES
'Taro understands English.'

c. *Tarō-ni/ga* *ninjin-ga* *tabe-rare-ru.*
Taro-DAT/NOM carrot-NOM eat-can-PRES
'Taro can eat carrots.'

d. *Tarō-ni/ga* *kono* *hon-ga* *yomi-yasui/nikui.*
Taro-DAT/NOM this book-NOM read-easy/difficult
'For Taro to read this book is easy/difficult.'

What is peculiar about *ga* is that there is no one-to-one correspondence between the nominative marking and its grammatical function. *Ga* marks not only subject arguments, but also non-subject arguments of a few simple stative predicates (e.g. *iru* 'have,' *dekiru* 'can do,' *tokui-da* 'be good at') and morphologically complex predicates formed by the potential morpheme *-(rar)e* 'can' and the "tough" morphemes *-yasui/nikui* 'easy/difficult,' as illustrated in (6b–d).

Another important point to note with respect to (6b–d) is that their subject arguments may bear either dative or nominative case. Examples (2) and (6b–d) illustrate that the nominative particle may mark more than one NP within a clause. Such multiple occurrence of a nominative-marked argument within a clause makes it impossible to define the nominative

[4] See Frellesvig (2010: 126–128) for historical discussion of the primary function of *no*.

particle *ga* as the subject marker and requires us to define it with no appeal to grammatical relations.

Second, the accusative particle *o* functions as a marker of direct objects (as in (6a)), but *o* also may serve as a marker of source and path arguments of motion verbs (Haig 1981; Miyake 1996), as exemplified in (7a–b):

(7) a. *Tarō-ga heya-o/kara de-ta.*
Taro-NOM room-ACC/ABL go.out-PST
'Taro went out of the room.' (source)
b. *Tarō-ga kaigan-o arui-ta.*
Taro-NOM beach-ACC walk-PST
'Taro walked along the beach.' (path)
c. *Chi-ga kizuguchi-*o/kara de-ta.*
blood-NOM wound-ACC/ABL go.out-PST
'Blood went out of the wound.' (source)

Source arguments as in (7a) may be marked by either the accusative or ablative particle, while path arguments as in (7b) may be marked only by the accusative particle. In (7c), when the subject argument is not volitional, the source argument may not be marked by *o* (Miyake 1996: 145). That is, not all source arguments of motion verbs may receive accusative case.

Third, the dative *ni* has a wide range of uses including the goal, recipient, source, experiencer, benefactive, causee, and addressee, as illustrated in (8):

(8) a. *Tarō-ga daigaku-ni dekaketa.*
Taro-NOM college-DAT go.out-PST
'Taro went out to college.' (goal)
b. *Tarō-ga Hanako-ni hon-o watashi-ta.*
Taro-NOM Hanako-DAT book-ACC hand-PST
'Taro handed a book to Hanako.' (recipient)
c. *Tarō-ga Hanako-ni(/kara) pen-o kari-ta.*
Taro-NOM Hanako-DAT(/ABL) pen-ACC borrow-PST
'Taro borrowed a pen from Hanako.' (source)
d. *Tarō-ni eigo-ga wakar-u.*
Taro-DAT English-NOM understand-PRES
'Taro understands English.' (experiencer)
e. *Tarō-ga musuko-ni hon-o katte-age-ta.*
Taro-NOM son-DAT book-ACC buy-give-PST
'Taro bought a book for his son.' (benefactive)
f. *Tarō-ga Hanako-ni hon-o kaw-ase-ta.*
Taro-NOM Hanako-DAT book-ACC buy-CAUS-PST
'Taro made Hanako buy a book.' (causee)
g. *Tarō-ga Hanako-ni hon-o yomu-yō susume-ta.*
Taro-NOM Hanako-DAT book-ACC read-COMP advise-PST
'Taro advised Hanako to read a book.' (addressee)

Fourth, the instrumental particle *de* started as a locative marker that specifies a location in which an event takes place and has acquired a wide range of meanings including instrument, manner, temporal duration, and material meanings (Mabuchi 2000: 18–28), as illustrated in (9):

(9) a. *Tarō-ga kōen-de sanpo-shi-tei-ta.*
Taro-NOM park-INSTR stroll.do-PROG-PST
'Taro was taking a walk in the park.' (location)

b. *Tarō-ga kagi-de doa-o ake-ta.*
Taro-NOM key-INSTR door-ACC open-PST
'Taro opened the door with a key.' (instrument)

c. *Tarō-ga sanjikan-de shigoto-o oe-ta.*
Taro-NOM three.hours-INSTR work-ACC finish-PST
'Taro finished his work in three hours.' (temporal duration)

d. *Tarō-ga kaze-de jugyō-o sōtai-shi-ta.*
Taro-NOM cold-INSTR class-ACC leave.early-do-PST
'Taro left class early because of a cold.' (cause)

The instrumental case has traditionally been defined as a marker of the semantic role of instrument, but it may mark a wide range of nouns (e.g. instrument, transportation, route, unit, manner, location, source, temporal duration, moved entity, material, cause, passive agent) in many languages including Japanese.

Finally, examples (10a–e) illustrate the rest of the case particles, *e* (allative), *made* (terminative), *kara* (ablative), *yori* (ablative), and *to* (comitative):

(10) a. *Tarō-ga Tōkyō-ni/e/made mukatta.*
Taro-NOM Tokyo-DAT/ALL/TERM head-PST
'Taro headed for Tokyo.'

b. *Tarō-ga san-ji-made sagyō-o tsuzuke-ta.*
Taro-NOM 3-o'clock-TERM work-ACC continue-PST
'Taro continued his work until 3 o'clock.'

c. *Tarō-ga Kyōto-kara jitaku-ni modot-ta.*
Taro-NOM Kyoto-ABL home-DAT return-PST
'Taro returned home from Kyoto.'

d. *Hanako-ga Tarō-yori sono shigoto-ni tekinin-da.*
Hanako-NOM Taro-ABL that job-DAT qualified-COP
'Hanako is more qualified for the job than Taro.'

e. *Tarō-ga Hanako-to eiga-o mi-ta.*
Taro-NOM Hanako-COM movie-ACC watch-PST
'Taro watched the movie with Hanako.'

3 Non-canonical Case Frames

SMJ has not only the set of case frames expected for standard accusative languages, but also case frames that deviate from them. These non-canonical case frames are borne by Dative-Subject, Multiple-Nominative, Genitive-Subject, Causative, and Desiderative Constructions.

First, (11a–e) illustrate Dative-Subject Constructions (DSCs), in which subject arguments optionally receive dative case, while non-subject arguments receive nominative case. It remains controversial how to assign nominative case to non-subject arguments (see Koizumi 2008 for a survey of generative accounts of DSCs in Japanese):[5]

(11) Dative-Subject Constructions

a. *Tarō-ni/ga musuko-ga i-ru.*
Taro-DAT/NOM son-NOM have-PRES
'Taro has a son.'

b. *Tarō-ni/ga ryōri-ga deki-ru.*
Taro-DAT/NOM cooking-NOM can.do-PRES
'Taro can do the cooking.'

c. *Tarō-ni/ga eigo-ga wakar-u.*
Taro-DAT/NOM English-NOM understand-PRES
'Taro understands English.' (= (6b))

d. *Tarō-ni/ga ninjin-ga tabe-rare-ru.*
Taro-DAT/NOM carrot-NOM eat-can-PRES
'Taro can eat carrots.' (=(6c))

e. *Tarō-ni/ga kono hon-ga yomi-yasui/nikui.*
Taro-DAT/NOM this book-NOM read-easy/difficult
'For Taro to read this book is easy/difficult.' (=(6d))

Examples (11c–e) may also bear a 'NOM–ACC' case frame. For example, in an imperative mood or with the auxiliary *-ō-to-suru* 'try to,' *wakaru* 'understand' can occur in the 'NOM–ACC' case frame, as illustrated in (12) (Sugioka 1984: 164–165; see also Haig 1979b):

(12) a. *Boku-no kimochi-o wakar-e.*
I-GEN feelings-ACC understand-IMP
'Understand my feelings.'

b. *Kimi-wa boku-no kimochi-o wakar-ō-to-shi-na-i.*
you-TOP I-GEN feelings-ACC understand-VOL-COMP-do-NEG-PRES
'You don't try to understand my feelings.'

These two environments force a dynamic interpretation of *wakaru* and motivate the use of a 'NOM–ACC' case frame. Likewise, potential and

[5] Potential constructions formed by *-(rar)e* 'can' and "tough" constructions formed by *-yasui* 'easy' and *-nikui* 'difficult' are lumped together under the rubric of DSCs in this chapter. See Inoue (1978, 2004) for a generative attempt to provide a full account of "tough" constructions.

some (but not all) "tough" constructions that take a transitive verb as their complement (e.g. 11d–e) may also bear a 'NOM–ACC' case frame.

Second, (13a–c) illustrate Multiple-Nominative Constructions (MNCs):

(13) Multiple-Nominative Constructions
  a. *Tarō-ga* *hahaoya-ga* *hyōban-ga* *ii.*
     Taro-NOM mother-NOM reputation-NOM good
     'Taro is such that his mother has a good reputation.' (=(2))
  b. *Tarō-ga* *butsuri-ga* *tokui/nigate-da.*
     Taro-NOM physics-NOM good.at/bad.at-COP
     'Taro is good/bad at physics.'
  c. *Boku-ga* *kuma-ga* *kowakat-ta.*
     I-NOM bear-NOM afraid.of-PST
     'I was afraid of bears.'

MNCs are divided into two subtypes, depending on whether the clause-initial subject argument is subcategorized by the predicate or not (Kuno 1973: ch. 4): (13a) is distinguished from (13b–c), in that the predicates in (13b–c) subcategorize for both the subject and the non-subject arguments, while the one in (13a) does not. A list of adjectives and nominal adjectives that require both of their arguments to bear nominative case is given in (14) (Kuno 1973: 81–82):

(14) a. Competence: *jōzu-da* 'be good at,' *negate/heta-da* 'be bad at,' *tokui-da* 'be good at, be proud of,' *umai* 'be good at'
  b. Feeling: *suki-da* 'be fond of,' *kirai-da* 'be hateful of,' *hoshii* 'want,' *kowai* 'be fearful of'
  c. *-Tai* derivatives (composed of *-tai* 'want' and a transitive verb stem): *yomi-tai* 'want to read,' *tabe-tai* 'want to eat'

It has been the standard practice within the generativist tradition to license nominative case in the presence of a tensed element since Chomsky (1981), but this raises the question of how to handle MNCs, since a clause may have only one tense marker (and therefore only one nominative-marked argument). MNCs have attracted much attention since the advent of the *Principles-and-Parameters Theory* (PPT) (Chomsky 1981, 1986b), since they require an elaboration/modification of the standard assumption about nominative case assignment in the PPT.

Third, examples (15a–c) illustrate Genitive-Subject Constructions (GSCs), which show up in dependent clauses such as relative clauses, (nominal and verbal) complement clauses, and adverbial clauses:

(15) Genitive-Subject Constructions
  a. *Tarō-no/ga* *nakushi-ta* *kagi-o* *mitsuke-ta.*
     Taro-GEN/NOM lose-PST key-ACC find-PST
     '(I) found the key that Taro lost.'

b. *Tarō-ga* *kanojo-no/ga* *dekake-ta-koto-o* *shira-nakat-ta.*
Taro-NOM she-GEN/NOM go.out-PST-NMLZ-ACC know-NEG-PST
'Taro didn't know that she went out.'

c. *Tarō-no/ga* *shin-da-ato,* *Hanako-ga* *nihon-ni* *modot-ta.*
Taro-GEN/NOM die-PST-after Hanako-NOM Japan-DAT return-PST
'After Taro died, Hanako returned to Japan.'

There is a restriction as to what may occur in those dependent clauses with genitive-marked subjects: no genitive-marked agentive argument may occur with an accusative-marked patientive argument in dependent clauses, as illustrated by (16a) (Harada 1971: 28):

(16) a. *Tarō-*no(/ga)* *isu-o* *kat-ta-koto-o* *Hanako-wa*
Taro-GEN(/NOM) chair-ACC buy-PST-COMP-ACC Hanako-TOP
shira-nakat-ta.
know-NEG-PST
'Hanako didn't know that Taro bought a chair.'

b. *Tarō-no/ga* *kat-ta* *isu-ga* *nusum-are-ta.*
Taro-GEN/NOM buy-PST chair-NOM steal-PASS-PST
'The chair that Taro bought was stolen.'

Example (16b) shows that an agentive argument may receive genitive case when it is not accompanied by an accusative-marked patientive argument in the dependent clause. This restriction is consistent with an observation that subjects of unaccusative verbs in relative clauses and nominal complement clauses are much more likely to receive genitive case than those of unergative and transitive verbs in the same environments (Kim 2009).

Harada (1971) makes an important observation that two "dialects" are available in SMJ, one that allows (16a) (Dialect A) and the other that does not (Dialect B). He goes on to argue that Dialect A is on the edge of losing its status as the majority, while Dialect B has been spreading among younger generations.[6] The ensuing debate concerning how to analyze GSCs has been under the assumption that what Harada terms Dialect A is obsolete.

Fourth, examples (17a–c) illustrate Causative Constructions (CCs), which are formed by attaching the causative morpheme *-(s)ase* to a verb stem. They bear case frames of the corresponding two-place (transitive) and three-place (ditransitive) verb constructions:

(17) Causative Constructions
a. *Tarō-ga* *Hanako-o/*ni* *gakkaris-ase-ta.*
Taro-NOM Hanako-ACC/DAT feel.disappointed-CAUS-PST
'Taro made Hanako feel disappointed.' (base predicate = unaccusative)

[6] It is more appropriate to analyze the two dialects as two successive stages in the diachronic change, but I will use Harada's terminology for expository purposes. His hypothesis is confirmed quantitatively by Nambu (2007). See Kinsui et al. (2011: 93–99) for related discussion.

b. *Tarō-ga* *Hanako-o/ni* *aruk-ase-ta.*
Taro-NOM Hanako-ACC/DAT walk-CAUS-PST
'Taro made/let Hanako walk.' (base predicate = unergative)

c. *Tarō-ga* *Hanako-*o/ni* *hon-o* *kaw-ase-ta.*
Taro-NOM Hanako-ACC/DAT book-ACC buy-CAUS-PST
'Taro made/let Hanako buy a book.' (base predicate = transitive)

Causatives of transitive verbs bear a 'NOM-DAT-ACC' case frame, while causatives of intransitive verbs exhibit variations in the causee case marking: causatives of unaccusative verbs (e.g. *shinu* 'die') only allow accusative causee marking, while causatives of unergative verbs (e.g. *oyogu* 'swim') allow either dative or accusative causee marking when the causees are animate.

The case alternation in (17b) has a semantic motivation: a volitional causee receives dative case, while a non-volitional causee receives accusative case (Shibatani 1976: 251–253). The semantic contrast may be revealed by adding an adverb *muriyari* 'forcibly' to (17b) as in (18):

(18) a. *Tarō-ga* *Hanako-o* *muriyari* *kaigan-e* *aruk-ase-ta.*
Taro-NOM Hanako-ACC forcibly beach-ALL walk-CAUS-PST
'Taro made Hanako walk to the beach forcibly.' (coercion reading)

b. *??Tarō-ga* *Hanako-ni* *muriyari* *kaigan-e* *aruk-ase-ta.*
Hanako-DAT
'Taro let Hanako walk to the beach forcibly.' (permission reading)

The low acceptability of (18b) indicates that the dative-marked causee in (17b) must be construed as volitional.

The prohibition on the accusative-marked causee in (17c) has often been attributed to the *Double-o Constraint* (DoC) (Harada 1973; Shibatani 1978). The DoC has attracted much attention in the Japanese linguistics literature and merits a brief digression here. The DoC bans examples (19a–c), each of which contains two accusative-marked nouns within a single verb phrase:

(19) a. *Tarō-ga* *Hanako-*o(/ni)* *hon-o* *kaw-ase-ta.*
Taro-NOM Hanako-ACC(/DAT) book-ACC buy-CAUS-PST
'Taro made Hanako buy a book.' (causative of a transitive verb)

b. *Tarō-ga* *eigo-*o(/no)* *benkyō-o* *shi-ta.*
Taro-NOM English-ACC(/GEN) study-ACC do-PST
'Taro studied English.' (light-verb construction)

c. *Tarō-ga* *otoko-*o(/no)* *ude-o* *sashi-ta.*
Taro-NOM man-ACC(/GEN) arm-ACC stab-PST
'Taro stabbed the man on the arm.' (inalienable possession construction)

Interestingly, scrambling, topicalization, and relativization of one of the accusative-marked nouns improves the grammaticality of (19b–c).[7] Compare (19b–c) with (20a–b), respectively:

(20) a. *Eigo-o* *Tarō-ga* *san-nen* *benkyō-o* *shi-ta.*
English-ACC Taro-NOM three-years study-ACC do-PST
'Taro has studied English three years.' (scrambling)

b. *Tarō-ga* *ude-o* *sashi-ta* *otoko*
Taro-NOM arm-ACC stab-PST man
'The man who Taro stabbed on the arm' (relativization)

Finally, (21) illustrates Desiderative Constructions (DCs), which are formed by attaching the desiderative morpheme *-tai* 'want' to a verb stem:

(21) Desiderative Constructions
Boku-ga *wain-o/ga* *nomi-takat-ta.*
I-NOM wine-ACC/NOM drink-want-PST
'I wanted to drink wine.'

What is intriguing about DCs is that when the desiderative morpheme takes a transitive verb as its complement, its non-subject argument may receive either accusative or nominative case. The case alternation is caused by whether the complement verb phrase is construable as an attributive predication of the subject argument or its eventive predication: in the former, the non-subject argument receives nominative case, while in the latter, it receives accusative case.

4 Generative Accounts of Case Assignment in Japanese

This section gives a brief survey of representative generative accounts of nominative, accusative, and dative case assignment in Japanese. These three cases constitute the core part of the SMJ case system and deserve special attention.

The generative accounts are divided into two stages. The first is represented by Kuroda (1965, 1978), Kuno (1973), and Shibatani (1978), which assign the above-mentioned three cases on the basis of phrase structure rules and/or grammatical relations, while the second stage is represented by Takezawa (1987), Heycock (1993), Watanabe (1996), Ura (2000), and Hiraiwa (2001), which assign/license *structural cases* such as nominative and accusative on the basis of phrase structural position and treat dative (and other oblique) cases under the rubric of *inherent cases*.

[7] See Hiraiwa (2010: 734–746) for further discussion and illustration of these and other strategies of salvation.

4.1 Classical Transformational Accounts

Kuroda (1965) is the first generative account of case assignment in Japanese. He adopts the distinction between the deep and surface structure and divides NPs in deep structure into unmarked and (case-)marked NPs. Under the assumption that two phrase structure rules in (22) obtain in Japanese, Kuroda (1965: 165–166) proposes that the case particles other than *ga* and *o* are attached to NPs before application of the two transformational rules in (23):

(22) a. S —> NP VP Aux
b. VP —> NP V

(23) Transformational insertion rules
a. Ø —> *ga* in ##NP ____
b. Ø —> *o* in NP ____ V

The rule in (23a) attaches *ga* to unmarked NPs that occur sentence-initially, while (23b) attaches *o* to unmarked NPs that occur immediately before the verb.

Kuroda (1978: 34) proposes to replace (23) with (24), in order to accommodate DSCs such as (11a), under the assumption that (25b) is the deep structure of (11a), repeated below as (25a):

(24) Mark the first unmarked NP with *ga* and mark any other unmarked NP(s) with *o*.

(25) a. *Tarō-ni/ga* *musuko-ga* *i-ru.*
Taro-DAT/NOM son-NOM have-PRES
'Taro has a son.' (= (11a))
b. *Tarō-ni* *musuko* *i-ru.*

The rule in (24) assigns the nominative particle to *musuko* 'son' (since it is "the first unmarked NP" in (25b)) and derives the 'DAT-NOM' case frame in (25a). One problem that Kuroda (1965, 1978) leaves unanswered is how to derive the 'NOM-NOM' case frame in (25a).

Another problem with Kuroda's account is that he does not uniquely identify what he means by the Aux (auxiliary) in (22a) except to suggest that the auxiliary is a tense marker or some other particle attached to the VP (Kuroda 1965: 167). In other words, Kuroda fails to identify the syntactic domain in which (23) or (24) applies. Kuroda (1978) leaves this problem unresolved and applies (24) to infinitival complement clauses of causative and potential constructions as well as finite clauses, under the assumption that (24) applies cyclically from the innermost to the topmost clause. This procedure makes case assignment in causative and potential constructions complicated (see Kuroda 1978: 30–41 for details).

Kuno (1973) follows Kuroda (1965) in dividing NPs in the deep structure into unmarked and (case-)marked NPs and assuming that unmarked NPs receive case particles by transformational insertion rules in (26) (Kuno 1973: 330):

(26) Transformational rules
  a. Indirect object marking: Attach *ni* to the second of three unmarked NPs, that is, the NPs that do not yet have a (case) particle.
  b. Subject marking: Attach *ga* to the subject NP.
  c. Object marking: Attach *o* to the first non-subject unmarked NP to the left of the main verb if it is [–stative], and *ga* if it is [+stative].

Three rules in (26) presupposes that (27a–c) are the deep structures of intransitive, transitive, and ditransitive sentences:[8]

(27) a. Intransitive sentence: NP V AUX
  b. Transitive sentence: NP NP V AUX
  c. Ditransitive sentence: NP NP NP V AUX

The sentence-initial NPs in (27) are subjects and are marked by *ga*. Both the second NP in (27b) and the third NP in (27c) are the first non-subject unmarked NP to the left of the main verb and are marked by *o* when the verbs are non-stative. The transformational rule in (26a) assigns *ni* to the second NP in (27c), which counts as the indirect object. The second NP in (27b) is marked by *ga* when the two-place verb is stative (e.g. *iru* 'have,' *wakaru* 'understand,' *dekiru* 'can do'). How the 'NOM-NOM' case frame of *iru* in (11a) is derived under Kuno's proposal:

(28) a. Deep structure: Tarō musuko iru
  b. Application of (26b): Tarō-ga musuko iru
  c. Application of (26c): Tarō-ga musuko-ga iru

The question that remains is how to derive the 'DAT-NOM' case frame borne by *iru* 'have.' In order to derive the 'DAT-NOM' case frame borne by the small number of two-place stative predicates, Kuno proposes the *ga/ni* conversion, a transformational rule that changes the first NP marked by *ga* to the one marked by *ni*, as shown in (29) (Kuno 1973: 88–90):

(29) *Ga/ni* conversion
  a. *Tarō-ga musuko-ga i-ru.*
  b. *Tarō-ni musuko-ga i-ru.*

What is peculiar about the *ga/ni* conversion is that it applies optionally when the two-place verb is stative and bears the 'NOM-NOM' case frame. This means that the *ga/ni* conversion may not apply when the verb is intransitive (and the NP marked by *ga* is the only argument of the verb) or when the object of a transitive verb is marked by *o*, as demonstrated by (30):[9]

[8] The linear order of grammatical relations in (27b–c) is 'Subject–(Indirect Object)–Direct Object.'

[9] The *ga/ni* conversion does not apply to two-place stative predicates such as *heta-da* 'be bad at' and *hoshii* 'want.' Kuno assumes that this is a matter of lexical idiosyncrasy.

(30) a. *Tarō-ga/*ni* *eki-e* *hashit-ta.*
Taro-NOM/DAT train.station-ALL run-PST
'Taro ran to the train station.'

b. *Tarō-ga/*ni* *isu-o* *kowashi-ta.*
Taro-NOM/DAT chair-ACC break-PST
'Taro broke the chair.'

Shibatani (1978: 235) posits the notion of subject as a theoretical primitive that requires no reference to phrase structural position and defines *ga* as the default subject marker as in (31b), which may be overridden by (31a):

(31) a. Assign *ni* to subjects of two-place predicates that are specified for assigning *ni* to their subjects.
b. Assign *ga* to subjects (this rule applies optionally when (31a) already applies).

The essential idea behind (31) is that *ni* is assigned to subjects lexically (given that its distribution is restricted), while *ga* is assigned to subjects syntactically.

In order to derive the 'DAT-NOM' case frame as illustrated in (11) and the 'NOM-DAT-ACC' case frame of ditransitive verbs, Shibatani (1978: 236–237) proposes (32a–b), which apply to direct objects, and (32c), which applies to indirect objects:[10]

(32) a. Assign *ga* to direct objects of two-place stative predicates.
b. Assign *o* to direct objects (this rule applies optionally when (32a) already applies and does not apply to sentences that contain existential and some other verbs).
c. Assign *ni* to indirect objects.

The rule in (32b) is designed to handle the case alternations in (33), in which the predicates comprise the nominalized continuative form of the transitive verb *suku/kirau* 'like/hate' and the copula:

(33) a. *Tarō-ga* *Hanako-ga/o* *suki-da.*
Taro-NOM Hanako-NOM/ACC liking-COP
'Taro likes Hanako.'

b. *Tarō-ga* *Hanako-ga/o* *kirai-da.*
hating-COP
'Taro hates Hanako.'

Furthermore, in order to describe the dative–nominative alternations in (11a–c) and the nominative–accusative alternations in (33a–b), Shibatani (1978: 235) proposes a rule that deletes any case particle followed by

[10] Shibatani (1978: 287–293) suggests that it is possible to replace the notions of direct and indirect objects with the semantic notions of "target (of an action/emotion)" and "recipient" in (32), but I keep using the notions of subject, direct object, and indirect object when summarizing his account of case assignment, since their replacement makes no empirical difference.

another one. The three steps in (34) shows how to derive the 'NOM-NOM' case frame from the 'DAT-NOM' case frame in (11a), while (35) shows how to derive the 'NOM-ACC' case frame from the 'NOM-NOM' case frame in (33a):

(34) a. Application of (31a) and (32a)
Tarō-ni musuko-ga i-ru.
b. Application of (31b) (optional)
Tarō-ni-ga musuko-ga i-ru.
c. Application of the rule of particle deletion
Tarō-~~ni~~-ga musuko-ga i-ru.

(35) a. Application of (31b) and (32a)
Tarō-ga Hanako-ga suki-da.
b. Application of (32b) (optional)
Tarō-ga Hanako-ga-o suki-da.
c. Application of the rule of particle deletion
Tarō-ga Hanako-~~ga~~-o suki-da.

In addition to (31) and (32), Shibatani (1978: 253–254) notes that when a subject receives the dative particle according to (31a), (32b) fails to apply, while when a direct object receives the accusative particle according to (32b), (31b) must apply and he generalizes this observation to (36):

(36) Obligatoriness of a nominative-marked NP (Shibatani 1978: 256)
A finite clause must contain at least one nominative-marked NP.

Finally, let us consider how Shibatani derives the case frames of causative constructions as in (17b) as an illustration of how Kuroda (1965), Kuno (1973), and Shibatani (1978) handle case frames of complex clauses. First, Shibatani proposes the two deep structures in (37) for (17b) under the assumption that *-(s)ase* has two subcategorization frames: one with a causer argument (*Tarō*) and he other with an extra "target" argument (*Hanako*) in addition to the causer argument:

(37) a. [Tarō Hanako$_i$ [Hanako$_i$ aruk] ase-ta]
b. [Tarō [Hanako aruk] ase-ta]

Application of (i) *equi NP deletion* (i.e. a rule that deletes the subject of a complement clause when it is coreferential with the subject or object of the main clause), (ii) *predicate raising* (i.e. a rule that combines the matrix predicate with the embedded predicate), and (iii) *tree pruning* (i.e. a rule that deletes the node of S (sentence) if S loses its subject or verb phrase) to (37a) yields (38a), while application of (ii) predicate raising and (iii) tree pruning to (37b) yields (38b):

(38) a. [Tarō Hanako aruk-ase-ta]
Subject/Agent Direct Object/Target
b. [Tarō Hanako aruk-ase-ta]
Subject/Agent Agent

The two causative constructions in (38) are different with respect to the role of the causee *Hanako*: it is a direct object (or a "target" in terms of semantic roles) in (38a), while it is a non-subject agent in (38b).[11]

Given (38a–b), Shibatani derives the 'NOM-DAT' case frame of (17b) from (31b) and another rule that assigns dative case to those agent arguments which do not function as subjects (Shibatani 1978: 298), while deriving the 'NOM–ACC' case frame of (17b) from (31b) and (32b).

To summarize this subsection, Kuroda (1965, 1978), Kuno (1973), and Shibatani (1978) lay the foundation for both generative and functional accounts of the SMJ case system in the following four respects. First, Kuno (1973) and Shibatani (1978) build on Kuroda's (1965) account of the nominative, accusative, and dative case particles and describe most, if not all, of the case frames of simple and complex clauses in SMJ. Second, Kuroda (1965) divides NPs into unmarked and (case-)marked and assigns nominative and accusative cases to the former ones syntactically (i.e. by transformational insertion rules). Both Kuno (1973) and Shibatani (1978) follow Kuroda (1965) in adopting the distinction between syntactic and lexical cases, but, unlike Kuroda, they treat those uses of dative case which mark recipient arguments of ditransitive verbs on a par with nominative and accusative cases and separate them from those uses of dative case which mark subjects of the small number of two-place stative predicates (e.g. *iru* 'have,' *wakaru* 'understand') and causee arguments of causative constructions.[12] Third, Shibatani (1978) identifies the syntactic domain in which the case assignment rules apply as a finite clause and defines nominative case as the default case (as in (36)). Although Shibatani does not theorize the relationship between a finite clause and the nominative case assignment, it receives a theoretical formulation within the framework of PPT (see Section 4.2 below). Finally, Kuno (1973), Kuroda (1978), and Shibatani (1978) derive causative, potential, desiderative, and other complex predicate constructions by reducing their underlying bi-clausal structure into a mono-clausal one through equi-NP deletion, verb/predicate raising, and tree pruning (i.e. deletion of the S node of the embedded clause).[13] This clausal reduction remains the key element in all the subsequent work on complex predicate constructions in SMJ, no matter what its theoretical formulation may look like.[14]

The polyfunctional nature of *ga*, *o*, and *ni* makes it challenging to provide a unified account of all their major uses. For example, *ni* receives a different

[11] The reason the semantic role of *Hanako* in (38a) is termed a "target" (not an agent) is that the subject of the complement clause is deleted by equi NP deletion.

[12] Sadakane and Koizumi (1995) also propose to treat dative case as used to mark recipient arguments of ditransitive verbs on a par with nominative and accusative cases.

[13] Kuno (1973) uses the terms "verb raising" and "AUX deletion" instead of "predicate raising" and "tree pruning," but since the auxiliary element is the indispensable element of any sentence, we may treat Kuno's (1973) account on a par with Shibatani's (1978).

[14] See Kuno (1973: 330–345), Kuroda (1978: 30–41), and Shibatani (1978: 120–156, 304–326) for further details on their classical transformational accounts of complex predicate constructions in SMJ.

treatment, depending on whether it marks indirect objects (i.e. recipient arguments of ditransitive verbs), subject arguments of some two-place stative predicates, or causee arguments of causative constructions. They leave the task for future studies, some of which will be reviewed in the next subsection.

4.2 Principles-and-Parameters Theory (PPT)

Takezawa (1987) is the first full-scale PPT account of the case system of SMJ. The aim of this subsection is to outline Takezawa (1987), which follows the spirit of Kuroda (1965) in making a distinction between nominative/accusative and dative (and all the other oblique) cases and formulates the relationship between a finite clause and the nominative case assignment within the framework of PPT (Chomsky 1981, 1986b).

In order to understand the outline of Takezawa (1987), it is essential to provide a brief outline of Chomsky's (1981) Case theory. There are three important principles proposed by Chomsky (1981) that underlie most PPT accounts of Case assignment (including Takezawa (1987)). First, PPT assumes that all NPs with lexical content are assigned *abstract Case* and distinguishes abstract Case from its overt morphological realization (*morphological case*).[15] Second, Case is assigned under government and the choice of Case is determined by its governor (i.e. Case assigner) as shown in (39):[16]

(39) Abstract Case assignment (slightly modified from Chomsky 1981: 170)
- a. NP is nominative if governed by a tensed INFL (when INFL contains AGR).
- b. NP is accusative if governed by a transitive verb.
- c. NP is oblique if governed by P.
- d. NP is inherently Case-marked as determined by properties of its governor.
- e. NP is genitive in $[_{NP}$ X] (X=N′ or VP).

All NPs with lexical content that have no abstract Case at S-structure are banned by the *Case Filter* (Chomsky 1981: 49):

(40) Case Filter: *NP if NP has phonetic content and has no Case

Third, PPT draws a distinction between *structural* and *inherent Case*: the former includes nominative and accusative and is assigned at *S-structure*, while the latter (e.g. dative, ablative, instrumental) is associated with theta-marking and is lexically assigned at *D-structure*.

15 Abstract Case is distinguished orthographically from morphological case by the use of an initial capital and this convention will be adopted throughout this subsection.

16 The notion of government is defined in terms of *c-command* and *m-command*. Specifically, α (governor) governs β when α c-commands/m-commands β: α c-commands/m-commands β if α does not dominate β and the first branching node/maximal projection (full phrasal category) that dominates α dominates β (Chomsky 1986b: 8). For example, nominative Case is assigned under m-command, while accusative Case is assigned under c-command.

The rule in (39a) links the nominative Case assignment with finiteness of a clause and may be construed as a theoretical formulation of Shibatani's (1978) observation that a clause must contain at least one-nominative-marked NP in Japanese (see (36)) (see Takezawa 1987: 72–83 for related discussion). Another point to note is that there is a parallelism between the PPT distinction between structural and inherent Case and Kuroda's (1965) account of nominative/accusative and oblique cases, in that he assigns nominative and accusative cases to unmarked NPs (i.e. NPs with no case marker in the deep structure), which are distinguished from (case-)marked NPs (i.e. those NPs which receive an oblique Case marker in the deep structure).

Given the assumption that SMJ is a *configurational language* (i.e. a language whose clauses contain a VP node) (see Saito and Hoji 1983 and Saito 1985: ch. 2 for theory-internal justification), Takezawa (1987) sets out to account for the case frames borne by DSCs and MNCs.

First, let us summarize Takezawa's account of DSCs by focusing on how he would handle (11a), repeated below:

(11) a. *Tarō-ni/ga* *musuko-ga* *i-ru.*
Taro-DAT/NOM son-NOM have-PRES
'Taro has a son.'

DSCs such as (11a) raise the question of how to explain the nominative marking of their non-subject arguments and the dative marking of their subject arguments. In order to answer this question, Takezawa (1987: 83–93) makes three proposals. The first is that two-place stative predicates such as *iru* 'have' in (11a) cannot assign any Case. This means that *iru* cannot assign accusative Case to its non-subject argument (*musuko* 'son' in (11a)) and that it must receive Case from elsewhere. The second proposal is that INFL moves down into a VP/AP in syntax in Japanese, so that it may govern non-subject arguments of DSCs. The operation in (41) shows how this operation (termed "INFL lowering") applies (adapted from Takezawa 1987: 84):

(41) NP INFL [$_{VP}$. . . .. V NP] —> NP [$_{VP}$. . . .. V-INFL NP]

The above operation yields the consequence that the lowered INFL is in a sister relation to the non-subject argument and governs it. This explains why *musuko* in (11a) receives nominative Case.

The third proposal is about the dative marking of the subject arguments of DSCs. It is important to note that (41) leaves the subject argument in (11a) Caseless (since it is not governed by the lowered INFL) and may cause a violation of the Case Filter if there is no way to assign Case to the subject argument. In order to solve this problem, Takezawa (1987: 90) proposes the following rule:

(42) The subject argument receives dative Case (*ni*) when it is not governed by a tensed INFL.

The rule in (42) assigns dative Case to the subject argument in (11a).[17] Takezawa states that this dative Case is distinct from the one assigned to recipient arguments of ditransitive verbs at D-structure and treats it as a postposition rather than a Case marker.

Before addressing the question of how to explain the dative–nominative alternation in (11a), Takezawa turns to MNCs. Let us consider how he would handle (13a) for illustration:

(13) a. *Tarō-ga* *hahaoya-ga* *hyōban-ga* *ii.*
Taro-NOM mother-NOM reputation-NOM good
'Taro is such that his mother has a good reputation.' (=(2))

What is notable about MNCs illustrated by (13a) is that neither *Tarō* nor *hahaoya* has any thematic relation with *ii* 'good' and that *hyōban* 'reputation' is the only thematic argument of the predicate. Takezawa (1987: 97–100) assumes that MNCs such as (13a) involve a multiple adjunction of IPs and goes on to propose that INFL has a potential to assign nominative Case to more than one NP in Japanese (see footnote 19). Example (43) is what Takezawa would propose as a partial phrase structure of (13a):

(43) $[_{\text{IP}}$ Tarō $[_{\text{IP}}$ hahaoya $[_{\text{IP}}$ hyōban $[_{\text{VP}}$ ii$]]]]$

Given the multiple adjunction of IPs, INFL assigns nominative Case to the three NPs, *Tarō, hahaoya*, and *hyōban* in (13a) (all of which occur in the specifier of IP).

Given the above account of MNCs, Takezawa (1987: 100) returns to the question of how to handle the dative–nominative alternation illustrated in (11a). He proposes that INFL must assign nominative Case to, at least, one NP, but that it optionally assigns nominative Case to other NP(s) in the same clause. The optional assignment of nominative Case accounts for the dative–nominative alternation as follows. First, when INFL assigns nominative Case only once, it must go to non-subject arguments of DSCs (otherwise they would not be able to receive any Case). Their subject arguments have no choice but to receive dative Case according to (42). On the other hand, when INFL assigns nominative Case more than once, subject (as well as non-subject) arguments receive nominative Case from the lowered INFL under the further assumption that the lowered INFL has an option of making a VP/AP transparent for government.

Heycock (1993) takes a different tack in explaining MNCs and their multiple-nominative case frame. She follows the spirit of Fukui (1986) in claiming that nominative Case in Japanese does not occupy a unique structural position (e.g. the specifier of IP) under the crucial assumption that there are an infinite number of VP-adjoined positions in which an

[17] Takezawa (1987: 91) argues in support of (42) that it also accounts for why the embedded subjects of morphological causatives of transitive verbs, benefactive constructions formed by an auxiliary verb *morau* 'receive,' and adversative passive constructions receive dative marking.

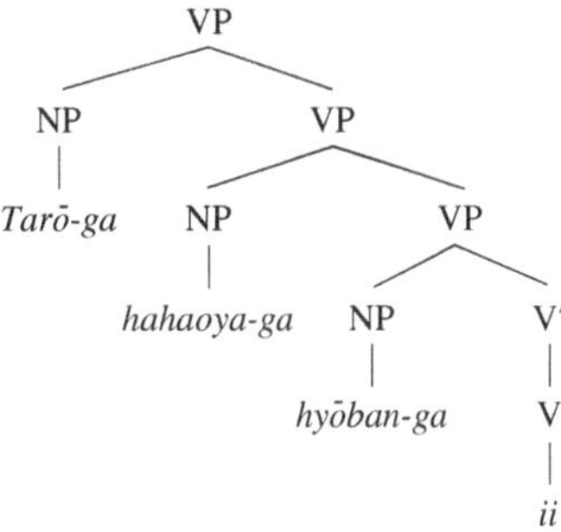

Figure 12.1 Phrase structure of (13a)

infinite number of nominative-marked NPs can appear. Figure 12.1 is the partial phrase structure of (13a):

(44) $[_{VP}$ Tarō-ga $[_{VP}$ hahaoya-ga $[_{VP}$ hyōban-ga $[_{V}$ ii$]]]]$

Her proposal is that layers of predication (as diagrammed in Figure 12.1) may be built up recursively, with a subject–predicate structure (e.g. *hyōban-ga ii, hahaoya-ga hyōban-ga ii*) functioning as the predicate licensing a further subject, and that nominative Case is available to license NPs in VP-adjoined positions. The recursive subject–predicate relation leads *Tarō* and *hahaoya*, both of which are not a thematic argument of *ii*, to receive nominative Case.

Heycock (1993: 172) further assumes that all theta-roles subcategorized by a lexical head are assigned within the smallest maximal projection of that head. This means that if a verb subcategorizes for two arguments (e.g. agent and patient arguments), they must occur within the domain of VP (i.e. the smallest maximal projection of V). This assumption yields the consequence that the subject argument of a simple sentence moves to adjoin to the VP, as shown in (45):

(45) $[_{VP}$ NP$_{i}$-ga $[_{VP}$ t_{i} V$]]$

The parallelism between (44) and (45) makes it possible to provide a configurational definition of *ga*: it marks any number of NPs that occur in VP-adjoined positions, whether they are theta-marked subjects or not.

What is novel about Heycock's proposal is that she formulates the subject–predicate relations that obtain in Japanese MNCs in phrase structural terms and provides a definition of nominative Case with no reference to INFL. This move obviates the need to appeal to the assumption made by Takezawa (1987) that INFL has a potential to assign nominative Case to more than one NP in Japanese, but leaves one important problem unsolved: how to assign nominative Case to non-subject arguments of DSCs. It is clear that Heycock's structural definition of nominative Case does not apply to them, since non-subject arguments of DSCs are VP-internal (Heycock 1993: 190–193).[18]

[18] Heycock (1993: footnote 20) acknowledges the problem, but she offers no solution.

To sum up this section, Takezawa (1987) maintains the PPT distinction between structural Case (i.e. nominative and accusative) and inherent Case (e.g. dative) and the government-based definitions of nominative and accusative Case in (39a–b) and derives the 'DAT-NOM' case frame of DSCs from the two technical assumptions: one, that Japanese requires INFL to move down to VP/AP when no Case assigner is available to non-subject arguments; and two, that dative Case is assigned to those subject arguments which are not governed by any tensed INFL. Takezawa further assumes that INFL may assign nominative Case to more than one NP in Japanese, in order to accommodate the multiple-nominative case frame of MNCs.[19] In contrast to Takezawa (1987), Heycock (1993) dissociates nominative Case assignment from INFL and incorporates the traditional observation (e.g. Kuno 1973: ch. 3; Takami and Kamio 1996) that MNCs involve a recursive layering of predications by assuming that MNCs involve a multiple application of VP adjunction as diagrammed in Figure 12.1 and assigning nominative Case to the VP-adjoined positions.

5 A Functional Account of Case Assignment in Japanese

This section outlines a functional account of non-canonical case frames borne by DSCs and MNCs in Japanese within the framework of Role and Reference Grammar (RRG) (Van Valin and LaPolla 1997; Van Valin 2005). RRG is a functionalist theory that assumes a direct mapping between the semantic representation of a sentence and its syntactic representation. DSCs and MNCs serve as a basis for comparison of the generative and functional frameworks.

5.1 A Brief Summary of Role and Reference Grammar

5.1.1 Syntactic Representation: Clause Structure

RRG represents clause structure not in terms of X-bar syntax but in terms of a semantically based model termed the *layered structure of the clause* (LSC). The LSC contains three layers: the *nucleus, core*, and *clause*. The nucleus contains the predicate, the core contains the nucleus plus the argument(s) of the predicate, while the clause contains the core plus its modifier(s).[20] In addition, some languages have a *precore slot* (PrCS), which is the position of *wh*-words in languages such as English and Icelandic, and a *left-detached position* (LDP), which is the position of the pre-clausal element (e.g.

[19] Takezawa's (1987) proposal to allow INFL to assign nominative Case to more than one NP is generalized and recast as *multiple feature checking* (Ura 2000) or as *multiple agree* (Hiraiwa 2001) within the framework of the Minimalist Program (Chomsky 1995), but the idea that nominative Case is assigned/licensed by a tensed element is shared by all of them.

[20] Adjunct modifies of the core (e.g. *slowly, yesterday*) occupy a clause-internal slot (termed the *periphery*), which, together with the core, constitutes the clause.

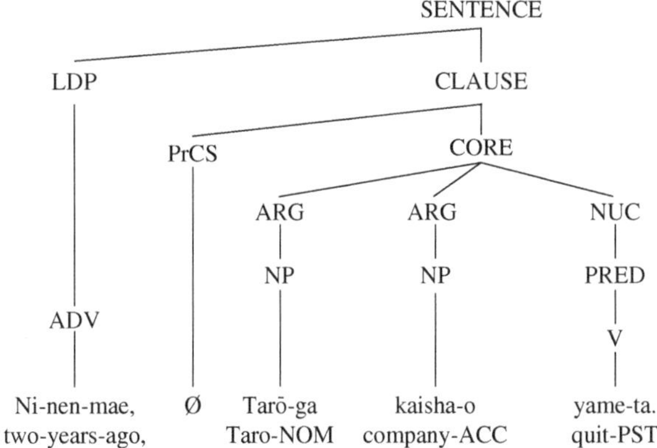

Figure 12.2 Formal representation of the LSC

a dislocated topic) that is often set off from the rest of the clause by an intonation break (cf. Chapter 18, this volume).[21] Figure 12.2 illustrates the LSC of a Japanese sentence with no element in the PrCS.

RRG dissociates auxiliary elements (e.g. aspect, negation, modality, mood, tense) from the LSC. These operators modify one of the above-mentioned three layers. For example, an aspectual marker modifies the nucleus, a root modal marker modifies the core, while a tense marker modifies the clause. They constitute a distinct level of representation (termed the *operator projection*) from the LSC and are ordered by the universal principle in (46) (Van Valin and LaPolla 1997: 72):

(46) Universal Operator Linear Precedence Rule
CLAUSE ⊃ CORE ⊃ NUCLEUS

5.1.2 Semantic Representation: Verbal Semantics

The above syntactic representation is coupled with the semantic representation of the clause, based on the decompositional lexical representation of the predicate in the nucleus. The decompositional system is based on the *Aktionsart* classes in examples (47a–f) (Van Valin 2005):

(47) a. State: *The boy is afraid.*
b. Activity: *The soldiers marched in the park.*
c. Achievement: *The balloon popped.*
d. Semelfactive: *The pencil tapped on the table.*
e. Accomplishment: *The ice melted.*
f. Active accomplishment: *The soldiers marched to the park.*

Semelfactive verbs denote a continuation of punctual events and pattern-like activity verbs (Smith 1997), while active accomplishment verbs are

[21] Some verb-final languages including Japanese have a *post-core slot* [PoCS] and a *right-detached position* [RDP], which is the position of the post-clausal element (e.g. an afterthought remark) (Van Valin and LaPolla 1997: ch. 2). These two slots are omitted for simplicity in Figure 12.2.

lexicalized telic uses of activity verbs. Examples (48a–f) are the causative counterparts of (47a–f), respectively:

(48) a. Causative state: *The dog frightens/scares the boy.*
b. Causative activity: *The sergeant marched the soldiers in the park.*
c. Causative achievement: *The cat popped the balloon.*
d. Causative semelfactive: *The teacher tapped the pencil on the table.*
e. Causative accomplishment: *The hot water melted the ice.*
f. Causative active accomplishment: *The sergeant marched the soldiers to the park.*

The twelve predicate classes in (47) and (48) are represented by the following decompositional system (termed *logical structure* (LS)) adapted from Vendler (1967), Dowty (1979), and Smith (1997) (Van Valin 2005: 45):

(49) Decompositional representations for *Aktionsart* classes

a. State	**predicate´** (x) or (x, y)
b. Activity	**do´** (x, [**predicate´** (x) or (x, y)])
c. Achievement	INGR **predicate´** (x) or (x, y), or INGR **do´** (x, [**predicate´** (x) or (x, y)])
d. Semelfactive	SEML **predicate´** (x) or (x, y), or SEML **do´** (x, [**predicate´** (x) or (x, y)])
e. Accomplishment	BECOME **predicate´** (x) or (x, y), or BECOME **do´** (x, [**predicate´** (x) or (x, y)])
f. Active accomplishment	**do´** (x, [$\textbf{predicate}_1$´ (x) or (x, y)]) & INGR $\textbf{predicate}_2$´ (z, x) or (y)
g. Causative	α CAUSE β, where α and β are logical structures of any type

State and activity are primitive predicates, while the other *Aktionsart* classes are built on these two primitive predicates, four operators (INGR (instantaneous change), BECOME (durational change), SEML (repetition of punctual events), and CAUSE (causation)), and their combinations.

A key component of the RRG linking system is the two-tiered system of semantic roles. The first tier is the decompositional representations of verbs in (49). The second tier comprises two *semantic macroroles: actor* (ACT) and *undergoer* (UND). They are generalized semantic roles that subsume a number of LS arguments for morphosyntactic purposes and correspond to the two major arguments of a transitive verb. The single argument of an intransitive verb can be either one, depending on the semantics of the verb (see below). Those LS arguments which are not an actor or undergoer are assigned non-macrorole [NMR] status. Examples (50a–f) illustrate the macrorole assignment:

(50) a. John [Effector, ACT] killed Bill [Patient, UND].
b. Bill [Patient, UND] was killed by John [Effector, ACT].
c. John [Effector, ACT] gave a book [Theme, UND] to Bill [Recipient, NMR].
d. John [Experiencer, ACT] knew the student [Theme, UND].
e. John [Effector, ACT] ran to the park.
f. John [Patient, UND] disappeared suddenly.

Examples (50a–b) show that passivization does not affect macrorole assignment: an actor may be realized either as an argument in active constructions or an adjunct in passive constructions.

The number of macroroles that a verb receives is determined by the *Default Macrorole Assignment Principles* [DMAP]:

(51) Default Macrorole Assignment Principles
 a. Number: the number of macroroles which a verb takes is less than or equal to the number of arguments in its LS:
  1. If a verb has two or more arguments in its LS, it will take two macroroles.
  2. If a verb has one argument in its LS, it will take one macrorole.
 b. Nature: for verbs which take one macrorole:
  1. If the verb has an activity predicate (**do´**) in its LS, the macrorole is actor.
  2. If the verb has no activity predicate (**do´**) in its LS, the macrorole is undergoer.

When the number of macroroles that a verb takes does not follow from the DMAP, it must be specified in the lexical entry of a verb by a feature (MRα) (where α is the number of macroroles). For example, when a two-place verb has only one macrorole (contrary to (51a1)), the verb has the feature (MR1) in its lexical entry. The principles in (51b) applies only when a verb receives one macrorole and it specifies which macrorole (actor or undergoer) it is.[22]

The relationship between LS arguments (i.e. argument positions in LS) and semantics macroroles is captured by the *Actor-Undergoer Hierarchy* (AUH) in Figure 12.3.

The AUH states that, given the LS of a multi-argument verb, the leftmost argument will be the actor and the rightmost argument will be the undergoer.[23]

5.1.3 Case Assignment

I adopt an RRG account of case assignment in (52–53) (adapted from Nakamura (1999a)). The former is the set of Optimality-Theoretic [OT] constraints for case assignment. The latter consists of the ranking of these OT

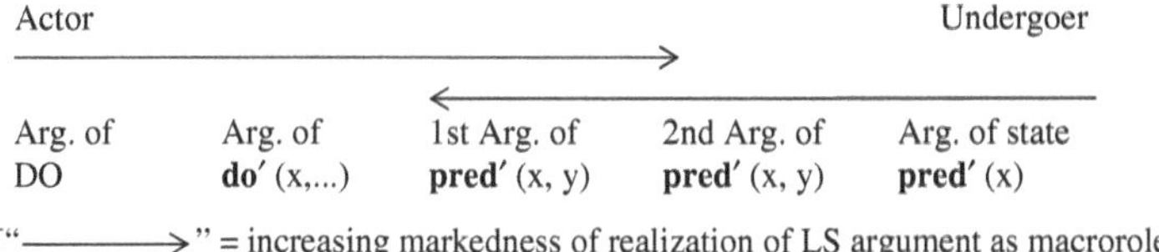

Figure 12.3 The Actor-Undergoer Hierarchy

[22] See Van Valin (1990) and Bentley (2006) for an RRG account of split intransitivity.

[23] These macroroles link up to language/construction-specific grammatical relations in most, if not all, languages (Van Valin and LaPolla 1997: ch. 6).

constraints and the minimal domain of case assignment (i.e. the one in which the OT constraints apply) for Japanese (see Van Valin and LaPolla 1997: 577–581 for a related proposal):

(52) OT constraints for case assignment
a. Some argument receives nominative case.
b. Non-macrorole core arguments receive dative case.
c. Undergoer arguments receive accusative case.

(53) a. Constraint ranking for Japanese: (52a) ≫ (52b) ≫ (52c)
b. Minimal domain of case assignment: Core

What is significant about (52a–c) is that they refer to macrorole status and the notion of core instead of referring to grammatical relations or phrase structural positions. The idea that non-macrorole core arguments (e.g. recipient arguments of ditransitive verbs) receive dative case as the default comes from Van Valin (1991). Another important point to note here is that (52a) and (53b) dissociate the nominative case assignment from the (finite) clause in the LSC and represent a crucial departure from the mainstream generative literature (see Section 4.2), which associates the nominative Case assignment/checking with a main (or an auxiliary) verb inflected for tense.

5.2 An RRG Functional Account of DSCs and MNCs

The first case frame to be considered is the 'DAT-NOM' case frame illustrated in (11a):

(11) a. *Tarō-ni/ga* *musuko-ga* *i-ru.*
Taro-DAT/NOM son-NOM have-PRES
'Taro has a son.'

The key to the RRG account of DSCs is the assumption that the dative-subject verbs receive only one macrorole contrary to (51a1) (Van Valin 1991). These verbs are irregular, but not with respect to case assignment. Rather, their irregularity lies in the number of macroroles: they receive one less macrorole than would be expected for a two-place verb. This marked macrorole assignment is captured by supplying the lexical entry of the dative-subject verb with the feature (MR1). The principles in (51b) dictate that it is an undergoer, since the verb *iru* has no activity predicate **do´** in its LS. The AUH requires *musuko* (the second argument of a two-place state predicate **have´**) to be associated with the undergoer. The remaining argument (*Tarō*) has no choice but to receive a non-macrorole status:

(54) LS: **have´** (Tarō, son) [MR1]

MR: Non-MR Undergoer

Given the macrorole assignment in (54), we can derive the 'DAT-NOM' case frame from the constraint ranking in (53a). Table 12.1 shows how the

Table 12.1 *OT evaluation of the case frame for (11a)*

	(52a)	(52b)	(52c)
NOM-NOM		*!	*
NOM-ACC		*!	
☞ DAT-NOM			*
DAT-ACC	*!		

evaluation proceeds when (53a) receives the pair of a non-macrorole core argument and an undergoer argument as the input.

Note that (52b) also applies to recipient arguments of ditransitive verbs and causee arguments of causative constructions, as illustrated in (55):

(55) a. *Tarō-ga* *Hanako-ni* *hon-o* *atae-ta.*
Taro-NOM Hanako-DAT book-ACC give-PST
'Taro gave a book to Hanako.'
b. *Tarō-ga* *Hanako-ni* *hon-o* *kaw-ase-ta.*
buy-CAUS-PST
'Taro made/let Hanako buy a book.' (=(17c))

The reason is that both the recipient and the causee arguments in (55) are non-macrorole core arguments.[24] Thus, (52b) gives a unified account of the dative case assignment in (11a) and (55a–b) (see Sadakane and Koizumi 1995 and Van Valin and LaPolla 1997: 376–384 for related discussion).

The second case frame to be considered in this subsection is the case frame borne by MNCs such as (13a):

(13) a. *Tarō-ga* *hahaoya-ga* *hyōban-ga* *ii.*
Taro-NOM mother-NOM reputation-NOM good
'Taro is such that his mother has a good reputation.'

What is peculiar about (13a) is that its syntactic subject has no thematic relation with the predicate *ii* 'good.' We may follow the spirit of Heycock (1993) in assuming that an iteration of a nominative-marked NP in MNCs is licensed by the recursive layering of subject–predicate relations in (56):

(56) a. [hyōban ii]
predication$_1$
b. [hahaoya [hyōban ii]]
predication$_2$
c. [Tarō [hahaoya [hyōban ii]]]
predication$_3$

24 The effector argument *Tarō* and the theme argument *hon* in (55a) are the highest-ranking and lowest-ranking arguments in terms of the AUH and receive an actor and undergoer status, respectively. The remaining argument *Hanako* becomes a non-macrorole. An analogous macrorole assignment holds for (55b) (Van Valin and LaPolla 1997: 532–537).

Layering in (56) suggests that each of the nominative-marked NPs is coupled with the (complex) predicate and that the leftmost nominative-marked NP (*Tarō*) is the subject of the whole sentence. This recursive layering of predications emerges when each of the nominative-marked NPs is licensed by virtue of the *characterization condition* (Takami and Kamio 1996: 224), according to which a non-argument NP may behave as the syntactic subject only when it is characterized by the rest of the sentence.

The question at hand is how to represent the recursive layering of predication relations in terms of the LSC. The *Complex Nucleus Formation* in (57) is the recast of the characterization condition in terms of the LSC:

(57) Complex Nucleus Formation (CNF) (adapted from Nakamura (1999b)): MNCs such as (13a) involve a reanalysis in which the innermost nominative-marked NP and the predicate combine to form a complex nucleus only when it may be interpreted as denoting an inherent attribute of the next innermost nominative-marked NP.

Given the CNF, we may propose (58) as the LSC of (13a):[25]

(58) [$_{\text{CLAUSE}}$ [$_{\text{CORE}}$ Tarō [$_{\text{CORE}}$ hahaoya [$_{\text{CORE}}$ hyōban [$_{\text{NUC}}$ ii]]]]]

The LSC in (58) describes a construction in which a core composed of *hyōban* 'reputation' and *ii* 'good' is reanalyzed as the first complex nucleus that licenses *hahaoya* 'mother' as its sole argument. This construction is, in turn, reanalyzed as the second complex nucleus that licenses the leftmost NP (*Tarō*) as its syntactic subject.[26]

Under the assumption that the minimal domain of case assignment is the core in Japanese, the LSC of (13a) in (58) allows us to derive the multiple-nominative case frame from (53a). The LSC in (58) shows that (13a) has three cores, each of which contains only one argument. The constraint ranking in (53a) requires that when a core contains only one argument, it must receive nominative case. The constraint ranking (53a) applies to the three cores in (13a) simultaneously and yields the multiple-nominative case frame.

The CNF-based RRG account of MNCs recasts Heycock's (1993) proposal (that MNCs involve an iteration of VP adjunction licensed by a recursive layering of predications) in terms of the LSC. The crucial difference between them, however, is that the RRG account derives the multiple-nominative case frames of MNCs and the 'DAT-NOM' case frames of DSCs in a unified way, while Heycock (1993) cannot do so, since her proposal to assign nominative case to VP-adjoined positions in MNCs does not extend to non-subject arguments of DSCs (see Section 4.2).

[25] I follow Kuno (1973: 75) in analyzing the leftmost nominative-marked NP of an MNC as receiving an exhaustive-listing (narrow focus; cf. ch. 13, this volume) interpretation when its complex predicate represents a generic statement. Since (13a) is not a generic statement, the sentence-initial nominative-marked NP in (13a) may receive a neutral-description interpretation.

[26] The CNF-based account extends to (13b–c) with no modification, since the combination of the second nominative-marked argument and predicate may be taken as an attributive predication of the clause-initial nominative-marked NP.

6 Conclusion

In this chapter, I have introduced in Section 2 the major uses of the nominative, accusative, dative, genitive, and other oblique case particles. I have surveyed in Section 3 those deviant case frames (from the standard accusative case patterns) which are borne by DSCs, MNCs, GSCs, CCs, and DCs. In Section 4, I have summarized the classical transformational and PPT accounts of case assignment in MSJ. In Section 5, I have provided an alternative functional account of DSCs and MNCs and their case assignment within the framework of RRG.

Although a large amount of work has been done about the Japanese case system and its realization in a variety of constructions (some of which have been surveyed in Section 3), many issues remain to be solved, including whether it is possible to maintain the generativist assumption that nominative case is assigned only in finite clauses (see Shibatani 1978: 256–259 for its initial formulation) and how to describe and classify the various uses of dative and other oblique cases. These two and other related questions await further research.[27]

27 One question that has received much attention since Kuroda (1965) is how to explain the case alternation illustrated in (17b) in such a way as to capture its semantic motivation. See Nakamura (2008: 105–108) for a macrorole-based account that dispenses with two distinct subcategorization frames.

13

Subjects and Topics

Yoko Hasegawa

1 Introduction

It is well known that Japanese has two postpositional particles that can mark the grammatical subject, as illustrated in (1), where *ga* is referred to as the nominative (subject) marker and *wa* as the topic marker.

(1) a. *Donarudo Toranpu ga/wa daitōryō ni shimei sareta.*
NOM/TOP president for was.nominated
'Donald Trump was nominated as president.'

In ordinary language, the terms *subject* and *topic* can both be loosely defined as discussion focal points. Therefore, they frequently overlap functionally: many subjects are also topics, and many topics are commonly expressed as subjects. However, in linguistics, *subject* and *topic* refer to drastically different concepts. Subject is a grammatical relation between a given constituent (typically an NP) and the predicate. That is, the scope of a subject is limited to a clause, or to a sentence if the sentence is mono-clausal. Topic, on the other hand, references a much broader notion. It is not unusual to consider the topic of a paragraph or of a chapter, or even of an entire book. In other words, the scope of a topic is a *discourse* (or a *text*), a sequence of sentences organized by a specific purpose. While the distinction between subject and topic is likely to be universally significant in verbal communication, it is grammaticalized (morphosyntactically distinguished) in Japanese.

The difference between how subject and topic function makes elucidation of *ga* and *wa* a considerable challenge because they sometimes contrast on different grounds. When a sentence is examined in isolation, *ga* and *wa* can often be used interchangeably; however, when that same sentence is embedded in a discourse, either *ga* or *wa* might not be usable. Another reason for explanatory difficulty is that the selection criteria for these particles are not mutually exclusive. In the same sentence, *ga* might be appropriate according to one criterion, but *wa* might be preferable according to another.

To put it differently, the distinction between *ga* and *wa* is primarily a matter of *information packaging* (Chafe 1976: 28), that is, how the message is sent, rather than the content of the message itself. Speakers present information in a linguistically structured way in order to provide the addressee with guidance on how to manipulate and integrate such information according to their beliefs about the addressee's knowledge and attentional state; for example, to highlight a constituent that should be paid special attention.

Nevertheless, elucidation of the difference between *ga* and *wa* is essential in Japanese linguistics because they have a partially overlapping distribution and explicating the differences between them has been a perennial problem. For more than two centuries, therefore, many researchers have investigated this fascinating issue.

Li and Thompson (1976) propose a linguistic typology based on how essential the role played by the subject and/or topic is in a given language. According to their proposal, both are prominent in Japanese:

(2) a. Subject-prominent: Indo-European, Finno-Ugric, Dyirbal (Australian), Indonesian
b. Topic-prominent: Chinese, Lahu (Lolo-Burmese), Lisu (Lolo-Burmese)
c. Both subject-prominent and topic-prominent: Japanese, Korean
d. Neither subject-prominent nor topic-prominent: Tagalog, Illocano (Philippines)[1]

The typical difference between subject and topic in English is illustrated in English in (3–4) and in Japanese in (5–6). As Chafe (1976: 49) points out, the (4b)-type sentences in English inevitably imply a contrast (e.g. the particular play vis-à-vis other plays), but the topic in topic-prominent languages does not. In (5b), the street in question is not necessarily contrasted with any other street.[2]

(3) a. *John made such efforts in vain!*
b. *But* *everyone* *praised John.*
SUBJECT PREDICATE

(4) a. *I want to see "The Secret in the Wings."*
b. *(As for) that play,* *Mary saw it yesterday.*
TOPIC COMMENT

(5) a. *Mata* *jiko* *desu* *ka?*
again accident COP INT
'An accident again?'

[1] Although highly innovative and influential, this typology must be regarded as preliminary. For example, both subject and topic are reported to be prominent in Tagalog (Schachter and Otanes 1982) as well as some other Austronesian languages in Indonesia (Masayoshi Shibatani, p.c.).

[2] A rudimentary notion of contrast exists whenever an entity is singled out and mentioned, for example, *kono michi* 'this street' in (5b). However, the speaker of (5b) does not necessarily contrast this particular street with others. Rather, the speaker is likely to encode 'this street' as the subject, that is, "this street has many accidents." Because what is contrasted is too indeterminate, we do not consider such a rudimentary notion as contrast in this chapter.

b.

Kono	*michi*	*wa*	*jiko*	*ga*	*ōi*	*desu*	*ne.*
this	street	TOP	accident	NOM	numerous	COP	SFP
TOPIC			COMMENT				

Lit. 'This street, accidents are numerous.'

In this chapter, rather than proceeding straight into abstract discussions of the nature of *ga* and *wa*, we shall first familiarize ourselves with concrete examples of various phenomena that pertain to them. We will then move on to more theoretical considerations. In addition to the function of subject, Section 2 discusses the main effects that *ga*-marking creates, and Section 3 is concerned with those of *wa*-marking. Section 4 continues with examination of additional functions of *wa*. Section 5 illustrates the topic-subject construction, a quintessential feature of *topic-prominent languages*. Section 6 is devoted to the behavior of *ga* and *wa* in dependent clauses; Section 7 reconsiders the characteristics laid out in Section 2–6 in terms of more abstract and systematic approaches. Section 8 provides a case study, followed by conclusions in Section 9.

2 The Subject

In modern linguistics, archetypal subjects are known to control the following grammatical phenomena (Keenan 1976).

(6) a. Reflexives: *John*$_i$ *praised himself*$_i$.
b. Deletion: *John*$_i$ *talked to Bill*$_j$ *for a while and then* $Ø_{i,*j}$ *left.*
c. Backward pronominalization: *When he*$_{i,\,?j}$ *got home, John*$_i$ *talked to Bill*$_j$.
d. Backward deletion: *On* $Ø_{i,\,*j}$ *arriving home, John*$_i$ *talked to Bill*$_j$.
e. Verb agreement: *John*$_i$ *hates*$_{i,\,*j}$ *them*$_j$.
f. Equi-NP deletion: *John*$_i$ *wants* $Ø_{i,\,*j}$ *to help Bill*$_j$.

2.1 *Ga* as the Subject Marker

Both *ga*-marked and *wa*-marked NPs generally fulfill the functions in (6):

(7) a. Reflexives

Maki$_i$	*ga/wa*	*jibun-jishin*$_i$	*o*	*hometataeta.*
	NOM/TOP	self	ACC	praised

'Maki$_i$ praised herself$_i$.'

b. Deletion

Maki$_i$	*ga/wa*	*shibaraku*	*Namiko*$_j$	*to*	*hanashi-te*	*kara*	$Ø_{i,\,*j}$
	NOM/TOP	for.a.while		with	talking	after	

tachisatta.
left

'Maki$_i$ talked with Namiko$_j$ for a while and then [$Ø_{i,\,*j}$] left.'

c. Backward pronominalization in Japanese is extremely awkward, if not ungrammatical.

d. Backward deletion

$Ø_{i, *j}$ uchi ni kaette, Maki$_i$ ga/wa Namiko$_j$ to hanashita.
home to returning NOM/TOP with talked
'Upon [$Ø_{i, *j}$] arriving home, Maki$_i$ talked with Namiko$_j$.'

e. Honorific verb agreement

Kōchō$_i$ ga/wa watashi$_j$ o goran ni natta$_{i, *j}$.
principal NOM/TOP I ACC looked (HON)
'The principal looked at me.'

f. Equi-NP deletion

Maki$_i$ ga/wa Namiko$_j$ ni $Ø_{i, *j}$ hanasu tsumori da.
NOM/TOP to talk intend
'Maki$_i$ intends to [$Ø_{i, *j}$] talk to Namiko$_j$.'

A topic can be a subject, but as shown in (4b) and (5b), it need not be. This is the most conspicuous case for distinguishing between the concepts of subject and topic. That is, with a non-subject topic, *wa* can mark non-subject NPs, but *ga* cannot. In (8), *sono eiga* 'that movie' is the direct object of *mimashita* 'saw'; therefore, it cannot be marked by *ga*.

(8) *Sono eiga wa/*ga senshū mimashita.*
that movie TOP/NOM last.week saw
'That movie, (I) saw (it) last week.'

2.2 *Ga* as a Focus-marker

As will be discussed later in Section 3.3, when some *attribute* (a characteristic or quality inherent in an entity) is to be described, the entity is typically presented with *wa*. When *ga* is used instead in such sentences, the NP-*ga* is understood to be the *focus*, that is, the most informative part, of the sentence because it is unpredictable in the given context (Lambrecht 1994: 207) as illustrated in (9). In English, in addition to manipulation of intonation, this notion of focus can be expressed most clearly with a *cleft construction* as in the translations of (9).[3]

(9) a. *Kono rapputoppu ga karui.*
this laptop NOM light
'It is this laptop that is light (weight).'

b. *Shigeru ga kangoshi da.*
NOM nurse is
'It is Shigeru who is a nurse.'

However, when a sentence describes a temporally transient state of affairs of an entity, a focal interpretation does not necessarily arise. Rather, such sentences are interpreted as unmarked in terms of information structure.

[3] *Cleft sentence* refers to a grammatical construction in which an original single clause – for example, *Jacob is a student* – is divided into two parts – for example, *[It is Jacob] [who is a student]*.

(10) a. *Kyō* *mo* *sora* *ga* *aoi.*
today also sky NOM blue
'The sky is blue again today.' Not 'It is the sky that is blue.'

b. *Shigeru* *ga* *nete iru.*
NOM is.sleeping
'Shigeru is sleeping.' Not necessarily 'It is Shigeru who is sleeping.'

When a question consists of an interrogative subject, the portion of the answer that corresponds to this unidentified entity is naturally the most informative, and, therefore, is marked by *ga*. In (11b), *watashi wa* is unacceptable because the sentence is not about the speaker him/herself, but, rather, about the event in which the speaker is a mere participant.

(11) a. *Dare* *ga* *kore* *o* *tsukuttan* *desu* *ka?*
who NOM this ACC made is INT
'Who made this?'

b. *Watashi* *ga/#wa* *tsukurimashita.*[4]
I NOM/TOP made
'I made it.' 'It's I who made it.'

In English, the future-tense markers *be going to* and *will* are interchangeable in many, if not most, contexts. However, if a lecturer enters your classroom and says, *Oh, I forgot to bring the projector*, and you decide to volunteer to bring it, you should say *I'll go get it*, not *#I'm going to go get it*, because the latter indicates that the activity is preplanned, not decided on site. This distinction can be captured by the use of *ga* and *wa*. In (12a), the use of *ga* conveys a decision made just at the time of the utterance, whereas the use of *wa* does not. On the other hand, in (12b), *wa*, but not *ga*, is appropriate if responding to the question, *Is everybody going to the lecture this evening?*

(12) a. *Watashi* *ga/#wa* *motte-kimasu.*
I NOM/TOP carry-come
'I'll go get (it).'

b. *Watashi* *#ga/wa* *ikimasu.*
I NOM/TOP go
'I'm going to go.'

3 The Topic

In this section, we examine the concept of topic, with which *wa* is commonly associated.

[4] The hashtag # indicates that the expression is grammatical and yet unacceptable for various reasons.

3.1 Identifiability

The following two sentences depict objectively the same situation:

(13) a. *Hon wa tsukue no ue ni aru.*
book TOP desk GEN top on exist
'The book is on [the top of] the desk.'

b. *Tsukue no ue ni hon ga aru.*
desk GEN top on book NOM exist
'There is a book on [the top of] the desk.'

Nevertheless, these two sentences are not interchangeable. *Hon wa* in (13a) cannot be used unless the speaker believes that the addressee can identify the referent (i.e. the book). This notion of *identifiability* is indispensable for topicality. By way of comparison, a subject need not be identifiable. English has a special sentence pattern referred to as the *there*-construction, which is used to introduce an unidentifiable entity into a discourse, as in the translation of (13b). Its Japanese counterpart uses the existential verb *iru* or *aru*.[5] When these verbs are used for this purpose, the subject uniformly occurs with the nominative *ga*, not with the topic marker *wa*.

In English, identifiable NPs are typically marked with the definite article *the*, as in (13a), and unidentifiable NPs by an indefinite article *a/an*, as in (13b). Notwithstanding such a distinction, identifiability is a supposedly universal cognitive category, whereas the definite article is a grammatical category, which can be idiosyncratic to a given language. In fact, among languages that employ definite articles (e.g. French, German, Greek, Italian), their use or non-use can vary considerably when depicting the same entity in the same situation (Lambrecht 1994: 79–87).

The referent of an interrogative NP – for example, *dare* 'who,' *nani* 'what' – is unknown to the speaker, that is, unidentifiable, so it cannot be marked by *wa*, although it can be marked by *ga*.

(14) a. *Dare ga/*wa kimashita ka?*
who NOM/TOP came INT
'Who came?'

b. *Nani ga/*wa miemasu ka?*
what NOM/TOP visible INT
Lit. 'What can be seen?' 'What can you see?'

[5] *Aru* and *iru* 'exist/be/stay/locate' are existential verbs. It is commonly explained that *aru* is used with an inanimate subject (something that is not alive and/or is unable to move independently) and *iru* with an animate one. This distinction, however, is a recent phenomenon. While *aru* has been a genuine existential verb throughout history, *iru* originally meant 'become motionless,' and contrasted with *tatsu* 'start moving' (Kinsui 1984). As the unique existential verb, *aru* was used for both animate and inanimate subjects until late Middle Japanese (the twelfth–sixteenth centuries). In the early twentieth century, *aru* could still be used with an animate subject, but *iru* had become dominant in such cases.

Likewise, the referent of an indefinite NP – for example, *dareka* 'someone,' *nanika* 'something' – is supposed to be unidentifiable by the speaker and/or the addressee, and can therefore be marked by *ga*, but not by *wa*.

(15) a.

Dareka	*ga/*wa*	*kimashita*	*ka?*
someone	NOM/TOP	came	INT

'Did someone come (here)?'

b.

Nanika	*ga/*wa*	*miemasu*	*ka?*
something	NOM/TOP	visible	INT

Lit. 'Is something visible?' 'Can you see something?'

The next three subsections discuss how this essential notion of identifiability is established.

3.1.1 Anaphoric Topics

In a discourse, the most common way to make a referent identifiable is by using the mechanism of *anaphora*. The following is the opening passage of *Momotarō* 'Peach Boy,' a popular Japanese folktale. It illustrates how anaphora typically works:

(16)

Mukashi mukashi	*aru*	*tokoro*	*ni*	*ojisan*	*to*	*obāsan*	***ga***
old.days	certain	place	in	old.man	and	old.woman	NOM

sunde imashita.	*Aru*	*hi*	*ojisan*	***wa***	*yama*	*e*
were.living	certain	day	old.man	TOP	mountain	to

shibakari	*ni,*	*obāsan*	***wa***	*kawa*	*e*	*sentaku*
gather.firewood	for	old.woman	TOP	river	to	washing

ni	*ikimashita.*
for	went

'A long, long time ago, there lived an old man and an old woman. One day, the old man went to the mountain to gather firewood, and the old woman went to the river to wash clothes.'

The old couple in (16) is first introduced into the discourse with *ga* (*ojisan to obāsan ga*), which serves as the antecedent. At this point, they are unidentifiable and translated into English with the indefinite article *an* (*an old man and an old woman*). Although the reader does not know these referents, they are nonetheless registered in the reader's mind. That is, they function as *hitching posts* for accumulation of new knowledge, to use Chafe's (1976: 44) metaphor. Once the referents are registered, the NPs can be marked with *wa* (*ojisan wa… obāsan wa…*), and in English the use of the definite article *the* is standard.

3.1.2 Generic Topics

In addition to anaphora, when the referent is *generic*, that is, a class of entities as a whole, rather than an individual member of the class, it is identifiable. In Japanese, generic NPs are uniformly marked with *wa*. In English, by contrast, they can be expressed with a plural NP (17a), with a singular NP with *the* (17b) or *a/an* (17c), or with a singular NP with no article (17d).[6]

(17) a. *Ari wa/#ga satō o konomu.*
ant TOP/NOM sugar ACC like
'Ants like sugar.'

b. *Nō wa/#ga ōku no nikutai-kinō o tsukasadoru.*
brain TOP/NOM many bodily-function ACC control
'The brain controls many bodily functions.'

c. *Rakuda wa/#ga mizu nashi de 3-shūkan ikirareru.*
camel TOP/NOM water without 3-weeks can.live
'A camel can live for three weeks without water.'

d. *Wain wa/#ga hakkōshu da.*
wine TOP/NOM fermented.liquor is
'Wine is (a kind of) fermented liquor.'

3.1.3 Unique Topics

Some entities are known by the speaker and addressee uniquely, and they are therefore identifiable.

(18) a. *Taiyō wa nishi ni shizumu.*
sun TOP west in set
'The sun sets in the West.'

b. *Maki wa konai to itta.*
TOP not.come QUOT said
'Maki said she won't come.'

Under normal circumstances, *taiyō* 'sun' in (18a) refers to our sun. In (18b), if Maki is not known by both interlocutors, or if they know more than one person whose name is *Maki*, the referent must be properly introduced into the discourse, as happens in this illustrative sentence: *Yesterday, I met Maki, a friend of mine*. The person, then, can be referred to as an anaphoric topic.

3.2 Staging

An explanation of *wa* as a special rhetorical device of *staging* is relevant at this point.[7] A written text can begin with an NP-*wa* even when the reader is certainly unable to identify the intended referent. For instance, (19) would appear as an opening sentence of a novel:

[6] As discussed in Section 2.2, when *ga* appears in sentences like (17), the NP is invariably interpreted as a focus element: *It's ants that like sugar, it's the brain that controls many bodily functions*, etc.

[7] The term *staging* is borrowed from Maynard (1987). Maynard defines her use of *staging* as the narrator's selection of an event participant whose point of view is taken as the basis of the narration. That is, the participant is selected as the protagonist, and the narrative is constructed as if the event were perceived by the person. Although Maynard's definition of *staging* is much broader than what is intended here, I nevertheless adapt this term because it provides the most illustrative image of this particular function of *wa*. The *wa*-marked entity at the beginning of a written discourse is, metaphorically speaking, placed on the theatrical stage as the protagonist.

(19) *Otoko* *wa* *kado* *o* *magaru* *to* *kyū ni* *tachidomatta.*
man TOP corner ACC turn when suddenly stopped
'The man stopped suddenly when [he] turned the corner.'

Although the man here is fictitious and therefore an unidentifiable entity, it is nonetheless more natural to mark *otoko* 'man' with the topic marker *wa*, rather than with the subject-marker *ga*. This stylistically specialized use of *wa* is limited to written texts. In spoken discourse, the speaker must supply some introductory passage – for example, *Kinō hen na hito ni attan dakedo...* 'Yesterday I ran into a strange man, and...' The speaker can then continue the story revolving around this person. Otherwise, the speech would sound strange, possibly incomprehensible. This function of *wa* is undoubtedly derived from the required identifiability of the *wa*-marked topic. The reader continues reading, believing that the entity will become identifiable.

3.3 Attribute Description

Participants in a described event need not be identifiable, as exemplified in (20a). However, when some *attribute* (e.g. tallness) is ascribed to an entity, the entity must be identifiable. Otherwise, the sentence would sound anomalous, for example (20b).

(20) a. *Tsūkōnin* *ga* *mado* *o* *kowashita.*
passerby NOM window ACC broke
'A passerby broke a window.'
b. #*Tsūkōnin* *ga* *se* *ga* *takai.*
passerby NOM hight NOM high
'A passerby is tall.'

Therefore, adjectival and nominal predicates normally co-occur with NP-*wa*, rather than NP-*ga*.

(21) a. *Kono* *rapputoppu* *wa* *omoi.* [adjectival predicate]
this laptop TOP heavy
'This laptop is heavy.'
b. *Shigeru* *wa* *kangoshi* *da.* [nominal predicate]
TOP nurse is
'Shigeru is a nurse.'

As discussed in Section 2.2, when *ga* marks the subject of such sentences, for example (9), the entity must be construed as a focal element.

4 Other Functions of *Wa*-marking

4.1 Contrast

Wa has a contrastive (CNT) function, in which case the NP does not have to be identifiable.

(22) a. *Ōzei no hito wa pātī ni kimashita ga, omoshiroi*
many people CNT party to came but interesting
hito wa hitori mo kimasendeshita. (Kuno 1972b: 270)
people CNT one.person even did.not.come
'Many people came to the party, but not a single one was interesting.'

b. *Tegami wa kimashita.*
letter TOP/CNT came
'The letter came.' [non-contrastive] or 'A letter came (but there was nothing else in the day's delivery).'

c. *Nani wa yurusarete, nani wa yurusarenain desu ka?*
what CNT permitted what CNT not.permitted is INT
'What is permitted, and what is not permitted?'

d. [Speaking about dangerous cities in the US]
Dono machi wa anzen desu ka?
which city CNT safe is INT
'Which city is safe?'

The first half of (22a), *ōzei no hito wa pātī ni kimashita* 'many people came to the party,' is unacceptable if it stands by itself because *ōzei no hito* is unidentifiable and yet is marked by *wa*. However, when a contrast is added by means of the second clause, the whole sentence becomes acceptable. Example (22b) is ambiguous. If *tegami* 'letter' is identifiable (e.g. when the interlocutors have been talking about a specific letter), the sentence is interpreted as consisting of a topic, but if *tegami* is not identifiable, the addressee automatically interprets the sentence as contrastive, inferring that something else has not arrived. With a strong emphasis on contrast, even interrogative subject NPs can be marked with *wa* as shown in (22c–d). Whether or not this (contrastive) use of *wa* is distinct from topic marking will be discussed later.

4.2 Negative-scope Marking

Wa can mark the *scope of negation* (NEG-SCP), that is, specifying what is negated.

(23) a. *Kenkyūsho wa yomimasen.*
research.book TOP/NEG-SCP not.read
'I don't read scholarly books.'

b. *Kenkyūsho wa kai wa shimasu ga yomi wa shimasen.*
research.book TOP buy CNT do but read NEG-SCP not.do
'As for scholarly books, I buy them but don't read them.'

In (23a), marking the direct object *kenkyūsho* 'research book' with the accusative particle *o* (unmarked in affirmative sentences) is possible, but when the sentence is negated, *wa*-marking sounds far more natural and idiomatic. *Kenkyūsho wa* here is thus ambiguous between the topic- and the negative-scope readings. If the interlocutors have been talking about scholarly books, *wa* is naturally understood as a topic marker. On the other hand, if the speaker of (23a) is responding to someone else's comment that the speaker is a diligent researcher, this utterance would politely negate such a praise by indicating that s/he buys scholarly books but does not necessarily read them. In other contexts, when reading is a topic of conversation, the utterance can imply that the speaker reads something other than scholarly books, and thus the NP is also contrastive. In this case, the *kenkyūsho* entity is introduced into the discourse by this very utterance.

In any case, *wa*-marking of an NP can enable the hearer to project negation early on when interpreting an utterance. This function is particularly significant because in Japanese a predicative negation marker does not appear until the very end of the clause.

In (23b), the first *wa* is normally construed as a topic marker, but the second and third occurrences of NP-*wa* cannot be topics because it is unlikely that the utterance is about buying and reading things in this context. While both the second and the third *wa* can be analyzed uniformly as contrastive, I prefer to consider the third *wa* as negative-scope marking because this function is most saliently perceived here.[8]

Negative-scope marking *wa* can appear freely with constituents other than NPs or internally to predicative elements (McGloin 1987: 173–174).

(24) a. *Tabe* *wa* *shinakatta.* [verb]
eating NEG-SCP did.not
'(I) didn't eat (it).'

b. *Kono* *kyōkasho* *wa* *atarashiku* *wa* *nai.* [adjective]
this textbook TOP new NEG-SCP not
'This textbook is not new.'

c. *Jōzu ni* *wa* *kakenai.* [adverbial]
well NEG-SCP cannot.write
'(I can write it, but) I can't write (it) well.'

d. *Zenbu* *wa* *dekinakatta.* [adverb]
all NEG-SCP could.not
'(I did some, but) I couldn't do (them) all.'

When a *wa*-marked constituent is not in a negative clause, it is understood to be contrastive:

(25) a. *Sono* *ryōri* *wa* *tabe* *wa* *shita.* [verb]
that dish TOP eating CNT did
'(I) tried [tasted] that dish (but I didn't like it).'

[8] I am aware of my considerable sensitivity to the effect of *wa*'s negative-scope marking. Negative clauses or sentences without *wa* – for example, *Hon o yomimasen* '(I) don't read books' – sound very unnatural to me, but I note that some native speakers do not share my intuition.

b. *Kono kyōkasho wa atarashiku wa aru.* [adjective]
this textbook TOP new CNT exist
'This textbook is new (but it has some undesirable features).'

c. *Jōzu ni wa kakeru.* [adverbial]
well CNT can.write
'I can write it eloquently (but that doesn't guarantee credibility).'

d. *?Zenbu wa dekita.* [adverb]
all CNT could.do
'I could do (them) all (but. . .).'

The speaker of (25a) unambiguously implies that s/he wishes to convey some message covertly that contrasts with her/his experience eating a particular type of meal; for example, s/he did not like it. While (25b) is easily interpretable in a similar way, (25c) requires more presupposition (i.e. contextual support); for example, evaluation of eloquence as an undesirable trait. I cannot think of any plausible context for (25d), however. These examples indicate that, whereas the negative-scope *wa* can co-occur freely with a constituent other than an NP, the use of *wa* with such a constituent is substantially restricted in affirmative clauses.

As I have discussed in this subsection, the distinctions among topic, contrast, and negative-scope marking are not clear-cut. Rather, one may wonder whether they are even distinct concepts. Nevertheless, the topic appears sufficiently different from the others because it must be identifiable, while the other two need not be. Furthermore, it is inconceivable that the marked entity is a topic when *wa* appears inside a predicate; for example, *tabe wa shita* 'tasted' in (25a). On the other hand, contrast and negative-scope marking are intertwined, as seen in (24–25). It is reasonable to consider that negative-scope marking is a subtype of contrast marking. These three concepts are mutually compatible, and when the NP is simultaneously the topic, contrastive, and with negation, *wa*-marking becomes stylistically obligatory.

5 The *Wa–ga* Construction

As mentioned in the chapter's introductory section, a single Japanese sentence can have both a distinct topic (NP-*wa*) and a subject (NP-*ga*). The topic in this construction delimits the applicability of the statement that includes the subject referent.

(26) a. *Maki wa zubanuketa sainō ga aru.*
TOP outstanding talent NOM exit
Lit. 'Maki, there is an outstanding talent.' 'Maki is an outstanding talent.'

b. *Watashi*	*wa*	*tomodachi*	*ga*	*ōi.*
I	TOP	friend	NOM	numerous

Lit. 'Me, friends are numerous.' 'I have many friends.'

c. *Sakana*	*wa*	*sake*	*ga*	*oishii.*
fish	TOP	salmon	NOM	delicious

'Of (all the various types of) fish, salmon is (the most) delicious.'

A commonly employed translation strategy into English for the *wa–ga* construction is *as for X*, for example, *As for Maki, there is an outstanding talent* for (26a). However, Chafe (1976: 50) cautions that this strategy is misleading because the original Japanese sentence does not carry contrastive connotation (i.e. vis-à-vis someone other than Maki), but *as for X* inevitably does so.

6 Dependent Clauses

6.1 Types of Dependent Clauses

There are three types of dependent clauses in Japanese: (i) subordinate clauses, (ii) noun-modifying clauses, and (iii) quotative clauses. Subordinate clauses usually augment the main clause with such additional information as time, condition, or reason. A statement asserts the content of the main clause, but not that of a subordinate clause. For example, in *When my father died, I inherited the house*, the speaker reports his/her inheritance, not the father's death.

Because the topic is the entity about which the speaker makes an assertion, subordinate clauses cannot contain a topic. In (27a), *Maki* is the topic as well as the subject, but when the sentence is converted into a subordinate clause, as in (27b), *Maki* is no longer the topic, although remaining as the subject of *katta* 'bought' and must be marked with *ga*.

(27) a. *Maki*	*wa*	*kabu*	*o*	*katta.*
	TOP	stock	ACC	bought

'Maki bought stocks.'

b. *[Maki*	*ga/#wa*	*kabu*	*o*	*katta*	*toki]*$_{\text{SUB}}$	*kaisha*	*wa*
	NOM/TOP	stock	ACC	bought	when	company	TOP

tōsan	*sunzen*	*datta.*
bankruptcy	right.before	was

'When Maki bought the stocks, the company was about to go bankrupt.'

Like subordinate clauses, noun-modifying clauses (relative clauses) do not assert their contents. Therefore, the topic marker *wa* does not occur in them.

(28) *[Watashi*	*ga/#wa*	*kinō*	*mita]*$_{\text{REL}}$	*eiga*	*wa*	*omoshirokunakatta.*
I	NOM/TOP	yesterday	saw	movie	TOP	was.not.interesting

'The movie I saw yesterday was not interesting.'

Quotative clauses – which represent utterances or thoughts of a person other than the speaker – are the exception to the rule of topic exclusion in dependent clauses. When an NP is marked with *wa* in the original, reported speech, *wa* can be maintained even when the clause is embedded into a larger, reporting clause. This is due to the fact that in a quotative sentence two voices (the original speaker's and the reporting speaker's) are represented, and each speaker's perspective (i.e. designation of a topic in this case) can be separately maintained. In (29b) *shiken wa muzukashikatta* 'the examination was difficult' is a quotative clause, and *Maki wa . . . to itta* 'Maki said that. . .' a reporting clause. Unlike (29b), *wa*-marking is anomalous in the conditional subordinate clause, as in (29c).

(29) a. *Shiken wa muzukashikatta.*
examination TOP was.difficult
'The examination was difficult.'

b. *Maki wa [shiken wa muzukashikatta]*$_{\text{QUOT}}$ *to itta.*
TOP examination TOP was.difficult QUOT said
'Maki said that the examination was difficult.'

c. *[Shiken ga/#wa muzukashikatta-ra]*$_{\text{SUB}}$ *gakusei wa (kōsu*
examination NOM/TOP if.difficult student TOP course

o) toranai.
ACC not.take
'If (its) examination is difficult, students won't take the course.'

When *wa* marks a contrast, rather than a mere topic, it can occur in subordinate clauses, as in (30b) or in noun-modifying clauses, as in (31b).

(30) a. *[Kuruma ga/#wa kowareta node]*$_{\text{SUB}}$ *mukae ni ikemasen.*
car NOM/TOP broke because pick.up for cannot.go
'Because (my) car broke down, (I) can't come [go] pick (you) up.'

b. *[Kuruma ga/wa kowarete-mo ōtobai ga aru node]*$_{\text{SUB}}$
car NOM/CNT broke-though motorcycle NOM exist because

mukae ni ikemasu.
pick.up for can.go
'Although (my) car broke down, (I) can come [go] pick (you) up because (I) have a motorcycle.'

(31) a. *[Watashi ga/#wa mita]*$_{\text{REL}}$ *eiga wa totemo bōryoku-teki datta.*
I NOM/TOP saw movie TOP very violent was
'The movie I saw was unusually violent.'

b. *[Watashi ga/wa mite Maki ga/wa minakatta]*$_{\text{REL}}$ *eiga*
car NOM/CNT seeing NOM/CNT did.not.see movie

wa totemo bōryoku-teki datta.
TOP very violent was
'The movie that I saw but Maki didn't see was unusually violent.'

6.2 Switch Reference

Nariyama (2002) investigates complex sentences with respect to the interaction between *ga*- and *wa*-marking of the subject on the one hand, and the referents of ellipted subjects on the other. She contends that, although Japanese does not have a switch-reference system proper,[9] such an interaction demonstrates a property analogous to switch reference. According to her analysis, while *ga* in a subordinate clause signals different subjects, as in (32a), *wa* in either the main or subordinate clause signals same subjects, as in (32b–c).

(32) a. *[Hanako$_i$ ga haitte kuru nari]$_{SUB}$ Ø$_j$ to o shimeta.*
NOM entering come as.soon.as door ACC closed
'Immediately after Hanako$_i$ entered (the room), Ø$_j$ closed the door.'

b. *[Ø$_i$ byōki na noni]$_{SUB}$ Hanako$_i$ wa kaisha e itta.*
sick COP although TOP company to went
'Although Ø$_i$ was sick, Hanako$_i$ went to work.'

c. *Hanako$_i$ wa [byōki na noni]$_{SUB}$ Ø$_i$ kaisha e itta.*
TOP sick COP although company to went
'Although Hanako$_i$ was sick, Ø$_i$ went to work.'

These are reasonable generalizations that capture well native speakers' intuitive speech-comprehension strategy based on their knowledge that (i) the domain of a topic (i.e. NP-*wa*) can span multiple clauses, whereas that of a subject (i.e. NP-*ga*) is intra-clausal, and (ii) a topic cannot appear in a subordinate/noun-modifying clause. Nevertheless, they are not strict rules because they can easily be overridden by other, more robust factors. For example, as Nariyama is aware, the *ga*-marked NPs in (33) are coreferential with the ellipted main-clause subjects due to the idiosyncrasies of the conjunctions utilized (cf. Hasegawa 1996 for the characteristics of *te*-linkage).

(33) a. *[Haha$_i$ ga terebi o mi nagara]$_{SUB}$ Ø$_i$ itta.*
mother NOM TV ACC watch while said
'My mother$_i$ said (something) while Ø$_i$ watched TV.'

b. *[Tarō$_i$ ga haitte ki-te]$_{SUB}$ Ø$_i$ denki o keshita.*
NOM entering come-TE light ACC switched.off
'Taro$_i$ came in, and Ø$_i$ switched off the light.'

Analogously, the *wa*-marked NPs in (34) are not coreferential with the elliped subjects.

(34) a. *[Ø$_i$ ayamattemo]$_{SUB}$ watashi$_j$ wa yurusanai.*
apologize.even I TOP not.forgive
'Even if Ø$_i$ apologizes, I$_j$ won't forgive (her/him$_i$).'

9 Switch reference is a morphosyntactic mechanism that indicates whether the subject of a dependent clause in complex sentences or clause chaining is the same as or differs from the main clause subject.

b. [Tanaka-san$_i$ wa kyonen kekkon shita]$_{SUB}$ to Ø$_j$ omou.
TOP last.year married QUOT think
'(I) think that Ms. Tanaka got married last year.'

The interpretation of (34a) is based on our daily experience, not on the lexico-syntactic information: when occurring in succession, *ayamaru* 'apologize' and *yurusu* 'forgive' are normally performed by different individuals. In (34b), fluent speakers of Japanese are aware that under ordinary circumstances, the subject referent of the verb *omou* 'think' in its non-past tense is the speaker him/herself, regardless of the subject of the quotative clause. Therefore, Nariyama's generalizations should be regarded as practical guidelines.

7 Event-reporting versus Topic-comment Sentences

Until now, we have assumed that *ga* and *wa* themselves designate various meanings. However, Shibatani (1990) cautions that these meanings are rather epiphenomenal, derived from the fundamental differences between two types of sentences (p. 263). What should be addressed, he continues, are the effects *ga* and *wa* bring to the whole sentence (p. 264).[10] At this point, this position may seem plausible given that when *wa* appears in a negative clause, its function is negative-scope marking, but when its appearance is in an affirmative clause, its function is to mark a topic or contrast (Section 4.2). This is admittedly a circular statement, even though the purpose of the previous sections is not theoretical rigor but, rather, to lay out all possible interpretations of *ga* and *wa* in various linguistic environments. In this section, we will re-examine the data more theoretically.

Shibatani attributes his idea of these two types of sentences to Daizaburo MATSUSHITA (1878–1935) and several other Japanese and European grammarians. I choose to discuss the issue invoking the theory of Franz Brentano (1838–1917), further developed by Anton Marty (1847–1914), whose works are more accessible to English-speaking readers.

7.1 Thetic versus Categorical Judgments

The notion of *subject* originated as a logical (semantic) term in ancient times. Aristotle (350 BCE, *Categories* Section 1) defined *subject* as what a statement is about, and *predicate* as what a statement says about its subject; for example, "S is P" or "S is not P." However, Brentano ([1874] 2009: 110) argued that the subject–predicate distinction must be defined in linguistic terms, not in cognitive terms. Therefore, although most

[10] Shibatani (1990) also points out that these two particles belong to different categories: *ga* being a case particle, and *wa* an adverbial particle.

sentences have a subject linguistically, not all sentences have a logical sense of subject. Some sentences – for example, *There is a dog* or *It's raining* – are deemed subjectless with respect to traditional subject–predicate structure. Since Kuroda's (1972) introduction of this Brentano–Marty theory to linguistic circles, sentences with the traditional sense of subject are said to represent a *categorical judgment*, whereas those without such a subject represent a *thetic judgment*.[11]

A categorical judgment requires two separate acts: the recognition of the referent of the subject, and then affirmation or denial of what the predicate attributes to the subject referent (i.e. there are two information units). Because both acts are judgments in themselves, this type is also called a *double judgment*. In other words, a categorical judgment represents a universally valid statement about the entire category (including singleton categories) referred to by the subject. A thetic judgment, on the other hand, is cognitively undivided (only one information unit), and it merely involves the recognition or rejection of the material of judgment.[12]

Kuroda (1972: 160) contends that *ga* is used in a non-topic or unmarked sentence that represents a thetic judgment; an event or state of affairs is taking place in which the referent of the *ga*-marked NP is involved, as in (35a). *Wa*, on the other hand, is used in a topical sentence that represents a categorical judgment about the referent of the *wa*-marked NP, as in (35b).[13]

(35) a. *Inu* *ga* *hashitte iru.*
dog NOM is.running
'A dog is running.'
b. *Inu* *wa* *hashitte iru.*
dog TOP is.running
'The dog is running.'

In (35a), the situation is such that the speaker witnesses an event of running. An act of running necessarily involves an actor, and this actor is recognized as a dog. It can be paraphrased as *There is a dog running*. When, on the other hand, the dog is not an arbitrary dog, but one with which the speaker is familiar, say Lassie, s/he would say *The dog is running* in lieu of *Lassie is running*, that is, (35b). Here, the speaker's interest is directed toward

[11] The term *thetic judgment* (a translation of *thetische Urteil*) was originally proposed by Johann Gottlieb Fichte (Martin 2010: 382).

[12] Sasse (1987: 566–567) lists the following as typical domains for thetic judgments:
1. Existential statements (presence, appearance, continuation, etc. positively or negatively)
2. Explanations (e.g. responses to the question *what happened?*)
3. Surprising or unexpected events
4. General statements (aphorisms, etc.)
5. Background descriptions
6. Weather expressions
7. Statements related to body parts

[13] In the Brentano–Marty theory of judgment, universal statements of the type *All humans are mortal* (equivalent to such negative existential statements as *There is no human who is not mortal*) constitute thetic judgments. However, as discussed in Section 3.1.2, such statements are uniformly expressed in Japanese with *wa*, that is, in the form of categorical judgments. It appears to be more plausible as well as more intuitive to consider universal statements as categorical judgments.

the particular dog that is not merely a participant in the running event. Hence (35b) is recognized as a categorical judgment.

To recapitulate, in this conceptualization, *ga* is construed to mark the syntactic subject of a sentence that represents a thetic judgment, whereas *wa* marks an entity qua logical subject in a statement of categorical judgment.

7.2 Functional Sentence Perspective

Another theoretical framework we should consider is the Prague School notion of *functional sentence perspective*.[14] Adopting it, Kuno (1972b: 269–270) characterizes *ga* and *wa* as follows:

(36) a. *Ga* as a subject marker indicates that its referent is new and unpredictable information. The sentence with *ga* is of the type of either *neutral description* or *exhaustive listing* [the latter is synonymous with the *focus construction* discussed in Section 2.2]. When the predicate represents a state (but not existence) or a habitual or generic action, only the exhaustive-listing interpretation is obtained.

b. *Wa* marks either *theme* [i.e. *topic* in our terminology] or *contrast*. The theme must be either anaphoric or generic, while there is no such constraint on the contrasted element.

These functions are illustrated in (37):

(37) a. *(What happened next?) Mary blamed John for the accident.* [neutral description]

b. *Mary (and only Mary) blamed John for the accident; among those under discussion, it was Mary who blamed John for the accident.* [exhaustive listing]

c. *Speaking of Mary, she blamed John for the accident.* [theme]

d. *Mary blamed John for the accident (but Susan didn't).* [contrast]

Kuno provides the following sentences with *ga* and *wa*:

(38) a. *Jon ga kimashita.* [neutral description or exhaustive listing]
NOM came
'John came.'

b. *Jon ga baka desu.* [exhaustive listing only]
NOM fool is
'(Among the people being discussed) John, and only John, is stupid.'
'It is John who is stupid.'

c. *Jon ga mainichi gakkō ni iku.* [exhaustive listing only]
NOM everyday school to go
'(Among the people being discussed) John, and only John, goes to school every day.' 'It is John who goes to school every day.'

[14] *Functional sentence perspective* is concerned with the distribution of communicative dynamism over elements of a sentence in terms of old (*theme*) and new (*rheme*) information (Firbas 1992).

When the predicate represents a state of affairs, for example (38b), or a habitual action, for example (38c), the sentence can receive only the exhaustive-listing interpretation (p. 271). Kuno continues that what is common between the *ga* for neutral description (the descriptive *ga*) and the *ga* for exhaustive listing is that the subject conveys new information (p. 272). Neutral descriptions "represent nothing but new information" (p. 298), whereas in sentences with exhaustive listing, the NP-*ga* is the focus of new information. Kuno's neutral description with *ga* corresponds fairly well to the concept of thetic judgment.

Deguchi (2012) argues that not all *wa*-sentences uniformly represent categorical judgments, nor do all *ga*-sentences represent thetic judgments. According to Deguchi, *ga*-sentences represent thetic judgments only in Kuno's neutral descriptions, but they involve categorical judgments in the exhaustive-listing interpretation. Likewise, *wa*-sentences involve categorical judgments only when they are thematic; when *wa* is contrastive, they involve thetic judgments.

One of the justifications that Deguchi provides is that the neutral-description *ga* and the contrastive *wa* appear in the same linguistic environments, as in (39), and so do the exhaustive-listing *ga* and the thematic *wa*, as in (40). While undoubtedly needing more scrutiny,[15] this approach merits serious consideration.

(39) Thetic judgment

a. *Ame ga futte iru.* [neutral description]
rain NOM is.falling
'It's raining.'

b. *Ame wa futte iru.* [contrastive]
TOP is.falling
'It's raining (but. . .).'

(40) Categorical judgment

a. *Jon ga sono hon o yonda.* [exhaustive-listing]
NOM that book ACC read
'It was John who read the book.'

b. *Jon wa sono hon o yonda.* [thematic]
TOP that book ACC read
'John read the book.'

To encompass both theories of thetic-categorical judgment and functional sentence perspective, let us use the terms *event-reporting* for thetic judgments and neutral descriptions, and *topic-comment* for categorical judgments and thematic sentences. Then, *ga* in an event-reporting sentence represents

[15] In particular, the contrastive *wa* interpretation of (39b) as a thetic judgment is questionable. To me, it appears to be more categorical than thetic. On the other hand, as discussed in Section 4.2, the negative-scope *wa* (which can be considered as a subtype of the contrastive *wa*) can introduce new, unidentifiable entities into the discourse. Therefore, it is reasonable to analyze the sentence with the negative-scope *wa* as representing a thetic judgment.

an unmarked, neutral subject, whereas *ga* in the context where a categorical judgment is expected, for example, to ascribe an attribute to an entity, the NP-*ga* is recognized as a focus. On the other hand, in a topic-comment (i.e. the traditional subject–predicate) sentence, *wa* marks the topic, whereas the contrastive *wa* appears to be totally dependent on the context. This generalization leads to the conclusion that neither *ga* nor *wa* itself determines in which of the two types a given sentence must be interpreted.

7.3 Contextual Effects

Shibatani (1990: 264) advises that the functions of *ga* and *wa* cannot be resolved without recourse to context, and that, historically, the function of *wa* was acknowledged as making the entity *emphatic*, and/or *separating* it from other entities.[16] He declines to posit two distinct *wa*'s (thematic and contrastive), nor two distinct meanings to ascribe to *wa*. The innate potential of *wa* to separate/isolate a given entity from others naturally makes it thematic, and when the context provides a contrast or covertly implies one, the emphatic force of *wa* makes that contrast even more significant.

While this is an elegant, very persuasive analysis, it cannot account for the fact that the use of *wa* is sometimes not sanctioned unless a strong contrast is involved, for example, (41):

(41) a.

#Dare	*wa*	*kimashita*	*ka?*
who	TOP	came	INT

'Who came?'

b.

Dare	*wa*	*kite,*	*dare*	*wa*	*konakattan*	*desu*	*ka?*
who	TOP	coming	who	TOP	came.not	is	INT

'Who came, and who didn't?'

According to Shibatani's account, (41a) must be legitimate in the first place, and then the contrastive effect becomes emphasized in (41b). However, (41a) by itself is quite anomalous.

For the function of *ga*, Shibatani (1990: 271) cites Nishiyama (1979) and points out that attributing the exhaustive-listing function to *ga* itself is untenable. Consider the following examples, adjusted by me:

(42) a.

Kyō	*wa*	*nani*	*ga*	*yasui?*
today	TOP	what	NOM	inexpensive

'What is inexpensive today?'

b.

Ninjin	*ga*	*yasui.*	*Sorekara*	*tamanegi*	*mo*	*yasui.*
carrot	NOM	inexpensive	and	onion	also	inexpensive

'Carrots are inexpensive. And onions are also inexpensive.'

c.

#Ninjin	*dake*	*ga*	*yasui.*	*Sorekara*	*tamanegi*	*mo*	*yasui.*
carrot	only	NOM	inexpensive	and	onion	also	inexpensive

Lit. 'Only carrots are inexpensive. And also onions are inexpensive.'

[16] For diachronic studies of *ga*, see Shibatani (1990: 347–357); for diachronic studies of *wa*, see De Wolf (1987) and Ueno (1987).

Dake 'only' is an incontrovertible exhaustive-listing marker. If *ga* has the same function, (42b) should be equally as odd as (42c). However, (42b) sounds quite natural. Shibatani argues that the exhaustive reading is derived from the combination of *ga*'s potential to mark focus and the Gricean implicatures, for example, if the second sentence in (42b) is absent, the addressee naturally supposes that only carrots are inexpensive via the Maxim of Quantity. This account regarding *ga* appears conclusive.

8 A Case Study

In this section, let us consider the distinction between *ga* and *wa* in a real discourse. Noda (1996: 108–117) maintains that the selection between *ga* and *wa* for subject marking depends upon the following factors:

(43) a. Thetic versus categorical judgment
b. Identifiability
c. Functional sentence perspective (new versus old information)
d. Syntagmatic consideration (main versus dependent clause)
e. Paradigmatic consideration (focus or contrast)

While identifiability is likely subsumed under the concept of categorical judgment, this is a practical guideline for disentangling the issues pertaining to *ga* and *wa* when we examine the following text drawn from a logic textbook, translated from English into Japanese by myself. At each point where either *ga* or *wa* must be chosen, a blank square is inserted. The proper filler of each square is discussed following each sentence.

(44) a. The Visor Television Company[1] shipped 1,000 television sets to a large department store chain. During the next three months, 115 of the sets[2] were returned.

b. *Baizā-terebi-gaisha* □[1] *terebi* *1,000-dai* *o* *ōte*
Visor-television-company TV 1,000-units ACC major

depāto *chēn* *ni* *shukka shita* *ga,* *3-kagetsu*
department.store chain to shipped but 3-months

inai ni *sono* *uchi* *115-dai* □[2] *henpin sarete kita.*
within that within 115-units were.returned

□[1] *Baizā-terebi-gaisha* 'Visor Television Company' is a fictitious entity and, therefore, unidentifiable. Recall that unidentifiable entities cannot be topics, that is, cannot be marked with *wa* (cf. Section 3.1). By contrast, the use of *ga* is justified (cf. Section 2.1). Indeed, many native speakers of Japanese would select *ga* here. Nevertheless, to me, *wa* is a more natural selection here than *ga* because of *wa*'s rhetorical effect of staging (cf. Section 3.2). This example illustrates that the choice between *ga* and *wa* can be based on stylistic preference, and not only on grammatico-pragmatic rules.

☐[2] *Ga* is more appropriate than *wa* because *115-dai* '115 units' is indefinite. *Wa* would be possible only if a strong contrast were intended, which is unlikely in this case.

(45) a. In each case[3], the picture reception[4] was good, but there was no sound[5].

b.

Sorera	*no*	*terebi*	☐[3]	*gazō*	☐[4]	*seijō*	*da*	*ga,*
those	GEN	TV		picture		normal	is	but
onsei	☐[5]	*denakatta.*						
sound		did.not.emit						

☐[3] *Wa* must be selected because *sorera no terebi* 'those TVs' is clearly anaphoric (cf. Section 3.1.1). Additionally, it is in the first component of the *wa–ga* construction (cf. Section 5).

☐[4] This clause is in the second part of the *wa–ga* construction, but the use of *ga* is anomalous. This irregularity is due to the salient contrast being expressed (cf. Section 4.1), that is, the picture reception was normal, *but* something else was not operating properly. Therefore, *wa* must be selected.

☐[5] Like 4, the use of *wa* is justifiable here because this is the second part of the contrast, indicating what was not working. However, I prefer *ga* for its focusing potential (cf. Section 2.2), that is, it was the sound that did not function properly. Here, again, some native speakers of Japanese might select *wa* because it does not violate any grammatical or pragmatic constraint.

(46) a. Examining the first group of ten returned sets, a plant inspection supervisor[6] noticed that, in every set, a particular wire[7] to the speaker had been improperly soldered.

b.

Seihin-kanri-kakarichō	☐[6]	*saisho no*	*10-dai*	*o*
product-control-supervisor		first	10-units	ACC

kensa shita	*tokoro,*	*izure mo*	*supīkā*	*e*	*no*	*haisen*
inspected	When	everyone	speaker	to	GEN	connection

no	*handa-zuke*	*ni*	*mondai*	☐[7]	*atta.*
GEN	soldering	In	problem		existed

☐[6] *Ga* must be selected because *seihin-kanri-kakarichō* 'plant inspection supervisor' is the subject of the subordinate clause (Section 6.1), *X ga Y o kensa shita tokoro* 'when X inspected Y.'

☐[7] *Ga* is naturally selected here because this is a typical instance corresponding to the English *there* construction (*there was a soldering problem*) with the existential verb *aru* (Section 3.1). However, the selection of *wa* is also reasonable because *mondai* 'problem' is already implied by the preceding sentence. Therefore, although the word *mondai* has not been previously explicitly mentioned, it can be construed as an anaphor, which is normally marked by *wa*.

(47) a. She also noticed that the same person – Bill Evans,[8] a fairly new employee – had done the soldering.

b. *Mata, saikin koyō sareta Biru Ebansu* □[8] *handa-zuke o*
and recently was.employed soldering ACC

okonatta koto mo kakunin sareta.
did fact also was.confirmed

□[8] This must be *ga* because the NP in a dependent, noun-complement clause (cf. Section 6.1), *the fact that Bill Evans did the soldering.*

(48) a. The supervisor[9] inspected the next group of returned sets and found the same improperly soldered wire in each.

b. *Kakarichō* □[9] *tsugi ni modotte kita terebi o kensa shi,*
supervisor next returned TV ACC inspection do.and

onaji mondai o hakken shita.
same problem ACC discovered

□[9] A prototypical case of the anaphoric *wa*.

(49) a. She[10] concluded that Bill Evans's faulty soldering[11] was the cause of the problem.

b. *Shitagatte, kakarichō* □[10] *Biru Ebansu no sagyō no ochido*
consequently supervisor GEN operation GEN failure

□[11] *mondai no gen'in da to no ketsuron ni itatta.*
problem GEN cause COP QUOT GEN conclusion to arrived

□[10] Anaphoric *wa*.

□[11] This must be *ga* because the NP is the subject of the dependent, noun-complement clause, . . . *to no ketsuron* 'the conclusion that. . ..'

This exercise has demonstrated how syntactic and pragmatic constraints intertwine with stylistic preferences, which naturally leads to idiolectal variations.

9 Conclusions

This chapter has examined the postpositional particles *ga* and *wa* when they mark the grammatical subject.

When the speaker wishes to comment on an entity that is already introduced into the discourse and is activated in the interlocutors' minds at the time of utterance, *wa* is the default choice. When, on the other hand, the speaker or the addressee or both cannot identify the entity, *ga* is likely to be selected. Because the referents of interrogative NPs (e.g. *dare* 'who') and indefinite NPs (e.g. *dareka* 'someone') are unidentifiable, the use of *wa* as a topic marker would be anomalous.

When the speaker ascribes an attribute (e.g. a physical characteristic) inherent to an entity, that entity must be identifiable (if not, the utterance is odd, for example, *A person is kind*) and, consequently, marked with *wa*. If *ga* appears in such a sentence, the NP is interpreted as the focus of attention, that is, *It is X that is Y*. When the sentence describes a transient state of affairs of an entity (e.g. the sky being clear), it is considered as event reporting, and *ga* is selected.

In order to characterize *ga* and *wa*, we need to identify the function of the sentence, for example, thetic versus categorical judgment, or commenting on the topic or reporting an event. That is, *ga* and *wa* are not essential in the determination of these functions. In fact, the marking of the subject with either particle is not obligatory. Especially in spoken Japanese, subjects frequently occur as bare NPs.

While the contrast between *ga* and *wa* is one of the most, if not the most, widely investigated topics in Japanese linguistics, uncertainties still remain:

A. As Deguchi (2012) questions, do all *ga*-sentences involve thetic judgments, and *wa*-sentences categorical judgments?
B. If both thematic and contrastive functions of *wa* are to be derived from *wa*'s characteristics of emphasis and separation, as Shibatani (1990) argues, then why is *wa* sometimes unacceptable without a strong implied contrast?
C. In terms of language processing, at what point in an utterance do native speakers determine the interpretation of *ga* and *wa*? This question is particularly significant in complex sentences.
D. When are their uses optional, and when obligatory?

In terms of materials for investigation, most researchers analyze easily interpretable sentences/passages constructed by native speakers, but large corpora and anomalous usage by non-native speakers can provide precious data as well.

14

Negation

Hideki Kishimoto

1 Introduction

There are multifarious ways of expressing negation in Japanese. One typologically notable fact about Japanese negation is that clausal negation is expressed by negative heads that appear following predicates, but not by negative adverbs (which are available in languages like English). Japanese has several distinct types of clause negators, including *nai* and *zu/nu*, that can appear in various kinds of clauses. Clausal negation is constrained by diverse syntactic and morphological restrictions depending on the clause type. Japanese also abounds with lexical negative expressions containing negative affixes, which behave differently from clausal negators.

This chapter provides an overview of how negation is expressed in Japanese by illustrating some important properties of negative expressions and is organized as follows: Section 2 shows how clausal negation is marked in various types of clauses. Section 3 is a discussion of negative scope and negative polarity items (NPIs). Section 4 discusses properties of lexical negative expressions comprising negative markers morphologically. Section 5 is a conclusion.

2 How Clausal Negation is Expressed in Japanese

Japanese has a number of clausal negative markers, illustrated in this section, that follow main predicates (except for the negative existential *nai*, which behaves as an independent predicate).

I am grateful to Yoko Hasegawa, Bjarke Frellesvig, and John Haig for valuable comments and suggestions on earlier versions of this chapter.

2.1 Negative *Nai*

Nai 'not' is most commonly used as a clausal negator. It appears with various kinds of predicates and serves to reverse the polarity of the proposition expressed in the clause.

(1) a. *Ken ga hashira-nakat-ta.*
NOM run-NEG-PST
'Ken did not run.' (verb+negation)

b. *Ken wa se ga takaku na-i.*
TOP height NOM high NEG-NPST
'Ken is not tall.' (adjective+negation)

c. *Ken wa gakusei de na-i.*
TOP student COP NEG-NPST
'Ken is not a student.' (nominal+negation)

d. *Tana ni hon ga na-i.*
shelf LOC book NOM NEG-NPST
'There are not books on the shelf.' (negative existential)

The examples in (1a–c) illustrate that *nai* works as a clausal negator, occurring after verbs, adjectives, and nominal predicates. In (1d), the negator stands on its own morphologically. In all cases, the negative *nai* displays adjectival inflection, which differs from the inflectional patterns of verbs.[1] The adjectival inflectional pattern of *nai* can be clearly seen by comparing *yoma-nai* 'read-not' and *kawaii* 'cute' in (2).

(2)

	*yoma-**na-i*** 'read-not'	*kawai-i* 'cute'
Mizen (Irrealis)	*yoma-**na-karo*** (*u* [will])	*kawai-karo* (*u*)
Ren'yō (Adverbal)	*yoma-**na-ku*** (*naru* [become])	*kawai-ku* (*naru*)
	*yoma-**na-kat*** (*tari* [CONJ])	*kawai-kat* (*tari*)
Shūshi (Conclusive)	*yoma-**na-i***	*kawai-i*
Rentai (Attributive)	*yoma-**na-i*** (*toki* [when])	*kawai-i* (*toki*)
Katei (Hypothetical)	*yoma-**na-kere*** (*ba* [if])	*kawai-kere* (*ba*)

In traditional Japanese grammar, *nai* is classified into three different categories, depending on the type of predicate it occurs with (Hashimoto 1935: 277–280). *Nai* combined with verbs is categorized as *jodōshi* 'auxiliary verb,' and *nai* combined with adjectives as *hojo-keiyōshi* 'auxiliary adjective.' (In the former, the preceding verb appears in the irrealis form, and in the

[1] The citation form of the most common negator is *nai*, which consists of the stem *na-* and the inflectional morpheme *-i*, which indicates the non-past tense. In traditional/pedagogical Japanese grammar, the negative auxiliary (occurring with verbs) is *-nai*, while in the linguistic tradition following Bloch (1946), the negative is treated as *-(a)nai* (often by assuming that it forms part of inflectional paradigms of verbs). Note that the negative existential *nai* in contemporary Japanese has been derived from *ara-nai* [be-NEG] – a negative expression which actually existed at an earlier stage – by deleting the verb part. This indicates that the verb stem and an epenthetic vowel constitute a unit that has undergone a syntactic process, thus suggesting that the negative auxiliary should be *-nai* (rather than *-anai*). Given this, it is reasonable to postulate that the epenthetic vowel *(a)* forms a verbal base with a consonant verb stem, while the negative *nai* is an independent category (i.e. auxiliary) agglutinated to verbs, as [V+*a*]-*na(i)* (cf. Shibatani 1990: 221–235).

latter, the adjective takes the adverbal form.) The existential *nai* is categorized as *keiyōshi* 'adjective,' because it behaves as an independent word.

The negative *nai* occurring after main verbs is a bound morpheme. When *nai* is separated from the verb by a focus particle (e.g. *wa, mo, sae*), the semantically empty verb *suru* 'do' is inserted to the left of it for morphological support.

(3) *Ken wa hashiri mo shi-nakat-ta.*
TOP run also do-NEG-PST
'Ken did not run as well.'

In cases where *nai* occurs with an adjective, no morphological support is added even when it is separated from the preceding host by a focus particle, as demonstrated in (4).

(4) *Ken wa isogashiku (mo) na-i.*
TOP busy also NEG-NPST
'Ken is not busy as well.'

The morphological status of the negative marker *nai* associated with adjectives is different from that attached to verbs.

The tripartite classification of *nai* in traditional grammar is solely based on morphological criteria. If distributional/syntactic criteria are taken into account, a different picture emerges. One way of evaluating the categorical status of *nai* is to put predicates in a small clause complement selected by *omou* 'think.'

(5) *Ken wa [Eri o {kawaiku/*hashira-naku}] omot-ta.*
TOP ACC {cute/run-NEG} think-PST
'Ken thought Eri {cute/not run}.'

In the small-clause construction, *omou* takes an adjective predicate as its complement. Thus, this construction can be used as a diagnostic to assess whether or not a given instance of *nai* is an adjective. Since *nai* associated with *hashiru* 'run' in (5) is a decategorized (or non-adjectival) grammatical negator, in spite of its adjectival conjugation, it cannot precede *omou*. Nevertheless, (6) shows that there are cases where *nai* can appear as a small-clause predicate in an adjectival construction. Specifically, *nai* appearing on negated adjectives is a negator that functions as an adjective categorically, that is, an adjectival negator.[2] The bound auxiliary *nai* associated with *warikireru* and *iru* behaves in the same way in the adjectival construction.

(6) *Ken wa [sore o {warikire-naku/ira-naku/omoshiroku naku}] omot-ta.*
TOP it ACC {be.satisfied-NEG/need-NEG/interesting NEG} think-PST
'Ken thought it {not satisfactory/not necessary/not interesting}.'

[2] With the type of negative adjective *nai* occurring with adjectives, unlike the genuine lexical adjective *nai* 'non-existent, empty' (see Section 4), an affirmative form can be derived by replacing *nai* with *aru*, and hence is referred here to as 'adjectival negator.'

The acceptability of embedding *warikire-nai* 'not satisfied' and *ira-nai* 'not need' under *omou* illustrates that *nai* here functions as an adjective. This shows that even the bound form *nai* (combined with verbs) – which is identified as an auxiliary verb – can be an adjective categorically. Given that *nai* inflects just like an adjective, it is plausible to hypothesize that the decategorized grammatical marker *nai* (combined with ordinary verbs) has been derived from the adjectival *nai* via grammaticalization; that is, the bound form of *nai* originates as an adjective, and *nai* appearing in *ira-nai* and *warikire-nai* represents the remnant use of the original adjectival *nai* (see Section 4).[3]

Furthermore, (7) illustrates that even if *nai* stands as an independent word, it does not necessarily serve as an adjective categorically.

(7) *Watashi wa [sore o {shikata ga naku/*naku}] omo-u.*
I TOP it ACC {doing.way NOM NEG/NEG} think-NPST
'I think it {unavoidable/not existing}.'

The traditional categorization classifying the existential *nai* as an adjective faces a problem, because (7) shows that the existential *nai* is not an adjective (Kishimoto 2007). On the other hand, *nai* included in *shikata ga nai* 'cannot help' is a genuine adjective, and thus does not have an affirmative form (**shikata ga aru* [doing.way NOM be] 'avoidable(?)').

The (inanimate) existential displays a morphological irregularity, in that the existential *nai* is the negative form of the existential verb *aru* 'be (inanimate),' but stands on its own (without combining with any predicate).

(8) *Tana ni hon ga ar-u.*
shelf LOC book NOM be-NPST
'There are books on the shelf.' (affirmative existential)

In contrast, a regular pattern is observed for another existential verb *iru* 'be (animate),' because its negative form is *i-nai* [be-NEG], where the verb *iru* is combined with the negative *nai*.

(9) *Asoko ni onnanoko ga {i-ru/i-na-i}.*
there LOC girl NOM {be-NPST/be-NEG-NPST}
'The girls are (not) there.'

These facts raise the question of how the negative existential *nai* is related to *aru*. Note that the existential *nai* must be a non-adjectival (or decategorized) negator, for it cannot stand as a small-clause predicate, as shown in (7). Given this, one reasonable account would be that the negative existential *nai* is derived from *ara-nai* by dropping the verb part, owing to the lack of the form **ara-* (for *aru*) (cf. Kato 1985: 31–32). This analysis gains support

[3] Hashimoto (1969: 326–346) (based on his lectures in 1931) suggests that the auxiliary *nai* has originated from an auxiliary in the Eastern province dialect of Japanese, while the possibility that it comes from an adjective is not excluded (cf. Frellesvig 2010: 401).

from the fact that the negative potential *ari-e-nai* [be-POT-NEG] does comprise the verb *aru*, and further, that the archaic negative existentials *ara-nu* and *ara-zu* include *ara-*.[4]

2.2 Older Negators

Clausal negation can be expressed by old negative auxiliaries like *zu* and *nu*. In classical Japanese, *nu* is the attributive form, and *zu* is the adverbal and conclusive form of the same auxiliary. In contemporary Japanese, due to a historical change of conjugation paradigms, *nu* and *n* (the reduced form of *nu*) fill the slot of the (non-past) conclusive, as well as the attributive form, while *zu* and *zu ni* are predominantly used to form adverbial clauses.

(10) a. *Watashi wa sore ga wakara-{n/nu}.*
I TOP that NOM understand-{NEG/NEG}
'I cannot understand that.'

b. *Wake ga wakara-zu(ni), watashi wa sō shi-ta.*
reason NOM understand-NEG I TOP so do-PST
'Without knowing the reasons, I did so.'

In contemporary Japanese, *zu* and *n(u)*, unlike *nai*, can be combined with only verbs.[5] Nevertheless, forms such as *ōkara-zu* 'not too many,' *sukunakara-zu* 'not too few,' and *supōtsuman-rashikara-nu (furumai)* 'unsportsmanlike (behavior),' which comprise *zu/nu* compounded with adjectives or adjectival suffixes, are found in archaic expressions, because *zu/nu* were allowed to combine with adjectives in classical Japanese.[6]

2.3 Polite Forms and Negation

In Japanese, politeness can be grammatically coded (cf. Chapter 26, this volume). There are two major ways of turning clauses into polite forms. One is to place *desu* at the end of clauses, and another is to add *masu*, which follows a verbal predicate in the adverbal form. Their basic paradigms are given in (11).

(11)

		Affirmative	Negative
V+*masu*	(NPST)	*yomi-**masu***	*yomi-**masen***
	(PST)	*yomi-**masen***	*yomi-**masen-deshita***
V+*desu*	(NPST)	NA	*yoma-na-i **desu***
	(PST)	NA	*yoma-nakat-ta **desu***

[4] The verbal form *ara-* is found in the negative existential *ara-hen* [be-NEG] in the Kansai dialect of Japanese.

[5] Negative *nai* used with verbs is a relatively new form introduced, presumably, at the end of the Late Middle Japanese period (c. 1200–1600), and started to be popularly used during the Edo period (1603–1868) (Frellesvig 2010: 401). *Nai* (occurring after verbs) began to replace *zu/nu* shortly after its introduction, but the replacement process is still under way. This is why *nai* and *zu/nu* can be used alternatively as clausal negators (despite their stylistic differences).

[6] This may be due to the fact that the *-kara(-zu)* form is derived from *-ku ara(-zu)*, which is a combined form of the adjective ending and *ari* 'be' (Martin 1975: 382).

Adj+*masu*	(NPST)	*yasashiku wa* ***ari-masu***	*yasashiku (wa)* ***ari-masen***
	(PST)	*yasashiku wa* ***ari-mashita***	*yasashiku (wa)* ***ari-masen-deshita***
Adj+*desu*	(NPST)	*yasashi-i* ***desu***	*yasashiku-na-i* ***desu***
	(PST)	*yasashikat-ta* ***desu***	*yasashiku-nakat-ta* ***desu***

The politeness marker *desu* can be either a genuine politeness marker or the polite form of the copula *da* 'be.' Politeness marker *desu* appears after predicates conjugated as adjectives, including the negative *nai*.

(12) a. *Sore wa {omoshiro-i/omoshiroku na-i} {desu/*deshita}.*
that TOP {interesting-NPST/interesting NEG-NPST} {POL/POL.PST}
'That is (not) interesting.'

b. *Ken wa hashira-na-i {desu/*deshita}.*
TOP run-NEG-NPST {POL/POL.PST}
'Ken {does/did} not run.'

The politeness marker *desu* does not have a past tense form, and tense is indicated by the preceding predicate, as in *omoshiro-i desu* [interesting-NPST POL] versus *omoshirokat-ta desu* [interesting-PST POL]. Verbal predicates can occur with *desu* only when they accompany *nai*, which has adjectival inflection, as in (12b).[7] If the verb is directly combined with *desu*, unacceptability results, as **hashir-u desu* [run-NPST POL] or **hashit-ta desu* [run-PST POL].

Politeness can also be expressed by using *masu* and its negative form *masen* (a combined form of *mas(u)+n(u)* (NEG)). *Masu/masen* can be hosted only by verbal predicates in the adverbal form.

(13) a. *Ken wa hashiri-{masu/mashita/masen/masen-deshita}.*
TOP run-{POL/POL.PST/NEG.POL/NEG.POL-POL.PST}
'Ken {does/did/does not/did not} run.'

b. *Sore wa utsukushiku (wa) ari-{masen/masen-deshita}.*
that TOP beautiful TOP be-{NEG.POL/NEG.POL-POL.PST}
'That {is/was} not beautiful.'

c. *Sore wa utsukushiku *(wa) ari-{masu/mashita}.*
that TOP beautiful TOP be-{POL/NEG.POL.PST}
'That {is/was} beautiful.'

The past form of the affirmative *masu* is *mashita*. The negative non-past form of *masu* is *masen*, but its past form is *masen-deshita*, where another past politeness marker *deshita* follows *masen*.[8] It is possible to combine *masu/masen* with non-verbal predicates, in which case the supportive verb *aru* 'be' in the adverbal form, that is, *ari-*, is inserted to the left of the politeness markers, as in (13b). The positive polite forms *ari-masu/ari-mashita* are not

[7] It is also possible to embed a verbal clause under *no desu* 'it is that. . .,' because *no* turns a verbal clause into a nominal.

[8] The form *masen-desu* is usually taken to be ill-formed, but it is commonly used in certain registers (e.g. *Tondemo gozai-masen-desu koto!* 'No kidding!') (p.c. Y. Hasegawa).

usable for adjectives unless they are preceded by focus particles like *wa*, *mo*, *sae*, etc. (at least in Standard Japanese), as shown in (13c). No such problem arises in the case of the negative form *masen*. The negative polite forms in (13b) are legitimate regardless of whether a focus particle intervenes between the adjective and the politeness markers.

The copula appears with not only nouns (e.g. *gakusei da* 'be a student') but also adjectival nouns (e.g. *shinsetsu da* 'be kind').[9] The polite copula *desu* inflects for the past tense, as in (14a), but does not have a negative form. When negated, the copular clause has the form in (14b), where the politeness marker *desu* follows the negator.

(14) a. *Eri wa gakusei {desu/deshita}.*
TOP student {COP.POL/COP.PST.POL}
'Eri {is/was} a student.'

b. *Ken wa gakusei de wa na-i {desu/*deshita}.*
TOP student COP TOP NEG-NPST {POL/POL.PST}
'Ken is not a student.'

c. *Ken wa gakusei de wa {na-i/nakat-ta} desu.*
TOP student COP TOP {NEG-NPST/NEG-PST} POL
'Ken {is/was} not a student.'

In (14b), *desu* serves as a genuine politeness marker, and thus does not inflect for tense. In this case, the preceding negative *nai* inflects for tense, as shown in (14c).

When the copular form is *de aru*, where the copula *de* is combined with the existential verb *aru*, *masu/masen* are used to express politeness.

(15) *Ken wa gakusei de (wa)*
TOP student COP TOP
{ari-masu/ari-masen/ari-mashita/ari-masen-deshita}.
{be-POL/be-NEG.POL/be-POL.PST/be-NEG.POL-POL.PST}
'Ken {is/is not/was/was not} a student.'

Since the copular expression *de aru* contains the verb *aru* alongside the copula *de*, it is possible to form polite sentences by adding the polite forms *masu/masen* at the clause end. The polite forms with the copula show the same morphological behavior as those associated with adjectival predicates, except that no focus particle is required in the affirmative polite form, as in *gakusei de (wa) ari-masu/mashita*, unlike the adjective case.

2.4 Modal Negation

Modal expressions can be divided into true modals (e.g. *darō* 'will,' *mai* 'will not,' *yō* 'will') and quasi-modals (e.g. *hazu ga nai* 'should not,' *beki da* 'should') (cf. Nitta 1991: 52–59). The former class of expressions does not

9 The term "adjectival noun" (coined by Martin 1975) refers to *keiyōdōshi* (i.e. *na*-adjective).

inflect. But the latter class does and often has negative forms. Note that the true modal *mai* 'will not' (which allegedly originated from the Old Japanese auxiliary *maji*) is a dedicated negative expression (with no overt negation marker), while many true modals do not have negative forms.

Japanese has a fairly large inventory of periphrastic quasi-modals, many of which are grammaticalized to varying degrees, and often show irregular syntactic behaviors. While some quasi-modals cannot be negated (e.g. *hō-ga ii/yoi* 'had better' versus **hō-ga yoku-nai*), others can be (e.g. *hazu da* 'must' versus *hazu {de/ga/(de) wa} nai* 'must not,' *-te ii/yoi* 'may' versus *-te wa ike-nai* 'may not'). Some quasi-modals like *sō da* 'likely' allow a negator to either precede or follow them.[10]

(16) *Ame ga <u>sukoshimo</u> {furi sō de na-i/fura-na(sa) sō da}.*
rain NOM at.all {fall likely COP NEG-NPST/fall-NEG likely COP}
'It is {not likely/likely not} to rain at all.'

When a negator follows the modal, it expresses a modal negation, but when it occurs in the reversed order, the negation of the proposition is expressed. In either case, *nai* can license negative polarity items (NPIs) like *sukoshimo* 'at all,' which are licensed only in negative contexts, as shown in (16).

By contrast, modal expressions like *ni chigainai* 'must' (< *chigai-nai* [discrepancy-NEG]) and *-te (mo) kamawanai* 'OK' (< *kamawa-nai* [care-NEG]) do not license NPIs, because *nai* included in the morphological sequence does not function as a clausal negator.

(17) *Ken wa <u>sukoshimo</u> {*hashit-ta/hashira-nakat-ta} ni chigaina-i.*
TOP at.all {run-PST/run-NEG-PST} DAT must-NPST
'Ken {must/must not} run at all.'

In this type of modal expression, the occurrence of NPIs is permitted only when the preceding clause is negative. If, on the other hand, *nai* included in modals functions as a clausal negator, *sukoshimo* is not licensed when the preceding clause is negative. Example (18) shows that *nai* appearing in *-te wa nara-nai* 'must' is a negator visible to the syntax, and cancels out the negative import of the preceding clause (if it is negative).[11]

(18) *<u>Sukoshimo</u> {hanashi-te/*hanasa-naku-te} wa nara-na-i.*
at.all {talk-GER/talk-NEG-GER} TOP become-NEG-NPST
'You {must/must not} talk at all.'

[10] The affirmative form *hazu ga aru* 'must' can be used only when a negator follows, as in *Sonna hazu wa aru mai* 'That cannot be true.'

[11] *Nebanaranai* 'must' (< *ne-ba-nara-nai* [NEG-COND-become-NEG]) carries an affirmative meaning, containing two negators (see Section 3.4). This modal does not allow the preceding clause to be negative. Similar behavior is observed for *zaru o e-nai* [NEG ACC obtain-NEG] 'cannot help.'

Modals sometimes show behavioral differences as to whether they can precede the modal *darō* 'will.' In particular, the negative presumptive *mai* does not allow *darō* to follow, unlike many other modal expressions, including ones formed with *nai*, which are allowed to precede *darō*.

(19) a. *Sonna koto wa {kamawa-n/kamawa-na-i/kamau-beki-de-na-i}*
that fact TOP {care-NEG/care-NEG-NPST/care-should-COP-NEG-NPST}
darō.
will
'(We){will not/will not/should not} care about that fact.'

b. **Sonna koto wa shiru-mai darō.*
that fact TOP know-may.not will
'(We) will not know that fact.'

The modal *darō* expresses a positive presumptive meaning, and *mai*, a negative presumptive meaning. Given that *mai* and *darō* are both presumptive modals, it is conceivable that they compete for the same slot syntactically, making it impossible for the two expressions to co-exist in a clause.

Some modals (e.g. *-te wa ike-nai* 'must not,' *-te wa nara-nai* 'must not') express prohibition. Notably, *-te wa dame da/desu* 'not good' expresses prohibition in a way similar to *-te wa ike-nai* 'must not,' *-te wa ike-masen* 'must not (polite form).'

(20) *Kore o tabe-te wa {dame desu/ike-masen/ike-nai}.*
this ACC eat-GER TOP {bad COP.POL/must-NEG.POL/must-NEG}
'You must not eat this.'

The expression *dame da/desu* can also be used to give a negative evaluation.

(21) *Kare no seiseki wa dame desu.*
he GEN score TOP bad COP.POL
'His scores are not good.'

If *dame da/desu* expresses a prohibitive meaning, it can license NPIs, as in (22a). When used as indicating a negative evaluation, *dame da/desu* does not work as a clausal negative marker, in which case it cannot license NPIs, as in (22b).

(22) a. *Kore shika tabe-te wa dame desu.*
this only eat-GER TOP bad COP.POL
'You must not eat except this.' (Prohibitive)

b. **Kare no seiseki shika dame datta (yō da).*
he GEN score only bad COP.PST seem COP
'(It seems that) only his scores were not good.' (Evaluative)

In addition, *dame da/desu* can express a prohibitive meaning without combining with any predicate, as in *Kore shika dame {da/desu}* 'Only this is OK.' In this case, the putative predicative meaning needs to be decided according to the context where it is used. Thus, the elliptical expression can be assumed to carry a meaning which may be represented approximately as "It is only this that you can X, where X = eat, use, touch, etc."

2.5 Negative Yes–No Questions

In Japanese, yes–no questions are derived from declarative clauses by simply adding an interrogative particle at the clause end. Yes–no questions can be direct or indirect questions (and of course, they can be either affirmative or negative).

(23) a. *Ken ga {ki-ta/ko-nakat-ta} no (desu ka)?*
Ken NOM {come-PST/come-NEG-PST} NMLZ COP.POL Q
'{Did/Didn't} Ken come?'

b. *Mari wa [Ken ga ki-ta {ka/kadōka}] shit-te i-ru.*
Mari TOP Ken NOM come-PST {Q/whether} know-GER be-NPST
'Mary knows whether Ken came.'

Direct yes–no questions are indicated by the question particle *ka* or *no* (< *no ka* or *no desu ka*), but indirect yes–no questions, which typically appear as embedded clauses selected by predicates like *shiru* 'know,' *tazuneru* 'ask,' etc., are indicated by *ka* or *kadōka* 'whether.' Note that *kadōka* can only be used in embedded yes–no questions.

In replying to direct yes–no questions, *hai* 'yes' or *iie* 'no' is used to confirm or disconfirm the status of information that the questioner inquires about. For non-negative direct yes–no questions, the answer is *hai* if an affirmative statement follows, and the answer is *iie* if a negative statement follows.

(24) Q: *Ken ga ki-mashita ka?*
Ken NOM come-POL.PST Q
'Did Ken come?'

A: *Hai, {ki-mashita/*ki-masen-deshita}.*
yes {come-POL.PST/come-NEG.POL-POL.PST}
'Yes, (he) {came/did not come}.'

B: *Iie, {*ki-mashita/ki-masen-deshita}*
no {come-POL.PST/come-NEG.POL-POL.PST}.
'No, (he) {came/did not come}.'

Hai and *iie* do not strictly correspond to *yes* and *no* in English, for answers to the negative yes–no question in (25) could be *hai* or *iie* regardless of whether the following statement is affirmative or negative.

(25) Q: *Ken ga ki-masen-deshita ka?*
Ken NOM come-NEG.POL-POL.PST Q
'Didn't Ken come?'

A: *Hai, {ki-mashita/ki-masen-deshita}.*
yes {come-POL.PST/come-NEG.POL-POL.PST}
'Yes, (he) {came/did not come}.'

B: *Iie, {ki-mashita/ki-masen-deshita}.*
no {come-POL.PST/come-NEG.POL-POL.PST}
'No, (he) {came/did not come}.'

A clausal negator used in yes–no questions indicates either the denial of the statement or the speaker's expectation that the non-negated statement is true. (The difference in meaning conveyed by the yes–no questions is often distinguishable by intonation.) When *nai* indicates the denial of the proposition, the answer is *hai* if a negative statement follows, and *iie* if an affirmative statement follows. When the negative marker encodes the speaker's expectation, the answer is *hai* if an affirmative statement follows, and the answer is *iie* if a negative statement follows.

The fact that how *hai* and *iie* are used is fixed according to the logical meaning encoded in yes–no questions is further confirmed by looking at examples containing negative and positive polarity items. First, observe how the hearer responds to the yes–no question in (26).

(26) Q: *Dare-ka* *ki-masen* *ka?*
someone come-NEG.POL Q
'Won't someone come?'
A: *Hai,* *ki-masu.*
yes come-POL
'Yes, (someone) will come.'
B: *Iie,* *ki-masen.*
no come-NEG.POL
'No, (no one) will come.'

To the yes–no question in (26), which contains a positive polarity item *dare-ka* 'someone,' the speaker must address the expectation that someone will come. Thus, the answer to the yes–no question is *hai* if the hearer knows that someone will come, and *iie* if this is not the case.

When the NPI *dare-mo* 'anyone' is included in yes–no questions, the answering pattern is reversed, as in (27).

(27) Q: *Dare-mo* *ki-masen* *ka?*
anyone come-NEG.POL Q
'Will no one come?'
A: *Hai,* *ki-masen.*
yes come-NEG.POL
'Yes, (no one) will come.'
B: *Iie,* *ki-masu.*
no come-POL
'No, (someone) will come.'

The yes–no question in (27), which includes the NPI *dare-mo* 'anyone,' expresses the meaning of 'Is it the case that no one will come?' Thus, if the situation where no one will come holds, the answer to the question is *hai*, but if this does not hold, the answer is *iie*. The difference in the propositional content conveyed by the negative yes–no question gives rise to the observed patterns of *hai-iie* answers.

2.6 Negation in Conjunctive Clauses

In Japanese, there are two negative *-te* conjunctive forms, that is, *naku-te* and *nai-de*, which can connect two clauses. Coordination is also possible with coordinating particles. Negated coordinate clauses show different scope properties, depending on how they are coordinated.

2.6.1 *Nai-de* versus *Naku-te*

The gerundive *-te* conjunctive forms, which can be affirmative or negative, specify a number of semantic relations, including "means, accompanying situation, reason/cause, temporal sequence, coordination" (see, for example, Nihongo Kijutsu Bunpō Kenkyūkai 2008; Yoshida 2012: 33–53). When the conjunctive *-te* is combined with negated verbs, two variants, that is, *naku-te* and *nai-de*, can be formed (see, for example, Masuoka and Takubo 1992: 187–188).[12]

(28) a. *Koko ni wa {ko-naku-te/ko-nai-de} yo-i.*
here LOC TOP {come-NEG-GER/come-NEG-GER} good-NPST
'It is all right not to come here.'

b. *Watashi wa isogashiku {naku-te/*nai-de} yo-i.*
I TOP busy {NEG-GER/NEG-GER} good-NPST
'It is all right for me not to be busy.'

The *nai-de* form can be derived only from verbs, but *naku-te* can be derived from either verbs or adjectives. One intriguing fact about *nai-de* and *naku-te* is that which form can be used is determined depending on the semantic relation expressed by the conjunctive *-te* clause.[13]

To be concrete, in cases where the conjunctive forms are taken to specify the relation of means or accompanying situation to the following clause, only the *nai-de* form (derived by combining *nai* with verbs) can be used.

(29) a. *Ken wa kagi o {tsukawa-nai-de/*tsukawa-naku-te},*
TOP key ACC {use-NEG-GER/use-NEG-GER}
doa o ake-ta.
door ACC open-PST
'Ken opened the door without using a key.' (Means)

b. *Ken wa raito o {tsuke-nai-de/*tsuke-naku-te},*
TOP light ACC {turn.on-NEG-GER/turn.on-NEG-GER}
benkyō-shi-te i-ru.
study-do-GER be-NPST
'Ken is studying without turning on the light.' (Accompanying situation)

[12] Kitagawa (1983) analyzes *naku-te* as the gerund form of the adjectival auxiliary and *nai-de* as the gerund form of the verbal auxiliary.

[13] *Naku-te*, but not *nai-de*, can be derived based on a copular expression, as in *gakusei/shizuka de naku-te* [student/quiet COP NEG-GER].

If the *-te* conjunctive clauses specify the semantic relations of cause/reason (while expressing the subject's judgments or emotional states) or coordination (with different subjects), both *nai-de* and *naku-te* can be used (cf. McGloin 1976: 373–381).

(30) a. *Kodomo ga yasai o {tabe-nai-de/tabe-naku-te},*
child NOM vegetable ACC {eat-NEG-GER/eat-NEG-GER}
komat-te i-ru.
worry-GER be-NPST
'(I am) worried because the children will not eat vegetables.'
(Reason/Cause)

b. *Ken ga {ko-nai-de/ko-naku-te} Mari ga ki-ta.*
NOM {come-NEG-GER/come-NEG-GER} NOM come-PST
'Ken did not come, but Mari came.' (Coordination)

Note that when reason/cause and coordinate meanings are expressed, not only verbs but also nouns and adjectives can occur in the *naku-te* form.

(31) a. *Ken ga akaruku-naku-te, watashi wa shinpai-shi-ta.*
NOM cheerful-NEG-GER I TOP worry-do-PST
'I was worried because Ken was not cheerful.' (Reason/Cause)

b. *Ken ga isogashiku-naku-te, Mari ga isogashikat-ta.*
NOM busy-NEG-GER NOM busy-PST
'Ken was not busy, but Mari was busy.' (Coordination)

Naku-te can be used in contexts where both verbs and adjectives can appear. The data suggest that when two clauses are connected by way of conjunctive *-te* forms, a variety of semantic relations are specified, but that there are semantic restrictions on the use of *nai-de* and *naku-te* forms.[14]

2.6.2 The Scope of Negation in Coordination

Two clauses containing subjects can be coordinated with the verb in the first conjunct appearing in either the adverbal form (*ren'yōkei*) or the *-te* form. There are also coordinate constructions where coordinating particles like *mo* and *tari* are attached to verbal constituents in their conjuncts. In the coordinate constructions, it is possible to place a negator in the second conjunct, but the negator may or may not take scope over the first conjunct.

In cases where a predicate in the adverbal form or the *-te* conjunctive form is used for coordination, the first conjunct is not interpreted in the negative if the second conjunct is negated.

(32) a. *Ken ga hashiri, Eri ga hashira-nakat-ta.*
NOM run NOM run-NEG-PST
'Ken ran and Eri did not run.'

b. *Ken ga hashit-te, Eri ga hashira-nakat-ta.*
NOM run-GER NOM run-NEG-PST
'Ken ran and Eri did not run.'

[14] For extensive discussion on the semantic/pragmatic as well as syntactic constraints on the use of the two forms, see, for example, Kitagawa (1976, 1983), McGloin (1976), Kuno (1978b).

In the two types of coordinate constructions in (32), *nai* takes scope only over the second conjunct.

Another form of coordinate structure can be constructed with particles used as coordinators (like *mo*). In (33), like (32), only the second conjunct contains a negator, but both first and second conjuncts are understood to be negated.

(33) *Ken ga hashiri mo Eri ga hashiri mo shi-nakat-ta.*
NOM run also NOM run also do-NEG-PST
'Neither Ken nor Eri ran.'

The data in (32) and (33) illustrate that the possibility of negating the first conjunct by a clausal negator in the second conjunct differs depending on the type of coordination involved.

2.7 Negative Imperatives and Exclamatives

In Japanese, both affirmative and negative clauses can be turned into imperatives, but they are subject to different imperative formation rules. Some imperative clauses behave as negated clauses even without overt negative markers. Exclamatives inherently carry negative meanings, and some of them behave like clauses containing a clausal negator.

2.7.1 Negative Imperatives

There are several ways of forming negative imperative clauses. (In contemporary Japanese, imperatives can be formed on verbs, but not on adjectives and adjectival nouns.[15]) Verbs inflect for *meirei-kei* 'imperative form.' Thus, affirmative imperatives can be formed by using this form, as in (34a), and it is also possible to construct affirmative imperatives by adding the imperative marker *nasai* to the verb in the adverbal form, as in (34b).

(34) a. *Tabe-ro!*
eat-IMP
'Eat!'

b. *Tabe-nasai!*
eat-IMP
'Eat!'

These strategies are not available for negative imperative formation. Negative imperatives are derived instead by adding the negative imperative particle *na* after the verb.

[15] Adjectival expressions can sometimes appear as imperatives, as exemplified in (i).

(i) *Shizuka ni!*
quiet COP
'Be quiet!'

The expression can be considered as an abbreviated form of the imperative *Shizuka ni shi-nasai!* [quiet COP do-IMP] 'Be quiet!'

(35) *Tabe-ru* *na!*
eat-NPST IMP
'Do not eat!'

In negative imperatives, the verb must appear in the non-past conclusive form. It is not possible to form a negative imperative with the verb in the past form, as **Tabe-ta na!* cannot be an imperative.[16]

Another strategy to form imperatives is to use the conjunctive *-te* forms of verbs. The verbal imperative in this form may be regarded as involving truncation of an auxiliary verb like *kudasai* (< *kudasaru* 'be given'). Both affirmative and negative imperatives can be formed by appeal to this strategy. Notably, the *nai-de* form, but not the *naku-te* form, can be used to derive this type of negative imperative.

(36) *{Tabe-te/Tabe-nai-de/*Tabe-naku-te}* *(kudasai)!*
{eat-GER/eat-NEG-GER/eat-NEG-GER} be.given.IMP
'(Do not) Eat!'

Imperative clauses can also be formed by adding *koto* 'fact' after the non-past, but not the past, form of the verb. When *koto* is involved in imperative formation, both affirmative and negative imperatives can be constructed.

(37) *Kore* *o* *{tabe-ru/*tabe-ta/tabe-na-i}* *koto!*
this ACC {eat-NPST/eat-PST/eat-NEG-NPST} fact
'(Do not) eat this!'

2.7.2 Exclamatives

Exclamatives formed with *ka* or *mon(o) ka* show some peculiar syntactic distributions. Some exclamatives behave as negated clauses syntactically, but others do not, as confirmed by the behavior of NPIs.

First, observe that in Japanese, exclamative clauses are most typically constructed by adding *ka* or *mon(o) ka* at the clause end.

(38) *Ken* *ga* *sonna* *tokoro* *ni* *ik-u* *{ka/mono* *ka}!*
NOM that.kind place LOC go-NPST {Q/thing Q}
'Ken will never go to that kind of place!'

Exclamatives with *ka* or *mon(o) ka* can be assumed to derive from rhetorical questions – a cross-linguistically common strategy for exclamative formation. The clause in (38) needs to be pronounced with a special intonation pattern so as to be qualified as an exclamative. Semantically, (38) makes the assertion that the described act will never be done.

Exclamatives differ from other types of clauses in that they intrinsically convey negative meanings, and cannot include clausal negators.

[16] An affirmative imperative like *Tabe na!*, formed by combining a particle *na* with the verb in the adverbal form, carries the same meaning as *Tabe nasai!*, but sounds like an informal and brusque colloquial speech.

(39) *Ken ga sonna tokoro ni ika-na-i {ka/mon(o) ka}!
NOM that.kind place LOC go-NEG-NPST {Q/thing Q}
'Ken will never go to that of kind place!'

While the exclamative clauses formed on *ka* or *mon(o) ka* are not compatible with clausal negators, they show a difference in acceptability when NPIs like *dare-ni-mo* 'to anyone' are included.

(40) a. {Sonna yatsu to/*dare-to-mo} hanas-u ka!
{that.kind guy with/anyone-with} talk-NPST Q
'I will not talk with {that kind of guy/anyone}!'
b. {Sonna yatsu to/dare-to-mo} hanas-u mon(o) ka!
{that.kind guy with/anyone-with} talk-NPST thing Q
'I will not talk with {that kind of guy/anyone}!'

Both exclamative expressions in (40) inherently carry negative meanings, but the NPI *dare-to-mo* 'with anyone' can appear in (40b), but not in (40a). This shows that only the exclamative with *mon(o) ka* projects negative scope, under which NPIs are licensed (see Section 3).

Moreover, clauses with *ka* and *mon(o) ka* can be exclamatives even when they include a wh-phrase *dare-ga* [who-NOM].

(41) a. Dare ga sonna tokoro ni ik-u {ka/mon(o) ka}!
who NOM that.kind place LOC go-NPST {Q/thing Q}
'Who will go to that kind of place! (= I will never go to that kind of place!)'
b. *Doko ni ik-u {ka/mon(o) ka}!
where LOC go-NPST {Q/thing Q}
'Where will I never go!'

Since (41a) contains a wh-phrase, it looks like a wh-question, but it is not. Rather, (41a) is an exclamation making the (strong) negative assertion that the speaker will never perform the described act. This type of exclamative can be formed only when *dare-ga* serves as a subject, and cannot be formed with other wh-phrases, as shown in (41b).

3 Syntactic Aspects of Negation

This section discusses syntactic aspects of negation, with particular attention to the syntactic behavior of negative polarity items (NPIs).

3.1 Kinds of Negative Polarity Items

Japanese has a fairly large inventory of NPIs. As previously noted, they are licensed under the scope of negation, and cannot appear in affirmative clauses, as illustrated in (42).

(42) *Sono eiga wa {kesshite/chittomo/sonnani} {omoshiroku nakat-ta/*
that movie TOP {never/least/very} {interesting NEG-PST/
**omoshirokat-ta}.*
interesting-PST}
'That movie was {never/least/not too/not very} interesting.'

Semantically, some NPI adverbs (e.g. *kesshite* 'never,' *sukoshimo* 'in the least,' *hitori-mo* 'even one') and the NPI particle *shika* 'only' occurring after Determiner or Postpositional Phrases (DPs/PPs) (e.g. *gakusei shika* 'only students') intensify the meanings of words they modify, and others (e.g. *kanarazushimo* '(not) necessarily,' *amari* '(not) too much,' and *sonnani* '(not) very much') weaken or soften them.[17]

There are several types of NPIs. NPIs can be derived by combining an indefinite pronoun with *mo* (e.g. *dare-mo* 'anyone' *nani-mo* 'anything,' and *doko-ni-mo* 'to anywhere'), as illustrated in (43a).

(43) a. *Ken wa nani-mo {*tabe-ta/tabe-nakat-ta}.*
TOP anything {eat-PST/eat-NEG-PST}
'Ken {ate/did not eat} anything.'
b. *Ken wa dochira-mo tabe-ta.*
TOP both eat-PST
'Ken ate both.'

Not all indefinite pronouns with *mo* behave as NPIs, however; for example, *dochira-mo* 'both,' *dore-mo* 'both,' and *itu-mo* 'always' are not NPIs. Thus, (43b), which includes *dochira-mo*, is well formed even though it is not a negative clause.

Furthermore, it is cross-linguistically observed that "minimizers" indicating the smallest natural number (i.e. "one") often serve as NPIs. In Japanese, minimizer expressions like *hito-ri mo* 'even one person' are NPIs.

(44) *Gakusei ga hito-ri mo {*ki-ta/ko-nakat-ta}.*
student NOM one-CL also {come-PST/come-NEG-PST}
'(Not) a single student came.'

While minimizers referring to "one" combined with *mo* 'also' generally serve as NPIs, NPIs combined with *to* 'even' do not necessarily have to refer to "one."

[17] *Amari* 'very' behaves as an NPI when it has a weakening sense, as in (i-a), but it does not when used in a strengthening sense, as in (i-b).
(i) a. *Ken wa amari {tabe-na-i/*tabe-ru}.*
TOP very {eat-NEG-NPST/eat-NPST}
'Ken (does not) eat very much.'
b. *Amari tabe-sugi-ru-to, futor-u yo.*
very eat-exceed-NPST-if get.fat-NPST SFP
'If you eat too much, you will get fat.'

(45) *Kono gakusei wa mik-ka to {*mot-ta/mota-naka-ta}.*
this student TOP three-day even {hold-PST/hold-NEG-PST}
'This student {could/could not} continue even for three days.'

Any number expression combined with *to* can serve as an NPI as long as it is conceived of as referring to the minimal or the least amount. In (45), *mik-ka* 'three days' is regarded (pragmatically) as the minimal length of time during which the students should continue working, and thus *mik-ka to* counts as an NPI (see, for example, Nihongo Kijutsu Bunpō Kenkyūkai 2007: 269–271).

NPIs are divided into two classes, according to whether they are licensed by a negator located in a higher clause. Many NPIs are subject to the so-called clause-mate condition. In (46a), the NPIs, constrained by the clause-mate condition, are not admitted, because they appear in the complement clause selected by the negated copula *de wa nai* '(It) is not the case that.' On the other hand, NPIs like *kanarazushimo (subete)* 'necessarily (all)' do not need to appear in the complement clause in which *nai* is located, as shown by the acceptability of (46b).

(46) a. **[Ken ga {nani-mo/kono hon shika} yon-da] no de*
NOM {anything/this book only} read-PST NMLZ COP
wa na-i.
TOP NEG-NPST
'It is not the case that Ken ate {anything/only this book}.'
b. *[Ken ga kanarazushimo subete no hon o yon-da]*
NOM necessarily all GEN book ACC read-PST
no de wa na-i.
NMLZ COP TOP NEG-NPST
'It is not necessarily the case that Ken read all the books.'

There are apparent exceptions to this generalization. As observed by Muraki (1978), complex negative expressions like *koto ga nai* 'have not experienced' and *kioku ga nai* 'have no memory' allow NPIs like *dare-ni-mo* 'to anyone' to appear in the noun-complement clause even if *nai* is located in the matrix clause.

(47) a. *Ken wa [[dare-ni-mo at-ta] (*toiu)] kioku ga na-i.*
TOP anyone-DAT meet-PST (that) memory NOM NEG-NPST
'Ken does not remember that he met anyone.'
b. *Ken wa [[dare-ni-mo awa-nakat-ta] (toiu)] kioku ga ar-u.*
TOP anyone-DAT meet-NEG-PST (that) memory NOM be-NPST
'Ken remembers that he did not meet anyone.'

A complex predicate like *kioku ga aru* invokes restructuring, whereby a bi-clausal constituent is reanalyzed as a single clause. Consequently, *dare-ni-mo*, which is constrained by the clause-mate condition, is licensed in (47a). This restructuring process is not instantiated when the complementizer *toiu* 'that' is introduced in the noun-complement clause. Thus, (47a) is not acceptable if *toiu* is present. In (47b), the presence or absence of the complementizer does not affect the grammaticality of the sentence, since the clausal negator is located inside the noun complement clause.

Another interesting property of NPIs is that many of them can occur as elliptical answers to questions.

(48) a. Q: *Minna ki-mashita ka?*
all come-POL.PST Q
'Did all people come?'
b. A: *Iie, {dare-mo/hito-ri mo/*hito-ri shika}.*
no {anyone/one-CL also/one-CL only}
'No, {no one/not one person/only one person}.'

Example (48a) is an affirmative question, which does not contain a clausal negator, and the elliptical answers do not contain any overt negator. Nevertheless, NPIs are allowed to occur in such elliptical answers because a negative meaning is expressed (implicitly). According to Watanabe (2004), this is one characteristic of "negative concord items (NCI)," which could be identified as a subclass of NPIs.

NPIs with the negative particle *shika* 'only' are distinguished from other NPIs (i.e. NCIs), in the sense that they cannot form elliptical answers, as in (48). Moreover, *shika*, in opposition to NPIs like *dare-mo* 'anyone,' cannot be iterated in a single clause.

(49) a. *Ken wa dare-ni-mo nani-mo age-nakat-ta.*
TOP anyone-DAT anything give-NEG-PST
'Ken did not give anything to anyone.'
b. **Ken wa kodomo ni shika hon shika age-nakat-ta.*
TOP child DAT only book only give-NEG-PST
'Ken gave only books to only children.'

The unacceptability of (49b) suggests that *nai* can license only one instance of *shika* per clause. DPs/PPs accompanying *shika* fall into the class of NPIs, but display a number of unique behaviors distinguishing them from other NPIs.

Finally, note that some alleged NPIs are licensed by predicates that do not project negative scope syntactically.

(50) *Sore wa zenzen {chiga-u/mu-imi-da}.*
that TOP at.all {differ-NPST/NEG-meaning-NPST}
'That is totally {different/meaningless}.'

The adverb *zenzen* 'at all' is often considered to be an NPI licensed under the scope of negation, but strictly speaking, it is not, because it is licensed by semantically negative predicates that do not project negative scope.

3.2 The Extent of Negative Scope

One interesting fact about clausal negation is that negative scope is projected syntactically. This fact can be easily confirmed by looking at where NPIs (e.g. *Ken shika* 'only Ken') – which are licensed under the scope of negation – can appear in the clause. In Japanese, negative scope extends over the entire clause in which a negator is located; in simple clauses, NPIs are licensed by a clausal negator, whether they occur in subject or object position.

(51) a. *Ken ga kore shika kawa-nakat-ta.*
NOM this only buy-NEG-PST
'Ken bought only this.'
b. *Ken shika hon o kawa-nakat-ta.*
only book ACC read-NEG-PST
'Only Ken bought the book.'

English differs from Japanese in that NPIs in subject position are not licensed by the clausal negator *not*, as in (52).

(52) a. **Anyone did not buy the book.*
b. *John did not buy anything.*

Example (53) illustrates that NPIs in the matrix clause are not licensed by a negator located in the embedded clause.

(53) **Eri shika [Ken ga ko-nakat-ta to] it-ta.*
only NOM come-NEG-PST that say-PST
'Only Eri said that Ken did not come.'

These facts indicate that the extent of negative scope is fixed structurally, and that it does not extend beyond the clause in which a clausal negator is located.

The absence of a subject–object asymmetry in the licensing of NPIs, as witnessed in (51), is a reflection of the fact that the *nai*, unlike English *not*, takes clause-wide scope. Kishimoto (2005: 68–84) suggests that the difference in the extent of negative scope between English and Japanese should be attributed to the presence or absence of Neg-head raising, as depicted in (54).[18]

(54) a. Japanese: [$_{TP}$ SUBJ [$_{NegP}$ [$_{VP}$ OBJ V-v] ~~Neg~~] **Neg**-T]
b. English: [$_{TP}$ SUBJ T [$_{NegP}$ **Neg** [$_{vP}$ V-v OBJ]]]

The scope of negation extends over the projection of the head in which Neg is included: TP in (54a) and NegP in (54b). In Japanese, a Neg-head is located in a structural position high enough to license

[18] TP (= Tense Phrase), NegP (= Negative Phrase), Neg-head (= Negative head).

a subject NPI by virtue of its head movement to T.[19] By contrast, in English, the scope of negation does not fall over the subject in TP due to the absence of Neg-raising.

The presence of Neg-head raising in Japanese is confirmed by the fact that *nai* resists addition of a focus particle to its right.

(55) **Ken* *ga* *hashira-naku* *mo* *ar-u.*
NOM run-NEG also be-NPST
'Ken also does not run.'

Note that it is possible to insert a focus particle like *mo* after adjectives (e.g. *kawaiku mo ar-u* [cute also be-NPST]) and verbs (e.g. *hashiri mo su-ru* [run also do-NPST]). Since focus particles cannot be placed inside complex words without a syntactic break, the unacceptability of (55) supports an analysis of the negative *nai* forming a complex head with tense (by virtue of Neg-head raising).[20]

The negator *nai* combined with verbs in matrix clauses generally takes clause-wide scope. Nevertheless, in the causative construction, where *nai* is embedded under the causative verb *suru* 'make,' the negative scope does not include the subject, that is, the causer.

(56) a. *Ken* *wa* *[Eri* *shika* *soko* *ni* *ik-e-naku]* *shi-ta.*
TOP only there LOC go-POT-NEG make-PST
'Ken caused only Eri to be able to go there.'

b. *Ken* *wa* *[Eri* *o* *soko* *ni* *shika* *ik-e-naku]* *shi-ta.*
TOP ACC there LOC only go-POT-NEG make-PST
'Ken caused Eri to be able to go only there.'

c. **Ken* *shika* *[Eri* *o* *soko* *ni* *ik-e-naku]* *shi-ta.*
only ACC there LOC go-POT-NEG make-PST
'Only Ken caused him to be unable to go there.'

Syntactically, the causative verb takes a clausal complement, and in the causative construction (56), the negator is located in the complement clause, as in [$_{TP}$ Subj [$_{TP}$... *naku*] *suru*]. Since the subject of the causative verb is located in the matrix rather than the embedded clause, it cannot be an NPI. The data show that the negator does not take clause-wide scope if it is deeply embedded in a complex predicate. This fact is naturally expected if scope is structurally defined, as often assumed.

19 This Neg-head raising analysis implies that when *nai* is an adjectival negator, it does not undergo Neg-raising (Kishimoto 2007, 2008), leading to the prediction that it will not take scope over TP. This is in fact the case, as shown in (i).

(i) **Kyō* *wa* *watashi* *shika* *isogashiku* *na-i.*
today TOP I only busy NEG-NPST
'Only I am busy today.'

The failure of *nai* occurring with the adjective predicate *isogashii* 'busy' to license an NPI subject with *shika* in (i) shows that an adjectival negator does not extend its scope over TP. For a comparison with another line of analysis taking subjects to stay within VP (e.g. Watanabe 2004; Kato 2000), see Kishimoto (2008).

20 When *nai* does not undergo Neg-head raising, it allows the addition of a focus particle to the right, as the acceptability of the double negative form *wakara-naku mo nai* [understand-NEG also NEG] 'not uncomprehensible,' where the lower *nai* (appearing next to the verb) does not undergo raising (see Kishimoto 2008).

3.3 The Focus of Negation

Negative clauses containing a clausal negator often have a prominent constituent to be negated, that is, the focus of negation, which may or may not be syntactically marked. One way of indicating this syntactically is to attach the topic marker *wa* to a constituent (cf. Chapter 13, this volume).

(57) *Ken ga kono ko wa home-naka-ta.*
        NOM this child TOP praise-NEG-PST
    'Ken did not praise this child.'

In (57), the *wa*-marked object is interpreted contrastively rather than thematically (cf. Kuno 1973: 37–61). Thus, (57) does not make a flat denial of the proposition that Ken praised the child, but rather asserts that this child does not belong to the group of people who Ken praised. This suggests that the *wa*-marked object counts as the focus of negation in (57) by virtue of the fact that the sentence is uttered with the presupposition that there is a set of alternatives to the individual referred to by the topic (McGloin 1976: 389–397).

The interpretation of quantified expressions is differentiated according to whether they count as the focus of negation. When a quantified subject like *zen'in* 'all' is focused, due to the presence of *wa*-marking, as in (58a), the sentence necessarily expresses partial negation, *nai* taking scope over the universal quantifier (not > all). In (58b), on the other hand, the quantifier (without *wa*-marking) does not necessarily count as the focus of negation.

(58) a. *Kono kaigi ni zen'in wa ko-nakat-ta.*
       this meeting LOC all TOP come-NEG-PST
       'Not all people came to this meeting.' (not > all)
    b. *Koko kaigi ni wa zen'in ga ko-nakat-ta.*
       this meeting LOC TOP all NOM come-NEG-PST
       'All people did not come to this meeting.' (all > not, not > all)

The preferred interpretation for (58b) is the one where the universal quantifier takes scope over negative *nai* (all > not), but the reverse 'not > all' interpretation is also possible.

Japanese has a complex negative form like *{wake/no} de wa nai* 'it is not the case that.' When this form is used, the negator takes scope over the complement clause, and a focused constituent is determined not syntactically but pragmatically.

(59) *[Ken ga hon o yon-da] {wake/no} de (wa) na-i.*
        NOM book ACC read-PST {reason/that} COP (TOP) NEG-NPST
    'It is not the case that Ken read the book.'

Example (59) can express a variety of meanings, depending on where focus falls, such as 'The event of Ken's reading the book did not take place,' 'It was not Ken that read the book,' and 'It was not the book that Ken read.'

3.4 Double Negation and Pleonastic Negation

In general, a clause may contain more than one negator, and double negation can be expressed by stacking negative markers. When two negators are used in a single clause, as in (60), the clause conveys an affirmative meaning, due to the fact that negating a negative clause logically entails an affirmative clause.

(60) a. *Ken* *wa* *hashira-naku* *(wa/mo)* *na-i.*
  TOP run-NEG (TOP/also) NEG-NPST
  'It is not the case that Ken will not run.'

b. *Reigai* *no* *na-i* *rūru* *wa* *na-i.*
  exception GEN NEG-NPST rule TOP NEG-NPST
  'There is no rule without exceptions.'

Although (60a) is taken to be affirmative semantically, it makes a weaker assertion, often implying a hesitation, because it signifies the possibility that Ken will run under certain conditions. No such weakening effect is observed for a different kind of double negative sentence in (60b), however. Logically, (60b) carries the same logical meaning as the affirmative clause *Rūru ni wa reigai ga ar-u* [rule LOC TOP exception be-NPST] 'there are exceptions to the rule,' but makes a stronger assertion than the positive clause.[21]

In general, the clausal negator *nai* expresses logical negation, but there are cases where it does not. In (61), the *before*-clause carries the same meaning regardless of whether the predicate is negated, suggesting that *nai* in the *before*-clause serves as a pleonastic negative marker (see, for example, Miyaji 1956).

(61) *Kare* *wa* *{nokku-shi-na-i/nokku-su-ru}* *mae-ni* *doa* *o*
  he TOP {knock-do-NEG-NPST/knock-do-NPST} before door ACC
  ake-ta.
  open-PST
  'He opened the door before he knocked.'

Cross-linguistically, pleonastic negation is fairly common; for instance, as noted in Horn (2010), in French, pleonastic negation appears in *before*-clauses, just as in Japanese, as in *avant qu'elle* ***ne*** *parle* 'before she speaks.'

3.5 NPIs in Non-negative Contexts

NPIs are usually licensed falling under the scope of a clausal negator. Nevertheless, the NPI *kore-ijō* can occur in certain non-negative contexts, including complement clauses taken by certain negative predicates that do not project negative scope.

[21] Modals like *nebanaranai* 'must' and *nakerebanaranai* 'must' include two negative markers morphologically (i.e. *ne* and *nai* for *ne-ba-nara-nai* and *nakere* and *nai* for *nakere-ba-nara-nai*) but carry positive meanings. Since these modals have strengthening effects, they belong to the second type of double negation.

3.5.1 Kore-ijō

The NPI *kore-ijō* 'anymore' patterns with the NPI *any* in English, which can sometimes be licensed without overt negation. Because *kore-ijō* behaves as an NPI, declarative clauses comprising *kore-ijō* give rise to a difference in acceptability, according to whether they contain a clausal negator.

(62) *Ken wa jiken-nitsuite kore-ijō {hanasa-nakat-ta/*hanashi-ta}.*
TOP accident-about anymore {speak-NEG-PST/speak-PST}
'Ken {did not talk/talked} about the accident anymore.'

Nevertheless, a clausal negator is not necessary for *kore-ijō* in certain syntactic contexts. It can occur in conditional clauses, *before*-clauses, and comparative clauses without overt negation.

(63) a. *[Kore-ijō {hashire-ba/hashir-u mae-ni}] Mari wa kitto*
anymore {run-if/run-NPST before} TOP surely
taore-ru darō.
fall.down-NPST will
'If/Before she runs anymore, Mari will surely fall down.'

b. *[Kore-ijō hashir-u yori] aruk-u hō-ga-i-i.*
anymore run-NPST than walk-NPST should
'You should walk rather than run anymore.'

Kore-ijō is not licensed in *after*-clauses and *when*-clauses, if they are not negated, however.

(64) **[Mari ga kore-ijō hanashi-ta {ato/toki}] Ken ga de-te it-ta.*
NOM anymore speak-PST {after/time} NOM go.out-GER go-PST
'{After/When} Mari spoke anymore, Ken went out.'

A comparison of the examples in (62–64) and their translations shows that *kore-ijō* behaves in exactly the same way as *any* in English, which can sometimes be licensed without overt negation.[22]

3.5.2 Negative Predicates

Simple negative predicates like *kobamu/kyohi-suru* 'refuse' and *hitei-suru* 'deny' express negative meanings intrinsically. They do not license NPIs like *sukoshimo* 'at all,' because they do not project negative

[22] *Kore-ijō* is not the only NPI that is allowed to occur in non-negative contexts. For instance, *(kibun ga) sugureru* 'feel better' behaves like such an NPI, although it does not show exactly the same syntactic behavior as *kore-ijō*.

(i) a. *Ken wa kibun ga {sugure-nakat-ta/*sugure-ta}.*
TOP feeling NOM {better-NEG-PST/better-PST}
'Ken {did not feel/felt} better.'

b. *[Tashōtomo kibun ga sugure-reba] kaet-te ii yo.*
a.little feeling NOM better-COND return-GER good SFP
'You can go home if you feel a little better.'

(Kibun ga) sugureru is licensed when it is associated with a clausal negator, but it is also allowed to occur without overt negation in conditional clauses (Kishimoto 2013: 140–142).

scope. Nevertheless, *kore-ijō* can be embedded felicitously in their complement clause, although it cannot appear in the matrix clause.

(65) a. *Mari wa [{kore-ijō/*sukoshimo} shōgen-su-ru] koto o*
TOP {anymore/at.all} testimony-do-NPST fact ACC
kyohi-shi-ta.
refuse-do-PST
'Mari refused [to testify {anymore/at all}].'

b. **Mari wa shōgen o {kore-ijō/sukoshimo} kyohi-shi-ta.*
TOP testimony ACC {anymore/at.all} refuse-do-PST
'Mari refused her testimony {anymore/at all}.'

Japanese abounds with complex predicates (see, for example, Kageyama 1993). *Kore-ijō* is allowed to appear in complement clauses taken by certain types of compound predicates, such as syntactic V-V compound verbs whose second verb is *-kaneru* 'cannot do' (denoting some kind of negation), as shown in (66).

(66) *Watashi wa [shigoto o kore-ijō hikiuke]-{kane-ru/*sokone-ta}.*
I TOP job ACC anymore accept-{cannot.do-NPST/fail-PST}
'I {cannot/failed to} accept jobs anymore.'

It is worth noting here that *-sokoneru* 'fail' does not license *kore-ijō*, even though it looks like a negative predicate.

Furthermore, observe that *tough*-adjectives, such as *-zuai*, 'hard,' *-gatai* 'hard' and *-nikui* 'difficult,' form complex adjectives permitting the occurrence of *kore-ijō*.

(67) *[Shigoto o kore-ijō*
job ACC anymore
*hikiuke]-{zura-i/gata-i/niku-i/*yasu-i}.*
accept-{hard-NPST/hard-NPST/difficult-NPST/easy-NPST}
'It is {hard/hard/difficult/easy} to accept jobs anymore.'

The *tough*-adjectives *-zurai, -gatai*, and *-nikui*, in opposition to *-yasui* 'easy,' express negative meanings inherently, so that they allow *kore-ijō* to appear in their complement clauses.

4 Lexical Negation

Japanese has a number of "lexical affixes" that express negative meanings. There are both negative prefixes (originated from Chinese) and negative suffixes (that have morphological affinity with clausal negators).

4.1 Negative Prefix

Japanese has a number of lexical prefixes that express negation, represented by *hi-* (非) 'negation,' *fu-* (不) 'negation,' *mi-* (未) 'incompletion,' and *mu-* (無) 'negation' (see, for example, Nomura 1973).[23]

[23] The prefix 不 is sometimes pronounced as [bu] (e.g. *bu-kiyō* [NEG-skillful] 'clumsy').

(68) a. *hi-*: *hi-jōshiki (na)* [NEG-common.sense] 'unreasonable,' *hi-seiki (no)* [NEG-proper] 'non-regular'
b. *fu-*: *fu-kigen (na)* [NEG-temper] 'sullen,' *fu-tashika (na)* [NEG-certain] 'uncertain'
c. *mi-*: *mi-keiken (no)* [NEG-experience] 'unexperienced'
d. *mu-*: *mu-kiryoku (na)* [NEG-power] 'apathetic'

All the prefixes in (68) have their roots in Chinese. Thus, they are most typically attached to Sino-Japanese words, but can sometimes be associated with native Japanese words (e.g. *fu-kakujitsu* [NEG-certain (SJ)] 'uncertain' versus *fu-tashika* [NEG-sure (NJ)] 'unsure').

In categorical terms, the negative prefixes are combined with nouns and adjectival nouns (or their roots), and often induce a change in the lexical category of the base. The categorical status of the expressions can be discerned most conspicuously by looking at how attributive forms are morphologically realized.

(69)

a.	*jōshiki*	***no***	*han'i*	→	*hi-jōshiki*	***na***	*hito*	
	common.sense	GEN	range		NEG-common.sense	COP	man	
	'the range of common sense'				'an unreasonable man'			(N → A)
b.	*tashika*	***na***	*shōko*	→	*fu-tashika*	***na***	*shōko*	
	solid	COP	evidence		NEG-solid	COP	evidence	(A → A)
	'solid evidence'					'weak evidence'		
c.	*kakokei*	***no***	*dōshi*	→	*hi-kakokei*	***no***	*dōshi*	
	past.form	GEN	verb		NEG-past.form	GEN	verb	
	'verbs in the past form'				'verbs in the non-past form'			(N → N)

Lexical negative expressions take different attributive forms, depending on whether they are categorized as nouns or adjectival nouns. When a given expression takes the *na* form, it is categorized as an adjectival noun, but when it takes the *no* form, it is categorized as a noun. The examples in (69) illustrate that the lexical-negative expressions do not necessarily match in category with the bases.

The negative *hi-*, *fu-*, *mi-*, and *mu-* are dedicated prefixes, which never assume the role of clausal negators, and do not license the occurrence of NPIs.

(70) a. **Sono kōshō shika mu-imi da.*
that negotiation only NEG-meaning COP
'Only that negotiation is meaningless.'

b. **Kare wa sukoshimo fu-kigen da.*
he TOP at.all NEG-temper COP
'He is ill-tempered at all.'

This illustrates that lexical affixes do not project negative scope syntactically even when they carry negative meanings.

4.2 Negative Adjectives with the Suffix *Nai*

Japanese has several types of lexical negative expressions formed with the addition of *-nai*. The negative *-nai* deriving a lexical negative expression functions as a suffix morphologically. As far as the complex negative adjectives with *nai* are concerned, there are two major sources. One type of morphologically complex adjectives is formed by combining *nai* with a noun, as in (71a), and the other, with a verb, as in (71b).[24]

(71) a. N+*nai*: *yurugi-nai* [shake-NEG] 'unshakable,' *sonshoku-nai* [inferiority-NEG] 'comparable,' *abunage-nai* [danger-NEG] 'without danger,' *nukari-nai* [fault-NEG] 'shrewd,' etc.

b. V+*nai*: *tsumara-nai* [clog-NEG] 'boring,' *tamara-nai* [bear-NEG] 'unbearable,' *suma-nai* [do.without-NEG] 'sorry,' *kudara-nai* [go.down-NEG] 'unbearable,' *uka-nai* [float-NEG] 'depressed,' etc.

The complex adjectives listed in (71) serve as single-word adjectives syntactically. Notably, they do not have affirmative forms; for example, *yarikire-nai* 'unbearable' and *abunage-nai* 'without danger' do not have affirmative counterparts **yarikireru* 'bear (?)' and **abunage-aru* 'dangerous (?).' There is also a minor type of complex negative adjectives, consisting of an adjective plus *nai*, such as *sewashi-nai* 'restless,' which has presumably been derived by compounding *sewashii* 'busy' with *nai*.

4.2.1 Noun-based Complex *Nai*-adjectives

A fairly large number of *nai*-adjectives belong to the type N+*nai*. Many, if not all, have periphrastic counterparts where the noun part is marked with nominative case (Kishimoto and Booij 2014).

(72) a. *Ken no shinnen wa [yurugi ga na-i].*
GEN faith TOP shaking NOM NEG-NPST
'Ken's faith is unshakable.'

b. *Ken no shinnen wa [yurugi-na-i].*
GEN faith TOP shaking-NEG-NPST
'Ken's faith is unshakable.'

With complex adjectives with the N+*nai* sequences, since *nai* is a genuine lexical adjective, no positive counterparts can be derived by replacing *nai* with *aru* regardless of whether the noun is case-marked (i.e. the hypothesized affirmative form **yurugi (ga) aru* [shaking NOM be] 'shaky(?)' is not acceptable).

The two variants of the complex adjectives with the N+*nai* sequence have essentially the same core meaning. This fact suggests that they should be created by the grammatical process of noun incorporation, as illustrated in (73).

(73) [TP N [A *na*-]*i*] → [TP [A N-*na*-]*i*]

[24] Owing to their idiomaticity, complex *nai*-adjectives often include elements that are no longer semantically transparent.

The resultant adjectives behave as single words, because incorporation is a process whereby two syntactically independent elements are formed into single lexical units. Accordingly, the two variants of the complex adjectives display a number of distinct syntactic behaviors, two of which are discussed below.

First, when the noun is marked with nominative case, it is possible for *nai* to accommodate a modifying expression, but when the noun appears without case marking, noun modification is not allowed.

(74) a. *Ken no shinnen wa [isasaka no yurugi] mo na-i.*
GEN faith TOP little GEN shaking also NEG-NPST
'Ken's faith is totally unshakable.'

b. **Ken no shinnen wa [isasaka no yurugi]-na-i.*
GEN faith TOP little GEN shaking-NEG-NPST
'Ken's faith is totally unshakable.'

Example (74b) is excluded, because the word-internal nominal element *yurugi* cannot be expanded to a phrase. No problem arises with noun modification in (74a), because the modified noun is a syntactically independent element.[25]

Secondly, the complex adjectives with the N+*nai* sequence show a difference with regard to the licensing of an NPI like *sukoshimo* 'at all,' depending on whether the component noun is case-marked or not.

(75) a. *Ken no shinnen wa (sukoshimo) yurugi ga nakat-ta.*
GEN faith TOP at.all shaking NOM NEG-PST
'Ken's faith has not been shaken (at all).'

b. *Ken no shinnen wa (*sukoshimo) yurugi-nakat-ta.*
GEN faith TOP at.all shaking-NEG-PST
'Ken's faith has not been shaken (at all).'

When the noun is case-marked, the complex adjective has a structure where the noun stands as an independent phrase lying outside the adjective *nai*, and the adjectival base *nai* serves as an operator to project negative scope. Example (75a) is acceptable, since the NPI *sukoshimo* is licensed by *nai*. On the other hand, if *nai* forms part of a complex word, it does not possess the ability to project negative scope; hence (75b) is not acceptable.

4.2.2 Verb-based Complex *Nai*-adjectives

Negative adjectives with the morphological sequence of V+*nai* generally do not carry the same meaning as their putative phrasal counterparts, in contrast with N+*nai* adjectives. For instance, the adjective *yarikirenai* 'unbearable' and its apparent phrasal counterpart *yarikire-nai* 'cannot

[25] As discussed by Kishimoto and Booji (2014), some complex adjectives (e.g. *shikata ga nai* [do.way NOM NEG] 'cannot help') do not allow even their case-marked nouns to expand to phrases, owing to lexicalization applying to the periphrastic variants with the 'N-NOM+*nai*' form.

finish' do not carry the same meaning. Moreover, the two expressions have different categorical status.

(76) a. *Ken wa [sono kettei o yarikirenaku] omot-ta.*
TOP that decision ACC unbearable think-PST
'Ken thought that decision to be unbearable.'

b. **Ken wa [sono shukudai o yarikire-naku] omot-ta.*
TOP that homework ACC can.finish-NEG think-PST
'Ken thought that homework to be unfinishable.'

The small clause complement of *omou* 'think' can accommodate an adjective, but not a negated verb (see Section 3.1). Then, the data show that while *yarikirenai* 'unbearable' is an adjective, *yarikire-nai* 'cannot finish' consists of the verb plus a grammatical negator. Needless to say, the phrasal expression *yarikire-nai* does have an affirmative variant *yarikireru* 'can finish,' since *nai* here functions as a clausal negator. If the adjective *yarikirenai* 'unbearable' is taken to be derived from the verbal expression *yarikire-nai* 'cannot finish,' a puzzling problem arises, because, under this analysis, it must be stated that an "adjective" can somehow be created out of a phrasal expression lacking categorical properties as an adjective.

The presence of complex adjectives with the V+*nai* sequence at first glance looks mysterious, but this does not come as a surprise if single-word V-*nai* adjectives are derived via lexicalization from phrasal expressions comprising the adjectival *nai*, not a negator, as depicted in (77).

(77) $[_{TP}$ $[_{AP}$ $[_{VP}$ V] *na*]-*i*] → $[_{TP}$ $[_{A}$ V-*na*]-*i*]

This view is reasonable, for there are a fairly large number of idiomatic expressions where *nai* combined with verbs serves as an adjective categorically (e.g. *warikire-nai* 'unsatisfied,' *te ni oe-nai* 'uncontrollable'), which can appear as in the small-clause clause selected by *omou*.

(78) *Ken wa [sore o {warikire-naku/te ni oe-naku}] omot-ta.*
TOP that ACC {satisfy-NEG/hand LOC carry-NEG} think-PST
'Ken thought that to be {unsatisfactory/uncontrollable}.'

Example (78) shows that *nai* appearing in *warikire-nai* and *te ni oe-nai* is an adjective and not a regular clausal negator. Note that these are phrasal adjectival expressions without affirmative variants (**warikireru* 'satisfy' is not acceptable in the intended sense). Moreover, *nai* must be independent of the verbs syntactically, for the verb part can be separated from *nai* by particles, as the acceptability of *warikire wa shi-nai* [satisfy TOP do-NEG] and *te ni oe wa shi-nai* [hand LOC carry TOP do-NEG] shows.

The presence of an auxiliary negator counting as an adjective (categorically) motivates the lexicalization process (77).[26] The process of

[26] To be more exact, the affixal *nai* appearing in negative adjectives has most likely been derived from lexical adjective *nai* via grammaticalization invoking the reduction process: word > clitic > affix (Hopper and Traugott 1993: 130–150). For an analysis of idiomatic adjectival V-*nai* expressions along this line, see Kishimoto (2009).

lexicalization, which reduces adjectival phrases to single-word adjectives, thus differs from the process deriving the adjectives of the N+*nai* type by incorporating a noun into the genuine adjective *nai*, although these operations both derive complex *nai*-adjectives.

Finally, negative expressions like *yurugi-nai/yuruga-nai* 'unshakable' and *nukari-nai/nukara-nai* 'shrewd' form apparent doublets. These expressions in fact have different sources. *Yurugi-nai* is formed from *yurugi ga nai*. Since **yurugi ga aru* is not acceptable, *yurugi-nai* must be derived by incorporating the noun *yurugi* 'shaking' into the adjective *nai* (NB: *yurugi* is a noun converted from the adverbial form of the verb *yurugu* 'shake').[27] *Yuruga-nai*, on the other hand, is an ordinary verbal expression. Thus, the affirmative form *yurugu* 'shake' is available, and the verb part can be separated from *nai*, as in *yurugi wa shi-nai* [shake TOP do-NEG].

4.3 Other Negative Suffixes

Japanese has several other types of lexical negative suffixes (and some of them no longer express negative meanings as a result of semantic shifts). Some representative suffixes include *zu, nu, nashi*, and *zaru*. A sample list of lexical negative expressions with *zu* is given in (79).

(79) a. *oya-shira-zu* [parent-know-NEG] 'wisdom tooth'
b. *seken-shira-zu* [world-know-NEG] 'greenhorn'
c. *haji-shira-zu* [shame-know-NEG] 'person without shame'[28]
d. *neko-ira-zu* [cat-need-NEG] 'ratsbane'
e. *tsuchi-fuma-zu* [soil-step-NEG] 'the arch (of a foot)'

The examples in (80) illustrate some cases of lexical negative expressions formed with the negative suffix *-nu*.

(80) a. *mi-shira-nu (hito)* [see-know-NEG (person)] 'unknown (person)'
b. *kaera-nu (hito)* [return-NEG (person)] 'a deceased (person)'
c. *nani-kuwa-nu (kao)* [any-eat-NEG (face)] 'an innocent-looking (face)'

Since, in classical Japanese, the negative *nu* is the attributive form of the negative auxiliary *zu*, the fixed (idiomatic) expressions formed with *nu* are used as noun modifiers in (80). Note also that in classical Japanese, the auxiliary *zu* has another attributive form *zaru*, and thus, some lexicalized expressions include *zaru*, as in (81).

[27] The deverbal noun is identical to the adverbal form of the verb in morphological form, but (i) provides a piece of confirming evidence that *yuruga-nai* and *yurugi-nai* have V-*nai* and N-*nai* forms, respectively.

(i) *Ken no shinnen wa {yuruga-nai-de i-ru/*yurugi-nai-de i-ru}.*
GEN faith TOP {shake-NEG-GER be-NPST/shaking-NEG-GER be-NPST}
'Ken's faith has not been shaken.'

Since the *nai-de iru* form can be formed only when the preceding element is a verb, it must be the case that *yuruga-nai* contains a verb, but *yurugi-nai* does not.

[28] *Hajishira-zu* can be used as an adjectival noun, meaning 'shameless.'

(81) a. *itsuwara-zaru (kimochi)* [deceive-NEG (feeling)] 'candid feeling'
b. *shir-are-zaru (sekai)* [know-PASS-NEG (world)] 'unknown world'

There are also lexical negative expressions derived by combining a noun with *nashi* 'without,' as exemplified in (82).

(82) a. *ikuji-nashi* [courage-without] 'coward'
b. *soko-nashi (no)* [bottom-without (GEN)] 'bottomless'

The compound expressions listed above are fixed expressions, which can be assumed to have been derived via lexicalization from their phrasal counterparts containing a clausal negator (e.g. *seken-shira-zu* 'greenhorn' versus *seken o shira-zu...* [world ACC know-NEG] 'not know the world...'). Needless to say, lexical negative expressions do not possess internal structures visible to the syntax, so the negative markers included in these expressions do not project negative scope, as the unacceptability of **sukoshimo seken-shira-zu* [at.all world-know-NEG] 'greenhorn at all' shows. Note also that many lexical negative expressions are completely lexicalized and constitute *bahuvrihi* compounds (one type of exocentric construction); for instance, *oya-shira-zu* 'wisdom tooth,' which comprises *oya* 'parents' and *shira-zu* (< *shiru* 'know (v)') 'knowing,' refers to a kind of *tooth*, that is, it denotes neither a kind of parent nor a kind of knowledge.

5 Concluding Remarks

This chapter has provided an overview of how negation is expressed in Japanese. Japanese has several distinct types of clausal negators, including *nai* and *zu/nu*. Negative expressions can be formed in various types of clauses. Clausal negators project negative scope, and NPIs are licensed under the scope of negation (although there are also NPIs that are allowed to appear in certain non-negative contexts). In Japanese, unlike English, the scope of clausal negation extends over the subject (in simple clauses), which can readily be ascertained by where NPIs are allowed to appear.

Negation can be expressed not only at the clause level but also at the lexical level. Lexical negations possess properties different from those of clausal negations. Japanese has both negative prefixes, which have a Chinese origin, and negative suffixes, many of which have the same morphological forms as clausal negators. This fact suggests that many of the lexical negative expressions with negative suffixes have probably emerged via lexicalization of periphrastic expressions. Notably, none of the lexical negative expressions project negative scope syntactically.

One important fact about Japanese negation is that the most common negator *nai* has adjectival inflection, which suggests that it has been derived from a lexical adjective, and this motivates a number of idiosyncratic properties of negation in Japanese. Remarkably, owing to the fact that the negative *nai* can be a lexical adjective, as well as a grammatical negator, Japanese has a fairly large inventory of complex negative adjective expressions that contain negative *nai* but lacks affirmative forms.

Research on Japanese negation has a long tradition, but still, there is much to be learned. Much more work needs to be done to find out precisely how the intricate system of negation works in Japanese. With a view to furthering our understanding on Japanese negation, it will be particularly fruitful to make cross-linguistic comparisons, which would allow us to uncover both universal and language-specific aspects of Japanese negation.

15

Tense and Aspect

Wesley M. Jacobsen

1 Introduction

A basic function of predicates in natural language is to position events and situations in time, and they do so in two main ways. One is by ordering them in time with respect to the time of other events, such as the time at which the predicate is uttered by the speaker, a category of meaning known as tense. In (1), for example, the event of the waitress setting coffee in front of me is ordered earlier than the time at which this sentence is being spoken, an ordering commonly called "past" tense.

(1) *Wētoresu ga watashi no mae ni kōhī o oi-ta.*
waitress NOM I GEN front LOC coffee ACC put-PST
'The waitress set the coffee in front of me.'

Predicates also interact with other elements in the sentence to define various kinds of structure that events or situations take as they unfold in time, such as whether they occur at a single point in time or at multiple points in time, or whether they are accompanied by some kind of change or occur continuously through time with no change, all of which fall under a category of temporal meaning known as aspect.[1] The event in (1), for example, defines an aspectual structure consisting of a series of activities of the waitress culminating in an endpoint at which a change occurs in the location of the coffee from not being in front of me to being in front of me.

Tense and aspect interact very closely, and it is not always apparent where the boundary between them lies, leading some native Japanese grammarians to question whether Japanese even has forms that express tense. This chapter will present an overview of the range of temporal meanings of both these kinds in Japanese, with a focus on understanding in what ways they are similar or distinct, and in what ways the expression

[1] In certain European traditions, this goes by the name Aktionsart.

of such meanings in Japanese shares universal characteristics seen across all languages and in what ways it exhibits unique characteristics.

2 Japanese and the Traditional Western Categories of Tense

In Western linguistic frameworks, tense has traditionally been understood in terms of a three-way distinction of past, present, and future, a distinction that many Western languages, including English, mark formally on the predicate. As seen in (2), however, Japanese does not make such a three-way distinction on the predicate itself.

(2) a. *Sengetsu made koko ni kōban ga at-ta.*
last.month until here LOC police.box NOM exist-PST
'There was a police box here until last month.'

b. *Asoko ni kōban ga ar-u.*
over.there LOC police.box NOM exist-NPST
'There is a police box over there.'

c. *Kono kōban wa ato 10 nenkan koko ni ar-u (darō).*
this police.box TOP more 10.years here LOC exist-NPST probably
'This police box will (probably) be here another 10 years.'

Unlike the three distinct forms seen in the English predicates *was/is/will be* in (2), Japanese makes only a two-way distinction, represented here in the *-u* and *-ta* endings of the predicate *ar-u* 'exist,' which we will in this chapter call the -RU and -TA forms of the verb.[2] As this example shows, the -TA form corresponds to the past tense form, whereas the -RU form combines both present and future meaning in a single "non-past" tense form. This two-way distinction in form is seen in all three predicate classes in Japanese, including adjectives (marked by the endings *-i* versus *-katta*) and the copula (*da* versus *datta*).

(3) a. *ōki-i* 'is large' vs. *ōki-katta* 'was large'
b. *shizuka-da* 'is quiet' vs. *shizuka-datta* 'was quiet'

How then does Japanese cover three tenses using only two tense forms? In (2), the -RU form of the verb *ar-u* 'exist' receives by default a literal present reading, and in order to receive a future reading requires the help of special forms such as temporal adverbs (e.g. *ato 10 nenkan* '10 more years') and sentence-final modals (e.g. *darō* 'probably'). But the verb *ar-u* is actually unusual in this respect. With most verbs, the opposite is true, as they receive by default a *future* reading in the -RU form and require special marking with adverbs and other forms to receive a present-like reading, as can be seen in the examples in (4).

[2] Depending on the form of the verb stem, *-u* alternates with *-ru* and *-ta* alternates with *-da*. The terms "-RU form" and "-TA form" subsume both alternating forms respectively.

(4) a. *Kinō* *eiga* *o* *mi-ta.*
yesterday movie ACC watch-PST
'Yesterday I watched a movie.'

b. *Eiga* *o* *mi-ru.*
movie ACC watch-NPST
'I'm going to watch a movie.'

c. *Mainichi* *eiga* *o* *mi-ru.*
every.day movie ACC watch-NPST
'I watch a movie every day.'

The behavior of the verb *mi-ru* 'watch' in (4) is typical of verbs indicating that something happens, called "eventive" predicates, as opposed to predicates that indicate unchanging situations, such as *ar-u* 'exist,' called "stative" predicates. Eventive predicates encompass a wide range of event types, including ones brought about by human control (e.g. *taberu* 'eat,' *yomu* 'read,' *aruku* 'walk') and ones occurring apart from human control (e.g. *shinu* 'die,' *tsuku* 'arrive,' *kumoru* 'become cloudy'), comprising well over 90% of the native Japanese verb corpus. The distinction between stative and eventive meaning is an aspectual one, associated with two very different ways in which situations unfold in time, as will be discussed in detail in Section 3.

Examples (2) and (4) provide our first major example of how tense and aspect interact: the default tense reading of the single form -RU depends on the aspectual character of the predicate, future in the case of eventive predicates, and literal present in the case of stative predicates, as summarized in Table 15.1.

To express tense in the non-default cases left blank in Table 15.1 requires some kind of special marking, such as the use of temporal adverbs for stative predicates to receive a future reading, as in (2c) or for eventive predicates to receive a present-like reading, as in (4c). The kind of present reading seen in (4c) is, however, somewhat unusual: it expresses a habitual present that does not necessarily mean that the event holds exactly at the time of speech. To express a "true present" meaning requires another form, the *-te-i(ru)* form, one of whose functions is to indicate that the event is literally in progress at the time of speech.

Table 15.1 *Default tense readings of -RU and -TA*

	Stative predicates	Eventive predicates
Past	-TA (e.g. *at-ta* 'was')	-TA (e.g. *mi-ta* 'watched')
Present	-RU (e.g. *ar-u* 'is')	—
Future	—	-RU (e.g. *mi-ru* 'will watch')

Table 15.2 *Full range of three tense readings with -RU and -TA*

	Stative predicates	Eventive predicates
Past	-TA (e.g. *at-ta* 'was')	-TA (e.g. *mi-ta* 'watched')
Present	-RU (e.g. *ar-u* 'is')	Adverb + -RU for habitual (e.g. *mainichi mi-ru* 'watch every day') OR -te-iRU for present progressive (e.g. *mite-i-ru* 'is watching')
Future	Adverb + -RU (e.g. *ato 10 nenkan ar-u* 'will be for 10 more years')	-RU (e.g. *mi-ru* 'will watch')

(5) *Ken wa (ima) eiga o mite-i-ru.*
TOP now movie ACC watch-PROG-NPST
'Ken is (now) watching a movie.'

With the aid of extra devices such as this, the full range of three tense readings becomes possible with both stative and eventive predicates, as summarized in Table 15.2.

The way *-te-i(ru)* is positioned in Table 15.2 might suggest that it is a third tense form alongside -RU and -TA. But this would not explain how the *-te -i(ru)* form itself is a -RU form with a contrasting -TA form *-te-i(ta)* illustrated in (6).

(6) *Ken wa yūbe uchi de eiga o mite-i-ta.*
TOP last.night home LOC movie ACC watch-PROG-PST
'Ken was watching a movie at home last night.'

The contrast between (5) and (6) is in fact just a special case of the contrast between literal present and past that -RU and -TA receive with stative predicates as seen earlier in (2). *-Te-i(ru)* does not therefore contribute any tense meaning beyond that already present in the -RU form, but rather contributes meaning of an aspectual kind, presenting a situation as unchanging in very much the same way that stative predicates do. The presence or absence of *-te-i-* introduces in this way a two-way aspectual distinction that cross-cuts the tense distinction between -RU and -TA, resulting in the four distinct predicate forms summarized in Table 15.3.

The literal present reading that *-te-i(ru)* receives in its -RU form is thus no more than a property it shares with stative predicates in general.

2.1 What Is It That Is Ordered by Tense?

As noted above, tense has traditionally been understood to order the situation expressed in a sentence with respect to the time that the sentence is spoken, or speech time. A past tense sentence such as (7a) encodes, for example, the order represented in (7b), where < means "occurs earlier than."

Table 15.3 *Cross-cutting tense and aspect patterns with -RU, -TA, and -te-i(ru)*

	Aspectual distinction	
Tense distinction	-RU (e.g. *Eiga o mi-ru* 'will watch a movie') -TA (e.g. *Eiga o mi-ta* 'watched a movie')	-te-i-RU (e.g. *Eiga o mite-i-ru* 'is watching a movie') -te-i-TA (e.g. *Eiga o mite-i-ta* 'was watching a movie')

(7) a. *2011 nen ni Tōhoku chihō de daishinsai ga oki-ta.*
2011.year TMP area LOC major.earthquake NOM occur-PST
'In 2011 a major earthquake occurred in the Tohoku area.'
b. time of earthquake < time of speech

Future tense, conversely, orders the time of speech earlier than the event expressed (time of speech < time of event), and present tense situates the time of speech and time of the event at the same time, or at least in an overlapping relationship with each other.

As pointed out by Klein (1994), however, this definition of tense encounters difficulty in explaining the past tense meaning of examples such as (8).

(8) *Hon no hyōshi wa aka dat-ta.* (adapted from Klein 1994)
book GEN cover TOP red COP-PST
'The cover of the book was red.'

Example (8) is not saying that the time of the book's being red occurs earlier than the time of speech, as this sentence could be true even if, as is likely, the book's cover is still red at the time of speech. Rather, the situation of the book being red is tied to a *particular* point in time that is under discussion in the previous context – for instance, at a point when I entered the room and saw the book lying on the coffee table. The particular point in time under discussion is what Klein (1994) calls "topic time," a renaming of what was called "time of reference" in an earlier classic study of tense by Reichenbach (1947), the term we will adopt in this chapter. In (8), what the so-called past tense orders as earlier than the time of speech is not the time of the situation itself, but rather this time of reference, although the time of reference is included within the overall time of the situation expressed – the book's cover being red.

This points to the need for not two but three basic elements in describing tense in natural language: the time of speech (S), the time of reference (R), and the time of the event or situation expressed by the predicate (E). In his system, Reichenbach distinguishes between "simple" tenses where R and E are identical or overlap and "complex" tenses where R and E are distinct from one another. An example of each of the three simple tenses present, past, and future is given in (9), with the ordering relationship between S, R, and E as indicated – = means "occurs at the same time as," ⊃ means "includes the time of," and ⊂ means "is included in the time of."

(9) a. *Aki wa ima uchi ni i-ru.* E ⊃ R ⊃ S
TOP now home LOC be-NPST
'Aki is at home now.'

b. *Aki wa 10 ji ni uchi o de-ta.* E = R < S
TOP 10:00 TMP home ACC leave-PST
'Aki left home at 10:00.'

c. *Aki wa 10 ji ni uchi o de-ru.* S < R = E
TOP 10:00 TMP home ACC leave-NPST
'Aki will leave home at 10:00.'

The time of reference in each of (9) is specified by temporal adverbs such as *ima* 'now' and *10 ji ni* 'at 10:00' and in each case coincides with the time at which the event occurs – the event is, as it were, being viewed from the point in time of the event itself.

But events are not always viewed from the point in time that they occur. There are cases where the event is viewed from another point in time separate from the event itself, that is, where R and E are not the same. These are what Reichenbach calls "complex" tenses and include the so-called English present perfect, past perfect, and future perfect, examples of which are given in (10) with their Japanese counterparts.

(10) a. *Aki wa (mō) uchi o dete-i-ru.* E < R ⊃ S
TOP already home ACC leave-RES-NPST
'Aki has (already) left home.'

b. *(Watashi ga denwa-shi-ta toki) Aki wa (mō) uchi o*
I NOM phone-do-PST time TOP already home ACC
dete-i-ta. E < R < S
leave-RES-PST
'At the time that I called, Aki had already left home.'

c. *(Watashi ga tsuku koro ni wa) Aki wa (mō) uchi*
I NOM arrive-NPST time TMP CTR TOP already home
o dete-i-ru (darō). E < R and S < R
ACC leave-RES-NPST probably
'At (by) the time I arrive, Aki will probably have left home.'

In each of these examples, the event of Aki leaving home is seen from the standpoint of a later point in time under discussion, so that E < R. In (10a), for example, the time referred to is the present moment of speech and the earlier event of Aki's leaving is viewed from that time of reference, as opposed to the simple past example in (9b). The time of reference R is here again specified by temporal adverbs or temporal adverbial clauses such as those headed by *toki* 'time' and *koro* '(about the) time.'

There are also sentences where the event is viewed from an earlier time than the event itself, that is, where R < E. Examples are the so-called prospective tenses seen in (11).

(11) a. *Aki wa uchi o de-yō.to-shite-i-ru.* S ⊂ R < E
TOP home ACC leave-VOL-do-PROG-NPST
'Aki is about to leave home.'

b. *(Sono toki) Aki wa uchi o de-yō.to-shite-i-ta.* R < S and R < E
that time TOP home ACC leave-VOL-do-PROG-PST
'(At that time) Aki was about to leave home.'

c. *(Sono koro ni wa) Aki wa uchi o de-yō.to-shite-iru*
that time TMP CTR TOP home ACC leave-VOL-do-PROG-NPST
(darō). S < R < E
probably
'At (by) that time, Aki will probably be about to leave home.'

In the case of complex tenses, the ordering relationship between E and S is not always specified. In both (10c) and (11b), for example, we cannot tell from the meaning of the sentence whether Aki's leaving home has, at the time of speech, actually occurred (E < S) or is yet to occur (S < E), even though the relationship between E and R and between S and R is clear in both cases.

We have so far assumed without question, following Reichenbach, that the various orderings of S, E, and R are matters of tense and are expressed using similar mechanisms of tense. But the Japanese examples show that there is a significant difference in the way that the ordering of E and R is expressed as compared to the ordering of S and R. As seen in (9), when R and E overlap (i.e. either E = R or E ⊃ R), the -RU and -TA forms are sufficient to express the order between S, R, and E. When E and R are distinct and do not overlap, however, as in (10) and (11), complex morphological forms such as *-te-i(ru)* and *-(y)ō.to-su(ru)* are required to distinguish those cases where R is ordered before E (R < E) from those where E is ordered before R (E < R).

These forms, however, do more than just order R and E with respect to each other. They also bind R and E together into a larger temporal structure of which the two are seen as subparts, and are in that sense *aspectual* forms. The *-(y)ō.to-su(ru)* form, for example, binds a future event (in the case of (11), Aki's leaving home) into a larger process that originates at the time of reference and is seen to lead inevitably toward that event. Whether that process is seen as a naturally occurring one or one that results from human intention is reflected in the two meanings "about to happen" and "try to do" that are encompassed in this form. The *-te-i(ru)* form, similarly, functions in (10) to bind an earlier event (here again, Aki's leaving home) to a later time of reference where a state resulting from the earlier event (here, Aki's being away from home) is seen to hold.

As a consequence, in both of these cases the event in question cannot be segregated neatly from an overarching event that encompasses the time of reference, sometimes making it difficult to determine how much of a time span is actually covered by E. The relationship between E and R thus involves temporal structure as well as temporal ordering, intertwining elements of both tense and aspect and calling into question Reichenbach's treatment of this relationship as straightforwardly a matter of tense. In his framework, Klein (1994) in fact departs from Reichenbach in treating ordering relationships between E and R as aspectual in nature, as opposed to ordering relationships between S and R, which he treats as belonging to the domain of tense.

It might appear that -RU and -TA on their own express purely tense relationships, since in all examples considered so far where -RU and -TA appear alone without aspectual forms attached (e.g. (9)) E and R are either identical or overlapping, and -RU and -TA seem to be concerned solely with differences in the ordering of R and S ($S < R$ or $S \subset R$ in the case of -RU and $R < S$ in the case of -TA). But even -RU and -TA exhibit uses that at times cross over the boundary into aspectual meaning. In the uses of -TA in (12), for example, E is distinct from and ordered earlier than R ($E < R$), even without the aid of extra aspectual forms.

(12) a. *Onaka* *ga* *sui-ta.* $E < R \supset S$
stomach NOM become.empty-PST
'I'm hungry.' Lit. 'My stomach has become empty.'

b. *Tadaima* *6-ji* *ni* *nari-mashi-ta.*
just.now 6:00 DAT become-POL-PST
'It is now 6:00.' Lit. 'It has just now become 6:00.'

c. *Aki* *wa* *mō* *uchi* *o* *de-ta.*
TOP already home ACC leave-PST
'Aki has already left home.'

The -TA form in these cases expresses a situation holding at the time of speech, here overlapping with the time of reference, integrating a prior event into a larger structure that encompasses the time of speech in a way different from the simple past use of -TA seen earlier in (9b). Evidence for this can be seen in temporal adverbs such as *tadaima* 'just now' in (12b) and *mō* 'already' in (12c) that bind the time of reference R to the time of speech. *Mō*, in particular, does this by imposing on the meaning of the predicate a separation between R and an earlier E, causing R in (12c) to overlap with S rather than E.[3]

Similar examples where R is disengaged from E can be seen with the -RU form as well, as in (13b), where the adverb *ima* 'now' binds R to S with the -RU form *kaer-u* 'return home,' as opposed to (13a), where *ashita* 'tomorrow' binds R to E in a standard future reading.

[3] See Jacobsen (2007) for a fuller treatment of the aspectual functions of the adverbs *mada* 'still' and *mō* 'already.'

(13) a. *Ashita uchi e kaer-u.* $S < R \supset E$
tomorrow home GOAL return-NPST
'I will return home tomorrow.'

b. *Ima uchi e kaer-u (tokoro da).* $S \subset R < E$
now home GOAL return-NPST point COP-NPST
'I'm returning home (about to return home) now.'

While ordering relationships among all three temporal primitives S, E, and R play a role in temporal meaning in Japanese, then, the relationship between E and R is unique in involving not only an ordering relationship but also a structural framework that encompasses the two, especially when E and R are disengaged from one another, combining elements of both aspectual and tense meaning. The relationship between S and R, by contrast, involves a more distinct ordering relationship, not entailing an overarching temporal structure binding the two together, and belongs therefore more centrally to the domain of tense, as argued by Klein. Although -RU and -TA exhibit both tense-like uses where E and R overlap and aspect-like uses where E and R are distinct, the latter are clearly peripheral, both in terms of frequency and in terms of their reliance on special marking in the form of adverbs or aspectual morphological forms. Japanese -RU and -TA may therefore be considered to have the primary function of marking relationships of tense.

2.2 -RU and -TA in Subordinate Clauses

The examples of -RU and -TA considered so far have all been in main clause contexts, but when these appear in subordinate clauses, they appear to exhibit a different kind of behavior from that in main clauses (Kuno 1973; Soga 1983; Ogihara 1999). In the subordinate *toki* 'when' clauses in (14), for example, -TA in (14a) marks an event that has yet to occur in the future and, conversely, -RU in (14b) marks an event that has already occurred in the past.

(14) a. *Tanaka-kun ni at-TA toki ni kono shorui o*
DAT meet-PST time TMP this document ACC
watashite-kudasai.
hand.over-please
'When you meet Tanaka (after meeting Tanaka), please give him these documents.'

b. *Kono sūtsukēsu wa konomae Rondon ni ik-U toki ni kat-ta.*
this suitcase TOP last.time London GOAL go-NPST time TMP buy-PST
'I bought this suitcase the last time I went to London (before going to London).'

Although this behavior of -RU and -TA has been used by some linguists in the native Japanese grammatical tradition to argue that -RU and -TA are not tense forms (see Teramura (1984) for a discussion), -RU and -TA in subordinate contexts in fact express relationships of temporal order no less than they do in main clause contexts. The difference is one of how the relationships of ordering are anchored. In main clause contexts, it is the time of speech that acts as the anchor for such ordering, whereas in subordinate contexts this function is taken over by the reference time R of the main clause itself, which in examples such as (14) is identical to the event time E of the main clause. -TA in (14a), therefore, orders the event of meeting Tanaka as past *relative* to the future time of handing Tanaka the documents, and -RU in (14b) orders the event of going to London as future *relative* to the past event of buying the suitcase. This is merely another kind of tense, a "relative tense" as opposed to the "absolute tense" anchored in the time of speech in main clause contexts.

The examples in (14) involve eventive predicates, but stative predicates, interestingly, tend to allow either an absolute tense or a relative tense perspective when they occur in subordinate *toki* 'when' clauses.

(15) *Nihon ni i-RU/ i-TA toki ni Fujisan ni nobot-ta.*
Japan LOC be-NPST be-PST time TMP Mt.Fuji GOAL climb-PST
'I climbed Mt. Fuji when I was in Japan.'

Either -RU or -TA is possible with the subordinate stative verb *i-ru* 'be' in (15), with no change in meaning, the former exemplifying relative present tense (the situation of being in Japan overlaps with the event of climbing Mt. Fuji) and the latter absolute past tense (the situation of being in Japan is ordered earlier than the time of speech).

While the meaning of the temporal conjunction *toki* 'when' is neutral to whether the subordinate event is ordered prior to or later than the main event, and thus allows either -RU or -TA on the subordinate verb, other temporal conjunctions have meanings that fix the relative order of the subordinate clause event and the main clause event. Examples are the temporal conjunctions *mae* 'before,' which orders the subordinate event later than the main event, *ato* 'after,' which orders the subordinate event prior to the main event, and *aida* 'while,' which puts the subordinate event in an overlapping relationship with the main event. Regardless of the absolute tense of the main predicate, therefore, *mae* is always preceded by a subordinate -RU form, *ato* by a subordinate -TA form, and *aida* by a subordinate -RU form with stative verbs and *-te-i(RU)* form with eventive verbs, exhibiting respectively a relative future, relative past, and relative present ordering relationship.

(16) a. *Nihon ni ku-RU mae ni nihongo o benkyō-shi-ta.*
Japan GOAL come-NPST before TMP Japanese ACC study-PST
'I studied Japanese before I came to Japan.'

b. *Yūgohan o tabe-TA ato de ofuro ni hair-ō.*
supper ACC eat-PST after TMP bath GOAL enter-VOL
'Let's take a bath after we eat supper.'

c. *Kodomo ga nete-i-RU aida ni ie no sōji o*
children NOM sleep-PROG-NPST while TMP house GEN cleaning ACC

shite-oi-ta.
do-put-PST
'I cleaned up the house while the children were sleeping.'

We saw in Section 2.1 that -TA in main clause contexts exhibits two possible orderings between E and R, either the normal simple past tense ordering where E = R (e.g. (9b)) or an aspectual-like ordering where E < R (e.g. (12)). A similar difference can be seen in subordinate uses of -TA as well, illustrated in (17).

(17) a. *Konna-ni nure-TA kōto de tenisu o suru no?*
this.much get.wet-PST court LOC tennis ACC do-NPST NMLZ
'We're going to play tennis on courts this wet (in a state of having become this wet)?'

b. *Kinō no ame de nure-TA kōto wa kesa wa*
yesterday GEN rain CAUS get.wet-PST court TOP this.morning CTR

kanzen-ni kawaite-i-ta.
completely get.dry-RES-PST
'The courts that got wet in yesterday's rain were completely dry this morning.'

The situation referred to by subordinate *nure-TA* 'get.wet-PST' in (17a) is that of the courts *being* wet, which is later than the event of the courts *getting* wet, and is one that overlaps in time with the time of reference of the main clause event of playing tennis. In (17b), by contrast, the situation referred to by subordinate *nure-TA* is that of the event itself of the courts *getting* wet in yesterday's rain, an event that is past relative to the time of reference of the main clause, namely *kesa* 'this morning' (see Kinsui 1994 for a fuller analysis of the behavior of -TA in subordinate contexts). Such examples provide evidence of a time of reference in the subordinate clause that is distinct from the time of the reference in the main clause, one that sometimes overlaps with the time of the subordinate event and at other times is distinct from the time of the subordinate event, overlapping instead with the time of reference of the main clause.

We have seen in this section that considerations of temporal order (tense) cannot be neatly divorced from considerations of temporal structure (aspect). The two are nevertheless independently defined concepts and it is not possible to fully reduce one kind of meaning to the other. In the next section we shift our focus to the temporal structure itself, the domain of aspect, in order to consider what kinds of temporal structure characterize the aspectual system of Japanese, and how unique or similar Japanese is with respect to other languages in how it expresses such temporal structure.

3 Aspect: Situation Aspect

Aspectual meaning – the temporal structure that situations take as they unfold in time – is sometimes expressed through grammatical forms such as *-te-i(ru)* and *-(y)ō.to-su(ru)* seen in Section 2, but is at other times inherent to the meaning of a predicate and not identifiable with any given grammatical form. Aspectual meaning of the first type, that expressed in grammatical forms, is what Smith (1997) calls "viewpoint aspect," as these forms function to impose a particular temporal viewpoint on the events expressed by the predicates to which they are attached. Aspect of the second type, lexical aspect, corresponds to what Smith calls "situation aspect." An example of situation aspect is the basic distinction existing between states and events, seen in Section 2 and illustrated in (18).

(18) a. *Tēburu no ue ni hon ga ar-u.*
table GEN top LOC book NOM exist-NPST
'There is a book on the table.'
b. *Akiko wa hoteru ni tomar-u.*
TOP hotel LOC stop.over-NPST
'Akiko will stay in a hotel.'

There is nothing about the *form* of the verbs *ar-u* and *tomar-u* that tells us that the first expresses a state and the second an event, but the distinction shows up in numerous ways in which the two behave differently. Their tense behavior is one example: states received a literal present meaning in the non-past -RU form, as in (18a), whereas events receive a future interpretation in that form, as in (18b). Another is in the way they interact with grammatical aspectual forms. Stative predicates, for example, do not co-occur with *-te-i(ru)*, but eventive predicates do, as seen in (19).

(19) *Akiko wa hoteru ni tomatte-i-ru.*
TOP hotel LOC stop.over-RES-NPST
'Akiko is staying in a hotel.'

The *-te-i(ru)* form is similar in this respect to the *-ing* form in English, which also cannot be used with stative verbs such as *is* in (18a), but can be used with eventive verbs like *stay*, as in the English gloss to (19).

Grammatical aspect forms such as *-ing* and *-te-i(ru)* turn out to be a useful diagnostic tool for categorizing predicates into various lexical aspectual categories, and play a central role in what are probably historically the two most influential studies of aspect in Japanese and English – Kindaichi (1950b) and Vendler (1957). These two studies, conducted independently from one another, point to a group of four aspectual categories that are in essential respects common to both languages. Following for convenience the terms used by Vendler,[4] the four categories are given in (20) with examples of predicates falling under each category and their behavior with *-te-i(ru)* and *-ing*.

(20) a. States: Do not accept *-te-i(ru)*; do not accept *-ing* (see (18a))
ar-u 'be, exist,' *i-ru* 'be, exist (of animate beings),' *deki-ru* 'be able to'

b. Activities: Take a *progressive* reading with *-te-i(ru)*; accept *-ing*
hashir-u 'run,' *oyog-u* 'swim,' *tabe-ru* 'eat,' *mi-ru* 'watch,' *hatarak-u* 'work'

Kakoi no naka de uma ga hashitte-i-ru.
corral GEN inside LOC horse NOM run-PROG-NPST
'Horses are running (around) in the corral.'

c. Achievements: Take a resulting state reading with *-te-i(ru)*; take a future (prospective) reading with *-ing*
tsuk-u 'arrive,' *shin-u* 'die,' *kekkon su-ru* 'get married,' *(mado ga) ak-u* '(window) opens,' *(denki ga) tsuk-u* '(lights) go on'

Denki ga tsuite-i-ru.
lights NOM go.on-RES-NPST
'The lights are on.' Lit. 'The lights are in a state of having gone on.'
Cf. *The lights are going on.* (future prospective)

d. Accomplishments: Take *either* a progressive or resulting state reading with *-te-i(ru)*; accept *-ing*
(shōsetsu o) kak-u 'write (a novel),' *(fuku o) ki-ru* 'put on/wear (clothes),' *(ie o) tate-ru* 'build (a house),' *(mado o) ake-ru* 'open (a window)'

Hanako wa kimono o kite-i-ru.
TOP kimono ACC put.on-PROG/RES-NPST
'Hanako is putting on/is wearing (Lit. has put on) a kimono.'

Activities, achievements, and accomplishments are all subcategories of eventive predicates and as such receive a default future reading in their bare -RU form, in contrast to the literal present reading that form receives with stative predicates. In addition to differences in their behavior with *-te -i(ru)* and *-ing*, the four categories exhibit differences in the range of temporal adverbs they allow. Adverbs expressing an interval of time such as *10 nenkan* 'for 10 years' are accepted by activities and states, but not by achievements and accomplishments. Adverbs expressing moments of time such as *sono shunkan ni* 'at that instant' are accepted by states and

[4] Vendler's states, activities, and achievements correspond respectively to Kindaichi's stative verbs, continuative verbs, and instantaneous verbs. Accomplishments are not given a category of their own in Kindaichi's framework, but their existence was noted by Kindaichi as predicates that sometimes exhibit the behavior of continuative verbs and sometimes of instantaneous verbs in their ability to take either a progressive or resulting state reading with *-te-i(ru)* (see the example of *(fuku o) ki-ru* 'put on/wear (clothes)' in 20D). Kindaichi also set up a fourth category he called simply "type 4 verbs," which cannot be used without *-te-i(ru)* attached in sentence-final position (e.g. *Gengonōryoku ga sugurete-i-ru* '(His/Her) linguistic ability is outstanding'). For our purposes, these may be seen as a special case of stative verbs where a verb has become lexicalized in the *-te-i(ru)* form, but will not be discussed further in this chapter.

achievements, but not activities or accomplishments. Adverbs expressing culmination within an interval such as *3 jikan de* 'in 3 hours' are accepted by achievements and accomplishments, but not states and activities.

These and numerous other tests that have been proposed for English, Japanese, and a wide range of other languages (see Dowty 1979) provide robust confirmation that these four categories are universally shared across all human languages and point to certain structural features uniquely distinguishing each category from the others, as schematized in (21).[5]

(21) States: ———————————— (e.g. *ar-u* 'exist')
Activities: ~~~~~~~~~~~~~~~~~ (e.g. *hashir-u*, 'run')
Achievements: ————(X)– – – – – – (e.g. *shin-u* 'die')
Accomplishments: ~~~~~~~(X)– – – – – – (e.g. *shōsetsu o kak-u* 'write a novel')

States are, first of all, perfectly homogeneous in their meaning, in a way that can be represented as a continuous line. They occur over intervals in such a way that, for any interval over which a state is seen to hold, the same state is seen to hold over any subinterval, no matter how small, down to an instant in time. Stative verbs can therefore be used either with adverbs indicating intervals of time or instants of time.

(22) *Sono hon wa {2 ji kara 5 ji made no aida/ 3 ji ni} tēburu*
that book TOP {2:00 from 5:00 until GEN interval/ 3:00 TMP} table

no ue ni at-ta.
GEN top LOC exist-PST
'That book was on the table from 2:00 to 5:00/at 3:00.'

Since speech time is no more than a special case of an instant of time, this characteristic of stative verbs accounts for why it is possible for them to receive a literal present reading in their -RU form, as noted in Section 2.

Activities are also homogeneous, but not perfectly so. They are made up of atomic subcycles (Dowty 1979; Bohnemeyer and Swift 2004), represented in (21) by tildes (~), which, when repeated over and over and viewed as an aggregate, as if through a wide-angle camera lens, converge to give the impression of a continuous line. In the activity of running, for example, one atomic subcycle consists of a foot coming off the ground, into the air, and onto the ground again, alternating with the other foot in such a way that both feet are never on the ground at the same time. An activity that occurs over an interval is thus seen to occur over smaller subintervals of that interval, but not, as in the case of states, down to a single point. As the camera lens zooms in on intervals that become successively smaller, a limit is reached at the point the intervals approach the size of

[5] The schematization used here is modeled after that used in Shirai (2000).

a subcycle, which is no longer itself internally homogeneous. Activities therefore may co-occur with temporal adverbs indicating intervals of sufficiently large size, but not ones expressing instants of time. To occur with instants requires the use of *-te-i(ru)*, which imposes a more perfectly homogeneous character on the activity predicate, as in (23b).

(23) a. *Yūji wa {8 ji kara 9 ji made/ 8 ji 15 fun kara 8ji han made/*
TOP {8:00 from 9:00 until/ 8:15 from 8:30 until/
**8 ji 20 pun ni} hashit-ta.*
8:20 TMP} run-PST
'Yuji ran from 8:00 to 9:00/from 8:15 until 8:30/*at 8:20.'

b. *Yūji wa 8 ji 20 pun ni hashitte-i-ta.*
TOP 8:20 TMP run-PROG-PST
'Yuji was running at 8:20.'

Achievements and accomplishments are, by contrast, inherently non-homogeneous, having at the center of their temporal structure a boundary, represented by (X) in (21), that marks a change between an earlier state of affairs and a later, different, state of affairs. In the case of achievements, the transition is one between the presence and absence of a particular state specified in the meaning of the verb, such as between the state of being alive and not being alive in the case of *shin-u* 'die.' With accomplishments, the boundary is one between an activity that leads up to a culminating point (the (X) in (21)), at which point the activity ceases, and a new state comes into existence. In the case of *shōsetsu o kak-u* 'write a novel,' for example, the activity of writing is bounded by an endpoint that marks both the termination of the activity of writing and the coming into existence of the novel as a finished product. Accomplishments are in that sense a composite category, made up of an activity component with an achievement structure superimposed upon it.

The (X) that forms the boundary with achievements and accomplishments is typically an instant without extension in time, as with predicates like *tsuk-u* 'arrive' and *shin-u* 'die,' but may sometimes consist of an interval that has some extension in time, as with predicates like *futor-u* 'become fat' and *tsukare-ru* 'become tired,' where the transition from one state to its opposite does not occur instantaneously. While achievements in their bare form typically highlight the change (X) itself, allowing the states that precede and follow to be defocused, accomplishments do not so easily allow their activity component to be defocused. This can be seen in the fact that adverbs indicating instants may occur with achievements, but not accomplishments, although both allow adverbs that indicate culmination over an interval, as seen in (24).

(24) a. *Densha wa {sono shunkan ni/ 2 jikan de} Kyōto ni tsui-ta.*
train TOP {that instant TMP 2.hours in} GOAL arrive-PST
'The train arrived in Kyoto at that instant/in two hours.'

b. *Sono* *sakka* *wa* {**sono* *shunkan* *ni*/ *3 kagetsu* *de*} *sono*
that author TOP {that instant TMP 3.months in} that
shōsetsu *o* *kai-ta.*
novel ACC write-PST
'That author wrote the novel *at that instant/in three months.'

Still, the composite character of accomplishments is reflected in the fact that two different readings are possible when *-te-i(ru)* is attached, either a progressive reading, a feature typical of activities, or a resulting state reading, a feature typical of achievements.

Although the inherent meaning of the predicate is central to the structural distinctions we have seen among the four Kindaichi/Vendler classes in (20), important contributions to such meaning may also come from elements within a clause other than the predicate alone. The meaning of accomplishments, for example, does not arise solely from the verb, but typically from a verb in construction with a direct object. In the case of *shōsetsu o kak-u* 'write a novel' the activity expressed by *kak-u* 'write' has no inherent endpoint contributing the (X) required for the accomplishment structure in (20d), but such an endpoint is imposed on the activity by the direct object *shōsetsu* 'novel' so that the writing can continue only up to the point that the novel comes into being and then ceases – the direct object "delimits" the activity of writing in the sense of Tenny (1994).

Temporal adverbs are another source of contributions to aspectual meaning from outside of the predicate. *Ochir-u* 'fall' is an achievement verb, and as such takes a resulting state reading with *-te-i(ru)* in default contexts such as (25a). But when the meaning of multiple occurrence is introduced by temporal adverbs, either by iteration of an event with the same subject, as in (25b), or with multiple subjects, as in (25c), the reading of *-te-i(ru)* shifts in the direction of the progressive meaning normally seen with activity verbs.

(25) a. *Jimen* *ni* *saifu* *ga* *ochite-i-ru.*
ground GOAL wallet NOM fall-RES-NPST
'There's a wallet lying (Lit. in the state of having fallen) on the ground.'

b. *Ano* *ko* *wa* *nandomo* *isu* *kara* *ochite-i-ru.*
that child TOP time.and.again chair from fall-PROG-NPST
'That child has been falling time and again from his/her chair.'

c. *Happa* *ga* *tsugitsugi to* *ochite-i-r-u.*
leaf NOM one.after.another fall-PROG-NPST
'Leaves are falling one after another.'

In structural terms, these adverbs have the effect of converting the (X) central to achievement structure in (20c) into multiple (X)'s that aggregate together in a way similar to the subcycles (~) in (20b), thereby conferring on the aspectual structure as a whole an activity-like quality.

There is another class of predicates that behave in certain respects like achievements and in other respects like activities but which do not appear in the Kindaichi/Vendler categories and do not fit neatly into any of the structures in (21). These predicates, called "semelfactive," allow a progressive reading with *-te-i(ru)*, but express events that do not have the extension in time of activities and instead express short, sometimes instantaneous, "atomic" events.[6]

(20′) e. Semelfactives: Take a *progressive* reading with *-te-i(ru)*; accept *-ing* *tatak-u* 'knock,' *hiramek-u* 'flash,' *mabataki su-ru* 'blink,' *kushami o su-ru* 'sneeze,' *seki o su-ru* 'cough'

Dareka	*ga*	*doa*	*o*	*tataite-i-ru.*
someone	NOM	door	ACC	knock-PROG-NPST

'Someone is knocking on the door.'

Semelfactives are like achievements in being short in duration and self-contained, but, unlike achievements, do not form a boundary between two different states – there is no difference in the state of affairs following a semelfactive event from what precedes it. In other respects, the aspectual shape of semelfactives and achievements are the same, as schematized in (21′), where (X) represents an atomic event that may approach an instant in extent.

(21′) Achievements: ——(X)━━━━ (e.g. *shin-u* 'die')
Semelfactives: ——(X)———— (e.g. *tatak-u* 'knock')

Because semelfactives involve no change in state, they do not receive the resulting state reading with *-te-i(ru)* that achievements do, but rather a progressive reading (see (20′e)) like activities or iterated achievements, where (X) is seen to occur multiple times.

The five categories of situation aspect – states, activities, achievements, accomplishments, and semelfactives – are foundational categories of lexical aspectual meaning in both English and Japanese, and are likely universal to all human languages. But while the categories themselves may be universal, lexically similar counterpart predicates do not necessarily fall under the same categories. One example of this is the class of motion predicates, including *ik-u* 'go,' *ku-ru* 'come,' and *kaer-u* 'return (home),' of which the English counterparts are activities, as seen in the freedom with which *-ing* may be attached, but the Japanese counterparts are achievements, as seen in the fact that they receive a resulting state, not progressive, reading with *-te-i(ru)*.

(26) a.

Tanaka	*wa*	*Tōkyō*	*ni*	*itte-i-ru.*	(< *ik-u*)
	TOP		GOAL	go-RES-NPST	

'Tanaka is in (Lit. has gone to) Tokyo.'

[6] The term "semelfactive" is due to Comrie (1976), but the existence of predicates like these was noted by Okuda (1978) in his criticism of Kindaichi's use of the feature "instantaneous" to characterize predicates that take a resulting state reading with *-te-i(ru)*.

b. *Sobo* *wa* *fuyuyasumi* *no* *aida* *uchi* *ni*
grandmother TOP winter.holiday GEN while home GOAL

kite-i-ru. (< *ku-ru*)
come-RES-NPST
'My grandmother is at (Lit. has come to) our home for the winter holidays.'

The focus of meaning of such motion predicates in Japanese is actually the point of arrival forming a boundary between being and not being in a certain place, as opposed to the activity leading up to the arrival. What is expressed as a progressive activity with the *-ing* form of such motion predicates in English is thus expressed as a simple future with the bare -RU form of the predicate in Japanese.

(27) *Doko* *e* *ik-U* *no?*
where GOAL go-NPST NMLZ
'Where are you going?' Lit. 'Where will you go?'

Another example of this kind of categorial mismatch is seen in verbs such as *know* and *have*, which are stative, but whose Japanese counterparts *shir-u* and *mots-u* are an achievement and accomplishment verb, respectively, expressing a *change* in state and meaning 'come to know' and 'grasp, take possession of,' as illustrated in (28).

(28) *Sakki* *terebi* *no* *nyūsu* *de* *sono* *jiken* *o*
just.now TV GEN news CAUS that incident ACC
shit-ta. (< *shir-u*)
come.to.know-PST
'I just learned (Lit. came to know) about that incident on the TV news.'

To express the stative sense of the English counterparts to these verbs requires that they be converted into states through the attachment of *-te-i(ru)*, yielding the resulting state meaning characteristic of achievements.

(29) *Tanaka* *sensei* *o* *shitte-i-mas-u* *ka.* (< *shir-u*)
professor ACC come.to.know-RES-POL-NPST Q
'Do you know (Lit. are you in a state of having come to know) Professor Tanaka?'

The usefulness of the *-te-i(ru)* form as a diagnostic for determining the lexical aspectual category of a predicate has been amply demonstrated in this section. But what is the basic function of *-te-i(ru)* itself and how does it combine such apparently distinct meanings as progressive and resulting state? *-Te-i(ru)* is an example of a grammatical form whose function is to impose a particular aspectual meaning, or "viewpoint," on the situational aspect structure already present in a predicate, and thus belongs to another kind of aspect called "viewpoint aspect."

4 Viewpoint Aspect: *-Te-i(ru)*

Viewpoint aspect – aspectual meaning that is associated with a particular grammatical form – interacts in specific ways with the inherent aspectual meaning of a predicate, and for that reason may be limited in its occurrence to predicates expressing certain types of situation aspect. *-Te-i(ru)*, in particular, interacts in one way with activity predicates and in another way with achievement predicates to produce what appear to be two different meanings, progressive with activities and resulting state with achievements.

(30) a. *Kodomo wa pūru de oyoide-i-ru.* (< *oyog-u*, progressive)
children TOP pool LOC swim-PROG-NPST
'The children are swimming in the pool.'

b. *Mado ga aite-i-ru.* (< *ak-u*, resulting state)
window NOM open$_{in}$-RES-NPST[7]
'The window is open.' Lit. 'The window is in a state of having become open.'

As (30) shows, regardless of which of these two meanings it takes, *-te-i(ru)* consistently exhibits a literal present reading in the -RU form, in contrast to the future reading that activities or achievements would receive in their bare form without *-te-i(ru)*.

(31) a. *Kodomo wa pūru de oyog-u.*
children TOP pool LOC swim-NPST
'The children will swim in the pool.'

b. *Mado ga ak-u.*
window NOM open$_{in}$-NPST
'The window will open.'

As noted in Section 2, *-te-i(ru)* exhibits in this sense the character of a stative predicate and shares with states a basic homogeneous character, regardless of which of these two readings it receives. In (30), for example, *oyoide-i-ru* 'be swimming' and *aite-i-ru* 'be open' are each seen to hold over an interval of time surrounding the time of reference (here, the same as the time of speech), and these situations are also seen to hold at any subinterval of that interval, no matter how finely divided, even to an instant. The function of *-te-i(ru)* is thus to impose on the time of reference the viewpoint of being included within an aspectually homogeneous interval.

But the particular way in which this interval is positioned with respect to the event expressed by the predicate differs in the case of activities versus achievements. Since activities are structurally homogeneous to begin with (even if not perfectly so), the interval imposed by *-te-i(ru)* can subsume the activity within itself, as schematized in (32), where the

[7] "Open$_{in}$" indicates that the verb is intransitive.

interval imposed by *-te-i(ru)* is indicated by the square brackets [] and the time of reference by R, resulting in a progressive reading that views the activity as ongoing throughout the interval.

(32) R
|
~~~~~[~~~~~~]~~~~~ (e.g. *Kodomo wa oyoide-i-ru* 'The children are swimming')

But with achievements, the existence of the (X) boundary that divides two states (e.g. being not open and open with *mado ga aku* 'window opens') creates an obstacle to imposing this interval: any interval containing this (X) will include subintervals in which different situations hold and will therefore not be homogeneous. The only possibility for placement of the interval imposed by *-te-i(ru)* is therefore either prior to (X) or after (X), but in no case including the (X) itself. The first of these possibilities is excluded because the *-te* in *-te-i(ru)* requires the event expressed by the preceding predicate to be "realized" (Soga 1983; McClure 1995), a historical relic of an older "perfective" meaning in this form, so that the only possibility is for the interval in question to be placed after the (X), yielding the resulting state meaning schematized in (33).

(33) R
|
—(X)—[——]—— (e.g. *Mado ga aite-i-ru* 'The window is open')

Accomplishments, by contrast, having an aspectual structure composed both of an activity and an achievement component, provide two possible sites for the placement of the interval presented by *-te-i(ru)*, resulting in either a progressive reading if the interval is positioned within the activity preceding (X) or a resulting state meaning if it is positioned within the state that follows (X), as schematized in (34) for the accomplishment *mado o akeru* 'open the window.'

(34) a. R
|
~~[~~~~]~~(X)—— (e.g. *Mado o akete-i-ru* '(S/he) is opening the window')

b. R
|
~~~(X)—[——]—— (e.g. *Mado o akete-i-ru* '(S/he) has opened his/her window; (s/he) has his/her window open')

Note that even for the progressive reading, the onset of the activity precedes the time of reference, fulfilling the requirement that *-te-i(ru)* express a realized state of affairs. The two apparently different readings that *-te -i(ru)* receives are therefore the result of a singular viewpoint meaning in this form – imposing a homogeneous aspectual structure over an interval surrounding the time of reference – interacting with different types of situation aspect inherent to the predicate to which it attaches (see Jacobsen 2016 for a fuller discussion).

Other uses of *-te-i(ru)* than the progressive and resulting state can for the most part be seen as variants of one or the other of these two basic meanings. Variants on the use of *-te-i(ru)* as a marker of resulting state are illustrated in (35). The standard use in (35a) carries the implication that the subject is at the time of reference in a state resulting from the event expressed by the predicate (here the state of being on the mountain resulting from *noboru* 'climb, ascend'), an implication that is not present in the so-called "experiential" use in (35b) or the "historical record" use in (35c).

(35) a. *Ken wa ima Fujisan ni nobotte-i-ru.*
TOP now Mt.Fuji GOAL climb-RES-NPST
'Ken is now atop Mt. Fuji (having climbed it).'

b. *Ken wa nido Fujisan ni nobotte-i-ru.*
TOP two.times Mt.Fuji GOAL climb-RES-NPST
'Ken has climbed Mt. Fuji twice.'

c. *Tabei Junko wa 1975 nen ni josei to shite hajimete*
TOP 1975 TMP woman as for.first.time

Eberesutosan ni nobotte-i-ru.
Mt.Everest GOAL climb-RES-NPST
'Junko Tabei ascended Mt. Everest in 1975 for the first time as a woman.'

The use in (35c) is remarkable for allowing a temporal adverb that specifies the time of the past event itself, an apparent example of two times of reference – one tied to the event, one to the time of speech – being incorporated into a single clause.

As for progressive meaning, a variant on the standard progressive use of *-te-i(ru)* in (36a) is the present progressive use in (36b), where a time adverb specifying the onset of the interval defined by *-te-i(ru)* is present.

(36) a. *Kyō wa yuki ga futte-i-ru.*
today TOP snow NOM fall-PROG-NPST
'Today it is snowing (Lit. snow is falling).'

b. *Asa kara yuki ga futte-i-ru.*
morning from snow NOM fall-PROG-NPST
'It has been snowing since morning.'

Other variants of the progressive include the various iterative uses of *-te -i(ru)* seen earlier in (25b, c). All variants on the progressive use have in common that the interval imposed by *-te-i(ru)* contains *within* it some portion of the activity or iterated event expressed by the predicate, as opposed to variants on the resulting state use, which are all characterized by the presence of the point or interval (X) defining achievement aspect positioned *outside* of and *prior* to the interval imposed by *-te-i(ru)*.

4.1 Viewpoint Aspect: Other Grammatical Forms

Unlike situation aspect, where the basic categories of meaning are universally shared by Japanese, English, and, so far as current research shows, all human languages, viewpoint aspect exhibits a high degree of language-specific idiosyncrasy, both in terms of the kinds and combinations of meanings that are expressed in aspectual forms and in terms of the morphological and syntactic patterns that are deployed to express those meanings. Limitations of space prevent a detailed treatment of the full scope of viewpoint aspectual forms in Japanese, so a few representative examples must suffice for our purposes in this chapter.

The most common formal device for expressing viewpoint aspect in Japanese is by means of one of two verb-linking patterns, either the gerund pattern V1-*te* V2 or the verb compound pattern V1-*i/e* V2, where V1 is the main verb and V2 a verb expressing aspectual meaning. The *-te-i(ru)* form is one example of the gerund pattern, and we have seen in Section 3 how it combines the two meanings of progressive and resulting state as special cases of imposing the viewpoint of an aspectually homogeneous interval on the inherent aspectual meaning of the main verb. Another gerund pattern that expresses resulting state is *-te-ar(u)*, differing from *-te-i(ru)* in that the state is one purposely brought about by intentional action, typically expressed by a transitive verb with an object that is promoted to subject position. In the case of verbs falling into intransitive/transitive pairs, the same state can therefore be expressed either in the form of V_{in}-*te-i(ru)* or V_{tr}-*te-ar(u)*, the former neutral as to how the state arose, the latter carrying the implication that the state was brought about for some intentional purpose, as in (37).

(37) a. *Mado ga aite-i-ru.*
window NOM $open_{in}$-RES-NPST
'The window is open.'

b. *Mado ga akete-ar-u.*
window NOM $open_{tr}$-RES-NPST
'The window is open (having been intentionally opened for a purpose).'

Interacting closely with the *-te-ar(u)* pattern is a third gerund pattern *-te-ok(u)* that presents an intentional action as one performed in preparation for some later purpose. Parallel to (37b), for example, is the construction with *-te-ok(u)* in (37c) that presents the situation expressed in (37b) from the standpoint of the action that brings about that situation as a result.

(37) c. *Mado* *o* *akete-oi-ta.* (< *akete-ok-u*)
window ACC open$_{tr}$-put-PST
'(I) opened the window (as preparation to some later purpose).'

In terms of the framework adopted in Section 2.1, (37c) and (37b) differ in whether the time of reference (R) overlaps with the time of the event (E) of opening the window, that is, E = R < S, as in (37c), or is separate from the time of the event and overlaps instead with the time of speech (S), that is, E < R ⊃ S, as in (37b).

Verbs appearing in the V2 position of these verb-linking patterns have independent meanings that are clearly related to the aspectual character expressed by these patterns. The stative character of *-te-i(ru)* and *-te-ar(u)*, for example, is related to the lexical character of the independent stative verbs *i-ru* 'be, exist (of animate beings)' and *ar-u* 'be, exist (of inanimate things),' and the preparatory character of *-te-ok(u)* bears a close affinity to the lexical meaning of the independent verb *ok-u* 'put, leave.' But certain elements of the independent lexical meaning, or constraints on that meaning, are typically removed, or "bleached," when these verbs are coopted as aspectual markers, as seen in the fact that *-te-i(ru)* and *-te-ar(u)* are not restricted to subjects that are animate or inanimate as are the corresponding independent verbs, or in the fact that *-te-ok(u)* is not limited to preparatory actions that involve physical positioning as does the independent verb *ok-u*, but is possible with a wider range of non-physical actions, such as *yonde-ok(u)* 'read (in advance).'

The idiosyncratic nature of viewpoint aspect can furthermore be seen in shifts away from the lexical meaning of the corresponding predicate in directions that are not purely aspectual. For example, the gerund pattern *-te-shimaw(u)*, derived from the independent verb *shimaw(u)* 'put (something) away,' functions to mark the aspectual meaning of completion of an event in its entirety, up through the concluding stage, but is also used to mark events that are beyond one's control or undesirable, as illustrated in (38).

(38) a. *Ashita* *no* *bun* *made* *shigoto* *o* *yatte-shimat-ta.* (< *shimaw-ta*)
tomorrow GEN part up.to work ACC do-put.away-PST
'I've completely done my work, even for tomorrow.'

b. *Kare* *no* *henna* *hyōjō* *ni* *omowazu* *waratte-shimat-ta.*
he GEN strange expression DAT unintentionally laugh-put.away-PST
'I couldn't help laughing at the strange expression on his face.'

c. *Shigoto* *ni* *kakas-e-nai* *pasokon* *ga* *kowarete-shimat-ta.*
work PURP do.without-POT-NEG computer NOM break$_{in}$-put.away-PST
'The computer that I cannot do without for my work has broken down.'

Idiosyncratic as such collocations of meaning may appear to be, they are nevertheless driven by a logic of their own. In the case of *-te-shimaw(u)*, the finality with which an event is completed leads to an implication that the event cannot be undone even if one willed it so, which in turn is a short step away from viewing the event as beyond the control of, and therefore contrary to the interests of, the speaker or someone the speaker identifies with.

A second verb-linking pattern commonly used in expressing viewpoint aspect is the compound pattern V1-*i*/*e* V2, V1 here occurring in the form of the infinitive verb stem. This pattern typically functions to present distinct stages of an event, as seen in (39), where *hajime-ru* 'begin$_{tr}$,' *tsuzuke-ru* 'continue$_{tr}$,' and *owar-u* 'end, finish' appear as V2 expressing the initial, medial, and final stages, respectively, of the event expressed in V1.

(39) *Densha no hassha beru ga nari {hajime-ta/tsuzuke-ta/owat-ta}.*
train GEN departure bell NOM ring- {begin-PST/continue-PST/finish-PST}
'The bell signaling departure of the train {began/continued/finished} ringing.'

Other compound-type aspectual patterns imposing a stage viewpoint in this way include V-*das-u* 'burst out V-ing,' V-*kake-ru* 'begin doing V (with implication of discontinuance),' and V-*age-ru* 'do V completely,' where a high degree of semantic bleaching can again be seen by comparison with the corresponding independent verbs *das-u* 'put out,' *kake-ru* 'put in contact with,' and *age-ru* 'raise.'

Verb linking of the gerund and compound type is, however, only the most frequent but not the exclusive means for imposing viewpoint aspect in Japanese, which exploits linguistic devices of a wide and varied range. These include lexical means such as adverbs (e.g. *mada* 'still,' which presents a situation as unchanged from before, and *mō* 'already,' which presents a situation as preceded by a change in state, represented by (X) in (21)), morphological patterns other than verb linking such as V*(y)ō.to.su-ru* 'try to V, be about to V' seen in Section 2, and syntactic patterns such as V-*ta koto ga ar-u* 'have the experience of (doing) V' and V-*ru koto ga ar-u* 'sometimes V.'

5 Conclusion

We have seen through the lens of Japanese how temporal meaning in language is concerned both with the positioning of events and situations in time with respect to other events and situations (the category of tense) and with the structure that events or situations describe as they unfold in time (the category of aspect), and how these two kinds of temporal meaning are closely interrelated. The description of tense requires reference to three primary elements – the time of speech (S), the time of the event expressed (E), and a time of reference (R), but ordering relationships among these, particularly between E and R, often have a structural component to them, so that tense shades into aspect. Temporal structure, conversely, as it unfolds along a one-dimensional timeline will contain within it constituent elements that are necessarily ordered in time, so that aspect shades into tense.

Relationships of order are particularly salient in the temporal structure defining achievement and accomplishment verbs, as the change in state (X) that centrally defines their structure inherently imposes a relationship of before and after between two states of affairs. Given such an interrelationship, it is not surprising that many temporal forms in Japanese exhibit both tense-like and aspect-like uses, such as *-te-i(ru)* which, while imposing an aspectually homogeneous interval on the meaning of predicate, also functions to order E prior to R with achievement verbs, or the -TA form, which exhibits both tense-like uses where R and E are ordered prior to S and aspect-like uses where R is disengaged from E and overlaps with S. Nevertheless, it is possible to distinguish among such forms those whose default function is to impose relationships of order, such as -RU and -TA, from those whose default function is to impose temporal structure, such as *-te-i(ru)*, and on that basis to identify the existence of both tense forms and aspect forms in Japanese. The fact that -RU and -TA exhibit uses in subordinate contexts where the ordering relationships are anchored in points in time other than the time of speech does not call for an aspectual treatment of these forms, as they function to impose relationships of order equally in such contexts as they do in main clause contexts.

Finally, aspectual meaning itself can be distinguished into two types: one that is inherent to the lexical meaning of predicates (situation aspect) and another that is associated with grammatical forms that impose a particular aspectual character on other predicates (viewpoint aspect). The structural categories that comprise situation aspect include two that are internally homogeneous in meaning (states and activities), two that include heterogeneous elements in their meaning (achievements and semelfactives), and one that is a composite category (accomplishments, which contains both an activity and an achievement component), and these five categories exhibit a remarkable uniformity not only between Japanese and English but also universally across all languages. Grammatical forms that express viewpoint aspect in Japanese, by contrast, exhibit a high degree of language-specific idiosyncrasy, in terms of both the kinds and combinations of meaning they express and the variety of lexical, morphological, and syntactic devices deployed to express such meaning.

16

Modality

Heiko Narrog

1 Modality and Related Categories in Japanese

This chapter provides a descriptive outline of modality in Modern Japanese, also suggesting areas for further study. The three main issues discussed are (i) definitions and subcategories of modality in Japanese (Sections 1 and 2), (ii) structural properties and interaction with other categories, especially negation and tense (Section 3), and (iii) history (Section 4).

1.1 Issues of Definition[1]

As a category label, *modality* has been a litter bin for all sorts of speaker-related grammatical categories and lexical expressions in Japanese linguistics. In the scope of this term, we find categories as widely different as topic and focus marking (e.g. particles *wa* and *mo*), tense (e.g. past tense *-ta*), politeness (e.g. *desu*/*-masu*), sentence moods (e.g. imperative and declarative), illocutionary marking (e.g. particles *yo* and *ne*), evaluative adverbs (e.g. *yappari* 'as expected'), and what I will call "modality proper," namely, expressions of possibility and necessity (e.g. *hazu*, *-(a)na-kereba naranai*).

There is one obvious culprit for the bloating of the category, namely definitions of modality in terms of *subjectivity*. Subjectivity itself is a rather ambiguous concept. In this context it is usually understood in terms of either speaker-deixis (relation to the *here* and *now* of the speaker) or

My research was supported by grant numbers 24520450 and 16H03411 from the Japanese Society for the Promotion of Science. I am grateful to the editor, the peer reviewer, and the copy-editor for helping me improve my chapter. All remaining errors are my own.

[1] For detailed discussions of the issue of the definition of modality, I would like to refer the reader to Narrog (2012: ch. 2.1) (English) and Narrog (2014) (Japanese).

speakers' attitudes and opinions. Speaker-deixis is a concept that can be fairly well delimited. Nevertheless, it is apparently not suitable to identify the intended forms and meanings, since tense, for example, is clearly speaker-deictic, as is spatial deixis, but nevertheless few scholars would like to say that tense is modality (although some actually do!). Instead, most scholars will want to treat tense as a category in its own right. On the other hand, the scope of the expression of "speakers' attitudes and opinions" can indeed hardly be delimited, and thus inevitably leads to the "litter bin" of categories cited above.

A much better way to define modality is in terms of factuality (or reality). Such a definition may look as in (1):

(1) Modality is a linguistic category referring to the factual status of a proposition. A proposition is modalized if it is marked for being undetermined with respect to its factual status, that is, it is neither positively nor negatively factual. (Narrog 2012: 6)

The denotation of this definition overlaps with that of traditional definitions of modality in logic as the expression of possibility and necessity (cf., for example, Wright 1951: 1). It has one disadvantage, though, namely, that there are many expressions of modality in natural language where it is difficult to decide whether they express possibility or necessity (e.g. the particle *darō* 'may, will' in Japanese).

Examples (2) and (3) indicate the scope of modality according to different definitions.

(2) *Kono mise wa yappari sugo.i ne.*
this shop TOP as.I.expected terrific.NPST SFP
'This shop IS terrific, isn't it?'

(3) *Ore wa mata shippai shita ka mo shire-na.i*
I TOP again failure did INT FOC know-NEG.NPST
'I may have failed again.'

According to the understanding of modality as the expression of subjectivity, each morpheme in sentence (2), except *mise* 'shop,' should be classified as modal. The adnominal demonstrative *kono*, the tense-ending of the adjective are speaker-deictic; topicalizing *wa* is an expression of the discourse-organization by the speaker (cf. Chapter 13, this volume); *yappari* and *sugoi* express the speaker's evaluation; and *ne* expresses that the speaker believes that the evaluation is shared with (or should be shared by) the hearer. In contrast, based on a view of modality in terms of factuality, sentence (2) is not modalized at all. Grammatically speaking, it simply states a fact, even if it is a fact presented from the speaker's perspective. But that is a property emanating from the basic speech setting in natural language that practically all sentences in natural discourse share.

In contrast, (3) does contain an expression of modality in terms of factuality, namely the periphrastic *ka mo shirenai*. Without *ka mo shirenai*, (3) would simply state a fact, "I have failed again." With it, the sentence expresses a state-of-affairs whose factuality is uncertain. The rest of this chapter will be based on this definition of modality in terms of factuality.

1.2 Short History of the Study of Modality in Japan

The very broad understanding of modality in traditional Japanese linguistics introduced in the previous section has its roots in the quirky history of a basically unrelated concept, namely that of "predication" (*chinjutsu*). Predication is a function of predicates that is needed for words to combine and form clauses. Adopting the term from European linguistics, specifically Heyse (1849), Yamada (1908: 156–159, 260–263) established it as a key concept in Japanese traditional grammar. However, starting with the influential writings of Tokieda (1941), who advocated a subjectivist stance to both the study of language and the study of subjective elements in language, this term took on an entirely different meaning. Tokieda tried to mechanically identify the subjective elements in sentences, and simultaneously claimed that they were decisive for the formation of sentences. *Chinjutsu* thus became almost synonymous with subjective elements of language. The term underwent some modifications, but a major break came in the late 1970s with a new influx of foreign students and the resulting need for Japanese language education for them, and with a heightened influence of Western, especially English linguistics. The term *chinjutsu* 'predication,' which was meanwhile far removed from its original meaning, was seamlessly replaced by the English word *modality*, a term that was notoriously opaque in itself.

Tellingly, the first use of the term *modality* in Japanese grammar that I am aware of, by Uyeno (1971), was for sentence-final particles (cf. Chapter 25, this volume), that is, typical *chinjutsu* elements, which also happened to be difficult to label with the categories then available in Western linguistics. A flood of publications from the late 1980s on – especially influential were Masuoka (1991) and Nitta (1991) – made *modality* a common staple of Japanese linguistic studies. This is in a nutshell how modality became a cover term for all kind of subjective elements in Japanese linguistics (see Kudo 1988, Narrog 2009b, and Onoe 2014a, 2014b for details of this history).

While the above understanding of modality is shared by the large majority of Japanese linguists, there have been groups of scholars with a different view. Most notably, the Gengogaku 'linguistic research' group of scholars promoted Russian linguistics, linking the category with the concept of both reality and sentenced moods (e.g. Okuda 1986). Scholars following Onoe (2001) combine a revival of Yamada's linguistics with modern cognitive linguistics, espousing the concept of reality as key for the definition. Since their definition of modality practically coincides with the one espoused in this chapter, the scope of their research is also largely identical with "modality proper."

1.3 Modality Proper

"Modality proper" refers to grammatical (i.e. grammaticalized) expressions that conform to the definition in (1). Adding these expressions to a clause will render an otherwise factual clause as undetermined with respect to its factual status. Epistemic expressions of possibility or necessity such as *ka mo shirenai* 'may/might' in (3) have this effect as their very meaning. In contrast, with non-epistemic expressions of possibilities or necessities, non-factuality is a side effect of a different intended meaning, such as a wish or an obligation. A constructed example is shown in (4).

(4) *Fusei* *wa* *yame.ru* *beki* *da.*
fraud TOP stop.NPST DEO COP
'Fraud must be stopped.'

The suffix *beki* usually expresses a necessity based on moral evaluation. The primary meaning is to express the moral evaluation and the obligation for future action that emerges from the moral obligation in the speaker's point of view. However, as an inevitable aspect of that meaning, the state-of-affairs, "stop the fraud" is non-factual.

Note that the fact that *beki* is a grammatical expression, that is, grammaticalized, is plainly visible from its status as a suffix, but there are other expressions where the degree of grammaticalization may be less clear. In any case, *ka mo shirenai* or *beki* are typical expressions of modality proper and since they will be the topic of the rest of the chapter from Section 2, I will not discuss them any further here.

1.4 Evidentiality

Evidentiality is a grammatical category defined as expressing source of information (cf. Aikhenvald 2004: 3). It has been established only fairly recently in Western linguistics. In contrast, in Japanese linguistics, the category's apparent exponents have been traditionally described and discussed in the same context as expressions of modality proper, namely as so-called *jodōshi* 'auxiliaries' with labels such as *suiryō* 'inference' or *denbun* 'hearsay.' Examples (5) and (6) list grammaticalized morphemes in Modern Japanese that fulfill the requirements for the definition of evidentiality in indicating a source of information.

(5) *yō* inferential
mitai inferential
-sō inferential

(6) *rashii* inferential and reportive
sō reportive

Other morphemes that have been notably associated with evidentiality in Japanese are quotatives (e.g. *-tte*) and the de-subjectivizing morpheme *-garu* (cf. Aoki 1986: 223–225), which we do not consider as evidential. Evidential meaning is also variously attributed to the topic marker *wa* or the stativizing aspect *-te iru*, but this does not concern us here. Important are those expressions that are clearly evidential. Among them, we find at least four inferential evidentials (*yō, mitai, -sō, rashii* in (5) and (6)) that out of contexts can loosely be translated as 'look(s) like.' Thus, the question arises as to what the semantic differences among them are. This question is not so relevant at this point though.[2]

What really matters here is the question whether these evidentials are part of the category of modality. The answer according to the definition in (1) is "yes": Japanese evidentials render a proposition non-factual in the same way that expressions of epistemic modality, for example, do, even if this is only a side effect of providing a source of information. This is shown in the constructed example (7).

(7) *Ano hito wa i-na.i [yō da/rashi.i].*
DEM person TOP be-NEG.NPST EVID COP/EVID.NPST
'That person is apparently not here.'

The factuality of "not being here" is relativized to the source of information (visual impression) and thus left undetermined. The same can be said of the other evidentials listed in (5) and (6) as well. Note, though, that Japanese evidentials all belong to a specific type of evidentials, so-called *indirect evidentials*. Cross-linguistically, there are also direct evidentials, which state sources for facts, for example, denoting something like "I have seen that. . .." They would not fall under the category of modality as defined here.

1.5 Mood

Mood is a very ambiguous term in Western linguistics. One common use is a label for a morphological category, namely verb inflections that typically, but not always, are the expression of, or have the same effect as, modality proper, that is, rendering propositions as non-factual (the term *irrealis* for the same thing is also widespread). This is the use that I wish to adopt in this chapter as well.

[2] A detailed attempt at an answer can be found in Narrog (2009a: ch. 10).

Japanese verbs have only a limited number of inflections. The ones listed in (8) render the proposition as non-factual in the majority of contexts and are, therefore, considered as the mood inflections of Modern Japanese.

(8) *-(y)ō* hortative
-e/-ro imperative

One could also make a case to add *-(r)u* as "declarative" here (e.g. Takahashi et al. 2005: 60, who also label *-ta* as declarative), but in my view this is a "Latin grammar" approach. The suffix *-(r)u* is used in so many contexts, most of them neutral with respect to mood (or to the factuality of the proposition), that it seems exaggerated to attribute a mood meaning to this morpheme. Also note that in certain contexts the past marker *-ta* has a counterfactual function that is mood-like, as in (9).

(9) *Sono toki damar.eba yo-kat.ta.*
DEM time be silent.COND good.VBZ-PST
'I should have kept my mouth shut then.'

The counterfactual reading is typically triggered by a past conditional setting with *-(r)eba*, as in this example, but it is also possible to obtain counterfactual readings if the conditional clause is not expressed and merely implied.

Besides this use of the past tense, one could argue that conditional forms such as *-(r)eba* and *-tara* themselves express a "conditional mood." Conversely, *-(y)ō*, which is often identified as a mood inflection, has some idiomatic uses in subordinate clauses that have no clear modal meaning.

1.6 Clausal Mood

The terms *clausal mood* or *sentence mood* or simply *mood* are occasionally used as an equivalent to the more common term in English linguistics, *clause type*. In Japanese, one can distinguish the following clausal moods (or clause types):

(10) Declaratives
Interrogatives
Directives

Declaratives as such are not modal in nature, since they are not intrinsically non-factual. But they are the clausal mood that contain the widest range of expressions of modality proper (cf. Section 3). They can also contain counterfactual predications. In contrast, directives are intrinsically modal, since they always render the proposition as non-factual. Subtypes of directives include imperatives, prohibitives, and hortatives. Finally, interrogatives are in between. Some of them, namely *yes-/no-*questions (e.g. *Did you steal my cheese?*) render the proposition as non-factual, while others, especially wh-questions, do not (in *Who stole my cheese?*, the factuality of someone having stolen cheese is presupposed).

Besides approaches to Japanese modality that categorically include clausal mood in modality (e.g. Masuoka 1991; Nitta 1991), Japanese also has a number of specific interrogative constructions, for example, "doubts" expressed by *no de wa nai ka* 'isn't it that?,' that have often been treated under the label of *modality* (see Narrog 2009a: ch. 11 for details on Japanese clausal moods).

1.7 Illocutionary Modulation

The term *illocutionary modulation* refers to grammatical marking that modifies illocutionary force, or contributes to relating an utterance to discourse. Japanese sentence-final particles or German so-called modal particles typically have such a function. The contrast between (11) and (12) illustrates this function in Modern Japanese.

(11) *Dōkyūsei ni Saitō-san te i.ta.*
classmate DAT QUOT be.PST
'We had a classmate called Saitō.'

(12) *Dōkyūsei ni Saitō-san te i.ta yo ne.*
classmate DAT QUOT be.PST SFP SFP
'We had a classmate called Saitō, didn't we?'

While the sentence in (11) is a mere statement, the sequence of final particles in (12), *yo ne*, adds a request for confirmation in order to keep the hearer engaged and ensure that speaker and hearer share the same information. It does not fully convert the utterance into an interrogative and does not affect the factuality of the statement, but it adds an element of speaker–hearer interaction. From the perspective of modality in terms of factuality (or reality) taken here, illocutionary modulation has the least to do with modality among all the categories discussed in this chapter. Sentence-final particles are discussed separately in Chapter 25. However, in traditional subjectivity- or speaker-stance-based concepts of modality (*chinjutsu*), Japanese sentence-final particles are typically treated as a core modal category.

2 Subcategories of Modality Proper in Japanese

Subcategorizations or classifications of modality are legion, even if modality is defined more strictly by factuality. Here we adopt a subcategorization that seems to suit the actual expression of modality in Modern Japanese. According to this classification, we have three major non-volitive types of modality, namely epistemic (based on knowledge), evidential (based on indirect evidence), so-called "dynamic" or participant-internal (based on the properties or functions of a participant in an event), and one major volitive one, namely deontic (based on rules and values), which is usually combined with teleological modality (modality based on goals). These subtypes are briefly discussed in turn in the following subsections.

2.1 Epistemic Modality

An epistemic modal expression predicates a possibility or necessity based on someone's world knowledge, typically the speaker's. Example (13) is a list of the representative grammaticalized expressions of epistemic modality in Japanese, ordered by "strength" of modality, that is, from necessity to possibility. After the expression itself, a semantic label and a possible translation are provided (actual translations will vary in context).

(13)	*hazu*	strong expectation	'should'
	ni chigai nai	high certainty	'there is no mistake that'
	darō	speculative	'will'
	ka mo shirenai	possibility	'may'

Like many languages, Japanese also has adverbs that express epistemic possibility such as *tabun* 'probably' or *moshi ka shite* 'perhaps.' The degree of likelihood they express and their correspondence to the grammaticalized markers and constructions in the verbal complex that are listed above has been the subject of some research (e.g. Kudo 2000; Sugimura 2000).

2.2 Deontic Modality

Deontic modality expresses a necessity or possibility in view of social rules or values. It is often used as a cover term for related notions that are expressed by the same morphemes and constructions, especially teleological modality, that is, necessity or possibility with respect to someone's goals. Example (14) is a list of representative expressions of deontic modality in Japanese.

(14)	*-nakereba naranai*	general obligation	'must'
	-(r)eba ii	advice	'you'd better do'
	-te wa naranai	prohibition	'must not'
	-te mo ii	permission	'may'
	hō ga ii	preference	'it's better to do'
	-zaru o enai	inevitability	'cannot help but'
	shika nai	singular choice	'there is only'

Compared with other types of modality, the expression of deontic modality is doubtless the most variegated. The list is not even complete (cf. Narrog 2009a: 167 for a more exhaustive listing). Furthermore, all expressions are periphrastic, that is, go across word boundaries, except *beki*, which is a clitic. Such expressions as *nakereba naranai* and *-te wa naranai* are conditional constructions ending on a negative evaluation, *naranai* 'Lit. does not become,' which has variants such as *ikenai* 'Lit. cannot go' and *dame* 'bad.'

2.3 Boulomaic Modality

Boulomaic modality expresses a necessity or possibility with respect to someone's volition or intentions. The four most common markers and constructions of boulomaic modality in Modern Japanese are listed in (15):

(15)	*-tai*	intention (1)	'want to do'
	tsumori	intention (2)	'want to, intend to'
	-te hoshii	desire (1)	'want someone to do something'
	-te moraitai	desire (2)	'want to get something done by someone'

A salient fact about boulomaic modal constructions is that they are typically bound to a certain person as subject. The two intention markers and constructions are basically bound to first person subjects in statements and second person subjects in questions. The desire constructions also typically express a speaker's wish; however, the "target of modality," that is, the person to implement the action, is a second or third person. There are various means to neutralize these person constraints, such as the de-subjectifying suffix *-garu* (cf. Makino and Tsutsui 1986: 443; Iori et al. 2000: 140–141).

2.4 Dynamic Modality

Like deontic modality, *dynamic modality* is also strictly speaking a cover term for a number of subtypes of modality, especially speaker-internal ability and possibility based on circumstances or the situation. Note that this kind of modality expresses only possibilities and not necessities. The main exponents are listed in (16).

(16)	*koto ga dekiru*	circumstantial possibility	'be possible, can'
	-(r)areru	potential	'can'
	-eru	logical possibility	'be possible'
	-kaneru	impossibility	'be impossible'

Note that traditional Japanese linguistics will not include these morphemes and constructions in the study of modality, because they allegedly lack subjectivity, which is definitional for the Japanese concept of *chinjutsu* or modality (see Sections 1.1–1.2). However, they render the factuality of a proposition as undetermined, and are therefore clearly modal as defined in this chapter. Furthermore, the claim that these markers and constructions lack subjectivity is highly questionable as well if they are analyzed in actual discourse (cf. Narrog and Horie 2005: 106–109).

2.5 Indirect Evidentials

The relationship between modality and evidentiality in Japanese was already discussed in Section 1.4. Only indirect evidentials fall under my definition of modality but all Japanese evidentials are indirect, so they can be treated as modal. Example (17) repeats the list of morphemes already provided in Section 1.4:

(17)	*-sō*	predictive appearance	'looks like'
	yō	present/past-oriented appearance	'looks like'
	rashii	distant appearance, reportive	'seem'
	sō	reportive	'it is said that, allegedly'
	mitai	(stylistic variant of *yō*)	

3 Structural Properties and Interaction with Other Categories

3.1 Morphological Properties

In terms of their morphological properties, the modal markers of Modern Japanese can be classified into suffixes and periphrastic constructions. Suffixes in turn can be divided into particles, that is, clitic-like suffixes that follow fully inflected and morphologically independent word forms, and derivational suffixes, that is, suffixes that follow word stems. First, (18) is a list of particles expressing modality proper.

(18)	Particles with adjectival inflection	*beki, rashii*
	Nominal adjectival particle	*mitai*
	Uninflecting particles	*sō* [reportive], *darō*

Example (19) is a list of derivational suffixes, that is, those that add to word stems.

(19)	Suffix with adjectival inflection	*-tai*
	Suffix with nominal adjectival inflection	*-sō* [inferential]
	Suffixes with verbal inflection	*-(r)areru, -(r)e-, -kaneru*

Most expressions of modality in Modern Japanese are periphrastic. They can be subdivided into expressions that center on one-word or multi-word expressions. The one-word expressions, which, of course, also occur in constructions with their linguistic context, are nominals. These nominals are also known as "formal nouns" (*keishiki meishi*) in traditional Japanese linguistics. Example (20) gives a list of grammaticalized modal nominals.

(20) *mono* 'thing,' that is, '[it] is the common thing to do,' *koto* 'thing/matter,' that is, 'it is the thing to do' [both deontic], *hazu* 'expectation' [epistemic], *yō* 'appearance' [evidential], *tsumori* 'intention' [boulomaic]

The multi-word periphrastic constructions are too large and numerous to list here. Especially famous, since Akatsuka (1992), are the conditional constructions ending on a negative evaluation (cf. Section 2.2 above). A list of the most important ones can be found in Narrog (2009a: 73).

If we deal with periphrastic constructions rather than suffixes, the question may be raised as to whether they are actually grammaticalized. Here, one can refer to an excellent study by Hanazono (1999) that through syntactic tests demonstrates grammaticalization of some representative periphrastic modals of Modern Japanese.

3.2 Modality and Clausal Mood (Clause Type)

All expressions of modality proper are compatible with declaratives. Examples (3), (4), and (7) above are all declarative sentences.

Non-epistemic modalities are, as a rule, also compatible with interrogatives. With the epistemics and evidentials, the matter is more complicated. With the exception of the narrow scope inferential *-sō* (cf. Sections 3.5–3.6 below), epistemic and evidential modal markers should be infelicitous in questions.[3] After all, epistemics and evidentials basically represent judgments based on the direct or indirect knowledge of the speaker. How, then, can a speaker question her/his own judgment? However, as the examples with the reportive *sō* in (21) and the inferential evidential *yō* in (22) show, if appropriate contexts are given, practically all epistemic and evidential markers can also be used in questions.

(21)

Ōshima Yūko	*mo*	*intai-s.uru*	*sō*	*des.u*	*ka?*
	FOC	retire-do.NPST	EVID	COP.NPST	INT

'Is it being said that Yuko Oshima also retires?'
(www.ztcizpnqixeh.exwweragi.xyz/)

(22)

Ikeda	*tōshu*	*wa*	*tukare.te*	*i.ru*	*yō*	*des.u*	*ka?*
	pitcher	TOP	tire-GER	be-NPST	EVID	COP.NPST	INT

'Does it look like Pitcher Ikeda is tired?' (Miyake 2006: 129)

Standard grammars do not present such examples, but searches on the Internet will deliver them in natural contexts. It seems that in both (21) and (22), it is not the speaker's judgment but the interlocutor's judgment that is questioned, and this fact may be the decisive factor that enables such usage. However, this is a question that needs further investigation.

Lastly, with respect to directives, no expression of modality proper can be directly used with imperative forms. However, we do find dynamic modality occurring in a complement clause embedded in an imperative (or other directive), and thus still in the scope of the imperative. Compare

[3] One more exception of a different kind from *-sō* that has been discussed repeatedly in the literature is *darō*. *Darō* often occurs in a construction followed by the interrogative particle *ka*, as in *darō ka*, but the prevailing opinion in the literature is that *darō* is not actually in the scope of *ka* (cf. Miyazaki 2002).

(23) with the imperative directly added to the modal expression in (24), which would be infelicitous for most speakers.

(23) *50 mētoru o* ***oyog-e.ru*** ***yō*** ***ni*** ***nari-nasa.i***
meter ACC swim-POT.NPST COMP to become-do.IMP
'Become able to swim 50 meters!'

(24) *#50 mētoru o* ***oyog-e-nasa.i***
meter ACC swim-POT-do.IMP
'Become able to swim 50 meters!'

3.3 Interaction with Tense

Japanese has basically two tenses: non-past, marked by *-(r)u* with verbs and *-i* with adjectives, and past, marked by *-ta* with verbs and *-kat.ta* with adjectives. However, *-(r)u* is more a multifunctional default verb ending than purely tense and thus not a reliable indicator of tense. *-Ta* as past is a more reliable indicator and therefore commonly used to test for tense. This will also be the case in this section.

First of all, all markers of modality proper except the epistemic *darō* can be marked with past tense *-ta*, and in all cases the past tense follows the modal marker, that is, seems to have scope over modality. In the case of *darō*, the lack of co-occurrence is, before questioning semantic compatibility, primarily morphologically conditioned: *darō* is the combination of the copular particle *da(r)-* with the inflection *-yō*, and the latter stands in a paradigmatic (i.e. mutually exclusive) relationship with *-ta* in Modern Japanese.

Now, the interesting question concerning modal markers in combination with past tense is what the past tense signifies, since, as a default, we would expect a modal expression to convey a speaker's judgment at the time of speech, and not in the past. So, the first question is whether the past actually scopes over the modal, as the order of morphemes indicates.

In most cases it clearly does, as the constructed example in (25) with deontic modality and that in (26) with epistemic modality illustrate:

(25) *Kinō kyū ni shukkin-shi-na.kereba* ***nar-ana-kat.ta.***
yesterday suddenly come.to.work-do-NEG.COND become-NEG.PST
'Yesterday I had to suddenly come to work.'

(26) *Kono toki mo watashi wa fui ni ut-are.ru ka mo*
this time FOC I TOP suddenly shoot-PASS.NPST INT FOC

shir-e-na-kat.ta.
know-POT-NEG.PST
'This time too, I could have been suddenly shot.'
(ŌOKA Shōhei: *Nobi*, 1952)

In (25) a deontic necessity that arose in the past is reported, and in (26) an epistemic possibility that existed in the past.

A second related issue that has been discussed in the literature, notably by Takanashi (2004, 2006: 85–95) and Narrog (2009a), is whether it is implied that the state of affairs was realized or not, if the modality is in the past tense. To put a complicated issue simply, practically all modal constructions are open with respect to this problem, that is, they both allow realization and non-realization. However, there is one group of modal constructions and markers across modal subcategories where non-realization is strongly implied. The constructed example with *beki* in (27) shows that this implication is difficult to cancel in many if not most contexts.

(27) ??*Kinō* *wa,* *shigoto* *o* ***suru*** ***beki*** ***dat.ta.*** *Da* *kara,*
yesterday TOP work ACC do DEO COP.PST COP because

shigoto-ba *e* *it.ta.*
work-place ALL go.PST
'I should have worked yesterday. Therefore, I went to my workplace.'

Nevertheless, this is an implication and not a meaning. Therefore, it is possible to find actual examples such as (28) where non-realization is in fact canceled in context.

(28) *Ōsaka* *wa,* *motomoto* *oashisu* *kokka* *to* *shi.te* ***hatten*** ***su*** ***beki***
TOP originally oasis state as do.GER develop do DEO

mono *de* *at.ta* *shi,* *jissai ni* *sō* *nat.te* *i.ta* *no*
thing ESS be.PST and actually this.way become.GER be.PST NMLZ

des.u *ga* ...
COP.POL.NPST but
'Osaka was originally supposed to develop as an oasis state, and actually it became just that, but...' (spoken, discussion)

Other modal markers and constructions that behave like *beki* are *-tai, -te hoshii* (boulomaic), *-reba ii* (deontic), and *hazu* (epistemic). They all have in common that in terms of strength of modality they are mid-scale (i.e. neither strong necessity nor mere possibility). Furthermore, they contain an evaluative element of desirability. With these modal constructions, the more common case is that the state-of-affairs is one of the past but the judgment of desirability of the present, as in (26). The contrast between past state-of-affairs and present desirability implies counterfactuality, that is, non-realization. However, infrequently, they can also be used to indicate a judgment in the past, as in (27), and then they are more likely to mark a state-of-affairs that was realized.

3.4 Interaction with Aspect

All Modern Japanese modal markers and constructions across subcategories investigated in Narrog (2009a) were able to scope over the stative *-te iru* and the completive *-te shimau*. On the other hand, only a limited number of modal markers and constructions, namely the dynamic and boulomaic ones, plus the evidential *-sō* and the deontic *nakereba naranai* can take scope under these aspectual constructions.

There are a number of interesting issues that emerge from the study of interaction of modality with aspect. One is that, as a rule, modality as such is stative, that is, designates a state of ability, of obligation, or of probability, and not dynamic events. Why, then, are there so many modal markers and constructions in Japanese that can be additionally stativized? While the full answer to this question is probably a little more complex, there is an obvious reply when looking at actual examples of use like (29):

(29) *Sentakushi* *ga* *mata* *fue.te* *shimat.ta* *node,* *yokei*
choice NOM again increase.GER CPV.PST because excessively

sagas-ana.kucha ***ik-e-naku*** ***nat.te*** ***i.ru.***
search-neg.TOP go-POT-NEG become.GER be.NPST
'As choices have increased, I now have to search around more.'
(spoken monologue)

In examples when a modal is further stativized, it is usually indicated that this state is only temporary or the result of some development (which also effectively means temporariness). Nevertheless, it seems that even this use of temporariness is ruled out with epistemic modal constructions. Thus, in contrast to (29), there is no **ka mo shirenaku natte iru* or **hazu de iru*. This may indicate that in contrast to dynamic, boulomaic, and some other narrow scope modal categories, epistemic modality does not have a temporality of its own at all.

Another issue of interest is the influence of stativity (or imperfectivity) in the proposition on the interpretation of modality. It has sometimes been claimed that stativity/imperfectivity of the proposition leads to an epistemic interpretation of modal markers, in contrast to a deontic or dynamic interpretation with a dynamic proposition (cf. Abraham and Leiss 2008: xii–xiv). Similar claims have been made for Japanese. There are a few cases where constructions such as *-te mo ii* and *nakereba naranai* receive quasi-epistemic readings, presumably with stative propositions. In a large-scale corpus study of this phenomenon, Narrog (2008: 295–303) showed that stative propositions are indeed conducive to quasi-epistemic interpretations but cannot force them. Example (30) shows a stative proposition embedded in the general deontic necessity construction receiving a quasi-epistemic interpretation. In contrast, (31) is an example of a stative proposition not evoking a quasi-epistemic interpretation.

(30) *Dāwin* *shinka-ron* *ga* *zettai-teki ni* *tadashi.i* *to*
evolution-theory NOM absolutely right-NPS QUOT

s.uru *nara,* *shinka* *wa* *ima* ***shinkō-chū*** ***de***
do COND evolution TOP now progress-during ESS

na.kereba ***nar-ana.i.***
not.be.COND become-NEG.NPST

'If Darwin's theory of evolution is absolutely right, then evolution must be in progress now.' (Essay, 1991)

(31) *[...]* *shikkari to* *yūzā* *o* ***mi.te*** ***i-na.i*** ***to*** ***ikena.i***
firmly user ACC look.GER be-NEG.NPST COND go.NEG.NPST

to *omoi-mas.u.*
QUOT think-HON.NPST

'[In the mobile [communication] market as well, fierce competition is taking place, and everything is decided by the customers. In this sense,] I think we must be firmly looking at the customers.'
(Newspaper, 1998)

3.5 Interaction with Negation

Cross-linguistically, a distinction between internal and external negation (e.g. Van Valin and LaPolla 1997: 46) is often made. This distinction is reflected formally on Japanese predicates by the distinction between internal negation suffix *-nai* 'not' and the external negation construction *no de wa nai* 'it is not [the case] that.' We will limit the discussion here to internal negation. The result with respect to interaction with expressions of modality is as follows. Taking into account suppletive constructions and cases where morpheme order and scope diverge, all non-epistemic and non-evidential modality markers and constructions can take scope under negation. Among the epistemic and evidentials (in their epistemic and evidential meaning), only the inferentials *yō, rashii,* and *-sō* can do the same, albeit infrequently. Conversely, all modal markers and constructions except for the dynamic modal *-eru* can take negation in their scope, if periphrastic and suppletive constructions are also taken into account (cf. Narrog 2009a: 192–194).

Cross-linguistically, a lot of irregularities occur in the combination of modality and negation (cf. Palmer 1995). In Japanese, as well, constructions of modality with negation are the biggest source of scope ambiguities in the verbal complex (cf. Narrog 2010: 226–229). One can logically distinguish the two cases in (32).

(32) a. The morpheme order MOD → NEG stands for both NEG[MOD] and MOD[NEG]
b. The morpheme order NEG → MOD stands for both MOD[NEG] and NEG[MOD]

Example (32a) is illustrated with a sentence with the deontic particle adjective *beki*.[4]

(33)

Shopan	*wa*	*ama.i*	*nante*	*karugarushiku*	*kuchi*
	TOP	sweet-NPST	EXM	lightly	mouth

ni	***s.u***	***beki***	***ja***	***na.i***	***to***	*omo.u*
to	do-NPST	DEO	ESS.TOP	not.be.NPST	QUOT	think-NPST

no	*sa.*
EMPH	SFP

'[I] think that one shouldn't say lightly that [the music of] Chopin is sweet' (FUKUNAGA Takehiko: *Kusa no hana*, 1956)

Because of a morphological constraint, *beki* 'should' in standard grammar can only be added to verbs and not adjectives, *beki* does not allow negation to precede (*-*(a)nai beki*), but only to follow. However, the actual interpretation is practically indistinguishable between *not* [*should*] (modality in the scope of negation) and [*not*] *should* [*not*] (negation in the scope of modality). One more modal suffix, the boulomaic *-tai* 'want to,' behaves just like *beki*.

The same phenomenon, but with the reverse morpheme order, that is, Case (32b), holds for *-(r)eba ii* 'you'd better.' This construction can only be preceded by negation, but the actual interpretation is ambiguous, as the example in (34) shows.

(34)

Kurōn	*ga*	*shinbun*	*ya*	*terebi*	*bangumi*	*o*	*gyūjit.te*
clone	NOM	newspaper	and	TV	program	ACC	control-GER

i.ru	*nara,*	*shinbun,*	*terebi*	*wa*	***mi-na.kereba***	***i.i.***
be-NPST	COND	newspaper	TV	TOP	see-NEG-COND	good.NPST

'If clones are [really] controlling newspapers and television, it's better not to look at them.' (KUWAHARA Ichiyo: *Ningen no kihon*, 1998)

Here as well, both 'it's better not to,' and 'it's not good to' are perfectly meaningful interpretations.

Besides *beki*, *-tai*, and *-(r)eba ii*, there are a couple of morphemes and constructions that allow negation to both follow and precede modality, but the interpretation is practically indistinguishable. For these constructions, both (32a) and (32b) apply. These are epistemic *hazu*, boulomaic *-te hoshii*, and the evidentials *yō* and *rashii*. Example (35) is with evidential *rashii* followed by negation.

[4] In terms of morphological distribution, *beki*, like *da* above, belongs to the group of particles, similar to case and sentence-final particles (cf. Narrog 1998: 18–22). However, *beki* (and *da*) inflect, and in terms of inflection, it is an adjective (although the inflection of *beki* follows Classical and not Modern Japanese rules).

(35) *Hayakawa* *wa* *warai-nagara* *mi.te* *i.ta* *ga,* *sukoshi*
TOP laugh-while see.GER be-PST but a.little

mo *keibetu-shi.te* *i.ru* *rashi.ku* *wa* *na.kat.ta.*
FOC contempt-do.GER be EVID TOP not.be-NPST
'Hayakawa laughed while watching but he didn't seem to look down on [him]' (MUSHANOKŌJI Saneatsu: *Yūjō*, 1920)

As in the case of modality and tense, all the constructions that display ambiguity are mid-scale in terms of strength of modality.

3.6 Modality Interacting with Modality

In English, there is the phenomenon of "double modality" in dialects (cf. Nagle 2003) and very regular co-occurrence of modals with semi-modals, as in *you may want to...* or *you will have to....* In Japanese, the same phenomenon is rather common. The following tendencies can be observed (cf. Narrog 2009a: 177–189).

(36) a. Participant-internal (traditional 'dynamic') modality does not embed other modality with the exception of dynamic modal markers embedding other dynamic modal markers as an apparent reinforcement of the same meaning.
b. Boulomaic modality can only embed dynamic modality and the inferential *-sō*.
c. Deontic modality can embed dynamic and boulomaic modality, and the inferential *-sō*.
d. Epistemic modality and evidentiality can in principle embed everything except for a few markers that resist embedding, especially the epistemic *darō* and the hearsay evidential *sō*.

Overall, nothing is really unexpected here. However, the behavior of *-sō* is striking: It can be embedded under a lot of other modal markers and constructions, thus indicating relatively narrow scope. On the other hand, it can also embed many other markers and constructions, thus indicating wide scope. Example (37) shows *-sō* from a recurring headline on a publisher's webpage, in which *-sō* embeds epistemic modal *ka mo shirenai*. Not all speakers of Japanese may be equally comfortable with this construction but it can be found fairly frequently on the Internet.

(37) *Ronguserā* *ni* ***nar.u*** ***ka*** ***mo*** ***shire-na-sa-sō-na*** *hon.*
longseller DAT become.NPST INT FOC know-NEG-NMLZ-EVID book
'Books that look like they might become longsellers.'
(www.hanmoto.com/longseller-76)

Without going into further detail, if one privileges the passive scope properties (i.e. the possibility of being embedded) over the active ones in

Table 16.1 *Layers of modal markers, as measured by their interaction*

Layer 1	*darō* (EPI), *sō* (EVID)
Layer 2	*ka mo sirenai, hazu* (EPI), *yō, rashii* (EVID)
Layer 3a	*beki* (DEO), *-(r)eba ii* (DEO)
Layer 3b	*-sō* (EVID), *nakereba naranai* (DEO), *-te hoshii* (BOU), *-tai* (BOU)
Layer 4	*-eru, -(r)areru, koto ga dekiru* (DYN)

Table 16.2 *Combined hierarchies*

Non-modal categories	Modal-related categories
	Illocutionary modification
	Moods (imperative, hortative)
	Epistemic modality (*darō*), (epistemic –*(y)ō*)
Tense	Evidentiality (*sō*)
	Epistemic modality (*ka mo shirenai*)
	Deontic modality (*beki, -(r)eba ii*)
(Internal) Negation	Evidentiality (*yō, rashii*)
	Epistemic modality (*hazu*)
Perfective/Imperfective aspect	Deontic modality (*nakereba naranai*)
	Evidentiality (*-sō*)
Phasal aspect[a]	Boulomaic modality (*-tai, -te hoshii*)
	Dynamic modality (*-eru, -(r)areru, koto ga dekiru*)
Benefactives voice	

[a] For phasal aspect, cf. for example, Dik (1997: 225) and Plungian (1999: 313). (Cf. Narrog 2012: 99)

case of contradiction, the following layers of scope of modal markers and constructions in Modern Japanese can be identified (Table 16.1).

Table 16.1 shows that the epistemic *darō* and the hearsay evidential *sō* have the broadest scope, and the dynamic modal markers and constructions in general the narrowest scope when interacting with other modal categories. The next section will provide some insight about scope properties in interaction with other (non-modal) categories.

3.7 Layering

When modal markers and constructions of various categories are tested for their combination not only with other modal markers but also with other categories – for example, tense, aspect, negation, benefactive, voice, illocutionary modification, and behavior in subordinate clause constructions – it is possible to arrive at a more accurate scope hierarchy of modal markers and constructions that reflects hierarchical clause structure beyond modality in Japanese, as in Table 16.2.

As indicated in Section 3.5, this hierarchy is necessarily a simplification from more complex behavior of individual markers and constructions that is sometimes contradictory. Besides apparent mismatch between "active" (embedding) and "passive" (embedded) scope properties, we also find individual mismatches, such as epistemic *darō* being more amenable to embedding in subordinate clauses than the hearsay evidential *sō*, while, on the other hand, it is only *sō* that can be marked with the past tense (cf. Narrog 2009a: 227–228).

4 Modality in Japanese Language History

Students of the history of Japanese know that the expression of modality in Modern Japanese is quite different from the expression of modality in, say, Classical Japanese. There has been almost a complete turnover in means of expression. This is shown in Table 16.3, which displays the means of expression of epistemic and evidential modal categories, which have been core modal categories in Japanese.

The only direct remnants of historical forms in Modern Japanese are the inflection *-(y)ō*, which is derived from the inflecting modal suffix *-(a)m-*, and the negative speculative particle *mai*, but since both of them are better

Table 16.3 *Epistemic, epistemic-evidential (inferential), and evidential markers through Japanese language history*

	Late Old Japanese (10th century)	Late Middle Japanese (late 16th century)	Modern Japanese (late 20th century)
Epistemic	*-(a)m-* 'future'**	*-(y)ō/-(y)ōz-* 'speculative'**	(*-(y)ō* 'speculative')**
	ram- 'speculative'	*rō* 'speculative'	*darō* 'speculative'
	-(a)ji 'negated future'**		*hazu* 'epistemic necessity/expectation'
	be- 'inevitability'*		*ni chigai na-* 'epistemic necessity/conclusion'
	maji 'negated inevitability'*	*maji(i)/mai* 'negated speculative'*	(*mai* 'negated speculative')**
			ka mo shire-na- 'epistemic possibility'
Inferential-Evidential	*meri* '(visual) appearance'		*rashi-* 'distant appearance'
	rashi 'certain appearance'		*yō/mitai* 'present- and past-oriented appearance'
	(*bera* 'appearance')	*sō* 'appearance'	*sō* 'predictive appearance'
	(*ge* 'appearance of state')	*ge* 'appearance of state'	
Hearsay-Evidential	*nari* 'reportive'		*rashi-* 'reportive'
	tef- 'reportive'		*sō* 'reportive'

* Also has deontic use.
** Also has boulomaic use.

categorized as mood than as modality proper in Modern Japanese, they are put into brackets in Table 16.3.

There are at least two further points of interest that emerge from the data displayed in the table. First, while practically all expressions of modality in Old and Late Old Japanese were "synthetic," that is, realized as suffixes on word stems and words as a whole, many Modern Japanese expressions are periphrastic. The Modern Japanese periphrastic expressions in Table 16.3 include the multi-word expressions *ni chigai nai* and *ka mo shirenai* as well as the nouns *hazu* and *yō*. Of course, there are many more periphrastic expressions in other areas of modality (cf. Section 2). Late Old Japanese had neither the periphrastic modal expressions in general nor those nouns to express core modality.

Second, it appears that there was a bottleneck in terms of expression in Middle Japanese. Most of the semantically finely differentiated modal endings that were characteristic for Old and Late Old Japanese became obsolete from the twelfth century on. One might expect that immediately new morphemes were grammaticalized with the same function, but that did not happen. Instead, a few morphemes, especially *-(y)ō*, with the Middle Japanese variant *-(y)ōz-*, and *maji(i)/mai* took on a high "functional load," that is, covered a large variety of meanings and functions. Most modern periphrastic expressions developed later, from the seventeenth century on.

The only modality and mood morphemes that have been present in the spoken language throughout history are Old Japanese *-(a)mu*, Modern *-(y)ō*, and its negative counterpart *ma(si)zi*, Modern *-mai*. The latter is much less prominent in Modern Japanese than the former, so I will focus on *-(y)ō* here. Formally, as indicated above, *-(a)mu/-(y)oo* has undergone salient changes. Morphologically, through loss of its own inflections, it has become an inflection itself, and phonologically, its sounds have changed considerably through the centuries, including condensation of sounds. These are typical grammaticalization changes.

But I want to draw attention here to the overall functional and semantic change of this morpheme, which is just as impressive. I will not try to give a full diachronic account here but instead contrast the meanings and functions of *-(a)mu* and Modern *-(y)ō* at two points in time, namely Old Japanese (Nara period) and Modern Japanese. The basis for the analysis of *-(a)mu* in Old Japanese is provided by Koji (1980), which is a very detailed corpus study of the suffixed inflected morphemes (so-called *jodōshi*) of the period. The analysis of *-(y)ō* in Modern Japanese is based on my own corpus data.

In Old Japanese, *-(a)mu* had basically two meanings, intention and prediction, and all other uses could be rather transparently derived from them in context. There are only relatively few examples where *-(a)mu* is used in fixed constructions. Example (38) shows a common collocation with the adjective *posi* or the verb *pori*, both meaning 'want.' In this construction, *-(a)mu* always indicates a wish.

(38) *nak.u* *kowe* *wo* *kik-am.aku* *pori* *to* ...
cry-ANP voice ACC hear-FUT-NMLZ want QUOT
'I [went out], wanting to hear [the cuckoo] sing' (*Man'yōshū* (MYS) 4209)

Eample (39) shows *-(a)mu* in its conditional form *-(a)me* at the sentence end. Here it always indicates a prediction of a possibility.

(39) *ter.u* *pi* *no* *mo* *wa* *ga* *sode* *pi-m.e* *ya* ...
shine-ANP sun GEN FOC I GEN sleeve dry-FUT-COND Q
'Would my sleeves dry even in the bright sun [if I cannot meet you]?' (MYS 1995)

In my count, there are only three such fixed constructions in Old Japanese.

In spoken Modern Japanese, *-(y)ō* is primarily a mood marker indicating hortative (*ikō!* 'Let's go!'). This alone is a remarkable change which I have described elsewhere in terms of subjectification or speech-act orientation (Narrog 2012: 130–132). But I want to draw attention to another fact here. Especially if we also include written language, there is a stunning number of fixed constructions involving *-(y)ō* in Modern Japanese. I will give just a few here. The examples are constructed unless otherwise noted.

Example (40) shows *-(y)ō* with the interrogative particle directed toward the hearer indicating a proposal, (41) in a construction with the complementizer *to* and certain mental verbs, indicating an intention, and (42) in a construction with the noun *yō* 'way,' in which the individual semantic contribution of *-(y)ō* is very vague and hard to pin down.

(40) *Odor.ō* *ka?*
dance-HORT Q
'Shall we dance?'

(41) *Mōshikom.ō* *to* *kime.ta.*
apply-HORT COMP decide-PST
'I decided to apply'

(42) *i.ō* *yō* *na.i* ...
say-HORT way not.be-NPST
'there is no way to say it'

I have counted twenty-four such "special" constructions, many more than there are in Old Japanese. They are the result of very complex historical forces at work. Due to the fact that it was used so widely in premodern Japanese, *-(a)mu/-(y)ō* appeared in many syntactic and pragmatic contexts. Some of them may have gained a life of their own, so to speak, through particularly frequent use in specific situations, like (40), for example. Others, that became uncommon in spoken language, survived in written language contexts, where they are not clearly connected anymore to productive usage, like (42).

This kind of development can be described in terms of "constructionalization," that is, the historical development of constructions (i.e. specific form–meaning mappings). In this sense, the development of *-(a)mu/-(y)ō* can be considered as an example of almost rampant constructionalization.

5 Conclusion

In this chapter, I have given an overview of the expression of modal categories in Japanese. Inevitably, the chapter had to start out with issues of definition and subcategorization, which are a notorious problem in this field, and which deserve considerable attention by themselves. I then concentrated on structural properties of modal expressions before giving a glimpse of their history. At some points throughout the chapter I have indicated areas of study that are still underdeveloped. Naturally, these also include topics that I have not been able to treat in any detail in the framework of this chapter, such as discourse properties of modality, or the role of adverbs in the expression of modality, or the relationship to the category of person. Despite having been a popular research topic in the past twenty or so years, there is still a lot to explore about modality in Japanese.

17

Logophoricity, Viewpoint, and Reflexivity

Yukio Hirose

1 Introduction

This chapter is concerned with the polysemous nature of the so-called reflexive pronoun *jibun* 'self' and related phenomena in Japanese. The word *jibun* may only be a simple lexical item, but a linguistic study of its use provides us with an important insight into how the self is conceptualized and expressed in Japanese. Drawing on pioneering works such as Kuno (1972a, 1978a), Kuroda (1973a, 1973b), Kuno and Kaburaki (1977), and Sells (1987) and more recent works such as Hirose (2000, 2002) and Oshima (2004, 2007), the present chapter argues that the use of *jibun* can be largely divided into three types: *logophoric, viewpoint,* and *reflexive.*

The logophoric use,[1] which is the most basic of the three, is the one in which *jibun* typically occurs in the indirect-discourse complement of a saying or thinking verb and refers to the original speaker of indirect discourse, as in (1), where *jibun* is coreferential with the matrix subject *Ken.*

(1) *Ken* *wa* *jibun* *wa* *ganko* *da* *to* *{itteiru/omotteiru}.*
    TOP self TOP stubborn COP QUOT {say/think}
    'Ken {says/thinks} that he [= *jibun*] is stubborn.'

The viewpoint and reflexive uses concern *jibun* as it appears outside the indirect-discourse context. Viewpoint *jibun* signals that the speaker is taking the perspective of its referent; thus in an example like (2), the book Ken lost is described from Ken's point of view, rather than from the speaker's own. Reflexive *jibun* serves as a reflexive marker to indicate coreference between the subject and object of a predicate, as in (3), just like the typical use of English reflexive pronouns.

[1] The notion of logophoricity was first introduced into linguistics by Hagège (1974).

(2) *Ken wa jibun ga tomodachi kara karita hon o nakushita.*
TOP self NOM friend from borrowed book ACC lost
'Ken lost a book that he [= *jibun*] borrowed from a friend.'

(3) *Ken wa jibun o hihanshita.*
TOP self ACC criticized
'Ken criticized himself [= *jibun*].'

I am not concerned here with how to describe syntactically the so-called binding relation between *jibun* and its antecedent, a question which has been tackled by numerous studies mainly in the tradition of generative grammar (for a useful survey, see Aikawa 1999).

In what follows, based primarily on my previous work on *jibun*, I examine each of the three uses from a cognitive semantic perspective and discuss the kind of self encoded in each use and its characteristics in relation to other subjectivity-related phenomena in Japanese.[2] The main points of this chapter are as follows. First, logophoric *jibun* represents the *private self*, that is, the speaker as the subject of thinking or consciousness, distinguished from the *public self* as the subject of communicating (see Section 2). Second, the meaning of *jibun* extends from logophoric to viewpoint to reflexive through the cognitive process of *objectification of self*, which is a metonymic conceptual shift from the self as the subject of consciousness to the self as the object of consciousness (see Sections 3 and 4). Third, viewpoint *jibun* represents the speaker's *objective self*, that is, the self that the speaker dissociates from his/her consciousness and projects onto another person (see Section 3). Fourth, reflexive *jibun* represents the objective self of the agent of an action, that is, the self that the agent (not the speaker) dissociates from his/her consciousness and treats like another person (see Section 4).

2 The Logophoric Use

The logophoric nature of *jibun* was first noted by Kuno (1972a), who proposed a theory called *Direct Discourse Analysis* in which *jibun* is assumed to be transformationally derived from first person pronominals like *boku* 'I (male)' and *watashi* 'I (formal or female).' Thus, according to this theory, the indirect-discourse sentence in (4) has an underlying structure like the direct-discourse sentence in (5).[3]

(4) *Ken wa jibun wa oyoge-nai to itta.*
TOP self TOP can.swim-NEG QUOT said
Lit. 'Ken said that self can't swim.'

[2] For a formal semantic approach to a similar three-way classification of *jibun*, see Oshima (2007, 2011).

[3] In a later work, Kuno (1978a: 213) postulates, instead of this transformational derivation, that when *jibun* is used in the subordinate clause of a verb denoting utterance, thought, or consciousness, it refers to the speaker or experiencer of that utterance, thought, or consciousness.

(5) *Ken wa "Boku wa oyoge-nai" to itta.*
TOP I TOP can.swim-NEG QUOT said
'Ken said, "I can't swim."'

Technical details aside, the Direct Discourse Analysis provides a way of capturing Japanese speakers' intuition that *jibun*, as well as *boku/watashi*, means a kind of "I." But what kind of "I" or self does *jibun* represent, compared to *boku/watashi*? This section deals with this and related questions.

2.1 Public versus Private Expression

It is argued in Hirose (2000) that the speaker has two different aspects called *public* and *private self*. The public self is the speaker as the subject of communicating, that is, the speaker who faces an addressee or has one in mind, while the private self is the speaker as the subject of thinking or consciousness, that is, the speaker who has no addressee in mind. The public and private self are the subjects of two different levels of linguistic expression called *public* and *private expression*. Public expression corresponds to the communicative function of language and private expression to the non-communicative, thought-expressing function of language. Thus public expression requires the presence of an addressee, whereas private expression does not.

There are linguistic expressions that inherently presuppose the existence of an addressee. Among such expressions in Japanese are: (a) certain sentence-final particles (e.g. *yo* 'I tell you,' *ne* 'you know'), (b) directives such as orders and requests (e.g. *tomare* 'Stop!,' *tomatte-kudasai* 'Please stop'), (c) vocatives (e.g. *ōi/oi* 'hey'), (d) responses (e.g. *hai/īe* 'yes/no'), (e) interactive adverbial phrases of various sorts (e.g. *sumimasen ga* 'Excuse me, but,' *kokodake no hanashi dakedo* 'between you and me'), (f) polite verb forms (e.g. *desu/masu*), (g) hearsay expressions (e.g. *(da)sōda/(da)tte* 'I hear'), and so on. These "addressee-oriented" expressions are themselves public expressions, and they also serve to make phrases and sentences containing them public expressions. On the other hand, phrases and sentences without addressee-oriented expressions are private expressions unless they are used by the speaker with the intention of communicating with another person (see Hirose 1995 for detailed discussion).

While public expressions involve communicative attitudes, private expressions correspond to mental states. Languages have many so-called modal expressions that represent mental states. In Japanese, for example, the copula *da*, as in *Ame da* 'It is raining,' indicates unmarked assertion; the modal expression *ni chigainai*, as in *Ame ni chigainai* 'It must be raining,' represents certainty; the modal *darō*, as in *Ame darō* 'It will be raining,' indicates conjecture; the interrogative particle *ka*, as in *Ame darō ka* 'Will it be raining?,' expresses uncertainty or doubt. All these expressions, unlike addressee-oriented expressions, are, by default, private expressions that characterize mental states.

Mental states are typically described in Japanese by verbs like *omou* 'think' followed by the stative aspectual verb *te-iru*. *Omou* and other mental-state verbs can take as a complement a reported clause marked by the quotative particle *to*. Because the level of linguistic expression that describes what one thinks, believes, doubts, or wishes must be private, a mental-state verb allows only a private expression as its reported-clause complement. Thus, consider the following examples, where angle brackets labeled *Priv* represent a private expression and square brackets labeled *Pub* represent a public expression.

(6) a. *Masao wa* <Priv *soto wa ame da*> *to omotteiru.*
TOP outside TOP rain COP QUOT think
'Masao thinks it is raining outside.'

b. *Masao wa* <Priv *soto wa ame ni chigainai*> *to omotteiru.*
TOP outside TOP rain must QUOT think
'Masao thinks it must be raining outside.'

c. *Masao wa* <Priv *soto wa ame darō ka*> *to omotteiru.*
TOP outside TOP rain will INT QUOT think
'Masao wonders whether it will be raining outside.'

(7) a. **Masao wa* [Pub *soto wa ame da yo*] *to omotteiru.*
TOP outside TOP rain COP SFP QUOT think
'Masao thinks "It is raining outside, I tell you."'

b. **Masao wa* [Pub *soto wa ame desu*] *to omotteiru.*
TOP outside TOP rain COP.POL QUOT think
'Masao thinks politely "It is raining outside."'

c. **Masao wa* [Pub *soto wa ame da tte*] *to omotteiru.*
TOP outside TOP rain COP EVID QUOT think
'Masao thinks "I hear it is raining outside."'

In (6) the reported clauses are private expressions because the underlined parts are modal expressions that represent mental states. In (7), on the other hand, the underlined parts are addressee-oriented expressions that mark the whole reported clauses as public expressions. Hence the unacceptability of the sentences in (7).

Unlike mental-state verbs, utterance verbs such as *iu* 'say' allow both public and private expressions as their reported clauses. For example, the reported clauses in (8) are public expressions, regarded generally as cases of direct discourse.

(8) a. *Masao wa Keiko ni* [Pub *soto wa ame da yo*] *to itta.*
TOP DAT outside TOP rain COP SFP QUOT said
'Masao said to Keiko, "It is raining outside, I tell you."'

b. *Masao wa Keiko ni* [Pub *soto wa ame desu*] *to itta.*
TOP DAT outside TOP rain COP.POL QUOT said
'Masao said to Keiko politely, "It is raining outside."'

c. *Masao wa Keiko ni* [Pub *soto wa ame da tte*] *to itta.*
TOP DAT outside TOP rain COP EVID QUOT said
'Masao said to Keiko, "I hear it is raining outside."'

Here the reported clauses convey not only Masao's communicative attitude toward Keiko but also his belief that it is raining outside. Focusing on the latter, we can report Masao's utterance as private expression, using so-called indirect discourse, as in (9).

(9) *Masao wa Keiko ni* <Priv *soto wa ame da*> *to itta.*
TOP DAT outside TOP rain COP QUOT said
'Masao said to Keiko that it was raining outside.'

These observations lead to the following hypothesis, first developed in detail in Hirose (1995) (cf. also Hirose 2000; Wada 2001).

(10) Direct discourse is a quotation of public expression, whereas indirect discourse is a quotation of private expression.

This means that while direct discourse can represent communicative attitudes of the original speaker, indirect discourse can represent only mental states of the original speaker. We will return to this hypothesis shortly.

2.2 Logophoric *Jibun* as a Word for Private Self

We should now notice that Japanese has separate words for public and private self. The private self is expressed by the word *jibun*. The public self, on the other hand, is referred to by a variety of words of self-reference such as *boku* 'I (male-casual),' *atashi* 'I (female-casual),' *watashi* 'I (male-formal, female-formal/informal),' *watakushi* 'I (very formal),' *ore* 'I (male-casual/vulgar),' *atai* 'I (female-vulgar),' and *oira/ora* 'I (male-vulgar)'; moreover, kinship terms like *otōsan/okāsan* 'father/mother' and the occupational title *sensei* 'teacher' are also used for the purpose of self-reference. Which word to use in a given situation depends on who the speaker is and whom he/she is talking to.

It must be emphasized here that *jibun* is a private expression, whereas first person pronominals like *boku/watashi* are public expressions. As argued in Hirose (2000) and Hasegawa and Hirose (2005), this point is confirmed by the acceptability contrast between examples like (11) and (12), which are meant to describe one's inner consciousness about oneself.

(11) *jibun wa ongaku ga sukida to iu ishiki*
self TOP music NOM like QUOT say consciousness
Lit. 'the consciousness that self likes music'

(12) ??*{boku/watashi}* *wa* *ongaku* *ga* *sukida* *to* *iu* *ishiki*
{I/I} TOP music NOM like QUOT say consciousness
'the consciousness that I like music'

While (11) is perfectly acceptable by itself, (12) sounds unnatural as it stands. This fact indicates that words like *boku/watashi* do not appear in inner or private description of consciousness, which in turn suggests that it is only when we communicate our thoughts to others that we can use these words to refer to ourselves. Thus, if (12) is used in a communicative situation in which the speaker reports his/her own consciousness to another person, it will become acceptable, as in (13).

(13) *{Boku/Watashi}* *ga* *{boku/watashi}* *wa* *ongaku* *ga*
{I/I} NOM {I/I} TOP music NOM

sukida *to* *iu* *ishiki* *o* *tsuyoku* *motsu-yōni* *natta*
like QUOT say consciousness ACC strongly have-to became

no *wa* *chōdo* *sono* *koro* *deshita.*
NMLZ TOP just that time COP.POL.PST
'It was just then that I became strongly conscious that I liked music.'

Compare this with the following, where (11) is embedded.

(14) *{Boku/Watashi}* *ga* *jibun* *wa* *ongaku* *ga* *sukida* *to* *iu*
{I/I} NOM self TOP music NOM like QUOT say

ishiki *o* *tsuyoku* *motsu-yōni* *natta* *no* *wa* *chōdo*
consciousness ACC strongly have-to became NMLZ TOP just

sono *koro* *deshita.*
that time COP.POL.PST
Lit. 'It was just then that I became strongly conscious that self likes music.'

Objectively, both (13) and (14) describe the same situation: at a certain point in the past, the speaker became strongly conscious that he/she liked music. The difference, however, is that this consciousness is represented directly within the inner, private domain in (14), but indirectly from the outer, public domain in (13). In other words, what makes it possible for *boku/watashi* to refer to the subject of consciousness in (13) is the speaker's external perspective as a reporter (i.e. public self). Example (12) above sounds odd as it stands because no such external perspective is explicitly given there.

It is worth considering here the ambiguous interpretation of *boku* in examples such as (15).

(15) *Yasuo wa boku ni jiko no sekinin ga aru to*
TOP I DAT accident GEN responsibility NOM exist QUOT
itta.
said
(a) 'Yasuo said, "I am responsible for the accident."'
(b) 'Yasuo said that I was responsible for the accident.'

In (15) *boku* can refer either to Yasuo, the referent of the matrix subject, or to the reporter, that is, the speaker of the whole sentence. In the former interpretation, the reported clause is direct discourse, as indicated by the English translation in (15a), while in the latter interpretation it is indirect discourse, as shown in (15b). Since the quotative particle *to*, unlike the English complementizer *that*, can freely introduce both direct and indirect discourse, it is much more difficult in Japanese than in English to distinguish syntactically between direct and indirect discourse (cf. Coulmas 1985). Herein lies the significance of the hypothesis, stated in (10), that direct discourse is a quotation of public expression, whereas indirect discourse is a quotation of private expression.

In terms of this hypothesis, we can say that since *boku* is a public expression, the ambiguity of (15) depends on whether it is the whole of the reported clause or just part of it that is a public expression. If so, the reported clause in (15) can be given the following two different representations.

(16) a. *Yasuo wa* [Pub *boku ni jiko no sekinin ga aru*] *to itta.*
b. *Yasuo wa* <Priv [Pub *boku*] *ni jiko no sekinin ga aru*> *to itta.*

In (16a) the whole reported clause is a public expression whose subject is Yasuo; that is, Yasuo is depicted in the role of the public self. In (16a), therefore, *boku*, representing the public self, must be associated with Yasuo. In (16b), on the other hand, since the reported clause is a private expression, Yasuo is depicted in the role of the private self. Hence *boku* cannot be associated with Yasuo; as a result, it is associated with the reporter, who depicts himself not in Yasuo's words but in his own words, based on his role as the public self.

By contrast, in (17) with the mental-state verb *shinjiteiru* 'believe,' *boku* is unambiguous, referring only to the reporter.

(17) *Yasuo wa boku ni jiko no sekinin ga aru to*
TOP I DAT accident GEN responsibility NOM exist QUOT
shinjiteiru.
believe
'Yasuo believes I am responsible for the accident.'

As seen in Section 2.1, mental-state verbs, unlike utterance verbs, do not allow public expressions as their reported-clause complements. This means that sentence (17) can have only one representation shown in (18), where the public expression *boku* is associated with the reporter for the same reason as in the case of (16b).

(18) *Yasuo wa* <Priv [Pub *boku*] *ni jiko no sekinin ga aru*> *to shinjiteiru.*

In order to say that Yasuo believes that he himself is responsible for the accident, we have to use the private expression *jibun*, as in (19).

(19) *Yasuo wa* <Priv *jibun ni jiko no sekinin ga aru*>
TOP self DAT accident GEN responsibility NOM exist

to shinjiteiru.
QUOT believe
'Yasuo believes he is responsible for the accident.'

Here *jibun* refers unequivocally to Yasuo. This fact is explained by saying that since *jibun* represents the private self and Yasuo in (19) is the subject of private expression, *jibun* must be associated with Yasuo.

It is such a use of *jibun* as in (19) that is termed logophoric. As should be clear by now, the present analysis enables us to account for this use without recourse to Kuno's Direct Discourse Analysis, mentioned at the beginning of this section; that is, the logophoric character of *jibun* follows naturally from the fact that it is a special word that represents the private self as distinguished from the public self.

Note in passing that in contrast to Japanese, English has a special word for public self, *I*, but no special word for private self, so that in English, personal pronouns are employed to represent the private self, depending on its grammatical person (and gender in the case of third persons). Japanese *jibun* can be used invariably to refer to any person's private self, as indicated in (20), whose English counterpart is (21).

(20) *{Boku/Kimi/Kare/Kanojo} wa jibun wa oyoge-nai to itta.*
{I/you/he/she} TOP self TOP can.swim-NEG QUOT said
Lit. '{I/You/He/She} said that self can't swim.'

(21) *{I/You/He/She} said that {I/you/he/she} can't swim.*

In (21) the private self is encoded differently as either *I* or *you* or *he/she*, depending on its grammatical person and gender, as seen from the public self (for a more detailed comparative analysis, see Hirose 2000).

2.3 The Public Use of Private *Jibun*

We might say, metaphorically, that the private self represented by *jibun* is the "naked" self, and it has a variety of formal and informal "clothes" to wear in public, including *boku, watashi, otōsan* 'father,' *sensei* 'teacher,' and so on. It is worth pointing out, however, that the word *jibun* could also be used to refer to the public self, as in (22).

(22) *Jibun wa sore ni-tsuite nanimo shiri-mase-n.*
self TOP it about anything know-POL-NEG
'I don't know anything about it.'

Because the polite auxiliary *masu* is employed here, this sentence is a public expression that requires the presence of an addressee. But such a public use of *jibun* has an unusual connotation: it is as if the speaker appeared in public without wearing any clothes. Thus, just as it is considered weird to be naked in public, so the use of *jibun* in reference to the public self sounds peculiar in ordinary conversation.

In fact, examples like (22) remind many Japanese of special situations such as those in the military where soldiers are talking to their superiors or those in sports clubs where junior male members (called *kōhai*) are talking to their seniors (called *senpai*). Probably in these situations it is tacitly assumed that one has to show one's real self to one's superior or senior, to whom one is expected to be loyal. Conversely, in ordinary situations there is a different tacit assumption related to politeness, namely, that one should not show one's real self in public; to use our metaphor again, one is supposed to wear some clothes in public. In effect, such a public use of *jibun* as that in (22) can be characterized as a special use showing one's loyalty which is motivated by its inheriting the naked-self character of private *jibun*.

It is interesting to note further that in contrast to (22), the following example sounds quite normal.

(23) *Jibun wa sore ni-tsuite nanimo shira-nai.*
self TOP it about anything know-NEG.NPST
'I don't know anything about it.'

This sentence is different from (22) only in that it does not contain the polite auxiliary *masu*. Because it has no addressee-oriented expressions in it, it is understood to be a private expression representing the inner consciousness of a private self. It is precisely for this reason that *jibun* sounds very natural in (23). Sentences of this kind can be used in the Japanese counterpart of so-called *free indirect discourse*,[4] as illustrated by examples such as (24).

(24) *Kazuo wa, sono jiken ni-tsuite kikare-ta toki, sukkari*
TOP the incident about be.asked-PST when quite

tōwakushi-ta. Jibun wa sore ni-tsuite nanimo shira-nai.
be.perplexed-PST self TOP it about anything know-NEG.NPST

Dakara nanimo ie-nai no da.
so anything can.say-NEG.NPST NMLZ COP.NPST

[4] In general, free indirect discourse is the same as ordinary indirect discourse in choice of person and tense, but resembles direct discourse with respect to word order and the interpretation of spatiotemporal deictic expressions such as *this, here*, and *now*. See, for example, Banfield (1982) and Fludernik (1993) for discussion of free indirect discourse in English.

Lit. 'When asked about the incident, Kazuo was quite perplexed. Self does not know anything about it. So (self) cannot say anything.'

The underlined sentences depict what the character Kazuo thought in his mind; thus, *jibun* refers to Kazuo's private self, and the non-past tense of the sentences reflects the "now" of his consciousness. In English, the underlined parts of (24) would be translated in free indirect style as in (25), where Kazuo's consciousness is expressed in the third person past tense.

(25) *When asked about the incident, Kazuo was quite perplexed. He didn't know anything about it, so he couldn't say anything.*

(For a more elaborate examination of free indirect discourse in Japanese and English, see Hirose 2000: 1650–1652 and Hirose and Hasegawa 2010: 25–29, 160–192.)

3 The Viewpoint Use

We now turn to the viewpoint use of *jibun*, which, as well as the reflexive use, appears outside the indirect-discourse context, as we saw in Section 1. But viewpoint *jibun*, unlike reflexive *jibun*, allows replacement with a pronominal like *kare* 'he,' as shown by the contrast between (26) and (27), where subscripts are used to indicate intended coreference between *kare* and *Ken*.

(26) *Ken$_i$ wa {jibun/kare$_i$} ga tomodachi kara karita hon o*
TOP {self/he} NOM friend from borrowed book ACC
nakushita.
lost
'Ken lost a book that he borrowed from a friend.'

(27) *Ken$_i$ wa {jibun/*kare$_i$} o hihanshita.*
Ken TOP {self/him} ACC criticized
'Ken criticized himself.'

The use of *kare* in (26), however, does not guarantee that the speaker takes Ken's point of view.[5]

[5] Logohoric *jibun* can also be replaced with *kare*, as exemplified in (i).

(i) *Ken$_i$ wa {jibun/kare$_i$} ga minna o tasuketa to omotteiru.*
Ken TOP {self/he} NOM everyone ACC saved QUOT think
'Ken thinks that he saved everyone.'

When *kare* is chosen here, its referent Ken is depicted not as the private self (as in the case of *jibun*) but as a third person from the speaker's external perspective as a reporter (cf. also the contrast between (13) and (14) discussed in Section 2.2). In the logico-philosophical or formal semantic tradition, the kind of opposition found between *jibun* and *kare* in indirect discourse is often discussed in connection with what is known as the *de se*/non-*de se* distinction; see Oshima (2011) for a detailed study of such phenomena in Japanese.

There is also a certain criterion for distinguishing the viewpoint use from the logophoric use: in the former use, unlike in the latter, the referent of *jibun* is not necessarily "aware" of the propositional content of the clause containing *jibun* (cf. Kuroda 1973b; Kuno 1978a; Sells 1987). Thus, in the logophoric example (1) in Section 1, the referent of *jibun*, Ken, is obviously aware that he is stubborn, because he himself says (or thinks) so, a fact deduced from the contradictoriness of such a sentence as (28). On the other hand, in the viewpoint example (2), Ken does not have to be aware that the book he lost is the one he borrowed from his friend, which we can see from the non-contradictoriness of (29).

(28) **Ken wa jibun wa ganko da to itteiru ga, sore ga*
TOP self TOP stubborn COP QUOT say but it NOM
jibun no koto da to wa kizuitei-nai.
self GEN thing COP QUOT TOP realize-NEG
'Ken says that he is stubborn, but he does not realize that it is about himself.'

(29) *Ken wa jibun ga tomodachi kara karita hon o nakushita*
TOP self NOM friend from borrowed book ACC lost
ga, sono hon ga tomodachi kara karita mono da to wa
but the book NOM friend from borrowed thing COP QUOT TOP
kizuitei-nai.
realize-NEG
'Ken lost a book that he borrowed from a friend, but he has not realized that the book is the one he borrowed from the friend.'

This contrast reveals that viewpoint *jibun* cannot mean the private self as the subject of thinking or consciousness. Then what self does it represent?

As argued in Hirose (2002), viewpoint *jibun* represents the speaker's *objective self*, the self that the speaker dissociates from his/her consciousness and projects onto another person. To illustrate the notion of objective self, let us first consider the interpretation of the following English sentence.

(30) *I dreamed that I was lonely.*

As was first pointed out by Lakoff (1968), this kind of sentence with the verb *dream* has two different readings which I refer to here as subjective and objective. In the subjective reading, the speaker experienced loneliness directly in the dream. In the objective reading, the speaker saw his/her alter ego being lonely in the dream. In Japanese, these two readings correspond to the two different sentences in (31), both of which involve the reflexive *jibun*.

(31) a. *Boku wa jibun ga sabishi-katta yume o mita.*
I TOP self NOM lonely-PST dream ACC saw
Lit. 'I had a dream that self was lonely.'

b. *Boku wa jibun ga sabishi-gatteiru yume o mita.*
I TOP self NOM lonely-be.showing.signs dream ACC saw
Lit. 'I had a dream of self showing signs of being lonely.'

In (31a), which is a subjective version, the predicate *sabishi-katta* 'was lonely' asserts the subject's direct experience of loneliness in the past; so *jibun* refers to the speaker as the subject of dreaming, which is itself an aspect of the speaker's private self. On the other hand, in (31b), which is an objective version, the emotive predicate *sabishi* 'lonely' is followed by the evidential expression *-gatteiru* 'be showing signs,' which normally indicates observable behavior on the part of someone other than the speaker. We can then say that *jibun* in (31b) refers to the self of the speaker that is objectified in the sense that it is placed on a level with (or on an equality with) others. This is what I call the speaker's objective self. In English, the use of the reflexive *myself* as in the following example permits only the objective reading; so it refers unambiguously to the speaker's objective self.

(32) *I dreamed of myself being lonely.*

The typical viewpoint use of *jibun* emerges when the speaker projects his/her objective self onto another person as a *situational subject*, that is, the most prominent participant in the situation involved.[6] Thus, consider an example like (33) (cf. Iida 1996; Oshima 2007).

(33) *Ken wa hon o jibun no migi-gawa ni oita.*
TOP book ACC self GEN right-side LOC put
Lit. 'Ken put the book on the right of self.'

Here Ken is the situational subject, and *jibun*, which is construed with *Ken*, represents the objective self the speaker has projected onto him. So the speaker is describing the situation from Ken's viewpoint, and not from his/her own viewpoint. This is why (33) means that the book was placed "on the right of Ken" from Ken's viewpoint. If *kare* 'he' is substituted for *jibun*, the location of the book can be interpreted from the speaker's viewpoint.

In what follows, I first outline Kuno's well-known analysis of viewpoint *jibun* in terms of his notion of empathy (Kuno 1978a, 1987; Kuno and Kaburaki 1977); I then show that the empathy phenomena involving *jibun* can be better accounted for by the notion of the speaker's objective self, which has both the "self as other" aspect and the "other as self" aspect.

[6] The situational subject thus defined is grammatically realized, by default, as the subject of a sentence (cf. Langacker 1987: 235). That is why viewpoint *jibun* normally takes a subject noun phrase as its antecedent; there are, though, exceptional cases in which it is bound to a non-subject noun phrase (see, for example, Iida 1996 and Aikawa 1999 for discussion).

3.1 Kuno's Empathy Theory

According to Kuno, *empathy* is the "camera angle" that the speaker takes to observe and describe a situation; more precisely, it is defined as "the speaker's identification, which may vary in degree, with a person/thing that participates in the event or state that he describes in a sentence" (Kuno 1987: 206). To illustrate, let us take as examples empathy phenomena observed in the use of (informal) verbs of giving in Japanese, *yaru* versus *kureru*.

(34) *Tarō ga Hanako ni okane o yat-ta.*
NOM DAT money ACC give-PST
'Taro gave money to Hanako.'

(35) *Tarō ga Hanako ni okane o kure-ta.*
NOM DAT money ACC give-PST
'Taro gave money to Hanako.'

Although these sentences would be translated into English in the same way, they are different with respect to the point of view of the speaker describing the situation in question (or, with whom the speaker is empathizing in describing the situation). In (34) the speaker is taking Taro's point of view, while in (35) he/she is taking Hanako's point of view. That is, when *yaru* is used, the speaker must empathize with the giver (subject) rather than the beneficiary (dative); when *kureru* is used, the speaker must empathize with the beneficiary rather than with the giver. In Kuno's theory this contrast is generally accounted for by assuming that *yaru* and *kureru* are subject to opposite conditions which are stated in terms of *empathy hierarchy*. Thus, *yaru* requires that the giver be placed higher than the beneficiary (giver > beneficiary), whereas *kureru* requires that the beneficiary be placed higher than the giver (beneficiary > giver).

Note in this connection that the giving verbs also mean "doing someone a favor" when they are immediately preceded by the (non-finite) *te*-form of another verb.

(36) *Tarō ga Hanako ni yubiwa o katte {yatta/kureta}.*
NOM DAT ring ACC buying {gave/gave}
Lit. 'Taro gave (the favor of) buying a ring to Hanako.'
'Taro bought Hanako a ring.'

In this case, too, the speaker's empathy must be with the giver, Taro, in the *yatta*-sentence and with the beneficiary, Hanako, in the *kureta*-sentence.

One interesting part of Kuno's theory is that just as we cannot see a scene from two or more different angles at the same time, so we cannot have more than one empathy focus in a single sentence; more precisely, "a single sentence cannot contain logical conflicts in empathy relationships" (Kuno 1987: 207). Bearing this in mind, let us look at the following examples with the first person pronominal *boku* 'I (male)' as subject or dative.

(37) *Boku ga Tarō ni tokei o katte {yatta/*kureta}.*
I NOM DAT watch ACC buying {gave/gave}
'I bought Taro a watch.'

(38) *Hanako ga boku ni tokei o katte {*yatta/kureta}.*
NOM me DAT watch ACC buying {gave/gave}
'Hanako bought me a watch.'

When *boku* appears as subject, as in (37), the giving verb must be *yaru*; by contrast, it must be *kureru* when *boku* appears as dative, as in (38). This is because another constraint is operative there to the effect that the speaker must place him/herself higher than others in the empathy hierarchy (speaker > others), a constraint called the *Speech Act Empathy Hierarchy*: "The speaker cannot empathize with someone else more than with himself" (Kuno 1987: 212). For instance, the choice of *yatta* in (37) and that of *kureta* in (38) place the speaker higher than Taro and Hanako, which is consistent with the Speech Act Empathy Hierarchy. On the other hand, the choice of *kureta* in (37) and that of *yatta* in (38) place Taro and Hanako higher than the speaker, but this is a violation of the Speech Act Empathy Hierarchy. Hence the unacceptability of *kureta* in (37) and *yatta* in (38).

By the same token, Kuno characterizes the reflexive *jibun* as an empathy expression on the basis of examples like (39).

(39) *Hanako$_i$ wa Tarō ga jibun$_i$ ni katte {kureta/*yatta} yubiwa o*
TOP NOM self DAT buying {gave/gave} ring ACC
nakushita.
lost
'Hanako lost the ring that Taro bought her.'

Here *jibun* is coreferential with the matrix subject *Hanako*, and appears in the same relative clause as *kureta* and *yatta*. While *kureta* is acceptable, *yatta* is not. Kuno accounts for this contrast by assuming in general that *jibun* is subject to the following "empathy constraint" (first proposed in Kuno and Kaburaki (1977: 636)): the speaker must empathize with the referent of *jibun* rather than other referents in the same clause. Given this constraint, *jibun* in (39) requires that the speaker empathize with its referent Hanako. But the verb *yatta* marks Taro (giver), not Hanako (beneficiary), as the target of empathy; hence its use results in a conflict of empathy foci. On the other hand, there is no contradiction between the empathy relationships required by *kureta* and *jibun*. I mention in passing that if *jibun* in (39) is replaced with the pronominal *kanojo* 'she,' both *kureta* and *yatta* are allowed; this is because third person pronominals like *kare/kanojo* 'he/she' are neutral with respect to the speaker's empathy.

3.2 Between the Speaker and Others

With Kuno's empathy theory in mind, let us come back to our hypothesis that viewpoint *jibun* represents the objective self of the speaker projected onto a situational subject. It is important to note that the objective self designated by *jibun* has intermediate characteristics between the speaker and others because from the perspective of the speaker it is placed on a level with others, but is nevertheless closer to the speaker.

We can then postulate a general empathy principle like (40) concerning a ranking of participants in a situation (cf. Hirose 2002).

(40) *Participant Empathy Hierarchy* (tentative)
When the speaker describes a situation, the participant to empathize with follows the hierarchy: speaker > objective self > others.

What this means is that if the speaker is a participant in the situation being described, he/she must empathize with him/herself more than any other participant; if not, he/she must empathize with the objective self (designated by *jibun*) more than any other participant. One advantage of this principle is that it unifies Kuno's Speech Act Empathy Hierarchy and empathy constraint on *jibun* in that it includes both the ranking of the speaker over others and the ranking of the objective self (designated by *jibun*) over others.

Another advantage of the Participant Empathy Hierarchy is that it can account for the acceptability contrast between *kureta* and *yatta* in sentences like (41), which poses a problem for Kuno's theory.

(41) *Akio$_i$ wa jibun$_i$ ga boku ni kashite {kureta/*yatta} hon o*
TOP self NOM me DAT lending {gave/gave} book ACC
nani yorimo taisetsuni-shiteita.
anything more.than treasured
'Akio treasured the book he lent me more than anything else.'

While *yatta* is completely unacceptable, *kureta* is quite acceptable. What is interesting about (41) is that *jibun*, which refers to Akio, occurs in the same relative clause as *boku*, which refers to the speaker. In Kuno's analysis, the Speech Act Empathy Hierarchy marks "boku" (the speaker) as the target of empathy, while the empathy constraint on *jibun* marks its referent (Akio) as the target; if so, there should arise a conflict of empathy foci. That is, Kuno's analysis incorrectly predicts that (41) should be unacceptable irrespective of *kureta* or *yatta*.[7] In the present analysis, on the other hand, the Participant Empathy Hierarchy requires that the speaker empathize with him/herself more than the objective self designated by *jibun*. This means that the relative-clause situation of (41) must

[7] Kuno (1987: 306) himself notices this kind of problem, suggesting in effect that the empathy constraint on *jibun* must be weaker than the Speech Act Empathy Hierarchy. But he does not explain why this should be so.

be described from the viewpoint of the beneficiary ("boku") rather than the giver (Akio), which is compatible with the empathy requirement of *kureta*, but not with that of *yatta*. Thus, examples like (41) provide empirical evidence that Kuno's two principles should be integrated into the Participant Empathy Hierarchy.

3.3 Empathy and Deconstruction of the Speaker

We have just seen that in the Participant Empathy Hierarchy the pronominal *boku*, which refers to the speaker, is higher than *jibun*, which refers to the objective self. However, this ranking of *boku* and *jibun* appears to be reversed in indirect discourse, as suggested by such sentences as (42).

(42) *Haruo wa jibun ga boku ni okane o kashite {yatta/*kureta}*
TOP self NOM me DAT money ACC lending {gave/gave}
to itteiru.
QUOT say
'Haruo says that he lent me money.'

Here *jibun* refers to Haruo, while *boku* refers to the speaker as reporter. The unacceptability of *kureta* in contrast to the acceptability of *yatta* means that in indirect discourse, *jibun* must be placed higher than *boku* in the relevant empathy hierarchy.

This kind of phenomenon was first observed by Kuno (1978a), who attempts to account for it in terms of the Direct Discourse Analysis, mentioned in Section 2; according to this analysis, *jibun* as it appears in indirect discourse (i.e. logophoric *jibun*) is derived from a first person pronominal like *boku* or *watashi* as used in direct discourse. Thus, (42) can be given a direct-discourse representation like (43), where *boku* refers to Haruo and *Akio* is assumed to refer to the speaker of (42).

(43) Haruo: *Boku ga Akio ni okane o kashite {yatta/*kureta}.*
I NOM DAT money ACC lending {gave/gave}
'I lent Akio money.'

This sentence is subject to the Speech Act Empathy Hierarchy, making "boku" (Haruo) the target of empathy. Since the acceptability judgment of (43) is exactly the same as that of (42), Kuno claims that it is at the level of direct-discourse representation that his empathy principles apply.

But the question remains of why *boku* should not be subject to the Speech Act Empathy Hierarchy when it appears in indirect discourse, as in (42); after all, if *jibun* in indirect discourse represents a speaker, so does *boku* in indirect discourse.

Our framework, on the other hand, allows us to account for such examples as (42) without recourse to the Direct Discourse Analysis. Recall from Section 2.2 that the speaker has two different aspects, public and private self, and that the reported speaker involved in indirect discourse is a private self, expressed in Japanese as *jibun*, whereas the reporting speaker is a public self, expressed as, say, *boku* or *watashi*. In this light, what (42) shows is that when a private and a public self compete with respect to empathy, the private self is given priority over the public self. In order to account for such examples, therefore, we have only to revise the Participant Empathy Hierarchy (40) in such a way that the notion of speaker is deconstructed into private and public self (Hirose 2002):

(44) *Participant Empathy Hierarchy*
When the speaker describes a situation, the participant to empathize with follows the hierarchy: private self > public self > objective self > others.

Given this revised version, we can say that the reason why logophoric *jibun* is higher than *boku* in the empathy hierarchy whereas viewpoint *jibun* is not is because the former represents the private self, whereas the latter represents the objective self. That is, the Participant Empathy Hierarchy (44) not only dispenses with the Direct Discourse Analysis, but also enables us to give a unified account of empathy phenomena concerning the logophoric and viewpoint uses of *jibun*.

3.4 The Duality of the Speaker's Objective Self

Kuno points out the unacceptability of *jibun* in sentences like (45) where it refers to a dead person (cf. Kuno 1972a).

(45) **Akio$_i$ wa, jibun$_i$ ga shinda toki, issen mo motte inakatta.*
TOP self NOM died when penny even having was.not
'Akio didn't have a penny when he died.'

In his empathy analysis, Kuno (1987: 256) accounts for this fact by proposing what he calls the *Aliveness Requirement*: "It is possible to describe an action or state with the camera angle only of a living person. (In other words, it is not possible to empathize with a dead person.)" In this connection, Whitman (1999) observes that the Aliveness Requirement applies also to the viewpoint use of picture noun reflexives in English, as witnessed by the contrast between (46a) and (46b).

(46) a. *The wind opened the album. Mary looked up from the floor. There on the first page was a picture of herself.*
b. *#The wind opened the album. Mary lay dead on the floor. There on the first page was a picture of herself.*

As pointed out in Hirose (2002), however, it is not necessarily correct to say that *jibun* cannot refer to a dead person. For example, if *Akio* in (45) is replaced with the first person pronominal *boku*, we get the following sentence, which sounds quite acceptable.

(47) *Boku*$_i$ *wa, jibun*$_i$ *ga shinda toki, issen mo motte inakatta.*
I TOP self NOM died when penny even having was.not
'I didn't have a penny when I died.'

Here *jibun* refers to the speaker, who is depicted as dead in the real world like Akio in (45). Of course, we are assuming that this "dead" speaker is alive in a fictitious world. But what matters to the Aliveness Requirement is not whether the speaker as locutionary agent is alive but whether the one talked about is dead, and this applies not only to (45) but to (47), where the speaker is talking about his dead counterpart in the real world. Thus, the Aliveness Requirement does not account for the acceptability difference between third person cases like (45) and first person cases like (47). Interestingly, a similar contrast is found with viewpoint uses of English reflexives: compare the third person discourse in (46b) with the following first person discourse, which is acceptable.

(48) *The wind opened the album. I lay dead on the floor. There on the first page was a picture of myself.*

What we need, therefore, is a more general principle or principles about the nature of viewpoint phenomena.

Recall here that the objective self designated by viewpoint *jibun* is the self that the speaker dissociates from his/her consciousness and projects onto another person. If so, it can be said to have both the "self as other" aspect and the "other as self" aspect. This duality leads to the following two principles, which are essential to objective-self projection by the speaker.

(49) *Principle of self-dissociation*
In order to dissociate themselves from their consciousness, speakers must get far enough away from themselves.

(50) *Principle of self-association*
In order to associate themselves with another person, speakers must get close enough to that person.

These two principles are motivated by our everyday experience that in order to see ourselves well, we need to keep ourselves at a distance, whereas in order to see others well, we need to get close to them.

With these principles in mind, let us now consider the acceptability contrast between (45) and (47). We will begin with the first person case of (47). Suppose, for the sake of argument, that there is a world after death, apart from the real world. It is then guaranteed by the principle of self-dissociation that the speaker in the world after death can observe him/herself in the real world, because he/she is far enough away from the objective self in the real world. That is why the speaker can talk about his/her dead counterpart in the real world, as in (47).

On the other hand, it follows from the principle of self-association that the speaker living in the real world cannot project his/her objective self onto a dead person, because the world after death is so far away from the real world that he/she cannot get close enough to that person. That is why the third person sentence (45) is unacceptable.

When we judge sentences like (45) to be unacceptable, we are tacitly assuming that the speaker is alive and talking in the real world. But if the speaker is a "dead" person who is talking about another dead person, or if the speaker is an omniscient narrator in a novel, then he/she can get close enough to the dead person, in which case the principle of self-association should be satisfiable. This is corroborated by the acceptability of the following sentence.

(51) *Akio$_i$ wa, jibun$_i$ ga shinde tengoku ni kuru toki, issen mo*
TOP self NOM dying heaven LOC come when penny even
motte inakatta.
having was.not
'Akio didn't have a penny when he died and came to heaven.'

As we can see from the use of the deictic verb *kuru* 'come,' the speaker of this sentence is in heaven, and is projecting his/her objective self onto the Akio who died and came to heaven. Unsurprisingly, the same also applies to viewpoint uses of English reflexives, as in (52).

(52) *John died and came to heaven the other day. When he got to the entrance, he was surprised. There on the wall was a large picture of himself.*

It is clear that the Aliveness Requirement is not adequate to capture the asymmetry in viewpoint between first person and third person cases, which is attributed to the duality of the speaker's objective self, that is, the "self as other" and "other as self" aspects.

Before concluding this section, it is worth noting that, as discussed in Hirose (2002), the notion of viewpoint is divided into two kinds, *personal* and *situational*: the former is the viewpoint from which to see persons (including oneself); the latter is the viewpoint from which to describe a situation. The principles of self-dissociation and self-association are concerned with personal viewpoint, the way speakers see themselves and others. On the other hand, the Participant Empathy Hierarchy, given in (44), is a general principle of situational viewpoint, dealing with which participant's viewpoint speakers take in describing the situation in question. The fact that the two different kinds of viewpoint are involved in the viewpoint use of *jibun* makes its behavior complicated.

4 The Reflexive Use

We now proceed to discuss the reflexive use of *jibun*, which serves to mark the reflexivity of one's action. Reflexive *jibun* must appear as the object of a predicate whose subject is its antecedent, as exemplified by (53).

(53) *Masao wa jibun o {semeta/hometa}.*
TOP self ACC {blamed/praised}
'Masao {blamed/praised} himself.'

In this section, we will see that the reflexive use is related to the viewpoint use in that it involves the process of objectification of self; that is, just as viewpoint *jibun* represents "the self that the speaker dissociates from his/her consciousness and projects onto another person," so reflexive *jibun* represents "the self that the agent of an action dissociates from his/her consciousness and treats like another person."

4.1 The "Subject–Self" Metaphor and the Objective Self

To begin with, notice that while the reflexive use is the primary function of English reflexive pronouns, it is just a derivative function for *jibun* (cf. Uehara 2003). The derivativeness of reflexive *jibun* is reflected in the fact that when *jibun* can be interpreted either logophorically or reflexively, as in (54), the logophoric interpretation (i.e. coreference with Masao) is preferred to the reflexive interpretation (i.e. coreference with Ken) without further contextual information.[8]

(54) *Masao$_i$ wa Ken$_j$ ga jibun$_{i/j}$ o semeta to omotteiru.*
TOP NOM self ACC blamed QUOT think
'Masao$_i$ thinks that Ken$_j$ blamed {him$_i$/himself$_j$}.'

The derivative nature of the reflexive use also manifests itself in the fact that English reflexives cannot always be translated as *jibun*. Thus, for example, physical actions such as hitting oneself and kicking oneself and psychological processes such as troubling oneself and bracing oneself cannot be naturally expressed in Japanese with *jibun*, as shown in the (b) examples of (55–57).

(55) a. *Ken {hit/kicked} himself.*
b. *??Ken wa jibun o {nagutta/tataita/ketta}.*
TOP self ACC {struck/hit/kicked}

(56) a. *Don't trouble yourself about that man.*
b. *??Anna otoko no koto-de jibun o nayamaseru na.*
that man GEN about self ACC trouble NEG.IMP

(57) a. *Ken braced himself.*
b. *??Ken wa jibun o hikishimeta.*
TOP self ACC braced

[8] This is because, as we hypothesize, the logophoric use is the most basic one for *jibun*. In this regard, very few Japanese dictionaries explicitly state whether it was the logophoric or the reflexive use that came first. But according to *Gogen Yurai Jiten*, an online dictionary of etymological origins of Japanese words (available at http://gogen-allguide.com/), *jibun* was first used as a first person pronominal in the ninth century (during the Heian period), and its reflexive use appeared in the medieval period (after the twelfth century). If this is correct, the historical development of *jibun* is consistent with our synchronic hypothesis. See Whitman (1999) and Mori (2008) for related discussion from a historical perspective.

The following questions immediately arise. First, how is reflexive marking by *jibun* in Japanese different from that by English *-self* forms? Second, why is it that *jibun* can be used with non-physical action verbs like those in (53), but not with physical and non-physical action verbs like those in (55–57)?

As argued in Hirose (2014), these questions can be answered by invoking what Lakoff calls the *Subject–Self* metaphor, according to which a person is divided into a Subject and one or more Selves (Lakoff 1996; Lakoff and Johnson 1999). The Subject is defined as the locus of consciousness, and the Self as the rest of the person, including the body, social roles, memories, past actions, and so on.[9] In this metaphorical model, the Subject is normally assumed to be inside the Self, in which case the Self physically corresponds to the body and psychologically to the mind; that is, one's consciousness is normally in one's body and mind. Now compare Lakoff's notion of Self with what I call the objective self. The Self in Lakoff's sense can refer to an objective aspect of a person,[10] whether it is located with or separated from the Subject. On the other hand, the objective self refers exclusively to that objective aspect of a person that is separated from the Subject and placed on a level with others.

Given this, the Subject–Self distinction can be largely divided into two conceptual models (Hirose 2014). One is the *Subject-in-Self* model, in which the Subject is located in the Self as a physical or psychological container, that is, the body or mind; the Self here is called the *container self*. The type of reflexive event depicted by this model is one in which the agent as Subject acts on his/her body or mind. The other conceptual model is the *Self-as-Other* model, in which the Self is separated from the Subject and placed on a level with others; the Self here is exactly what I call the objective self. This model covers those reflexive events in which the agent as Subject acts on his/her Self as if it were someone else. When we say the reflexive use of *jibun* represents the objective self of an agent, that means it agrees with the Self-as-Other model, but not with the Subject-in-Self model.

Let us now return to the examples in (55–57) and consider why *jibun* is unacceptable there. Beginning with (55), we note that when one hits or kicks oneself, one's Subject is usually considered to be inside one's Self, that is, one's body. This situation matches the Subject-in-Self model, but not the Self-as-Other model; thus the Self in this case cannot be expressed by *jibun*. The same explanation applies to sentences such as (58) and (59).

9 Note that "Subject" and "Self" in Lakoff's sense are used with a capital letter. As discussed by Lakoff, there are many English expressions about the self whose meanings cannot be adequately explained without the Subject–Self metaphor; just to mention a few, the semantic contrast between *If I were you, I'd hate me* and *If I were you, I'd hate myself*, and idiomatic expressions such as *You need to step outside yourself, I was beside myself, I got carried away*, and so on. For details, see Lakoff (1996) and Lakoff and Johnson (1999: 267–289).

10 An objective aspect of a person is "that which is observable by everyone," as suggested to me by Kevin Moore (personal communication).

(58) a. *Ken washed himself.*
b. **Ken wa jibun o aratta.*
TOP self ACC washed

(59) a. *Ken stretched himself out on the bed.*
b. **Ken wa beddo no ue-de jibun o nobashita.*
TOP bed GEN on self ACC stretched.out

As discussed by Haiman (1983) and Kemmer (1993), in body actions like washing oneself and stretching oneself out, the agent and the object acted on are viewed as conceptually inseparable. This is because, in terms of the Subject–Self metaphor, when these actions are carried out, one's Subject is normally taken to be inside one's Self. Hence the unacceptability of (58b) and (59b).[11] Similarly, in psychological processes such as troubling oneself and bracing oneself, one's Subject can be said to be inside one's Self in the sense that in these cases one's consciousness is usually in one's mind. This does not fit in with the Self-as-Other model, so *jibun* is not allowed in (56) and (57). In Japanese, the container self is generally denoted by words for body or body parts or words related to mind, as illustrated by the following examples.

(60) a. *Ken wa karada o aratta.*
TOP body ACC washed
Lit. 'Ken washed body.'
b. *Ken wa beddo no ue-de karada o nobashita.*
TOP bed GEN on body ACC stretched.out
Lit. 'Ken stretched body out on the bed.'

(61) a. *Anna otoko no koto-de {atama/kokoro} o nayamaseru na.*
that man GEN about {head/mind} ACC trouble NEG.IMP
Lit. 'Don't trouble {head/mind} about that man.'
b. *Ken wa {kimochi/ki} o hikishimeta.*
TOP {feelings/spirits} ACC braced
Lit. 'Ken braced {feelings/spirits}.'

On the other hand, in non-physical domains involving mental abilities such as perception, memory, imagination, and cognition, we can get outside ourselves and look at ourselves as if we were someone else; namely, the Subject can easily detach the Self and put it on a level with others. This is the kind of situation depicted by the Self-as-Other model, and the Self in question is precisely the objective self. The objective self is no longer a physical or psychological container for the Subject, but corresponds to abstract entities such as a mental image of oneself, social roles, memories, beliefs, past actions, values, day-to-day behavior, and so on, which the Subject can treat as external objects. Thus, when one blames or praises

[11] These sentences sound worse than those in (55b), because the degree of conceptual inseparability of the two participants involved is greater in the former than in the latter (see Section 4.2).

oneself, one's Self is construed to be separated from one's Subject and placed on a level with others. This is why *jibun* can be used reflexively in examples like (53). By the same token, *jibun* is acceptable in the following sentences, which all describe "self-conscious" actions in which we treat ourselves as if we were someone else.

(62) *Masao* *wa* *jibun* *o*
TOP self ACC
{keibetsushita/osaeta/hagemashita/sonchōshita/nagusameta}.
{despised/suppressed/encouraged/respected/comforted}
'Masao {despised/suppressed/encouraged/respected/comforted} himself.'

Unlike *jibun* in Japanese, English *-self* forms can represent both the container self and the objective self. This is because they are general terms for objective aspects of a person, so it does not matter to them whether the Self is located with or separated from the Subject.

4.2 The Double-*Jibun* Reflexive Construction

It is interesting here to compare the unacceptable sentences in (55b) with the acceptable ones in (63), which have the additional phrase *jibun de* 'by self.'

(63) *Ken wa jibun de jibun o {nagutta/tataita/ketta}.*
TOP self by self ACC {struck/hit/kicked}
'Ken {hit/kicked} himself by himself.'

As observed by McCawley (1972) and Aikawa (1998), verbs of hitting and kicking do not allow *jibun* as such, but do allow it when it co-occurs with *jibun de*, as in (63). We will see below that this *jibun de jibun* construction – call it the double-*jibun* reflexive construction – serves to reinforce the Self-as-Other model.

Generally, *jibun de* means "by one's own agency" and implies "without the help of others," as illustrated by an example like (64a). Its function is to emphasize the agent's independence and separation from others, so it may be referred to as an "emphatic agentive marker." When *jibun de* highlights the agent's separation from others, it also has a meaning close to "alone," which itself is expressed in Japanese by *hitori de*, as in (64b). Interestingly, *by oneself* in English has both senses of *jibun de* and *hitori de*, as shown in (65).

(64) a. *Ken wa jibun de kita.*
TOP self by came
Lit. 'Ken came by self (= by his own agency, without the help of others).'
b. *Ken wa hitori de kita.*
TOP one.person by came
'Ken came alone.'

(65) *Ken came by himself.* (= (64a) and (64b))

Now, what happens when *jibun de* occurs with reflexive *jibun*? To answer this question, we need to consider again the Self-as-Other model.

A moment's reflection reveals that *jibun de*, when applied to this model, emphasizes the Subject's separation from the Self, which is placed on an equality with others. Thus, the double-*jibun* reflexive construction creates more distance between Subject and Self than the unmarked, single-*jibun* reflexive construction; in this sense, it serves to reinforce the Self-as-Other model.

By employing the double-*jibun* reflexive construction, we can construe actions normally incompatible with the Self-as-Other model in such a way that they agree with the model; this is possible, of course, due to the above-mentioned function of *jibun de*. Thus, sentences like (63) evoke images in which one hits or kicks oneself as if one were someone else. Similarly, the unacceptable examples in (56b) and (57b) become acceptable when *jibun-de* is added, as in (66).[12]

(66) a. *Anna otoko no koto-de jibun de jibun o nayamaseru na.*
that man GEN about self by self ACC trouble NEG.IMP
'Don't trouble yourself by yourself about that man.'

b. *Ken wa jibun de jibun o hikishimeta.*
TOP self by self ACC braced
'Ken braced himself by himself.'

When we trouble ourselves or when we brace ourselves, we are not normally viewing ourselves as if we were someone else, which means that the Self is co-located with the Subject. In this case, as can be seen from the oddity of (56b) and (57b), *jibun* is not appropriate to use to describe the situation, since it represents the "self as other." But on the other hand, it is also possible in some cases to treat ourselves as another (even if unconsciously) in troubling ourselves or bracing ourselves. This situation can be described by using the double-*jibun* reflexive construction, where *jibun de* serves to distance the Self from the Subject, thereby placing it on a level with others. Thus, (66a) and (66b) imply, respectively, "Don't trouble yourself as if you were troubling someone else" and "Ken braced himself as if he were bracing someone else." Generally in these cases, as compared with cases of Subject-in-Self such as (61a) and (61b), one's worry or one's feelings are much harder to control, just as it is harder to control others.

In contrast to (63) and (66), double-*jibun* reflexive sentences like the following are odd.

(67) a. ??*Ken wa jibun de jibun o aratta.*
TOP self by self ACC washed
'Ken washed himself by himself.'

[12] The judgments of examples such as (66) are subtle and may vary among speakers. If so, that may have something to do with how speakers construe the psychological processes of troubling oneself and bracing oneself, namely, to what extent one's Self is construed to be separated from one's Subject in these processes, as will be discussed immediately below.

b. **Ken wa beddo no ue-de jibun de jibun o nobashita.*
TOP bed GEN on self by self ACC stretched.out
'Ken stretched himself out by himself on the bed.'

This is because it is rather difficult to conceive of a situation in which one washes oneself as if one were washing someone else, or stretches oneself as if one were stretching someone else.

To recapitulate, the double-*jibun* reflexive construction is an emphatic version of the single-*jibun* reflexive construction, reinforcing the Self-as-Other model.[13]

5 Conclusion

In this chapter, I have argued from a cognitive semantic perspective that *jibun* has three distinct but related uses – logophoric, viewpoint, and reflexive – which encode different selves. The logophoric use is the most basic of the three and represents the private self, that is, the speaker as the subject of thinking or consciousness, distinguished from the public self as the subject of communicating. The logophoric use semantically extends to the viewpoint use through the cognitive processes of objectification of self and its projection onto another. As a result, viewpoint *jibun* represents the speaker's objective self, that is, the self that the speaker dissociates from his/her consciousness and projects onto another person. The speaker's objective self has both the "self as other" aspect and the "other as self" aspect, and this duality is the very essence of viewpoint *jibun*. The reflexive use emerges when objectification of self applies not to the speaker but to the agent of an action. Thus reflexive *jibun* represents the agent's objective self, that is, the self that the agent dissociates from his/her consciousness and treats like another person. This is why reflexive constructions with *jibun* are semantically constrained by the conceptual model of "self as other."

It has been noted in typological studies that reflexives in many languages can be used not only as reflexive markers but also as viewpoint and/or logophoric expressions (see, among others, Culy 1997; Huang 2000; Oshima 2007). Japanese *jibun* is one such typical example. I therefore hope that this chapter not only advances our understanding of the polysemous nature of *jibun*, but also contributes from a cognitive semantic perspective to typological research into how logophoricity, viewpoint, and reflexivity are distinct but related to one another. In particular, it remains to be investigated whether reflexives in other languages that are polysemous like *jibun* have the same directionality of semantic extension, and if so, whether the same cognitive processes are involved there.

[13] In addition to *jibun*, Japanese has other reflexives such as *jishin, mizukara, onore*, and *ware*. For a detailed semantic analysis of them, see Hirose (2014).

18

Word Order and Extraction: A Functional Approach

Mitsuaki Shimojo

1 Introduction

Japanese is known for its structural flexibility, best exemplified by flexible word order, in spite of the canonical ordering of SOV, and by a high degree of extractability in complex sentences. Yet this does not mean that these syntactic phenomena are unconstrained. This chapter examines both flexibility and constraints and surveys functional approaches to word order variations involving pre-predicative and post-predicative (postposed) elements, and extends the discussion to constraints on relativization, topicalization, and wh-question formation.

Constraints can be observed at different levels. Some are observable in terms of whether a given sentence or phrase is grammatical or acceptable for speakers. Extraction constraints discussed in this chapter are typically of this type, as the acceptability can be evaluated relatively easily even when given without a particular context. Other constraints are better described as discourse preferences. A sentence may be grammatical or acceptable when it is given by itself; however, it may not be preferred or it may even be unacceptable in particular contexts. These constraints may be observable in a minimal discourse, such as question–answer pairs. However, such constraints are often operative only when they are examined in extended discourse. Word order variations in Japanese span this type of constraint when acceptable variations are differentiated in discourse and certain word orders are preferred in a given context.

Within generative grammar, constraints on word ordering and extraction are described by the theory of movement such that movement is disallowed under certain conditions. In functional approaches, on the other hand, these phenomena are related to the focus structure of sentences. The distribution of information in sentences such as pragmatic presupposition and assertion (Lambrecht 1994: 52) is closely connected with constraints on these phenomena, and, in particular, the placement of focus, which is the asserted part of the sentence, affects acceptability in word ordering and extraction. Furthermore, unlike languages such as English, Japanese allows extraction in a broad range of complex sentences, and the range of extractability correlates with flexible placement of focus in such sentences. At the same time, construction-specific functional properties are essential for proper description of extractability. Topicalization, for example, must hold a topic–comment relationship such that the sentence represents a comment about the topic.

The functional characterization as described above is essentially related to the way language is used in discourse because the focus structure of a sentence is based on context. Assuming that a sentence serves a communicative purpose in a given discourse, the assertion part of the sentence plays an important role in the purpose because it represents important information "which the hearer is expected to know or believe or take for granted as a result of hearing the sentence uttered" (Lambrecht 1994: 52). With the above premise in mind, the first half of this chapter discusses constraints on non-canonical word order, followed by discussions on extraction constraints in complex sentences.

2 Non-canonical Word Ordering

Japanese is canonically verb-final, and SOV is the unmarked order for a transitive sentence. It is in this basic order that a native speaker would find a sentence most natural without particular contexts. However, non-canonical word ordering is possible. This section presents descriptions of word order variations known as scrambling (Saito 1985) and right dislocation (Tanaka 2001).

2.1 Pre-predicative Ordering

With respect to scrambling, which involves pre-predicative word ordering, Japanese exhibits considerable flexibility. Shibatani (1990: 260) gives the range of variations for a ditransitive sentence as shown in (1).

(1) a. *Tarō ga Hanako ni sono hon o yatta.* (basic order)
  NOM to that book ACC gave
  'Taro gave the book to Hanako.'
 b. *Hanako ni Tarō ga sono hon o yatta.* (fronting of the indirect object)
 c. *Sono hon o Tarō ga Hanako ni yatta.* (fronting of the direct object)
 d. *?Hanako ni sono hon o Tarō ga yatta.* (fronting of both indirect and direct object)
 e. *?Sono hon o Hanako ni Tarō ga yatta.* (fronting of both indirect and direct object)
 f. *Tarō ga sono hon o Hanako ni yatta.* (fronting of the direct object)

Shibatani suggests that the awkwardness in examples (1d–e) is caused by more than one constituent being fronted. It should be noted that, while they may be awkward if given by themselves, these sentences are not ungrammatical and acceptability improves in appropriate contexts. In other words, non-canonical orderings are possible but restricted in the sense that they require specialized contexts.[1]

2.1.1 Non-canonical Word Order and Flow of Information

In general, pre-predicative non-canonical ordering in Japanese observes the principle that given information precedes new information (Kuno 1978a: 54). The principle is given in (2).

(2) Flow of information principle
Elements in a sentence that does not contain emphatic stress or morphologically marked focus elements are ordinarily arranged in the order "less important information first and more important information last."
(Kuno 1995: 222)[2]

Since Japanese is a verb-final language, this principle implies that most important or focal information appears in the position immediately preceding the verb. This is demonstrated by the examples in (3–4), assuming that no intonational prominence is placed on any phrase of the question.

(3) a: *Jirō wa Hanako to Bosuton ni itta?*
TOP with to went
'Did Jiro go to Boston with Hanako?'
b: *Un, Bosuton ni itta yo.*
yeah to went SFP
'Yeah, (he) went to Boston.'
b′: **Un, Hanako to itta yo.*
yeah with went SFP
'Yeah, (he) went with Hanako.' (Kuno 1978a: 52)

(4) a: *Jirō wa Bosuton ni Hanako to itta?*
TOP to with went
'Did Jiro go to Boston with Hanako?'
b: **Un, Bosuton ni itta yo.*
yeah to went SFP
'Yeah, (he) went to Boston.'
b′: *Un, Hanako to itta yo.*
yeah with went SFP
'Yeah, (he) went with Hanako.' (Takami 1995: 222)

[1] Non-canonical ordering has also been studied in terms of sentence processing. While sentence processing clearly represents an area in which constraints affect sentence forms, this chapter differentiates the processing-based constraints and grammatical constraints. See Miyamoto (2008) and references cited therein for sentence-processing studies in Japanese.

[2] Because Japanese is not a stress language, "stress" in (2) should be interpreted as intonational prominence.

The difference in acceptability between the two answers in (3–4) relates to what information is meant to be focal in the question, that is, important for questioning. The unacceptable answer in (3b′) suggests that in (3a) *Bosuton ni* 'to Boston,' which is in the immediately pre-verbal position, represents the focus of the question. On the other hand, the unacceptability of (4b) suggests that *Hanako to* 'with Hanako' in the question is meant to be more important, that is, the focus.

In addition, the examples above suggest a basic principle with respect to omission, given in (5).

(5) Pecking order of reduction principle
Reduce less important information first, and more important information last. (Kuno 1995: 219)

Example (3b) is acceptable despite the omission of *Hanako to* and (4b′) is acceptable despite the omission of *Bosuton ni* because these are not the foci of the questions. In contrast, the unacceptability of (3b′) and (4b) results from reduction of more important information instead of less important information. Also, (3–4) show that importance of information correlates with word ordering.

Given the discussions above, it is important to consider the difference between canonical and non-canonical ordering with respect to the functional characterization. In (3–4), although both (3b′) and (4b) are marked as unacceptable by the respective authors, (3b′) is more acceptable, at least for some speakers. In other words, for (3a) even without intonational prominence, it is easier to interpret *Hanako to* than *Bosuton ni* as the focus for (4a). Essentially, this contrast relates to the difference between the canonical word order in (3) and the non-canonical order in (4). Consider examples in (6–7) from Kuno (1995: 224–225). Both are meant to carry no intonational prominence.

(6) a: *Tarō wa yoru Naomi ni denwasuru.*
TOP night to call
'Taro calls up Naomi at night.'
b: ?*Ken wa asa denwasuru.*
TOP morning call
'Ken calls up (Naomi) in the morning.'

(7) a: *Tarō wa Naomi ni yoru denwasuru.*
TOP to night call
'Taro calls up Naomi at night.'
b: **Ken wa Erika ni denwasuru.*
TOP to call
'Ken calls up Erika (at night).'

Kuno indicates that (6b) is noticeably more acceptable than (7b) despite the omission of the entity which corresponds to the immediate pre-verbal element in (a) in both cases, and this contrast is due to the canonical word order in (6a). In (6a), *Naomi ni* in the immediately pre-verbal position is in the unmarked (i.e. canonical) position; thus, it is not required to be focal, and (6b) is rendered acceptable if the non-focal reading of (6a) is obtained. In (7a), on the other hand, *yoru* 'night' is in the marked (i.e. non-canonical) position which is immediately pre-verbal and therefore required to be focal. The relevant principle is given in (8):

(8) Markedness principle for discourse rule violations
Sentences that involve marked (or intentional) violations of discourse principles are unacceptable. On the other hand, sentences that involve unmarked (or unintentional) violations of discourse principles go unpenalized and are acceptable. (Kuno 1995: 211)

The "unmarked violation" is exemplified by (6a). For (6b) to be acceptable, the immediate pre-verbal element *Naomi ni* in (6a) must be non-focal, which violates the Flow of Information principle in (2). However, this violation is acceptable because (6a) represents the canonical order. In other words, the immediately pre-verbal position is the *default* position for a focal element in the canonical order and the other positions in the sentence may be focal, as in the case of *yoru* 'night' in (6a). In (7a), on the other hand, *yoru* 'night' is non-canonically in the immediately pre-verbal position; therefore, violation of the Flow of Information Principle is not acceptable, hence the unacceptability of (7b).

The Markedness Principle in (8) also predicts the observation in (1). Perceived unnaturalness in those cases in which two arguments are fronted is expected because those sentences represent greater degree of markedness and therefore require more specialized contexts to meet the flow of the information principle.

2.1.2 Preposing of Argument: OSV

The preceding section gave an overview of pragmatic properties related to non-canonical word order. This section focuses on preposed arguments with particular reference to objects in the OSV order.

It is common in discourse-configurational languages (Kiss 1995: 6) that preposed elements of a sentence exhibit pragmatic prominence such as topic or focus. Word order is often restricted by the position of topic or focus, hence, rigid focus structure, as in French, Italian, Sesotho, and Toba Batak (Van Valin 1999: 514). However, as shown in (9), the pragmatically specialized nature of a left-detached element (*yesterday*) and a preposed element (*what*) is observed even in English, which is considered to be a language of rigid syntax and flexible focus structure.

(9) *Yesterday, what did John give to Mary in the library?*

The critical property of the left periphery is that the left edge of a sentence is commonly ambiguous in terms of topic and focus, not only because both topic and focus may be placed in the left periphery of the same sentence, but also because the same phrase may have both topic- and focus-like properties. It is common across languages for a topic to represent a contrastive or switched topic, which has focus-like properties, and for a focus to represent a contrastive or restrictive focus, a specific type of focus that has some topic properties (Erteschik-Shir 2007: 48–51). Not all languages require a preposed topic or focus; however, in Japanese, a topicalized argument or adjunct is usually placed in the sentence-initial position, detached from the clause.[3]

Given the cross-linguistic observation outlined above, a question arises with respect to pragmatic properties of preposed (non-topicalized) arguments in Japanese. Such arguments are formally distinguished from topicalization of an object since preposing maintains the case marker, as exemplified by (10):

(10) a. *Tarō ga hon o katta.* (basic order)
NOM book ACC bought
'Taro bought a book.'
b. *Hon o Tarō ga katta.* (preposing of the object)
c. *Hon wa Tarō ga katta.* (topicalization of the object)

Ishii (2001: 97) shows that a subject wh-question is awkward if the object is preposed as shown in (11b), but if the object is referential with a demonstrative pronoun, as in (11c), the OSV ordering with a subject wh-phrase is noticeably more acceptable. This observation is expected if the object of OSV represents information which is less important for the purpose of the utterance than the wh-phrase, which is the focus of the question.

(11) a. *Dare ga okane o nusunda no?*
who NOM money ACC stole INT
'Who stole (some) money?'
b. *#Okane o dare ga nusunda no.*
c. *Sono okane o dare ga nusunda no?*
that money ACC who NOM stole INT
'Who stole that money?'

Ishii's observation is consistent with Imamura's (2014: 229) findings in his analysis of the Balanced Corpus of Contemporary Written Japanese.[4] Imamura measured referential distance (Givón 1983: 13–14) for objects in 3,273 cases of O[accusative]-S[nominative] sequence in the corpus and found the following: objects in 2,676 cases (81.8%) represent information given in the preceding discourse, that is, discourse-old information (Prince

[3] A topic-marked argument or adjunct may appear in-situ, and such topics are explicitly contrastive. Also, there are "base-generated" topics (e.g. *Petto wa inu ga ii* 'As for pets, dogs are good'), for which there is no corresponding topic-less sentence.

[4] See Maekawa et al. (2014) for detail of the corpus.

1992: 303–304). Among those, 2,600 objects (79.4%) are coreferential with entities within ten preceding clauses, and 2,449 objects (74.8%) are coreferential with entities within five preceding clauses. Furthermore, objects in 1,724 cases (52.7%) are coreferential with entities in the immediately preceding clause. Overall, these findings suggest the pragmatic prominence of these objects; preposed (non-topic) objects tend to represent continuing information from the preceding discourse.[5] This further suggests that preposed (non-topic) objects are functionally similar to a topic because the topic of a sentence normally represents presupposition, not part of assertion, and continuing information typically relates to the presupposition which is relevant to the utterance in question.

2.2 Post-predicative Ordering (Postposing)

While the basic word order in Japanese is verb-final, postposing of an element is allowed in spoken Japanese, particularly in informal speech. In general, post-predicative elements (which are structurally part of the preceding unit) consist of two types: those considered to be a speaker's afterthought ("pause type") and those considered to be part of a planned utterance, produced within a single intonation contour, typically without a noticeable pause after the predicate ("no-pause type"). It is reasonable to assume that the pause type is used for confirmation (Kuno 1978a: 68), resolution of ambiguity (Hinds 1982: 197), or a remedy for an incomplete utterance caused by the speaker's memory or production difficulties (Maynard 1989: 37). In these cases, the speaker realizes during production of the utterance that the hearer may not be able to comprehend the intended message without the added information. K. Matsumoto (1995: 244) reports that given information tends to constitute the final part of an intonation unit (which includes the preceding part of the utterance) and new information is placed in a separate intonation unit.

Our concern here is the planned postposing as it raises a question as to the functions of such postposing. A prevailing view is the principle of "important information first." Postposing is used to give recoverable or supplementary information (Kuno 1978a: 68), defocus familiar or easily deducible information (Clancy 1982: 69), and convey important or urgent information first (Simon 1989: 189). It should be noted that this principle of more important information first does not contradict Kuno's (1995: 222) Flow of Information Principle (more important information last), which was discussed earlier. The former states that less important information is placed after the predicate and the latter states that more important information is placed immediately before the predicate. Therefore, the two principles complement each other and capture the flow of information for a whole sentence including the postposed element.

[5] While continuing information may be considered topical, such information is not necessarily encoded as a topic phrase.

Given the range of characterizations above, relative importance of information claimed by Takami (1995: 228) best captures the basic property of postposing.

(12) Functional constraints on postposing in Japanese
The elements placed after the main verb are limited to those other than the elements which represent the most important information in the sentence. (translation mine)

First, Takami's principle predicts the unacceptability of (13b, 14b). The focus of the wh-question *dare o* cannot be postposed. Likewise, in an answer to the question, the element which represents the focus *Tarō o* cannot be postposed.

(13) a.

Hanako	*wa*	*dare*	*o*	*mita*	*no?*
	TOP	who	ACC	saw	INT

'Who did Hanako see?'

b. *Hanako wa mita no, dare o?*

(14) a.

Tarō	*o*	*mita*	*yo.*
	ACC	saw	SFP

'(Hanako) saw Taro.'

b. **Mita yo, Tarō o.*

In (15), the postposing is acceptable if the post-predicative element is the topic. The predication is more important than the topic itself for the purpose of the utterance. However, with the nominative marking (i.e. exhaustive listing *ga* (Kuno 1973: 38) in this case; cf. Chapter 13, this volume), the postposing of the narrow-focus subject is not acceptable.

(15)

Sekaiichi	*no*	*daitokai*	*da*	*yo,*	*Tōkyō*	*wa/*ga.*
best.in.the.world	GEN	metropolis	COP	SFP		TOP/*NOM

'Tokyo is the best metropolis in the world.' (Kuno 1978a: 70)

In all unacceptable cases above, the information expressed by the post-predicative elements is not recoverable, supplementary, or familiar; thus, the unacceptability is expected. However, as Takami (1995: 231) points out, postposing is often possible with the broad focus, where postposed elements are not recoverable, supplementary, or familiar, hence, encode important information.

(16) a.

Akegata	*yatto*	*umaremashita,*	*otokonoko*	*ga.*
dawn	finally	was.born	boy	NOM

'A boy was born finally at dawn.' (p. 219)

b.

Watashi	*itta*	*no,*	*kekkonshitai*	*tte.*
I	said	SFP	want.to.marry	QUOT

'I said "(I) want to marry (you)".' (p. 232)

Takami's principle in (12) predicts the acceptable postposing in (16) because it is reasonably assumed in these cases that the pre-verbal elements express more important information than the post-verbal elements. It is natural to interpret that the baby's long-awaited birth is more important and newsworthy than the baby's gender, and likewise, the speaker's action of saying is more important than what was said. Notice that in these cases, information expressed post-verbally is not recoverable, supplementary, or familiar; therefore, the acceptable postposing is not predicted on these terms.[6]

The properties of postposing summarized thus far have empirical support as follows. In Japanese conversation examined by Shimojo (2005, Section 3), post-predicative elements were commonly subjects (83 out of 110 cases; 75%) and only eighteen cases (16%) were objects. Because subjects are more likely to represent continuing information than objects (Walker, Cote, and Iida 1994: 6–7), postposed elements tend to represent more continuing, that is, given, information. Also, for post-predicative elements, the average referential distance was shorter, that is, more recently given, and cataphoric continuity was lower than for overtly expressed pre-predicative elements (pp. 83, 105–114). In addition, in 70% of the cases, there was no post-nominal marking for the post-predicative elements. *Wa* (topic) and *ga* (nominative) were used much less frequently (19% and 11%, respectively), and there was no case of *o* (accusative) (p. 203).

These findings together point to both anaphoric continuity and cataphoric discontinuity of post-predicative elements. In other words, information expressed post-predicatively tends to be accessible by the preceding discourse or possibly in the speech situation (hence in line with the recoverability/familiarity accounts), but simultaneously, tends to be discontinued in the subsequent discourse; that is, the information is relatively unimportant in the given discourse. Furthermore, the co-occurrence with omission of post-nominal marking supports Takami's principle. In the same conversation data, omission of post-nominal marking itself was associated with cataphoric discontinuity; therefore, the functional compatibility accounts for frequent absence of post-nominal marking for postposed elements (ibid.: Section 6.4).

3 Extraction and Subjacency

Non-canonical word ordering discussed in the preceding sections has commonly been described in the theory of movement in syntactic analyses. Extraction such as wh-question formation is a related phenomenon which has also been discussed in terms of movement.

Since Ross's (1967) discovery of the so-called island constraints, constraints on extraction as shown in (17) have drawn much attention.

[6] Takami (1995: 237–244) shows that the principle in (12) applies to postposing of noun modifiers and adverbial clauses as well.

(17) a. John believes [$_{NP}$ the rumor [$_{S}$ that Mary lost her cell phone]].
*What does John believe [$_{NP}$ the rumor [$_{S}$ that Mary lost __]? (complex NP)
b. John talked to [$_{NP}$ the neighbor [$_{S}$ who bought the house recently]].
*What did John talk to [$_{NP}$ the neighbor [$_{S}$ who bought __ recently]]? (complex NP)
c. John ate a sandwich after [$_{S}$ Mary made an omelet].
*What did [$_{S}$ John eat a sandwich after [$_{S}$ Mary made __]]? (adjunct)
d. [$_{S}$ That John ate the sandwich] was obvious.
*What was [$_{S}$ [$_{S}$ that John ate __] obvious]? (subject)

Beginning with Chomsky (1973: 247), there have been further reformulations of the original proposal and the constraints have been subsumed under the general structural principle of Subjacency given in (18).

(18) Extraction cannot cross more than two bounding nodes (NP, S) in a single movement.

While there has been much theory-internal debate with respect to the status of the subjacency condition (see Yoshimura 1992 and references cited therein), there have also been proposals external to the formalist's theories, such as semantic and pragmatic approaches (Erteschik-Shir 1973; Erteschik-Shir and Lappin 1979; Haig 1996; Kuno 1987; Kuno and Takami 1993; Shimojo 2002; Van Valin 1996; Van Valin and LaPolla 1997), cognitive and performance-based proposals (Deane 1992; Hofmeister 2007; Kluender 1990; Kluender and Kutas 1993), and parsing and expectation-based claims (Chaves 2013).

These studies claim that the constraints are sensitive to a range of factors beyond pure structural grounds. While the subjacency account is incompatible with theories that do not posit movement, there are languages without overt movement that display constraints similar or identical to those of subjacency. For example, Lakhota blocks wh-questions formed within a complex NP despite its wh-in-situ characteristics (Van Valin 1996: 36–37). The movement-based account requires covert movement in wh-in-situ languages (Chomsky 1986a: 152–155) so that subjacency applies in languages such as Lakhota. Wh-in-situ in Japanese has also been analyzed in terms of covert movement (Lasnik and Saito 1984). Unlike Lakhota, on the other hand, Japanese allows a wh-question in complex NPs and subjacency does not apply.[7]

[7] Besides Japanese, there are other languages which do not obey subjacency yet exhibit construction-specific restrictions and/or constraints under certain semantic and pragmatic conditions. These languages include Chinese (Jin 2013), Danish (Erteschik-Shir and Lappin 1979; Jensen 2001), Korean (Hong 2003), and Swedish (Allwood 1982).

4 Focus-structure-based Approach

For the discussion of functional approaches to extraction constraints, this chapter uses the focus-structure-based principle claimed in Role and Reference Grammar (RRG) (Van Valin and LaPolla 1997; Van Valin 2005), which is a monostratal theory and does not posit any movement operation.[8]

RRG combines structural and pragmatic grounds to capture both language-internal and cross-linguistic variations in extraction restrictions. The relevant pragmatic property is represented in the focus structure projection of a sentence, which indicates the domain of the sentence that actually represents or may represent the focus or pragmatic assertion (Lambrecht 1994: 52). The principle given in (19) states that an extracted element or a wh-phrase in-situ must function within the domain of a sentence which may represent a focus.

(19) General restriction on extraction constructions
The displaced element (or the *in-situ* question word in a language like Lakhota) must be linked to an argument position in the semantic representation of a clause within the PFD [potential focus domain] of the IF [illocutionary force] operator. (Van Valin 1996: 54)

With respect to focus structure for complex sentences, the cross-linguistic concern is to what extent the focus domain is extended into subordinate clauses. Languages such as Polish restrict the focus domain to matrix clauses only, and in other languages such as English, the focus domain includes certain types of subordinate clauses (Van Valin 1996: 49). In RRG, language-internal variation in terms of the focus domain is described structurally as in (20).

(20) The potential focus domain in complex sentences
The potential focus domain extends into a subordinate clause if and only if the subordinate clause is a direct daughter of the clause node which is modified by the illocutionary force operator. (Van Valin 2005: 275)

For example, an object complement clause, which is a direct daughter of a clause node, is within the potential focus domain (PFD), where a focal element may appear. In contrast, an adverbial subordinate clause, which is in the periphery to the core, is excluded from the PFD. Figure 18.1 shows the contrast between the two types of subordination with respect to the scope of the PFD, which is represented by the dotted line.

The cross-linguistic and language-internal observations in terms of focus domains correlate with extraction restrictions. First, languages such as

[8] In the present discussion of functional approaches, the term "extraction" and related terms such as "wh-question formation," "relativization," "topicalization," and "displaced element" are used only for expository purposes, without assuming any movement. Likewise, a gap in examples is used only to show the place in which the displaced element functions.

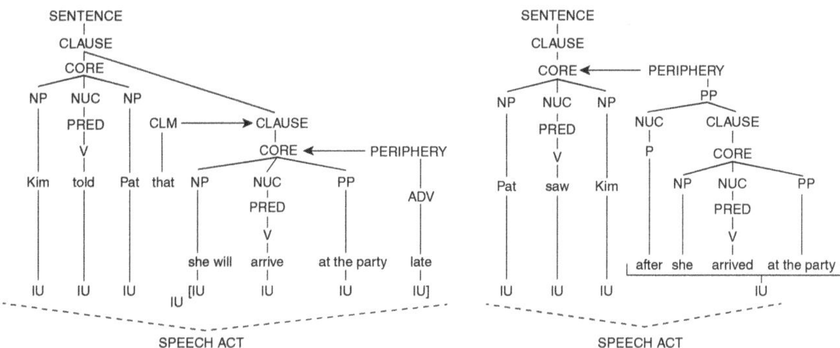

Figure 18.1 PFD in English complex sentences (Van Valin 2005: 214–216)

Polish, which restrict the focus domain to matrix clauses and prohibit extraction out of tensed subordinate clauses, are the most inflexible type. Languages like English and Lakhota are more flexible, allowing extraction out of a subordinate clause within the PFD. Thus, extraction is possible out of an object complement clause (e.g. *Where did John tell Mary that he will arrive* __?), but not out of an adverbial subordinate clause (e.g. **Where did John see Mary after he arrived* __?). Languages such as Danish, Japanese, and Swedish represent the other extreme of the scale because they allow extraction out of a greater range of subordinate clauses. The scale of cross-linguistic variations is illustrated in (21).

(21) Range of extractability: Cross-linguistic variations

Matrix clause only:	Polish
Subordinate clauses: direct daughter of clause only:	English, Lakhota
More subordinate clauses:	Danish, Japanese, Swedish

5 Extraction in Japanese

This section employs the focus-structure-based approach outlined above to discuss three types of extraction in complex sentences in Japanese: wh-question formation, relativization, and topicalization. While wh-questions have traditionally been associated with movement, there are varied analyses for topicalization. Hoji (1985: ch. 3) and Saito (1985: ch. 4) claim that a topic may be base-generated in the topic position (hence, no movement) but there is also topicalization by movement. The base-generation analyses follow Kuno's (1973: 254) proposal for base-generated topic constructions. Kuno relates topicalization to relativization, arguing that relative clauses are derived from a deep structure containing a topic sentence by deletion of the coreferential topic.

In the functional analyses, these three types of extraction share the focus-structure-based property as stated in the principle in (19). Topicalization and relativization are discussed together for their relevance to the aboutness condition, and wh-question formation is discussed separately due to the focus property of wh-phrases.

5.1 Possible Extraction in Complex Sentences

First, extraction which is unacceptable in English but possible in Japanese is exemplified by the following:

(22) Wh-question formation in a relative clause

Seifu	*wa*	*[dare*	*ga*	*sekkeishita]*	*dorōn*	*o*	*kōhyōshimashita*	*ka?*
government	TOP	who	NOM	designed	drone	ACC	announced	INT

'The government announced the drone who designed?'

(23) Relativization out of a relative clause

[seifu	*ga*	*[__*	*sekkeishita]*	*dorōn*	*o*	*kōhyōshita]*	*enjinia*
government	NOM		designed	drone	ACC	announced	engineer

'the engineer who the government announced (s/he) designed the drone'

(24) Topicalization out of a relative clause

Sono	*enjinia*	*wa*	*[seifu*	*ga*	*[__*	*sekkeishita]*	*dorōn*	*o*
that	engineer	TOP	government	NOM		designed	drone	ACC

kōhyōshita]	*hito*	*da.*
Announced	person	COP

'The engineer is the person who the government announced (s/he) designed the drone.'

Furthermore, the extensive range of possible extraction is exemplified by the following wh-questions formed in different types of subordinate clause: a noun complement, a sentential subject, and an adjunct clause (relativization and topicalization out of these subordinate clauses are also possible; see Shimojo (2002: 70–71) for noun complements and sentential subjects).[9]

[9] It has been observed (Lasnik and Saito 1984: 244) that wh-adverbials such as *naze* 'why' cannot be used in a complex NP, as shown in the following:

**Jon*	*wa*	*[Tarō*	*ga*	*naze*	*kinō*	*katta]*	*hon*	*o*	*karita*	*no?*
	TOP		NOM	why	yesterday	bought	book	ACC	borrowed	SFP

'John borrowed the book which Taro bought yesterday why?'

The unacceptability seems to have a bearing on the adsentential nature of such adjunct questions. Van Valin (2002: 169) points out that the answers to *who/what/how* questions involve some change in the original sentence but "the answer to a *why* question would normally be a *because*-clause which is added to the unchanged original sentence." This adsentential nature makes it difficult to obtain an interpretation which relates the matrix clause to *why* in the subordinate clause such that the former is immediately relevant to or about the latter (see Section 4.3).

(25) Wh-question formation in a noun complement

Jon wa [dare ga dorōn o sekkeishita] to iu jōhō o
TOP who NOM drone ACC designed COMP information ACC

utagatteimasu ka?
doubt INT
'John doubts the information that who designed the drone?'

(26) Wh-question formation in a sentential subject

[Dare ga dorōn o sekkeishita koto] ga yosōgai deshita ka?
who NOM drone ACC designed NMLZ NOM unexpected was INT
'It was unexpected that who designed the drone?'

(27) Wh-question formation in an adjunct clause

[Pātī ni dare ga kita toki] Jon ga deteikimashita ka?
party to who NOM came when NOM left INT
'John left when who came to the party?'.

5.2 Focus Domain in Complex Sentences

The focus-based principle outlined earlier predicts the relationship between the focus domain and a possible extraction site. This prediction is borne out in Japanese because the potential focus domain includes subordinate clauses. This is demonstrated by the following tests.

Only the asserted part of an utterance can be negated. If the constituent can be negated in a conversational exchange, then it is in the potential focus domain. Example (28) shows the negation test applied to a relative clause. The possibility of negation shows that the information expressed by the relative clause may be interpreted as part of the assertion.

(28) The negation test

A: *Seifu ga [dorōn o sekkeishita] enjinia o kōhyōshita.*
government NOM drone ACC designed engineer ACC announced
'The government announced the engineer who designed the drone.'

B: *Iya, misairu da.*
no missile COP
'No, a missile.

In English, an adjunct wh-question is ambiguous in a complex sentence in which the PFD extends over the subordinate clause (Van Valin and LaPolla 1997: 626). In (29a), *when* can be interpreted as modifying either the matrix clause or the object complement. However, ambiguity is not the case with a subordinate clause which is outside a PFD, as in (29b).

(29) a. *When$_{i/j}$ did Skinner say __$_i$ that Krycek would be at the missile silo __$_j$?*
b. *When$_{i/*j}$ did Skully interview the witness __$_i$ who saw the alien spacecraft in the silo __$_j$?*

In contrast, the corresponding Japanese sentences are both ambiguous as shown in (30), which indicates that both the object complement and the relative clause may be within a PFD.[10]

(30) a. *Itsu Kuroichekku ga kakunōko ni iru to Sukinā ga itta?*
when NOM silo in exist QUOT NOM said
'When$_{i/j}$ did Skinner say __$_i$ that Krycek would be at the missile silo __$_j$?'
b. *Itsu kakunōko de uchūsen o mita mokugekisha to*
when silo in spacecraft ACC saw witness with
Sukarī ga menkaishita?
NOM intervewed
'When$_{i/j}$ did Skully interview the witness __$_i$ who saw the alien spacecraft in the silo __$_j$?'

On the other hand, the PFD excludes the left-detached position (LDP) and the right-detached position (RDP), which contain a sentence-initial topic and a sentence-final (postposed) topic respectively. The focus domain includes the precore slot (PrCS), which contains a sentence-initial narrow-focus (such as an exhaustive-listing *ga* phrase), and the postcore slot (PoCS), which contains a postposed focus. (Examples of postposed topic and focus were given earlier in (15) and (16), respectively.) Figure 18.2 shows the layered structure of the clause with respect to the PFD.

Japanese uses post-nominal markings that correlate with the information structuring of the sentence. A topic marked with *wa* is outside the PFD. If a subject is not topicalized, hence within the PFD, it is marked with *ga*, whether it is a narrow focus (PrCS) or part of a broad focus (referential phrase (RP)). The direct evidence of a detached position being outside of the PFD comes from the observation that a wh-question word cannot be topicalized, as shown in (31).[11]

(31) *Dare ga/*wa sono uchūsen o mimashita ka?*
who NOM/*TOP that spacecraft ACC saw INT
'Who saw the spacecraft?'

[10] However, ambiguity depends on the linear position of the wh-word. If it is contained within the subordinate clause, it is interpreted as modifying that clause only (e.g. *[Kuroichekku ga itsu kakunōko ni iru] to Sukinā ga itta?*), and if it appears after the subordinate clause, it modifies the matrix clause only (e.g. *[Kuroichekku ga kakunōko ni iru] to itsu Sukinā ga itta?*).

[11] Miyagawa (1987: 188) states that the use of *wa* with a wh-phrase is acceptable only when it is contrastive such that an identifiable set of referents is presupposed in the immediate conversational context and every member of this set is exhaustively represented in the wh *wa* question.

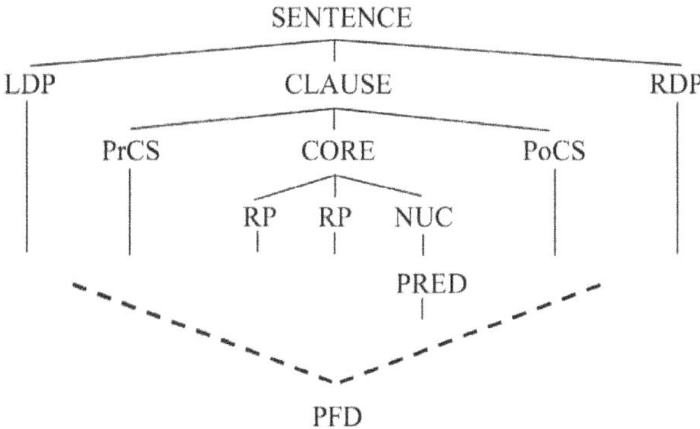

Figure 18.2 Layered structure of the clause and PFD

Also, as shown in (32), it is slightly more awkward to negate information expressed by an element which is part of the topic than to negate information expressed by non-topic, which was given earlier in (28).[12]

(32) A: *[Dorōn o sekkeishita] sono enjinia wa seifu ni*
drone ACC designed that engineer TOP government by

kōhyōsareta.
was.announced
'The engineer who designed the drone was publicized by the government.'

B: *?Iya, misairu da.*
no missile COP
'No, a missile.'

The functional principle given in (19) predicts that an extraction site is not permitted within a topic phrase, which is outside the PFD, and this is shown by (33–35). These topicalized complex NPs are not felicitous when no particular presupposition for the sentence is present (e.g. when the sentence is given out of the blue).

(33) *[Dare ga shuppanshita] hon ga/*wa yoku ureru?*
who NOM published book NOM/*TOP well sell
'Do books that who published sell well?'

(34) *[[__ shuppanshita] hon ga/*wa yoku ureru] joyū*
published book NOM/*TOP well sell actress
'the actress who books that (she) publishes sell well'

(35) *Sono joyū wa [__ shuppanshita] hon ga/*wa yoku ureru.*
that actress TOP published book NOM/*TOP well sell
'The actress, books that (she) publishes sell well.'

[12] The negation given in (32b) is only mildly awkward and this is predicted by the contrastive property of *wa*-marked topic, which contains a focal element, as discussed below.

However, the extraction in these examples is possible if the topic is intended to be overtly contrastive. In (33), the topicalized *books* may be contrasted with books published by others. The topicalization in (34–35) may be interpreted as contrastive with other merchandise or other activities of the actress. The required contrast for possible extraction further supports the principle in (19) because contrast inherently contains focus. Erteschik-Shir (2007: 48–51) states that contrast is contextually constrained to occur only if a contrast set is available. Contrast is represented by singling out a subset of a whole and separating it from the remaining subset; therefore, the singled out subset represents a subordinate focus. In RRG terms, a topic which allows an extraction site within cannot be in the detached position outside the PFD; it must be a topicalized focus since it is within the PFD of the sentence.[13]

5.3 Extraction Restrictions in Complex Sentences

5.3.1 Relativization and Topicalization

Despite the high degree of extractability, extraction in Japanese is not free from restrictions. Examples of unacceptable topicalization and relativization are given in (36) and (37), respectively.

(36)	**Sono*	*kuruma*	*wa*	*keisatsu*	*ga*	*[__*	*nusunda]*	*otoko*	*o*	*taihoshita.*
	that	car	TOP	police	NOM		stole	man	ACC	arrested

'The car, the police arrested the man who stole (it).'

(37)	**[keisatsu*	*ga*	*[__*	*nusunda]*	*otoko*	*o*	*taihoshita]*	*kuruma*
	police	NOM		stole	man	ACC	arrested	car

'a car which the police arrested the man who stole (it)'

These cases of unacceptable extraction are not predictable by the focus-based principle in (19) since relative clauses in Japanese are within a PFD as discussed earlier. What is relevant here is the aboutness condition, (38):

(38) Pragmatic-aboutness condition on topicalization and relativization
The sentence fragment following a topical element in the precore slot or a restrictive relative clause must be pragmatically interpretable as being about the precore slot element or the head noun.
(Van Valin and LaPolla 1997: 627)

The constraints are observed when it is difficult to obtain the interpretation that the sentence or the relative clause is about the displaced entity. In other words, when a subordinate element is relativized or topicalized,

[13] Topicalized foci are either in the precore slot if it is a narrow focus, as in (33), or a CORE-internal referential phrase if it is a part of a broad focus, as in (34–35). See Shimojo (2011: 281–285) for discussion of marked use of the topic marker, which involves a mismatch between the inherent focus structure of the topic marker and the contextually determined focus structure of an utterance. Such a mismatch yields a particular implicature due to focus shifting caused by the inherent property of the topic marking.

the intervening matrix clause as well as the subordinate clause (the extraction site) must be relevant to the displaced topic or the relative clause head. This general principle which relates to the notion of relevance is valid for extraction from a NP in English (Kuno 1987: 23).

(39) a. *Who did John write a book about?*
b. *?Who did John destroy a book about?*
c. *?Who did John lose a book about?*

Examples (39b–c) show degraded extractability. In these cases, it is difficult to interpret that the sentence is about the displaced element. As Chaves (2013: 308) puts it, while the action of writing is immediately relevant to the book's topic, destroying or losing the book is not. In RRG, this aboutness principle relates to the principle of focus domain in (19) because the verbs in (39b–c) are informationally distinctive, not being directly relevant to the book's topic, and therefore draw the focus to be the actual focus domain, preventing the object NP from being the actual focus (Van Valin 2005: 288–289).

The aboutness condition is further evidenced by the contrast in (40).

(40) a. **[keisatsu ga [_ nusunda] otoko o taihoshita] kuruma* (cf. (36))
police NOM stole man ACC arrested car
'a car which the police arrested the man who stole (it)'
b. *[[_ kiteiru] yōfuku ga yogoreteiru] shinshi*
wearing clothes NOM dirty gentleman
'a gentleman who the clothes that (he) is wearing are dirty'
(Kuno 1973: 239)

Example (40a) is unacceptable because the car is not immediately relevant to the action of arresting; a car would be directly relevant if it was the cause of the arrest. In (40b), on the other hand, the state of being dirty is immediately relevant to the person, who is in fact dirty. Put differently, "the clothes are dirty" may be taken as *a statement about* the gentleman, but "the police arrested the man" is not *a statement about* the car (Kuno 1973: 250). The corresponding topicalization of (40a–b) shows the same contrast in acceptability.

Because Japanese allows so-called gapless relative clauses, in which the head noun is relatable to the relative clause only semantically or pragmatically (Y. Matsumoto 1997), the truncation diagnostic in (41) serves as a useful means to see how relatable a head noun is to the matrix clause.

(41) The truncation test for aboutness
Relativization and topicalization out of embedded clauses are possible if the relative or topic construction is acceptable even without the embedded clause in which the extracted NP functions. (Shimojo 2002: 77)

In essence, if the displaced NP is relevant to the matrix clause, the intended relevance should be inferable or at least not contradictory even if the clause containing the extraction site is omitted. The truncated versions of (40a–b) are given in (42a–b).

(42) a. *#[keisatsu ga otoko o taihoshita] kuruma*
police NOM man ACC arrested car
'a car which the police arrested the man (who stole (it))'

b. *[yōfuku ga yogoreteiru] shinshi*
clothes NOM dirty gentleman
'a gentleman who the clothes (that (he) is wearing) are dirty'

The possible interpretation of the truncated version in (42a) is the stolen car as the cause of the arrest, which is not the intended meaning of the original (cf. 40). On the other hand, the possible reading of (42b) is consistent with the meaning of the original version.

Inoue (1976) claimed a subject bias in extraction, and N. Hasegawa (1985: 292) proposed as a structural principle that the relativization or topicalization out of a relative clause is allowed if the displaced phrase is the subject of the (lower) relativized clause and the head of the relative clause is the subject of the embedding clause. Although it has since been shown that this is problematic as a principle (see Shimojo 2002: 74–75 and the references cited therein), the said subject bias, if taken as a tendency, is not so inconsistent with what the pragmatic-aboutness condition predicts. Assuming a subject represents the target of predication, the displaced element functions as (part of) the target of predication if the displaced element is the subject of the embedded relative clause which is in turn the subject of the embedding clause. The example of an acceptable extraction in (40b) represents this structure.

However, it should be noted that the subjecthood does not automatically satisfy the required aboutness because aboutness is also affected by lexical choice. This point is demonstrated by the relativization in (43). While this example represents the optimal structure per N. Hasegawa (1985), the verb choice for the inner relative clause affects the extractability.

(43) *[[__ kaita/*yonda] hon ga eigaka sareta] Jon*
wrote/*read book NOM into.a.movie was.made
'John who a book which (he) wrote/*read was made into a movie'

Truncation of this example results in *[hon ga eigakasareta] Jon*. Possible readings of this truncation are John as the author/editor/translator, etc. of the book (as translated as 'John whose book was made into a movie'), not a mere reader, and this does not include the reading of *[[__ *yonda] hon ga eigaka sareta] Jon*.

5.3.2 Wh-questions

Unlike relativization and topicalization, wh-questions in complex sentences in Japanese are generally acceptable; yet restrictions have been observed in particular types of relative clauses.

(44) a. ?*[*Dare* *ga* *Hanako* *ni* *kureta*] *inu* *ga* *shindeshimatta?*
who NOM to gave dog NOM ended.up.dying
'The dog that who gave to Hanako died?' (Haig 1979a: 90–91)

b. ?**kono ko* *wa* [__ *Hanako* *ni* __ *kureta*] *inu* *ga* *shindeshimatta.*
this child TOP to gave dog NOM ended.up.dying
'This child, the dog which (he) gave Hanako died.'

Given the unacceptability of the corresponding topicalization, Haig claimed that a question must be about the questioned NPs, which essentially relates restrictions on wh-questions to the aboutness condition discussed earlier. In fact, Kuno (1987: 23) has proposed the topichood condition for extraction, which subsumes wh-questions in English such as (39b–c). However, restrictions observed in Japanese wh-questions are of a different nature from those in relativization and topicalization, which are conditioned on aboutness. Consider (45):

(45) a. **Sono yōfuku* *wa* [__ *kiteita*] *shinshi* *ga* *yukuehumei* *da.*
that clothes TOP was.wearing gentleman NOM missing COP
'The clothes, the gentleman who was wearing (them) is missing.'
(N. Hasegawa 1981: 281)

b. [__ *Nani* *o* *kiteita*] *shinshi* *ga* *yukuefumei* *na* *no?*
what ACC was.wearing gentleman NOM missing COP INT
'The gentleman who was wearing what is missing?'

The unacceptable extraction in (45a), and unacceptable truncation **yōfuku wa shinshi ga yukuehumei da* 'the clothes, the gentleman (who was wearing (them)) is missing,' show that the topicalized element *yōfuku* is not immediately relevant to the gentleman's missing. Despite this, the corresponding wh-question is acceptable, and this undermines the claim which relates wh-words to aboutness. In this regard, Van Valin and LaPolla (1997: 627–629) argue that the function of a displaced wh-word is focus, and therefore, it must function in the PFD. This claim is valid for wh-questions in Japanese despite the wh-in-situ characteristics. What influences extractability in Japanese wh-questions is lexical semantic factors which interact with the PFD.

As discussed thus far, the default range of PFD is language-specific. The structural constraint in (20) represents the default range of PFD in languages like English, while in Japanese, the PFD excludes only detached positions. Yet in both languages, the PFD interacts with lexical semantic factors, as Van Valin and LaPolla (1997: 630) state "lexical semantic factors may also influence the potential focus domain, both in terms of preventing a position in the potential focus domain from being the actual focus domain and of overriding the principle [in (20)] and permitting the actual focus domain to be in structural configurations where it would otherwise be impossible."

An object complement is part of the PFD by default since it is a direct daughter of the clause node. However, as shown in (46a), extraction is blocked by the so-called non-bridge verbs, which denote a particular manner, such as *murmur, whisper*, and *shout*, unlike bridge verbs such as *say, think*, and *believe* (Erteschik-Shir 1973: 84; Takami 1992: 47). In RRG terms, these semantically highlighted verbs shift the focus and reduce the PFD away from the complement clause, hence blocking the wh-question (Van Valin 1996: 50). The same argument applies to an unacceptable extraction when a bridge verb is used with a manner adverb, as shown in (46b). The manner adverb causes the same focus shifting, preventing the object complement from being the actual focus domain.

(46) a. *What did John say/*murmur/*whisper that Mary had bought?*
b. **What did John say angrily that Mary had bought?*

Analogous lexical semantic factors are responsible for restrictions on wh-questions in Japanese. However, wh-question formation is affected only in a certain type of relative clause. First, consider Y. Hasegawa's (1989) proposal cited in (47), with respect to different readings of a wh-question formed in a relative clause.

(47) Two possible readings of a wh-question formed in a relative clause
(i) Narrow reading: what is questioned, that is, the wh-phrase, is what is to be identified by the question.
(ii) Broad reading: what is questioned is NOT what is to be identified by the question. What is to be identified is represented by the relative clause head noun.

According to Y. Hasegawa, the interpretation depends on two separate factors: referability of the head noun and inherent topic-worthiness of the wh-expression. The former bears immediate relevance on the present discussion. Now consider the contrast between (48) and (49).

(48) Q: *[Dare ga kaita] shōsetsu ga yoku uremasu ka?*
who NOM wrote novel NOM well sell INT
'Novels that who writes sell well?'

A: *Murakami Haruki desu.*
COP
'(It's) Haruki Murakami.'

A′: *[Murakami Haruki ga kaita] shōsetsu desu.*
NOM wrote novel COP
'(It's) the novel which Haruki Murakami writes.'

(49) Q: *[Dono kyōju ga suisenshiteiru] hito ga saiyōsaresō*
which prof. NOM recommending person NOM likely.to.be.hired
desu ka?
COP INT
'A person that which professor has recommended is likely to be hired?'

A: **Suzuki-kyōju desu.*
Suzuki-prof. COP
'(It's) Prof. Suzuki.'

A′: *[Suzuki-kyōju ga suisenshiteiru] hito desu.*
Suzuki-prof. NOM recommending person COP
'(It's) the person that Prof. Suzuki has recommended.'
(Nishigauchi 1986: 74)

Wh-questions as in (48) have a narrow-reading, because the relative head *shōsetsu* is non-referential, and therefore, what is to be identified by the question is who it is that sells his/her novels, rather than particular novels which the writer publishes. On the other hand, wh-questions as in (49) have a broad-reading, because the head noun *hito* is referential, that is, what is to be identified by the question is who the candidate is, and this identification of the person is done by way of identifying the recommender of the candidate. Thus, the short answer, which supplies just the value for the wh-word, is awkward, as in (49). As expected, for wh-questions such as (49) to be felicitous, there must be a shared assumption in the context that there is a set of candidates and each of them is recommended by a professor. The purpose of the wh-question is to identify a particular candidate via identifying a particular candidate-recommender pair; therefore, the question is synonymous with *which*-questions such as "which candidate is most likely to get the position?"

The distinction between narrow reading and broad reading sheds light on why constraints are observed in some wh-questions. A narrow reading contains a single focus, since what is questioned, that is, the wh-phrase, is what is to be identified. On the other hand, a broad reading represents two foci because what is to be identified by the question, that is, the relative clause head noun, represents a focus of the question, and this focus element is additional to the canonical focus of the question. In other words, wh-questions which represent a broad-reading are functionally complex, and it is this type of wh-questions that are subject to restrictions.

Haig's example given earlier in (44a) is a broad-reading question with the referential head noun *inu*, which represents what is to be identified by the question; thus, this question is synonymous with *which dog died?* In this particular wh-question, there is an additional referential noun *Hanako* in the relative clause that makes the relative clause focused and prevents the head noun, one of the foci of the question, in the PFD from being the actual focus domain. Therefore, this case is analogous to the English examples in (46), where the default range of PFD is reduced away from the extraction site and the actual focus is shifted to a semantically highlighted element. This argument is supported by the fact that the wh-question in (44a) becomes perfectly acceptable if *Hanako ni* is not overtly expressed, as shown in (50).

(50) *[Dare ga kureta] inu ga shindeshimatta?*
who NOM gave dog NOM ended.up.dying
'The dog that who gave (Hanako, you, etc.) died?'

As we observe in (51), broad-reading wh-questions become increasingly awkward, if there is gradient acceptability for a speaker, as more referential expressions intervene with the foci of the questions. The gradient acceptability correlates with the degree of lexical semantic highlighting.

(51) a. *[Dare ga okutta] hon ga nakunatta no?*
who NOM sent book NOM lost INT
'The book that who sent had been lost?'

b. *??[Dare ga Tarō ni okutta] hon ga nakunatta no?*
who NOM to sent book NOM lost INT
'The book that who sent to Taro had been lost?'

c. **[Dare ga sono yūbinkyoku de Tarō ni okutta] hon ga nakunatta no?*
who NOM that post.office at to sent book NOM lost INT
'The book that who sent to Taro at the post office had been lost?'

Furthermore, if the wh-expression is kept adjacent to the relative head NP, the restriction is ameliorated even if there are other referential expressions in the relative clause. In (52b–c), the double foci of the question are adjacent, and therefore, the foci are contiguous as the actual focus domain and the preceding referential phrases in the relative clause are readily interpreted as presupposition, that is, non-focus within the PFD, and therefore, do not influence the PFD with respect to the actual focus.

(52) a. *[Dare ga okutta] hon ga nakunatta no?*
who NOM sent book NOM lost INT
'The book that who sent had been lost?'

b. *[Jon ga dare ni okutta] hon ga nakunatta no?*
NOM who to sent book NOM lost INT
'The book that John sent to whom had been lost?'

c. *[Jon ga sono yūbinkyoku de dare ni okutta] hon ga nakunatta no?*
NOM that post.office at who to sent book NOM lost INT
'The book that John sent to whom at the post office had been lost?'

On the other hand, the acceptability of a narrow-reading of the wh-question is not affected by additional referential phrases in the relative clause, as in (53b–c). The wh-question is not blocked in these cases because the relative head noun does not represent a focus of the question; hence, the additional referential phrase in the relative clause does not influence the PFD with respect to a focus of the question.

(53) a. *[Dare ga dasu] shōsetsu ga yoku uremasu ka?*
who NOM publish novel NOM well sell INT
'Novels that who publishes sell well?'

b. *[Dare ga Amerika de dasu] shōsetsu ga yoku uremasu ka?*
who NOM America in publish novel NOM well sell INT
'Novels that who publishes in America sell well?'

c. *[Dare ga Amerika de Jeri Pāneru to dasu] shōsetsu ga*
who NOM in with publish novel NOM

yoku uremasu ka?
well sell INT
'Novels that who publishes with Jerry Pournelle in America sell well?'

6 Conclusion

This chapter has provided an overview of functional approaches to constraints on non-canonical word order and extraction in Japanese. These phenomena share the focus structure as the basis of functional characterization. The use of non-canonical word ordering is associated with particular contexts such that most important information is presented in the position which immediately precedes the predicate and a post-predicative entity represents less important information. Given the verb final property of Japanese, postposing is particularly a marked option and it not only follows the principle of information flow above but also tends to be used under the very specific discourse conditions of anaphoric continuity (i.e. high topicality) and cataphoric discontinuity (i.e. low importance).

Extraction restrictions have commonly been studied with the assumption that such restrictions are structurally definable, as in the case of subjacency-based accounts. From the functional viewpoint, although the three extraction constructions discussed in this chapter represent different functions, there is a common property that the displaced element or the wh-in-situ must function in the assertion part of a sentence. While there is an obvious connection between a wh-element (which is focal) and assertion, relativization and topicalization share the property that "the clause in which the displaced NP functions is always *about* the referent of the NP" (Van Valin and LaPolla 1997: 627). In other words, such a clause functions as predication about the displaced element, and "predication and 'assertion about' are fundamentally related notions" (1997: 629). This functional principle is valid for Japanese, despite its radical difference from other languages with respect to possible range of focus domain. This offers an important implication for the universality of the principle, particularly because it is assumed (Van Valin 1996: 55) that the constraints are ultimately derivable from Grice's (1975) cooperative principle and the maxim of quantity.

The cross-linguistic variations in extraction are captured in terms of how deep into the sentence structure assertion may be represented. By default, a matrix clause is always within the potential focus domain; thus, it is a possible extraction site across languages. Some languages (e.g. English) extend the potential focus domain to those subordinate clauses that are tightly connected to the matrix clause, as a direct daughter of a clause. In Japanese, the potential focus domain is extended further to include other subordinate clauses; yet, even in Japanese, detached topic positions are excluded. This exclusion is an important corroboration of the functional principle since a topic does not represent assertion. In Kempson's (1975: 190) terms, a topic represents part of the pragmatic universe of discourse which is neither assertible, deniable, nor queriable without violating the quantity maxim. Extraction is allowed in a topic only if the topic is focal (i.e. overtly contrastive), and this conforms to the Gricean explanation.

Part IV

Grammatical Constructions

19

Nominalization

Masayoshi Shibatani

1 Introduction

Studies on nominalization, in both Western and Eastern grammatical traditions, have largely concentrated on lexical nominalizations, neglecting grammatical nominalizations, despite their theoretical importance and far-reaching implications to the descriptive practice. This imbalance is due to the fact that while lexical nominalizations (e.g. English *kill-er*) typically involve distinct morphology and their lexical status as nouns is relatively clear-cut, grammatical nominalizations (e.g. [I know] *that John recklessly shoots trespassers*; [I saw] *John shoot trespassers; John's recklessly shooting trespassers* [angered the entire community]; *To shoot trespassers* [is unacceptable]) vary considerably in form, some of which display structural properties similar to clauses, and their nominal status is less fully realized compared to lexical nominalizations (e.g. *a/the shooting* [of trespassers]; *those terrible shootings* [of trespassers], but not **a shooting trespassers* [is unacceptable]).[1]

The Japanese grammatical tradition is no exception to this general trend. In the context of Japanese there have been two historical developments that have contributed to the failure to properly recognize grammatical nominalizations and their roles in grammar. One is a terminological issue, which nonetheless has had a profound effect on the thinking of Japanese grammarians. One of the major functions of grammatical nominalizations is that of modifying a noun. Because of this, the monk Tōjō Gimon (1785–1843) named a nominalized verbal form *Rentaigen* (adnominal word). This term has gained wide currency in the name of *Rentaikei* (adnominal form), used today in the paradigms of verb conjugation, where the nominalized form is recognized as a conjugated verbal form along with finite (*Shūshikei*) and other forms. The term *Rentaikei* and placing *Rentai*

[1] See Lees (1963) for an early, comprehensive treatment of English nominalizations.

forms in the verb paradigm have led many grammarians to believe that these forms in both Classical and Modern Japanese are simply conjugated forms of verbs associated with the function of noun modification rather than distinct grammatical nominalization structures with different usage patterns, one of which is modification of a noun.

The other confounding issue has to do with a formal distinction between a finite verb form and its nominalized counterpart. In Old Japanese, there was a formal distinction for many verbs between a finite verb form (*Shūshikei*) and its nominalized counterpart labeled as *Rentaigen* by Tōjō. These two forms, however, began to merge in the eighth century and the merger of the two was completed by the middle of the sixteenth century, when nominalized structures supplanted finite sentences. This process, known as insubordination/desubordination in the current literature, obliterated the historical formal distinction between *Shūshikei*, for example *otsu* 'fall.PRS,' and *Rentaikei* forms, for example *otsu-ru* 'falling,' resulting in single modern forms based on the latter, for example *ochi-ru* 'fall-PRS/falling.' This loss of the formal distinction between finite and nominalized forms of verbs has led many grammarians to believe that grammatical nominalizations are just regular clauses, rather than independent structures or constructions with functions and syntactic properties distinct from those of clauses and sentences.

The two issues touched on here are, of course, related. The lack of formal distinction between finite verb forms and their nominalized counterparts in Modern Japanese and maintaining the label for the latter suggesting a modification function have had a profound effect on generations of Japanese grammarians. Had Tōjō given a more neutral term to what we consider to be grammatical nominalizations, such as *Juntaigen* (quasi-nominal), the term coined by Yamada Yoshio (see below), and had grammarians paid more attention to grammatical functions, both semantic and syntactic, than just to formal appearances of linguistic structures, which may vary over time and from one language to another, Japanese grammar would have had a countenance quite different from what it is purported to be.

2 What is Nominalization?

Nominalization is a *metonymic process* that yields constructions, including both words and phrasal units, associated with a denotation comprising substantive or entity concepts that are metonymically evoked by the nominalization structures, such as events, facts, propositions, and resultant products (*event nominalizations*), and event participants (*argument nominalizations*) or other concepts closely associated with the base forms. As products, nominalizations are like nouns by virtue of their association with an entity-concept denotation; both denote thing-like concepts, a property that provides a basis for the referential function of a noun phrase headed by these nominals.[2] Verbal constructions, including verbs, verb phrases, and clauses, on the other hand, are associated with relational concepts (time-stable or transient properties pertaining to an entity) and play a predication function. They differ crucially from nouns and nominalizations in not being associated with things and thing-like entity concepts and thereby in being unable to play a referential function.

Metonymic expressions may denote a variety of entity concepts that are closely associated with the concepts denoted by the original words or larger structures, and it is the speech context that determines and selects the denotation most relevant to the context per Gricean maxims of conversation, one of which (the Maxim of Relevance) requires speakers to be contextually relevant at the time of the utterance. For example, *the United States* may metonymically denote a variety of entities closely associated with the country by this name, but only a contextually relevant interpretation would be intended by the speaker and would be chosen by the hearer – for example, the sitting US president in *the United States decided to attack the Islamic State's forces inside Syria*, or a US women's soccer team in *the United States defeated China 1–0 to advance to the semifinals of the 2015 FIFA Women's World Cup*. Likewise, the lexical nominalization *half-pounder*, based on the noun *half-pound*, may denote a hamburger in a fast-food restaurant, or a can of tobacco in a smoke shop. While many lexical nominalizations, listed as nouns in the lexicon, tend to have more uniform denotations, grammatical nominalizations, which are created for the nonce, do not have fixed denotations, and speech context plays an important role in determining and selecting the denotation most consistent with the context.

3 Lexical Nominalizations

3.1 Sino-Japanese Agentive Formatives

The division between lexical and grammatical nominalizations is based on the lexical status of the resultant nominalizations, the former creating nouns[3] and the latter yielding structures larger than words. Like the English suffixes *-er* (*employer*), *-ee* (*employee*), and *-ist* (*pianist*), morphology often indicates the types of entities denoted by the derived forms. Japanese has the native agent-deriving formative *-te*, as in *hanashi-te* 'speaker,' *kaki-te* 'writer.' But more productive agent-deriving formatives occur in the Sino-Japanese vocabulary; for example, *-nin* (*kanri-nin* 'custodian'), *-shu* (*unten-shu* 'driver'), *-sha* (*happyō-sha* 'presenter'), *-shi* (*sōjū-shi* 'operator'), and *-ka* (*ensō-ka*

[2] *Denotation* refers to the relationship between a linguistic form and concepts connected with it, while *reference* is the denotation-mediated relationship between a linguistic form and a real (or imaginary) world entity.

[3] But see below, where we argue that one type of lexical nominalization produces sublexical compound formatives. We also suggest that lexical and grammatical nominalizations form a continuum without a clear-cut division between the two.

'performer'). Notice that while nominalization is usually understood as a process that derives a noun from a verb or parts of speech other than nouns,[4] this is not actually the case even in English, where the so-called agentive suffix *-er* derives nominalizations from nouns quite freely, as in *villager, New Yorker, left-fielder*. While these are not strictly agentive, they denote entities that are closely associated with the meaning of the base forms. Whether a derived form denotes an agent or non-agentive entity simply depends on the nature of the base form; verb-based nominalizations denote an entity most closely associated with activities, namely an agent, whereas noun-based ones denote other types of entities metonymically evoked in close association with the denotations of the base nouns.

Sino-Japanese forms such as *shusseki-sha* 'attendee,' *kussaku-shu* 'driller,' *sōjū-shi* 'operator,' and *katsudō-ka* 'activist' derive nouns denoting people from verbal nouns, which are nouns denoting activities by themselves and which form verbs in combination with the verb *suru* 'do'; for example, *shusseki* 'attending/attendance' and *shusseki-suru* 'to attend.' The change from verbal noun to noun is arguably a case of category change, although verbal nouns form a subcategory of nouns. But these noun-deriving formatives, like the English suffixes *-er* and *-ist*, may also attach to simple nouns yielding new nouns such as, *hikoku-nin* 'defendant,' *higai-sha* 'victim,'[5] *eiyō-shi* 'nutritionist,' and *shōsetsu-ka* 'novelist.'

A major difficulty in dealing with these agentive formatives is their category status. Since they do not occur as freestanding forms, it appears reasonable to treat them as suffixes. In the case of the native form *-te*, it is clearly related to the freestanding word *te* 'hand.' But there is sufficient divergence in meaning between the two to warrant treatment of *-te* as a suffix. The problem is more difficult in the case of Sino-Japanese forms, in which agentive formatives *-sha, -shu, -shi*, and *-ka* frequently attach to forms that are not free forms, as in *wa-sha* 'speaker,' *ka-shu* 'singer,' *gi-shi* 'technician,' and *ga-ka* 'painter.' Although the Chinese characters employed in these forms convey their basic meanings clearly (*wa-* 'speech,' *ka-* 'song,' *gi-* 'skill,' *ga-* 'painting'), they do not have syntactic autonomy. While it is tempting to treat these as frozen complex words, many of these formatives are highly productive. For example, *wa-* of *wa-sha* 'speaker' is involved in many complex words whose meanings have something to do with speaking, as in *wa-jutsu* 'speech technique,' *wa-dai* 'discussion topic,' *dan-wa* 'discourse,' etc.

Whether or not forms such as *wa-sha* and *ga-ka*, involving two bound formatives, are derived from base forms in a similar way to such forms as

[4] Cf. Payne (1997: 223): "operations that allow a verb to function as a noun. Such operations are called nominalizations, and can be described with a simple formula: V → N."

[5] Despite our labeling of these suffixes as agentive, there are forms marked by *-nin* and *-sha* with a patientive reading as in these two examples, where *hi* in the base forms marks passivity. See Ono (2016) for an extensive discussion of "agentive nominals."

kenkyū-sha 'researcher' and *ginkō-ka* 'banker,' whose base forms are free morphemes, is a challenging question that applies to a very large number of Sino-Japanese as well as native complex words, as we shall see below (Section 3.3). One real issue pertaining to the topic of this chapter is whether these are a case of nominalization or compounding. If recognized as compounds, we would be seeing a type of compound formation associated with meanings similar to metonymically motivated nominalizations,[6] while compounds in general denote a far greater range of meaning beyond what is metonymically evoked.

3.2 *Sa-* and *Mi-*nominalizations

In the realm of the native nominalization processes much controversy surrounds the suffixes *-sa* and *-mi* for adjective and nominal adjective roots,[7] as well as stem-based nominalizations to be discussed in the next section. Between *-sa* and *-mi*, the former is by far the more productive, attaching to all types of adjective roots, and to nominal adjective roots to a lesser extent.

(1) *sa*-nominalization
  a. Native adjective roots: *ama-sa* 'sweetness,' *uma-sa* 'tastiness,' *kanashi-sa* 'sadness'
  b. Sino-Japanese nominal adjective roots: *kirei-sa* 'prettiness,' *benri-sa* 'handiness,' *idai-sa* 'greatness'
  c. Foreign loan nominal adjective roots: *tafu-sa* 'toughness,' *hādo-sa* 'hardness,' *kyūto-sa* 'cuteness'

Nominalization by *-mi*, on the other hand, is very low in productivity and attaches only to a few dozen native adjectival roots.

(2) *mi*-nominalization
  ama-mi 'sweetness/sweetener,' *uma-mi* 'tastiness,' *kanashi-mi* 'sorrow,' *atataka-mi* 'warmth'

There are two issues pertaining to these nominalizations. One is the possible meaning difference between *mi-* and *sa*-nominalizations. As a comparison between (1a) and (2) reveals, a number of adjectival roots can take either *-sa* or *-mi*. In general, the productive *-sa* forms denote more abstract characteristics, states, or degrees, while *-mi* forms tend to be associated with more concrete meanings denoting more tangible states or

[6] Indeed, it is not uncommon that a language resorts to compounding where other languages make use of derivational morphology. The Colombian language Boro, for example, derives new words via nominalizing classifiers, as in *mútsɨɨtsɨ-ba* 'pear-apple leaf,' *mútsɨɨtsɨ -he* 'pear-apple tree' *mútsɨɨtsɨ-báju* 'pear-apple grove,' where English resorts to compounding as in the translations of these examples.

[7] We divide the class of *Keiyōdōshi* (adjectival verb) in Japanese school grammar into two classes in this study; nominal adjectives (*kirei* 'pretty,' *jūdai* 'important') take the copula *da* in a prediction function and *na* exclusively in a modification function, while the adjectival nouns (*shiawase* 'happiness,' *kenkō* 'health') may function as a noun, and take *da* in a predication function and *na* or *no* in a modification function.

concrete objects; for example, *tsuyo-sa* 'strength' versus *tsuyo-mi* 'strong points.' This difference is reflected in the appropriateness of the following expressions.

(3) a. *Amasa/?Amami o shiraberu.*
sweetness/sweetener ACC examine
'Check on the sweetness.'

b. *?Kanashisa/kanashimi o wakachiau.*
sadness/sorrow ACC share
'Share the sorrow.'

(4) a. *Kare no omosa/?omomi o hakaru.*
he GEN heavinesss/importance ACC weigh
Lit. 'Weigh his weight.'

b. *Kare no ?omosa/omomi ga yoku wakaru.*
he GEN heaviness/importance NOM well understand
'(I) understand his weight (figurative)/importance well.'

A contentious issue on the derivation of *mi*-nominalizations, for which there is no ready answer, has to do with the possibility that some of them are derived from verbs ending in a *m*-consonant via stem nominalization involving *-i/-Ø* discussed in the next section. There are a handful of verb stems that are derived from adjectival roots by the addition of an *-m* ending, as in *ita-m-* (*ita-* 'painful,' *itamu* 'to hurt'), *kurushi-m-* (*kurushi-* 'agonizing,' *kurushimu* 'to be tormented'), and *tanoshi-m-* (*tanoshi-* 'joyful,' *tanoshimu* 'to enjoy'). Nominal forms such as *itami* 'pain,' *kurushimi* 'torment,' and *tanoshimi* 'enjoyment,' therefore, could have been derived either directly from the adjectival roots *ita-*, *kurushi-*, and *tanoshi-* via *-mi* suffixation, as suggested by the renditions *ita-mi, kurushi-mi*, and *tanoshi-mi*, or from the *m*-derived verbal stems via stem nominalization involving *-i/-Ø* suffixation, as in the renditions *ita-m-i, kurushi-m-i*, and *tanoshi-m-i* similar to the derivation of other *m*-ending verbal roots that have no associated adjectival roots, for example, *kubom-i* 'cavity/pit,' *uram-i* 'grudge,' *hasam-i* 'scissors.'

3.3 Stem *-i/-Ø* Nominalizations

The stem nominalization in terms of *-i/-Ø* suffixation produces a high number of theoretically challenging nominal forms from verbal roots and stems.[8] Verbal roots and stems ending in a consonant take the *-i* suffix (e.g. *odor-* > *odor-i* 'dancing/dance'), whereas those ending in a vowel have no overt marker (e.g. *kake-* > *kake* 'betting'). While the following discussion dwells on derivations based on verbal roots, this process applies to derived verbal stems as well, for example, *nak-ase* (cry-CAUS) and *ijime-rare* (bully-

[8] This derivation possibly applies to adjective roots, yielding nouns such as *aka* 'red color,' *shiro* 'white color,' *waru* 'a bad person,' *waka* 'a young lord/young fellow,' which occur both independently as nouns and as compound formatives like nominalized forms based on verbal roots. See Section 4.1 for a related discussion on these.

PASS) as found in the compounds *nakase-dokoro* 'scene to make the audience cry' and *ijimerare-kko* 'child prone to be bullied.'

Major issues involved in this highly productive process revolve around the lexical status of derived nominals. While the derivation itself appears to apply to a great many native verbal roots, there are severe restrictions on the use of many of the resulting nominals. Nishio (1961), a seminal paper on this topic, and subsequent studies (e.g. Shin 2013) identify three groups on the basis of whether or not they can function as freestanding nouns.[9]

(5) a. Freestanding forms: *ijime* 'bullying,' *asobi* 'playing,' *tsuri* 'fishing,' *kanashimi* 'sorrow'
   b. Semi-freestanding forms – those that can be used as a freestanding noun only in restricted syntactic environments such as modification context: *(yoi) hataraki* '(good) work,' *(hōchō no) kire* 'sharpness (of a kitchen knife),' *(kizu no) naori* 'healing (of a wound)'
   c. Bound forms – those that can function only as members of compounds: *(hi)-yake* '(sun) burn,' *(haya)-oki* '(early) rising,' *ochi-(ba)* 'falling (leaf)'

Differences in the usage patterns are illustrated below:

(6) a. Freestanding form: *ijime* 'bullying'

Ijime *o* *yame-ro.*
bullying ACC stop-IMP
'Stop bullying.'

b. Semi-freestanding form: *hataraki* 'working'

**Hataraki* *o* *kitai* *shiteiru* *yo.*
work ACC expectation doing SFP
Lit. '(I) am expecting a work, you know.'

b′. *Ii* *hataraki o kitai shiteiru yo.*
good
'(I) am expecting a good work (from you), you know.'

c. Bound form: *kae* 'changing'

**Kae* *o* *shita.*
changing ACC did
'(We) did changing.'

[9] Nishio (1961) mentions a possibility that these stem nominalizations result from the so-called *Ren'yōkei* (adverbal) form of verbs via a conversion process, recognizing at the same time that *Ren'yōkei* forms themselves were possibly nominalizations in their origin. Yumoto (2016) follows this suggestion without offering any evidence for the correctness of the conversion analysis or for her assumption that forms such as *dashi-ire* 'putting in and taking out' have the internal structure like $[[V]_{VN}\text{-}[V]_{VN}]_{VN}$ (see the relevant discussions in the main text below). This chapter considers the basic function of the *-i/-Ø* suffixation to be a nominalization process that was once more prevalent applying to both stems and phrasal units (see Section 4.1) and that continues to function in Modern Japanese as a stem-based lexical nominalization process that directly captures the relationship between forms like *warau* 'to laugh' such as *warai* 'laughter' and *ageru* 'to raise' such as *(suso) age* (hemline raising) 'hemming.' As for so-called *Ren'yōkei* forms, we analyze them as an adverbal-use of stem nominalizations, just as *Rentaikei* (adnominal) forms are no more than a modification-use of grammatical argument nominalizations (see Section 5).

c′. *Seki no kae o shita.
seat GEN
'(We) did changing of the seats.'

c″. Seki-gae o shita.
seat-changing
'(We) did seat-changing (in a classroom).'

A major function of nominals derived by the stem nominalization is forming compounds, in which both constituents of the compounds may be derived nominals, as in (7a), or just one of them may be such a form, as in (7b), where the first constituents are regular nouns and the second are derived nominals, and as in (7c), in which the first constituents are derived nominals and the second regular nouns.

(7) a. *tachi-yomi* 'standing-reading,' *tsumami-gui* 'picking-eating,' *kiri-uri* 'cutting-selling'
b. *yuki-doke* 'snow-melting,' *ara-sagashi* 'flaw-searching,' *hige-sori* 'beard-shaving'
c. *yomi-mono* 'reading-thing,' *uke-zara* 'receiving-plate,' *kaeri-jitaku* 'returning-preparation'

Notice that forms in (7a) do not have idiomatic complex verbs associated with them (**tachi-yomu* 'standing-read,' **tsumami-guu* 'picking-eat,' **kiri-uru* 'cutting-sell').[10]

While the process of compound formation itself is not nominalization, the following discussions center on these compounds because of the important role that derived nominals play in this process. Derived nominals play a role both compound internally and externally. Those compounds that contain derived nominals internally as their constituent members must be distinguished from cases where compound verbs as a whole undergo nominalization, as in the following forms, which look similar to the forms in (7a):

(8) *tabe-aruki* 'strolling around for eating' (< $[\text{tabe-aruku}]_V$ 'eating-walk/to stroll around while eating here and there'), *mi-mawari* 'patrolling' (< $[\text{mi-mawaru}]_V$ 'seeing-go.round/to go around checking on things'), *yobi-modoshi* (< $[\text{yobi-modosu}]_V$ 'calling-return/to call back')

Both simple and compound forms of nominalizations under discussion acquire the function of naming the following types of concepts, all derived metonymically from the lexical meanings of the base forms (plus those of the partner constituents in the case of compounds):

(9) a. Process/Activity: *nagare* 'flowing,' *ugoki* 'movement,' *ake-shime* 'opening and closing,' *mawashi-yomi* (rounding-reading) 'reading by circulating reading materials in a group,' *yama-nobori* 'mountain climbing,' *hito-goroshi* (person-killing) 'manslaughter'

[10] Google search yields some forms like these, but their low frequency compared with genuine compound verbs in (8) indicates that some speakers sporadically apply back formation to derive these.

b. State/Characteristic person: *hare* 'fine weather,' *yū-yake* (evening-burning) 'sunset glow,' *jikan-gire* 'time expiration,' *ame-agari* (rain-stopping) 'after the rain,' *hanashi-zuki* (talk-liking) 'a talkative person,' *Tōkyō-umare* 'a Tokyo-born'
c. Agent/Natural force: *suri* 'pick pocket,' *tasuke* 'helper,' *hito-goroshi* 'killer,' *uso-tsuki* (lie-telling) 'liar,' *arashi* 'storm,' *hubuki* 'snow storm'
d. Instrument/Chemical agent: *hasami* 'scissors,' *hakari* 'scale,' *neji-mawashi* 'screwdriver,' *tsume-kiri* 'nail cutter,' *ha-migaki* 'tooth paste,' *shimi-nuki* 'stain remover'
e. Patient: *yatoi* 'employee,' *tsukai* 'errand runner,' *tsumami* 'what is picked/hors d'oeuvre,' *tsure* 'one taken along/companion'
f. Resultant product: *kōri* 'ice,' *kasumi* 'haze,' *age* 'thin fried-tofu,' *kan-gae* 'thought,' *kashi* 'loan,' *shirase* 'message'
g. Game name: *tako-age* 'kite flying,' *karuta-tori* 'playing Japanese cards,' *nawa-tobi* 'rope skipping'
h. Sports technique: *seoi-nage* (Jūdō), *ōsoto-gari* (Jūdō), *uwate-nage* (Sumō), *oshi-dashi* (Sumō)
i. Location: *hanare* 'detached room/house,' *nagashi* 'sink,' *watashi* 'landing pier'

Reflecting their entity-denotation function, freestanding forms, both simple and compound, behave like other basic nouns syntactically, such as heading an NP functioning as a subject or object and modifying another noun together with the particle *no*. Of these nouns, compound forms that denote activities behave like members of the verbal noun subclass, which, in addition to functioning as nouns, verbalize in compound with the verb *suru* 'do.' Observe the parallelism between the activity-denoting compounds *uo-tsuri* (fish-hanging) 'fishing' and the Sino-Japanese verbal noun *benkyō* 'study' below:

(10) Verbal noun

a. *Benkyō wa tanoshii.*
study TOP fun
'Studying is fun.'

b. *Tarō wa benkyō o tanoshinde iru.*
TOP study ACC enjoy.GER is
'Taro is enjoying studying.'

c. *Tarō wa asokode benkyō-shite iru.*
TOP there study-do.GER is
'Taro is studying there.'

(11) Compound verbal noun

a. *Uo-tsuri wa tanoshii.*
fish-hanging TOP fun
'Fishing is fun.'

b. *Tarō wa uo-tsuri o tanoshinde iru.*
TOP fish-hanging ACC enjoy.GER is
'Taro is enjoying fishing.'

c. *Tarō wa asokode uo-tsuri-shite iru.*
TOP there fish-hanging-do.GER is
'Taro is fishing there.'

On the other hand, freestanding non-compound forms like *sawagi* 'commotion,' *nerai* 'aim,' and *tomari* 'overnight stay,' though based on action verbal roots, do not verbalize with *suru*. Many of these, however, allow the verbalized forms when they are compounded. *Asobi* 'playing,' for example, functions as a freestanding noun (12a), but its verbalized version *asobi-suru* does not occur. When compounded with another form, it yields a verbal noun and allows a *suru* verb form, as in (12d).

(12) a. *Asobi wa kodomo ni mo otona ni mo jūyō da.*
playing TOP child for also adult for also important COP
'Playing is important for both children and adults.'

b. **Tarō wa asobi-shite iru.*
TOP playing-do.GER is
Lit. 'Taro is doing playing.'

c. *Tarō wa asonde iru.*
TOP play.GER is
'Taro is playing.'

d. *Tarō wa saikin yo-asobi-shite iru.*
TOP lately night-playing-do.GER is
'Taro is lately staying out late at night.'

Kageyama (1993), an important and influential work in this area of research, analyzes the stem nominalization as a process deriving verbal nouns from verbs, which, he claims, involves the following change in the feature specifications of lexical entries:

(13) *yomu* 'to read' [-N, +V, -A] – Nominalization → *yomi* 'reading' [+N, +V, -A]

This analysis, followed by some subsequent studies such as Yumoto (2016), entails a few stipulations. First, activity-denoting nominalized forms, while treated as verbal nouns by Kageyama, do not allow *suru*-verbalized forms in their non-compound, simple form, as seen in (12b). Kageyama (1993: 182–183) suggests that their verbalization yielding forms like *asobi-suru* 'do playing,' *yomi-suru* 'do reading,' and *nobori-suru* 'do climbing' is blocked because there already exist basic verbs with the same meaning, namely *asobu* 'to play,' *yomu* 'to read,' and *noboru* 'to climb' (see (12c)).

Such a blocking account, however, is suspect since there are cases where the *suru*-verbalization is permitted even when more basic synonymous words exist. We noted in (8) that there are compound verbs that yield nominalizations, as in *tabe-aruku* 'stroll around eating here and there' → *tabe-aruk-i* 'strolling around eating here and there.' These compound-based nominalizations, as long as they denote activities, can easily combine with *suru*, yielding verb forms despite their meanings are essentially the same as those of the original compound verbs: *tabe-aruku* → *tabe-aruki* → *tabe-aruki-suru* 'do strolling around eating here and there,' *mi-mawaru* → *mi-mawari* → *mi-mawari-suru* 'do going round checking,' *ake-watasu* → *ake-watashi* → *ake-watashi-suru* 'do handing over after vacating a property,' etc.[11] The simple answer to Kagayama's problem about ill-formed expressions like **asobi-suru* 'do playing,' **yomi-suru* 'do reading' is simply that *asobi*, *yomi*, etc. are not verbal nouns by themselves (see below).

A much more fundamental problem with Kageyama's analysis has to do with his assumption that the basic function of the stem nominalization is a derivation of nouns with an activity sense, namely verbal nouns. This is a curious position considering that this process yields forms with a variety of meanings as shown in (9); those that denote activities are just a subset of the totality of the nominalizations under consideration. Kageyama considers those forms denoting concepts other than activities to have been derived secondarily from verbal nouns via what he calls *meaning expansion* that has the effect of turning the feature specification of verbal nouns into that of simple nouns; that is, [+N, +V, -A] → [+N, -V, -A]. However, this does not apply to forms denoting states or things/people associated with them, because they do not obtain from action verb roots via verbal nouns – they never form a verbal noun by themselves or in compound; for example, *kumori* 'cloudy weather,' *ame-agari* 'after the rain,' *katamari* 'lump,' *Tōkyō-sodachi* 'one grew up in Tokyo.'

Kageyama's analysis seems to be motivated by two considerations. One is his impression that nominalized forms denoting activities are more prevalent and are seemingly more systematically related to the meanings of the base verb roots. But this is also true with the forms denoting states, as in (9b), which are just as numerous and are fairly systematically related in meaning to change-of-state process verbs. The difference in the size of word groups is a function of our worldly experiences and a need for naming them, not what grammar determines. It is only subsets of routinely occurring states, processes, and activities that involve a type of people constantly associated with them, that produce resultant objects, that require special tools, and that take place in particular locations or in specific games or sporting events. The relative scarcity of certain types of nominalized forms such as those denoting instruments and locations is

[11] Many compound verb forms of this type do not yield activity-denoting stem nominalizations, for example, *tazune-aruku* 'walk around making inquiries' > **tazune-aruki*. These naturally do not yield *suru* verbal forms, for example, **tazune-aruki-suru*. There are only nine hits in Google searches for the form *tazune-aruki o* (walk-around-making-inquiries ACC) and three hits for *tazune-aruki ga* (walk-around-making-inquiries NOM), and one hit for *tazune-aruki-suru* (do walk-around-making-inquiries) and two different hits for *tazune-aruki-shita* (did walk-around-making-inquiries).

simply a reflection of the paucity of the types of activities name-worthy for ordinary people that are associated with a specialized tool or a specially designated place.

Linguistic signs – words and sentences – are connections between a series of speech sounds (or structure/form) and a concept. When a form involving a nominalization like [sake-nomi] (wine-drinking) is associated with the concept "drinker," we have a word with such a connection, and the meaning of the word is defined in terms of this connection. There are other compounds involving presumably the same nominalized form [nomi] (drinking). The form [ikki-nomi] (one gulp-drinking) 'drinking in one gulp' has a connection with a concept of drinking alcoholic beverage in one gulp. This word, denoting an activity concept, verbalizes in combination with *suru*. The words [sake-nomi] and [ikki-nomi] are two different words with separate connections with two different concepts, an agentive concept for the former and an activity concept for the latter. There is no reason to assume that the former is secondarily derived from the form-activity connection.

The same is the case even when a single form displays different types of form–concept connection. Take [tachi-nomi] (standing-drinking), which is connected with the activity concept of drinking while standing. There are places dedicated to such an activity. It appears that some people are beginning to establish a connection between the form [tachi-nomi] with the concept of establishments that let customers drink while standing (i.e. folksy stand bars), as seen in an expression like *tachi-nomi ni yotte kaeru* '(I) go home after stopping at a *tachi-nomi* place.' While it appears that the noun [tachi-nomi] denoting a location is being newly formed, it does not mean that it is derived from the existing activity-denoting verbal noun by altering its connection with a drinking activity (say, changing the feature specification of [+N, +V, –A] of the [nomi] component to [+N, –V, –A]). It simply means that a new metonymically motivated connection is being established with an existing form; that is, a new word – a new connection between an old form and a new concept in this case – is being formed, and that is how polysemy arises. Indeed, in this type of nominalization, there is no morphological evidence that one form is secondarily derived from another unlike cases of derivation involving morphological alterations, as in the case of the English *-er* suffixation.

Metonymy is a powerful cognitive process that allows a variety of form–concept connections, increasing the expressive power of a language with limited resources. It takes advantage of our knowledge that many things in the world occur in close association. Verbal-based nominalization, both the lexical type under discussion and the grammatical type to be discussed presently, evokes various concepts intimately related to what the verbal bases denote, namely states, processes, activities, attendant participants such as agents and patients, resultant products, as well as instruments and locations constantly associated with particular activities. Thus, nominalizations based on change-of-state process verb roots[12] denote resultant states, as in [kumori] 'cloudiness,' [usu-[gumori]] 'lightly clouded state,' resultant products as in [kori] 'stiffness,' [kata-[kori]] 'shoulder stiffness,' but never activities or agents, though they may denote things including people associated with the denoted states; for example, *hage* 'a bald person,' *Tōkyō-sodachi* 'one grew up in Tokyo.'

Action and action-process verb roots may yield forms denoting agents as in [tasuke] 'helper' and [sake-[nomi]] 'drinker,' or activities as in [yama-[nobori]] 'mountain climbing' and [hito-[dasuke]] 'helping people.' Some other forms in this group may name both activities and agents, as in [hito-[goroshi]] 'manslaughter' or 'killer' and [hebi-[tori]] 'snake catching' or 'a snake catcher.'

Action-process verb roots such as *age-* 'fry' and *hos-* 'dry' may produce forms that denote either activities or resultant products, as in [kara-[age]] 'frying with light coating' or 'fried stuff with light coating' and [ichiya-[boshi]] 'drying overnight,' (*ika no*) [ichiya-[boshi]] '(squid) dried overnight.' Like this, the meanings of derived forms, both freestanding single nouns and compounds, are to a great extent predictable based on the semantics of the verb roots (and the partner constituents in the case of compounds), but there are too many irregularities to allow simple algorithms in arriving at the meaning of the nominalization-based nouns.

As seen earlier, many based on action verb roots allow both activity and agent/instrument readings. But many similar forms have only one reading. Forms like *yama-nobori* 'mountain-climbing,' *uo-tsuri* 'fish-catching,' and *sumi-yaki* 'charcoal-making' only denote activities, whereas *uta-utai* 'song-singing,' *e-kaki* 'picture-drawing,' and *sumō-tori* 'sumo-taking' name only agents and not activities such that while *yama-nobori-suru* 'do mountain-climbing' is possible, **uta-utai-suru* 'do song-singing' is not. The lack of the agentive form of *yama-nobori*, for example, might be attributed to the fact that there is a Sino-Japanese word with that meaning, namely *tozanka* 'mountain climber.' But agentive forms *uta-utai, e-kaki*, and *sumō-tori* are possible despite the existence of Sino-Japanese counterparts, namely *kashu* 'singer,' *gaka* 'painter,' and *rikishi* 'sumo wrestler.'

Finally, Kagayama's analysis, as represented by his rule given in (13) above, appears to be motivated by a desire to predict the category status of compounds. Forms like *asobi* 'playing' and *yomi* 'reading' yield verbal noun compounds when they occur as the right-hand member of compounds, as in *[yo-asobi]-suru* 'do late-night playing,' and *[tachi-yomi]-suru* 'do reading while standing.' By recognizing verbal nouns like $[\text{asobi}]_{VN}$ and $[\text{yomi}]_{VN}$, Kageyama can predict the category status of the compounds containing them as their heads. But there are numerous cases where the category status of compounds of the similar type cannot be determined by the

[12] The classification of verb roots employed in this chapter is as follows: *State* (e.g. *wakaru* 'understand'), *Process* (*nagareru* 'flow'), *Change-of-state process* (*kōru* 'freeze'), *Action* (*aruku* 'walk'), and *Action-process* (*korosu* 'kill').

category status of the right-hand-side members. A case in point are those involving derived nominals that can occur only as compound formatives without a word status associated with part-of-speech categories, which are properties of (free) words.[13] For example, *ok-i* 'rising,' *ne* 'sleeping,' and *hik-i* 'subtracting/pulling' do not occur as freestanding nouns or verbal nouns. Yet, when they form compounds like [haya oki]$_{VN}$, [haya ne]$_{VN}$, and [ne biki]$_{VN}$, they form verbal nouns. Thus, there is no reason to assume that forms like *asobi* 'playing,' *ijime* 'bullying,' and *yomi* 'reading,' some of which occur as freestanding nouns but not as verbal nouns, are verbal nouns derived via Kagayama's rule. It is entirely circular to recognize all these as verbal nouns because they form compound verbal nouns, as in Yumoto's (2016: 322) representation of *dashi-ire* 'putting in and taking out' as [[V]$_{VN}$-[V]$_{VN}$]$_{VN}$.

Bound compound formatives like the ones found in [[tachi] [nomi]]$_{VN}$ (standing-drinking) 'drinking while standing' and [[kaki] [age]]$_{N}$ (scrambling-frying) 'stuff deep-fried after scrambling the material in the dough,' are like a huge number of Sino-Japanese compound formatives, which have no word status. For example, both components of words like [[doku]$_{?}$-[ritsu]$_{?}$]$_{VN}$ (alone-stand) 'independence,' [[chū]$_{?}$-[ritsu]$_{?}$]$_{N}$ (middle-stand) 'neutrality,' and [[doku]$_{?}$-[shin]$_{?}$]$_{N}$ (alone-body) 'bachelor,' are transparent in meaning thanks to the Chinese characters used, and they recur as components of numerous other compounds but never function as independent words warranting part-of-speech classification.

A corollary of the above is that the word category of these nominalized forms is determined by the meaning and the external morphosyntactic properties of the entire words, whether they are single freestanding forms or compounds. In particular, nominalization-based compound formatives, like many Sino-Japanese compound formatives, do not determine the word category of the entire compound even when they function as a semantic head determining the meaning of the compound.[14]

A more reasonable analysis of stem nominalization is to regard it as a process that derives forms with a function of denoting things and thing-like entities, namely sublexical nominalization units. A nominalization

[13] The term "part of speech" refers to WORD categories and does not apply to roots and suffixes, which are not words. One may classify different roots as "verb roots," "adjective roots," and suffixes as "causative suffix" and "passive suffix," depending on their morphological and functional status, but verb roots, for example, need to be clearly distinguished from verbs. Verb roots become verbs when they are inflected for tense or mood, as in *yorokob-u/yorokon-da* 'rejoice-PRS/rejoice-PST' and *yorokob-e* 'rejoice-IMP,' and they become nouns when they undergo the stem nominalization discussed here, as in *yorokob-i* 'pleasure,' when they have a word status as in this example. Similarly, adjective roots are not adjectives by themselves; they become adjectival predicates when they form words with the *-i* tense suffix (e.g. *tsuyo-i* 'be strong'), nouns when suffixed by *-sa* (*tsuyo-sa* 'strength'), or adverbs when suffixed by *-ku* (*tsuyo-ku* 'strongly'). In this way, Japanese inflecting roots are "precategorical" in the sense that their part of speech is not predetermined.

[14] Typically Japanese compounds are right-headed semantically, as in *tachi-nomi* 'drinking while standing' and *yama-aruki* 'mountain walking,' or are of the dvandva type, in which the components are equal in rank contributing equal weight to the meaning of the compound; for example, *ake-shime* 'opening and closing,' *age-sage* 'raising and lowering.'

such as [asob-i]$_{\mathrm{NMLZ}}$ may form a noun by itself, as in [[asob-i]$_{\mathrm{NMLZ}}$]$_{\mathrm{N}}$ 'playing,' or form compounds with another constituent, as in [[yo]$_{\mathrm{N}}$-[asob-i]$_{\mathrm{NMLZ}}$]$_{\mathrm{VN}}$ (night-playing) 'staying out late at night,' [[asob-i]$_{\mathrm{NMLZ}}$-[shigoto]$_{\mathrm{N}}$]$_{\mathrm{N}}$ (playing-work) 'casual work,' and [[das-i]$_{\mathrm{NMLZ}}$-[ire-Ø]$_{\mathrm{NMLZ}}$]$_{\mathrm{VN}}$ (taking out-putting in) 'putting in and taking out.' The advantage of this analysis is that a large number of nominalized forms that occur only as bound compound formatives receive a natural analysis. By labeling these formatives as [. . .]$_{\mathrm{NMLZ}}$, we are analyzing them as nominalization structures independent from a part-of-speech classification.

What about those that occur both as freestanding nouns and as compound formatives? Do we assign part-of-speech labels to the compound formatives on the basis of the freestanding forms? It depends on the status of the relevant freestanding forms, which raises several issues that are subtle yet fundamental in morphological analysis. The most basic issue has to do with the question of when two similar-looking forms are deemed related. Since speakers' knowledge about words differs from one person to another, this question does not receive uniform answers. In the mind of Japanese speakers who know the word *tachibasami* [tachi-hasami] (cutting-scissor) 'scissors for cutting clothing material,' it is likely that the second component [hasami] is related to the commonplace word *hasami* 'scissors.' But it is most likely that a large majority of Japanese speakers do not know that *hasami* itself is a nominalized form of the verb root *hasam-* 'pinch/bind.' Representing this word as [[hasami]$_{\mathrm{NMLZ}}$]$_{\mathrm{N}}$ has only a historical or etymological value. Reasonable representations for these forms, then, would be [hasami]$_{\mathrm{N}}$ for *hasami* and [[tachi]$_{\mathrm{NMLZ}}$-[hasami]$_{\mathrm{N}}$]$_{\mathrm{N}}$ for *tachibasami*, assuming that speakers know that the first constituent [tachi] is related to the verb root *tat-* 'cut/sever' and that it recurs in the language. Otherwise, this word could be analyzed as [tachi-[hasami]$_{\mathrm{N}}$]$_{\mathrm{N}}$, where *tachi-* is treated like a prefix of some sort, or simply as [tachibasami]$_{\mathrm{N}}$ if no connection between this and the word *hasami* 'scissors' is recognized, which is unlikely.

There is another etymologically related form [hasami] used in *kami-basami* (paper-pinching) 'paper holder' and *sentaku-basami* (laundry-pinching) 'clothes pin.' People are most likely not to connect this [hasami] to *hasami* 'scissors,' but are instead likely to know that it is related to the verb *hasamu* 'to pinch/bind' and to the form found in other compounds such as [hasami-uchi] 'pincer attack' and [ita-basami] (board-binding) 'dilemma of being in the middle of two opposing parties.' If so, these forms can be represented as [[kami]$_{\mathrm{N}}$-[hasami]$_{\mathrm{NMLZ}}$]$_{\mathrm{N}}$, [[sentaku]$_{\mathrm{VN}}$-[hasami]$_{\mathrm{NMLZ}}$]$_{\mathrm{N}}$, [[hasami]$_{\mathrm{NMLZ}}$-[uchi]$_{\mathrm{NMLZ}}$]$_{\mathrm{N}}$, and [[ita]$_{\mathrm{N}}$-[hasami]$_{\mathrm{NMLZ}}$]$_{\mathrm{N}}$.

A fair number of freestanding nouns derived by the stem nominalization, such as *age* 'thin fried tofu,' *shirase* 'news/message,' and *ochi* 'punch line,' which sufficiently diverge in meaning from the etymological verb roots, can safely be analyzed as simply as [age]$_{\mathrm{N}}$, [shirase]$_{\mathrm{N}}$, [ochi]$_{\mathrm{N}}$, and so on. In between these and those whose morphological connections with verbs and compound formatives are quite transparent are forms like *hakari* 'scale,' *nejimawashi* 'screwdriver,' and *suri* 'pickpocket,' which are likely represented in the speaker's mind as simple, underived nouns. But they can be connected to the relevant verb forms upon slight reflection. Our analysis makes a clear distinction between nouns that are underived and those derived by the stem nominalization process in terms of the representations of $[\text{inu}]_{\text{N}}$ 'dog' and $[\text{mizu}]_{\text{N}}$ 'water' versus $[[\text{ijime-}\emptyset]_{\text{NMLZ}}]_{\text{N}}$ 'bullying' and $[[\text{asob-i}]_{\text{NMLZ}}]_{\text{N}}$ 'playing.'

Lexical nominalizations play important roles in word formation in Japanese, both in simple and in compound form. While the meaning of the derived forms is predictable to a large extent from the meaning of the base forms, there are many gaps and idiosyncrasies since word creation is largely need-based and because the meaning and external morphosyntactic properties are liable to individual changes as the words mature in age. Both native and Sino-Japanese compounds involving bound formatives, whether they are derived nominals or not, present an interesting challenge to the theory of word formation that takes a head component as a determinant of the word category of the entire compound.

4 Grammatical Nominalizations

While lexical nominalizations create nouns either by themselves or in combination with another nominal, grammatical nominalizations are nominal structures larger than words. Like bound compound formatives, grammatical nominalizations are not subject to part-of-speech classification, contrary to the term *Meishika* (noun-forming) used in the literature. Similar to lexical nominalization, grammatical nominalization produces structures that denote metonymically evoked entity (thing-like) concepts. Because of this entity-denoting function, shared by all nominal forms, grammatical nominalizations head an NP, the most telling syntactic property of nominals. In addition, they may function as a modifier in an NP, or they play an adverbial function, typically in conjunction with an adverbial particle (see below). These are all uses of grammatical nominalizations, not what grammatical nominalizations are per se, contrary to the claim that grammatical nominalization produces noun phrases.[15]

4.1 Stem and *Sa*-nominalizations

Before turning to the discussions of the prevalent types of grammatical nominalizations, let us briefly look at some phenomena that suggest that the stem nominalization studied above may have been a productive

[15] Givón (2009: 66) contends, "Nominalization is the process via which a *finite verbal clause* – either in its entirety or only the subject-less verb phrase – is converted to a *noun phrase*."

grammatical nominalization process in the past. The *sa*-nominalization also produces grammatical nominalizations that have a limited range of use in Modern Japanese.

Japanese has an evidential marker, *sō*, which marks information obtained typically based on visible evidence about certain states and properties. It attaches to adjectival nouns such as the native word *shiawase* 'happiness' and the Sino-Japanese form *kenkō* 'health,' which, like other nouns, require the copula *da* for predication. Adjective roots denoting states and properties also take *sō* as in (15b):

(14) a. *Takashi wa shiawase da.*
TOP happy COP
'Takashi is happy.'

b. *Takashi wa shiawase=sō da.*
happy=EVID
'Takashi looks happy.'

(15) a. *Takashi wa kashiko-i.*
TOP smart-PRS
'Takashi is smart.'

b. *Takashi wa kashiko-Ø=sō da.*
smart-NMLZ-EVID COP
'Takashi looks smart.'

It is not clear whether the adjective root *kashiko-* 'smart' in (15b) is inherently nominal or has been nominalized via stem nominalization. Since all adjective roots end in a vowel, Ø-stem nominalization would apply producing the form identical with the root form. We tentatively assume that adjective roots undergo Ø-stem nominalization, as indicated in the gloss for (15b). Either way, they follow the pattern of adjectival nouns, suggesting that the *sō* evidential attaches to nominals denoting property concepts, or conversely, what can be marked by the *sō* evidential is nominal.

Now, this *sō* evidential also attaches to verbal-based stem nominalizations. For example,

(16) *[Ame ga kyūni furidash-i]=sō da.*
rain NOM suddenly fall.start-NMLZ=EVID COP
'Rain appears to start falling suddenly.'

When verbal-based nominalizations are involved, the *sō* evidential points to a circumstance with a visible sign about an imminent occurrence of a process or action. Our point here is that these kinds of *i-*/*Ø-*nominalizations are not words but have structures like a VP or a clause, indicating that the stem nominalization also produces grammatical nominalizations with structures larger in size than words. This is also seen with the desiderative predicates derived via suffixation of *-ta*, which conjugate like adjectives (e.g. *yomi-ta-i* 'want to read').[16]

(17) *Takashi ga [hon o yomi-ta-Ø]=sō ni shiteiru.*
NOM book ACC read-DES-NMLZ=EVID PRT is.doing
'Takashi looks like wanting to read a book.'

Grammatical nominalizations derived by both stem and *sa*-nominalizations also have an adverbial use in combination with the particle *ni*, occurring in a position where an NP headed by a verbal noun occurs:

(18) a. *Takashi wa [shiryō no* $[shūshū]_{VN}]_{NP}$ *ni toshokan ni itta.*
TOP material GEN collecting PRT library to went
'Takashi went to the library for collecting material.'

b. *Takashi wa [hon o yom-i] ni toshokan ni itta.*
read-NMLZ
'Takashi went to the library for reading books.'

c. *Takashi wa [hon o yomi-ta-sa] ni toshokan ni itta.*[17]
book ACC read-DES-NMLZ
'Takashi went to the library out of his desire of reading books.'

While these usage patterns of the relevant nominalization structures are highly productive in Modern Japanese, they are atypical as nominalizations in that they do not head an argument NP, nor do they modify a noun like more typical grammatical nominalizations to be discussed next. But the usage patterns seen above suggest that both stem and *sa*-nominalizations may once have been productive processes that have become more restrictive lexical processes in recent history. They also indicate that lexical and grammatical nominalizations form a continuum.

4.2 Verbal-based Grammatical Nominalizations

YAMADA Yoshio (1873–1958) was perhaps the first to study Japanese grammatical nominalizations in some detail. But his seminal study has not received the critical appraisal it deserves, nor has any attempt to extend his work beyond its limitations succeeded in drawing far-reaching theoretical implications that a proper analysis of grammatical nominalizations

[16] There is an interesting gap in the pattern for mono-moraic adjective roots such as *yo-* 'good' and *na-* 'non-existent.' These do not allow **yo-Ø=sō da* and **na-Ø=sō da*; instead they require *sa*-nominalized forms, as *yo-sa=sō da* 'looks good' and *na-sa=sō da* 'looks non-existent.'

[17] One should not expect from facts like this that all these nominal forms behave alike in all contexts. They are different kinds of nominal forms, after all – lexical verbal nouns, *-i/-Ø* verbal stem nominalizations, and *-sa* adjectival stem nominalizations. Even members of the same lexical category may not behave all alike, as demonstrated by Ross's (1973) *nouniness squish* capturing the cline of nouniness among various types of nominals: *that* clauses > *for to* clauses > embedded questions > Acc *ing* complements > Poss *ing* complements > action nominals > derived nominals > underived nominals.

is bound to make. In his monumental *Nihonbunpōron* [Theory of Japanese Grammar] (1908), Yamada recognized the following types of grammatical nominalizations, which he termed *Juntaigen* (quasi-nominal) after the term *Taigen* (nominal).

(19) a. True grammatical nominalization

[Yorokobu] wa yoku, [ikaru] wa ashi.[18]
rejoicing TOP good getting.angry TOP bad
'Rejoicing is good, and getting angry is bad.'

b. Abbreviated grammatical nominalization

[Ikareru] wa kare ni shite, [yorokobu] wa ware nari.
angry.one TOP he COP do-GER rejoicing.one TOP I COP
'The angry one is he, and the one rejoicing is I.'

c. Clausal grammatical nominalization

[Hito no yorokobu] o mireba ureshi.
person GEN rejoicing ACC when.seeing delighted
'When (I) see people rejoicing, I feel delighted.'

d. Purposive grammatical nominalization

[Hana o mi] ni iku.
flower ACC seeing PRT go
'(I) will go to see flowers.'

Despite his definition of grammatical nominalizations as "the adnoninal forms of conjugating words [verbs and adjectives] used in the nominal status" (1908: 707), the revered guru of modern Japanese grammatical studies fails to grasp the true nature of what he terms "abbreviated grammatical nominalizations" illustrated in (19b). Likely influenced by the term *Rentaikei* (adnominal form), Yamada describes these nominalizations as involving

> conjugating words [e.g. *ikareru* 'angry (one)'] **that modify substantive concepts**. What is modified here, however, has been absorbed in the conjugating words and cannot be recognized in external form. In order to understand these, *hito* [person], *mono* [person], *mono* [thing], etc. must be added after the relevant conjugating words.
>
> (ibid., my translation; emphasis added)

This interpretation is curious in view of the fact that the same verbal-based forms *yorokobu* 'being glad/one who is glad' is seen in what Yamada calls "true grammatical nominalizations" in (19a) and "clausal grammatical nominalizations" in (19c), where he apparently would not consider those forms to be modifying a substantive concept.

When Yamada defined grammatical nominalizations as words "conjugated" in the so-called adnominal form that function like nominals,

[18] Yamada's examples are in Classical Japanese form.

he seems to have had in mind the syntactic properties of these forms, such as their functioning as sentence subjects and objects, rather than the more basic-meaning function that all nominals bear, namely the function of denoting substantive concepts. Had Yamada taken this fundamental function of nominals more seriously, he would have analyzed forms such as *ikareru* 'angry one' and *yorokobu* 'one who is glad' in (19b) as directly bearing the nominal, entity-denoting function, denoting entities that are metonymically evoked by these forms – a person who is being angry and one who is glad, in this case. While inventing the new term *Juntaigen* (quasi-nominal), Yamada still falls victim of the traditional term *Rentaikei* (adnominal form) reflecting an adnominal modification function. Had he considered the *Rentaikei* as representing a derivation, rather than a verbal conjugation, that yields nominalization structures with a nominal denotation function, he would have had a more straightforward analysis that connects the meaning function of nominalizations to their syntactic functions consistent with how nouns in general function in grammar. In other words, it is the sharing of the function of denoting substantive concepts that makes nominalizations and nouns pattern syntactically alike.

The essential difference between Yamada's true nominalizations (19a) and abbreviated nominalizations (19b) is, then, whether the structure denotes an event – or a state-of-affairs more broadly – or it denotes more concrete substantive entities. What Yamada calls "clausal nominalizations" in (19c) are also event nominalizations with a modifier, which specifies an event participant in this case. We will subsequently take up the question of whether or not these nominalizations are indeed clauses.

4.2.1 Event Nominalizations

Grammatical nominalizations denote either abstract concepts like processes or activities, and concepts closely related to them, including such abstract ones as facts and propositions, or concrete substantive entities such as event participants and resultant objects, just as lexical nominalizations denote these in a more codified manner.

Event nominalizations have clause-like internal structures, often with a full array of NP arguments overtly expressed. They have, however, external syntagmatic properties like nouns in that they head an NP, playing the syntactic function of arguments of a clause as well as a semantic referential function. Bear in mind that grammatical categories are determined on the basis of external properties, not by the internal properties, meaning that even if a structure is clause-like internally, it does not follow that the structure in question is a clause. Event nominalizations denote the following kinds of concepts:

(20) a. State-of-affairs/Circumstance

[Haha ga you][19] *no o itsumo mitemashita kara...*
mother NOM getting.drunk PRT ACC always watched because
'Because I always watched my mother getting drunk...'

b. Fact

Masako wa [otto ni sonna onna ga ita]
TOP husband LOC such woman NOM existing

no o shitta.
PRT ACC learned
'Masako learned that (her) husband had such a woman.'

c. Time, place, reason/Cause

[Watashi ga umareta] no wa Saitama – sono inaka
I NOM was.born PRT TOP that rural

machi ni aru shakuya datta.
town in exist rental.house was
'Where I was born was a rental house in a rural town in Saitama.'

d. Event participant

Hora, [sensei ga izen kingyo no e o
look teacher NOM before gold.fish GEN picture ACC

kaita] no ga aru deshō.
drew PRT NOM exsist COP.CNJ
Lit. 'Look; there is that the teacher drew a picture of a gold fish sometime ago, isn't there?'/'Look; there's a picture of a gold fish that the teacher drew some time ago, isn't there?'

e. Resultant product

[Sobo no katte iru jūshimatsu ga saezuru] no
grand.mother GEN keep society.finch NOM chirp PRT

o kiita.
ACC heard
'(I) heard the society finch chirp that (my) grandmother keeps.'

These constructions are interesting in that the bracketed nominalization structures are syntactic arguments, but what they denote, namely events, are not semantic arguments of the main clause predicates. What exists in (20d) and what was heard in (20e) are not events; rather it is an event participant (a painting of a goldfish that exists in the former, and a resultant product (a chirping sound) that was heard in the latter. Indeed, nowhere in the entire structure of (20e) is there an NP denoting the thing that was heard.

[19] By bracketing as [haha ga you] as in this example and the others below, we are indicating the basic nominalization structures, which take the particle *no* only in their NP-use in central dialects, including Tokyo Japanese (see below). The structure containing *no* can be represented as [[haha ga you]$_{NMLZ}$ no]$_{NMLZ'}$.

In some circles (e.g. Keenan 1985; Kuroda 1992c), constructions like (20d) are analyzed as *internally headed relative clauses* (cf. Chapter 21, this volume), assuming (i) that these are relative clauses, and (ii) that a head nominal exists within relative clauses unlike regular relative clause constructions, where a head exists externally in the main clause. A problem with the first assumption is that it is not at all obvious that these structures play the function of relative clauses, which is either to restrict the denotation of the head noun (restrictive relatives) or to identify the head noun in terms of additional information about it (non-restrictive or appositive relatives). The second assumption that in these structures an argument internal to the "relative clause" is the argument of the main-clause predicate is also problematic. In (20e) there is no NP within the "relative clause" that can serve as a main-clause argument, and thus the proposed analysis cannot handle such a construction.

Furthermore, the lack of such an NP internal to the nominalization structures in (20a–c) is seen from a comparison between them and the synonymous constructions below, where an NP argument of the main clause predicates is explicitly coded:

(21) a. *[Haha ga you] jōkyō o itsumo mitemashita*
mother NOM getting.drunk scene ACC always watched
kara...
because
'Because I always watched the scene that my mother was getting drunk...'

b. *Masako wa [otto ni sonna onna ga ita] jijitsu o shitta.*
TOP husband LOC such woman NOM existing fact ACC learned
'Masako learned the fact that (her) husband had such a woman.'

c. *[Watashi ga umareta] basho wa Saitama – sono inaka machi ni aru shakuya datta.*
I NOM was.born place TOP that rural town in exist rental.house was
'The place where I was born was a rental house in a rural town in Saitama.'

Whatever analysis is offered to these cases, the proposal to analyze forms like (20d) as internally headed relative clauses divides the phenomenon into two or more sub-phenomena, while the metonymy-based analysis treats it uniformly. All these constructions contain nominalization structures that, like lexical nominalizations discussed earlier, metonymically evoke concepts such as situations that result from an event, circumstantial matters like time, location, and reason for an event, event participants, as well as resultant product closely associated with the event. In these constructions, nominalization structures function as syntactic arguments as a subject or object precisely because they evoke and stand for thing-like entities just like nouns do. The metonymic relation seen here between the nominalization structures and what they stand for parallels the ordinary metonymic patterns such as *furo ga waita* (bath NOM has.boiled) 'the bath has boiled/the bath is ready' and *Bētōben o kiku* 'listen to Beethoven,' where the metonymically evoked entities, not what the syntactic arguments literally denote, serve as the semantic arguments of the verbs.

Take notice, at this juncture, that nominalization is not a morphological concept or process. Accordingly, nominalization structures are not necessarily associated with a morphological marker, though many may be. The English nominalization process known as "conversion" does not involve a morphological marker ($[\text{cook}]_V$ > $[\text{cook}]_N$). One type of the English "factive nominals" typically take *that* as a marker, but may not in some contexts; *I know [John is honest]*$_{\text{NMLZ}}$. In Chinese, while argument nominalizations (see next subsection) involve a morphological marker, event nominalizations have no such marker (*[tā dǎ rén]*$_{\text{NMLZ}}$ *shì bú duì=de* '[That he hits people] is not right'). While in many languages verbs undergo a morphological alteration under nominalization, in both English and Chinese verbal forms are no different from finite verb forms.[20] These structures are recognized as nominalizations not because of morphological properties but because of their nominal denotations and external syntagmatic properties that may be morphologically indicated in some other languages.

In our analysis, nominalization structures analyzed and labeled as $[\ldots]_{\text{NMLZ}}$ are grammatical constructions of various sizes in the sense of Construction Grammar. Grammars contain various constructions that are smaller or larger in size than words that are not categorizable as words such as Noun or Verb or phrasal units such as NP or VP, though they may function as constituents of these units. For example, the conjoined structures [$10 to Pat] and [$5 to Kim], as well as the entire coordinate structure [$10 to Pat and $5 to Kim] in *I gave $10 to Pat and $5 to Kim* are neither NPs nor any other known phrasal categories because they are not constituents in other contexts. Similarly, *extremely expensive and in bad taste* in *This dress is extremely expensive and in bad taste* is a grammatical construction that functions as predicative complement like an adjectival phrase (*extremely expensive*) and a prepositional phrase (*in bad taste*), but it is neither an AP nor a PP. A view that grammatical units must be morphemes, words, or familiar phrasal categories such as NP and VP is based on a limited observation about possible grammatical constructions. These points are further

[20] In the case of Japanese, there is a possibility of analyzing the verbal-based nominalizations of the type seen in this section as involving nominalized verb forms (so-called *Rentaikei*) that are identical in form to the finite verb forms (*Shūshikei*) due to a historical process merging the two. This is the position taken by Japanese school grammar that recognizes separate *Rentaikei* and *Shūshikei* forms though they are identical in form, except for the copula *da* accompanying an adjectival noun and a nominal adjective in a predicative function.

demonstrated by another type of grammatical nominalization that we call *argument nominalization*, to which we now turn.

4.2.2 Argument Nominalizations

Event nominalizations may evoke event participants, as seen in (20d). When the structure contains two NP arguments, a possible ambiguity arises regarding which of the arguments points to the intended denotation, as in the following example attributed to S.-Y. Kuroda:

(22) *Gakusei* *wa* *[shifuku* *ga* *dorobō* *o* *oikakete iru]*
student TOP plainclothes.police NOM thief ACC chasing

no *o* *tsukamaete,* *nejifuseta.*
PRT ACC catching tackled.down

Lit. 'The student caught and tackled down that a plainclothes police was chasing a thief.'

This sentence can be disambiguated by leaving empty an argument position within the nominalization structure, as below:

(23) a. *Gakusei wa [Ø dorobō o oikakete iru] no o tsukamaete, nejifuseta.*
'The student caught and tackled down the one that was chasing a thief.'
b. *Gakusei wa [shifuku ga Ø oikakete iru] no o tsukamaete, nejifuseta.*
'The student caught and tackled down the one that a plainclothes police was chasing.'

Unlike the event nominalizations discussed in the preceding subsection, which may evoke a variety of concepts metonymically related to the basic events denoted by the structures, these nominalizations are dedicated to denoting event participants, whose semantic roles are indicated by the position of a gap. The subject argument nominalization has a gap in subject position, as in (23a), and the nominalization structure as a whole denotes an entity acting as an agentive participant. The object argument nominalization, on the other hand, creates a gap in object position and denotes a patientive participant, as in (23b). Again, the entire nominalization structures marked by the particle *no* function as syntactic objects of the main-clause verbs. They can bear these grammatical functions precisely because they denote substantive concepts just like any noun.

As in other cases of metonymy, the actual denotation/reference of an argument nominalization is determined by context, as in (24) below, where there are two argument nominalizations, *jukushita (no)* and *sukoshi katamena (no)*, which can potentially refer to a variety of ripe things (e.g. mangoes, bananas, tomatoes) and things that are slightly hard (mangoes, avocados, pasta), respectively. The context and the Gricean Maxim of Relevance, however, tell us that the author is referring to the mountain persimmons given to him.

(24) *Yama no mura no Natanoshō ni chūzai shiteita*
mountain GEN village GEN LOC residence was.doing

toki, yama-gaki ga dekiru to, mura no
time mountain-persimmon NOM bear.fruit when village GEN

ie kara moratta koto wa aru. Keredomo, ***jukushita***
house from received NMLZ TOP exist however ripen(ones)

no o sonomama kuu ka sukoshi ***katamena*** *no wa, kawa*
PRT ACC as.is eat INT a.little hard(ones) PRT TOP skin

o muite hoshi-gaki ni suru ka datta.
ACC peel dried-persimmon DAT do INT was

(MIZUKAMI Tsutomu, *Kokyō* 'Hometown')

'During my residency at a police substation in Natanoshō, a mountain village, when the season of mountain persimmons arrived, I indeed received some from villagers. However, I ate ripened ones as they are, or slightly hard ones, I peeled them and made dried persimmons.'

Because these nominalizations in central dialects of Japanese, including Tokyo Japanese, are marked by the particle *no*, and because their interpretations depend on context, Kinsui (1995) and some others treat this particle as a pronominal *no*, which heads a nominalization and which functions as an anaphor. Such an analysis, however, does not extend to comparable nominalization structures in some other dialects that have not developed a particle similar to *no*. Observe the following from the Izumo dialect in Western Japan.

(25) a. *[Okke na]*$_{NMLZ}$ *wa umai.* (Izumo dialect)
big COP TOP tasty
'A/the big one is tasty.'

a´. *[Ōki na]*$_{NMLZ}$ *no wa umai.* (Central dialect)
big COP PRT TOP tasty
'A/the big one is tasty.'

b. *Kono [yaita]*$_{NMLZ}$[21] *o goshinahai.* (Izumo dialect)
this grilled ACC give.me
'Give me this grilled one, please.'

b´. *Kono [yaita]*$_{NMLZ}$ *no o kudasai.* (Central dialect)
this grilled PRT ACC give.me
'Give me this grilled one, please.'

Notice that these Izumo forms without *no* receive exactly the same referential interpretations appropriate to the context as the *no*-marked central dialect forms, indicating that *no* actually does not play a role in

[21] These nominalizations, like regular nouns, can also be modified by nouns; [sakana no [okke na]$_{NMLZ}$]$_{NP}$ ga tsureta 'Lit. A big one of fish got caught,' [sakana no [yaita]$_{NMLZ}$]$_{NP}$ o goshinahai 'Lit. Give me a grilled one of fish, please.' Cf. [sakana no [nimono]$_{N}$]$_{NP}$ 'Lit. cooked food of fish/cooked fish,' [nasu no [tsukemono]$_{N}$]$_{NP}$ 'Lit. pickles of eggplants/pickled eggplants.'

determining reference in argument nominalization. In other words, there is nothing like a pronominal *no* in Japanese.[22]

Another very popular analysis of these argument nominalizations is deriving them from relative clause constructions, which are said to undergo deletion of their head nouns when their identity is obvious from the context. For example, (26b) would be derived from (26a) in this analysis.

(26) a. *Kono [[yaita] **sakana**] o kudasai/goshinahai.*
this grilled fish ACC please.give.me
'Give me this grilled fish, please.'

b. *Kono [[yaita] (**no**)] o kudasai/goshinahai.*
PRT
'Give me this grilled one, please.'

The problem here is that a full deletion account must refer to context anyway; that is, when does the deletion apply? Our point is that, if we have to refer to context, let the context do the whole work of determining the reference of an argument nominalization without recognizing a pronominal *no* or positing an unexpressed head noun, a practice that goes against Ockham's razor.

5 Structures and Their Use

Grammatical structures, whether words or units larger in size than words, function differently depending on their uses. Nominals, including nominalizations, have two major uses, an NP-use and a modification-use. Observe these two uses of the noun *inu* 'dog.'

(27) a. NP-use/Referential function

$[[\text{inu}]_{N}]_{NP}$ *wa chūjitsu na dōbutsu da.*
dog TOP loyal animal COP
'Dogs are loyal animals.'

b. Modification-use/Restrictive function[23]

$[[\text{inu}]_{N}$ $[\text{koya}]_{N}]_{N}$ (noun compound)
shack
'kennel'

In (27a) the noun $[\text{inu}]_{N}$ heads an NP and plays a referential function at the NP level, referring to a type of animal in the real world. In (27b) the same noun functions as a modifier of the head noun, restricting the denotation of the latter to its subset. The important point here is that the structure

22 See Section 6 on the true role of the nominalization particle *no* seen here.

23 Japanese nouns do not syntactically modify nouns directly, as in English, which allows non-compound, syntactic modification by nouns, as in $[[\text{cotton}]_{N}$ $[\text{shirt}]_{N}]_{NP}$ and $[[\text{car}]_{N}$ $[\text{smell}]_{N}]_{NP}$.

does not change its grammatical category under different uses. In particular, nouns do not become adjectives even when they play a modification function.[24]

Nominalizations, qua quasi-nominals, behave like regular nouns in allowing both NP- and modification-use. The examples in the preceding subsections all demonstrate the NP-use of grammatical nominalizations, where they play a referential function as the head of an NP. The following examples show the parallelism observed in the usage pattern between a regular noun and an argument nominalization.

(28) a. NP-use/Referential function

[[[Hanako ga Ø katte-kita]$_{NMLZ}$ no]$_{NMLZ'}$]$_{NP}$ *o minnade tabeta.*
NOM buying-came PRT ACC by.everyone ate

Lit. 'We ate all together what Hanako bought and came.'

b. Modification-use/Restrictive function

[[Hanako ga Ø katte kita]$_{NMLZ}$ ringo]$_{NP}$ *o minnade tabeta.*
apple

Lit. 'We ate all together the apples that Hanako bought and came.'

So-called relative clauses (e.g. (28b)) involve two nominal structures, both with an entity denoting function, whereby a modifying nominalization denotes a subset of the denotation of the head noun. In this way, a construction with a restrictive function is characterized by a modifying structure that specifies a subset of the denotation of the head noun. Our analysis of so-called relative clauses is entirely consistent with the treatment of restrictive relative clauses in Formal Semantics, which would analyze a structure like *apples that Hanako bought* as denoting the intersection of the two sets of objects specified as {x | x are apples} and {x | Hanako bought x}. The only difference is that we would define the second set in terms of the entities that are evoked by the nominalization structure, namely as {x | x are what Hanako bought}.

Event nominalizations also permit two uses:

(29) a. NP-use/Referential function

[[[Takashi ga kekkonshite ita]$_{NMLZ}$ no]$_{NMLZ'}$]$_{NP}$ *o*
NOM had.been.married PRT ACC

daremo shiranakatta.
even.a.single.person did.not.know

'No one knew that Takashi had been married.'

b. Modification-use/Identification function

[[Takashi ga kekkonshite ita]$_{NMLZ}$ [jijitsu]$_{N}$]$_{NP}$ *o daremo shiranakatta.*
fact

'No one knew the fact that Takashi had been married.'

[24] If the noun *car* in *a car smell* has turned to an adjective, we would expect it to be modified by an adverb, for example, *newly*. It is modified by an adjective as *a new car smell*, indicating that *car* remains noun under its modification-use.

Example (29b) involves a nominalization as an appositive modifier that identifies the head noun as one that the nominalization structure denotes, namely the fact that Takashi had been married.

Yamada (1908: 1461–1462) correctly recognizes the two uses of nominalizations shown in (28–29), but he then curiously suggests that these nominalizations become special types of clause, as if nominalizations somehow turn into clauses under the two uses. He tells us that the nominalizations in an NP-use can be called *Juntaiku* (nominalization clause), and those in a modification-use *Rentaiku* (adnominal clause). Yamada's move is in line with the Western grammatical tradition that identifies the nominalization structure in (29b) as a relative CLAUSE.[25] The use of an event nominalization in example (29b) is known as a content CLAUSE in traditional grammar. Our analysis, however, reveals that there exist nothing like relative clauses and content clauses apart from a modification-use of argument and event nominalizations, respectively. Indeed, there is nothing that indicates that these nominalization structures turn into clauses or sentences under the two uses for them.

Those who identify so-called relative clauses and complement or subordinate clauses as clauses fail to make a clear distinction between internal and external properties of grammatical constructions, and to properly understand how structures are defined and categorized. Many grammatical nominalizations have verbal syntax structure internally. For example, the English event nominalization [that [John recklessly shoots trespassers]] contains a finite verb that agrees with the subject, an adverb that modifies the verb, and the verb *shoots* is followed by a direct object in exactly the same way as the sentence *John recklessly shoots trespassers*. However, these verbal properties are structure internal, while the category of a structure is determined by external morphosyntactic properties. Lexical nominalizations like *(We built that) building, (Those terrible) shootings (are deplorable)* are categorized as nouns on account of their denoting entities, such as physical objects and abstract entities such as events and facts, and external morphosyntactic properties. We would not categorize them as verbs even though they internally contain the verbs *build* and *shoot*, as [[[build]$_{V}$-ing]$_{NMLZ}$]$_{N}$ and [[[shoot]$_{V}$-ing]$_{NMLZ}$]$_{N}$. The structure [that [John recklessly shoots trespassers]] in an expression like *[That John recklessly shoots trespassers] is well known* denotes an abstract entity of fact, like a noun *fact* denotes an abstract entity concept. It also has an important external syntactic property of heading a subject or object NP, a major hallmark of nominals.

The reason why nominalizations behave syntactically like nouns is because they denote substantive concepts like nouns. Clauses and

[25] Comrie and Horie (1995) tell us that relative clauses are no different from ordinary sentences with an anaphoric gap.

sentences perform functions different from the entity denoting function. Clauses complete a predication of verbal structures by ascribing relational concepts to the referent of a subject nominal. Sentences, on the other hand, perform various types of speech acts such as asserting that the predication made by a clause is true (declarative sentences), questioning whether or not the predication is true (yes–no questions), ordering (imperative sentences). The structure [John recklessly shoots trespassers] is a clause when it is used to ascribe a verbal property to the referent of the subject noun. The structure [John recklessly shoots trespassers] is a sentence when it is used in making an assertion about the clausal predication. The nominalization structure [(that) [John recklessly shoots trespassers]], on the other hand, bears a function of denoting an abstract entity such as a fact and a proposition, which are not asserted as in sentences but are only presupposed. In this way, grammatical constructions are defined in terms of their functions and morphosyntactic properties, not by morphology or formal similarities to other structures.

6 Nominalization Particle *No*

The grammar of nominalizations of most modern Japanese dialects has evolved from that of Classical Japanese via two prominent historical changes. One is the merger of nominalized verbal (verbs and adjectives) forms and their finite counterparts, as already discussed. The other is the rise of so-called *Juntaijoshi* (nominalization particle) starting in the late sixteenth century in the case of central dialects, which began to use the particle *no* to mark one use of grammatical nominalizations. Many other, but not all, dialects have also developed similar particles for this function: *to* or *tsu* in Kyūshū, *so* in Yamaguchi Prefecture, *ga* in Hokuriku (Toyama and Ishikawa Prefectures) and Kōchi Prefecture in Shikoku, and the compound form *ga-n* in Niigata Prefecture, etc. While the term *Juntaijoshi* itself is non-committal to its function, many scholars consider these particles to be nominalizing particles or nominalizers that create nominalization structures (Horie 2008; Frellesvig 2010, etc.). That these particles are independent from the nominalizing process is clearly seen from the data in those dialects that have not developed such particles, as in the Izumo dialect seen above (see (25)), where nominalizations occur without a particle.

There is one verbal form in many varieties of Modern Japanese that distinguishes between the finite and the nominalized form. It is the copula *da* that supports predication by a nominal adjective or adjectival noun, whose finite form is *da* and whose nominalized form is *na*. Observe the following, where we can clearly see that the nominalization structure in (30c) obtains independently from the particle *no*:

(30) a. *Ano* *hana* *wa* *kirei* ***da***.
that flower TOP pretty COP
'That flower is pretty.'

b. *Ano* [kirei **na**]$_{\text{NMLZ}}$ *no* *o* *katte*. (NP-use)
COP PRT ACC buy.GER
'Buy (me) that pretty one.'

c. *Ano* [kirei **na**]$_{\text{NMLZ}}$ *hana o katte*. (Modification-use)
'Buy (me) that pretty flower.'

The usage pattern of nominalizations above shows that the so-called *Juntaijoshi* occurs only when nominalizations are used as NP-heads and that it is not really a nominalizing particle.[26] Its true function is to mark the referential use of nominalizations as the heads of NPs. The historical fact that this *no* first developed in the NP-use of argument nominalizations corroborates this conclusion. Argument nominalizations tend to denote concrete things that play a referential function in discourse more readily than abstract concepts such as events and facts that event nominalizations denote.

A tantalizing question remains regarding the connections between the markers of NP-use of nominalizations, *Juntaijoshi*, across different dialects (*no/n, ga, ga-n, to, tsu, so*) and the so-called genitive particles found in possessive constructions; for example, *Takashi* ***no*** *hon* 'Takashi's book' in modern central dialects, *nushi* ***ga*** *musuko* 'your son' in the Kumamoto dialect, and Classical Japanese forms *Hitomaro* ***ga*** *uta* 'Hitomaro's poems' and *oki* ***tsu*** *shiranami* 'white waves of the open sea.' The exploration of this question will lead us to recognize another type of nominalization, namely nominal-based nominalizations, which would obviate the so-called genitive particles and which would answer the question posed above. Space limitation, however, prevents us from exploring this new line of inquiry concerning the function of so-called genitive particles.[27]

7 Conclusion

Despite its importance in both grammar descriptions and theoretical studies, there has been a general neglect in the study of nominalizations in the field. A consequence of this neglect has been widespread misunderstanding of the true nature of so-called subordinate clauses in general and

[26] A true nominalizing particle/nominalizer occurs in both NP- and modification-use. Compare the occurrence of *no* in (30b–c) and that of the Chinese nominalizing particle *de*, which occurs in all the contexts in which an argument nominalization is used; for example, *[[Ø zái nár diáo yú]=de (shì Xiǎo Wáng)]* 'The one fishing over there (is Little Wang)' (NP-use) and *[[Ø zái nár diáo yú]=de hái-zi (shì Xiǎo Wáng)]* 'The child who is fishing over there (is Little Wang)' (modification-use).

[27] See Shibatani (2017), a vastly expanded version of this article, addressing this and other pertinent questions. Shibatani and Shigeno (2013) deal with parallel nominalization phenomena in Ryukyuan, close sister languages of Japanese.

so-called relative clauses, in particular, which have long been analyzed in a wrong-headed way. This chapter has tried to show that a proper understanding of lexical and grammatical nominalizations has far-reaching implications for the analysis of these complex constructions as well as for the general theory of grammar.

Lexical nominalization derives a large number of nouns from both verb and adjective roots and stems, as well as from nouns. A high number of nominalizations derived by stem nominalizations function only as compound formatives, without achieving lexical status. Many compounds in both Sino-Japanese and native strata consist solely of this kind of pre-lexical compound formatives. Their theoretical implication is that the lexical category of many compounds cannot be determined by the category of their constituents, forcing a theory of morphology to allow exocentric structures, which are generally ostracized in Formal Linguistics.

Grammatical nominalizations, yielding structures larger in size than words, are similar to nouns and lexical nominalizations in bearing an entity-denoting function. As a corollary of this function, grammatical nominalizations behave syntactically like nouns by heading NPs. The treatment of the nominalizations in NP-use as headless relative clauses (Andrews 2007, etc.) or as nominalizations derived from relative clauses is putting the cart before the horse.[28] This misguided practice, popular in the field, has no doubt been caused by the imbalance in the past studies, which have tended to focus on relative clauses, almost entirely ignoring nominalizations and their roles in grammar.

Comrie and Thompson (2007: 378) recognize a connection between nominalizations and relative clauses, but they describe it as "a somewhat more rare function of nominalization: as a relative clause modifying a head noun," despite the fact that such a connection is found even in English, which uses wh-forms to mark argument nominalizations, as in Figure 19.1.[29]

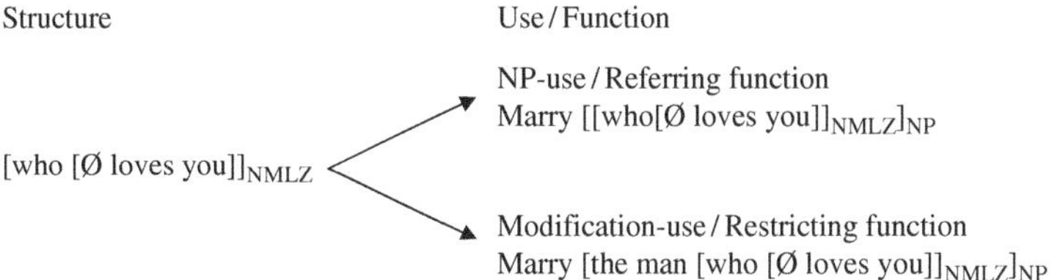

Figure 19.1 Two uses/functions of English argument nominalization

[28] Sneddon (1996: 300) remarks about Indonesian nominalizations thus: "Nominalization occurs when the head noun [of a relative clause] is elipted . . . The yang [nominalization] phrase then functions like a noun."

[29] See Shibatani (2009) for a cross-linguistic survey of the extensive use of nominalizations as modifiers in relative constructions.

There is even more striking similarity between Japanese and English. Both have developed a special marker for an NP-use of nominalization, *no* in central dialects of Japanese, as discussed above, and English *one*, as used for argument nominalizations in NP-use; cf. *You should marry [who [Ø loves you]]* and *You should marry* ***one*** *[who [Ø loves you]]*.

We have also shown that so-called relative clauses are neither clauses/sentences nor independent structures apart from a use of nominalizations as modifiers. The same applies to so-called content clauses that identify head nouns (*the fact [that John is already married]*). Treating these as clauses or sentences, as in the past studies, fails to distinguish between internal and external properties of grammatical structures. Structure-internal similarities do not guarantee that we are dealing with similar grammatical structures, whose category status must be determined on the basis of their functions and external morphological and syntagmatic properties. Sentences, clauses, and nominalizations differ in both function and external properties, as described in Section 5. Sentences and clauses, on the one hand, and nominalizations, on the other, are as different as a turkey in the wild and a roast turkey on the dinner table despite the obvious internal structural resemblances between the two.

20

Clausal Noun Modification

Yoshiko Matsumoto

1 Introduction

"Noun-modifying clause constructions" (NMCC), in which a clause combines with a noun, are commonly observed in many languages, including Japanese. Among the instances of this construction, it is fair to say that attention has most commonly been focused on the "relative clause construction" (RCC), perhaps because of its wide distribution across languages and its frequent uses within a language.

The RCC is generally considered to be syntactically defined, and is characterized by a reference-binding relationship between the head noun (HN) and the relative pronoun or a syntactic gap in the modifying (i.e. relative) clause. For example, in English *the book {which/that/Ø} the student enjoyed*, the semantic relationship of the HN to the RC is strictly determined by the syntax. This feature distinguishes the RCC from other types of NMCC in English, such as the noun complement clause construction (NCCC). In contrast to an RCC, a NCCC *the fact that the student enjoyed the book*, for example, has no clause-internal gap. There is a common assumption that, in any language, constructions that share some of the semantic and structural features of RCs are structurally distinct from other constructions, such as NCCCs.

However, the premise of structural distinctions among instances of the NMCC is not always supported within a specific language. As will be illustrated in more detail in the following sections, Japanese arguably exhibits one single construction that covers a range of different interpretations including not only what would have been expressed in English as RCCs and NCCCs, but also by such constructions as infinitival, gerundive, and participial clauses (e.g. *things to do, the result of practicing everyday*, and *burnt toast*).

Attention to this characteristic of the Japanese NMCC and the existence of instances that cannot plausibly be categorized as RCCs or NCCCs invites rethinking of the assumed structural distinctions within noun-modification and consideration of alternative analytical and theoretical approaches to the construction. This chapter examines a variety of instances of one general construction – a clause combined with a noun – under the rubric of the NMCC. The investigation focuses on the construal of the construction, as it lacks explicit markings that guide interpretation, and takes the approach that no single factor but, instead, an aggregate of factors, including structural, semantic, and pragmatic information, determines a successful construal.

The study of the Japanese NMCC not only provides information about Japanese, but can also afford further understanding of languages beyond Japanese. As suggested in cross-linguistic studies, the phenomenon of having a single construction covering a wide range of interpretations can be observed to a varied degree in a number of (but not all) geographically related languages in Eurasia, and even among some dialects of typical European languages. A single NMCC that covers a range of semantic relationships between the HN and modifying clause that is broader than that of RCCs is termed a general noun-modifying clause construction (GNMCC). In Japanese, the NMCC and the GNMCC are coterminous (Matsumoto, Comrie, and Sells 2017), while in English the NMCC would include the distinct constructions of RCCs and NCCCs.

In the following, some basic characteristics of the Japanese NMCC are illustrated in Section 2. Section 3 offers a summary of past and present syntactic and descriptive studies that provide background to the study of the NMCC from the perspective presented in this chapter. Section 4 illustrates crucial factors for construal which motivate an alternative perspective, and in Section 5, a summary of the studies integrating pragmatics and a range of examples of the construction are provided. Section 6 addresses related issues and provides suggestions for future directions of study.

2 The Basic Characteristics of the Japanese Noun-modifying Clause Construction

The basic structure of the NMCC in Japanese can be schematically represented as in (1).

(1) [[. . . Predicate (finite/adnominal)] Noun]

The modifying clause predicate (a verb, an adjective, or a noun+copula) is in the adnominal form, but in present-day Japanese it is virtually identical to the finite form since the adnominal form has supplanted the original finite form, except in the case of nominal adjectives in the non-past form (see Chapter 4, this volume). Speech act modal expressions, such as sentence-final particles, usually do not appear in the modifying clause unless they are followed by the quasi-quotation marker *toiu* (also represented as *toyuu*) or its variants (often glossed as a complementizer), or are used innovatively. A verb can be the sole element of the modifying clause, as it can be in a main clause, since arguments are not required to be overtly expressed in the main clause, as "referential density" (Bickel 2003) in Japanese is reported as moderate (Noonan 2003: 6). That a modifying clause has the basic structure of a well-formed main clause, especially with regard to the argument array, implies that a missing argument in a modifying clause is not necessarily associated with the HN.

The crucial property of the NMCC in Japanese is that there is no explicit indication of the relation between the two main constituents, the modifying clause and the HN. The simplified examples in (2–3) show some of the typical varieties of the construction.

(2) *[hon o kat-ta] gakusei*
book ACC buy-PST student
'the student [who bought the book]'

(3) *[gakusei ga kat-ta] hon*
student NOM buy-PST book
'the book [that the student bought]'

In (2–3), the HN is interpreted as playing the role of an argument internal to the clause; the subject of *katta* 'bought' in (2) and the direct object in (3). Semantically, the HN in (2) is construed as the buyer and in (3) as the goods.

The HN of (4) *mise* 'store' is interpreted as the location where the event of the student's buying occurred, an adjunct of the modifying verb.

(4) *[gakusei ga kat-ta] mise*
student NOM buy-PST store
'the store [where the student bought (x)]'

It is worth pointing out that, depending on the context, the interpretation of the construction in (2) can be different from what is given above, as indicated in the English translations:

(2) *[hon o kat-ta] gakusei*
book ACC buy-PST student
a. 'the student [who bought a book]'
b. 'the student [from whom (x) bought a book]'
c. 'the student [for whom (x) bought a book]'
etc.

Similarly in example (4) *[gakusei ga katta] mise*, the interpretation could be 'the store that the student bought,' in which the HN is an argument. If it is known that the particular student is extremely affluent with the ambition of owning properties, this interpretation could be possible and even be intended, but the more commonly shared knowledge of the world that students are not regularly wealthy would lead to the interpretation in which the HN is an adjunct, as given in (4). The direct object, which represents what was bought at the store, is assumed known or not relevant in the context.

Further, in (3) *[gakusei ga katta] hon*, 'the book that the student bought,' the modifying clause verb has a missing element (the direct object), which is interpreted to be associated with the HN. However, in a well-known book title given in (5), there is no missing argument in the clause for the HN to be associated with, yet the construction presents no problem for successful construal. In contrast, there is no obvious well-formed construction in English to translate this in some form of NMCC, perhaps except for some dialect versions like 'the book where/such that you get smart.'

(5) *[atama no*[1] *yoku-naru] hon*
head GEN good-become book
'the book [(by reading) which (one's) head gets better (i.e. one becomes more intelligent)]'

Example (6) *[hon o katta] uwasa* 'the rumor that (x) bought a book' presents a different kind of construal of the relation between the clause and the HN.

(6) *[hon o kat-ta] uwasa*
book ACC buy-PST rumor
'the rumor [that (x) bought a book]'

The HN is not interpreted as an argument or an adjunct of the modifying predicate, despite the fact that structurally the modifying clause in (6) is exactly the same as in (2), which would be categorized as a "relative clause" in the English translation. Because of the semantics of the HN *uwasa* 'rumor,' the modifying clause in (6) is interpreted to specify the content of *uwasa*. The English translation is given in the form of a noun complement construction, unlike the RC in (2). The fact that there is a clear division of constructions in English to express the above examples, while one single general structure is used in Japanese, leads us to question whether the same categorical division as commonly used in English should be adopted in the analysis of Japanese noun modification. The concept of RC may be used as a comparative concept (Haspelmath 2010: 672–673), but that does not necessarily imply that it should be realized as a structurally distinct construction in any particular language, and it does not exclude the possibility of having a single construction expressing a wider range of meanings than can be expressed as RCs.

Example (7) adds yet another example of the wide application of the single form of the construction.

(7) *[hon o kat-ta] otsuri*
book ACC buy-PST change (tender minus price)
'the change [from (x) buying a book]'

[1] The genitive case in a noun-modifying clause can mark the subject.

The elements expressed in the modifying clause are identical to those in (2) and (6), but (7) receives a different interpretation from either of them because of its HN *otsuri* 'change (tender minus price).' The HN is neither an argument of the modifying clause predicate, nor is its content specified by the clause. The meaning of *otsuri* suggests that the change came about as a consequence of the commercial transaction of buying a book. The past form of the modifying predicate also plays a role in leading to the interpretation that the past event conditioned the result of producing the change. If the predicate were in the non-past form, the most likely interpretation of the construction would be that it is the change (that came about from some unmentioned past transaction) that will be used for the purpose of buying a book.

As we speak of a construction that has a broad range of interpretations involving the language users' structural, semantic, pragmatic, and world knowledge, it is absolutely important to note that it does have its constraints. The constraints are not syntactically characterized and the construal of the construction is not unequivocally guided by syntax, but the semantic coherence between the two juxtaposed main constituents needs to be inferred by the construers and, accordingly, the acceptability of instances of the construction is constrained by the aggregate of factors necessary for construal. This is reminiscent of novel Noun+Noun compounds in English (Downing 1977), but the fact that one constituent is a clause in the Japanese NMCC creates different conditions (Matsumoto 2014: 561–562 for more detail).

3 Syntactic Approaches and Descriptive Approaches

The conceptual approach to the NMCC in this chapter places more importance on semantic and pragmatic factors than do syntactic and descriptive approaches, which preceded it and influenced its inception.

3.1 Syntactic Approaches: Generative Grammar and Functional Syntax

The development of generative grammar prompted a surge of syntactic studies of Japanese RCs and, to a lesser degree, noun complementation, especially from the 1970s to early 1990s. The majority of the work in the generative framework has focused on (transformational) rules and constraints on "relative clauses" in Japanese; for example, whether Japanese RCs were generated by a movement rule, as in English RCs (N. Hasegawa 1981; Saito 1985; Kuroda 1992c; Kameshima 1990), or by a deletion of the embedded target noun (along with its case marker) under coreference with the HN (Nakau 1971; Okutsu 1974; Inoue 1976; Shibatani 1978). Okutsu and Inoue discussed the deletability of an embedded target NP depending on its case marker, partly inspired by the *Noun Phrase Accessibility Hierarchy* proposed by Keenan and Comrie's cross-linguistic investigation of RCs (1977).

Island constraints (Ross 1967), that is, syntactic constraints on the extractability of an embedded noun, have been claimed as one of the crucial indicia for the existence of syntactically governed RCs, as movement rules are considered particularly sensitive to these constraints. Japanese, unlike English, was largely understood as not having island constraints in general. However, there are situations in which the extractability of a noun from a complex NP in Japanese has been argued to illustrate such features as subject/non-subject asymmetry, that is, the extraction out of an NP in subject position is allowed, while the extraction out of an NP in non-subject position is not (N. Hasegawa 1985). We will consider related examples in Section 4.

Whether RCs (or the more general NMCC) involve syntactic movement is still a debated issue even within the generative grammar tradition. While the extraction-based analysis continues to be advocated (Whitman 2013), others, such as Hoji (1985) and Murasugi (2000), argue against a movement analysis. Murasugi, in particular, applying Kayne's (1994) antisymmetry analysis, states that Japanese does not have RCs as they are virtually indistinguishable from sentential modifiers in pure complex NPs.

The type and scope of data considered in studies that adopt the syntactic approach are much more narrowly drawn than the data used in the descriptive or semantic and pragmatic approaches: syntactic arguments generally employ introspective data, presumably because they are considered to represent linguistic competence and contribute to theoretical development. Instances of NMCC that are likely to be viewed as outside of the scope of syntactic accounts will be examined in the following sections.

From the perspective of functional syntax, Kuno (1973: 243–260) argued in his influential analysis of Japanese RCs that relativization involved theme deletion rather than simply the deletion of a coreferential NP. Specifically, what is relativized in his formulation is a thematic NP (i.e. NP+topic marker *wa*), not NP+case marker. This observation was based on four points of parallelism claimed between relativization and thematization: (i) when a case marker attached to the noun can be replaced by the topic marker *wa* (i.e. thematization of a noun without an attendant case marker), the noun can be the target of relativization, (ii) both constructions (under appropriate conditions) allow resumptive pronouns, (iii) a target in adverbial clauses, complex NPs, and sentential subjects can undergo thematization and relativization, and (iv) topic constructions with no corresponding themeless sentences have corresponding RCs. The association between the two constructions was attractive since it is intuitively plausible that the content of the RC provides a description *about* the HN. However, Kuno's proposal was not free of counterexamples

(Muraki 1970 discussed in Kuno 1973: 253–254 based on Kuno's manuscript; J. D. McCawley 1976 [1972]: 303–306; Matsumoto 1991: 391–395). A comparative chart of these two operations provided by Teramura (1992 [1975–1978]: 243) indicates that thematization is more restricted. The basic concept, nonetheless, was adopted by some movement-based syntactic analyses as an "aboutness relation" on relativization (Saito 1983: 314ff; Kameshima 1990).

3.2 Descriptive Approach

Martin (1975) and Teramura (e.g. 1992 [1975–1978]) are particularly notable for their insightful, in-depth descriptive analyses of instances of the NMCC. Martin's work, being part of a reference grammar of Japanese, provides ample natural data that are accessible to readers, including those who are not familiar with Japanese. Teramura's influential work, the majority of which is written in Japanese, offers detailed analyses of naturally occurring instances from various written sources. The classification of NMCCs that Teramura proposed – *uchi no kankei* 'inner relation' and *soto no kankei* 'outer relation' – has become well recognized among Japanese specialists.

Teramura did not directly address the developments within syntactic theories, but, reflecting the influence of structural linguistics, generative grammar, and traditional Japanese linguistics (by Mikami (1963), Sakuma (1952 [1940]), and Tokieda (1941)), he examined a wide range of instances and presented systematic analyses of Japanese noun modification (*rentai shūshoku*). One of his contributions is his bipartite classification of the construction in terms of the relations of the (semantically substantial) HN (*soko no meishi* 'base noun' in his term) to the modifying clause; namely, inner relation and outer relation. According to Teramura, the relationship between the HN and the modifying clause in the inner relation construction is solely structural, and such construction is comparable to the RC construction in English. It is created by a noun being extracted out of the sentence to become the HN, that is, the HN is in a case relation with the modifying clause predicate; specifically, the two constituents of the construction could form a sentence with the appropriate case marker for the HN. On the other hand, in the outer relation construction, the HN is required to be of a semantically special type, and the clause supplements the content of the meaning designated by the HN.

Instances of the outer relation NMCC are further categorized by Teramura into four types, depending on whether the HN expresses (i) speech and thought, (ii) facts and abstract concepts, (iii) sensation, or (iv) relational concepts. The outer relation instances can be compared to noun complement clauses in English, but the types of nouns that can be the HN are much broader than the English counterparts, as suggested above. The examples in (8) were provided by Teramura as a minimum pair of the two types of relations that share the same modifying clause. The example of the outer relation noun modification, (8b), is of the third type, that is, content of sensation.

(8) a. *[sakana* *o* *yaku]* *otoko* <inner relation>
fish ACC grill man
'[a man [who grills fish]]'

b. *[sakana* *o* *yaku]* *nioi* <outer relation/sensation>
fish ACC grill smell
'[the smell [of grilling fish]]'

Teramura, however, pointed out some unresolved issues, noting various instances in his data that did not clearly fit into the proposed bipartite classification. One of such cases is given as (5) in Section 2 [*[atama no yoku naru] hon]* 'the book where you become smarter; the book (by reading) which (one's) head gets better.' The major constituents in (5) neither form a sentence by a simple "insertion" of the HN with the appropriate case marker, nor can they fit into one of the four types of the outer relation construction, as the HN is not semantically so specified. Teramura refers to these examples as *"truncated" inner relation constructions*. We will see more examples in the following sections.

In a similar vein, example (9), a simplified version of an attested example discussed by Shirakawa (1986), presents another related difficulty. Shirakawa ultimately concluded that (9) is an instance of the outer relation construction because of the impossibility of converting the construction into a sentence by adding a case marker to the HN, but he also pointed out that the HN *wan-rūmu* 'one room' is not a semantically specialized noun of one of the four types of the outer relation modification.

(9) *[[Futatsu* *no* *heya* *no* *shikiri* *o* *toriharat-ta]* *wan-rūmu]* *ni*
two GEN room GEN divider ACC remove-PST one-room DAT

natte-iru.
become-PRF
'(It) has become [one room [which (resulted from) removing the divider between two rooms]].

Another issue is illustrated by (10), from a transcribed conversation, containing the HN *dōki* 'motive.' The HN is classified as an outer relation noun (relational), but Teramura also noted that constructions with nouns such as *dōki* as the HN could be converted to a sentence with the case marker *de* (i.e. *sono dōki de kimuchi o hajimeta* 'I started kimchee with that motive') and therefore they could also be classified as inner relation.

(10) *[[Kimuchi* *hajimeta]* *dōki]?*
kimchee started motive
'(My) motive [(for) having started (making) kimchee]?'

Teramura also made an observation regarding the use of *toiu* (referred to earlier as the quasi-quotation marker) in the outer relation instances; specifically, with respect to the co-occurrence conditions for *toiu*. In contrast to some other prominent contemporaneous studies of complementation that focused on the concepts of factivity and presupposition following Kiparsky and Kiparsky (1968) (e.g. Kuno 1973: 214; Josephs 1976), Teramura's analysis was based on the semantic type of the HN and the modality expressed in the modifying clause. For example, if the HN is *iken* 'opinion' and the clause conveys an assertion, *toiu* must be used for example, *kore wa dameda toiu iken* [this TOP is.not.good toiu opinion] 'the opinion that this is not good.' In some cases, for example, instances with a HN of fact, the use is optional, and in others, for example, instances with a HN of sensation, *toiu* is not used, for example, **sanma o yaku toiu nioi* [saury (fish) ACC grill *toiu* smell] '(intended) the smell of grilling a saury' (Teramura 1992: 204). Some others, such as N. A. McCawley (1978) and Terakura (1983), emphasized the propositional attitude of the speaker in the choice of *toiu* and presented more epistemologically based analyses. More recent discussions on functions and use of *toiu* from the discourse and cognitive perspectives are found in Masuoka (1997a: 32–38), Maynard (1992a), and Matsumoto (1998).

Martin's work in his chapter on "adnominalizations" in his reference grammar (1975) has not received as much attention as Teramura, but offers a comparable classification of the NMCC. Martin categorized nouns that become *epithemes* (i.e. HNs) into two major groups: those that are "extruded" from the sentence, and those that are "intruded," which he names "post-adnominals." With regard to the first group, he stated that "a noun phrase referring to the time (when), the place (where), the agent (who or by whom), the object (that or which is affected), the beneficiary (for whom), the reciprocal (with/against whom), the instrumental (with which), the ablative (from what/whom), etc., is pulled out to be embedded as an adjunct to a new predicate" (1975: 619). The idea is comparable to Teramura's inner relation type.

The "intruded" epithemes, which "come from outside the adnominalized sentence" are classified into three subtypes: summational (or synoptic), resultative (or creational), and transitional (or relational, or conjunctive). According to Martin, the summational epithemes refer to a situation, a fact, a report, an experience, a similarity, a hope, a thought, a sense, etc., and the situation or fact is elaborated in the adnominalized sentence. The resultative epithemes refer to a resultant thing or state, a product, a percept, etc., and the adnominalized sentence is the creative (or perceptive) process from which the result stems. The transitional epithemes refer to relative time or place, to a cause or reason, a purpose, or a degree, etc. These three subtypes occupy approximately the domain of Teramura's outer relation type.

Martin and Teramura thus presented similar classifications of the constructions. The extruded or the inner-relation type was described as strictly structural in contrast to the semantic treatment of the other type. In particular, the extruded or inner-relation type posited a sentence, that is, predication, as the basis of explaining attributive modification. While this offered a tangible guideline for acceptable constructions, there were unresolved questions, some of which were mentioned above, and importantly, the conflation of predication and attribution was a well-known problem pointed out by Bolinger (1967) in his seminal study of English adjectives. These issues figure prominently in the alternative approach that integrates semantic and pragmatic information into the analysis of the construction. In the next section, we will examine more cases for which consideration of semantic, pragmatic, and non-linguistic contextual information plays a significant role in the understanding of the construction.

4 Crucial Factors for Construal: Semantics, Pragmatics, and Real-world Knowledge

Structural conditions, for example, verb valence, are certainly important factors in understanding the relationship between the modifying clause verb and the HN, but other information also contributes crucially to the construal of a NMCC. We will discuss several examples to illustrate how non-structural information is crucially involved in determining the construal of a construction. (More detailed discussions are found in Matsumoto 1996b, 1997, 2007, among others, from which the following examples are cited, unless otherwise noted.)

The first set of examples were also given in Section 1. Among them, (2, 6, 7) are structurally identical except for the HNs, and the same is true of (3–4). They are repeated here as (11–13) and (14–15).

(11) *[hon o kat-ta] gakusei*
book ACC buy-PST student
'the student [who bought the book]'

(12) *[hon o kat-ta] uwasa*
book ACC buy-PST rumor
'the rumor [that (x) bought a book]'

(13) *[hon o kat-ta] otsuri*
book ACC buy-PST change (tender minus price)
'the change [from (x) buying a book]'

Given that these constructions are identical at the level of basic structure and, indeed, have the same modifying clause, the semantic information (including frame semantic information) supplied by the HN becomes most crucial in understanding the distinction among the three. It should be noted that the importance of semantics is relevant not only to examples (12–13), which are categorized as instances of the "outer relation" construction in Teramura's terms (or a noun complement construction and an "other" construction, respectively). It is equally relevant to examples such as (11), which is considered as an "inner relation" instance and an RCC, that is, a construction that is often considered to be defined purely structurally or syntactically. The meaning of *gakusei* 'student' supports the interpretation that the HN designates an entity that can be the buyer of the book, as given in (11).

Similarly, the choice of interpretation seems to closely reflect the construer's knowledge of the semantic information, real-world knowledge, and the context of the expressions used. The interpretation of the HN in (15) as a location is easy to understand, although it is an adjunct rather than a missing argument of the modifying verb as in (14). The semantic and pragmatic knowledge that *mise* 'store' is a likely location for a commercial event is an important factor for this interpretation; another factor may be that a student would not regularly be supposed to have financial means to purchase a store.

(14) *[gakusei ga kat-ta] hon*
student NOM buy-PST book
'the book [which the student bought]'

(15) *[gakusei ga kat-ta] mise*
student NOM buy-PST store
'the store [where the student bought (x)]'

This semantic and pragmatic precedence in choosing a preferred interpretation is also demonstrated by (16) from an actual conversation. The HN *katei-kyōshi* 'tutor' designates, in the preferred interpretation (16a), neither the subject nor an ordinary adjunct of the modifying clause (intransitive) verb *ukaru* 'pass (an exam, etc.),' but an element that can be interpreted as the condition or cause for what is described in the clause, as such consequence can be brought about by some condition. A similar relation was discussed in (5) *atama no yoku-naru hon* 'the book where you become smarter.' This interpretation is partly but crucially due to the real-world knowledge that a tutor is commonly sought and hired to assist someone to pass a high school entrance exam, rather than someone who has to pass such an exam. Another crucial factor is the meaning of the modifying clause verb, which can give rise to the role of condition that brought about the change of state. As the interpretation relies on some specific knowledge about the situation of high school entrance exams, this preference in interpretation is expected to vary depending on the construer's understanding of the relevant sociocultural conditions.

(16) *[[Kōkō nyūshi ni zettai ukaru] katei-kyōshi]*
high.school entrance.examination DAT absolutely pass tutor

o sagashite-iru n desu kedo...
ACC searching.for-PROG NMLZ COP but

a. Preferred: '(I) am searching for [a tutor [(with whose assistance) (x) can pass the high school entrance exam]], but...'
b. ??'(I) am searching for [a tutor [(who) can pass the high school entrance exam]], but...'

Similar effects of pragmatic and real-world knowledge in construal are also observed in the judgment of examples that are presented to illustrate syntactic constraints such as the subject–object asymmetry of extractability of an embedded NP. Comrie (1998: 71–72), referring to examples and arguments against subject–object asymmetry presented in Haig (1996: 84–85), emphasizes that constraints on extraction of a noun are pragmatic rather than syntactic. Haig argued specifically for the superiority of the functional concept of the "aboutness condition" over syntactic conditions, but regardless of the specific condition, it seems clear that what makes (17) appear unacceptable (or highly questionable) is not syntax, since a change in pragmatic conditions – as illustrated by (18) – makes the construction uncontroversially acceptable, although it has the same syntactic structure. The acceptability of (18) relies significantly on people's knowledge of the famous story of the dog Hachikō, whose loyalty continued after the master's death. The presentation of the examples is based on Comrie's representation.

(17) *?[[katte ita] kodomo ga shindeshimatta] inu*
keeping was child NOM died dog
'*the dog$_i$ [that the child$_j$ [that —$_j$ was keeping —$_i$] died'

(18) *[[Kawaigatte ita] hito ga nakunatta] inu ga maiban*
taking.care.of was person NOM died dog NOM every.evening

eki made kainushi o mukae ni kita.
station to master ACC greet to came
*'The dog$_i$ [that the person$_j$ [who —$_j$ was keeping —$_i$] died] came to the station every evening to greet his master.'

A naturally occurring example in which the indirect object is extracted out of a NP is provided in (19). This construal is supported by pragmatic and real-world knowledge that there is a custom of sending summer gifts to people, including business clients, and that a sender would be upset if such a gift arrived broken at the addressee.

(19) *[[[[Watashi ga okutta] o-chūgen] ga kowarete-ita] tokuisaki]*
I NOM sent HON-summer.gift NOM broken-was client
ga aru n desu ga...
NOM exist NMLZ COP but
Lit. 'There is a [client [(to whom) the summer gift [(which) I sent [was broken]]]], but...'

Cf. *[[Watashi ga **tokuisaki ni** okutta] o-chūgen] ga*
I NOM client DAT sent HON-summer.gift NOM
kowarete-ita. (Matsumoto 1997: 100–101)
broken-was
Lit. 'The summer gift [(which) I sent to a client was broken].'

The importance of pragmatics in the analysis of NMCCs was also demonstrated in a detailed examination of island effects in Japanese by Shimojo (2002). Investigating conditions under which island effects are "observed" in Japanese, he concluded that the controlling factors are not syntactic but are a multitude of related functional and cognitive factors, such as processing difficulties and maintaining focus. In other words, a successful construal is hindered if the specific instances present functional and cognitive difficulties. It is interesting to note in passing that much attention has been directed to a pragmatic and processing point of view in understanding island effects in English also (Hofmeister and Sag 2010).

Simple instances of the NMCC without involving embedding can be difficult to construe if they are not supported semantically and pragmatically. The following example (20) is problematic for Japanese speakers as a possible NP, according to the results of an informal experiment (Matsumoto 1997: 83).

(20) *??[[Tōkyō o tabeta] tomato]*
ACC ate tomato
'the tomato [that ate Tokyo]'

Unless the construers could imagine a horror movie-like scenario in which a monster tomato consumed the city of Tokyo, the construction was not comprehended. Since what was presented in the construction did not match the construer's understanding of the lexical meanings or their knowledge of the (regular) real world, some construers thought that they had either wrongly heard the accusative marker *o* instead of the locative marker *de* or that the speaker had misspoken. In contrast, the English counterpart, given as the translation, provides one undisputable interpretation, guided by its syntax, in which the tomato is the agent and Tokyo is the patient of eating. What is significant in this example is that, even if an argument position (i.e. the subject in this example) is available (i.e. missing in the clause) to be associated with the HN, without semantic and pragmatic support such interpretation is unattainable in Japanese. While in many prototypical instances all syntactic, semantic, and pragmatic conditions are met to reach a single acceptable interpretation, giving the impression that the necessary information is the syntactic (or structural) information alone, the examples above illustrate that when they are in competition, semantics and pragmatics take precedence over the syntax in construal and in judging the acceptability of the construction.

5 Construal of the Noun-modifying Clause Construction

5.1 Approach Based on Semantics and Pragmatics

The discussion in the previous sections suggests the benefit of an analytical model of construal that crucially incorporates semantic and pragmatic information. The theoretical foundation for the investigation of Japanese NMCCs in semantic and pragmatic terms was provided by the establishment of pragmatics in linguistics and of frame semantics (e.g. Fillmore 1982) in the late 1970s to 1980s. Both theoretical approaches investigated meaning beyond the truth value of propositions by incorporating contextual and encyclopedic knowledge in interpreting texts and other human communication. The development of pragmatics made it possible to approach language from a functional perspective, recognizing its complexity in terms of cognition, speech context, and sociocultural background. Just as the analysis of speech acts no longer needed to rely on posited linguistic materials, as was once proposed in the framework of transformational grammar (Ross 1970), the relationship between the two main constituents of a Japanese NMCC can be described without the aid of notional expressions (and deletion thereof) by directly appealing to the semantic and pragmatic information available in the text and context. Frame semantics, being an influential concept in the construction of meaning and grammar, allowed analyses that reference frame elements that reflect various components of the lexical meaning that are part of the frame evoked by a linguistic item.

In the context of those theoretical developments emerged a grammatical analysis of adnominal clauses in Japanese that significantly incorporated semantic and pragmatic factors (Matsumoto 1988a). The initial account was followed by a more detailed study of Japanese NMCCs which elaborated on the frame semantic-based construal mechanism and emphasized the semantic and pragmatic coherence (or non-coherence) between the two juxtaposed main constituents, which lack explicit marking of their relation (Matsumoto 1997). In this framework, the coherence of an instance of the NMCC that is morphosyntactically well formed is inferred through the integration of frames and frame elements evoked by the linguistic items of the construction with the support of the construer's world-view. For example, (5) *atama no yokunaru hon* 'the book where you become smarter' given earlier, is coherent, even though the HN is not associated with the notional subject or an adjunct, because the modifying clause predicate *yoku-naru* 'gets better' evokes a change-of-state frame, and in that frame we can identify the role of a condition that brings about the change. In order for this interpretation to be obtained, the construer's world-view needs to support the situation given in the construction, that is, (reading) books is understood to develop people's intellectual capacity.

Matsumoto (1997) presented three possible patterns in which the single structure of NMCC is likely to be construed classified by which constituent plays the role of anchor (or host) in the semantic integration of the construction. They are: the "Clause Host" (CH) type, the "Noun Host" (NH) type, and the "Clause and Noun Host" (CNH) type. These were presented not as definitive subcategories but only for expository purposes to illustrate that NMCC construal is not based on a simple association of the constituents but is systematic.

In CH-type instances, for example, (2–5) above, the modifying clause hosts the HN, that is, a member of the category denoted by the HN participates in the frame evoked by the predicate of the modifying clause. Although these instances resemble RC constructions, the "gap" in the clause is not syntactic but is conceived as a semantic element in a conceptual structure evoked by the predicate. Therefore, the semantic relation between the HN and the clause can be more extended than a syntactic or structural analysis could support, for example, (5), (9), and (16). The HN could represent a frame element specific to the particular modifying predicate (e.g. commercial event frame elements) or other elements, such as location, cause, and consequence, motivated by various characteristics of the predicate, such as being an agentive action, punctual action, volitional action, etc.

In NH type instances, for example, (6), the HN hosts the modifying clause, that is, what is described in the modifying clause participates in the nominal frame evoked by the HN. Instances of the HN in the NH-type pattern (e.g. *uwasa* 'rumor,' *jijitsu* 'fact,' *denpō* 'telegram') semantically function as content taking in Japanese in a similar way as the HNs of noun complement clause constructions do.

In the instances that are observed to present the CNH-type construal pattern, for example, (7) and (8b), both the modifying clause and the HN are said to host reciprocally, that is, the HN evokes a frame in which what is expressed by the modifying clause participates, while what is denoted by the HN can participate in the frame evoked by the modifying clause predicate. The semantics of the HN in this integration type is not content taking, but relational in a broad sense in that such nouns (e.g. *kekka* 'result,' *nioi* 'smell,' *nokori* 'remainder) are meaningful specifically in relation to some entity or event, and the modifying clause can describe such an event or a state. Unlike in the NH type, in which there is no involvement of the HN in the state or the event described in the modifying clause (e.g. in *hon o katta uwasa* 'the rumor that (x) bought a book,' the rumor has no position internally in the event of book buying), the denotatum of a CNH-type HN can participate in the event described in the modifying clause (e.g. in *sakana o yaku nioi* 'the smell of grilling fish,' the smell can be identified as a byproduct of the event). Instances such as (10) *kimuchi hajimeta dōki* '(my) motive for having started (making) kimchee,' which presents a problem for Teramura's bipartite classification in that they present features of the inner relation and of the outer relation constructions, are of the CNH type in this frame-semantic-based framework. The similarity and the difference between the CNH-type and the CH-type integration patterns are observed in examples such as (8b) *[sakana o yaku] nioi* 'the smell of grilling fish' and (9) *[futatsu no heya no shikiri o toriharat-ta] wan-rūmu* 'one room (which resulted) from removing the divider between two rooms.' Both HNs represent the consequence of the event given in the modifying clause, yet while the HN of the CNH type (8b) is semantically relational in the sense described above, the HN of the CH type (9) is a regular noun without the special semantic specification of being relational, and is understood as the consequence of the event described in the clause in the linguistic and non-linguistic context.

The integration of frame-semantic and pragmatic principles into the grammatical analysis of Japanese NMCCs made it possible to discuss a wide range of instances that share one structure under one rubric without discounting some non-prototypical instances and without forced categorization boundaries. The semantic- and pragmatic-focused approach to Japanese NMCCs is also found in more recent studies by researchers such as Kato (2003: 2207–2297), who argues against Teramura's bipartite categorization and proposes a pragmatic-based construal process, Masuoka (1997a: 25–46, 167–180), who advocates a conceptual schema analysis in order to account for the extensive semantic relationships observed between the HN and the modifying clause of the structurally undifferentiated NMCC, and Nakayasu (2003), who investigates further conditions of Japanese NMCC construability by considering multiple factors of the language user's cognition and world-view. Matsumoto (2007) provides a more cognitively based analysis of NMCC instances, inspired by the idea of conceptual blending (e.g. Fauconnier and Turner 2002).

5.2 Possible Relations Construed between the Head Noun and the Modifying Clause

Below are some instances of NMCCs that illustrate the possible semantic relations between the two constituents. Unless otherwise noted, the examples are drawn mostly from naturally occurring instances cited for the three types of construal patterns by Matsumoto (e.g. 1997, 2007), which provide more instances and analyses.

5.2.1 Clause Host Type

When the HN is not a noun that evokes a nominal frame, it is likely that the denotatum of the HN participates in the event or state described in the modifying clause. Such examples are considered to be of the Clause Host (CH) type. The denotatum of the HN can in some instances participate as a core element of the frame evoked by the modifying clause predicate (e.g. 21), but it can also be a non-core member, typically motivated by some general characteristic of the modifying clause predicate (e.g. 22). In terms of grammatical relations, the core elements are (usually considered as) arguments (e.g. subject, direct object) and the non-core elements are adjuncts.

The HN of (21) – the headline of a newspaper article on a baseball game between the Tokyo-based team (the Giants) and the Osaka-based team (the Tigers) – was interpreted to instantiate a core role of the frame evoked by *yaburu* 'beat,' either the beater or the beaten, depending on the non-linguistic context in which it was used.

(21) [[Event/State] Core Role]
[[yaburu] kyojin]
beat the.Giants (Tokyo-based baseball team)
a. 'the Giants, [who will beat (every team/the opponent)]' [The Tokyo edition]
<Beater; Subject>
b. 'the Giants, [whom (our home team) will beat]' [The Osaka edition]
<Beaten; Direct Object>

(22) [[Event/State] Non-Core Role]
[[petto ga shin-da] tomodachi] o hagemash-itai . . .
pet NOM die-PST friend ACC encourage-want
'(I) want to encourage [the friend [whose pet died]]. . .' (Web forum: *Chiebukuto* 2013/11/01)
<Possessor; Genitive>

Example (22) shows that the HNs can instantiate an NP position that is very low in Keenan and Comrie's Accessibility Hierarchy (1977) of relativization SU > DO > IO > OBL > GEN > OCOMP. (Elicited examples in which the HN instantiates the role of object of comparison, that is, OCOMP, are given in Matsumoto 1997: 99.)

Further, the HN can instantiate a role whose relation to the modifying clause predicate cannot be reduced to what can be expressed by case markers, but the relationship between the two constituents is construable and the modifying clause presents an attributive description of the HN. For example, we have discussed earlier how (5) is construed as coherent with a common world-view by regarding the denotatum of the HN as instantiating the role of condition identified in the change-of-state frame evoked by the modifying clause predicate *yoku-naru* 'gets better.' In turn, the modifying clause is understood to represent the state that is the consequence (Matsumoto 2007: 133–134). The English translations are mostly literal translations.

(23) [[Consequence (Event/State)] Condition]
[[atama no yoku-naru] hon]
head GEN good-become book
'the book (by reading which) (x's) head gets better'

(24) [[Condition (Event/State)] Consequence]
[[Hon'yakushita] o-kane], zenbu tabe-chatta no?
translated money all eaten-have Q
'Have you eaten your way through all the money (which you earned by) (your) having translated (x)?'

In (24), the description given in the modifying clause 'having translated (something)' may make the role of consequence available since the perfect form describes a past event. When it is construed in juxtaposition with the HN *o-kane* 'money,' which evokes a commercial transaction frame, it can be understood as representing a service that is provided in exchange of money (Matsumoto 2007: 140–142). This interpretation needs to be supported by the construer's understanding of the world.

(25) [[Event/State] Reverse Condition]
[[Futoranai] okashi] wa nai kashira.
gain.weight-not sweets TOP exist.not I.wonder
'I wonder if there aren't any sweets (even though (x) eats which) (x) doesn't gain weight.'

As somewhat twisted variations of the consequence-condition relation, (25) represents an object (sweets) that brings out normally unexpected effects, rather than the sweets that cause you not to gain weight.

(26) [[Purpose (Event/State)] Requisite]
[[shimekiri ni maniawasu] hayai hitsuryoku]
deadline at make.it.meet fast the.power.of.the.pen
'the brisk writing (which is necessary for) (x) to meet the deadline'

(27) [[Requisite (Event/State)] Purpose]
[[Te o araw-anakute ii] oyatsu] nai?
hand ACC wash-not.GER O.K. snack exist.not
'Isn't there a snack (in order to eat which) (x) don't have to wash hands?'

(28) [[Part] Whole]
[[Go-fun-kan de suji ga ieru] kabuki] wa kirai.
five-minutes-period by plot NOM can.tell TOP dislike
'(I) dislike a kabuki play (whose) plot can be told in five minutes'

(29) [[Whole] Part]
[[Nuimono o suru] te] mo yasume-nai.
sewing ACC do hand even rest-not
'(She) does not rest even (her) hand (with which she) is sewing.'

In (29), the 'hand' expressed by the HN is not what is sewing, but the hand is the relevant part of the person who is sewing. The relationship between the HN to the clause in this example is the opposite of the part–whole relationship that is illustrated in (28).

5.2.2 Noun Host Type

Examples under the Noun Host (NH) type are instances in which the HN can evoke a nominal frame that has a role or "frame element" that represents the content of what is denoted by the noun and in which the content element is described in the modifying clause. (A noun that can evoke a nominal frame can behave as a regular noun and participate in a construction construed as a CH type, for example, *kinō kiita uwasa* [yesterday heard rumor] 'the rumor that (I) heard yesterday.')

(30) [[Content] Communication]
[[Tōnyō ga akka-shite gan ni natta] hanashi]
diabetes NOM become.aggravated cancer DAT become story

nado tsuizo kiita koto ga nai.
such.as ever heard NMLZ NOM not.exist
'(I) have never heard of a story (that/in which) diabetes became aggravated to become a cancer.'

(31) [[Content] Thoughts and Feelings]
[[Bakana koto o shita nā, tte] ki] ga mōretsuni shita
stupid thing ACC did SFP QUOT feeling NOM intensely did

wake yo.
NMLZ SFP
'(I) had an intense feeling that (I) had done something stupid.'

(32) [[Content] Abstract Concept]
. . . [[atama o tataku] kuse] ga aru . . .
head ACC hit habit NOM exist
'. . . have the habit of hitting (my) head. . .'

5.2.3 Clause and Noun Host

If the HN denotes some relational concept or an instantiation of such a concept that is dependent on some event or state, it is likely that what is described in the modifying clause provides such event or state. On the one hand, the relational concept denoted by the HN calls for propositional content on which it is relationally dependent; on the other, it participates in a frame evoked by the modifying clause predicate. The HN of the construction (33), *gen'in* 'cause' is a general relational term, while the HN of (34), *otsuri* 'change' is a concept more specific to a commercial event frame.

(33) [[Event/State] Relational Concept]
sorede, kono, [[shippai-shita] gen'in] wa da na ...
and this failed cause TOP is SFP
'and, this, the cause for (x's) having failed is...'

(34) *[[kodomotachi ga dagashi o kat-ta] otsuri] o ...*
children NOM candy ACC buy-PST change ACC
'[the change [(from) children buying candy]]...'

The same HN can be used to express different construal patterns such as those presented below. The difference between (36) and (37) is that the content of the result is given in the modifying clause in (36), whereas the content is given in the main clause in (37) and the cause of such result is described in the modifying clause.

(35) Clause Host
[[Ishi kara kii-ta] kekka] o tsutae-ta.
doctor from hear-PST result ACC relay-PST
'(I) relayed the result which (I) heard from the doctor.'

(36) Noun Host
Kinō tabesugi-ta node [[kyō nanimo tabe-rare-nai] kekka]
yesterday overeat-PST because today anything eat-POT-NEG result

ni nat-ta.
DAT become-PST
'Because (I/you/he/etc.) overate yesterday, it became [the result [that (x) cannot eat anything today]].'

(37) Clause and Noun Host
[[Kinō tabesugi-ta] kekka] kyō nanimo tabe-rare-nai.
yesterday overeat- PST result today anything eat-POT-NEG
'As [a result [of having overeaten yesterday]], (x) cannot eat anything today.'

6 Concluding Remarks: Related issues and Future Studies

We have discussed instances of the NMCC in Japanese that demonstrate a wide range of semantic relations between the modifying clause and the head noun. While in some other languages these interpretations are expressed by distinct constructions such as RCCs, NCCs, and others, the instances discussed above demonstrate that in Japanese one single construction can be employed for an extensive array of relations. In the absence of an explicit marking of the relation between the noun and the modifying clause, semantic and pragmatic information and real-world knowledge are crucial to the construal of the construction. To determine what may be the most satisfactory explanation of the Japanese NMCC, further studies are required, but it is clear that any explanation must address the wide range of meanings covered by the single construction.

The phenomenon in Japanese of having one single noun-modifying construction covering a broad range of interpretations – that is, the GNMCC – has cross-linguistic implications. The Eurasian languages investigated in Matsumoto et al. (2017) share similar properties to Japanese, such as low referential density. They also show variations in the extent to which they exhibit a GNMCC.

We have seen that Japanese differs from European languages such as English with regard to having a GNMCC. However, variations within European languages such as Greek, German, and English demonstrate to some degree a GNMCC: Greek colloquial relative clauses with the invariant marking *pou/pu* (Maling 1977; Haberland and van der Auwera 1990; Nikiforidou 2005), German *wo* (van Riemsdijk 2003), and certain English relatives that are signaled by *where* and *that* (Matsumoto 1989) as in the attested example *Here is a snack that/where you don't have to wash your hands.*

In Greek, German, and English, the referential density is high, unlike in Japanese. Yet, without explicit marking of the semantic relationship between the constituents, the construal seems to rely on semantic, pragmatic and real-world information. By the same token, the lack of syntactically imposed constraints allows a wide range of semantic relationships between the head noun and the clause, which cannot easily be expressed by the normative RCCs. More cross-linguistic investigation would provide further information as to what properties of a language are significant in determining whether and to what degree it has a GNMCC.

This chapter has focused on the important features of the basic structure of the Japanese NMCC, but there are other relevant aspects of the construction that have been studied and that can be further investigated. I only briefly mention a few, and reference should be made to the cited works.

One issue is about the form of the modifying clause predicate. Unless it is followed by the quasi-quotation marker *toiu*, it is normally – or, perhaps, normatively – in the merged adnominal/finite form, unaccompanied by the sort of speech act expressions that can be used in a main clause. However, in many attested instances, performative honorific forms and other speech act elements are observed in the subordinate clause in certain communicative contexts (e.g. Maynard 2008b: 73–75; Matsumoto 2009, 2010). These observations suggest that (i) the historical merger of adnominal and finite forms of predicates may be the source of the observed main clause phenomena in subordinate clauses (Horie 2017), and that (ii) constructions that are considered to be "deviant" may, in fact, be pragmatically motivated genre-sensitive constructions (Matsumoto 2010).

A second issue worthy of further investigation is the function of the modifying clause final *toiu* and its variants. As mentioned in Section 3.2, *toiu* does not function simply as a complementizer, such as English *that*. We have mentioned earlier studies by N. A. McCawley (1978) and Terakura (1983), which discussed *toiu*'s functions beyond the concerns of factivity. More recent studies, such as (Masuoka 1997a: 32–38; Maynard 1992a; Matsumoto 1998), focus on the pragmatic effects of using *toiu*.

Another important topic previously noted is NMCCs with HNs that are semantically abstract or light, such as *toki* 'time,' *tame* 'purpose,' *koto* 'matter' (Teramura 1992 [1978]; Takara 2012). These NMCCs function similarly to adverbial clauses (e.g. *itta toki* [went time] 'when I went') or complement clauses (e.g. *itta koto* [went matter] 'that I went'). The ubiquity of NMCCs in Japanese is likely to be associated with such functional versatility.

Continuing and extending the study of NMCCs with light heads, the pragmatic effect of using them without a main clause has been explored (e.g. Horie 2008), and the genre-sensitivity of NMCCs with more substantial HNs that stand alone has been investigated (Tsubomoto 2009; Matsumoto 2015). Those studies relate NMCC issues – which might otherwise have been seen as peripheral or fragmentary instances – to broader topics of linguistic investigation.

How the construction is acquired by children and by second language learners is another important issue for investigation. Recently, some studies have started investigating acquisition across the entire range of NMCCs in Japanese (e.g. Ozeki 2008; Yabuki-Soh 2012). More studies with a broad scope supported by sophisticated experimental methods will certainly elucidate our understanding of the acquisition process.

The process of construing NMCCs in general is another very interesting and intriguing issue. Cognitive linguistic approaches, such as blending of cognitive domains (Fauconnier and Turner 2002), can provide further insights to constructions such as the NMCC in which no explicit marking of the domain connection is provided. At the same time, recent developments in computational linguistics and natural language processing may shed light on the process of NMCC construal (e.g. earlier investigations by Baldwin 1998), while further investigation within FrameNet (Baker and Fillmore 2010) may be able to illuminate how a network of concepts can explicate the coherence in the construction.

There is ample room for the NMCC to be further investigated to yield more insights in the areas mentioned above, among others. Past studies of NMCCs demonstrated that this construction in Japanese does not necessarily behave in the same way as similar constructions in more commonly studied languages. Such studies, as well as studies of the topic construction in Japanese, also illustrated that the analysis of Japanese can provide a fresh perspective on linguistic phenomena that are either considered well known or that may not previously have been recognized as important.

21

Internally Headed Relativization and Related Constructions

Kyoko Hirose Ohara

1 Introduction

This chapter discusses the so-called internally headed relativization (IHR) construction in Modern Japanese in comparison with other constructions that are related to it either formally or semantically. Describing and accounting for the nature of IHR involves not only structural, semantic, and pragmatic examinations but also typological and diachronic considerations. The internally headed relative clause (IHRC) is recognized as one type of relative clause. This chapter focuses on a common use of IHRC, the narrative IHRC, which has been studied extensively since Kuroda's pioneering work (1992a [1974–1977]).

An important research question concerning IHRC has been how to make sense of the relationship between the IHRC and the externally headed relative clause (EHRC). Syntactically IHRCs and EHRCs both behave externally as NPs, and semantically IHR sentences and the corresponding externally headed relativization (EHR) sentences have the same propositional content. Nevertheless, they seem to have different functions. Another question involving IHR is how to account for its restricted occurrence.

1.1 Internally Headed Relativization

Sentences such as (1) and (2) have structures that suggest the literal translations in (1a) and (2a), respectively, but in fact have the meanings shown in (1b) and (2b):

(1) *[[Ringo ga tēburu no ue ni atta]$_{S1}$ no] o Midori wa totta]$_{S2}$*
apple NOM table GEN top LOC existed NMLZ ACC TOP took
a. 'Midori picked up [that there was an apple on the table].'
b. 'There was an apple on the table, and Midori picked (it) up.'

(2) *[[[Ringo ga tēburu no ue ni atta]$_{S1}$ no] ga ochita]$_{S2}$.*
NMLZ NOM fell.off

a. '[That there was an apple on the table] fell.'
b. 'There was an apple on the table, and (it) fell off.'

The morpheme *no*, which follows S1 in (1–2), can be used as a nominalizer, hence the pseudo-translations in (1a) and (2a).[1] The direct-object referent of the main predicate in (1) must be an entity and not a proposition. The same is true for the subject referent in (2). Hence, the meanings shown in (1b) and (2b).

In both (1) and (2), a valence requirement of the main predicate corresponds to an NP inside S1, namely, *ringo* 'apple,' which is underlined. Also, the case marking on the nominalized clause (i.e. S1 plus *no*) coincides with that required by the main predicate for the role of the valence requirement: In (1) it is the accusative *o* and in (2) it is the nominative *ga*.

These two properties, namely, a valence requirement of the main predicate appearing inside S1 and the case marking on the nominalized clause matching that required by the main predicate for the valence participant, have led researchers to characterize these types of sentences as involving IHRCs (Kuroda 1992b; Ohara 1996; inter alia). Traditionally, the IHRC has been defined as a nominalized clause pertaining to a target NP which occurs inside the clause. It is commonly recognized as one type of relative clause and is attested in a number of languages (Andrews 1985 [1975]; Keenan 1985). The term IHRC can mean different things in different languages, as we will see in Section 2. Unless otherwise noted, in this chapter IHR and IHRC refer to those in Japanese.

As is well known, Japanese also has externally headed relative clauses (EHRCs) and much study has been done on them (Matsumoto 1997). The schematic representations of EHRCs and IHRCs are given in Figure 21.1.

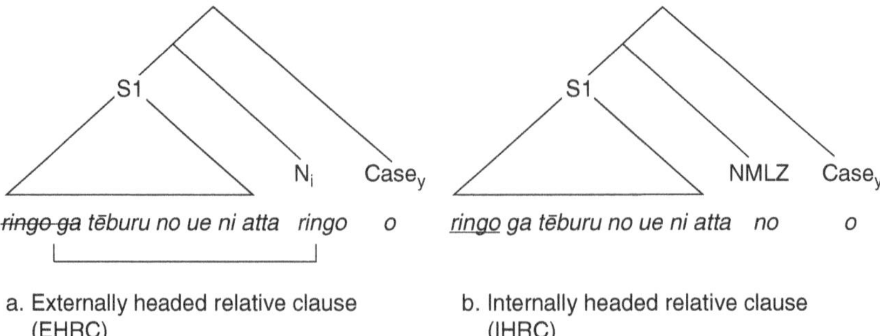

Figure 21.1 Two types of relative clause

[1] In Japanese, a strict verb-final language, the predicate of the subordinate clause, whether the clause is embedded or not, precedes the main predicate. Throughout this chapter I will call the subordinate clause Sl and the main clause S2 based on the order of the predicates.

At first glance, the two structures seem parallel to each other. They are, however, crucially different in two respects: (i) whether or not the target of relativization appears inside S1, and (ii) what kind of constituent can follow S1. With EHRCs, the target of relativization and its case marker are phonetically missing inside S1. On the other hand, in IHRCs, the target is present in S1. Second, in EHRCs, the head noun N_i follows S1. In contrast, it is the nominalizer *no* that always follows an IHRC.

Example (3a) gives the structural description of EHR sentences. The crossed out NPi-case$_x$ represents the phonetically missing target of relativization and its case marker, or a "gap," in the relative clause. The head noun N_i is coindexed with the target of relativization. Case$_y$, which is attached to the complex NP as a whole, indicates the role of the NP in the main clause S2.

(3) EHR sentences
  a. [. . . [[. . . ~~NP$_i$-case$_x$~~. . . V1]$_{S1}$ N$_i$] case$_y$. . . V2]$_{S2}$
  b. *[[~~Ringo~~ ~~ga~~ tēburu no ue ni atta]$_{S1}$ ringo] o Midori wa*
  apple NOM table GEN top LOC existed apple ACC TOP
  totta.
  took
  'Midori picked up the apple [that there was ~~an apple~~ on the table].'

The structural description of IHR sentences is given in (4). NP$_i$-case$_x$ is phonetically present in S1; NP$_i$ represents the target and case$_x$ is appropriate for the role of NP$_i$ within S1. Strictly speaking, the term *target* is generally used to refer to the role of NP$_i$ in S1. Throughout this chapter, however, I will refer to NP$_i$, which corresponds to a valence requirement of V2, as the "target NP." Case$_y$ after the nominalizer indicates the role of NP$_i$ in S2. Sentence (1) above exemplifies IHR.

(4) IHR sentences
  [. . . [[. . . NP$_i$-case$_x$. . . V1]$_{S1}$ *no*] case$_y$. . . V2]$_{S2}$

I will mention "external syntax of S1." In the case of EHRCs, this refers to the syntactic role that the sequence S1 plus the head noun N_i plays within the larger sentence. In the case of IHRCs, it refers to the syntactic role played by the sequence S1 plus *no*. Also, I will refer to the sequence S1 plus *no* in IHR sentences as "the (*no*-)nominalized clause." Throughout this chapter, "the external marking on S1" refers to case$_y$, shown in (3a) and (4).

The reader may have noticed that the EHR sentence (3b) and the IHR sentence (1) are translated differently into English. As will be discussed in Section 3, they are typically used under different pragmatic circumstances. I have purposely avoided using ordinary restrictive relative clauses for the translations of the IHR sentences in order to reflect this fact.

1.2 Salient Properties of IHR

IHR sentences possess properties that are peculiar with respect to what we know about relativization.

1.2.1 Restricted External Marking

The IHRC is restricted in its external marking. It is typically marked by either the nominative *ga* or the accusative *o*, as in (5a–b). *No*-nominalized clauses marked with the dative (5c) or the instrumental (5e) are not usually construed as IHRCs, although IHRCs externally marked with the allative (5d), the ablative (5f), or the comitative (5g) are possible:

(5) a. Nominative

[[ōkami ga ori kara tōbō shita] no] ga niwatori
wolf NOM cage ABL ran.away NMLZ NOM hen

o osotta.
ACC attacked

'The wolf ran away from the cage, and (it) attacked the hen.'

b. Accusative

[[Tarō ga hashittekita] no] o Hanako ga tukamaeta.
NOM came.running NMLZ ACC NOM caught

'Taro came running, and Hanako caught (him).'

c. Dative

**[[Hanako ga kekkonshita] no] ni Midori wa kabin o ageta.*
NOM married NMLZ DAT TOP vase ACC gave

Intended: 'Hanako got married, and Midori gave a vase to (her).'

d. Allative

[[Mi o irete Yūsaku ga tazuneru] no] e Mitsugu wa
body ACC put NOM ask NMLZ ALL TOP

odayakani hanashita. (MIYAO Tomiko, *Kyara no kaori*)
calmly spoke

'Yusaku earnestly asked, and Mitsugu spoke calmly to (him).'

e. Instrumental

**[[Pen ga ofisu ni atta] no] de Tarō wa atena*
pen NOM office LOC existed NMLZ INSTR TOP address

o kaita.
ACC wrote

Intended: 'A pen was in the office, and Taro wrote the address with (it).'

f. Ablative

Jimukan wa [[shorui ga mada dekiteinai] no] kara
secretary TOP papers NOM yet not.completed NMLZ ABL

katazukeyō to shita. (Mihara 1994: 86)
tried.to.finish

'The paperwork was not done yet, and the secretary decided to finish (it) first.'

g. Comitative

[[Tomodachi ga Amerika kara nihon ni ichiji kikoku shiteita]
friend NOM ABL Japan ALL was.on.a.home.leave

no] to jū-nen buri ni saikaishita.
NMLZ COM after.10-years.of.absence saw.again

'A friend of mine was in Japan on a home leave from America, and I saw (him) after 10 years of absence.'

This kind of limited external marking is peculiar in light of commonly held views of relativization. Comrie (1989: 153) notes that the role of the head noun in the main clause makes little or no difference to the possibility of forming relative clauses. The accessibility hierarchy proposed by Keenan and Comrie (1977: 63–88) characterizes accessibility of an NP to relativization, which pertains to the role of the target within the relative clause, but what we are concerned with here is the role of the whole NP in the main clause. Hirose and Ohori (1992: 4–5) suggest that the reason why *no*-nominalized clauses marked with the dative *ni* or the instrumental *de* are not usually construed as IHRCs has to do with processing constraints. That is, there exist clausal conjunctions *noni* 'although' and *node* 'because,' which look just like the nominalizer plus the dative or the instrumental, respectively, and this may be responsible for limited occurrences of IHRCs marked externally with the dative *ni* or the instrumental *de*. Note that S2 in (6b) explicitly contains a pronoun marked with the instrumental *de*.

(6) a. Concessive clausal-conjunction *noni* 'although,' cf. (5c):

[Hanako ga kekkonshita] noni, Midori wa o-iwai o
NOM married although TOP gift ACC

agenakatta.
did.not.give

'Although Hanako got married, Midori did not give a wedding gift.'

b. Causal clausal-conjunction *node* 'because,' cf. (6e):

[Pen ga ofisu ni atta] node, Tarō wa ***sore***
pen NOM office LOC existed because TOP that

de *gāru furendo ni tegami o kaita.*
INSTR girl friend DAT letter ACC wrote

'Because there was a pen in the office, Taro wrote a letter to his girlfriend with that.'

1.2.2 The Target of Relativization

EHRCs in Japanese are used not only restrictively (i.e. to help identify the head noun referent) but also non-restrictively (i.e. to add a piece of parenthetical information about the head noun referent):

(7) a. EHRC – Restrictive

[[*Taiheiyō* *ni* *iru*] *kuzira*] *wa* *ōkii.*
Pacific Ocean LOC exist whale TOP large
'Whales that are in the Pacific Ocean are large.'
('Pacific Ocean whales are large.')

b. EHRC – Non-restrictive

[[*Honyūrui* *dearu*] *kuzira*] *wa* *sakana* *to* *wa* *kotonaru.*
mammal COP whale TOP fish COM TOP different
'Whales, which are mammals, are different from fish.'

Thus, the target of relativization of EHRCs can be a proper noun as in (8a). IHRCs also allow proper-noun targets as in (8b), although the typical function of IHRCs is neither restrictive nor non-restrictive in the usual sense, as will be discussed later.

(8) a. EHRC

[[Furimukikakeru] *Senkichi]* *o,* *Tami* *ga* *karada* *de* *tometa.*
about.to.turn.back ACC NOM body INSTR stopped.
'Tami stopped Senkichi, who was about to turn back, with her body.'

b. IHRC

[[Senkichi *ga* *furimukikakeru]* *no]* *o,* *Tami* *ga* *karada*
NOM about.to.turn.back NMLZ ACC NOM body
de *tometa.* (MUKŌDA Kuniko, *A un*)
INSTR stopped.
'Senkichi was about to turn back, and Tami stopped (him) with her body.'

Furthermore, IHR differs from EHR in allowing multiple-targets (Kuroda 1992a: 155). In (9), for example, the subject *Jiro* and the direct object *Saburo* of S1 are both taken as the direct object of V2:

(9) *[[Jirō* *ga* *Saburō* *o* *onbu shiyō to shiteiru]* *no]* *o*
NOM ACC try.to.carry.on.one's.back NMLZ ACC
Tarō *wa* *futari-tomo* *okizari ni shita.*
TOP two.people-both left.behind
'Jiro was trying to carry Saburo on his back, and Taro left both (of them) behind.'

The multiple-target phenomenon appears to be unique to Japanese IHRCs (cf. Section 2.1.2).

1.2.3 IHR as Bi-clausal Sentences

An IHRC plus the nominalizer, unlike an EHRC plus a head noun, cannot be used in isolation as a simple referring expression. Just as one can refer to a person using a lexical noun as in (10b), one can equally well use an EHRC followed by a lexical head for the same function, as in (10c). An IHRC followed by the nominalizer *no*, in contrast, cannot be used alone as a referring expression as shown in (10d). This illustrates that *no*-nominalized IHRC can only be used in combination with another clause and that IHR sentences are bi-clausal.

(10) a. Q: *Dare ga kawa ni ochimashita ka?*
who NOM river DAT fell.into Q
'Who fell into the river?'

b. A: *Keikan.* (lexical noun)
policeman
'A policeman.'

c. *[[Dorobō o oikaketeita] keikan].* (EHRC+lexical head)
thief ACC chased policeman
'The policeman who was pursuing a thief.'

d. *[[*Keikan ga dorobō o oikaketeita] no].* (IHRC+NMLZ)
policeman NOM thief ACC chased NMLZ
Intended: 'The policeman who was pursuing a thief.'

1.3 The Status of the Post-relative *No* in IHR

So far I have assumed that the post-relative *no* in IHR is a nominalizer, but this is not the only possible analysis. *No* in Modern Japanese is polyfunctional between the genitive case marking, nominalizing, and so-called "pronominal" uses (11).[2]

(11) a. *Sakana <u>no</u> hone* (genitive)
fish GEN bone
'bone of fish'

b. *Kuniko wa [[sakana o yaku] <u>no</u>]* (NMLZ)
TOP fish ACC grill NMLZ
ga jōzuda.
NOM is.good.at
'Kuniko is good at grilling fish.'

c. *Fugu no mise de [[kara-age ni shita] <u>no</u>] ga*
globefish GEN restaurant LOC deep.fried PRO NOM
deta.
appeared
'In a globefish restaurant, I was served deep-fried ones (=globefish).' (pronominal)

It might be argued that the post-relative *no* in IHR is the pronominal rather than the nominalizer. That is, it might be possible that the post-relative *no* is coindexed with the target NP inside S1. This would mean that IHRCs are externally headed, with the pronominal as the external head:

(12) An alternative analysis of IHR

[... [[... NP_i-$case_x$... V1]$_{S1}$ no_i] $case_y$... V2]$_{S2}$
no_i: pronominal

[2] Japanese grammarians generally believe these uses to be historically related.

I ignore the possibility that *no* in IHR could be the genitive case marker, since the genitive *no* cannot follow a predicate. Kuroda argues that the post-relative *no* in IHR is indeed the nominalizer against the pronominal analysis of Martin (1975). He observes that the post-relative *no* behaves differently from the pronominal *no* in two respects. First, the pronominal *no* is generally replaceable by its explicit antecedent even though it would be wordy:

(13) a. *Asoko ni aru ringo wa aokute, [[koko ni aru]*
there LOC exist apple TOP green-and here LOC exist
no] wa akai.
PRO TOP red
'The apple which is there is green, and the one here is red.'
=b. *Asoko ni aru ringo wa aokute, [[koko ni aru] ringo] wa akai.*
'The apple which is there is green, and the apple here is red.'

In IHR, *no* is not replaceable by the same noun as the target inside S1:

(14) a. *[[Aoi ringo ga sara no ue ni aru] no] o*
green apple NOM plate GEN top LOC exist ACC
Tarō wa totte,...
TOP took-and
'There was an apple on the plate, and Taro picked (it) up, and...'
b. **[[Aoi ringo ga sara no ue ni aru] ringo] o Tarō wa totte,...*

Second, the pronominal *no* may not be used in reference to somebody who is conventionally shown deference linguistically. That is, stylistically the pronominal *no* does not harmonize with honorific expressions, as shown in (15b):

(15) a. *Asoko ni tatteiru kodomo o soko ni*
there LOC standing child ACC there LOC
suwarasete, [[mukō ni tatteiru] no] o koko
sit-CAUS far.over.there LOC standing PRO ACC here
ni suwarasete kudasai.
LOC sit-CAUS please
'Please have the child standing over there sit there near you and have the one standing far over there sit here.'
b. **Asoko ni tatteirassharu go-rōjin o soko ni*
standing.HON HON-elderly.person ACC there LOC
oyobishite,
HON.have.come
[[mukō ni tatteirassharu] no] o koko ni oyobishite kudasai.
PRO ACC here LOC HON.have.come please

Intended: 'Please have the honorable elder standing over there come there near you and the one standing far over there come here.'

The target NP in IHR, in contrast, can be used in reference to somebody who is linguistically shown deference, again suggesting that the post-relative *no* is not pronominal, as shown in (16):

(16) *Tarō wa [[sensei ga hikōjō ni otsuki ni natta] no] o*
TOP teacher NOM airport LOC arrive.HON.PST NMLZ ACC
sassoku kuruma de hoteru e otsureshita. (Kuroda 1992b:] 159)
immediately car INSTR hotel ALL bring.HON.PST
'The teacher arrived at the airport, and Taro took (him) immediately to the hotel by car.'

In addition to the contrasts above discussed by Kuroda, the pronominal *no* and the *no* in IHR also behave differently with respect to modifiers. The pronominal allows a modifier immediately preceding it, just like lexical nouns, as seen in (17). On the other hand, the post-relative *no* in IHR does not, as shown in (18).

(17) a. *Asoko ni aru ringo wa aokute, [[koko ni aru] [ōkii] no] wa akai.*
there LOC exist apple TOP green.and here LOC exist big PRO TOP red
'The apple which is there is green, and the big one here is red.'
b. *Asoko ni aru ringo wa aokute, [[koko ni aru] [ōkii] ringo] wa akai.*
'The apple which is there is green, and the big apple here is red.'

(18) *[[Aoi ringo ga sara no ue ni aru] [ōkii] no] o Tarō wa totte, ...*
green apple NOM plate GEN top LOC exist big NMLZ ACC TOP took.and
Intended: 'There was a big apple on the plate, and Taro picked (it) up, and...'

Based on these contrasting properties, I conclude that the post-relative *no* in IHR is the nominalizer and not the pronominal. In other words, IHR does not involve an external head. Incidentally, the contrast between (17) and (18) suggests separate phrase structures for noun modification and the IHRC in Japanese:

(19) a. Noun modification
NP → (MOD)* – N
N: noun (including the pronominal *no*)
*(Kleene star): any number of occurrence including zero
b. IHRC
NP → S – NMLZ
NMLZ: nominalizer *no*

No is not the only morpheme which functions as a nominalizer in Japanese. There is a closed class of grammaticalized nouns which are generally called *keishiki meishi* 'formal nouns' and such grammaticalized nouns can be used as sentence nominalizers. In fact, some have argued that sentences such as (20a) below, whose S1 is nominalized by *tokoro* 'place' instead of *no*, can also be characterized as IHR (cf. 5b). I regard (20a) as an instance of another highly idiomatic grammatical construction with its own semantic and pragmatic constraints on the form, even though sometimes it is possible to replace *no* in IHR with *tokoro* and get acceptable results as in the case of (20a). Moreover, there are sentences in which *tokoro* is not followed by any case marker, as in (20b). I therefore focus on analyzing IHR with a *no*-nominalized clause as S1 and will not discuss *tokoro* any further.

(20) a. *[[Tarō ga hashittekita] tokoro] o Hanako wa tsukamaeta.*
NOM came.running place ACC TOP caught
'Hanako caught the situation in which Taro came running.'

b. *[[ie e kaetta] tokoro], saifu o gakkō ni*
home ALL returned place wallet ACC school LOC
oitekita koto ni ki ga tsuita.
left NMLZ DAT realized
'When I got home, I realized that I had left my wallet at school.'

2 Comparison with IHRCs in Other Languages

Several proposals have been made regarding the correlation between typological characteristics and the existence of IHRCs in a language. Culy (1990: 199), for example, proposes the following three correlations: if the language in question has IHR, then (i) the language also uses nominalized sentences in other constructions; (ii) it has SOV word order; and (iii) it is a pro-drop language. Although Japanese fits these descriptions, some of the properties of Japanese IHRCs do not perfectly coincide with commonly accepted characteristics of IHRCs.

2.1 Japanese IHRCs from a Typological Perspective

Let us examine Japanese IHRCS with respect to the four properties exhibited by IHRCs in other languages, namely, (i) the "nominalized" status of IHRCs, (ii) lack of a relative marker to identify the target, (iii) structural resemblance to complementation, and (iv) the position of the IHRC within a sentence.

2.1.1 The "Nominalized" Status of IHRCs

Just like IHRCs in other languages, Japanese IHRCs are nominalized clauses. As we saw in Section 1.3, the morpheme *no*, which follows an IHRC, should be analyzed as a nominalizer (cf. (19b)).

2.1.2 Target Identification

As with IHRCs in other languages, there is no marker to identify the target inside a Japanese IHRC. In the following example, either the subject (*gakusei-tachi* 'students') or the object (*CIA no supai* 'CIA spy') can be the target:

(21) *Sono omawari wa [[gakusei-tachi ga CIA no supai o kumifuseta]*
that cop TOP students NOM GEN spy ACC hold.down
no] o uchikoroshita.
NMLZ ACC killed.by.shooting
'The cop shot and killed {the students who held down the CIA spy/the CIA spy who the students held down/both the students and the spy.}
(Kuroda 1992a : 153)

Here, both the subject and the object (students and the CIA spy) can equally well be construed as the target. The target of Japanese IHRCs is morphosyntactically underdetermined inside S1, just as in other languages.

In Japanese IHR, pragmatic contexts play a role in narrowing down the range of possible targets. In (22a), although *tsukamaeta* 'caught' can take either *neko* 'cat' or *nezumi* 'mouse' as its required valence participant, the most natural interpretation is the one in which Taro caught the cat and not the mouse. If, however, an adverbial phrase such as *saki-ni* 'ahead' is added as in (22b), the interpretation in which Taro caught the mouse before the cat did becomes stronger. In (22c), the quantifier *ni-hiki-tomo* 'both of the two' determines the identity of the target.

(22) a. *Tarō wa [[neko ga nezumi o oikaketeiru] no] o tsukamaeta.*
TOP cat NOM mouse ACC chasing NMLZ ACC caught
'The cat was chasing the mouse, and Taro caught (the cat/mouse).'
b. *Tarō wa [[neko gan ezumi o oikaketeiru] no] o saki-ni tsukamaeta.*
'The cat was chasing the mouse, and Taro caught (the mouse) before the cat did.'
c. *Tarō wa [[neko ga nezumi o oikaketeiru] no]o ni-hiki-tomo tsukamaeta.*
'The cat was chasing the mouse, and Taro caught both the cat and the mouse.'

The multiple-target phenomenon such as (9) and (22c), in which both the subject and the object of S1 are taken as the target, seems to be peculiar to Japanese IHRCs.

2.1.3 Relation to Complementation

Just like IHRCs in other languages, Japanese IHRCs structurally resemble complement clauses. In addition to being used in IHR, a *no*-nominalized clause can be used for sentential complementation. When V2 is a verb of physical action requiring its object argument to be a concrete entity such as *tsukameru* 'catch,' the *no*-nominalized clause is understood as an IHRC (23a). When V2 is a verb of knowledge such as *shitteiru* 'know,' on the other hand, the nominalized clause is construed as a complement clause. Note that (23b) does not mean "Hanako knew Taro, who came running."

(23) a. *Hanako wa [[Tarō ga hashittekita] no] o tsukamaeta.*
'Taro came running, and Hanako caught (him).'
b. *Hanako wa [[Tarō ga hashittekita] no] o shitteita.*
'Hanako knew that Taro came running.' not 'Hanako knew Taro, who came running.'

A question arises as to whether it is legitimate to analyze IHRCs as grammatically distinct from complement clauses. That is, it may be argued that the lexical semantics of V2 determines the relevant reading and that therefore there is no need to posit two separate constructions. I argue that IHRCs are indeed grammatically distinct from complement clauses. First, a conjoined sentence may not occupy the position of an IHRC (24a), whereas it may occupy the position of a complement clause (24b):

(24) a. **Tarō wa [[ringo ga sara no ue ni ari, nashi*
TOP apple NOM plate GEN top LOC exist pear
ga bon no ue ni aru] no] o totte, ...
NOM tray GEN top LOC exist NMLZ ACC take.and
Intended: 'An apple was on the plate and a pear was on the tray, and Taro picked (them) up, and...'
(Kuroda 1992b: 170)
b. *Tarō wa [[ringo ga sara no ue ni ari, nashi ga bon no ue ni aru] no] o omoidashita.*
remembered
'Taro remembered that an apple was on the plate and that a pear was on the tray.'

Second, an IHRC (25a) may not contain an adverbial particle such as the topic marker *wa*, but a complement clause (25b) may:

(25) a. **Tarō wa [[ringo wa sara no ue ni aru] no] o totte,...*
(Kuroda 1992b: 171)
b. *Reizōko ni wa nanimo nakatta ga, Tarō*
fridge LOC TOP anything not.exist but
wa [[ringo wa sara no ue ni
aru] no] o omoidashita.
'There was nothing in the fridge, but Taro remembered that an apple was still on the table.'

The discussion above suggests that IHR sentences should indeed be treated as structurally different from complementation.

2.1.4 The Position of S1 within the Whole Sentence

Whereas IHRCs in other languages may occupy any place within a sentence, Japanese IHRCs tend to occur sentence-initially. Furthermore, the event described in S1 precedes the S2 event, as in (26):

(26) *[[Akanbō ga nakikakeru] no] o hahaoya wa yasashiku dakiageta.*
baby NOM about.to.cry NMLZ ACC mother TOP gently held
'The baby was about to cry, and the mother gently held (it) in her arms.'

The temporal sequence that Japanese IHR typically describes is also at variance with characterizations of IHRCs in other languages.

3 A Constructional Analysis of IHR Sentences

In this section it will be shown that although IHR has the same propositional content as EHR, the two types of sentences have distinct pragmatic characteristics. In particular, by focusing on S1 of each type of sentence, we will see that the IHRC functions to report an event, while the EHRC serves to modify the head noun.

In analyzing IHR, we take a constructional approach, in which a grammatical construction is defined as a pairing of syntax with semantics and pragmatics (cf. Fillmore, Kay, and O'Connor 1988; Ostman and Fried 2005; Goldberg 2013). That is, in this approach, a grammatical construction is partly characterized by the pragmatic circumstances under which the sentence is used. Put differently, a grammatical construction can be dedicated to certain pragmatic functions. It is important to stress that we are dealing with only the CONVENTIONALIZED pragmatic constraints and not the CONVERSATIONAL pragmatic constraints, which can be uncovered only by discourse analysis. By conventionalized pragmatic constraints we mean pragmatic functions that DEMAND a certain discourse context, while conversational pragmatic constraints are those which are IMPOSED by a discourse context. We will see that IHR advances a narrative by reporting two events which share a participant. Furthermore, it will be shown that seemingly puzzling structural and semantic properties of IHR sentences correlate with this narrative-advancing function.

3.1 Pragmatically Motivated Morphosyntax of IHRCs

Even though the propositional contents of IHR and EHR sentences are the same, the morphosyntactic behavior of S1 of IHR and that of EHR are distinct in some important ways. By the Principle of No Synonymy, which states "if two constructions are syntactically distinct, they must be semantically or pragmatically distinct," we assume that the differences are correlated with different pragmatic relations (Goldberg 1995: 3, 67).

3.1.1 The Morphosyntax of IHRCs

When IHRCs display morphosyntactic behavior different from that of EHRCs, they behave like coordinated clauses. In Japanese, subject case marking in modifier clauses such as EHRCs can alternate between the nominative *ga* and the genitive *no* as shown in (27a). This phenomenon is called *ga-no* conversion. The subject case marking in S1 of clauses coordinated by the clausal conjunction *ga* 'and/but,' on the other hand, must be the nominative as in (27b). Example (27c) shows that subjects of IHRCs must take the nominative *ga*, exactly as in S1 of *ga*-coodinated clauses.

(27) a. EHRC (modifier clause)

[[Tarō *ga/no* *sewa shiteita]* *inu]* *ga*
NOM/GEN was.taking.care.of dog NOM
yatto *genki ni natta.*
finally got.well
'The dog that Taro was taking care of finally got well.'

b. *Ga*-coordinated S1 clause

*[Tarō ga/*no* *inu o* *sewa shiteita]* *ga, sono inu wa yatto*
NOM/*GEN dog ACC was.taking.care.of but that dog TOP finally
genki ni natta.
'Taro was taking care of the dog, and the dog finally got well.'

c. IHRC

[[Tarō *ga/*no* *inu o sewa shiteita]* *no]* *ga* *yatto genki ni natta.*
NOM/*GEN NMLZ NOM
'Taro was taking care of the dog, who finally got well.'

The S1 of *ga*-coordinated clauses, in contrast to EHRCs, disallows wh-questions. Although the EHRC in (28a) allows one of its constituent NPs to be replaced by a *wh*-word, the S1 in (28b) does not. IHRCs are subject to the same restriction as the S1 of *ga*-coordinated clauses:

(28) a. EHRC

[[Dare *ga* *kattekita]* *ringo]* *o* *Hanako* *ga* *tabemashita* *ka?*
who NOM bought apple ACC NOM ate Q
'Who bought the apple which Hanako ate?'

b. *Ga*-coordinated S1 clause

**[Dare ga ringo o kattekita] ga Hanako ga tabemashita ka?*
Intended: 'Who bought the apple, and Hanako ate it?'

c. IHRC

**[[Dare ga ringo o kattekita] no] o Hanako ga tabemashita ka?*
Intended: 'Who bought the apple, and Hanako ate (it)?'

The fact that IHRCs resemble *ga*-coordinated clauses with respect to *ga-no* conversion and with respect to *wh*-questions suggests that IHRCs are structurally like coordinated clauses, rather than like modifying clauses.

According to the approach we are adopting, if two sentences exhibit distinct structural properties in spite of having the same propositional content, then the difference can be ascribed to their distinct pragmatic properties. In Japanese, EHRCs can be used either restrictively or non-restrictively (cf. (7)). Both types of EHRCs modify and describe some property of the head noun referent.

On the other hand, what is characteristic of clauses coordinated by *ga* is that both clauses make assertions. It can thus be said that the predicate of

IHRCs also makes an assertion, in contrast to EHRCs. Assertion can be defined as follows:

(29) ASSERTION: The proposition expressed by a sentence which the hearer is expected to [come to] know or take for granted as a result of hearing the sentence uttered. (Lambrecht 1994: 52, bracketed words are mine)

3.1.2 The Event-reporting Function of IHRCs

When the predicate of a clause is construed as making an assertion, the clause can be either of the following two types: *event-reporting sentences* (also called *neutral description, thetic sentences*, or *sentence-focus structures*) or *topic-comment sentences*. What is meant by *event* here includes temporally bounded states and situations. Whereas event-reporting sentences prototypically have to do with information about SITUATIONS, topic-comment sentences convey information about ENTITIES.

In Japanese the two types of sentences are distinguished formally by whether or not the topic marker *wa* appears inside the sentence. In event-reporting sentences *wa* is not allowed, while in topic-comment sentences *wa* is allowed, and it marks the topic expression, that is, the subject of the subject–predicate paradigm.

Examples (30b) and (31b) are instances of event-reporting and topic-comment sentences, respectively. Since event-reporting conveys information about situations, it is often used in reply to questions such as "What's the matter?," "What happened?," and "Guess what?" Topic-comment sentences, on the other hand, are about entities, and they may thus be used in reply to "How's Masako?" or "What happened to Masako?" Since Japanese allows NP ellipsis, answers to these questions would normally not contain explicit topic NPs, as shown by the parentheses in (31b). If answers contain explicit topic expressions, however, they are marked by *wa*.

(30) a. Q: *Dō* *shita* *no?*
how happened SFP
'What's the matter?'

b. A: *Masako* *ga* *iede shita.* (event-reporting)
NOM ran.away.from.home
'Masako ran away from home.'

(31) a. Q: *Masako* *wa* *dō?*
TOP how
'How's Masako?'

b. A: *(Masako* *wa)* *iede shita.* (topic-comment)
TOP
'She ran away from home.'

Supporting evidence for the argument that IHRCs are event-reporting comes from the fact that their syntactic subject NP corresponding to the "subject" of the subject–predicate paradigm is marked by the nominative *ga* and not by *wa*, as in (32):[3]

(32) a. *[[Haha ga/*wa sētā o okuttekureta] no] ga kyō todoita.*
mother NOM/TOP sweater ACC sent NMLZ NOM today arrived
'Mother sent me a sweater, and (it) arrived today.'

b. *[[Tsuma ga/*wa sakana o tsuttekita] no] o otto ga ryōri shita.*
wife NOM/TOP fish ACC fished NMLZ ACC husband NOM cooked
'The wife caught a fish, and the husband cooked (it).'

It has been observed that predicates appearing in event-reporting sentences tend to be dynamic predicates which refer to temporally bounded situations. Similarly, the predicates of IHRCs tend to be dynamic. That is, V1 in an IHRC typically denotes a transitory activity but not a durable state. Example (33b) contains a predicate denoting a durable state (being kind) and thus is unacceptable:

(33) a. *[[Shinsetsuna] kanrinin] o watashi wa heya e manekiireta.*
kind manager ACC I TOP room ALL invited.inside
'I invited the kind manager into my room.' (EHRC)

b. **[[Kanrinin ga shinsetsuna] no] o watashi wa heya e manekiireta.*
NMLZ
Intended: 'The manager is kind, and I invited (him/her) into my room.' (IHRC)

The sentences in (34) demonstrate that among stative predicates only those that denote temporally bounded situations qualify as V1 in IHRC. Such a predicate allows an interpretation in which a situation existed temporarily, ENABLING another event to occur or setting a stage for a subsequent situation (cf. Section 5).

(34) *[[Kodomo no koro no akutaigo ga atama ni nokotteita] no] ga tsui kuchi e deta.*
child GEN days GEN bad.words NOM head LOC remained NMLZ NOM by.mistake mouth ALL came.out
'In her head had remained bad words from her childhood days, and she uttered (them) by mistake.' (TANABE Seiko, *Uba tokimeki*)

[3] It is important to note that *wa* is not allowed in EHRCs either, as shown in (32b), but for a different reason.

(32) b'. *[[Tsuma ga/*wa tsuttekita] sakana] o otto ga ryōri shita.*
'The husband cooked the fish which the wife had caught.'

Occurrence of *wa* is said to be a 'main clause' phenomenon and this is why *wa* is not allowed in EHRCs, which are not main clauses but are embedded clauses. IHRCs, on the other hand, are not embedded and are similar to coordinated clauses structurally, in disallowing *ga-no* conversion and *wh*-questions, as we have seen in Section 3.1.1. In other words, *wa* is not allowed in IHRCs because of their event-reporting function, while it is disallowed in EHRCs because they are not main clauses.

To summarize, the primary function of the IHRCs is event-reporting and not modifying the target as it is for EHRCs. Construing the predicate of IHRCs as making an assertion just like the predicate of coordinated clauses allows us to understand why they resemble coordinated clauses morphosyntactically. First, *wh*-questions are allowed in EHRCs but not in IHRCs, because questioning a constituent of EHRCs helps identify the head noun referent and thus is in accordance with EHRCs' function of modifying the head noun.[4] In contrast, trying to identify the target NP referent by questioning would conflict with IHRCs' primary function of presenting an event as a whole. Furthermore, the unacceptability of (33b) may also be seen as motivated by the event-reporting function of the IHRCs, since intrinsic or static properties do not qualify as scenes to be reported.

3.2 Narrative-advancing Constructions in Japanese and English

The continuative relative construction in English, discussed by Jespersen, for example, has a function similar to that of the IHR construction in Japanese. The English continuative relative construction is exemplified in (35):

(35) a. *He gave the letter to the clerk, who then copied it.* (Jespersen 1965: 113)
b. *She had quite a long argument with the Lory, who at last turned sulky.*
c. *She said it to the Knave of Hearts, who only bowed and smiled in reply.*
d. *The Queen began staring at the Hatter, who turned pale and fidgeted.*
(Lewis Carroll, *Alice in Wonderland*)

The continuative relative construction is a construction that establishes a temporal link between two states of affairs. Unlike restrictive and non-restrictive relatives, continuative relatives advance a narrative within a sentence. They are generally paraphrasable as coordinated sentences, using *and (then)* and replacing the relative pronoun with an appropriate referential pronoun:

(36) a. *I gave the form to Mary, who immediately lost it.* (continuative relative)
b. *I gave the form to Mary, and then she immediately lost it.* (*and*-conjunction)

This paraphrasability by *and (then)* shows that the order of the two clauses is iconic to the order of events and that each of the two clauses makes an assertion.

The continuative relative in English and IHR in Japanese are similar in function. Although they differ in their clause order and target-identification mechanism, the two constructions have the same function of advancing a narrative in the two clauses.

[4] This, however, cannot account for the fact that in languages such as English wh-questions are disallowed in EHRCs.

4 Relativization and Clause-linkage

This section investigates the relation between IHR and the concessive bi-clausal sentences. It will be argued that the concessive construction should indeed be treated as distinct from IHR.

4.1 The Concessive Construction

In Modern Japanese, there are other sentences which closely resemble IHR. Just like S1 in typical IHR, S1 in these sentences is followed by the sequence *no ga* or *no o*, as indicated by the underline.

(37) Concessive bi-clausal sentences

a. *[Rei-nen da to asa-yū sukōru ga aru]*
every-year COP CONJ morning-evening squall NOM exist
no ga kotoshi wa hotondo ame ga furanai.
this-year TOP scarcely rain NOM fall-NEG
'Whereas every year we have a squall in the morning and in the evening, this year it has scarcely rained.' (*Asahi Newspaper*)

b. *Kare wa [kesseki shita hō ga ii] no o muri o shita.*
he TOP absent had.better.be pushed.oneself.too.hard
'Whereas he should have stayed home, he pushed himself too hard.' (Lê 1988: 86)

If these sentences were to be analyzed as IHR, then they should exhibit the two defining properties of the IHR construction. However, they do not. In (37a) there is no NP inside S1 which corresponds to a valence requirement of V2. The valence requirement of V2 is satisfied within S2 by the nominative-marked NP *ame* 'rain.'

In (38), *Noriko* inside S1 is construed as the subject of V2 *naru* 'become,' but the external marking on S1 is *o*, not the expected nominative *ga*. I will call these types of sentences *concessive sentences*, due to the adversative semantic relation between the situations described in the two clauses.

(38) *[Saisho wa Noriko ga shutai deatta] no o itsunomanika Tatsuo to*
first TOP NOM leader was eventually from
gyaku no ichi ni natta.
opposite GEN place LOC became
'At first Noriko was the leader, but eventually (she) got the opposite place from Tatsuo.' (Lê 1988: 85)

Should concessive sentences be considered instances of the same grammatical construction as IHR? Some analysts have proposed that the answer is indeed "yes." Here I will argue against such a view.

First, while IHR sentences do not allow the so-called contrastive *wa* in S1 and S2, concessive sentences do. In that case, two phrases to which *wa* attaches are made foci of contrast. In (39a), the two *wa*-marked adverbials, *mukashi* 'old days' in S1 and *ima* 'now' in S2, are the foci of contrast. In (39b), *wa* is attached to the locative of S1 *Amerika de* 'in America' and to the grammatical subject of S2 *watashi* 'I,' making them the foci of contrast. The writer is contrasting the different ways in which the book was designed: in America by somebody versus in Japan by herself.

(39) a. *[Mukashi wa ichi-nen o hatsuka de kurasu yoi otoko*
old.days TOP one-year ACC twenty-days LOC work happy guy
datta] no ga ima wa ichi-nen roku-basho dearu.
was now TOP one-year six-tournaments COP
'Whereas in the old days they [sumo wrestlers] were happy fellows working 20 days a year, nowadays there are 6 tournaments a year.'
(*Asahi Newspaper*)

b. *Kono hon wa [Amerika de wa e-hon no ōkisa de*
this book TOP LOC TOP picture-book GEN size COP
shuppans-are-ta] no o watashi wa itsumo beddo saido ni
publish-PASS-PST I TOP always bed side LOC
ok-areru hon ni natte hoshii to omotta.
put-PASS book GOAL become want COMP thought
'Whereas in America the book had been published in the size of a picture book, I thought I wanted (it) to be a book which would always be kept by the bed.' (*Asahi Newspaper*)

On the other hand, attaching *wa* to two phrases in S1 and S2 of IHR results in unacceptable sentences, as shown by (40a′) and (40b′).

(40) a. *[[Kinō ringo o okuttekudasatta] no] ga kyō tsukimashita.*
yesterday apple ACC send-HON-PST NMLZ NOM today arrived
'(You) sent me apples yesterday, and I received (them) today.'

a′. **[[Kinō wa ringo o okuttekudasatta] no] ga kyō wa tsukimashita.*
TOP NMLZ NOM TOP

b. *Tarō wa [[kinō ringo o kattekita] no] o kyō tabeta.*
TOP apple ACC bought NMLZ ACC today ate
'Taro bought an apple yesterday, and he ate (it) today.'

b′. **Tarō wa [[kinō wa ringo o kattekita] no] o kyō wa tabeta.*
TOP NMLZ ACC TOP

As we have seen in Section 3, IHR functions to advance a narrative within a sentence. The unacceptability of the contrastive *wa* in IHR sentences suggests that the discourse function of IHR may not be compatible with that of emphasizing a contrast in propositions. That function, on the other hand, is congruent with the concessivity expressed by concessive sentences: they emphasize a contrast between propositions (cf. Section 4.2.2).

Furthermore, the concessive meaning is CONVENTIONALIZED in concessive sentences. The fact that the contrastive *wa* is allowed in concessive sentences does not, by itself, entail any such conventionalization. One might argue that the concessivity found in them is just a CONVERSATIONAL implicature, and that the contrastive *wa*, when it is used, strengthens such a reading. The examples in (41), however, show that the concessive relation is not cancelable and thus is indeed conventionalized in this sentence type:

(41) a. *[Rei-nen da to asa-yū sukōru ga aru] no ga*
every-year COP CONJ morning-evening squall NOM exist
kotoshi wa hotondo ame ga furanai.
this-year TOP scarcely rain NOM fall-NEG
'Whereas every year we have a squall in the morning and in the evening, this year it has scarcely rained.'

a′. *#Rei-nen sukōru ga aru kara kotoshi hotondo ame ga furanakute*
because
tōzen dakedo.
follows but
Intended: 'From the fact that we have a squall every year it follows that it has scarcely rained this year, but…'

b. *Kare wa [kesseki shita hō ga ii] no o muri o shita.*
he TOP absent had.better.be pushed.oneself.too.hard
'Whereas he should have stayed home, he pushed himself too hard.'

b′. *#Kesseki shita hō ga ii koto to muri o suru koto wa mujunshinai*
COMP and TOP conflict.NEG
kedo.
but
Intended: 'Being in a condition such that one should stay home and pushing oneself too hard do not conflict with each other, but…'

It thus follows that if we define a grammatical construction as a conventionalized pair of form and meaning, then the concessive clause-linkage must be recognized as a grammatical construction distinct from IHR (cf. Fillmore, Kay, and O'Connor 1988). In the concessive construction, the sequences *no ga* and *no o* are used as devices for connecting two clauses, although they are not fully lexicalized into clausal conjunctions yet (cf. Horie 1993: 313). I tentatively treat them as subtypes of the same grammatical construction. The structure of the concessive construction is thus schematized as (42):

(42) The concessive construction

$$S1\left\{\begin{matrix} no - ga \\ no - o \end{matrix}\right\}S2$$

no-ga, no-o: clausal conjunctions (CONJ)

4.2 IHR versus Concessive Clause-linkage

Let us now compare the structural, semantic, and pragmatic properties of IHR and the concessive construction.

4.2.1 Structural Comparison

Based on the coordination-subordination and embeddedness distinction, IHRCs are categorized as [+dependent, +embedded] (cf. Van Valin 1993: 118). IHRCs cannot be used on their own to refer to anything and must be used in combination with another clause. In this sense, IHRCs are distributionally dependent. Moreover, the *no*-nominalized S1 fulfills a syntactic valence requirement of V2 and is thus embedded within S2.

The syntactic relation between S1 and S2 of the concessive construction, on the other hand, can be described as [+dependent, –embedded]. S1 of concessive sentences is distributionally dependent, since it cannot stand alone. It is not, however, embedded in S2, because S1 is not a syntactic argument of V2. The concessive construction is therefore more coordination-like than IHR. At the same time, IHRCs, even though they are embedded in that they externally function as NPs, syntactically behave like coordinated clauses with respect to certain syntactic processes such as *wh*-questions and *ga-no* conversion (Section 3.1.1). S1 of concessive sentences also exhibits a coordination-like behavior with respect to the same syntactic phenomena. For example, while EHRCs allow one of their constituent NPs to be replaced by a *wh*-word (28a), as illustrated in (43), IHRC and S1 of concessive sentences do not, just like S1 of coordinated sentences (28b).

(43) a.

**[[Dare*	*ga*	*ringo*	*o*	*kattekita]*	*no]*	*o*	*Hanako*	*ga*
who	NOM	apple	ACC	buy.came	NMLZ	ACC		NOM

tabemashita	*ka?*	(IHRC)
ate	Q	

Intended: 'Who bought the apple, and Hanako ate (it)?'

b.

**[Mukashi*	*wa*	*dare*	*ga ringo o*	*katte ita]*	*no ga*	*ima*	*de*	*wa*
old.days	TOP	who		used.to.buy		nowadays	LOC	TOP

Hanako	*no*	*yakume*	*desu*	*ka?*	(S1 of a concessive sentence)
	GEN	duty	COP	Q	

Intended: 'Whereas in the old days who used to buy apples, nowadays it is Hanako's duty?'

4.2.2 Semantic Comparison

IHR is characterized by a valence requirement of the main predicate appearing inside S1. In discourse-structure terms, this marks participant continuity. IHR advances a narrative by reporting two events which share a participant and the target NP referent corresponds to such a participant.

In concessive sentences, it is not obligatory to have a valence requirement of the main predicate inside S1 but it can be present (e.g. (38)). Even when there is no shared NP between the two clauses, concessive sentences may contain a *wa*-marked topic NP, whose scope spans both S1 and S2 (e.g. (37b)). It is also possible to identify a discourse topic shared by the two clauses of concessive sentences, even if it is not explicitly realized as a topic NP. In (39a), for example, both of the clauses are about sumo wrestlers. The concessive construction is thus always characterized by topic continuity. IHR, on the other hand, is characterized by participant continuity.

We saw in Section 2.1.4 that a temporal sequence is often expressed by IHR. It is typically observed in concessive sentences as well. Furthermore, in concessive sentences, the contrastive *wa* often attaches to a time adverbial in each of the two clauses, emphasizing a contrast in the situations holding at the two different time frames, as in (39a).

4.2.3 Pragmatic Comparison

Even though IHRCs are embedded inside S2, the syntactic behavior of IHRCs with respect to *wh*-questions argues for the view that V1 of IHRCs makes an assertion, just like that of coordinated or main clauses (Section 3.1.1). Since S1 of the concessive construction behaves similarly to IHRCs and S1 of coordinated clauses, V1 of concessive sentences can also be construed as making an assertion.

To summarize, syntactically, the concessive construction is more coordination-like than IHR, since S1 in the concessive construction is not embedded within S2. Semantically, the concessive construction expresses topic continuity, while IHR is characterized by participant continuity. However, the concessive construction often involves a temporal sequence just like IHR. Finally, in both constructions V1 is construed as making an assertion.

5 Summary and Future Directions

This chapter has been concerned with describing and accounting for the nature of the IHR construction in Modern Japanese, focusing on its narrative-advancing use. We have examined IHR in comparison with EHR, coordinated sentences, and concessive sentences. There remain, however, issues such as those pertaining to the target identification mechanism and the semantic relations between the contents of the two clauses in the IHR construction.

We have seen that in the IHR syntax underdetermines the possible range of targets, and the target is ultimately construed by available semantic and pragmatic information (cf. (9)). It thus seems possible to say that, in IHR, the target is construed by semantic frames evoked by the two clauses (cf. Fillmore and Baker 2010).

Kuroda proposed a "relevancy condition," whereby acceptability of IHR sentences depends on the IHRC's pragmatic relevance to the main clause (Kuroda 1992b: 147). It seems, however, that the condition is too vague to account for the semantic restriction on V1. It is not too difficult to imagine a context in which the situations described in the two clauses are relevant to each other but still there are many pairs of situations that cannot be expressed by the construction. In (44a), for example, it may be that the reason why I invited the student to my office was that the student is smart and I wanted to discuss something with him/her. The two situations described in the sentence may thus be construed as relevant to each other, but it is nonetheless unacceptable. I propose that the notion of ENABLEMENT describes the semantic relation between the two clauses more precisely than that of RELEVANCE. That is, in the IHR construction, the situation described in S1 sets the stage and enables the S2 event to occur. In (44b), the situation in which the bright student was talking with people outside my office enabled me to invite him/her to my office, and the sentence is acceptable. In other words, the situation in which the student was talking was a necessary condition for my inviting him/her.

(44) a. **[[Gakusei ga yūshūna] no] o kenkyūshitsu e yonda.*
student NOM bright NMLZ ACC office ALL invited
Intended: 'The student is bright, and I invited (him/her) to my office.'

b. *[[Yūshūna gakusei ga rōka de hito to hanashiteiru]*
bright student NOM corridor LOC people COM was.talking
no] o kenkyūshitsu e yonda.
NMLZ ACC office ALL invited
'The bright student was talking with others in the corridor, and I invited (him/her) to my office.'

It may be argued that the relation of CAUSE-RESULT characterizes the semantic relation between the two clauses in the IHR construction even more precisely than the notion of ENABLEMENT. It is not, however, difficult to find IHR sentences in which the S1 is not necessarily a CAUSE of the S2 event. In (45), for instance, your sending me a birthday card does not always result in its arriving today. That is, the fact that you sent me a card is not a sufficient condition for it to arrive today.

(45) *[[Otanjōbi kādo o okuttekudasatta] no] ga kyō tsukimashita.*
birthday card ACC sent NMLZ NOM today arrived
'You kindly sent me a birthday card, and (it) arrived today.'

ENABLEMENT may be paraphrased as CAUSE TO BE POSSIBLE or MAKE IT POSSIBLE. In this sense, semantic relations characterized as ENABLEMENT include situations described as CAUSE-RESULT. The notion of ENABLEMENT, however, can also cover cases such as (45). I thus contend that the CAUSE-RESULT relation is too narrow and RELEVANCE is too broad and that the notion of ENABLEMENT captures the semantics of the IHR construction better than CAUSE-RESULT or RELEVANCE.

The IHR construction is not the only clause-linking construction in Japanese in which the ENABLEMENT relation is involved. Other such constructions include *te*-linkage and *tokoro*-linkage, exemplified in (46). In *te*-linkage, two clauses are connected by a verbal suffix *-te*. In *tokoro*-linkage, clauses are linked by the clausal conjunction *tokoro*. In both of the sentences in (46), the situation described in S1 establishes a temporal setting for the subsequent event.

(46) a. *Te*-linkage

Kōshi *ga* *kaijō* *ni* *tsui***te** *kōen* *ga* *hajimatta.*
lecturer NOM meeting.place LOC arrive-TE lecture NOM began
'The lecturer arrived at the meeting place, and the lecture began.'

b. *Tokoro*-linkage

Sensei *ni* *mēru* *o* *dashita* **tokoro**, *sassoku* *henji* *o* *itadaita.*
teacher DAT email ACC sent CONJ immediately reply ACC got
'I sent email to my professor, and I immediately got a reply.'

In conclusion, we have seen in this chapter that a constructional approach, which regards subtle semantic and pragmatic factors as an important part of the characterization of grammatical constructions, is useful to understanding the interactions between the syntax, semantics, and pragmatics of the IHR construction. Consideration of these factors allows the IHR to be described as an independent construction with unique pragmatic, syntactic, and semantic characteristics. Overlap in one or another of these three areas, propositional equivalence in the case of the EHR construction, coordinating temporal sequencing in the case of *ga*-coordination, or disallowing *wh*-words in the case of the concessive construction show how the IHR is related to, though distinct from, such constructions.

22

Benefactives

Nobuko Hasegawa

1 The Basic Facts on *Ageru* and *Kureru* 'Give'

Japanese is rich in grammatical phenomena, such as honorifics, in which the speaker's status and his/her relation with the addressee or the participants of the expressed proposition play a crucial role in the grammaticality or acceptability of an utterance. Benefactives[1] are such a phenomenon, illustrated by the following examples with the "giving" verbs *ageru* and *kureru*. Compare (1), English examples, with (2) and (3), Japanese counterparts.

(1) a. *Hanako gave {you/Taro} flowers.*
  b. *{You/Taro} gave Hanako books.*
  c. *I gave you flowers.*
  d. *You gave me books.*

(2) a. *Hanako ga {anata/Tarō} ni hana o {ageta/kureta}.*
  NOM you DAT flower ACC gave
  'Hanako gave {you/Taro} flowers.'

  b. *{Anata/Tarō} ga Hanako ni hon o {ageta/kureta}.*
  you NOM DAT book ACC gave
  '{You/Taro} gave Hanako books.'

Portions of this chapter have been presented at various places including graduate seminars and linguistic workshops at Kanda University of International Studies, the 6th FAJL at Humboldt University, and the 146th LSJ at Ibaraki University. I would like to thank the participants for helpful questions and comments. I have benefited much from the discussions with Naoko Okura. I am thankful to Yukio Hirose and John Haig for comments. And I am particularly grateful to Yoko Hasegawa for inviting me to contribute to this volume and for various comments and suggestions. Part of the research reported here is supported by JSPS Research-in Aids for scientific research No. 23320089.

[1] The definition of "benefactives" or what constructions are to be subsumed under this term may vary among grammarians and/or grammatical components and subfields of linguistics. That is, any expression that has to do with "for/for the sake of/on behalf of/owing to someone or something" or with beneficial effects on someone/something may be considered as some sort of "benefactive." In this chapter, however, we will pay attention only to structural aspects of the construction with "giving" predicates, *give* in English, *ageru* and *kureru* in Japanese, and their relevance to the interpretation that may arguably be relevant to syntactic structures and operations.

(3) a. *Watashi ga {anata/Tarō} ni hana o {ageta/*kureta}.*
I NOM you DAT flower ACC gave
'I gave {you/Taro} flowers.'

b. *{Anata/Tarō} ga watashi ni hon o {*ageta/kureta}.*
you NOM I DAT book ACC gave
'{You/Taro} gave me books.'

In English, when expressing a giving event, the verb *give* can be used irrespective of the relation of the giver or the receiver to the speaker; that is, the speaker, the addressee, or a third person – *Hanako* and *Taro* – can assume either the giver or the receiver role. In contrast, in Japanese, as the unacceptability of the use of *kureru* in (3a) and that of *ageru* in (3b) shows, once the speaker (i.e. the first person) is involved as a participant in the giving event, *ageru* must be used when s/he is the giver and *kureru* if s/he is the receiver.

Furthermore, it is not only the presence of the speaker as a participant that matters in the choice of *ageru* and *kureru*. The situations in (2), which may appear to be basically the same as English (1a–b), are not objective descriptions of the events. The choice of *ageru* or *kureru* reflects the relations between the speaker and the event participants – *you*, *Hanako*, and *Taro*. With *ageru*, the speaker stands on the side of (or empathizes with) the giver (i.e. the subject), while s/he empathizes with the receiver (the indirect object) with *kureru*.[2] Considering the giving event as the most typical benefactive event, the above fact shows that Japanese cannot express the giving event neutrally or objectively, disregarding the speaker's empathetic view or subjective evaluation of the event in question.[3]

What is particularly notable in Japanese in terms of the use of *ageru/ kureru* is that these predicates not only serve as a main predicate meaning 'give' as shown in (2–3), but also function as a kind of auxiliary, making

[2] The use of *ageru* and *kureru* is one of the most important topics in Japanese language studies. It is often explained in terms of the speaker's "in-group" and "out-group" or the relative closeness to the speaker, as illustrated in Kuno (1973: 139) and Y. Hasegawa (2015: 165), or the speaker's empathy, as in Kuno (1978a: 141) and Kuno and Kaburaki (1977: 628). The speaker is considered to be the center of the spectrum of the human relations and the relationship with others is subjective and flexible, being altered depending on how the speaker considers the given situation. In a giving event, if the giver is more in-group than the receiver according to the speaker's view, *ageru* is used, and *kureru* is employed in the opposite situation, the receiver being more in-group than the giver. *Morau* 'receive' has the same "empathy or in-group" hierarchy or relation as *kureru*; that is, *morau* is acceptable when the speaker empathizes more with the receiver (the subject) than the giver (the indirect object) in the event, though, these predicates differ in whether the receiver shows up as a subject as in the case of *morau* or as an indirect object as in *kureru*. This means that the same event can be described either with *kureru* or with *morau* but their syntactic structures are different: *ageru/kureru* is the giving event, and *morau*, the receiving event. We will not deal with *morau* in this chapter.

[3] If the giving event is of a formal kind, it may be possible to express it neutrally with the predicates such as *juyo-suru, sazukeru* 'bestow.' One of the reviewers of this chapter provides *zōtō-suru* 'give a present,' *ataeru* 'give,' as possible neutral predicates; however, with the first person as a receiver, the use of these predicates still sound infelicitous. The giving event can be described as a receiving event with a predicate of the 'receive' kind: *morau, ukeru, uketoru*, etc. 'receive.' We will not discuss *morau* 'receive' in this chapter; however, given that *morau* 'receive' has a structure quite different from *ageru* and *kureru*, including it would take us too far afield.

any event expressed by the predicate that they attach to a "benefactive" construction in terms of the speaker's point of view. Observe (4–5):

(4) a. *Watashi wa otōto ni yūhan o tsukutte-ageta.*
I TOP brother DAT dinner ACC make-gave
'I cooked my brother dinner.'

b. *Chichi wa watashi ni hon o yonde-kureta.*
father TOP I DAT book ACC read-gave
'Father read me a book.'

(5) a. *Watashi wa otōto no shukudai o tetsudatte-ageta.*
I TOP brother GEN homework ACC help-gave
'I helped with my brother's homework (for him).'

b. *Haha wa itsumo watashi o shinjite-kureta.*
mother TOP always I ACC believe-gave
'Mother always believed in me (and I benefitted from it).'

The presence of *ageru* and *kureru* indicates that the subject of the predicate provides some favorable effects on the affectee of the event, which is described in terms of the speaker's subjective point of view. The difference in the use of *ageru* and *kureru* is basically the same as what has been observed in (2–3). That is, as is obvious from where the first person pronoun *watashi* 'I' appears, in the (a) examples with *ageru*, the speaker empathizes with the subject and in the (b) examples with *kureru*, the speaker's empathy is not with the subject but with the affectee of the event.

There is an interesting difference between (2–3) and (4–5), however. In the former, being a main predicate, *ageru* and *kureru* syntactically require the presence of an indirect object or a recipient GOAL argument of the main verb. On the other hand, in the latter examples, it is not clear whether *ageru* or *kureru*, being an auxiliary type, requires such an argument. It looks as though the affectee, DATIVE *ni*-phrase, is called for by the presence of *ageru* and *kureru*, since the predicates, *tsukuru* 'make, cook' in (4a) and *yomu* 'read' in (4b), do not need, or rather they may not allow, a DATIVE *ni*-phrase, which is shown in (6).

(6) a. *Watashi wa {Ø/??otōto ni} yūhan o tsukutta.*
I TOP brother DAT dinner ACC made
'I cooked my brother dinner.'

b. *Chichi wa {Ø/?*watashi ni} hon o yonda.*
father TOP I DAT book ACC read.PST
'Father read me a book.'

Here, Ø means null, that is, without a *ni*-phrase. Without a *ni*-phrase, these sentences simply describe the events objectively, 'I cooked dinner' and 'Father read a book.' With the *ni*-phrase, the activity gains the direction;

the referent of the *ni*-phrase is the receiver of the activity, implying basically the same as what is expressed in (4) but the speaker's viewpoint or judgment on the occurrence of the expressed event is intended to be quite objective.[4] Nonetheless, given that the speaker is specifically mentioned to be the referent of the participant of the activity, it seems rather odd to describe it without *ageru* or *kureru* in (6).

With respect to the occurrence of the DATIVE *ni*-phrase, examples (5) yet differ from (4) in that no *ni*-phrase is allowed irrespective of *ageru/kureru* or of how objectively the events are intended to be described. Observe (7):

(7) a. **Watashi wa otōto ni (otōto no) shukudai o*
I TOP brother DAT brother GEN homework ACC

tetsudatta/tetsudatte-ageta.
helped/help-gave
'I helped with my brother's homework (for him).'

b. **Haha wa itsumo watashi ni (watashi o)*
mother TOP always I DAT I ACC

shinjita/shinjite-kureta.
believed/believe-gave
'Mother always believed in me (and I benefitted from it).'

These predicates – *tetsudau* 'help,' *shinjiru* 'believe' – simply do not allow the presence of the *ni*-phrase, irrespective of the presence or absence of *ageru* or *kureru*, even if the expressed event has some favorable effects on the participants of the events.

Given the above facts, the following questions naturally arise.

(8) a. How does the main verb *ageru/kureru* differ from the auxiliary counterpart in terms of argument structure and structural representation?
b. What is responsible for the occurrence of the *ni*-phrase? ((2–3) versus (4) versus (5))
c. Is it possible to formally represent the speaker's empathy or point of view in syntax? If so, how?

These questions will be taken up in this chapter. We will first consider (8a–b), by referring to classical analyses of *ageru/kureru* (Nakau 1973: ch. 7; Inoue 1976: ch. 2; Shibatani 1978: ch. 3, 1994b, etc.): the auxiliary use of these predicates is analyzed as a higher predicate that takes a sentence as a theme object. We will then present a more recent approach to the "giving" or benefactive construction: an applicative approach (N. Hasegawa 2006, 2007a; Pylkkänen 2008: ch. 2; Okura 2009: ch. 3, 2011). Then at the onset of

[4] Thus, the sentences like (6) do not seem appropriate as ordinary conversational utterances, where the speaker's subjective evaluation of events is expected. They would be acceptable in narrative writing or in the situation where the speaker describes the events very objectively, say, in the description of the act of a defendant in courts, for example.

Section 3, the question of (8c) will be explored incorporating recent proposals concerning clause structure (Rizzi 1997; Speas and Tenny 2003; Haegeman and Hill 2014, etc.). Then, the syntactic phenomenon of first person (speaker) deletion will be discussed and analyzed with the proposed structure of *ageru/kureru.*

2 The Syntactic Representation of *Ageru*

Given the similarity between English (1) and Japanese (2–3), apart from the empathy characteristics, *ageru* and *kureru* can be analyzed as being structurally similar to or the same as *give*. That is, they are all three place predicates and they need three arguments, AGENT (SOURCE), GOAL (RECIPIENT), and THEME, which are syntactically represented as subject, indirect object, and direct object, respectively.

In an early stage of generative syntax, Standard Theory, a primary concern was how lexical information (i.e. argument structure) is to be structurally represented. In such a framework, the predicate used as an independent verb and used as an auxiliary are considered to share the same argument structure, which, consequently, gives rise to similar syntactic structures. The difference between the two is specified with respect to how the THEME role is categorically assumed; a noun phrase (NP) for the independent predicate and a sentence (S) for the auxiliary counterpart. Examples such as (9) (see also (2–4)) can be structurally represented without any problem (cf. Nakau 1973: ch. 7; Inoue 1976: ch. 2; Shibatani 1978: ch. 3, etc.).

(9) a. *Hanako ga Tarō ni hon o ageta.*
NOM DAT book ACC gave
'Hanako gave Taro a book.'

b. *Hanako ga Tarō ni hon o yonde-ageta.*
NOM DAT book ACC read-gave
'Hanako read Taro a book.'

c. Hanako$_i$ ga Tarō ni [$_S$ PRO$_i$ hon o yonde]-ageta.

The D-structure of (9b), with the giving verb, *ageru*, used as an auxiliary, is something like (9c), which clearly indicates that the theme role of *ageru* is filled by an embedded sentence *[PRO hon o yonde]*, whose subject is phonologically null but identified with the subject of the higher predicate, *ageru*.

A problem with the analysis in (9c) is immediately detected, however. If the *ni*-phrase is given by the auxiliary *ageru*, just like the *ni*-phrase of the main predicate *ageru* of (9a), how can it explain the fact observed in (4) versus (5) and (7); namely, a *ni*-phrase is allowed with predicates such as *tsukuru* 'make, cook,' *yomu* 'read,' etc. on the one hand, but it is not allowed with *tasukeru* 'help,' *shinjiru* 'believe,' etc. on the other? Obviously, what controls the occurrence of a *ni*-phrase as a beneficiary is not *ageru* per se; the event type of the preceding predicate also has something to do with it.

A careful scrutiny of what predicates allow a *ni*-phrase reveals a dichotomy that closely coincides with what predicates allow the double object construction (DOC) in English.[5]

(10) a. *They cooked dinner for me.* a´. *They cooked me dinner.*
b. *He made a dress for his daughter.* b´. *He made his daughter a dress.*
c. *He read the book for his children.* c´. *He read his children the book.*
d. *She sang a song for her pupils.* d´. *She sang her pupils a song.*
e. *She bought a car for his son.* e´. *She bought his son a car.*

(11) a. *He closed the door for her.* a´. **He closed her the door.*
b. *She swept the garden for her mother.* b´. **She swept her mother the garden.*
c. *They cleaned the room for their children.* c´. **They cleaned their children the room.*
d. *She killed the centipede for me.* d´. **She killed me the centipede.*

As is clear from (10) and (11), the construction that involves a *for*-benefactive phrase can be paraphrased with DOC if the beneficiary, the referent of the *for* phrase, is considered to be a sort of possessor of the referent of the direct object as the result of the event. Given the similarity between the DOC of English and the *ageru* construction in Japanese, the analyses of the former would be quite suggestive when analyzing the latter.

2.1 The Structural Representation of DOC, Applicative Phrase

The DOC has been one of the most popularly investigated constructions in syntactic investigations. The construction provides a challenge to a syntactic theory that claims that a predicate can assign at most one objective case. As long as the two objects of DOC are considered to be Case-assigned by one verb, this problem is easily solved (but see Larson 1988). Recent considerations of the relation between arguments or semantic roles that appear in a sentence (i.e. syntactic representation of arguments) and event types (i.e. lexical conceptual representation of predicates) have opened up a different way to approach this problem, however. The verbal projection part of syntactic structure is now considered to be itself a representation of the lexical conceptual or semantic structure (LCS) of an event, where a concrete predicate may occupy a sub-verbal head of a verbal complex and a theta role (argument) occupies a designated theta position in the syntactic

5 Shibatani (1996) examines benefactive constructions in various languages, including DOC of English and *ageru* of Japanese, pointing out that, though prototypical cases exist, whether particular occurrences of such constructions are allowed may vary among languages. English DOC, which does not make use of any particular benefactive marking, seems to exhibit a prototypical benefactive case.

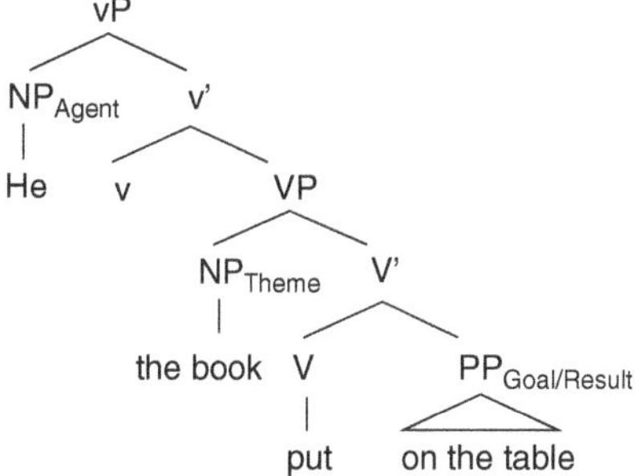

Figure 22.1 Syntactic structure of LCS (e.g. *He put the book on the table*)

representation (see Hale and Keyser 1993; Pylkkänen 2008: ch. 2). Though various executions are possible within such a framework, what is expressed in the LCS (12), a typical three-place predicate, *put*, for example, can be represented as Figure 22.1 in syntax.

(12) lexical conceptual structure (LCS) of *put*:
[x ACT-ON y] CAUSE [y BECOME [y BE-AT z]]
where x = AGENT, y = THEME, z = GOAL

As the LCS (12) shows, *put* is an accomplishment verb, where an AGENT (x) acts on a THEME (y), affecting y in such a way that it changes its positon or state (z). This LCS representation is mirrored in the syntactic structure in Figure 22.1, where the VP domain basically corresponds to the change of place/state part, the BECOME-BE area of the LCS, being a complement of a higher portion of verbal (vP) domain, which indicates that the eventuality in the VP is caused by the AGENT at the specifier position of vP.[6] The vP–VP structure provides designated argument positions in the way specified in Figure 22.1: AGENT is given to the specifier position of v, THEME to the specifier position of V, and GOAL to the complement position of V. In short, this approach assumes the following: (i) the structure of an event that may correspond to a single predicate involves a layered verbal projection with multiple sub-heads, which may be phonetically null, as with little-v in English; (ii) theta roles are not assigned by a single predicate but are considered to be items that occupy designated positions in the layered structure of the verbal projection; and (iii) the verbal projection as a whole gives rise to a particular single event that may correspond to a predicate as a lexical item.[7]

[6] For the role of the little-v category, see Chomsky 1995: ch. 4; Collins 1997: ch. 2; N. Hasegawa 1999, 2001, 2007b, etc. See also Pylkkänen 2008, whose Voice category is basically equivalent to little-v.

[7] What is stated here is how the predicate and its argument structure are syntactically represented. As for syntactic derivation, the following steps are needed: the verb *put* raises to little-v, which then assigns Accusative Case to the THEME NP, *the book*. This vP–VP structure will be taken as a complement of the higher functional structure, TP (or IP), and the subject NP will be raised to the TP domain, receiving Nominative Case. Being embedded under the TP projection, the event expressed in the verbal projection is anchored in the real world. TP then appears as a complement of a yet higher functional projection, CP, which is the level that mediates the propositional content (TP) to the superordinate structure, the main clause if that CP constitutes an embedded sentence, or the discourse or information structure with a particular speech act force if it itself is a main clause. We will come back to these functional projections, the C system (CP) in particular, in Section 3.

Then, the question regarding DOC or the benefactive construction is how it is represented. Recall the grammatical contrast between (10) and (11), which shows that DOC is possible if the three arguments involved constitute the interpretation that the act of an agent results in a situation where the THEME argument is possessed by what is expressed as an indirect object. Within the framework of construction grammar, which advocates the thesis that a particular syntactic construction has a construction-specific meaning, Shibatani (1996: 173) presents (13) as the 'give' DOC scheme (cf. Goldberg 1995: ch. 6).

(13) Structure: [NP_1 NP_2 NP_3 give]
Semantics: NP_1 cause NP_2 to have NP_3.

That is, the indirect object, NP_2, is not a GOAL but a possessor or recipient of NP_3 in DOC. In fact, it has been noted that although the dative construction and DOC are close in meaning, they are different and the dative GOAL phrase can appear in DOC (e.g. Larson 1988). Observe (14):

(14) a. *He sent a book to me.* a´. *He sent me a book.*
b. *He sent a book to my address.* b´. **He sent my address a book.*

As the ungrammatical (14 b´) shows, an inanimate locational phrase cannot constitute DOC.

Based on this kind of fact, two different GOAL-related positions are proposed: upper GOAL and lower GOAL (e.g. Miyagawa and Tsujioka 2004; Pylkkänen 2008: ch. 2). In these proposals, the lower GOAL is equivalent to the GOAL positon in Figure 22.1, where the *to*-dative phrase takes place, and the upper GOAL is given by the verbal projection, Applicative Phrase (ApplP), which takes place just above VP and below vP. This upper GOAL position is designated for the possessor/recipient of DOC, NP_2 of (13).[8] In this system, DOC, say (14), is represented as in Figure 22.2. Note that Applicative head is phonologically null in English, just as is little-v head.

The verb *sent* will eventually move up to the Appl-head then to the little-v head in the course of derivation and two objective Cases are given through this derivation.

2.2 The Structural Representation of *Ageru* as Applicative

Adopting the Applicative approach to the English DOC given above, Okura (2009: ch. 3, 2011) proposes that the auxiliary use of *ageru* is

[8] Applicative phrases or applicative projections have been discussed not only in the context of DOC but with regard to various syntax-morphology phenomena of diverse language types where another argument shows up in addition to what is ordinarily assumed with particular predicates. See Baker 1988: ch. 5; Marantz 1993: ch. 7; Shibatani 1996; Pylkkänen 2008: ch. 2, etc. for more general discussion on applicatives.

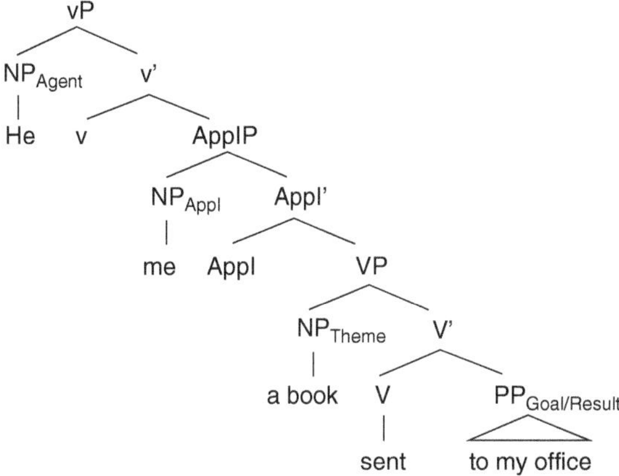

Figure 22.2 Structure of the double object construction with Applicative

a lexical representation of Applicative (see also N. Hasegawa 2006). Note that Japanese is a head final language with agglutinative characteristics, and the verbal sub-heads, whose counterparts in English are usually not clearly marked or phonologically null, often appear with phonological matrix. For example, little-v, which is null in English as shown in Figures 22.1 and 22.2, shows up as transitivizers *-os, -as, -s, -e*, etc. or intransitivizers, *-are, -re, -ar*, etc. in Japanese, as exemplified in *kow-as(u)* 'break-transitive,' *shim-e(ru)* 'close-transitive,' etc. and *kow-are(ru)* 'break-intransitive,' *shim-ar(u)* 'close-intransitive,' etc., respectively (see N. Hasegawa 1999: ch. 3, 2001, 2007b, and Nishiyama 2000 for relevant discussion). Thus, it is not surprising to see that the Appl-head, which is phonologically null in English, shows up with the phonological content in Japanese, *ageru*.[9]

Okura (2009: ch. 3) provides several pieces of evidence that support an Applicative analysis of *ageru*. We will go over just a couple of them. First, with *ageru*, two *ni*-phrases are possible with a change of location transitive, such as *okuru* 'send,' the Japanese counterpart of (14c), while only one *ni*-GOAL is allowed without *ageru*. Furthermore, when two *ni*-phrases occur, the order should be the possessor of the theme object, the higher GOAL, first and the pure-GOAL phrase, the lower GOAL, next.[10] That is, the presence of *ageru* gives rise to a possessor positon above the theme object.

(15) a. *?*Tarō wa Hanako ni hon o kenkyūshitsu ni okutta.*
NOM DAT book ACC office DAT sent
'Taro sent Hanako a book to the office.'

[9] We will discuss in Section 2.3 the difference between the presence and absence of the phonologically realized marking of Applicative, which has to do with the question (8b).

[10] Since Japanese exhibits relatively free word order, the order may not be too rigid. However, the preferred order shown in (15b) is robust. See Miyagawa and Tsujioka (2004) for more discussions on two GOAL positions in Japanese.

b. *Tarō wa Hanako ni hon o kenkyūshitsu ni okutte-ageta.*
NOM DAT book ACC office DAT send-gave
'Taro sent Hanako a book to the office.'

c. *?*Tarō wa kenkyūshitsu ni hon o Hanako ni okutte-ageta.*
NOM office DAT book ACC DAT send-gave
'Taro sent Hanako a book to the office.'

Another piece of evidence has to do with the difference in the categorical status of the two *ni*-phrases. If the possessor, the upper-GOAL *ni* phrase, is clefted, deleting *ni* is preferred, whereas the lower-GOAL *ni* phrase, the locational GOAL, needs *ni* when clefted. Observe (16), the clefted sentences of (15b).[11]

(16) a. *Tarō ga hon o kenkyūshitsu ni okutte-ageta no wa*
NOM book ACC office DAT send-gave NMLZ TOP
{Hanako/??Hanako ni} da.
DAT COP
'It was {Hanako/??to Hanako} that Taro sent a book to the office.'

b. *Tarō ga Hanako ni hon o okutte-ageta no wa*
NOM DAT book acc send-gave NMLZ TOP
*{*kenkyūshitsu/kenkyūshitsu ni} da.*
office DAT COP
'It was {*the office/to the office} that Taro sent Hanako a book.'

This difference indicates that the *ni*-phrase occurring with *ageru* with the possessor interpretation is an NP with DATIVE *ni*, not a mere GOAL phrase, which would be a PP.

Applying the Applicative analysis of DOC, illustrated in Figure 22.2, to Japanese benefactives, Figure 22.3 obtains as the basic structure of *ageru* (and *kureru*). The only difference, apart from the positions of phrasal heads, head final in Japanese and head initial in English, is that the lexical predicate, *ageru*, occupies the Applicative head.

In this structure, Accusative *o* is given to the THEME object and, crucially, DATIVE *ni* is given to the possessor applicative argument at the specifier position of ApplP, whose head is *ageru* (*kureru*). Note crucially that the *ni*-phrase under VP is a PP locational GOAL phrase.

Figure 22.3 is not only for the auxiliary version of *ageru* (*kureru*) but also for their main verb use. The difference is that the auxiliary version is simply an Applicative head, which takes place with another predicate (V) that functions as the predicate of eventuality to be

[11] See Machida (1996), for relevant discussion on two different GOAL phrases and their behavior in cleftability. See also Okura (2009: ch. 3, 2011).

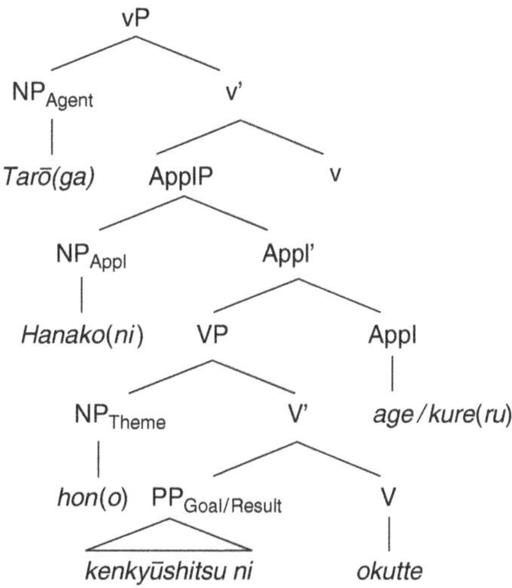

Figure 22.3 Applicative analysis of benefactives for Japanese

expressed, whereas the main verb version occupies the V head, which then moves to the Appl-head.[12] This is the answer to the question (8a), raised in Section 1: "How does the main verb *ageru/kureru* differ from the auxiliary counterpart in terms of argument structure and structural representation?"

Figure 22.3 also provides an answer to the question (8b): "What is responsible for the occurrence of the *ni*-phrase?" That is, ApplP head provides a position for it. Nonetheless, it does not explain why there are *ageru/kureru* sentences without a *ni*-possessor phrase, such as (5), repeated here as (17).

(17) a. *Watashi wa otōto no shukudai o tetsudatte-ageta.*
I TOP brother GEN homework ACC help-gave
'I helped with my brother's homework (for him).'

b. *Haha wa itsumo watashi o shinjite-kureta.*
mother TOP always I ACC believe-gave
'Mother always believed in me (and I benefitted from it).'

We will take up this question next.

2.3 Lexical versus Non-lexical Applicative Head

The Applicative analysis of *ageru* provided in Figure 22.3 is basically the same as the one for DOC of English, that is, Figure 22.2. The crucial difference, however, is that the Appl head of English is phonetically null

[12] Thus, in principle, two *ageru*'s, that is, *agete-ageru*, the sequence of V *age-* 'give' and Applicative *age-* is possible.

and that of Japanese is lexically realized as *ageru/kureru*. This difference is responsible for another important difference between the two languages: namely, the Applicative in English is confined to DOC, generating an indirect object of the possessor reading, whereas that in Japanese gives rise to the benefactive construction in a wide range, including not only what is equivalent to DOC of English but also the benefactives without a *ni*-possessor GOAL phrase.

As briefly touched upon in Section 2.2, the theoretical underpinning of the Applicative analysis of DOC assumes that arguments that appear in a sentence are licensed in a verbal complex, such as vP-ApplP-VP of Figure 22.1 and 22.2. Furthermore, though the entire verbal complex in Japanese corresponds to a single verb in English, whether each of the sub-heads takes a phonologically identifiable form or remains as an abstract entity without morphophonological specification depends on languages and types of predicates. Many sub-heads are phonologically marked in Japanese, whereas English makes use of abstract entities.

In principle, syntactic structure represents what is expressed and it should not matter whether a relevant head is abstract (phonologically null) or takes a morphophonologically identifiable form. However, to the extent that linguistic representation is to be used not only in constructing logical propositions but also in conveying the propositions (ideas) to others and exchanging and sharing them with others, it does matter whether or not what is conceptually represented involves audible or visible entities. In English, where Applicative is abstract, the presence of the possessor (beneficiary) object is the only indication of the benefactive construction. Naturally Applicative is allowed only when its specifier position is lexically filled with a possessor NP. That is, with an Applicative head being abstract, unless it licenses a possessor (beneficiary) NP at its specifier position (and subsequent case marking on it), its existence would be undiscernible to the hearer (reader) and would be useless in conveying what is to be expressed. This is the reason why Applicative is allowed only in the DOC construction in English.

In Japanese, on the other hand, a concrete lexical item, *ageru/kureru*, marks the benefactive construction even without a possessor (beneficiary) NP at the specifier position of Applicative.[13] Thus, practically any event may show up with *ageru/kureru*, as long as it has a benefactive effect to those assumed in the given context. Note, nonetheless, that if an NP

[13] In short, what the abstract sub-head generates is more restricted than what the corresponding lexical one gives rise to. This is true also for little-v. As briefly mentioned in Section 2.2, English does not make use of lexicalized little-v, which explains why English does not exhibit transitive–intransitive alterations and the pair is strictly confined to a limited class, that is, the change of state verbs, such as *break, open, bend*. On the other hand, Japanese, being rich in morphological markings, allows various transitive–intransitive pairs. With clear morphological markings, not only the change of state verbs but emergent unaccusatives, which are strictly intransitives without transitive counterparts in English, are allowed to have transitive counterparts, as in *oki(ru)* 'occur, happen' versus *ok-os(u)* 'make happen,' *araw-are(ru)* 'appear' versus *araw-as(u)* 'make appear,' *ki-e(ru)* 'disappear, vanish,' *ke-s(u)* 'make disappear,' etc.

occupies the specifier position of Applicative, it has to syntactically receive DATIVE *ni*-Case, being interpreted just like the possessor object of DOC of English. This is the answer to the question (8b) – When an Applicative head itself gives rise to an NP in its specifier position, the *ni*-possessor phrase is possible.

2.4 The Structural Determination of the Beneficiary

With the lexical Applicative predicate, Japanese does not require the lexical presence of a beneficiary argument. It may be specifically generated as the Applicative "possessor" argument with *ni*, it may show up as a beneficiary adjunct PP, *no tame ni* 'for the sake of,' it may be a direct object or the genitive argument of the direct object, or it may even not be mentioned at all but understood to be someone in the discourse. These examples follow.

(18) a. *Tarō wa Hanako ni yūhan o tsukutte-ageta.*
TOP DAT dinner ACC make-gave
'Taro cooked Hanako dinner.'

b. *Tarō wa Hanako no tameni heya o sōji-shite-ageta.*
TOP Hanako for room ACC clean-do-gave
'Taro cleaned the room for the sake of Hanako.'

c. *Tarō wa Hanako o shinjite-ageta.*
TOP ACC believe-gave
'Taro believed Hanako (for her).'

d. *Tarō wa Hanako no shukudai o tetsudatte-ageta.*
TOP GEN homework ACC help-gave
'Taro helped Hanako with her homework.'

e. *Tarō wa isshōkenmei hataraite-ageta.*
TOP earnestly work-gave
'Taro worked hard (for someone understood in discourse).'

Note that when there is more than one possible beneficiary, the one structurally higher seems to win out. That is, the indirect object is the beneficiary in (19), not the direct object.

(19) *Tarō wa Hanako ni Jirō o shōkai-shite-ageta.*
TOP DAT ACC introduce-do-gave
'Taro introduce Jiro to Hanako (for her).'

Examples (18–19) indicate that the choice of the beneficiary is not determined by pragmatics but is syntactically determined. Let us assume that the item that resides at or moves to the specifier positon of ApplP receives the beneficiary interpretation. As a syntactic operation, movement obeys minimality in general and the one higher in the structure or closer to the

Applicative projection is the one that moves, not the one that is farther away or below. This is the reason why the indirect object, *Hanako*, is determined to be a beneficiary, not the direct object, *Jirō*, in (19). If no indirect object exists, the direct object can (overtly or covertly) move to the specifier position of ApplP, which is the case with (18c), where the direct object *Hanako* moves from the theme position to the specifier of ApplP, gaining the beneficiary interpretation. Similarly, in (18d), the genitive *Hanako*, being detached from the object NP, covertly moves to the specifier of ApplP.[14]

2.5 The Choice of *Age-ru* and *Kure-ru*: The Role of the Empathy Hierarchy

With the presence of the lexical applicative head, *ageru* or *kureru*, as shown in Figure 22.3, benefactives obtain. However, its mere existence does not yet answer question (8c). Is it possible to represent the speaker's empathy or point of view in syntax? As discussed in Section 1, the choice of *ageru* or *kureru* is not simply due to a particular referent or person feature like the first, second, or third person but is relative to the degree of closeness to the speaker among the participants of the event. Syntax is not suited to encoding such relative relations. It seems best to leave the choice of *ageru* and *kureru* to pragmatic interpretation along the lines of Kuno and Kaburaki (1977) (see also Chapter 17, this volume). That is, syntactic representations such as Figure 22.3 would be subject to some sort of a well-formed condition regarding Empathy Hierarchy.

3 The Speaker Feature and *Kureru*

In Section 2, we have taken up how the benefactive construction is represented in syntax, providing an analysis for the benefactive predicate, *ageru* and *kureru*, and a beneficiary argument. That is, we have mainly been concerned with the structure of the verbal complex, vP-ApplP-VP. In Section 2.5, we conceded that the choice of *ageru* and *kureru*, which cannot be determined simply by syntactic person features, is not a matter of syntax per se and thus some pragmatic condition relating to the speaker's empathy would be needed. This does not mean that syntax does not say anything about the speaker (or the addressee). There are in fact various syntactic phenomena that specifically involve the speaker and the addressee. For example, the constructions with specific illocutionary force need

14 Here, Possessor Ascension (PA) is assumed to be at work in Japanese. N. Hasegawa (2007b, 2011) argues that Japanese makes use of PA quite freely, pointing out that Kuno's (1973: ch. 3) Subjectivization, which makes the genitive NP of the subject become a major subject, is just one example of the wider and freer operation of PA. It has been noted in N. Hasegawa (2006: Section 4) incidentally that PA plays an important role in determining the target of non-subject honorification, which is supposed to have a similar structure as the benefactive construction.

to refer to the speaker and/or addressee: imperatives are possible only when the subject is the addressee and only the speaker subject may be deleted in certain registers; for example, subject deletion in diaries and informal writings in English (Haegeman 1990).

Turning to Japanese, besides benefactives, there are various phenomena whose account requires the reference to the speaker (and the addressee). It is well known that sentient predicates, such as *samui* 'cold' and *kanashii* 'sad,' require the speaker (the first person) subject in reportive style, as pointed out by Kuroda (1973a), and certain speech act modalities require the addressee or the speaker subject, as extensively discussed in Nitta (1991).[15] See (20).

(20) a. *{Watashi/*Anata/*Tarō} wa {samui/ ureshii/ kanasii}.*
I/you TOP cold/happy/ sad
'{I am/*You are/*Taro is} {cold/happy/sad}.'

b. *{Omae/*Boku/*Kare} wa koko de tabako o suu na.*
you/I/he TOP here at cigarette ACC smoke NEG.IMP
'Don't {you/*I/*he} smoke cigarettes here!'

c. *{Watashi/*Anata/*Hanako/Watashi to Hanako} ga iki-mashō.*
I/you and NOM go-shall
'{I/*You/*Hanako/Hanako and I} shall go.'

Until recently, those phenomena specifically relevant to the speaker and the addressee have not attracted mainstream attention in theoretical syntactic research. However, in recent studies, where the syntactic encoding of clause types and functions has been taken up, such phenomena have invited serious consideration. For example, Rizzi (1997) and those advocating so-called Cartography provide the structural and conceptual foundation for dealing with the phenomena at the interface between syntax and discourse or information structure, considering the C system or the CP area "as the interface between a propositional content (expressed by the IP) and the superordinate structure (a higher clause or, possibly, the articulation of discourse, if we consider a root clause)" (p. 283). In this approach, the CP area involves several sub-heads or sub-projections that refer to the concepts such as illocutional force, topic, focus, etc., which are relevant to information structure or discourse. Rizzi (p. 297) proposes Figure 22.4 for the C system, where everything above IP (i.e. TP) constitutes the area that has been considered as CP.

Adopting the spirit of Rizzi's view, Zanuttini (2008) provides an analysis of imperatives where the addressee feature is posited in the projection of CP, which is further extended in N. Hasegawa (2009, 2010). Speas and Tenny (2003) propose the Speech Act phrase (SaP) in the realm of

[15] Tenny (2006) takes up the phenomena like (20a), and N. Hasegawa (2009, 2010a) and Ueda (2007, 2009) those of (20b–c), providing structural analyses of these phenomena, where the speaker and the addressee features in the main clause CP play crucial roles. The discussion on *kureru* is along the line of these analyses.

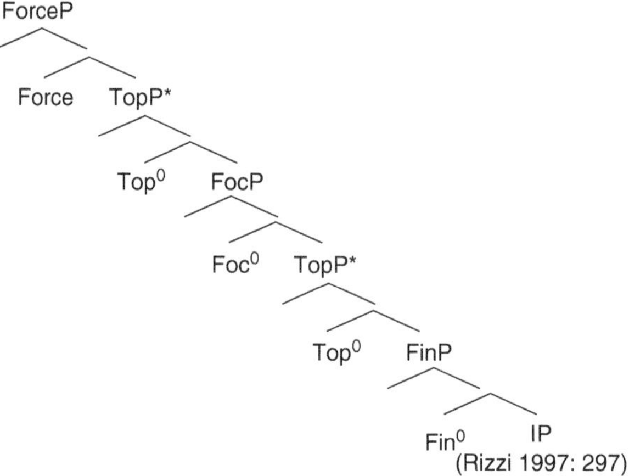

Figure 22.4 Structure of the C system

C system and Tenny (2006) analyzes the sentient predicate phenomena (20a) with SaP (see also Haegeman and Hill 2014 for a cartographic structure with a SaP).

In N. Hasegawa (2009, 2010a), I account for the phenomena that involve the speaker and the addressee such as imperatives and those like (20b–c) where the features [±speaker] [±addressee] in the C system agree with the corresponding speech act modalities, (Polite, Negative) Imperative markers, *nasai, na*, and imperative inflection, Propositive *mashō*, etc. (cf. Zanuttini, Pak, and Portner 2012 for an analysis of similar phenomena in Korean). Dealing with different phenomena, these recent attempts are not necessarily mutually compatible in detail, and it is beyond the scope of this chapter to carefully examine them. However, what is common to these attempts is that the speaker plays an important role in the occurrence of these discourse-related phenomena, and the syntactic presence of the feature relevant to the speaker is responsible for accounting for them. Here, I will simply assume Figure 22.5 as a relevant structure, abstracting away from details.[16]

In what follows, I would like to point out that the phenomenon with *kureru* is yet another instance that crucially makes use of this sort of structure (i.e. the structure with the speaker feature incorporated in the C system). Once the speaker is involved as a participant of an event, there are cases where the use of the beneficiary predicate *kureru* is mandatory and the specific interpretation is forced, which is made available from

[16] In short, what Figure 22.5 shows is that there is a layer, that is, Speech Act phrase (SaP), which may well be part of the C system. We will not deal with how the entire CP is structured here, incorporating Figures 22.4 and 22.5. What is crucial here is simply that the CP area, the interface between a propositional content and its superordinate field, hosts the [±Speaker][±Addressee] features, which are considered responsible for various speaker–addressee phenomena. In Figure 22.5, only the [+Speaker] feature is marked, which is relevant to the following discussion.

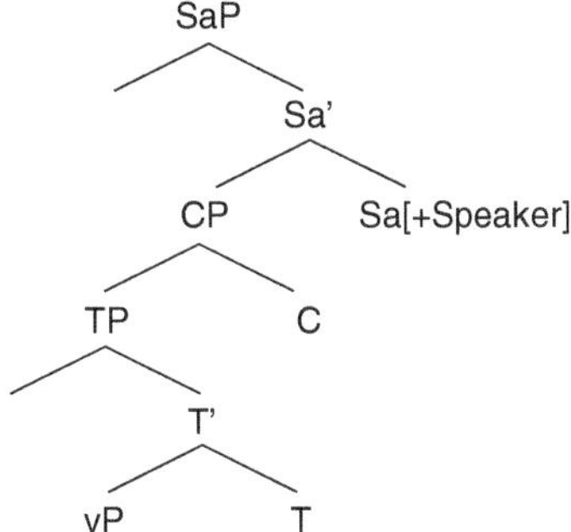

Figure 22.5 Speech act phrase in syntactic structure

Figure 22.5, showing that such phenomena would be subject to syntactic consideration.

3.1 The First Person Deletion and *Kureru*

It has widely been assumed that Japanese is a free pronoun drop language and any item that is contextually recoverable may drop as Kuno's (1978a: 8) "principle for deletion" suggests. Such a view is compatible with the fact that the null argument (Ø) in the following examples may refer to anyone or anything that is identifiable in a given context.

(21) a. Ø *hon* *o* *katta.*
book ACC bought
'(I/you/he/they, etc.) bought a book.'

b. *Hanako* *ga* Ø *katta.*
NOM bought
'Hanako bought (it/them).'

This fact has often been analyzed in terms of topic deletion, as in Kuno (1978a) in the Standard Theory framework or in Huang (1984) and N. Hasegawa (1985) in the government and binding framework. In such 'topic deletion' analyses, the item that discoursally functions as a topic is topicalized (i.e. moves to the topic position of the C system) and then deleted, provided that the deleted topic is contextually recoverable (i.e. the principle of deletion is satisfied). This results in a sentence with a phonologically unrepresented topic, which binds a trace, giving rise to a sentence with a null argument, such as (21).

Under this view, among the discoursally identifiable items, the speaker seems to be the most easily identifiable and it seems natural that it would be freely deleted. However, speaker deletion is not as free as expected. Observe (22).

(22) a. In response to the question of why {I am/(s)he is/they are} here:
Hanako ga Ø shōtai-shita (no desu).
NOM invite-did (it is that)
'Hanako invited {*me/ him/ her/ them}.'

b. In response to the question of how {I/ s(he)/ they} got to know the news:
Hanako ga Ø oshieta (no desu).
NOM told (it is that)
'Hanako told (it) to {*me/him/her/them}.'

What is to be observed here is that the acceptability of the null object depends on its person feature – it can refer to the third person but not to the first person, even though the first person is to be easily identifiable in the context.[17] Given the topic deletion analysis of null arguments, it is a mystery why only the third person is subject to topicalization (and deletion), while the first person is not. To resolve this problem, I argue in N. Hasegawa (2007a) that a topic is [–Speaker] and topicalization does not apply to the first person. The view that the topic phrase has the [–Speaker] feature accords with Kuroda's (1992a) claim that a sentence with the topic *wa* expresses categorical judgment (cf. Chapter 13, this volume), which is "the cognitive act of apprehending something as substance and attributing to it a certain property perceived in a situation" (Kuroda 1992a: 22–23). That is, the speaker himself/herself is not subject to such apprehension as a substantial entity and, thus, cannot be a topic. Naturally, the first person cannot be a topic nor be subject to topic deletion.[18]

[17] One of the reviewers pointed out that first person object deletion is possible in the following discourse.

(i) a. *Dare ga Ø nagutta no?*
who NOM hit.PST Q
'Who hit you?'

b. *Hanako ga Ø nagutta.*
NOM hit.PST
'Hanako hit me.'

There is a clear contextual difference between the acceptable (ib) and the unacceptable first person object deletion in (22), however. Namely, (ib) has a structure that is basically identical with the preceding question sentence, whereas there is no such linguistically represented antecedent sentence for (22). The deleted object in (ib), which refers to the addressee of (ia), namely the speaker of (ib), can be recovered as part of the linguistically repeated parallel structure, not from the context. The null object in (22), on the other hand, without a corresponding parallel structure, has to recover its reference purely from the context as a topic, which cannot be done where the first person is concerned. I, thus, consider the null object in (ib) is a different process from that observed in (22). Note, incidentally, that it has been widely accepted in syntactic research that the linguistic presence or absence of the antecedent would differentiate deletion and anaphoric processes; for example, VP ellipsis, which requires the linguistic antecedent with the parallel structure, versus *do it* anaphora, which is allowed contextually without a corresponding linguistic antecedent (see Hankamer and Sag 1976). The question here is why topicalization of the object and its subsequent deletion cannot apply to the first person object in (22), to which we will turn shortly.

[18] This claim leads to the conclusion that the *-wa* in *watashi-wa* is not a topic but something else. My claim is that it is, if not contrastive, an instance of what is generated at SaP, indicating "the speaker," not a topic. That is, Topic has the [–Speaker] feature, while SaP has [+Speaker]. Both items are marked *-wa*, taking place in the area of the C system. See N. Hasegawa (2007a: Section 2) for relevant discussion.

This does not mean that the first person object cannot be null, however. With the predicate *kureru*, as shown in (23), the null object can refer to the first person under the same context as (22).[19]

(23) a. *Hanako ga Ø shōtai-shite-kureta.*
NOM invite-do-gave
'Hanako invited {me/you/him/them, etc.}.'

b. *Hanako ga Ø tasukete-kureta.*
NOM help-gave
'Hanako helped {me/ you/ him/ they, etc.}.'

The above fact suggests that the speaker object deletion be conditioned by the presence of the Applicative head *kureru*, which then refers to the speaker feature of the C system. We can assume something like Figure 22.6. for the structure and mechanisms of the null first object deletion phenomena.

That is, for speaker object deletion two steps are required: the feature [+Speaker] of Sa at the C system of the utterance agrees with that of the benefactive Applictive predicate *kureru*, and the [+Speaker] feature on *kureru* agrees with the [+Speaker] feature of the beneficiary argument, *watashi*, at the specifier of Applicative Phrase, which is (perhaps covertly) raised from the THEME object position. Through these two steps, the object is identified as the speaker, which is then allowed to be null, phonetically deleted.[20, 21]

[19] In both examples in (23), the deleted object can refer not only to the first person but also to anybody with whom the speaker can empathize more than with the subject *Hanako*. We are not concerned with this reading, however. What is at issue here is that if the speaker is to be deleted, the presence of the benefactive predicate *kureru* is mandatory. Note that with an act that is not of the benefactive type, say *naguru* 'hit,' *keru* 'kick,' the benefactive *kureru* is incompatible; naturally, the speaker cannot be deleted but has to be lexically specified instead.

(i) *Hanako ga {*Ø/ watashi o} nagutta.*
NOM I ACC hit.PST
'Hanako hit me.'

The null object in (i) is allowed if it refers to someone other than the speaker who is identifiable in the given context.

[20] I will leave it open exactly where the verbal complex, *tasukete-kureta*, resides in the structure through this derivation. Since Japanese is a head final language, it is difficult to determine exactly where a verbal complex is in the structure, particularly given a syntactic theory where abstract movement or feature agreement is allowed. I tentatively assume that the verbal complex may overtly move to T, while the [+Speaker] agreement with the Sa head may take place covertly. In any case, what is to be done in Figure 22.6 is that the [+Speaker] feature at Sa, at the Appl head, and at the specifier of ApplP are in the configuration where the feature sharing, which may be due to movement or agreement, is expected to take place structurally.

[21] The null argument phenomenon taken up in this section is only a part of what Japanese exhibits. To discuss the entire phenomenon of null arguments in Japanese would take us too far afield. What is to be noted here is that the first person null object is licensed by Applicative head, which is marked [+Speaker]. Concerning deletion of other persons and of the subject, see Kuno (1978a: ch. 1) and N. Hasegawa (1985) for deletion via topicalization, N. Hasegawa (2007a) for first person deletion in a wider perspective involving more detailed description and analysis of what is discussed here, and N. Hasegawa (2009, 2010a) for subject deletion that has to do with pro-drop phenomena in general as well as those in specific clause types.

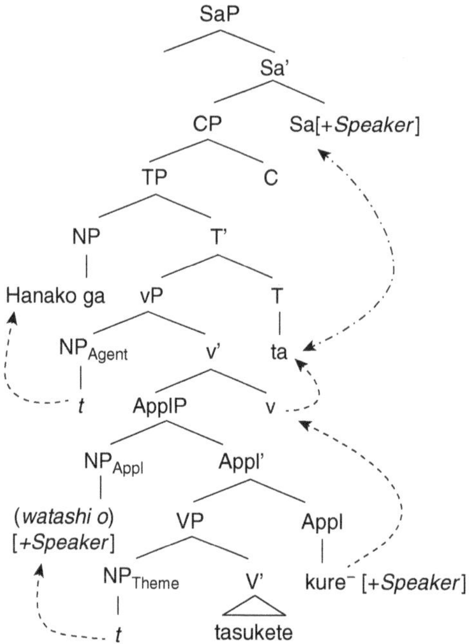

Figure 22.6 The structure and the interpretation procedure of *kureru*

3.2 First Person Deletion in the Embedded Context

The crucial relevance of the [+Speaker] feature at CP is clearly seen in the contrast observed in (24), where *i* refers to Hanako, the matrix subject, *j* refers to someone in discourse but not the speaker, and *k* refers to the speaker. The reading *j*, which is available in both examples, irrespective of the presence of *kureru*, is a case of topic deletion and is irrelevant to the present discussion.

(24) a. *Hanako*$_i$ *ga* *[Tarō* *ga* *Ø*$_{*i/j/*k}$ *tasuketa* *to]* *itta.*
NOM NOM helped QUOT said
'Hanako$_i$ said that Taro helped Ø$_{*i/j/*k}$.'

b. *Hanako*$_i$ *ga* *[Tarō* *ga* *Ø*$_{i/j/*k}$ *tasukete-kureta* *to]* *itta.*
NOM NOM help-gave QUOT said
'Hanako$_i$ said that Taro helped Ø$_{i/j/*k}$.'

What needs to be considered is the availability of the reading *i*, the subject of the main clause, and the reading *k*, the speaker. The unavailability of the reading *k* in (24a) is expected given that the null object cannot refer to the speaker without *kureru*. But the fact that the null object may not refer to the speaker, that is, the unavailability of the reading *k*, even in (24b) is somewhat surprising, if *kureru* is considered simply able to refer to the speaker as its lexical characteristic.[22] The reading that *kureru* makes possible is the reading *i, Hanako*, the subject of the main clause. This means that the feature [+Speaker] on *kureru* is sensitive to syntactic structure; namely, what is the immediate superordinate controller of the C system in question. The speaker of the subordinate clause is *Hanako*, not the speaker of the entire utterance, and the [+Speaker] feature of *kureru* picks up the speaker of the embedded *to*-clause (the C system), namely, *Hanako*.

What is shown in the above is the structural "minimality" or "closeness" of what the [+Speaker] feature refers to, the closest speaker. [+Speaker] on the Applicative head *kureru* refers to the [+Speaker] feature on Sa of the closest C system, the embedded C system, which then refers to the subject of the main clause event, not to the speaker of the entire utterance, the [+Speaker] of the main clause CP. The fact that interpretation is crucially dictated by the structural closeness indicates that syntactic structure and syntactic operation (e.g. feature checking or agreement) are at work in determining who the beneficiary is.

4 Summary

Benefactives involve the speaker's view of the expressed proposition. In this chapter, taking up *give* in English and *ageru/kureru* in Japanese as representative cases of benefactives, we have considered how these predicates and the role of the speaker are structurally represented, adopting recent theoretical developments in the attempt at structurally representing some aspects of information structure and discourse. What is presented here is rather coarse, and more careful and detailed execution is definitely called for. However, it seems apparent that benefactives need syntactic consideration. Through such attempts, we may be able to gain more insight into syntax-pragmatics phenomena, which then invites productive consideration of what syntactic mechanisms need to be refined. Approaching benefactives offers both syntax and pragmatics challenging problems concerning how these subfields of linguistic research may develop further, mutually learning from each other.

[22] As one of the reviewers pointed out, the *k* reading, the reading that refers to the speaker, may be available in the sense of Kuno's (1988) "blended quasi-direct discourse," where the direct quote from what Hanako says is expressed in the form of indirect quote. The unavailability of the *k* reading is more clearly detected if the matrix predicate is changed to *omotteiru* 'think,' whose complement clause may not be a direct quote.

23

Passives

Shoichi Iwasaki

1 Introduction

A passive sentence (1a) is often contrasted with an active sentence (1b).

(1) a. *A dog was chased by a cat.* (passive)
 b. *A cat chased a dog.* (active)

This passive–active pair has a direct counterpart in Japanese as in (2).

(2) a. *Inu ga neko ni oikake-rare-ta.* (passive)
 dog NOM cat DAT chase-PASS-PST
 'A dog was chased by a cat.'
 b. *Neko ga inu o oikake-ta.* (active)
 cat NOM dog ACC chase-PST
 'A cat chased a dog.'

In (2b), Agent (*neko* 'cat') appears as the subject with the nominative particle *ga* and Patient (*inu* 'dog') as the direct object with the accusative particle *o*. In contrast, in (2a) Patient appears as the subject and Agent is coded as an oblique NP with *ni*. The verb-final nature of Japanese places the verb at the end in both types of sentence. Another notable difference between English and Japanese passives is the verb morphology. In English, the verb *chased* (active voice) is changed to *was chased* (passive voice) in the passive sentence. In Japanese, the verb *oikake-ta* 'chased' is changed to *oikake-rare-ta* 'was chased.'

This simplistic comparison of active and passive in the two languages may suggest that the difference may be reduced to typological differences. However, the Japanese passive structure presents many intriguing properties not present or apparent in English. Before we begin our discussion, we should note that *-rare-* is a verbal marker of passive in Japanese. The consonant *(r)* appears after vowel verbs (see Chapter 1 for verb categories) such as *oikake-* 'chase' and *mi-* 'see,' while *-are-* directly follows

Table 23.1 *Passive forms*

	Active form		Passive form	
Vowel verbs	*oikake-ru*	'chase'	*oikake-rare-ru*	'be chased'
	mi-ru	'see'	*mi-rare-ru*	'be seen'
Consonant verbs	*yom-u*	'read'	*yom-are-ru*	'be read'
	shin-u	'die'	*shin-are-ru*	n/a
Irregular verbs	*ku-ru*	'come'	*ko-rare-ru*	n/a
	su-ru	'do'	*sa-re-ru*	'be done'

consonant verbs such as *yom-* 'read' and *shin-* 'die.' This form will be cited as *rare* below. The non-past, affirmative active and passive forms of vowel and consonant verbs as well as irregular verbs are presented in Table 23.1.[1]

Below, we begin in Section 2 with a discussion of the traditional tripartite distinction of Japanese passives from the structural perspective: direct, indirect, and *ni-yotte* passives. We examine the important semantico-pragmatic notion of adversity associated with the passive in Section 3, then examine passives from a functional point of view in Section 4. We survey the use of passive in discourse in Section 5. We summarize the discussion in Section 6.

2 Direct, Indirect, and *Ni-yotte* Passives: Syntactic Structures

Since the early days of generative analysis of Japanese in the 1970s, passives have been categorized into two types according to their syntactic profiles: direct and indirect (e.g. N. McCawley 1972). Example (3) is a direct passive, while (4) and (5) are indirect passives. (Examples are from Howard and Niyekawa-Howard 1976: 202.)

(3) (direct passive)
Tarō wa sensei ni shikar-are-ta.
TOP teacher DAT scold-PASS-PST
'Taro was scolded by the teacher.'

(4) (indirect passive–transitive based)
Tanaka-san wa sensei ni kodomo o shikar-are-ta.
TOP teacher DAT child ACC scold-PASS-PST
Lit. 'Speaking of Tanaka-san, (her) child was scolded by the teacher.'

[1] Though not discussed in this chapter, it is well known that *-rare-* also marks spontaneous, potential, and honorific meanings (Shibatani 1985). Among these four different meanings, the potential is believed to be the oldest. However, currently the potential form is in the process of changing to a form distinct from that of the other meanings. Thus, the potential is expressed by a shortened form for consonant verbs: *yom-eru* (potential) versus *yom-are-ru* (passive, honorific) for *yomu* 'read.' For vowel verbs, both long and short forms are available for the potential: *oikake-rare-ru* and *oikake-re-ru*, but only the long form, *oikake-rare-ru*, is available for 'passive' and 'honorific.' In Modern Japanese, the spontaneous meaning is restricted to occur with limited verbs, such as *omow-are-ru* 'some idea occurs to me' for *omou* 'think.'

(5) (indirect passive – intransitive based)

Tarō	*wa*	*ame*	*ni*	*fur-are-ta.*
	TOP	rain	DAT	fall-PASS-PST

'Taro was rained on.'

Direct passives have associated active sentences (*sensei ga Tarō o shikatta* 'the teacher scolded Taro' for (3)), while indirect passives do not. The active voice of *shikar-are-ta* 'was scolded' in (3–4) is *shikat-ta* 'scolded,' which takes only two arguments (e.g. *sensei ga kodomo o shikatta* 'the teacher scolded a child'), and thus *Tanaka-san* in (4) is an "extra" argument and *kodomo* 'child' is a "retained" object (i.e. not promoted to subject). The active voice of *fur-are-ta* 'was rained on' in (5) is *fut-ta* 'rained,' an intransitive verb, and takes only one argument (*ame ga futta*), thus *Tarō* is again superfluous. (The nature of these extra arguments will be discussed in Section 3.) Indirect passives, for example, (4), are construed to have an underlying structure consisting of the matrix and an embedded clause as in (4′), where *sensei* 'teacher' is the subject of *shikar-* 'scold' in the embedded clause, while *Tanaka-san* is the matrix subject.

(4′) [Tanaka-san [sensei kodomo shikar] -are-ta]

Kuroda (1965) proposes that the embedding structure also underlies direct passives, as shown in (3′) for (3). Since both direct and indirect passives have identical "deep structures," this view is named the "uniform theory." In this theory *-rare-* is considered a two-place predicate requiring a subject and a complement-clause object.

(3′) a. [Tarō [sensei Tarō shikar] -are-ta]
b. [Tarō [sensei (gap) shikar] -are-ta]

Tarō in the embedded clause in (3′a) will be deleted under identification with the matrix subject, leaving a gap in the embedded clause, as shown in (3′b). Thus, the direct passive is sometimes called a "gapped" passive, while the indirect passive a "gapless" passive.

N. McCawley (1972) and Kuno (1973), however, propose that (3) is produced by a simple permutation applied to a transitive sentence (*sensei ga Tarō o shikatta* 'the teacher scolded Taro'), and consider *-rare-* a suffix. Since the direct and indirect passives come from different structures and the nature of *-rare-* is different, this view is named the "non-uniform theory." Strong support for the non-uniform theory comes from the interpretation of the reflexive pronoun, *jibun* 'self,' which has been shown by independent evidence to take the subject (either matrix or embedded) as its antecedent. An interesting observation is that *jibun* is ambiguously interpreted when it appears in an indirect passive (6) with the retained object *jibun no koto o*, but not so in a direct passive (7) with an oblique NP *jibun no uchi de*. The following examples are from Kuno (1973: 307).

(6) *Mary wa John ni jibun no koto o jiman-s-are-ta.* (indirect)
TOP DAT self GEN matter ACC brag-do-PASS-PST
'Mary suffered from John's bragging about self's matter.' (self = John or Mary)

(7) *Mary wa John ni jibun no uchi de koros-are-ta.* (direct)
house LOC kill-PASS-PST
'Mary was killed by John in self's house.' (self = Mary, not John)

Two possible interpretations of (6) can be accounted for by positing two different underlying structures, (6´a) and (6´b).

(6´) a. Mary wa [**John**$_i$ **John**$_i$ no koto jiman s] -are-ta
> Mary wa **John**$_i$**-ni jibun**$_i$-no-koto-o jiman s-are-ta
b. **Mary**$_j$ wa [John **Mary**$_j$ no koto jiman s] -are-ta
> **Mary**$_j$ wa John-ni **Mary**$_j$-no-koto-o jiman s-are-ta
> **Mary**$_j$ wa John-ni **jibun**$_j$-no-koto-o jiman s-are-ta

When reflexivization applies to (6´a), the second *John* is replaced by *jibun* under identity with the embedded subject, resulting in (6). When the embedded clause contains two different NPs (*John* and *Mary*) as in (6´b), reflexivization cannot apply, but after the clause is raised, it can because the second *Mary* now finds its antecedent in the matrix clause subject; the embedded *Mary* is replaced by *jibun* under identity with this matrix subject, resulting again as in (6).

Two possible underlying structures for the direct passive in (7) can also be assumed. For (7´a) after passivization with *-rare-* and permutation of two NPs (*John* and *Mary*), the second *Mary* can be replaced by *jibun* under identity with the new matrix subject. For (7´b), once the active sentence is passivized, the second *John* is no longer coreferential with the new matrix subject and cannot undergo reflexivization. This argument assumes that passivization applies prior to reflexivization.

(7´) a. John ga **Mary**$_i$ o **Mary**$_i$ no uchi de koroshita
> (passivization) **Mary**$_i$ wa John ni **Mary**$_i$ no uchi de koros-areta
> (reflexivization) **Mary**$_i$ wa John ni **jibun**$_i$ no uchi de koros-areta
b. **John**$_j$ ga Mary o **John**$_j$ no uchi de koroshita
> (passivization) Mary wa **John**$_j$ ni **John**$_j$ no uchi de koros-areta
> (reflexivization) Mary wa **John**$_j$ ni ***jibun**$_j$ no uchi de koros-areta

The only way to make the final derivation for (7´b) felicitous is to change *jibun* 'self' to *kare* 'he.' This is the main argument to support the non-uniform theory.

However, Howard and Niyekawa-Howard (1976: 228) point out that the ungrammaticality of the last derivation in (7´b) does not have to be construed in the way the non-uniform theory advocates claim. Assuming that (7) also has an underlying structure as (7´c), similar to (6´a–b), the second *John* will be replaced by *jibun* under identity with the embedded subject.

At the same time the second *Mary* finds its antecedent in the matrix subject and can undergo reflexivization.

(7′) c. Mary wa [**John** Mary **John** no uchi de koros] -areta
 > (reflexivization-1) Mary wa [**John**$_i$ Mary **jibun**$_i$ no uchi de koros] -areta
 > (reflexivization-2) **Mary**$_j$ wa **John**$_i$ ni **jibun**$_j$ o **jibun**$_i$ no uchi de korosareta

Howard and Niyekawa-Howard (1976: 229) propose the "reflexive coreference constraint," which does not allow two reflexive pronouns with two different antecedents in a sentence. If this is correct, the non-uniform theory will lose its strongest supporting argument. Kuroda (1979: 307) further supports the uniform theory arguing that there is no ambiguity in either the direct (7) or the indirect (8) passives, nullifying the non-uniform advocates' argument.

(7) *Mary wa John ni jibun no uchi de koros-are-ta.* (direct)
 TOP DAT self GEN matter ACC kill-PASS-PST
 'Mary was killed by John in self's house.' (self = Mary, not John)

(8) *Mary wa John ni jibun no heya de atama o war-are-ta.* (indirect)
 room LOC head ACC split-PASS-PST
 'Mary got her head split by John in self's room.' (self = Mary, not John)

Ishizuka (2012) adds her argument for the uniform theory from a different perspective (the minimalist approach) by claiming that the indirect passive contains a gap as in direct passive. The derived passive subject corresponds to an original oblique argument with the genitive *no*, dative *ni*, or ablative *kara*. According to her analysis (2012: 84), an indirect passive sentence with an intransitive verb such as (9a) is derived from an underlying structure (9b). The dative *ni* phrase in (9b) is promoted to the nominative *ga* phrase in (9a).

(9) a. *Naomi ga Ken ni donar-are-ta.* (indirect passive)
 NOM DAT yell-PASS-PST
 'Naomi was yelled at by Ken.'
 b. *Ken ga Naomi ni dona-tta.* (active)
 NOM DAT yell-PASS-PST
 'Ken yelled at Naomi.'

Currently, intense discussion still continues among formalists regarding the proper syntactic description of the two types of passive (see Hoshi 1999; Huang 1999; Fukuda 2006, 2015; Goro 2006; inter alia). While Kuroda maintains that both direct and indirect passives are derived from the same underlying structure, he suggests that another type of passive, the *ni-yotte* passive, has a different underlying structure. The examples below are from Hoshi (1999: 191, 194).

(10) *Sensei* *ga* *gakusei* *ni* *hihans-are-ta.* (direct)
teacher NOM student DAT criticize-PASS-PST
'The teacher was criticized by a student.'

(11) *Sensei ga gakusei ni* *kurasu* *de* *nak-are-ta.* (indirect)
class LOC cry-PASS-PST
'The teacher was adversely affected by a student crying in his/her class.'

(12) *Sensei ga gakusei* *ni-yotte* *hihans-are-ta.* (*ni-yotte* passive)
by criticize-PASS-PST
'The teacher was criticized by a student.'

According to Kuroda (1979), both direct and indirect passives require the subject be "affected" by the state of affairs described in the embedded clause (see the discussion of "affectedness" and "adversity" in Section 3 below), but the *ni-yotte* passive does not. That is, both (10) and (11) indicate that the teacher was psychologically affected by the student's action in her class, while (12) reports the event objectively. This difference accounts for the grammaticality difference between (13) and (14); *kaikai* 'opening (e.g. of a political session),' being an event (or an abstract notion), is not something that can be potentially affected psychologically by the chairman's act of declaring the opening of the meeting (Inoue 1976: 77), compared to *sensei* 'teacher' being affected by the students' act of criticizing him/her.

(13) **Kaikai* *ga* *gichō* *ni* *sengens-are-ta.* (*ni* direct passive)
opening NOM chair DAT declare-PASS-PST
Lit. 'Opening (of a session) was declared by Chair.'
'A session was called to order by Chair.'

(14) *Kaikai ga gichō* *ni-yotte* *sengens-are-ta.* (*ni-yotte* passive)
by declare-PASS-PST

Kuroda (1979: 336–337) proposes that the *ni-yotte* passive is derived by transformation applied to the active sentence in a way similar to how the direct passive is derived under the non-uniform theory. Thus, (13) can be described as (13′) and sentence (14) as (14′). (Representations here are slightly modified from Kuroda's original.)

(13′) NP_1 $(NP_2\ NP_3\ V_2)_{S2}$-*rare-ru*
a. NP_3 will be deleted if it is identical with NP_1. (= direct passive)
b. NP_3 will be retained if it is different from NP_1. (= indirect passive)

(14′) NP_1 NP_2 V-ru → NP_2 NP_1 *ni-yotte* V-*rare-ru*

In summary, under the uniform theory, the direct and indirect passives are treated equally with a special semantic interpretation of the passive subject, while the *ni-yotte* passive has a different structure and no special interpretation is required for its subject. Under the non-uniform theory, the *ni* direct passive and the *ni* indirect passive have different structures, though the former has an underling structure similar to the *ni-yotte* passive of Kuroda's theory.

The crucial difference between the two theories is how the direct passive is positioned vis-à-vis indirect passive and *ni-yotte* passive. To reconcile the two competing theories, Hoshi (1999: 212–213) proposes a structure which involves the theta subject generated in the deep structure and movement of PRO as shown in (15).

(15) [NP_1 [PRO_i [NP_2 t_i V]] -rare-ta]

NP_1 in this structure is a theta subject (i.e. an argument) specified by the passive verb *rare-* as in the indirect passive structure. Though the indirect passive does not involve movement, this structure assumes that PRO undergoes a movement from the object position shown as t_i to the subject position of the complement clause. In other words, Hoshi's proposal attempts to capture both the nature of theta subject for indirect passive and movement for direct passive to account for all the facts discussed by other researchers. Hoshi also notes that the distinction between the *ni* direct passive and *ni-yotte* passive finds a similar distinction between the "get" passive and "be" passive in English (1999: 199–200).

3 Adversity Passive

Semantically Japanese passives can be divided into the "neutral" (or "pure" or "simple") passive and the "adversity" (or "adversative" or "affective") passive. This distinction, briefly noted in the syntactic description above, is based on a recognition of a special semantico-pragmatic interpretation associated with the passive subject for the adversity passive and a lack thereof for the neutral passive. Adversity is characterized as "an implication of disadvantage for the subject" (Kuroda 1965: 160), "the connotation of suffering or inadvertent effect on the part of the main subject" (Kuno 1973: 302–303), or "a strong emotional implication for the subject" (Howard and Niyekawa-Howard 1976: 209). There has been a debate whether the semantic distinction (neutral versus adversative) and the syntactic distinction (direct versus indirect) are related. Both uniform and non-uniform theories adopt a position that the higher verb *rare*, a full-fledged two-place predicate verb, is responsible for this special effect. However, proponents of the non-uniform theory claim that direct passives do not bear this special semantic connotation because the *rare* that appears in this type of passive is not a verb, but a suffix.

Kuroda (1979), who adopts the uniform theory, takes the position that *rare* in both types of passive has this connotation based on his uniform analysis, and claims that *rare* in the *ni-yotte* passive does not have this connotation. He, adds, however, that the "affectivity cannot be characterized in a simple way by means of a putative semantic feature or bundle of semantic features such as adversity" (1979: 336), and leaves the precise definition of affectivity unresolved.

Kuno (1983) proposes a new way of understanding affectivity based on the degree of involvement of the referent of the passive subject, thereby allowing different gradations of adversity associated with passives (both direct and indirect).[2] Compare (16a) and (17a) (from Howard and Niyekawa-Howard (1976: 211) and Kuno (1983: 192), respectively).

(16) a. *Tanaka wa Yamada ni yūshoku ni yob-are-ta.* (passive)
TOP DAT dinner to invite-PASS-PST
'Tanaka was invited by Yamada to dinner.'

b. *Yamada wa Tanaka o yūshoku ni yon-da.* (active)
TOP ACC dinner to invite-PST
'Yamada invited Tanaka to dinner.'

(17) a. *Hawai daigaku wa Satō sensei ni yame-rare-ta.*
university TOP teacher DAT resign-PASS-PST
'The University of Hawaii had Professor Sato quit.'

b. *Satō sensei wa Hawai daigaku o yame-ta.*
teacher TOP university ACC resign-PST
'Professor Sato resigned from the University of Hawaii.'

Examples (16a) and (17a) are both direct passives relatable to (16b) and (17b), respectively. According to the non-uniform theory, neither sentence should bear the sense of adversity. Indeed, (16a) is interpreted as neutral. However, (17a) does express adversity on the part of the University of Hawaii (i.e. the UH administrators, colleagues, and students); the university suffered from Professor Sato's departure, that is, if it were a happy occasion for the people involved at UH, (17a) could not be used. Kuno (1983: 205) proposes the following generalization to account for this discrepancy: The lower the degree to which the passive subject is involved in the event or psychological state expressed by the complement clause, the stronger the sense of adversity and, conversely, the higher the degree of involvement, the weaker the sense of adversity. Since Tanaka is directly involved in the invitation event in (16a), this direct passive bears little adversity, and while the University of Hawaii is not involved in the event of Professor Sato's departure in the same way as Tanaka was involved in the invitation event, the adversity meaning is highlighted. Kuno also observes that a direct passive like (17a) cannot be rendered as a passive in English (**UH was quit by Professor Sato*). These observations suggest that when the embedded clause is higher in transitivity in the sense of Hopper and Thompson (1980), passive is more neutral, and when it is lower, it is more adversative. This explains why intransitive verbs usually impart adversity (see below).

Washio (1993: 51–55) uses the term "adversity by exclusion" (cf. Wierzbicka 1979) to account for a similar effect found in passive sentences.

(18) *John ga Mary ni kami o kir-are-ta.*
NOM DAT hair ACC cut-PASS-PST

[2] Kuno in this publication (1983) changed his position from the non-uniform to the uniform theory.

a. Lit. 'John was cut his hair by Mary.'
b. Lit. 'John was cut her hair by Mary.'

This sentence is ambiguous as to the possessor of the hair, it could be John's or Mary's. Washio notes, "[i]f the subject is excluded in a passive structure ... the subject receives an adversative interpretation in Japanese" (1993: 54). That is, if the hair belongs to Mary, John is interpreted as experiencing stronger adversity compared to the situation where the hair belongs to him. Iwasaki (2013: 161) further notes that when the hair belongs to John in a situation like (18), John has a potential control over Mary's attempt to cut his hair, but if the hair belongs to Mary, his potential intervention is weaker; Mary could have cut her hair when John was not around. This latter situation will create a special psychological adversity (e.g. because John secretly admired Mary's long hair) which is qualitatively different from more direct or physical adversity signaled by the verb *kiru* 'cut.' Between the two readings (psychological and physical adversity), interpretation (18a) is easier for native speakers to obtain (Ishizuka 2012: 114). In other words, to get the second interpretation, (18b 18b), native speakers need to be given some relevant contextual information, such as John's secret admiration toward Mary's hair.

Shibatani (1994) explains the adversity effect in his "integration approach," which applies not only to Japanese adversity passives but also to other linguistic phenomena such as possessor raising and ethical dative observed in other languages. He notes, "these constructions involve no theta-roles such as possessor and the affectee roles; instead I maintain that the meanings suggested by these roles are imputed to these constructions as a way of integrating the extra-thematic nominals into clausal semantics" (p. 468). He further states, "when the semantic integration of an extra-thematic argument is possible on the account of the body-part and the possessor relationship, no additional semantic support is required, but when such an account is not possible, semantic augmentation is required that doctors up the relevance of the referent of the extra-thematic argument to the described scene" (p. 468). This explains why (18) is readily interpreted as (18a), where the extra-thematic argument (John) is the possessor of the inalienably possessed body-part (hair). If this interpretation is blocked somehow (e.g. John still wears long hair), the recipient of the sentence must work harder to recognize the relevance between the extra-thematic argument (John) and Mary's hair. One potential relevance between them is, as already suggested above, John's secret admiration of Mary's hair.

Shibatani's integration approach also explains the subtle difference between (19) and (20), and a special circumstance we need to come up with for (21).

(19) *Boku wa inu ni ude o kam-are-ta.*
I TOP dog DAT arm ACC bite-PASS-PST
'I was bitten by a dog.'

(20) *Boku wa inu ni* *musuko* *o* *kam-are-ta.*
son ACC bite-PASS-PST
'I was adversely affected by a dog biting (my) son.'

(21) *Boku wa* *dorobō* *ni* *sensei* *no* *hon* *o* *nusum-are-ta.*
thief DAT teacher GEN book ACC steal-PASS-PST
'I was adversely affected by a thief stealing (my) teacher's book.'

Examples (19–20) are sometimes called "possessive passive" because there exists a possessor–possessed relationship between the subject and the retained object. Example (20) clearly implies psychological adversity on the part of the subject-speaker, but (19) has only physical adversity, with a possible psychological adversity through implicature. Example (21), on the other hand, is not a possessive passive because the subject is not the owner of the teacher's book. For this sentence to be felicitous, we need to imagine the circumstances in which this sentence may be used; for example, the speaker had borrowed a book from the teacher, and someone stole it while it was temporarily in the speaker's possession. This indirect relationship between the speaker and the book imparts stronger psychological adversity.

Indirect passives based on intransitive verbs are known to impart adversity meaning strongly. The explanations given by Kuno, Washio, and Shibatani above can account for this fact (*John wa ame ni furareta* 'John was rained on'). However, it is crucial to give the right prompt to have native speakers accept some "difficult" interpretation. Consider (22).

(22) *Ken* *wa* *Naomi* *ni* *hashir-are-ta.*
TOP DAT run-PASS-PST
'Ken was adversely affected by Naomi's running.'

In Ishizuka's experiment (2012: 218–219), many participants judged the sentence as ungrammatical, but if they can imagine that Naomi's running was an unexpected action for Ken (e.g. there is an agreement between Ken and Naomi that the event should not happen), the acceptability rate would go up.

Note that the verb *hoeru* 'bark (at)' has two argument structurers: 'bark' (intransitive) and 'bark at' (transitive). Example (23a) can be interpreted either way. If a dog sees Naomi and barks "at" her, as indicated by (23b), the situation will create direct, physical adversity (and psychological adversity by implicature), but if a dog barks without involving Naomi's existence (23c), the situation would create psychological adversity. It is impossible to interpret that the neighbor's dog barked "at" Naomi directly at night when she was in bed.

(23) a. *Naomi* *ga* *inu* *ni* *hoe-rare-ta.*
NOM dog DAT bark-PASS-PST
'Naomi was barked at by a dog.'

b. *Naomi ga yomichi de inu ni hoe-rare-ta.*
street.at.night LOC dog DAT bark-PASS-PST
'Naomi was barked at by a dog on a street at night.'

c. *Naomi wa yūbe 12 ji ni beddo ni hait-ta ga,*
TOP last.night o'clock at bed LOC enter-PST but

tonari no inu ni hoe-rare-te netsuke-nakat-ta.
next.door GEN dog DAT bark-PASS-CONJ fall.asleep-NEG-PST
'Last night, Naomi went to bed at 12 o'clock, but she was adversely affected by the next door's dog barking and could not fall asleep.'

Before completing this section, we must mention the "benefactive" construction (cf. Chapter 22, this volume) which contrasts with the adversity passive. Consider the sentences below.

(24) *Hanako no musume ga sensei ni homer-are-ta.* (direct passive)
GEN daughter NOM teacher DAT praise-PASS-PST
'Hanako's daughter was praised by (her) teacher.'

(25) *Hanako no musume ga sensei ni home-te-morat-ta.* (direct benefactive)
praise-CONJ-BEN-PST
'Hanako's daughter benefitted from (her) teacher praising her.'

Examples (24–25) are "direct passive" and "direct benefactive," respectively. In these cases (and if we follow the non-uniform theory), there is no psychological affectivity in relation to the subject, Hanako's daughter. They are both objective statements. The role of these constructions is to reverse the Agent perspective to the Patient perspective. If the psychological affectivity exists, it must be attributed to the speaker of these sentences, not the subject. Now compare (24′) and (25′).

(24′) (Indirect Passive)
Hanako wa musume o sensei ni home-rare-ta.
TOP daughter ACC teacher DAT praise-PASS-PST
'Hanako was adversely affected by teacher's praising of her daughter.'

(25′) (Indirect Benefactive)
Hanako wa musume o sensei ni home-te-morat-ta.
praise-CONJ-BEN-PST
'Hanako benefited by (her) daughter being praised by (her) teacher.'

In (24′) (indirect passive) and (25′) (indirect benefactive), there is the mother–daughter relationship between the extra-thematic NP and the retained object; what affects her daughter will also affect the mother psychologically. The benefactive interpretation is clear in (25′) due to the benefactive auxiliary, *morat-ta*. The same interpretation is also possible for (24′) due to the positive evaluation encoded in the verb *homeru* 'praise.'

However, (24′) may be interpreted as having a negative effect on the part of the extra-thematic NP (*Hanako*) due to the meaning of *rare*, which can indicate a negative feeling, for example, 'Hanako was embarrassed because the teacher praised her daughter when she knows that her daughter does not deserve praise.'

Finally compare (24″) and (25″).

(24″) (Strong Indirect Passive)

Hanako	*wa*	*Reiko*	*no*	*musume*	*o*	*sensei*	*ni*	*home-rare-ta.*
	TOP		GEN	daughter	ACC	teacher	DAT	praise-PASS-PST

'Hanako was adversely affected by Reiko's daughter being praised by the teacher.'

(25″) (Strong Indirect Benefactive)

Hanako wa Reiko no musume o sensei ni	*homete-morat-ta.*
	praise-CONJ-BEN-PST

'Hanako was benefited by Reiko's daughter being praised by (her) teacher.'

We may call (24″) and (25″) "strong indirect passive" and "strong indirect benefactive," respectively. Since the mother–daughter relationship does not exist in these cases between the extra-thematic noun (Hanako) and the retained object, Reiko's daughter, the relevance of Hanako vis-à-vis Reiko's daughter must be pragmatically established. To understand these sentences, the addressee must make a reasonable assumption about a special relationship that exists between Hanako on the one hand and Reiko and her daughter on the other. If, for example, Reiko is Hanako's favorite sister, it is easy to interpret both sentences as having a positive psychological effect on Hanako. Example (24″), however, can be also interpreted differently; if Reiko's and Hanako's daughters are rivals in class, their mothers may be psychologically affected when the teacher praised the daughter of the other. That is, (24″) is interpreted as "Hanako was disappointed because her daughter's rival in class, Reiko's daughter, was praised by the teacher. Hanako thinks her daughter should be recognized over Reiko's."

To conclude this section, we consider the interaction between the verb's semantics and the nature of adversity indexed by the passive construction. Verbs may be divided into three categories in terms of the types of adversity: neutral, negative, and positive. Verbs in the passive form with *rare* may convey positive or neutral meanings, but they all allow negative interpretation. If the verb has negative connotation, such as *kenasu* 'criticize,' its passive form *kenas-are-ru* always has the negative meaning. If a positive tone needs to be added, the benefactive form must be used *kenashite morat-ta* (e.g. I begged him to criticize me in front of others in order to reveal my evil intention for whatever purpose). On the other hand, *homerareru* 'be praised' with the positive connotation is interpreted positively without a context, but it is possible to consider a situation where "being praised" is evaluated negatively (see the discussion surrounding (25″)). Verbs with

Table 23.2 *Semantic types of verbs and their passive forms*

Semantic type of verbs	Verbs	Semantic type of *rare*
Neutral	*yomu* 'read,' *nomu* 'drink,' *aruku* 'walk'	neutral, negative,
Positive	*homeru* 'praise,' *uyamau* 'respect,' *aisuru* 'love'	positive, neutral, negative
Negative	*kenasu* 'criticize,' *kirau* 'hate,' *naguru* 'hit'	negative

neutral semantic content may be interpreted neutrally, but it is always possible to interpret them negatively. Thus, we can safely say that the passive morpheme always potentially expresses negative affect, or adversity. However, actual interpretation may be modified in the discourse context, as summarized in Table 23.2.

4 Functional Perspective

In this section passives are examined from a functional perspective. This perspective has already been adopted in the discussion of adversity passive in Section 3, and is expanded further here. A functional perspective departs from the structural perspective considered in Section 2 in that rather than being concerned with the structural relationship between active and passive sentences, it recognizes the passive as one type of "construction" (cf. Fillmore 1988; Goldberg 1995) which co-exists with the active voice construction. The construction approach tries to understand any construction as an aggregate of the form and semantic-pragmatic indices. This does not mean that the insight gained from the structural analysis will be completely abandoned, but rather it will guide our discussion. To be more specific, the direct, indirect, and the *ni-yotte* passives are based on three different constructions though obviously related morphologically and semantically. In the functional approach, passives are divided into the eventive and stative passives (Iwasaki 2013: 153–164). The eventive type depicts specific happenings that affect Patients, while the stative type depicts a scene as perceived objectively by a human observer, or a generic fact as conceived by a human cognizer.

4.1 The Eventive Passive

The eventive passive may be either direct or indirect structurally. The direct type has a related active sentence which contains an accusative- or dative-marked object, while the indirect type contains an extra-thematic NP. The related active sentence may take the form of (i) [AGT-ga PAT-o V_{ACT}] or (ii) [AGT-ga PAT-ni V_{ACT}]. The Agent is coded as an oblique phrase with *ni*, [PAT-ga/wa AGT-ni V_{PASS}] in the passive. Patients in (26) and (27) are an affected direct object in a transitive event and an object of emotional activity, respectively.

(26) a. *Tarō ga Jirō o ijimete-i-ru.* (active)
NOM ACC bully-PROG-NPST
'Taro is bullying Jiro.'

b. *Jirō ga Tarō ni ijime-rarete-i-ru.* (passive)
NOM DAT bully-PASS-PROG-NPST
'Jiro is being bullied by Taro.'

(27) a. *Tarō ga Hanako o aishite-i-ru.* (active)
NOM ACC love-PROG-NPST
'Taro loves Hanako.'

b. *Hanako ga Tarō ni ais-arete-i-ru.* (passive)
NOM DAT love-PASS-PROG-NPST
'Hanako is loved by Taro.'

The particle *o* can also mark the path or departure point for movements, as in (28), and the substance of speech activity, as in (29), but the active sentences with these *o* marked NPs do not have passive counterparts.

(28) a. *Inu ga kōen o aruk-u.* (active)
dog NOM PARK ACC walk-NPST
'A dog walks the park.'

b. **Kōen ga inu ni aruk-are-ru.* (passive)
park NOM dog DAT walk-PASS-NPST
'The park is walked on by a dog.'

(29) a. *Tarō ga henna koto o i-u.* (active)
NOM strange thing ACC say-NPST
'Taro says strange things.'

b. **Henna koto ga Tarō ni iw-are-ru.* (passive)
strange thing NOM DAT say-PASS-NPST
'Strange things are being said by Taro.'

The difference between (26–27) and (28–29) is that the *o*-marked NP is an affected Patient in the former and not in the latter. Notice also that the *o*-marked NPs in (28–29) are inanimate or abstract. This suggests that active sentences with higher transitivity can be expressed in a direct passive, and those with lower transitivity cannot. This also explains why some sentences with a *ni*-marked NP such as (30a) have a passive counterpart (30b), but not others, such as (31).

(30) a. *Yopparai ga Tarō ni butsukat-ta.* (active)
drunkard NOM DAT bump.into-PST
'A drunkard bumped into Taro.'

b. *Tarō ga yopparai ni butsukar-are-ta.* (passive)
NOM drunkard DAT bump.into-PASS-PST
'Taro was bumped into by a drunkard.'

(31) a. *Densha ga eki ni tomat-ta.* (active)
train NOM station LOC stop-PST
'A train stopped at the station.'
b. **Eki ga densha ni tomar-are-ta.* (passive)
station NOM train DAT stop-PASS-PST
'A station was stopped at by a train.'
c. *Yoshiko ga Tarō ni at-ta.* (active)
NOM DAT meet-PST
'Yoshiko met Taro.'
d. **Tarō ga Yoshiko ni aw-are-ta.* (passive)
NOM DAT meet-PASS-PST
'Taro was met by Yoshiko.'

Since most ungrammatical passives so far have inanimate subjects, for example, (31b), we might stipulate that the passive cannot have an inanimate subject. However, human Agent and human Patient do not guarantee a passive counterpart, as shown in (31d). At the same time, when an inanimate NP is conceived as having some (real or metaphorical) agency, the passive counterpart exists (Iwasaki 2013: 156–157). In (32), high transitivity of the active sentence (or event) allows the passive counterpart.

(32) a. *Kaze ga kami o tobashi-ta.* (active)
wind NOM paper ACC blow.away-PST
'The wind blew away (a sheet of) paper.'
b. *Kami ga kaze ni tobas-are-ta.* (passive)
paper NOM wind DAT blow.away-PASS-PST
'(A sheet of) paper was blown away by the wind.'

A sentence with a donatory verb (e.g. *ataeru* 'bestow,' *okuru* 'present'), a communication verb (e.g. *tsutaeru* 'report,' *hōkoku suru* 'report'), or a request verb (e.g. *motomeru* 'request') with a direct object (Theme) and an indirect object (Goal), [AGT-ga THM-o GOAL-ni V_{ACT}], can find direct passive counterparts, as in (33):

(33) a. *Giin ga daihyō ni hanataba o okut-ta.* (active)
Diet.member NOM delegate DAT bouquet ACC present-PST
'A Diet member presented a bouquet to the delegate.'
b. *Daihyō ga giin ni/kara hanataba o okur-are-ta.* (passive)
DAT/ABL give-PASS-PST
'The delegate was presented a bouquet by/from a Diet member.'
c. *Hanataba ga giin *ni/kara daihyō ni okur-are-ta.* (passive)
'A bouquet was presented to the delegate by a Diet member.'

d. *Hanataba ga giin ni okur-are-ta.* (passive)
'A bouquet was presented to the Diet member.'
(Not) 'A bouquet was presented by the Diet member.'

e. *Hanataba ga giin ni-yotte daihyō ni okur-are-ta.* (passive)
'A bouquet was presented to the delegate by a Diet member.'

There are several notable features found in passive sentences with donatory, communication, and request verbs. First, GOAL is usually a human and THEME an inanimate/abstract entity. Therefore, the THEME subjects are an inanimate subject, as in (33c).

Second, when either THEME or GOAL is a passive subject, the Agent of a donatory, communication, and request event may be marked by *kara* 'from' in addition to the dative *ni* in a passive sentence; that is, [PAT-ga AGT-ni/kara THM-o V_{PASS}] (33b) or [THM-ga AGT-*ni/kara GOAL-ni V_{PASS}] (33c). Impossibility of [THM-ga AGT-*ni GOAL-ni V_{PASS}] can be described as a consequence of a general constraint which prohibits two identical particles in sequence, named the double *ni* constraint by Ishizuka (2012: 64). Alternatively, we might describe from a more functional point of view that the passive morpheme assigns the argument structure as [THM-ga ORG-kara GOAL-ni V_{PASS}] (ORG = origination point) following the argument structure for motion verbs, [THM-ga ORG-kara GOAL-ni V_{MOTION}], for example, *tsuki ga higashi kara nishi ni ugoita* 'The moon moved from east to west.' This explanation, if correct, suggests that passive-like sentences are not derived from a corresponding active sentence as assumed in the formal tradition, but are constructed independently.

Third, when there is only a *ni*-marked NP in a passive sentence with a donatory/communication/request verb as in (33d), it is interpreted without a context as the goal with no ambiguity. Thus (33d) means 'A bouquet was presented *to the Diet member*,' not '*by the Diet member*' (cf. Ishizuka 2012: 66).

Fourth, the most typical donatory verbs, *ageru* 'give' and *kureru* 'give (to me),' do not have passive forms, **agerareru*, **kurerareru*. This is because these verbs are highly speaker oriented; in the case of *ageru* the speaker must have a great empathy with the subject (Agent) (the subject must be the speaker him/herself or someone close to him/her), and in the case of *kureru* with the indirect object (GOAL) (see Kuno and Kaburaki 1977; Kuno 1987). It is therefore impossible to give empathy to Patient in the passive construction.

Ni-yotte can be used to mark Agent to avoid the double *ni* constraint as shown in (33e). However, the use of *ni-yotte* is not only to avoid this constraint. Observe an active and passive pair shown in (34).

(34) a. *Kaikai ga gichō ni-yotte sengens-are-ta.* (passive)
opening NOM chair by declare-PASS-PST
Lit. 'Opening (of a session) was declared by Chair.'
'A session was called to order by Chair.'

b. *Gichō ga kaikai o sengenshi-ta.* (active)
chair NOM opening ACC declare-PST
'Chair declared opening (of a session).'

This pair seems to indicate that *ni-yotte* is employed when the passive subject is inanimate as in (34a). However, observe the next pair.

(35) a. *Kono kōen wa shimin no bokin ni-yotte tsukur-are-ta.*
this park TOP residents GEN fundraising by make-PASS-PST
'This park was made possible by residents' fundraising effort.' (passive)

b. **Shimin no bokin ga kono kōen o tsukut-ta.* (active)
make-PST
'Residents' fundraising effort made this park.'

Passive sentence, (35a), does not have an active counterpart, (35b). In other words, passive sentences may not be a result of conversion from an active sentence, but are produced from scratch, perhaps, based on a similar argument structure underlying (36a).

(36) a. *Chiri ya koishi ga taiki to no masatsu ni-yotte moetsuki-ru.*
dust and gravel NOM atmosphere with GEN friction by burn.up-NPST
'Dust and gravel burn up from the friction between them and the atmospheric air.'

Example (36a) is not a passive sentence as *moetsukiru* 'burn up' is in the active voice. Here, the *ni-yotte* phrase indicates a cause for burning of dust and gravels. Example (36a) is taken from the original shown in (36b) with two instances of *ni-yotte*. Notice both *ni-yotte* phrases mark a cause, but only in the first instance does it appear with a verb in the passive voice.

(36) b. *Chikyū no inryoku* <u>*ni-yotte*</u> ***hikiyose-rare-ta***
earth GEN gravity by pull-PASS-PST
sorera no chiri ya
those GEN dust and
koishi ga taiki to no
gravel NOM atmosphere with GEN
masatsu <u>*ni-yotte*</u> ***moetsukiru***
friction by burn.up
genshō ga nagareboshi dearu.[3]
phenomenon NOM shooting.star COP
'Shooting stars are a phenomenon in which the dust and small pebbles attracted by the earth's gravity burn up because of the friction between them and the atmospheric air.'

[3] Miyake Yoshinobu, 1998. www.relnet.co.jp/relnet/brief/r12-19.htm

Comparing *hikiyoseru* (TR) 'pull/attract' and *moetsukiru* (INT.) 'burn up' after the *ni-yotte* phrase, we may conclude that the passive morphology is sometimes employed because there is no intransitive counterpart of a transitive verb. That is, *moetsukiru* is an intransitive verb, but no intransitive counterpart exists for *hikiyoseru* (i.e. **hikiyoru*). Therefore, the passive morpheme was employed to coin the intransitive counterpart (*hikiyose-rare-ru*) in an ad hoc way.

At this point it is instructive to review the history of the *ni-yotte* passive. According to Kinsui (1997: 770), *ni-yotte* is a compound particle consisting of the particle *ni* and the conjunctive form of the verb *yoru*, which means 'to approach, to go via, to lean against.' This compound particle has the meanings of (i) cause/reason and (ii) means/way. It is already found in the poetry from the eighth century with meaning (i). Notice *ni-yotte* in (36b) discussed above has this cause/reason implication. Kinsui (1991, 1997) further notes that the particle, *ni-yotte* (or its older form *ni-yori* or *ni-yorite*), was used more frequently in the translation of Chinese texts or sentences written in the Chinese style. In the early nineteenth century *ni-yotte* was adopted as the agent marker in a passive sentence when translators of Dutch texts started to translate *door*, the Agent marker in a passive sentence, originally 'through,' directly. Thus, the origin of *ni-yotte* is old, but its use as the Agent marker in a passive is relatively new. The translation method adopted in the nineteenth century also brought a new, hitherto uncommon, type of passive; passive sentences with an inanimate subject. Even in modern Japanese, *ni-yotte*'s distribution is skewed. It is used more in formal writing (a descendant of translation style), but is rarely used in informal speech (We will discuss this point further in Section 5.)

4.2 The Stative Passive

The stative passive, as noted earlier, depicts a scene as perceived objectively by a human observer, or a generic fact as conceived by a human cognizer. From a historical perspective, Japanese passives were for the most part constructed with animate (especially human) subjects. However, passives with inanimate subjects were also found in historical texts (Kinsui 1991). One typical example of such passive is to depict a static scene perceived by a human observer. What is described is not an action or event, but a state that resulted from some prior events and actions (1991: 3–5). Static scenes are usually depicted by the construction V_{int}-*te iru* (where V is intransitive) in modern Japanese (e.g. *mado ga aite-iru* 'the window is open'). Note in passing that Japanese has many morphologically related transitive–intransitive pairs, such as *moeru* 'burn (INT.)' versus *moyasu* 'burn (TR.),' *ochiru* 'fall (INT.)' versus *otosu* 'drop (TR.)' (Jacobsen 1992b). If a transitive verb is used in the V-*te iru* construction, the aspectual meaning changes to progressive (e.g. *mado o akete-iru* '(someone) is opening the window'). Now not all transitive verbs have an intransitive counterpart (e.g. *oshinagasu* 'push away'). For such verbs, the passive form is used and put in the V-*te iru* construction (e.g. *oshinagas-arete-iru* '(something) has been pushed away').[4] See a few examples below (from Iwasaki 2013: 162–164).

(37) *Kono kōen wa takusan no ki ni kakom-arete-i-ru.*
this park TOP many GEN tree DAT surround-PASS-PROG-NPST
Lit. 'This park is being surrounded by many trees.'

Not only static scenes, but also generic statements (either individuated or universal, (38–39), respectively) can be expressed with stative passive.

(38) *Kono hon wa wakamono ni yoku yom-arete-i-ru.*
this book TOP young.people DAT well read-PASS-PROG-NPST
'This book is widely read by young people.'

(39) *Remon ni wa bitamin shī ga takusan fukum-arete-i-ru.*
lemon LOC TOP vitamin C NOM plenty contain-PASS-PROG-NPST
Lit. 'In a lemon, plenty of vitamin C is contained.'

Notice, formally (37–39) are direct passives, but (40) is an indirect passive, but no adversity meaning is present here. They are simply objective statements.

(40) *Kono e wa ōkuno hito ni sono na o*
this painting TOP many person DAT its title ACC
shirarete-iru.
know-PASS-PROG-NPST
'This painting, its title is known by many people.'

5 Discourse Perspective

In this section, we will examine how passive sentences are used in actual discourse contexts in the framework of "the multiple grammar model" (Iwasaki 2015). As will be made clear, passives are used in radically different ways in formal writing (e.g. newspaper editorials, academic papers) and informal conversations. First, I will point out the difficulty of identifying a passive sentence structurally as direct or indirect in discourse. Then, I will discuss differences found between passives used in the two different modes of language use. Finally, I will make a comment on the multiple grammar model and the passive construction.

Example (41a), taken from a newspaper article, has the Patient-subject (*seiji-handan* 'the political decision') marked by *ga* and the oblique-agent (*kokumin* 'the people in the nation') marked by *ni*, and they are relatable to an active object and active subject in (41b), respectively. In other words, (41a) is a direct passive from the structural point of view.

(41) a. *Chūkyōshin-tōshin o mu ni kisu yōna*
Central.Council.for.Education-report ACC nullify like
seiji-handan ***ga***, *kokumin* ***ni*** *ukeire-rare-ru darō ka.*
political-decision NOM citizen DAT accept-PASS-NPST SPEC INT

[4] In some contexts, it is possible to interpret this with the progressive aspectual meaning, '(something) is being pushed away.' This is an eventive passive.

'Will a political decision which could nullify the Central Council for Education's report be accepted by the people of the nation?'

b. *Kokumin* **ga** *Chūkyōshin-tōshin o mu ni kisu yōna seiji-handan* **o**
NOM ACC
ukeire-ru darō ka.
accept-NPST
'Will the people of the nation accept a political decision which could nullify the Central Council for Education's report?'

As we will see shortly, however, an agent is often unexpressed, or unexpressable. The agent in the next example can be construed as people in general though not overtly coded. This type of passive is called an "agentless passive" or "short passive." Discourse-oriented studies of passives confirm this type of passive to be an unmarked type, suggesting "agent defocusing" to be the main function of passive (Shibatani 1985: 830–831).

(42) a. *Jimintō* *ga* *"Jibuntō"* *to*
Liberal.Democratic.Party NOM self.party QUOT

yayus-arete-ki-ta *yuen* *de aru.*
ridicule-PASS-come-PST reason COP-NPST

'(That) is the reason why the Liberal Democratic Party has been cynically called the "Liberal Selfish Party".'

b. *(Hitobito* *ga)* *Jimintō* *o* *"Jibuntō"* *to* *yayushite-ki-ta.*
people NOM LDP ACC self.party QUOT ridicule-come-PST
'(People) have been calling the Liberal Democratic Party the "Liberal Selfish Party".'

In (42a) the passive subject (Patient) is marked with *ga*. This is important because if a Patient were marked by *o*, it would be interpreted as a retained object and the sentence would be an indirect passive. In other words, case marking of a Patient NP is a crucial information for identifying different types of passive.

In (43a), the Agent is *Furansu kokumin* 'French people,' which does not appear overtly, but is recoverable from the context. Crucially the retained object (*kenpō no hijun* 'ratification of the EU Constitution') appears with the particle *o* in this sentence. In other words, this is an indirect passive, in which, according to the traditional analysis of passive, the Patient (*Shiraku Futsu daitōryō* 'French President Chirac') assumed to be affected negatively by the Agent's act of rejecting the EU Constitution.

(43) a. *Shiraku* *Futsu* *daitōryō* *wa* *ōshūrengō (EU)* *kenpō* *no*
France president TOP European Union (EU) constitution GEN

hijun *o* *kokumin-tōhyō* *de* *hiketsu-sare* ...
ratification ACC natonal-vote by rejection-do.PASS.ADV
'French President Chirac was negatively affected by the rejection of the EU Constitution by the vote, and...'

b. *(Furansu kokumin ga) ōshūrengō (EU) kenpō no*
(France people NOM) European Union (EU) constitution GEN

hijun o kokumin-tohyō de hikestsu shi ...
ratification ACC natonal-vote by rejection-do:ADV
'French people rejected the EU Constitution by vote, and...'

Structurally identifiable indirect passives such as (43a), however, are actually not very frequent in editorials. If a Patient is marked by a non-case particle such as *wa* (topic marker) or *mo* 'also,' the sentence becomes potentially ambiguous between the two readings from a purely structural point of view. Consider (44).

(44) *kabushiki ya saiken <u>wa</u> shōken-torihiki-hō nado de*
stock and bond TOP securites-regulation-law etc. with
kisei s-arete-i-ru.
control do- PASS-PROG-NPST
'Stocks and bond are controlled by the Security Control Regulations.'

This sentence could be related to either of (45).

(45)
a. *kabushiki ya saiken <u>ga</u> shōken-torihiki-hō nado de kisei s-arete-i-ru.* (direct)
NOM
'Stocks and bond are controlled by the Security Control Regulations.'
b. *kabushiki ya saiken <u>o</u> shōken-torihiki-hō nado de kisei s-arete-i-ru.* (indirect)
ACC

'(Investors are adversely affected by their stocks and bonds being) controlled by the Security Control Regulations.'

Before proceeding, we should note that except for *Shiraku Futsu daitōryō* 'French President Chirac,' none of the passive subjects in the examples used in this section are an individuated human noun: *Seiji-handan* 'political judgment' (abstract), *Jimintō* 'LDP' (a group – a non-individuated third person), and *kabushiki ya saiken* 'stocks and bonds' (inanimate). Later, I will show that these types of Patient are typical in editorials.

As seen above, it is not always easy to make the direct–indirect passive distinction in formal written discourse as appearance of a retained object, and *ga* marking on the Patient subject are the only clues available to identify indirect passive. This problem is more pronounced in informal talk because NPs in general are often un-expressed, and even when a patient NP is expressed, the crucial particles may be un-expressed, as shown in (46) taken from a conversation about a major earthquake in Los Angeles.

(46) *Tatemono __ yuras-arete-ru yōna.*
building shake-PASS-PROG.NPST seem
'It felt like the building was being shaken.'

In (46) no case particle appears after *tatemono* 'building.' Notice if *o* appears, the sentence is identified as an indirect passive, but if *ga* appears, it is identified as a direct passive. Without such a structural clue, we cannot determine structural identity of this passive. A few lines after (46) in the same conversation, two similar passives appear with a particle after *tatemono* 'building,' as in (47).

(47) a. *Tatemono o yuras-arete-ru yōna.*
building ACC shake-PASS-PROG.NPST like
'(It was) like buildings are shaken.'
b. *Tatemono ga kowas-are-ru.*
building NOM destroy-PASS-PROG.NPST
'Buildings are destroyed.'

Example (47a) can be identified structurally as an indirect passive with a retained object (*tatemono o*), while (47b) as a direct passive with the nominative marked Patient (*tatemono ga*). Consequently, (47a) is construed to express adversity, and (47b) is not. However, from a pragmatic point of view, the distinction between the two sentences is very subtle if there is one at all. The two sentences below also appear in the same data.

(48) a. *Kir-are-chau-n desu yo ne.*
cut-PASS-COMP-NMLZ COP SFP SFP
'(The phone lines) were cut.'
b. *Denwa-gaisha ni kirarete-shimau.*
telephone.company by cut-PASS-COMP.NPST
'(The phone lines) were cut by the phone company.'

The speaker is explaining the difficulty of calling Japan from Los Angeles after the earthquake. Both have the same passive form (*kirarechau* and *kirareteshimau* [5] 'is cut'), but the semantic Patient (*denwa kaisen* 'telephone line') for *kiru* 'cut' does not appear. Thus, it is possible to reconstruct them either as (49a) or (49b).

(49) a. *Denwa kaisen ga denwa-gaisha ni*
telephone line NOM telephone-company DAT
kirarechau/kirarete-shimau. (direct)
will.be.cut
'Telephone lines are disconnected by telephone companies.'
b. *Boku ga denwa kaisen o denwa-gaisha ni kirarechau/kirarete-shimau.*
I NOM (indirect)
'I am adversely affected by the telephone lines that are disconnected by the telephone company.'

In other words, (48a–b) are potentially either direct or indirect. What the ongoing discussion demonstrates is that the traditional distinction

[5] *Kir-are-chau* is a contracted form of *kir-arete-shimau*. Both mean 'being cut completely' or 'being cut inconveniently,' and are analyzed as (cut-PASSIVE-COMPLETIVE AUXILIARY).

Table 23.3 *Overt and non-overt Patients in speech and writing*

Patient	Conversation (spoken)	Editorial (written)
Overt	5 (10.0%)	101 (61.9%)
RC Head	2 (4.0%)	38 (23.3%)
Non-overt	43 (86.0%)	24 (14.8%)
Total	50 (100%)	163 (100%)

between the direct and indirect, or adversity or neutral passives is not useful when analyzing passives in real discourse context, calling for a new look at the passive construction. It turns out that it is informative if we examine the features of Patient and Agent in the passive construction. I examined the total of fifty passives in seventeen conversational interactions and the total of 163 passives in thirty-four newspaper editorials.[6] First, I examined the number of overt and non-overt Patient and Agent in the two modes. The results are shown in Tables 23.3 and 23.4.

RC Head in Table 23.3 means that the patient is expressed as a head of a relative clause construction, as shown in (50) (*hito* 'people') and (51) (*rikiryō* 'the talent'). Thus, RC Head is a case of overt Patient.

(50)

Mō	*[tojikome-rare-ta]*	*hito*	*ga*	*ita-n*	*da*	*tte?*
already	trap-PASS-PST	people	NOM	be.PST-NMLZ	COP	EVID

'I hear that there were people who were trapped inside.'

(51)

Sōgō-teki-na	*gaikō*	*no*	*kōjō*	*o*
comprehensive	foreign-diplomacy	GEN	improvement	ACC

hakaru	*shikumi*	*to*	*kankyō*	*o*	*tsukuru*
persue	mechanism	and	environment	ACC	make

koto	*ga*	*Koizumi*	*shushō*	*no*	*yakuwari*
NMLZ	NOM		prime.minister	GEN	role

deari	*[motomer-are-ru]*	*saidai*	*no*	*rikiryō*	*da*	*to*
COP	seek-PASS-NPST	biggest	GEN	talent	COP	QUOT

mo	*ieyō.*
also	say.POT

'We can say that making a system and environment to promote a comprehensive foreign diplomacy is the talent expected most for Prime Minister Koizumi.' (*Sankei* 7/12/2005)

As seen in Table 23.4, passives used in the two modes are very different for the use of overt Patient; the Patient in the spoken mode is usually unexpressed (86.0%). In contrast, it is often expressed in the written mode

[6] The conversational data come from the Northridge Earthquake conversation data (Iwasaki 1997) and the corpus created by Tsuyoshi Ono of University of Alberta. The editorial data come from four different major newspapers published in July and October of 2005.

Table 23.4 *Overt and non-overt Agents in speech and writing*

Agent	Conversation (spoken)	Editorial (written)
Overt	5 (10.0%)	16 (9.9%)
Non-overt	45 (90.0%)	147 (90.1%)
Total	50 (100%)	163 (100%)

Table 23.5 *Semantic types of Agent and Patient*

	Patient		Agent	
	Conversation	Editorial	Conversation	Editorial
a) First person	30 (60.0%)	4[a]	1	0
b) Second person	2	0	1	0
c) Individuated third person	1	18 (11.0%)	8	3
d) Non-individuated third person	0	28 (17.2%)	5	94 (58.9%)
e) Non-specific human	9 (18.0%)	2	26 (81.3%)	55 (33.7%)
f) Inanimate	3	16 (9.8%)	1	1
g) Abstract	5 (10.0%)	95 (58.2%)	8	11
TOTAL	50 (100%)	163 (100%)	50 (100%)	163 (100%)

[a] *First person Patient only appears in direct quotation in editorials.*

including the RC head (85.2%). On the other hand, passives used in the two modes are similar for the use of non-overt Agents (90.0% for spoken and 90.1% for written discourse). These results suggest that there are both differences and similarities between the uses of the same passive construction in spoken and written contexts.

To understand the difference further, the semantic type of Patient and Agent in the two modes were compared. The seven semantic types of patient and agent used for this purpose are as follows:

- first person (speaker)
- second person (addressee)
- individuated third person (referential individual third person, e.g., Mr. Sato.)
- non-individuated third person (e.g. a company, a committee, a group etc.)
- non-specific human ('they,' that is, people in general)
- inanimate (including places)
- abstract (including events).

The results are shown in Table 23.5.

Several facts become apparent from the tables above. First, the passive Agent is usually "non-specific human" (e) in conversations and either "non-individuated third person" (d) or "non-specific human" (e) in editorials. In other words, a passive construction is generally used when the Agent does not have a clearly distinguished identity. This is related to the fact that Agents are expressed overtly only about 10% of the time in both spoken and written discourse (Table 23.4), confirming the Agent defocusing function of passive proposed by Shibatani (1985). From the multiple-grammar point of view, Agent defocusing is a common core function distributed across different genre grammars.

In contrast to the similarity found in the Agent types, conversational-spoken and editorial-written modes show drastic differences in the Patient types. For spoken mode, the only significant type of Patient is first person (60.0%) (a). Observe (52) below. The notional Patient for the passive verb (*wakaku*) *mirare-* 'be seen (as young)' is the speaker herself, but is not coded overtly. Likewise, the Patient for *kigae sa-se-rarete* 'be made to change into a different outfit' in (53) is the speaker himself, but is not coded overtly.

(52) M: *betsu-ni, chikaku ik-ana-kya, shimi toka sobakasu,*
not.particularly close go-NEG-COND spots etc. freckles
wakar-anai ja nai?
see-NEG MOD
'Unless they come closer, they won't see the spots and freckles, right?'

A: *u= [n].*
'yes'

M: *[de], wakaku* ***mi-rare****-n da kedo,*
and young see-PASS-NMLZ COP but
'so they think I am young, but'

(53) U: *jūdō-gi o, ta- hayaku motte-koi toka tte.*
judo-clothes ACC FS fast bring etc. QUOT
'(He said) bring your judo-gi now!'

M: *@@[@@]* (laughter)

U: *<@ [nan]ka @>, kigae* ***sa-se-rarete*** *[sa].*
somehow change.clothes do-CAUS-PASS SFP
'Somehow, I was made to change into a different outfit.'

In contrast, in written text, the Patient is mostly 'abstract concepts' (58.2%) such as 'a solution' in (54), or 'non-individuated third person' (17.2%), such as 'interns' in (55).

(54) *Rokkakokoku kyōgi no wakugumi o tsūjita*
6-nation council GEN framework ACC go.through
kaiketsu ga motome-rarete kita koto o
solution NOM seek-PASS come.PST NMLZ ACC
wasurete wa naranai.
forget TOP become.NEG

'We should not forget that a solution via the system of dialogue among six countries has been sought out.'

(55) *Kanari no kenshūi ga hakkyū no mama zatsumu o shiir-are*
many GEN intern NOM low.wage GEN still chore ACC force-PASS
'Many interns are forced to do chores with low salary, and...'

To summarize the findings so far, passives in conversation tend to have non-overt first person Patient, while those in editorials tend to have an overt Patient, which is either abstract or non-individuated third person referents. This difference is a result of the distinct demands called for in each mode. For conversational language, one of the most important needs is to express subjectivity through utterances, or more accurately, the speech is organized around the speaker for consistent and easy organization of discourse (egocentric constraint). When an event is described from the non-volitional, non-controlling first person Patient's perspective in a passive sentence, he/she puts him/herself at the mercy of the volitional and controlling participant, that is, Agent. This is amplified when the Agent is non-specific, non-individuated as the Patient cannot confront this type of faceless entity. Thus, although case marking will not reveal the structural nature of the passive, it is possible to interpret these passives as showing pragmatic adversity.

On the other hand, editorial written texts which are free from the egocentric constraint of the spoken language can use the passive for a purpose other than expressing adversity. As noted already, most passives in editorial texts can be classified as the direct passive as the Patient (passive subject) is usually overt (76.4%), and 35.5% of the overt subjects are marked by the particle *ga* as shown in Table 23.6. Furthermore, though structurally ambiguous, the particles *wa* and *mo* can be understood as replacing *ga* (not *o*)[7] from the contextual information, eliminating a possibility of retained object interpretation. Thus, except when the Patient is unmarked due to noun phrase ellipsis or identity with the head-noun position in the relative clause construction, most passives can be identified as direct passive. This is a consequence of objectivity-focus in editorial writing. This combined with the fact that the Patient in editorials is either 'abstract concepts' or 'non-individuated third person' suggests

Table 23.6 *Patient–subject marking particles*

	Conversation	Editorial
ga	4	58 (35.5%)
wa	2	31 (19.0%)
mo	0	10
Others	0	2
No marking	44 (88.0%)	62 (38.0%)
Total	50	163

[7] According to the National Language Research Institute's report (1964), the subject is marked by *wa* 61.1%, while the direct object only 4.7%. Thus, it is safe to assume most *wa*-marked Patients can be analyzed as the subject, that is, *ga*-marked noun phrase.

that passives in editorials are used mainly to express objective facts concerning abstract or general concepts.

We have discussed the following points in this section.

- The passive construction has a core function of Agent defocusing. This is the function found in both newspaper editorials and conversations.
- In conversation, the passive construction is used to express subjectivity (adversity in particular) with the speaker as the Patient, though not expressed overtly. This is a consequence of speech as an egocentric linguistic mode.
- In editorials, the passive construction is used to make an objective statement by placing an overt abstract concept or non-individuated third person in the subject position. This is a consequence of editorial writing as an objectivity-focused mode.

From the perspective of the multiple-grammar model, the danger of examining one mode of language is obvious; if we examine only one particular mode of language use, we understand only the partial outline of grammar. By comparing different modes of language, we understand different pragmatic needs that shape grammar differently, and at the same time we understand the common core of grammar. The multiple-grammar consists of two or more component grammars (or genre grammars) which develop partially independently according to the needs of the specific mode and genre. This suggests that a language works to separate component (genre) grammars as distinct. If this is the nature of language, why is this so? The answer may be that a language must maximize the limited resources for various purposes. Since the environments are critically different for conversation and editorials, or more broadly for interaction-oriented and expository-oriented language use, the same structure may function differently. If a language is too rigid and does not allow this flexibility, it would become a very restricted system.

6 Conclusion

The passive construction has prompted many linguists working on Japanese to scrutinize its structure and functions. It is natural to attempt to relate a passive sentence to its active counterpart as they could refer to the same propositional content. This tradition may be challenged from a more functional perspective. One idea is to conceive the passive as a distinct construction that co-exists with a separate active construction, that is, the synonym relation. The passive construction with the three subtypes of direct, indirect, and *ni-yotte* passive (and all other constructions) needs to be explored in real discourse contexts in order to evaluate all the previous research results. Since the passive is one of the most widely studied grammatical structures, it is possible to consolidate different views and consider the nature of grammar in a fresh perspective.

24

Conditionals

Seiko Fujii

1 Introduction

This chapter gives an overview of Japanese conditionals, laying out different types of constructions and the relations among them as well as characterizing their forms, meanings, and functions. Bearing this general mission in mind, and given the limited space, this chapter presents my view on the major issues and parameters involved in explicating and characterizing Japanese conditionals.

One of the important issues, as in many other languages, is to show the multifaceted families of conditional constructions bearing significant variations both in form and in function. To this end, the first major parameter to consider is the distinction between predictive versus non-predictive conditionals and between content versus non-content conditionals (see Sections 3.1 and 5). This chapter addresses conditional constructions as used in different linguistic domains (or mental spaces): content, epistemic, speech-act, and meta-linguistic (Dancygier and Sweetser 2005). The predictive and content conditionals alone yield a rich variety. The non-predictive and non-content conditionals also offer intriguing variations within and beyond Japanese.

Analyses of conditionals require forays into neighboring semantic domains, due to their polysemous nature. Most notably, conditionals must be understood alongside such related adverbial constructions as temporals, causals, and concessives. This issue is in fact essential as we compare Japanese with other languages. One of the parameters to be discussed is the speaker's epistemic stance, which is crucial in distinguishing what are normally regarded as temporals from most

I thank the editor of this handbook, Dr. Yoko Hasegawa, for her guidance, feedback, and support throughout the process. I am also grateful to Dr. Wesley Jacobsen for peer-reviewing this chapter and offering valuable comments, and to Dr. John H. Haig for proofreading and improving the manuscript. My gratitude extends to Charles J. Fillmore and Russell Lee-Goldman for our earlier collaborations, advice, discussions and beyond. Any remaining errors are my own.

typical (hypothetical) predictive conditionals. (The same principle applies to distinguishing concessives from concessive conditionals.) This distinction, however, is shown to be neutralized to some extent in Japanese, or less grammaticalized than in some languages like English. The speaker's epistemic stance will also be shown to contribute to constructing different shades of predictive conditionals. To clarify the contrast between ordinary (non-concessive) conditionals and concessive conditionals, we must attend to how the semantic relationship between the antecedent P and the consequent Q corresponds to the speaker's background assumption(s) about the P–Q contingency.

This chapter also discusses the interesting antecedent-only construction, *If* P, for example, *ittara* (go.if 'If (subject) goes'). The forms and functions of bare antecedent clauses and their constructionalization (or insubordination) are described and related to ordinary bi-clausal conditionals and to idiomatic modal expressions (e.g. *-tara ikenai* 'if ~, then bad' (shouldn't)) and their constructionalization (Integrated Evaluative Conditional Constructions).

This chapter further examines the use of Japanese conditional constructions as discourse markers, as when truncated antecedent forms such as *nara* 'if,' *dattara* 'COP.if,' or *da to* 'COP if' are used utterance-initially. These usages are connected to the (inter-)subjectivity of conditional constructions.

Japanese conditional constructions can be marked with a variety of clause-linking morphemes including *-(e)ba, tara, to, nara, -te.wa, -te.mo.* These variations, taken together with the tense, aspect, and modality of the antecedent and consequent clauses, are dealt with in the course of exploring the above-mentioned topics.

2 A Variety of Conditional Constructions in Japanese

By way of introduction to the variety of conditionals in Japanese and their descriptions, let us begin by briefly looking at the form (this section) and function (Section 3) of the major conditional constructions.

2.1 Major Conditional Markers

Representative constructions for expressing conditionality in Japanese are shown in (1); each is a clause-linking construction featuring a conditional clause-linking morpheme at the end of the antecedent clause. The major conditional markers include particles such as *to* and *nara*, verb conjugation forms (optionally combined with another morpheme) *-tara, -(r)e-ba, -te.wa*, and *-te.mo*, and function nouns such as *baai* 'case' and *toki* 'time':

(1) clause-linking morphemes

	to	
	(no) nara	
	-(r)e-ba	
	-tara	
	-te-wa	
P (antecedent clause)	*-te-mo*	Q (consequent clause)
	baai (ni/wa)	
	toki (ni/wa)	
	to suru to	
	to sureba	
	to shitara	

Also included in (1) are the complex linkers (called *fukugōji* 'complex morphemes'), *to suru to* and *to sureba*. Here, the quotative particle *to* precedes *suru* 'do.'

To attaches to the conclusive form of the P predicate (e.g. *iku to* 'if go,' *miru to* 'if see'), and *ba* to the hypothetical form (e.g. *ike-ba* 'if go,' *mire-ba* 'if see'). *Tara* involves the past tense *ta*-form of the P predicate (e.g. *itta.ra* 'if go,' *mita.ra* 'if see'), though it derives from the irrealis form of the completive auxiliary *tari*. In *-te-wa and -te-mo*, the focus particle *wa* or *mo* attaches to the *te*-form of the P predicate. These linkers require the verb to take on specific forms, resulting in tenseless clauses.

Nara, on the other hand, can take either the non-past form (*miru nara*) or the past form (*mita nara*), and thus the *nara* clauses are tensed. Similarly, *baai* (*ni/wa*) and *toki* (*ni/wa*) can take either the non-past form or the past form. The semantic functions of tensed forms in such clauses are not necessarily the ordinary "tense" (i.e. a past tense antecedent clause does not necessarily convey a past event or state), but are more often aspectual and/or modal. The complex conditional linkers (*to suru to, to sureba*, etc.) take the quotative marker *to* and thus can be preceded by tensed clauses.

Another characteristic of *nara* is that it can take an antecedent clause furnished with the nominalizer *no* (i.e. P *no nara*). A similar nominalized antecedent, with the *tara* linker, is possible: P *no dattara*. The tensed *nara* antecedent, and its nominalized antecedents (*no nara, no dattara*) exhibit less dependence on the Q consequent clauses in their interpretations.

Nara is noteworthy in its capacity to take not only a clause but also an NP alone (e.g. *kuruma nara* 'if (it's by) car').[1] A similar construction is also possible with the complex conditional forms (NP) *dattara*, (NP) *da to*, etc., where combination of the copula *da* and *tara* or *to* has been constructionalized.

[1] This description applies to the surface form in present-day Japanese. Both the meaning of the construction 'if (it's) NP' and the historical provenance of *nara* (from the copula *nari*) suggest that the construction involves copular predication (i.e. NP *nara* is actually a conditional form of NP *da*). It is thus unsurprising that *nara* can be preceded by an NP.

The major conditional constructions shown in (1) and described above are illustrated in (2–3):

(2)	*Kuruma*	*de*	*iku*	*to*	*go.jikan*	*kurai*	*kakaru*	*deshō.*
	car	by	go	if	five.hours	about	take	MOD
			iku nara					
			iku no nara					
			ikeba					
			ittara					
			ittemo					
			iku baai					
			iku to suru to/iku to sureba/iku to shitara					

'If (you) go by car, it will take (you) about five hours.'

(3)	*Kuruma*	*nara*	*go.jikan*	*kurai*	*kakaru*	*deshō.*
	car	if	five.hours	about	take	MOD
		da to				
		datta.ra				

'It will take (you) about five hours by car.'

2.2 Multifaceted Conditional Constructions

A number of studies have attempted to characterize the different forms of Japanese conditionals introduced in the preceding section (e.g. Kuno 1973; Hinds and Tawa 1975–1976; McGloin 1976–1977; Akatsuka 1983, 1992; Fujii 1989, 1990, 1992a, 1993, 2012; Masuoka 1993; Jacobsen 1992a, 2002a, 2002b; Arita 2007; Maeda 2009; Hasegawa 2015; inter alia). Japanese reference grammars and textbooks for Japanese as a second/foreign language also attempt to differentiate these conditional types semantically to some extent. The wide range of these analyses and descriptions reflects the complexity of Japanese conditional expressions.

In addition to the variation shown above regarding the forms and morphologies of conditional markers, conditional constructions vary with respect to their meanings and functions. This variation is by no means unique to Japanese; many other languages, including English, exhibit variations (see Fillmore 1987, 1990 for English). Japanese conditionals nevertheless offer not only the validation of those types that are generally found cross-linguistically but also intriguing types and uses that do not exactly fit among the general types.

To do justice to all these issues with precise descriptions is beyond the scope of this chapter, but this chapter presents the major types of Japanese conditionals showing the rich spread of multifaceted constructions, for both those types that reflect cross-linguistic tendencies and those that do not.

3 Major Functional Types of Conditional Constructions

Let us first review the major functional types of conditional constructions, the major ones of which will be elaborated on in later sections.

3.1 Predictive Conditionals (Hypothetical Conditionals)

Predictive conditionals, illustrated in (4–5), are taken to be the prototypical variety of conditional in most languages:

(4) *Sōki ni shujutsu o sureba/shitara tabun yoku naru*
early at operation ACC do.COND perhaps well become
darō.
MOD
'If (she) has an operation at an early stage, she will perhaps recover.'

(5) *Sōki ni shujutsu o shiteireba/shiteitara tabun yoku natteita*
do.ASP.COND perhaps well become.ASP.PST
darō.
MOD
'If (she) had had an operation at an early stage, she would have perhaps recovered.'

This variety includes predicative conditionals whose reference time is future in both P and Q (4) and ones whose reference time is past in both P and Q (5). (There are other variations, omitted here.) They have also been referred to (in many previous studies and grammar reference books) as hypothetical conditionals; the latter type, with past reference time, is also referred to as a counterfactual conditional.

In predictive conditionals and in the generic type shown in the following subsection, the speaker uses the conditional construction because s/he assumes (in her/his background world knowledge) a causal contingency relation between P and Q. The "causal" relations here should be understood in terms of everyday thinking, including experiential links, tendencies and co-occurrence, and perceived correlations, and not limited to precise causality in a technical sense.

Such predictive conditionals convey a P–Q contingency relation at the propositional level. In terms of Sweetser (1990), this is the content domain of conceptualization, or within content mental-spaces in the terms of Dancygier and Sweetser (2005).

3.2 Generic Conditionals

One of the general functions of conditional constructions is to convey timeless, generic principles of contingency relations between P and Q, as illustrated in (6):

(6) *Kono shikkan wa sōki ni shujutsu o sureba/suru to*
this disease TOP early at operation ACC do.COND
50% ijō kaifuku kanō da.
more cure possible COP
'This disease is more than 50% curable if one has an operation at an early stage.'

As mentioned above, this generic type often conveys the speaker's assumption about a causal relation between P and Q. The P–Q relations, however, encompass various kinds of experiential links, perceived correlations, and co-occurrences; they also extend to habitually co-occurring contingencies of events or states, resulting in a related functional type – habitual conditionals. Examples (7–8) illustrate present and past habituals, respectively:

(7) a. *Chichi wa asa okiru to suguni inu no*
father TOP morning get.up COND immediately dog GEN
sanpo ni dekakeru.
walk for go.out
'When the father wakes up in the morning, he takes the dog(s) for a walk.'
b. *Asa denki ga tsukeba niwa no inu*
morning light NOM turn.on.COND backyard GEN dogs
ga issei ni hoe-hajimeru.
NOM at.once bark-start
'When the lights are turned on in the morning, the dog(s) in the backyard start to bark all at once.'

(8) a. *Chichi wa asa okiru to suguni inu*
father TOP morning get.up COND immediately dog
no sanpo ni dekaketa.
GEN walk for went.out
'When the father woke up in the morning, he would immediately take the dog(s) for a walk.'
b. *Asa denki ga tsukeba niwa no inu*
morning light NOM turn.on.COND backyard GEN dogs
ga issei ni hoe-hajimeta.
NOM at.once bark-started
'When the lights were turned on in the morning, the dog(s) in the backyard would start to bark all at once.'

Generic and habitual conditionals belong to a conceptual and constructional ground where conditionals and temporals are neutralized in Japanese (as in many other languages).

3.3 Temporal Contingency Conditionals

One of the crucial characteristics of Japanese conditionals is their interaction with temporal expressions, or, put differently, their capacity to convey meaning that is normally regarded as temporal. Constructions marked with conditional linkers, such as (9), can naturally render either a hypothetical interpretation or a temporal interpretation in Japanese.

(9) *Nihon e ittara denwa shimasu.*
Japan to go.COND call do.POL
'If/When (I) come to Japan, (I will) call (you).'
a. Hypothetical interpretation: 'If I come to Japan, I will call you.'
b. Temporal interpretation: 'When I come to Japan, I will call you.'

Polysemy in conditional–temporal constructions is by no means unique to Japanese, and can be found in many languages including German and Dutch. English, on the other hand, makes a clear distinction by the choice of *if* or *when*.

3.4 Non-content Conditionals: Epistemic Conditionals

Conditional constructions are also often used in what is known as epistemic conditionals, as illustrated in (10):

(10) *Yoku natta {(no)nara□ / n dattara} kitto sōki ni*
well became NMLZ.COND / NMLZ COP.COND surely early at
shujutsu o shita no darō.
operation ACC did NMLZ MOD
'If she has recovered, she must have had an operation at an early stage.'

In this epistemic use, the speaker takes a certain situation or state expressed in P and conveys her/his reasoning that her/his assumption of P leads to the conclusion Q. In such epistemic conditionals, note that the causal chain (and the temporal order) in the physical world (content domain) is seemingly reserved, and thus the P–Q contingency conveyed by using a conditional construction is not in terms of the content but rather of the speaker's epistemic reasoning process, which is most likely abductive or inductive rather than deductive.

It is noteworthy that *nara* is most typically used (Fujii 1993; Tsunoda 2004; Arita 2007) for epistemic conditionals, and that the nominalized P antecedents are preferentially used to convey epistemic conditionality.

3.5 Non-content Conditionals: Speech-act Conditionals

Conditional constructions are also used to preface a speech-act to be carried out in Q, as illustrated in (11):

(11) *Shujutsu o go-kentō deshitara kochira ni kanō*
operation ACC consider COP.COND here in possible
iryō kikan risuto ga arimasu.
medical institution list NOM exist.POL
'If (you) are considering having an operation, here is the list of hospitals (that can deal with it).'

In a speech-act conditional, the speaker refers to a certain situation in P (most likely a situation or state that the speaker can assume in a given context), and then, within the context of P, the speaker carries out a certain speech act, namely Q. Here again, the P–Q contingency conveyed by a conditional construction does not address the content but rather the speaker's speech-act process.

3.6 Speech-act Qualification

As illustrated in (12–15), Japanese conditional antecedents (appearing utterance-initially and containing a conditional marker at the end) are frequently used in discourse to qualify the speech act expressed in Q, including an ordinary statement as in (13–15).

(12) ***Yoroshikereba*** *onamae o oshiete itadakemasu ka.*
all.right.COND name ACC tell receive.POT.POL Q
Lit. 'If it is all right (with you), can I receive your name?'
'May I ask your name, if you don't mind?'

(13) ***Hontō no koto o yuu to*** *kinō ikanakatta no.*
true GEN thing ACC say COND yesterday go.NEG.PST SFP
Lit. 'If/When (I) tell the truth, I did not go yesterday.'
'To tell you the truth, I did not go yesterday.'

(14) ***Sotchoku ni itte shimaeba*** *mō dō demo ii tte kanji.*
frankly say.ASP.COND by.now I.don't.care QUOT feel
Lit. 'If (I) speak frankly, I really don't care, I feel.'
'Frankly speaking, I don't give a damn.'

(15) ***Ketsuron o iimasu to*** *saru mo kuraku naru*
conclusion ACC say.POL COND monkey also dark.become
to shiryoku ga teika shimasu.
COND eye.sight NOM decrease do.POL
Lit. 'If (I) tell (you) the conclusion, monkeys' eyesight capacities also decrease when it gets dark.'
'In conclusion, monkeys' eyesight capacities also decrease in the dark.'

These uses can be regarded as belonging to the overall category of speech-act conditionals in a cross-linguistically applicable typology of conditionals.

For example, (12) is a typical speech-act conditional prefacing a request. This use and its pragmatic functions, however, goes beyond that of the typical speech-act conditionals originally proposed by Sweetser (1990) based on English, extending to, for example, prefaces of simple descriptive statements. Such uses yield a large group of semi-formulaic antecedent expressions that are pervasive in discourse for speech-act qualification, mitigation, coherence, textual organization, and rhetorical purposes. This type, while regarded as a special type of speech-act conditional, merits special attention as a type of Japanese conditional that functions as a discourse marker.

3.7 Conditional Discourse Markers

In the preceding section, we took up the issue of conditional constructions used at the left-periphery as discourse markers. The type shown in the preceding section contains a lexical predicate, often (but not limited to) a verb of communication such as *yuu* 'say,' in the antecedent clause. Japanese conditionals also offer intriguing utterance-initial examples of truncated antecedent constructions. They are illustrated in (16–17).

(16) *Sō ka. Nara atchi mo tetsudatte yaru ze.*
so Q if that too help BEN SFP
'I see. If so/Then I will (offer to) help with that, too.'

(17) a. *Asu San Furanshisuko de kaigi. Japan taun de*
tomorrow in meeting in
tabeyō kana.
eat.VOL SFP
'I will have a meeting in San Francisco tomorrow. I'm thinking about having (dinner) in Japan Town.'

b. *Dattara Kinokuniya de hon katte kite kurenai?*
COP.COND in book buy come BEN.NEG
'If so/Then, would you please buy me a book in Kinokuniya?'

3.8 Conditional Modal Constructions

Conditional modal constructions constitute another important main type. Japanese deontic modal expressions are known to use constructions featuring conditional markers, such as *-tara, to, -(r)eba*, as illustrated in (18–20).

(18) *Kore nondara dame desu yo.*
this drink.COND bad COP SFP
'Drinking this is bad./You must not drink this.' (prohibition)

(19) *Kore nomanakereba ikenai yo.*
this drink.NEG.COND bad SFP
'It is bad not to drink this./You must drink this.' (obligation)

(20) *Kore* *nomanai* *to* *ikenai* *yo.*
this drink.NEG COND bad SFP
'It is bad not to drink this./You must drink this.' (obligation)

Example (18) with *tara* conveys the deontic function of prohibition, and (19–20) that of obligation.

3.9 Antecedent-only Conditionals

What is noteworthy in Japanese is that the antecedent-only utterances, without the main clause, can still clearly convey the same function of obligation, as shown in (21–22), to the extent that such P-only utterances can be considered constructionalized as antecedent-only constructions or reduced constructions (Fujii 1993, 2004). Section 8 will elaborate on these modal conditionals and antecedent-only conditionals.

(21) *Kore* *nomanakereba.*
this drink.NEG.COND
'not to drink this.' → 'You must drink this.' (obligation)

(22) *Kore* *nomanai* *to.*
this drink.NEG COND
'not to drink this.' → You must drink this.' (obligation)

4 Conditionals as Mental-space Builders

At this point, we briefly consider what conditionals are used for in general.

4.1 Are Conditionals Topics in Japanese?

Conditionals have been observed to share certain properties with topics. One of the most influential claims comes from Haiman (1978), who proposes that "Conditionals are Topics." This issue has been of interest for Japanese conditionals, especially in the context of the development of the topic marker *wa*. To examine this issue in Modern Japanese, Jacobsen (1992a: 155) gives an extensive review of aspects of topic and conditionals, and reaches the conclusion that "These considerations make it apparent that topical and conditional meaning should be treated as independent, if occasionally converging, parameters of meaning."

4.2 Conditionals as Mental-space Builders and Counter-identity Conditionals

A more comprehensive approach to conditionals, which can also incorporate their topic-like properties, considers them as important grammatical devices for building mental spaces. The theory of conditionals by Dancygier and Sweetser (2005), in particular, has been constructed based on the mental-space theory.

Fujii (1996) explored linguistic devices for building mental spaces (i.e. mental-space builders) including conditionals, comparing English and Japanese. The hypothesis examined and the thesis presented is that while English grammar easily accommodates mono-clausal conditional expressions, the Japanese counterpart often requires conditional linking morphology and syntax, and that this contrast in the mechanisms for expressing conditionality is systematic and reflects a general divergence between the two languages.

There are mono-clausal conditionals in English where an element in contrast in the sentence introduces a hypothetical space, by taking the place of another entity (either person or object). For example, in sentence (23), the subject – *MY advisor* – presents a hypothetical mental space, by substituting for somebody else (your advisor) in the other individual's situation. In other words, the speaker's advisor (my advisor) is hypothetically introduced into the hearer's advisor's situation.

(23) *You are so lucky. MY advisor wouldn't have been so patient.*

The hypothetically introduced individual, *my advisor* in this case, has prosodic salience.[2] This is a variety of the counterfactual sentence type which Goodman (1983: 6) refers to as *counter-identicals.*

The Japanese counterpart of (23) is given in (24):

(24) *Boku* *no* *adobaizā* ***dattara/nara*** *kesshite* *sonnani*
I GEN advisor COP.COND never to.that.extent
gaman *wa* *shite-kurete-inakatta* *(darō)* *yo.*
patience TOP do-BEN-ASP.NEG.PST (MOD) SFP
'My advisor wouldn't have been so patient.'
'If (it had been) my advisor, he/she wouldn't have been so patient.'

In English conditionals, when expressed as a mono-clausal sentence (23), the verbal morphology, which takes the tense-aspect-modality of the consequent clause of a bi-clausal conditional, sets up a hypothetical mental space, though the intonation placed on the contrasted element (MY advisor) also contributes to it. In Japanese, on the other hand, the antecedent marked with *dattara* or *nara* sets up a contrastive hypothetical mental space.

In our review of major functional types of conditionals in Japanese in Sections 3 and 4, we have at the same time encountered variation in form. The sections that follow elaborate on major constructional types laid out in the overview sections above and explore the important and intriguing issues that those constructions present.

[2] Fillmore (1987), analyzing another example, notes this prosody.

5 Predictive Conditional Constructions

Dancygier and Sweetser (2005) establishes the analysis of conditionals based on the idea that the antecedent clause sets up a mental space in the sense of Fauconnier (1985). While there are different types of mental space that conditional constructions can evoke, "[o]ne of the most important reasons for setting up mental spaces is to imagine alternatives: in a mental space where we imagine some eventuality, what do we imagine as the results of that eventuality?" (Dancygier and Sweetser 2005: 31). Such prediction, involving the conceptualization of alternatives and imagination of the possible results, is conveyed by a conditional construction in many languages. We call this general type of conditionals *predictive conditionals*. Examples (4–5), shown in Section 2, illustrate such predictive conditionals in Japanese:

(4) *Sōki ni shujutsu o sureba/shitara tabun yoku naru darō.*
early at operation ACC do.COND perhaps well become MOD
'If (s/he) has an operation at an early stage, s/he will perhaps recover.'

(5) *Sōki ni shujutsu o shiteireba/shiteitara tabun yoku natteita*
do.ASP.COND perhaps well become.ASP.PST
darō.
MOD
'If (s/he) had had an operation at an early stage, s/he would have perhaps recovered.'

5.1 Alternativity, Causality, and Invited Inference

By using conditional constructions, people can talk about alternative worlds. The antecedent P sets up one of the alternatives that the speaker chooses to refer to, and the Q clause states the consequent that P should lead to (or the unreal P would have led to) based on the speaker's assumption of experientially linked chains of events (causal or contingent).

One of the characteristics of such predictive conditionals is that the other unstated alternative, namely ~P, is also evoked, leading in people's everyday cognition to the inference of "~P leading to ~Q." Such an invited inference applies to Japanese predictive conditionals. In (4) above, for example, the stated prediction "If she has an operation at an early stage, she will perhaps recover" invites the inference that if she does not have an operation at an early stage, she perhaps will not recover. In (5), the stated P–Q for an imaginary alternative past world "If she had had an operation at an early stage, she would have perhaps recovered" implies that since she did not have an operation at an early stage, she perhaps did not recover. In short, this is the kind of conditional where *if P, then Q* gives rise to the implicature that *if not P, then not Q* in Japanese as in many other languages.

5.2 The Speaker's Epistemic Stance in Predictive Conditionals

In talking about alternative worlds, the speaker takes a certain epistemic stance toward the actuality (and/or certainty) of P, and in some cases of Q as well. The speaker's epistemic stance is the speaker's assumption about the actuality of P, or the kind of commitment the speaker has to the proposition expressed (Fillmore 1990). The epistemic stance that the speaker encodes can be one of the three kinds: neutral, positive, or negative, as proposed by Fillmore (1990) and in turn explicated by Dancygier and Sweetser (2005: 45). To illustrate neutral and negative epistemic stances, let us take examples with English predictive conditionals, with the three basic construction types shown in (25). (Positive epistemic stance will be dealt with in the next subsection.)

(25) a.	If P-present, Q-*will*-future *If you ask him, he'll do it.*	neutral stance future predictive, hypothetical
b.	If P-past, Q-*would* *If you asked him, he'd do it.*	distanced, negative stance future predictive, contrary-to-expectation hypothetical
c.	If P-pluperfect, Q-*would have* *If you had asked him, he would have done it.*	distanced, negative stance past counterfactual

For neutral-stance conditionals, one basic pattern is (25a), where 'backshifting' – that is, the use of simple present forms with future reference – occurs in the antecedent clause for future predictions. For distanced stance, (25b), P-past paired with Q-*would* is used. For past-reference distanced stance (25c), P-pluperfect paired with Q-*would have* is used. Combinations of these modal and tense morphologies in P and Q are required, if both P and Q appear, in English predictive conditional constructions.

5.3 Predictive Conditionals and Their Overlap with Temporals in Japanese

In Japanese predictive conditionals (illustrated in Section 3.1 above), by contrast, the uses of modality, tense, and aspect are more variable. Within the Q clause, the use of epistemic modal auxiliaries (e.g. *darō* or *deshō* 'will,' 'would') is possible but not strictly required. The antecedent clauses, when marked with *to*, *-(r)eba*, and *-tara* require a fixed verb form and are tenseless, as discussed in Section 2. Thus, whichever linking form the antecedent clause takes, the verbal morphology is not uniquely associated with a particular type of conditional construction.

5.3.1 Neutral versus Positive Epistemic Stance: Conditionals and Temporals

English *if* and *when* are used to distinguish between an irrealis antecedent, which encodes the speaker's neutral or negative stance, and a realis antecedent, which encodes the speaker's positive stance. For example, compare sentences (26–27):

(26) *If I come to Japan, I will call you.* neutral stance

(27) *When I come to Japan, I will call you.* positive stance

The use of *if* in (26) reveals that the speaker does not commit herself/himself to the truth of the antecedent (neutral stance), whereas in (27) the use of *when* reveals that the antecedent is taken for granted by the speaker (positive stance).

In the Japanese equivalent (here, using *tara*), this epistemic distinction is not necessarily signaled by linguistic form, yielding potential ambiguity between the two interpretations manifested in (26–27).

(28) *Nihon e it<u>tara</u> denwa shimasu.*
Japan to go.COND call do.POL
'If/When (I) go to Japan, (I will) call (you).'
a. Conditional interpretation with neutral epistemic stance:
= (26) *If I come to Japan, I will call you.*
b. Temporal interpretation with positive epistemic stance:
= (27) *When I come to Japan, I will call you.*

Tara and *to* constructions, in general, can be used with a neutral stance in hypothetical conditionals, and can also serve as markers of temporal clauses with a positive stance (though there are certain other important semantic and pragmatic conditions on each construction). We note not only that the same clause-linking morphemes can be used for either neutral or positive stance, but also that both epistemic meanings can be expressed without making obligatory distinctions in the tense/aspect/mood verbal morphology.

As explicated by Jacobsen (2002a), one pattern that tends toward a hypothetical interpretation with neutral, rather than positive epistemic stance is where the antecedent clause is stative and non-perfective, as in (29a). This can be contrasted with (29b), containing an event predicate with change of state, which can be interpreted as either neutral or positive.

(29) a. *Hima ga attara asobi ni iku.* (ibid.: 5)
free.time NOM have play for go
'If I have some free time I'll come over for a visit.'
b. *Hima ni nattara asobi ni iku.* (ibid.)
free.time DAT have play for go
'If/when my time frees up (I become free), I'll come over for a visit.'

5.3.2 Neutral versus Positive Epistemic Stance: Concessive Conditionals and Concessive Temporals

Exactly the same point as made in the previous section can be made with respect to concessive conditionals using *temo*.

(30)

Asu	*ame*	*ga*	*fut**temo***	*ensoku*	*ni*	*ikimasu.*
tomorrow	rain	NOM	fall.CC-COND	excursion	DAT	go.POL

'Even if it rains tomorrow, we will go on a picnic.'
(CC-COND: concessive conditional)

(31)

Kono	*chihō*	*de*	*wa*	*haru*	*ni*	*nat**temo***	*yuki*	*wa*
this	area	LOC	TOP	spring	DAT	become.CC-COND	snow	TOP

tokenai.
melt.NEG

'Around here, even when spring comes, the snow does not melt.'
#'Even if spring comes...'

In (30), the speaker's epistemic stance is most likely neutral. The speaker in (31), on the other hand, most likely takes a positive stance toward the antecedent event "spring comes." Here again, there *are* certain ways to encode this epistemic distinction, but it is safe to say that the *temo* construction itself does not specify the value of the speaker's epistemic stance and thus can accommodate either a neutral or positive epistemic stance.

5.3.3 Negative versus Positive Stance: (Concessive) Conditionals and Temporals with Past-reference

The second contrast to be considered is between negative and positive stance. This boundary is perhaps considered extremely clear-cut epistemologically, especially for past specific events/states. At least in English, this distinction can never be obscured in linguistic manifestation; they are clearly manifested with different clause connectives (*if* versus *when*) and with different tense/aspect/mood verbal morphology on both the antecedent and the consequent. Even this distinction, however, can sometimes be blurred in Japanese.

Temo can be used in cases where the antecedent event is assumed to be true in the past. This creates ambiguity between past counterfactual concessives and past factual concessives. Example (32) can mean either "Although he had an operation, he did not recover" (conveying the speaker's positive stance) or when spoken with the right intonation or followed by some pragmatic particle such as *yo*, "Even if he had had an operation, he would not have recovered" (conveying the speaker's negative stance).

(32)

Shujutsu	*o*	*shitemo*	*naoranakatta.*
operation	ACC	do.CC-COND	recover.NEG.PST

'Although he had an operation, he did not recover.'
or 'Even if he had had an operation, he would not have recovered.'

Similar potential ambiguities can also be observed in ordinary conditionals between past counterfactuals (negative) and past temporals (positive), though again there is always a way to disambiguate them in language use.

5.3.4 Grammatical Devices for Encoding the Speaker's Epistemic Stance in Conditional Constructions in Japanese

How then can the various types of the speaker's epistemic stance be conveyed in Japanese conditionals? First, as in English but to a lesser extent, past tense and aspectual morphology can be used in Japanese for expressing distanced epistemic stances. The use of stative aspect (both grammatical and lexical) tends to convey a distanced negative stance and/or enhance the sense of hypotheticality. These phenomena have been explicated most thoroughly by Jacobsen (2002a). As for the aspectual marking, the *te-iru* (*te-ita*) formation is regularly used.

In addition to the use of tense and aspect, Japanese conditionals make use of a variety of other grammatical devices shown in (33) for expressing distanced epistemic stances (see Fujii 2009 for illustrations):

(33) a. tense, aspect on the antecedent and the consequent
b. epistemic modal expressions on the consequent
c. adverbs in the antecedent
d. clause-linkers: consequent-clause-final connectives
e. negative polarity items (scalar expression) conveying negative valuation and in turn implicating epistemic distancing
f. nominalized antecedent
g. final pragmatic particles such as *yo*
h. intonation
i. choice of clause-linker (for the antecedent)

6 Non-content, Non-predictive Conditionals

Work in pragmatics has also analyzed non-content conditionals. Speech-act, meta-linguistic, and epistemic conditionals are all most frequently non-predictive in function, unlike content domain conditionals. Such non-predictive conditionals are typically not used to imagine and set up alternative worlds that would lead to different consequences, and thus do not normally result in invited inferences as typically understood (unlike the predictive conditionals discussed in Section 5).[3] To draw an example

[3] This, however, is a matter of tendency of distributional correlation, not a strict constraint on each construction, and thus only captures speech-act conditionals and clear epistemic conditionals. As Dancygier and Sweetser (2005: 124, etc.) point out, certain epistemic conditionals involve predictivity and alternativity (thus giving rise to invited inferences). As was also pointed out by Hasegawa (2015: 230), "[s]trictly speaking, all content conditionals are also inferential because conditionality itself is inferential." Therefore, there are many cases where content predictive conditionals involve and manifest epistemic reasoning, and vice versa.

from English, *If you need any help, my name is Chris* (Dancygier and Sweetser 2005: 114) does not implicate that the speaker's name is not Chris if the addressee does not need help.

These general characteristics concerning the contrast between content and non-content conditionals apply to Japanese conditionals. Japanese differs (from English), however in how non-content, non-predictive conditionality is constructionally marked.

6.1 Epistemic Conditionals

More explicit coding of abductive reasoning is necessary in Japanese epistemic conditionals than in English (Fujii 1993, 2012, etc.). This is constructionally manifested in at least two ways: First, epistemic reasoning is coded by an evidential or epistemic modal expression on the consequent clause. Second, the antecedent of epistemic conditionals is also typically marked by a specific conditional clause-linker that constructs a tensed clause.

Japanese epistemic conditionals typically require the consequent clause to be furnished with an epistemic modal expression such as *no da* (e.g. 34a), *to yuu koto da* 'that means' (34b), and *hazu da* 'ought to' (34c). It is very difficult to construct epistemic conditionals without such modal expressions in the consequent clause, especially with past reference.

(34) a. *Teika de katta no nara, kuraun shoten de*
full.price with bought NMLZ COND Crown book.store at
kawanakatta no da ne.
bought.NEG NMLZ COP SFP
'If you paid full price, you did not buy it at Crown Books.'

b. *Teika de katta no nara, kuraun-shoten de kawanakatta to yuu koto da.*
bought.NEG QUOT NMLZ COP
'If you paid full price, you did not buy it at Crown Books.'

c. *Denki ga tsuiteiru (no) nara, mō kaetteiru hazu da.*
light NOM is.on NMLZ COND already be.home ought.to
'If the light is on, they ought to be home already.'

In contrast, as shown in (35), English epistemic conditionals do not require any special linguistic encoding of epistemic reasoning on the consequent clause, although epistemic modals do readily occur in Q-clauses (e.g. *must; if I know* P, *I conclude* Q; or *if it is true that* P, *then I would guess* Q).

(35) a. *If you paid full price, you did not buy it at Crown Books.*
b. *If the light is on, they are home already.*
c. *If it's live, it's on channel five.*

It is noteworthy that this phenomenon is consistently found with epistemic causals as well as conditionals: In comparing epistemic causals in English and Japanese (e.g. constructions linked with *because* and with *kara*, respectively), epistemic modal expressions tend to be required or at least preferred on Q-clauses in Japanese. These modal expressions encode the speaker's reasoning of a condition, cause, or reason based on abductive inference from a given consequence.

Second, the antecedent of an epistemic conditional, especially when the temporal and causal order of P–Q is reversed (i.e. the temporally/causally-prior clause comes second), is typically marked by a specific form of conditional clause-linkage: (i) a nominalized conditional, *no nara* [nominalizer + linker] (e.g. 34), *no dattara* [nominalizer + copula + linker]; (ii) by *nara* rather than other conditional linkers (*reba, to, tara*); or (iii) by a complex linker, *to sureba, to shitara, to suru to* [quotative + let/suppose/assume + linker], which involves transparent lexemes that set up an epistemic mental-space. English *if* antecedents, on the other hand, can readily host not only predictive conditionals but also non-predictive conditionals.

Recall that, among the several conditional linkers, *nara* is the only morpheme that forms a finite clause, permitting free choice of tense within the antecedent clause independently of the main clause. Another important characteristic of *nara* is that, unlike other conditional linkers, it does not require P to be temporally prior to Q. Moreover, nominalizing the antecedent clause (via *no*) makes P disjoint from Q, conveying that the speaker takes P for granted for the sake of cognitive reasoning. Therefore, in the most typical, clearest cases of epistemic conditionals, where the causal and temporal order of P and Q is reversed (i.e. P temporarily follows Q; or P is the consequence inferred from the premise Q), the preferred constructions are those in which P and Q clauses are disjoint and bear independent tense. *Tara* and *ba* are not used because they cannot accommodate the reversed temporal order of P and Q; *to* is not used for the same reason, and also because its consequent cannot accommodate the act of presenting the speaker's subjective epistemic judgment.

The use of the *to suru* construction is especially characteristic of conditionals that involve epistemic reasoning, since such epistemic meanings are explicitly encoded by the transparent lexeme "Y *to suru*," which immediately precedes the conditional morpheme in P, and means 'let/suppose/assume Y.' ('X *o* Y *to suru*' [X ACC Y QUOT do] means 'let X be Y,' or 'suppose X to be Y,' for example, X *o 5 to suru* 'Let X be 5.')

Example (36), a sentence taken from the Balanced Corpus of Contemporary Written Japanese, has two antecedent clauses using *to shitara* and *to sureba*; these P clauses present two pieces of evidence, on the basis of which the writer draws the conclusion stated in Q.

(36) *Moshi* *isha* *no* *sewa* *ni* *natteinai* ***to***
supposedly doctor GEN care DAT be.under.NEG QUOT
shitara *kusuri* *ni* *issai* *tayotteinai* ***to*** ***sureba***
make.COND medicine on at.all depend.NEG QUOT make.COND

genson	*no*	*onsen*	*chiryō*	*ga*	*kō*	*o*
this.village	GEN	hot.spring	treatment	NOM	success	ACC
sōshiteiru	*koto*	*wa*	*machigainakatta.*			
make-ASP	NMLZ	TOP	no.doubt-PST			

'If (she) didn't go to (or get checked out by) doctors, and if (she) didn't rely on medicine at all, then it {was absolutely certain/must be the case} that the hot spring treatment from this village was effective.'

6.2 Speech-act Conditionals

Speech-act conditionals in Japanese also tend to be expressed with the *nara* antecedent and especially with a nominalized conditional antecedent, *no nara* (nominalizer + linker) or *no dattara* (nominalizer + copula + linker), as seen in (37):

(37) a.

Ryūgaku	*shiteita*	*no*	*nara,*	*dōshite*	*motto*	*eigo*
study.abroad	was.doing	NMLZ	COND	why	more	English
o	*renshū shite*	*konakatta*	*no.*			
ACC	practice	came.NEG	SFP			

'If (it is true that) you were studying abroad, why didn't you practice English more?'

b.

Ryūgaku shiteita	*n*	*dattara,*	. . .
	NMLZ	COP.COND	

c.

Ryūgaku shiteita	*no*	*de*	*areba,*	. . .
	NMLZ	COP	COND	

As shown in (38) and (11) (repeated from Section 3), however, other conditional linkers (*tara* and *ba*) are readily used for speech-act conditionals, while *to* cannot be used for this type of speech-act conditional. *To* is incompatible with a consequent that enacts a speech act and in general with the intersubjective construction of conditionality.

(38)

Oguai	*ga*	*warui*	*yō*	*deshitara/naraba*	*mōsugu*
phycial.condition	NOM	bad	MOD	COP.COND	soon
orimasu	*kara*	*dōzo.*			
get.off.POL	because	please			

'If you are not feeling well, I am getting off soon, so please take my seat.'

(11)

Shujutsu	*o*	*go-kentō*	*deshitara*	*kochira*	*ni*	*kanō*	*iryō*
operation	ACC	consider	COP.COND	here	in	possible	medical
kikan	*risuto*	*ga*	*arimasu.*				
institution	list	NOM	exist				

'If (you) are considering having an operation, here is the list of hospitals (that can deal with it).'

Note that these *tara* and *ba* conditionals involve the copula *da* in the antecedent. Given that *nara* (most typically used for speech-act conditionals) is also etymologically a copular form, along with typical speech-act uses of other linkers, the speech-act property of conditionals may be associated with the presence of the copula *da* rather than those other linking morphemes.

6.3 Disjoint P- and Q-clauses

In English, whereas predictive conditionals in content mental spaces are strictly subject to the requirements of formal and semantic *concordance* (Fillmore 1990: 140) or *epistemic coherence* (Dancygier and Sweetser 2005: 45–54) between the two linked clauses, non-predictive conditionals are not. In this way, P- and Q-clauses in non-content non-predictive conditionals can be disjoint either formally or semantically, unlike predictive conditionals, which require particular pairings of tense/aspect morphology and semantic relations. Though the grammatical devices differ, Japanese non-content, non-predictive conditionals are also expressed by constructions that accommodate disjoint P- and Q-clauses, where the construal of temporal ordering and/or causal links between the two events in the content domain is not required (Fujii 2012). This dimension of disjoint P- and Q-clauses also relates to the intersubjectivity of conditionals to be discussed below.

6.4 Subjectivity and Intersubjectivity in Conditionals

In addition to the different domains of conceptualization – and different types of mental spaces – in which the P–Q dependency is established and communicated, what is key to the uses of this type of speech-act conditional is its intersubjective construction of conditionality.

Speech-act conditionals are intersubjective at least in two respects. Recall that, in a speech-act conditional, the speaker refers to a certain situation in P, most likely a situation or state that the speaker can assume in a given context, and asks the addressee to confirm by stating the conditional antecedent. And then, within the context of P, the speaker carries out a certain speech act, namely Q. The act of performing a speech act in Q itself is obviously intersubjective in nature. More importantly, however, what the speaker does with the antecedent is to set up, clarify and share the context with the addressee as a condition for his/her speech act. In doing so by means of a conditional clause, the speaker not only refers to conditions upon his/her speech act, but also invites the addressee to consider the validity of P, letting the addressee determine the effect of the speaker's speech act. These processes of speech-act conditionals are intersubjective.

6.5 Phenomenal Conditionals and Meta-propositional Conditionals

The variety of conditionals that have been analyzed and discussed thus far by attending to different domains of conceptualization (content versus non-content conditionals) can be related to – and is compatible with – the two types of conditionals proposed by Jacobsen.

Jacobsen (2002b: 361) proposes two types of conditionals: phenomenal conditionals and meta-propositional conditionals. Phenomenal conditionals are defined as "a conditional construction where the predicates in the antecedent and consequent clauses represent events literally ordered in time in such a way that the consequent event is dependent on the prior occurrence of the antecedent event." Meta-propositional conditionals, on the other hand, are defined as "a conditional construction where a temporal dependence occurs between antecedent and consequent clauses at the level of higher-order predications of stating, deducing, judging, deciding, requesting, etc., under which the predicates in the antecedent and consequent clauses are subordinated and treated as items of information rather than events."

The preceding discussions have adopted the theoretical and analytical framework based on Dancygier and Sweetser (2005), alluding to the terms "content" and "non-content" so as to cover the general classes of conditionals. The content type of conditional by its nature pertains to P and Q events and the P–Q contingency at the propositional level. The non-content type, which attends to the P–Q dependency at the levels of epistemic reasoning, speech-acts, and meta-linguistic or meta-metaphorical conceptualization, is meta-propositional.

These two frameworks of analysis agree with respect to the temporal ordering and aspectual relations of the P and Q clauses: these are integral to the definition of content and phenomenal conditionals. On the other hand, in non-content conditionals as in meta-propositional conditionals, the temporal P–Q dependencies are construed at the level of higher-order predication of epistemic reasoning, speech-acts, and meta-linguistic or meta-metaphorical conceptualization, whereas the temporal entities that P and Q refer to do not directly contribute to the higher-order predication.

One of Jacobsen's (2002b) major purposes in establishing these two types of conditions is to show when hypothetical readings arise (or not) in Japanese conditionals, and more importantly, to argue that hypotheticality is not a definitional component of conditionals. This perspective on conditionals is clearly shared and has guided the analyses of my studies, as seen in this chapter, which explores types of conditionals that do and do not involve hypotheticality and attempts to arrive at a theory of conditionals that captures them all.

7 Concessive Conditionals and Ordinary (Non-concessive) Conditionals

Yet another crucial issue in dealing with Japanese conditionals concerns the contrast between ordinary (non-concessive) conditionals and concessive conditionals. The functional categories of ordinary and concessive conditionals might appear to be obvious as long as we consider them to be emic categories (i.e. well defined within Japanese) which are rooted in the speaker's linguistic cognition. These categories, which convey ordinary versus counter connections of P and Q (often referred to in Japanese linguistics by *junsetsu* and *gyakusetsu*), indeed appear to be clear emic categories. Within such conceptualization of these categories, the *temo* construction exemplifies concessive conditionals, whereas the *tara/ba/to/nara* constructions form the category of ordinary (non-concessive) conditionals.

This assumption, however, does not hold as we examine such uses of *temo* as (39) and compare them with the English counterparts that would be used to convey the same meaning in the same context (40):

(39) a.

Koko de	*matteitemo*	*basu*	*wa*	*kimasen*	*yo.*
here	waiting.CC-COND	bus	TOP	come.NEG	SFP
Achira de	*omachi ni naranai*	*to.*			
over.there	wait.HON	QUOT			

< you wait here > *temo* < bus won't come >
expected: P → ~Q (bus will come)

b.

San Furanshisuko	*ni*	*ittemo,*	*kēburukā*	*ni*	*wa*	*noranai*
	to	go.CC-COND	cable.car	DAT	TOP	ride-NEG
hō ga ii desu	*yo.*					
had.better	SFP					

< you go to San Francisco > *temo* < don't ride a cable car >

c.

Tanaka-san	*ni*	*attemo*	*kono*	*koto*	*wa*
	DAT	meet.CC-COND	this	matter	TOP
himitsu ni siteoite	*kudasai.*				
keep.this.secret	please				

< you see Mr. Tanaka > *temo* < please keep this secret >

(40) a. *If you wait here, the bus won't pick you up. But if you wait at that other bus stop over there, it will.*
(in this context) *#Even if you wait here, the bus won't pick you up. But if you wait at that other bus stop over there, it will.*

b. *If you go to San Francisco, don't ride a cable car.*
#Even if you go to San Francisco, don't ride a cable car.

c. *If you see Mr. Tanaka, please keep this secret.*
#Even if you see Mr. Tanaka, please keep this secret.

Why would concessive conditionals using *even if* not be used in these contexts for expressing what is conveyed by Japanese concessive conditionals with *temo*? It is because a scalar interpretation is necessary for *even if* but *not* for *temo* (Fujii 1989). It is quite common for *temo* to occur without scalar entailments, and without the property of referring to an end point (or an end point of scalar entailment in a scalar model). In the absence of these properties, unconditionality of the consequent and paradoxicality are attained without appealing to scalar entailment in Japanese.

8 Conditional Modal Constructions and Antecedent-only Constructions, "If P"

8.1 Conditional Modal Constructions

Deontic modal constructions use conditional constructions in Japanese. Among the deontic modal constructions that inherit from a conditional construction are those expressing necessity and possibility, obligation and permission, positive advice and prohibition, hopes and wishes, and so forth (see (41) for partial illustration).

(41) a. *Kore nondara ii desu yo.*
this drink.COND good SFP
'Drinking this would be good for you.' (suggestion/recommendation)

b. *Sugu naottara ii desu ne.*
soon recover.COND good SFP
'(We) hope (you) will recover soon.' (wish)

c. *Kore nondara dame yo.*
this drink.COND bad SFP
'Drinking this is bad./You must not drink this.' (prohibition)

d. *Kore nomanakereba ikenai yo.*
this drink.NEG.COND bad SFP
'It is bad not to drink this./You must drink this.' (obligation)

e. *Kore nondemo ii desu yo.*
this drink.CC-COND good SFP
'It is O.K. to drink this./You may drink this.' (permission)

f. *Kore nomanakutemo ii desu yo.*
this drink.NEG.CC-COND good SFP
'It is O.K. not to drink this./You don't have to drink this.' (free choice, permission)

Akatsuka's (1992) seminal work on Japanese conditionals took these modal expressions, showing that "Japanese Modals are Conditionals" (the title of Akatsuka 1992). Akatsuka's main proposal was that "the key to understanding the present issue is the speaker's attitude, 'I want it to happen/not to happen.' Japanese has grammaticalized [this] in the idiomatic conditional form, 'if p, q,' where q is the speaker's evaluative judgement, DESIRABLE/UNDESIRABLE, toward the realization of p" (1992: 2–3).

8.2 Construction Types and Constructional Schemes: Capturing both Productive Compositional Patterns and (Semi-)idiomatic Expressions

Fujii (1993, 2004) presented an analysis of conditional modal constructions to capture both productive compositional general patterns and (semi-)idiomatic expressions. To this end, I posit two orthogonal constructional units: Construction Types and Constructional Schemes. First, conditional constructions form a family of constructions consisting of formally distinguishable Construction Types (illustrated in (42)), namely the full bi-clausal construction (a), integrated evaluative construction (b–c), and reduced construction (d). Second, these construction types share a certain Constructional Scheme when they convey the same modal function – such as the Constructional Scheme for "obligation" shown in Figure 24.1.

(42) a. Full Bi-clausal Conditional Construction
Hayaku ikanai to sensei ni mo mihanasarete shimau yo.
early go.NEG COND teacher by also give.up.PASS ASP SFP
Lit. 'If you don't go soon, you will be given up on even by your teacher.'
'If you do not go soon, your teacher will give up on you.'

b. Integrated Evaluative Conditional Construction
Hayaku ikanai to taihen da yo.
early go-NEG COND troublesome COP SFP
'If you don't go soon, it will be troublesome.'

c. Fixed idiomatic deontic modal
Hayaku ikanai to ikenai yo.
early go.NEG COND bad SFP
Lit. 'If you don't go soon, it will be bad.'
'You must go soon.'

d. Reduced Conditional Construction
Hayaku ikanai to.
early go-NEG COND
Lit. 'If you don't go soon.'
'You must go soon.'

PRAG/SEM: 'obligation'

SYN: CLAUSE 1 – NEG – LINKER SEM: conditional antecedent PRAG: negatively evaluated	SYN: unspecified (full-fledged clause, bare predicate, or null) PRAG/SEM: negative evaluation

Figure 24.1 Constructional Scheme for "obligation" (An example of Constructional Scheme)

The semantic structures of these schemes as applied to grammaticalized modal conditionals can be accounted for in terms of modal logic shown in (43).

(43) a. □A if and only if ~ <> ~A
     b. O p = ~P ~p

Example (42b) (including idiomatic modal expressions (42c)) semantically conveys the modal function (here obligation). A full bi-clausal conditional (42a) can convey the same pragmatic function (obligation) via pragmatic implicature. The antecedent alone, (42d), also clearly conveys the same obligation, and has moreover been constructionalized to do so. Well-entrenched antecedent-only reduced constructions, however, are not available uniformly for all conditional linkers in Japanese. The reduced construction for obligation, for example, can be lexically instantiated with *(r)eba*, *to*, or *te-wa*, but not with *tara* (Fujii 1992b).

9 Conditional Discourse Markers

Let us now examine utterance-initial uses of antecedent conditional constructions as (inter-)subjective discourse markers in Japanese. I will discuss two major groups of conditional left-periphery constructions based on Corpus of Spontaneous Japanese (CSJ) and the Balanced Corpus of Contemporary Written Japanese (BCCWJ).

9.1 Antecedent Conditional Morphemes Used as Discourse Markers

First we examine truncated antecedent constructions used as discourse markers, such as *nara* 'if,' *dattara* 'if (it) is,' *sō dattara* 'if (it) is so,' analogous to English 'if so' or 'then.' Conditional markers as typical for a head final language appear at the end of the antecedent clause, as in "P-*tara (-reba, to, nara)* Q." They are typically bound morphemes. In (44–46), however, *nara* 'if,' *da to-sitara* 'if (it) is,' or *dattara* 'if (it) is' appear as free unbound markers.

(44)

Sō	*ka.*	*Nara*	*atchi*	*mo*	*tetsudatte*	*yaru*	*ze.*
so	Q	if	that	too	help	BEN	SFP

'I see. If so/Then I will (offer to) help with that, too.'

(45)

Da	*to*	*shitara…*	*dono yōni*	*hōkoku*	*o*	*sureba*	*yoi mono*
COP	QUOT	make.COND	how	report	ACC	do.COND	good

yara.
wonder
'Then (if it is the case), I wonder how I should make a report.'

(46) a. *Asu San Furanshisuko de kaigi. Japan taun de tabeyō kana.*
tomorrow in meeting in eat.VOL SFP
'I will have a meeting in San Francisco tomorrow. I'm thinking about having (dinner) in Japan Town.'

b. *Dattara Kinokuniya de hon katte kite kurenai?*
COP.COND in book buy come BEN.NEG
'If so/Then, would you please buy me a book in Kinokuniya?'

This general phenomenon has been observed and studied most frequently in causal (e.g. *dakara* 'so') and concessive connectives (e.g. *ga, demo* 'but'). My analysis of BCCWJ shows that a variety of other utterance-initial uses of conditional antecedent constructions make pervasive use of clause-linking morphemes.

The utterance-initial uses can be categorized into three types with respect to their formal compositions. Type 1 is a clause-linking morpheme used utterance-initially, for example, *to, nara*; Type 2 is copular *da* plus a clause-linking morpheme, for example, *dattara, da to, da to-suru-to*; Type 3 is a pronoun (*sō*, etc.), copular *da*, and clause-linking morpheme, for example, *so dattara, sō da to suru to*. Functionally, all of these conditional discourse markers are used to anaphorically refer to some content in the prior discourse.

9.2 Antecedents Containing Lexical Predicates: Speech-act Modifiers, Rhetorical Connectors

Whereas the above group does not contain any full predicate (except for the bare copular *da* or *sō da*), the second group of left-periphery expressions contains lexical predicates (mainly verbs), such as *yuu* 'say, speak,' as seen in (13–15) repeated below:

(13) ***Hontō no koto o yuu to*** *kinō ikanakatta no.*
true GEN thing ACC say COND yesterday go.NEG.PST SFP
Lit. 'If/When (I) tell the truth, I did not go yesterday.'
'To tell you the truth, I did not go yesterday.'

(14) ***Sotchoku ni itte shimaeba*** *mō dō demo ii tte kanji.*
frankly say.ASP.COND by.now I.don't.care QUOT feel
Lit. 'If (I) speak frankly, I really don't care, I feel.'
'Frankly speaking, I don't give a damn.'

(15) ***Ketsuron o iimasu to*** *saru mo kuraku naru to*
conclusion ACC say.POL COND monkey also dark.become COND
shiryoku ga teika shimasu.
eye.sight NOM decrease do.POL
Lit. 'If (I) tell (you) the conclusion, monkeys' eyesight capacities also decrease when it gets dark.'
'In conclusion, monkeys' eyesight capacities also decrease in the dark.'

The verb *yuu* 'speak' collocates extremely highly with conditional constructions (Fujii 2013). There is a large group of utterance-initial antecedent expressions containing verbs of communication that are used as speech-act modifiers, by which the speaker qualifies the upcoming main utterance. Analogous expressions in English include sentential adverbs such as *frankly* and *honestly*, or gerundive (*speaking frankly*) or infinitival constructions (*to be honest with you*).

With these left-periphery speech-act modifiers, the speaker qualifies her/his own utterance that follows and thus constructs conditionality intra-subjectively. This intra-subjective single-subject property accounts for the frequent use of *to* conditionals as speech-act modifiers, which is distinct from the inter-subjective property that we discussed for typical speech-act conditionals.

This speech-modifier antecedent with the verb *yuu* 'say' can also be treated as a partially filled construction containing an embedded interrogative construction, as schematized in (47):

(47) [[$_{\text{INT CONSTRUCTION}}$ [wh-word] . . . [interrogative particle *ka*]] *to ieba*]
Lit. 'if (I) say [embedded INT construction]'
'if (one asks and) (I) tell (you) [embedded INT construction]'

This interrogative construction embedded in the conditional antecedent is used rhetorically in discourse to raise a question and preface the consequent, which the speaker proceeds to state (as an answer to that question). This and many other partially filled left-periphery constructions serve as rhetorical connectors in discourse.

Many of the above-discussed groups can be analyzed as speech-act conditionals, but their functions crucially vary among these groups, and differ from typical speech-act conditionals in English.

10 Conclusions

This chapter has given an overview of the complex family of Japanese conditional constructions, characterizing for each their forms, meanings, and functions. The complexity of Japanese conditional constructions can be seen in their rich variety of meaning and usage, and intricate morphosyntactic connections to one another and to non-conditional constructions.

By comparing the Japanese constructions with their English counterparts, this chapter has shown the detailed ways in which conditional constructions can both differ from one another as well as overlap and be extended in complex ways. The descriptive challenge of characterizing the high degree of variation in Japanese conditional marking (Section 2.1) should expand and enrich, it is hoped, our understanding of what "conditional" meaning is and how it can be realized formally. The high degree of diversity, overlap, and neutralization among these functional and semantic categories reveals the breadth of possibility for the general study of form–meaning mappings.

This is not unique to Japanese conditionals, but Japanese is uniquely positioned to illustrate many of the relevant phenomena with its wide range of conditional constructions. To summarize briefly, on the functional side, we have seen the overlap of conditionals with temporals, the overlap of concessive conditionals with temporals (Section 5.3), and the contrast between conditionals and concessive conditionals (Section 7). We investigated the connection to epistemic stance, as well as the content/non-content contrast as it applies to Japanese as contrasted with English (Section 6). Furthermore, these functional varieties exhibit different P–Q dependencies and conditionality, which are constructed subjectively and inter-subjectively.

On the form side, we saw great variation as well. In addition to the basic issues of antecedent marking, we touched on the issues of clause-integration and insubordination, which are important in understanding modal conditionals and antecedent-only conditionals. Taken together with utterance-initial uses of conditional antecedents as discourse markers, Japanese conditionals prove to be a rich constructional ground for the development of discourse and pragmatic markers at both the left and the right periphery.

In sum, as noted by Fillmore (1988), it is exactly these complexities and the rich variety of conditional constructions that continue to draw us back into the study, both theoretical and empirical, of the "Mysteries of Japanese Conditionals."

Part V

Pragmatics/ Sociolinguistics

25

Sentence-final Particles

Emi Morita

1 Introduction

This chapter provides an overview of the research on what have been called "sentence-final particles" (SFPs).[1] These particles are small lexemes that have neither denotational nor referential meaning, and are found mainly (but not always) at the utterance-final position in spoken Japanese, where their use is widespread. Examples of such usage may be seen below, in a naturally occurring conversation between a mother (M) and her four-year-old boy (C). As these particles are not translatable, I have left the particle as it appears in the English vernacular translation.

(1) M: *kondo* *dare* *to* *isshoni* *iko-k* ***ka***.
next-time who with together go.VOL SFP
'Who should we go next time with (***ka***)?'

C: *kondo* *wa* *ojī-chan* *to* *It-chan* *to* *obā-chan*
next-time TOP grandpa with (name) with gramma

to *Shōta* *to* *Mako-chan* *de* *ikō* ***yo***.
with (name) with (name) with go.VOL SFP
'Next time, let's go (***yo***), with grandpa and It-chan and grandma and me and Mako-chan.'

M: *sō* *da* ***nē***, *sō* *shiyo-k* ***ka***.
so COP SFP so do.VOL SFP
'That's right (***ne***). Shall we do that (***ka***)?'

In the above excerpt of naturally occurring conversation, each utterance ends with a particle – here, *ka, yo, ne,* and *ka*. Spoken Japanese employs numerous such particles – for example, *ne, na, yo, sa, ya, no, wa, ze, zo, i,*

[1] Depending on the scholar, sometimes these lexemes are called *pragmatic particles, interactional particles*, or *discourse markers*, reflecting their differing views regarding such lexemes' use in spoken Japanese. I have used the term *sentence-final particles* for the title of this chapter, as it has been the most commonly used term, but my own view of the applicability of this term is discussed in Section 3.3.

kashira(n), tomo, tte, ke[2] – and if we include particles from different regional dialects, such as *nō, chā, tai, bai,* and many others, the list becomes much longer. Some of these particles have emerged through the process of grammaticalization; for example, the complementizers *mon(o), koto* and the conjunctives *kara* and *tara* also now appear at the final position of utterances, shifting away from their original grammatical functions. Some of these particles may be combined to form particle clusters, such as *none, yone,* and *kana.* As the ubiquity of these particles in the corpus of spoken Japanese indicates, the importance of these particles as a linguistic resource for everyday conversation is immeasurable. Accordingly, these particles have drawn linguists' attention and numerous studies have been made to explicate their meanings and pragmatic functions.

These particles are sometimes given misleadingly simple descriptions in Japanese language grammar books and textbooks. For example, it is often said that *ne* "expresses confirmation or agreement" depending on the state of knowledge of the speaker and the hearer (e.g. Masuoka and Takubo 1989: 48); or that *yo* "marks strong conviction or assertion" (e.g. Makino and Tsutsui 1986: 543). Such shorthand descriptions may seem handy as a reference and may even seem reasonable among native speakers; however, in-depth studies have shown that such simplistic descriptions hardly cover the complexity of the relevant phenomena, and that these particles are not the type of linguistic items that can be understood as having invariant meanings with a fixed interpretation.

Moreover, ever since the earliest studies of such particles in modern Japanese were published about a century ago, the development of the research into these particles has not necessarily been done by building onto preceding studies, but rather by discovering the diversity of roles and functions that such particles may have in spoken Japanese.[3] Such discovery has resulted in a good deal of controversy and confusion, as the wide variety of meanings and functions that have become attributed to each of these particles varies considerably among scholars, making it difficult to grasp the essential work that the various particles are doing in actual speech.

The aim of this chapter is to provide an overview of some of the major approaches to the investigation of these particles, in order to demonstrate how diversified this field of inquiry has become. In the second half of the chapter, I will discuss some as-yet neglected and unsolved issues impacting this research field and propose an approach that is capable of reconciling some of the major controversies.

[2] Whether all of these particles should be classified as sentence-final particles, as part of verb conjugation, or as modal auxiliaries is debatable, depending on how one chooses to parse and define the suffixes. Saji (1991: 15), for example, claims that "ending forms" such as *kashira(n)* contain the verb *shiranu* 'don't know,' to which *ka* is added for the expression of recollection, and thus should not be considered as a "sentence-final particle."

[3] For a representative list of studies that have been done on such particles, see Togashi (2004).

2 Various Approaches to the Sentence-final Particles (SFP)

2.1 Syntagmatic Approach: Grammatical Nature

In traditional Japanese linguistics (e.g. Tokieda 1941; Watanabe 1968), researchers categorized the lexicon into two functional categories. *Shi* was the category of "content words" – words deployed for *jojutsu* 'predication,' necessary to convey propositional meaning – and *ji* was the category of 'function words,' used for *chinjutsu* 'modality' (cf. Chapter 16, this volume), allowing speakers to express their personal attitude toward what has been propositionally described. It is interesting to note that in the pioneer days of Japanese linguistics, SFPs were a much debated topic and their social functions – that is, establishing a relationship between interlocutors through language – were emphasized. For Tokieda especially the most important elements to study in the Japanese language are those related to the expression of subjective stances – a notion that is still important for current functional linguistics (e.g. Iwasaki and Yap 2015). It was within this context that Tokieda (1951) discussed SFPs and described the particle *ne*, for example, as an expression of subjective stance which locates the listener in a "cooperative relation." Tokieda's emphasis on the use of such particles for constructing relationships between interlocutors by conveying speakers' voices and emotions and adding subjective stance or a displayed attitude toward the proposition of the sentence continues to be employed in Japanese functional linguistics.

Watanabe (1968) classified SFPs based on their concatenation processes with other predication forms, focusing on the order in which particles may appear and what grammatical form of the predicate these particles can attach to. SFPs were categorized as either part of building the propositional content or exerting more interpersonal effects. Conversely, H. Suzuki (1976) suggested that SFPs should be classified not so much based on grammatical restriction, but rather on how the relationship between the speaker and the listener is indicated by them. These particles' grammatical status is, however, not completely considered to be extra-propositional, as some particles, such as *ne*, are often described as an *obligatory* element of an utterance in some situations (e.g. Kamio 1990: 62).

2.2 Epistemic Approach: Sharedness, Accessibility, and Management of the Information/Knowledge State

Numerous studies maintain that SFPs, particularly *ne* and *yo*, reflect their speakers' assumptions regarding the relative sharedness or accessibility of information (e.g. Oso 1986; Maynard 1997). Among such studies, Kamio's "territory of information" theory is probably the most influential, especially for the succeeding studies of sentence-final particles. Kamio (1979) first introduced the notion of territory of information as a concept to indicate the relative psychological distance between a speaker and/or hearer (X) with regard to the information being conveyed (I). He found that different linguistic forms are considered by native speakers as sounding either natural or unnatural depending on how they see (I) as relating to (X). Among other expressions, he discussed the use of *ne* as evidence for his theory, for example, in the following contrastive examples:

(2) a.	*anata*	*wa*	*1957*	*nen*	*6-gatsu*	*22-nichi*	*umare*	*desu.*	
	you	TOP		year	June	22nd	born	COP	
b.	*anata*	*wa*	*1957*	*nen*	*6-gatsu*	*22-nichi*	*umare*	*desu*	***ne.***
	you	TOP		year	June	22nd	born	COP	SFP

'Your birthday is June 22, 1957 ***ne/Ø.***'

The only difference between (2a) and (2b) is *ne* at the end. According to Kamio (1990: 4), (2b) is natural, and (2a) is only possible in such cases as a doctor talking to an amnesiac patient. This is because information such as one's own birthday "belongs" in the most epistemically primary and immediate sense, to the addressee of the utterance. *Ne*, claims Kamio, must be used when the claim being put forth falls within the addressee's territory of information. Kamio argues that in cases where information is proximate to both the speaker and the listener, *ne* (or its variations, *nē* or *na*) must appear, as demonstrated below derived from Kamio (1990: 26):

(3)	*Ii*	*tenki*	*desu*	***nē.***
	good	weather	is	SFP

'It's nice weather ***nē.***'

Kamio argues that (3) without the SFP sounds unnatural or strange, that is, *ne* is virtually obligatory. He further claims that even when the speaker and the addressee do not share the same information, the speaker can optionally use *ne* to make the utterance sound polite, treating the information as if it belongs to both of them, and thereby expressing solidarity (1990: 65).

Other studies also hypothesize that *ne* and *yo* indicate an acknowledgment of epistemic disparity regarding the information being conveyed between a speaker and a hearer. Izuhara (2003) argues that *ne, yo*, and *yone* request some modification in addressee's cognition in order to persuade the addressee to adopt the same cognitive state as that of the speaker. Saigo (2011: 53) hypothesized *ne* or *yo* is added depending on how the emerging figure, that is, what the speaker is going to assert, should be treated by the addressee (e.g. as known or acceptable in the case of *ne*; as new or controversial in the case of *yo*), and directs an appropriate response by the addressee.

Hayano (2011: 60–61) focused on assessment sequences in naturally occurring conversation, and examined how *yo* is used to actively negotiate "epistemic authority" between participants as they talk, claiming that "the distribution of information is often not objectively discernible prior to and independent of the interaction." Observing how *yo* is used in such assessment sequences, she claims that *yo* is a marker of epistemic primacy to differentiate the intensity of the *yo*-speaker's assessment from that of the co-participant's.

2.3 Cognitive Approach: Signaling Mental Processing

A quite different approach toward understanding the role of SFPs is taken by Takubo and Kinsui (1997), who propose that the particles *yo* and *ne* appear as the result of a verification process that takes place within the cognitive interface between the two different mental discourse subdomains inside each individual's mind. According to their Discourse Management Model, the "mental discourse domain" is divided into two components, an I-domain and a D-domain. The I-domain is linked to temporary memory, and information that is acquired through "indirect experience" is posited to be stored there. Conversely, the D-domain is linked to long-term memory and said to be filled with information that is acquired through direct experience. Takubo and Kinsui argue that *ne* is a marker indicating that the speaker is currently in the process of incorporating information from the I-domain into the D-domain. For example (Takubo and Kinsui 1997: 754):

(4)	*anata*	*wa*	*Jon Sumisu-san*	*desu*	***ne.***
	you	TOP		COP	SFP

'You are John Smith, aren't you?'

Here, the speaker's not-yet-verified assumption that the hearer is John Smith has been taken out of the I-domain. After the verification procedure, the speaker incorporates the proposition into the D-domain. They argue that because *ne* shows that the speaker is in the process of verifying the assumption, it serves to invite the contribution of the hearer who can provide the ultimate evidence for the truth of proposition. Thus they argue that *ne*'s often-associated meaning of "confirmation" is only a side-effect of this more basic manifestation of cognitive processing.

2.4 Performative Approach: Associations with Modality

Based on generative semantics and performative analysis, Uyeno (1971) argues that SFPs reflect how speakers wish their hearers to evaluate and react to their propositions. For example, *ne* is used for "practices of rapport," which implies that "the option of judgment on the given information is left to the addressee" (p. 130), and as result *ne* "softens the declarative nature of the sentence" and "gives the effect of humbling the speaker and being polite to the addressee" (p. 131); while the particle *sa* implies "the obviousness of the matter expressed. The effect with an ordinary statement is that it is a matter of course which may in turn yield an insulting or scornful effect" (p. 97).

Some studies using this approach attribute these effects to the illocutionary force that they are thought to create. Nakano (1995) compared the degrees of illocutionary force attributed to different particles along a continuum of how strongly the speaker "pressures" the listener to accept the content of the message. According to Nakano, *na, ne, sa*, and *yo* are distributed within a continuum of forcefulness from weaker to stronger.

Focusing more on participants' joint cooperation than on individuals' acts of illocutionary forcefulness, Cook meanwhile proposes that *ne* indexes an "affective common ground" between interlocutors. By using *ne*, claims Cook, "the speaker can solicit, confirm, or refer to these feelings that are supposedly shared among the interlocutors" (1992: 519). Cook further notes that "the relation between a cultural value and an effective feature works two ways. In one way, the cultural value is encoded by the linguistic feature, and in the other, the use of this feature reinforces the cultural value" (1992: 534). In Cook's approach, the meanings and/or functions of Japanese particles are both context-sensitive and, at the same time, are themselves context-creating, for the promotion and accomplishment of collaborative, mutually intelligible talk.

2.5 Intonations of Sentence-final Particles

Another factor that complicates the analysis of SFPs is their intonational variations. Eda (2001) maintains that prosody can cue speakers' communicative intentions independently, and argues that the variations in the meanings of *ne* are attributed to sentence-final intonation patterns. Izuhara (1994) specifically analyzes the communicative functional difference of *ne* and *nē*, focusing on intonational variation. Koyama (1997) argues that *ne* fundamentally indicates the sharing of psychological or cognitive states between the speaker and the hearer, and that intonation adds another layer of functional meaning; for example, a rising intonation already indicates attention-seeking and addressing, so when *ne* occurs in this intonation pattern, it seeks the matching cognitive status between the speaker and the listener, in the manner of a confirmation check. Sugito, Inukai, and Sadanobu (1997: 18), however, argue that we still need empirical evidence for the iconicity of intonation, that is, whether there is a schematic sign system between intonational patterns and understanding meaning.

2.6 Speech Style

SFPs are also often impressionistically associated with certain speech styles. For example, frequent occurrences of sentence-internal and sentence-final particles have also been said to be associated with informal speech (Shibatani 1990: 386)[4] or with being childish (Kataoka 1995: 441). On the other hand, the use of these particles is said to indicate a positive communication style, as it shows intimacy. Ikeda discusses how deploying *ne* and *yo* may have the effect of politeness by displaying the speaker's attitude of getting closer to his or her interlocutor. According to Ikeda, *ne* has been claimed to convey the impression of friendliness, however, the over-use of these particles may give an impression of an "over-familiar attitude" (1995: 103).

Kataoka (1995), who examined young Japanese women's letter writing, argues that the use of SFPs incorporates the addressor's and the addressee's relative social standings, such as age difference, politeness, and asymmetry of information, and are in turn supposed to construct power/solidarity relations in particular groups by the way in which they index such inter-group feelings as familiarity, reciprocity, and pride.

The fact that speakers of Japanese may derive such impressionistic readings of these particles points out the need for research analyzing the way such utterances are produced and how these particles contribute to the creation of such impressions. Nagasaki's study (1998), however, reports that the particle *sa*, which appears in conversation in a rough manner today, seems to have appeared also in polite conversation in the Edo period. This suggests that the association with speech styles is not an inherent characteristic of SFPs.

2.7 Sociolinguistic Approach: Associations with Gender

As SFPs are often associated with characteristics of speech styles, they are further connected to certain stereotypes of social identity, such as gender, age, and social status. A more detailed discussion of this topic is discussed in Okamoto (Chapter 29, this volume), but here I will briefly discuss the claims made for the SFPs as gender markers. McGloin (1990: 37), for example, claims that *wa* and *no* are feminine particles, with *wa* expressing strong emotional feeling and *no* creating conversational rapport between the speaker and the hearer. Such practices, she claims, are considered to be both positive politeness strategies and "a very important aspect of women's speech in Japanese." Correspondingly, Masuoka and Takubo (1989: 201) state that *yo* is a masculine expression that expresses strong assertion and is used to demand the listeners' action or response. Compared to *yo, zo* and *ze* are said to be used for even stronger insistence, and McGloin (1990: 29) supports Reynolds's (1985: 25) contention that "there is a direct correlation between degrees of assertion expressed by these particles and their speaker's 'power in society.'"

[4] An interesting historical fact about these particles is that the use of some particles was at one time considered to be "uneducated" and their use was prohibited at an elementary school in Kanagawa province in the 1960s (Hashimoto 2002). Although this so-called "*ne-sa-yo* prohibition movement" did not affect Japanese speakers' use of these particles, it indicates that there exists strong association between these particles with speech style.

However, Komatsu (1988) has examined the use of SFPs in the dialogue of NATSUME Soseki's novel *Sanshirō* (published in 1909) and *kokkeibon*, the Edo-period humorous prose fiction *Ukiyoburo* (written by SHIKITEI Sanba between 1809 and 1813) and found that what are often considered to be male particles (e.g. *zo, ze*, and *na*) or female particles (*wa* and *no*) are both used by male and female characters, suggesting that whatever the pragmatic functions of these particles are, they are not inherently associated with gender per se. Komatsu also discovered that certain particles, such as *ze*, were not found in the speech of upper-class women of that period, and claims that the masculinization of certain endings seem to have started by this time; while gradually decreasing occurrences of N+*yo, noyo*, and *wa* are found in male characters' speech of the period, paving the way for the feminization of those endings.

Starting from the late 1880s, the forms used by young females of that time became the target of criticism (Komatsu 1988: 105), and thus the association of certain forms of particle usage with certain "types" of people took place. Importantly, work in this field shows that there seems to be little semantic or pragmatic continuity between today's so-called "feminine" particles and the same forms as they were used by both males and females in the Edo period, as use of them by young women, even in the Meiji period was felt to be "bizarre" by their contemporaries (Komatsu 1988: 103; Kinsui 2003: 146).

Thus, it is important to historically situate the notions of particles as gender-markers, as their associations with certain types of people has been sociohistorically constructed as if they really were so differentially associated (Inoue 2006). This process of association is probably best understood within the theoretical construct of *yakuwarigo* 'role language' (Kinsui 2003). Kinsui introduces the notion of role language to refer to suites of speech features that have become closely related to an image of certain persona, claiming further that the development of these particles is evidenced at the time when the social structure is changing and different social persona are beginning to appear or fade. Such association, he claims, results in more or less fixed linguistic stereotypes, and the stereotypes are reinforced by their use in fiction of various art forms and media for the easy portrayal of certain characters and roles, hence becoming even more widely ingrained in the minds of Japanese speakers. The historical studies of Komatsu (1988) and Kinsui (2003) strongly suggest that certain SFPs that are now recognized as "gendered" particles took this route of development.[5] According to Kinsui, the higher the "degree of role-language" used, the more concrete persona, such as "wise old man" or "lady from upper class," is evoked (Kinsui 2003: 67). Indeed, the fact that many native speakers of Japanese often do associate

[5] However, it is important to note that such change in the pragmatic function, that is, being associated with a specific role or a character, did not happen to all particles.

certain SFPs as being either masculine or feminine suggests the culturally deep-seated nature of role-language in Japanese and the existence of a strong language ideology, as notions of "strongly feminine" or "moderately feminine" (e.g. Okamoto 1995: 301) seem to correlate with such degree of role-language.

Sadanobu's (2011) notion of "character language (*kyara-go*)" encompasses such virtual role-language, but looks as well at the manifold ways in which people create a displayed "character" in everyday life. Sadanobu elaborates that, in real life, Japanese speakers are also constantly *acting out* certain characters using not only linguistic resources – such as SFPs, vocabulary, and grammar – but also gesture, intonation, and even ways of inhaling, even though such character- (or identity-) building may not necessarily evoke a concrete or pre-defined role in Kinsui's sense. Individual people creatively combine elements to enact a character depending on the immediately pertaining conversational context, claims Sadanobu, and this explains why we see to such an extent the individual variation in the use and non-use of various particles.

While many recent studies on gendered language (e.g. Okamoto and Shibamoto 2004) have explored real language practices and demonstrated that the use and non-use of gendered linguistic resources appear to be Japanese speakers' active choices, undertaken in order to communicate desired images of self in particular interactional contexts, many other studies still treat each of the particles as being related to unique gender identities (to different degrees). Reporting on such particles' frequency of appearance in conversation, Ide and Yoshida (2002: 463) state that "Some sentence-final particles characterize male or female speech because of their exclusive use by one sex or the other." Yet we have seen much evidence to support the understanding that very few particles are used exclusively by one gender. There thus seems to be a discrepancy between Japanese speakers' language ideology – that is, how women should speak, etc. – and the actual ways we find such particles being used.

SFPs' habitus being both in fiction and in reality needs to be recognized in research, and the study of SFPs should carefully distinguish whether we are talking about real language use, fictionalized characterizations, or understandings drawn from Japanese language ideology.

2.8 Problems and Unsolved Issues

As should be obvious from the foregoing brief overview, an extraordinary range of different approaches and conclusions reveal the still unsettled nature of our understanding of SFPs. One problem vexing the current field of Japanese particle research is that as soon as one tries to assign a particular "meaning" to each particle or to explain its function from one dimension, one finds numerous counterexamples or inapplicable cases. Moreover, there is as yet no one encompassing meta-explanation as to how it is that so many different reasonable, but sometimes contradictory, explanations can seem to accurately describe the meaning and action of the same single particle in one set of data but not in another. We are thus left with a disparate list of various possible meanings, functions, and ways to interpret intentions. A consideration of all these different approaches, *when taken together*, makes it difficult to understand the fundamental work that must be going on in order to make these SFPs so ubiquitous in speech, yet so varied in their apparent use and meaning. In order to have a comprehensive understanding of these SFPs, it will be necessary to reconcile the contradictory yet potentially enlightening analyses that we have been considering thus far. Such reconciliation would help clarify some of the important and as-yet-unresolved issues that emerge when one examines the current research field of Japanese SFPs as a whole. Such a comprehensive meta-explanation for the use and ubiquity of particles in spoken Japanese, then, must be able to coherently account for the following pragmatic, syntactic, and semantic problems that characterize their use:

- Children as young as 18 months are able to correctly use particles, even prior to the development of a basic vocabulary and grammar, or an understanding of adult social norms such as politeness or epistemicity. Conversely, accurate and fluent use of SFPs by adult learners of Japanese as a foreign language appears to be one of the most difficult skills for them to master. What might this apparent paradox suggest to us about the underlying real-world pragmatics of such SFPs?
- Empirical evidence shows overwhelmingly that SFPs do not always appear sentence finally in actual talk and that some of them do appear at virtually any position within an utterance. In order to understand the syntactic promiscuity of SFPs, how might we have to broaden our analysis of these particles' syntactic role so as to better comprehend the actual data, and be able to account for why a particular particle appears in its particular position in a particular utterance and in another position altogether in a different utterance by the same speaker?
- As can be seen in the literature review above, for each of these particles, numerous possible meanings, interpretations, and connotations have been proposed – many of which contradict each other, yet almost all of which resonate as partly correct to the ear of a native Japanese speaker. Clearly, each of these different analyses are capturing something of what these particles mean (or could mean). A question then becomes: Is there some core semantics associated with each of these non-denotational particles that is not only recognized as such by Japanese speakers, but could also coherently give rise to a variety of secondary and derived meanings, such as have been proposed for each of these particles?

In the following section, I will propose one possible approach to the study and analysis of these particles that may allow for a more comprehensive way of accounting for and understanding these three seemingly paradoxical pragmatic, syntactic, and semantic phenomena characteristic of the reality of Japanese particle use.

3 Toward a Unifying Account of the Semiotics of Sentence-final Particles

Having now reviewed most of the major approaches that have been taken in the study of SFPs to date, in the following section I want to explore some of the readers potential explanatory benefits that may be derived from taking a "meta-explanatory" approach to the phenomenon of SFPs and interaction more generally in the attempt both to reconcile many of the various interpretations suggested thus far and to help possibly shed some light on a way forward in addressing the three as yet unresolved research questions noted above.

3.1 Interactional Approach: Examining the Practices of Situated Interaction

The interactional approach to the study of SFPs differs from other approaches in that it employs the methodology of Conversation Analysis (CA) (e.g. Heritage 1984; Schegloff 1996). CA holds that the moment-to-moment back-and-forth of face-to-face human interaction is the primordial site of human sociality and meaning-making and is therefore the most fundamental data to be captured and analyzed for an understanding of human language practice (Sacks, Schegloff, and Jefferson 1974).

In such face-to-face interaction, CA maintains, talk is co-organized and co-constructed by the participants involved, each of whom must be constantly attentive to what communicative action their interlocutor is doing in the present moment, as well as to what immediately following action of their own is now being made relevant, required, possible, or pre-empted by the action that their interlocutor has now introduced into the talk as an issue needing to be dealt with in the immediately following moment.

Accordingly, the focus is on examining what people are *doing* by using various resources, including linguistic features, that they use with one another, and only then deriving what meanings have come to be associated with the use of those linguistic features and other communicative signs. Such an approach may be particularly appropriate for the study and understanding of Japanese SFPs, since such particles often attach to such conversational *actions* as suggesting (e.g. *ikō yo* 'let's go *yo*'), giving orders (*yamete yo* 'stop it *yo*!'), thanking (*arigato ne* 'thank you *ne*'), and apologizing (*gomen ne* 'sorry *ne*'), etc., where conveyance of propositional information is not the primarily accomplished task.

In the CA perspective, particles are akin to tools or resources that conversationalists draw upon to accomplish and negotiate the ever-present social world of doing things. We may still identify their conventionally determined connotations and meanings, but it is their precise deployment of those items within the sequences of actual conversation that is the primary site of collaborative meaning-making, and that is thus the focus of investigation.[6]

Observing the sequential development of particle-marked utterances, Morita (2005) proposes that the basic function of such particles is as a resource for accomplishing some relatively *fundamental actions* in negotiating talk's contingency. In examining the co-construction of talk-in-interaction that has been captured within naturally occurring conversation, the study concludes that, overwhelmingly, *ne* is a resource with which those participants explicitly create a sanctioned space in which participants can negotiate issues of interactive *alignment* in the moment, and that concrete contextual meanings are derived by thematizing such general interactional agenda between turns at particular points of interaction. The data presented below illustrates how the deployment of a particle is sensitive to the development of the action sequence, as opposed to adding some interpretational instruction to the "proposition."

(5) ((S has explained that he does not know his neighborhood very well because he leaves home very early and comes home very late. After that, S describes that area.))

1 S: *dakara apāto ōi n desu yo.*
so apartment many NMLZ COP.POL SFP
'So, there are many apartment buildings.'

2 Y: *fūn.*
'I see.'

3→K: ( ) *kurai toki ni uchi dete kura(h)kuna(h)tte=*
dark time at home leave.TE dark-become.TE

4 *=ka(h)ette kuru(h) n da(h).*
return.TE come NMLZ COP
'(You) leave when it is still dark and come home when it gets dark.'

[6] One could instead examine the use of SFPs in novels, monologues, or constructed sentences in idealized contexts and then derive some "rules of use." But those instances, for example, author-created works of fiction and in controlled experiments, are not equivalent to one another. More importantly, such creations are artificially fabricated or impoverished in a way that is far more simplified than is the case when we examine recordings of everyday talk-in-interaction, which is the natural habitat of human language. If a theory of Japanese SFP use is to be applicable in all the possible instances, an analysis based on invented sentences, or one concerned with the exchange of information in static idealized contexts, will not be as fully persuasive as one grounded in actual interaction, which reveals far more complex dynamics, and a manifold of interactional concerns that participants must confront and deal with in real-time. Therefore, observing SFPs in ordinary talk-in-interaction first seems to be most sensible. Only then we can see what type of contextual effect is further created in deploying them when they appear in drama or in soliloquy (Hasegawa 2010), for example, for such forms of language use are derived from the talk-in-interaction as specialized adaptations.

5 (.6)
6→ [((looks up)) **ne** [:?
SFP
7→ S: [((looks up)) [sō
'yes'
8 (.) *de ima nanka makkura desu yo.*
and now TOP dark COP.POL SFP
'And now, it's completely dark.'
9 K: *un, sō desu yo ne, goji nante ne:.*
yeah so COP.POL SFP SFP five.o'clock TOP SFP
'Yeah, it must be *ne*, (if it is) five o'clock *ne*.'

When K's talk reaches its completion, there is a short silence (line 5). K's turn in lines 3–4 is not understood by S as a turn that requires a specific next action. As there is no uptake from S at this point, K's utterance winds up hanging in the air. It is at this moment that K explicitly thematizes S's alignment as an interactionally relevant issue by moving his gaze toward S and adding *ne* (line 6) – thereby making it explicit that an action that has not yet happened, should happen now, if S is to display his interactional alignment to K's previous turn.

This segment shows how *ne* is utilized to deal with contingency issues of the sequence and how it highlights *alignment* as an interactional issue at the precisely needed moment, and provides for the recipient a sanctioned space for immediately resolving the issue. Indeed, S's understanding of *ne*'s work here is evidenced in the subsequent sequential development of the talk, where S quickly moves to an aligned action by not just giving a confirming response, but also connecting his talk to the *ne*-attached turn in such a way that covers up the gap. Note here that *ne* was supplied after the original turn was completed. This shows that whether to attach *ne* or not depended *neither* on the proposition nor the information conveyed in the utterance. Rather, *ne* was added due to an immediately arising exigency in the maintenance of the ongoing talk. Thus, when taking an interactional approach to analyze these particles, the semantics of any particle should be examined and understood as a meaning-making resource that is directed not so much at instructing the listener how to interpret the proposition of the utterance, but rather at providing possibilities for participants' next relevant action in the ongoing co-construction of the conversational interaction itself.

When the social act that one is doing is co-constructing face-to-face interaction, one must be able to draw upon a wealth of different interactional tools and resources at a split-second's notice in order to deal successfully with the almost infinite possibilities and contingencies that are being manifested in the moment. Words and, particularly, non-denotational, non-referential tools like these particles are thus interactional resources that each have their own particular range of *affordances* that they are best equipped to do.

This concept of *affordances* refers to the set of action possibilities made relevant by different objects in an animal's (or human's) environment (Gibson 1977). Just as a Japanese folding fan affords grasping with one hand to accomplish various actions, "what other persons afford, comprises the whole realm of social significance for human beings" (Gibson 1979/1986: 128). It is this view of SFPs as resources for *accomplishing particular actions within and relevant to* the unfolding moment-to-moment action of interactional talk that I want to suggest may be the most productive way to grasp these SFPs. By discovering how conversationalists themselves display their understandings of such SFPs' affordances, or underlying pragmatic functions, to one another in the course of actual talk, we may then be in a much better position to understand and evaluate the variety of proposed (and sometimes contradictory) theories as to what these SFPs mean.

One may thus say that one of the primary action affordances of *ne* is its ability to explicitly thematize underlying alignment issues, and that this is its core semiotic function, or use. But such affordances – even principal ones – do not exhaust all the possible real-world uses or meanings of *ne*, just as the core affordance of a Japanese folding fan for creating breeze does not determine or delimit all of the possible uses to which a fan can be put.[7]

The analysis of naturally occurring conversational data shows that affordances of a given particle can be connected to different pragmatic meanings when analyzed in a specific sequential position in a specific interactional context accomplishing certain kinds of tasks, and resolving certain kinds of problems, at the moment that such necessities arise in the course of the immediately unfolding talk-in-interaction.

3.2 Acquisition of Sentence-final Particles

Let us now turn our attention to the question of how children learn to use SFPs in their communicative interactions with others. Despite the lack of consensus among linguists about the basic functions and meanings of these SFPs, it has been empirically established that Japanese children start using them productively between age 1.6 and 2.0 even before they reach the two-word stage. Child first language acquisition research reveals that children acquire five to seven different SFPs within three months since the first appearance of a SFP (usually *ne* or *yo*) (Clancy 1985: 428).

[7] As an analogy to the current state of SFP studies, imagine that in the attempt to understand a Japanese folding fan, researchers have come up with a long list of functions, each of which may be said to be appropriate in its analytically chosen context; for example, to use as a prop in dancing, hiding the mouth when laughing or talking in whispers, symbolizing the boundary at the tea ceremony. One may also describe that females use a fan more often than men do, and that using a folding fan is not child-like behavior, etc. All these descriptions may be true within their contexts, but here we want to understand what the most basic function (or *affordance*) of a Japanese folding fan *is*, prior to all the auxiliary uses to which it can be put.

Focusing on *yo*, Morita (2016) has observed that from the beginning it appears in a variety of action types, such as suggesting (*ikō yo* 'let's go *yo*'), reporting (*ochita yo* 'it dropped *yo*'), rejecting (*iyada yo* 'don't want *yo*'), and warning (*sawattara akan yo* 'don't touch *yo*') – all of which are acts of seeking some relevant next action from another party interactively. Moreover, in her study of the early spontaneous use of *yo*, a 1.9-year-old child made a suggestion (using the volitional form of the verb 'go') alternatively with and without *yo*, showing that the child has not necessarily learned the phrase *ikō yo* as a fixed phrase, but is using *yo* as a differentiated linguistic resource that he can use or not use, appropriate to his particular situation (2016: 152).

The fact that Japanese children seem to understand the most basic functions of these SFPs very early suggests that such acquisition is a part of learning human interaction, that is, how one mobilizes the other interlocutor through their use of language, as opposed to analyzing the particular SFP as a lexeme within a sentence independently (as most second language learners of Japanese have to do). Children's early mastery of their use, too – before even the development of a fully fluent vocabulary and other grammatical items – suggests that those novices must first come to understand the collaborative products of action that can be accomplished by them, and in so doing, internalize the interactional practices that they are used to accomplishing. Another important fact about the acquisition of SFPs is that they are not observed in Japanese autistic children's speech (Watamaki 1997). This is to be expected, given that SFPs are in essence interactional linguistic symbols that point beyond the speakers' own experience, intentions or desires, and toward communicative situations in which other persons are recognized as intentional beings like oneself, and in which the natural recursivity of interactional co-construction is fully recognized.

Japanese children are involved in various social interactions every day even from the pre-linguistic stage (where these particles are frequently used), and they learn the conventional use of these particles as an integral part of learning culture-specific ways of sharing and manipulating the attention of others as social-cognitive practice (Tomasello 2003). In this process, Japanese children are discovering the *affordances* of the particles. For as children pass the nine-month mark and begin to initiate joint-attentional interactions with their peers and caretakers, they learn to "view complex events from various perspectives that connect either more or less well with the current joint attentional scene" and thus to "conceptualize, categorize, and schematize events" (Tomasello 1999: 159). For example, Japanese children learn how, in stating their own opinion or desire, they must take into account the perspective of their interlocutors. In order to be effective, then, they must also learn the culture-specific strategies and resources of how to successfully involve other participants. Such actions are enabled by the affordance of SFPs.

Once children discover the affordance of these "content-free" particles like *ne* or *yo*,[8] they find that such particles are extremely useful tools for communicative interaction. Moreover, rather than acquiring SFPs as parameters for different schemas, for example, "when attached to a request, it indicates insisting" or "when attached to an evaluation, it indicates epistemic authority," what children seem to be learning here is the most basic affordance of the symbol, which is the building of the joint attention frame for the talk's contingency. This is the affordance that is at the base of all later individual variants, such as the ones (correctly, if only partially) invoked by most previous analyses of, say, *ne* and *yo*. As young children internalize these symbols, they cognitively represent one way that "the current situation may be attentionally construed by 'us,' the users of the symbol" (Tomasello 2003: 13). Thus, evidence from early acquisition encourages us to understand (and to seek to discover) the fundamental affordance of any given SFP, upon which all later uses are built.

Yet such a learning process is only possible when learners find themselves an active part of a genuinely ongoing "participation framework," that is, the interactional roles taken up by the different interlocutors of conversation, wherein both the learner and other participants must rely on SFPs to successfully co-create the talk-in-interaction. It is thus the *development of social cognition* – and not the learning the lexeme's functions per se – that is needed for successful understanding and mastery of SFPs. That is why the native-like use of SFPs is one of the hardest skills to acquire for the second language learners, as students of JFL do not have opportunities to find the affordance of SFPs *experientially* – which is the only way that they can be appropriately understood. Conversely, people who learned the particles as part of their native language need never attempt to analyze them in isolation, for they only know (and need to know) what the particles afford them to do, given the immediate conversational context that they find themselves in. That is why these are linguistic items which are extremely difficult to reduce to a single isomorphic meaning, such that even native speakers have difficultly explaining them.

3.3 Sentence Final versus Interjectional Use

Another unsolved issue in studies of SFPs regards their positions within utterances. And here, too, I will suggest that an interactional approach to particle study can help provide a more comprehensive understanding. Although I have been using the traditional term *sentence-final particles* throughout most of this chapter, particles such as *ne* or *sa* often occur at internal positions within an utterance. Thus, observing naturalistic data raises a question for the dichotomy of the terms *shūjoshi* 'sentence-final particles' and *kantōjoshi* 'insertion particles.' Consider the following utterance:

[8] Morita (2012b) has argued that the primary function of *yo* is to indicate the speaker's stance of *dependence* on the interlocutor that the current *yo*-marked conversational move or action needs in some way to be interactionally registered by the interlocutor.

(6) ((H, a female graduate student talking to her friend M as she reaches to the food on a low table))[9]
H: *ii* *yo* ***ne*:::,**① *gohan ga oishikute* ***ne*::,**② *kono machi tte* ***ne*:?**③
good SFP? SFP? food SBJ tasty SFP? this town TOP SFP?
'It's nice *ne*, because the food is delicious *ne*, speaking of this town *ne*?'

In this utterance, it is not clear which are "sentence-final particles" and which are "insertion particles," given that a sentence-final particle, by definition, should end the sentence. But right before the last *ne*③ is the topic marker *tte*, which suggests some comment should follow. That comment (*gohan ga oishikute ii yo ne*), however, actually comes before this segment. Furthermore, it is not clear whether to analyze *yo ne*① as an insertion particle that is attached to the predicate, and which should come at the end of the sentence. One cannot simply dismiss such cases as disfluencies or anomalous, as word orders like the above are not uncommon in spoken Japanese. Thus, in real conversational data, the very notion of "sentence" itself becomes questionable (e.g. Morita 2005, 2007, 2008b). If one is to study the functions of these particles by examining natural spoken data, the term 'sentence-final particle' itself thus comes into question.

Indeed, Morita (2008a) found that these particles may occur not only in utterance-internal position, but also in breaking up a semantically coherent noun phrase. Consider the next example of naturalistic data.

(7) ((M and H are discussing what to eat in Los Angeles. M has been giving several recommendations on food and just finished one topic.))
1 M: *ato wa doko: ga e- ii ka na:** other TOP
where NOM FRG good SFP SFP
'Where else would be good, I wonder...'
2 (.4)
3 → H: *e,* *sono* ***sa*** *kankoku no otōfu tteiu hanashi wa*
IP that SFP Korea GEN tofu QUOT story TOP
uwasa o miminishita
rumor ACC heard
4 *n da kedo*
NMLZ COP but
'Eh, that ***sa*** rumor about the Korean tofu, I heard but...'
5 M: ↑*un.* 'Yeah.'
6 H: *sore tte nani?* that TOP what
'What is it?'
7 *o- ni- nihon no otōfu to onaji na no?* FRG
FRG Japan GEN tofu as same COP:ATT SFP
'Is it the same as Japanese tofu?'

9 For more detailed analysis of this segment, please refer to Takagi, Hosoda, and Morita (2016: 300).

What kind of conversational or interactional work, then, might these utterance-internal particles be doing? What was claimed in early studies about the main function of SFPs being to "end a sentence" (e.g. Watanabe 1968: 128) is not necessarily completely unreasonable, if we consider that these particles demarcate not just sentences but all and any possible meaningful units for interaction (Morita 2008a). In other words, when the talk is linearly unfolding little by little in real time, the speaker may mark some segment in a prosodically salient way with particles, so that the recipients are able to recognize which specific segment they should particularly attend to. When the particle appears at the end, the whole action is something to which the recipient is expected to give some response. But the speaker may bring attention to a certain move, which is less than a concrete action by demarcating a part of the talk (Morita 2008a).

In the above examples, by marking with *ne* or *sa*, the speaker can let her recipient know the nature of the emerging action at the earliest possible point. Especially when the speaker starts a somewhat disjunctive action, highlighting a move to increase the projectability (Tanaka 1999) is a useful strategy for maintaining the inter-subjective understanding of the ongoing action. In this sense, whether the demarcated segment is a complete utterance or part of the utterance is just a matter of length, for both are interactionally relevant units (Morita 2008a), and its affordance should be the same whether it occurs in utterance-final position or in medial position. For this reason, Morita (2005, 2008a, 2008b) suggests calling these particles "interactional particles" without separating them into sentence-final and interjectional.

We see such a situation being played out in the talk above when H starts her new turn in line 3 in (7). She interpolates *sa* after the adnoun *sono* 'that' – breaking up a semantically coherent noun phrase (since *sono* is an adnoun, grammatically, a noun should follow immediately). If the insertion of particles was for conveying "information" bit by bit, this would be an odd place to do so, as it breaks up a semantically coherent unit. This demarcation of the adnoun *sono* with *sa* is not random. Rather, precisely at this point in the interaction, H highlights the emergent move (adumbrated with discourse deixis *sono*) that is re-directing the talk back to something that had been discussed previously. H, by so doing, lets M know about the nature of her intended move at the earliest possible place in the interactional sequence. At this interactional juncture, where M is displaying her engagement in searching for a new topic of food, H's changing the topic back to an already discussed topic is a sensitive operation, as it will block M's move. The insertion of *sa* here,[10] however, helps negotiate such interactional concerns as the conversation unfolds moment-by-moment.[11] Thus from

[10] Morita (2005: ch. 5) argues that the core affordance of *sa* is to indicate the "prospective non-negotiability" of the conversational action being proffered at that moment.

[11] For more detailed analyses of such demarcation practices, see Morita (2008a).

an interactional perspective, these particles are linguistic resources to demarcate interactionally relevant units of talk, whether they occur at the end of the utterance or within an utterance. At the end of each segment, different particles' affordances will highlight different interactional concerns relevant for that segmented move. Thus, the analysis of the functions of particles should also pay attention to their positions within the talk as their occurrences are by no means random.

3.4 Reconciliation of the Different Higher-level Analyses Offered for these Particles

Another issue in the current state of SFP studies is the manifold descriptions of interpretations and functions of SFPs proposed by various scholars, without any overarching explanation to connect them. Assuming that each of the hypotheses proposed so far have captured some aspects of SFPs' functions, the question then becomes: How do the participants in the conversation know *which* of these possible meanings or functions (of *ne*, say, or of *yo*) should be evoked in the particular interactional moment? One possible approach is to identify the *core affordance* of the SFP, then explain how that fundamental function could make various contextual meanings derivable therefrom. For example, the basic function of *ne* as a negotiation tool for resolving inter-turn contingency problems, which I have shown in Section 3.1, can be connected to various higher-level interpretations that have been offered by other theorists. *Ne*, which at its most basic level affords the thematization of interactive alignment, may then (depending on how and where it is employed) lead to impressionistic interpretations of "stance taking" that invoke such higher-order concepts as sociality, politeness, neediness, coerciveness, and (according to certain ideologies) femininity.

Let us see how this can be so by examining the following passage, which is taken from a posting to an online discussion forum entitled "Words that bother me" on *Hatsugen Komachi*, a Japanese website that is mainly targeted to women.

(8) The thing that has been bothering me is that my boyfriend, who is 30 years old, the same age as me, uses *ne* in his emails, as in: "We had good time today *ne*" or "Because you have been saying that you wanted to go *ne*." Honestly, I feel like telling him: "How old are you?" or "Are you a girl from the old generation?" But I cannot tell him this, since I am afraid that it would hurt him (because he uses it so regularly). But because he is a grown-up man, I wish that he wouldn't use it. (Posted on March 30, 2009 on *Hatsugen Komachi*)

Here, a Japanese woman is complaining about her boyfriend's use of *ne* in phrases such as *Kyō wa tanoshikatta ne* 'We had a good time, didn't we?' If this statement were to be presented out of context, it might not necessarily be judged as sounding feminine by most native Japanese speakers – yet the author of this posting thinks that the use of *ne* is not appropriate for a 30-year-old man, and that it sounds like a young girl's talk.

As seen in Section 2.7, certain ways of using SFPs are often judged in terms of femininity and masculinity, and this is widely shared or treated as common knowledge among Japanese speakers in general. The association of SFPs with gender is deep-seated, and very often unquestioned. But how is it that such an association is only reasonable in some cases and not in others (e.g. in the case of Example (5), we do not necessarily judge K's additional *ne* as feminine)?

Let us first examine the most basic context for what the participants are going to establish. SFPs draw special attention to the participation framework that is being co-constructed by the conversationalists at that moment and *ne* specifically thematizes alignment as the interactional agenda. Recall use of *ne* as a targeted criticism in (8), a boyfriend making an assessment of the date *Kyō wa tanoshikatta* and then adding *ne* to that assessment creates a space for the recipient to display her stance toward the projected second assessment. But when the first assessment is articulating something jointly experienced, the second assessment claim on the part of the recipient, in her capacity as a "co-enjoyer," is thereby made a particularly relevant next action. Such use of *ne* may be instrumental for establishing both participants' membership as co-experiencers and for solidarity building. Yet when the validation of alignment is continually emphasized, such action may come to be perceived as either needy or perhaps even coercive.

Moreover, when a higher order of language ideology is operational in the interpretation of lower-level (turn- and discourse-level) events, and such behavior is checked against the language ideology held by the recipients, it may then be evaluated and perceived positively or negatively; for example, as per the author of this web posting, repeated use of *ne* was judged as typical behavior of young girls. Such meta-linguistic discourse about the use of *ne* suggests that her particular speech community shares such sociolinguistic conventions that determine the appropriate amount and type of explicit alignment solicitation acceptable for various social identities (e.g. young and old, male and female) and for different social roles. At the same time, it shows that the derived meaning of *ne* changes considerably depending on the position where *ne* occurs. For example, if *ne* occurs in the second assessment, it would mark that the assessment is occasioned rather than proffered as an independent opinion, therefore it would indicate affiliative stance. If the second assessment contains the same evaluative term, the aligned stance is even more emphasized and even suggests presumption of affective common ground. The additional intonational emphasis could further add a layer of an emotional tone, thereby further connected to readings such as solidarity or friendliness.

Accordingly, if such behavior does not agree with one's language ideology, the same behavior could be judged as overly friendly. In other words, it is not a person's inclusion within some pre-given gendered membership category (or any other higher-order social category) that determines a speaker's use of *ne*, though the use of *ne*, through its association with the negotiation of interpersonal alignment, may come to be heard as appropriate for certain socially constructed identities and types. It is for this reason that so many seemingly incongruous understandings of SFPs such as *ne* can simultaneously, if only partially, hold true.

Thus, it should be emphasized that there is no definitive account of how *ne* is always interpreted. Rather, as an affordance, *ne* gives rise to a number of different understandings, each of which, in turn, provides the grounds for multiple possible paths of higher-level interpretation. But more importantly, such impressionistic interpretations may be possible after adding many layers of other factors, such as composition of the turn, prosody, sequential position, and societal language ideology of the person who evaluates.[12]

4 Conclusion, Outstanding Issues and Future Research Direction

This chapter has provided a brief overview of various approaches to SFPs, showing that although it is a popular topic in Japanese pragmatics, the analyses of these particles are by no means in consensus. Here I have attempted to suggest a future research direction to help reconcile this fragmentation in a productive and comprehensive way. I have proposed that describing the affordance of these particles will relieve us from listing 'meanings' and 'functions' – each of which only apply in limited cases – and that a detailed analysis of interactional context will enable us to understand how such 'meanings' and 'functions' could be derived. Observing the actual occurrences of these particles in natural conversation reveals, and will keep revealing, how people employ them as a way of managing various interactional issues, and that these particles are first and foremost an invaluable resource with which to structure social actions.

[12] See Morita (2012a) for more detailed discussion of how different sociopragmatic meanings are derived based on this example.

26

Linguistic Politeness

Michael Haugh

1 Introduction

The academic study of the interpersonal dimensions of language use, in particular, the role of language in displaying respect and consideration for the feelings of others, has traditionally come under the umbrella of linguistic politeness research.[1] While politeness research as a field was initially grounded in Anglo-American pragmatics (Lakoff 1973; Leech 1983; Brown and Levinson 1987), work by Japanese linguists that critiqued these early theories (Matsumoto 1988b; Ide 1989) had a major impact on thinking in the field. It is now widely acknowledged that while a concern for what others think of us may well be universal to the human condition, the ways in which we can use language to conceptualize such feelings, and the various linguistic practices by which we indicate appropriate levels of consideration for the feelings of others, is subject to considerable cultural diversity.

The use of honorifics in Japanese is often taken to be a case in point. While it was claimed by Brown and Levinson (1987: 179–181) that what motivates honorifics is a concern for avoiding imposition on others, or what they have termed "negative face," it has subsequently been argued that negative face cannot account for all the various ways in which honorifics can be used to display respect and consideration in Japanese (Matsumoto 1988b: 405; Ide 1989: 230; Ohashi 2003: 269). Indeed, the Japanese honorific system is more complex than Brown and Levinson's model claims, as the use of such forms is governed not only by the (perceived) relationship of the speaker with the addressee but with the referent as well. Moreover, style shifts can indicate changes in the perception of the relationship that holds, in that moment at least, between the speaker and referent, for instance.

[1] Politeness researchers generally acknowledge the importance of non-verbal aspects of interaction. However, the discussion in this chapter will be centered primarily on linguistic politeness, given the overall focus of this handbook.

Japanese is not, of course, unique in having a complex system of morpho-syntactic forms that index varying degrees of formality, deference, social distance, and so on. However, it is one of the most comprehensively studied honorifics systems in pragmatics, and linguistics more broadly. For that reason it is perhaps not surprising to many that "politeness" in Japanese has been largely equated with the use of honorifics in both lay and academic discourses (Okamoto and Shibamoto Smith 2016: 126).

Yet one consequence of this emphasis on the study of honorifics is that the other ways in which "politeness" may be accomplished in Japanese have tended to be neglected. While there is no doubt that honorifics play an important role in accomplishing "politeness" in Japanese, it has been long argued that honorifics have a much broader range of functions than indexing "politeness," and that "politeness" can be expressed linguistically in all sorts of ways that go well beyond the use of honorifics in Japanese (Oishi 1975: 65; Minami 1987a: 143). Displays of respect and consideration for the feelings of others, and polished forms of self-presentation, can be accomplished through a whole range of different linguistic and non-linguistic means in Japanese that include but are not limited to the use of honorifics.

In this chapter, the aim is to demonstrate that although the study of honorifics has an important role to play in politeness research, Japanese linguists have more to offer politeness research than that. The chapter begins, in Section 2, by reviewing the major academic traditions that have contributed to our understanding of "politeness" in Japanese, and developments within those traditions, in particular, since the 1970s. In Section 3, the epistemological challenges that politeness researchers face when working across languages are considered, both in relation to delimiting the object of study and in choosing which analytical lens to use in studying this object. It is suggested that linguistics has much to offer in that respect, both in allowing us to carefully examine the (meta)language that underpins different conceptualizations of "politeness" and in contributing to the study of the interactional practices by which "politeness" arises. This position is further illustrated, in Section 4, through analyses of "politeness" in naturally occurring interactions. It is argued that paying close attention to the linguistic formulation of the participants' turns-at-talk, along with their sequential positioning, can offer us considerable insights into interpersonal dimensions of language use. The chapter concludes with a brief discussion of possible future directions for politeness researchers who have a particular interest in the Japanese language.

2 Academic Traditions in the Study of "Politeness" in Japanese

There are two major academic traditions that have contributed to our understanding of "politeness" in Japanese. The first stems from the long-standing study of honorifics (*keigo*) and relational expressions (*taigū hyōgen*) in the national language studies (*kokugogaku*) tradition. The second is the more recent emergence of the study of "politeness" (*poraitonesu*) in the linguistic pragmatics tradition. While there have been some attempts to foster greater cross-fertilization between these two traditions (e.g. Pizziconi 2004: 269), they have proceeded largely in parallel. This is partly because the former tradition is only accessible to those who can read Japanese and there are very few translations or detailed summaries of extant work in the national language studies tradition available in English or other languages. But it is also partly because the analytical concerns of scholars in the different traditions have, historically at least, been somewhat different.

2.1 Honorifics and the "National Language Studies" (*Kokugogaku*) Tradition

While lay observations about the use of honorifics in Japanese stretch back to the earliest written works in Japanese in the eighth century, the systematic study of honorifics by scholars in the national language studies tradition emerged more recently in the late nineteenth century. Early work on *keigo* 'honorifics' (Lit. respect language) by Japanese scholars was focused primarily on morphosyntactic variation across different categories of honorifics. Studies of the broader notion of *taigū hyōgen* 'relational expressions' (Lit. expressions of treatment), namely, "a speaker's expressive choice of linguistic forms which reflect his/her regard for determined objects and people, and his/her assessment of the relation with an addressee" (Pizziconi 2004: 271), initially developed in parallel. However, the study of honorifics increasingly came to dominate the field from the early twentieth century onwards. This was due in part to the growing influence of structural linguistics, which favors the study of language as an abstract system, and in part to the ideological influence of pre-war Japanese nationalists (Tsujimura 1992: 134). The emphasis on honorifics as a key pillar of "politeness" in Japanese has been further reinforced through two highly influential government reports from the Council for National Language in 1952 and 1998 (Okamoto and Shibamoto Smith 2016: 125).

Honorifics in Japanese are generally classified in two ways. The first is based on the focus of the honorific form in question, that is, whether it is directed at an addressee or a referent. There are generally held to be three types of honorific operations on referents: persons can be either elevated or lowered, and objects or events can be "beautified." The second way in which honorifics are classified is on the basis of the typical function of these forms, that is, to show "politeness" (*teineigo*), respect (*sonkeigo*) or humbleness (*kenjōgo*). The former set of distinctions is generally utilized by linguists, while the latter are quasi-lay distinctions that are often

Table 26.1 *Categories of* keigo

<table>
<tr><td colspan="5">Keigo</td></tr>
<tr><td>Focus of deference</td><td>addressee honorifics *taisha keigo*</td><td colspan="3">referent honorifics *sozai keigo*</td></tr>
<tr><td>Honorification type</td><td colspan="2">beautifying expressions *bika hyōgen*</td><td>higher-rank expressions *jōi hyōgen*</td><td>lower-rank expressions *kai hyōgen*</td></tr>
<tr><td>Linguistic form</td><td colspan="2">'polite forms' *teineigo*</td><td>'deferential forms' *sonkeigo*</td><td>'humble forms' *kenjōgo*</td></tr>
</table>

(Pizziconi 2011: 48, adapted from Tsujimura 1992: 227)

employed in the teaching of Japanese as a second language. Notably, beautifying expressions cross-cut these two major axes of classification in that they are treated as a type of referent honorific, on the one hand, and as "polite forms," on the other. These major categories are illustrated in Table 26.1.

Traditionally work on honorifics has been carried out using sociolinguistic methods, such as surveys, including interviews and questionnaires, and participant observation. Such studies have indicated a shift in the major function of honorifics over the past century from marking differences in hierarchical status to marking varying degrees of social distance or intimacy. Notably, the focus of much of this work has been on Modern Standard Japanese, as defined in Chapter 1 of this volume, with only passing recognition of the extent to which there is regional variation in honorific forms and the use of such forms in Japan (Nakai 2005: 110).

Since the 1970s, however, there has also been a move back to studying the broader notion of *taigū hyōgen* 'relational expressions.' This body of work encompasses the study of expressions through which speakers indicate their evaluation of various kinds of interpersonal relations, including not only honorifics but also expressions showing affection, rudeness, contempt, and so on. The interpersonal effects of honorifics are thus held to go beyond simply indicating deference or respect. Oishi (1975: 65), for instance, proposes that the social effects of honorifics also include indicating reverence, distance, formality, dignity, grace/good manners, irony, contempt/disdain, and endearment.

Subsequent work has focused on the various factors that underlie the use and interpretation of such forms. Kikuchi (1997: 42–43), for instance, suggests the use of honorifics is dependent on: (a) the relationships between the speaker, addressee, and referent (including relative social position, familiarity, in-group/out-group status); (b) the context in which the interaction is taking place; (c) the topic of the interaction; and (d) psychological factors (including the speaker's intentions and feelings). Minami (1987a: 66), on the other hand, has proposed that rather than directly encoding deference, the various interpersonal effects of honorifics and relational expressions are mediated through forms of consideration that reflect the speaker's evaluation of the addressee or referent, along with perceived norms of usage. He also goes well beyond the traditional focus on honorifics in including interjections and response tokens, turn-final particles, different speech act formulations and indirect or round-about expressions as forms of relational expressions.

Notably, this latter strand of research in the relational expressions tradition resonates with many of the themes that have subsequently emerged in politeness research in the linguistic pragmatics tradition, as we shall see in the following section.

2.2 Politeness and the Linguistic Pragmatics Tradition

Politeness research is now generally held to have developed in two waves. The first wave encompasses studies in early linguistic pragmatics from the 1970s to the late 1990s, which were largely motivated by, or developed in reaction to, the seminal work of Lakoff (1973), Leech (1983), and Brown and Levinson (1987). Work in this first wave was grounded in the epistemological assumptions and methods of structuralist forms of linguistics, in which linguistic structure is abstracted out from usage, and theorized with respect to underlying pragmatic principles (e.g. politeness maxims) or psychological wants (e.g. positive and negative face). These studies thus generally used isolated sentences, often made up by the researchers themselves, to illustrate their claims.

The second wave in politeness research started to gain momentum in the early 2000s (Eelen 2001; Mills 2003; Watts 2003), but has its origins in the distinction between "first order," lay understandings of participants themselves (so-called politeness1), and "second order," technical understandings of theorists (so-called politeness2), which was proposed by Watts, Ide, and Ehlich (1992). Work in this second wave is grounded in the epistemological assumptions and methods of post-structuralist forms of linguistics, in which it is assumed that linguistic structure cannot be examined apart from its natural ecological habitat. Two key assumptions underpinning this second wave of politeness studies are that the proper focus of politeness researchers is the first-order understandings of participants themselves, and that "politeness" is not inherent in the use of linguistic forms but is a contextual judgment or evaluation that can be disputed by those participants. For that reason there has been a methodological shift toward examining "politeness" as it arises in stretches of naturally occurring discourse, or what is commonly known as the *discursive turn* in politeness research.

In the remainder of this section, the ways in which politeness researchers have taken up these respective assumptions in studies of "politeness" in Japanese are briefly reviewed.

2.2.1 First-wave Studies of 'Politeness' in Japanese

A key assumption of first-wave approaches as they were taken up by scholars studying "politeness" in Japanese is that "politeness" arises through the normative use of linguistic forms and strategies, in particular honorifics, in ways that reflect underlying social structures. Studies of "politeness" in Japanese in the first wave were particularly influenced by Brown and Levinson's (1987) face-saving view of politeness. According to Brown and Levinson, "politeness" arises through the use of various kinds of strategies that reduce the threat of speech acts, such as requests or refusals, to either positive face (the desire to have a positive social image) or negative face (the desire to be free from imposition). The degree to which a particular speech act threatens the hearer's face is claimed to be a function of the relative power of the hearer over the speaker, the social distance between participants, and the absolute ranking of the degree of imposition of that act. Politeness strategies, including the use of honorifics, are selected by speakers depending on the degree of (perceived) face threat of that (speech) act in that context.

Early studies frequently applied Brown and Levinson's (1987) theory in examining how particular kinds of speech acts are performed "politely" in Japanese, often in the context of comparative studies with English. The most commonly studied speech acts include requests (e.g. Fukushima 2000; Rinnert and Kobayashi 1999), refusals (e.g. Kinjo 1987; Yokoyama 1993), disagreement (e.g. Beebe and Takahashi 1989), and apologies/thanks (e.g. Ide 1998; Kumatoridani 1999). This wave of studies generally relied on data elicited through discourse completion tests in order to allow researchers to control for the effects of sociolinguistic variables, such as age, gender, and so on. However, studies that rely on this kind of data have subsequently been critiqued for confounding people's beliefs about what they should do (i.e. perceptions of prescriptive norms), and what they do themselves in real-life interactions (i.e. actual usage) (Okamoto 2010b: 88).

While a number of studies have employed Brown and Levinson's theory, the degree to which it is able to adequately account for "politeness" in Japanese has been challenged by a number of Japanese scholars. It has been suggested, for instance, that rather than orienting to a concern for negative face, Japanese are more concerned about their "place" (*ba*) within groups (Matsumoto 1988b: 405), and their respective roles or statuses (Ide 1989: 230). The view that the use of honorifics reflects these two concerns underpinned the highly influential proposal by Ide (1989) that "politeness" in Japanese is primarily a matter of "discernment" (*wakimae*). On this approach, the use of certain honorifics is considered to be sociopragmatically obligatory, dependent on social factors such as status difference and degree of intimacy. Some scholars have thus argued that differences in power and social distance can account for the use of different honorific forms in Japanese (Fukada and Asato 2004; Usami 2002), and so Brown and Levinson's (1987) theory is applicable to Japanese. However, while perceived differences in such variables may indeed have an influence on the use of honorifics, it does not explain why honorifics are needed in the first place in the absence of any discernible face threat (Pizziconi 2003: 1479).

Finally, consistent with the assumption of first-wave theorists that politeness can be linked with the normative use of particular forms, a distinction is made between "polite" and "plain" speech styles. However, given honorifics can be directed at addressees and referents, the "polite" and "plain" styles can arise through two different combinations with respect to addressee and referent honorifics (Hasegawa 2015: 267). The "polite" speech style arises when addressee honorifics are used, either with or without referent honorifics being used in the same utterance (Examples (1) and (2) respectively). The "plain" speech style, in contrast, arises when addressee honorifics are not used, either with or without referent honorifics being used in the same utterance (Examples (3) and (4) respectively).

(1) +HON, +POL
irassharu *n* *desu* *ka.*
go.HON NMLZ COP.POL Q

(2) -HON, +POL
iku *n* *desu* *ka.*
go.PLN NMLZ COP.POL Q

(3) +HON, -POL
irassharu *no?*
go.HON NMLZ

(4) -HON, -POL
iku *no?*
go.PLN NMLZ

In seminal work, Ikuta (1983) noted that in some cases speakers may shift between these polite and plain speech styles, a phenomenon that has subsequently become a significant focus of attention by politeness researchers. Building on this work, Usami (2002: 185) argues that "politeness" arises at the level of discourse as it is tied to shifts in speech styles across utterances, rather than being tied to the speech styles of individual utterances in isolation. She proposes that marked speech level shifts either give rise to positive or negative politeness, rudeness, or various discourse effects (e.g. indicating that one is talking to oneself). One challenge for this account of "politeness," however, is how to establish what counts as marked or unmarked usage (Okamoto 2010b: 81–82). Usami's (2002) approach is to establish this empirically through ascertaining the frequency of particular speech levels, and the extent to which they vary according to the relative power and social distance that is presumed to hold between participants in different activity types. This necessarily involves collecting large amounts of conversation in relatively controlled settings, an approach that while empirically sound, does require considerable time and effort on the part of the researcher.

An important point about the concept of politeness that has emerged from these earlier studies is that politeness may be conceptualized both as a form and as an effect, echoing Leech's (1983: 83–84) earlier distinction between "absolute politeness" and "relative politeness." *Polite forms* are particular linguistic forms or expressions, such as honorifics, which are considered to vary in their degree of "politeness." It is presumed that the relative level of "politeness" of these so-called polite forms can be established through comparing these forms across contexts. *Polite effects*, on the other hand, arise when the addressee believes the speaker is being polite. The addressee may, of course, come to believe that the speaker is being polite for a variety of reasons other than the use of polite forms, and the use of polite forms does not necessarily lead to polite effects. These two points have subsequently become the subject of considerable debate in more recent studies of "politeness" in Japanese.

2.2.2 Second-wave Studies of "Politeness" in Japanese

A key assumption from the second wave of politeness research taken up by scholars studying "politeness" in Japanese is that social structures and interpersonal relations are themselves co-constructed through the use of various kinds of linguistic forms, including honorifics, and it is this which enables users to take various kinds of affective stances. Rather than assuming that particular power or social distance relations hold between participants and that these determine, at least in part, what is the most appropriate honorific form to use in that situation, it is argued that power, social distance, and so on are themselves co-constructed in interaction through the use of particular linguistic forms and strategies. Second-wave theories of "politeness" have been taken up in studies of "politeness" in Japanese within two distinct strands of research.

The first strand encompasses studies addressing the indexical nature of honorifics. Based on analyses of the use of honorifics in naturally occurring interactions, scholars have observed that actual usage of honorifics does not always reflect perceived norms about how they should be used (Okamoto 2011; Geyer 2013). Echoing the claims made in earlier studies of relational expressions in the national language studies tradition, there is a growing body of work that suggests that honorifics do not straightforwardly encode deference or respect. In fact, they can be used to accomplish various pragmatic effects, including backgrounding information (Cook 2006: 281), indexing self-directed talk, such as exclamatory and soliloquy-like utterances (Hasegawa 2010: 160), and indexing affective stances, including sarcasm (Okamoto 2002), psychological distance (Pizziconi

2003: 1490), empathy (Ikuta 1983: 40), and so on. Speech style shifts can also mark different genres or speech activities (Cook 1996a: 193), thereby allowing participants to co-construct different identities (Dunn 2005: 218). On this view, "politeness" is just one of the many different affective stances that can arise through the use of honorifics.

One debate that has emerged from such work is the extent to which participants can use honorifics that deviate from claimed normative usage, a debate that has implications for Ide's (1989) distinction between discernment and strategic politeness. On the one hand, some scholars have argued that since speech style shifts occur in various kinds of institutional settings where a particular speech style would be normatively expected, such as that between a student and a teacher, this constitutes evidence that honorifics can be used strategically (Cook 2006: 286). It follows that discernment and strategic politeness are not mutually exclusive (Okamoto 2010b: 87). Others have argued, however, that speech style shifts in such contexts do not constitute evidence of deviance from "politeness" norms, but rather are involved in accomplishing other pragmatic effects, such as marking instances of soliloquy (Hasegawa 2012: 263) or backgrounding information (Cook 2006: 281). Ultimately, however, such debates turn not only on the specifics of empirical analysis (Cook 2012), but also on how one defines "politeness" in the first place.

While much of the research on speech style shifts has left the conceptualization of "politeness" in Japanese somewhat open-ended, a second strand of research has emerged where it is argued that the moral underpinnings of "politeness" be grounded in the understandings of cultural insiders or what is sometimes referred to as an "emic" perspective (Pike 1990: 28). These latter studies echo some of the themes initially proposed by Japanese scholars critical of Brown and Levinson's approach, including the emphasis said to be placed on role (Ide 1989: 230) and one's "place" within a social group (Matsumoto 1988b: 405) amongst Japanese. However, second-wave theorists analyze "politeness" as it arises in extended stretches of discourse rather than at the utterance level, thereby treating place or roles as dynamic and contextually sensitive constructs that arise through interaction (Haugh and Obana 2011: 175), and so are inevitably subject to variation across both users and over time.

Requests have become the object of particular attention amongst scholars of Japanese. Building on previous research that has questioned the applicability of Brown and Levinson's notion of negative face in explaining how requests are formulated and evaluated by speakers of Japanese (Matsumoto 1988c: 405; Pizziconi 2003: 1485), Gagné (2010) argues, drawing from meta-pragmatic interviews with Japanese speakers, that requests are not so much conceptualized in terms of possible imposition on the autonomy of others (negative face), but rather in terms of potential trouble (*meiwaku*) for the addressee. *Meiwaku* literally refers to "the feeling or status of being troubled and uncomfortable due to the deeds of another party," but also "connotes a sense of 'debt' – a reflexive force of debt that returns to oneself" (2010: 131). Japanese informants reported in conceptualizing requests that what drives their choices about whether they refrain from making a request or consider using more indirect ways of making the request in question is their view of themselves as "'mature social adults' (*shakaijin*) who should not cause 'trouble' (*meiwaku*) for others" (ibid.).

Ohashi (2003: 270–271) also suggests that what underpins evaluations of requests as "polite" is a sense of potential indebtedness (*ongi*) to the other drawing from field notes and recordings of naturally occurring interactions. The emic notion of *on(gi)* is a complex one according to Lebra (1976: 91):

> *on* is a relational concept combining a benefit or benevolence given with a debt or obligation thus incurred ... From the donor's point of view, *on* refers to a social credit, while from the receiver's point of view, it means a social debt. An *on* relationship, once generated by giving and receiving a benefit, compels the receiver-debtor to repay *on* in order to restore balance.

It follows that making a request invariably invokes a debt–credit equilibrium, which needs to be balanced through thanking, reciprocating a benefit, or by acknowledging one's indebtedness through formulaic expressions such as *yoroshiku onegaishimasu*, 'Lit. please treat this matter as you think fit' (Ohashi 2003: 270).

Another perspective on the relationship between requesting and "politeness" in Japanese is offered by Obana (2016: 268), who suggests that speakers can display that a request is not licensed by their role through speech style upshift. She draws data to support her argument from the Tokyo University of Foreign Studies BTS Corpus of Spoken Japanese.

(5) JFC05:	*Onegai*	*ga*	*at-te*	*denwashi-ta*	*n*	*desu*	*kedo...*
	request	NOM	have-GER	phone-PST	NMLZ	COP.POL	but

'I wanted to ask you a favor and so contacted you'

(Obana 2016: 269)

What is of particular note here is that this pre-request is formulated using addressee honorifics despite the two participants being close friends who normally use the plain form with each other. In using addressee honorifics in delivering this preliminary to the request, the participant thereby displays that this request lies outside of his role.

A third emic perspective on requests in Japanese is offered by Fukushima (2004), who proposes that making pre-emptive offers that anticipate the needs of others constitutes a display of attentiveness, and that such displays are open to evaluation as "polite." In other words, allowing the other person to avoid having to make a request in the first place through making a pre-emptive offer is a recognizable means of being "polite" in Japanese. For example, in the following interaction reported in

Haugh (2007: 95), the mother notes to herself that she has not brought along a handkerchief. This prompts her daughter to pass a handkerchief to her mother to use. Given the mother did not actually make any request here, the pre-emptive offer can be regarded as a demonstration of attentiveness.

(6) M: mother, D: daughter

M:	*Mama,*	*hankachi*	*mot-te-ki-ta*	*to*	*omot-ta*
	mother	handkerchief	carry-GER-come-PST	QUOT	think-PST
	n	*da*	*kedo...*		
	NMLZ	COP	but		

'I thought I had brought a hankie along but...'

D: ((passes her handkerchief to her mother))

M: *a,* *dōmo.*
'ah thanks' (Haugh 2007: 95)

However, while displaying attentiveness through making pre-emptive offers may be evaluated positively, it may also be evaluated negatively as meddling (*osekkai*) (Fukushima and Haugh 2014: 171). Demonstrations of attentiveness evidently may be evaluated in different ways by participants.

In reviewing these various approaches to "politeness" in this section, it has become apparent that the way in which we define our object of study is no straightforward matter. While multiple understandings of "politeness" are perhaps inevitable, these different perspectives can sometimes mask the fact that we, as analysts or theorists, are not necessarily talking about the same thing. These issues become even more acute when working across languages such as Japanese and English, an issue to which we shall now turn to consider.

3 Concepts and the Role of Metalanguage in Politeness Research

One of the key challenges in politeness research is that the use of terms from English to define pragmatic objects in other languages can create ambiguity as to what we are in fact analyzing. The use of different sets of analytical terms is not just a problem of translation across the scientific metalanguage of different languages. What counts as the object of study is influenced by how we conceptualize it, which is influenced, in turn, by the words we use and the broader fields of meaning they inhabit. For example, when we study "politeness" in Japanese or "Japanese politeness," it is not always clear what in fact is our object of study. Are we studying (1) a scientific concept from English as it manifests itself in Japanese, (2) an analogous scientific concept from Japanese, or (3) a lay concept in Japanese that is analogous to lay concepts in English? Moreover, given scientific notions are invariably drawn from lay concepts (Eelen 2001; Watts, Ide and Ehlich 1992), there is the additional complication of potential vacillation between so-called first-order, lay notions, such as *politeness* in English and *teinei* in Japanese, and second-order, scientific conceptualizations of "politeness." It is clear, then, that not only do politeness researchers always need to be explicit about their own object of study, but that they need to consider the extent to which their understandings are reconcilable with those of other researchers.

At the core of such questions is the issue of *whose* understanding we are in fact analyzing. All the above notions are clearly legitimate objects of study, but it is important to make clear whether we are analyzing the understanding(s) of the participants, a theorist, or both. While in first-wave studies second-order understandings of "politeness" of theoreticians were considered paramount, in second-wave studies of politeness research the pendulum shifted firmly across to lay, first-order understandings of participants. In recent times, however, it has been suggested that these two perspectives are not, in fact, mutually exclusive, and that ultimately politeness researchers need to engage with the understandings of both users and observers.

A move to grounding politeness research in the understandings of both users and observers does, however, necessitate careful consideration of the analytical lens we use to study and, ultimately, theorize politeness. In theorizing politeness we are ultimately seeking to elucidate the moral bases for the converging and diverging understandings of politeness that can be observed to arise amongst users and observers. In other words, what are the moral grounds for particular users or observers to be evaluating the (linguistic) behavior of others or themselves as "polite"?

The growing body of work on the notion of *teinei(na)*, a common translation of *polite*, in Japanese and how it both converges and diverges with the concept of *polite(ness)* in different varieties of English is rather instructive in that respect. For instance, in a multivariate analysis of terms associated with *polite* and *teineina* amongst speakers of American English and Japanese respectively, Ide, Hill, Carnes, Ogino, and Kawasaki (1992) found that while there was some overlap, being friendly was not associated with being polite in Japanese as summarized in Table 26.2.

Table 26.2 *Terms associated with (American English)* polite *and (Japanese)* teineina

polite	teineina
respectful	*keii no aru*
considerate	*omoiyari no aru*
pleasant	*kanji no yoi*
friendly	
appropriate	*tekisetsuna*

(Adapted from Ide et al. 1992: 291)

In a related study, Pizziconi (2007) used multidimensional scaling techniques to compare the lexical fields of *polite* and *teineina* amongst speakers of British English and Japanese, respectively. Amongst British English speakers, three main clusters were found: (1) *polite, well-mannered, courteous*, (2) *nice, kind, friendly*, and (3) *appropriate, educated*, with *considerate* lying between the first two clusters. Three main clusters also emerged amongst Japanese speakers. However, these were constituted somewhat differently: (1) *teineina, reigitadashii* ('appropriate,' 'well-mannered'), *jōhinna* ('refined,' 'genteel'), (2) *shinsetsuna* ('kind'), *omoiyari no aru* ('considerate'), *seijitsuna* ('sincere,' 'decent'), and (3) *kenkyona* ('modest'), *herikudaru* ('humble'), *enryogachina* ('reserved,' 'restrained'), with *wakimae* ('discerning') lying between the first and third clusters.

It is clear from such studies that when we talk of *politeness* in different varieties of English, or *teineisa* in Japanese, these two words have somewhat different underlying conceptual structures. To complicate matters further, we cannot assume, of course, that the other concepts that make up this meaning field are equivalent across these languages. It has been argued, for instance, that the notions of *omoiyari no aru* in Japanese and *considerate* in English do not necessarily always refer to the same thing (Travis 1998). This is because *omoiyari (no aru)* itself lies within its own distinct meaning field, albeit one that overlaps in some respects with that of *teineina*.

Linguists arguably have much to offer in helping politeness researchers to unpack the kinds of complex meta-linguistic and conceptual issues that arise when undertaking politeness research across different languages. It is important to bear in mind, however, that what underpins politeness is not simply the abstracted understanding of a concept that emerges when one studies the meanings of words across aggregated populations of speakers of a language. Individual users of a language may invoke situated understandings that are influenced by their own personal histories and experiences of the concept in question (Shimizu 2000: 225). In politeness research we are interested not only in abstracted and aggregated understandings of relevant concepts, but also in situated understandings of the various evaluative concepts that are invoked by users and observers in grounding their evaluations of a particular (linguistic) behavior as polite.

In this section, it has been suggested that we need to unpack the concepts and related metalanguage that underpins our study of politeness across languages, including in Japanese. Without paying due attention to differences in the way in which we conceptualize politeness across languages, we are left without a clear understanding of what constitutes our object of study. Given language plays a key role in the way in which we conceptualize such phenomena, linguists clearly have an important contribution to make to politeness research. We now move to consider the role these kinds of evaluative concepts might play in the accomplishment of politeness in interaction.

4 Politeness in Interaction

A polite stance can, of course, be indexed through the use of particular honorifics in situated contexts, including through various speech style shift practices. However, this is not the only way in which politeness can be accomplished in Japanese. In this section, we focus on two distinct practices by which participants can indicate an orientation on their part to issues of politeness in addition to their use of honorifics. The first practice involves the reciprocation of thanking, and the role repetition plays in negotiating the debt–credit equilibrium (Ohashi 2013). The second practice involves attenuating upshots in ways that allow colleagues to delicately negotiate their respective roles and entitlements in the workplace (Haugh 2015). The focus in this section on discursive practices is not meant to be taken as suggesting that such linguistic forms are not important, but rather that we should not limit ourselves to the study of honorific forms in advancing our understanding of politeness in Japanese. Indeed, it will become apparent that close analytical attention needs to be directed to the linguistic formulation of these turns-at-talk if we are to get a proper grasp on our object of study.

The first example is taken from a recording of a telephone conversation that forms part of a broader study on thanking in Japanese (Ohashi 2013). The conversation has been transcribed using conversation analysis (CA) conventions (Jefferson 2004), although it has been simplified somewhat in order to draw attention to the most salient aspects of the interaction for this analysis. Prior to the call, Ken, who is good friends with Akiko's husband, offered to lend his car to Akiko's family, as he had heard that they needed a larger car to take a trip. Ken cleaned the car and delivered it to Akiko's family for them to use on the trip. Akiko has just called to thank Ken prior to taking the trip.

(7) A: Akiko, K: Ken

1 A: *moshi mo [shi dōmo::]*
hello hello thanks

2 K: *[a:: dōmo]*
ah thanks

3 A: *hontō ni arigato ne=*
really thank.you SFP
'Really thank you so much.'

4 K: *=ie ie tondemonai*
no no not.at.all
'No not at all.'

5 A: *un soide konaida wa arigato ne*
uh and other.day TOP thank.you SFP
'And also the other day, thank you.'

6	K:	*iya*	*iya*	*i[ya]*			
		no	no	no			
		'No, no no.'					
7	A:	*[tōi]*	*tokoro*	*kara*	*kite*	*kurete*	
		far	place	from	come-GER	BEN-GER	
		'For coming such a long distance.'					
8	K:	*iya*	*iya*	*zenzen,*	*de*	*daijōbu*	*sō?=*
		no	no	not.at.all	and	alright	appear
		'Not at all, is the car okay?'					
9	A:	*=kaiteki*	*kaiteki*				
		comfortable	comfortable				
		'(It's) comfortable, comfortable.'					

(adapted from Ohashi 2013: 83–84)

While neither of the participants here uses any honorifics, enabling them to index a relatively close relationship as family friends of similar age, the exchange here clearly involves an orientation on the part of both participants to issues of politeness. After the initial mutual greeting (lines 1–2), Akiko launches a thanking turn (line 3) where the illocutionary force indicating device, *arigato* 'thank you,' is upgraded through an adverbial (*hontō ni* 'really'). While the object of this thanks is not specified by Akiko, through the turn-final *ne*, she treats this object as already known (i.e. Ken lending the car to Akiko's family). More importantly, she also displays her concern about the impact of this thanking on their ongoing "interpersonal alignment" (Morita 2012a: 304). Ken's response where he disagrees with the need for such thanking (line 4) indicates what this display of concern on Akiko's part may involve, namely, the "social disquietude" that she feels as the benefactee of Ken's offer. Ken's disagreement fosters affiliation through mitigating Akiko's implicit stance that she is a benefactee who has created an imbalance in their ongoing interpersonal relationship.

Akiko follows with another thanks directed at Ken (line 5), although this time it is explicitly formulated as distal, that is, for a previous event *konaida* 'the other day' (as opposed to immediate thanking for a service or object received in the current here-and-now). In doing so, she frames this current turn as a second thanking, one which indicates her ongoing sense of gratitude to Ken for his offer. Second thanking, that is, thanking for a prior service or offer when encountering the benefactor after the event in question is a practice by which participants reconstitute their roles as benefactee–benefactor in order to demonstrate that prior services are not forgotten. Once again, the turn-final *ne* indicates her "social disquietude" about the implications of this apparent imbalance in their relationship (Morita 2012a: 304), a display that occasions another disagreement with the need for such "thanking" from Ken (line 6).

Akiko goes on to specify the object of her second thanking, namely, Ken bringing the car over to them by explicitly construing herself as the beneficiary, through the benefactive verb *kureru* 'give,' of an action that likely brought trouble to him (line 7). Once again, Ken disagrees with the need for this display of concern on her part, before shifting the topic by inquiring whether the car meets their needs (line 8).

In the course of this sequence, then, we can see the two participants pivoting between their respective roles as benefactee and benefactor. Notably, Akiko uses repetition to emphasize her stance as benefactee, and to acknowledge her indebtedness to Ken, while Ken downplays his role as benefactor by denying her indebtedness to him. Through this repeated "acknowledging benefit/debt-denigrating credit" adjacency pair, the two participants orient to the potential (im)propriety of allowing an imbalance in the debt–credit equilibrium to continue (Ohashi 2013: 84). In other words, politeness is interactionally accomplished through reciprocating concern for the respective positions of each other in relation to the debt–credit equilibrium that is being invoked in the course of this sequence.

While reciprocation and repetition lie at the core of the way in which politeness is accomplished in the above interaction, in the next excerpt, the participants orient to issues of politeness, (im)propriety, and the like through leaving things unsaid. Prior to this excerpt, Satomi and Matthew, two colleagues in a Japanese importing company based in Australia, have been talking about what information needs to be included on the label of a particular fruit juice product. While Satomi has a slightly higher rank in the company than Matthew, she is not his supervisor and so decisions are often made by them jointly. Just prior to where this excerpt begins they have been discussing whether to include information about the lycopene content of the juice. While Matthew, who is responsible for marketing has suggested they include information about the lycopene content, Satomi, who is responsible for designing labels, has just pointed out that if they include that information, they will need to do the same for the amount of lemon.

(8) S: Satomi, M: Matthew

33	S:	*ja:*	*remon*	*wa*	*tte*	*koto*	*ni*	*natta*	*toki*	*ni*
		then	lemon	TOP	QUOT	thing	to	became	time	in
		'When we are asked, "well, how about lemon?"'								
34	M:	*un*								
		'Yeah.'								
35	S:	*nante*		*shi-tara*						
		how		do-COND						
		'How can we'								
36	M:	*shiraberu?*								
		find.out								
		'(Should we) find it out?'								

37 (2.5)
38 S: *dō shi-yō ka*
how do-VOL Q
'What should we do?'
39 (3.0)
40 S: *un sō. dakara atashi koko no e ni wa*
hmm that.way therefore I here GEN picture in TOP
41 *kaka-nakat-ta n da yo=*
write-NEG-PST NMLZ COP SFP
'Hmm, yeah, that's why I didn't put it on this picture.'
42 M: *=u::n*
'yeah'
43 S: *bunshō de hidari-gawa ni kaitoi-ta n da yo*
paragraph at left-side in put-PST NMLZ COP SFP
'I put that in a paragraph on the left.'
44 M: *u::n*
'Well.'
45 (20.0)
46 M: *at-ta hō ga ii to omou n dat-tara*
have-PST way NOM good QUOT think NMLZ COP-COND
47 *kantanni shiraberareru to omou n da kedo*
easily can.find QUOT think NMLZ COP but
48 *<hitsuyō na no kana:> kore mo*
necessary NMLZ wonder this also
'If you think [that information] should be there, then I can easily find it out, but I wonder if this is really necessary.'
49 S: *HONto ni chotto desho (.) go-pāsento miman dakara ne*
really little probably 5-percent under so SFP
'It's really a small amount, isn't it? It's under 5%.'
50 M: *iya iya iya motto (.) motto aru motto aru*
no no no more more have more have
'No, no, no, more. It has more. It has more.'
51 S: *↑a sō↓ na no?*
oh that.way COP NMLZ
'Ah, is that really?'
52 M: %they are organic%
53 S: *a sō na no*
oh that.way COP NMLZ
'Ah, is that so?'

54 M: *desho (.)* *ja:*
probably then
'It is, isn't it? So'

55 S: *a:* *sō* *da* *ne* *ja:* *shirabe-te* *sa:*
oh that.way COP SFP then find.out-GER SFP
'Ah, that's right, then you find it out, and'

56 M: *un*
'Yeah.' (adapted from Watanabe 2009: 178–181)

Satomi raises the problem that if they are going to include lemon juice content on the label they will need to find out this information. She formulates the problem as contingent using an "asking conditional" that constitutes an implicit challenge to Matthew's stance, on the one hand, and yet invites him to "engage in joint decision making about the proposed plan" (Stevanovic 2013: 519), on the other. Notably, the upshot of this asking conditional is left "designedly ambiguous" (Mori and Nakamura 2008: 53), thereby leaving space for Matthew to make a decision. In this way, Satomi indexes a low degree of entitlement to be making such a decision on her own, thereby accomplishing her implicit challenge as open to evaluation as polite by Matthew. He responds, in turn, with a proposal that they find out this information (line 36), although in being formulated as a question rather than being asserted, Matthew decreases his degree of commitment to his prior stance that they should include information about lycopene content on the label. In this way, he reciprocates Satomi's orientation to a low degree of entitlement to be making this decision on his own.

However, rather than responding to Matthew's question, Satomi goes on to muse, in line 38, about what they should do through a soliloquy-like utterance (Hasegawa 2010). Her response thus constitutes a form of delayed repetition (Mori 1999: 80) whereby she frames her stance as dispreferred. She then goes on to offer an account as to why she didn't include the lycopene content in her previous design (lines 40–41, 43), with the upshot of this account being left attenuated. The turn-final *yo* here frames this account as one that be "acknowledged and acted upon" (Morita 2012b: 1721). In doing so, Satomi subtly indicates her doubt about Matthew's proposal.

A long period of silence follows (line 45) before Matthew finally responds that if they think this information about lemon juice content needs to be included it should be relatively easy to find out (lines 46–47). However, he also muses in line 48 whether this is necessary through a soliloquy-like utterance (Hasegawa 2010) that leaves open space for Satomi to respond. Satomi then implies that these things need not be included on the label through suggesting it is not worth finding out the lemon juice content because it is likely only a small amount (line 49). However, this assumption is soundly rejected by Matthew (line 50). This is treated as new information by Satomi (lines 51, 53), and Matthew responds with the epistemic auxiliary, *deshō*, whereby he indexes relative certainty about this claim as well as his assumption that the recipient is likely to know this and so agree (Kamio 1997: 77–78). Thus, what is initially framed as a correction of Satomi's apparently incorrect assumption is subsequently construed as something on which they likely both agree. This allows for the decision that they go ahead and find out the lemon juice content to be one reached by mutual agreement. Indeed, it is Satomi who explicates this upshot (line 55), notably with a turn-final *sa* that indicates this proposed course of action is "non-negotiable" (Morita 2005: 26).

In the course of this sequence, then, the two colleagues are negotiating their respective decision-making entitlements through a number of features of both their own turn design and their responses to the other participant's prior turns. In this way, they reciprocate the orientation to this decision-making process as a delicate one, which reflects, in turn, a concern for not overstepping their respective deontic entitlements in relation to making decisions (Stevanovic 2013: 519).

What arguably underpins the accomplishment of politeness in the two examples discussed here is the negotiation of their respective roles (Haugh and Obana 2011: 175; Long 2010: 1060), and a display of mutual concern for each other's entitlements with respect to these roles. These analyses are, of course, only partial, and not meant to cover all the different ways in which politeness may arise in Japanese. However, what they suggest is that by closely examining the ways in which the linguistic composition of talk-in-interaction is carefully calibrated by participants, we can observe the ways in which they display their concern not only for the situational contingencies and demands of conversational interaction itself, but also with issues of propriety, appropriateness, and politeness. Attention to linguistic form, including but not limited to the use of honorifics, is thus evidently an important locus of concern for politeness researchers.

5 Summary and Future Directions

In surveying work to date on interpersonal dimensions of the use of Japanese, it has become apparent that there are two quite distinct traditions. On the one hand, there is the long-standing national language studies tradition of studying honorifics and relational expressions. On the other hand, we have witnessed the more recent emergence of the study of politeness in the linguistics pragmatics tradition. While the respective objects of study, and preferred methods of analysis, in those two traditions have been somewhat different, the influence of the former is apparent from the heavy emphasis placed on the role of honorifics and speech style shift amongst politeness researchers in the latter tradition.

In this chapter it has been suggested that while such research is indeed valuable, it should be complemented by studies that focus on how politeness is conceptualized in Japanese and the ways in which it is interactionally accomplished. It has been argued that linguists have much to offer this endeavor, with respect both to analyzing the metalanguage that underpins the varied notions of politeness in Japanese and to analyzing the role that the specific linguistic composition of talk-in-interaction plays in the interactional accomplishment of politeness.

Looking forward, there remains much to be done in this space. While researchers focusing on the study of relational expressions have noted the importance of analyzing expressions that come under the broad umbrella of "impoliteness," there have only been a limited number of studies to date that have focused on such phenomena in Japanese. The ways in which participants may laminate ostensibly affiliative, "polite" stances onto ostensibly disaffiliative, impolite stances in Japanese have also been relatively neglected, including phenomena that come under the umbrella of "mock impoliteness" and "mock politeness" in the linguistic pragmatics tradition. It is thus becoming increasingly evident that the study of linguistic forms and their interpersonal functions in Japanese by (im)politeness researchers necessarily includes, but should not be limited to, the study of honorifics.

27

Speech Style Shift

Haruko Minegishi Cook

1 Introduction

This chapter overviews research on Japanese speech style shift between so-called "addressee honorifics," the *desu/masu* form, and its non-honorific counterpart, the plain form,[1] and shows that speech style shift is not a simple rule-based linguistic operation but rather a dynamic, creative, and complex pragmatic phenomenon.[2] Scholars have investigated functions of the *desu/masu* and plain forms and social and/or psychological factors that trigger a shift between the two forms. Since the mid-1960s, speech style shift has been extensively discussed in the literature on Japanese sociolinguistics and pragmatics published in English.

As "there is no socially unmarked form" in Japanese (Matsumoto 1988c: 418), the verbal in the main clause must be marked either with the addressee honorific form or the plain form. The addressee honorific form is called *teineitai* 'polite style' in Japanese, and the plain form, *jōtai* 'ordinary style.' It is generally assumed that the social meaning of *teineitai* is politeness to the addressee while that of *jōtai* is non-politeness. In this chapter, however, I refer to the addressee honorifics as the *desu/masu* form because the term *teineitai* or polite form is misleading in the sense that this implies that the function of this form is solely a marker of politeness.[3] As discussed below, the *desu/masu* form does not always express politeness to the addressee but indexes a wide range of social meaning. The addressee honorific forms are the morpheme *-mas*, which is suffixed to the verb stem,

I am grateful to Shigeko Okamoto and Yoko Hasegawa for helpful comments on earlier drafts of this chapter.

[1] Although speech style shift involves not only a shift between *desu/masu* and plain forms but also other linguistic features (cf. Jones and Ono 2008), this chapter focuses on the most widely discussed speech style shift in the literature, namely that between the *desu/masu* and plain forms.

[2] In more recent years, scholars have investigated the acquisition of speech style shift by L2 learners of Japanese. This body of research, however, is beyond the scope of this chapter.

[3] The addressee honorific form is also referred to as [+distal] or "formal style" while the plain form is also called [–distal] or "*da*-style."

Table 27.1 *Three predicate types and gerund in the* desu/masu *and plain forms*

Clause type	*Desu/masu* form		Plain form	
Verbal	Verb stem-*mas-u* (present) Verb stem-*mas-en* (negative) Verb stem-*mashi-ta* (past) Verb stem-*mashi-te* (gerund)		Verb stem-*(r)u* (present) Verb stem-*nai* (negative) Verb stem-*ta* (past) Verb stem-*(t)te* (gerund)	
Adjectival	Adj +	copula *des-u* (present) *deshi-ta* (past) *deshi-te* (gerund)	Adj	 *-i* (present) *-kat-ta* (past) *-kute* (gerund)
Nominal	Nom +	copula *des-u* (present) *deshi-ta* (past) *deshi-te* (gerund)	Nom +	copula *da* (present) *dat-ta* (past) *de* (gerund)

and the copula *des*. Table 27.1 shows morphological variants of the *desu/masu* and plain forms.

The marking of the *desu/masu* or plain form does not affect the referential meaning of a sentence as shown in Example (1).

(1) a. *Tarō* *wa* *gakusei* ***desu***. [*desu/masu*]
TOP student COP
'Taro is a student.'

b. *Tarō* *wa* *gakusei* ***da***. [plain]
TOP student COP
'Taro is a student.'

In (1a) the copula is in the *desu/masu* form (*desu*), while in (1b) it is in the plain form (*da*). The referential meanings of (1a) and (1b) are identical, but the social meanings differ. The usual analysis is that (1a) shows politeness to the addressee whereas (1b) does not.

The social meaning of "politeness" is indicated by the predicate form in the main clause, while the predicate in a subordinate clause remains in the plain form. Example (2a) is considered polite while (2b) is not because the main clause verb in (2a) is in the *desu/masu* form, and that in (2b) is in the plain form even though the copula in the subordinate clause in (2a) is in the plain form.[4]

(2) a. *Watashi wa [Tarō ga gakusei* ***da****] to* ***omoimasu***. [*desu/masu*]
I TOP NOM student COP QUOT think
'I think that Taro is a student.'

b. *Watashi wa [Tarō ga gakusei* ***da****] to* ***omou***. [plain]
I TOP NOM student COP QUOT think
'I think that Taro is a student.'

[4] However, it is a stylistic option to mark the subordinate clause verbal with the *desu/masu* form, which is considered very formal.

This chapter is organized as follows: Section 2 reviews earlier studies on speech style shift, followed by Section 3, which discusses a widely assumed view, that of the *desu/masu* form as a marker of distance. Section 4 presents more recent studies on speech style shift from the indexical perspective. Section 5 discusses the distinction between naked and non-naked plain forms, a subject that has not been widely researched. Section 6 explores how speech style shifts serve as linguistic resources for construction of social realities in various social contexts, and Section 7 concludes the chapter.

2 The *Desu/Masu* Form as a Marker of Politeness: Rule-based Analysis

In the *Kokugogaku* 'Japanese language studies' tradition in Japan, Japanese grammarians discuss the *desu/masu* forms in the context of the study of *keigo* 'honorifics.' They are concerned with the taxonomy of *keigo* (e.g. Oishi 1975) or with how *keigo* functions as what they call *taigū-hyōgen* 'expressions of considerateness' (e.g. Minami 1987a; Kikuchi 1994). For example, Minami pursued the questions of what *keigo* indicates and what functions *keigo* has in human communication. He claimed that the functions of addressee honorifics are the opening and closing of social relationships, the maintenance of social relationships, and expressions of aesthetic value.

In the Western linguistics paradigm, the basic assumption of previous studies on speech style is that the *desu/masu* form is a marker of politeness and that there is a one-to-one relationship between the speech style and the context of its use. Scholars who take this view proposed a rule-based analysis. Martin (1964: 408), who analyzed factors that influence the speaker's choice, proposed that the speaker chooses the polite style (*desu/masu* form) when he or she speaks to someone outside his or her group, or to a higher-status person in terms of social position, age, or sex.

Niyekawa's proposal of speech levels (1991: 41–47) exemplifies the rule-based view of Japanese speech styles. According to her proposal, there are four speech levels in Japanese: the neutral speech style level and three polite-speech styles. While the neutral speech style level (N-level) corresponds to an informal relationship, the *desu/masu* form is associated with the three polite speech style levels (P-levels). The P-0 level incorporates only the *desu/masu* form, and the P-1 and P-2 levels combine the *desu/masu* form and referent honorifics. While the N-level is equated with informal contexts such as conversations between family members or close friends, the P-levels are associated with formal relationships. However, examining naturally occurring speech, we find that most speakers are not single speech-level speakers in a given social situation. It is not uncommon for speakers to change speech styles throughout the course of talk with the same addressee in the same setting.

Ide (1982a) discussed speech style shift in terms of *wakimae* 'discernment.' Her rule-based approach to politeness proposed the following social rules in Japanese society.

(3) Ground rules:
Rule 1 – Be polite to a person of a higher social status
Rule 2 – Be polite to a person with power
Rule 3 – Be polite to an older person
Overriding rule: Be polite in a formal setting (1982: 366–371)

Ide explains that these rules operate when the speaker uses the polite speech-level marker, the *desu/masu* form, in talking to an addressee of a higher social status, an addressee with more power, and/or an older addressee. She claims that the notion of politeness in Japanese society is best described by *wakimae*, which is obligatory. In this perspective, the use of the *desu/masu* and plain forms is regulated by social rules (*wakimae*), and any usage that deviates from the rules is perceived as a violation or incorrect usage. This prescriptive view is often adopted in *keigo* 'honorifics' usage books written for native Japanese speakers as well as Japanese language textbooks for learners of Japanese as a foreign language. However, this static, rule-based analysis does not capture the dynamic nature of human interaction.

The rule-based analysis does not adequately account for many usages of the *desu/masu* and plain forms. Assuming that the *desu/masu* form is a marker of politeness and the plain form is one of non-politeness, Usami (2002) investigated seventy-two dyadic conversations between newly acquainted people in order to see how the social dimensions of age and gender affect speech style shift. She found that the dominant speech style in this context is the *desu/masu* form but that age difference can at times trigger a shift to the plain form. In other words, an older speaker may speak to a younger speaker using the plain form. Usami interprets such a shift to the plain form as a display of "positive politeness" (Brown and Levinson 1987) in a power relationship between interactants. Although we do not know the age of the interactants in each of the dyads in this study, a shift to the plain form could be interpreted as a sign of a status difference.

Other studies report that not only an older speaker but also a younger speaker can shift to the plain form in a power relationship (e.g. Cook 2006; Okamoto 1999, 2011; Saito 2010). For example, in a conversation between a professor and a student, the student can use the plain form in exclamatory expressions and soliloquy-like remarks. In Example (4), which comes from my study of academic consultations in Japanese universities, the student freely shifts to the plain form in such contexts.[5] The professor

[5] Examples (4–9) of this chapter are drawn from my previous work or my own data. These data are all naturally occurring discourse.

asks the student a question in line 1 using the *desu/masu* form. According to the notion of *wakimae*, this use of the *desu/masu* form is interpreted as the professor's indexing his sense of place in the formal setting, an academic consultation. However, we note a "violation" of *wakimae* in this segment, namely the student's use of the plain form in lines 6 and 7, where he makes soliloquy-like remarks.

(4) P (professor), S (student)[6]

1 P: *Ano ichiban:: kore ga sono: mondai da tte iu,*
well most this NOM that problem COP QUOT say
sō iu na- nante iu ka sō iu no arimasu ka?
so say wh- what say Q so say NMLZ exist Q
'Uh this one is the number one problem, is there any sort of- that sort of thing?'

2 S: *E:tto* ((coughs))
well
'Well'

3 P: *Nan- ste- e: Pinkā to sono Binsu no koko kore ga*
what- st- uh and that Vince GEN here this NOM
tadashii toka ne, sō iu no
correct etc. SFP so say NMLZ
'Wel- Ste- uh this one by Pinker and Vince is correct, it's that sort of thing'

4 S: *Ee:to*
'Well'

5 P: *Mata koko wa okashii toka* ((sniffling)) (3.0)
also this TOP strange etc.
'Or this part is strange, etc.'

6 → S: *Doko datta kke na* (12.0) ((sniffling and turning pages of the book))
where COP SFP SFP
'Where was it, I wonder.'

7 → S: *Ano:: nan- nan datta kke na*
well wha- what COP SFP SFP
'Uh, I wonder what- what that was.'

8 → P: *Kore ronbun to shite wa sugoi nagai ronbun da yo ne* ( )
this thesis as TOP very long thesis COP SFP SFP
'As for theses, this is a very long one, right? ( )'

Does the student in this example act in an impolite manner, violating the social etiquette of Japanese society? In this example, the professor does not react negatively to the student's utterances that end in the plain form in lines 6 and 7. Instead, he shifts his utterance to the plain form in line 8 to align his stance to that of the student. By so doing, the two participants

[6] Example (4) is drawn from my data but was not included in my previous publications.

construct a more personal relationship momentarily. This fact suggests that the student's use of the plain form does not necessarily index impolite attitude to the professor.

Similarly, Saito (2010), who studied interactions between a superior and subordinates in a small company, found that the subordinates use the plain form in interaction with their superior but when they speak to each other they orient to the informational content. These studies provide evidence that rigid social rules cannot fully explain the intricacies of social life. The rule-based analysis views the participants of a speech event as passive observers of socially agreed-upon rules. Participants in most social events, however, are active agents who create their identity and other social dimensions in discursive practice.

The social rules presented by Niyekawa (1991) and Ide (1982a) are, in fact, a part of the widely accepted language ideology of honorifics in Japanese society. We need to distinguish actual practice from language ideology when discussing speech style shift.

3 The *Desu/Masu* Form as a Marker of Distance and *Soto*

3.1 Interpersonal or Psychological Distance

Some scholars claim that the *desu/masu* form is a marker of interpersonal or psychological distance (Hinds 1978a; Ikuta 1983; Jorden and Noda 1987). Based on his findings from interview data, Hinds (1978a) claims that the *desu/masu* form is chosen when there is a perceived social distance between interlocutors. Ikuta (1983), who studied a TV interview program, proposes that the *desu/masu* form indicates [+distance], and the plain form [–distance] in interpersonal relationships. She asserts that speakers obligatorily choose one of the forms according to the social situation, but they can shift to a level appropriate to their momentary feelings. The explanation that the *desu/masu* form indexes interpersonal or psychological distance is in line with the notion of "negative politeness" (Brown and Levinson 1987) and explains why the *desu/masu* form is a polite form. This analysis, however, does not account for uses of the *desu/masu* form when this form does not mark interpersonal or psychological distance. For instance, a mother can often speak in the *desu/masu* form when she serves food to her children as shown in Example (5). This is a family conversation between the mother and her five-year-old son, H. The mother talks to H using the plain form most of the time. In this example the mother and H are talking about diving beetles which eat killifish in lines 1 to 3. They are speaking in the plain form. But in line 4, prefacing with the discourse marker *sa*, which announces a new activity follows, the mother shifts to the *desu/masu* form asking H what kind of jam he wants to eat.

(5) [Family O] (lines 4–7 appeared in Cook 1997: 702; glosses are added.)

1 H: *Medaka tte ii?* [plain]
killifish QUOT good
'Is killifish good?'

2 M: *Sō ne. Ma yoku wa nai ka.* [plain]
so SFP well good TOP NEG Q
'Well, it is not that good.'

3 *Demo nanka, medaka taberarechattara iya ja nai.* [plain]
but somehow killifish eat.if no.good NEG
'But if diving beetles eat killifish, that not good.'

4 M: *Sa jamu desu ka?* [*desu/masu*]
well jam COP Q
'well, (you) want jam?'

5 M: *Apurikotto jamu desu ka, choko desu ka?* [*desu/masu*]
apricot jam COP Q chocolate COP Q
'(Do you want) apricot jam or chocolate?'

6 H: *Boku wa jamu da na.* [plain]
I TOP jam COP SFP
'I want jam.'

7 M: *Hai hai.*
'Yes, yes.'

Why does she shift to the *desu/masu* form in this instance? It would seem strange if the mother were distancing herself when serving food to the children, for the mealtime is a time of sharing among family members. How "interpersonal distance" is employed in interaction is highly complex. As we can see from this example, the notion of interpersonal or psychological distance does not fully capture the complexity of *desu/masu* usages. I will return to this example in Section 4.2.

3.2 *Uchi* and *Soto*

Some scholars (e.g. Makino 2002; Sukle 1994) directly link the *desu/masu* and plain forms to *soto* 'outside/out-group' and *uchi* 'inside/in-group,' respectively, an important cultural distinction in Japanese society (Bachnik and Quinn 1994; Lebra 1976). The *uchi/soto* 'inside/outside' orientations organize Japanese self, society, and language. While *uchi* evokes the notions of familiarity, proximity, inclusion, certainty, and control, *soto* evokes unfamiliarity, distance, exclusion, uncertainty, and lack of control (Quinn 1994). Although this distinction exists in every society, because it organizes the self, society, and language, it is particularly meaningful within Japanese society. *Uchi/soto* defines different sets of behavioral patterns (Bachnik and Quinn 1994; Lebra 1976).

Makino (2002: 123) considers the plain form as the form "primarily used when speaking with a person or persons in *uchi* space, a space in which casual communication takes place" and the *desu/masu* form as the form "primarily used when speaking with a person or persons in *soto* space, a space in which formal interactions take place." That is, mutual *desu/masu* exchanges indicate a polite, formal, or "outside" (*soto*) relationship between the interlocutors, whereas mutual plain form exchanges indicate an informal or "inside" (*uchi*) relationship.

Sukle (1994) investigates directives in four different locations (a railway ticket window, a post office window, a neighborhood vegetable market, and a middle-class family).[7] He found that the frequency of the *desu/masu* form used in directives is proportionate to the degree of distance between interlocutors appropriate to the location. In other words, at a railway ticket window and a post office window, which are both considered to be *soto* 'out-group/outside' contexts, only the *desu/masu* form occurred whereas in family conversation, which is a typical *uchi* 'in-group/inside' context, the plain form was mainly used. Relating the *desu/masu* and plain forms to the notions of *soto* and *uchi*, respectively, however, cannot explain the non-reciprocal use of these forms (also see Matsumoto and Okamoto 2003 for criticism of Sukle 1994). For example, in a situation in which a professor speaks to a student in the plain form while the student speaks to the professor in the *desu/masu* form, it is rather confusing to say that the two interlocutors create the *uchi* and *soto* space simultaneously in the same interaction. This problem arises from directly linking the linguistic forms (the *desu/masu* and plain forms) to contextual features (*soto* and *uchi*).

In sum, some previous studies have assumed that the *desu/masu* and plain forms are directly linked to only one social meaning and have not taken into account that these forms are indexical in nature.

4 Indexical Approach

An indexical approach to speech style shift considers the *desu/masu* and plain forms to be indexes and the social meanings of these forms to come in part from the social dimensions in which the forms are used. This approach can explain a wide range of social meanings associated with these forms and how the linguistic forms as indexes evoke a certain social context in speech situations.

4.1 Indexicality

I will briefly discuss the notion of indexicality and the view of honorifics as indexical signs (Silverstein 1976a). Indexical signs by nature have multiple (and often ambiguous) social meanings because a part of the

[7] In his study, Sukle (1994) included the request form, *-te kudasai*, in the *masu* form.

meaning of an index lies in the context in which the index occurs. Thus, the meaning of an index varies from context to context. This, however, does not mean that linguistic forms that function as indexes are entirely dependent upon their context in sense making. Rather, as a linguistic sign, an index is directly associated with a certain social dimension and further enriched by the context of actual use. Let us consider, for example, the semiotic functions of the deictic word *I*. The first person pronoun *I* has a typical and schematic core meaning that is directly linked to the current speaker at the time of utterance. This core meaning helps to index different situational meanings in actual speech situations. When the speaker changes, the deictic word *I* acquires a different situational meaning. When the current speaker is Bill, *I* points to Bill, but when the speaker changes to Mary, *I* indexes Mary. As exemplified by the personal pronoun *I*, the core meaning of an index is schematic and underspecified, but enriched by actual use.

To capture the fluidity and multiplicity of indexical meaning, a two-step model of indexicality has been proposed by Ochs (1990, 1996, 2002) in which indexes are divided into direct and indirect indexes. She claims that – cross-linguistically – acts and stances (epistemic and affective stances) are directly indexed by linguistic forms, and other social dimensions are entailed (i.e. indirectly indexed) in the context. In other words, the act or stance directly indexed by a linguistic form can further index a range of situational meanings mediated by the local ideology and/or other co-occurring linguistic and non-linguistic features. A model of indexicality that directly links honorifics to affective stance but makes other dimensions of social context entailments mediated by local ideology and other co-occurring features can capture the multiplicity and fluidity of the social meaning of honorifics.

Drawing on Ochs's model of indexicality, I have proposed that the *desu/masu* form directly indexes the affective stance of self-presentation (or on-stage acting in role) and that this core meaning helps constitute a variety of social meanings in different social situations (Cook 1996a, 1997). The notion, "self-presentational stance" is defined as the self that presents an on-stage display of a positive social role to the addressee. It is the particular affective stance of presenting oneself to other(s) when one is literally or figuratively "on stage" and being watched by others. In Japanese, the terms, *shisei o tadasu* 'to hold oneself up,' or *kichin to suru* 'to do something neatly' describe this affective stance. This analysis is consistent with Maynard's proposal (1993) that the *desu/masu* form is more likely to be used when the speaker's awareness of the addressee becomes high. Thus, the affective stance of self-presentation is characterized by the speaker's heightened awareness of the addressee. In what follows, I will illustrate how the affective stance of self-presentation can evoke a range of social meanings.

4.2 Social Meanings of the *Desu/Masu* Form

In this section, I explain how the social meanings of the *desu/masu* form are context dependent and vary from context to context or even from moment to moment. This is because as an indexical sign, the core meaning of the *desu/masu* form takes on a particular aspect of the context in which it is used and evokes social meaning(s) *via* association with the contextual aspect.

The self-presentational stance directly indexed by the *desu/masu* form can indirectly index the social identity of a person in charge or a responsible person. Going back to Example (5), we see the mother speaks to the child in the *desu/masu* form when offering food. When the norm of the speech style in family conversation at home is the plain form, why does she shift to the *desu/masu* form in this example? Apparently, the mother's use of the *desu/masu* form does not index a display of politeness to the child. Given the analysis that the direct index of *desu/masu* form is a self-presentational stance, which is in this case the mother's on-stage role in the household, the *desu/masu* form in Example (5) highlights the social identity of the "mother" who is responsible for providing food to the family in the household. By shifting to the *desu/masu* form in this example, she underscores her role as a mother. In other words, she is saying, "As a mother who is in charge of providing food to the family, I am asking you whether you want jam or chocolate." As parents have a responsibility to discipline a child, they sometimes shift to the *desu/masu* form when they do so. In the several different data of family conversations I examined, it was found that mothers often shift to the *desu/masu* form when offering or serving food to the family members. Furthermore, as Example (6) shows, fathers tend to shift to the *desu/masu* form when performing acts that are considered as parental responsibilities. Although these instances of shift to *desu/masu* can simultaneously index other situational meanings such as attention getting, these shifts underscore the role of parents in the household. In Example (6), the parents and their three-year-old daughter A are enjoying eating fruits after the meal (lines 1–10). They are talking in the plain form, but A climbs on the dinner table. In line 11 the father shifts to the *desu/masu* form and tells his child that climbing on the table is not good behavior.

(6) [Family M] (line 11 appeared in Example (6) in Cook 1997: 703; glosses are added.)

1 M: *Hayai wa ne, uchi wa kudamono o taberu no ga ne*
fast SFP SFP us TOP fruit ACC eat NMLZ NOM SFP
'We eat fruits fast, don't we?'
[plain]

2 F: ((laugh))

3 A: *Un*
'Yeah.'

4 M: *Minna mono mo iwazu ni zun zun taberu kara* [plain]
all thing even say.NEG rapidly eat so
'We eat (fruits) rapidly without saying a thing.'

5 A: *Mō saikō* [plain]
already happy
'Already happy.'

6 M: *Mō saikō* ((laugh)) [plain]
already happy
'Already happy.'

7 F: ((laugh))

8 A: *A-chan chaikō* [plain]
happy
'I'm happy.'

9 F: *Saikō* [plain]
happy
'Happy.'

10 M: *Honto ni uchi wa kudamono o taberu no ga hayai*
really we TOP fruit ACC eat NMLZ NOM fast
((laugh)) [plain]
'Really, we eat fruits fast.'

11 ((A gets up on the table))
F: *Otsukue no ue, ogyōgi warui desu yo, sore wa.*
desk GEN TOP manner bad COP SFP that TOP
'On top of the desk, that's bad manners, that is.' [desu/masu]

Here the presentational stance of the father's *desu/masu* form highlights his social identity as the "father" who is responsible for disciplining the child. It is not the case, however, that in every instance when the parents provide food or discipline the child, they shift to the *desu/masu* form. This is because parents are not following a rigid rule but are active agents who create social contexts with linguistic resources. The important point is that parents choose to shift to the *desu/masu* form when they engage in acts in which they are responsible for or in charge of the household. The social meaning of the *desu/masu* form that young Japanese children first experience, then, is someone who is acting in a responsible manner rather than politeness.

The *desu/masu* form can index a person in charge or responsible person outside of family conversation as well. If the *desu/masu* form is used in the context of a workplace or institution, then it can index an identity associated with the workplace or institution. For example, in faculty meetings in secondary schools, teachers predominantly use the *desu/masu* form, particularly in on-stage talk (official and transactional talk), in contrast to use of the plain form in off-stage talk (Geyer 2008: 102), and in college speech club meetings, members speak mostly in the *desu/masu* form to the audience while shifting to the plain form when displaying their emotions

(Dunn 1999). In these cases, the direct index of the *desu/masu* form, affective stance of self-presentation, evokes a person in charge, which is interpreted as the speaker's institutional identity.

How does the indexical account of the *desu/masu* form explain the social meaning of politeness to the addressee? The use of the *desu/masu* form indexes politeness to the addressee in an interaction between adult speakers in a distant relationship (Ikuta 1983) and in speech to an older and/or more powerful addressee (Ide 1982a). The speaker's stance of self-presentation (*shisei o tadasu* 'to hold oneself up') is interpreted as a polite act to an older and/or more powerful addressee.

Indexical meanings of a linguistic form are fluid and multiple, mediated by the situational, cultural, or ideological contexts in which the form is used. Therefore, the core meaning of the *desu/masu* form, affective stance of self-presentation, can simultaneously index more than one social meaning. The *desu/masu* form used by the teachers in faculty meetings, for example, can simultaneously index the institutional identity of "teacher" as well as politeness to the addressees and the formality of the meeting.

Furthermore, Okamoto's study (2011) suggests that a speaker's language ideology can color the use and interpretation of the *desu/masu* and plain forms. Assuming that these forms are indexical signs, Okamoto analyzed speech style shifts in six pairs of dyadic conversation. Each pair consists of an older and a younger speaker. Unlike the dominant language ideology that the younger speaker should talk to the older speaker using the *desu/masu* form, she found wide inter- and intra-speaker variations in the use of these forms. For example, in a conversation between a university professor and his former student, the professor's main clause predicates are marked 54% with *desu/masu* and 46% with the plain form. Okamoto analyzes that the professor's frequent shifts between the two forms is an indication of his ambivalent feelings about the relationship with his former student. In other words, on the one hand, he perceives the interlocutor as his own student, but, on the other hand, he recognizes that she is now a graduate student in a different university, which obscures the hierarchical relationship he used to have with this student. Okamoto concludes that as active agents, speakers choose forms based on their stance toward the dominant language ideology and specific contextual dimensions.

In sum, the indexical approach can account for a number of social meanings the *desu/masu* form indexes in speech contexts as well as a creative aspect of language use.

5 Naked and Non-naked Plain Forms

Most studies on Japanese speech style shift consider binary shifts between the *desu/masu* and plain forms and characterize the plain form as a marker of informal and casual speech. However, the plain form is not always informal or casual. Newspaper articles, academic papers, and other similar genres are typically written in the plain form. Maynard (1993) proposes two types of plain forms, namely *naked* and *non-naked plain forms*. The naked plain form is an instance of the plain form without any discourse marker such as a sentence-final particle. Maynard (1982: 178) points out that the naked plain form is used "when the awareness of the other momentarily lapses." Thus, the naked plain form is typically used in soliloquy. She explains that the speaker uses the non-naked plain form when talking to an addressee in a close relationship in a casual situation because in such a context, the speaker feels the distinction between the self and the addressee becomes non-distinct (i.e. low awareness of the other).

Building on Maynard's proposal, I further developed the notions of naked and non-naked plain forms (Cook 2002, 2008). I observed that in casual conversations, most instances of the plain form co-occur with a linguistic and/or non-linguistic element that has something to do with the speaker's feelings, moods, or attitude such as a sentence-final particle, vowel lengthening, rising intonation, coalescence, a certain voice quality, and laughter, among others. Following Ochs (1996), I call these linguistic elements "affect keys." Thus, the non-naked plain form is defined as the plain form that co-occurs with an affect key/keys. In my analysis, informality and psychological closeness are indexed by the affect key of the non-naked plain form rather than claiming that the distinction between the self and the addressee becomes non-distinct. In contrast, the naked plain form is devoid of emotion due to the absence of an affect key, and instead, it foregrounds the content of an utterance/sentence. This is a case of a detached speech style, which "suppresses the direct involvement of an agent in an action" (Chafe 1982: 45). This analysis accounts for the use of the naked plain form in newspaper articles and scientific papers as well as in soliloquy. The writer of a newspaper article or a scientific paper focuses on the referential content of the article or paper, and the speaker utters a soliloquy at the moment when he/she orients solely to his/her psychological state, not addressing the interlocutor. The naked plain form is also used in listing items and summarizing the previous turn, for the speaker orients to the referential content in these instances. Examples (7) and (8) illustrate the use of the naked plain form to list items and to summarize the previous turn.

Example (7) comes from an elementary school classroom interaction. The teacher poses a review question as to what one should do in writing a poem and nominates students.

(7) [T: teacher, Ka: Kato, H: Hashimoto, Ki: Kishiro] (Example (4) in Cook 2002: 157–158)

1 T: *Hai, katō-san.*
'Yes, Kato-san.'

2 → Ka: ((stands up)) *Hai nani ni tsuite kaku ka kimeru.*
yes what about write Q decide
'Yes, we decide what to write about.'

3 T: ((writes on the board.))
((one line is omitted))

4 *Tsugi. Hashimoto-kun.*
next
'Next, Hashimoto-kun.'

5 → H: ((stands up)) *Hai, shi o tōshite tsutaeru koto o iu.*
yes poem ACC through convey thing ACC say
'Yes, we say things we want to convey through poems.'

6 T: ((writes on the board))
Kishiro-san.

7 → Ki: ((stands up)) *Kanjita koto, kizuita koto o memo ni toru.*
felt thing noticed thing ACC memo in take
'Jot down what we felt and noticed.'

The turns in lines 2, 5, and 7 are responses to the teacher's question regarding the content of the lesson (i.e. how to create a poem), and it is in these turns that the students use the naked plain form. Here the naked plain form foregrounds the informational content of the students' anwers. Similar uses of the naked plain form are reported in academic consultation sessions between a professor and a student (Cook 2006; Okamoto 1998). The student's answer to the professor's question is sometimes in the naked plain form. In addition, the professor and the student may use this form in repeating each other's prior turn. In these instances, the naked plain form indexing the speaker's detached stance toward his/her utterance highlights the content of the utterance.

A similar usage of the detached speech style is found in the interviewer's summary/evaluation turn in TV interview programs. Often the interviewer repeats the interviewee's utterance using the naked plain form (Cook 2002, 2008; Ikuta 2008). The interviewer also uses the naked plain form to prompt and/or extend the interviewee's response (Nazikian 2007). Example (8) illustrates the use of the naked plain form in the interviewer's speech. While in line 1 the interviewer asks a question in the *desu/masu* form, in lines 3 and 6 he summarizes in the naked plain form the interviewee's statement. Since one of the important responsibilities of the interviewer is to convey the content of the interviewee's opinion to the TV audience in a clear manner, it makes sense to use the naked plain form, which foregrounds informational content in the summary turn.

(8) The interviewer (I) is interviewing a female customer (C) in a yakitori restaurant. (Example (3) in Cook 2002: 157)

1 I: *Ano yakitori no miryoku wa dō iu toko desu ka?*
uh GEN appeal TOP what kind place COP Q
'Uh what is yakitori's appeal?'

2 C: *A, yappari yasukute oishii n de, oishii kara.*
uh after all cheap delicious NMLZ COP delicious because
'Uh it's after all inexpensive and delicious, because it's delicious.'

3 → I: *Yasukute oishii.*
cheap delicious
'It's inexpensive and delicious.'

4 *Jibun de anō tsukutchaō nante ki wa?*
self by uh make what desire TOP
'Don't you want to make it yourself?'

5 C: *Arimasen.*
exist.NEG
'I don't.'

6 → I: *Nai.*
exist.NEG
'You don't.'

In sum, the studies which discuss the naked plain form indicate that at least in institutional talk, the naked plain form does not occur randomly, but occurs in utterances which focus on the content rather than the interpersonal relationship.

6 Speech Style Shift as a Linguistic Resource

6.1 On-stage and Off-stage

The *desu/masu* and plain forms serve as linguistic resources for constructing social dimensions (e.g. Cook 1996b; Enyo 2015; Geyer 2008, 2013). As briefly mentioned in Section 4.2, in institutional settings, the *desu/masu* form indexes on-stage talk, whereas the non-naked plain form indexes off-stage talk. Dunn's study (1999), which analyzed speech style shift in students' reports given in a meeting of a college speech club, demonstrates that students in her study use the *desu/masu* form to index on-stage talk whereas the plain form indexes off-stage talk. Dunn found that while the meeting is rather formal and students' reports are public expressions, which are expressed by the *desu/masu* form, sometimes the students shift to the plain form to express their private feelings. She explains these shifts by *omote* 'front' and *ura* 'back,' Japanese cultural notions related to *soto* and *uchi*.[8] She does not, however, directly link the

[8] For further discussion on the notions of *uchi/soto* and *omote/ura*, see Lebra (1976) and Bachnik and Quinn (1994).

desu/masu and plain forms to *omote* and *ura*, respectively. Rather, she analyzes that the *desu/masu* and plain forms help constitute the *omote* and *ura* contexts through indexical association. In faculty meetings in secondary schools, the *desu/masu* forms tend to occur when the content of the talk is transactional and likely to appear in the minutes (Geyer 2008: 102). Such use of the *desu/masu* form organizes the structure of the meeting so that the participants of the meeting pay attention to what is official and important, while the plain form allows the participants to spontaneously reveal their true feelings. Similarly, in movie club meetings at a university, reciprocal uses of the *desu/masu* form frame on-stage talk (Enyo 2015). In Japanese universities, students form a hierarchical relation based on class standings, in particular when they participate in a club for extracurricular activities. This hierarchical relation is referred to as *senpai-kōhai* 'senior-junior' in Japanese, and it is linguistically realized by a non-reciprocal use of the *desu/masu* and plain forms, among others. Enyo (2015) found that although students in different class standings use the *desu/masu* and plain forms non-reciprocally to maintain the hierarchical relation in off-stage talk, they exchange *desu/masu* forms regardless of their class standing in on-stage talk. The reciprocal use of *desu/masu* forms, which indexes on-stage talk, plays a crucial role in foregrounding the official nature of the meeting and backgrounding the *senpai-kōhai* relation in the club meeting.

In an elementary school, the *desu/masu* form constructs the classroom activity called *happyō* (Cook 1996b). In the *happyō* activity, a student presides over the class, gives a presentation, and asks students questions while the teacher observes the activity without participating in it. Students who are engaged in the *happyō* activity are literally on-stage, but the teacher as an observer is off-stage. Example (9) illustrates how the student who is presiding over the *happyō* activity shifts between the two forms to indicate the on- and off-stage contexts.

(9) [T: teacher, S: student, C: class] (Example (4) in Cook 1996b: 76; the names of the participants are changed and glosses are added.)

1 S: *De shitsumon san wa ēto shitsumon ni to onaji de*
and question 3 TOP eh question 2 with same COP

tōmē no fukuro ni gomi- tōmē no fukuro o
transparent GEN bag in garbage transparent GEN bag ACC

gomibukuro ni zembu matomete dashite imasu. [*desu/masu*]
garbage. bag in all together put.out

'And question 3 is the same as question 2, and garbage in clear bags – they put out all in garbage bags.'

2 T: *Kore wa bunbetsu shite aru wake?* [plain]
this TOP sort.out do.exist

'Is this sorted out, burnable and unburnable?'

3 S: *Shitenai* ((low voice)) [plain]
'It is not.'

4 T: *Koko wa bunbetsu shinai.* [plain]
here TOP sort.out do.NEG
'Here (they) do not sort out.'

5 S: *Bunbetsu shinai.* [plain]
sort.out do.NEG
'(They do) not sort out.'

6 *Mō matomete zembu dashichau.* [plain]
well together all put.out
'(They) put it all out.'

7 T: (not clear)

8 S: ((turns to the whole class)) *Ii desu ka* [*desu/masu*]
good COP Q
'Is it OK?'

9 C: *Hāi.*
'Yes.'

In Example (9), the class is studying the garbage problem in Tokyo. S (male student) is presiding over the *happyō* activity and standing in front of the class, while T is standing in the back of the classroom, observing the class activity. In line 1, using the *desu/masu* form, S presents to the class his observation as to what type of plastic bags are used for garbage. But the subsequent exchanges between T and S are all marked in the plain form. In line 2, T asks him a clarification question. After S responds to her question, T repeats S's response to display her understanding of his response. Then in lines 5 and 6, S repeats his response and adds more detail on how garbage is put out. The use of the plain form here indexes that S and T are taking the off-stage stance. Then, in line 8, S turns to the whole class, resuming the *happyō* activity, which is signaled by the shift to *desu/masu* form. This example demonstrates that in the elementary classroom, the on-stage activity, *happyō*, is indexed by the *desu/masu* form whereas the off-stage exchanges are marked by the plain form.

Happyō is a routine classroom activity in Japanese elementary schools. By participating in it, Japanese elementary school students are socialized into a way of constructing on-stage identity through the use of *desu/masu* forms. There is evidence that Japanese children learn the social meaning of the *desu/masu* form as self-presentational stance quite early in life – by the age of three (Cook 1997). Thus, by the time they go to elementary school, they already know when to display self-presentational stance in a culturally appropriate way in and around the home environment. Engaging in the *happyō* activity in the classroom adds another social context in which such a display is appropriate and further strengthens the indexical link between the *desu/masu* form and self-presentational stance.

6.2 Style Shifts in Literary Essays

Style shifts between the two forms organize the structure of essays and novels as well. Drawing on Bakhtin's (1981) theoretical concept of *heteroglossia* (multi-voicedness), Maynard (1993, 2008a), who investigated style shifts in literary essays and novels, demonstrates that Japanese writers utilize style shifts as a linguistic resource to create different "voices" in their story world. Most Japanese literary essays and novels are written either primarily in the plain form (base-line plain) or primarily in the *desu/masu* form (base-line *desu/masu*).[9] The base-line *desu/masu* style is addressive whereas the base-line plain style is non-addressive (Maynard 2008a: 99). In other words, in essays and novels that take the base-line *desu/masu* style the writer directly addresses readers, whereas in those that take the base-line plain style the writer takes on the descriptive mode. Within these two frameworks, shifts may occur in essays and novels. Table 27.2 summarizes eight styles that Maynard proposes. The writer may mix and match these eight styles in writing an essay or novel.

Example (10), which comes from Maynard (2008a), shows how in a base-line plain style essay, various styles are mixed to create multiple "voices" (Bakhtin 1981). This example is drawn from a series of essays by Sadao Shōji that appeared in the weekly magazine *Shūkan Asahi*. The particular essay is titled "Going to eat a 100-yen udon noodle dish."

Table 27.2 *Eight writing styles*

Base-line: plain[a]	
1. Emotive plain form	Foregrounds emotivity – use of the plain form, accompanied by particles, spoken-style vocabulary, sound change, etc.
2. Emotive *desu/masu* form	Foregrounds addressivity with emotivity – use of *desu/masu* form, accompanied by particles and other emotive features
3. Addressive *desu/masu* form	Foregrounds addressivity
4. Supra-polite	Special writing genre – use of *desu/masu*, (extensive) honorifics, and polite vocabulary
Base-line: *desu/masu*	
1. Emotive plain form	Foregrounds emotivity – use of the plain form, accompanied by particles, spoken-style vocabulary, sound change, etc.
2. Non-addressive plain form	Often used in sentences with subordinate information
3. Emotive *desu/masu* form	Foregrounds addressivity with emotivity – use of *desu/masu* form, accompanied by particles and other emotive features
4. Supra-polite	Special writing genre – use of *desu/masu* and (extensive) honorifics and polite vocabulary

[a] *Maynard calls this category "the base-line da style." The base-line plain form is basically what is called "naked plain form," and emotive plain form is "non-naked plain form."(Maynard 2008a: 99)*

[9] Maynard uses the term "*da* style" instead of "plain form."

(10) (Example (1) in Maynard 2008a: 101; glosses are added.)

1 P *Hyaku-en no udon o tabe ni itta.* [base-line *da*]
100-yen GEN ACC eat for went
'I went out to eat 100-yen *udon* noodle dish.'

2 P *Ii desu ka hyaku-en desu yo.* [emotive *desu/masu*]
ok COP Q 100-yen COP SFP
'Are you paying attention? It is 100 yen.'

3 P *Ikkai no shokuji ga hyaku-en de sumu wake desu.*
one.time GEN meal NOM 100-yen COP complete COP
'It's that one meal costs only 100 yen.' [addressive *desu/masu*]

4 "*Fūn, sorya yokatta ne.*"
well that.TOP good.PST SFP
'"I see, that's nice."'

5 P *Datte?*
'You say?'

6 P *Dōmo jijō ga yoku nomikomete-nai yō da na.*
apparently situation NOM well understand-NEG seems COP SFP
'It seems that you don't quite understand the situation.' [emotive *da*]

7 P *Tsumari desu, hirumeshi o kui ni iku.*
after.all COP lunch ACC eat for go
'In other words, I go out for lunch.' [emotive desu/masu, base-line *da*]

8 P *Hyaku-en no udon o taberu.* [base-line *da*]
100-yen GEN ACC eat
'I eat a 100-yen *udon* noodle dish.'

9 P *Dōdō to yōji de shiiha shinagara mise o deteiku.*
proudly toothpick with pick.tooth doing shop ACC leave
'I come out of the shop proudly, picking my teeth with a toothpick.' [base-line *da*]

10 P *Hyaku-en de kō yū koto dekiru wake desu.*
100-yen with this.kind thing able COP
'It's that you can do this for 100 yen.' [addressive *desu/masu*]

11 "*Fūn, sorya yokatta ne.*"
well that.TOP good.PST SFP
'"I see, that's nice."'

12 P *Ano nē imadoki nē, tatoeba nē, teishokuya no raisu*
well SFP now.a.days SFP for.example SFP eatery GEN rice
datte nē, nihyaku-en na wake desu. [emotive *desu/masu*]
COP SFP 200-yen it.is
'Listen, this day and age, for example, a plateful of cooked rice costs 200 yen at restaurants where Japanese set entrees are served.'

13 P *Teishokuya e itte raisu dake tabete, dōdō to yōji de*
eatery to go rice only eat proudly toothpick with
shiiha shinagara mise o deteiku koto ga dekimasu ka.
pick.tooth doing shop ACC leave NMLZ NOM possible Q
[addressive *desu/masu*]
'Can you go to that kind of restaurant and eat rice only and come out proudly picking your teeth with your toothpick?' Shōji (2003: 54)

Here in line 3, the sentence ends in the *desu/masu* form, which addresses the reader. The instances of the *desu/masu* form in lines 2, 7, and 12 are addressive and emotive because these co-occur with the sentence-final particles *yo* and *nē* (in lines 2 and 12), and in line 7, *desu* itself functions like a sentence-final particle. Maynard writes, "These particles enhance the feelings that the writer is repetitiously breaking news of great importance with an urgent concern that the reader 'gets it'" (Maynard 2008a: 102). In a base-line plain style essay like this one, a shift to the *desu/masu* form signals the writer's appearance to the reader. The writer directly talks to the reader. The sentences in lines 7, 8, and 9 are in the base-line plain style. These sentences are referred to by the demonstrative *kō yū* 'this kind' in line 10. In this sense, the sentences in 7, 8, and 9 are like subordinate clauses embedded in the sentence in line 10. Furthermore, in line 6, the sentence is in the emotive plain form ending in the sentence-final particle *na*, which adds a soliloquy-like quality to this sentence. In sum, in this short segment, various "voices" (Bakhtin 1981) are constructed by the manipulation of the *desu/masu* and plain forms. It includes the voice that describes the content of the story (base-line plain form), the voice that directly talks to the reader (addressive *desu/masu*), the voice that directly talks to the reader with emotion (emotive *desu/masu*), and the voice that talks to himself (emotive plain form). The writer skillfully utilizes style shifts as a linguistic tool to create his/her story world.

7 Conclusion

This chapter reviewed studies on speech style shifts. The *desu/masu* and plain forms have long been linked to the social meanings of politeness and non-politeness, respectively. The notion that the *desu/masu* form is polite is reinforced by the fact that the *desu/masu* form is called *teineitai* 'polite style' in Japanese and is widely accepted as a dominant language ideology in Japanese society. Earlier studies, which did not examine naturally occurring data, assumed the dominant language ideology and attempted to explain the speech style shift by pragmatic rules. More recently, studies on speech style shifts based on naturally occurring data, however, found that the *desu/masu* and plain forms not only index politeness and non-politeness but also evoke a wide range of other social meanings in the speech context. These studies, which are mostly done from the constructivist perspective, examined social contexts, including homes, schools, workplaces, TV interviews, and literary essays, and they contributed to our knowledge that speech style shift is not static and prescriptive, but is a dynamic and creative linguistic resource available to speakers of Japanese and utilized in a wide range of social contexts.

Thus, in scholarly endeavors, it is important to differentiate language ideology from actual practice (cf. Okamoto and Shibamoto-Smith 2004). In other words, it is critical to investigate how speakers use speech style shift in different social situations without looking through the lens of the language ideology. But at the same time, it is reported that speakers of Japanese are affected by the language ideology of speech style. For example, Okamoto (2011) illustrates that speakers' use of the plain form is limited when talking to addressees older than themselves. For this reason, it is also indispensable to examine the role of folk notions of the *desu/masu* and plain forms (cf. Geyer 2016) and the ways folk notions influence patterns of speech style shift. Future research needs to examine both perspectives (i.e. speech style shift as a linguistic resource to construct a desired social context and how the language ideology of speech style shift affects speakers' linguistic behavior).

28

Discourse/Conversation Analysis

Polly Szatrowski

1 Introduction

This chapter reviews four waves of research on discourse/conversation analysis focusing on spoken Japanese in spontaneous conversation.[1] The first wave was concerned with discourse/conversation units. The second analyzed devices, strategies, utterance functions, and discourse structure. The third consisted of research that applied Conversation Analysis (CA) developed by Sacks, Schegloff, and Jefferson (1974) and other analysts of English conversation to Japanese. The fourth wave has analyzed the use of language together with gesture, gaze, and other multimodal aspects of face-to-face conversation. I will highlight some of the research done in these four areas, as well as focus on several themes including ellipsis/zero anaphora, aizuchi 'back channel,' turn-taking, co-construction, and gaze and body movements.

2 Discourse/Conversation Units

2.1 Discourse Structure and Anaphora

Hinds (1978b) was one of the first discourse analysts to use casual Japanese conversation as data to answer questions such as what is the relation between zero anaphora and discourse structure. He defined zero anaphora as NP deletion, taking "a neutral stance on whether the noun phrases in question have been deleted or are simply not present in the abstract/deep structure" (pp. 136–137). Hinds proposed the paragraph, "a connected series of sentences, or sentence fragments, all of which relate to the same topic" (p. 154), as a unit for spoken discourse.

[1] I based these waves on chronological order and themes that like waves have continued through time. Note that spontaneous conversation does not include made-up or role-play conversation.

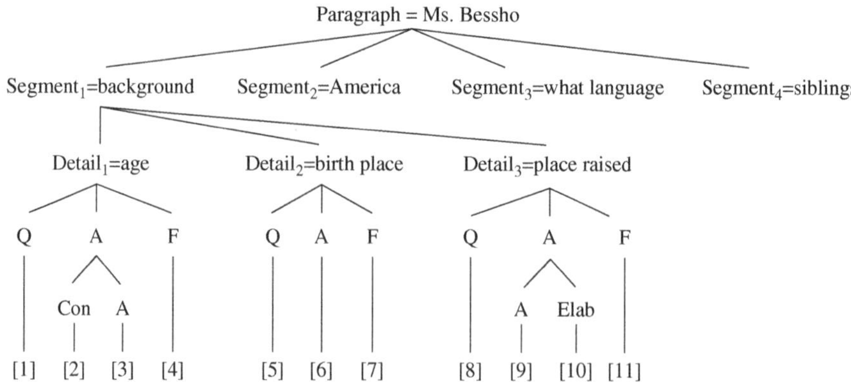

Figure 28.1 Discourse structure of interview including (1) (Hinds 1978b: 160)[3]

The interview in (1) (pp. 156–157) has the structure shown in Figure 28.1.[2] It illustrates Hinds's two conditions for zero anaphora: the deleted noun phrase (i) is in the discourse registry and (ii) is "uniquely" the paragraph topic (p. 161). Zero anaphora occurs after the first sentence by the interviewer (A) because the interviewee's name *Bessho-san* has been entered into the discourse registry, and no other topics are introduced in (1). Zero anaphora may also be used when segment topics and detail topics are assumed to be known by the addressee. Thus, *Bessho-san* is ellipted in subsequent segments related to her going to America, her siblings, etc.

(1) 1A *Bessho-san, toshi wa ikutsu desu ka?*
'Ms. Bessho, how old are (you)?'
2B *Toshi?*
'How old?'
3B *Nijū shichi.*
'Twenty seven.'
4A *Nijū shichi?*
'Twenty seven?'
5A *Doko de umaremashita?*
'Where were (you) born?'
6B *Ano ne, anō, Ehimeken no Ōmishima tte iu chitcha na shima de umaremashita.*
'Um, on a small island in Ehime Prefecture called Ōmishima.'
7A *Sō?*
'Really?'
8A *Anō, soko de sodatta no?*
'Uh, did (you) grow up there?'

[2] Cited examples have been altered and romanization and English translations added for consistency. Transcription conventions are given at the end of this chapter.

[3] Q = question, A = answer, F = feedback, Con = confirmatory question, Elab = elaboration

9B *Mm, soko wa umareta dake de,*
'Uh huh, (I) was born there, and'
10B *sugu Hyōgoken no Takarazukashi tte iu tokoro ni utsurimashita.*
'then (I) moved right away to a place in Hyōgo Prefecture called Takarazuka.'
11A *A sō?*
'Oh really?'
12A *Sore kara Amerika ni itta wake?*
'And then (you) went to America?'

Upon hearing that *Bessho-san* is an only child, A changes the topic to her own family, and subsequently from her family to herself as shown in (2) (p. 162). Hinds notes that these topic changes correlate with the explicit NPs *uchi* 'my family' and *atashi* 'I.'

(2) 38A *Ū, ja, uchi to hantai ne.*
'Wow, my family is just the opposite.'
39A *Uchi wa jūnin.*
'(In) my family there are ten.'
40B *Wa, suggoi ne.*
'Wow, (that)'s something.'
41B *Ja, hitori gurai hette mo ii wake ne.*
'Well, (you) could get rid of one with no trouble, huh.'
42A *Sō, atashi nanka shinda hō ga yokatta gurai.*
'Yeah, it probably would have been better if I died or something.'
43B *Masaka.*
'Don't be silly.'

Hinds analyzed instances where the speaker repeated a NP even when the conditions for zero anaphora had been met, as a stalling or confirming device. Thus, he explained ellipsis/zero anaphora on the discourse level using topic-related structures such as paragraphs, details, and segments.

2.2 Units of Conversation

Minami (1987b) points out the need to determine criteria for discourse units in any analysis that uses discourse data. The data for his study were audio-recorded by the Kokuritsu Kokugo Kenkyūjo (presently called the National Institute for Japanese Language and Linguistics) in 1963 from 6:00am to 10:00pm at a home in Matsue City, Shimane Prefecture. The communicative functions and participants in these spontaneous conversations between members of the family and visitors are highly varied compared to Hinds's data. Minami (1981: 89) proposed the six criteria for discourse units shown in (3), where b–f apply within the unit.

(3) a. Distinct pause before or after the unit.
 b. Continuity.
 c. Consistent participants (speakers, listeners).
 d. Consistent communicative function (e.g. greeting, business talk, chatting, direct expression of emotion).
 e. Consistent style (e.g. formal, informal, polite).
 f. Consistent topic (e.g. everyday life, small talk, gossip).

Minami (1997 [1983]: 335) generalized these criteria to apply to discourse units in written as well as spoken genre. Discontinuities (changes) in one or more of the criteria in (4) can be used to identify units across genre.

(4) a. Form actually expressed
 b. Participants
 c. Topic
 d. Linguistic communicative function
 e. Expressive attitude (pretense)
 f. Language used
 g. Medium
 h. Overall structure

For example, Minami identified three units in (5) (1997 [1983]: 352–353), based on discontinuities in criteria b–d for units ① and ②, and b–e for units ② and ③.

(5)	①	D	*Yūbin.*	'Mail.'
		A	*Hai.*	'Yes.'
	②	A	*N:to XXX n:a Kajita*	'U:hm XXX [inaudible speech] u:h Kajita (person's name)'
		B	*N:.*	'Uh hu:h.'
		A	*Kajita anta XXX ageta?*	'Did you give XXX to Kajita?'
		B	*Ageta yo.*	'(I) gave (it), you know.'
		A	*Ha:.*	'Ooh.'
		B	*A kōden o ne:.*	'Oh the funeral gift, you kno:w.'
		A	*A: a:.*	'O:h o:h.'
		B	*Sanbyaku-en yūbin de okutta.*	'(I) sent (it) by mail for ¥300.'
		A	*A: koko mo XXX yūsō-shimashita.*	'O:h I also sent XXX.'
		B	*So:?*	'Rea:lly?'
		A	*Yūbin-shita.*	'(I) mailed (it).'
		B	*So:.*	'Is that so:.'

③ C	*Gomen kudasai.*	'Excuse me.'
A	*Ara irasshai. Ara a irasshai.*	'Oh welcome. Oh ah welcome.'
B	*A: irasshaimase.*	'O:h welcome.'
A	*A ha.*	'Oh yes.'
A	*Ma: ma ma.*	'We:ll well well.'
C	*Dōmo ohisashū gozaimashit-(e)a.*	'(It) has been a long while (since I saw you).'
B	*Ya:ya XXX. Dōmo gomen kudasaimase.*	'We:ll well XXX. Hello.
	Maimai dōmo XXX.	I'm always grateful to you XXX.'
C	*Gomen kudasai. Itsumo arigatō gozaimasu.*	'Hello. (I) am always grateful.'

2.3 Conversational Units and the Functions of Connective Expressions

Sakuma (1987) proposed the units *bundan* and *wadan* 'grammatico-semantic paragraphs' in written and spoken conversational texts, respectively. Sakuma's analysis is more comprehensive than Hinds's paragraph, because it includes connectives, demonstratives, repetition, ellipsis, topic, and predicate expressions. She also identified topic sentences that express the main information and give coherence to the *bundan/wadan*, and thesis sentences that give the theme and unify the overall text. *Bundan/wadan* have seven coherency functions that roughly correlate with the Beginning (topic presentation, introduction of a problem, preface), Middle (connection with the preceding while introducing the following, often single sentence *bundan*), and End (conclusion, raising an issue, afterthought) of the text.

The *wadan* in (6), an excerpt from a conversation among three female college students, are indicated by circled numbers (Sakuma 2003: 108–109). The main topic is the international student, Mr. R. The main speaker N has the initiative and uses many referential utterances, S gives referential utterances to add supportive explanation, and M, who gives back channel and asks questions, is in the listener role.

(6) ④ 20 N *De mo, ano R-san tte iu hito wa, [myō ni tomodachi ni naritagaru hito na no.* 'But, as for that person called Mr. R, [it's that (he) is a person who strangely wants to become friends.'

21 M [*Un.*
['Uh huh.'

22S *Sonna kanji.*
'(He) gives that kind of impression.'

23 M [*R-san?*
['Mr. R?'

24S [*Nanka, un tomodachi ga inai n da to ka i[tte.*
['Somehow, uhm, (he) says like "it's that (I) don't have (any) friends."'

25 N [*Un.*
['Uh huh.'

⑤ 26 N *Sore de ne, ano, pātī, derannaku tte,*
'So, you know, uhm, (he) says that (he) can't go to the party, and'

27 M *Un.*
'Uh huh.'

28 N *kakioki o shite tta no, [kare.*
'it's that (he) left a note, [he.'

29 M [*At, un, un, un.*
['Oh, yeah yeah yeah.'

⑥ 30 N *De, sore ni ne, "Watashi, sukoshi, teian arimasu" tte kaite atte,*
'And, in addition, you know, he wrote "I, have a small suggestion," and'

31 N *de, "Sensei mo, keiken ga sukunai shi,"*
'and, "Teacher (you) also, have limited experience (teaching non-native speakers), and what's more,"'

32 N *ano, "Watashi-tachi mo, nihongo o shaberu kikai ga sukunai kara,"*
'uhm, "We too, have few chances to speak Japanese so,"'

33 N *tomodachi ni nareba,*
'if (you) become (my) friend,'

34 N *sore ga, ikkyo ryōtoku [da yo" tte koto o enen to kaite at[te,*
'that would be (like) killing two birds with one stone, [I tell you" was written on and on, [and'

35 M [{LAUGH}

36 M [*Un, un, un.*
['Yeah, yeah, yeah.'

37 N *A, naruhodo ne to ka omotte.*
'Oh, I see, you know is what I thought, and.'

⑦ 38S *Ryō ni sunde ru tte itta k[ke.*
'Did (he) say that he lived in a dormitory?'

39 N [*Un.*
['Yeah.'

40 M *K-juku ga motte n no?*
'Is it that K School has (a dorm)?'

41S *Un, sō mitai.*
'Yeah, (it) appears so.'

Based on the topic/core sentences (underline), connective (double underline) and demonstrative (wavy underline) expressions, Sakuma determined the following topics and main speakers for each of the *wadan*:

④ "Mr. R/Friends" (N), ⑤ "Party/Note" (N), ⑥ "Was written/Teacher/I (we)/ Friends" (N), ⑦ "Dormitory/K School" (S, M).[4] With the exception of ⑦, all the *wadan* begin with N's connective expressions and end with other participants' back channel and agreement. ⑦ is a connecting *wadan* that continues ⑥ while introducing ⑧ (about classes offered at K School).

Building on Ichikawa's (1978) analysis of seven types of connective expressions in written discourse,[5] Sakuma (2002) proposed the three major context developing functions for connective expressions in (7). Her analysis was based on 749 connectives in approximately three hours of data from two casual conversations, a discussion, and a television interview.

(7) a. Topic introducing (a1 Beginning, a2 Rebeginning)
b. Topic continuing (b1 Repeating, b2 Deepening, b3 Advancing, b4 Encouraging, b5 Returning, b6 Inserting, b7 Diverting, b8 Interrupting, b9 Changing, b10 Summarizing)
c. Topic ending (c1 Ending, c2 Internal ending)

In (6), N begins ④ with the connective expression in 20 N *Demo* 'but' (E. Transitional) and demonstrative *ano* 'that' to change the talk (b9) to Mr. R. ⑤ starts with 25 N *Sore de ne* 'So, you know,' and ⑥ with 30 N *De* 'And,' and *sore ni ne* 'in addition' (all C. Additive) to advance the talk (b3). Thus, connective expressions are important indicators of *wadan* and cohesion.

3 Discourse/Conversation Features, Strategies, and Structure

3.1 Features of Japanese Conversation

Maynard (1989) investigated features of spoken Japanese in dyadic conversations between college students including fragmentation of talk, final particles, fillers (e.g. *nanka* 'well,' *uuuun* 'uhh'), ellipsis, postposing, metacommunication remarks, utterance co-creation, and question as a conversational elicitor. She noted that Japanese conversation was fragmented; for example, syntactic clauses were "broken into a number of smaller units bounded by pauses or skipped beats … mostly marked by distinct intonation contour" (p. 23) which she called Pause-bounded Phrase Units (PPUs). PPUs, indicated by "/" in (8) (p. 142), are "mostly accompanied by pause-predicting tone and/or pause-warning decreased speed, along with occasional stressed, rising intonation … frequently followed by particles which function to elicit listener response" (p. 24).

(8) 1A *De, Ichikawa tte yatsu ga in ja nai?/*
'And uh, you know the guy Ichikawa?'

[4] As is often the case in casual conversation, there are no thesis sentences in (6).

[5] A. Causative, B. Adversative, C. Additive, D. Contrastive, E. Transitional, F. Paraphrasing, G. Supplementary, H. Sequential.

2B *Un un.*
'Uh huh.'

3A *Aitsu ga ne/*
'That guy. . .'

4B *Shūshoku*
'Getting a job'

5A *Shinai mitai./*
'(He) doesn't seem to do that.'

Maynard proposed four reasons for postposing: (i) to add presupposed information for listener comprehension, (ii) to compensate for memory or production difficulties, (iii) to background postposed information and foreground earlier non-postposed information, and (iv) to qualify a statement (e.g. express doubt/hesitation) for social or other reasons. Her first reason is similar to Hinds's (1982) claim that postposing may be used to reinsert an ellipted element to make sure the listener can follow, and her third reason to Clancy's (1982: 69) claim that postposing can be used to defocus "familiar or easily deducible information."[6]

The co-creation in (8) foreshadows research in Section 4.3 Co-construction. In 4B, B predicts the word *shūshoku* 'getting a job' from the previous discussion, and together A and B create the sentence *Aitsu ga ne shūshoku-shinai mitai* 'It seems like that guy, you know, isn't going to get a job.'

3.2 Strategies in Japanese Conversation

3.2.1 Conflict Strategies in Japanese Conversation

Jones (1990: 21) defines strategies as "ways in which speakers try to achieve an interactional goal." Table 28.1 summarizes the conflict strategies Jones found in formal and informal conversations in a variety of settings. She distinguished between explicit strategies, which express the conflict directly, and inexplicit strategies, which do not mention the conflict. Jones found that the canonical, least confrontational strategies such as (1) Acknowledgment/Opposition and (2) Self-disparagement/Opposition and Citing Authority (no examples given) were rare in her data. In contrast, explicit conflict strategies such as (3) Opposition/ Explanation, (4) Opposition with Apology, (5) Blunt Opposition, and (8) Discourse Markers (e.g. *shikashi, (da) kedo, keredo, kedomo, tada, demo, datte* all meaning 'but,' *Sō deshō ka* 'Might it be so?,' *dakara* 'and so; that's why,' *mō* 'already,' *tashika ni* 'certainly') were more common.

Implicit strategies included (9) Veiled Opposition (organizing "discourse to indicate opposition without expressing it explicitly"), (10) Ignoring

[6] Studies by Koike (2003) on intonation and grammar, by Szatrowski (2005) on information management, interaction, and discourse structure, and by Couper-Kuhlen and Ono (2007) on cross-linguistic incrementing practices have developed postposing research further.

Table 28.1 *Strategies used in Japanese conflicts*

Explicit	Implicit	
Verbal		Non-verbal
1. Acknowledgment/Opposition	9. Veiling Opposition	15. Changing Rhythm
2. Self-disparagement/Opposition	10. Ignoring Conflicts	16. Frequent Laughter
3. Opposition/Explanation	11. Dropping Conflicts	17. Marked Prosody
4. Opposition with Apology	12. Switching Speech Style	18. Silence
5. Blunt Opposition	13. Repetition and Parallelism	19. Dropping Conflict by Withdrawing from the Conversation
6. Compromise	14. Disfluencies	
7. Concession		
8. Discourse Markers of Opposition		

Conflicts, (11) Dropping Conflicts, (12) Switching Speech Style, (13) Repetition and Parallelism (e.g. self-repetition for emphasis and other-repetition to show support), and (14) Disfluencies (Jones 1990: 90–92). Non-verbal strategies include (15) Changing Rhythm, (16) Frequent Laughter, (17) Marked Prosody, (18) Silence, and (19) Withdrawing from the Conversation.

Jones demonstrated that when conflict is not situationally ratified, that is, acknowledged as appropriate in the context (as in television debate), it is often reframed as play. This turns the conflict into a non-conflict, by allowing for a non-confrontational interpretation on another level (Bateson 1972).

3.2.2 The Structure and Strategies Used in Japanese Invitation Conversations

I (Szatrowski 1993a, 1993b) analyzed the structure of and strategies used in invitation conversations in twenty hours of tape-recorded spontaneous phone conversations building on previous research on units in conversation by Minami (1981) and Sakuma (1987). Reinterpreting Sakuma's (1987) content (topic)-based *wadan* as action-related "stages" in conversational interaction, I use the term *wadan* 'stage' to refer to a unit (utterance or sequence of utterances) produced through the interaction between Information Presenter(s) and Supporting Participant(s), and identified *wadan* based on the participants' goals, distribution of utterance functions, and prosody.[7] I demonstrated that Japanese invitation conversations consist of Invitation *Wadan* and Answer *Wadan* which are characterized by the utterance functions shown in (9). Other utterance functions that are used by both Information Presenter(s) and Supporting Participant(s) are given in (10) (Szatrowski 1993a).

[7] An Information Presenter(s) is the primary speaker(s) who uses utterance functions on the left side of (9), and a Supporting Participant(s) supports the Information Presenter using the functions on the right. Due to space limitations, prosody is not covered. Suzuki (2009) uses a similar approach to analyze consultation discourse.

(9)

	Utterance Function	Information Presenter	Supporting Participant
1	Attention request	✔	
2	Agreement request	✔	
3	Information presentation	✔	
4	Expressions of will	✔	
5	Directive	✔	
6	Invitation	✔	
12	Attention display		
j	Agreement	✔	
7	Information request		✔
12	Attention displays		
a	Continuer		✔
b	Recognition		✔
c	Confirmation		✔
d	Interest		✔
e	Emotion		✔
f	Sympathy (agreement)		✔
g	Comment		✔
h	Negating		✔
i	Concluding		✔

(10)

	Utterance Function	Information Presenter	Supporting Participant
8	Discourse markers	✔	✔
9	Repeat request	✔	✔
10	Repeat	✔	✔
11	Relation-building, etiquette	✔	✔
12	Attention display		
k	Self-directed	✔	✔

In invitations, where the goal of the inviter is to invite and the goal of the invitee is to answer, *wadan* can be identified at places where the primary speaker's goals change, that is, from invitation to answer or vice versa. This corresponds to changes of footing from Information Presenter to Supporting Participant or vice versa, that is, alternation in the use of the utterance functions from the left side and right side of (9). In Invitation *Wadan*, where the inviter's goal is central, the inviter becomes the Information Presenter using 1–6 and 12j, while the invitee becomes the Supporting Participant using 7 and 12a–i. In Answer *Wadan* the invitee's goal is central, and the utterance functions are reversed. The invitee becomes the Information Presenter, using 1–5 and 12j (excluding 6 Invitation), and the inviter becomes the Supporting Participant, using 7 and 12a–i.

The Invitation *Wadan* in (11) is an example of a relatively passive Supporting Participant.[8] The Information Presenter (inviter N) uses two Self-directed Attention Displays and a Discourse Marker in 1N, and Information Presentation utterances in 3N, 5N, and 7N, and the Supporting Participant (invitee G) responds with Continuer Attention Displays.

(11) Invitation to a tea ceremony [inviter N (27, female) calls invitee G (25, female)]

Invitation *Wadan* 1:		N	G
1 N	*Eee, a sore kara ne?* 'Um, oh, then, you know?'	8+8+k	
2G	*Un.* 'Uh huh.'		a
3 N	(0.5) *ano:* (0.4) *kondo ne?* 'U:::h next, you know?'	3	
4G	*Un.* 'Uh huh.'		a
5 N	*ochakai ga aru no yo. Uchi no shusai no.* 'It's that there will be a tea ceremony, you know. Sponsored by my group.'	3	
6G	*U:n.* 'Uh hu:h.'		a
7 N	*Shichi-gatsu no mikka. Nichiyōbi.* '(It will be on) the third of July. Sunday.'	3	

(Szatrowski 1993b: 22)

The Supporting Participants (invitee A in the Invitation *Wadan* in (12), and inviter B in the Answer *Wadan* in (13)) are more active, using Information Requests in addition to Attention Displays.[9]

(12) Invitation to come out drinking [inviter B (20's, female) calls invitee A (20's, female)]

Invitation *Wadan* 1:		A	B
19B	*Ano ne?* 'Uhm you know?'		1
20A	*U:n.* 'Uh:m.'	a	
21B	*ima T to nonde ru ka mo:.* 'now (I)'m drinking with T you kno:w.'		3
22A +	*Doko de?*	7	

[8] In (11) to (14) utterance functions are given on the right under participant letters.

[9] 7/e means both 7 and e. + and – indicate utterances that take a positive or negative attitude, respectively, toward the achievement of the invitation. * indicates "utterances of compassion" defined below.

		'Where?'		
23B		*Suzume:.*		3
		'The Sparro:w.'		
24B		[*Kichi* #Beginning of place name		3
25A	+	[*Doko no:.*	7	
		['(The) [one which is] whe:re.'		
26B		*Kichijōji.* #Place name		3
27A	–	*Maji:.*	c/e	
		'You're kidding.'		
28B	–	*Soide ne:[:?*		8+1
		'And, you kno:[:w?'		
29A		[*U:n.*	a	
		['Uh hu:h.'		
30B	–	*T ga ne[:?*		3
		'T, you kno[:w?'		
31A		[*U:n.*	a	
		['Uh hu:h.'		
32B	–	*A to ocha de mo shitai tte iu ka [mo:.*		3
		'says that (s/he) would like to have tea with you, you [kno:w.'		
33A	–	[*Nan da yo. sore.*	7/e	
		['What (do you mean), I tell you. (by) that.'		
34B	–	{LAUGH}		

(13) Invitation to come out drinking (continuation of (12))

			A	B
Answer *Wadan* 1:				
35A	*	(0.5) *Ii kedo sā,*	3	
		'(0.5 (It)'s okay, but you know.'		
36B		*U:n.*		a
		'Uh hu:h.'		
37B	–	*Boroboro?*		7
		'(Are you) worn out?'		
38A	–	(0.5) *Chotto ne[:,*	3	
		'A bit, you kno[:w.'		
39B		[*U:n.*		a
		['Uh hu:h.'		

The use of *wadan* 'stages' reflects the structure of Japanese invitations in which Supporting Participants cooperate in the construction of *wadan* with the Information Presenter. In contrast, English speakers tended to take independent turns as in the telephone invitation in (14) (Davidson 1984: 108–109) in which I indicate the *wadan* and utterance functions for comparison.

(14) Invitation to watch television

Invitation *Wadan* 1:		C	D
1C	*°Gee I feel like a real nerd°*	3	
2C	*You c'n ahl come up here,*	3/6	
Answer *Wadan* 1			
3	(0.3)		
4D	*Nah that's alright*		3
5D	*wil stay down he[re.*		3
Invitation *Wadan* 2			
6C	*[We've gotta color T.V:,*	3	
Answer *Wadan* 2			
7D	*tch.hh I know but u-*		3
8D	*we're watchin:g the Ascent 'v Ma:n,*		3
9D	*.hh en then the phhreview:*		3
10D	*so: y' know wil miss something if we come over*		3

The turn units in 1C–2C, 3–5D, 6C, and 7D–10D are roughly equivalent to solo *wadan*, in which the inviter C produces the Invitation *Wadan* and the invitee D the Answer *Wadan*. Thus, English turns tended to be solo productions. In contrast, Japanese invitations were produced by a multiple of participants, and both passive (10) and active (12) Supporting Participants got more involved in the construction of *wadan* than in English, where listeners often remained silent.

There were also differences in the use of strategies in the conversational development of Japanese and American English invitations. I observed that Japanese inviters used a *Kikubari* 'Consideration' Strategy that made it easier for the invitee to refuse when the invitee showed a negative attitude or did not show interest in the invitation. For example, they gave reasons for refusing, negative evaluations, or information disadvantageous for achieving the invitation as in 45 N and 80 N (Invitation to go to Hawaii) and 25 N (Invitation to a Tea Ceremony) in (15) (Szatrowski 1993b: 32, 33, 18).

(15) 45 N *Kono mae itta bakkari da shi ne? Sore ni nē?*
'(You) just went (there) recently, didn't you, in addition.'
80 N *Mā muri da to omotta kedo ne?*
'Well (I) thought it wouldn't be possible, but, you know?'
25 N *Jikan nai ka.*
'(You) don't have the time, huh.'

In contrast, English inviters used a strategy of "Winning the Invitee Over" when they pursued the invitation further by giving subsequent versions and inducements as in 6C in (14) and (16) in order to encourage the inviter to accept.

(16) a. *Got plenty a' roo:m.* (Invitation to Stay Over)
b. *I got lotta stuff,=I got be:er en stuff 'n* (Invitation to Come Over)
c. *It's rilly intresti:ng:.* (Invitation to Learn About Computers)
(Davidson 1984: 105, 108)

There were also differences in the invitees' strategies. Japanese invitees used an *Omoiyari* 'Compassion' Strategy when they gave reasons for accepting, positive evaluations, or information advantageous for achieving the invitation to preface utterances that displayed a negative attitude toward the invitation as in 35A in (13). In contrast, Americans tended to refuse more directly as in (14).

Differences in the structure of Japanese and English conversation and the meaning of listening in silence versus *aizuchi* 'back channel' can lead to cross-cultural miscommunication. It is common for American inviters to give information about their invitation in turns during which the invitee listens in silence, and for Japanese inviters to present this information bit by bit and expect response from their invitees. By listening in silence, non-native Japanese invitees can give the impression that they are not interested in a Japanese invitation. Japanese inviters may interpret this lack of back channel as a sign of disinterest and use the Consideration Strategy in order to make it easier for the invitee to refuse. This in turn can make the American invitee feel like the inviter does not want him/her to come. Miscommunication results because Americans do not intend to convey disinterest by listening in silence, and Americans may interpret Japanese inviters' utterances of consideration as distancing compared to American inviters' subsequent versions and inducements.

4 Applications of Conversation Analysis (CA)

The third wave of research applied conversation analytic research on English conversation (Sacks et al. 1974; and others) to Japanese. Strict adherents to this approach included Mori (1999), Tanaka (1999), Hayashi and Mori (1998), Lerner and Takagi (1999), and Hayashi (2003), while other researchers, for example, Furo (1998), Ono and Yoshida (1995), and Szatrowski (2000a, 2005, 2007), were more inclusive of other approaches.

4.1 Connective Expressions Used in Negotiation of Agreement and Disagreement

Mori (1994) studied the connective expressions used in conversational excerpts involving agreements and disagreement, adhering to basic notions of CA (Conversation Analysis) by focusing on sequences and turns within sequences. Her results are summarized in Tables 28.2 and 28.3 (Mori 1999: 200–201).

Table 28.2 *The workings of "causal" markers*

	Agreement (recipients)	Disagreement (recipients)	Pursuit (speaker)
datte	Justifying the prior speaker's assertion	Introducing an account for a stronger, asserted disagreement	Justifying one's own prior assertion
dakara	Introducing a consequence or an example of a circumstance described by the prior speaker		Rephrasing the prior utterance or replacing an unclear referent
kara	Providing weaker or partial support	Marking the preceding clause as an account, creating an inference of unstated disagreement	Marking the end of supplementary talk, equivocally projecting the repetition of the initial assertion or the recipient's collaborative completion

Table 28.3 *The workings of "contrastive" markers*

	Disagreement (recipients)	Pursuit (speaker)
demo	Marking a shift in perspective, introducing a qualification or a limitation of the proffered opinion or evaluation	Reintroducing, or re-emphasizing one's initial assertion
kedo	Mitigating a disagreeing response, creating an inference of unstated partial agreement	Acknowledging a potential problem in one's own assertion, marking the end of a self-qualifying segment while de-emphasizing the preceding clause

Mori claims that previous studies did not specify "what brings the speaker to a circumstance where s/he has to justify her/himself or challenge others through the use of *datte*" (1999: 148). She notes that the use of *datte* in (17) differs from uses analyzed previously by Jones (1990) and Maynard (1992b) in disagreements. Although the sequence involves agreement, Mori concludes that E uses *datte* in 2E to create an alliance and display group disagreement regarding the issue of women having to serve tea in an office.

(17) 1Y *Demo oyatsu no jikan mendokusai ne, are ne.*
'But snack time is a bother, isn't it, that (thing we all know about), you know.'

2E *Sō da yo. Datte sa:, hito ni yotte sa:, chigau jan konomi ga.*
'That's right, I tell you. Because, you kno:w, depending on the person, you know, isn't it different, (their) preference.'

3E *Kōhī wa burakku toka sa:, miruku dake toka sa:=*
'Coffee (should) be black, or you know, only (with) milk (in it) or you know='

4 M *Sō.*
'Right.'

5 M *=Usume no kōhī toka,*
'=Thin coffee or,'

6E *Sō.*
'Right.'

7 M *de zekkai* <sic> *ni naninani buchō wa ocha shika nomanai kara toka.*
'and Manager so-and-so absolutely won't drink anything except green tea, so or.'

8E *Sō sō.*
'Right right.'

9Y *Urusai urusai.*
'(It)'s annoying (it)'s annoying.' (Mori 1994: 158)

4.2 Syntactic, Intonational, and Pragmatic Resources in Turn-taking

Furo (1998) and Tanaka (1999) applied Ford and Thompson's (1996) (hereafter F&T) study of syntactic, intonational, and pragmatic resources in English turn-taking to Japanese. F&T questioned Sacks et al.'s (1974: 702) claim that turns are constructed primarily from "unit-types" (sentential, clausal, phrasal, and lexical constructions) that project the unit-type and its completion, by investigating the role of pragmatics and intonation in addition to syntax. They operationalized syntactic completion as a complete clause in its discourse context with an overt or directly recoverable predicate that may include elliptical clauses, answers to questions, and back channel (pp. 143–145). Syntactic completion was evaluated incrementally (often in relation to a previous predicate), and the unit between two syntactic completion points was not necessarily a complete syntactic unit, as shown in (18), where a "/" indicates syntactic completion.

(18) V . . . *made my Dad feel comfortable/, said that he's gonna have this sa:me operation/ when he's- in about (0.2) twenty years/ cause he had bad knees/ from football/ n-in high school/* (p. 144)

F&T identified intonational completion after a final intonation contour (a marked rise or marked fall). Pragmatic completion by definition (i) had a final intonation contour (i.e. every pragmatic completion point was necessarily intonationally complete) and (ii) was interpretable as a complete action in the interactional sequence. Speaker change was noted at any point another speaker took a full turn or back channel turn (includes laughter onset) (p. 152).

Tanaka (1999) operationalized syntactic completion differently. She distinguished between analytical syntactic completion which requires only that "within its prior context, no further talk is syntactically projected" and conversational syntactic completion where "intonation is taken into account to exclude points which fall within agglutinated expressions, unless there is a prosodic break ... at that point" (1999: 70). In (19) the slashes indicate that there are only three conversational syntactic completions after the acknowledgments in 2, 4, and 5.[10]

(19)	1G	... *Sensei*	*ga*	*dareka*	*suki na*	*hito*	*ga*	*dekita*[*ra*			
		teacher	NOM	someone	like COP	person	NOM	be.realized-COND			
		'... if teacher had fallen in love with someone'									
	2( )							[*N./>*			
								'Uh huh.'			
	3G	*dekita**	*tte**	*yo*[*katta**	*ja nai*	*ka**	*to:.* *>				
		be.realized-PERF	QUOT	good-PERF	COP-NEG	INT	QUOT				
		'(then that) would have been good (for her) too, it would seem'									
	4( )			[*N::./>*							
				'Uh hu::h.'							
	5( )	*N::./>*									
		'Yeah'									
	6G	*Dakara...*									
		'Therefore...' (Tanaka 1999: 75; asterisks added by Szatrowski)									

Applying F&T's criteria for syntactic completion could conceivably include the points I marked with an *. In that case, it is significant that the acknowledgments in 2 and 5 would come at points of syntactic completion.[11] The acknowledgment in 4 occurs after the adjectival root, *yo-* 'good,' at the precise moment the main point is conveyed. This suggests that places that are "fused morpohologically through agglutination" (which Tanaka excluded) may be oriented to as syntactically complete in some way.

Furo followed F&T's criteria for the most part. She marked syntactic completion after predicates, increments (post-predicate words and phrases) and back channel, and intonational completions after final rising or falling intonation. Furo identified pragmatically complete utterance(s) when they did a recognizable action (e.g. a question) in (i) single unit turns (single sentence turns, back channel, etc.) and (ii) multi-unit turns (e.g. stories). She also included all full turns and back channel turns in her analysis of speaker change.

The results for F&T's study on English and Furo's and Tanaka's studies on Japanese are summarized in Table 28.4.

Rows 1–3 show that syntactic completions were the most numerous in all three studies, but the gap between that and intonation and pragmatic

[10] / = syntactic completion, > = pragmatic completion, and ? = intonational completion.

[11] See Lerner and Takagi (1999) for a discussion of co-participatory completions occurring in similar positions.

Table 28.4 *Overall results for Ford and Thompson (1996), Furo (1998), and Tanaka (1999)*[a]

		English	Japanese	
		Ford and Thompson (1996)	Furo (1998)	Tanaka (1999)[b]
1	S Completion (S)	798	853	422
2	I Completion (I)	433	695	411
3	P Completion (P)	422	659	347
4	I that were ¬ S	5 (1.2%)	6 (0.9%)	64 (16%)
5	S that were ¬ I	370 (46.4%)	164 (19.2%)	75 (18%)
6	I&S	428	689	347
7	I that were S	98.8%	99.1%	84%
8	S that were I	53.6%	80.8%	82%
9	I that were ¬ P	11 (2.5%)	36 (5.2%)	
10	P & I	422	659	
11	I that were P	97.5%	94.8%	
12	P that were I	100%	100%	
13	P & S	417		
14	P that were S	98.8%		
15	CTRP (I&P&S)	417	659	325
16	CTRP that were S	52.3%	77.3%	77%
17	All SC	279	729	191
18	SC at ¬CTRP	81(29%)	175 (24%)	
19	CTRP with ¬SC	219 (52.5%)	105 (15.9%)	42 (13.9%)
20	SC & CTRP	198	554	149 full turn CTRPs
21	SC at CTRP	71%	76%	
22	CTRP with SC	47.5%	84.1%	78% full turn CTRPs
23	S with SC		630 (73.3%)	
24	I with SC		559 (80.4%)	
25	P with SC		554 (84.1%)	

[a] CTRP = Complex Transition Relevance Place, S = syntactic, I = intonational, P = pragmatic, SC = speaker changes, BC = back channel, ¬ = 'not.' No data were available for blank cells.

[b] In the Tanaka (1999) column, all the numbers given for S completion are "conversational syntactic completion points." Tanaka found 877 "analytic syntactic completion points" in her data.

completions was somewhat less than English for Furo, and considerably less for Tanaka (due to operationalization differences). In rows 4–8, very few intonation completions were not syntactically complete in English and Furo's Japanese data, but Tanaka found more (row 4). More syntactic completions were intonationally complete in Japanese (81%; 82%) than in English (54%) (row 8). In rows 9–14, F&T and Furo found few intonational completions that were not pragmatically complete (row 9), and all pragmatic completions were intonationally complete by definition (row 12). F&T noted that most pragmatic completions were also syntactically complete (row 14).

Complex Transition Relevance Places (CTRP) are points where intonational and pragmatic completion select syntactic completion points. The percentage of syntactic completions that were CTRPs was lower in English (52%), than in Japanese (77%; 77%) (row 16). The percentage of speaker changes that occurred at CTRPs (English 71%, Japanese 76%) (row 21) was similar across languages. However, row 22 shows that fewer CTRPs had speaker changes in English (48%) than in Japanese (84%, 78%). Furo showed further that the percentage of speaker changes increased from syntactic completions (73%), to intonational completions (80%), to pragmatic completions (84%) (rows 23–25).

F&T (1996) concluded that CTRPs are better predictors of speaker change than syntactic completion points alone. Approximately half (47.5%) of the CTRPs in their English data had speaker changes, and 71% of the speaker changes occurred at CTRPs. They demonstrated that speaker change did not occur at about half (52.5%) of the CTRPs and about a third of the speaker changes (29%) occurred at non-CTRPs due to interactional factors.

Tanaka's results in Table 28.4 differ because they are based on "conversational syntactic completions." Unlike F&T and Furo, Tanaka counted speaker change as a percentage of full turns, rather than full and back channel turns. She also excluded minimal acknowledgments like those in 2 and 4 in (18) because they perform different interactional work, and often occur in overlap. In addition, she did not require pragmatic completions to be intonationally complete, and concluded that pragmatic completion (rather than CTRPs) is the best predictor of speaker change.

Furo developed F&T's analysis further by giving the breakdown for full turn speaker changes and back channel speaker changes shown in Table 28.5. (F&T did not indicate the breakdown, and Tanaka excluded some back channels.) Furo's results show that while 76% of all speaker changes occurred at CTRPs (Table 28.4), 90% of full speaker changes and only 59% of back channel speaker changes occurred at CTRPs (Table 28.5). Further investigation of the unit types where back channel versus full speaker changes occur is likely to reveal significant differences between English and Japanese. In addition, Furo found that there were eight motivations for speaker changes at non-CTRPs: "(1) collaborating with others, (2) adding information, (3) asking questions/clarification, (4) showing surprise, (5) correcting the previous utterance, (6) showing strong agreement,

Table 28.5 *Number of different types of SC occurring at CTRPs and ¬CTRPs*

	CTRP		¬CTRP		Total
Full SC	356	90.4%	38	9.6%	394 (54%)
BC SC	198	59.1%	137	40.9%	335 (46%)
All SC	554	76.0%	175	24.0%	729

(7) showing disagreement, (8) introducing a new topic" (1998: 47). Cases where there was no speaker change at a CTRP included (1) overlap, (2) rush-throughs, and (3) self-selection after a pause.

The question of which resources are most influential for turn-taking should be of interest to linguists with a background in conversation analysis who also specialize in syntax, prosody (intonation), or pragmatics. In particular, the task of finding appropriate and possibly universal criteria is a challenge. In comparing and contrasting languages such as English and Japanese, on the one hand, operationalization should be as similar as possible, but, on the other, one needs to pay attention to large differences in the languages; for example, differences in word order and the extensive use of back channel in Japanese as compared to English.

4.3 Co-construction

Co-construction (Maynard's (1989) co-creation) is a practice found in spoken conversation. However, researchers have varied in their position on whether Japanese speakers do or do not finish each other's sentences. In regard to projectability, researchers have argued that while in English it is "easy" to predict what is coming, in Japanese speakers have to "wait and see" (Fox, Hayashi, and Jasperson 1996: 213) or "wait to say" (Szatrowski 2002).

Ono and Yoshida (1995: 116) define co-construction as "a syntactic unit (i.e. phrase, clause, and sentence) produced by more than one speaker, in which the utterance by the first speaker is taken by the second speaker as a part of his/her unit," and argue that Japanese speakers do not complete one another's sentences. They give examples where the second speaker adds a postpositional element (e.g. *Ichimarukyū* '(the building) 109' + *no mae de* 'in front of'), the verb to a clause started by the first speaker, a main clause to a subordinate clause, and a subordinate clause to a main clause. They claim that co-construction is rare because "it seems impolite to finish another speaker's sentence or to provide additional information unexpressed by the first speaker" (p. 120), and propose a pragmatic constraint in Japanese against another speaker intruding on the speaker's territory of information (Kamio 1994). They conclude that co-construction is allowed in the case of assumed world knowledge or an event that both speakers co-experienced. It is also possible in cases where these conditions are violated if information in the second speaker's utterance was mentioned previously as in (20) (p. 125), or if the second speaker turns the first speaker's utterance into a question as in (21) (p. 126).

(20) H *Sō yuu chūtohanpa na kanji de kō yatchatta tte iu no ga boku wa*
'(He) did (it) by halves, I'
S *ikenai to omou.*
'think (it's) bad.'

(21) H *Morioka kara mata densha ni notte ichijikan gurai no tokoro*
'From Morioka, riding on a train again, a place which is about one hour (away)'
O *itta no?*
'(you) went (to)?'

In contrast, Hayashi and Mori (1998) claim that "We [Japanese] *do* 'finish each other's sentences'" to negotiate, "achieve, and display to each other, *concurrent understanding*" (Goodwin and Goodwin 1987: 3) as in (22) (p. 81), manage participant alignment (agreement or disagreement) as in (23) (p. 84), and organize "assisted explaining" (Lerner and Takagi 1999). In (22), the participants have been recalling going to a makeup workshop as teenagers, and use co-construction to make their independent prior experiences into collective experiences. In (23), K and S use co-construction to indicate that they agree that they like to brush their teeth and to align together against two other participants who dislike brushing their teeth (Hayashi and Mori 1998: 81).

(22) 1 M → *Nanka, [konna shikyōhin mora [tte kaette kite sa::,*
'Right, like this sort of sample, (we) receive them and go home'
2 N *[an*
3T → *[Sō, kuru n da yo ne::.*
'Right, and come back.'

(23) 1 K *Tada nanka mo tsurutsuru shite nai to:* (0.3) *i [ya da kara::*
'But, uhm, because (I) don't like it if (the surface of my teeth) isn't smooth,
2S *[Sō desu yo nyoue::.* <sic>
'I agree.'
3 K → *Yappari tetteiteki ni::* (0.3)
'You know, thoroughly,'
4S → *Migakimasu yo ne::.*
'(We) brush (them), right?'

Hayashi and Mori object to Ono and Yoshida making the claim that co-construction is rare in Japanese compared to English because "even if some practice does not occur very frequently in some set of transcripts in one language, we cannot prematurely conclude that that practice is 'rare' in that language" (p. 89). They indicate further that a "speaker's private territory" is not static, but rather "is a contingent achievement that is negotiated moment-by-moment by multiple participants in ongoing social interactions" (pp. 90–91), and suggest that it is more constructive to examine what aspects of social interaction allow for co-construction.

I (Szatrowski 2007) take the middle ground, by on the one hand taking Ono and Yoshida's pragmatic constraint seriously, and on the other situating co-construction in the interactional context. I observed four co-construction types: (1) participants align together in addressing other participants, (2) the latter speaker completes the co-construction on the former speaker's footing, (3) the latter speaker completes the co-construction on his/her own footing as (a) an Information Presenter or (b) Supporting Participant (see Section 3.2.2). I demonstrated how co-construction allows speakers to use elements related to perspective (deictic verbs, honorifics, pronouns) and subjectivity (person restriction with subjective predicates including adjectives/nominals of emotion, predicates of desire and will, verbs related to sensation, sensory perception, cognition, and thinking) (Iwasaki 1993; Masuoka 1997b) to penetrate/display private territory. Structures that participants co-construct in interaction as shown in (24) may violate sentence level grammars.

(24) a. 58A *Mā itte mo ii n da kedomo,* +59B *mata iku no wa mendokusai?*
58A 'Well, it's that (it)'s okay if (I/you) go,' +59B 'but is going (away from the speaker) again a bother?'

b. 1F *Kinō chotto yō ga atte, Kamakura e* +2G *oide ni natta n desu ka.*
1F 'Yesterday (I/you) just had some business, and to Kamakura' +2G 'it's that (you) went (HONORIFIC)?'

Further research on how co-construction is elicited or offered, and on the role of non-verbal behavior (Szatrowski 2000a; Hayashi 2003) and prosody should prove fruitful.

5 Multimodal Discourse/Conversation Approaches

The most recent wave of research includes analysis of language together with gesture, gaze, and other multimodal resources in face-to-face conversation. I will focus on two studies in research on storytelling in spontaneous conversation that has highlighted the use of multimodal resources (Koike 2001, 2009, 2010, 2014; Hayashi, Mori, and Takagi 2002; Karatsu 2004, 2012; Szatrowski 2010).

Koike (2010) analyzes how the use of language and the body mutually elaborate one another for the recovery of ellipsis and cuing action. In the storytelling in (25) (2010: 67–71), Fujio uses gaze and gestures to indicate the characters ellipted in his story (empty parentheses ( )), and to indicate the action being done through his telling. Prior to (24), Taku mentions that recently he and Seiji had some delicious *okonomiyaki* 'Japanese-style pancake.' In line 15 he adds that it was the time when he stood up (a common friend) Ruri and laughs. Taku's utterance is a possible beginning for a funny story, but Fujio is the one who tells the story of how Taku stood up Ruri, and he does so in a more serious tone.

(25) Fujio's Story

15 Taku *Kono mae itta toki yan. Ruri-san futta toki ya. {U he he he he}*
'(It)'s the time when (we) went (to eat *okonomiyaki*) the other day. (It)'s the time when (I) stood up Ruri. {LAUGH}'
16 (1.0)
17 Fujio → *Nanka ne? burēdo-suru tte yuute [te ne?*
'You know? () (was) saying () will (go) [do] rollerblading, and, you know?'
18 Taku [*{He he he he}*
['{LAUGH}'
19 Fujio → *Shimasen ka tte koe kakete kite Ruri-san ni.*
'() asked "Won't () do (it with ())?" [to] Ruri, and,'
20 (1.0)
21 Fujio → *Nde [itte:,*
'And [() went, and,'
22 Seiji [*E? So yatta n.*
['What? Is it that (it) was so?'
23 Fujio → *Un. Nde itte:, hona ikimasho ka: yuute ne:, kite:, Taku-, Nakai-sensē mo:,*
'Yeah. And, () went, and () said well then shall (we) go, you know, and () came, and Taku-, Mr. Nakai also,'
24 Seiji °*Un.*°
'°Uh-huh.°'
25 Fujio *Kite, Taku-san kēhen nā yuttara Ruri-san honja Taku-san ni kakemasho ka:, yuttara:, metchamecha daibakushō shite ru n desu yo Ruri-san ga.*
'Came, and when () said Taku hasn't come, has he, and when Ruri said well then shall () call Taku, and it's that () is laughing out loud, Ruri is.'
26 Taku *{Ha ha [ha ha}*
'{LAUGH}'
27 Seiji [°*Un.*°
['°Uh-huh.°'
28 Fujio → *Nani ka na: omotara nondon nen [tte iu.*
'When () wondered what is (going on), it turns out that (Lit. (the situation) is that) it's that () is drinking.'
29 Taku [*{Ha ha ha}*
['{LAUGH}'

It is significant that Fujio is pointing at Taku while gazing at Seiji in lines 17 and 19 (Figure 28.2).[12] His gaze at Seiji suggests that Seiji is the addressed recipient of the story, in this case the only participant that

[12] The parts of utterances where a body movement is sustained are indicated with a dashed underline.

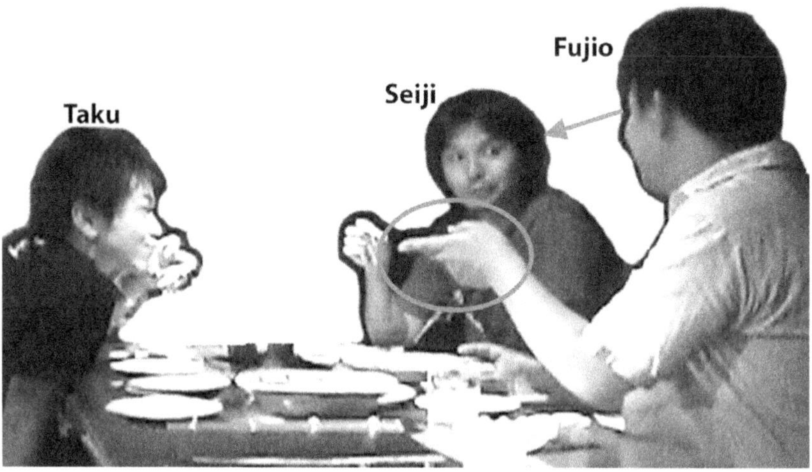

Figure 28.2 Fujio looks at Seiji while pointing at Taku (lines 17, 19) (Koike 2010: 70)

Figure 28.3 Fujio maintains his gaze at Seiji while pointing at himself (lines 21, 23) (Koike 2010: 70)

does not know the story. Fujio's pointing indicates that the ellipted information in the parentheses is as follows: 'You know? (he = Taku) (was) saying (he = Taku) will (go) [do] rollerblading, and, you know? (he = Taku) asked "Won't (you = Ruri) do (it with (me = Taku))?" [to] Ruri, and.'

Next, still gazing at Seiji, Fujio points at himself during lines 21 and 23 (Figure 28.3). His pointing indicates that "I" (= Fujio) is the ellipted information in these clauses, making the English translation 'And (I) went, and, Yeah. And, (I) went, and (I) said well then shall (we) go, you know, and (I) came, and Taku-, Mr. Nakai also.'

Subsequently, Fujio continues to gaze at Seiji and points at Taku again in line 28 (Figure 28.4). Once again his pointing indicates that

Figure 28.4 Fujio maintains his gaze at Seiji while pointing at Taku (line 28) (Koike 2010: 70)

the ellipted information relates to Taku ('When (I = Fujio) wondered what is (going on), it turns out (Lit. (the situation) is that) it's that (he = Taku) is drinking.')

Koike also demonstrates how Fujio's pointing and gaze cue the action behind his story. "Fujio portrays Taku as an irresponsible selfish villain who stood up Ruri and other friends because he was drinking, despite the fact that Taku was the one who first invited Ruri to go rollerblading" (Koike 2010: 72). Fujio shows his accusatory attitude toward Taku in his pointing at Taku, gaze at Seiji, and body posture. Although Taku is present and is the principal character of Fujio's story, Fujio creates an alliance with Seiji by turning his upper body and head toward Seiji throughout the story. This strengthens his accusation of Taku.

Coming full circle from Hinds's analysis of ellipsis and discourse structure in the 1970s, Koike contributes new insight to research on ellipsis and storytelling. Specifically, she demonstrates how grammar and actions are constructed through a multitude of mutually elaborating verbal and non-verbal resources (Goodwin 2003).

Karatsu (2012) investigated the overall process of storytelling focusing on patterns of use; for example, how a story becomes worth telling, shared and influenced by the participants. Her analysis focuses on social and conversational circumstances, storytellability, and how they affect the participants' lives as summarized in Figure 28.5.

For example, the storyteller establishes the groundwork and obtains the interest of story recipient(s) using a confirmation request as in 13k in (26) and 3c in (27). In (26) (Karatsu 2012: 71), after the prospective storyteller Kayo obtains her recipient Yoko's recognition of the referent, she tells a humorous story about how a professor and the lady were caught by surprise when they saw each other at a bar.

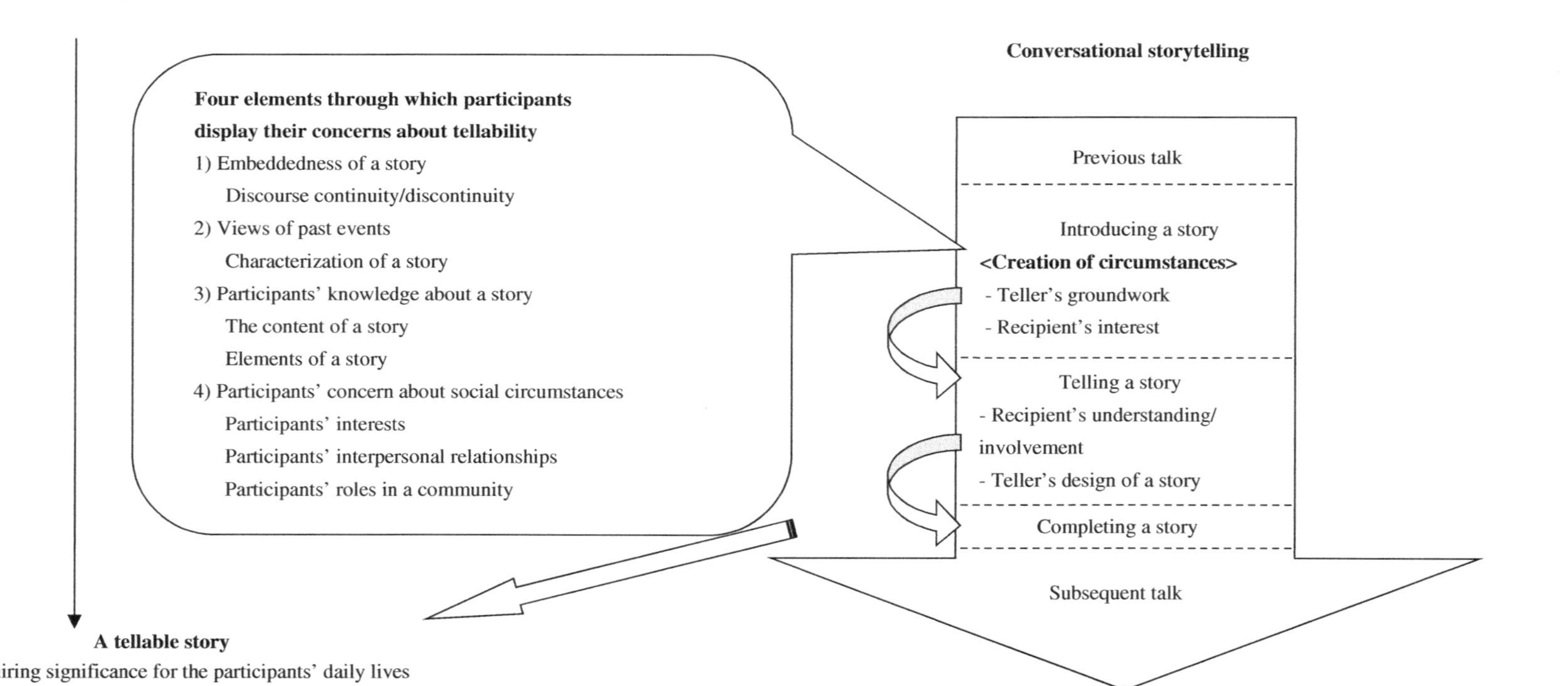

Figure 28.5 Storytelling and the participants' concerns about the tellability of a story (Karatsu 2012: 5)

(26) 13 K *.hhh Kyonen made sa, uketsuke ni ita (.) ano (.) kenkyūshitsutō no uketsuke ni ita obasan iru jan.*
.'hhh until last year uhm you know, at the reception desk (.) uhm (.) there is the lady who was at the reception desk in the lab building, isn't there.'
14Y *Hai. Hai. [Hai.*
'Yes. Yes. [Yes.'
15 K *[Ano obasan ga ite e:: to ka (.)*
['That lady was (at the bar) and (she says) "Wo::w" or something (.)'

In contrast, in (27) (Karatsu 2012: 71–72 and Karatsu 2004: 135–136, 139), the prospective storyteller Chie's confirmation request is met by a claim by her recipient Aki that the situation is not comparable to a story Aki had just told (about a boy who said he preferred to be asked about his scar rather than to be stared at). Chie accompanies her confirmation request in 3C with the gesture in Figure 28.6[13] (Karatsu 2004: 135) where she strokes her hair lightly two times to evoke Aki's memory of when she (=Chie) dyed her hair. However, instead of acknowledging the event, Aki tilts her head in 4A and indicates that Chie's prospective story is not an appropriate sequel (second story) to Aki's previous story. Then, in 8A Aki overlaps Chie's response (7C) to Beniko's question (6B), and begins to tell Chie's story while leaning forward with her arm extended across the table pointing at Chie (Figure 28.7). In this way, initially Aki prevents Chie's story from moving forward, and the participants use gestures and pointing to negotiate if, how, and by whom the story will be told.

(27) 1C *Kimi warui. Kikarenai [to.*
'(I) would feel strange. [If (I) were not asked.'
2A *[Kikarenai to:?*
['If (you) were not asked?'
3C *Un. Dakara, kami no ke sā, midori iro ni someta koto atta jan. [Ichiji.*
'Yeah. So, my hair, you know, (I) had the experience of dying (my hair) green, didn't I.
[(At) one time.
4A *[@Sore zenzen chigau n ja [nai?@ {hi hi hi}*
['@Isn't it that that's totally different?@ {LAUGH}'
5C *[{hu hu}*
['{LAUGH}'
6B *@·Itsu·@ desu ka. [sore.*
'@·When·@ (was it). [that.'
7C *[<? kedo @sa,@>*
['<? but @you know,@>'
8A *[A, nanka ne, kami midori iro ni sometara ne, nanka ne,*
['Oh, somehow, you know, when (you/she) dyed (your/her) hair you know, somehow, you know,'

[13] The participants in (27) from left to right (as viewed from the camera) are Aki, Beniko and Chie.

Figure 28.6 Chie strokes her hair lightly two times during her confirmation request in 3C (Karatsu 2004: 139)

Figure 28.7 Aki begins to tell Chie's story while pointing at Chie in 8A (Karatsu 2004: 139)

These excerpts illustrate the patterns in the process of storytelling shown in Figure 28.8 (Karatsu 2012: 72).

Other research on multimodality in Japanese conversation includes studies of head nodding, gaze, and back channel (Maynard 1987; Szatrowski 2000b, 2003; Aoki 2011), and gaze and facial displays in subunit construction within turn construction units (Iwasaki 2011).

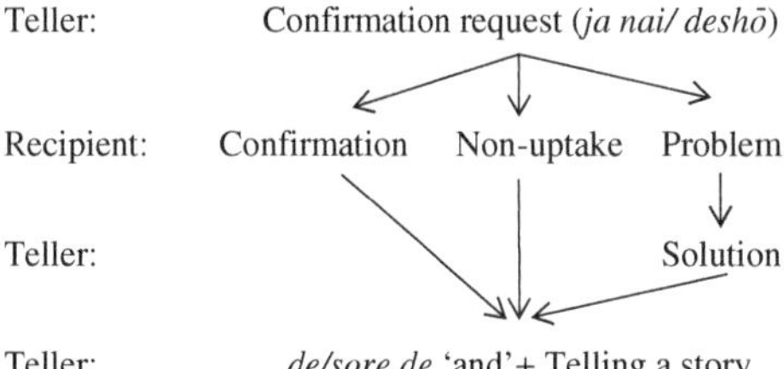

Figure 28.8 Interactional sequences after the teller's confirmation request (Karatsu 2012: 72)

6 Conclusion

Recent studies have explored other conversational genre including university lectures (Sakuma 2010), talk about food (Szatrowski 2014), interviews (Kumagai and Kitani 2010), and casual conversation among native and non-native Japanese speakers (Ohba 2012; Tsutsui 2012). It is important to note that the data for this research comes from spontaneous conversation, not made-up conversations or role play. Unsettled issues include the role of social context, identity, gender, and the need for research on overall conversational development and prosody. There is also a need to include a Japanese version of the transcription. There is no question but that use of Japanese writing in transcriptions would make this research more accessible to native speakers of Japanese, non-English speaking researchers of Japanese, researchers in countries that use Chinese characters in their writing system, etc. Prosody is another area that deserves more concern, and is crucial for the interpretation of conversational data.

Transcription Conventions

? rising intonation, not necessarily a question
: lengthening of the preceding sound
.hh in-breath
tch saliva click
@ @ laughing voice
° ° quieter voice
· · louder voice
< ? > indecipherable or slightly audible speech
(0.7) length of pause in seconds
[overlapping utterances
= = latched utterances, no gap
{} non-linguistic sounds such as laughter
note about the data

29

Language, Gender, and Sexuality

Shigeko Okamoto

1 Introduction

Japanese language and gender research has advanced greatly in the last four decades. During the course of this development, the field as a whole – involving English, Japanese, and other languages – has witnessed a major shift in direction since the early 1990s. In this introduction I summarize the important aspects of this radical turn in the field as a whole and then in Japanese language and gender research specifically in order to situate the latter in the broader development of the field. The ensuing three sections focus on Japanese and are organized as follows: research on the construction of linguistic gender norms (Section 2), research on situated language practice (Section 3), theoretical issues raised by the findings of these previous studies (Section 4), and conclusion (Section 5).

1.1 Shifting Directions in Language and Gender Research in General

Earlier research on language and gender placed its primary focus on gender differences, mapping linguistic forms straightforwardly to women or men as a whole based on the assumption that a particular linguistic form is a "direct index" (Och 1992) of gender. Reconsidering this static approach, since the early 1990s scholars have started exploring an alternative approach, taking a more critical view of the relationship between language and gender. It is argued that the binary of women and men is not a given, but rather is ideologically constructed, and that real women and men differ socially and contextually and cannot be assumed to always behave in the same way. From this standpoint, numerous studies have examined the intersection of gender with other social variables (e.g. age, class, ethnicity, sexuality, social setting) in language use and

I thank Yoko Hasegawa, Emi Morita, Shigeko Kumagai, and Cindi SturtzSreetharan for valuable comments.

interpretation (see, e.g., Ehrich, Meyerhoff, and Holmes 2014 for an overview of current research). In particular, examining the intersection of gender with sexuality is increasingly recognized as vital in accounting for the linguistic practice of not only sexual minorities but also heterosexual speakers.

These empirical studies found extensive diversity and complexity in language use and interpretation that challenge any attempt to directly link linguistic forms to gender. To cope with this challenge, the notion of indirect index (Ochs 1992)[1] has been proposed and the relationship between a linguistic form (e.g. honorifics) and a particular social group (e.g. women and/or middle-class) is viewed as indirect and socially constructed, mediated through qualities and stances (e.g. politeness, refinement) stereotypically associated with that social group (Eckert 2008). The link is therefore ideologically based and certain kinds of links become normative, but may be contested or negotiated in specific local interactional contexts.

The notion of indirect index is imperative for a social constructionist view of language and gender (or other social groups) – a view that assumes that language is not simply a reflection of gender, but may serve as a resource for constructing identities/personae[2] in specific local contexts (e.g. Bucholtz and Hall 2005). That is, language is viewed as social practice in which women and men, regarded as members of macro-level distinct categories, use language variously in order to construct diverse gender and sexuality identities. It is thus crucial to consider how macro-level normative categories are related to micro-level interactions in local contexts, as is increasingly recognized in the field.

1.2 Shifting Directions in Japanese Language and Gender Research

Japanese language and gender (and sexuality) research has also taken a parallel turn since the early 1990s. The primary focus in earlier research was on gender differences, or differences between *joseigo* 'women's language' and *danseigo* 'men's language,' characterized in terms of a set of features, such as those listed in Table 29.1.[3]

While the earlier research served as a valuable starting point, its static approach of mapping linguistic forms directly to gender raised many questions, in particular the following two inter-related questions: (a) whether the differences between *joseigo* and *danseigo* characterized primarily based on researchers' introspections or self-report survey data are empirically observable in situated interactions, and (b) what those differences between *joseigo* and *danseigo* represent, if they are not entirely supported by empirical evidence.

[1] Cf. Hasegawa (2010), who points out the limitations of Ochs's theory of indirect indexing.

[2] The notion of identity is used here in the sense of a context-dependent, fluid, and relationally understood social persona rather than what is invariably associated with an individual (Bucholtz and Hall 2005).

[3] Table 29.1 is based on previous studies, including Ide (1982b) and Shibamoto Smith (2003).

Table 29.1 *Example features of* joseigo *and* danseigo

Linguistic features	*Joseigo*	*Danseigo*
First person pronouns	*atashi*	*boku, ore, washi*
Second person pronouns	*anata*	*kimi, anata*
Sentence-final particles	*wa, wa yo, wa ne, kashira*	*ze, zo*
Honorifics	women's use > men's use	men's use < women's use
Interjections	*ara, mā*	*oi, kora*
Directives	gerundive (e.g. *Itte* 'Please go') or with honorific (e.g. *Itte kudasaru?* 'Would you go?'	imperative (e.g. *Ike* 'go')
Stylistic features	gentle, polite, refined	direct, forceful, rough

Prompted by the first question, researchers began investigating the actual speech of socially diverse women and men and have demonstrated extensive within-gender diversity in their speech.[4] This diversity invites the second question. And it has been claimed that *joseigo* and *danseigo* correspond to linguistic gender norms rather than accurate descriptions of how women and men use language in real-world situations. Scores of researchers then have examined a wide variety of metapragmatic discourse, addressing the question of how such norms are constructed in Japanese society. In the following, I first review the research on the second question, and then that on the first question.

2 The Construction of Linguistic Gender Norms in Japanese Society: Evidence from Metapragmatic Discourse

A large number of previous studies as a whole show that linguistic gender norms have been actively constructed in Japanese society. These studies have examined metapragmatic discourses, or comments, on women's and men's speech in a variety of genres. Such comments may be given explicitly as in self-help books or online blogs, or implicitly through the stratified representation of characters' speech in fictional worlds, such as novels and films (Okamoto and Shibamoto Smith 2008: 93). They are by nature prescriptive rather than descriptive. But the need to examine metapragmatic discourses closely is increasingly recognized because they reveal native speakers' beliefs and attitudes toward language structure and use (e.g. Agha 2003: 242).

The construction of linguistic gender norms as part of general behavioral norms has a long history in Japan, dating back to early premodern times and it is focused primarily on women's language use, as women's behavior has been regulated much more explicitly and intensely than men's. In this section, I discuss notable findings of the previous studies

[4] Note that Hasegawa (2010) found in her data of soliloquy that the female subjects' use of gendered speech was fairly uniform.

on this topic. In doing so, I pay special attention to two aspects of linguistic gender norms: (a) stylistic features as characterized in terms of such qualities and stances as gentleness, politeness, and elegance, and (b) specific linguistic features such as personal pronouns and sentence-final particles that are linked to those qualities and stances (see Okamoto and Shibamoto Smith 2008 for a discussion of these two aspects of linguistic gender norms).

2.1 Premodern Japan

Evidence suggests the existence of linguistic gender norms since ancient times. For example, documents (e.g. stories, diaries) from the Heian period (794–1185) indicate that women were expected to speak gently in a quiet voice and in a reserved manner, and also to use *kana* syllabary and Japanese-origin words (*wago*), rather than *kanji* and Sino-Japanese words (*kango*), which were reserved for men (e.g. Endo 1997: 23–29). Such expectations continued to be upheld in the Middle Ages, as evidenced in genres, such as *Kyōgen* plays and women's conduct books, that began to emerge during this period.

In the feudal Edo-period (1603–1867), women's language use (and other aspects of their behavior) began to be more explicitly regulated under the patriarchal social system combined with the ideology of *danson-johi* 'male supremacy, female inferiority' derived from Confucianism and Buddhism (Nakamura 2007a: 47). A large number of conduct manuals and ethics books for women were written and many of them included remarks on *fugen*, lit. 'women's language,' emphasizing that women should speak in a reserved, gentle, polite, and refined manner. Some of these books also gave detailed instructions about specific linguistic features, such as to be taciturn, to speak in a low voice, to use *wago* rather than *kango*, and to use the (polite) prefix *o-* and indirect reference terms for certain objects. Many of these features resemble the features of *nyōbō kotoba* 'court ladies' language,' or a variety emerged in the Middle Ages among women working in the imperial palace, which suggests a class-based ideology in that *nyōbō kotoba* was considered an ideal model for women's speech.

2.2 Modern Japan

Did the concept of ideal women's language use change along with the development of modern Japan? Some important aspects concerning specific linguistic features did (see below), but qualities and stances expected of women seem to have hardly changed in that women continued to be taught, directly or indirectly, to speak in a reserved, gentle, polite, and refined manner through a variety of avenues in the now nationally available media – for example, ethics textbooks, magazines, and characters' dialogs in novels (e.g. Satake 2004).

These instructions also referred to specific linguistic features, such as honorifics and *wago*, that were recommended in premodern Japan. However, there was one significant difference from premodern times. That is, "Standard Japanese" (SJ), defined as the speech of Tokyoites in middle class or above, began to be incorporated into the concept of ideal women's language. And it has been claimed that modern Japanese women's language, or SJ-based *joseigo*, is a product of Japan's modernity, totally severed from the concept of (ideal) women's speech in premodern Japan (e.g. Inoue 2002: 410–411). However, it has also been argued that it is neither completely severed nor handed down faithfully from premodern times and that it is the result of a more complex process in which the modern ideology of SJ is integrated into the age-old ideology of femininity that women should speak gently, politely, and elegantly (Okamoto 2008: 95–96; Okamoto and Shibamoto Smith 2016: 216–224). To put it differently, when the (women's version of) Tokyo dialect is "taken out" from its region and repositioned in the national context as SJ, it is no longer viewed simply as a regional dialect in that SJ and other dialects came to be stratified and reinterpreted, or "resemiotized" (e.g. Agha 2003: 251), with SJ, or its women's version, as being proper, polite, and gentle (or not rough), and feminine.

Research also shows that before and during the war in the 1930s and early 1940s, the term *fujingo* or *joseigo* 'women's language' began to be used frequently by scholars, and that it was regarded as polite, gentle, and elegant, and hence a sign of the superiority of Japanese culture. Women were then taught to speak in a feminine manner, using specific linguistic features such as honorifics and personal pronouns in SJ forms (Washi 2004: 83–87). According to Nakamura (2007a: 239–244), such sentence-final forms as *te yo* and *da wa* that were part of Meiji schoolgirls' language, or *teyo dawa kotoba*, were excluded from the grammar books of *kokugo* 'national language' during the Meiji period because they were considered rough and vulgar. But as the use of these sentence-final forms spread to a larger group of women (in the middle class and above) in fiction, especially in novels, and presumably also in reality, they began to be elevated in status and included as part of *joseigo* in the grammar books of *kokugo* published during this period. This is an excellent example of resemiotization through recontextualization.

2.3 Contemporary Japan

These efforts to gender linguistic norms hardly came to an end in the supposedly democratic post-war Japan. Explicit instructions on women's speech are given in many forms. For example, numerous self-help books on women's speech stress the importance of speaking politely, gently, and elegantly. They also place an enormous emphasis on speaking beautifully, which is touted as a way to make a (heterosexual) woman beautiful and attractive (to men). These qualities are then linked to specific linguistic features such as honorifics, certain sentence ending forms, hedges, and a variety of ways of making indirect speech acts, with examples given in SJ forms (see Okamoto 2010a for examples). These observations indicate that in self-help books, feminine ways of speaking are regarded as linguistic capital, or resources, that can be used to create a desired context rather than simply reflecting the context toward the construction of identities, or "better" persona.

We also sometimes encounter direct comments in letters-to-the-editor in newspapers and magazines that often criticize women's "unfeminine" speech. The rapid propagation of the Internet today is especially conducive to such metapragmatic activities. Analyses of blogs reported by Okamoto and Shibamoto Smith (2016: 248–257) illustrate that many writers criticize women who use rough and vulgar language, although others express disagreement. They also observed blogs that comment on men's speech, criticizing or approving men who speak gently and politely, that is, speak "like women" or like *okama* 'effeminate gay men.'

Indirect, or implicit, comments are also actively made through the representation of characters' speech in novels, children's stories, *manga*, films, TV dramas, and so forth (e.g. Satake 2003). It has been reported that, although female characters' diverse speech patterns are well represented, heroines and/or socially desirable characters tend to use *joseigo* while secondary and peripheral characters use regional dialects or *danseigo* (Kinsui 2003: 54–57). For example, Okamoto and Shibamoto Smith's (2008: 97–102) analysis of a TV drama (*Tenka* 2004) shows that even when the setting is in regional Japan (Sendai, Tohoku), the young heroine who grew up in the area speaks in SJ-based *joseigo*, while the secondary and peripheral female characters use Tohoku dialect or a mixture of *joseigo* and the dialect. Kumagai (2010: 52) argues that when contrasted with the image of SJ associated with white-collar Tokyoites, Tohoku dialect is not understood simply as a regional dialect, but is associated with images such as farmers, countrified people, or rough and unfeminine women. That is, Tohoku dialect is overlaid by stratified meanings vis-à-vis SJ.[5]

Examining *manga*, Chinami (2010: 78–79) notes that, although female characters use diverse speech patterns, overall, stereotypical feminine patterns are assigned to young women in the mainstream society. Based on her analysis of popular TV shows for children broadcast in Okinawa between 2008 and 2010, Takahashi (2011: 68) concludes that SJ-based *joseigo* is reserved for heroines who can be the objects of male love, while *danseigo* is assigned to old women, "bad" or "mentally weak" women, and foreigners. These studies suggest that the use of SJ-based *joseigo* is one

[5] In recent years, there have been more TV dramas and films in which heroines use regional dialects. However, those heroines are somewhat "marked," as discussed below. It remains to be seen whether the increased use of dialects by heroines has any lasting impact on changing the stratified meanings of SJ and dialects or whether it is a temporary phenomenon simply for entertainment.

aspect of the portrayal of a woman's desirability as a heterosexual woman, which is also gauged in terms of other aspects of their personae, including their age, class, and regionality. Shibamoto Smith and Occhi (2009) present a somewhat more complicated example. Analyzing a TV drama series (*Wakaba* 2005), they conclude that, due to the gradient association of modernity with SJ, Kansai dialect (KD, hereafter), and other dialects, romantic heroines are most likely to use SJ-based *joseigo* and occasionally KD. This suggests that SJ is woven into the concept of heteronormative femininity, but that it is possible to construct femininity using a regional dialect to some extent, as far as represented speech is concerned.

Dialogs in novels, films, and so forth translated from other languages into Japanese also offer numerous examples. To cite one recent example, in comparing the English and Japanese versions of a popular computer game (*Fire Emblem Awakening* 2012), in which the game player can choose either the male or the female protagonist, Elisa Salomone in her unpublished study conducted in 2016,[6] found that in the English version there is no difference in the speech of male and female protagonists (e.g. *You know who I am*), whereas in the Japanese version the male character uses stereotypical *danseigo* forms without honorifics (e.g. *Ore wa dare da* 'Who am I?'), while the female character uses *joseigo* forms, including honorifics (e.g. *Watashi wa dare desu ka* 'Who am I?'). Research also shows stratified representations of the speech of different kinds of female characters. As is well known, in *Gone with the Wind*, the heroine uses SJ-based *joseigo* while the black slaves use a pseudo-countrified, or pseudo-Tohoku, dialect (Kinsui 2003: 186–187). Kumagai (2010: 60) also offers similar examples, including the Japanese translation of the American TV comedy show *I Love Lucy*, in which the heroine, a white middle-class housewife, normally uses *joseigo*, but uses a pseudo-Tohoku dialect when she disguises herself as a lower-class woman in the slums. Kumagai (2010: 61) points out that the perpetual assignment of the pseudo-Tohoku dialect to characters in the lower social strata reproduces and reinforces the negative image of Tohoku dialect and its speakers.

Research on male characters' speech also shows diversity, but heroes tend to use SJ-based *danseigo* (e.g. Takahashi 2011: 55). Examining a TV drama series (*Haken no hinkaku* 'The Dignity of the Temp' 2007), Occhi, SturzStreetharan, and Shibamoto Smith (2010: 421) conclude that, although the representation of romantic heroes' masculinity is more complex than the use of SJ *danseigo*, involving other social variables (e.g. regionality and occupation), there is a tendency for successful romantic heroes to use SJ or, on a more limited basis, KD, suggesting the strongest tie between SJ and (heteronormative) masculinity.

Several studies concern the pronouns *ore* and *boku* (e.g. Kinsui 2003: 118–126), the former being associated with stronger and more aggressive

[6] This study was reported in a term paper by one of the author's students.

images of masculinity than the latter. According to Nakamura (2007b: 63–64), for instance, in the 1939 translation of *Gone with the Wind*, the two male protagonists, Rhett Butler and Ashley Wilkes, both use *boku*, but in the 1994 version, Rhett uses *ore*, while Ashley, who is more gentlemanly than Rhett, still uses *boku*. This suggests the development of differentiated (indexical) meanings of *boku* and *ore* according to the different forms of masculinity. Sato (2010: 113–116) offers similar examples from her analyses of novels in which gentler men use *boku*, and tough, assertive men use *ore*. She also observes that the same character may shift between *boku* and *ore* depending on the context, as illustrated by the male protagonist in a novel (*Yasashii ongaku* 'Gentle Music' 2008) using *ore* in interactions with his girlfriend and *boku* in interactions with the parents of his girlfriend as well as in the first person narrative part of novel. Thus, *boku* and *ore* may be used as semiotic resources for constructing different forms of masculinity.

In sum, although there have been some notable changes, particularly related to SJ, the normative idea of how (ideal) women and men should speak has been tirelessly produced and reproduced in the long history of Japan. Note, however, that the dominant ideology of linguistic femininity and masculinity is neither fixed nor universally accepted. Because hegemony is never complete (e.g. Gal 1998: 321–323), it may be contested or negotiated, giving rise to diverse uses and interpretations of gendered linguistic forms – a topic taken up in Section 4.

3 Diversity in Situated Language Practice

Efforts to sustain linguistic gender norms continue, as seen in the preceding section. But how do real women and men speak in situated practice? Researchers have addressed this question by examining the actual speech of socially diverse women and men and have found wide within-gender diversity in speech. These studies illustrate the importance of considering the intersection of gender with other social variables in language use – variables such as the speaker's age, occupation, region, and sexuality, as well as other aspects of the context, such as the interlocutor, speech activity/act, and setting.

3.1 Women's Situated Speech

Studies offer plenty of evidence for women's diverse language use. Analyzing audio-recorded conversations, Okamoto and Sato (1992), one of the earliest studies on the topic, consider the intersection of gender with age and report that (SJ-speaking) young women used sentence-final forms associated with *joseigo* less frequently than (SJ-speaking) older women and instead used masculine forms more frequently. Additionally, they note that young women used strongly masculine forms[7] (e.g. the pronoun *ore*, the particle *zo*, imperatives) occasionally to index particular aspects of the context, such as friendship, emotions, and certain speech acts (see Section 4). More recently, Mizumoto (2006) analyzed audio-recorded conversations with respect to the use of feminine sentence-final particles by SJ-speaking women in three age groups (20s, 30s, 40s). She found that the use of some particles (e.g. *wa yo ne* and Noun *yo*) was greater among women in the oldest age group, while the use of some other particles (e.g. *wa, da wa*, and *kashira*) was hardly observed among women in any age group.

Matsumoto's (2004) study focuses on middle-aged women in a particular social group, namely, (SJ-speaking) mothers in the middle- and upper-middle classes. Her analyses of their audio-recorded conversations demonstrate wide inter-speaker and intra-speaker variation. That is, except for one woman who consistently employed a stereotypical feminine style, they used forms considered masculine to a greater or lesser extent, which Matsumoto links to a variety of meanings related to their personae, friendship, speech acts, and emotion. Focusing on young women, Miyazaki's (2004) ethnographic study of the speech of SJ-speaking junior high school students addresses the intersection of gender with age and social group. She found that girls in less school-oriented groups tended to use *ore* and *boku*, while more school-oriented girls used *atashi* and also *uchi*.

Okada's (2008) study concerns the intersection of gender with occupation and activity type. Based on the analyses of video-recorded interactions involving a female boxing coach training male boxers, Okada found that the coach frequently used direct imperatives – forms normatively associated with masculine speech – and argued that the use of such forms was required in situations that involved fast moment-by-moment changes in boxers' body movement. Focusing on women in positions of authority, Smith (1992) considers the intersection of gender with profession and power/position and reports that in giving directives, these women did not defeminize their speech, but rather used strategies normatively associated with women (e.g. the Passive Power strategy and the Motherese strategy). Takano (2005), also focusing on women in positions of authority, analyzes their speech with regard to 630 directives obtained from a large body of audio-recorded interactions at nine workplaces. He concludes that these women skillfully deploy gender-appropriate strategies, such as polite and deferential directives accompanied by various solidarity-building approaches. As discussed by Smith and Takano, their findings suggest that these professional women are not free from the gender norms and use feminine, that is, polite and gentle, speech styles as a strategy to deal with the conflict between their position and their gender.

If *joseigo* is based on SJ, how do female dialect users speak? How does gender interact with regionality? Although research on this matter is quite

[7] See Okamoto and Sato (1992) for the distinction of strongly and moderately masculine forms.

limited, Sunaoshi's (2004: 193–199) ethnographic study, for example, found that farmwomen in Ibaraki did not use *joseigo* forms and instead used stereotypically masculine forms, including the pronoun *ore* and the phonologically coalesced form *ē* instead of *ai* and *oi* (e.g. *ja nē* rather than *ja nai* 'it is not'). Okamoto (2016) analyzed six audio-recorded dyadic informal conversations: two involving women living in relatively rural areas in Yamagata (one between young women and the other between elderly women), two involving SJ-speaking young women, and two involving SJ-speaking young men. The results show that all four Yamagata women used certain stereotypically masculine forms, in particular phonological form *nē* (e.g. *wagaranē* 'I don't know'; *konē gā* 'don't (they) come?'), extensively – in fact, as frequently as the SJ-speaking young men did, whereas the SJ-speaking young women used those forms only infrequently in certain contexts (see Section 4). The Yamagata women also used masculine sentence-final forms quite frequently. Interestingly, the two older Yamagata women used *ora* to refer to themselves while the two young Yamagata women used *atashi*, suggesting the influence of the standard language ideology.

Research on women's speech must also take into consideration sexual orientation and sexual identification. Abe's (2010) ethnographic study, for example, examined the intersection of gender with sexuality and speech activities. Lesbian women at lesbian bars that Abe observed used masculine personal pronouns and sentence-final particles particularly when they were quarreling or angry. Abe (personal communication), on the other hand, examines one of the least studied groups of speakers, namely transsexual women, and observes wide inter- and intra-speaker variation with regard to the use of the first person pronouns (*watashi, ore*, and *jibun*), sentence-final forms, and honorifics.

3.2 Men's Situated Speech

Though not extensive, there have been a number of studies on men's situated language use. Smith (1992), for example, found a normative pattern in that professional men used direct and forceful directives more frequently than professional women did. Examining eight mixed-sex dyadic conversations, Itakura and Tsui (2004) found a normative pattern in three of them in which the male speaker dominated using a self-oriented style, supported by the female speaker's other-oriented style. Sato (2011), on the other hand, reports that while examining same-sex conversations, the transcribers criticized one speaker in one of the male dyads as being "too quiet and unmanly." In this conversation, one of the men used a dominating style in the topic management, which was supported by the other man who asked questions, gave supportive feedback, and produced much shorter turns. The latter is the man who was criticized as unmanly. Considering this finding in relation to Itakura and Tsui's finding,

Sato suggests that the interpretation is not simply a matter of gender or power, but involves gender norms in that the same supportive style may be interpreted differently depending on the gender of the speaker.

Miyazaki's (2004) aforementioned study included seventeen SJ-speaking junior high school boys. According to her report, the majority of the boys used the first person pronoun *ore* and a couple of them also used two other masculine forms, *oresama* or *washi*. But one boy, who was considered "weird," used *boku* and *atashi*. Interestingly, another boy was reported to use *boku* when talking with powerful boys, and *ore* when talking with gentle boys and girls, suggesting the intersection of gender with power relationships.

SturtzStreetharan's (2009) study concerns the intersection of gender with regionality and age. Analyzing eight audio-recorded informal conversations of men living in Osaka and Hyōgo, she observed a large age difference in that the six young men frequently used the masculine pronouns *ore* and *omae* 'you,' while the fourteen older men used them only infrequently and instead used *boku, watashi*, or *wareware* 'we.' SturtzStreetharan's (2004) study involves the intersection of gender with regionality and speech acts. She found that the Kansai men in the study used stereotypically masculine sentence-final forms only infrequently and that when they did, it was for achieving particular goals, such as expressing strong disagreements or joking.

The intersection of gender with sexuality (and other social variables) is another important issue. Analyses of the speech of *gei tarento* 'gay talent,' or gay celebrities, on TV reality shows,[8] for example, offer numerous examples of non-normative language use. Maree (2013) terms such language use as *onē kyara kotoba*, 'language of effeminate gay media personalities' and regards it as a linguistic commodity distributed in the (media entertainment) market. *Onē kyara kotoba* is characterized by the use of a stylized feminine speech style along with some incongruent elements (e.g. scathing remarks, occasional uses of strongly masculine styles) to bring about comical effects.

In summary, studies reviewed in Sections 2 and 3 demonstrate the importance of considering the intersectionality of gender with other social variables in language use and interpretation. We have seen that in both norm construction and situated practice, gender is intertwined with other variables, including age, class, occupation/position, regionality, and sexuality. Studies have also shown that gender interacts not only with other demographic aspects of the speaker, but also with a variety of features of the ongoing interactional context, including the interlocutor, speech activity/act, emotion, and setting.

One issue that calls for special attention is the intersection of gender with sexuality. Heteronormativity, or the normative alignment of sex, gender,

[8] Although talk in TV reality shows is, strictly speaking, not the same as spontaneous naturally occurring conversation. But it is not fully scripted, either, blurring the distinction between the two.

and sexuality, is widely taken for granted as natural, but studies have shown that it is not natural and rather requires serious reexamination regarding its significance for both sexually normative and non-normative speakers. For example, we have seen examples of gays' and lesbians' complex use of gendered speech styles, illustrating how they position themselves vis-à-vis the heteronormative social order. Several studies have also indicated the importance of sexuality for the speech of heterosexual women and men by showing that metapragmatic comments, made directly or indirectly, often assume heteronormativity and link stereotypical SJ-based *joseigo* to young, beautiful women deserving of male attention.

I emphasize, however, that the foregoing discussion does not mean that the speech of individuals in particular demographic categories (e.g. SJ-speaking middle-aged, middle-class mothers) is predictable. That is, however finely such categories are identified, a perfectly predictable model of their speech is unattainable because language cannot be directly linked to social categories, which makes it possible for members of the same category to use different speech styles in like situations (as illustrated by the diverse speech styles used by the SJ-speaking middle-aged, middle-class mothers observed by Matsumoto 2004). As a corollary, stereotypically gendered linguistic forms may be interpreted as indexing a multitude of meanings, some of which may even be incompatible with each other. I pursue these issues further in the following section.

4 Theoretical Issues: Relating Norms and Practice

I have reviewed research on the construction of linguistic gender norms and research on situated language practice. But how are norms, or macro-level social forces, and situated practice, or micro-level social interactions, related to each other? Considering this question is essential for a better understanding of the relationship between language and gender because, as Eckert (2008: 463) puts it, "[i]t is in the links between the individual and the macro-sociological category that we must seek the social practices in which people fashion their ways of speaking, moving their styles this way or that as they move their personae through situations from moment to moment, from day to day, and through the life course." In this section, I address this matter in relation to the following two issues that emerge from the findings of the previous studies: (a) variable and multiple indexical meanings; and (b) limitations of treating SJ-based *joseigo*/*danseigo* as linguistic gender norms.

4.1 Variable and Multiple Indexical Meanings

As noted earlier, the notion of indirect indexing plays a crucial role in accounting for the diverse social meanings of the same linguistic form used in specific social contexts. Eckert argues:

> [T]he very fact that the same linguistic variables may stratify regularly with multiple categories – for example, gender, ethnicity, and class – indicates that their meanings are not directly related to these categories but to something that is related to all of them. In other words, variables index demographic categories not directly but indirectly (Silverstein 1985), through their association with qualities and stances that enter into the construction of categories. (Eckert 2008: 455)

For example, Japanese honorifics may be indirectly linked to women through their association of the stereotypical quality of politeness with this social group, but the same quality may also be associated with higher social classes. And when politeness is linked to gender and class, it may further evoke meanings such as gentleness, formality, refinement, and elegance, which may further be interpreted as indexing even negative meanings, such as pretentiousness and aloofness in certain contexts. The meanings of linguistic forms are thus continually interpreted and reinterpreted in context (Silverstein 2003: 193) and hence are potentially multiple and variable. Eckert (2008: 455) introduces the notion of indexical field to capture this complexity and argues that "the meanings of variables are not precise or fixed but rather constitute a field of potential meanings – an indexical field, or constellation of ideologically related meanings, any one of which can be activated in the situated use of the variable."[9]

This indexical approach allows us to account for the diverse uses and interpretations of gendered linguistic forms. Drawing on the findings of previous studies as examples, I explicate how the same form may be interpreted with multiple and varying meanings in specific contexts.

4.1.1 Meanings of Stereotypically Feminine Forms

Although stereotypical SJ-based *joseigo* forms are ideologically associated with qualities such as gentleness, politeness, and elegance, the findings of previous studies suggest that they may be construed as indexing a wide range of additional or differing meanings in specific contexts. For example, research shows that heroines, especially young, attractive women, in fiction tend to use *joseigo* sentence-final forms extensively – in fact, much more frequently than real women do (e.g. Mizumoto 2006: 88). This suggests that in fiction these forms are further linked to (heterosexual and attractive) young women rather than to women in general. In situated practice, in contrast, research shows that such feminine forms are hardly used, especially by young women. In addition, the results of surveys show that many people, particularly men, associate stereotypical feminine forms with adult women (e.g. Mizumoto 2006: 80). In other words, in real-world contexts, stereotypical feminine speech is interpreted as indexing older, or adult, (SJ-speaking) women. Feminine speech styles employed by women in positions of authority observed by Smith (1992) and Takano

[9] See Chapter 25 of this volume for a related discussion on the diversity of meanings concerning sentence-final particles.

(2005) also illustrate their context-bound meanings in that their strategic use may be interpreted as indexing not simply women's powerlessness, but rather their ambivalent identities with regard to power – that is, being simultaneously powerless (as women) and powerful (as supervisors).

A number of studies offer examples in which the use of stereotypical feminine speech styles is "marked" in some way. Chinami's (2010: 78–80) aforementioned study of the speech of characters in *manga*, for example, found that female characters in higher social echelons sometimes used the normative feminine speech patterns in ways that can be interpreted as indexing aggression (e.g. *Monku wa nai wa yo ne* 'You have no complaint, do you?') or sarcasm (e.g. *Yosomi suru hito wa yoso ni itte kurete ii wa* 'It is all right for those who are not paying attention to please go elsewhere'). Chinami points out that when stereotypical feminine forms are used excessively, the politeness and refinement are further construed as sarcasm. A similar example is offered by Matsumoto's (2004: 248) study of the actual speech of a middle-aged woman who used a stylized, or "stereotypical old-fashioned forms of upper-middle class female speech" (*nani ka o-mise mo roku ni aitemasen koto yo* 'it somehow seems that the stores are hardly open') in an otherwise much less feminine speech. This speaker, explains Matsumoto, used such a style "ironically for humorous effect." This interpretation suggests that (stylized) polite and gentle speech is mockingly used as a parody for entertainment and at the same time for distancing the speaker herself from the stereotypical feminine persona associated with this style (see also Inoue 2006 for similar examples).

Exaggerated, or stylized, forms of feminine speech, or *onē kyara kotoba*, are also used by gay media personalities on TV shows, but the meanings of these feminine forms substantially differ from the women's use of such forms seen above. Here, the stylized speech blatantly crosses gender boundaries. This may be construed as indexing these performers' non-normative gender and sexuality identities by challenging the heteronormative gender order, although ironically, it may also serve to reinforce it by the very act of crossing that must assume the existence of gender boundaries. Furthermore, it may also index their identities as gay entertainers who "sell" such a speech style as a linguistic commodity to bring about comical effects. Such comical effects are induced by combining an exaggerated feminine style with some incongruent elements, such as scathing comments (e.g. *Marude osu no azarashi yo ne* 'just like a male seal, I tell you, right,' a comment on the look of the transsexual addressee; Maree 2013: 184) and exaggerated masculine speech styles that are occasionally thrown in (e.g. *Baka, dēto ja nē yo, kono yarō!* 'Stupid, it's not a date, damn you!'; Okamoto 2016: 28). Comical effects are also augmented by the act of crossing not only gender boundaries, but also boundaries between the subculture, or queer community, and the mainstream public space, or TV shows – namely in contexts where such crossing is not expected (Maree 2013). In this case, argues Maree, crossing gender boundaries can be viewed not as a challenge to but as acceptance of the heteronormative gender order. These observations thus indicate that qualities such as (hyper) politeness and gentleness can be further linked to multiple meanings, including non-normative gender and sexuality identities, professional identities as *gay tarento*, and humorousness.

4.1.2 Meanings of Stereotypical Masculine Forms

The foregoing observation suggests that the interpretation of gendered speech varies depending on what is considered the relevant norm for the speech of individuals interacting in specific local contexts. I pursue this matter further in this section with examples concerning the interpretation of stereotypical masculine forms.

As we saw earlier, young women have been found to use stereotypically masculine forms more than older women in situated practice. The young women who hardly used stereotypical feminine forms in Okamoto's study (1995: 313) reported that they think they consider what is called men's language as *wakamono no kotoba* 'the language of young people.' Their use of masculine forms then may be reinterpreted as indexing meanings such as youth and modernity as well as solidarity. Matsumoto (1996a: 460–461), in examining women's magazines and TV commercials, points out that the use of forms stereotypically considered masculine in these contexts may index cuteness or immaturity, as stereotypical women's speech is associated with properly socialized adult women. In Matsumoto's (2004: 246) aforementioned study of middle-aged mothers, one of them used both stereotypical feminine and masculine forms, which Matsumoto interprets as a way to construct a complex persona that recognizes the constraints of being a traditional adult woman while attempting to avoid the "covert stigma" attached to images of such traditional women.

Research also shows that, although some SJ-speaking young women use strongly masculine forms, such as the pronoun *ore*, the vowel-coalesced form *ē*, the particles *zo*, and direct imperative forms, their use is quite limited in frequency and contexts (e.g. in certain speech activities/acts, such as protesting, criticizing, and joking). And when they use these forms, they are often delivered with giggling and qualifiers (e.g. *shiranē yo mitaina* 'like I don't know') as though they were attempting to mitigate the force of such forms. That suggests that the use of these forms is marked as an anomaly for them, and that they are aware of the (dominant) speech norms for women. Yet, they break the norms, which may be linked to such meanings as solidarity and certain speech acts (e.g. protest, criticism).

However, there are also many cases in which SJ-speaking women use stereotypically masculine forms, particularly strongly masculine forms, without any mitigating devices. For example, the lesbians observed by Abe (2010: 213–217) blatantly crossed linguistic gender boundaries without any qualifiers. Their use of masculine forms may be interpreted as indexing multiple meanings, including their non-normative gender and sexuality identities, solidarity among lesbians, and certain speech activities (e.g. quarreling). In other words, the forcefulness and assertiveness of these forms may be further linked to these multiple meanings. Okada's (2008) study provides yet another interesting example. As seen earlier, the female boxing coach in training sessions used direct imperatives. They were delivered without any mitigating devices. Okada suggests that "a different standard regarding language and gender may apply to the boxing domain," and that "women (or anyone) can use imperative if they are required by the boxing (or athletic) situation" (2008: 183). In another words, gender norms may not be relevant to (or at least suspended in) this particular context – a possibility that deserves further exploration. The forcefulness of imperatives, then, seems unlikely to be further interpreted as indexing such meanings as solidarity or non-normative gender and sexuality identity, as seen in the case of female students and lesbians discussed above.

The relevance of norms in terms of SJ-based *joseigo* is a key issue for dialect-speaking women. As seen earlier, the women in the Tohoku area observed by Sunaoshi (2004) and Okamoto (2016) used forms considered stereotypically masculine, including strongly masculine forms. Their use of these forms is not limited to special contexts, nor is it mitigated with giggling and qualifiers, indicating that it is nothing to be marked as unusual and that using SJ-based *joseigo* forms is not regarded as the norm for them, at least for interactions in the local context. Accordingly, their speech seems unlikely to be interpreted as impolite, rough, and unfeminine in the local context. However, it may be perceived as such from the standpoint of SJ *joseigo*. In fact, according to Kumagai (2010: 53–54), such a perception seems to be on the rise even within the local community, as indicated by a survey conducted in Fukushima, Tohoku, which found that local respondents expressed reservations toward the use of *ore* by high school girls, and that boys reported that they do not wish to go out with a girl who uses *ore*. This again suggests the underlying ideological assumption that SJ is more suitable for (heterosexual) femininity.

Men's use of stereotypical masculine speech is variable and multiple in its situated meanings. In the case of the speech of SJ-speaking young men examined in Okamoto's (2016) study, for example, masculine forms, such as the pronoun *ore*, the particle *ze*, and the vowel-coalesced form *ē*, were used frequently, but without any qualifiers. Their use of these forms then may be seen as an index of normative masculinity. On the other hand, SturtzStreetharan's (2009) finding of the large age difference in the use of *ore* and *omae* by KD-speaking men suggests that these pronouns index not only masculinity but also regionality and youth in this local context. The finding of SturtzStreetharan (2004) that the use of masculine sentence-final forms by KD-speaking men was limited to the context involving certain speech activities, such as disagreeing and joking, suggests that the use of these forms is not normal for them and that the forcefulness and assertiveness associated with these forms may be further linked to certain speech activities as well as regionality. SturtzStreetharan (2017) looked at the speech of two Kansai comedians in an all-male TV reality show (*Junjō Gakuen Otokogumi* 'Academy of Devotion: Men's Team' broadcast in 1998 and 1999), in which they played teacher roles in a mock high school classroom. The comedians used strongly masculine forms along with KD, which, according to SturtzStreetharan, contributed to generating comedic effects because such language use is not expected in the (real) classroom and in the public space like a nationally televised TV show.

An infinite number of examples such as these can be found, but those discussed above seem sufficient to demonstrate that, although on the surface, different speakers – whether they are SJ-speaking men, KD-speaking men, female boxing coaches, or women in Yamagata – all use stereotypically masculine forms without any qualifiers, but their meanings emerge in a unique way in each context, as speakers position themselves variously vis-à-vis what she/he believes to be linguistic gender norms.

4.2 Beyond *Joseigo/Danseigo* as Linguistic Gender Norms

The foregoing observations raise the question of whether the SJ-based *joseigo* and *danseigo* are in fact apprehended by real women and men as the norms for their speech in situated practice. Particularly with regard to certain feminine sentence-final particles, such as *wa, da wa*, and *kashira*, we have seen studies indicating that even SJ-speaking women use them only infrequently in situated practice, particularly in recent years. This suggests that these forms may not be perceived as what real women, including SJ-speaking women, are expected to use. Yet, characters, especially heroines, in fictional worlds use them extensively, which suggests, as pointed out by Kinsui (2003: 38–39), that they serve as *yakuwarigo* 'role language' for certain types of characters in fiction (rather than as women's language).

Furthermore, it has been pointed out that it is possible to construct femininity and masculinity without recourse to SJ-based *joseigo* or *danseigo*. As seen earlier, studies have indicated that in fictional worlds, KD seems to be seen as more fitting for protagonists' speech than other regional dialects. In situated practice, on the other hand, the outlook seems rather different. In the case of the speech of Yamagata women examined by Okamoto (2016), for example, their extensive and unqualified use of forms normatively considered masculine suggests that they do not necessarily consider SJ-based *joseigo* as the model to which they aspire. Yet they seem to be concerned about gender norms in terms of qualities such as gentleness and politeness in that they use a number of resources available in their own dialect that seem to bring about such qualities (see below for example resources).[10]

Pointing out that in her native regional dialect, linguistic forms exclusively used by women hardly exist, Chinami (2007: 2) asserts that *onna kotoba* 'women's language' simply means a tendency not to use forms considered rough. And studies suggest that styles that are not rough, but polite, gentle, and refined, that is, *onnarashii hanashikata* 'feminine ways of speaking,' can be achieved in many ways without necessarily resorting to SJ *joseigo* forms. In other words, linguistic norms for women (and also for men) need to be seen in a broader and more fluid sense than SJ-based *joseigo* (and *danseigo*) forms. Terms such as *joseigo* (or *onna kotoba*) and *danseigo* (or *otoko kotoba*) suggest static linguistic categories due to the morpheme *go* 'language,' as in *nihongo* 'Japanese language.' In contrast, *onnarashii* or *otokorashii hanashikata* suggests a process through which speakers construct diverse forms of femininity and masculinity by making use of a variety of linguistic resources available to them. And it is the latter that deserves more attention in the investigation of linguistic gender norms.

This brings us to another related matter, that is, the need to consider the construction of (diverse forms of) femininity and masculinity not only at the level of individual linguistic forms such as personal pronouns and sentence-final particles, but also the level of discourse in which multiple and concerted linguistic (as well as extralinguistic) resources are employed as a strategy for effecting diverse personae. Takano's (2005) aforementioned study, for example, demonstrates that directives used by women in positions of authority involved a polite and rapport-building approach accompanied by a number of co-occurring "contextualization strategies," such as the use of supportive moves, attention getting, and terms of address. The dialect-speaking women examined in Okamoto's (2016) study used a host of discourse-level strategies that can be interpreted as polite and feminine, in particular positive politeness strategies, such as supportive back channels, laughter or giggling, repetitions, and certain speech acts (e.g. offering; praising; empathetic agreements) as well as some negative politeness strategies (e.g. self-deprecating expressions, such as *nan ni mo hodai gossō nē gen domo* 'There is no great food (to offer you)') throughout the conversations examined. Matsumoto's (2004: 248) analysis of the speech of middle-aged mothers show that while they often used (moderately) masculine styles, they also used feminine morphological forms as well as other strategies associated with feminine speech, such as (supportive) repetitions and agreements.

[10] This, however, does not mean that these dialect-speaking women are entirely free from the ideology of SJ as being polite, formal, and so forth, because they may use SJ-forms (e.g. honorifics) in conversations taking place in formal situations or outside the local area. This is an issue that requires closer attention.

As seen earlier, research shows that *onnarashii hanashikata* (rather than SJ-based *joseigo*) as an ideology still continues to be conceptualized largely in relation to qualities and stances such as politeness, gentleness, and refinement, while *otokorashii hanashikata* is conceptualized in relation to qualities such as forcefulness, assertiveness, and even roughness, although these conceptualizations may be starting to change. At the same time, speakers' understandings of specific linguistic forms to be used for *onna-* or *otokorashii hanashikata* seem much more complex than SJ-based *joseigo* and *danseigo* and require further investigation.

5 Conclusion: Toward Further Research

There is no doubt that Japanese language and gender research has made great advances, but equally evident is the need for further research to address a number of gaps yet to be filled. With regard to linguistic gender norms, the question of how speakers understand how women and men should speak in specific contexts requires more scrutiny by examining socially diverse native speakers' views expressed through metapragmatic activities carried out in various forms. Considering the possibility of differing views informed by competing ideologies is vital for a better understanding of the variable and fluid nature of linguistic gender norms that may affect use and interpretation.

With regard to situated language practice, it is imperative to examine more socially diverse speakers interacting in diverse social situations. The concept of normative masculinity, for example, seems to be in flux in contemporary Japan (e.g. Nakamura 2007b) and needs close examination of how it manifests in actual language use. The intersection of gender with regionality and sexuality in situated practice is another understudied topic that poses many questions yet to be answered. How do women and men in regional Japan consider and express femininity and masculinity? To what extent are they constrained by the standard language ideology related to gender? In fact, the question of how speakers conceptualize femininity and masculinity and express them linguistically in specific contexts is relevant to SJ speakers as well as dialect speakers. More in-depth investigation of the relationship between macro-level social forces and micro-level linguistic practice is called for. Such research also entails the need for more attention to the relevance of sexuality to language practice, or the question of how and to what extent heteronormativity constrains or affects both sexually normative and non-normative speakers in situated practices.

Another important and understudied topic is the possibility of each speaker employing different linguistic strategies, or interactional styles, depending on the context (e.g. at home, at work). Exploring this issue will help clarify the way socially diverse women and men position themselves toward what they understand as their expected ways of speaking in specific contexts.

Furthermore, whether it is represented speech in fiction or actual speech practice, more study is called for with regard to the way multiple linguistic resources are employed, both locally at specific points in an interaction and globally throughout a particular interaction, in order to meet specific interactional goals.

Finally, although space does not permit me to discuss methodological issues extensively, the directional shift in the field since the 1990s also included changes in the methodology for data collection and analysis from primary reliance on researchers' introspections or self-report survey data to the incorporation of attested discourse data and to analyzing the data quantitatively and/or qualitatively by means of a discourse analytic method, Conversation Analysis, and/or ethnographic studies. Further methodological sophistication is called for in order to advance theory-guided and empirically grounded research

References

BLS Proceedings of the Berkeley Linguistics Society
CLS Proceedings of the Chicago Linguistic Society
CSLI Proceeding of the Canadian Second Language Institute
JKL *Japanese/Korean Linguistics*
JP *Journal of Pragmatics*
LI *Linguistic Inquiry*

NINJAL Tokyo: National Institute for Japanese Language and Linguistics

Abe, Hideko. 2010. *Queer Japanese: Gender and Sexual Identities through Linguistic Practices*. Macmillan.

Abercrombie, David. 1967. *Elements of General Phonetics*. Atherton.

Abraham, Werner and Elisabeth Leiss (eds.). 2008. *Modality-Aspect Interfaces: Implications and Typological Solutions*. Benjamins.

Agha, Asif. 2003. The social life of cultural value. *Language & Communication* 23, 231–273.

Ahn, Mikyung and Foong Ha Yap. 2014. On the diachronic development of Korean SAY evidentials and their extended pragmatic functions. *Diachronica* 31, 299–336.

Aikawa, Takako. 1998. Nature of local *zibun* 'self' and reflexive-marking in Japanese. *Reports of the Keio Institute of Cultural and Linguistic Studies* 30, 17–52.

1999. Reflexives. In Natsuko Tsujimura (ed.), *The Handbook of Japanese Linguistics*, 154–190. Blackwell.

Aikhenvald, Alexandra. 2004. *Evidentiality*. Oxford University Press.

Akatsuka, Noriko. 1983. Conditionals. *Papers in Japanese Linguisitics* 9, 1–33.

1992. Japanese modals are conditionals. In Diane Brentari et al. (eds.), *The Joy of Grammar*, 1–10. Benjamins.

Akinaga, Kazue. 1985. Kyōtsūgo no akusento [Accent of Standard Japanese]. In NHK (ed.), *Pronunciation and Accent Dictionary*, 70–116. Nihon Hōsō Shuppan Kyōkai.

Akita, Kimi. 2009. A grammar of sound-symbolic words in Japanese: Theoretical approaches to iconic and lexical properties of mimetics. Ph.D. dissertation, Kobe University.

2012. Toward a frame-semantic definition of sound-symbolic words: A collocational analysis of Japanese mimetics. *Cognitive Linguistics* 23, 67–90.

2013. Constraints on the semantic extension of onomatopoeia. *The Public Journal of Semiotics* 5, 21–37.

Akita, Kimi and Natsuko Tsujimura. 2016. Mimetics. In Taro Kageyama and Hideki Kishimoto (eds.), *The Handbook of Japanese Lexicon and Word Formation*, 133–160. Gruyter.

Akita, Kimi and Takeshi Usuki. 2016. A constructional account of the "optional" quotative marking on Japanese mimetics. *Journal of Linguistics* 52, 245–275.

Aldridge, Edith. 2011. Analysis and value of *Hentai Kanbun* as Japanese. *JKL* 20, 1–15.

Allwood, Jens. 1982. The complex NP constraints in Swedish. In Elisabet Engdahl and Eva Ejerhed (eds.), *Readings on Unbounded Dependencies in Scandinavian Languages*, 15–32. Almqvist & Wilsell.

Andrews, Avery. 1975/1985. *Studies in the Syntax of Relative and Comparative Clauses*. Garland.

2007. Relative clauses. In Timothy Shopen (ed.), *Language Typology and Linguistic Description*, 206–236. Cambridge University Press.

Aoki, Haruo. 1986. Evidentials in Japanese. In Wallace Chafe and Johanna Nichols (eds.), *Evidentiality. The Linguistic Coding of Epistomology*, 223–238. Ablex.

Aoki, Hiromi. 2011. Some functions of speaker head nods. In Jürgen Streeck et al. (eds.), *Embodied Interaction: Language and Body in the Material World*, 83–105. Cambridge University Press.

Arche, María. 2006. *Individuals in Time*. Benjamins.

Arisaka, Hideyo. 1959 [1940]. *On'inron* [Phonology]. Sanseidō.

Arita, Setsuko. 2007. *Nihongo jōkenbun to jiseisetsusei* [Japanese conditional sentences and tensed clauses]. Kurosio.

Aso, Reiko. 2010. Hateruma. In Michinori Shimoji and Thomas Pellard (eds.), *An Introduction to Ryukyuan Languages*, 189–227. ILCAA.

2015. Hateruma Yaeyama grammar. In Patrick Heinrich et al. (eds.), *The Handbook of the Ryukyuan Languages*, 423–448. Gruyter.

Bachnik, Jane and Charles Quinn (eds.). 1994. *Situated Meaning: Inside and Outside in Japanese Self, Society, and Language*. Princeton University Press.

Baker, Collin and Charles Fillmore. 2010. A frame approach to semantic analysis. In Brent Heine and Heiko Narrog (eds.), *Oxford Handbook of Linguistic Analysis*, 313–339. Oxford University Press.

Baker, Mark. 1988. *Incorporation: A Theory of Grammatical Function Changing*. University of Chicago Press.

Bakhtin, Mikhail. 1981. *The Dialogic Imagination*. University of Texas Press.

Baldwin, Timothy. 1998. The analysis of Japanese relative clauses. ME thesis, Tokyo Institute of Technology.

Banfield, Ann. 1982. *Unspeakable Sentences: Narration and Representation in the Language of Fiction*. Routledge.

Beebe, Leslie and Tomoko Takahashi. 1989. Sociolinguistic variation in face-threatening acts: Chastisement and disagreement. In Miriam Eisenstein (ed.), *The Dynamic Interlanguage: Empirical Studies in Second Language Variation*, 199–218. Plenum.

Beeching, Kate and Ulrich Detges (eds.). 2014. *Discourse Functions at the Left and Right Periphery: Crosslinguistic Investigations of Language Use and Language Change*. Brill.

Bentley, Delia. 2006. *Split Intransitivity in Italian*. Gruyter.

Benveniste, Emile. 1958/1971. *Problems in General Linguistics*. University of Miami Press.

Bickel, Balthasar. 2003. Referential density in discourse and syntactic typology. *Language* 79, 708–736.

Blevins, Juliette. 1995. The syllable in phonological theory. In John Goldsmith (ed.), *Handbook of Phonological Theory*, 206–244. Blackwell.

Bloch, Bernard. 1946. Studies in colloquial Japanese I: Inflection. *Journal of the American Oriental Society* 66, 97–109.

1950. Studies in colloquial Japanese IV: Phonemics. *Language* 26, 86–125.

Bohnemeyer, Jürgen and Mary Swift. 2004. Event realization and default aspect. *Linguistics and Philosophy* 27, 263–296.

Bolinger, Dwight. 1967. Adjectives in English: Attribution and predication. *Lingua* 18, 1–34.

1972. Accent is predictable (if you're a mind-reader). *Language* 48, 633–644.

1973. Essence and accident: English analogs of Hispanic *ser-estar*. In Braj Kachru et al. (eds.), *Issues in Linguistics: Papers in Honor of Henry and Renée Kahane*, 58–69. University of Illinois Press.

Bossong, Georg. 1985. *Differentielle Objectmarkierung in den neuiranischen Sprachen*. Narr.

Brentano, Franz. [1874] 2009. *Psychology from an Empirical Standpoint*, trans. Antos Rancurello et al. Routledge.

Brinton, Laurel. 1996. *Pragmatic Markers in English: Grammaticalization and Discourse Functions*. Gruyter.

2010. Discourse markers. In Andreas Jucker and Irma Taavitsinen (eds.), *Historical Pragmatics*, 285–314. Gruyter.

Brown, Alan. 1985. Review of "The History of the Japanese Written Language" by Yaeko Sato Habein. *Pacific Affairs* 58, 532–533.

Brown, Penelope and Stephen Levinson. 1987. *Politeness: Some Universals in Language Usage*. Cambridge University Press.

Bucholtz, Mary and Kira Hall. 2005. Identity and interaction: A sociocultural linguistic approach. *Discourse Studies* 7, 585–614.

Carlson, Gregory. 1977. Reference to kinds in English. Ph.D. dissertation, University of Massachusetts, Amherst. [Published by Garland, 1980.]
Chafe, Wallace. 1976. Givenness, contrastiveness, definiteness, subjects, topics, and point of view. In Charles Li (ed.), *Subject and Topic*, 25–56. Academic Press.
1982. Integration and involvement in speaking, writing, and oral literature. In Deborah Tannen (ed.), *Spoken and Written Language: Exploring Orality and Literacy*, 35–53. Ablex.
Chaves, Rui. 2013. An expectation-based account of subject islands and parasitism. *Journal of Linguistics* 49, 285–327.
Chinami, Kyoko. 2007. Hon'yaku-manga ni okeru josei tōjō-jinbutsu no kotoba-zukai: Josei jendā hyōshiki o chūshin ni [Language use of female characters in translated manga: On female gender indexes]. *Nihongo to jendā* 7 www.gender.jp/journal/no7/02_chinami.html.
2010. Manga: Jendā hyōgen no tayōna imi [Manga: Diverse meanings of gender expressions]. In Momoko Nakamura (ed.), *Jendā de manabu gengogaku* [Linguistics taught through gender], 73–87. Sekai Shisōsha.
Chomsky, Noam. 1973. Conditions on transformations. In Stephen Anderson and Paul Kiparski (eds.), *A Festschrift for Morris Halle*, 232–285. Holt, Rinehart and Winston.
1981. *Lectures on the Government and Binding*. Foris.
1986a. *Knowledge of Language: Its Nature, Origin, and Use*. Praeger.
1986b. *Barriers*. MIT Press.
1995. *The Minimalist Program*. MIT Press.
Clancy, Patricia. 1982. Written and spoken style in Japanese narratives. In Deborah Tannen (ed.), *Spoken and Written Language: Exploring Orality and Literacy*, 55–76. Ablex.
1985. The acquisition of Japanese. In Dan Slobin (ed.), *The Crosslinguistic Study of Language Acquisition. Vol. 1: The Data*, 373–524. Erlbaum.
Clark, John and Colin Yallop. 1990. *An Introduction to Phonetics and Phonology*. Blackwell.
Clements, George. 1990. The role of the sonority cycle in core syllabification. In John Kingston and Mary Beckman (eds.), *Papers in Laboratory Phonology I: Between the Grammar and Physics of Speech*, 283–333. Cambridge University Press.
Collins, Chris. 1997. *Local Economy*. MIT Press.
Comrie, Bernard. 1976. *Aspect: An Introduction to the Study of Verbal Aspect and Related Problems*. Cambridge University Press.
1989. *Language Universals and Linguistic Typology*. University of Chicago Press.
1998. Rethinking the typology of relative clauses. *Language Design: Journal of Theoretical and Experimental Linguistics* 1, 59–85.
Comrie, Bernard and Kaoru Horie. 1995. Complement clauses versus relative clauses: Some Khmer evidence. In Werner Abraham et al. (eds.),

Discourse Grammar and Typology: Papers in Honor of John W.M. Verhaar, 65–75. Benjamins.

Comrie, Bernard and Sandra Thompson. 2007. Lexical nominalization. In Timothy Shopen (ed.) *Language Typology and Syntactic Description. Volume 3*, 334–381. Cambridge University Press.

Cook, Haruko. 1992. Meaning of non-referential indexes: A case study of the Japanese sentence-final particle *ne*. *Text* 12, 507–539.

1996a. Japanese language socialization: Indexing the modes of self. *Discourse Processes* 22, 171–197.

1996b. The use of addressee honorifics in Japanese elementary school classroom. *JKL* 5, 67–81.

1997. The role of the Japanese *masu* form in caregiver-child conversation. *JP* 28, 695–718.

2002. The social meanings of the Japanese plain form. *JKL* 10, 150–163.

2006. Japanese politeness as an interactional achievement: Academic consultation sessions in Japanese universities. *Multilingua* 25, 269–292.

2008. Organization of turns, speech styles and postures in a Japanese elementary school. In Junko Mori and Amy Ohta (eds.), *Japanese Applied Linguistics: Discourse and Social Perspectives*, 80–108. Continuum.

2012. A response to "Against the social constructionist account of Japanese politeness." *Journal of Politeness Research* 8, 269–276.

Coulmas, Florian. 1985. Direct and indirect speech: General problems and problems of Japanese. *JP* 9, 41–63.

2003. *Writing Systems. An Introduction to Their Linguistic Analysis*. Cambridge University Press.

2013. *Writing and Society*. Cambridge University Press.

2016. *Guardians of Language. Twenty Voices through History*. Oxford University Press.

Couper-Kuhlen, Elizabeth and Bernd Kortmann. 2000. Introduction. In Couper-Kuhlen, Elizabeth and Bernd Kortmann (eds.), *Cause–Condition–Concession–Contrast: Cognitive and Discourse Perspectives*, 1–8. Gruyter.

Couper-Kuhlen, Elizabeth and Tsuyoshi Ono. 2007. 'Incrementing' in conversation. A comparison of practices in English, German and Japanese. *Pragmatics* 17, 513–552.

Croft, William. 2001. *Radical Construction Grammar*. Oxford University Press.

Cruttenden, Alan. 1997. *Intonation*, 2nd edn. Cambridge University Press.

Cuenca, Maria Josep. 2013. The fuzzy limits between discourse marking and modal marking. In Liesbeth Degand et al. (eds.), *Discourse Markers and Modal Particles: Categorization and Description*, 191–216. Benjamins.

Culy, Christopher. 1990. The syntax and semantics of internally headed relative clauses. Ph.D. dissertation, Stanford University.

1997. Logophoric pronouns and point of view. *Linguistics* 35, 845–859.

Dancygier, Barbara and Eve Sweetser. 2005. *Mental Spaces in Grammar: Conditional Constructions*. Cambridge University Press.

Davidson, Donald. 1967. The logical form of action sentences. Reprinted in Donald Davidson (1980), *Essays on Actions and Events*, 105–122. Oxford University Press.

Davidson, Judy. 1984. Subsequent versions of invitations, offers, requests, and proposals dealing with potential or actual rejection. In Maxwell Atkinson and John Heritage (eds.), *Structures of Social Action: Studies in Conversation Analysis*, 102–128. Cambridge University Press.

Davis, Stuart. 1989. On a non-argument for the rhyme. *Journal of Linguistics* 25, 211–217.

2011. Quantity. In John Goldsmith et al. (eds.), *The Handbook of Phonological Theory*, 103–140. Wiley-Blackwell.

De Wolf, Charles. 1987. Wa in diachronic perspective. In John Hinds et al. (eds.), *Perspectives on Topicalization: The Case of Japanese Wa*, 265–290. Benjamins.

Deane, Paul. 1992. *Grammar in Mind and Brain: Explorations in Cognitive Syntax*. Gruyter.

Degand, Liesbeth. 2014. 'So very fast very fast then': Discourse markers at left and right periphery in spoken French. In Kate Beeching and Ulrich Detges (eds.), *Discourse Functions at the Left and Right Periphery: Crosslinguistic Investigations of Language Use and Language Change*, 151–178. Brill.

Degand, Liesbeth, Bert Cornillie, and Paola Pietandrea (eds.). *Discourse Markers and Modal Particles: Categorization and Description*. Benjamins.

Deguchi, Masanori. 2012. Revisiting the thetic/categorical distinction in Japanese. *Poznań Studies in Contemporary Linguistics* 48, 223–237.

Detges, Ulrich. 2015. Review of "Liesbeth Degand et al. (eds.) Discourse Markers and Modal Particles. Categorization and Description." *Functions of Language* 22, 132–141.

Diesing, Molly. 1992. *Indefinites*. MIT Press.

Diewald, Gabriele. 2013. "Same same but different": Modal particles, discourse markers and the art (and purpose) of categorization. In Liesbeth Degand et al. (eds.), *Discourse Markers and Modal Particles: Categorization and Description*, 19–46. Benjamins.

Diffloth, Gérard. 1972. Notes on expressive meaning. *CLS* 8, 440–447.

Dik, Simon. 1997. *The Theory of Functional Grammar. Part 1: The Structure of the Clause*. Gruyter.

Dixon, R.M.W. 1979. Ergativity. *Language* 55, 59–138.

Dore, Ronald. 1965. The legacy of Tokugawa education. In Marius Jansen (ed.), *Changing Japanese Attitudes toward Modernization*, 99–131. Princeton University Press.

Downing, Laura. 2011. Bantu tone. In Marc van Oostendorp et al. (eds.), *The Blackwell Companion to Phonology* 5, 2730–2753. Wiley-Blackwell.

Downing, Pamela. 1977. On the creation and use of English nominal compounds. *Language* 55, 810–842.

Dowty, David. 1979. *Word Meaning and Montague Grammar*. Reidel.
Dryer, Matthew and Martin Haspelmath. 2013. *The World Atlas of Language Structures Online*. Max Planck Digital Library. http://wals.info/
Duanmu, San. 2009. *Syllable Structure*. Oxford University Press.
Dunn, Cynthia. 1999. Public and private voices: Japanese style shifting and the display of affective intensity. In Gary Palmer and Debra Occhi (eds.), *Languages of Sentiment: Cultural Constructions of Emotional Substrates*, 107–127. Benjamins.
2005. Pragmatic functions of humble forms in Japanese ceremonial discourse. *Journal of Linguistic Anthropology* 15, 218–238.
Eckert, Penelope. 2008. Variation and the indexical field. *Journal of Sociolinguistics* 12, 453–476.
Eda, Sanae. 2001. A new approach to the analysis of the sentence final particles *ne* and *yo*: An interface between prosody and pragmatics. *JKL* 9, 167–180.
Eelen, Gino. 2001. *A Critique of Politeness Theories*. St. Jerome.
Ehrich, Susan, Miriam Meyerhoff, and Janet Holmes (eds.). 2014. *The Handbook of Language, Gender, and Sexuality*. Blackwell.
Endo, Orie. 1997. *Onna no kotoba no bunkashi* [A cultural history of Japanese women's language]. Gakuyō.
Enyo, Yumiko. 2015. Contexts and meaning of Japanese speech styles: A case of hierarchical identity construction among Japanese college students. *Pragmatics* 25, 345–367.
Erteschik-Shir, Nomi. 1973. On the nature of island constraints. Ph.D. dissertation, MIT.
2007. *Information Structure: The Syntax–Discourse Interface*. Oxford University Press.
Erteschik-Shir, Nomi and Shalom Lappin. 1979. Dominance and the functional explanation of island phenomena. *Theoretical Linguistics* 6, 41–86.
Evans, Nicholas. 2007. Insubordination and its uses. In Irina Nikolaeva (ed.), *Finiteness. Theoretical and Empirical Foundations*, 366–431. Oxford University Press.
Evans, Nicholas and Honoré Watanabe (eds.). 2016. *Insubordination*. Benjamins.
Fauconnier, Gilles. 1985. *Mental Spaces: Aspects of Meaning Construction in Natural Language*. MIT Press.
Fauconnier, Gilles and Mark Turner. 2002. *The Way We Think: Conceptual Blending and the Mind's Hidden Complexities*. Basic Books.
Fayol, Michel and Jean-Pierre Jaffré. 2014. *L'ortographe*. Pressses Universitaires de France.
Fernald, Theodore. 2000. *Predicates and Temporal Arguments*. Oxford University Press.
Fillmore, Charles. 1982. Frame semantics. In Linguistic Society of Korea (ed.), *Linguistics in the Morning Calm*, 111–138. Hanshin.

1987. Varieties of conditional sentences. *Proceedings of the Third Eastern States Conference on Linguistics*, 163–182. Ohio State University.

1988. The mechanisms of "Construction Grammar." *BLS* 14, 35–55.

1990. Epistemic stance and grammatical form in English conditional sentences. *CLS* 26, 137–162.

Fillmore, Charles and Collin Baker. 2010. A frames approach to semantic analysis. In Heine Bernd and Heiko Narrog (eds.), *The Oxford Handbook of Linguistic Analysis*, 791–816. Oxford University Press.

Fillmore, Charles, Paul Kay, and Mary Catherine O'Connor. 1988. Regularity and idiomaticity in grammatical constructions: The case of Let Alone. *Language* 64, 501–538.

Firbas, Jan. 1992. *Functional Sentence Perspective in Written and Spoken Communication*. Cambridge University Press.

Fludernik, Monika. 1993. *The Fictions of Language and the Languages of Fiction: The Linguistic Representation of Speech and Consciousness*. Routledge.

Foley, William and Robert Van Valin. 1984. *Functional Syntax and Universal Grammar*. Cambridge University Press.

Ford, Cecilia and Sandra Thompson. 1996. Interactional units in conversation: Syntactic, intonational, and pragmatic resources for the management of turns. In Elinor Ochs et al. (eds.), *Interaction and Grammar*, 134–184. Cambridge University Press.

Fox, Barbara, Makoto Hayashi, and Robert Jasperson 1996. Syntactic projectability in Japanese conversation. Resources and repair: A cross-linguistic study of syntax and repair. In Elinor Ochs et al. (eds.), *Interaction and Grammar*, 185–237. Cambridge University Press.

Fraser, Bruce. 1999. What are discourse markers? *JP* 31, 931–953.

Frellesvig, Bjarke. 2010. *A History of the Japanese Language*. Cambridge University Press.

Frellesvig, Bjarke and John Whitman. 2008. *Proto-Japanese: Issue and Prospects*. Benjamins.

Frellesvig, Bjarke, Stephen Horn, and Yuko Yanagida. 2015. Differential object marking in Old Japanese: A corpus based study. In Dag Haug (ed.), *Historical Linguistics 2013: Selected Papers from the 21st International Conference on Historical Linguistics*, 195–211. Benjamins.

Fromkin, Victoria. 1971. The non-anomalous nature of anomalous utterances. *Language* 47, 27–52.

Fudge, E.C. 1969. Syllables. *Journal of Linguistics* 5, 253–286.

Fujii, Seiko. 1989. Concessive conditionals in Japanese: A pragmatic analysis of the S1-TEMO S2 construction. *BLS* 15, 291–302.

1990. Counterfactual concessive conditionals in Japanese. *JKL* 1, 353–367.

1992a. On the clause-linking TO construction in Japanese. *JKL* 2, 3–19.

1992b. On the idiomaticity of conditional constructions in Japanese. *Proceedings of the Fifteenth International Congress of Linguists*, 59–62. Les Presses de L'université Lavel.

1993. The use and learning of clause-linkage: Case studies in Japanese and English conditionals. Ph.D. dissertation, University of California, Berkeley.

1996. Mental-space builders: Observations from English and Japanese conditionals. In Masayoshi Shibatani and Sandra Thompson (eds.), *Topics in Semantics and Pragmatics*, 72–90. Benjamins.

2000. Incipient decategorization of MONO and grammaticalization of speaker attitude in Japanese discourse. In Gisle Andersen and Thonstein Fretheim (eds.), *Pragmatic Markers and Propositional Attitude*, 85–118. Benjamins.

2004. Lexically (un)filled constructional schemes and construction types: The case of Japanese modal conditional constructions. In Mirjam Fried and Jan-Ola Östman (eds.), *Construction Grammar in a Cross-Language Perspective*, 121–155. Benjamins.

2012. On conditional constructions. In Harumi Sawada (ed.), *Constructions and Meanings*, 107–131. Hituzi.

2013. Conditional constructions as discourse markers in Japanese: Toward a typology of their form and function. *Language Information Text* 20, 87–101.

Fukada, Atsushi and Noriko Asato. 2004. Universal politeness theory: Application to the use of Japanese honorifics. *JP* 36, 1991–2002.

Fukuda, Shinichiro. 2006. Japanese passive, external arguments, and structural case. *UCSD Linguistics Papers* 2, 86–133.

2015. Review: Tomoko Ishizuka. The passive in Japanese: A cartographic minimalist approach. *Linguistic Variation* 15, 291–298.

Fukui, Naoki. 1986. A theory of category projection and its applications. Ph.D. dissertation, MIT.

Fukushima, Saeko. 2000. *Requests and Culture: Politeness in British English and Japanese*. Lang.

2004. Evaluation of politeness: the case of attentiveness. *Multilingua* 23, 365–388.

Fukushima, Saeko and Michael Haugh. 2014. The role of emic understandings in theorizing im/politeness: The metapragmatics of attentiveness, empathy and anticipatory inference in Japanese and Chinese. *JP* 74, 165–179.

Fukuzawa, Yukichi. 1873. Moji no oshie [Instruction in writing]. http://project.lib.keio.ac.jp/dg_kul/fukuzawa_title.php?id=73

Furo, Hiroko. 1998. Turn-taking in Japanese conversation: Grammar, intonation, and pragmatics. *JKL* 7, 41–57.

Gagné, Nana. 2010. Reexamining the notion of negative face in the Japanese socio-linguistic politeness of request. *Language and Communication* 30, 123–138.

Gal, Susan. 1998. Multiplicity and contention among language ideologies: A commentary. In Bambi Schieffelin et al. (eds.), *Language Ideologies: Practice and Theory*, 317–331. Oxford University Press.

Gendai Nihongo Kenkyūkai. 1997. *Josei no kotoba: Shokuba hen* [Female corpus: In work place]. Hituzi.
Geyer, Naomi. 2008. *Discourse and Politeness: Ambivalent Face in Japanese.* Continuum.
2013. Discernment and variation: The action-oriented use of Japanese addressee honorifics. *Mulitlingua* 32, 155–176.
2016. Constructing appropriateness in Japanese institutional discourse: A case of (non-use of) honorifics. Paper presented at the American Association for Applied Linguistics Conference. Orlando, FL.
Gibson, James. 1977. The theory of affordances. In Robert Shaw and Johen Bransfold (eds.), *Perceiving, Acting, and Knowing: Toward an Ecological Psychology*, 67–82. Erlbaum.
1979/1986. *The Ecological Approach to Visual Perception.* Erlbaum.
Giriko, Mikio. 2009. Nihongo ni okeru go-ninshiki to heibangata akusento [Word recognition and unaccented pattern in Japanese]. Ph. D. dissertation, Kobe University.
Givón, Talmy. 1979. *On Understanding Grammar.* Academic Press.
1983. Topic continuity in discourse: An introduction. In Talmy Givn (ed.), *Topic Continuity in Discourse*, 5–41. Benjamins.
1984. *Syntax, Vol. I.* Benjamins.
2009. *Genesis of Syntactic Complexity.* Benjamins.
Givón, Talmy and Masayoshi Shibatani (eds.). 2009. *Syntactic Complexity.* Benjamins.
Gnanadesikan, Amalia. 2009. *The Writing Revolution: Cuneiform to the Internet.* Wiley-Blackwell.
Goldberg, Adele. 1995. *Constructions: A Construction Grammar Approach to Argument Structure.* University of Chicago Press.
2013. Constructional approaches. In Thomas Hoffman and Graeme Trousdale (eds.), *The Oxford Handbook of Construction Grammar*, 15–31. Oxford University Press.
Goldsmith, John. 2011. The syllable. In John Goldsmith et al. (eds.), *The Handbook of Phonological Theory*, 164–196. Wiley-Blackwell.
Goodman, Nelson. 1983. *Fact, Fiction, and Forecast.* Harvard University Press.
Goodwin, Charles. 2003. Pointing as situated practice. In Sotaro Kita (ed.), *Pointing: Where Language, Culture and Cognition Meet*, 217–241. Erlbaum.
Goodwin, Charles and Marjorie Goodwin. 1987. Concurrent operations on talk: Notes on the interactive organization of assessments. *IPRA Papers in Pragmatics* 1, 1–54.
Goody, Jack. 1968. Introduction. In Jack Goody (ed.), *Literacy in Traditional Societies*, 1–26. Cambridge University Press.
Goro, Takuya. 2006. A minimalist analysis of Japanese passives. *Minimalist Essays* 91, 232.
Gottlieb, Nanette. 1995. *Kanji Politics. Language Policy and Japanese Script.* Kegan Paul.

2011. Playing with language in E-Japan: Old wine in new bottles. In Nanette Gottlieb (ed.), *Language in Public Spaces in Japan*, 71–85. Routledge.

Greenberg, Joseph. 1963. Some universals of grammar with particular reference to the order of meaningful elements. In Joseph Greenberg (ed.), *Universals of Human Language*, 73–113. MIT Press.

(ed.). 1978. *Universals of Language*: Stanford University Press.

Grice, Paul. 1975. Logic and conversation. In Peter Cole and Jerry Morgan (eds.), *Syntax and Semantics 3: Speech Acts*, 41–58. Academic Press.

Gussenhoven, Carlos. 2004. *The Phonology of Tone and Intonation*. Cambridge University Press.

Haberland, Hartmut and Johan van der Auwera. 1990. Topic and clitics in Greek relatives. *Acta Linguistica Hafniensia* 22, 127–157.

Haegeman, Liliane. 1990. Understood subjects in English diaries. *Multilingua* 9, 157–199.

Haegeman, Liliane and Virginia Hill. 2014. The syntactization of discourse. In Raffaella Folli et al. (eds.), *Syntax and Its Limits*, 370–390. Oxford University Press.

Haga, Yasushi. 1954. *Chinjutsu to wa nanimono?* [What is chinjutsu?]. *Kokugo Kokubun* 23, 47–61.

Hagège, Claude. 1974. Les pronoms logophoriques. *Bulletin de la Société de Linguistique de Paris* 69, 287–310.

Haig, John. 1979a. What relative clauses are about. *Papers in Linguistics* 12, 57–109.

1979b. Real and apparent multiple subject sentences. *Papers in Japanese Linguistics* 6, 87–130.

1981. Are traversal objects objects? *Papers in Linguistics* 14, 69–101.

1996. Subjacency and Japanese grammar: A functional account. *Studies in Language* 20, 53–92.

Haiman, John. 1978. Conditionals are topics. *Language* 54, 564–589.

1983. Iconic and economic motivation. *Language* 59, 781–819.

Haiman, John and Sandra Thompson (eds.). 1998. *Clause Combining in Grammar and Discourse*. Benjamins.

Hale, Kenneth and Samuel Keyser. 1993. On argument structure and the lexical expression of syntactic relations. In Kenneth Hale and Samuel Keyser (eds.), *The View from Building 20*, 53–109. MIT Press.

Hamano, Shoko. 1988. The syntax of mimetic words and iconicity. *Journal of the Association of Teachers of Japanese* 22, 135–149.

1998. *The Sound-Symbolic System of Japanese*. CSLI.

Hanazono, Satoru. 1999. Jōkenkei fukugō yōgen keishiki no nintei [The recognition of complex predicate forms based on conditionals]. *Kokugogaku* 197, 39–90.

Handschuh, Corinna. 2014. *A Typology of Marked-S Languages*. Language Science.

Hankamer, Jorge and Ivan Sag. 1976. Deep and surface anaphora. *Linguistic Inquiry* 7, 391–426.
Hansen, Maj-Britt Mosegaard and Jacqueline Visconti (eds.). 2009. *Current Trends in Diachronic Semantics and Pragmatics*. Emerald.
Harada, Shin-Ichi. 1971. *Ga-no* conversion and idiolectal variations in Japanese. *Gengo Kenkyu* 60, 25–38.
1973. Counter equi NP deletion. *Annual Bulletin* 7, 113–147. Research Institute of Logopedics and Phoniatrics.
Haraguchi, Shosuke. 1977. *The Tone Pattern of Japanese: An Autosegmental Theory of Tonology*. Kaitakusha.
1991. *A Theory of Stress and Accent*. Foris.
2003. The phonology-phonetics interface and syllabic theory. In Jeroen van de Weijer et al. (eds.), *The Phonological Spectrum. Vol. 2: Suprasegmental Structure*, 31–58. Benjamins.
Harris, Roy. 2000. *Rethinking Writing*. Athlone.
Hasegawa, Nobuko. 1981. A lexical interpretive theory with emphasis on the role of subject. Ph.D. dissertation, University of Washington.
1985. On the so-called "zero pronouns" in Japanese. *The Linguistic Review* 4, 289–341.
1999. *Seisei nihongogaku nyūmon* [Introduction to Generative Japanese Linguistics]. Taishūkan.
2001. Causatives and the role of v: Agent, causer, and experiencer. In Kazuko Inoue and Nobuko Hasegawa (eds.), *Linguistics and Interdisciplinary Research. Proceedings of the COE International Symposium*, 1–35. Kanda University of International Studies.
2006. Honorifics. In Martin Everaert and Henk van Riemsdijk (eds.), *The Blackwell Companion to Syntax, Vol. 2*, 493–543. Blackwell.
2007a. Ichininshō no shōryaku: Modaritī to kureru [The deletion of the first person: Modality and kureru 'give']. In Nobuko Hasegawa (ed.), *Nihongo no shubun-genshō: Tōgo-kōzō to modaritī* [Main clause phenomena in Japanese: Syntactic structure and modality], 331–369. Hituzi.
2007b. The possessor raising construction and the interpretation of the subject. In Simin Karimi et al. (eds.), *Phrasal and Clausal Architecture: Syntactic Derivation and Interpretation*, 62–99. Benjamins.
2009. Agreement at the CP level: Clause types and the 'person' restriction on the subject. *The Proceedings of the 5th Workshop on Altaic Formal Linguistics* 5, 131–152. MIT.
2010. CP ryōiki kara no kara-shugo no ninka [Licensing null-subjects from the CP area]. In Nobuko Hasegawa (ed.), *Tōgo-ron no shintenkai to nihongo kenkyū: Meidai o koete* [New developments in syntactic theory and research in Japanese: Beyond proposition], 31–65. Kaitakusha.
2011. Shoyūsha-bunri to bun-kōzō: Shudaika kara no hatten [Possessor ascension and clausal structure: An extension from subjectivization]. In Nobuko Hasegawa (ed.), *70-nendai seisei-bunpō saininshiki: Nihongo*

kenkyū no chihei [Re-acknowledgement of the 70s generative grammar: The horizon of research in Japanese], 85–121. Kaitakusha.

Hasegawa, Yoko. 1989. Questioning vs. identifying: A functionalist analysis of the [a candidate that which professor recommended was hired?] construction in Japanese. *BLS* 15, 138–149.

1996. *A Study of Japanese Clause Linkage: The Connective TE in Japanese*. CSLI and Kurosio.

2010. *Soliloquy in Japanese and English*. Benjamins.

2012. Against the social constructionist account of Japanese politeness. *Journal of Politeness Research* 8, 245–268.

2015. *Japanese: A Linguistic Introduction*. Cambridge University Press.

Hasegawa, Yoko and Yukio Hirose. 2005. What the Japanese language tells us about the alleged Japanese relational self. *Australian Journal of Linguistics* 25, 219–251.

Hashi, Michiko, Akina Kodama, Takao Miura, Shotaro Daimon, Yuki Takakura, and Ryoko Hayashi. 2014. Nihongo gobi hatsuon chōon jittai: X-sen maikurobīmu nihongo hatsuon dētabēsu o mochiite [Articulatory variability in word-final Japanese moraic nasals: An X-ray microbeam study]. *Onsei Kenkyū* 18, 95–105.

Hashimoto, Norinao. 2002. Ne sa yo undō to sono shūhen [Ne-sa-yo movement and its surrounding]. Paper presented at the sociolinguistic conference, Chiba, Japan.

Hashimoto, Shinkichi. 1935. *Shin-bunten: Bekki, jōkyūyō* [New grammar: Separate volume, advanced]. Fuzanbō.

1969. Jodōshi no kenkyū [Studies on auxiliaries]. In *Joshi-jodōshi no kenkyū* [Studies on particles and auxiliaries], 225–420. Iwanami.

Hashimoto, Shiro. 1966. Kodaigo no shijitaikei: Jōdai o chūshin ni [The system of demonstratives in archaic Japanese: Focusing on Old Japanese]. *Kokugo Kokubun* 35/36, 329–341.

Haspelmath, Martin. 2010. Comparative concepts and descriptive categories in crosslinguistic studies. *Language* 86, 663–687.

Hattori, Shiro. 1954. On'in-ron kara mita nihongo no akusento [A phonological view of Japanese accent]. *Kokugo Kenkyū* 2, 2–50.

Haugh, Michael. 2007. The co-constitution of politeness implicature in conversation. *JP* 39, 84–110.

Haugh, Michael. 2015. *Im/politeness Implicatures*. Gruyter.

Haugh, Michael and Yasuko Obana. 2011. Politeness in Japanese. In Dániel Kádár and Sara Mills (eds.), *Politeness in East Asia*, 147–175. Cambridge University Press.

Hawkins, John. 1986. *A Comparative Typology of English and German*. Helm.

Hayano, Kaoru. 2011. Claiming epistemic primacy: *Yo*-marked assessments in Japanese. In Tanya Stivers et al. (eds.), *The Morality of Knowledge in Conversation*, 58–81. Cambridge University Press.

Hayashi, Makoto. 2003. *Joint Utterance Construction in Japanese Conversation*. Benjamins.

Hayashi, Makoto and Junko Mori. 1998. Co-construction in Japanese revisited: We do finish each other's sentences. *JKL* 7, 77–93.

Hayashi, Makoto, Junko Mori, and Tomoyo Tagaki. 2002. Contingent achievement of co-tellership in a Japanese conversation. In Cecilia Ford et al. (eds.), *The Language of Turn and Sequence*, 81–122. Oxford University Press.

Hayata, Teruhiro. 1999. *Onchō no taiporojī* [Typology of tone]. Taishūkan.

Hayes, Bruce. 1995. *Metrical Stress Theory: Principles and Case Studies*. University of Chicago Press.

Heinrich, Patrick. 2012. *The Making of Monolingual Japan*. Multilingual Matters.

Heritage, John. 1984. *Garfinkel and Ethnomethodology*. Polity.

Heycock, Caroline. 1993. Syntactic predication in Japanese. *Journal of East Asian Linguistics* 2, 167–211.

Heyse, Johann Christian August. 1849. *Theoretisch-praktische deutsche Grammatik oder Lehrbuch der deutschen Sprache*. 5. Völlig umgearbeite und sehr vermehrte Ausgabe [Theoretical-practical German Grammar, or Textbook of the German Language, 5th entirely revised and greatly enhanced edition]. Sahn. (Reprint by G. Olms, Hildesheim, 1972.)

Hibiya, Junko. 1999. Variationist sociolinguistics. In Natsuko Tsujimura (ed.), *The Handbook of Japanese Linguistics*, 101–120. Blackwell.

Hidaka, Mizuho. 2005. Hōgen ni okeru bunpō-ka [The regional differences of the grammaticalization]. *Nihongo no Kenkyū* 1, 77–91.

Higashiizumi, Yuko. 2015. Periphery of utterances and (inter)subjectification in Modern Japanese: A case study of competing causal conjunctions and connective particles. In Andrew Smith et al. (eds.), *New Directions in Grammaticalization Research*, 135–156. Benjamins.

Higurashi, Yoshiko. 1983. *The Accent of Extended Word Structures in Tokyo Standard Japanese*. Educa.

Hinds, John. 1978a. Conversational structure: An investigation based on Japanese interview discourse. In John Hinds and Irwin Howard (eds.), *Problems in Japanese Syntax and Semantics*, 79–121. Kaitakusha.

(ed.). 1978b. *Anaphora in Discourse*. Linguistic Research.

1982. *Ellipsis in Japanese Discourse*. Linguistic Research.

Hinds, John and Wako Tawa. 1975–1976. Conditions on conditionals in Japanese. *Papers in Japanese Linguistics* 4, 3–11.

Hinton, Leanne, Joanna Nichols, and John Ohala. 1994. *Sound Symbolism*. Cambridge University Press.

Hiraiwa, Ken. 2001. Multiple agree and the defective intervention constraint. *MIT Working Papers in Linguistics* 40, 67–80.

2010. Spelling out the double-*o* constraint. *Natural Language and Linguistic Theory* 28, 723–770.

Hirako, Tatsuya. 2016. Izumo hōgen ni okeru kakujoshi 'ga' to 'no' ni tsuite [On the case particles "ga" and "no" in the Izumo dialect]. In Nobuko Kibe (ed.), *Shōmetsu kikihōgen no chōsa hozon no tame no sōgōteki kenkyū: Izumo hōgen chōsa hōkokusho* [General study for research and conservation of endangered dialects in Japan: Research report on Izumo dialect], 69–78. NINJAL.

Hirayama, Teruo. 1951. *Kyūshū hōgen onchō no kenkyū* [Studies on tone in Kyūshū dialects]. Gakkaino Shishin-sha.

1968. *Nihon no hōgen* [The Japanese dialects]. Kōdansha.

1998. *Tottori ken no kotoba* [The Tottori dialect]. Meiji.

Hirose, Kyoko and Toshio Ohori. 1992. Japanese internally headed relative clauses revisited. Paper presented at the annual meeting of the Linguistic Society of America, Philadelphia.

Hirose, Yukio. 1995. Direct and indirect speech as quotations of public and private expression. *Lingua* 95, 223–238.

2000. Public and private self as two aspects of the speaker: A contrastive study of Japanese and English. *JP* 32, 1623–1656.

2002. Viewpoint and the nature of the Japanese reflexive *zibun*. *Cognitive Linguistics* 13, 357–401.

2014. The conceptual basis for reflexive constructions in Japanese. *JP* 68, 99–116.

Hirose, Yukio and Hasegawa Yoko. 2010. *Nihongo kara mita nihonjin: Shutaisei no gengogaku* [Japanese people as seen from the Japanese language: The linguistics of subjectivity]. Kaitakusha.

Hirschberg, Julia and Gregory Ward. 1995. The interpretation of the high-rise question contour in English. *JP* 24, 407–412.

Hockett, Charles. 1955. *A Manual of Phonology*. Waverly.

1958. *A Course in Modern Linguistics*. Macmillan.

Hofmeister, Peter and Ivan Sag. 2010. Cognitive constraints and island effects. *Language* 86, 366–415.

Hofmeister, Philip. 2007. Retrievability and gradience in filler-gap dependencies. *CLS* 43, 109–123.

Hoji, Hajime. 1985. Logical form contraints and configurational structures in Japanese. Ph.D. dissertation, University of Washington.

Hong, Sun-ho. 2003. On island constraints in Korean. In Gregory Iverson and Sang-Cheol Ahn (eds.), *Explorations in Korean Language and Linguistics*, 107–125. Hankook.

Hooper, Joan and Sandra Thompson. 1973. On the applicability of root transformations. *LI* 4, 465–497.

Hopper, Paul and Sandra Thompson. 1980. Transitivity in grammar and discourse. *Language* 56, 251–299.

Hopper, Paul and Elizabeth Traugott. 1993/2003. *Grammaticalization*. Cambridge University Press.

Horie, Kaoru. 1993. From zero to overt nominalizer *no*: A syntactic change in Japanese. *JKL* 3, 305–321.

1998. Functional duality of case-marking particles in Japanese and its implications for grammaticalization: A contrastive study with Korean. *JKL* 8, 147–159.

2002. Verbal nouns in Japanese and Korean: Cognitive typological implications. In Kuniyoshi Kataoka and Sachiko Ide (eds.), *Culture, Interaction, and Language*, 77–101. Hituzi.

2008. Grammaticalization of nominalizers in Japanese and its theoretical implications: A contrastive study with Korean. In Elena Seoane and Maria Jose Lopez-Couso (eds.). *Rethinking Grammaticalization: New Perspective for the Twenty-first Century*, 169–187. Benjamins.

2012. The interactional origin of nominal predicate structure in Japanese: A comparative and historical pragmatic perspective. *JP* 44, 663–679.

2017. The attributive-final distinction and the manifestation of "main clause phenomena" in Japanese and Korean NMCs. In Yoshiko Matsumoto et al. (eds.), *Noun-Modifying Clause Constructions in Languages of Eurasia: Rethinking Theoretical and Geographical Boundaries*, 45–57. Benjamins.

Horie, Kaoru and Prashant Pardeshi. 2009. *Gengo no taiporojī. Ninchi ruikeiron no apurōchi* [Linguistic typology. A cognitive typological approach]. Kenkyūsha.

Horie, Kaoru and Heiko Narrog. 2014. What typology reveals about modality in Japanese: A cross-linguistic perspective. In Kaori Kabata and Tsuyoshi Ono (eds.), *Usage-Based Approaches to Japanese Grammar*, 109–133. Benjamins.

Horn, Laurence. 2010. Multiple negation in English and other languages. In Laurence Horn (ed.), *The Expression of Negation*, 111–148. Gruyter.

Hoshi, Hiroto. 1999. Passives. In Natsuko Tsujimura (ed.), *The Handbook of Japanese Linguistics*, 191–235. Blackwell.

Howard, Irwin. 1978. *Problems in Japanese Syntax and Semantics*. Kaitakusha.

Howard, Irwin and Agnes Niyekawa-Howard. 1976. Passivization. *Japanese Generative Grammar: Syntax and Semantics* 5, 201–238.

Huang, James. 1984. On the distribution and reference of empty pronouns. *Linguistic Inquiry* 15, 531–574.

1999. Chinese passives in comparative perspective. *Tsing Hua Journal of Chinese Studies* 29, 423–509.

Huang, Yan. 2000. *Anaphora: A Cross-Linguistic Study*. Oxford University Press.

Hyman, Larry. 1977. On the nature of linguistic stress. *Studies in Stress and Accent. Southern California Occasional Papers in Linguistics* 4, 37–82.

1985. *A Theory of Phonological Weight*. Foris.

2006. Word-prosodic typology. *Phonology* 23, 225–257.

Ichikawa, Takashi. 1978. *Kokugo kyōiku no tame no bunshōron gaisetsu* [Introduction to Japanese discourse analysis for Japanese education]. Kyōiku.

Ide, Risako. 1998. "Sorry for your kindness": Japanese interactional ritual in public discourse. *JP* 29, 509–529.

Ide, Sachiko. 1982a. Japanese sociolinguistics: Politeness and women's language. *Lingua* 57, 357–385.

1982b. Taigū hyōgen no danjosa [Gender differences in interpersonal expressions]. In Tetsuya Kunihiro (ed.), *Nichieigo hikaku kōza 5: Bunka to shakai* [A comparative study of Japanese and English 5: Culture and society], 105–169. Taishūkan.

1989. Formal forms and discernment: Two neglected aspects of universals of linguistic politeness. *Multilingua* 8, 223–248.

1992. On the notion of *wakimae*: Toward an integrated framework of linguistic politeness. In Mejiro Linguistic Society (ed.), *Mosaic of Language: Essays in Honour of Professor Natsuko Okuda*, 298–305. Mejiro Linguistic Society.

Ide, Sachiko and Megumi Yoshida. 2002. Sociolinguistics: Honorific and gender differences. In Natsuko Tsujimura (ed.), *The Handbook of Japanese Linguistics*, 444–480. Blackwell.

Ide, Sachiko, Beverley Hill, Yukiko M. Carnes, Tsunao Ogino, and Akiko Kawasaki. 1992. The concept of politeness: An empirical study of American English and Japanese. In Richard Watts et al. (eds.), *Politeness in Language. Studies in its History, Theory and Practice*, 281–297. Gruyter.

Igarashi, Yosuke. 2014. Typology of intonational phrasing in Japanese dialects. In Sun-Ah Jun (ed.), *Prosodic Typology II: The Phonology of Intonation and Phrasing*, 525–568. Oxford University Press.

2015. Intonation. In Haruo Kubozono (ed.), *Handbook of Japanese Phonetics and Phonology*, 525–568. Gruyter.

Igarashi, Yosuke, Ken'ya Nishikawa, Kuniyoshi Tanaka, and Reiko Mazuka 2013. Phonological theory informs the analysis of intonational exaggeration in Japanese infant-directed speech. *Journal of Acoustical Society of America* 134, 1283–1294.

Iida, Masayo. 1996. *Context and Binding in Japanese*. CSLI.

Ikeda, Yutaka. 1995. Shūjoshi to teineisa [Sentence-final particles and politeness]. *Gengo* 24, 102–103.

Ikuta, Shoko. 1983. Speech level shift and conversational strategy in Japanese discourse. *Language Science* 5, 37–53.

2008. Speech style shift as an interactional discourse strategy: The use and non-use of *desu/-masu* in Japanese conversational interviews. In Kimberly Jones and Tsuyoshi Ono (eds.), *Style Shifting in Japanese*, 71–89. Benjamins.

Imamura, Satoshi. 2014. The influence of givenness of heaviness on OSV in Japanese. *Proceedings of the 28th Pacific Asia Conference on Language, Information and Computation*, 224–233. Chulalongkorn University.

Inagaki, Kayoko, Giyoo Hatano, and Takashi Otake. 2000. The effect of kana literacy on the speech segmentation unit used by Japanese young children. *Journal of Experimental Child Psychology* 75, 70–91.

Inoue, Kazuko. 1976. *Henkei bunpō to Nihongo* [Transformational grammar and Japanese]. Taishūkan.

1978. "Tough sentences" in Japanese. In John Hinds and Irwin Howard (eds.), *Problems in Japanese Syntax and Semantics*, 122–154. Kaitakusha.

2004. Japanese "tough" sentences revisited. *Scientific Approaches to Language* 3, 75–111. Kanda University of International Studies.

Inoue, Miyako. 2002. Gender, language, and modernity: Toward an effective history of Japanese women's language. *American Ethnologist* 29, 392–422.

2006. *Vicarious Language: Gender and Linguistic Modernity in Japan.* University of California Press.

Iori, Isao, Hiroshi Matsuoka, Kumiko Nakanishi, Toshihiro Yamada, and Shino Takanashi. 2000. *Shokyū o oshieru hito no tame no nihongo bunpō handobukku* [Handbook of Japanese grammar for teachers of basic Japanese]. Surī Ē Nettowāku.

Irwin, Mark. 2011. *Loanwords in Japanese.* Benjamins.

Ishihara, Shinichiro. 2007. Major phrase, focus intonation, multiple spell-out. *The Linguistic Review* 24, 137–167.

2015. Syntax-phonology interface. In Haruo Kubozono (ed.), *Handbook of Japanese Phonetics and Phonology*, 569–618. Gruyter.

Ishihara, Shinichi. 2004. An acoustic-phonetic descriptive analysis of Kagoshima Japanese tonal phenomena. Ph.D. dissertation, Australian National University.

Ishii, Yasuo. 2001. Presuppositional effects of scrambling reconsidered. *Linguistics and Interdisciplinary Research: Proceedings of the COE International Symposium*, 79–101. Kanda University of International Studies.

Ishizuka, Tomoko. 2012. *The Passive in Japanese: A Cartographic Minimalist Approach.* Benjamins.

Itakura, Hiroko and Amy Tsui. 2004. Gender and conversational dominance in Japanese conversation. *Language in Society* 33, 223–248.

Ito, Junko and Armin Mester. 2015. Word formation and phonological processes. In Haruo Kubozono (ed.), *Handbook of Japanese Phonetics and Phonology*, 363–395. Gruyter.

Iwasaki, Noriko, Peter Sells, and Kimi Akita (eds.). 2017. *The Grammar of Japanese Mimetics: Perspectives from Structure, Acquisition and Translation.* Routledge.

Iwasaki, Shimako. 2011. The multimodal mechanics of collaborative unit construction in Japanese conversation. In Jürgen Streeck et al. (eds.), *Embodied Interaction: Language and Body in the Material World*, 106–120. Cambridge University Press.

Iwasaki, Shoichi. 1993. *Subjectivity in Grammar and Discourse.* Benjamins.

1997. The Northridge earthquake conversations: The floor structure and the "loop" sequence in Japanese conversation. *Journal of Pragmatics* 28, 661–693.

2013. *Japanese: Revised Edition*: Benjamins.

2015. A multiple-grammar model of speaker's linguistic knowledge. *Cognitive Linguistics* 26, 161–210.

Iwasaki, Shoichi and Foong Ha Yap. 2015. Stance-marking and stance-taking in Asian languages. *JP* 83, 1–9.

Iwata, Seizi. 2005. Locative alternation and two levels of verb meaning. *Cognitive Linguistics* 16, 355–407.

Izuhara, Eiko. 1994. Kandōshi, kantōjoshi, shūjoshi *ne, nē* no intonēshon [Intonation of interjectional, insertion, and sentence-final particles ne and nē]. *Nihongokyōiku* 83, 97–107.

2003. Shūjoshi *yo, yone, ne* saikō [Reconsidering sentence final particles yo, yone, and ne]. *The Journal of Aichi Gakuin University* 51, 1–15.

Izutsu, Katsunobu and Mitsuko Izutsu. 2013. From discourse markers to modal/final particles: What the position reveals about the continuum. In Liesbeth Degand et al. (eds.), *Discourse Markers and Modal Particles: Categorization and Description*, 217–236. Benjamins.

Jackendoff, Ray. 1983. *Semantics and Cognition*. MIT Press.

2010. *Meaning and the Lexicon*. Oxford University Press.

Jacobsen, Wesley. 1992a. Are conditionals topics? – The Japanese case. In Diane Brentari et al. (eds.), *The Joy of Grammar*, 131–160. Benjamins.

1992b. *The Transitive Structure of Events in Japanese*. Kurosio.

2002a. On the interaction of temporal and modal meaning in Japanese conditionals. *JKL* 10, 3–17.

2002b. Multiple times and multiple worlds: Modal and temporal meaning in BA, TEMO, TEWA, and NARA conditionals in Japanese. *JKL* 11, 352–366.

2007. Reference time, temporal adverbials, and the tense/aspect interface in Japanese. In Bjarke Frellesvig et al. (eds.), *Current Issues in the History and Structure of Japanese*, 1–26. Kurosio.

2016. Lexical meaning and temporal aspect in Japanese. In Taro Kageyama and Hideki Kishimoto (eds.), *The Handbook of Japanese Lexicon and Word Formation*, 531–558. Gruyter.

Jakobson, Roman and Morris Halle. 1962. Phonology and phonetics. In Roman Jakobson (ed.), *Selected Writings I: Phonological Studies*, 464–504. Mouton.

Jefferson, Gail. 2004. Glossary of transcript symbols with an introduction. In Gene Lerner (ed.), *Conversation Analysis: Studies from the First Generation*, 13–23. Benjamins.

Jensen, Anne. 2001. Sentence intertwining in Danish. In Elisabeth Engberg-Pedersen and Peter Harder (eds.), *Ikonicitet og struktur*, 23–39. Preprint from Netværk for Funktionel Lingvistik, Department of English, University of Copenhagen.

Jespersen, Otto. 1924/1965. *The Philosophy of Grammar*. Norton.

Jin, Dawei. 2013. Information structure constraints and complex NP islands in Chinese. *Proceedings of the 20th International Conference on Head-Driven Phrase Structure Grammar*, 110–120. CSLI.

Jones, Kimberly. 1990. Conflict in Japanese conversations. Ph.D. dissertation, University of Michigan.

Jones, Kimberly and Tsuyoshi Ono (eds.). 2008. *Style Shifting in Japanese*. Benjamins.

Jorden, Eleanor and Mari Noda. 1987. *Japanese: The Spoken Language*. Yale University Press.

Josephs, Lewis. 1976. Complementation. In Masayoshi Shibatani (ed.), *Syntax and Semantics 5: Japanese Generative Grammar*, 307–369. Academic Press.

Kageyama, Taro. 1993. *Bunpō to gokeisei* [Grammar and word formation]. Hituzi.

2004. Keidōshi kōbun to shite no 'Aoi me o shiteiru'-kōbun [Physical attribute sentences as a light verb construction]. *Nihongo Bunpō* 4, 22–37.

2006a. Property description as a voice phenomenon. In Tasaku Tsunoda and Taro Kageyama (eds.), *Voice and Grammatical Relations*, 85–114. Benjamins.

2006b. Gaikō-fukugōgo to jojutsu no taipu [External argument compounding and types of predication]. In Takashi Masuoka et al. (eds.), *Nihongo-bunpō no shinchihei* [New horizons in Japanese grammar], 1–21. Kurosio.

2007. Explorations in the conceptual semantics of mimetic verbs. In Bjarke Frellesvig et al. (eds.), *Current Issues in the History and Structure of Japanese*, 27–82. Kurosio.

2009. Kōzō-seiyaku to jojutsu-kinō [Structural constraints and predication functions]. *Gengo Kenkyu* 136, 1–34.

2010. Variation between endocentric and exocentric word structures. *Lingua* 120, 2405–2423.

Kageyama, Taro and Michiaki Saito. 2016. Vocabulary strata and word formation processes. In Taro Kageyama and Hideki Kishimoto (eds.), *The Handbook of Japanese Lexicon and Word Formation*, 11–50. Gruyter.

Kameshima, Naoko. 1990. On aboutness conditions. *JKL* 1, 255–267.

Kamimura, Takaji. 1937. Koshikijima hōgen no kenkyū [A study of the Koshikijima dialect]. *Mantetsu Kyōiku Kenkyūsho Kenkyū Yōhō* 11, 319–348.

1941. Koshikijima hōgen no akusento [The accent of the Koshikijima dialect]. *Onseigaku Kyōkai Kaihō* 65/66, 12–15.

Kamio, Akio. 1979. On the notion speaker's territory of information: A functional analysis of certain sentence-final forms in Japanese. In George Bedell et al. (eds.), *Explorations in Linguistics: Papers in Honor of Kazuko Inoue*, 213–231. Kenkyūsha.

1990. *Jōhō no nawabari riron: Gengo no kinōteki bunseki* [Territory of information: Functional analysis of language]. Taishūkan.

1994. The theory of territory of information: The case of Japanese. *JP* 21, 67–100.

1997. *Territory of Information*. Benjamins.

Karatsu, Mariko. 2004. Verbal and nonverbal negotiation in Japanese storytelling. In Polly Szatrowski (ed.), *Hidden and Open Conflict in Japanese Conversational Interaction*, 121–161. Kurosio.

2010. Sharing a personal discovery of a taste: Using distal demonstratives in a storytelling about kakuni 'stewed pork belly.' In Polly Szatrowski (ed.), *Storytelling across Japanese Conversational Genre*, 113–143. Benjamins.

2012. *Conversational Storytelling among Japanese Women: Conversational Circumstances, Social Circumstances and Tellability of Stories*. Benjamins.

2014. Repetition of words and phrases from the punch lines of Japanese stories about food and restaurants: A group bonding exercise. In Polly Szatrowski (ed.), *Language and Food: Verbal and Nonverbal Experiences*, 185–207. Benjamins.

Kataoka, Kuniyoshi. 1995. Affect in Japanese women's letter writing: Use of sentence-final particles *ne* and *yo* and orthographic conventions. *Pragmatics* 5, 427–453.

Kato, Shigehiro. 2003. *Nihongo shūshokukōzō no goyōronteki kenkyū* [Pragmatic study of modifying structures in Japanese]. Hituzi.

Kato, Yasuhiko. 1985. *Negative Sentences in Japanese*. Sophia Linguistica 19. Sophia University.

2000. Interpretive asymmetries of negation. In Laurence Horn and Yasuhiko Kato (eds.), *Negation and Polarity*, 62–87. Oxford University Press.

Kawahara, Shigeto. 2006. A faithfulness ranking projected from a perceptibility scale: The case of [+voice] in Japanese. *Language* 82, 536–574.

2016. Japanese has syllables: A reply to Labrune (2012). *Phonology* 33, 169–194.

Kawakami, Shin. 1956. Buntō no intonēshon [Sentence-initial intonation]. Reprinted in 1995 in *Nihongo Akusento Ronshū* [A collection of papers on Japanese accent], 76–91. Kyūko Shoin.

1957. Tōkyōgo no takuritsu kyōchō no onchō. [Tonal prominence in Tokyo Japanese]. Reprinted in 1995 in *Nihongo Akusento Ronshū* [A collection of papers on Japanese accent], 76–91. Kyūko.

1963. Bunmatsu nado no jōshōchō ni tsuite [On phrase-final rises]. Reprinted in 1995 in *Nihongo akusento ronshū* [A collection of papers on Japanese accent], 274–298. Kyūko.

1977. *Nihongo onsei gaisetsu* [Outline of Japanese phonetics]. Ōfūsha.

Kayne, Richard. 1994. *The Antisymmetry of Syntax*. MIT Press.

Keenan, Edward. 1976. Towards a universal definition of subject. In Charles Li (ed.), *Subject and Topic*, 303–334. Academic Press.

1985. Relative clauses. In Timothy Shopen (ed.), *Language Typology and Syntactic Description, Vol. 2*, 141–170. Cambridge University Press.

Keenan, Edward and Bernard Comrie. 1977. Noun phrases accessibility and universal grammar. *LI* 8, 63–99.

Kemmer, Suzanne. 1993. *The Middle Voice*. Benjamins.

Kempson, Ruth. 1975. *Presupposition and the Delimitation of Semantics*. Cambridge University Press.

Kibe, Nobuko. 2000. *Seinanbu kyūshū nikei akusento no kenkyū* [Studies on the two-class-accent dialects of southwest Kyūshū]. Benseisha.

2010. Intonēshon no chiikisa: Shitsumonbun no intonēshon [Regional differences in intonation: Intonation in interrogative sentences]. In Takashi Kobayashi and Koichi Shinozaki (eds.), *Hōgen no hakken – Shirarezaru chiikisa o shiru* [Discovery of dialects – To find unknown regional differences], 1–20. Hituzi.

Kikuchi, Yasuto. 1994. *Keigo* [Honorifics]. Kadokawa.

1997. *Keigo* [Honorifics]. Kōdansha.

Kim, E. 2009. Gendaigo no rentaishūshokusetsu ni okeru joshi *no* [The particle *no* in the modificational construction in modern Japanese]. *Nihongo Kagaku* 25, 23–42.

Kindaichi, Haruhiko. 1950a. "Gooku" to "gōku": Hikionsetsu no teishō [Gooku and gōku: In support of the lengthening mora]. *Kokugo to Kokubungaku* 27, 46–59.

1950b. Kokugo dōshi no ichibunrui [A classification of Japanese verbs]. *Gengo Kenkyu* 15, 41–63. Reprinted in Haruhiko Kindaichi (ed.), 1976, *Nihongo dōshi no asupekuto* [Aspect in Japanese verbs], 5–26. Mugi.

1953. Fuhenka jodōshi no honshitsu: Kyakkanteki hyōgen to shukanteki no betsu ni tsuite [The essential nature of the conjugationless auxiliaries: On the distinction between objective and subjective expressions]. *Kokugo Kokubun* 22, 149–169.

1964. Watashi no hōgen kukaku. In Nihon Hōgen Kenkyūkai (ed.), *Nihon no hōgen kukaku* [The classification of Japanese dialects], 71–94. Tōkyōdō.

1966. Kyōtsūgo no hatsuon to akusento. In Nippon Hōsō Kyōkai (ed.), *Nihongo Hatsuon Akusento Jiten*, 5–30. Nippon Hōsō Shuppan Kyōkai.

1967. Onsetsu, mōra oyobi haku [Syllable, mora, and beat]. In *Nihongo on'in no kenkyū* [Studies in Japanese phonology], 58–77. Tōkyōdō.

1978. Giongo/gitaigo gaisetsu [Outline of mimetic words]. In Tsuruko Asano (ed.), *Giongo/gitaigo jiten* [Dictionary of phonomimes/phenomimes], 3–25. Kadokawa.

1985. Kyōtsūgo no hatsuon to akusento [Pronunciation and accent in the common language]. In Nippon Hōsō Kyōkai (ed.), *Nihongo Hatsuon Akusento Jiten* [Japanese pronunciation and accent dictionary], 5–36. Nippon Hōsō Shuppan Kyōkai.

1998. Kyōtsūgo no hatsuon to akusento [Pronunciation and accent in the common language]. In NHK Hōsō Bunka Kenkūyjo (ed.), *Nihongo hatsuon akusento jiten* [Japanese pronunciation and accent dictionary], 90–122. Nippon Hōsō Shuppan Kyōkai.

Kindaichi Haruhiko and Akinaga Kazue (eds.). 2001. *Shin meikai nihongo askusento jiten* [New easy-to-understand Japanese accent dictionary]. Sanseidō.

Kinjo, Hiromi. 1987. Oral refusals of invitations and requests in English and Japanese. *Journal of Asian Culture* 11, 83–106.

Kinsui, Satoshi. 1984. "Iru, aru, oru": Sonzai hyōgen no rekishi to hōgen. *Eureka* 16, 284–293.

1991. Judōbun no rekishi ni tsuite no ichi kōsatsu [An observation about the history of passive]. *Kokugogaku* 164, 1–14.

1994. Rentaishūshoku no *~ta* ni tsuite [On ~ta as a noun modifier]. In Yukinori Takubo (ed.), *Nihongo no meishi shūshoku hyōgen* [Noun modifying expressions in Japanese], 29–65. Kurosio.

1997. The influence of translation on the historical development of the Japanese passive construction. *Journal of Pragmatics* 28, 759–779.

2003. *Vācharu nihongo: Yakuwarigo no nazo* [Virtual Japanese: The mysteries of role language]. Iwanami.

Kinsui, Satoshi, Yoshiyuki Takayama, Tomohide Kinuhata, and Tomoko Okazaki. 2011. *Nihongoshi 3: Bunpōshi* [A History of Japanese 3: A History of Japanese Grammar]. Iwanami.

Kiss, Katalin. 1995. Introduction. In Katalin Kiss (ed.), *Discourse Configurational Languages*, 3–27. Oxford University Press.

Kiparsky, Paul and Carol Kiparsky. 1968. Fact. In Manfred Bierwisch and Karl Erich Heidolph (eds.), *Recent Advances in Linguistics*, 143–173. Mouton.

Kishimoto, Hideki. 2005. *Tōgokōzō to bunpō kankei* [Syntactic structures and grammatical relations]. Kurosio.

2007. Negative scope and head raising in Japanese. *Lingua* 117, 247–288.

2008. On the variability of negative scope in Japanese. *Journal of Linguistics* 44, 379–435.

2009. On the formation of lexicalized negative adjectives. In Yoko Yumoto and Hideki Kishimoto (eds.), *Goi no imi to bunpō* [Lexical meanings and grammar], 47–64. Kurosio.

2013. Verbal complex formation and negation in Japanese. *Lingua* 135, 132–154.

Kishimoto, Hideki and Geert Booij. 2014. Complex negative adjectives in Japanese: The relation between syntactic and morphological constructions. *Word Structure* 7, 55–87.

Kita, Sotaro. 1997. Two-dimensional semantic analysis of Japanese mimetics. *Linguistics* 35, 379–415.

2001. Semantic schism and interpretive integration in Japanese sentences with a mimetic: A reply to Tsujimura. *Linguistics* 39, 419–436.

Kitagawa, Chisato. 1976. *Naku-te* to *nai-de* [Naku-te and nai-de]. *Nihongokyōiku* 29, 57–67.

1983. On the two forms of negative gerund in Japanese. *Papers in Linguistics* 16, 89–126.

Kitamura, Masanori. 2008. "Odoroki/Kangai" o arawasu monoda-bun no kōzō henka – Kinsei ikō o chūshin ni [Structural changes of monoda sentences expressing "surprise/exclamation" since the seventeenth century]. *Kokubungaku* 92, 448–464.

Klein, Wolfgang. 1994. *Time in Language*. Routledge.

Kluender, Robert. 1990. A neurophysiological investigation of wh-islands. *BLS* 16, 187–204.

Kluender, Robert and Marta Kutas. 1993. Subjacency as a processing phenomenon. *Language and Cognitive Processes* 8, 573–633.

Kobayashi, Hideki. 2004. *Gendai nihongo no kango-dōmeishi no kenkyū* [A study of Sino-Japanese verbal nouns in present-day Japanese]. Hituzi.

Koike, Chisato. 2001. An analysis of shifts in participation roles in Japanese storytelling in terms of prosody, gaze and body movements. *BLS* 27, 353–370.

2003. An analysis of increments in Japanese conversation in terms of intonation and grammar. *JKL* 11, 67–80.

2009. Interaction in storytelling in Japanese conversations: An analysis of story recipients' questions. Ph.D. dissertation, UCLA.

2010. Ellipsis and action in a Japanese joint storytelling series. In Polly Szatrowski (ed.), *Storytelling across Japanese Conversation Genre*, 61–111. Benjamins.

2014. Food experience and categorization in Japanese talk-in-interaction. In Polly Szatrowski (ed.), *Language and Food: Verbal and Nonverbal Experiences*, 159–183. Benjamins.

Koizumi, Masatoshi. 2008. Nominative objects. In Miyagawa Shigeru and Mamoru Saito (eds.), *The Oxford Handbook of Japanese Linguistics*, 141–164. Oxford University Press.

Koji, Kazuteru. 1980. *Man'yōshū jodōshi no kenkyū* [Studies of the auxiliaries in the Man'yōshū]. Meiji.

Kokoma, Katsumi. 2014. "Jiyūdo" koso nihon kanji no miryoku [The appeal of Japanese characters because of the degree of freedom]. In Tomokazu Takada and Shoichi Yokoyama (eds.), *Nihongo moji hyōki no muzukashisa to omoshirosa* [Difficulties and pleasures of Japanese writing], 34–53. Sairyūsha.

Kokuritsu Kokugo Kenkyūjo. 1964. Gendai zasshi 90-shu no yōji yōgo [Words and characters used in ninety modern magazines], Part III.

Komatsu, Toshio. 1988. Tōkyōgo ni okeru danjosa no keisei: Shūjoshi o chūshin to shite [Development of sex difference in Tokyo dialect: With a focus on sentence-final particles]. *Kokugo to Kokubungaku* 11, 94–106.

Konishi, Izumi. 2015. Hiroshima-shi hōgen no taikaku hyōji [The accusative marking in the Hiroshima city dialect]. *Kokugo Kyōiku Kenkyū* 56, 13–24.

Kori, Shiro. 1997. Nihongo no intonēshon: Kata to kinō [Japanese intonation: Its patterns and functions]. In Tetsuya Kunihiro et al. (eds.), *Nihongo onsei 2: Akusento intonēshon rizumu to pōzu* [Sound in Japanese 2: Accent, intonation, rhythm, and pause], 169–202. Sanseidō.

Koyama, Tetsuharu. 1997. Bunmatsushi to bunmatsu intonēshon [Sentence-final particles and sentence-final intonation]. In Onseibunpō Kenkyūkai (ed.), *Bunpō to onsei* [Grammar and sound], 97–119. Kurosio.

Kratzer, Angelika. 1995. Stage-level and individual-level predicates. In Gregory Carlson and Francis Pelletier (eds.), *The Generic Book*, 125–175. University of Chicago Press.

Krifka, Manfred, Francis J. Pelletier, Greg Carolson, Alice ter Meulen, Bennaro Chierchia, and Godehard Link. 1995. Genericity: An introduction. In Gregory Carlson and Francis Pelletier (eds.), *The Generic Book*, 1–124. University of Chicago Press.

Kubozono, Haruo. 1988. The organization of Japanese prosody. Ph. D. dissertation, University of Edinburgh. [Published by Kurosio 1993.]

1989. The mora and syllable structure in Japanese: Evidence from speech errors. *Language and Speech* 32, 249–278.

1993. Nihongo no onsetsu-ryō [Syllable weight in Japanese]. In Shōsuke Haraguchi (ed.), *Nihongo no mōra to onsetsu kōzō ni kansuru sōgō kenkyū (2)* [Integrated research on Japanese mora and syllable structure (2)], 72–101. Osaka Gaikokugo Daigaku, Nihongo Gakka.

1995a. Constraint interaction in Japanese phonology: Evidence from compound accent. *Phonology at Santa Cruz (PASC)* 4, 21–38.

1995b. *Gokeisei to on'in kōzō* [Word formation and phonological structure]. Kurosio.

1997. Lexical markedness and variation: A non-derivational account. In Brian Agbayani and Sze-Wing Tang (eds.), *Proceedings of the 15th West Coast Conference on Formal Linguistics*, 273–287. CSLI.

1999. Mora and syllable. In Natsuko Tsujimura (ed.), *The Handbook of Japanese Linguistics*, 31–61. Blackwell.

2006a. Where does loanword prosody come from? A case study of Japanese loanword accent. *Lingua* 116, 1140–1170.

2006b. *Akusento no hōsoku* [Laws of accent]. Iwanami.

2006c. The phonetic and phonological organization of speech in Japanese. In Mineharu Nakayama et al. (eds.), *The Handbook of East Asian Psycholinguistics. Volume II Japanese*, 191–200. Cambridge University Press.

2007a. Tonal change in language contact: Evidence from Kagoshima Japanese. In Tomas Riad and Carlos Gussenhoven (eds.), *Tones and*

Tunes. Vol. 1: Typological Studies in Word and Sentence Prosody, 323–351. Gruyter.

2007b. Focus and intonation in Japanese: Does focus trigger pitch reset? In Shinichiro Ishihara (ed.), *Interdisciplinary Studies on Information Structure*, 1–27. Universitätsverlag Potsdam.

2008. Japanese accent. In Shigeru Miyagawa and Mamoru Saito (eds.), *The Oxford Handbook of Japanese Linguistics*, 165–191. Oxford University Press.

2010. Accentuation of alphabetic acronyms in varieties of Japanese. *Lingua* 120, 2323–2335.

2011. Japanese pitch accent. In Marc van Oostendorp et al. (eds.), *The Blackwell Companion to Phonology, Vol. 5*, 2879–2907. Wiley-Blackwell.

2012a. Introduction: Special issue on varieties of pitch accent systems. *Lingua* 122, 1325–1334.

2012b. Varieties of pitch accent systems in Japanese. *Lingua* 122, 1395–1414.

2012c. Word-level vs. sentence-level prosody in Koshikijima Japanese. *The Linguistic Review* 29, 109–130.

2015a. Diphthongs and vowel coalescence. In Haruo Kubozono (ed.), *Handbook of Japanese Phonetics and Phonology*, 215–249. Gruyter.

2015b. Japanese dialects and general linguistics. *Gengo Kenkyu* 148, 1–31.

2016. Diversity of pitch accent systems in Koshikijima Japanese. *Gengo Kenkyu* 150, 1–31.

2017. Accent in Japanese phonology. *Oxford Research Encyclopedia of Linguistics* (online encyclopedia).

2018. Postlexical tonal neutralizations in Kagoshima Japanese. In Haruo Kubozono and Mikio Giriko (eds.), *Tonal Change and Neutralization*, 27–57. Gruyter.

Kubozono, Haruo and Takeru Honma. 2002. *Onsetsu to mōra* [Syllables and moras]. Kenkyūsha.

Kudo, Hiroshi. 1988. Bunpō ronsō. In Haruhiko Kaneda (ed.), *Nihongo hyakka jiten* [Encyclopedia of Japanese], 152–159. Taishūkan.

2000. Fukushi to bun no chinjutsuteki na taipu [Adverbs and predicative sentence types]. In Takurō Moriyama et al. (eds.), *Modaritī* [Modality], 164–234. Iwanami.

Kulikov, Leonid and Nikolaos Lavidas. 2014. Introduction. *Linguistics* 52, 871–877.

Kumagai, Shigeko. 2010. Hōgen no rekishi: Wakai josei ga Tōhoku-ben o tsukai-nikui wake [A history of dialects: The reasons why it is difficult for young women to use Tohoku dialect]. In Momoko Nakamura (ed.), *Jendā de manabu gengogaku* [Linguistics taught through gender], 50–65. Sekai Shisōsha.

Kumagai, Tomoko and Naoyuki Kitani. 2010. *Sansha mensetsu chōsa ni okeru komyunikēshon* [Communication in three-party survey interviews]. Kurosio.

Kumatoridani, Tetsuo. 1999. Alternation and co-occurrence in Japanese thanks. *JP* 31, 623–642.

Kuno, Susumu. 1972a. Pronominalization, reflexivization, and direct discourse. *LI* 3, 161–195.

1972b. Functional sentence perspective: A case study from Japanese and English. *LI* 3, 269–320.

1973. *The Structure of the Japanese Language*. MIT Press.

1978a. *Danwa no bunpō* [The grammar of discourse]. Taishūkan.

1978b. *Shin nihon bunpō kenkyū* [A new study of Japanese grammar]. Taishūkan.

1987. *Functional Syntax: Anaphora, Discourse and Empathy*. University of Chicago Press.

1988. Blended quasi-direct discourse in Japanese. In William Poser (ed.), *Papers from the Second International Workshop on Japanese Syntax*, 75–102. CSLI.

1995. Null elements in parallel structures in Japanese. In Reiko Mazuka and Noriko Nagai (eds.), *Japanese Sentence Processing*, 209–33. Erlbaum.

1983. Shin Nihon bunpō kenkyū [A new study of Japanese grammar]. Taishūkan.

Kuno, Susumu and Etsuko Kaburaki. 1977. Empathy and syntax. *LI* 8, 627–672.

Kuno, Susumu and Ken-ichi Takami. 1993. *Grammar and Discourse Principles: Functional Syntax and GB Theory*. University of Chicago Press.

Kurihara, Sayoko. 2009. Shūjoshika shita "shi" [On shi grammaticalized as a sentence-final particle]. *Gakushūin Daigaku Kokugo Kokubungakkaishi* 52, 1–15.

Kuroda, S.-Y. 1965. Generative grammatical studies in the Japanese language. Ph.D. dissertation, MIT.

1972. The categorical and the thetic judgment: Evidence from Japanese syntax. *Foundations of Language* 9, 153–185.

1973a. Where epistemology, style, and grammar meet: A case study from Japanese. In Stephen Anderson and Paul Kiparsky (eds.), *A Festschrift for Morris Halle*, 377–391. Holt, Rinehart and Winston.

1973b. On Kuno's direct discourse analysis of the Japanese reflexive zibun. *Papers in Japanese Linguistics* 2, 136–147.

1974–1977/1992. Pivot-independent relativization in Japanese. *Japanese Syntax and Semantics: Collected Papers*, 114–174. Kluwer.

1978. Case marking, canonical sentence patterns, and counter equi in Japanese. In John Hinds and Irwin Howard (eds.), *Problems in Japanese Syntax and Semantics*, 30–51. Kaitakusha.

1979. On Japanese passive. In G. Bedell et al. (eds.), *Explorations in Linguistics: Papers in Honor of Kazuko Inoue*, 305–347. Kaitakusha.

1992a. Judgment forms and sentence forms. In S.-Y. Kuroda (ed.), *Japanese Syntax and Semantics: Collected Papers*, 13–77. Kluwer.

1992b. Pivot-independent relativization in Japanese. In S.-Y. Kuroda (ed.), *Japanese Syntax and Semantics: Collected Papers*, 114–174. Kluwer.

1992c. What happened after the movement of NPs in Japanese in La Jolla? In S.-Y. Kuroda (ed.), *Japanese Syntax and Semantics: Collected Papers*, 293–314. Kluwer.

Labrune, Laurence. 2012a. *The Phonology of Japanese*. Oxford University Press.

2012b. Questioning the universality of the syllable: Evidence from Japanese. *Phonology* 29, 113–152.

Ladd, Robert. 2008. *Intonational Phonology*. Cambridge University Press.

Ladefoged, Peter. 1982. *A Course in Phonetics*. Jovanovich.

Ladefoged, Peter and Ian Maddieson 1996. *The Sounds of the World's Languages*. Blackwell.

Ladusaw, William. 2000. Thetic and categorical, stage and individual, weak and strong. In Laurence Horn and Yasuhiko Kato (eds.), *Negation and Polarity*, 232–242. Oxford University Press.

Lakoff, George. 1968. Counterparts, or the problem of reference in transformational grammar. Reproduced by the Indiana University Linguistics Club, Bloomington, Indiana.

1996. Sorry, I'm not myself today: The metaphor system for conceptualizing the self. In Gilles Fauconnier and Eve Sweetser (eds.), *Spaces, Worlds, and Grammar*, 91–123. University of Chicago Press.

Lakoff, George and Mark Johnson. 1999. *Philosophy in the Flesh: The Embodied Mind and Its Challenge to Western Thought*. Basic Books.

Lakoff, Robin. 1973. The logic of politeness; or minding your p's and q's. *CLS* 9, 292–305.

Lambrecht, Knud. 1994. *Information Structure and Sentence Form: Topic, Focus, and the Mental Representations of Discourse Referents*. Cambridge University Press.

Langacker, Ronald. 1987. *Foundations of Cognitive Grammar, Volume I: Theoretical Prerequisites*. Stanford University Press.

1991. *Concept, Image, and Symbol. The Cognitive Basis of Language*. Gruyter.

Larson, Richard. 1988. On the double object construction. *LI* 19, 335–391.

Lasnik, Howard and Mamoru Saito. 1984. On the nature of proper government. *LI* 15, 235–289.

Lass, Roger. 1984. *Phonology: An Introduction to Basic Concepts*. Cambridge University Press.

Laver, John. 1994. *Principles of Phonetics*. Cambridge University Press.

Lê, Van Cu. 1988. *"NO" ni yoru bun umekomi no kōzo to hyōgen no kinō* [The Structure and function of sentence embedded by *no*]. Kurosio.

Lebra, Takie. 1976. *Japanese Patterns of Behavior*. University Press of Hawai'i.

Lee, Yeonsuk. 1996. *"Kokugo" to iu shisō* [An ideology called "kokugo"]. Iwanami.

Leech, Geoffrey. 1983. *Principles of Pragmatics*. Longman.

Lees, Robert. 1963. *The Grammar of English Nominalizations*. Mouton.

Lerner, Gene and Tomoyo Takagi. 1999. On the place of linguistic resources in the organization of talk-in-interaction: A co-investigation of English and Japanese grammatical practices. *JP* 31, 49–75.

Levin, Beth and Malka Rappaport. 1986. The formation of adjectival passives. *LI* 17, 623–661.

Levin, Beth and Malka Rappaport Hovav. 1995. *Unaccusativity*. MIT Press.

Levin, Beth and Malka Rappaport Hovav. 2005. *Argument Realization*. Cambridge University Press.

Li, Charles and Sandra Thompson. 1976. Subject and topic: A new typology of language. In Charles Li (ed.), *Subject and Topic*, 457–489. Academic Press.

Lieber, Rochelle. 1983. Argument linking and compounds in English. *LI* 14, 251–286.

Liberman, Mark and Janet Pierrehumbert. 1984. Intonational invariance under changes in pitch range and length. In Mark Aronoff and Richard Oerhle (eds.), *Language Sound Structure*, 157–233. MIT Press.

Lieberman, Philip. 1977. *Speech Physiology and Acoustic Phonetics*. Macmillan.

Linell, Per. 1979. *Psychological Reality in Phonology: A Theoretical Study*. Cambridge University Press.

Long, Christopher. 2010. Apology in Japanese gratitude situations: The negotiation of interlocutor role-relations. *JP* 42, 1060–1075.

Lurie, David. 2011. *Realms of Literacy: Early Japan and the History of Writing*. Harvard University Press.

Mabuchi, Yoko. 2000. Kakujoshi "de" no imikakuchō ni kansuru ichikōsatsu [A note on the historical development of the case particle "de"]. *Kokugogaku* 51, 15–30.

Machida, Nanako. 1996. On the notion of affectedness and the null beneficiary in benefactive constructions in Japanese. *Academia* 61, 203–224.

Maeda, Naoko. 2009. *Nihongo no fukubun* [Complex sentences in Japanese]. Kurosio.

Maekawa, Kikuo. 1994. Intonational structure of Kumamoto Japanese: A perceptual validation. *Proceedings of 1994 International Conference on Spoken Language Processing*, 119–122. Acoustical Society of Japan.

1997a. Akusento to intonēshon: Akusento no nai chiiki [Accent and intonation: accentless areas]. In Ryoichi Sato et al. (eds.), *Shohōgen no akusento to intonēshon* [Accent and intonation in various dialects], 97–122. Sanseidō.

1997b. Nihongogimonshigimonbun no intonēshon [Intonation in Japanese wh-questions]. *Bunpō to onsei* [Grammar and sound], 45–53. Kurosio.

1999. Contributions of lexical and prosodic factors to the perception of politeness. *Proceedings of the 14th International Congress of Phonetic Science*, 1573–1576. International Phonetic Association.

2003. Corpus of spontaneous Japanese: Its design and evaluation. *ISCA & IEEE Workshop on Spontaneous Speech Processing and Recognition* 4, 7–22.

2006. Analysis of language variation using a large-scale corpus of spontaneous speech. *Proceedings of the International Symposium on Linguistic Patterns in Spontaneous Speech*, 15–37. Taipei.

Maekawa, Kikuo and Norimichi Kitagawa. 2002. Onsei wa paragengo jōhō o ikani tsutaeru ka [How does speech transmit paralinguistic information?]. *Cognitive Studies: Bulletin of the Japanese Cognitive Science Society* 9, 46–66.

Maekawa, Kikuo, Hideaki Kikuchi, Yosuke Igarashi, and Jennifer Venditti. 2002. X-JToBI: An extended J_ToBI for spontaneous speech. *Proceedings of the 7th International Conference on Spoken Language Processing*, 1545–1548. International Speech Communication Association.

Maekawa, Kikuo, Makoto Yamazaki, Toshinobu Ogiso, Takehiko Maruyama, Hideki Ogura, Wakako Kashino, et al. 2014. Balanced corpus of contemporary written Japanese. *Language Resources and Evaluation* 48, 345–371.

Makino, Seiichi. 2002. When does communication turn mentally inward? A case study of Japanese formal-to-informal switching. *JKL* 10, 121–135.

Makino, Seiichi and Michio Tsutsui 1986. *A Dictionary of Basic Japanese Grammar*. Japan Times.

Maling, Joan. 1977. A non-recoverable deletion. *The CLS Book of Squibs*, 66–67.

Marantz, Alec. 1993. Implications of asymmetries in double object construction. In Sam Mchombo (ed.), *Theoretical Aspect of Bantu Grammar*, 113–150. CSLI.

Maree, Claire. 2013. *"Onē kotoba"-ron* [A theory of *onē* language]. Seidosha.

Martin, Samuel. 1952. *Morphophonemics of Standard Colloquial Japanese*. Linguistic Society of America.

1964. Speech levels in Japan and Korea. In Dell Hymes (ed.), *Language in Culture and Society*, 407–415. Harper and Row.

1975. *A Reference Grammar of Japanese*. Yale University Press.

1987. *The Japanese Language through Time*. Yale University Press.

Martin, Wayne. 2010. Fichte's logical legacy: Thetic judgment from the Wissenschaftslehre to Brentano. In Violetta Waibel et al. (eds.), *Fichte and the Phenomenological Tradition*, 379–406. Gruyter.

Masuoka, Takashi. 1987. *Meidai no bunpō* [Grammar of propositions]. Kurosio.

1991. *Modaritī no bunpō* [The grammar of modality]. Kurosio.

(ed.). 1993. *Nihongo no jōkenbun hyōgen* [Conditional expressions in Japanese]. Kurosio.

1997a. *Fukubun* [Complex sentences]. Kurosio.

1997b. Hyōgen no shukansei to shiten [Subjectivity and perspective of expressions]. *Nihongogaku* 11, 28–34.
2004. Nihongo no shudai: Jojutsu no ruikei no kanten kara [Topics in Japanese: From the perspective of predication types]. In Takashi Masuoka (ed.), *Shudai no taishō* [Contrastive studies of topics], 3–17. Kurosio.
2008. Jojutsu ruikeiron ni mukete [Toward a typology of predications]. In Takashi Masuoka (ed.), *Jojutsu ruikeiron* [A typology of predications], 3–18. Kurosio.
Masuoka, Takashi and Yukinori Takubo. 1989. *Kiso nihongo bunpō* [Basic Japanese grammar]. Kurosio.
1992. *Kiso nihogo bunpō* [Basic Japanese grammar]. Kurosio.
Matras, Yaon. 2009. *Language Contact*. Cambridge University Press.
Matsumoto, Kazuko. 1995. Fragmentation in conversational Japanese: A case study, *JALT Journal* 17, 238–253.
Matsumoto, Yoshiko. 1988a. Semantics and pragmatics of noun-modifying constructions in Japanese. *BLS* 14, 166–175.
1988b. Reexamination of the universality of face: Politeness phenomena in Japanese. *JP* 12, 403–426.
1989. Japanese-style noun modification . . . in English. *BLS* 15, 226–237.
1991. Is it really a topic that is relativized? Arguments from Japanese. *CLS* 27, 388–402.
1996a. Does less feminine speech in Japanese mean less femininity? In Natasha Warner et al. (eds.), *Gender and Belief Systems: Proceedings of the 4th Berkeley Women and Language Conference*, 455–467. Berkeley Women and Language Group.
1996b. Interaction of factors in construal: Japanese relative clauses. In Masayoshi Shibatani and Sandra Thompson (eds.), *Grammatical Constructions: Their Form and Meaning*, 103–124. Oxford University Press.
1997. *Noun-Modifying Constructions in Japanese: A Frame-Semantic Approach*. Benjamins.
1998. The complementizer *toyuu* in Japanese. *JKL* 7, 243–255.
2004. Alternative femininity: Personae of middle-aged mothers. In Shigeko Okamoto and Janet Shibamoto Smith (eds.), *Japanese Language, Gender, and Ideology: Cultural Models and Real People*, 240–255. Oxford University Press.
2007. Integrating frames: Complex noun phrase constructions in Japanese. In Susumu Kuno et al. (eds.), *Aspects of Linguistics: In Honor of Noriko Akatsuka*, 131–154. Kurosio.
2009. Pragmatics of performative honorifics in subordinate clauses. In Bruce Fraser and Ken Turner (eds.), *Language in Life, and a Life in Language: Jacob Mey: A Festschrift*, 289–297. Emerald.
2010. Interactional frames and grammatical descriptions: The case of Japanese noun-modifying constructions. *Constructions and Frames* 2, 136–157.

2014. Nihongo meishi shūshokusetsu kōbun – tagengo tono taishō o fukumete. *Nihongo fukubun kōbun no kenkyū* [Noun-modifying clause constructions in Japanese: With comparisons to other languages]. In Takashi Masuoka et al. (eds.), *Studies on Japanese Complex Sentence Constructions*, 559–590. Hituzi.

2015. Partnership between grammatical construction and interactional frame: Stand-alone noun-modifying construction in invocatory discourse. *Constructions and Frames* 7, 289–314.

Matsumoto, Yoshiko and Shigeko Okamoto. 2003. The construction of the Japanese language and culture in teaching Japanese as a foreign language. *Japanese Language and Literature* 37, 27–48.

Matsumoto, Yoshiko, Bernard Comrie, and Peter Sells (eds.). 2017. *Noun-Modifying Clause Constructions in Languages of Eurasia: Rethinking Theoretical and Geographical Boundaries*. Benjamins.

Matsumura, Akira. 1971. *Nihon bunpō daijiten* [A comprehensive dictionary of Japanese grammar]. Meiji.

Matsuura, Toshio. 2014. *Nagasaki hōgen kara mita go-onchō no kōzō* [Word prosodic structure from the perspective of Nagasaki Japanese]. Hituzi.

Maynard, Senko. 1987. Thematization as a staging device in Japanese narrative. In John Hinds et al. (eds.), *Perspectives on Topicalization: The Case of Japanese Wa*, 57–82. Benjamins.

1989. *Japanese Conversation: Self-contextualization through Structure and Interactional Management*. Ablex.

1992a. Where textual voices proliferate: The *toyuu* clause-noun combination in Japanese. *Poetics* 21, 169–189.

1992b. Speech act declaration in conversation: Functions of the Japanese connective *datte*. *Studies in Language* 16, 63–89.

1993. *Discourse Modality: Subjectivity, Emotion and Voice in the Japanese Language*. Benjamins.

1997. *Japanese Communication: Language and Thought in Context*. University of Hawai'i Press.

2008a. Playing with multiple voices: Emotivity and creativity in Japanese style mixture. In Kimberly Jones and Tsuyoshi Ono (eds.), *Style Shifting in Japanese*, 91–129. Benjamins.

2008b. *Maruchi janru danwaron* [Multi-genre discourse studies]. Kurosio.

Mazuka, Reiko, Yosuke Igarashi, and Kenya Nishikawa. 2006. Input for learning Japanese: RIKEN Japanese Mother-Infant Conversation Corpus. *Technical report of IEICE*, TL2006–16, 106(165), 11–15.

McCawley, James. 1968. *The Phonological Component of a Grammar of Japanese*. Mouton.

1976 [1972]. Relativization. In Masayoshi Shibatani (ed.), *Syntax and Semantics 5: Japanese Generative Grammar*, 295–306. Academic Press.

1977. Accent in Japanese. In Larry Hyman (ed.), *Studies in Stress and Accent*, 261–302. University of Southern California Department of Linguistics.

1978. What is a tone language? In Victoria Fromkin (ed.), *Tone: A Linguistic Survey*, 113–131. Academic Press.

McCawley, Noriko A. 1972. A study of Japanese reflexivization. Ph. D. dissertation, University of Illinois at Urbana-Champaign.

1978. Another look at *no, koto* and *to*: Epistemology and complementizer choice in Japanese. In John Hinds and Irwin Howard (eds.), *Problems in Japanese Syntax and Semantics*, 178–212. Kaitakusha.

McClure, William. 1995. *Syntactic Projections of the Semantics of Aspect*. Hituzi.

McGloin, Naomi. 1976. Negation. In Masayoshi Shibatani (ed.), *Syntax and Semantics 5: Japanese Generative Grammar*, 371–419. Academic Press.

1976–77. The speaker's attitude and the conditionals *to, tara,* and *ba*. *Papers in Japanese Linguistics* 5, 181–191.

1987. The role of wa in negation. In John Hinds et al. (eds.), *Perspectives in Topicalization: The Case of Japanese Wa*, 165–183. Benjamins.

1990. Sex difference and sentence-final particles. In Sachiko Ide and Naomi McGloin (eds.), *Aspects of Japanese Women's Language*, 23–42. Kurosio.

McGloin, Naomi and Yumiko Konishi. 2010. From connective particle to sentence-final particle: A usage-based analysis of *shi* "and" in Japanese. *Language Sciences* 32, 563–578.

Mihara, Ken-ichi. 1994. *Iwayuru shuyōbu naizaigata kankeisetsu ni tsuite* [On so-called internally headed relative clauses]. *Nihongogaku* 7, 80–92.

Mikami, Akira. 1953. *Gendai gohō josetsu* [Modern Japanese usage: An introduction]. Tōkō. Reproduced by Kurosio, 1972.

1963. *Nihongo no kōzō* [The structure of Japanese]. Kurosio.

Miller, Roy. 1967. *The Japanese Language*. University of Chicago Press.

Mills, Sara. 2003. *Gender and Politeness*. Cambridge University Press.

Milsark, Gary. 1974. Existential sentences in English. Ph.D. dissertation, MIT. Published by Garland, 1979.

Minami, Fujio. 1974. *Gendai Nihongo no Kōzō* [The structure of Modern Japanese]. Taishūkan.

1997. *Gendai nihongo no kenkyuu* [Research on Modern Japanese]. Sanseido.

1981. Nichijō kaiwa no wadai no suii – Matsue tekusuto o shiryō to shite [Topic transition in everyday conversation – Using the Matsue transcription as data]. In Fujiwara Yoichi, Sensei Koki, Shukuga Ronshū, and Kankō Iinkai (eds.), *Hōgengaku ronsō 1 – Hōgen kenkyū no suishin* [Discussions related to dialects 1 – Advances in dialect research], 87–112. Sanseidō. Reprinted in Fujio Minami (1997), *Gendai nihongo kenkyū* [A study of Modern Japanese], 307–334. Sanseidō.

1983. Danwa no tan'i [Units of discourse]. *Nihongo kyōiku shidō sankōsho 11 – Danwa no kenkyū to kyōiku I* [Reference guide for Japanese language education 11 – Discourse research and education I], 90–112. Ōkurashō. Reprinted in Fujio Minami (1997), Gendai nihongo kenkyū [A study of Modern Japanese], 335–356. Sanseidō.

1987a. *Keigo* [Honorifics]. Iwanami.

1987b. *Danwa kōdōron* [Discourse behavior theory]. *Danwa kōdō no shosō – Zadan shiryō no bunseki* [Aspects of discourse behavior – Analysis of conversation data], Kokugo kokugoken hōkoku [National Language Research Institute report] 92, 5–35. Sanseidō.

Mithun, Marianne. 1984. The evolution of noun incorporation. *Language* 60, 847–894.

Miyagawa, Shigeru. 1987. Wa and the wh phrase. In John Hinds et al. (eds.), *Perspectives on Topicalization: The Case of Japanese Wa*, 185–217. Benjamins.

Miyagawa, Shigeru and Takae Tsujioka. 2004. Argument structure and ditransitive verbs in Japanese. *Journal of East Asian Linguistics* 13, 1–38.

Miyaji, Yutaka. 1956. Hitei hyōgen no mondai [Problems of negative expressions]. *Gengo Seikatsu* 97, 49–51.

Miyake, Kazuko. 2014. Denshi media no moji hyōki [Writing style in computer mediated communication]. In Tomokazu Takada and Shoichi Yokoyama (eds.), *Nihongo moji hyōki no muzukashisa to omoshirosa* [Difficulties and pleasures of Japanese writing], 183–198. Sairyūsha.

Miyake, Tomohiro. 1996. Nihongo no idōdōshi no taikaku-hyōji ni tsuite [On the accusative marking of motion verbs in Japanese]. *Gengo Kenkyu* 110, 143–168.

2006. Jisshōteki handan ga arawasareru keishiki – *yōda, rashii* o megutte [About forms that express evidential judgment – yōda and rashii]. In Takashi Masuoka et al. (eds.), *Nihongo bunpō no shinchihei* [A new horizon in Japanese grammar], 119–136. Kurosio.

Miyamoto, Edson. 2008. Processing sentences in Japanese. In Shigeru Miyagawa and Mamoru Saito (eds.), *The Oxford Handbook of Japanese Linguistics*, 217–249. Oxford University Press.

Miyazaki, Ayumi. 2004. Japanese junior high school girls' and boys' first person pronoun use and their social world. In Shigeko Okamoto and Janet Shibamoto Smith (eds.), *Japanese Language, Gender, and Ideology: Cultural Models and Real People*, 92–109. Oxford University Press.

Miyazaki, Kazuhito 2002. Ninshiki no modaritī [Epistemic modality]. In Kazuhito Miyazaki et al. (eds.), *Modaritī* [Modality], 121–171. Kurosio.

Mizumoto, Terumi. 2006. Terebi dorama to jisshakai ni okeru josei bunmatsushi shiyō no zure ni miru jendā firuta [The gender filter as seen in discrepancies in women's use of sentence-final forms in television dramas versus real society]. In Nihongo Jendā Gakkai (ed.), *Nihongo to jendā* [Japanese language and gender], 73–94. Hituzi.

Moravcsik, Edith. 1978. Universals of language contact. In Joseph Greenberg (ed.), *Universals of Human Language*, 94–122. Stanford University Press.

Mori, Junko. 1994. Functions of the connective datte in Japanese conversation. *JKL* 4, 147–163.

1999. *Negotiating Agreement and Disagreement in Japanese. Connective Expressions and Turn Construction*. Benjamins.

Mori, Junko and Kanae Nakamura. 2008. Negotiating agreement and disagreement in Japanese: An analysis of designedly ambiguous turn completion points. In Junko Mori and Amy Snyder (eds.), *Japanese Applied Linguistics. Discourse and Social Perspectives*, 52–79. Continuum.

Mori, Yuichi. 2008. Jiko-hyōgen no dainamizumu: *jibun, ware, onore* o chūshin ni [The dynamism of self-expression: With special reference to *jibun, ware*, and *onore*]. In Yuichi Mori et al. (eds.), *Kotoba no dainamizumu* [The dynamism of language], 295–309. Kurosio.

Morita, Emi. 2005. *Negotiation of Contingent Talk: The Japanese Interactional Particles Ne and Sa*. Benjamins.

2007. Shūjoshi/kantōjoshi no kubetsu wa hitsuyō ka [Is distinction between final particle and interjectional particle necessary?]. *Gengo* 36, 44–52.

2008a. Highlighted moves within an action: Segmented talk in Japanese conversation. *Discourse Studies* 10, 513–537.

2008b. Sōgokōi ni okeru kyōchō no mondai – Sōgokōi-shi *ne* ga meiji suru mono [Issues of alignment in interaction: Functions of the Japanese interactional particle ne and its sociopragmatic implications]. *The Japanese Journal of Language in Society* 10, 42–54.

2012a. Deriving the socio-pragmatic meanings of the Japanese interactional particle *ne*. *JP* 44, 298–314.

2012b. "This talk needs to be registered": The metapragmatic meaning of the Japanese interactional particle *yo*. *JP* 44, 1721–1742.

2016. Kaiwa no hajime no ippo: Kodomo ni okeru sōgokōishi *yo* no shiyō [First steps in conversation: Children's use of the interactional particle yo]. In Akira Takada et al. (eds.), *Kosodate no kaiwa bunseki: Otona to kodomo no sekinin wa dō sodatsu ka* [Conversation analysis of child care: How adults' and children's "responsibility" develops], 145–170. Shōwadō.

Moriya, Tetsuharu and Kaoru Horie. 2006. What is and what is not language-specific about the Japanese modal system? A comparative and historical perspective. In Barbara Pizziconi and Mika Kizu (eds.), *Japanese Modality: Exploring Its Scope and Interpretations*, 87–114. Macmillan.

Muller-Gōtama, Franz. 1994. *Grammatical Relations: A Cross-linguistic Perspective on their Syntax and Semantics*. Gruyter.

Muraki, Masatake. 1970. Presupposition, pseudo-clefting and thematization. Ph.D. dissertation, University of Texas, Austin.

1978. The *sika nai* construction and predicate restructuring. In John Hinds and Irwin Howard (eds.), *Problems in Japanese Syntax and Semantics*, 155–177. Kaitakusha.

Murasugi, Keiko. 2000. An antisymmetry analysis of Japanese relative clauses. In Artemis Alexiadou et al. (eds.), *The Syntax of Relative Clauses*, 231–263. Benjamins.

Nagasaki, Yasuko. 1998. Edogo no shūjoshi *sa* no kinō ni kansuru ichi kōsatsu [On the function of sentence final particle sa in language of Edo]. *Kokugogaku* 192, 13–26.

Nagle, Stephen. 2003. Double modals in the southern United States: Syntactic structure or syntactic structures? In Roberta Facchinetti et al. (eds.), *Modality in Contemporary English*, 349–371. Gruyter.

Nakai, Seiichi. 2005. Hōgen no keigo: Nihongo keigo no chiikisei [Honorifics in dialects: The regional character of Japanese honorifics]. *Nihongogaku* 24, 110–123.

Nakamura, Momoko. 2007a. *"Onnakotoba" wa tsukurareru* ["Women's language" is constructed]. Hituzi.

2007b. *Sei to nihongo: Kotoba ga tsukuru onna to otoko* [Gender and Japanese: Women and men constructed through language]. Nihon Hōsō Shuppan Kyōkai.

Nakamura, Wataru. 1999a. Functional Optimality Theory: Evidence from split case systems. In Michael Darnell et al. (eds.), *Functionalism and Formalism in Linguistics* 2, 253–276. Benjamins.

1999b. An Optimality-Theoretic account of the Japanese case system. *Studies in Language* 23, 607–660.

2008. Fluid transitivity and generalized semantic macroroles. In Robert Van Valin (ed.), *Investigations in the Syntax-Semantics-Pragmatics Interface*, 101–116. Benjamins.

Nakano, Nobuhiko. 1995. Shūjoshi *sa* to *na* no hataraki ni tsuite [On sentence-final particles sa and na]. In *Tsukishima Hiroshi hakushi koki kinen kokugogaku ronshū*. Kyūko.

Nakau, Minoru. 1973 [1971]. *Sentential Complementation in Japanese*. Kaitakusha.

Nakayasu, Minako. 2003. Toward a cognitive explanation of Japanese noun modification. In Yoshihiko Ikegami, Victoria Eschbach-Szabo, and André Wlodarczyk (eds.), *Japanese Linguistics: European Chapter*, 261–270. Kurosio.

Nambu, Satoshi. 2007. Teiryōteki bunseki ni motozuku *ga/no* kōtai saikō [Reconsideration of ga/no conversion based on a quantitative analysis]. *Gengo Kenkyu* 31, 115–149.

Nariyama, Shigeko. 2002. The WA/GA distinction and switch-reference for ellipted subject identification in Japanese complex sentences. *Studies in Language* 26, 369–431.

Narrog, Heiko. 1998. Nihongo dōshi no katsuyō taikei [The inflection system of Japanese verbs]. *Nihongo Kagaku* 4, 7–30.

2008. The aspect-modality link in the Japanese verbal complex and beyond. In Werner Abraham and Elisabeth Leiss (eds.), *Modality-Aspect Interfaces – Implications and Typological Solutions*, 279–307. Benjamins.

2009a. *Modality in Japanese – The Layered Structure of the Clause and Hierarchies of Functional Categories*. Benjamins.

2009b. Modality, *modaritī* and predication – The story of modality in Japan. In Barbara Pizziconi and Mika Kizu (eds.), *Japanese Modality: Exploring its Scope and Interpretation*. Macmillan.

2010. The order of meaningful elements in the Japanese verbal complex. *Morphology* 20, 205–237.

2012. *Modality, Subjectivity, and Semantic Change. A Cross-Linguistic Perspective*. Oxford University Press.

2014. Modaritī no teigi o megutte [On the definition of modality]. In Harumi Sawada (ed.), *Modaritī I: Riron to hōhō* [Modality I: Theory and methods], 1–23. Hituzi.

Narrog, Heiko and Kaoru Horie. 2005. Hanashikotoba ni okeru kanō hyōgen [Potential expressions in spoken language]. In Masahiko Minami (ed.), *Gengogaku to nihongo kyōiku* [Linguistics and Japanese language education] IV, 99–110. Kurosio.

Nazikian, Fumiko 2007. Shift of speech style and perspective in interview talk: Representing the other speaker and engaging audience. Paper presented at the 17th Pragmatic and Language Learning Conference. Honolulu.

Newman, Paul. 1968. Ideophones from a syntactic point of view. *Journal of West African Languages* 5, 107–117.

NHK Hōsō Bunka Kenkyūjo (ed.). 1998. *Nihongo hatsuon akusento jiten* [Japanese pronunciation and accent dictionary]. Nihon Hōsō Shuppan Kyōkai.

Nihongo Kijutsu Bunpō Kenkyūkai. 2007. *Gendai nihongo bunpō 3: Tensu, asupekuto, kōhi* [Modern Japanese grammar 3: Tense, aspect, and affirmative-negative]. Kurosio.

2008. *Gendai nihongo bunpō 6: Fukubun* [Modern Japanese Grammar 6: Complex clauses]. Kurosio.

Niinaga, Yuto. 2014. A grammar of Yuwan, a Northern Ryukyuan language. Ph.D. dissertation, University of Tokyo.

Niinaga, Yuto and Shinji Ogawa. 2011. Kita-ryūkyū Amami Yuwan hōgen no akusento taikei [The accent system of the Amami Yuwan dialect in North Ryukuan]. *Proceedings of the 143rd meeting of the Linguistic Society of Japan*, 238–243. Linguistic Society of Japan.

Nikiforidou, Kiki. 2005. Conceptual blending and the interpretation of relatives: A case study from Greek. *Cognitive Linguistics* 16, 169–206.

Nishi, Amane. n.d. Writing Japanese with the Western alphabet. *Meiroku zasshi, Vol. 1.1*. Quoted from the English translation by William Braistead. University of Tokyo Press, 1976, 3–20.

Nishigauchi, Taisuke. 1986. Quantification in syntax. Ph.D. dissertation, University of Massachusetts, Amherst.

Nishio, Toraya. 1961. Dōshi ren'yōkei no meishika ni kansuru ichi kōsatsu [A study concerning nominalization by verb adverbal forms]. *Kokugogaku* 43, 60–81.

Nishiyama, Kunio. 2000. Jita-kōtai to keitairon [Transitive-intransitive alterations and morphology]. In Tadao Maruta and Kazuyoshi Suga (eds.), *Nichi-eigo no jita no kōtai* [Transitive-intransitive alterations in Japanese and English]. Hituzi.

Nishiyama, Yuji. 1979. Shinjōhō, kyūjōhō to iu gainen ni tsuite [On the concepts of new and old information]. In Kazuko Inoue (ed.), *Nihongo no kihon-kōzō ni kansuru rironteki, jisshōteki kenkyū* [Theoretical and experimental studies of basic structures of the Japanese language]. International Christian University.

Nitta, Tetsuo. 2012. Fukui-ken Echizen-chō Kokonogi hōgen no akusento [Accent of the Kokonogi dialect in Echizen Town, Fukui Prefecture]. *Onsei Kenkyū* 16, 63–79.

Nitta, Yoshio. 1991. *Nihongo no modaritī to ninshō* [Modality and person in Japanese]. Hituzi.

Niyekawa, Agnes. 1991. *Minimum Essential Politeness: A Guide to the Japanese Honorific Language*. Kodansha International.

Noda, Harumi. 1997. *No (da) no kinō* [Functions of *no (da)*]. Kurosio.

Noda, Hisashi. 1996. *"Wa" to "ga"* ["Wa" and "ga"]. Kurosio.

Nogita, Akitsugu and Noriko Yamane. 2015. Japanese moraic dorsalized nasal stop. *Phonological Studies* 18, 75–84.

Nomura, Masa-aki. 1973. Hitei no settōgo *mu-, fu-, mi-, hi-* no yōhō [Usage of the negative prefixes mu-, fu-, mi- and hi-]. *Kokuritsu Kokugo Kenkyūjo Ronshū: Kotoba no Kenkyū* [Kokuritsu Kokugo Kenkyūjo reports: Studies on language] 4, 31–50. Shūei.

Noonan, Michael. 2003. A crosslinguistic investigation of referential density. Presented as a talk handout at the meeting of the Association for Linguistic Typology at the University of Cagliari in September 2003. http://crossasia-repository.ub.uni-heidelberg.de/190/

Obana, Yasuko. 2016. Speech level shifts in Japanese: A different perspective. The application of symbolic interactionist role theory. *Pragmatics* 26, 247–290.

Occhi, Debra, Cindi L. SturzStreetharan, and Janet S. Shibamoto Smith. 2010. Finding Mr. Right: New looks at gendered modernity in Japanese televised romances. *Japanese Studies* 30, 409–425.

Ochs, Elinor. 1990. Indexicality and socialization. In James Stigler et al. (eds.), *Cultural Psychology: Essays on Comparative Human Development*, 287–307. Cambridge University Press.

1992. Indexing gender. In Alessandro Duranti and Charles Goodwin (eds.), *Rethinking Context: Language as an Interactive Phenomenon*, 335–358. Cambridge University Press.

1996. Linguistic resources for socializing humanity. In John Gumperz and Stephen Levinson (eds.), *Rethinking Linguistic Relativity*, 407–437. Cambridge University Press.

2002. Becoming a speaker of culture. In Claire Kramsch (ed.), *Language Socialization and Language Acquisition: Ecological Perspectives*, 99–120. Continuum.

Ogihara, Toshiyuki. 1999. Tense and aspect. In Natsuko Tsujimura (ed.), *Handbook of Japanese Linguistics*, 326–348. Blackwell.

Ohala, John. 1984. An ethological perspective on common cross-language utilization of F0 of voice. *Phonetica* 41, 1–16.

Ohara, Kyoko Hirose. 1996. A constructional approach to Japanese internally headed relativization. Ph.D. dissertation, University of California, Berkeley.

Ohashi, Jun. 2003. Japanese culture specific face and politeness orientation: A pragmatic investigation of *yoroshiku onegaishimasu*. *Multilingua* 22, 257–274.

2013. *Thanking and Politeness in Japanese. Balancing Acts in Interaction*. Macmillan.

Ohba, Miwako. 2012. *Sesshoku bamen ni okeru sansha kaiwa no kenkyū* [Research on three-party conversations in contact situations]. Hituzi.

Ohori, Toshio. 1995. Remarks on suspended clauses: A contribution to Japanese phraseology. In Masayoshi Shibatani and Sandra Thompson (eds.), *Essays in Semantics and Pragmatics*, 201–218. Benjamins.

(ed.). 1998. *Studies in Japanese Grammaticalization: Cognitive and Discourse Perspectives*. Kurosio.

Oishi, Hatsutaro. 1975. *Keigo* [Honorifics]. Chikuma.

Okada, Misato. 2008. When the coach is a woman: The situated meanings of so-called masculine directives in a Japanese boxing gym. In Junko Mori and Amy Snyder Ohta (eds.), *Japanese Applied Linguistics: Discourse and Social Perspectives*, 160–187. Continuum.

Okamoto, Shigeko. 1995. “Tasteless” Japanese: Less “feminine” speech among young Japanese women. In Kira Hall and Mary Bucholtz (eds.), *Gender Articulated: Language and the Socially Constructed Self*, 297–325. Routledge.

1998. The use and non-use of honorifics in sales talk in Kyoto and Osaka: Are they rude or friendly? *JKL* 7, 141–157.

1999. Situated politeness: Manipulating honorific and non-honorific expressions in Japanese conversation. *Pragmatics* 9, 51–74.

2008. Nihongo ni okeru josei no kotoba-zukai ni taisuru “kihan” no saikōsatsu [Rethinking the “norms” for Japanese women’s speech]. In Shinji Sato and Neriko Doerr (eds.), *Bunka to kotoba no “hyōjun” o tou* [Examination of the Linguistic and Cultural “Standard”], 83–105. Akashi.

2010a. "Kotoba-bijin ni naru hō": Josei no hanashikata o oshieru jitsuyōsho no bunseki ["How to become a language beauty": Analyses of self-help books that teach women how to talk], *Nihongo to jendā* 10, 1–25.

2010b. Politeness in East Asia. In Miriam Locher and Sage Graham (eds.), *Interpersonal Pragmatics*, 71–100. Gruyter.

2011. The use and interpretation of addressee honorifics and plain forms in Japanese: Diversity, multiplicity, and ambiguity. *JP* 43, 3673–3688.

2016. Variability and multiplicity in the meanings of stereotypical gendered speech in Japanese. *East Asian Pragmatics* 1, 5–37.

Okamoto, Shigeko and Shie Sato. 1992. Less feminine speech among young Japanese females. In Kira Hall et al. (eds.), *Locating Power: Proceedings of the 2nd Berkeley Women and Language Conference*, 478–488. Women and Language Group, University of California, Berkeley.

Okamoto, Shigeko and Janet Shibamoto Smith (eds.). 2004. *Japanese Language, Gender, and Ideology: Cultural Models and Real People*. Oxford University Press.

2008. Constructing linguistic femininity in contemporary Japan: Scholarly and popular representations. *Gender and Language* 2, 87–112.

2016. *The Social Life of the Japanese Language: Cultural Discourses and Situated Practice*. Cambridge University Press.

Okamoto, Shinichiro. 2002. Politeness and the Perception of Irony: Honorifics in Japanese. *Metaphor and Symbol* 17, 119–139.

Okuda, Yasuo. 1978. Asupekuto no kenkyū o megutte I, II [On the study of aspect]. *Kokugo Kyōiku* 53, 33–44; 54, 14–27.

1986. Genjitsu, kanō, hitsuzen [Reality, possibility, necessity]. *Kotoba no Kagaku* 1, 181–212.

Okura, Naoko. 2009. Applicative and little verbs: In view of possessor raising and benefactive constructions. Ph.D. dissertation, Kanda University of International Studies.

2011. Jueki-kōbun to kinō-hanchū to shiteno "ageru" [Benefactives and "ageru" as a functional category]. In Nobuko Hasegawa (ed.), *70-nendai seisei-bunpō saininshiki: Nihongo kenkyū no chihei* [Re-acknowledgement of the 70s generative grammar: The horizon of research in Japanese], 231–252. Kaitakusha.

Okutsu, Keiichiro. 1974. *Seisei nihongo bunpōron: Meishiku no kōzō* [On generative Japanese grammar: The structure of noun phrases]. Taishūkan.

Olson, David. 1977. From utterance to text: The bias of language in speech and writing. *Harvard Educational Review* 47, 257–286.

Onishi, Miho. 2013. Bunmatsu ga meishi de owaru hōkoku in'yō hyōgen [Reporting and quoting expressions with a sentence-final noun]. *Goyōron gakkai ronbunshū* 15, 25–32.

Onishi, Takuichirō and Akiko Matsumori. 2012. Japanese dialects: Focusing on Tsuruoka and Ei. In Nichokas Tranter (ed.), *The Language of Japan and Korea*, 313–348. Routledge.

Ono, Naoyuki. 2016. Agentive nominals. In Taro Kageyama and Hideki Kishimoto (eds.), *Handbook of Japanese Lexicon and Word Formation*, 599–629. Gruyter.

Ono, Tsuyoshi and Eri Yoshida. 1992. A study of co-construction in Japanese: We don't finish each other's sentences. *JKL* 5, 115-129.

Onodera, Noriko. 2004. *Japanese Discourse Markers: Synchronic and Diachronic Discourse Analysis*. Benjamins.

2011. The grammaticalization of discourse markers. In Heiko Narrog and Bernd Heine (eds.), *The Oxford Handbook of Grammaticalization*, 614–624. Oxford University Press.

2014. Setting up a mental space: A function of discourse markers at the left periphery (LP) and some observations about LP and RP in Japanese. In Kate Beeching and Ulrich Detges (eds.), *Discourse Functions at the Left and Right Periphery: Crosslinguistic Investigations of Language Use and Language Change*, 92–116. Brill.

Onoe, Keisuke. 2001. *Bunpō to imi I* [Grammar and meaning I]. Kurosio.

2014a. *Chinjutsuron 1* [Predication theory 1]. In Nihongo Bunpō Gakkai (ed.), *Nihongo bunpō jiten* [Dictionary of Japanese grammar], 405–408. Taishūkan.

2014b. *Modaritī 1* [Modality 1]. In Nihongo Bunpō Gakkai (ed.), *Nihongo bunpō jiten* [Dictionary of Japanese grammar], 627–629. Taishūkan.

Oshima, David. 2004. *Zibun* revisited: Empathy, logophoricity, and binding. *University of Washington Working Papers in Linguistics* 23, 175–190.

2007. On empathic and logophoric binding. *Research in Language and Computation* 5, 19–35.

2011. *Perspectives in Reported Discourse: The De Re/De Dicto Distinction, Indexicality, and Presupposition*. VDM Verlag Dr. Müller.

Oso, Mieko. 1986. Goyō bunseki: Kyō wa ii tenki desu ne – Hai, sō desu [Error analysis: It's a fine day today ne]. *Nihongogaku* 5, 91–94.

Ostman, Jan-Ola and Mirjam Fried. 2005. The cognitive grounding of constructional grammar. In Jan-Ola Ostman and Mirjam Fried (eds.), *Construction Grammars: Cognitive Grounding and Theoretical Extensions*, 1–13. Benjamins.

Ozeki, Hiromi. 2008. *Daiichi daini gengo ni okeru nihongo meishiku shūshokusetsu no shūtoku katei* [The acquisition process of Japanese noun-modification in the first and the second language acquisition]. Kurosio.

Palmer, Frank. 1995. Negation and the modals of possibility and necessity. In Joan Bybee and Suzanne Fleischman (eds.), *Modality in Grammar and Discourse*, 453–471. Benjamins.

Parker, Steve. 2008. Sound level protrusions as physical correlates of sonority. *Journal of Phonetics* 36, 55–90.

Payne, Thomas. 1997. *Describing Morphosyntax: A Guide for Field Linguists*. Cambridge University Press.
Pellard, Thomas. 2015. The linguistic archaeology of the Ryukyu islands. In Patrick Heinrich et al. (eds.), *The Handbook of the Ryukyuan Languages*, 13–37. Gruyter.
Pierrehumbert, Janet. 1980. The phonology and phonetics of English intonation. Ph.D. dissertation, MIT.
Pierrehumbert, Janet and Mary Beckman. 1988. *Japanese Tone Structure*. MIT Press.
Pike, Kenneth. 1943. *Phonetics*. University of Michigan Press.
1947. *Phonemics*. University of Michigan Press.
1990. On the emics and etics of Pike and Harris. In Kenneth Pike and Marvin Harris (eds.), *Emics and Etics. The Insider/Outsider Debate*, 28–47. Sage.
Pirani, Laura. 2008. Bound roots in Mandarin Chinese and comparison with European "semi-words." In Marjorie Chan and Hana Kang (eds.), *Proceedings of the 20th North American Conference on Chinese Linguistics* 1, 261–277. Ohio State University.
Pizziconi, Barbara. 2003. Re-examining politeness, face and the Japanese language. *JP* 35, 1471–1506.
2004. Japanese politeness in the work of Fujio Minami. *SOAS Working Papers in Linguistics* 13, 269–280.
2007. The lexical mapping of politeness in British English and Japanese. *Journal of Politeness Research* 3, 207–241.
2011. Honorifics: The cultural specificity of a universal mechanism in Japanese. In Dániel Kádár and Sara Mills (eds.), *Politeness in East Asia*, 45–70. Cambridge University Press.
Plungian, Vladimir. 1999. A typology of phasal meanings. In Werner Abraham and Leonid Kulikov (eds.), *Tense-aspect, Transitivity and Causativity: Essays in Honor of Vladimir Nedjalkov*, 311–321. Benjamins.
Poser, William. 1984. The phonetics and phonology of tone and intonation in Japanese. Ph.D. dissertation, MIT.
1990. Evidence for foot structure in Japanese. *Language* 66, 78–105.
Prince, Ellen. 1992. The ZPG letter: Subjects, definiteness, and information status. In William Mann and Sandra Thompson (eds.), *Discourse Description: Diverse Linguistic Analyses of a Fund-Raising Text*, 295–325. Benjamins.
Pustejovsky, James. 1995. *The Generative Lexicon*. MIT Press.
Pylkkänen, Liina. 2008. *Introducing Arguments*. MIT Press.
Quinn, Charles. 1994. *Uchi/soto*: Tip of a semiotic iceberg? "inside" and "outside" knowledge in the grammar of Japanese. In Jane Bachnik and Charles Quinn (eds.), *Situated Meaning: Inside and Outside in Japanese Self, Society, and Language*, 247–294. Princeton University Press.

Ramus, Franck, Marina Nespor, and Jacques Mehler. 1999. Correlates of linguistic rhythm in the speech signal. *Cognition* 73, 265–292.

Reichenbach, Hans. 1947. *Elements of Symbolic Logic*. Macmillan.

Reynolds, Katsue. 1985. Female speakers of Japanese. *Feminist Issues* 5, 13–46.

Rinnert, Carol and Hiroe Kobayashi. 1999. Requestive hints in Japanese and English. *JP* 31, 1173–1201.

Rizzi, Luigi. 1997. The fine structure of the left periphery. In Liliane Haegeman (ed.), *Elements of Grammar: Handbook of Generative Syntax*, 281–331. Kluwer.

Rogers, Henry. 2000. *The Sounds of Language*. Pearson.

2005. *Writing Systems. A Linguistic Approach*. Blackwell.

Ross, John. 1967. Constraints on variables in syntax. Ph.D. dissertation, MIT.

1970. On declarative sentences. In Roderick Jacobs and Peter Rosenbaum (eds.), *Readings in English Transformational Grammar*, 222–272. Ginn.

1973. Nouniness. In Osamu Fujimura (ed.), *Three Dimensions of Linguistic Theory*, 137–257. TEC.

Sacks, Harvey, Emanuel A. Schegloff, and Gail Jefferson. 1974. A simplest semantics for the organization of the turn-taking for conversation. *Language* 50, 696–735.

Sadakane, Kumi and Masatoshi Koizumi. 1995. On the nature of the "dative" particle ni in Japanese. *Linguistics* 33, 5–33.

Sadanobu, Toshiyuki. 2011. *Nihongo shakai nozoki kyarakuri: Kao-tsuki, karada-tsuki, kotoba-tsuki* [Mechanisms for viewing Japanese language society]. Sanseidō.

Saegusa, Reiko. 2013. Meishi kara fukushi, setsuzokushi e [From nouns to adverbs, conjunctions]. *Hitotsubashi Daigaku Kokusai Kyōiku Sentā Kiyō* 4, 49–61.

Saigo, Hideki. 2011. *The Japanese Sentence-Final Particles in Talk-in-Interaction*. Benjamins.

Saito, Junko. 2010. Subordinates' use of Japanese plain forms: An examination of superior-subordinate interactions in the workplace. *JP* 42, 3271–3282.

Saito, Mamoru. 1985. Some symmetries in Japanese and their theoretical consequences. Ph.D. dissertation, MIT.

Saito, Mamoru and Hajime Hoji. 1983. Weak crossover and move α in Japanese. *Natural Language and Linguistic Theory* 1, 245–259.

Saito, Tsuyoshi. 1977. *Meiji no kotoba. Higashi kara nishi e no kakehashi* [The language of Meiji Japan. A bridge from east to west]. Kōdansha.

Saji, Keizo. 1991. *Nihongo no bunpō no kenkyū* [A study of Japanese grammar]. Hituzi.

Sakaguchi, Itaru. 2001. Nagasaki hōgen no akusento [The accent of the Nagasaki dialect]. *Onsei Kenkyū* 5, 33–41.

Sakai, Mika. 2015. Tōgo ron [Syntax]. In Yuta Mori et al. (eds.), *Koshikijima hōgen kijutsu bunpōsho* [A descriptive grammar of the Koshikijima dialect], 91–118. NINJAL.

Sakuma, Kanae. 1940/1952. *Gendai nihongohō no kenkyu* [Studies on the rules of Modern Japanese]. Kōseisha.

1941. *Nihongo no tokushitsu* [Characteristics of Japanese]. Ikuei. Reproduced by Kurosio, 1995.

Sakuma, Mayumi. 1987. "Bundan" nintei no ichi-kijun (I) – Teidai hyōgen no tōkatsu [A parameter of sentence paragraph (I) – Summary of theme]. *Bungei Gengo Kenkyu Gengohen* 11, 89–135.

2002. Setsuzokushi/shijishi to bun rensa [Conjunctions/demonstratives and sentence chains]. In Hisashi Noda et al. (eds.), *Nihongo no bunpō 4: Fukubun to danwa* [Japanese grammar 4: Subordinate clauses and discourse], 117–189, 219–223. Iwanami.

2003. Bunshō/danwa ni okeru "*dan*" no tōkatsu kinō [Coherence functions of grammatico-semantic paragraphs in written texts and spoken discourse]. In Mayumi Sakuma (ed.), *Bunshō/danwa* [Written text/spoken discourse], 91–119. Asakura.

(ed.). 2010. *Kōgi no danwa no hyōgen to rikai* [Expression and comprehension of Japanese lecture discourse]. Kurosio.

Sampson, Geoffrey. 1985. *Writing Systems*. Stanford University Press.

Sasaki, Kan. 2006. Kaku [Case]. In Mayumi Kudō et al. (eds.), *Hōgen no bunpō* [The grammar of dialects], 1–46. Iwanami.

Sasse, Hans-Jürgen. 1987. The thetic/categorical distinction revisited. *Linguistics* 25, 511–580.

Satake, Kuniko. 2003. Terebi-*anime* no rufu-suru "onna-kotoba/otoko-kotoba" kihan [Norms for women's language and men's language promulgated through TV anime]. *Kotoba* 24, 43–59.

2004. "Onna kototoba/otoko kotoba" kihan no keisei-Meijiki jakunensha muke zasshi kara [The formation of norms for "women's language and men's language" from magazines for young people in the Meiji era]. *Nihongogaku* 23, 64–74.

Sato, Kazuyuki. 2003. Sōron [Overview]. In Teruo Hirayama (ed.), *Aomori no kotoba* [The Aomori dialect], 1–42. Meiji.

Sato, Kyoko. 2010. Ren'ai shōsetsu: Kotoba de tsukuru shinmitsuna kankeisei [Romance novels: The intimate relationship constructed by language]. In Momoko Nakamura (ed.), *Jendā de manabu gengogaku* [Linguistics taught through gender], 107–121. Sekai Shisōsha.

2011. Normative masculine verbal behavior among Japanese youth. In Kyoko Sato et al. (eds.), *Kotoba no jijitsu o mitsumete: Gengokenkyu no riron to jishō* [Observing facts of language: Theory and attestation in linguistic research], 350–358. Kaitakusha.

Sato, Takuzo. 2003. Aoi me o shite iru-gata kōbun no bunseki [An analysis of Aoi me o shite iru constructions]. *Nihongo Bunpō* 3, 19–34.

Schachter, Paul and Fe Otanes. 1982. *Tagalog Reference Grammar*. University of California Press.

Schegloff, Emenuel. 1996. Turn organization: One interpretation of grammar and interaction. In Elinoa Ochs et al. (eds.), *Interactions and Grammar*, 52–133. Cambridge University Press.

Schiffrin, Deborah. 1987. *Discourse Markers*. Cambridge University Press.

Seeley, Christopher. 1991. *A History of Writing in Japan*. Brill.

Sells, Peter. 1987. Aspects of logophoricity. *LI* 18, 445–479.

2017. The significance of the grammatical study of Japanese mimetics. In Noriko Iwasaki et al. (eds.), *The Grammar of Japanese Mimetics: Perspectives from Structure, Acquisition and Translation*, 7–19. Routledge.

Shattuck-Hufnagel, Stephanie and Alice Turk. 1996. A prosody tutorial for investigators of auditory sentence processing. *Journal of Psycholinguistic Research* 25, 193–247.

Shibamoto Smith, Janet. 2003. Gendered structures in Japanese. In Marlis Hellinger and Hadumod Bußmann (eds.), *Gender Across Languages, Volume 3*, 201–225. Benjamins.

Shibamoto Smith, Janet and Debra Occhi. 2009. The green leaves of love: Japanese romantic heroines, authentic femininity, and dialect. *Journal of Sociolinguistics* 13, 524–546.

Shibatani, Masayoshi. 1976. Causativization. In Masayoshi Shibatani (ed.), *Syntax and Semantics 5: Japanese Generative Grammar*, 239–294. Academic Press.

1978. *Nihongo no bunseki* [An analysis of Japanese]. Taishūkan.

1985. Passives and related constructions: A prototype analysis. *Language* 61, 821–848.

1990. *The Languages of Japan*. Cambridge University Press.

1994a. An integrational approach to possessor raising, ethical datives, and adversative passives. *BLS* 20, 461–486.

1994b. Benefactive constructions: A Japanese-Korean comparative perspective. *JKL* 4, 39–74.

1996. Applicatives and benefactives: A cognitive account. In Masayoshi Shibatani and Sandra Thompson (eds.), *Grammatical Constructions: Their Form and Meaning*, 157–194. Oxford University Press.

2009. Elements of complex structures, where recursion isn't: The case of relativization. In Talmy Givn and Masayoshi Shibatani (eds.), *Syntactic Complexity: Diachrony, Acquisition, Neuro-cognition, Evolution*, 163–198. Benjamins.

2017. Nominalization. In Masayoshi Shibatani, Shigeru Miyagawa, and Hisashi Noda (eds.), *Handbook of Japanese Syntax*, 271–332. Gruyter.

Shibatani, Masayoshi and Taro Kageyama. 1988. Word formation in a modular theory of grammar. *Language* 64, 451–484.

Shibatani, Masayoshi and Hiromi Shigeno. 2013. Amami nominalizations. *International Journal of Okinawan Studies* 4, 107–138.

Shimizu, Hidetada. 2000. Japanese cultural psychology and empathic understanding: Implications for academic and cultural psychology. *Ethos* 28, 224–247.

Shimoji, Michinori. 2015. Ryūkyū shohōgen ni okeru yūhyō shukaku to bunretsu jidōshi sei [Marked nominative and split intransitivity in Ryukyuan dialects]. *Hōgen no Kenkyū* 1, 103–132.

2016. *A Grammar of Irabu, a Southern Ryukyuan Language*. Kyūshū University Press.

Shimojo, Mitsuaki. 2002. Functional theories of island phenomena: The case of Japanese. *Studies in Language* 26, 67–123.

2005. *Argument Encoding in Japanese Conversation*. Macmillan.

2011. The left periphery and focus structure in Japanese. In Wataru Nakamura (ed.), *New Perspectives in Role and Reference Grammar*, 266–293. Cambridge Scholars Publishing.

Shin, Chen. 2013. Nihongo ren'yōmeishi no jiritsusei no dankai ni tsuite [On the levels of the independence of Japanese infinitive-derived nouns]. *Dai 4 kai kōpasu nihongogaku wākushoppu yokōshū* [Proceedings of the fourth workshop of corpus Japanese linguistics], 151–158. NINJAL.

Shinohara, Kazuko and Ryoko Uno (eds.). 2013. *Chikazuku oto to imi: Onomatope kenkyū no shatei* [Approaching sound and meaning: The range of studies in sound symbolism]. Hituzi.

Shinzato, Rumiko. 2006. Subjectivity, intersubjectivity, and grammaticalization. In Satoko Suzuki (ed.), *Emotive Communication in Japanese*, 15–33. Benjamins.

2007. (Inter)subjectification, Japanese syntax and syntactic scope increase. *Journal of Historical Pragmatics* 8, 171–206.

2011. From a manner adverb to a discourse particle: The case of *yahari, yappari* and *yappa*. *Journal of Japanese Linguistics* 27, 17–44.

2014. From degree/manner adverbs to pragmatic particles in Japanese: A corpus-based approach to the diachronic parallel developments of *amari, bakari,* and *yahari*. In Andreas Jucker and Irma Taavitsainen (eds.), *Diachronic Corpus Pragmatics: Intersections and Interaction*, 77–105. Benjamins.

2015. Two types of conditionals and two different grammaticalization paths. In Sylvie Hencil et al. (eds.), *Final Particles*, 157–180. Gruyter.

Shinzato, Rumiko and Satoko Suzuki. 2007. From quotative conditionals to emotive topic markers: A case of *tteba* and *ttara* in Japanese. *JKL* 15, 173–183.

Shirai, Yasuhiro. 2000. The semantics of the Japanese imperfective *-teiru*: An integrative approach. *JP* 32, 327–361.

Shirakawa, Hiroyuki. 1986. Rentai-shūshoku-setsu no jōkyō-teiji kinō [Noun-modifying clauses for circumstance presentation]. In *Bungei Gengo Kenkyu* [Studies in language and literature], 1–18. Tsukuba Institute of Literature and Linguistics.

1996. Sentence ending with -kedo. *Hiroshima Daigaku Nihongo Kyōiku Gakka Kiyō* 4, 9–17.

2009. *Iisashi no kenkyū* [A study of Japanese suspended clauses]. Kurosio.

Shōji, Sadao. 2003. Hyakuen udon o tabe ni iku [Go to eat 100 Yen udon noodle]. *Shūkan Asahi* (February 14), 54–55.

Shopen, Timothy (ed.). 2007. *Language Typology and Syntactic Description. Vol II. Complex Constructions*. Cambridge University Press.

Sibata, Takesi. 1958. *Nihon no hōgen* [Japanese dialects]. Iwanami.

Sibata, Takesi and Ritei Shibata. 1990. Akusento wa dōongo o dono teido benbetsu shiuruka: Nihongo eigo chūgokugo no baai [How much can accent distinguish homophonous words: Japanese, English, and Chinese]. *Keiryō Kokugogaku* 17, 317–327.

Silverstein, Michael. 1976a. Shifters, linguistic categories and cultural description. In Keith Basso and Henry Selby (eds.), *Meaning in Anthropology*, 11–55. University of New Mexico.

1976b. Hierarchy of features and ergativity. In R.M.W. Dixon (ed.), *Grammatical Categories in Australian Languages*, 112–171. Australian Institute of Aboriginal Studies.

1985. Language and the culture of gender: At the intersection of structure, usage, and ideology. In Elizabeth Mertz and Richard Parmentier (eds.), *Semiotic Mediation: Sociocultural and Psychological Perspectives*, 219–259. Academic Press.

2003. Indexical order and the dialectics of sociolinguistic life. *Language & Communication* 23, 193–229.

Simon, Mutsuko. 1989. An analysis of the postposing construction in Japanese. Ph.D. dissertation, University of Michigan.

Smith, Carlota. 1997. *The Parameter of Aspect*. Kluwer.

Smith, Janet. 1992. Women in charge: Politeness and directives in the speech of Japanese women. *Language in Society* 21, 59–82.

Sneddon, James. 1996. *Indonesian: A Comprehensive Grammar*. Routledge.

Soga, Matsuo. 1983. *Tense and Aspect in Modern Colloquial Japanese*. University of British Columbia Press.

Speas, Peggy and Carol Tenny. 2003. Configurational properties of point of view roles. In Anna Maria DiSciullo (ed.), *Asymmetry in Grammar*, 315–344. Benjamins.

Spring, Ryan and Kaoru Horie. 2013. How cognitive typology affects second language acquisition: A study of Japanese and Chinese learners of English. *Cognitive Linguistics* 24, 689–710.

Steriade, Donca. 2003. Syllables in phonology. In William Frawley (ed.), *International Encyclopedia of Linguistics, Vol. 4*, 190–195. Oxford University Press.

Stevanovic, Melisa. 2013. Constructing a proposal as a thought: A way to manage problems in the initiation of joint decision-making in Finnish workplace interaction. *Pragmatics* 23, 519–544.

Street, Brian. 1995. *Social Literacies*. Longman.

SturtzSreetharan, Cindi. 2004. Japanese men's conversational stereotypes and realities: Conversations from the Kanto and Kansai regions. In Shigeko Okamoto and Janet Shibamoto-Smith (eds.), *Japanese Language, Gender, and Ideology: Cultural Models and Real People*, 279–289. Oxford University Press.

2009. "Ore" and "omae": Japanese men's use of first- and second person pronouns. *Pragmatics* 19, 253–278.

2017. Academy of Devotion: Performing status, hierarchy, and masculinity on reality TV. *Gender and Language* 11, 165–185.

Sugahara, Mariko. 2003. Downtrends and post-FOCUS intonation in Tokyo Japanese. Ph.D. dissertation, University of Massachusetts, Amherst.

Sugioka, Yoko. 1984. Interaction of derivational morphology and syntax in Japanese and English. Unpublished Ph.D. dissertation, University of Chicago.

Sugimura, Yasushi. 2000. Gendai nihongo ni okeru gaizensei o arawasu fukushi no kenkyū [A study of adverbs expressing probability in Modern Japanese]. Ph.D. dissertation, Nagoya University.

Sugito, Miyoko, Takashi Inukai, and Toshiyuki Sadanobu. 1997. Bun no kōzō to purosodī [Sentence structure and prosody]. In Onsei Bunpō Kenkyūkai (ed.), *Bunpō to onsei* [Grammar and speech], 3–20. Kurosio.

Sukle, Robert. 1994. *Uchi/soto*: Choices in directive speech acts in Japanese. In Jane Bachnik and Charles Quinn (eds.), *Situated Meaning: Inside and Outside in Japanese Self, Society, and Language*, 113–142. Princeton University Press.

Sunaoshi, Yukako. 2004. Farm women's professional discourse in Ibaraki. In Shigeko Okamoto and Janet Shibamoto Smith (eds.), *Japanese Language, Gender, and Ideology: Cultural Models and Real People*, 187–204. Oxford University Press.

Suzuki, Hideo. 1976. Gendai nihongo ni okeru shūjoshi no hataraki to sono sōgō shōsetsu ni tsuite [The function of sentence final particles in modern Japanese and their correlation]. *Kokugo to Kokubungaku* 11, 58–70.

Suzuki, Kyoko. 2009. *Kinō bunkei ni motozuku sōdan no danwa no kōzō bunseki* [An analysis of the structure of consultation discourse based on functional sentence patterns], Waseda University Monograph 11a. Waseda University Press.

Suzuki, Ryoko. 2006. How does "reason" become less and less reasonable? In Satoko Suzuki (ed.), *Emotive Communication in Japanese*, 35–51. Benjamins.

2007. (Inter)subjectification in the quotative *tte* in Japanese conversation. *Journal of Historical Pragmatics* 8, 207–237.

Suzuki, Satoko. 2008. Expressivity of vagueness: Alienation in the Verb-*tari suru* construction. *Japanese Language and Literature* 42, 157–169.

Sweetser, Eve. 1990. *From Etymology to Pragmatics*. Cambridge University Press.

Syromiatnikov, Nikolai. 1981. *The Ancient Japanese Language*. Nauka.

Szatrowski, Polly. 1993a. *Nihongo no danwa no kōzō bunseki – Kan'yū no danwa no sutoratejī no kōsatsu* [Structure of Japanese conversation – Invitation strategies]. Kurosio.

1993b. *Bessatsu shiryō – Nihongo no kan'yū no danwa shiryōshū* [Separate volume – Data corpus of Japanese invitations]. Kurosio.

2000a. Kyōdō hatsuwa ni okeru sankasha no tachiba to gengo/higengo kōdō no kanren ni tsuite [Relation between participant status and verbal/nonverbal behavior in co-construction]. *Nihongo Kagaku* [Japanese Linguistics] 7, 44–69.

2000b. Relation between gaze, head-nodding and *aizuti* "back channel" at a Japanese company meeting. *BLS* 26, 283–294.

2002. Syntactic projectability and co-participant completion in Japanese conversation. *BLS* 28, 315–325.

2003. Gaze, head nodding and *aizuti* "back channel utterances" in information presenting activities. *JKL* 11, 119–132.

2005. Jōhō shori, sōgo sayō, danwa kōzō kara mita tōchi to higengo kōdō to no kankei [The relation between postposing and non-verbal behavior from the point of view of information management, interaction and discourse structure]. In Hideya Kushida et al. (eds.), *Katsudō to shite no bun to hatsuwa* [Sentences and utterances as activities], 159–208. Hituzi.

2007. Subjectivity, perspective and footing in Japanese co-construction. In Nancy Hedberg and Ron Zacharski (eds.), *Topics on the Grammar-Pragmatics Interface: Essays in Honor of Dr. Jeanette K. Gundel*, 313–339. Benjamins.

(ed.). 2010. *Storytelling across Japanese Conversational Genre*. Benjamins.

(ed.). 2014. *Food and Language: Verbal and Nonverbal Experiences*. Benjamins.

Takagi, Tomoyo, Yuri Hosoda, and Emi Morita. 2016. *Kaiwabunseki no kiso* [Basics of conversation analysis]. Hituzi.

Takahashi, Keiko and Yuko Higashiizumi. 2013. Use of Sino-Japanese nouns as adverb: Evidence from the Balanced Corpus of Contemporary Written Japanese. *The 3rd Corpus Nihongo-gaku Workshop Yokōshū*, 195–202. Association for Computational Liguistics.

Takahashi, Minako. 2011. Rōkaru hīrō sakuhin ni okeru josei tōjō-jinbutsu no hanashi kotoba [Female characters' speech in programs about local heroes]. *Kotoba* 32, 55–72.

Takahashi, Taro, Hisakazu Kaneko, Akihiro Kaneko, Michiko Sai, Tai Suzuki, Jun'ichi Suda, and Hirotake Matsumoto. 2005. *Nihongo no bunpō* [Japanese grammar]. Hituzi.

Takami, Ken-ichi. 1992. *Preposition Stranding: From Syntactic to Functional Analyses*. Gruyter.

1995. *Kinōteki kōbunron ni yoru nichieigo hikaku: Ukemibun kōchibun no bunseki* [A comparison of Japanese and English in functional theories: An analysis of passive and postposing constructions]. Kurosio.

Takami, Ken-ichi and Akio Kamio. 1996. Topicalization and subjectivization in Japanese: Characterizational and identificational information. *Lingua* 99, 207–235.

Takanashi, Shino. 2004. Hyōka no modaritī keishiki no Ta-kei ni tsuite – *beki-datta, nakute-wa ikenakatta, zaru-o enakatta* [The Ta-form of valuative modality – beki-datta, nakute-wa ikenakatta, zaru-o enakatta]. *Nihongo Bunpō* 4, 38–54.

2006. Hyōka no modaritī to kibō hyōgen – *Ta*-kei no seishitsu o chūshin ni [Valuative modality and expression of desires – the Ta-form in the focus]. In Takashi Masuoka et al. (eds.), *Nihongo bunpō no shinchihei* [A new horizon in Japanese grammar] 2, 77–97. Kurosio.

Takano, Shoji. 2005. Re-examining linguistic power: Strategic uses of directives by professional Japanese women in positions of authority and leadership. *JP* 37, 633–666.

Takara, Nobutaka. 2012. The weight of head nouns in noun-modifying constructions in conversational Japanese. *Studies in Language* 36, 33–72.

Takeuchi, Lone. 1999. *The Structure and History of Japanese: From Yamatokotoba to Nihongo*. Longman.

Takeuchi, Shiro and Michio Matsumaru. 2015a. Honshū hōgen ni okeru tadōshi bun no shugo to mokutekigo o kubetsu suru sutoratejī: Kansai hōgen to miyagi ken tome hōgen no bunseki [The strategy for distinguishing between the subjects and direct objects in transitive sentences: An analysis of the Kansai dialect and the Tome dialect of Miyagi Prefecture]. A paper read at the symposium of Aspec, Voice and Case. NINJAL.

2015b. Kansai hōgen no toritate sei to bunretsu jidōshi sei [Focusing and split intransitivity in the kansai dialect]. *Proceedings of the 151st Conference of the Linguistic Society of Japan*. Kyoto, Japan.

Takezawa, Koichi. 1987. A configurational approach to case-marking in Japanese. Ph.D. dissertation, University of Washington.

Takubo, Yukinori. 1987. Tōgo kōzō to bunmyaku jōhō [Syntactic structures and contextual information]. *Nihongogaku* 6, 37–48.

Takubo, Yukinori and Satoshi Kinsui. 1997. Discourse management in terms of mental spaces. *JP* 28, 741–758.

Talmy, Leonard. 2000. *Towards a Cognitive Semantics. Vol. II: Typology and Process in Concept Structuring*. MIT Press.

Tamori, Ikuhiro. 1980. Co-occurrence restrictions on onomatopoeic adverbs and particles. *Papers in Japanese Linguistics* 7, 151–171.

Tamori, Ikuhiro and Lawrence Schourup. 1999. *Onomatope: Keitai to imi* [Onomatopoeias: morphology and meaning]. Kurosio.

Tamura, Hiroshi and Takashi Kitazawa. 2011. Teinei hyōgen "~masu desu" no hensen ni tsuite: Kokkai kaigiroku 63 nenkan no kiroku kara [History of Japanese polite expression "~masu desu" in 63 year session records in the Diet]. *Tokyo Gakugei Daigaku Kiyō* 62, 1–12.

Tanaka, Hidekazu. 2001. Right-dislocation as scrambling. *Journal of Linguistics* 37, 551–579.

Tanaka, Hiroko. 1999. *Turn-Taking in Japanese Conversation. A Study in Grammar and Interaction*. Benjamins.

Tanaka, Katsuhiko. 1978. *Gengo kara mita minzoku to kokka* [Nation and state in the light of language]. Iwanami.

Tanaka, Yukari. 1993. Tobihane intonēshon no shiyō to imēji [Usage and image of jumping intonation]. *Proceedings of the 56th Conference of the Dialectological Circle of Japan*, 59–68.

Taylor, Yuki. 2015. The evolution of Japanese *toka* in utterance-final position. In Sylvie Hencil, Alexander Haselow, and Margje Post (eds.), *Final Particles*, 141–156. Gruyter.

Tenny, Carol. 1994. *Aspectual Roles and the Syntax-Semantics Interface*. Kluwer.

2006. Evidentiality, experiencers, and the syntax of sentience in Japanese. *Journal of East Asian Linguistics* 15, 245–288.

Terakawa, Kishio. 1941. *Hyōjun nihongo hatsuon hikaku jiten* [Standard Japanese comparative pronunciation dictionary]. Kōnan Shinbunsha.

Terakura, Hiroko. 1983. Noun modification and the use of *to yuu*. *Journal of the Association of Teachers of Japanese* 18, 23–55.

Teramura, Hideo. 1975–1978. Rentai-shūshoku no shintakusu to imi [Syntax and semantics of noun modification]. *Nihongo Nihonbunka* 4–7, 71–119, 29–78, 1–35, 1–24. Osaka University of Foreign Studies. Reprinted in *Teramura Hideo ronbunshū*, 1992, 157–320. Kurosio.

1984. *Nihongo no shintakusu to imi 2* [Syntax and meaning in Japanese 2]. Kurosio.

Terao, Yasushi. 2002. *Iimachigai wa dōshite okoru?* [Why do speech errors occur?]. Iwanami.

Thompson, Sandra and Ryoko Suzuki. 2011. The grammaticalization of final particles. In Heiko Narrog and Bernd Heine (eds.), *The Oxford Handbook of Grammaticalization*, 668–680. Oxford University Press.

Togashi, Junichi. 2004. Gendai nihongo shūjoshi kenkyū bunken mokuroku [Bibliography on Japanese sentence-final particles]. *Tsukuba Nihongo Kenkyū* 9, 69–90.

Tojo, Misao. 1966. *Kokugo no hōgen kukaku* [The classification of the dialects of the national language]. Tōkyōdō.

Tokieda, Motoki. 1941. *Kokugogaku genron* [The principles of Japanese linguistics]. Iwanami.

1951. Taijin kankei o kōsei suru joshi, jodōshi [Particles and auxiliary verbs that construct interpersonal relationships]. *Kokugo Kokubun* 20, 1–10.

Tomasello, Michael. 1999. *The Cultural Origins of Human Cognition*. Harvard University Press.

2003. *Constructing a Language: A Usage-Based Theory of Language Acquisition*. Harvard University Press.

Toratani, Kiyoko. 2006. On the optionality of *to*-marking on reduplicated mimetics in Japanese. *JKL* 14, 415–422.

2013. Constructions in RRG: A case study of mimetic verbs in Japanese. In Brian Nolan and Elke Diedrichsen (eds.), *Linking Constructions into Functional Linguistics*, 41–66. Benjamins.

2015. Iconicity in the syntax and lexical semantics of mimetics in Japanese. In Masako Hiraga et al. (eds.), *Iconicity: East meets West*, 125–141. Benjamins.

2017. The position of *to*/Ø-marked mimetics in Japanese sentence structure. In Noriko Iwasaki et al. (eds.), *The Grammar of Japanese Mimetics: Perspectives from Structure, Acquisition and Translation*, 35–72. Routledge.

Tranter, Nicolas. 2012. *The Languages of Japan and Korea*. Routledge.

Traugott, Elizabeth. 1995. The role of the development of discourse markers in the theory of grammaticalization. Paper presented at ICHL XII, Manchester.

2010. Exploring pragmatic particles at the right periphery. Keynote speech at the 4th International Conference on Language, Cognition and Discourse. National Taiwan University. http://homepage.ntu.edu.tw/~gilntu/cldc/2016/files/cldc2010_program.pdf

2014. On the function of the epistemic adverbs *surely* and *no doubt* at the left and right peripheries of the clause. In Kate Beeching and Ulrich Detges (eds.), *Discourse Functions at the Left and Right Periphery: Crosslinguistic Investigations of Language Use and Language Change*, 72–91. Brill.

Traugott, Elizabeth and Richard Dasher. 2002. *Regularity in Semantic Change*. Cambridge University Press.

Travis, Catherine. 1998. *Omoiyari* as a core Japanese value: Japanese-style empathy? In Angeliki Athansiadou and Elzbieta Tabakowska (eds.), *Speaking of Emotions. Conceptualization and Expression*, 55–81. Gruyter.

Treiman, Rebecca and Brett Kessler. 1995. In defense of an onset-rime syllable structure for English. *Language and Speech* 38, 127–142.

Trubetzkoy, Nikolai. 1969 [1939]. *Principles of Phonology*, trans. Christiane Baltaxe. University of California Press.

Trudgill, Peter. 2011. *Sociolinguistic Typology: The Social Determinants of Linguistic Complexity*. Cambridge University Press.

Tsubomoto, Atsuro. 2009. Sonzai no rensa to bubun/zentai no sukīma: "Uchi" to "soto" no aida [Chaining of existence and part/whole schema]. In Atsuro Tsubomoto et al. (eds.), *"Uchi" to "soto" no gengogaku* [Linguistics of "inside" and "outside"], 299–351. Kaitakusha.

Tsujimura, Natsuko. 2001. Revisiting the two-dimensional approach to mimetics: A reply to Kita (1997). *Linguistics* 39, 409–418.

2005. A constructional approach to mimetic verbs. In Mirjam Fried and Hans Boas (eds.), *Grammatical Constructions: Back to the Roots*, 137–154. Benjamins.

2014. Mimetic verbs and meaning. In Franz Rainer et al. (eds.), *Morphology and Meaning*, 303–314. Benjamins.

Tsujimura, Toshiki. 1992. *Keigo ronkō* [The Theory of (Japanese) Politeness]. Meiji.

Tsujioka, Takae. 2002. *The Syntax of Possession in Japanese*. Routledge.

Tsukamoto, Hideki. 1997. Goitekina gokeisei to tōgotekina gokeisei: Nihongo to chōsengo no taishō [Lexical and syntactic word formation: A comparative study of Japanese and Korean]. *Nihongo to chōsengo, Vol. II* [Japanese and Korean, Vol. II], 191–212. Kurosio.

Tsunoda, Mie. 2004. *Nihongo no setsu bun no rensetsu to modality* [Connection of clauses and sentences and modality in Japanese]. Kurosio.

Tsunoda, Tasaku. 1996. The possession cline in Japanese and other languages. In Hilary Chappell and William McGregor (eds.), *The Grammar of Inalienability: A Typological Perspective on Body Part Terms and the Part-whole Relation*, 563–630. Gruyter.

Tsutsui, Sayo. 2012. *Zatsudan no kōzō bunseki* [Structural analysis of Japanese casual conversation]. Kurosio.

Ueda, Kazutoshi. 1895. Hyōjungo ni tsukite [On Standard Japanese]. *Teikokubungaku* 1, 14–23.

Ueda, Yukiko. 2007. Nihongo no modaritī no tōgo-kōzō to ninshō-seigen [The syntactic structure of modality in Japanese and person restrictions]. In Nobuko Hasegawa (ed.), *Nihongo no shubun-genshō: Tōgo-kōzō to modaritī* [Main clause phenomena in Japanese: Syntactic structure and modality], 261–294. Hituzi.

2009. Person restriction in CP-domain in Japanese. *The Proceedings of the 5th Workshop on Altaic Formal Linguistics*, 345–359. MIT.

Uehara, Satoshi. 1998. *Syntactic Categories in Japanese: A Cognitive and Typological Introduction*. Kurosio.

2003. *Zibun* reflexivization in Japanese: A Cognitive Grammar approach. In Eugene Casad and Gary Palmer (eds.), *Cognitive Linguistics and Non-Indo-European Languages*, 389–404. Gruyter.

Uemura, Yukio. 1989. Nihongo no intonēshon [Intonation in Japanese]. *Kotoba no Kagaku* 3, 193–220.

Ueno, Noriko. 1987. Function of the theme marker wa from synchronic and diachronic perspectives. In John Hinds et al. (eds.), *Perspectives on Topicalization: The Case of Japanese Wa*, 221–263. Benjamins.

Ujiie, Yoko. 1992. *No desu* bun no seiritsu to sono haikei: Nihongoshi to no taiwa [The establishment of the no desu sentence, and its background: A dialogue with Japanese language history]. In Tsujimura Toshiki, Kyōju Koki, Kinen Ronbunshū, and Kankō Iinkai (eds.), *Tsujimura Toshiki kyōju koki kinen: Nihongoshi no shomondai*, 554–72. Meiji.

UNESCO. 1957. *World Illiteracy at Mid-Century*. UNESCO. http://unesdoc.unesco.org/images/0000/000029/002930eo.pdf

Unger, Marshall. 1996. *Literacy and Script Reform in Occupation Japan*. Oxford University Press.

United States Education Mission to Japan. 1946. *Report of the United States Education Mission to Japan*. Tokyo: GHQ/SCAP. Quoted from Japanese Government website at: http://www.mext.go.jp/b_menu/hakusho/html/others/detail/1317419.htm

Ura, Hiroyuki. 2000. *Checking Theory and Grammatical Functions in Universal Grammar*. Oxford University Press.

Usami, Mayumi. 2002. *Discourse Politeness in Japanese Conversation: Some Implications for a Universal Theory of Politeness*. Hituzi.

Uwano, Zendo. 1984. Rui no tōgō to shiki hozon [Merger of accent types and the preservation of pitch register]. *Kokugo Kenkyū* 47, 1–53.

1997. Fukugō meishi kara mita nihongo shohōgen no akusento [Accent of various dialects of Japanese seen from the viewpoint of compound nouns]. In Tetsuya Kunihiro et al. (eds.), *Accent, Intonation, Rhythm and Pause*, 231–270. Sanseidō.

1999. Classification of Japanese accent systems. In Shigeki Kaji (ed.), *Cross-linguistic Studies of Tonal Phenomena: Tonogenesis, Typology and Related Topics*, 151–186. ILCAA.

2000. Amami hōgen akusento no shosō [Aspects of accent in the Amami dialect]. *Onsei Kenkyū* 4, 42–54.

2012a. Three types of accent kernels in Japanese. *Lingua* 122, 1415–1440.

2012b. Enu-kei akusento towa nani ka [What is an N-pattern accent?]. *Onsei Kenkyū* 16, 44–62.

Uyeno, Tazuko. 1971. A study of Japanese modality – A performative analysis of sentence particles. Ph.D. dissertation, University of Michigan.

Van Riemsdijk, Henk. 2003. East meets West: Aboutness relatives in Swiss German. In Jan Koster and Henk van Riemsdijk (eds), *Germania et alia: A Linguistic Webschri for Hans den Besten*. University of Groningen. http://odur.let.rug.nl/~koster/DenBesten/contents. htm

Van Valin, Robert. 1990. Semantic parameters of split intransitivity. *Language* 66, 221–260.

1991. Another look at Icelandic case marking and grammatical relations. *Natural Language and Linguistic Theory* 9, 145–194.

1993. A synopsis of role and reference grammar. In Robert Van Valin (ed.), *Advances in Role and Reference Grammar*, 1–164. Benjamins.

1996. Toward a functionalist account of so-called extraction constraints. In Betty Devriendt et al. (eds.), *Complex Structures: A Functionalist Perspective*, 29–60. Gruyter.

1999. A typology of the interaction of focus structure and syntax. In Ekatarina Raxilina and Yakov Testelec (eds.), *Typology and Linguistic Theory: From Description to Explanation*, 511–524. Jazyki Russkoj Kul'tury.

2002. The development of subject-auxiliary inversion in English wh-questions: An alternative analysis. *Journal of Child Language* 29, 161–175.

2005. *Exploring the Syntax-Semantics Interface*. Cambridge University Press.

2013. Lexical representation, co-composition, and linking syntax and semantics. In James Pustejovsky et al. (eds.), *Advances in Generative Lexicon Theory*, 67–107. Springer.

Van Valin, Robert and Randy LaPolla. 1997. *Syntax: Structure, Meaning, and Function*. Cambridge University Press.

Vance, Timothy. 1987. *An Introduction to Japanese Phonology*. State University of New York Press.

1995. Final accent vs. no accent: Utterance-final neutralization in Tokyo Japanese. *Journal of Phonetics* 23, 487–499.

2008. *The Sounds of Japanese*. Cambridge University Press.

Venditti, Jennifer. 2005. The J_ToBI model of Japanese intonation. In Sun-Ah Jun (ed.), *Prosodic Typology: The Phonology of Intonation and Phrasing*, 172–200. Oxford University Press.

Venditti, Jennifer, Kkazuaki Maeda, and Jan P.H van Santen. 1998. Modeling Japanese boundary pitch movements for speech synthesis. *Proceedings of the Third ESCA Workshop on Speech Synthesis*, 317–322. NSW, Australia.

Venditti, Jennifer, Kikuo Maekawa, and Mary E. Beckman. 2008. Prominence marking in the Japanese intonation system. In Shigeru Miyagawa and Mamoru Saito (eds.), *Handbook of Japanese Linguistics*, 456–512. Oxford University Press.

Vendler, Zeno. 1957. Verbs and times. *The Philosophical Review* 66 (2), 143–160. Reprinted in Zeno Vendler (ed.), *Linguistics in Philosophy* (1967), 97–121. Cornell University Press.

1967. *Linguistics in Philosophy*. Cornell University Press.

Venetzky, Richard. 1995. How English is read: Grapheme-phoneme regularity and orthographic structure in word recognition. In Insup Taylor and David Olson (eds.), *Scripts and Literacy*, 111–129. Kluwer.

Viberg, Åke. 1983. The verbs of perception: A typological study. *Linguistics* 21, 123–162.

Von Wright, George. 1951. Deontic logic. *Mind* 60, 1–15.

Vovin, Alexander. 1997. On the syntactic typology of Old Japanese. *Journal of East Asian Linguistics* 6, 273–290.

2003. *A Reference Grammar of Classical Japanese Prose*. RoutledgeCurzon.

2005–2009. *A Descriptive and Comparative Grammar of Western Old Japanese*, 2 volumes. Global Oriental.

Wada, Minoru. 1942. Kinki akusento ni okeru meishi no fukugō keitai [Compound forms of nouns in Kinki accent]. *Onseigaku Kyōkai Kaihō* 71, 10–13.

Wada, Naoaki. 2001. *Interpreting English Tenses: A Compositional Approach*. Kaitakusha.

Walker, Marilyn, Sharon Cote, and Masayo Iida. 1994. Japanese discourse and the process of centering. *Computational Linguistics* 20, 193–231.

Warner, Natasha and Takayuki Arai. 2001. Japanese mora-timing: A review. *Phonetica* 58, 1–25.

Washi, Rumi. 2004. "Japanese female speech" and language policy in the World War II Era. In Shigeko Okamoto and Janet Shibamoto Smith (eds.), *Japanese Language, Gender, and Ideology: Cultural Models and Real People*, 76–91. Oxford University Press.

Washio, Ryuichi. 1993. When causatives mean passive: A cross-linguistic perspective. *Journal of East Asian Linguistics* 2, 45–90.

Watamaki, Toru. 1997. Jiheishōji ni okeru kyōkankaku kakutoku hyōgen joshi *ne* no shiyō no ketsujo: Jirei kenkyū [Lack of the particle ne in conversation by a child with autism: A case study]. *Hattatsu Shōgai Kenkyū* 19, 146–157.

Watanabe, Akira. 1996. *Case Absorption and WH-Agreement*. Kluwer.

2004. The genesis of negative concord: Syntax and morphology of negative doubling. *LI* 35, 559–612.

Watanabe, Minoru. 1953. Jojutsu to chinjutsu: Jutsugo bunsetsu no baai [Proposition and modality in predicate clauses]. *Kokugogaku* 13/14, 20–34.

1968. Shūjoshi no bunpōronteki ichi – jojutsu to chinjutsu saisetsu [The function of Japanese final particles]. *Kokugogaku* 72, 127–135.

Watanabe, Yasuhisa. 2009. Face and power in intercultural business communication. Ph.D. dissertation, Griffith University.

Watts, Richard. 2003. *Politeness*. Cambridge University Press.

Watts, Richard, Ide Sachiko, and Ehlich Konrad. 1992. Introduction. In Richard Watts et al. (eds.), *Politeness in Language. Studies in its History, Theory and Practice*, 1–17. Gruyter.

Whaley, Lindsay. 1997. *Introduction to Typology*. Sage.

Whitman, John. 1999. Personal pronoun shift in Japanese: A case study in lexical change and point of view. In Akio Kamio and Ken-Ichi Takami (eds.), *Function and Structure: In Honor of Susumu Kuno*, 357–386. Benjamins.

2013. The prehead relative clause problem. *Proceedings of WAFL* 8, 361–380.

Wierzbicka, Anna. 1979. Are grammatical categories vague or polysemous? [The Japanese "adversative" passive in a typological context]. *Research on Language & Social Interaction* 12, 111–162.

Wrona, Janick. 2012. The early history of *no* as a nominalizer. In Bjarke Frellesvig et al. (eds.), *Studies in Japanese and Korean linguistics*, 201–220. LINCOM.

Yabuki-Soh, Noriko. 2012. Japanese noun-modifying constructions in L2 learners' writing: The NPAH revisited. *Studies in Language Sciences* 11, 96–113.

Xiong, Ying. 2009. *Kagi ga doa o aketa. Nihongo no museibutsu shugo tadōshibun e no apurōchi* [The key opened the door. An approach to inanimate subject transitive sentences in Japanese]. Kasama.

Yakame, Hiromi. 2008. *Nihongo keiyōshi no kijutsuteki kenkyū* [A descriptive study of Japanese adjectives]. Meiji.

Yamada, Yoshio. 1908. *Nihonbunpōron* [Theory of Japanese grammar]. Hōbunkan.

Yamashita, Hitoshi. 2011. Japan's literacy myth and its social functions. In Patrick Heinrich and Christian Galan (eds.), *Language Life in Japan: Transformations and Prospects*, 94–108. Routledge.

Yanagida, Yuko and John Whitman. 2009. Alignment and word order in Old Japanese. *Journal of East Asian Linguistics* 18, 101–144.

Yokoyama, Sugiko. 1993. *Nihongo ni okeru Nihonjin no Nihonjin ni taisuru kotowari to Nihonjin no Amerikajin ni taisuru kotowari no hikaku* [A comparison of refusals made by Japanese toward native speaker Japanese and non-native speaker Americans]. *Nihongo Kyōiku* 81, 141–151.

Yomikaki Nōryoku Chōsa Iinkai. 1951. *Nihonjin no yomikaki nōryoku* [Survey of reading and writing proficiency of the Japanese]. Tokyo Daigaku Shuppanbu.

Yoshida, Etsuko. 2015. Bunpō to danwa no intāfeisu: Kodoku na if setsu o megutte. [The interface between grammar and discourse: Centering on isolate *if*-clause]. *Papers from the 32nd National Conference of the English Linguistic Society of Japan*, 179–185. English Linguistic Society of Japan.

Yoshida, Taeko. 2012. *Nihongo-dōshi te-kei no asupekuto* [The aspect of *te*-verbs in Japanese]. Kōyō.

Yoshimura, Kyoko. 1992. LF subjacency condition in Japanese. *Coyote Papers: Working Papers in Linguistics* 8, 143–162.

Yoshizawa, Norio. 1960. Intonēshon [Intonation]. In National Institute for Japanese Language and Linguistics (ed.), *Hanashikotoba no bunkei, Vol. 1* [Spoken sentence patterns, Vol. 1], 249–288. Shūei.

Yumoto, Yoko. 2016. Conversion and deverbal compound nouns. In Taro Kageyama and Hideki Kishimoto (eds.), *Handbook of Japanese Lexicon and Word Formation*, 311–345. Gruyter.

Zanuttini, Rafaella. 2008. Encoding the addressee in the syntax: Evidence from English imperative subjects. *Natural Language and Linguistic Theory* 26, 185–218.

Zanuttini, Rafaella, Miok Pak, and Paul Portner. 2012. A syntactic analysis of interpretive restrictions on imperative, promissive, and exhortative subjects. *Natural Language and Linguistic Theory* 30, 1231–1274.

Zec, Draga. 2007. The syllable. In Paul de Lacy (ed.), *The Cambridge Handbook of Phonology*, 161–194. Cambridge University Press.

Index